D1744578

SOUTH AFRICAN HUMAN RESOURCE MANAGEMENT

THEORY & PRACTICE
Fourth Edition

Ben Swanepoel (Editor), Barney Erasmus,

Heinz Schenk

JUTA

South African Human Resource Management

First published 1998
Second edition 2000
Third edition 2003
Fourth edition 2008
Reprinted 2009
Reprinted 2010
Reprinted 2012

© Juta & Co Ltd, 2008
PO Box 14373, Lansdowne, 7779, Cape Town

ISBN 978-0-70217-750-7

Disclaimer
All rights reserved. No part of this publication may be reproduced or
transmitted in any form or by any means, electronic or mechanical,
including photocopying, recording, or any information storage or retrieval
system, without prior permission in writing from the publisher. Subject to
any applicable licensing terms and conditions in the case of electronically
supplied publications, a person may engage in fair dealing with a copy of this
publication for his or her personal or private use, or his or her research or
private study. See Section 12(1)(a) of the Copyright Act 98 of 1978.

Project management: Sharon Steyn
Editing: Wendy Priilaid
Proofreading: Lee-Ann Ashcroft
Cover design: Marius Roux
Indexing: Sanet le Roux
Design and typesetting by Mckore Graphics
Illustrations by Mckore Graphics
Printed and bound in the Republic of South Africa by Academic Press

The authors and the publisher have made every effort to obtain permission
for and to acknowledge the use of copyright material. Should any
infringement of copyright have occurred, please contact the publisher, and
every effort will be made to rectify omissions or errors in the event of a
reprint or new edition.

THE AUTHORS
(and contributors)

Prof Ben Swanepoel, at the time of developing this fourth edition, was on sabbatical (and unpaid) leave from the University of Southern Queensland (USQ) where he is a member of the Faculty Business (and a former Head of Department and acting Head of School). He is a former president of IRasa (Industrial Relations Association of South Africa) and also used to be a part-time commissioner of the CCMA. Ben has authored and co-authored numerous books in South Africa and articles internationally. For a number of years now, he has also been privileged to gain international academic leadership and managerial experience.

Prof Barney Erasmus, at the time of developing this fourth edition, was Vice-Principal: Operations of the University of South Africa. Having formerly achieved success in roles such as Head of the Centre for Business Management, Head of the Department of Business Management, and later also Director of the School of Management Sciences, Barney was seconded to his current role during 2006. He is registered with the South African Board for Personnel Practice, has authored and co-authored numerous books and articles in the fields of human resource development, labour relations and human resource management, and acts as consultant in these fields as well as in general management.

Prof Heinz Schenk, at the time of developing this fourth edition, was acting as Director: Programmes of the College of Economic and Management Sciences of the University of South Africa. Heinz has proven his managerial capabilities through having successfully occupied roles such as Executive Director: Human Resource Management at the former Technikon Southern Africa, and also as Head of Department: Human Resource Management at the University of South Africa (from which position he has now been seconded to his present role). He is registered as an industrial psychologist and also as a (generalist) Master Practitioner of the South African Board for Personnel Practice, where he serves on the education committee and also as a registered mentor. He has co-authored and contributed to various textbooks in the broad field of HRM.

Marius van Wyk, former Professor of Labour Law and Business Ethics at the Graduate School of Business Leadership of the University of South Africa, whose expertise and dedicated contributions as co-author of the previous three editions of this book was invaluable, sadly passed away before work on this fourth edition commenced. His continued involvement in this ongoing project has indeed been enormously missed.

Contributors (to the fourth edition)

Maggie Holtzhausen is a lecturer in the Department of Human Resource Management of the School of Management Sciences of the University of South Africa and acts as consultant, specialising in labour relations and human resource development.

Professor Mahamed Rajah is a Labour Relations and Labout Law specialist at the Graduate School of Business Leadership of the University of South Africa, a well-known consultant in the field and a highly sought-after expert of alternative dispute resolution (also a CEDR accredited commercial mediator and a part time commissioner of the CCMA).

Gary Watkins, founder of Workinfo.com in 1998, agreed to collaborate and make available for use with the book, some of the highly valued information provided by Workinfo.com. Workinfo.com is the online legal and human resources portal of the management consultancy, Workplace Performance Technologies (Pty) Ltd. It is a subscription service (http://www.workinfo.com) providing pro forma policies and procedures, employment legislation on employment equity, human resources, industrial relations, and training and development. It also offers various related free facilities to subscribers, including a comprehensive database of online job descriptions and free downloads for members. Workinfo.com, with its joint venture partners, Perrott, Van Niekerk, Woodhouse and Matyolo Inc., owns and manages the premier case law portal Case Law CC (http://www.caselaw.co.za).

Contributors (to previous editions)

The first edition of this book on South African HRM saw the light a decade before this fourth edition. Over this period, and as part of the development of the three previous editions, various people have made contributions (as co-authors of some chapters and/or as contributing authors in more minor ways) as indicated in each of these three publications (1998, 2000 and 2003).

PREFACE

Developing this fourth edition has been rather peculiar in more ways than one. Having gone abroad to expand horizons and gain international experience, initially for a limited period, which became more prolonged, I had not intended to develop a further edition of this book. Demand in the market, however, led to my being approached to bring out this fourth edition. Initially the idea was to do so in 2006, and this was later postponed to 2007. Work and life pose challenges to all of us, and as a result the project had to be postponed yet again. Ultimately we could only manage to bring out this edition during 2008, a time generally, and a year specifically, that brought to our country some very interesting dynamics at a macro level.

South Africa has been undergoing 'deep change' since the first edition of this book was written during the years 1995 to 1997. Our society has been challenged with macro-level transformation issues, probably to a degree very few other societies have been experiencing over the last two decades. The people of South Africa must stand up to these challenges. In fact, our people have to bring about the required change and transformation. These challenges occur and are required in multiple dimensions and across a multitude of spheres of our society. People are always central to these. Human resource management (or HRM) is about people and the work that they do in and for organisations. This book and edition has therefore become part of a time and situation of change and challenge – and quite appropriately so, this book itself also reflects and revolves around various HRM-related changes and challenges.

Initially, due to all the changes and challenges that have emerged over time, it was thought that it would be more appropriate to publish a new book on South African HRM. This also at some stage formed the departure point in the process of working on what came to be this fourth edition. However, events such as the passing on of Marius van Wyk, Barney Erasmus and Heinz Schenk both being called upon to fill higher-level managerial leadership roles, and my own life and work dynamics (such as spending a number of years overseas – gaining great international experience but not really keeping in touch with a fast- and deep-changing South Africa – and agreeing to take on further managerial roles at work when restructuring took place), it became quite a daunting challenge to change this book into a fourth edition. The work has been done and the product is in your hands.

This fourth edition reflects the most recent prominent international trends in how the field of HRM is evolving. Most notably this includes a shift reflected in how we define HRM and the concomitant demarcation of the scope and foci of this field of theory and practice. HRM is not limited to the work of the 'staff function', traditionally better known as the 'personnel function' of organisations. HRM is much more than that – because it is the work of *all* managers to manage the human resources of and in our organisations. Furthermore, as this book now clearly shows, HRM can no longer be limited to a field of theory and practice that revolves around employees in their employment relationships. The work of organisations today gets done in many different ways, including through employing people (as employees), but also through alternative arrangements (such as making use of *independent contract work*). As will be found, these changes are reflected in ideas and issues dispersed throughout this edition of this book. While these are some of the important shifts, they are not the only changes.

Apart from having restructured the book (chapters/parts), a number of chapters are basically completely new. Users of this book will find these changes to be applicable especially to the chapters in Part 1 and Part 2, and also to Part 6 and 7 in a sense. The structure of parts 3, 4 and 5 remains more or less the same. Throughout the book, including in the three parts just mentioned, all chapters have been thoroughly updated though (except, of course, for those that are basically brand new). The structure and flow of this edition of the book now looks as follows:

Part 1 consists of three chapters that, together, aim at 'setting the agenda' for South African HRM. It lays the conceptual and contextual foundations and, as in previous editions, emphasises the importance of making sure we get the context right. As readers will learn (in these three chapters, and also throughout the book), we now also broaden the context of South African HRM. This we do by locating the book more in the Africa context as well.

Part 2 consists of three chapters that revolve around strategising, designing and planning – all aimed, together, at preparing the work environment.

Part 3 contains the two chapters devoted to how we can go about sourcing talent for our organisations – and, as will be learned, this goes beyond recruitment and selection typically covered by most HRM books to include finding and engaging the services of non-employee working people (such as consultants and/or temporary employment services such as labour brokers).

Part 4 consists of six chapters that are geared towards finding appropriate ways of empowering the human resources of organisations. These include themes related to motivation, leadership, the enhancement/development of work performance and careers – and South Africa's huge challenge pertaining to human resource development.

Part 5 revolves around what we regard as the 'reward and care' challenge facing our organisations and, as readers will find, we start to push some boundaries again by arguing for care way beyond the workforce to include aspects like 'corporate citizenship' and efforts at enhancing sustainability.

The three chapters (not two, as in previous editions) of *Part 6* now revolve around all the challenges pertaining to labour and employee relations, including (unlike previous editions) how to fairly terminate employment relationships.

Part 7 contains the three final chapters of this book. These are not the same as in previous editions and indeed cover *key aspects of the HRM challenge* of our time, including some related to leading *change and transformation*, and how we manage HRM-related information. The final chapter is called 'Pushing boundaries – going beyond ...', and as readers will find, this title signals more than one thing, including crossing national boundaries, and also extending into realms traditionally not included in most books of this kind in the field of HRM.

In this book all gender references, such 'he', 'his', 'herself', etc, can be taken to imply the other gender equivalent, such as 'she', 'her', 'himself', etc.

While there is a significant degree of change to this book, as in life, some things remain largely the same: change and continuity, the way life is. We stick to the holistic and strategic approach that has been there since the inception of this uniquely South African textbook. Also, I want to stress again that this is not an American textbook adapted with injecting some South African flavour. This book is, therefore, still a book written by South Africans for South Africans. It took me years overseas to realise that I am, in the first instance, an African. I may be a global citizen in the true sense of the word, but I remain an African. Not only was I born in Africa (in Namibia, or South West Africa as it was known then – to be more precise), but today I also realise more than ever before that Africa was also born in me. I love Africa, and this fourth edition is regarded as a very modest attempt to make a tiny and very humble contribution not only to South Africa (as has been the case in the past with previous editions), but also to start doing so through making this book more 'Africa' relevant. It will be found that this edition contains ample new material to make this book the first of its kind with a 'dash of Africa ingredients' injected into the 'recipe'. The development of this aspect of the fourth edition then also brought about a yearning to expand and deepen research and other work in the evolving field of HRM 'into Africa'. It may well be that such work will in future serve as input to further editions of this book – or entirely different publications, perhaps.

For now, let us remain focused on the current edition: Had it not been for the sabbatical leave (granted by USQ), this edition would not have seen the light – at least not in its present form. I am thus very grateful for this. As I write this preface I am on unpaid leave, and the future is uncertain in terms of my own (working) life. Flexibility in terms of work arrangements is a key trend internationally – as shown also in the book – and this is also something presently being explored by me. While sabbatical (and unpaid) leave are/were great and important, change and flexibility beyond this might be appropriate – only time will tell what will evolve. In this I am thus actually experiencing some of the changes (such as working 'internationally', working in flexible ways, and also working in uncertain situations) that are indeed reflected in this book. I am sure many people who would be reading this book will also be able to identify and relate their own worlds (of work) with what they read. It is still, therefore, a book which seeks the nexus of the theory and practice of HRM.

Different people have helped make this fourth edition a reality. They must be thanked, including employees of Juta, like Phillip Liebenberg and Sharon Steyn. Wendy Priilaid has also made huge contributions, even though not as an employee. This very product of Juta thus reflects the alternative ways of arranging for work of organisations to get done (as also covered in this book), including through employees – and non-employee workers like myself (and Barney and Heinz), and also Wendy. It has been a team effort, and the team must be thanked. I also wish to thank others who have helped (with some typing), like my wife, Sonia. At times help was even offered 'free of charge' – voluntary 'charity work' almost in a sense. Here I specifically thank Chris O' Reilly. My thanks also to Gary Watkins for agreeing that we could use very valuable material of workinfo.com.

Lastly I wish to extend a word of thanks to all of those who have found this book to be so worthwhile in the past, that it is still regarded as something essential for the future. It is sincerely hoped that this fourth edition will add the value it is intended to: helping people of South Africa mainly – and to a lesser extent other people of Africa – to become better at managing the work and working people in and of our organisations. It is only through 'better' (suited) HRM that we will be able to make this country (and continent) a success and a better place for all. HRM is about improving lives – not only of working people, but also of ordinary citizens and communities who use the (improved) products/services of (better performing) organisations, made possible through enhanced capacity and contributions of the people who do the work of and in our organisations.

Ben J Swanepoel
(Editor)

TABLE OF CONTENTS

PART ONE

SETTING THE HRM AGENDA: CONCEPTUAL AND CONTEXTUAL PERSPECTIVES

1 THE HUMAN RESOURCE MANAGEMENT CHALLENGE: AN INTRODUCTION

LEARNING OUTCOMES

After studying this chapter, you should be able to:

- define human resource management (HRM);
- explain what forms the foundation of HRM;
- explain what is meant by the 'societal embeddedness' of organisations, management and HRM, and how this relates to sustainability;
- demonstrate why and how HRM is central to value creation through analysing the process of organisational value creation from an open-system, supply chain perspective;
- show how HRM adds or creates value by using an outline of the process and scope of HRM work;
- briefly demonstrate the complex nature of HRM through showing how HRM interplays with numerous variables;
- explain why HRM involves various role players; and
- provide a brief evolutionary perspective of HRM.

1.1 HUMAN RESOURCE MANAGEMENT: FOUNDATION AND DEFINITION

Human resource management (or HRM, which is the abbreviation we will use throughout this book) is rooted in work as a human activity. While work can take on many forms, we refer to the work people engage in as a socio-economic activity, and also mainly so in an organisational context.

Work is central to life, and most people, as adults, have to engage in some form of work to be able to earn and make a living. Today millions of people do so by working in and for organisations. Modern-day society is very much organisation driven, and organisations require work to be done. Thus, most organisations need people to do work and millions of people depend on organisations to be able to work and make a living. We can almost say that it is the working people who make organisations, and society, work! This is the foundation of HRM and also the reason why this is such an important field of theory and practice.

HRM has been defined in many different ways. It is thus important that we clarify right from the outset what we mean by this concept in this book. We take the same approach as that taken in the *Oxford Handbook of Human Resource Management* (Boxall, Purcell & Wright 2007).

We regard HRM as being focused on all aspects pertaining to the management of the work and the people doing it, of and in organisations. Most people working in and for organisations do so as employees. An employee is a person who engages in an employment relationship with that organisation (also referred to as an employer in such contexts). While traditionally a number of books on HRM limit the focus and scope of HRM to those people who work as employees of organisations, we believe this has become too narrow.

While we recognise that in any organisation most of the people doing the work will indeed be doing so as employees in employment relationships, we also know that increasing use is made of alternative ways to arrange to get the work done. Non-employees frequently help, and some work may be subcontracted or outsourced. Managing such issues forms part of the management of 'the human resources function' of organisations, simply because the work of the organisation is still done by people. We would thus like to define HRM as follows:

> *Human resource management* is that part of the management of organisations that is concerned with all aspects that relate to, and interplay with, the work and the people who do the work of and in organisations.

From this definition it should be clear that we regard HRM to be firmly embedded in organisations and management. Unlike some books on the subject, we do not regard HRM as the work domain of some specialist practitioners who form part of some kind of 'HR department'. We regard the 'HR function' as broader. We stick to the roots of the concept of an HR function as conceived by E. Wight Bakke (1958: 5–6) some five decades ago, as quoted by Kaufman (2007: 34):

> The general type of activity in any function of management ... is to use the re-sources effectively for an organizational objective ... The function which is re-lated to the understanding, maintenance, development, effective employment, and integration of the potential in the resource 'people' I shall call simply *the human resource function*.

All managers thus manage human resources. As Bakke (1958: 4) already stated five decades ago in his seminal lecture (Kaufman 2007: 34): "The first thing we ought to be clear on is that there is nothing new about the managerial function of dealing with people ... Like other sub-functions of management ... it has been *carved out of* the *general* managerial function, not *put into* it."

We thus believe that even though some people specialise in HRM work, HRM is an integral part of all managerial work. We furthermore work from the premise, as explained in the next section, that organisations, management and HRM make up an integral part of modern-day society. It is therefore essential for anyone interested in how organisations, economies and societies function to learn more about HRM. Across the globe HRM is recognised as a challenging, dynamic and evolving field of theory and practice – including in South Africa and on the African continent.

1.2 ORGANISATIONS AND MANAGEMENT AS EMBEDDED SOCIETAL PHENOMENA: THE SUSTAINABILITY CHALLENGE OF HRM

1.2.1 Organisations and management

The immediate context in which HRM is practised is that of 'the organisation'.[1] It is thus important that we try to further clarify this contextual setting. We fully concur with what Watson (2007: 108) says: "HRM processes are organizational processes. They occur within all work organizations and they cannot be understood separately from the way in which we understand organizations themselves. The same can be argued about management more broadly."

We all come into contact with organisations regularly. Most of us were born in or with the aid of organisations (hospitals), and we are educated with the aid of other organisations (such as schools and universities). Most of the food we consume would not have been available in that form had it not been for organisations that make and distribute it. We can see organisations and their outputs and outcomes all around us almost every day, and yet we hardly ever think about what organisations entail or how they operate or function. In order to understand HRM, we must have some understanding of organisations. We now thus briefly take a closer look at what organisations essentially are.

An organisation can be described as people and other resources that are put together in a coordinated way in order to achieve specific outcomes, ends or goals. Organisations are thus purposeful societal entities and are generally formally established. Watson (2007: 109) refers to organisations as "authoritatively coordinated human enterprises". All organisations have some reason for being, (or *raison d'être*) which would in turn relate directly to some needs in society.

Fundamentally organisations exist because of the needs, wants or desires of society and its people. Resources are purposefully mobilised so that the vast range of needs and interests of modern-day society can be met. There are many kinds of organisations that not only serve different purposes, but also seek different resultant outcomes from their existence and operations. Schools are there to help us educate our children. Private schools typically cater for the need to educate our children but they also seek appropriate return on what they have invested into these operations. Hospitals are there to help and care for the unhealthy among us. Public and private hospitals do not seek all the exact same outcomes even though they exist to serve the same purpose (private hospitals also seek profits from their services). These are just two examples of different types of organisations with different purposes and interests.

Some business enterprises strive to make a profit out of what they do (such as Pick 'n Pay, Absa, SABMiller, Anglo Platinum, MTN and Medi-Clinic). Some are government organisations (such as local authorities or municipalities) and others are really parastatal institutions or state-owned enterprises (SOEs), such as Eskom and the SABC. Some other organisations are formed and operated by volunteers, and are not profit seeking (such as churches, trade unions and welfare institutions). All organisations will generally continue to exist only if the particular societal needs are being met and served by them, and in many instances only if this is better than what

---

1 Please note that in this book when we refer to organisation/s, we mean so mainly in the formal or official sense – ie formally established organisations. We generally also tend to use the term 'organisation' interchangeably with such terms as 'firm', 'company', enterprise', and so on – unless we specify otherwise for any particular reason.

other organisations can achieve. The continued existence of organisations is basically a function of the extent to which they can be successful. This is broad and generally stated. They must at least be successful at delivering the goods (we use this term to denote the products and/or services delivered) and meeting the relevant societal needs. We need to clarify further what we mean by 'successful' (see figure 1.1).

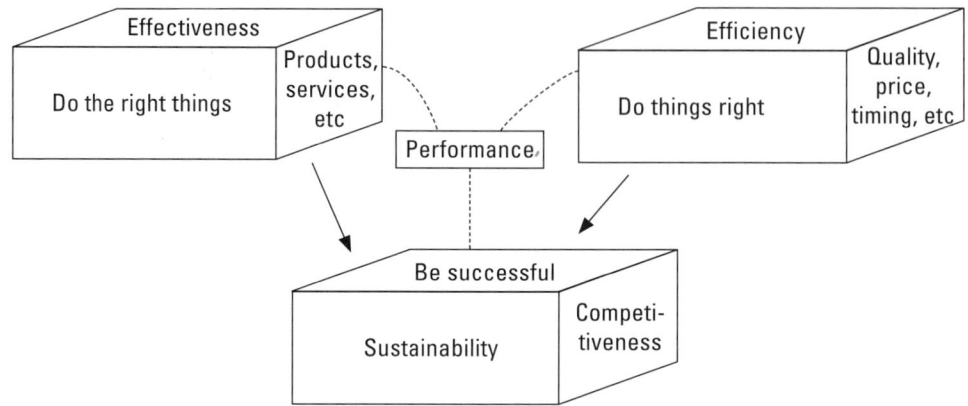

Figure 1.1: Organisational success

Organisations can be said to be successful if they deliver the right goods in the right way. The former is known as the *effectiveness* of organisations, and the latter as their *efficiency*. The 'right goods' refer to the actual products and/or services that any particular organisation provides (for instance the education, the health care, the radio and television programmes, electricity, the minerals that are mined, the beer, the cellphones or the groceries). As explained, the provision of such goods constitutes the basic *raison d'être* of any such social entity. Effectiveness is not sufficient, though. All organisations also have to 'do things right'. This means that, in providing these right goods, they must also function in such ways that all the stakeholders of the organisation – in particular the customers, consumers or users of these goods – are optimally satisfied with these products and/or services, and with the other organisational outcomes. For example, the nature and quality of the goods must be right, and they must be provided at the right price, at the right time, at the right place. Customer satisfaction is thus essential – but that is still not sufficient.

Stakeholders of an organisation are essentially those who have a stake or an interest in it. Organisations have many stakeholders, such as the government, the banks, the suppliers (other organisations from whom things that are needed in order to be able to deliver the goods are bought), other similar and perhaps competing organisations, and the employees and their trade unions. From a stakeholder perspective of organisations and management, all these stakeholders must be satisfied with the organisational outcomes, as far as this is possible. The diverse interests of the wide range of stakeholders often differ though, which can lead to some tensions and paradoxes.

If the customers and other stakeholders are optimally happy, the chances of organisational survival and continued existence are generally good. We can take this a step further and say that at the minimum an organisation must be able to survive, but the aim would be to make it thrive. The better an organisation performs (the better it can be at being effective and efficient), the more it will be able to thrive rather than merely survive. The effectiveness, efficiency and performance of organisations are thus central to organisational success. Organisational success is beneficial to society because it implies that the needs of society are being met and useful purposes are being served. This means that through successful organisations, contributions are made and value is added to the quality of life of the members of society.

Being successful does not just happen. In organisations the people and other resources are put together to achieve this aim of serving a useful purpose successfully. People must 'make it happen'. The single most important resource of any organisation must therefore be its people. People do all the work of organisations, even if they use other things like technology to do so. Some people are specifically given the role, task and responsibility to make sure that all that is required to bring about organisational success is attended to. These people are generally referred to as the managers in organisations. This is quite a challenging role to fulfil because organisations are complex and the interests of all stakeholders are not always aligned. Thus, in order to deliver the right goods in the right ways, people and other resources are brought together, by managers, in and as organisations (see figure 1.2) that are striving to survive and thrive through serving useful purposes as best as they possibly can.

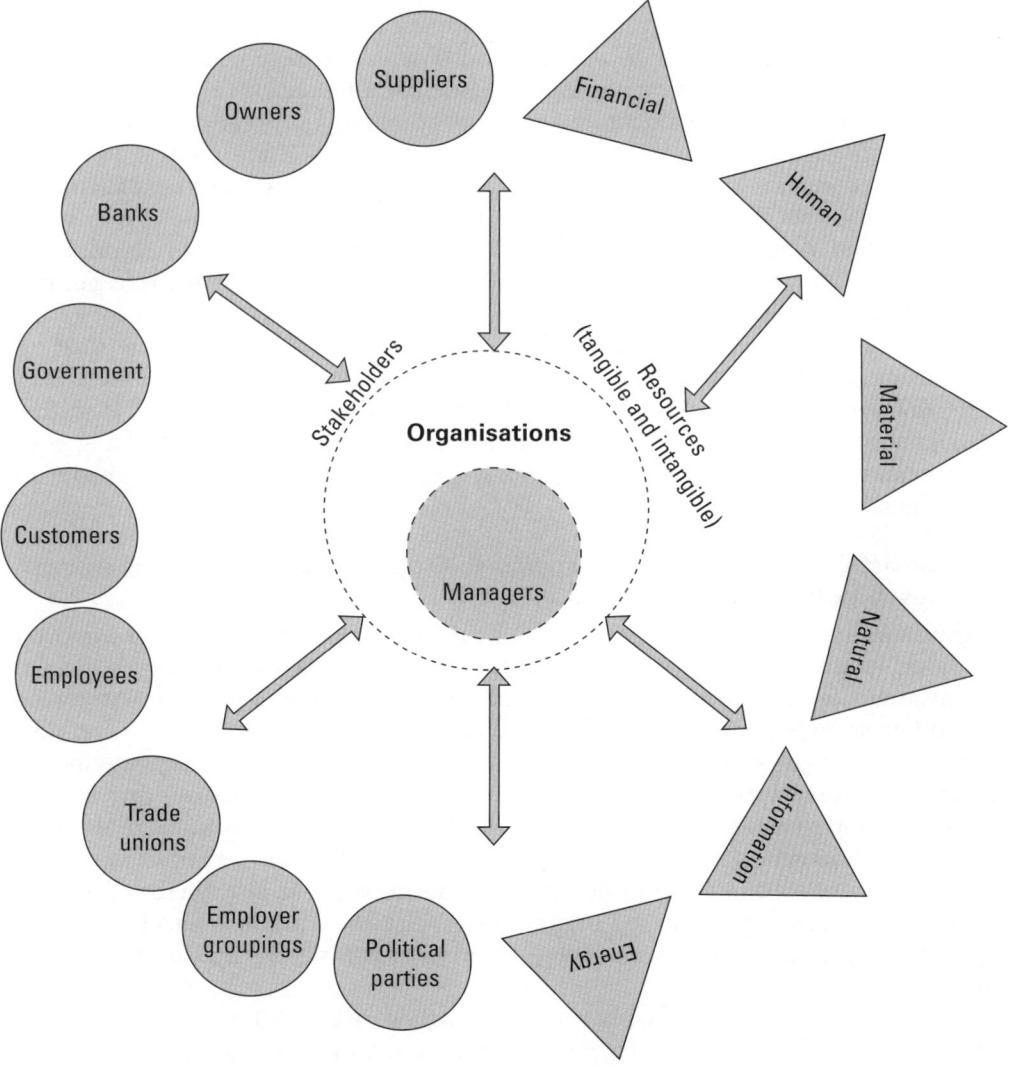

Figure 1.2: Organisations, managers, resources and stakeholders

A lot of work has to be done to ultimately be successful, for example, in delivering the educational and health-care services mentioned earlier, and people do all that work. Schools need teachers and administrative support staff to help our children learn and develop. Hospitals need health-care professionals like doctors, nurses and various other types of people to perform all the work required to care for patients. Companies that manufacture products like food or beverages require people to do all the work related to the actual manufacturing processes. Retail organisations such as Shoprite or Spar require, among others, people to keep shelves stocked, to work as cashiers, and to serve the customers in many other ways. It is most common to refer to the people who work for such organisations as personnel, staff or human resources, and they play a fundamental role in the performance and success of organisations generally – and in fact of national economies and entire societies. In general we can thus say that 'the people factor' is at the very core of not only organisations and management, but also of economic activity, and of all societies worldwide. HRM specifically revolves around this 'people factor' and how working people can best help bring about organisational success and a better quality of life, not just for customers or the shareholders of a company, but also for themselves and their families, and their communities.

This book thus fits into the field of organisation and management studies. Samson and Daft (2005: 11) say that management is the "attainment of organisational goals in an effective and efficient manner through the planning, organising, leading and controlling of organisational resources". Stone's (2005: 5) definition of management magnifies the human factor or dimension of managerial work when management is defined as the "art of getting things done through people". Perhaps this is a little over-simplified though, because organisations need various kinds of resources, as mentioned before. Nevertheless it does make the point that to manage is to get work done through people and that organisations cannot exist or survive without this.

Some resources are tangible (for example land, buildings, machinery, water, money, equipment) and some are intangible (for example energy, and the knowledge, skills and attitudes of working people). All of these resources have to be utilised, brought together in a coordinated way and transformed into needs-satisfying goods while balancing the interests of all organisational stakeholders. This is the role and task of management.

1.2.2 Societal embeddedness, the sustainability challenge and the human resource factor

Organisations, management and the work of managers are thus extremely important and also relatively complex societal phenomena. This is even more so because organisations are an intrinsic part of broader society, and hence closely intertwined with other aspects of our world. We are living in an era whereby it is increasingly acknowledged that organisations have a tremendous impact on society, way beyond the products/services they serve to provide. Organisations, for instance, provide work and hence opportunities for millions of people to be able to work, earn and make a living. Unfortunately, however, organisations can also have negative impacts on society. This may include the pollution of planet Earth, but also the quality of life of the people working in and for organisations, and their families and friends. This brings us to the sustainability challenge faced by organisations and management in our modern world.

The role of organisations in terms of our world's sustainability challenge has now become a prime focus worldwide. Just over half a decade ago, Dunphy, Griffiths and Benn (2003: 3) made a clear, generic case:

We are faced with an extraordinary situation. Never before in the history of the world has the viability of much of the life on this planet been under threat from humanity; never before have so many of the world's people experienced such material wealth and so many others lived in abject poverty; never before have so many had such interesting and fulfilling work and so many others such degrading work or no work at all. If we are to live healthy, fulfilling lives on this planet in the future, we must find new life-affirming values and forge new patterns of living and working together.

Organisations and managers thus now have a broader mandate than merely delivering 'the goods'. It is not only about the products/services and the customers. It is very much also about the working people and society at large. It is about how we build places where we work together and add value that will last for all our offspring who will have to live together, sharing what our planet has to offer. As such we, as managers, become stewards of that which this world offers us – the natural resources and our place of habitat. Dunphy et al (2003: 67) refer to the organisation's "connection with its key stakeholders and the notion of a social and ecological contract negotiated by management with these stakeholders". In a sense this is almost becoming the 'licence to operate' for modern-day organisations and managers. The same authors propagate the centrality of the human dimension in the strive towards sustainability. They refer to "human sustainability" and say that any organisation should accept

> responsibility for the process of contributing to and upgrading human knowledge and skill formation within the organization itself ... because it makes good business sense to develop the intellectual and social capital of the workforce ... This upgrading is also valuable for its own sake and reflects the organization's commitment to treating people as having value in their own right. It also contributes to a society where human capabilities are enhanced ... and this ... improves the quality of life in society as a whole (Dunphy et al 2003: 70).

It seems therefore that we are at some threshold in the history of mankind and in this book we want to locate human resource management firmly within this context. There are huge challenges and amidst all the flux and turmoil of our fast-changing world, 21st century managers must deal with issues that are complex and comprehensive in scope, and that directly interface with life generally and with the very sustainability of our precious planet Earth. In the end the human factor is central to these challenges. We, the people of this planet, are the human resources of the world. We work in and for organisations, or we set up and develop organisations (that we own, perhaps). If we are managers, we have to manage these organisations and the people that work with us. As such we can make a huge difference between ruining our world, or helping to create a sustainable world for the generations we leave behind. The way in which we manage our organisations, and particularly our human resources, is therefore crucial.

Let us summarise the management challenge of our time: through organisations, managers are challenged to purposefully bring together a vast array of resources, including people, in a rather uncertain and challenging environment, with the aim of delivering needs-satisfying goods as effectively and efficiently as possible, to the best possible satisfaction of all stakeholders, and with the distinct challenge to do all of this in ways that enhance sustainability of our societies and planet Earth.

Our view is that it is through HRM that such a holistic approach to organisations and management can and should help bring about improved quality of life and sustainability. We hold this view for two reasons primarily:

- Firstly, only people can really make the difference between a sustainable or unsustainable world and HRM is that part of management and organisations that revolves around the people.
- Secondly, all managers, per definition, manage human resources, making HRM *the* generic managerial task and challenge.

We are not hereby downplaying other aspects of management. While we regard HRM as the key challenge of managerial work and organisations of our era, we acknowledge that management entails much more. It includes such things as research and development, marketing, public relations and the management of logistics and organisational operations. However, irrespective of whether someone is an operations manager, or a logistics, marketing or public relations manager in an organisation, as a manager he or she will generally be working through and with other people to get the work done. This is why the management of human resources is central to all managerial work, as we have said: all managers manage human resources. We now take a closer look at HRM from a system and supply chain perspective.

1.3 HRM IN THE VALUE CHAIN: AN 'OPEN SYSTEM, SUPPLY CHAIN' PERSPECTIVE

A system can basically be regarded as a set of interconnecting and interdependent things or parts, arranged in a united way to work together as a whole. From what we have already said it should be quite clear that organisations can be regarded as systems. Clegg, Kornberger and Pitsis (2005: 504), in their book *Managing and Organizations*, say a system involves "a stable set of relationships between inputs, transformation processes, and outputs". Distinction is made between open and closed systems. A closed system is a system that is insulated from the environment outside of it, and thus is not influenced by it. By contrast, an open system is in constant dynamic interaction with the environment outside of it, and as such it is influenced by the environment and in turn it also influences its external environment. We regard organisations as open systems, which is clear from what we have said thus far. Organisations can also be viewed as operating like a 'chain of interconnected nodes' that create value through developing products and/or services that are valued by others.

Michael Porter (1985) developed the concept of the value chain. Essentially, the value chain is a way of conceptualising and categorising the activities of organisations which, together and as a process, creates value as inputs are converted into products and/or services that are sold to make a profit ('margin' in Porter's terms). In the original value chain as conceptualised by Porter (see figure 1.3), a distinction is made between 'primary activities' and 'support activities' (possibly signalling that the latter may in a sense be 'secondary').

The organisational *infrastructure* relates to the formal structures, systems and routines related to planning, information, finance, quality control and compliance, etc. *Procurement* is said to revolve around acquiring all the required resources or inputs. *Technology development* refers to the hardware, software, skills, know-how, and so on, and the equipment related to the resources, processes and activities, or the goods (products/services). *Human resource management* is explained to involve all those activities required to recruit, employ, develop, reward and manage the people in

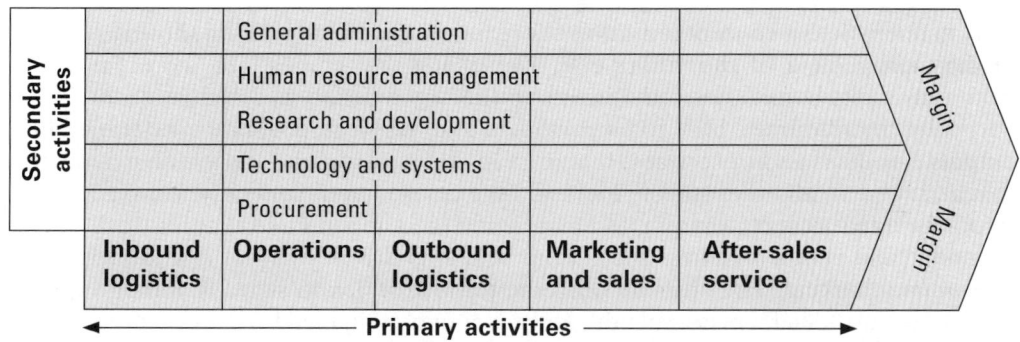

Figure 1.3: The organisational value chain of Porter (Smit et al 2007)

the organisation. Based on Johnson, Scholes and Whittington (2008: 110), the primary activities can be described as follows:

- *Inbound logistics*: activities pertaining to receiving, storing and distributing the inputs that are to be transformed into outputs, including such things as materials handling and transportation.
- *Operations*: activities that actually transform the inputs into the final outputs as products and/or services, including machining, assembling and packaging.
- *Outbound logistics*: activities relating to collecting, storing and distributing the products/services to the customers.
- *Marketing and sales*: those activities that make prospective users of the outputs aware thereof and that induce them to actually purchase, such as advertising, promotion and selling.
- *Service*: activities that maintain or enhance the value of the goods (products and/or services), such as repairs and general after-sales services.

We basically regard these activities as another way of categorising the work that organisations are required to do in order to convert inputs into outputs. If work is central to the value chain, as it is, people are too. We therefore do not go along with Porter's original conceptualisation that categorised HRM is a 'support activity'. It is an integral part of the process of creating value and not a mere support function or activity. It is not secondary to management, it is indeed central to it. Human resources should thus be put in the mainstream of management thinking, theory and practice, as far as we are concerned.

Without human resources none of the activities can happen. People think about and consider what the market needs or wants. People make choices about what products and services to develop and deliver, and also how to do these things (people devise the strategies, operational technologies and so forth). People in organisations determine what other resources or inputs to acquire and how best to go about doing so. People do the work to convert or transform these inputs into the actual services and/or products as they go down in the mines, work on the production lines and service the customers. People do the selling and distribution to get these products/services to actually be acquired and used by customers. Only people can choose to make the difference beyond creating customer value (people in organisations make decisions about such things as corporate social responsibility, ethical business conduct and contributions to society and sustainability generally).

Figure 1.4 is thus our adaptation of Porter's classic value chain picture, in combination with an open-system conceptualisation of organisations. HRM is being shown as central to the management of everything else. Everything that comes into the organisation from outside its boundaries – the inputs to the organisation as a system, including in particular the resources, have to be combined and transformed, and hence turned into outputs (products and/or services) that are valued by customers, and yielding outcomes that add value to all other stakeholders and the environment generally. Unlike Porter's value chain that reflects 'margin' as an outcome (keeping in mind that his work has an economic and competitiveness focus), our model is driven by what is known as *triple bottom line* thinking. The ultimate outcome towards which to strive is adding value in three domains: social, environmental, and economic or financial.

Figure 1.4 is intended to be a simplified conceptualisation. As the real world is very complex, it shows, in the tradition of the value chain and hence in an almost linear fashion, a process of value creation through the flow of work activities of organisations. It puts the people factor right in the centre of everything, though, and it incorporates a multiple stakeholder view with a distinct incorporation of a sustainability focus. The key point is that we put people and hence HRM at the very core of the process of value creation (also see 'A case at hand').

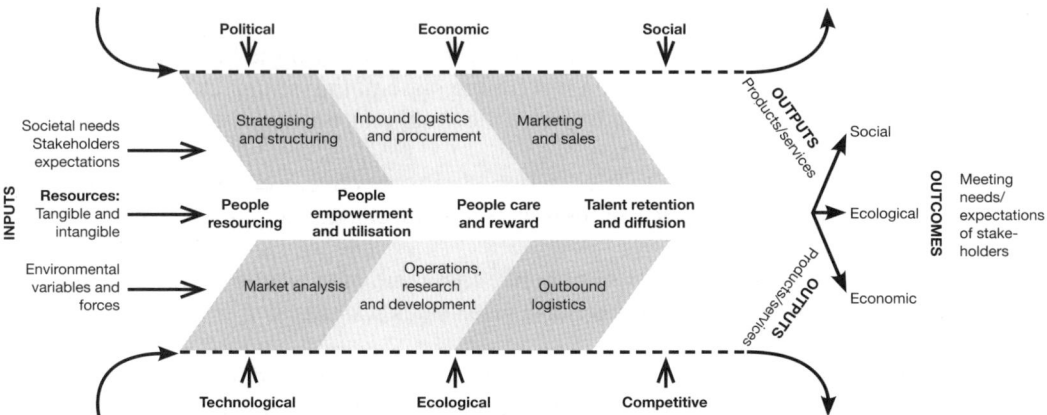

Figure 1.4: Human resource management: central to organisational value creation

A CASE AT HAND

People, HRM and competitiveness at SABMiller

Our people

One of SABMiller's five values is that our people are our enduring advantage and our aim is therefore to be a global and local employer of choice. We have a strong culture of performance management and employees at every level are empowered and accountable for achieving clear goals. In this they are supported with world-class training and development. Being a learning and self-refreshing organisation is one of the priorities for the business.

Source: http://www.sabmiller.com/Annual_Report_2007/8_sustainable/sustaindevreport.html

Figure 1.4 reflects the centrality of HRM to the organisational efforts of converting inputs into value-adding outputs and outcomes. The organisation itself is reflected as being open, hence the dotted lines that signal the organisational boundaries that set it apart from the bigger system within which it exists and functions. In the next section we return to this model with some further explanation. For now, keep in mind that organisations can in this way be thought of as value-creating entities in society.

No such organisation as a value-creating entity exists or operates in isolation, though. From an open-system perspective there are systems within systems. Organisations as systems thus form subsystems of the bigger system of a country, or society, and the world at large. Each such system is meant to create and add value, and in reality numerous organisations are thus interconnected to form webs of supply chains. We thus have different value chains (viewing each organisation as a value chain) that interconnect with other such value chains to form what is often referred to as a supply chain. These webs of interconnected value chains thus ultimately function together to develop and move the goods (products and/or services) from being bundles of natural and other resources (including what is known as raw materials) into finished products/ services as ultimately used and experienced by the end users or customers. At each point in the supply chain, value is supposed to be added and different organisations, through their own value chains, thus add value at each point. Throughout these supply chains, different organisations thus engage in exchanges with each other as they buy and sell up or down the value stream. From an open-system perspective, there are all these different interconnected value-adding systems, all of which are subsystems of the bigger system and each of which has its own subsystems (such as procurement, operations and marketing), all of which have to be managed. The important thing is that in all these supply chains, people are the key. This is echoed by a senior supply chain management professional at Accenture South Africa, Haley Walters (see exhibit 1.1).

EXHIBIT 1.1: Supply chain success depends on the quality of working people

Supply chain management head at Accenture South Africa, Haley Walters, says: "Behind every world-class supply chain is a world-class workforce. Companies with well-trained, knowledgeable employees operate more efficiently and seize market opportunities more readily."

Source: http://www.accenture.com/Countries/South_Africa/About_Accenture/Newsroom/News_Releases/ DrivingBuilding.htm

---

1.4 HOW HUMAN RESOURCE MANAGEMENT ADDS VALUE: PROCESS AND SCOPE OF WORK

Referring to figure 1.4, we see that the inputs from outside the organisation include and are founded on the needs of society and the expectations of all the stakeholders of the organisation. There are many environmental variables and forces outside the organisation that impact on and interact with it. These we categorise, for conceptual purposes, as PESTEC (political, economic, social, technological, ecological and competitive). The required resources are brought into the organisation in order to develop and deliver the needs-satisfying products and/or services and other outcomes, as is shown in that graphical presentation.

We regard strategising as the starting point in organisational value creation. Strategising refers to the making of strategy, which is based on strategic thinking. An easy way to simplify and understand 'strategy' and 'strategic' is to think of them in relation to tactics. As when playing a game of chess, there is an overall game plan (strategy), but as the game progresses certain moves (tactics) are made depending on what the opposition is doing. If one thinks and acts tactically, it is of short-term nature but geared to fit with the strategy. *Tactics* refer to actions, manoeuvres or ploys that have a shorter time horizon, and *strategy* refers to the long-term and overall situation. There thus has to be consideration of the long term – what the organisation must achieve and stand for; in other words, its purpose. This is closely intertwined with market analysis because, per definition, the reason for being of the organisation is linked to the market – the needs and wants of those who will be using the products and services of the organisation. As figure 1.4 reflects, people resourcing is right there with these starting points of organisational value creation. This is so because it will be the people that will think strategically and determine long-term direction for the organisation in terms of such things as what products/services should be delivered to whom, why and how. People will make the strategic decisions about what the organisation stands for, who or what it is and why it is there. If we are talking about a one-person business enterprise, these things are typically done implicitly by the owner or entrepreneur. The human factor is right there. As soon as it is contemplated that perhaps one or more other persons may be needed to help build this enterprise, HRM kicks in.

With *people resourcing* we essentially refer to all that needs to be done in order to secure for the organisation the right work services and people with the required work potential and talent, at the right place and at the right time to help ensure organisational success. This will include thinking strategically about the overall needs of the organisation over the long term in respect of its work and concomitant working people. The total 'work and people system' of the organisation (also referred to as the HR architecture) must be considered – what it should look like and entail, and so forth: how the *work* will be *organised* (including all the work in relation to managing the people), what work will be outsourced and what will constitute the core workforce of the organisation, and what the general approach would be towards managing employees as well as other working people. This should flow over into strategic and at times more operational *workforce planning*, where the focus is more on what types of jobs we have and what numbers of what kinds of working people will be needed if the organisation is to achieve its goals and mission. People resourcing naturally also includes the activities associated with actually finding and engaging the relevant people, such as the *recruitment*, *selection* and *appointment* of new employees. This may, however, also include entering into contracts with other organisations that provide specialised services using their own staff, such as outsourcing security work or cleaning services, or making use of the labour provided by temporary employment services firms.

People who have been made part of the organisation and its work in some or other way should then be afforded the opportunities to contribute to and help make the organisation more successful, which we refer to as *people empowerment and utilisation*. Such people should feel and be empowered to add value in terms of what the organisation has to achieve, and to the quality of their own lives. The *work and organisational environment* should be such that working people can perform well in their work, are *motivated* to be productive, and enjoy what they do. This must therefore include *leadership* that empowers the working people appropriately. Helping people to improve their *work performance* and *develop* their *careers* is just as crucial and in this regard the key is *training and developing* working people. We have to unlock the potential of people and help them live their own dreams. These activities should be aimed at aligning organisational needs with such personal aspirations and potential.

This brings us to that group of HRM activities we refer to as *people care and reward*.

One of the most basic needs relates to *health and safety*, and in the workplace we need to ensure that good care is taken of this. However, aligned with the holistic approach we follow in this book, we believe that more than mere occupational health and safety is at stake. It is part of HRM to ensure we do things to help improve the *general well-being* of our working people. In fact, from a *sustainability* perspective we go further than this – we want to say that organisations should also take into consideration the *well-being* of those *people* and parts of *society* from where we actually source our working people, such as their families and communities. Basic care must surely start with making sure our working people are *paid*, and paid fairly. As explained earlier, in modern-day society one of the reasons people work is to be able to make a living. It is thus of critical importance that we make sure that we *reward* people appropriately in return for the value they add to our organisations. Part of this category of HRM activities is ensuring we develop *healthy relations* with our working people as well as those people and organisations that might act as their *representatives*. This includes *trade unions* in particular. Even when relationships with working people have to cease, we have to do everything we possibly can to make sure that such things are handled in a decent and fair way, and with dignity. We must never forget that the people who formerly worked in and for our organisations can be very powerful in terms of building or destroying such organisations' brand as an employer and place of work. The way in which we *terminate the services of employees* can play a very important role in this.

This leads us to another facet of HRM that we refer to as *talent retention and diffusion*. This is not so much a category of specific activities similar to those introduced thus far. Rather it can be regarded as a culmination of whatever we ultimately do when we manage our human resources appropriately. You will recall that in the first category of people resourcing we referred to securing the right working potential and services which working people might have to offer our organisation. If we do this and we actually get these people to work in and for the organisation, it is essential that we do whatever we can to retain their services. The people who do good work, perform well, are productive and add good value should thus preferably be kept. Generally speaking, if we do well in terms of people empowerment and utilisation and also employee reward and care, the chances are better that we will not lose our highly regarded talent and high-performing working people. There are, however, numerous factors way beyond the organisation's control that may lead to situations where we part company. It may even be specifically decided to bring this about. When this happens we would like to think of it as a process of the organisation actually diffusing back into society human beings who are better groomed and equipped to add value elsewhere compared to before they engaged working with our organisation. We thus send people back into the world who have been empowered to add value, either as working people in and for other organisations in the web of value and supply chains, or perhaps in other capacities (such as owners of their own businesses).

From the foregoing you should already have developed a good grasp of the scope of work covered by the HRM subsystem of organisations. It is quite comprehensive and actually entails more than we have covered thus far in this section. The global world in which we live and work is fast changing, and a lot of variables and forces are at play. Not only do we have to manage human resources within national boundaries, but there are also variables beyond national issues and challenges that HRM has to factor in. Many factors thus interplay with organisations and the people who work in and for them, which makes change in and of organisations inevitable. Moving any organisation from a present to a future, more desirable state requires change dynamics anyhow. The mere fact that organisations are in motion towards future accomplishment means change is taking place all the time. This is similar to what happens to human beings. We are constantly changing – from conception to the completion of the full cycle of life. As we experience and learn more (and this happens all the time even though some may not realise it), we undergo change. HRM without the *change management* ingredient would thus be incomplete and inadequate. We believe that the championing of organisational change is part and parcel of HRM because it is people who bring about change in organisations. In South Africa we are in a particular phase where change and transformation are crucial for our future. That is also why the whole approach of this book is to gear HRM towards infusing holistic thinking and practice into management and organisations, making sustainability and quality of life become central to the dynamics and strive of organisations. Not only should HRM be geared towards adding value to the organisation's efforts to deliver needs-satisfying products/services through high-performing working people (as individuals or as groups), but the aim should also be to add value to the people themselves, and to their quality of life, as well as, more broadly, to society and to our precious planet from an ecological perspective.

From such a holistic perspective we can only expect things to be complex when it comes to HRM. It is, in this context, important that we become more aware of all the variables that play a role in the management of human resources. We now briefly explore some of these variables.

1.5 VARIABLES THAT INTERPLAY WITH HRM: A GLIMPSE OF THE HRM COMPLEXITY ISSUE

When people and organisations come into interaction for work purposes, there are a lot of variables or issues at play. These can have an impact on the actual work performed, on the working people, and on the value added by them, as well as the value derived by them. Figure 1.5 reflects a visual presentation of this complex interaction and some of the variables at play.

We will now very briefly take a look at some of these variables and issues, all of which may contribute to the dynamics of managing human resources in organisations. We start off by looking at two crucial areas, namely the actual nature of the work and the kind of work relationship that may be involved.

1.5.1 The work relationship and the work

All people who perform work in an organisational context have some kind of a relationship with that organisation. Many or perhaps even most form an employment relationship; in other words, an employer–employee relationship. Certain unique rights and duties go along with these types of relationships because they have various dimensions. These include formal (legal) and informal dimensions, individual and collective dimensions, and also economic, social and time-related dimensions. We will go into more detail later in the book. It is very important at this point to be aware, though, that the type of relationship will have an important bearing on the HRM dynamics.

There are different types of employment relationships. Some variables are reflected in the work, and workers are typified, for instance, as casual workers, temporary or fixed-term versus permanent staff, full- or part-time work, probationary employees, and even perhaps people performing some work as part of their studies, such as when universities arrange for work experience as part of work-integrated learning schemes. There are other schemes as well, such as learnerships. Some people may even work in

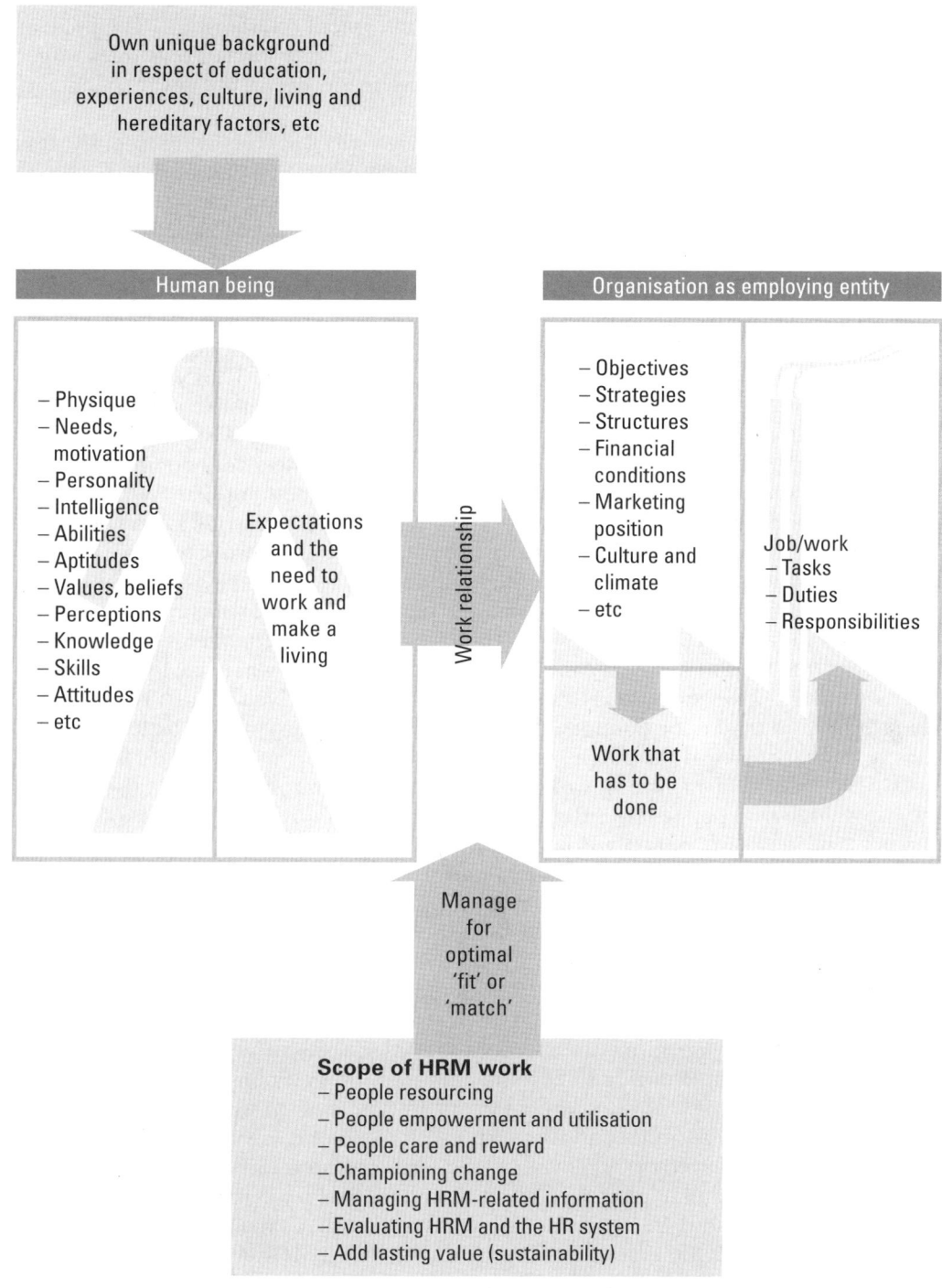

Figure 1.5: The interface: people, organisations and work

and for another organisation as an independent contractor, perhaps as a consultant or as a member of a labour broking firm to whom some of the work may have been outsourced. There are also volunteers.

There are thus different kinds of work relationships. HRM is primarily, but not exclusively, concerned with people working in employment relationships. The issue at hand is how the organisation can best make use of available human resources to get the work done as successfully as possible. Work has, in any event, not always been part of an organisational or employment context.

Work became a kind of a specialised economic activity only relatively recently. It is only since the advent of the industrial society about 200 years ago that work has evolved into a predominantly paid-for activity in an employment and formal organisation context. Work in pre-industrial societies (eg hunting/gathering and agrarian societies) had a different meaning and role primarily related to human needs satisfaction for survival purposes, and mostly within a mere subsistence mindset. As we explain again later, in the era following the Industrial Revolution and with the advent of capitalist-industrialist societies in particular, work became a full-blown economic activity as part of the processes of manufacturing systems and mass production. Thus we have today a society where people work for a variety of reasons, including to make a living.

Work, and what derives from it, thus seems to be playing a significant role in defining who we are in modern-day society. It is, for instance, very common to find people who meet each other for the first time asking something like 'What do you do for a living?'. Likewise, people tend to ask children from a young age what they would like to become when they are grown up. Although people work to make a living, they also tend to do so in order to define and determine what they want out of life. In some sense work has therefore become the medium through which people tend to define who they are. The type of work we do and the type of monetary reward that flows from that tend to have a big impact on what we can buy, where we live, whom we interact with, how we spend our leisure time, and so forth. Even though the extrinsic rewards of work tend to be dominant in our modern-day, (too) materialistically driven society, to varying degrees people also tend to derive intrinsic rewards from their work. The mere fact of having work or a job has become important – also from a socio-psychological perspective. Being out of work is often regarded and experienced as something negative, not only from the rational economic perspective, but also from the point of view of the psychological and moral or ethical dimensions that have come to be associated with work. To work is generally regarded as good – or at least as better than being idle all the time. On the other hand, there have been cases where people would rather not work than perform certain types of work or working for or in a specific organisation. From an HRM perspective we want the work of or in an organisation to be the opposite.

Whenever people work for organisations, all these sorts of aspects of work might be at play. When people decide to become educated for a certain type of career or be trained for a specific type of work, these factors are somehow at stake. When we design a particular job or work role, and when people look for work, or apply for a job, or when they are interviewed or employed, or perhaps dismissed for whatever reasons – it should be understood that much more is at stake than just a job or merely work, or an employment relationship. Because work as such is so central to mankind, the implications and dynamics of work are crucial to people's quality of life. HRM as a set of practices, processes and so on that intervenes with people as working beings in an organisational context becomes so much more meaningful as a field of theory and practice when we think about it in this way. HRM has a direct impact on quality of life and on sustainability. It is quite safe to say that each and every person who might have a choice would prefer to have a better rather than a worse quality of life. Defining what makes a better quality of life is, however, a relative thing because individuals differ in terms of what they want out of life. This brings us to the human nature of working people.

1.5.2 The working people – 'human beings'

Working people are human beings that bring with them into the organisation all the qualities of *homo sapiens*. These include demographic variables such as age, gender, race and ethnic roots, cultural background and language. It goes beyond that, though, to include personal attributes related to personality and certain personality traits, personal values, perceptions, attitudes, needs, interests and preferences, and even something like emotions. Most importantly, these people have certain aptitudes, abilities and competencies. They bring into the organisation certain knowledge, skills, know-how and intelligence, as well as various physical attributes, such as height, weight, and so forth.

Let us briefly take a closer look at what some of these variables or personal attributes are about.

Abilities, aptitudes and attitudes

- An *aptitude* can be said to refer to a person's natural inborn capacity or capability to learn something or to develop a certain level of performance or skill in future.
- *Abilities*, on the other hand, can be taken to refer to innate or learned general traits that enable people actually to do something.
- An *attitude* can be defined as the degree of positive or negative feeling a person has towards a particular object, such as a place, thing, situation or other person.

These kinds of variables are at the very core of the dynamics we encounter when it comes to work and working people. For instance, we want to employ people who have the *ability* to do good work and perform in a superior manner. That is not enough, though, as superior work performance is not guaranteed by having the right knowledge, skills and general know-how. The other key ingredient is *attitude*. People must have a positive attitude towards the work and the organisations and its people because if they do not, there will be a lack of motivation to perform well. In this regard, *aptitude* plays an important role, because people who work in areas for which they have a natural aptitude will generally become high performing faster.

Perceptions and values

- *Perception* refers to those (mainly cognitive and mental) processes that enable us to interpret, give meaning to and understand our internal and external environments.
- *Personal values* can be described as the explicit or implicit conceptions of the desirable held by an individual. Values are concerned with what 'should be' and form the normative standards by which human beings are influenced when choosing between alternatives.

These variables are mostly not espoused, even though they are fundamental to the way people behave. As we will stress again in the next section, communication is vital when it comes to people working together in organisations. Perceptions play a central role in how we interpret information and our work environment. Similarly, the personal values of people guide them in terms of judging what they believe is appropriate and what is not. This will happen in the workplace as well. A prime example may be one's inclination to behave or act ethically. Another one might be the value placed on fairness. As you will learn as you read further, these sort of variables interplay very strongly with HRM dynamics.

Personality, emotions and intelligence

- *Intelligence* generally refers to the individual's mental ability or cognitive capacity to use the intellect, to think, to solve problems, to reason, to learn and to understand.
- *Emotion* is the complex experiencing of feelings, accompanied by some characteristic physiological states, and finds expression in certain behavioural patterns with a particular function. Emotions are characterised by feeling and it is this affective experiencing which gives 'colour' to emotions, for example joy, anger, fear, etc. These feelings can be experienced as pleasant, unpleasant or mixed.
- In a broad sense, *personality* can be taken to refer to the way in which the biological, physical, social, psychological and moral traits of an individual are organised into a whole, and also to the relatively stable set of behavioural patterns which flow from the dynamic interaction between individuals and their environment in a particular situation.

As can be imagined, variables like these make people very complex beings who bring all of these complexities into the workplace. It is no wonder, therefore, that a discipline like psychology exists, and that it has subdisciplinary fields, for example personality psychology and personnel psychology (with entire books on 'work psychology'). All of these variables (and there are others) that belong to the working person as a human being are thus rather complex in themselves and not always easy to understand, let alone define or interpret as to how they may impact work and HRM dynamics. Let us take the last one mentioned above as an example.

The concept *personality*, although often used very loosely, is difficult to define. Various experts have approached it from different theoretical perspectives and one therefore cannot provide a single, definitive description of what it entails. The term is, in fact, often misused. You may well have overheard somebody describing someone else as having 'absolutely no personality' or as having a 'good' or 'nice' personality. These are vague generalisations used to sum people up, often wrongly so. Many view the term 'personality' as an aggregate or sum total of almost all the characteristics or traits peculiar to any individual, thus constituting the individual's identity and unique nature. While some good understanding of different personalities or personality traits, for example, are important and can be helpful in terms of how we go about managing human resources, the purpose and focus of this book is not to go into this in any depth. Rather, it is important to stress that being aware of individual differences and becoming more knowledgeable about them will help to improve HRM.

In a similar vein it can be said that being aware of and becoming more knowledgeable about variables and issues pertaining to organisations as societal entities will also be very important. We now turn to this category of variables.

1.5.3 The organisation

You will no doubt already be well aware that organisations are rather complex. We have already explained that from an open-system point of view, organisations are part of larger systems and in turn have different subsystems that interact. There are numerous variables at play in organisations that add to the dynamics and complex challenges related to the management of human resources. We now take a brief look at some of them.

1.5.3.1 Strategies and management of organisations

The strategies determine the long-term direction of the organisation and this leads directly to the kind of work to be done and the types of people needed. In the case of business organisations, the strategic choices made determine in which industries or sectors they will be operating and competing, and it is well known that certain industries have in common certain human resource dynamics not shared by others. Strategies try to align the organisation with its external environmental dynamics. The variables from outside thus also interplay with management and HRM, including the laws of the country and other socio-political and economic dynamics. We elaborate on these below and in the next two chapters, and also on some of the strategy-related aspects in chapter 4 in particular. For now, a few examples should suffice.

A turnaround strategy (when profits are declining and something needs to be done to rescue the organisation) may mean cost reduction in various areas, including those associated with human resources, which may lead to retrenchments. A decision to grow aggressively by diversifying and entering new markets may mean that different competencies are required, hence different kinds of human resources and perhaps new ways of managing our people. The market dynamics and financial state of firms naturally also interplay directly with HRM, such as when new competitors take away market share, which may lead to lower turnover (a drop in sales), and this may force the scaling down of operations (and perhaps the reduction of staff).

1.5.3.2 Organisational structures

Part of management's task is to organise the work of the organisation. This usually includes some form of division of labour, usually done through structuring work into different positions or work roles as well as different organisational units (for example departments, sections or divisions). This typically may also involve some form of hierarchy, ranging from the most senior managers at top management level to the lowest-level non-managerial employees. There may also be a decision to outsource some work (for example security, food or cafeteria facilities, etc). Various decisions in this regard directly interplay with the work, the working people and the management hereof.

One common example relates to what we often read or hear about, namely the restructuring of organisations. This generally refers to rationalising or changing the structural configurations of organisations and often it includes downsizing. This may lead to doing away with some parts or aspects of the organisation, which may also result in redundancy.

1.5.3.3 Group dynamics

Most people spend the greater part of their time at work working within a group context rather than as individuals. In fact, one of management's major organisational functions is to group tasks and people together. The dynamics underlying the formation, development and functioning of groups form a vast and complex field of study. A group in an organisation refers to a collection of relatively regularly interacting people who perceive themselves as belonging together in some or other sense because of the common objectives they share and because their behaviour can influence each other as well as the achievement of their objectives.

We thus see that group members are per definition interdependent, and their interaction is purposeful. As such they are engaged in specific relationships that require some goal-directed behaviour. Although there are shared objectives, the group members all differ from one another (in accordance with variables such as those mentioned in the previous section) in some respects, bringing about the seeds for interpersonal dynamics in intra-group as well as inter-group contexts. There can, for example, be conflict within as well as between groups. All of these things clearly make an integral part of the management of people at work.

1.5.3.4 Communication

In an organisational context, communication can be described as the processes by which working people transmit and receive information and exchange messages and try to make sense of it. Communication is often referred to as the lifeblood of human relations. How often does one hear of a lack of communication? This means more in terms of quality rather than quantity. In other words, it is often not so much about how much we communicate, but more about how well we do so. When people work together, an appropriate quantity and especially quality of communication is expected. If not, relationships can break down, which may result in counterproductive work.

Many obstacles or barriers can harm the quality of communication, and consequently, HRM. Apart from semantic problems, other factors such as physical distractions (for example noise) and organisational structures that are too bureaucratic may influence communication. There are many more such potential barriers.

Communication in processes and practices like recruitment, selection and managing the working people of and in organisations is absolutely essential.

1.5.3.5 Decision-making dynamics

Decision making is one of the most fundamental management tasks. In organisations it typically refers to the identification and choice of alternatives, usually regarding objectives, priorities and/or courses of action and so forth in order to address issues that somehow relate to achieving some organisational objectives.

For example, managers have to decide which business/industry to be in or which business strategies to follow. Some decisions are more complicated and require more information, experience and knowledge, while others are relatively simple and routine, requiring little information or specialised knowledge. Irrespective, decisions are made by people, and usually in groups. Decision making is therefore exposed to all of the diversity dynamics pertaining to individuals in organisations, as discussed in section 1.5.2. The risk propensity of individual managers can, for example, influence the extent to which decision-making powers are delegated or decentralised to lower levels. This may impact on the sense of empowerment that others experience which in turn may influence things like job satisfaction and productivity levels.

1.5.3.6 Power and politics

Power and politics exist in all organisations.

Power generally refers to the ability to control things or the way things happen. Formal authority is one form of power, which refers to the right to seek or obtain compliance. This is often called legitimate power.

In organisations, therefore, the element of power often relates to the ability of some people to exert control over or influence the behaviour or decisions of others. When people use their power or shrewd ways to influence others or processes in order to achieve that which they prefer (often purely for themselves and sometimes even in conflict with the goals of the organisation), we talk of organisational politics.

People who play 'power and politics' in organisations try to gain control over certain resources and develop alliances with others who are powerful to help them get what they want. Empire building takes place when one or more persons decides to gain more power by increasing their influence and role within the organisation, such as getting greater resource control. So, for example, the head of a specific department may decide to work deliberately towards gaining greater control over aspects such as budgets and other areas of decision making within the organisation by always helping or supporting his or her superiors, inflating work requirements, employing more people and building up the department. In times of financial difficulties this may have various implications – even perhaps retrenchment for those who were employed based on inflated workload needs.

1.5.3.7 Organisational culture

As is the case with so many concepts, there is a lack of consensus among theorists, researchers and practitioners regarding the precise definition of organisational culture. We propose the following one:

> *Organisational culture* can broadly be defined as the shared understanding that exists among the working people of an organization regarding 'the way things work and are done around here'.

It basically refers to a set or system of shared features such as beliefs, values, assumptions, expectations, norms, sentiments, symbols, rituals, and so on. For example, if the belief that the customer is always right is shared by all in a particular retail organisation, and one of the salespeople is overheard quarrelling with an unhappy customer, such a person might perhaps expect some informal reprimand of 'we don't do that sort of thing here!'.

New working people normally gradually learn about an organisation's culture. The role played by the induction process (see also chapter 8) can help in this regard, and it plays a part throughout a person's working relationship with an organisation. In fact, organisational cultures can even lead to some working people feeling that they do not fit in, causing them to resign.

1.5.4 The country – and beyond national boundaries

Organisations and the way the working people are managed will, of course, be influenced by what goes on in the country in which they exist. The state of the economy, the political stability, the relevant laws and so forth can all interplay strongly with HRM dynamics. These aspects are so important that we devote chapters 2 and 3 to them to develop some common perspective of the South African situation and the implications for the way we manage our people in this country. For now it should suffice to mention, for example, that when the ANC government came to power after the first-ever democratic elections in South Africa in 1994, a key to transforming our society was to come up with a completely overhauled labour legislation dispensation. As you will learn, a whole stream of new laws impacting directly (and some less directly) on the way we manage our people (and more broadly, our organisations) was rolled out, and these now still play a major role in terms of HRM dynamics and challenges in our country. South Africa does not exist in isolation, though – no country does.

In today's global world, countries are connected, and organisations and supply chains across different countries are interconnected. All we have to do to appreciate this is to look at the place of manufacturing of products that we buy. Companies often decide to enter international markets and expand in this way. The Shoprite Group is a well-known example (see exhibit 1.2) on the African continent.

EXHIBIT 1.2: Example of a South African organisation that operates in international markets

The Shoprite Group is Africa's largest food retailer, with headquarters in Bellville in the Western Cape, South Africa. It operates 698 retail outlets in South Africa and a further 129 in the rest of Africa and beyond. These include Angola, Botswana, Ghana, Lesotho, Malawi, Mozambique, Namibia, Swaziland, Tanzania, Uganda, Zambia and Zimbabwe. It has also extended its services to the Indian Ocean islands of Madagascar and Mauritius and, most recently, to Nigeria, the world's fifth-largest oil producer. The Group also operates in India, and is continuing its implementation of a strategic expansion programme to maintain its position as the leading food retailer on the African continent.

Source: Extracted and adapted from www.shoprite.co.za

It is not only the outputs (products/services) of organisations that impact across national boundaries, but also the inputs as well as the outcomes (see figure 1.4). It is well known that organisations sometimes make strategic decisions to relocate their manufacturing facilities to countries other than where their headquarters are situated. These decisions are driven, most of the time, by human resource related variables. If organisations set up operations in other countries, they typically draw on those countries' human resources. As such they also provide job opportunities (interplaying with local labour market dynamics) and help play a direct role in that country's economy. Exhibit 1.3 takes exhibit 1.2 a little further, and illustrates the point just made in the case of the Shoprite Group.

EXHIBIT 1.3: Doing business in Africa and beyond – adding value internationally

Shoprite Holdings sees as its primary objective operating its business in a way that will not only be beneficial to the Group in the long term but also to the communities in which it operates and to the individual consumers of whose daily lives it has become such an inseparable part. It provides employment to more than 69 000 people within the vast geographic sweep of its operations, and creates career opportunities across a broad spectrum through extensive training and advancement from within. In recruitment it gives preference to local people, most frequently from disadvantaged communities.

   Through its operations it stimulates growth, and creates employment and career opportunities both within its own business and those of its suppliers, helps small entrepreneurs participate in the economy and strives to correct the social imbalances of the past by investing in the community's aspirations and development. Although as a South African company, this approach applies first and foremost to its operations at home, it adheres to the same business philosophy wherever it trades in Africa and beyond.

Source: Extracted and adapted from www.shoprite.co.za

We must thus realise that as the world increasingly becomes 'a global village', international issues are at play more seriously. This holds particularly true for the management of our organisations and the working people. As a clear recent example we can cite what Mkhabela (2008: 5) reports:

> South African companies operating elsewhere in Africa must draw up a code of conduct for their operations on the continent, Foreign Affairs Director-General, Ayanda Ntsaluba said in an interview ... Ntsaluba's call came as the Human Sciences Research Council (HSRC) said preliminary findings of its research on South African operations revealed a bad picture, particularly regarding labour standards ... the dominant picture was positive, but there were 'a few

elements' ... among the issues the government had advised companies to take into account ... [one of which] was the need to establish partnerships with entities in host countries and to adopt a developmental business approach.

1.5.5 Variables and complexity in human resource management: concluding remarks

As can clearly be understood from the foregoing, there are numerous variables that impact on the dynamics of the work relationship. HRM can thus be viewed as a dynamic interventionary process aimed at integrating, balancing and synchronising a host of variables in order to help make work relationships such that working people are content and productive, and add appropriate value to the organisation and its products and/or services, as well to other organisational outcomes. Our philosophy of HRM is based on the belief that the commitment of working people to perform their work in a superior manner to contribute to an organisation's success is very closely intertwined with the extent to which their own needs and personal objectives will be met through their work relationship with that organisation. HRM is thus aimed at capturing, enhancing and developing human talent and potential to improve the quality of life for organisational success on the one hand, and individual success and happiness of the working people on the other. Appreciating the diversities locked up in people and organisations and the world in which they come together and interact in specific work relationships makes it easier to realise the complexities of the HRM challenge. These complexities can hardly be overestimated and this is also why HRM cannot be left to the human resource specialists alone, but neither can it be left to generalist managers with no specialist assistance.

1.6 HRM REQUIRES MANAGERS AND SPECIALISTS TO ENGAGE

As mentioned before, all managers per definition work with other people to accomplish goals. As such, all managers are involved in HRM. Having said this, especially in larger organisations there often develops the need for the services of specialist human resource practitioners ('HR specialists'). In smaller companies in particular, HRM often remains the sole work of the line of generalist managers. Sometimes, however, the services of certain 'HR specialists' are secured by means of independent contractual arrangements (for example through recruitment agencies and/or labour relations consultants). Irrespective of whether the services of the HR specialists are sourced from outside or inside the organisation, the work has to be done together. In this regard the specialists and the line managers should thus act like partners. Consider, for example, the following:

- When an employee resigns, the manager is normally one of the first to know about this and must consider whether or not to replace this person.
- If it is decided not to abolish the job, somebody else must be found to do it. The manager will be responsible for making the final decision about whom to appoint but he/she might seek some help from HR specialist staff regarding where to look for potentially suitable people, and also how to attract them. He or she might also seek specialist assistance in terms of making a final choice regarding whose work services to secure.
- Should a person be employed, an employment relationship will be established and the specialist HR staff might help with the legal aspects pertaining to the employment contract and letter of appointment. The manager will

usually introduce the new employee to his or her colleagues and working environment.

- The manager, as time goes by, usually not only appraises the progress and performance of the employee, but may also provide some on-the-job training. The HR practitioners might champion the development of performance appraisal systems and give advice where necessary. Similarly, the HR staff may not only help develop the manager's competencies as an on-the-job trainer, but they may be able to advise about or offer alternative training opportunities for the newly appointed employee.

- The HR staff may devise and administer the remuneration and reward system of the organisation, but the manager also usually recommends relevant performance-related pay increases (apart from the general increases for all workers negotiated with trade unions) or bonuses when merit pay for superior work performance is involved.

- The HR staff may be instrumental in setting up career-development systems and processes, but the manager and the employee discuss career prospects, possible future transfers or promotion prospects, and so forth.

- The manager is responsible for dealing with issues related to grievances, poor work performance or disciplinary matters but there might well be need for some assistance and advice from specialist HR staff if such issues become complicated. The managers also often have to engage and communicate with employee representatives (for example shop stewards of the trade unions), and yet often the more large-scale negotiations with trade unions involve both line managers and some specialist HR staff.

- The responsibility for safety and health in the workplace also lies with the manager, who has to ensure that conditions are conducive to the employee's safety and general well-being. At the same time, however, organisations typically employ occupational health and safety specialists to help develop appropriate policies, systems and practices regarding this important aspect at places of work.

From the foregoing examples it should be quite clear that HRM involves line managers as well as specialist HR practitioners. This is the reality, and the reasons why more than one party engaging in this managerial work are to be found in the complexity of the HRM challenge. While we stress this point and hence justify the need for specialist HR practitioners, we emphasise again that this book is based on the premise that HRM is, in the final analysis, the responsibility of all managers. To this end there has to be a partnership between line managers and HR practitioners. We concur with the views of Stone (2005: 5): "Managers manage people and the management of human resources is primarily a line or operating management responsibility. However, the degree to which HRM activities are divided between line or operating managers and the HR manager (and their departments) varies from organisation to organisation."

Deciding on who plays what role in respect of HRM is thus largely a matter of choice at organisational level. The decision whether there should be in-house HR practitioners or whether such specialist services should be outsourced has to be made. If the former, as is the case in most of the larger organisations, their exact role and whether they will be organised into a human resource department or not must also be decided upon. We return to these aspects in chapter 5. For now we just state that, increasingly, should there be in-house HR specialist units and people, the emphasis must be on their ability to really add value.

As mentioned previously, our approach is aligned with this recent trend in the evolution of HRM whereby it is increasingly being recognised as a general management task and responsibility (see, for example, Hornsby & Kuratko (2005); Huselid, Becker & Beatty (2005); Purcell & Hutchinson (2007)). Boxall and Purcell (2008: 4) put it thus: "As an essential organisational process, HRM is an aspect of all management jobs."

HRM is thus an evolving field of theory and practice. In ending off this chapter we now provide a brief evolutionary perspective of the development of this exciting and dynamic field.

1.7 MANAGING WORK AND PEOPLE: A BRIEF EVOLUTIONARY PERSPECTIVE OF HRM

Kaufman (2007: 20) says the following:

> Viewed as a generic activity involving the management of other people's labor in production, human resource management (HRM) goes back to the dawn of human history. The first visible roots of the HRM function as practiced today in modern business organizations appeared in the late nineteenth century more or less contemporaneously in England, France, Germany, and the United States. Japan experienced a broadly similar development a decade or so later.

Few areas of research, teaching or writing have evoked as much semantic debate as in the field to do with the management of people who perform work in a context of enhancing others' interests. Terms or concepts used to describe this field include labour management, employment management, personnel management, personnel administration, manpower management, industrial relations, labour relations, human resource (or resources) management, managing human resources, the strategic managing of human resources and employment relations. It seems this semantic confusion may stem partly from international and historical contextual differences, and we thus now trace some developments from an international-historical perspective.

Firmly into the 21st century, and looking back in time, it seems that not only life in general but working life in particular is significantly different from what it used to be. We can probably quite safely say that in another 50 years or so things will yet again look very different from what they do now. That is just the way life is – things change over time, but as we all know – some also stay the same.

1.7.1 Before and subsequent to the Industrial Revolution

Before the Industrial Revolution most people were engaged in home crafts or agriculture. The Industrial Revolution changed daily life and the world of work dramatically as technological developments led to the establishment of factories that employed people to work. Thus working life was removed from the family or household context.

The origins of personnel or human resource management actually date back to those efforts by employers who over the years tried to devise ways to look after their workers better. For example, Robert Owen (1771–1858), a Scottish textile manufacturer, spent company profits on efforts to improve the living and working conditions of his labour force at New Lanark, Scotland. This included the provision of villages for workers near their places of work, schooling facilities, as well as decent health and sanitation facilities in his cotton mill factories (Beach 1980; Cuming 1989).

In 1794, Albert Gallatin established the first profit-sharing scheme at his glass works factory in Pennsylvania (Cherrington 1983: 15).

1.7.2 The 19th and 20th centuries: from welfare to administration to personnel management – to human resource management

In the first half of the 19th century, numerous factories mushroomed, to the extent that at some stage during that period only about 50% of American workers were engaged in agriculture (Cherrington 1983; Beach 1980).

During the late 19th and early 20th century, three important changes came about: a massive growth in factory-type work; serious efforts to improve the general welfare of factory workers; and scientific management to improve production levels.

Frederick W. Taylor, known as the father of scientific management, started conducting research into scientific techniques to elicit higher output and higher profits (and higher wages) through a differential piece-rate wage incentive system. He propagated using scientific methods to study work and working conditions to identify the best working methods (tools, equipment, machinery and process) and to employ people to fit these unique job requirements. Scientific management protagonists, such as Taylor, the Gilbreths and Henry Grant, thus advocated clearly defined jobs with concomitant organisational structures. Managers' approach was to drive for productivity and to get as much out of the working people as possible, using scientific management principles. Needless to say, workers suffered in many cases.

The welfare phase thus gained momentum in the UK as well as in the US during the 20th century in particular. Specialists came to the fore, and employment and welfare sections or departments were established, staffed with welfare workers and employment managers. The focus was on providing facilities and programmes (related to aspects such as health and recreation) aimed at improving the general welfare of the factory workers. Recruitment and selection assistance was also an important task. This was the birth of the paternalism paradigm that was central to the field of per-sonnel administration and which also dominated the personnel management field in earlier periods. Apart from the welfare-related work and recruitment and selection, the focus of this function was rather administrative and aimed at supporting the workers who were managed along scientific management lines. The Welfare Workers Association was formed in the UK in 1913, and evolved into the UK's Institute of Personnel Management in 1946 (Cherrington 1983; Cuming 1989). By 1915 the first official training programme for these employment managers was launched in the US (Beach 1980: 15).

By this time industrial psychological research had also paved the way for the use of sophisticated selection tests, such as the first large-scale group intelligence tests, the Army Alpha and Beta tests, which were used for the first time in 1917 in the US (Cherrington 1983: 15). Hugo Munsterberg's seminal book, *Psychology and Industrial Efficiency*, was also published in 1913, which arguably laid solid foundations for the fields concerned with applying psychological knowledge to the management of work and people at work.

In a similar spirit, Elton Mayo and some colleagues at Harvard University conducted their well-known 'Hawthorne Studies' at the Western Electric Company in Chicago from 1924 to 1933. Their work on the role of aspects such as lighting, rest pauses and group norms in work performance levels laid the foundation for the 'human relations movement'. This movement emphasised that too impersonal, task-orientated, rational and scientific approaches were of little value in the field of people management. The 'softer' or social aspects of workers as human beings required more attention. These developments marked the beginning of the era of applying behavioural sciences in the workplace. This school of thought propagated that workers were not to be regarded as just other 'factors of production' (like materials, money and natural resources).

During the 1950s and 1960s various behavioural scientists were influential in the evolution of the human relations school of thought. Humanistic psychologists such as Abraham Maslow, Chris Argyris, Douglas McGregor and Frederick Herzberg deserve mentioning. These developments gave momentum to the development of personnel management as a field of theory and practice that required specialists. The concepts *personnel administration* and particularly *personnel management* became more and more widely published and used.

It seems that during this period the focus somehow slipped away from the people management task of line managers as research became more and more specialised, shifting to the specialists and their work – those researching and practising personnel management, the specialists who performed personnel management as a staff function in organisations. The personnel function and specialists, what their work entailed and how they functioned in these personnel departments seem to have become the central focus for quite a period of time then as a consequence of, as Bakke (1958: 34) explained, their having been 'carved out of management', as quoted earlier in this chapter. In some cases that is still so today, as reflected in the definitions, scope and vocabulary articulated in many HRM textbooks, projecting 'HR' or the 'HR function' as the separate work of the people specialising in the 'personnel' field.

Personnel management as a staff function was largely regarded at the time as a reactive function which had to serve or support other functions within the context of pre-existing organisational strategies and structures. The other functions (such as production and marketing) would keep the personnel department informed of its needs regarding employees, and the latter then had to see to it that, through the use of specialised knowledge, these needs were satisfied by means of recruitment, selection, training, compensation and administrative work.

In the 1960s Miles published an article in the *Harvard Business Review*, explicitly distinguishing between 'human relations' and 'human resources'. Human relations was claimed to emphasise the 'human' aspect, the 'softer' issues of supportive, friendly people management whereby employees' feelings and needs were emphasised. Human resources was claimed to emphasise the potential value of the 'resource' aspect in terms of workers' potential talents, qualities and abilities that could contribute to the business goals of organisations. According to Kaufman (2007), we can actually trace the concept of human resource management to a lecture in the late 1950s by E. Wight Bakke.

More comprehensively, Becker's work, *Human Capital*, probably cemented further foundations for the 'resource' part of human resource management. Frederick Herzberg's *Work and the Nature of Man* in turn made key contributions to the 'softer', 'human' side of the concept and the field. Rensis Likert's work again contributed to the 'harder', 'resource' side, emphasising the quantification of things through the development of the first 'human resource accounting systems'.

By the very late 1970s human resource management as a concept became more widely diffused. Somewhere between the late 1970s and the early 1980s the rechristening of personnel management to human resource management took place in the US. As the second last decade of the 20th century unfolded, increasingly volatile and competitive environments put pressure on organisations, and many innovative HRM practices, geared towards reducing costs and increasing flexibility in these fast-changing environments, came from line and top management rather than from the so-called HR experts (Strauss, in Towers 1992: 27–29). As such the seeds were sown for the next wave, later increasingly commonly referred to as strategic human resource management.

By the 1990s the case was quite clear that the HRM challenge was too complex and too important to leave all of it for the HR departments of organisations. The work of Barney (1991) and others on the resource-based view of the firm probably contributed to paving the way for putting human resources on the radar screen of strategy makers and scholars. The intangible resources (scarce, hard to imitate and so on) of firms that increasingly came to be recognised as key to gaining competitive advantage, brought human resources squarely into the realm of top management interest. A plethora of publications linking strategy and human resources started to appear during the 1990s. A few examples will help illustrate the point: *Strategy and the Human Resource* (Starkey & McKinlay 1993); *Strategic Prospects for HRM* (Tyson 1995); *Strategy and Human Resources* (Greer 1995); *Human Resource Strategy* (Tyson 1995); *Strategic Human Resource Management* (Lundy & Cowling 1996). Most of these were US and UK publications, but linked to the legacies of colonialism and the role of foreign multinational companies operating in numerous other countries, including South Africa and other African countries, we saw a spill-over of these developments and a spread of this trend almost worldwide (even though the take-up varied in terms of speed and scope).

Towards the turn of the century the pressure was mounting for HR specialists to become more concerned with mainstream business and adding value directly to organisational competitiveness – to become business partners, so to speak. At the same time HRM as a line management responsibility increasingly (re)gained prominence. The implications hereof were clearly articulated by one of the US's most prominent scholars in the field at the turn of the century, Dave Ulrich: "When HR professionals add value, however, the distinction between line and staff blurs. HR professionals ... act in ways that complement rather than compete with the roles of line managers. HR professionals ... do more than advise: They actually ... act to get business results" (Ulrich 1998: 17).

1.7.3 HRM in the 21st century: quo vadis?

Whereas most experts would agree that *human resource management* is the concept that has replaced *personnel management*, there is still considerable debate in the Western world regarding what HRM means and entails. To some, HRM is still a rather loosely used concept – simply a more modern or trendy name for what has traditionally been termed 'personnel management'. There are others who argue, quite convincingly, that it is at least partly symbolic of the changing focus and content of this field of theory and practice as it has evolved over time. At the other end of the spectrum, some others still regard HRM as 'anti-industrial relations' and 'anti-union'. While this debate lingers on, things are becoming increasingly complex in a globalised world. The need for 'superior HRM' in this millennium is a non-negotiable challenge across the globe, and also particularly in South Africa and on the Africa continent.

The dawn of the 21st-century knowledge economy and information society, driven by the information technology revolution and concomitant increasing globalisation of the world, is bringing some signs of a new vocabulary entering the field. These include concepts such as 'human performance technology', 'knowledge management', 'knowledge capital', 'knowledge resources', 'knowledge assets', 'workforce management', 'talent management', 'people management', and also 'human capital' management. Willcoxson (2003: 72) argues that we are witnessing a shift in the locus of economic power that is as profound as that which was seen at the time of the Industrial Revolution, and that knowledge has now displaced labour, money and materials "as the key input into an organisation's income-generating process". Whether "labour" has come to be "displaced" is open to debate at the very least and arguably stretching things too far. The world is still filled with factories, mines and so forth, and basic industrial era-type work still abounds. We at least need some healthy scepticism among practising managers and scholars in the field of management broadly, but also particularly among those in HRM. The issue of semantics is less important, though.

Of greater importance as we move further into the 21st century are probably the pressures to make our planet sustainable, the changing competitive landscapes that go along with economic power shifts away from the once-dominant US, and also in particular the shifting profile of the people that will be (and already are) the source from which we will draw our organisations' human resources. As time goes by, organisations will increasingly have to deal with multiple generations in the pool of human resources from where our working people will come. By about 2017 it is conceivable that we could have people from four or even perhaps five different generations working side by side in our organisations, causing all sorts of opportunities as well as challenges (and perhaps problems if not managed properly). Hankin (2005: 48) and Tulgan (2004: 13–15) describe these five workforce generations (as adapted below). As we briefly reflect on them, keep in mind that these are gross generalisations merely meant to identify some shifts in demographic profiles of workforces over time.

The Silent Generation: born 1922 to 1945

The Silent Generation is the most traditional: working fathers, family people, and strong work ethics. They have gone through some really tough times and have seen some negative things in this world, but they have learned to survive. Discipline and authority are important. Having worked under command-and-control regimes for so long, they tend to be hard working and loyal workers who play by the rules, favouring established systems and ways of work that have proved to serve them well over many years. They have the most years of experience and are said to be 'wisdom keepers' and natural leaders and mentors (even if they do not hold managerial positions). In South Africa most of what they have known was apartheid. What they like to hear in our workplaces is this message: 'Welcome to our family. Give us your best, and we'll do our best to take good care of you.'

The Baby Boomers: born 1946 to 1964

The Baby Boomers probably now make up the bulk of our labour force. In the West in particular they took the steadily increasing affluence that their parents created and were enjoying after World War II and ran with it. Education became a top priority for the Boomers and for their children, but in South Africa the majority of them were prevented from enjoying proper education or economic prosperity. While family values and ties are most important, in our country these are the people who really fought most of 'the struggle'. They do not fear and tend to take on risk. Most of the women were homemakers while most of the men were the family breadwinners, making for generally strong gender-based role stereotyping. Boomers are inclined to be surrounded by issues from their ageing parents on one side and their adult children on the other, with many facing challenges pertaining to parenting their elderly parents who may be in declining health. They thus face stresses, time demands and money constraints, all of which require organisational support and understanding. They were not too young when the technology revolution dawned and are less 'high-tech' driven generally. Women of this generation led the charge for flexible working time. Boomers increasingly feel the heat and are less keen to keep up with the frenetic pace, having had their fair share of many rounds of 're' issues at work (*re*structuring, *re*-engineering, *re*sizing, *re*trenchment, etc). This is the message they want to hear at work: 'Welcome to the club. We want to put your competence to work for our customers and owners, and we reward you accordingly.'

Generation X: born 1965 to 1976

Generation X is considered a generation raised with a silver spoon and some sense of entitlement. Many have much less political interest than the Baby Boomers and as a result are often viewed as slackers with less involvement in and more pessimistic views about politics and other issues. When they started entering the workforce during the 1980s they were seen to be less loyal and were often labelled as job-hoppers. On the other hand, some Generation Xers are hard-core traditionalists – optimistic and hard working, and still with some narrow-minded belief in gender roles and stereotypes. They tend to try to sidestep rules, and many seem to be impatient for results. They are quite at ease with risk and became the free-agent workforce of our time. The high rate of divorce and increased number of working mothers impacting on the Generation Xers led to them being often characterised by traits of independence, resilience and adaptability. This group formed part of the technology revolution. Many show innovativeness and are open to learning. As adolescents and young adults in South Africa, most saw the end of apartheid coming and they have lived through a lot of change. For the majority of South Africa's people the feeling is that 'this is our time'. Generally they are more adaptable, have travelled more than their predecessors and are naturally more inclined to work better in multicultural settings.

Baby Boom Echo (Generation Y): born 1977 to 2000

The first wave of the Baby Boom Echo, also referred to as 'Gen-Y', is now entering the world of work in large numbers and will become a key force through the first quarter of the 21st century. Some refer to these people as the bedrock of the 'what's-in-it-for-me workforce'. Most have been raised with the idea that they can do anything and as such they are seen as a largely self-confident group, and can be very demanding. Technology is what they have known and 'high-tech' is almost second nature to them. Most have always known about Aids. In South Africa the majority did not really experience the height of apartheid or its effects in the political sphere, and have had the opportunity to vote for their leader/s. They have lived through the change and want rapid improvement for all. Many seem to feel that this is now 'their turn', while others feel they are paying the price for the 'sins' of prior generations. They tend to be global citizens, and are generally very open-minded and at ease with 'multi' things (multicultural, multitasking, multiskilling, etc). It seems like some affinity is developing between the Silent Generation and this generation, which could mean that mentor relationships between a member of the Silent Generation and an Echo could work well.

Millennium Generation: born since 2000

Some (like Marston 2007) do not distinguish between Gen-Y and those born since 2000, while most others do. Those who do, say that all the people from this group are the babies born since the turn of the 21st century and as such this is a distinct generation. We are not so sure what their mindset will be as we are forming these as we go. Historical, political and entertainment events will influence them in major ways. These people will enter our organisations in about a decade's time. According to Hankin (2005), the Millennials who will enter the workplace will be even more comfortable with diversity. In South Africa we can only hope that they will be the group of people who will only know a 'normal' society free of any form of prejudice. Whether that will be the case is up to us, though, and that is part of our HRM challenge.

As we all have to work together to help unfold this millennium to make it a better time for all who work and live in our country, we need to be proactive in adding value in multidimensional ways. While the semantics or jargon of the field may remain an area for debate, it is much more important that we tackle the real and substantial issues, such as managing diversity and social inclusiveness challenges. While 'fads' and the 'fashionable jargon of the day' may come and go, the substance of our actions and practices will be the test of whether we have risen to the challenges of our time. Globalisation is a mighty force and no country can ignore it. It brings with it a complex array of challenges, including forces that drive the need to be competitive and capitalise on diversity. In Africa in particular, we are faced with human resource related challenges of gigantic nature that include the need to become more competitive and socio-economically inclusive, and to embrace diversity, something we will only be able to achieve if we develop and empower *all* our people. As will be shown in the next two chapters, here in South Africa we face some peculiar challenges that relate directly to the lack of equity and the dire need to develop a more inclusive society.

This millennium is only in its infancy and as we strive towards making this the century of the Africa Renaissance, the management of our human resources will no doubt be one of our most crucial challenges. This holds at all levels. This is the case simply because people are at the core of life on our continent and our planet. While Africa has been referred to as 'the hopeless continent', we also know that as a world we have come at a crucial junction. Much of what we can achieve in the years and decades ahead will determine the sustainability of our country, our continent and indeed of planet Earth. The field revolving around the management of people who have to work in and for organisations will continue to evolve, but it has now become widely recognised that this very field must hold the key to our future.

This time the pressure is really on to make a significant and lasting difference. What we call this field is less important than what we do and how we do it. This book is intended to make some contribution to some of the challenges we face regarding how we manage our people and our organisations – not only in South Africa and Africa, but also in other parts of the world. In the last chapter we return to some 'futuristic' perspectives. For now, let us take a glimpse of what we can expect in the rest of the book.

1.8 AN OUTLINE OF THIS BOOK

We started off in this chapter by introducing you to HRM generally. The next two chapters are much more uniquely South African, while making the connections with our continent. Chapter 2 gives an overview of the broader South African context in which we manage the human resources of and in our organisations. In chapter 3 we zoom in on the the need to conform with the transformational legislative framework that governs HRM in South Africa – and specifically on what has arguably become the key transformational challenge of South Africa during this first decade of the 21st century, namely the empowerment of our people. In chapters 4, 5 and 6, we cover aspects of HRM from strategic and planning angles. Chapters 7 and 8 cover the challenge to find, attract and secure the talent and services of working people.

Chapters 9 to 14 have to do with how we can go about empowering and optimally utilising our working people through stimulating their motivation through leadership and enhancing their work performance and their careers, and in particular also through human resource development. Chapters 15 to 17 revolve around what we can do to care for and enhance the general well-being and quality of life of our working people and communities. Because social justice is so central to HRM, and labour relations (especially trade unions) play such an important role in South African organisations and in our society generally, we devote chapters 18, 19 and 20 to themes relating to labour and employee relations. The final chapters of this book are devoted to some contemporary issues and challenges that somehow urge us to push the boundaries of HRM as a field of theory and practice.

SELF-EVALUATION QUESTIONS

1 'Organisations are central to HRM.' Argue why you agree/disagree with this statement, and provide a brief explanation of what organisations are and why they exist.
2 'HRM stands separately from management, even though there used to be some distant relationship between these two fields of theory and practice.' Do you agree or disagree? Why? Use an open system, supply chain perspective to develop your argument.
3 'HRM has nothing to do with "sustainability".' Analyse and critically discuss.
4 Outline the scope and process of HRM.
5 'HRM is the domain of the specialist, because human beings are so complex.' Analyse and critically comment on this statement.
6 'Work as we know it today, in an organisational context and as a socio-economic activity, is central to HRM.' Argue whether this is correct or not.
7 Name and briefly explain variables that might interplay with the management of working people.
8 Summarise how HRM has evolved over time.

2 SOUTH AFRICAN HUMAN RESOURCE MANAGEMENT IN CONTEXT

LEARNING OUTCOMES

After studying this chapter, you should be able to:

- demonstrate a clear grasp of the historical development of HRM in South Africa across seven phases;
- engage in meaningful dialogue about aspects of South Africa's contemporary socio-political economy, relating these to the international context and Africa particularly, and indicating how these contextual dynamics might generally interplay with HRM in our country; and
- discuss issues pertaining to South Africa's fraternity of human resource practitioners.

2.1 INTRODUCTION

In chapter 1 we laid the foundations to help you grasp what HRM is about. This book, however, is about HRM in South Africa. As we have explained before, it is important to take into consideration the context within which we manage the work and people doing it, as also emphasised by Paauwe and Boselie (2007). You now know that our focus is on the context of formal organisations, particularly on such organisations in South Africa.

This chapter is thus intended to introduce you to the South African context of HRM. As you will see, we refer to the broader context of Africa because South Africa is part of this continent and, may we add, a most significant part.

We start off with an overview of the historical development of HRM in South Africa. This is followed by a section on South Africa's socio-political and economic situation. This chapter ends with information of relevance to those who may be interested in becoming specialist human resource practitioners in South Africa.

2.2 SOUTH AFRICAN HUMAN RESOURCE MANAGEMENT IN HISTORICAL CONTEXT: SYNOPTIC REFLECTIONS

Any textbook on South African HRM would be incomplete without some reflection on how this field has evolved over time in our country. The risk in trying to address this theme relates to such aspects as scope and depth of coverage, as well as the lens through which historical aspects are viewed. While being aware of these challenges, we cannot say that we have been able to overcome all of them. However, we at least provide a historical contextual picture, something lacking in other South African HRM textbooks.

2.2.1 The world of work in pre-industrial South Africa

South Africa was mainly an agrarian society prior to the discovery of diamonds in 1867 and gold in 1872, and most of the country's inhabitants were engaged in household and agrarian activities. The San people, probably the first inhabitants of South Africa, were, for example, highly competent hunters. The Khoikhoi, who lived at the Cape when the first Europeans came ashore in 1488, were nomadic herdsmen and also proficient hunters. These indigenous peoples bartered their cattle in exchange for the copper, beads, iron and tobacco offered by the early European visitors. Later, some of the Khoikhoi became the servants and slaves of the Dutch settlers.

As more and more immigrants settled at the Cape after Jan van Riebeeck arrived in 1652 to set up a refreshment post, trade between these groups increased. The Khoikhoi provided fresh vegetables and fruit. More people were required to help to build the growing settlement (colony). Many of the passing crewmen stayed on, and the first Cape community thus came to include skilled people like millers, bakers and blacksmiths.

Because the settlers needed more and more help with work, and the Khoikhoi people were reluctant to work for them, Van Riebeeck, who was well acquainted with the slave trade in the East, arranged for the first shipment of slaves from Angola in 1658. Gradually, more slaves were imported from places like West Africa, the East, Madagascar and Mozambique. They worked hard to maintain gardens and buildings, chopping trees and working on farms for six days a week, without pay. Working conditions were poor and these people were often punished, for example by taking away their tobacco rations, if they did not perform or behave as required. In this way the Cape Colony joined in the East African slave trade.

Finnemore and Van der Merwe (1992: 17) state that "by the end of the 18th century slavery had become an integral part of the Cape Colony. The nomadic Boer farmers carried these ideas into the interior, where manual labour was expected to be done by blacks who rendered their services to the farmer in return for squatting rights". The basic relationship was thus mainly one of slavery – of master and servant. Slaves, as the property of whoever bought them at auctions, had to obey their masters and work hard without obtaining much in return. Slavery was eventually officially abolished in 1834 (Nel & Van Rooyen 1993: 54), and the first real formal regulation of some form of individual employment relationship came into being with the Masters and Servants Act of 1841.

Later the Masters and Servants Act 15 of 1856 repealed the Act of 1841 and increased the strict legalistic and paternalistic nature of 'worker management' in South Africa. Servants were subjected to a host of rules and Acts dealing with aspects such as failure to commence work on an agreed date, intoxication, disobedience, unauthorised absence from work, substandard work performance, negligence and the use of abusive language. In terms of Act 15 of 1856, these offences were punishable by imprisonment with or without hard labour for a period of not more than one month (Nel & Van Rooyen 1993: 54). The 'personnel', or rather servants, were thus managed in a very strict, inhumane way without any real concern about their protection or well-being.

2.2.2 People and work in the period following the South African 'industrial revolution'

The discovery of diamonds and gold brought about South Africa's own industrial revolution in the late 1860s and 1870s, which changed life and the world of work in our country.

Mining- and engineering-related skills to mine diamonds and gold were in great demand. Other industries, such as building, engineering and the railways, developed around the mining industry. The supply of the required competencies came from mainly the UK (and hence there was the influx of the British settlers) and other European countries. These highly skilled people were paid well because of the great demand for their services and know-how. The local inhabitants were used for the less-skilled tasks in these industries. In this way there was a movement away from traditional, mainly agrarian and household activities as people entered into formal employment relationships with the growing number of industrial types of organisations.

During December 1881, the first trade union was established in South Africa, namely the Amalgamated Society of Carpenters and Joiners of Great Britain. Membership was limited exclusively to the British skilled workers (excluding blacks as well as non-English-speaking whites), preventing others from entering these skilled jobs. Mechanisation increased as mining owners broke down the many skilled jobs into smaller, simpler units in order to be able to employ cheaper, unskilled or semi-skilled labour to do this work at lower costs. This was resisted by the trade union movement. Strict control was thus very much the watchword of people management during these times, and rules and regulations on the mines were extensive.

A regulation which required miners who came off duty to be searched and stripped led to the first official strike in South Africa, which took place on the Kimberley diamond fields in 1884. In 1897 white miners went on strike when attempts were made to lower their wages in line with those of black mine workers. The late 1800s and early 1900s were therefore characterised by the legalistic management of people, strict control and a lack of flexibility, with little concern for the workers' needs and their long work hours. All of these circumstances resulted in increased unionisation and spiralling levels of conflict in the world of work and people management in our country. There were seven strikes recorded between 1904 and 1908 in South Africa (Nel & Van Rooyen 1993: 57), and "during the period of 1915 to 1917, there was a fourfold increase in worker representation through trade unions" (Nel 1993: 59). Trade unions thus played a prominent role in sensitising management in South Africa to the needs of workers. Most of the dissatisfaction on the mines can also be traced back to the strong racial undertones characterising people management practices at the time.

As secondary industries (mainly manufacturing) grew along with the expanding mining industry, and in line with 'scientific management' thinking, mass production increased and the need arose for predominantly semi-skilled workers in industries such as furniture, clothing and shoe manufacturing. Many white females and black males were prepared to do this type of work for lower wages than those paid to skilled labourers. Whereas whites in the mining industry were largely to be found in supervisory positions, there was a greater mix of race groups on the shop floors of these manufacturing organisations (Finnemore & Van der Merwe 1992: 22). The spectrum of people who had to be managed throughout industrialised South Africa was thus basically multiracial and multicultural (due to the presence, for example, of former slaves and indentured labourers of Asiatic and Chinese origin) and not limited only to males. Although there were efforts during the late 1920s and in 1930 to establish a culture of non-racialism in South African industrial relations (for example the multiracial conference of 1930, which resulted in the establishment of the South African Trades and Labour Council which called unsuccessfully for the inclusion of blacks under the Industrial Conciliation Act) (Finnemore & Van der Merwe 1992: 22), race continued to play a dominant role in all people-management issues in South Africa. Various labour-related Acts made sure of this. For example, in terms of the

Industrial Conciliation Act 11 of 1924, later repealed by Act 36 of 1937, blacks were excluded from the definition of 'employee'.

Partly due to the high cost of industrial action and the rise in trade unionism in South Africa, awareness of the necessity for greater sensitivity towards the needs, welfare and rights of employees gradually increased during the first three to four decades of the 20th century. The Industrial Conciliation Act 36 of 1937 and the Wage Act 44 of 1937 can, for example, be viewed partly as attempts by government to provide, among others, for the welfare and rights of certain groups of workers and to remove the need to belong to trade unions (Nel & Van Rooyen 1993: 62). Although union membership figures generally kept on growing (black workers, for example, organised and went on to form the Council for Non-European Trade Unions in 1941, claiming 158 000 individual members and 119 union members in 1945), managers gradually began to realise that people are not the same as other production factors and cannot simply be treated and controlled like 'extensions of the machine'. In South Africa, as in other parts of the world, it became clear that people as employees needed some form of special treatment.

2.2.3 Isobel White and the advent of personnel management in South Africa[1]

South Africa was indeed fortunate that Isobel White, the wife of a professor appointed as chair of classics at Rhodes University College in Grahamstown in 1938, accompanied her husband to settle in South Africa. Isobel White can be regarded as 'the mother of South African personnel management'.

Towards the end of 1940, Mrs White gave her first six lectures at Rhodes University College, at that time a residential college of the University of South Africa. As an industrial psychologist holding an MA degree from St Andrew's University, she began to conduct research in the personnel field during the 1940s, published extensively and addressed various meetings in order to propagate and publicise the need for 'welfare officers' in larger factories in South Africa. In October 1941 she addressed a special joint meeting in Port Elizabeth of the South African Institute of the Boot and Shoe Industry, and the Port Elizabeth (Shoe Trade and Training Industry) Managers and Foremen's Association, on 'human problems of management'. She emphasised, for example, the need for a new attitude towards labour, the training and follow-up of new employees, the need for cooperation between management and non-management staff, and the importance maintaining employee health, proper nutrition and good working conditions for the working people.[2]

In recognition of her pioneering work in South Africa, Isobel White was elected to the Fellowship of the Institute of Personnel Management of Great Britain (then called the Institute of Labour Management) in 1943. She went on to establish a Factory Welfare Board in Port Elizabeth in 1944, working towards the improvement of the general environment of factory workers. She also worked on aptitude tests and recruitment methods during that time. She relentlessly tried to sensitise management for the need to have welfare workers and personnel officers as support staff for workers.

Mrs White felt that the time was right to work more formally towards the establishment of an official personnel management training course at tertiary level. In this regard she realised that South Africa had its own unique situation and that a course in personnel management in South Africa had to have its own character. In 1944/1945 she wrote on this subject, as depicted in exhibit 2.1 (White 1944–45: 144).

EXHIBIT 2.1: Early comments on the industrial population in South Africa

"There are many more problems involved in planning a course of personnel management training in this country than there are in Great Britain due to the character of the industrial population and the attitude to work of the people as a whole. During the agricultural depression of 1932 there was a decided drift of the poorer and less successful European farmers and their families to the towns, and these began to drift into industry. They are the "poor white" type and have come into both skilled and semi-skilled jobs in industry. On the whole they are Afrikaans speaking and there is no long tradition of industrial background, so that the pride in craftsmanship has to be built up. Many foremen are still overseas men.

Alongside the white industrial workers, but segregated from them, there are the coloured girls who are often employed on similar types of work machining in the footwear and clothing industries, biscuit packing, sweet wrapping, etc. Coloured girls are employed a great deal in factories in the Cape, but not nearly so much in factories in the Eastern Province and on the Reef owing to the population distribution. In Natal many Indian boys and men are employed in industry, where in Great Britain we would use girls and women. African native men are used for packing, factory sweeping, etc. This all adds to the problem of the personnel officer as he cannot, by law, mix these different races in the factory. Messrooms, cloakrooms and lavatories all have to be quadrupled, different exits and clocking arrangements have to be provided. The personnel officer must be familiar also with the racial background of the various groups and with their taboos, as well as be fluent in Afrikaans."

Mrs White strongly advocated the introduction of an obligatory scheme of welfare supervision, and in January 1944 she instituted a special postgraduate Diploma in Personnel Welfare and Management at Rhodes University College. Recognition for this diploma was obtained from the Institute of Labour Management in Great Britain. At the end of 1944, the first two graduates qualified for this diploma and went into industry.

As more and more of these personnel specialists worked in factories throughout South Africa, it was felt necessary to establish some forum for interaction among them. Through Mrs White's work, a local branch of the Institute of Personnel Management (UK) was formed in Port Elizabeth in 1945, with others following later in Johannesburg, Cape Town and Durban.

The foregoing shows that early personnel management in South Africa had quite a strong welfare orientation or focus, as well as an approach to hand these concerns over to specialist staff.

By 1955 there were signs of a gradual shift from a 'welfare' orientation to 'human relations'. Extracts from Isobel White's address delivered to a one-day conference of the Port Elizabeth branch of the SA Institute of Personnel Management, on Tuesday, 9 August 1955 (the first conference of this kind in South Africa), serve to illustrate this shift in thinking (White 1955: 1–2). (See exhibit 2.2.)

As early as 1955, personnel management in South Africa thus started to focus on issues beyond 'welfare'. In the same address, for example, White refers to the importance of training all supervisors of people in "the understanding of human beings and on leadership". The role of line managers was thus already acknowledged then. Other aspects that featured strongly include wage incentives, merit-rating schemes, selection and training of supervisors, motivation of people, attending to morale problems and grievance handling. The human relations movement was thus also propagated in South Africa at that stage. White (1955: 4–6), for example, stated that the

> worker is a human being who is also a member of a team … It is now clear that the most important single factor in determining output is the emotional attitude

EXHIBIT 2.2: Isobel White's address to IPM in 1955

"In the past the emphasis has been placed on the Welfare aspects, on the housing of the worker, on establishing standards of good cloakrooms and their equipment, washing facilities and good general working conditions. Attention was given to the provision of adequate lighting, protective clothing, rest pauses, and canteen facilities. The personnel manager in earlier days was very much concerned with recreation, social clubs, arranging holiday camps and other activities concerned with the maintenance of health. Students in training were taught the importance of these welfare aspects, were encouraged to undertake research in them. They were taught how to educate and convince employers on the need for expenditure on these activities in order to get a more efficient and contented staff. Now it is true that many of these "welfare activities" are admirable in themselves, but they dealt exclusively with the individual worker in relation to his environment, not with the individual in relation to the group whether co-workers, supervisors or management. Much of the work included in this category has now been covered in our factory legislation and we take these standards for granted ... Nothing will illustrate the great change in emphasis of which I have spoken more than the successive changes of name which have occurred since the foundation of the Institute in 1909 from Institute of Welfare Workers to Institute of Labour Management and finally to its present title. Today we have moved away from the conception of the factory as a kind of hygienic cowshed where the cows, if given every physical condition that is conducive to content will produce an ever-increasing volume of milk, to one where we realise that we are employing human beings who react in different ways not only to each other but to those who are leading them. The Personnel Manager has, therefore, become much more concerned not so much with the battle for staff comfort ... but with the human relations side of this job. The function of the Personnel Manager thus becomes:

- Recruitment
- Employment
- Incentives
- Morale"

Source: White, IHB (1955)

of the worker towards his work and his workmates ... The main problem is how to apply the carrot and stick theory when jobs are open to choice ... The modern manager, therefore, is not so concerned with machines and materials, but with handling people. The need for social skills is a further reason for the interest shown in problems of motivation and morale today ...

Meanwhile the National Party came to power in 1948, and the apartheid policy had direct implications for South African organisations and the people working for and in them. Various pieces of legislation were enacted to ensure an 'apartheid system of people management' in South African organisations. This system represented an embodiment of the macro-political thinking of white Afrikaner rulers of the time, as expressed in the Senate by Dr HF Verwoerd in 1954 (Cunningham et al 1990: 2.11):

Natives will be taught from childhood to realise that equality with Europeans is not for them ... What is the use of teaching a Bantu child mathematics when it cannot use it in practice? ... That is absurd ... Education must train people in accordance with their opportunities in life ... the opportunities are ... manual labour.

Separate labour-related legislation was thus enacted for blacks in South Africa, such as the Black Labour (Settlement of Disputes) Act 48 of 1953. The foundations were thus cemented at the time for South African 'personnel management' to be developed around racial discrimination. Interest in the personnel field grew quite rapidly in South Africa during the 1940s and 1950s. The Johannesburg branch of the Institute of Personnel Management, for example, expanded so fast that it was registered as the South African Institute of Personnel Management in 1959.

2.2.4 Antecedents to the 'labour relations' era

Personnel management as a field of study, research and practice in South Africa had already become relatively well established by the time South Africa attained Republic status. On 20 October 1964, all provincial units of the Institute of Personnel Management joined forces to form a single national body, retaining the name South African Institute of Personnel Management.

The focus was the people who specialised in this field. Estimates from early research (Langenhoven & Verster 1969) indicate that by 1964 South African organisations probably had a ratio of 'personnel' staff to total number of employees of 0,97:100. Research (Langenhoven & Verster 1969; Marx 1969) indicated that at the time the majority of organisations did not have separate personnel departments and that the emphasis in 'personnel work' was on administrative or clerical, routine type of work, and also on paternalistic, welfare-related activities. Most of the people performing work in the personnel field at the time did not have formal qualifications but of those who did, most were graduates in the social sciences.

Most importantly, by the end of the 1960s, with the majority of workers being black, it became increasingly clear that change was inevitable regarding the ways in which working people were managed in South African organisations. While most of the personnel specialists were white, the workforces of organisations were predominantly black, especially the unskilled and lower-skilled sectors. The realisation was dawning that African workers especially had been suppressed and too strictly controlled for far too long, particularly by means of legal restrictions in keeping with the preceding two decades of apartheid rule. This realisation came along with the growth in unionisation of our workforces of the time. As Friedman (1987: 33) states: "None of the African union movements before the 1970s endured because none could turn worker support into a permanent source of power ... By the 1970s new pressures were building which forced those in power to concede that they could no longer simply resist unionism: by then a new generation of unions was beginning to grow."

The period from 1969 to 1979 saw a significant growth in the 'collectivism' of black workers. In the year 1973 we had the greatest outbreak of strikes in the country since World War II. Friedman (1987: 40) states that "between 1965 and 1971, less than 23 000 African workers had struck. In the first three months of 1973, 61 000 stopped work. By the end of the year, the figure had grown to 90 000 and employers had lost 229 000 shifts".

The strikes stressed the fact that the system and approach to the management of black workers in South African organisations was totally deficient and that too little proper interaction was taking place between them and management (Nel & Van Rooyen 1993: 68). Labour legislation was reviewed, and the Black Labour Relations Regulation Amendment Act 70 of 1973 followed as a result. Liaison committees were increasingly established in South African workplaces not only to try to improve communication with black workers, but also to reinforce paternalistic personnel management, as in most cases these structures were set up by employers who decided how they were to operate (Friedman 1987: 56).

In July 1973 the Institute of Personnel Management (Southern Africa) (having changed its name from the South African Institute of Personnel Management on

2 February of the same year) published the first edition of *People & Profits*. In this edition, an article appeared about black advancement efforts by the Anglo American Corporation (*People & Profits* 1973: 9–12). This testified to an awareness that changes to our system of managing the working people of South Africa were seriously needed. Pressures were mounting to make improvements, such as to train black workers and enhance their career opportunities, to engage them meaningfully in the workplace and to improve welfare generally.

By 1975, Langenhoven came up with an early South African definition (Langenhoven 1975: 7) of the field: "Personnel management is one of the responsibilities of management and the full-time function of personnel specialists in regard to the human resources of the organisation to develop, apply and manage a complete network of interdependent processes and systems with a view to achieving the organisation's and its people's objectives, with due consideration to the concepts, principles and techniques of the behavioural sciences and the practical requirements of the situation."

As can be seen, this definition purported personnel management to be largely the work of the 'specialists'. It also underplayed the collective dimension of trade unions – despite the fact that organised labour was becoming an increasingly powerful force in our country.

A wave of serious strikes on the Witwatersrand in 1976 again pointed to the inadequacy of our country's labour relations dispensation. Professor Nic Wiehahn of the University of South Africa was appointed as adviser to the then Minister of Labour, Fanie Botha. In May 1977 he was appointed chairman of a commission of inquiry into South African labour legislation. Following the publication of the White Paper on Part 1 of the Wiehahn Commission's report in 1979, the remainder of the report, and the subsequent changes in South Africa's labour legislation, irreversible changes took place in the context of work and people management in South Africa. This made labour relations very prominent in our country because even though apartheid was still the order of the day in society generally, we were no longer going to have a dual workforce system. Effectively, workplace apartheid had to be dismantled.

Meanwhile the notion of human resources was also heard of from time to time. In 1978, for example, Lombard (after returning from the US) published an article in the *South African Journal of Labour Relations* entitled "Human resources management: A new approach for South Africa" (Lombard 1978: 12–24).

During mid-1978 there were efforts to 'professionalise' personnel work in South Africa (Langenhoven 1978; Whyte 1978), and by 1979 personnel management in our country showed some interesting characteristics, according to Verster (1979). These included that many organisations had separate personnel departments headed by a personnel manager or personnel director, and the ratio of personnel specialists to total staff was about 1,26:100. By that time the three key areas of focus were found to be the upgrading of black workers, employee training and industrial relations.

2.2.5 People management during the last years of the 'old' South Africa: the labour relations phase

The South African government's acceptance of the Wiehahn Commission's recommendations marked the beginning of an era where black employees were no longer to be excluded from the statutory labour machinery of our country. This effectively saw the dawn of a non-apartheid labour dispensation. This also, in many respects, paved the way for the dismantling of apartheid in society at large. Some have argued that the labour arena formed the testing grounds for a post-apartheid society that had to come.

Although collectivism in the form of (predominantly black) trade unionism was already a permanent feature in South Africa by 1980, the Wiehahn developments gave further impetus to this aspect of people management. Labour or industrial relations hence occupied centre stage throughout the 1980s and into the 1990s.

Trade union membership figures increased throughout the 1980s, and along with union organising efforts came the signs of increasing adversarialism in the relationships between (especially black) employees and their trade unions on the one side, and employers (and mostly white managers) on the other. The unions displayed a great deal of militancy, and industrial action became a frequent challenge to be managed in our organisations. Whereas for the ten-year period 1970 to 1979 the number of reported strikes stood at 179, the corresponding number for the five-year period 1983 to 1987 was 3 135. Statistics also revealed that South Africa lost more person-days to strike action over the period 1985 to 1990 than during the entire preceding 75 years.

Meanwhile in October 1983, the 'professionalisation' of the personnel field in South Africa was pushed one step further with the inauguration of the South African Board for Personnel Practice (SABPP). In June 1983 it was reported *(IPM Manpower Journal* 1983: 4–5) that "[t]he Registrar for the Board, Mr Wilhelm Crous, said that he was 'overwhelmed' by the response ... the Board was now 'truly launched', and will play a 'meaningful role' in South Africa's fields of personnel, training and industrial relations".

Meanwhile organised labour gained prominence and the Congress of South African Trade Unions (Cosatu) was born on 30 November 1985. It had an initial membership of 33 trade unions and since its inception it had been instrumental in the transformation of South African society. During the 1980s, much of South Africa's organised labour unrest was socio-politically linked. The majority of South Africa's people were disenfranchised politically, and the trade unions and labour relations became the only legitimate platform to air the views of millions of South Africans. People management in South African organisations thus became very politicised during the 1980s. Strike action peaked in 1987, with 1 148 recorded strikes and 5 825 231 person-days lost. Labour relations, and in particular organised industrial conflict and strike management, thus became prominent features of the people management scene in South African organisations.

The importance of people to the success (or failure) of South African organisations became increasingly apparent and with this came an enhanced role played by the personnel and labour relations specialists of organisations. Hall (1985: 6), for instance, found that by the mid-1980s most people management-related issues had been transferred to the personnel and industrial relations sections of organisations. Hill (1987: 6–9) proposed the adoption of a "strategic approach to human resources management" by South African organisations and, also in 1987, the first local comprehensive academic textbook on the personnel field was published. In this publication the authors held that, due to the rapid developments in industrial relations in South Africa over the preceding decade, employers had been compelled to "resort to the employment of industrial relations specialists to cope with the new demands ...", and that "... the task of the industrial relations manager may come to be as important as that of the human resource manager" (Gerber, Nel & Van Dyk 1987: 315–316). Industrial or labour relations thus became a distinct and extremely important aspect of organisations and management during the 1980s – and it almost developed as something akin to, or even perhaps apart from, human resource management.

By the end of the 1980s the South African economy was in recession due to, inter alia, political instability, disinvestment and sanctions imposed by overseas countries, and rising labour unit costs (lower labour productivity and higher wages). Poor economic growth had resulted in large-scale unemployment, and job creation had become one of the major challenges. Against the background of the gloomy economic situation, the socio-economic backlogs suffered by the majority of black South Africans were increasingly accentuated. South Africa was in the midst of political and socio-economic turmoil – a situation felt by virtually every employer and employee.

On 2 February 1990, South Africa's State President, FW de Klerk, announced the government's intention of trying to resolve South Africa's socio-political problems through negotiations with all stakeholders. A number of organisations (such as the African National Congress (ANC), the South African Communist Party (SACP), and the Pan Africanist Congress (PAC)) were unbanned, and restrictions imposed on various other organisations (including Cosatu) during the latter part of the 1980s were lifted. The stage was set for a major transformation of the country and the idea of a 'new South Africa' and a 'post-apartheid era' echoed throughout the land. This also brought along certain dynamics and challenges that spilled over into the world of work and people management as the people and organisations are intrinsic to and in fact the backbone of society. Some people had extremely high expectations of the future, while others experienced uncertainty and fear.

South African organisations became increasingly aware that they had to exhibit the role of being more socially responsible. In March 1990, Wilhelm Crous, the then executive director of IPM (SA), for instance, stated that as we were resolving political problems, other areas of pressing concern, such as unemployment, housing, education, training and health, had to be addressed (Crous 1990: 3). Consequently, during the early 1990s many of the personnel-related publications dealt with these types of issues. Aspects like conflict, intimidation and violence (spilling over from the community) also became pressing concerns for organisations in the early 1990s. These were 'people issues' and the human resource specialists were thus drawn right into the broader societal challenges at the time. Increasingly it was realised that our challenges were huge and that more cooperation was needed.

Aspects like 'social contracts' at national level and joint decision making at the organisational level became increasingly apparent. From early 1992, representatives of business and labour engaged in bilateral negotiations with the aim of setting up a national, tripartite economic forum. Eventually the National Economic Forum was formally launched on 29 October 1992. In this regard, Botha pointed out that "human resource practitioners have played an important role" (Botha 1992: 7).

Priority areas of people management now included such things as affirmative action, discrimination and white resistance; labour relations (with particular reference to shop-floor relationships and bargaining levels); business literacy; education and training; social responsibility and violence (SPA Consultants 1992: 6–24). In 1994, the Human Sciences Research Council (HSRC) found that managers in South Africa had begun to realise anew that the quality and well-being of the workforces of organisations are key influences on their productivity. This led to an even greater awareness of the importance of 'the human resource function' (in the narrow sense) of organisations and, consequently, to an apparent improvement in its status generally. Human resource practitioners in South Africa were also apparently being expected to participate more and more in the general strategic management of organisations. Some discerned signs that HRM was increasingly devolved from the human resource specialists, to line managers. Many organisations were starting to downsize their in-house human resource departments or functions with more use being made of independent external HR consultants. The HSRC report also emphasised that an enhanced focus on human resource development was required. Many South African organisations were in the process of large-scale change and had been compelled to adapt to a changing environment. It was thus anticipated that organisational change and development would increase in relative prominence in terms of the competence and role of HR specialists, and that labour relations would remain important. Community upliftment and social investment were also predicted to increase in importance, with less emphasis on administrative skills. The ability to conceptualise, resolve problems, negotiate/mediate/facilitate and communicate was to become progressively more important, according to the HSRC. Also, it was predicted that entrepreneurial and business skills as well as strategic thinking abilities of HR specialists were to grow in relative importance.

2.2.6 Democratic South Africa's first decade: transforming the country's HRM landscape

Soon after the 1994 'political miracle', the development of a new labour policy regime for South Africa was kickstarted by the Department of Labour's first five-year Ministerial Programme of Action (1994–1999). A stream of new labour-related laws provided the impetus for a renewed awareness of what the 'people-centred philosophy' of the new government meant for South African organisations.

On 5 May 1995 the National Economic, Development and Labour Council (Nedlac) came into existence through Act 35 of 1994. Nedlac was basically to facilitate the social dialogue between the representatives of the major stakeholders and role players, namely labour, business, government and the 'socially excluded' (such as the unemployed) on all socio-economic and labour matters. In particular, one of Nedlac's functions in terms of the statute was to seek to reach consensus on proposals regarding labour market policy and labour legislation before any of these were introduced through Parliament.

One of the first pieces of labour legislation that went this route was the Labour Relations Act 66 of 1995, which eventually came into operation during November 1996. Other new labour-related statutes that followed included the South African Qualifications Authority Act 58 of 1995, the Basic Conditions of Employment Act 75 of 1997, the Employment Equity Act 55 of 1998, the Skills Development Act 97 of 1998 and the Skills Development Levies Act 9 of 1999. Needless to say, this whole period posed organisations (and consultants) with serious challenges relating to adapting to the new legislation. The legal dimension of the employment relationship thus became of primary concern, again ensuring that the industrial relations (IR) aspect of people management in our country remained at the forefront.

By 1997 the unionisation of South African workers stood at about 3,2 million, but strike activity reached its lowest level since peaking in 1987. Some espoused the view that this signalled a downward spiral related to the collective dimension of people management in the country – but it turned out to have been the proverbial calm before the storm. Strike activity rose sharply in 1998 to the highest level since democracy was achieved in 1994, again still keeping labour relations as a key focus of people management in South Africa. Various commentators ascribed the 1998 jump in industrial action activity to dissatisfaction of millions who felt that even though they had put the ANC in power (Cosatu and its membership base being in alliance with the ANC), they had not yet experienced, at the time, any real improvement in their quality of life. One key contributing factor at the time was related to a lack of growth in work opportunities. Unemployment from 1994 through to 1998 showed a clear overall trend of increasing.

The first cycle (1994–1998) of the Department of Labour's initiatives to reform our labour dispensation was aimed at developing a new policy framework with concomitant institutions (through legislation). The second cycle had to include actually executing the change, alongside further developing the new regime and its institutions. Capacity building of the state apparatus became very important. Implementation thus posed challenges, also specifically relating to labour market dynamics. The unemployment problem our country faced became increasingly pertinent.

Implementing the new regime meant hard work to transform South Africa's landscape for people management. In accordance with the South African Qualifications Authority Act 58 of 1995 for example, the South African Board for Personnel Practice (SABPP) initiated the establishment of a standards generating body (SGB) for the human resources field about mid-way through 1998. A steering committee was established in August 1998 with the task of establishing such an SGB for eventual alignment of HRM qualifications with the National Qualifications Framework (NQF). The SGB for 'human resource management and practices' was eventually formally established as part of NSB 03 (The National Standards Body for Business, Commerce and Management Studies) during 1999. This SGB essentially adopted the definition of HRM from earlier editions of this book, and gave the following, description of HRM as guide to the definition and domain of the 'HRM and practices' subfield:

- all the decisions, strategies, factors, principles, operations, practices, functions, activities and methods related to the management of people as employees in any type of organisation, including SMMEs and virtual organisations;
- all the dimensions related to people in their employment relationships, and all the dynamics that flow from it (including the realisation of the potential of individual employees in terms of their aspirations);
- all activity aimed at adding value to the delivery of goods and services, as well as to the quality of work life of employees, and hence helping to ensure continuous organisational success in transformative environments.

Making the new dispensation work entailed a lot of 'learn as we go'. The second Ministerial Programme of Action of the Department of Labour hence involved a 15-point plan to address specific labour market problems as perceived at the time. The Department (Department of Labour 2004: 11–12) summarised the "key elements of this Fifteen Point Programme" for the period 1999 to 2004 as having encompassed the following:

- the government's commitment to seek an appropriate balance between labour market flexibility, efficiency, and equity through skills development, promotion of employment equity, extension of coverage to vulnerable groups, addressing unintended negative consequences of existing labour market policies, and strengthening social dialogue
- the need for a proper alignment of policies in order to promote economic efficiency, growth and development which can result in employment generation and increased labour absorption, following up on Job Summit resolutions, designing social safety nets and active labour market policies, promoting increased productivity, and monitoring economic developments with respect to their impact of employment and conditions of employment
- restructuring the Department of Labour to enhance its ability to execute its mandate in a manner compatible with the attainment of the Fifteen-Point Programme of Action.

By February 2001 the National Skills Development Strategy was launched and during the period 1999 to 2004 various Sector Education and Training Authorities

(SETAs) were established as part of the drive to enhance skills development in the country. This period also saw the President of the country at the time, Thabo Mbeki, instructing the Department of Labour to review the labour policies in order to be able to address issues and problems. This led to amendments to various aspects of the labour legislation through processes of consultation via Nedlac.

Nedlac also played a key role in facilitating the social partners to cooperate on developing some shared vision for reducing poverty, enhancing job creation and stimulating economic growth (Department of Labour 2004). On 7 June 2003 an historic deal was signed by all the social partners at the conclusion of a growth and development summit (GDS), committing all to seek to address three themes (South Africa 2004: 17):

■ More jobs, better jobs, decent work for all
■ Advancing equity, developing skills, creating economic opportunities for all and extending services
■ Addressing the investment challenge

A fourth theme required the Department of Labour to ensure that the GDS Agreement was to be prominent in the next Ministerial Programme of Action (2004–2009), in order to help ensure its implementation.

As can be gathered, at a more macro level the captains of business and industry, the leaders of trade unions (the workers' representatives) and the government, together with other stakeholders, were re-committing themselves to working together to transform the world of work and people management in the country by the end of our first decade of democracy. At organisational level this obviously posed concomitant challenges of implementing new people-management policies and practices that were aligned with the ongoing change.

2.2.7 Democratic South Africa's second decade: entering a watershed period?

The changing context we faced as we entered the second decade of post-apartheid South Africa in 2004, as perceived by the Department of Labour (2004: 19–20), speaks for itself in exhibit 2.3.

South Africa faced some serious challenges as we entered the country's second decade of democracy. Most of the labour-related challenges (reflected in exhibit 2.3) persisted throughout the first half of this period. The prevailing broader socio-political and economic context of South Africa by 2008, though, provided dynamics and uncertainties that pose some serious challenges to all engaged in the field of managing organisations, work and working people in our country. We elaborate on these in section 2.3 below as well as in chapter 3. For now we just want to stress that the crux is that we have to create a sustainable society and, as the old Chinese proverb says, if we give a man a fish we feed him for the day, but if we can teach him how to fish, we are feeding him for a lifetime. The message from this probably holds the key for our future.

Our challenge revolves largely around empowerment of our people to enable them to develop a sustainable future. We return to this theme in chapter 3, and throughout the book. For now we first ponder our contemporary socio-political and economic situation in a bit more detail.

Firstly, our economy reveals dual characteristics. On the one hand we have an advanced industrialised economy which is well developed, employs people who are skilled, is technologically driven, upholds labour standards, and is globally competitive. Alongside this first economy we have a developing-country economy, which in many cases is structurally disconnected from the first. High levels of income poverty, and limited access to knowledge, technology and markets characterise this second economy. It is also characterised by poor labour standards and informal work relations.

The *second* challenge facing us is structural unemployment, which is possibly the starkest indicator of the welfare challenge facing our society. There are two notable features of the country's unemployment crisis: firstly that the unskilled are simultaneously most likely to be the first to lose their jobs in periods of employment contraction, and least likely to be hired in periods of employment expansion. Secondly, the youth currently constitutes about 70% of the unemployed, giving us a dominant, identifiable cohort within this group of long-term unemployed individuals.

The *third* challenge relates to inequalities and discrepancies in terms of ownership, shareholding and management, which remain dominated by white males. Black people, women and people with disabilities remain marginalised in relation to meaningful and influential participation in the economy.

The *fourth* challenge relates to the changing nature of work. This is evident in the increased propensity among employers to switch from permanent and full-time employment toward atypical forms of employment such as casual labour, part-time employment, temporary and seasonal work. Externalisation in the form of outsourcing and subcontracting is also on the rise as the pressures of greater international competitiveness are felt by domestic firms.

The *fifth* challenge relates to cross-border and domestic migration. The latter refers to the phenomenon whereby (mostly unskilled) people from rural areas migrate to urban areas in search of employment. The former relates to refugees who leave their home countries to settle in South Africa, hoping to find employment.

The *sixth* challenge is that of a shortage of very specific skills required by domestic firms in order to both expand production and increase their global competitiveness. This challenge does not only require that we train less-qualified people to acquire these skills, but also that re-orientation and retraining of those who have qualifications is undertaken.

The *seventh* challenge relates to strengthening our labour market institutions and increasing their capacity to carry out their mandates.

The *eighth* challenge relates to the management of HIV and Aids in the workplace in such a way that workers who are infected and affected are not unfairly discriminated against on the basis of their HIV status. Allied to this is the challenge of preventing Aids from adversely affecting workplace productivity. In addition, the pandemic's deleterious impact in terms of a potential reduction of supply of skilled workers is noted.

The *ninth* challenge relates to ensuring that the labour market has an efficient and effective system of occupational health and safety fully integrated with a system of compensation for occupational injuries and diseases across government. The growth of the informal economy introduces a particular challenge in this regard.

The *tenth* challenge relates to ensuring the development and implementation of effective instruments for constant review of the impact of labour market policies in the economy.

The *eleventh* challenge is that of ensuring that key economic policies of government are in harmony with one another and are mutually reinforcing in promoting growth, reducing unemployment and eradicating poverty.

Source: Slightly adapted extract, Department of Labour (2004: 19–20)

2.3 SOUTH AFRICA'S CONTEMPORARY SOCIO-POLITICAL ECONOMY: SNAPSHOTS IN A GLOBAL CONTEXT

In this section our focus is on the contemporary situation of our country as the context in which we manage working people, work and organisations. The challenges and complexities facing South African organisations cannot be separated from broader international developments. In particular we have to be mindful of developments in Africa. We therefore start off by looking at some international dynamics with an emphasis on Africa before we look at the South African situation as such. In turning to our country specifically, we start off with the 'socio' component of our 'socio-political economy', followed by some 'economic' reflections, and end this section with some brief observations about some of our country's political dynamics.

2.3.1 Africa and beyond: a glimpse of some shifting international competitive landscapes and dynamics

It is generally accepted that the world has experienced multifaceted and revolutionary change over the last three decades or so. From the perspective of world politics and international power relations, an era has dawned where generally the world out there has a rapidly growing appreciation and acceptance of more democratic systems. The oppressive, authoritarian and communistic systems that were common for a long period in the world's history have been making way for democracies. A shift is also taking place from a largely bipolar world order towards a multipolar one.

For many years the US and the Soviet Union, as the two world 'superpowers' with their distinctive systems of free enterprise and state socialism respectively, have taken centre stage in debates over world politics and economics. Instead of this bipolar order we now have a situation where different power blocs are developing – the confederation of major European countries, the European Union, as well as a shift of economic power towards the East Asian bloc. China in a sense almost seems to be becoming the leader of the pack of BRIC countries (Brazil, Russia, India and China) that are coming to the fore as international economic powers.

Simultaneously and integrated herewith, the information communication technology revolution keeps moving ahead at a relentless pace. Information flow and shrinking distance have become crucial variables in transactions between countries and organisations that do business across national boundaries and continents. Technology has helped create a platform for more free trade and for faster-moving economic transactions and systems across the world. Globalisation is thus in full swing as we witness how international trade and the free flow of money, information and even people and their cultures is creating an interconnected, almost integrated, world.

Because of these and other developments – such as the formation of regional and subregional economic trade blocs and concomitant more free trade between nations (further facilitated by developments such as the establishment of the World Trade Organization (WTO)) – it is becoming increasingly difficult for governments to retain control over information and money flows, which impacts negatively on their ability to maintain systems of nation-state sovereignty.

We almost have what some refer to as a 'global village' where internationalisation means new markets and increasingly greater challenges to compete across national boundaries – as organisations and as countries. Companies from almost all countries are setting up operations that include business and work in other countries. Thus South

African organisations now have to compete not only with the providers of products and services from other countries on our local markets, but also with others in markets within other countries. Our business leaders have to decide whether or not they are interested in setting up operations or trading beyond the boundaries of South Africa. These developments interconnect these countries more closely and hence place the working people in any one country in competition with those of others. These dynamics can often create pressures to downgrade wages and working conditions, something also relevant to African organisations (see exhibit 2.4).

EXHIBIT 2.4: The Ramatex saga in Namibia – as seen by Herbert Jauch, 8 April 2005

Over the past few weeks, Ramatex made headlines again as its subsidiary Rhino Garments reportedly plans to retrench Namibian workers due to an apparent lack of orders from its customers in the US.

While the allegations of closure were refuted by Ramatex and the Namibia Food and Allied Workers Union (NAFAU), Ramatex workers in the meantime observed signs of a pending factory closure. To understand why Ramatex is behaving the way it does, why it came (temporarily) to Namibia, it is crucial to look at three interrelated issues:

1 The developments in the global textile industry, especially the end of the WTO's Agreement on Textiles and Clothing (ATC) and the 'Chinese attraction';
2 The global Ramatex company strategy; and
3 The special incentives offered to Ramatex in Namibia.

Global developments

When the international Multi-Fibre Arrangement (which provided for a complicated host of quotas for textile and clothing products) came to an end in 1994, it was followed by the Agreement on Textiles and Clothing (ATC) within the framework of the World Trade Organization (WTO). This agreement paved the way for the gradual phasing out of quotas and other measures aimed at protecting local textile and clothing industries (particularly in the industrialised countries). These quotas came to an end on 31 December 2004 and basically 'freed' global textile companies from shifting production to countries whose quotas were not yet filled. We need to remember that Ramatex essentially came to Namibia to benefit from the provisions of the Africa Growth and Opportunity Act (AGOA), which granted duty-free access to the US market for companies that produce in African countries, 'approved' by the US government. As tariffs on clothing and textile products as well as country quotas are removed, companies like Ramatex have no special incentive to stay in a particular country like Namibia as they will be able to choose their production sites anywhere in the world.

The end of the quotas at the beginning of this year already had severe implications for Africa's textile industry. In Lesotho alone, more than 22 000 textile workers lost their jobs as the global corporations relocated their production. Likewise, Kenya is about to lose 20 000 jobs in the textile industry, and even Asian countries (such as Bangladesh, Sri Lanka and Indonesia) are likely to lose millions of jobs in the clothing and textile sector. This is where China moves to the centre stage.

China has become a main attraction as a production site and potential market for global capital. Already by 2002, 30 million of the world's 43 million workers in export processing zones (EPZs) were employed in China. In that year, China already accounted for over 20% of the world's exports in clothing, and its share is expected to rise to about 50% within a few years. It already supplies 70% of all Japanese and Australian clothing imports.

China offers the full manufacturing chain from the production of cotton to the final products, and is able to meet the demands of the global clothing and sportswear chains. It also offers extremely fast manufacturing and transportation times and cheap electricity, and has reached high levels of productivity. This means that few countries can compete as, during peak times, Chinese workers are forced to work seven days a week and up to 14 hours a day!

>>

«

This is a classic example of the race to the bottom as far as labour and environmental standards are concerned. It is therefore highly questionable if it is in Africa's interest to enter this downward spiral. It also seems to be an illusion to think that Namibia, Lesotho, Kenya or any other African country will be able to compete with China under the current rules of the globalisation game.

Ramatex's strategy

A visit to the Ramatex website provides a glimpse into the company's global strategy. The initially Malaysia-based company expanded production into China in 1997. In 2001 it started operations in Namibia, expanding them in 2002. In 2003, Ramatex returned its focus to Asia with expansions in Cambodia and China. In 2004, this trend continued as the company extended further in Cambodia and especially in China, where it plans further expansions in 2005. This is in line with global trends and if international experiences are anything to go by, Ramatex's stay in Namibia will be only of a temporary nature. Ramatex's investments have little to do with South–South cooperation as they were not designed to assist Namibia's industrialisation efforts. The company seeks temporary competitive advantages around the globe.

Namibia's special incentives

Namibia provided infrastructure of over N$100 million in the initial stages alone. Ramatex was provided with subsidised water and electricity, and despite signing a recognition agreement with NAFAU in September 2002, the company never increased its low wages and essentially condemned its workers to a life in poverty. It also seems that no systematic skills transfer to Namibian workers has taken place as the company provided only some initial training and instead opted to import thousands of production workers from Asia. This meant that Namibia did not even take maximum advantage of the potential job opportunities associated with Ramatex. Furthermore, there are no indications of a programme to ensure technology transfer, which could have contributed to the development of Namibia's own textile industry in the medium term. Such technology transfer was crucial, for example, during the initial industrialisation in South-East Asia.

For Ramatex Namibia may just have been a temporary location in line with the company's global strategy, which included a shift towards China once the clothing and textile quotas came to an end.

Source: Adapted and shortened extract from Jauch (2005)

In this competitive global economy, management must continuously seek ways of improving the performance of organisations in order to compete, survive and hopefully thrive. Within this context of global competition and free trade, countries are tied via their business economic structures into a state of vigorous competition for foreign investment to stimulate growth. At the same time (or rather as a result of this), the capacity to work has become a more fluid, yet also a key source of competitive advantage in what can almost be termed a global labour market. These dynamics are directly relevant to the management of human resources in South African organisations, including those that operate beyond our borders in Africa and elsewhere. The state of affairs in Africa as such is therefore also very relevant for South African organisations and their managers.

According to the World Bank (www.worldbank.org), the countries of Africa can be divided into three categories along an economic continuum: the major oil-exporting economies of Africa host a little more than a quarter of the continent's population, just over another third of Africa's people live in a further group of countries that generally showed a diversified but sustained economic growth of at least 4% over the last decade or so, and a third group of countries, also hosting just over a third of the total African population, are countries that are conflict prone and resource poor, showing strong volatility and afflicted or emerging from conflicts, or simply trapped in slow economic growth of less than 4% ('Spreading and sustaining growth in Africa'

2007). We might thus detect some general clusters and trends, but we also have to be careful not to generalise too much, as Africa as a continent is vast and with countries that are very diverse (see table 2.1). The question we might ask is this: how are things going in Africa? Before we dwell on this it may be useful to glance over some of the statistics in table 2.1. Population is given in millions and gross domestic product (GDP, which measures the size of the economy in terms of monetary value of output delivered/produced) in terms of billions of dollars (US), except where expressed in millions of dollars. Illiteracy levels are given as the percentage of the population of 15 years of age and older who cannot read/write.

EXHIBIT 2.5: Some Africa 'Fast Facts – Halfway to 2015' – according to the World Bank

- While most countries in sub-Saharan Africa are off track to halve poverty and hunger by 2015, countries such as Ghana, Mozambique, Tanzania and Uganda are making solid progress toward achieving the MDGs.
- Ethiopia's poverty headcount as of 2005 was 39%; as of 2004, Zambia's was 68% and in Sierra Leone 70% of citizens fell below the poverty line.
- Africa's economic growth has risen from 2.1% in the 1990s to an average 5.6% in 2003–07. Challenges are greatest in a group of about 20 countries characterized by low or negative growth, and include enhancing security, providing private sector growth opportunities, and building basic government capacity to put international aid to good use. What Africa needs is a long period of sustained growth.
- Aid to Africa has risen, although much of it is in the form of debt relief. Overall aid flows from DAC and multilateral donors to the region climbed to over $40 billion in 2006, representing an increase of $6.9 billion in real terms over 2005 levels and $12.4 billion over 2004 amounts. Aid remains essential for most countries in the region. New donors like China are growing in importance.
- Some countries in Africa have made strong progress in strengthening development strategies and institutional frameworks for implementation. Good candidates for scaled-up aid include Burkina Faso, Ghana, Madagascar, Mozambique, Rwanda and Tanzania; while Mali could use a moderate increase.
- Ten of the 11 countries worldwide with under-five mortality rates over 200 per 1 000 are in sub-Saharan Africa, including Angola and Sierra Leone. Only two of the 33 fragile states have achieved or are on track to reduce under-five mortality by two-thirds by 2015.
- Malnutrition reduces school achievement and results in inferior cognitive abilities that can persist through life. In rural Zimbabwe, childhood nutritional deficits due to civil war in the late 1970s and drought in 1982–84 led to late school entry and an estimated 14% reduction in lifetime earning.
- Of all births recorded in the region, only 45% were attended by skilled personnel in 2006 – an increase of just one percentage point since 1992. Sub-Saharan Africa has the highest maternal mortality rate among all developing regions.
- The region's proportion of population living with HIV has declined by a full percentage point since 2000.
- Eighteen of 37 countries in the region for which data exist are not on track to achieve gender parity in primary and secondary education.
- Eighty percent of countries in the region with available data show poor progress on improved sanitation and 44% of the population still lacks access to clean water.
- In 2007, gross concessional flows from multilateral development banks crossed $12 billion. Africa received 44% of these flows in 2007, up from 37% in 2000.

Source: 'Africa's progress on development goals linked to growth, environment' (2008).

Overall, from an economic and socio-political perspective, Africa seems to be in a better position now, almost a decade into the 21st century, than it has been since independence. Table 2.1 shows the economic growth, for instance, between 2003 and 2006. While this is so we should not forget that poverty is still extremely rife on the continent, and HIV/Aids rates the worst in the world. Also, infrastructure is seriously lagging behind in general, and corruption is still claimed to be prevalent in many African countries. Still, the first seven or so years of the 2000s seem to be a cause for greater hope and optimism on and for the continent. Africa is generally a resource-rich continent and on the back of the commodities boom and a period of sustained global economic growth, the demand for and prices of resources and commodities such as iron ore, copper, platinum, timber and oil have been on the rise, and foreign direct investment into Africa has increased. Politically we are also finding some encouraging trends generally.

Over the past decade or so we have witnessed a broadening of democracy in Africa with more and more countries engaging in multiparty democratic elections, and also more outcomes of new leaders coming into power (compared to a general tendency in the past of authoritarian regimes clinging to power). There has been a trend of fewer incidents of political instability on the continent, and cases of armed conflict also showed a downward trend. From an economic point of view, things are looking more encouraging, as reflected in table 2.1. There have thus been more and more people signalling the message that perhaps many African countries seem to have turned the corner and might well be gaining momentum on a path of steadier and stronger economic growth. Over the past decade, Africa has been just about on par with the rest of the world in terms of economic growth rates, having shown an average growth rate of almost 5,5% ('Spreading and sustaining growth in Africa' 2007). Despite these encouraging trends there have also been warnings about the stark realities still in Africa. Most countries in Africa do not seem to be quite on track and target to achieve the set of eight MDGs (millennium development goals) that were set to be achieved by 2015, including the first one of halving extreme poverty by 2015 (see exhibit 2.5 for some 'Fast Facts' regarding Africa by April 2008).

From exhibit 2.5 we can thus develop a feel of where Africa generally is, and where it seems to be heading. Table 2.2 contains a little more detail about our own region and the people of the Southern African Development Community (SADC) countries. The people of southern Africa are, as can be seen, very diverse, and the numbers are vast. In this probably lies our potential strength, but simultaneously also – if not managed properly – probably our single biggest problem. We have a huge challenge to develop and empower our people in the region (as on the rest of the continent, of course).

Table 2.1: Countries of Africa – some basic statistics

	Popu-lation	Illiteracy	GDP 2003	GDP 2006
SOUTHERN AFRICA				
Angola	16,4m	32,6%	13,8	47,3
Botswana	1,8m	18,8%	7,5	10,8
Lesotho	1,8m	17,8%	1,1	1,6
Madagascar	19,1m	29,3%	5,4	5,4
Malawi	13,2m	35,9%	1,7	2,2
Mauritius	1,3m	15,6%	5,2	6,4
Mozambique	20,1m	48,3%	3,6	5,9
Namibia	2,1m	15,0%	4,2	6,5
Seychelles	0,08m	8,2%	$703m	$682m
South Africa	47,4m	17,6%	165,4	256,4
Swaziland	1,1m	20,4%	1,9	2,6
Zambia	11,9m	32,0%	4,3	12,1
Zimbabwe	13,1m	7,6%	11,0	8,2
EAST AFRICA				
Burundi	7,8m	40,7%	$595m	$955m
Comoros	0,6m	43,0%	$319m	$386m
Djibouti	0,8m	28,7%	$625m	$761m
Eritrea	4,5m	38,6%	$751m	1,0
Ethiopia	72,7m	53,7%	6,6	13,3
Kenya	35,1m	26,4%	14,3	23,6
Rwanda	9,2m	35,1%	1,68	2,4
Somalia	8,5m	–	–	–
Sudan	37,0m	39,1%	17,8	37,6
Tanzania	39,5m	30,6%	10,3	13
Uganda	29,9m	33,2%	6,3	9,4
CENTRAL AFRICA				
Cameroon	16,7m	32,1%	12,5	18,6
Central African Republic	4,1m	51,4%	1,0	1,5
Chad	9,9m	74,3%	2,6	6,8

	Popu-lation	Illiteracy	GDP 2003	GDP 2006
Congo-Brazzaville	4,1m	13,4%	3,5	8,4
Dem. Republic of Congo	59,3m	32,8%	5,6	8,4
Equatorial Guinea	0,5m	13,0%	2,9	9,2
Gabon	1,4m	n/a	6,0	9,5
São Tomé e Principe	0,2m	15,1%	$60m	$73m
WEST AFRICA				
Benin	7,8m	65,3%	3,5	4,5
Burkina Faso	13,6m	78,2%	4,1	6,2
Cape Verde Islands	0,5m	21,3%	$797m	1,054
Côte d'Ivoire	18,5m	51,3%	13,9	17,3
Gambia	1,6m	56,3%	$366m	$506m
Ghana	22,5m	42,1%	7,6	11,3
Guinea-Bissau	1,6m	53,9%	$239m	$313m
Guinea Conakry	9,2m	37,3%	3,6	3,2
Liberia	3,4m	40,2%	$442m	$664m
Mali	13,2m	81,0%	4,3	6,0
Niger	14,4m	71,3%	2,7	3,4
Nigeria	144,7m	28,1%	57,6	121,1
Senegal	11,9m	60,7%	6,4	9,2
Sierra Leone	5,6m	64,9%	$703m	1,3
Togo	6,3m	46,8%	1,8	2,3
NORTH AFRICA				
Algeria	33,3m	30,1%	68	124,1
Egypt	75,4m	28,6%	82,4	103,3
Libya	5,9m	15,3%	23,4	48,9
Mauritania	3,2m	48,8%	1,2	2,8
Morocco	30,5m	47,7%	43,7	56,9
Tunisia	10,2m	25,7%	25,0	30,0

Source: Country Reports (2008)

Table 2.2: SADC people profile

	Pop, 2006 (growth pa) [est. 2015]	Age structure	Ethnic groups	Languages	Literacy % 15+ can read/ write	Population % above poverty line (% em- ployed)	Popula- tion % (urban- cities)	HIV/ Aids % adult pre- valence
Angola	16,4 million (2,7%) [20,9 million]	0–14: 43,7% 15–64: 53,5% +65: 2,8%	Ovimbundu: 37%; Kimbundu; 25%; Bakongo: 13%; Mestico (mixed European and native African): 2%; European: 1%; other 22%	Portuguese (official), Bantu and other African languages	Total: 67,4% Male: 82,9% Female: 54,2%	30% (50%)	53% (17%)	3,9%
Botswana	1,8 million (–0,4%) [1,7 million]	0–14: 35,8% 15–64: 60,3% +65: 3,9%	Tswana: 79%; Kalanga: 11%; Basarwa: 3%; other, including Kgalagadi and white: 7%	Setswana: 78%; Kalanga 8%; Sekgalagadi: 3%; English (official): 2%; other 9%	Total: 81,2% Male: 80,4% Female: 81,8%	69,7% (76,2%)	57% (n/a)	37,3%
Democratic Republic of the Congo	59,3 million (3,0%) [77,9 million]	0–14: 47,6 15–64: 49,9% +65: 2,6%	Over 200 ethnic groups, majority Bantu, four largest tribes: Mongo, Luba, Kongo (Bantu), Mangbetu-Azande (Hamitic): about 45%	French (official), Lingala (a lingua franca trade language), Kingwana (dialect of Kiswahili), Kikongo, Tshiluba	Total: 65,5% Male: 76,2% Female: 55,1%	n/a (small)	32% (17%)	4,2%
Lesotho	1,8 million (-0,3%) [1,7 million]	0-14: 35,7% 15–64: 59,3% +65: 5,0%	Sotho: 99,7%; white, Asian, and other: 0,3%	Sesotho, English (official), Zulu, Xhosa	Total: 84,8% Male: 74,5% Female: 94,5%	51% (55%)	19% (n/a)	28,9%

>>

	Pop, 2006 (growth pa) [est. 2015]	Age structure	Ethnic groups	Languages	Literacy % 15+ can read/ write	Population % above poverty line (% employed)	Population % (urban-cities)	HIV/ Aids % adult prevalence
Malawi	13,2 million (2,2%) [16,0 million]	0–14: 46,1% 15–64: 51,2% +65: 2,7%	Chewa, Nyanja, Tumbuka, Yao, Lomwe, Sena, Tonga, Ngoni, Ngonde, Asian, European	Chichewa (official): 57,2%; Chinyanja: 12,8%; Chiyao 10,1%; Chitumbuka: 9,5%; other: 10,4%	Total: 62,7% Male: 76,1% Female: 49,8%	47% (n/a)	17% (n/a)	14,2%
Mauritius	1,3 million (0,7%) [1,3 million]	0–14: 23,5% 15–64:69,8% +65: 6,7%	Indo-Mauritian: 68%; Creole: 27%; Sino-Mauritian: 3%; Franco-Mauritian: 2%	Creole: 80,5%; Bhojpuri: 12,1%; French: 3,4%; English (official): 1%; other: 4%	Total: 84,4% Male: 88,4% Female: 80,5%	90% (90,8%)	42% (n/a)	0,1%
Mozambique	20,1 million (1,7%) [23,5 million]	0–14: 44,7% 15–64: 52,5% +65: 2,8%	African (Makhuwa, Tsonga, Lomwe, Sena and others): 99,7%; Europeans: 0,06%; Euro-Africans: 0,2%; Indian: 0,1%	Emakhuwa: 26,1%; Xichangana: 11,3%; Portuguese: (official; spoken by 27%): 8,8%; Elomwe: 7,6%; Cisena: 6,8%; other: 39,4%	Total: 47,8% Male: 63,5% Female: 32,7%	30% (79%)	35% (7%)	12,2%
Namibia	2,1 million (1,0%) [2,2 million]	0–14: 37,7% 15–64: 58,6% +65: 3,8%	Ovambo: 50%; Kavangos: 9%; Herero: 7%; Damara: 7%; White 6%; mixed 6,5%; Nama: 5%; Caprivian: 4%; Bushmen: 3%; other: 3%	English (official): 7%; Afrikaans (common language of most of the population/60% of whites); German: 32%; indigenous languages (Oshivambo, Herero, Nama)	Total: 85% Male: 86,8% Female: 83,5%	65,1% (94,7%)	35% (n/a)	21,3%

	Pop, 2006 (growth pa) [est. 2015]	Age structure	Ethnic groups	Languages	Literacy % 15+ can read/write	Population % above poverty line (% employed)	Popula-tion % (urban-cities)	HIV/Aids % adult pre-valence
Seychelles	0,09 million (n/a) [n/a]	0–14: 25,4% 15–64: 68,5% +65: 6,1%	Mixed French, African, Indian, Chinese and Arab	Creole: 91,8%: English (official): 4,9%; other: 3,3%	Total: 91,8% Male: 91,4% Female: 92,3%	n/a (n/a)	n/a (n/a)	n/a
South Africa	46,9 million (0,1%) [47,3 million]	0–14: 29,1% 15–64: 65,5% +65: 5,4%	Black African: 79%; white; 9,6%; coloured: 8,9%; Indian: 2,5%	Zulu: 23,8%; Xhosa: 17,6%; Afrikaans: 13,3%; Pedi: 9,4%; English: 8,2%; Tswana: 8,2%; Sotho: 7,9%; Tsonga: 4,4%; other: 7,2%	Total: 86,4% Male: 87% Female: 85,7%	50% (75,8%)	59% (30%)	21,5%
Swaziland	1,1 million (–0,4%) [1,1 million]	0-14: 40,3% 15–64: 56,1% +65: 3,6%	African: 97%; European: 3%	English (official, government business conducted in English); siSwati (official)	Total: 81,6% Male: 82,6% Female: 80,8%	31% (60%)	24% (n/a)	38,8%
Tanzania	39,5 million (2,1%) [47,1 million]	0–14: 43,9% 15–64: 53,3% +65: 2,8%	*Mainland:* African: 99% (mainly Bantu from over 130 tribes); Asian, European and Arab: 1%; *Zanzibar:* Arab, African, mixed Arab and African	Kiswahili (of-ficial); Eng-lish (official, language of commerce, administra-tion, and higher education); Arabic; many local languages	Total: 69,4% Male: 77,5% Female: 62,2%	64% (n/a)	24% (7%)	8,8%

	Pop, 2006 (growth pa) [est. 2015]	Age structure	Ethnic groups	Languages	Literacy % 15+ can read/ write	Population % above poverty line (% employed)	Population % (urbancities)	HIV/ Aids % adult prevalence
Zambia	11, 9 million (1,7%) [13,8 million]	0–14: 45,7%; 15–64: 51,9% +65: 2,4%	African: 98,7%; European: 1,1%; other: 0,2%	English (official); major vernaculars: Bemba, Kaonda, Lozi, Lunda, Luvale, Nyanja, Tonga, plus some 70 other indigenous languages	Total: 80,6% Male: 86,8% Female: 74,8%	14% (50%)	35% (11%)	16,5%
Zimbabwe	13,1 million (0,6%) [13,8 million]	0–14: 37,2% 15–64: 59,3% +65: 3,5%	Shona: 82%; Ndebele: 14%; other black: 2%; mixed/ Asian: 1%; white: under 1%	English (official); Shona; Sindebele (Ndebele); numerous minor dialects	Total: 90,7% Male: 94,2% Female: 87,2%	20% (20%)	36% (12%)	24,6%

Source: South Africa & SADC Media Facts (2008)

While there is a global competitive landscape that somehow impacts on all organisations in the world, South African, southern African and African organisations face certain shared, peculiar and indeed pressing, yet somehow also encouraging, circumstances. While most other countries and their local organisations across the globe do not share in these same circumstances, those in Africa at least are connected in some unique way and have more in common. The people of Africa, spurred on by us in South Africa, must find their own ways of improving life for all on this continent, and through ways that enhance sustainability – and in all of this, HRM is central. As we settle into the first decade of the 21st century it seems that we might indeed be on our way doing just that – finding our own ways of making things better. As Nicky Oppenheimer, Chairman of De Beers said (2007):

> The international agenda has moved on ... Interest in Africa has cooled as Iraq, Afghanistan and global warming have heated up ... Africa is succeeding – not in spite of the international community's apathy or unreliability, but because of it. It has forced African countries to become more self-reliant and to take responsibility ... Today, for every African failure there is a steady stream of successes, and for every African autocrat, many more democrats. Sound domestic policy always counts more than external assistance in creating conditions for growth,

stability and prosperity. More and more, that is the African norm. Failure is the deviation.

Despite facing very serious challenges – such as the fact that our continent accounts for almost two-thirds of all the world's HIV/Aids cases, our vast food insecurities on the continent (with agricultural production only about a third of what Asia's levels of production are) and the fact that more than 250 million of Africa's people today live in urban slums – Oppenheimer (2007) argues that we are no longer the "hopeless continent" and that we are on the road to success. He attributes Africa's general progress to five main reasons which we now share.

Three of these include the macro-level shifts in Africa towards democracy and liberal economic reform, Africa catching up with globalisation (while Africa's share of global capital flows declined fivefold during post-independence years to just about 1%, foreign direct investment and remittances from Africa's Diaspora are spiralling upwards at quite a pace), and the China–Africa connection.

China's rising prominence (together with Brazil, Russia and India) in the world's socio-economic order, and its dramatically enhanced presence in Africa is an important driving or pulling force, and Oppenheimer adds that this now poses a serious challenge to the once supreme Western aid-development model. China's trade with Africa is said to have increased more than fivefold in six years (from $10 billion to $55,6 billion in 2006) and while the World Bank spent $2,3 billion in all of sub-Saharan Africa in 2005, China is said to have committed more than $8 billion in lending to Nigeria, Angola and Mozambique alone in that same year (also see exhibit 2.6).

Another reason for Africa's rise out of the doldrums, Oppenheimer (2007) argues, relates to the fact that Africa no longer waits for external parties to help mediate and resolve conflicts but instead brokers its own peace deals on the continent, using its own peace-building and peace-keeping mechanisms. This, Oppenheimer asserts, comes from the 1994 birth of our own democracy here in South Africa, made possible through negotiations, consultation and mediated communication during the early 1990s. From South Africa's end to apartheid thus also stems Oppenheimer's fifth reason for Africa's turnaround on the road to success: our newfound democracy liberated our citizens as well as our businesses, says Oppenheimer (2007): "Since 1994, South African annual trade with Africa has increased fivefold to over $7 billion, while the investment stake of South African firms in Africa has increased by an estimated $1 billion per year." South Africa's role in Africa is thus not to be underestimated.

A recent report of the International Monetary Fund (IMF) concluded that South Africa is the economic powerhouse of Africa, and showed that growth in our own country gives a significant spill-over to other African countries. About 1% growth in South African GDP, sustained over five years, is correlated with just below 0,5% or even up to almost 0,75% growth in the rest of Africa ('SA is a significant engine of growth for Africa').

The role of South African companies for and in Africa thus seems crucial. A survey conducted between May and November by Unido (the UN Industrial Development Organisation), capturing data from 1 216 foreign firms with assets of about $19,6 billion (no mining, oil and gas companies were included), revealed that "South African investors in the region were largely in food, beverages, finance, marketing and communications ... had the highest numbers of graduates, paid the highest average wages ... spent the most on employee training ... Six of the top 10 spenders ... are South African ... Of the $39 million ... total spent on training, $13.4 million is spent by South Africans" ('SA firms play vital role in Africa').

EXHIBIT 2.6: China in Africa: Giant from the East coming to replace the West?

China is extraordinary in many ways. It has a population of over 1,4 billion (almost a fifth of the world's total) and covers a landmass of over 9,5 billion square metres, and yet it has only 7% of the world's arable land and fresh water, only 2% of the world's oil and 3% of its forests. It is using up more than half of the world's cement, a third of its steel and over a quarter of its aluminium, and it has swallowed over 80% of the increase in the world's copper supply since 2000 – and its people gobble up more than half of the world's pork. China is spending 35 times as much on importing crude oil as it did in 1999, and demand for oil keeps growing. China has been in existence for over 5 000 years and is also the world's oldest centralised state.

The resurgence of this 'giant' in Africa is thus attracting huge attention, and not only transforming the continent's political, economic and social landscapes, but apparently also sending shivers to the Western governments, hitherto the dominant forces in Africa.

Even though Europe organised an African summit in April 2000, it was the Forum on China–Africa Cooperation (FOCAC) summit later the same year in Beijing, and a second follow-up ministerial meeting of FOCAC in Addis Ababa in 2003, that made the difference. The FOCAC summits were different. In contrast with the big shows, the charity business and other high-profile humanitarian diplomacy promoted by the West, the United Nations, NGOs and the international financial institutions, China ensured that deeds preceded words. China today stands in sharp contrast to the Western governments, whose inconsistencies and lack of tangible results in their African development efforts are rather too obvious.

China has surprised everyone. It has created a *fait accompli*, not storming Africa as would have been expected from a 'dragon', but getting into it in a powerful but cautious way. China's money flowing into Africa is a clear and significant sign of its determination to meet words with deeds on the continent. A symbolic signal in this regard is the fact that in 2007, with over US$9 billion worth of investment, it dwarfed the World Bank's money flow into Africa of no more than US$2,5 billion. There are more than 800 000 Chinese people currently living and working and running their businesses in Africa – with over 800 small and medium businesses involved in manufacturing, and bidding for construction of railways, ports, hospitals, administrative buildings and other facilities.

China, which has lifted at least 400 million of its people out of poverty, has come up with an economic and political development model that produced tangible results in terms of poverty alleviation and national control of assets – a model that works without the involvement of foreign advisors, institutions or bilateral tutors.

The China–Africa issue cannot be restricted to its bilateral dimension. Many other issues abound and call for discussion. Among these are the vexing question of African immigrants in relation to the African Diaspora's impact on the continent's development, as well as Africa's stance on the war on terror. Beijing matters to all 48 African countries that have diplomatic ties with China, but even the remaining four which still have diplomatic relations with only Taiwan, cannot ignore the China factor.

This unfolding evolution brings to the fore various questions that call for debate, including assessing the consequences of China's entry into Africa – good or bad, threats or opportunities.

Sources: Adapted and extracted from Gaye (2008: 13–18) primarily; and McBride (2008: 13), to a much lesser extent

Of the more than 300 large multinational corporations operating in sub-Saharan Africa, 13% were South African (with 26% being French and 11% having originated in the UK). Various South African multinational organisations (like the MTN Group (see exhibit 2.7), the Shoprite Group, various mining companies, SABMiller and numerous others) are making huge contributions to our continent with operations and interests across Africa (and beyond). The management of these organisations and in particular also how the work and working people are managed as part of these businesses, are thus fulfilling crucial roles on our continent. Irrespective, however, of whether you or your organisation actively operates in Africa beyond South African borders, we all are part of the continent, and the African context thus remains very important for all of us who practice (teach or research) HRM in South Africa.

EXHIBIT 2.7: MTN: in Africa – and beyond

The MTN Group's vision is "To be the leading provider of telecommunications in emerging markets", and its strategy is embedded in the belief "that information and communication technologies (ICTs) are an indispensable catalyst for economic development; one that affords developing countries the opportunity to leapfrog many stages of modernisation from a technological perspective".

Launched in 1994, the MTN Group is a multinational telecommunications group, operating in 21 countries in Africa and the Middle East. As at the end of December 2006, MTN recorded more than 40 million subscribers across its operations in the regional areas of South and East Africa, West and Central Africa, and the Middle East and North Africa.

As part of its platform for continued growth, a priority for MTN and an important component of the company's vision is making a significant and real contribution to the economies of the territories in which it operates. In line with this, up to December 2005, MTN's investment in cellular infrastructure in its operating territories had already exceeded R30 billion – a significant contribution also to the New Partnership for Africa's Development (NEPAD) goals for ICT development for the continent.

The MTN Group operates in Botswana, Cameroon, Côte d'Ivoire, Nigeria, Republic of Congo (Congo-Brazzaville), Rwanda, South Africa, Swaziland, Uganda, Zambia, Iran, Afghanistan, Benin, Cyprus, Ghana, Guinea Bissau, Guinea Republic, Liberia, Sudan, Syria and Yemen.

Source: Adapted extracts from http://www.mtn.com/mtn.group

2.3.2 South Africa and its people: some brief contemporary reflections

Any country at any given point in time is a product of its history. We are no different. Our country's peculiar and complex socio-politico-economic landscape is as a result of our historical development (outlined in earlier sections). Our situation is thus not simple to capture or cover, especially not in a book such as this one. At the risk of oversimplifying and being incomplete, we nevertheless attempt, in this section, to provide some snapshot of how we see some of the variables and dynamics in South Africa that interplay with the ways in which we manage our organisations, our work and our working people.

We believe that one aspect really dominates the overall impression one gets of our country when taking a helicopter view. This issue we would like to label as 'inequitable inequalities' for the moment. This concept consists of two terms that we believe should be combined. *Inequitable* means unfair or unjust. *Inequality* means lack or absence of equality. *Equality* is derived from the term *equal*, which literally means being the same in value, status, size, and so forth – a term derived from Latin *aequalis*, from *aequus*, ('even' or 'level').

Inequality, inequity and 'inequitable inequalities' have been central features of this country since long before the advent of apartheid almost half a century or so ago. Over the centuries there have been different groups who have benefited more than others, different groups of 'winners', and also then, 'losers'. While we now have to face huge challenges directly brought about by the legacies of the apartheid system, there has been a culmination of a multitude of other and highly complex factors and forces, which created the situation as we have it today. We have had some issues pertaining to inequality and inequity since the first Europeans arrived here, and in all likelihood long before that too. The pressures and demands facing modern-day South Africa as part of a global economy – where competitiveness is key – must thus be considered against the background of this major challenge our country faces, and which, if not handled appropriately, might well become the key threat of our time, we believe. Please note that this challenge (or problem if not addressed appropriately) is multidimensional, even though racial inequalities and inequities apparently seem to tend to dominate agendas in South Africa. The racially based perspective is understandable given that we are merely 15 years down the road since apartheid (which was around for about 45 years) was dismantled. We have some other serious inequalities and inequities in our society too, though – gender inequalities for one. The key one, however, and the one that might well become the most important to tackle in order to develop sustainable stability and prosperity in our country, relates to the 'haves and the have-nots' of and in South Africa. As we show in the next chapter, we have to empower our people in the broadest and deepest sense possible throughout our country, so that we can ultimately have a situation of equity and fairness generally, and a decent quality of life for all our people.

2.3.2.1 South African society: a snapshot

Perhaps a good starting point of orientation might be to try and get a snapshot of South Africa as society. A clever way of doing this might be to reflect on South Africa as a single small village with only 100 inhabitants. This is what Markinor did. According to a research document compiled by Markinor we would then look like what is portrayed in exhibit 2.8.

2.3.2.2 South Africa's population

This book centres around people. Let us now take a closer look at the people of South Africa. From table 2.3 we can see that our country's total population was about 47 million people by 2005. Based on MacFarlane (2007), a 'guesstimate' would hint that in 2008 our population probably stood at about, or just over, 48 million. In comparison with some other African countries (also see table 2.1), our official population is a little less than two-thirds of that of Ethiopia, just less than a third of that of Nigeria, while being more than double than that of Ghana and more than 10 times greater than the population of Eritrea, Africa's youngest independent country.

EXHIBIT 2.8: The South African Village: a snapshot according to Markinor

"If we were a single village with only 100 inhabitants, what would it look like? What would the people be like? A research document compiled by Markinor attempts to answer these and other questions:

Characteristics and behaviour of the people in the village
- Thirty-three are younger than 16
- Five are older than 65
- Two were born during the last year
- Thirteen are HIV positive
- Seventy-eight are black; 11 are white; eight are coloured and three are Indian
- Twenty-three speak Zulu in their homes; 17 speak Xhosa; 14 speak Afrikaans, 10 speak Tswana, another 10 speak English, eight speak Sepedi, another eight speak Sesotho, and the other 10 speak one of the other four official languages or another language
- Seventy-three are Christians, of which 52 are Protestant or Catholic and 21 belong to the ZCC/ the Church of Shembe or another African Independent Church

>>

<<

The infrastructure in the village

- Seventy-six homes have electricity
- Seventy have television
- Sixty-eight have tap water in the house or on the stand/in the yard
- Thirty-one have hot water from a geyser
- Thirty have a motor vehicle
- Seventeen have a landline telephone in working order
- Eighty own, rent or use a cellphone
- Fifty do NOT use any banking service
- Forty-one have a savings account
- Thirty-six have an ATM card

If the village only consisted of 100 adults (i.e. those who are 16 years and older)

- Forty-two are employed (full-time or part-time)
- Twenty-six are unemployed and looking for work
- Forty-nine are poor (the total household income per month is below R2 499)
- Four earn an income of R300 000 per year or higher
- Fourteen earn an income of R100 000 per year or higher
- Twenty-five earn incomes of R50 000 per year or higher
- Sixty-eight do not have matric
- Eight have a university/technikon degree
- Thirty-nine are married; nine are living together; seven are widowed; two are divorced or separated, and 43 are single

They spend their money as follows:

- R21 out of every R100 on food
- R17 out of every R100 on housing and municipal services
- R4 out of every R100 on clothing and footwear
- R9 out of every R100 on income tax

If the village consisted of voters only (those 18 years and older) the following would be true:

- Sixty-three will vote for the ANC if there were an election tomorrow; 13 for the Democratic Alliance; nine for other parties, and 15 do not know, will not say or will spoil their ballot papers
- For 20 there is no political party that represents their views
- Forty-five believe democracy will only survive in South Africa with a single strong opposition party that can keep the governing party on their toes
- Seventy-two are happy with how the current government promotes gender equality, and 73 give the government credit for distributing welfare payments to those who are entitled to it, i.e. old-age pensions, disability payments and child maintenance grants
- Sixty-nine think the government is not doing well with reducing unemployment and job creation, and 69 say that reducing the crime rate does not get enough attention; 59 think more should be done about fighting corruption in government, and 54 feel the right people are not always appointed in government positions; 53 think the government should do more to control the cost of living
- Forty-four believe that everybody, irrespective of income, should pay for water, electricity and other basic services
- Fifty-four think the country is going in the right direction
- Fifty-five think that the children of South Africa have a bright future
- Seventy-seven are very or fairly confident of a happy future for all races
- Sixty want to know more about AsgiSA (Accelerated and Shared Growth Initiative for SA)

<<
- Seventy-one believe we are on course with the preparations for the Fifa Soccer World Cup in 2010
- Forty-seven feel that South Africa has an obligation to help with conflict resolution in Africa
- Forty would vote for Jacob Zuma if we directly elected our president

Sources: Ipsos Markinor Khayabus, Demographic Detail. November 2007; Ipsos Markinor. Socio-Political Trends. November 2007; BMR. Income and Expenditure Model. 2008 update; AMPS 2007."

Source: 'A breakdown of the South African Village' (2008)

Table 2.3: Total population of South Africa, 2005 ('000)

	Male	Female	Total	% breakdown by population group
Black African	18 209	18 965	37 206	79,2%
Coloured	2 039	2 106	4 148	8,8%
Indian/Asian	599	553	1 153	2,5%
White	2 191	2 165	4 367	9,3%
Total	23 089	23 834	46 971	100,0%
% breakdown by sex	49,2%	50,7%	100,0%	

Note: Due to rounding, figures do not always add up.
Source: Slightly adapted from Barker (2007: 15), as based on official statistics

By international standards South Africa's population grew rather rapidly for quite some time – at a rate of approximately 2,3% over the last two decades of the 20th century. However, the growth rate has been declining quite quickly more recently, with an estimated growth rate of only 0,7% for the 2000–2010 period (Van Aardt 2004, as quoted in Barker 2007: 15). There have been forecasts of an even slower rate of growth (even as low as 0,1%) for the period up to 2015. This can be ascribed to HIV/Aids, declining fertility rates and also the brain drain, or loss of skilled people due to emigration (Barker 2007), among other things. South Africa's white population is showing slightly negative growth and this is projected to become more negative into the second decade of the 21st century. The growth rate for the black African population, while slowing down, is a little less than 1%, as is that of the Indian/Asian population. The growth rate of the coloured population is slowing down at a faster rate and projected to get close to 0% by about 2020 (the same low growth rate that is projected for the Indian/Asian population by that time).

HIV/Aids is a key contributing factor to slower population growth in South Africa as it is spreading rapidly, with estimates of up to 13% of the population being HIV positive. According to Barker (2007: 23), it can be as high as 15–20% among adults. This factor is having the most drastic impact on the structure of the black African population group. We elaborate more on the crucial HIV/Aids challenge in chapter 17. Another key factor that is contributing especially to the now negative growth of the white population is that of net migration. Owing to the skills and HRM-related challenges facing South Africa, it is worth elaborating a little on South Africa's brain drain, in accordance with Barker (2007: 23–28).

Unfortunately, policy changes implemented in 2003 meant that from then onwards we could no longer determine the extent of emigration from South Africa and hence official data on net migration is only available until 2003 (Barker 2007). From a macro-perspective we thus do not really know how many people of what calibre we might be losing to other countries. For a country in need of skills to help grow the economy, this does not make good sense. Table 2.4 gives an indication of the trend of net loss of working people, and in particular skilled people, by South Africa over the three years 2001 to 2003. Please note also that data deficiencies disguise the real figures and that some (like Meyer et al 2000 and Myburgh 2004) have argued rather persuasively that the real emigration figures could be about three times greater than the official ones of Statistics South Africa (SSA). SSA itself has said that the real number of emigrants is probably about double the official statistics.

Table 2.4: South African immigration and emigration: net gain/loss

Occupation	2001	2002	2003
Engineers and technologists	−412	−430	−639
Accountants and related	−475	−488	−703
Management	−696	−764	−1 313
Clerical	−1 217	−1 093	−1 870
Artisans and apprentices	−293	−239	−356
All economically active persons	−6 638	−6 280	−9 529

Source: Barker (2007: 25)

There is another dimension to people migration in our part of the world. This relates to the illegal immigrants who come into South Africa from other countries up north on our continent, and there are millions. This can be ascribed to a number of factors, including the relative states of wellness of different African countries (such as political and/or socio-economic). However, according to a report which the auditor general presented to South African parliament during 2008, people-management problems in the South African Police Service (SAPS) are also at play in terms of the 'crisis' related to the poor state of border control in South Africa (Gerardy 2008: 1):

> South Africa's borders are a shambles. There are just 19 police officers to con-trol 3 600km of coastline and 283 officers to control its nearly 5 000km-long land border. There should be 448 officers controlling the coastline and 970 officers on the land border. As a direct result, there are between three and five million illegal immigrants in the country ... Air border security has also been compro-mised. Instead of 18 permanent staff and two fieldworkers per province, there have only been temporary secondments from other units ... [A] damning inter-nal memorandum on security at OR Tambo International Airport was leaked to media ... The report also slammed failures by the Border Control Coordinating Committee, which is responsible for security at OR Tambo. Last year, a Musina-based home affairs official told Argus Weekend the country was facing a 'human tsunami' from thousands of fleeing Zimbabweans.

These things spill over into our country's labour market dynamics because South Africans compete with people from other countries for jobs. In addition, these dynamics cause all sorts of other issues which impact on the quality of life of South African people as well as these illegal immigrants (and their families, of course). Nare (2008: 12), for instance, reported about how illegal Zimbabwean migrants are apparently exploited (he investigated this through experiment near Mopani, which is about 40 kilometres south of Musina), and how these working people become the subject of xenophobia among South African people:

> [M]any of the people on the streets are unemployed when employment seems to be in abundance on the farms. The belief held by many of the unemployed South Africans ... is that working on farms is exclusively reserved for Zimbabweans, whom farmers claim will work very long hours for little money ... There is a lorry parked ... that must be filled to the brim with tomatoes that must reach Johannesburg by tomorrow morning. This means ... work until 10pm ... Those who fill more than 10 crates ... are eligible for a permanent job, or so we're told ... The farmers are well aware of the conditions from which these people flee ... While the economic chaos continues in my country, migrant workers will continue to cross the border ... As a husband and a father, if faced with the same situation, I would probably do the same.

It should thus be clear that even though our focus is on the management of working people in South Africa, we cannot ignore issues related to cross-border dynamics in this day and age. The people of South Africa, and of other countries on this continent, are the people of Africa. As we have shown, the implications for our country's people, including in particular the working people of our country – those who are able (and willing) to work – are real. This brings us to South Africa's economic active population (EAP).

2.3.2.3 South Africa's EAP – and the unemployed

The EAP (economic active population or total labour force) is defined as "the total number of people over the age of 15 years who present their labour for the production of economic goods and services, whether employed or not" (Barker 2007: 9). According to the same author (2007: 10–11), South Africa's total labour force was estimated at 16,8 million people in 2005. Between 300 000 and 400 000 people enter the labour market every year, of which many do not find work. For quite some time South Africa has experienced problems with economic growth that was not high enough compared to the growth of people entering the job market. This brings us to the issue of unemployment. South Africa has a very high number of people who are unemployed, and this is one of our country's main challenges as we move further into the 21st century.

Unemployment can be defined in different ways. In South Africa we have a strict and an expanded definition. The former says that an unemployed person is one who wants work, is seeking work, but is without work (Barker 2007). The stricter and official definition of SSA excludes those people who have become discouraged to seek work. In our view this is flawed and can disguise the real problems that we have. People without work cannot make a meaningful living or contribute towards the success of our country. Figure 2.2 (taken from Barker 2007) reflects our country's unemployment levels from 1994 to 2005 according to SSAs strict definition. While according to this we had an unemployment rate of 26,7% in 2005, the more realistic expanded definition would say that our unemployment rate in 2005 stood at 38,8% (Barker 2007: 180).

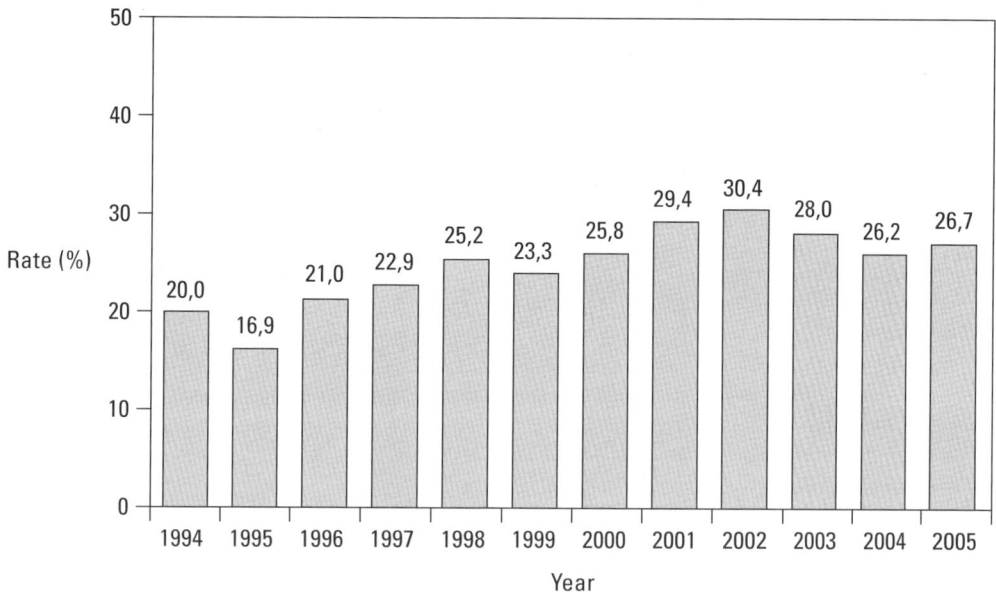

Figure 2.2: Unemployment rates in SA (strict definition): 1994–2005
Source: Barker (2007: 179), based on figures published by Statistics South Africa

Our country's unemployment rate is much higher among the black African economic active population than among whites (SSA, September 2005). The official unemployment rate for blacks was in the region of 32% in 2005, and about 5% among whites (see figure 2.3). However, this picture is changing. Barker (2007: 235) points out, for instance, that between 2001 and 2005, black employment increased by 5,2% per annum, whereas the employment of whites stagnated at 0,3% per annum. In the early 2000s 'jobless growth' was identified as one of our country's major challenges. As mentioned earlier, while the economy might be growing (see also the section below), concomitant growth in opportunities to work is not happening at the same pace. The growth of South Africa's EAP is faster than the growth in job opportunities.

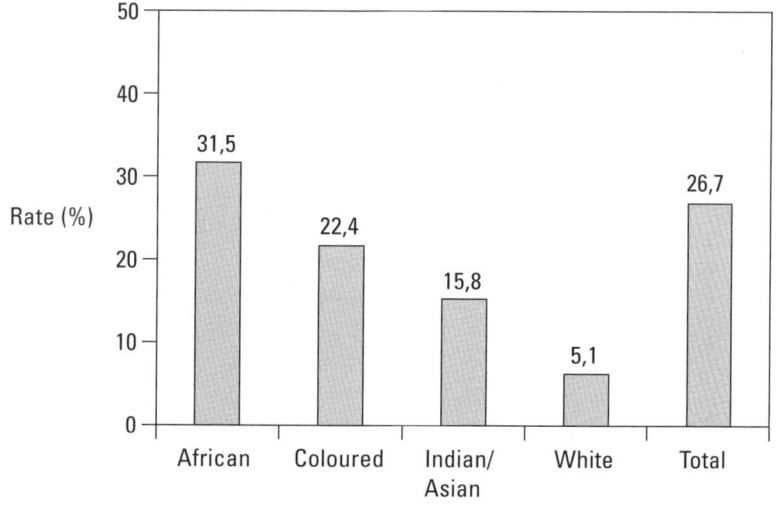

Figure 2.3: Unemployment rates in SA by population group, 2005
Source: Barker (2007: 235), based on figures published by Statistics South Africa

We also need to mention that over the last four or so decades, the participation of women in the labour market has increased significantly. According to Barker (2007: 2), women constituted 23% of the South African EAP in 1960, and 45% in 2005. The Labour Force Participation Rate (LFPR) is the proportion of the total population in the age group 15 to 65 that works or wants to work, and in South Africa the LFPR for women has increased over time, whereas it has declined for men (Barker 2007: 12–14). Lastly, as we will show below, HIV/Aids is impacting on the EAP of South Africa, particularly due to the age group which this pandemic is hitting the hardest. The demand for skilled people is becoming more pressing while the supply of appropriately skilled people does not seem to match that, and the brain drain is another important contributing factor. This brings us to issues such as education and health.

2.3.2.4 Health and education

South Africa's population also shows notable differences between especially the black and white population groups. Two primary factors seem to be contributing to this: the brain drain and HIV/Aids. We have an ageing and shrinking white population in South Africa (found in many developed countries). According to Barker (2007: 15–16), the age distribution of our black population is typical of a developing country (we have a young and expanding black population in which about 58% are between 15 and 65 years of age). According to research by the HSRC (MacFarlane 2005), HIV/Aids is the highest among blacks in the country, standing at about 12,9% in 2002. It is the second highest rate among the whites, at less than half of that rate (6,2%). MacFarlane (2005) elaborates about this in our black population group saying that "it is clear that there is an abnormally high death rate in the 30–39 age group. Since HIV typically affects sexually active people between the ages of 20 and 29, and further since the average time from infection to death is five years, this rapidly increasing death rate must largely be the result of HIV/Aids". Barker (2007) also points to the fact that among the white people in South Africa there is a relatively small proportion who are in the age groups 25–39, which aligns well with emigration statistics because especially young, usually skilled working people tend to be those leaving the country.

In terms of the education levels, only 34% of the black EAP had a matric or higher qualification in 2005, whereas this percentage was 64% for other population groups (Barker 2007: 233–234). There have, however, also been some heartening developments in educational levels over time. Whereas less than 5% of the black 'labour force' had at least a Grade 10 qualification in 1970, 34% had at least a Grade 12 qualification in 2005.

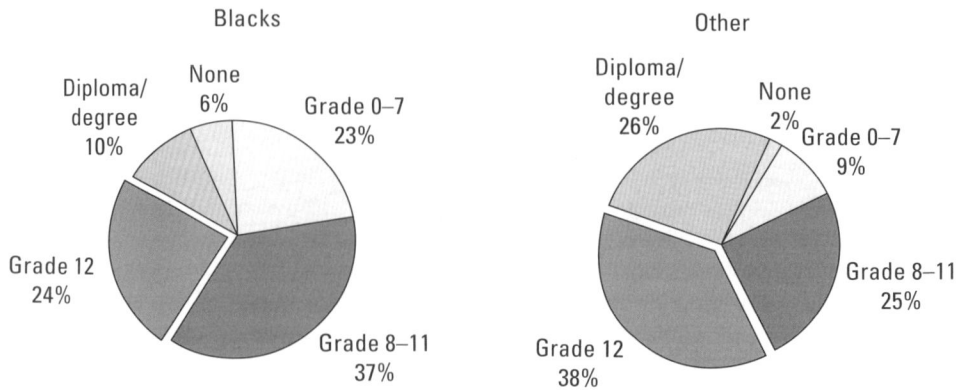

Figure 2.4: Educational level of South Africa's EAP by population group, 2005
Source: Barker (2007: 234) based on figures published by Statistics South Africa

Clearly, one of our country's most pressing challenges must thus relate to the development of our people, in particular those who have been deprived of that for so long. In this book we therefore devote two chapters to human resource development, reflecting in some sense the importance of this issue for and in our country. The foundation for human resource development, however, has to do with the education of our children. In terms of education, Kane-Berman (2007) reports that after almost a decade and a half of democracy in our country

> [T]here has been scant improvement in black education ... Only 30% of children (of all races) aged between five and six are attending early childhood development centres ... Among pupils in grade 6 the desired level of reading mastery stands at 20% ... There were fewer university-entrance matric passes among all races last year ... than in 1994 ... Africans account for most of these matriculants ... [R]esults have shown virtually no improvement in the past twelve years ... [F]igures tell us that the number of Africans obtaining university-entrance matric certificates was not much higher after 13 years of democratic rule than after 50 years of Bantu Education (which came into operation in 1955) ... all the more alarming if one remembers that discriminatory funding no longer applies ... The education minister, Naledi Pandor, was therefore right when she recently said that the poor performance of the schooling system could not simply be dismissed as the legacy of apartheid ... [S]he blamed the crisis in public education on other factors, including tolerance of neglectful parents and of mediocre officials and teachers ... "No education before liberation" was the slogan. Tragically education after liberation leaves much to be desired.

Enhancing human capacity in South Africa, through education, training and the like, will be key to unlocking sustainable growth and the enhancement of quality of life in our country. Developing our people is thus of prime importance – but it is not a challenge in isolation. There are numerous other important societal features of South Africa that interplay with the management of our working people, their work, and the organisations where they work. As you work further through this book, this will hopefully become clearer.

2.3.2.5 Some last words – for now: and South Africa's 'violent crime' factor

While as a country we have achieved much since the fall of apartheid in 1994, we are still also a society challenged with some seriously negative dynamics. Exhibit 2.9 presents some contemporary 'Fast Facts' about South Africa, as reported by the South African Institute of Race Relations (MacFarlane 2007). This gives a superficial and overall 'feel' of the state of South African society generally. Probably one of the most disturbing negative aspects at this stage of our journey towards 'a better life for all', and something affecting virtually all of South Africa's people, relates to the last point in exhibit 2.9: the excessive rates of crime and violence in South Africa.

Altbeker (2007: 13) says that "... the unavoidable, irreducible reality is that every single piece of reliable data tells us that South Africa ranks at the very top of the world's violent crime".

Crime and violence, and in particular 'violent crime', have become seriously disturbing aspects of our country and these phenomena spill over to working people and organisations in a very real way. In fact it threatens our whole society. The back cover of Altbeker's book (2007) sums up the magnitude and impact:

EXHIBIT 2.9: South Africa in brief: Fast Facts – July 2007

The 'big picture' reveals a mix of success and failure in South Africa's socio-economic performance.

DEMOGRAPHIC patterns show that between 1995 and 2006 the South African population grew from 41m to 48m people. The population growth rate is slowing, primarily due to the impact of HIV/AIDS. Also attributable to HIV/AIDS is a marked drop in life expectancy. This decrease from 56 years in 2000 to 51 years in 2006 is projected to fall further to 50 years by 2010.

HEALTH is a pressing concern in the face of the HIV/AIDS pandemic. The overall HIV infection rate was 11% in 2006. The spread of tuberculosis (TB) is closely associated with HIV infection, and in 2004 some 66% of all TB cases were co-infected with HIV. Malaria has been well controlled, with the number of cases and fatalities dropping rapidly since 2000. Some 93% of Africans were without medical aid in 2005.

The ECONOMY grew by 5.1% in 2005 and 5% in 2006. The agricultural and mining sectors, however, shrank by 13.1% and 0.7% respectively in terms of their contribution to GDP. The tertiary sector accounted for 66.4% of GDP in 2006. Gross fixed capital formation rose to R320.6 billion in 2006, an increase of 22% on the previous year. GDP per head also increased to close on R36 000 in 2006.

BUSINESS and EMPLOYMENT data reveal that the unemployment rate was 25.6% in 2006. Africans accounted for 88.7% of all unemployed people. The number of people living on less than $1 per day increased by 122.6% between 1996 and 2005. Acute poverty peaked in 2002, and has since declined marginally, largely because of social grants and job growth.

EDUCATION remains a concern, especially as fewer matriculants obtained university entrance passes in 2006 than in 2005. Higher education remains an important determinant of economic status, for 62% of those earning R8 001 or more in 2006 held a tertiary qualification.

LIVING CONDITIONS have improved overall, and 88% of households had access to clean water in 2005. The number of households residing in formal dwellings rose by 2.46 million, or 38%, between 1995 and 2005. However, over the same period those households living in informal dwellings rose by 223%. This is largely because demand for formal housing outstripped even this impressive supply. Demand was driven by rapid urbanisation and a drop in household size.

Violent CRIME escalated between 2005/06 and 2006/07. There was a reduction in rape and burglary of households, but murder and aggravated robbery rose sharply, along with burglary of businesses.

Source: MacFarlane (2007)

Crime is tearing South Africa apart! Whether it is hijacking or rape, a home robbery or a husband's explosion of rage, violence is so common that few lives have been left untouched by it. The result is a society deformed by its fears. Closeted behind locked doors and high walls, panic buttons at the ready, members of the middle class live lives haunted by fear. The poor, who are both more likely to be victimised and less able to secure themselves, are just as traumatised.

There are, on average, 50 murders every single day in South Africa (Altbeker 2007). The same author (2007: 37–30) explains that to the more or less 19 000 murders per year we can add about half a million cases of "… assault, serious assault and attempted murder recorded by the police every year … roughly 200 000 robberies and aggravated robberies … 55 000 rapes … 300 000 burglaries and 85 000 stolen cars … before we even think about the ocean of crimes that go unreported or unrecorded". These are absolute figures. For comparison purposes it is better to look at 'per capita' statistics.

In this regard, Altbeker (2007) says that in 2006 we had 41 murder victims per 100 000 people, compared to less than one per 100 000 in Japan, and similar figures for

Western Europe of less than two, and about five in the US. In China and India he says, "reported murder rates are between 3 and 6 per 100 000" (Altbeker 2007: 42).

Newmarch's (2008: 2) comments are in line with Altbeker's, and emphasise the seriousness of the situation and the implications for South Africa's organisations and people, also as customers and workers:

> While most of the country's challenges are manageable, crime has emerged as the one factor which consumers and businesses feel powerless to tackle ... [the] South African business community has been seriously affected ... This ranges most seriously from the debilitating, demoralising effects of violent, personalised attacks on employees and customers of all socio-economic and demographic groups on the streets, in their cars and homes, to the organised and random theft of billions of rands of company's assets ... Companies had to deal with trauma and skills depletion from death, injury or emigration as a result, and have to invest abnormally in protecting people and assets ...

To anyone serious about improving quality of life in our country, reading this must give some serious food for thought. Reading about it is one thing – living with it is the real challenge! All of these things impact directly on the people of South Africa – and this is the very source from which we draw our skills and talents to work and build the economy of our country.

Gumede (2007: 325) quite rightly says that the violent crime "... negatively affects economic growth, as both black and white skilled workers migrate because they feel unsafe in their homes and workplaces ...".

We have left the issue of violent crime as the last bit of this section, not to reflect that it is the least important, but rather because we feel this might in some sense be a determining issue, hence having it as a 'last word' in terms of our country's people.

Having reflected more on the 'socio' aspects thus far, we now turn our attention to some of our country's 'economic'-related dynamics.

2.3.3 South Africa's economic situation: some relevant observations[2]

Before we look at how our economy is doing or performing, let us take a brief look at the structure of our economy.

2.3.3.1 Structure of the South African economy

Traditionally our country's economy has been driven by the primary sector (agriculture, fishing, forestry, quarrying and mining), based on our wealth of mineral resources and favourable agricultural conditions. Over the past four decades the economy's structural make-up (in terms of output of different sectors – see table 2.3) has shifted, however, first to the secondary sector (manufacturing, construction and utilities such as water and electricity), and then to the tertiary sector (wholesale and retail trade, tourism, transport, communication and services). The tertiary sector dominates our economy today and within this sector, the financial, real estate, insurance, business services, communications and transport sectors accounted for about half of value added in 2006. As we move deeper into the 21st century, indications are that we are increasingly taking up aspects that form part of a 'knowledge-based economy', with more emphasis on, for example, technology and e-commerce.

Economic output is commonly measured in terms of gross domestic product (GDP), and table 2.5 illustrates how our economy's output has shifted across the various sectors over the last (almost) half a century.

Table 2.5: Structure of the South African economy in terms of sectoral contribution to GDP growth

Sector	Relative size 1960 (%)	Relative size 2006 (%)	Contribution to growth (% points)
Agriculture, forestry and fishing	10,6	2,4	–0,3
Mining	11,8	7,0	0
Manufacturing	19,0	16,1	0,8
Electricity, gas and water	2,3	1,9	0,1
Construction	2,8	2,3	0,4
Wholesale and retail trade, catering and accommodation	13,2	12,3	0,9
Transport, storage and communication	9,4	8,4	0,5
Finance, insurance, real estate and business services	10,0	19,5	1,6
Community, social and personal services	15,7	18,6	0,6
Total value added	94,9	88,6	4,6
Taxes on products less subsidies	5,1	11,4	0,4
GDP at market prices	100	100	5,0

Note: Total may not add up to 100 due to rounding
Source: South African Reserve Bank (in 'Economic Profile South Africa 2007')

With a GDP of four times that of our neighbouring countries, South Africa is commonly referred to as the 'economic powerhouse of Africa'. Our country's GDP represents almost a quarter of that of the continent as a whole. We are the leaders on the continent in industrial output (40% of total output) and mineral production (45%), and we generate most of the African continent's electricity (over 50%). South Africa's major strengths in relative terms probably relate to physical and economic infrastructure, natural mineral and metal resources, and our strong manufacturing (and of late also construction) sector. Our economy shows strong growth potential in the tourism, higher value-added manufacturing and service sectors. South Africa is well known for its banking and financial services sector. Our banking regulations are ranked with the best in the world, and as a sector rated among the top 10 globally. The JSE is the 18th largest exchange in the world market capitalisation. Having said all this, the next question relates to how our economy is performing.

2.3.3.2 Performance of the South African economy – in context

The performance of South Africa's economy must be considered against the ultimate aim of economic policy, namely to improve the welfare of the population at large. This requires economic growth which must be achieved in the context of a highly competitive global economy. How well we can compete relates to numerous and complexly interwoven factors. The same thus holds for how well our economy performs. Naturally our economic performance is thus connected with how well the world economy (and/ or parts thereof) performs. In all of this, competitiveness is central.

When it comes to competitiveness at a macro level the main goal of economic policy must be to enhance the ability of any country to develop a domestic economic situation that shows acceptable improvements in the real standards of living of the population of the country. This has to be achieved in a global economy that is highly competitive and it must include an acceptable fair distribution of the improvement of living standards across the whole population. Obviously one key aspect in this regard must be to provide work opportunities to all those members of the population who can and want to work. We have seen in previous sections that in South Africa we have been battling to get some of these things right, and that is the case despite relatively good economic growth over the past half a decade or so.

On the back of a world economy that has recorded real growth of approximately 5% per year for the period 2004 to 2006, the real growth of the African continent was around 5,5% for the same three successive years. Similarly, South Africa recorded increased real GDP at a rate of 5% in 2006, broadly in line with growth in 2005 and 2004. This rate of economic growth over three consecutive years was last witnessed in South Africa over the period from 1979 to 1981. During 2007, signs started to surface that a global economic slowdown was probably unavoidable, spurred on by things like disruptions that originated in the US sub-prime mortgage market, as well as in the international markets for structured investment products. According to the South African Reserve Bank (2008), global growth thus seemed to have lost some momentum in the final quarter of 2007 and in early 2008, with concomitant uncertain but less optimistic global economic prospects. Real economic growth in South Africa for 2007 as a whole nevertheless amounted to 5,1%, slightly lower than the rate of 5,4% recorded in 2006 (SA Reserve Bank 2008). This means that for four successive years (2004–2007) South Africa has experienced an economic growth rate of 5% or higher. An important contributing factor to our improved economic performance has been improved productivity levels, notably labour productivity which has improved especially since the late 1990s (Barker 2007). This has coincided with higher wages and increasing unit labour costs (the cost of a unit of labour to produce one unit of output), as Barker (2007: 125) explains: "Unit labour costs in South Africa have been increasing quite rapidly … However, when one considers real wages, the increase in labour productivity in recent years has exceeded the real wage increases."

There is thus more to competitiveness and economic performance than the actual growth rate of GDP, and a key factor is the productivity of working people, as well as what they get for that in return (pay). This makes the whole issue of the distribution of the wealth generated through economic growth, and hence the improvement of people's living standards, central to economic performance. However, the prices of goods (whether these rise and at what rate) also comes into the picture ('real' wage increases refer to wage increases after taking inflation into consideration – as opposed to nominal wage increases).

Let us briefly dwell on the role played by the prices of goods (products and services) when it comes to the improvement of living standards. The rise in living costs is commonly measured by the consumer price index (CPIX), and it is known as consumer inflation. This aspect is especially important in a country like South Africa where we have many unemployed and poor people who have to battle to make a living.

South Africa's consumer inflation was on a downward trend from 2002 to 2005, but has been increasing again since 2006/2007. Consumer inflation averaged 6,8% in 2003 and 4,3% in 2004. According to the IMF (2006), our inflation had again risen to 4,6% in 2006, though. During 2007, consumer inflation increased further and according to the South African Reserve Bank (2008), it accelerated even more into 2008, moving towards double-digit figures. Food price increases recorded double-digit rates, greatly spurred on by rising prices of petrol, among other things.

Other aspects playing a role in uplifting living standards include the exchange rate of the South African rand (which generally showed a deteriorating trend over the last decade and a half or so) as well as interest rates, which were on the rise from 2005/ 2006 and into 2007. All of these things impact on the living standards of South Africa's people, as the ability to buy goods is affected. Of particular concern must be those less fortunate in our society, who must bear much of the brunt of, for instance, increases in the price of life's necessities like food (see exhibit 2.10).

From exhibit 2.10 it should be clear that economic growth and performance can only really be interpreted and considered in the context of how the 'fruits' thereof are adding value to people's lives. In this context, economic performance only makes sense if we look at outputs and how these are distributed, and if we consider these things in a global as well as a local context. Economic performance includes, per definition, how economic output is put to use to enhance people's quality of life. In all of this, the economies of countries are linked in this global age and that is also why it is essential for companies and countries to strive towards being competitive globally.

The economic performance of any country is thus relative and hence we must consider the competitiveness of countries from a comparative perspective. By going into the websites of the IMD (www.imd.ch/wcc) and particularly the World Economic Forum (WEF) (www.weforum.org), one can learn a great deal about international comparative ratings of various countries' competitiveness.

According to the Global Competitiveness Index of the World Economic Forum, South Africa's overall ranking slipped from 40th place (out of 117 countries) in 2005 to 45th in 2006 (out of 125 countries), and then it went back up one place to number 44 (out of 128) in 2007. The top-performing African country over these three years

---

EXHIBIT 2.10: The poor suffer as food prices spiral – in South Africa, Africa and beyond

Global price increases have created more hungry people worldwide than ever before – and a rise in urban hunger, according to the United Nations' World Food Programme ... cost of our food has doubled in just the last eight, nine months ... we are seeing food on the shelves, but people being unable to afford it ... [t]he need for stable food supplies in Africa is especially serious ... Protesters blocked roads with barricades and burning tyres ... as violent demonstrations over the high cost of food in West Africa spread to once prosperous Ivory Coast (Powell 2008: 3).

"Is it not said 'a hungry man is an angry man'?" commented Simon Nkwenti, the head of a teachers' union in Cameroon, after riots that killed dozens of people there ... Anger over high food and fuel costs has spawned a rash of violent unrest across the globe in the past six months. People have taken to the streets from dusty Mauritania to steamy Mozambique. There have been tortilla riots in Mexico, villagers have clashed with police in eastern India and hundreds ... have marched for cheaper food in Indonesia ... Sub-Saharan Africa is particularly vulnerable ... For African households, even a small rise in the price of food can be devastating when meals are a family's main expense (Musa 2008: 2).

According to Farber (2008: 4), South African experts such as Professor Carel van Aardt of the University of South Africa and Dr Miriam Altman of the Human Sciences Research Council are warning that "South Africa could be facing a disaster as food and petrol price increases rock the economy – unless urgent measures are taken". And, said Farber, "Health Minister Manto Tshabalala-Msimang added her voice to concerns over spiralling food and petrol prices, warning that the effect on the health of the poor and vulnerable will be devastating".

Sources: Farber (2008); Musa (2008); and Powell (2008)

---

has been Tunisia with positions of 37, 30 and 32 over these same three years. Another less comprehensive (in terms of countries included) annual study of the international competitiveness of countries is published by IMD as the World Competitiveness Scoreboard. South Africa was ranked number 50 (out of 55 countries) in 2007, down 12 places from number 38 in 2006, according to the World Competitiveness Scoreboard. Although these different studies use different criteria as they measure competitiveness, collectively the sets of criteria reflect similar aspects being measured. Owing to its comprehensiveness, we stick to the WEF studies here.

The WEF uses nine pillars as the drivers of the competitiveness of countries (institutions, infrastructure, macro economy, health and primary education, higher education, market efficiency, technological readiness, business sophistication and innovation). Since 1998 the WEF has published *The Africa Competitiveness Report*. The fourth one in 2007 ranked Tunisia first of all African countries, followed by South Africa and Mauritius.

The WEF ratings, as expected, rate South Africa as faring poorly on aspects such as health and education (except for our country's management schools/education, for which we are ranked 19th out of the 128 countries), labour market flexibility (126th) and also on rankings related to crime and violence, and police services. Another disturbing development is the drop in South Africa's ranking on infrastructure from 35th place in 2006 to 50th in 2007. This was ascribed to the country's electricity supply problems that became increasingly evident during 2007 and 2008, as well as deficiencies in telecommunication infrastructure.

From an international and comparative perspective, we can see that although South Africa is performing better than any other sub-Saharan country, there still is a lot of room for improvement. Most of our challenges can somehow be related to human resources and especially the issue of social justice, or more precisely, distributive justice (these concepts are expanded upon in the next chapter). South Africa's economy has grown well, and Gumede (2007: 115) mentions that 12 years after democracy our country's economy was 33% bigger than in 1994 and that "jobs grew from about 9,5 million in 1995 to 12 million in 2006". He adds, however, that "... for four million people, a job is still a distant dream", and he sums up our situation and challenge as follows (Gumede 2007: 115): "Since 1994, almost 8,4 million people gained access to water, 3,8 million to electricity, two million to housing and 6,4 million to sanitation. However, inequality is more prevalent than ever, with the poor truly having become more impoverished, while rich amassed even greater fortunes." Similarly, Van der Westhuizen (2007: 322) explains:

> But, due to the bias in ANC government economic policies, the elite and upper middle classes have been deracialised. The upper classes became increasingly racially representative, while intra-racial inequality worsened. The white proportion of the top income group moved from 73 per cent in 1995 to between 61 and 55 per cent in 2000, while the black component increased from 18 per cent in 1995 to 31 per cent in 2000. In the second highest income group, blacks accounted for 61 per cent by 2000, up from 46 per cent in 1995. Whites had moved from 38 to 17 per cent ... Overall, inequality worsened, especially within racial groups ... This trend of deracialising the upper echelons had started under the NP, as the white population's share of national income dropped from 71 per cent in 1970 to 52 per cent in 1996 ... creating a black middle class accelerated under the ANC ...

Boyle (2008: 8) also reports that the latest official statistics in South Africa show that "the poorest 10th of the nation gets just 20 cents of every R100 that flows to households. Families in the richest 10th get R51". Various analysts, such as the South African Institute of Race Relations (MacFarlane 2005) and Barker (2007), concur that the widening of the gap between the rich and the poor in our country is now most prominent within the black population, and much less so between the racial groups. It has therefore clearly become a class issue, and it is well known that class struggles can and have led to revolutions. This is therefore an urgent and extremely serious feature of South Africa as we move closer to the fourth episode of elections in our country.

If we want to succeed as a country to really transform society to be a better place for all, we will thus have to pay urgent attention to aspects like these and concomitant issues such as poverty, unemployment, and crime (most notably violent crime). Almost a decade ago already, Westcott (1999: 21) warned "that the many empowerment initiatives ... served to deracialise the gaps ... the ranks of the rich have expanded to include a select bank of black industrialists. The poor remain poor, unskilled, uneducated and unemployed. This is South Africa's time bomb and contains the seeds of a potential class revolution". These very same issues we still find are being uttered from various circles and on numerous platforms today. We have known of this challenge as key to our future for a long time, and in this lies also the greatest challenge to our country's political leadership at this point in time. Gumede (2007: 427–429) puts it thus:

> And herein lies the country's future dilemma. The absence of economic and so-cial delivery, or at least the cushioning of hardship and misery while the masses wait for benefits of the economy to trickle down to them, could feed a grassroots revolt ... The ideal of the ANC and like-minded progressives – white and black – of creating a good society appears to be collapsing ... an equitable society that shows compassion for the poor while providing economic opportunities for all its citizens ... Right now there is a deep leadership void at the centre of South Africa's politics.

This brings us to the South African political scene.

2.3.4 Politics, policy and the state: notable shifts, key challenges and big uncertainties

Our country has come a long way since our new democracy was founded in 1994 with a government of national unity (GNU) that governed the country initially until 1996. The electoral results of 1994 gave the ANC a majority of the vote of 63,12% and we had Nelson Mandela as the first President of our 'new South Africa'. Our new democracy's next round of multiparty elections followed in 1999 and in the tradition of a true liberation movement, Mandela's successor as leader of the ANC and also President of the country became the then Deputy, Thabo Mbeki. The ANC (with its alliance parties of the South African Communist Party and the Confederation of South African Trade Unions) nearly hit the two-thirds majority mark in the 1999 elections, winning with 66,35%. The most recent elections in 2004 yielded the ANC victorious with 69,69% of the national vote. Clearly, the ANC came to dominate the political landscape rather dramatically. While some have argued that there were some signs effectively resembling those of one-party states, it also became increasingly clear during the third term of ANC-led democracy that within the ANC (and hence as part of the tripartite political alliance), tensions and division linked to policy and leadership shifts were mounting. This came to a high when Thabo Mbeki was recalled by the ANC and had to step down as the President of South Africa during September 2008.

From sections 2.2.6 and 2.2.7 we already know about some of the key relevant policy related changes and challenges that faced our country's ANC government during the first 15 years of our relatively young democracy. We particularly know that we have had, and still have, some persisting challenges that must be addressed, with social and distributive justice issues being squarely central to these. As South Africa move closer to the 2009 elections, though, a certain sense of uneasiness and a number of uncertainties have been creeping progressively into our political situation, linked very much with the socio-economic dynamics of the country.

Initially the framework governing policy and legislative reform was the Reconstruction and Development Programme (RDP). This was clearly underpinned by a people-central philosophy with some strong socialist democratic undertones. Growth, Employment and Redistribution (GEAR) later became the economic policy framework, while the essence of the RDP still had to be adhered to. With Thabo Mbeki at the helm, efforts were increasingly launched to modernise the ANC and the state, as well as the broader policy framework.

By July 2005, the South African government's Accelerated and Shared Growth Initiative for SA (AsgiSA) was launched by President Thabo Mbeki. The President often referred to our country's dual economy and in response hereto, partly at least, there was an acknowledgement that more had to be done to propel the country forward. This formed part of President Mbeki's drive to make our country a developmental state. AsgiSA's main aim was set to halve unemployment and poverty by 2014. An essential principle of AsgiSA was said to be the fact that economic growth could not be chased at any cost, and that it had to be sustainable and shared among all of South Africa's people. The increasing divide between the rich and the poor was thus central to this policy development, and in developing AsgiSA it was concluded that interventions to accelerate growth in a shared manner must be precision driven and based on South Africa's unique weaknesses (see exhibit 2.11) as brought about by previous strategies and policies of government.

EXHIBIT 2.11: Weaknesses of South Africa and initiatives to counter: AsgiSA

The six weaknesses unique to South Africa that have been identified:
- The overvaluation and volatility of the South African currency;
- An inadequate national infrastructure;
- A shortage of skilled labour;
- Barriers to entry, limits to competition, and limited new investment opportunities;
- A cumbersome regulatory environment; and
- Deficiencies in state organisation, capacity and leadership.

AsgiSA has initiatives which fall into six broad categories to address these constraints:
- Substantially investing in infrastructure;
- Targeting economic sectors with growth potential;
- Developing the skills of South Africans;
- Building up small businesses to bridge the gap between the formal and informal economies;
- Improving public administration; and
- Creating a macroeconomic environment more conducive to economic growth.

Source: Economic Profile South Africa 2007

In the introductory section of the HSRC publication, *State of the Nation: South Africa 2004–2005,* Daniel, Southall & Luchtman (2005: xxxi) stated that "the African National Congress (ANC) is in the throes of shifting from the Growth, Employment and Redistribution (GEAR) strategy to a more interventionist, developmental state". Roger Southall, in his introduction to the HSRC's similar but next publication (2005–2006), explains that since the previous publication the change has become "sufficiently explicit ... to have initiated the beginnings of a serious debate about the changing nature and role of the state as the second Mbeki presidency unfolds" (Southall 2006: xvii). The idea has been for South Africa to apply some lessons learned from the Asian-styled transformation politics and policies based on the principles of the (capitalist) 'development state'. It was felt that we needed a strong state that had to become more of an active interventionist to correct some market failures (including in particular the problems we have been experiencing pertaining to jobless growth and unemployment). AsgiSA identified six weaknesses unique to South Africa, and six broad categories of initiatives to address these problems (see exhibit 2.11).

The state apparatus (the three tiers of government and also including the state-owned enterprises (SOEs) or parastatals like Eskom and the SABC) were to become key to this shift and challenge, and capacity building throughout the public service had therefore to be a priority in this regard. Over time, many questions have, however, arisen regarding the capacity of the state apparatus to deliver. Herein lie also the seeds of the uncertainties and blends of optimism and pessimism that have come to feature so strongly in our country's socio-political and economic landscape as the fourth election period approaches. 'Delivery' has become a burning point: is this regime delivering what the people are, and have been, expecting?

The year 2006 was going to be a year of celebrating the tenth anniversary of the adoption of the Constitution of the Republic of South Africa. That year was also going to see our country's second general municipal elections (the first round having been in 2000). The lack of capacity to deliver at local government level and the increasingly frustrated people at grassroots level whose expectations have become unmet, culminated in large-scale protests in South Africa during the period leading up to these municipal elections – with many elements of violence.

Atkinson (2007: 58) captures it thus: "According to the Minister for Provincial and Local Government, Sydney Mufamadi, in 2005 protests were recorded in 90 per cent of the 136 municipalities identified as needing urgent assistance. The estimate by Minister for Safety and Security Charles Nqakula, was higher: in the 2004/05 financial year, there had reportedly been 5085 legal protests and 881 illegal protests ..."

Southall (2007) thus argues that while the state organs have become a key area of focus for transformation through affirmative action, there has unfortunately been a lack of emphasis on enhancing the capabilities of the working people of these public institutions. This, it is argued, might well be leading to compromising the effectiveness and efficiency of these organisations in terms of delivery. Southall (2007: 8) explains:

> The principal issue at stake is whether the drive for representativeness is compatible with efficiency and effectiveness ... The ANC opted for a short-term strategy of middle-class replacement through on-the-job affirmative action rather than choosing to invest in human capacity over the long term. The outcome has been a low level of administrative performance and the extensive abuse of their powers and positions by many self-serving public servants.

Many uncertainties thus started to surface, including issues related to corruption in government circles and especially how widespread these have become. One thing became certain, though: there was rising dissatisfaction with a perceived lack of delivery of what the people at grassroots needed, expected and wanted for long. These seem to have been making the masses increasingly disillusioned as they see some of those who were supposed to 'deliver' (those working in the state apparatus, the politicians, government officials and public servants) driving in new cars and living in comfort and even luxury. These things have also brought about much tension within the ANC, and its alliance partners.

There are thus increasing uncertainties and diverse perspectives as to the extent to which the ANC-led government has been succeeding in what it had to achieve. While President Mbeki each year, through his 'State of the Nation' addresses, tried to reassure South Africa's people of the successes being achieved, as his second term unfolded there were more and more people in the ANC who started to question the President's style and the direction of policy. The very 'soul of the ANC' came to be questioned as it has had to transform itself from having been a liberation movement into a modern political party. Some have found it disturbing and argued that very 'silently' almost the ANC have apparently become less of a democratic organisation itself, being more controlled by the centre (President Mbeki and his presidency) and having gradually moved away from socialist foundations to a more liberal-democratic framework (Southall 2007). As Gumede (2007) also shows, there have been mounting pressures to renew and reposition things in the ANC/Cosatu/SACP alliance as part of the 'battle for the ANC's soul'. Together herewith, inevitably, came the internal struggles for the succession of leadership – of the ANC as South Africa's dominant political party, and also then for the President of the country – with 'elections 2009' looming. All of this became intertwined with a situation by 2008 where "... social tensions are rising as South Africa moves away from a racially-polarised society to an increasingly class-divided society ... Against this background, the battle for succession ... [which] the party denies in public ... in reality [is] being manifestly fought out in the corridors of government and in the full glare of the media, with bitterly opposed camps competing ..." (Southall 2007: 21).

These two opposing camps referred to were reflected in the elections of the ANC leadership at the end of 2007. Jacob Zuma, with the full backing of the SACP and Cosatu (among others), and seen as representative of the 'have-nots', replaced Thabo Mbeki (seen increasingly as representing the 'haves' in the ANC and the country) as President of the ANC – even though Mbeki was still the President of South Africa. During September 2008 political intrigue and turmoil reached extreme levels when Thabo Mbeki was recalled by the ANC and had to step down as the president of South Africa. Kgalema Motlanthe was appointed and sworn in as interim President of the country and numerous resignations followed with a new Cabinet that was sworn in on 26 September 2008. Mbeki filed a case with the Constitutional Court and there were strong rumours about a possible break-up of the ANC and the forming of a new political party. Letsoalo (2008: 2) for instance reported as follows:

> With only months to go before elections, serious cracks have emerged in the ANC. The axing of Thabo Mbeki has strengthened these centrifugal forces. A growing number of ANC members ... want to join a new political party that disgruntled ANC leaders are planning ... Although there has been no formal an-nouncement, the *Mail & Guardian* understands plans ... are at an advanced stage ... An ANC source said many senior leaders did not want to go public with their

support for the new party at this stage because they were afraid of being vilified as "sell-outs". One provincial premier raised fears that the launch of the new party could ignite violence.

Towards the end of 2008 the formation of a new political party, COPE ("Congress of the People") was announced by former ANC leaders. The confusion, tension, uncertainty and angst brought about by these political dynamics, fully intertwined with the socio-economic realities of South Africa have meant that as the country moved closer to the 2009 elections, it became less and less certain what sort of country we are and should be, and where we are heading not only politically but also socio-economically. One thing was rather certain: the change and challenges ahead were very real.

2.3.5 South Africa's socio-political economy: concluding remarks

The socio-political economy of South Africa makes up a significant part of the 'bigger picture' and framework within which HRM is practised in our country. While politically there are many uncertainties and concerns, socio-economically there can be little doubt that 'the show must go on': we have to work harder and smarter at building a better South Africa for all. The framework within which to do this has largely been established and, although this may change as we see changes in the political realm, the legal framework established over the past decade and a half will go a long way to guiding and governing the way we manage the work systems and working people of our organisations in the years to come. No doubt, in all of this, all people involved in the management of human resources in our organisations will have a key role to play – in particular also the fraternity of HR practitioners. This makes for another important contextual setting for HRM in South Africa, not least because as we move deeper into the first decade of the 21st century, we have also had tensions, uncertainties and shifts in the country's human resource practitioner fraternity.

2.4 SOUTH AFRICA'S FRATERNITY OF HUMAN RESOURCE PRACTITIONERS: CHANGE, CONTINUITY – OR BOTH?

By now you will have an enhanced grasp of what the broader context entails within which we have to manage human resources in South Africa. 'We' in the previous sentence reflects those people involved in managing human resources. From Chapter 1 you know that when it comes to this field there are predominantly two groups of people who are directly involved with managing the human resources in our organisations – the general line managers, and those who prefer to specialise in the people management field. Naturally there are many groups of people involved with the human resource side of organisations (but not necessarily as part of the organisation as such), like trade unions, HRM consultants, labour brokers and employment agencies. Irrespective of this, we now shift our attention to those who prefer to specialise in HRM. More specifically, our focus in this section is on those who want specialise to the extent that they want to become 'professionals' in the field, so to speak. This is an important context within which to look at HRM, because there are so many who choose HRM as a specialised career in South Africa (and in the world), and also because these HR practitioners play such an important role in our organisations and in society generally.

From early sections in this chapter we know how the field of HRM has evolved in South Africa. As the move towards engaging people who specialised in 'personnel work' gained momentum, we know that local branches of the Institute for Personnel Management (IPM) of the UK were established in South Africa. By 1946 these evolved into the South African Institute of Personnel Management. On 2 February 1973 this became the Institute of Personnel Management (Southern Africa) and from within the IPM (SA) was born the South African Board for Personnel Practice (SABPP). According to Whyte (1990: 33), there was a groundswell of opinion and feeling during the mid 1970s, "expressed by the members of the personnel fraternity" of South Africa, that they wanted to embark on a path towards making personnel management a 'profession'. Consequently, in 1976 an Ad Hoc Committee on Professional Recognition for Personnel Practitioners was established, paving the way for the eventual establishment of the SABPP on 15 October 1982. Whyte (1990: 33) explained the reasoning behind setting up the SABPP: "Just like chartered accountants and professional engineers have to be 'registered', and every profession needs to have set standards (related to education and training of new entrants, registration and professional conduct) which are fully credible and are hence set by an impartial body, the need arose for a similar body and registration process in the personnel field."

We are now more than 25 years down that path and not there yet in terms of official professional status. We have thus witnessed a lot of change in the country from the early days of the IPM in the mid 1940s through the 1970s and into the 1980s, and also in respect of the work and challenges of the people of the HR practitioner fraternity. However, some things seem to stay with us. The 'struggle' to professional status received renewed impetus as we moved through the first decade of the 21st century in South Africa. During 2006 a document entitled the *Human Resources Professions Bill* was drafted and tabled with the aim of getting legislation in order to statutorily regulate 'the HR professions'. In the definitions section of this draft document, this has been described as follows:

> 'Human Resources Professions' means those occupations requiring prolonged training and formal qualification which specialise in general human resources; compensation management; education, training and development; employee safety, health and wellness; industrial relations; information systems and administration; planning, recruiting and selection; organisation development; research and development, related to human resources of an organisation or business.

It can be seen that the spectrum of 'human resource professions' is reflected as being pretty broad. Into the new millenium there were some interesting developments relating to potential fragmentation, proliferation and even some hostility and tensions within this broad fraternity of HR practitioners in the South Africa. So, for instance, the Human Resource Council of South Africa (HRCOSA) was established in the early 2000s in an attempt to bring together under one umbrella the broad range of associations that evolved in the fraternity of people who were specialising in some or other aspect of the management of human resources. These associations now include, for example (and apart from the IPM and SABPP), the Employee Assistance Professionals Association (EAPASA) (www.eapasa.org); the Association for Personnel Service Organisations of South Africa (www.apso.co.za); the Industrial Relations Association of South Africa (IRasa) (www.irasa.org.za); the South African Forum of ASTD (www.astd.co.za) and the Association of Mining Industries Human Resource Practitioners (AMIHRP).

In the SABPP's *Annual Report 2007/2008*, it is stated that it was becoming "... deeply concerned that a climate of antagonism among the organisations in the HR field" was "damaging the human resources profession" in South Africa. The SABPP thus organised a seminar under the banner 'Professionalising HR – A Time for Action' for 8 June 2007 in order to address these negative developments among South Africa's fraternity of HR practitioners. Well into 2008 the SABPP's efforts to harmonise things continued (as reflected also in exhibit 2.12), even though it seemed as though some sort of waiting game might have come into play regarding the statutory professionalisation drive. This drive has thus been prolonged and by mid-2008 some might well have developed concerns and uncertainties about progress and momentum in this regard.

As Swanepoel (2008) argues, though, the very fact that it is a debatable issue as to what extent it is possible or even perhaps desirable to regard HRM as the same as other professions, such as in medicine, law, engineering or accounting, makes the extreme slow progress over a period of more than three decades quite understandable. Regardless of whether there is statutory recognition and/or regulation of specialist practice in this field, the two main bodies that have been and still are the key role players are the IPM and the SABPP. It is therefore also good, as reflected in exhibit 2.12, that these two traditionally closely aligned bodies are taking the lead in collaborating to ease out possible negative dynamics. The clarification of roles in this regard, and as reflected in exhibit 2.12, lies at the heart of this effort.

In concluding this section we want to emphasise the important role played by the SABPP in South Africa. Exhibit 2.13 reflects some of the important work and role of the SABPP, and anyone serious about formally studying in the field and becoming a recognised and respected specialist in the field of HRM will do well to visit their website (www.sabpp.co.za) and establish contact. Becoming and remaining a valued HR practitioner is challenging and rewarding, and apart from engaging the SABPP, any such people should seriously consider what is stated also in exhibit 2.12 in relation to the roles of the IPM and the SABPP. Being in contact with the appropriate organisations (hence also including others as mentioned earlier, such as IRasa, for instance) and networking with fellow specialising HR practitioners in South Africa (and beyond, through international bodies) is very important, as is reading extensively to stay current with developments in the field.

EXHIBIT 2.12: The SABPP and the IPM – some tensions or greater cooperation?

"The IPM visited the Board on the 18th of January to explore ways in which the IPM and the SABPP could cooperate in the interest of the profession and the larger collective by seeking solutions for the challenges of our country. Present on the day for IPM: Elijah Litheko, Sam Tsima, Penny Abbott and Marius Pheiffer. Present for SABPP: Elizabeth Dhlamini-Kumalo, Pat Naves, Marietta van Rooyen and Huma van Rensburg.

After a preliminary round it was very clear that the intention of both bodies was to find synergies, to support one another and to stand together on important issues. The first order of business was to clarify the roles of the SABPP and the IPM.

The role of the SABPP

(IPM established SABPP to be the standards body in 1982)

1 The Board is the national professional registering body for HR
   Setting standards
   Setting criteria for each registration level
   Evaluating individuals
   Registering individuals in one of five levels
   Evaluating and registering RPL candidates
   Accrediting tertiary institutions so that students can register

>>

<<

Representing HR to tertiary institutions to ensure that the curricula meet the needs of industry

Enforcing a Code of Ethics

Enforcing Continued Professional Development

Doing research through the HRRI

Determining specialist categories and criteria

2   The Board is also the national statutory quality assurance body (ETQA) for HR

Accrediting Providers

Registering Assessors and Moderators

Placing learning credits on the NLRD

Certificating learners for qualifications achieved

Representing HR with SAQA and with SETAs, CHE and Umalusi

Meeting SAQA's requirements in terms of the Act.

The role of the IPM

The Portal to thought leadership in people management

- Provides members with easy access to the latest information, knowledge, expertise, training and development, systems and processes and networks in people management.
- Creates platforms and opportunities for HR professionals and members to network.
- Creates communities of learning such as "Knowledge Exchange Groups" for specialized learning and knowledge sharing.
- Provides members with access to solution providers via workshops/seminars, IPM magazine, annual convention and exhibition
- Brings HR professionals together through branch networks nationally
- An association for HR professionals with continental and international links
- Facilitates capacity building within the HR fraternity and continuous professional development and high level refinement of HR practices
- Contributes to organizational sustainability
- Contributes to and influences national strategic issues
- Initiates and participates in domestic, continental and global research projects.

An IPM representative came up with a suggested dual motto:

> "No HR professional can operate effectively without being registered through SABPP, as this registration sets the standard. No HR practitioner can operate effectively without a network, which is offered through the IPM."

Both groups agreed to inform their own bodies of the many suggestions made on possible future areas of cooperation and support."

Source: Taken from 'Across the Board – a communication from the SA Board for Personnel Practice', March 2008

EXHIBIT 2.13: The SABPP: what it stands for and what it has done to prepare for statutory recognition

SABPP's mission: To establish, direct and sustain a high level of professionalism and ethical conduct in personnel practice.

SABPP's strategy: To promote, direct and influence the development of the human resources profession; to review competency standards for the education, training and conduct of those engaged in the profession; to advise involved parties on the development and attaining of those competencies and to evaluate such attainment.

SABPP's value statement: Our actions are guided by the following values:

- The SABPP is committed to objectivity, fairness, consistency and integrity in all its functions

<<

- The quality assurance system of the SABPP ETQA strives to contribute to the economy of South Africa
- The SABPP links the achievement of quality to equity and the fostering of innovation and diversity
- With a customer-centred focus the SABPP will work in a consultative and cooperative mode with partners and stakeholders
  - offering service excellence
  - being professional in all our dealings
  - building and maintaining trust and confidentiality
- The SABPP strives to facilitate the delivery of high quality HR practice.

IN PREPARATION FOR STATUTORY RECOGNITION

After the establishment in 1982, the Board immediately began working for statutory recognition. A draft Personnel Practice Bill was published 4 October 1985. The then Minister of Manpower declined to table the Bill in Parliament. We remain convinced that HR would have been years further in its development had this initiative been accepted by Government.

To consolidate the position of HR in the difficult new NQF environment, the Board took various steps to ensure standards and quality. A Standards Generating Body for Human Resource Management and Practice (SGB for HRMP) was initiated. We convened and funded the first plenaries in 1998 and the SGB was formally accredited by SAQA and published in *Government Gazette* of 11 February 2000. We currently have a representative on the SGB Board and we still support them. This SGB has since registered a framework of qualifications on the NQF and has written over 50 unit standards for the HR field. Based on the work of the SGB, the Board did an extended exercise of consultation and deliberation and announced new professional registration levels aligned to the NQF in 2002.

The Board applied for ETQA status in 1997 and was accredited by SAQA in November 2002. We are currently one of the few ETQAs that receive no part of the levy funds to fund its ETQA service to the country. In 1998 the Board started a series of meetings with the different organisations in the HR field and formed a loose Alliance of these organisations. In November 2002 these efforts culminated in the formal establishment of the HR Council of South Africa (HRCOSA). The Board is a member together with some 25 other HR-related organisations.

The Board strongly supports statutory recognition and mandatory registration of HR Practitioners. We have an extended network of Mentors throughout the country that will assist the Board with the huge task of registering thousands of HR people. A series of conferences "HR Crossroads" were held in Johannesburg, Cape Town and Durban which addressed questions critical to the future of HR practice in South Africa: should the HR professional be held accountable to the state and business, including investors, for the HR practices of the organisation and what do employers require that HR professionals are able to do?

These conferences were addressed by Government, Business, Academia, IPM, HRCOSA and SABPP. The proposed Human Resource Profession Act is now out for comment and can be viewed on this website.

Source: Taken from the SABPP website www.sabpp.co.za, April 2008

2.5 CONCLUSION

In this chapter you had the opportunity to learn about the broad South African context of HRM. We have placed South African HRM in an appropriate context in terms of time and broader societal dimensions. It is very important to know 'where one is from' – for had it not been for history, 'one would not have been'. We thus started off this chapter by exposing you to South African HRM as seen through a historical lens. We then proceeded to provide you with some contemporary glimpses of the broader socio-economic and political context of South Africa – as these relate to human resources in our country as well, and also as appropriately located in the context of Africa and the world more globally. In the last section, we shared some dynamics pertaining to the challenges faced by the fraternity of people and bodies involved with the field of HRM in a specialised way. In the next chapter we zoom in and become more focused to address the more detailed aspects of the HRM challenge of our era. That challenge, as you will discover, is multidimensional and relates to conformance as well as performance.

SELF-EVALUATION QUESTIONS

1 Write an essay in which you give an overview of the historical development of South African HRM.
2 Explain the role of Isobel White in the historical development of personnel management in South Africa.
3 Write brief notes that outline the following: 'Democratic South Africa's first decade: transforming the country's "HRM landscape"'.
4 Write a five-page essay about the following: 'South Africa's contemporary "socio-political economy" and HRM in our country'.
5 Analyse and critically discuss this statement: 'The human resources of South Africa, and how people are managed in our organisations, hold little implications for things like "performance" and "competitiveness". These are dictated by international politics and regional location. We are part of Africa, a continent which the rest of the world does not really care about at all.'
6 Describe the nature and role of the SABPP in terms of HRM in South Africa. What about the IPM? Are there any other such relevant bodies in South Africa, and if so, which are they?

ENDNOTES

1 This section is based largely on personal notes of IHB White (kindly supplied to the author by the IPM (SA)), on publications by IHB White, and on a personal interview with IHB White conducted by Ben Swanepoel during the late 1990s.
2 This section is based on and contains material adapted from the 'Economic Profile South Africa 2007'.

3 BEYOND CONFORMANCE: HRM FOR SOCIO-ECONOMIC INCLUSIVENESS

LEARNING OUTCOMES

After studying this chapter, you should be able to:

- explain what is meant by the 'HRM conformance' challenge, and describe the legislative framework impacting on HRM in South Africa;
- engage in informed dialogue about the meaning of the 'HRM empowerment agenda', explain various related concepts, issues and perspectives, and debate the challenges we face in South Africa in this regard, including affirmative action and employment equity; and
- explain issues pertaining to diversity management.

3.1 INTRODUCTION

As you know by now, politics, economics and broader social dynamics are closely intertwined, in South Africa as elsewhere. Political empowerment was achieved in 1994 when all of South Africa's people gained the status of having equal opportunities to vote for whom they wanted to govern their country. This was a wonderful achievement, but it did not automatically translate into a situation where all of our country's people had equal opportunities in the socio-economic sphere. Quality of life is very much influenced by access to 'socio-economic goods' such as work and income-earning opportunities, welfare benefits and education.

From the first two chapters we know that one of South Africa's persistent challenges has been to create a society in which all of our people are better off in terms of the socio-economic dimensions of the country. Although a lot has been achieved to date, a number of pressing problems are persisting, not least of which being directly related to distributive justice, and in particular the skew distribution of wealth in our country. As our society has been transforming, some have benefited a lot while others have been left behind.

Sunter and Ilbury (2008: 30), in reflecting on South Africa's possible future scenarios within a global context, explain that the key rules of the game that will be determining for our future include our ability to create social harmony or cohesion, which in turn will require our economy to be inclusive. They elaborate to issue a stern, almost disturbing, warning as they try to explain:

> South Africa's economy is currently anything but inclusive. Its development since 1994 is more akin to a change in the membership of an existing, exclusive club. This brings to mind Karl Marx's rule of the game that if you alienate the masses, you can expect a revolution (Sunter & Ilbury 2008: 30).

Since the birth of our democracy, the ANC government has been rolling out a stream of new laws to transform South Africa into a society where the 'socio-economic goods' are distributed more fairly across the spectrum of the country's people. There is, however, a serious need for accelerated and enhanced achievement in this regard, as shown in chapter 2. We have a comprehensive legislative framework imposing compliance-related challenges on organisations, but we seem to be falling short of really utilising these to our full benefit. Instead, it seems as though during the past decade and a half there has been an increasing reluctance to conform to some new laws. From the perspective of HRM specifically, conformance to a whole range of new laws has become a central task. However, as we will show in this chapter, we believe we have to go beyond a conformance mindset and focus on enhancing performance through empowerment.

We should not merely conform to the new legislative regime, but develop a way of thinking and acting that reflects our embracing this legislative regime to really empower and engage the full spectrum of our country's diverse people. Such an approach will be important if we want to enhance performance and create opportunities to improve the quality of life of more and more people. We have to strive towards having a just and fair society in which we embrace the diversity of our country's people so that all can have opportunities to meaningfully participate and contribute towards 'a better life for all'.

In this chapter we first introduce you to the legislative framework within which HRM in South Africa has to be practised. This sets the broad framework or parameters for the conformance challenge pertaining to the management of our country's human resources. However, it also serves as the foundation and sets the tone for how we can go about making our society and economy more inclusive, and capitalise on the diversity of our people.

Throughout the rest of this book you will also come across some legal aspects pertaining to the management of human resources. In this chapter we can merely introduce you to a legislative framework that drives the HRM conformance challenge. Because this book is not a 'book of law', though, we merely introduce you to the framework of relevant laws, doing no more than sensitising you in terms of some of the spectrum of legal issues that may be encountered in relation to the work and working people in our society. Law is, of course, a highly specialised profession and hence it would be important to have access to relevant legal advice and assistance regarding all laws that interplay with the management of work, and the people who do the work in and for our organisations.

Apart from introducing you to the legislative framework for HRM in South Africa, our prime concern is how we can leverage relevant legislation as a platform to empower more and more people of our country. Our people empowerment challenge is huge, but it goes beyond a conformance mindset – it requires one of 'performance'. In the second part of the chapter we thus go into a little more detail regarding the affirmative action and other empowerment initiatives we should engage in. We end off the chapter with a brief reflection on some of the challenges pertaining to the management of diversity.

3.2 THE HRM CONFORMANCE CHALLENGE: SOUTH AFRICA'S LEGISLATIVE FRAMEWORK

South African HRM is governed by many sources of law. These include the common law, the law of contract (including the contract of employment and the contract for the provision of services), various statutes, collective agreements entered into between employers and trade unions, international labour standards (such as, for example, the various Conventions of the ILO), workplace practices, customs and traditions, and lastly, the values enshrined in the Bill of Rights contained in our Constitution. There is a vast range of statutes that have a potential impact on how we manage work and working people, including, generally, the Employment Equity Act, The Promotion of Equality and Prevention of Unfair Discrimination Act, the Labour Relations Act, the Basic Conditions of Employment Act, the Occupational Health and Safety Act, the Compensation for Occupational Injuries and Diseases Act, the Unemployment Insurance Act, the Skills Development Act, and the Broad-Based Black Economic Empowerment Act.

In a book of this nature it is obviously neither possible nor the aim to provide a detailed discussion of the provisions of Acts like these. There are numerous books that do this, given the specialised nature of law generally, and also law related to labour. This section is intended to merely make you aware of the existence of these sources of law and to develop a general feel for the overall legal framework that drives the conformance dimension of HRM in our country. Naturally, from the perspective of managing human resource related organisational risk, the whole issue of legal compliance becomes very important. In this regard you are strongly advised to consult appropriate specialist sources like legal publications and/or qualified legal professionals when encountering law-related issues. Note, however, that the view we propagate is that the legal framework should be used to drive strategies and practices that go beyond the risk and conformance aspects embedded in the rules of the HR game in South Africa. We think it offers the parameters of the *risks* related to non-conformance, as well as the opportunities to excel and perform superiorly.

In considering the laws relevant to HRM, it is important to remain mindful that the dominant relationship in this field, and the one that is governed by labour law, is the employment relationship. While HRM includes the management of work and the people doing it in terms of other relationships as well (such as via labour brokers or temporary employment service providers), people and their work in the context of employment relationships are much more prominent. You will thus find that we are particularly concerned about labour law when it comes to HRM.

The existence of so many sources of rules governing work and the management of working people means that we also need rules to determine which source of law will take precedence in instances where different rules may come into conflict. Figure 3.1 reflects an example of a hierarchy of sources as discussed in the sections below. For example, common-law principles may be amended by the contract of employment, which, in turn, must comply with the Basic Conditions of Employment Act. The provisions of the latter Act may be superseded by a collective agreement in terms of the Labour Relations Act.

3.2.1 Constitutional law

Chapter II of South Africa's Constitution guarantees all people of our country certain basic rights. Nobody (including parliament) may infringe upon those rights that are regarded as indispensable in a democratic society affirming the democratic values of human dignity, equality and freedom. The only exception is when such an infringement or limitation of the right in question can be brought under the general limitation clause of the Constitution (section 36). Therefore, any action that is in contravention of the constitutionally guaranteed rights can be challenged on those grounds. Furthermore, any Act of parliament can be similarly challenged and, indeed,

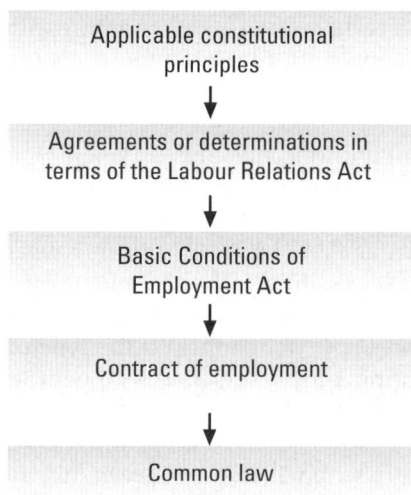

Figure 3.1: Hierarchy of sources of labour law rules

be declared null and void, should it be found to be unconstitutional. The principle is that sovereignty no longer belongs to parliament – it resides in the Constitution, which gives the Constitutional Court the authority to overrule parliament. Section 23 of the Constitution, for instance, guarantees everyone in South Africa the right to fair labour practices. This has far-reaching implications for HRM. The Constitution contains numerous other provisions that impact on how we manage work and working people in our country, including freedom of expression and association, protection against servitude, forced labour and discrimination, as well as property rights and the right to pursue a livelihood.

3.2.2 Common law

The common law of South Africa is Roman-Dutch law, that is, the legal system that Jan van Riebeeck brought to the Cape in 1652. In general one can say that the common law is applicable in all cases except in those instances where it is superseded by a particular statute. For instance, in common law there is no duty on an employer to grant any leave to an employee; this has been changed by the Basic Conditions of Employment Act, which prescribes certain minimum leave requirements.

Our common law regards the contract of employment as a contract of letting and hiring; the worker lets his or her labour potential to the employer (the lessee), who in turn pays the worker for it. It is thus a reciprocal agreement between an employer and an employee. A contract of employment exists when the parties have concluded an agreement conforming to the requirements of *locatio conductio operarum* (Grogan 2007: 18).

There are also other forms of contract through which an organisation (as a legal entity) can engage people to do its work. Grogan (2007: 18) explains that the contract for the provision of services opens up the avenue for getting people to perform work as independent contractors in accordance with the requirements of *locatio conductio operis*. This is a different working relationship, though, than the employment relationship between employee and employer. Probably the single most important distinguishing trait of the employment relationship is the element of control that the employer has over the employee – if this is lacking, the worker is likely to be regarded not as an employee but rather as an independent contractor. As Grogan (2007: 17) says, the "independent contractor of the common law is not an employee. Nor, to take other examples, are partners or agents, even though one of the parties may work for the other".

We have statutory definitions that tell us when someone can be regarded as an employee generally. The common law is thus the baseline in this regard. In South Africa we can look at definitions in the Basic Conditions of Employment Act as well as in the Labour Relations Act (LRA) – both introduced to you below. There have been numerous court cases dealing with the issue of what type of contract is at play in the course of one party performing work on behalf of (or for) another party. This is so because different laws apply depending on the type of contract. The labour laws of our country generally apply only when there is a contract of employment proper. As we have said before, most of HRM relates to the management of working people as employees, which makes employment relationships between employers and employees the dominant relationship with which we concern ourselves.

Grogan (2007: 22) draws on findings of our country's Labour Appeal Court (LAC) and summarises the main differences between the contract of employment

Table 3.1: Contracts of employment proper versus 'contracts of work' (independent contractors)

Locatio conductio operarum	Locatio conductio operis
The object is the rendering of personal services between employer and employee	The object is the production of a certain specified service or the production of a certain specified result
The employee renders service at the behest of employer	The independent contractor is not obliged to perform work personally unless otherwise agreed
The employer may decide whether it wishes to have employee render service	The independent contractor is bound to perform specified work or produce a specified result within a specified or reasonable time
The employee is obliged to obey lawful, reasonable instructions regarding work to be done and manner in which it is to be done	The independent contractor is not obliged to obey instructions regarding manner in which task is to be performed
Terminated by the death of the employee	Not terminated by the death of the contractor
Terminates on completion of the agreed period	Terminates on completion of the specified work or production of the specified result
Additional factors may be: An employee pays PAYE/SITE tax and UIF The employee is entitled to paid annual leave, paid sick leave, etc. And possibly (but not necessarily) other benefits such as pension, provident or medical aid The employee works the hours stipulated by the employer	Additional factors may be: The independent contractor is usually a provisional taxpayer and does not pay UIF for him- or herself Independent contractors must make their own financial provision for annual leave, sick leave, etc, and provide their own benefits Independent contractors regulate their own working hours, and are bound usually only by the deadline date specified in the contract

Sources: Grogan (2007: 22); Jackson (www.labourguide.co.za)ww

proper and what the LAC calls a 'contract of work'. These are depicted in the first six points of difference in table 3.1. The 'additional factors' in the same table are further differences that might help determine the type of relationship, according to Jackson (www.labourguide.co.za). Note, however, as Grogan explains, "[t]he courts have frequently held that the classification of contracts is a matter of substance, not merely form ... The true nature of the contract is determined from the relationship between the parties".

Irrespective of the type of contract and working relationship, the general common-law requirements for a valid contract to come into existence must be present. These are:
- there must be consensus between the contracting parties regarding the contents of the agreement and the intention to contract;
- both parties must have contractual capacity;
- performance in terms of the contract must be possible at the time of the conclusion of the contract;
- the contract must be lawful in the sense that it must not offend the prevailing good morals of society; and
- while formalities, such as reducing the contract to writing are generally not required, in those cases where compliance with formalities is a prerequisite for the validity of a particular contract (such as an apprenticeship contract), those formalities must be complied with.

When there is a contract of employment proper, the parties to it have certain common-law rights and duties (generally speaking, the rights of the one party constitute the duties of the other party, and vice versa). These are summarised in table 3.2.

Table 3.2: Common-law duties of employers and employees

Employee's duties	Employer's duties
- to enter and remain in service; - to maintain reasonable efficiency; - to further the employer's business interests; - to be respectful and obedient; - to refrain from misconduct; and - not to compete in his or her private capacity with the business of his or her employer.	- to receive the worker into service and to retain him or her; - to pay the worker's wages; - to provide safe working conditions; - not to expect the worker to do work inconsistent with his or her status; and - to provide work for the worker.

The rest of section 3.2 (and its subsections) covers primarily our country's labour laws (thus applicable only where employment relationships are at stake). We do go beyond that as well, though, especially towards the last subsection. We are generally interested also in laws that are applicable to work and working people beyond employment relationships structured through contracts of employment. As we move beyond conformance to a performance mindset, we thus broaden the HRM agenda to our broad-based black economic empowerment (BBBEE) challenge which is geared towards an embracement of the full diversity of our country's people.

3.2.3 The Basic Conditions of Employment Act 75 of 1997

Under common law the parties are essentially free to agree to whatever terms and conditions they deem fit in terms of how they want to structure their employment relationship (within limits of the law, reasonableness and good morals, though). However, over the years the contractual freedom of the parties has been restricted by the legislature, due mainly to power imbalances inherent in any employment relationship. For many years, though, only the minority of people of South Africa received legal protection against these power imbalances. The object of the Basic Conditions of Employment Act (BCEA) is to lay down minimum conditions of employment to protect all employees in the absence of collective agreements and/or relevant sectoral determinations regulating such conditions.

The BCEA regulates minimum conditions in respect such things as working time (including meal intervals, daily and weekly rest periods, overtime), work on Sundays and public holidays, leave (annual, sick, maternity and family responsibility) and primarily process (how and when) aspects related to pay/remuneration and notice periods when employment is terminated. The purpose can thus be thought of as advancing social justice and economic development through establishing and enforcing certain basic conditions of employment.

Basically, the BCEA kicks in as a default option (when there is no collective agreement for instance) and acts as a safety net in recognition of the much weaker power position of any individual employee, compared to an employer. In industries, sectors and areas where, for example, a collective agreement caters for an issue such as hours of work, these collectively bargained-for provisions will prevail over the corresponding provisions of the BCEA – as long as these conditions are at least as favourable as those set out by the BCEA.

Thus, any actual condition of employment, such as working hours, that is less favourable than the minimum specified in the BCEA will be regarded as null and void, and will be replaced by the relevant provisions of the BCEA. For example, suppose that, in terms of her common-law contract of employment, an employee is expected to work more than ten hours a week overtime, this stipulation will be of no force or effect because the Act lays down a maximum of ten hours a week overtime.

The BCEA does not specify minimum wages, the determination of which is left to a body such as the Employment Conditions Commission, which, after thorough investigation, determines wages (and, incidentally, other minimum conditions of employment) on an *ad hoc* and local basis.

The Basic Conditions of Employment Act 75 of 1997 came into effect on 1 December 1998 in respect of the private sector and as from I May 2000 it became applicable to South Africa's public sector. On 1 August 2002, the Basic Conditions of Employment Amendment Act (11 of 2002) became effective. The BCEA applies to all employers and employees, except for members of the South African Secret Service (SASS), the National Intelligence Agency (NIA) and the South African National Defence Force (SANDF), as well as unpaid charity workers. Some provisions of the BCEA are not applicable to certain categories of employees. Provisions governing hours of work, for instance, do not apply to senior managerial employees (defined as employees who have the authority to hire, discipline and dismiss other employees, and to represent the employer externally and internally).

3.2.4 The Occupational Health and Safety Act 85 of 1993 (OHSA)

The Occupational Health and Safety Act 85 of 1993 (OHSA) came into operation on 1 January 1994. While this Act is still applicable in its current form as this edition of our book is going to print, it is under review. A new proposed National Occupational Health and Safety Bill has seen the light and, once promulgated, will replace OHSA (and the Mines Health and Safety Act).

The objectives of the OHSA are to "provide for the health and safety of persons at work and for the health and safety of persons in connection with the use of plant and machinery; the protection of persons other than persons at work against hazards to health and safety arising out of or in connection with the activities of persons at work; [and] to establish an advisory council for occupational health and safety..." (long title of the Act).

The ambit of the OHSA is wider than any other labour statute. In addition to covering the private as well as the public sectors, it is also applicable to persons in private households; in fact, this Act covers persons who are exposed to hazards or occupational disease or who are injured through the use of machinery or through exposure to hazardous substances, even though such exposure or injury did not occur in the context of an employment relationship. The major exclusions from the ambit of the Act are the mining industry (only in respect of matters provided for in the Mine Health and Safety Act 29 of 1996), and certain vessels as defined in the Merchant Shipping Act 57 of 1951. In terms of the new Bill, it is foreseen that the new legislation will apply to all persons who conduct businesses; who work (whether as an employee or self-employed); and every person whose health and safety may be affected by work activities.

The OHSA makes the following provisions for the achievement of its objectives:

- The establishment of an Advisory Council for Occupational Health and Safety.
- Every employer must provide and maintain, as far as is reasonably practicable, a working environment that is safe and without risk to the health of his or her employees, as well as other people affected by the operations of the business.
- Every supplier or manufacturer of items used in a workplace must ensure that such items do not pose a safety or health risk.
- Every employer must inform his or her workforce (and the appointed health and safety representatives) of hazards at the workplace.
- All employees must
  - take reasonable care for the health and safety of themselves and of other persons who may be affected by their acts or omissions;
  - carry out any lawful order given to them, and obey the health and safety rules and procedures laid down by their employer;
  - report any unsafe or unhealthy situation which comes to their attention; and
  - report any incident which may affect their health or which has caused an injury to themselves.
- The Act provides that every employer who employs more than 20 employees at any workplace must appoint health and safety representatives, and spells out the functions of such representatives.
- One or more health and safety committees must be established in respect of each workplace where two or more health and safety representatives have been designated. The functions of health and safety committees are spelled out in the Act.
- Certain incidents must be reported to an inspector.
- Occupational diseases must be reported to the chief inspector.
- Wide powers of inspection, entry, enquiry and seizure are conferred on inspectors.
- A wide range of actions (or lack of actions) are declared offences and can incur criminal penalties.

The health and safety of people working in and for our organisations are very important. It really is the baseline of looking after the general well-being of our working people.

Relevant aspects of the OHSA and the Mine Health and Safety Act are discussed in greater detail in chapter 17, a chapter that goes way beyond conforming to basic health and safety legislation.

3.2.5 The Compensation for Occupational Injuries and Diseases Act 130 of 1993

The Compensation for Occupational Injuries and Diseases Act (COIDA) came into operation on 1 March 1994.The purpose of this Act is to "… provide for compensation for disablement caused by occupational injuries or diseases sustained or contracted by employees in the course of their employment, or for death resulting from such injuries or diseases …" (long title of the Act). Should an employee die as a result of an accident, injury or disease, the compensation will be paid to his or her dependants.

The rationale of the Act is to provide employees (or their dependants in the case of the employee's death) with compensation without their having to prove fault on the part of their employer or any other person (or the absence of fault on the employee's part) and to create a fund from which such compensatory payments can be financed. The logic behind this scheme is that employees are frequently unable to prove fault on the part of their employer (which makes a damages claim impossible), or that the injury/death could be the result of fault on the part of the employee him- or herself (which would likewise be fatal for any civil claim for damages). By removing the fault requirement, which is an essential element of a civil claim for damages, employees are guaranteed some compensation, provided that the injury, illness or death arose out of and in the course of their employment (employees who are being transported to or from work by a person appointed by the employer to do so are also regarded as being at work). Furthermore, by instituting a fund, employees are protected from the possibility of their employer being insolvent or otherwise unable to compensate them. The fact that the COIDA caps the amount of compensation which can be awarded and provides for intercession by the fund on behalf of the employer (an employee is precluded from instituting a claim against his or her employer or any other third party), protects employers from potentially ruinous claims (although the caps on compensation can be seen as a definite disadvantage from the employee's point of view).

The COIDA covers all employees, including seasonal or contract workers, as well as directors who have a contract of employment. The COIDA also covers members of the permanent force of the SANDF, as well as members of the South African Police Service (SAPS). It applies to independent contractors and domestic workers as well.

In terms of the COIDA every employer must do the following:

- register with the Compensation Commissioner and supply particulars regarding his or her business and employees;
- keep records of wages, time worked and payment for overtime and piecework, and retain these records for a period of four years;
- submit to the Commissioner in prescribed form, by the end of March each year, the total salary bill for the preceding financial year;
- report any accident within seven days and any occupational disease within 14 days of its coming to his or her attention; and
- pay an assessed amount into the Compensation Fund (no contributions may be deducted from employees' pay).

The Commissioner determines annually the percentage of total salary bill that must be paid by every employer into the Compensation Fund. The Commissioner may decide that different percentages should apply to different employers or to different groups of employers, based, inter alia, on the claims history of an employer or particular group of employers. It is therefore in the interest of employers to introduce measures to decrease the likelihood of accidents and occupational diseases which may result in an unfavourable claims history, as this may in turn cause an increase in the assessed rate for that employer or sector.

Benefits are payable to three categories of claimants:

- employees who have suffered temporary disability;
- employees who are permanently disabled; and
- the dependants of employees who have died as a result of their injuries or occupational disease (occupational diseases are listed in a schedule to the Act).

Claims for compensation must be lodged within 12 months after the accident or illness occurred or after the employee died. Compensation will not be payable if temporary disablement lasts for three days or less, or if an accident is the result of the serious and wilful misconduct of the employee (unless the accident results in the serious disablement of the employee or the employee dies as a consequence thereof). Employees may apply for increased compensation if the accident in which they were injured or the occupational disease they contracted was caused by the employer's negligence.

3.2.6 The Unemployment Insurance Act 63 of 2001

The Unemployment Insurance Act (UIA) came into operation on 1 April 2002. The main purpose of the Act is to provide for the payment of benefits for a limited period to those contributors who are ready and willing to work, but who are unable to find work for whatever reason.

This Act is peculiar in that it does not contain a definition of an employee. Instead it works with the concept of a 'contributor' (see below), which is central to the scheme envisaged by the Act. Employees who qualify as contributors contribute 1% of their earnings to the Unemployment Insurance Fund (UIF), while their employers contribute an equal amount. When such contributors become unemployed, fall ill for lengthy periods, or give birth to or adopt a child, they may apply for UIF benefits. The dependants of deceased contributors may also apply for benefits.

The UIF thus provides financial assistance to contributors or their dependants during periods of unemployment, illness (which must be a listed illness), during pregnancy or on the adoption of a child under two years of age, and also when a contributor dies.

Only persons who are contributors are covered by the Act. The Act does not apply to the following categories of people:

- Employees working less than 24 hours per month for a particular employer, and their employees
- Employees receiving remuneration according to learnership agreements as registered according to the Skills Development Act 97 of 1998, and their employers
- Employers and employees employed in the national and provincial field of government
- Persons who enter the Republic for the purpose of carrying out a contract of service, apprenticeship or learnership within the Republic, where, upon termination thereof, the employer is required to repatriate that person to his or her country of origin, and their employers.

Domestic and seasonal workers and their employers fell under the Act from 1 April 2003. Previously, employees who earned in excess of an amount stipulated by the Minister were also not regarded as contributors. With effect from 1 April 2002, the Act was amended to bring these employees within the ambit of the Act. The maximum for contributors is currently set in excess of R100 000 per year, and is amended annually. The UIF is administered by the Department of Labour.

In terms of the Act, persons who may be contributors, but who are however not entitled to benefits include:

■ Contributors receiving a monthly state pension/grant or benefits in terms of the Compensation for Occupational Diseases Act.
■ Contributors refusing acceptable appropriate available work.
■ A person who has voluntarily resigned from work.

The Act imposes duties on employers, namely that they must:

■ provide the street address of their business and its branches;
■ supply a list of all their employees with all their details as specified by the Act (including their remuneration) and of those employees who qualify as contributors (employers must keep their employee database up to date);
■ deduct monthly contributions from every employee who is a contributor and submit these (together with the employer's contributions) to the Unemployment Insurance Commissioner not later than seven days after the end of each month;
■ inform the Commissioner before the seventh day of each month of any changes from the previous month with regard to information previously furnished.

Normally, contributors or their dependants are paid benefits at a rate calculated on a sliding scale ranging from 38% for the highest-paid to 58% for the lowest-paid workers of their total weekly or monthly earnings (schedule 2 of the Act). Contributors will not be granted benefits if they worked for less than 13 weeks in the 52-week period preceding their unemployment. Various categories exist for claiming benefits, namely:

■ Illness benefits
■ Maternity benefits
■ Adoption benefits
■ Dependant's benefits
■ Unemployment benefits

For a more detailed discussion of these and other details of the UIA, visit the website of the Department of Labour at www.labour.gov.za

3.2.7 The Labour Relations Act 66 of 1995

The Labour Relations Act (LRA) provides the framework for the collective dimension (as pertaining to trade unions) of people and their work. Things like the right to join trade unions and the onus on employers to engage with trade unions through collective bargaining (under certain conditions) are regulated by this Act. You will recall from chapter 2 that the majority of South Africa's working people were excluded from this law's predecessor for decades. The LRA thus came as another piece of legislation to include all employees and to regulate many important aspects pertaining to employees and employers. Grogan (2007b: 14) explains:

> ... unlike most statutes, its aim goes much further than simply to enunciate

rights, confer powers, create institutions or prohibit or regulate specific conduct. The professed aims disclose rather that the LRA is intended to be an instrument of social change aimed, in particular, at purging the labour dispensation of past inequities and injustices, and extending democracy into the economic sector. It is in that spirit that the specific provisions of the Act must be read.

Provisions of this Act are not limited to the collective dimension. It also, for instance, deals with the dismissal of employees and dispute resolution. The LRA consists of nine chapters (and various schedules). *Chapter one* outlines the purpose, application and interpretation of the LRA. The overall purpose of the LRA is stated as being "… to advance economic development, social justice, labour peace and the democratisation of the workplace". This it intends to achieve by fulfilling a range of objectives, which we can summarise as follows:
- to give effect to and regulate the fundamental rights conferred by the Constitution;
- to give effect to obligations incurred by the Republic as a member state of the International Labour Organization;
- to provide a framework within which employees and their trade unions, employers and employers' organisations can:
  - collectively bargain to determine wages, terms and conditions of employment and other matters of mutual interest, also at sectoral and workplace level; and
  - formulate industrial policy;
- to promote employee participation in decision making in the workplace; and
- to facilitate the effective resolution of labour disputes.

Chapter two deals with freedom of association and with general protections in this regard – such as the right of employees to join trade unions and take part in their activities. *Chapter three* deals with collective bargaining. It covers aspects such as the organisational rights of trade unions, structures for collective bargaining (such as bargaining and statutory councils), and collective agreements. *Chapter four* of the LRA contains lengthy provisions regarding strikes, lockouts and other forms of industrial action. *Chapter five* deals with workplace forums as structures that can facilitate worker participation through joint consultation and joint decision making. *Chapter six* contains stipulations regarding trade unions and employers' organisations, such as those relating to their registration and regulation. *Chapter seven* provides for structures and processes for dispute resolution, and *Chapter eight* deals with unfair dismissal. *Chapter nine* contains various general provisions as well as definitions.

You know from the first two chapters of this book that the collective dimension of the employment relationship as related to trade unions is very prominent in our country. So too, however, is the right to fair treatment of all individuals. The LRA covers both dimensions, although the collective one features more prominently in this specific Act. The LRA is only enforceable in South Africa, and only in relation to parties that fall within its scope. The Labour Court (and the Commission for Conciliation Mediation and Arbitration (CCMA)) may, however, assume jurisdiction if an employee works in another country while the employer is based in South Africa, or if the contract was concluded in South Africa, or when the parties implicitly or expressly accepted the jurisdiction of South African courts. Regarding the parties covered, the LRA is clear that it is concerned with *employers* and *employees* and their employment relationships, including, in one case, applicants for employment. Section 200A of the Labour Relations Amendment Act 12 of 2002 establishes that a person is presumed to be an 'employee' if he or she works for, or renders services to another party, and if any one or more of a number of factors are present (and if the person earns below certain levels) (Nel et al 2007: 87), namely if:

- the way in which a person should work is controlled or directed by the other party;
- the person's hours of work are controlled or directed by the other party;
- the other party is an organisation and the person who performs such work can be regarded as part of that organisation;
- the person has worked for the other party for at least an average of 40 hours per month during the last three months;
- the person is economically dependent on the other party for whom the work is performed;
- the other party provides the person doing the work with the required tools or equipment;
- the person works for or renders services to that other party only.

Members of the NIA, SSS and SANDF are expressly excluded from the ambits of the LRA. According to Grogan (2007b: 17), the "Labour Court has held that judicial officers are impliedly excluded", the Constitutional Court has held that military personnel are at least free to form and join trade unions, and apart from all these exceptions, all employees have the statutory right to join trade unions and take part in unions' lawful activities, including lawful strikes.

You will find that in various parts throughout this book we may refer to aspects pertaining to the LRA, most notably in chapters 18, 19 and 20.

3.2.8 The Employment Equity Act 55 of 1998

From the preamble (see exhibit 3.1) to the Employment Equity Act (EEA) it is clear that it aims to redress the effects of South Africa's unfortunate past. It recognises, though, that anti-discriminatory measures would be insufficient to achieve this aim. It essentially aims to bring about a diverse workforce broadly representative of South Africa's demographics (as covered in chapter 2).

The two main aims of the EEA to achieve equity in South African workplaces are by:

- promoting equal opportunity and fair treatment in employment through the elimination of unfair discrimination; and
- implementing affirmative action measures to redress the disadvantages in employment experienced by designated groups, in order to ensure their equitable representation in all occupational categories and levels in the workforce.

The EEA provides for two main pillars in its legislated structure to achieve employment equity. Two separate chapters of the Act exist, each one dealing with one pillar. Chapter II deals with *unfair discrimination*, and is applicable to all employers and employees (that is, white males are also protected against unfair discrimination, and all employers, irrespective of their size, are prohibited from unfairly discriminating against employees and job applicants). Chapter III deals with *affirmative action* and is applicable only to 'designated employers' and people from 'designated groups' (that is, only employers who meet certain requirements are under a duty to implement affirmative action measures, and able-bodied white males cannot be the beneficiaries of affirmative action measures).

> **EXHIBIT 3.1: Preamble to the Employment Equity Act**
>
> **Recognising**
> - that as a result of apartheid and other discriminatory laws and practices, there are disparities in employment, occupation and income within the national labour market; and
> - that those disparities create such pronounced disadvantages for certain categories of people that they cannot be redressed simply by repealing discriminatory laws,
>
> Therefore, in order to –
> - promote the constitutional right of equality and the exercise of true democracy;
> - eliminate unfair discrimination in employment;
> - ensure the implementation of employment equity to redress the effects of discrimination;
> - achieve a diverse workforce broadly representative of our people; and
> - promote economic development and efficiency in the workforce; and
> - give effect to the obligations of the Republic as a member of the International Labour Organisation
>
> BE IT ENACTED by the Parliament of the Republic of South Africa as follows: ...

The only categories of employees who are wholly excluded from the Act are members of the SANDF, the NIA and the SASS. People working for these organisations could bring unfair discrimination matters before the Constitutional Court, or lodge complaints with the Human Rights Commission. The anti-discriminatory provisions of the EEA apply to all other employers and employees, whereas the affirmative action provisions apply only to 'designated employers' and members of 'designated groups'.

The EEA imposes particular conformance duties on relevant employers, including that they must compile employment equity plans and report on progress in this regard to the Director-General of Labour.

In light of the overall significance of the EEA in terms of the key HRM challenge of our time, we deal with the implications more elaborately in section 3.3 of this chapter.

3.2.9 Legislation pertaining to human resource development

From chapter 2 in particular, we know that the development of our people is central to unlocking the growth potential of South Africa. The sad history of our country means that we unfortunately have masses of people whose potential is totally untapped simply because they have been deprived from their opportunities related to their education and development. Since 1994 the overhauling of South Africa's labour dispensation has included a stream of new laws being promulgated and enacted pertaining to the development of our people. The earliest new law was the South African Qualifications Authority Act 58 of 1995, which had put the South African Qualifications Authority (SAQA) and the National Qualifications Framework (NQF) in place.

The purpose was to have an integrated national framework for dealing with South Africa's people's learning achievements and to:
- facilitate access to and mobility and progression with education, training and career-path development for and of our people;
- enhance the quality of education and training in the country; and
- accelerate the redress of past unfair discrimination and thereby contribute to the full personal development of all learners and the socio-economic development of the nation at large (Nel et al 2008).

The Skills Development Act 97 of 1998 (SDA) and the Skills Development Levies Act 9 of 1999 (SDLA) followed on from the SAQA Act (SAQAA). We thus have a very comprehensive set of laws pertaining directly to the development of South Africa's people and we cover the implications hereof more comprehensively in chapters 13 and 14. For now we merely want you to become aware of these laws that bring along with them quite a number of conformance requirements. We would like to stress again, however, that the challenge is rather much more to use these laws as mere platforms from which to launch initiatives that are aimed at really empowering our people.

The Skills Development Act (SDA) came into effect on 1 February 1999. The goals of the SDA basically include to:

- provide for a skills development strategy and system which is flexible, accessible, decentralised, demand led and based on partnerships between the public and private sectors;
- increase the levels of investment in human resource development and improve return on those investments;
- encourage employers to make the workplace an active learning environment where employees can acquire new competencies, and new entrants to the labour market can gain work experience;
- improve the competency levels of the workforce in order to promote their employability and labour market mobility as well as their levels of responsibility, which should in turn also improve their quality of life and enable employers to achieve rising levels of productivity and competitiveness;
- ensure good standards of quality of training and development in the workplace;
- encourage people to take part in learnerships and other training programmes;
- improve employment prospects of people who were previously disadvantaged by redressing these disadvantages through education, training and development;
- assist work seekers to find work, help retrenched people to re-enter the labour market and simultaneously help employers find qualified people to work for them; and
- provide and regulate employment services.

The aims can thus be taken to include enabling people to enter and remain in employment, even if this means being self-employed. As can be deduced, human resource development efforts of such magnitude require a large investment, thus a system of financing was necessary.

The Skills Development Levies Act (SDLA) provides for a system whereby all employers who are not exempted (see chapter 13) must pay monthly skills development levies that are basically determined as a percentage of the employer's total monthly payroll (called a 'leviable amount'). The levy is basically payable by employers who have a payroll in excess of R250 000 per year or those who are registered for employee tax purposes with the South African Revenue Service (SARS).The actual calculation of these levies can be quite complex and generally it is wise to make use of tax consultants to assist with this. Interest is charged on late payments of these levies, and failure to pay the levies is an offence and can lead to a fine on conviction. The collection of the levies is administered by SARS. Employers who provide training to employees can then apply to receive grants in terms of the SDLA. Further details of the SDA and the SDLA are covered in chapters 13 and 14.

3.2.10 The Broad-Based Black Economic Empowerment Act 53 of 2003[1]

Sections 3.2.9 and 3.2.10 introduced specific pieces of legislation that are geared towards the empowerment of people to allow and enable them to make more meaningful contributions to the socio-economics of our country. Laws like the UIA,

COIDA and OHSA have less to do with economic performance and are geared more towards the distribution of foundational 'social goods' one would expect citizens of countries to have access to – like health and safety, compensation when injured at work, and assistance when unemployed. The legislative framework hence provides for some 'maintenance' and some 'empowerment' laws.

According to Cheadle Thompson and Haysom Inc (2005: 1.5), the Black Economic Empowerment Commission was established in 1997 under the chairmanship of Cyril Ramaphosa in order "to review developments in empowerment and to make recommendations to government".

Drawing on some other sources, Cheadle et al (2005: 1.5) go on to explain:

> The report of the Commission was submitted to government in March 2001. The commission report identified problems in the approach taken to black economic empowerment by the public and the private sectors and it recommended the adoption of an integrated national black economic empowerment strategy and the enactment of legislation dealing specifically with black economic empowerment. Significantly, the commission moved away from a narrow definition of black economic empowerment that "focuses on the entry and transaction activities of black people in business" to a definition that sees black economic empowerment as an integrated and coherent socio-economic process. In terms of this latter definition, black economic empowerment is not only concerned with ownership of businesses by black people but also the management and control of those businesses. Following this definition, one of the purposes of black economic empowerment is "to ensure broader and meaningful participation in the economy by black people to achieve sustainable development and prosperity". The commission provided much of the impetus and preliminary thinking on the issues now contained in the BBBEE Act and in the strategy document on BEE issued by the Department of Trade and Industry. Both the strategy document and the Act adopt the approach recommended by the commission – hence the focus on 'broad-based black economic empowerment', rather than just 'black economic empowerment'.

During March 2003, South Africa's Department of Trade and Industry published its *Strategy for Broad-Based Black Economic Empowerment* (BBBEE). Herein it was explained that a systematic and comprehensive approach to transforming our society was required because apartheid politics systematically restricted the majority of South Africa's people from meaningfully participating in our country's economy. The BBBEE strategy explicitly recognised that vast inequalities have persisted in South Africa despite all the transformational efforts up to that point in time. It was also acknowledged at the time that these conditions might hold very negative consequences in terms of political and social stability:

> The South African economy is performing well ... South Africa has enjoyed 10 years of consistent economic growth. Much has been achieved since 1994. Unfortunately, the extent to which this growth has been shared equitably amongst all South Africans is not yet adequate for the requirements of a stable, integrated and prosperous society. (*Strategy for Broad-Based Black Economic Empowerment*, 2003)

The strategy made it clear that it was aimed beyond redressing past imbalances "to situating BEE as a powerful tool to broaden the country's economic base and accelerate growth, job creation and poverty eradication" (*Strategy for Broad-Based Black Economic Empowerment*, 2003). Subsequent to issuing this strategy, the Broad-Based Black Economic Empowerment Act 53 of 2003 became effective on 21 April 2004, with the purpose essentially of establishing a legislative framework to facilitate and promote black economic empowerment in a comprehensive ('broad') sense.

BBBEE is described in the Act as meaning the economic empowerment of all of South Africa's black people ('black' being a generic term used to denote black Africans, coloureds and Asians/Indians) through diverse but integrated socio-economic strategies that include, but are not limited to:

- increasing the number of black people that manage, control and own enterprises and productive assets;
- facilitating ownership and management of enterprises and productive assets by workers, cooperatives, communities and other collective enterprises;
- human resource and skills development;
- achieving equitable representation in all occupational categories and levels of our workforces;
- preferential procurement; and
- investment in enterprises that are owned or managed by black people.

In the strategy document that preceded the publication of the BBBEE Act, the government lists the following as some of its policy objectives for broad-based black economic empowerment:

- a substantial increase in the number of black people who have ownership and control of existing and new enterprises in the priority sectors of the economy that government has identified in its micro-economic reform strategy;
- an increasing proportion of the ownership and management of economic activities vested in community and broad-based enterprises (such as trade unions, employee trusts, and other collective enterprises) including cooperatives;
- increased ownership of land and other productive assets, improved access to infrastructure, increased acquisition of skills and participation in productive economic activities in underdeveloped areas. These include the 13 nodal areas identified in the government's *Urban Renewal Programme* and the *Integrated Sustainable Rural Development Programme*.

There has been a fair share of debate on whether the Act will be effective in ensuring that empowerment will indeed be broad based. Blade Nzimande, secretary-general of the SACP, was quoted as saying the following in 2004 (Cheadle Thompson & Haysom Inc 2005: 1.7):

> With few arguable exceptions, we believe that most of the celebrated BEE deals have had a neutral and probably negative impact on addressing the real transformational challenges of our economy. The dominant approach is to implement a narrow BEE, focusing on the advancement of a black minority through equity acquisitions and individual promotion into the senior manage-ment ranks ... BEE must principally be about addressing the needs of the over-whelming majority of our people – black workers and the poor – the basic economic empowerment of millions of our people through access to jobs and through the provision of affordable and reliable electricity, housing, transport, telecommunications and so on.

Since the promulgation of the BBBEE Act drafts of 'Codes of Good Practice', comments have been received and taken on board, and on 9 February 2007 the Codes were issued. The flexible approach that had been envisaged by the strategy seems to some extent to have been replaced by the codes which emphasise "alignment and consistency between charters and codes" (Cheadle Thompson & Haysom Inc 2005: 1.11). According to the same publication, a recurring theme in the codes is that one industry should not be disadvantaged over another by allowing some charters to be more stringent than others. The codes thus seek to level the playing field for all entities operating within the South African economy by providing clear and comprehensive criteria for the measurement of BBBEE.

Charters that have been developed are agreements between the parties to seek to achieve the specified levels of empowerment. The negotiation of a charter by stakeholders in the sector does not in itself bind the government to implement that charter. In order to be binding on organs of state and public entities, a charter must be converted into a sector code. A charter will only be gazetted as such if it is consistent with the codes in terms of definitions and principles, including principles underlying the measurement of the different elements of the generic scorecard. If a charter includes additional elements or if it deviates from the targets and weightings given to the elements in the generic scorecard, it must fully justify the deviation.

The generic scorecard (see below) set out in the codes is very simple. It lists the seven elements of BBBEE, gives each a weighting out of 100, and stipulates the relevant code to which one must have reference for measuring each element of the scorecard.

Element	Weighting	Code series reference
Ownership	20 points	100
Management control	10 points	200
Employment equity	15 points	300
Skills development	15 points	400
Preferential procurement	20 points	500
Enterprise development	15 points	600
Socio-economic development initiatives	5 points	700

BBBEE	Status qualification	BBBEE recognition level
Level One Contributor	≥ 100 points on the generic scorecard	135%
Level Two Contributor	≥ 85 but < 100 points on the generic scorecard	125%
Level Three Contributor	≥ but < 85 on the generic scorecard	110%
Level Four Contributor	≥ 65 but < 75 on the generic scorecard	100%
Level Five Contributor	≥ 55 but < 65 on the generic scorecard	80%
Level Six Contributor	≥ 45 but < 55 on the generic scorecard	60%
Level Seven Contributor	≥ 40 but < 45 on the generic scorecard	50%
Level Eight Contributor	≥ 30 but < 40 on the generic scorecard	10%

From the foregoing it should be rather clear that this piece of legislation has brought HRM even more into the mainstream of South Africa's efforts to transform our society towards a better life for all. The BBBEE Act can in a sense also be seen as an integrating mechanism and the umbrella or pinnacle piece of our country's legislative regime aimed at societal transformation. The stage has thus been set to move into an empowerment mode in our country in order to arrive ultimately at a situation whereby the full spectrum of diversity of our country's people is embraced, and all people have equitable equality of opportunity in our country.

3.3 BEYOND CONFORMANCE TO PERFORMANCE: EMPOWERING PEOPLE TOWARDS EQUITABLE EQUALITY

Thus far in this chapter we have introduced you to a broad framework of sources of law that interplay with how we manage our human resources. These laws require organisations to make sure they comply with all relevant provisions – this is the HRM conformance challenge as we see it. We believe that we cannot legislate growth and development in reality, though. The perspective we take is that through the legislation a platform for performance has been created – performance through empowerment. It is a question of whether we embrace this opportunity and leverage the platform, and this requires a 'change of heart and mind', we believe – a different way of thinking and doing as we manage our people and our organisations.

In this section we turn our attention to the possibilities to leverage the legislative platform to become catalysts for performance through empowering people and embracing the diversity of the people of South Africa. During the apartheid era, the 'human resource' was almost limited to the 'white human resource' while basically regarding 'black labour' as 'a cheap and abundant commodity' or 'factor of production', and hence almost as a cost element. We must now make a shift of paradigm to embrace the reality that all people have the potential to be a source of superior performance and hence competitive advantage. The sheer diversity of South Africa's people holds a key to leveraging performance if managed appropriately. We have to embrace this and empower our people as best as we possibly can so that we can grow through including as many people as possible to be productive participants in our socio-economic endeavours. Before we focus in more detail on what this challenge entails, we need to clarify some concepts as we use them in this book.

3.3.1 Clarifying some concepts and considering some perspectives

We have already used concepts such as 'empowerment' and 'affirmative action', and yet we have not defined them. We have also used the notion of 'distributive justice' before. We now try to briefly clarify some of these issues or concepts, and how we prefer to use these in this book.

3.3.1.1 Distributive justice and employment or work opportunities

The dilemma facing our country, as you know by now, seems to largely revolve around distributive justice. We are growing our economy and developing our democracy, but too many are not getting a fair 'piece of the pie'.

Distributive justice may be defined as the fairness of societal rules regulating how social goods (such as welfare benefits, infrastructure, fixed assets, education, work opportunities and the ability to earn income) are distributed among the members and groups within society at large.

From section 3.2 you know that some of the most basic steps taken to improve distributive justice patterns and restore equity in our country relate to having laws such as the BCEA, COIDA and UIA. These help ensure that employees are given certain minimum conditions of employment (getting a 'fair deal', in general terms), are compensated when they are injured at work (which is just fair), and receive some assistance when they fall out of employment (something which we experience so much in South Africa – unemployment). Paying people something when they do not have work is one way of helping to distribute the income or wealth generated in a country, and it helps to facilitate some redistribution from the 'haves' to some of the 'have-nots'. Arguably a better way, though, would be to find ways of creating opportunities for people to enable them to work and earn their own income. We are thus talking employment here – even self-employment, perhaps.

In the context of employment we can think about the distribution of work as a social commodity. Because work is so central to life, it should be easy to appreciate why this social commodity is so highly sought after. Keep in mind now that *work* refers to more than 'a job'. By the latter we mean when someone is actually employed by someone else. When we create job opportunities we actually grow the work requirements of organisations in a way that requires us to employ new people. This is an important way of distributing opportunities to earn income. In this respect employment opportunities are no different from other social goods of which all members of society wish to have their fair share, such as health care, clean water, electricity, safety, education and old-age pensions.

One other area of employment that has a different connotation is that of self-employment – when people engage in productive work and earn, but they do not do so in the context of being employed by another party. We return to this aspect later.

3.3.1.2 Affirmative action

The concept of affirmative action is often taken to merely refer to the employment context. However, from our definition of distributive justice above, we can say that, although affirmative action has historically been most closely associated with the workplace, it can be taken to actually encompass a much larger field. Indeed, land redistribution, reformation of the educational system, the awarding of government tenders and subsidies to organisations owned by historically disadvantaged people, and the distribution of radio licences can all be said to be examples of where affirmative action can be instituted. It depends on how we define it.

The concept of affirmative action is used in many different guises and it is not always readily apparent what people mean when employing it. The comments on affirmative action in exhibit 3.2 are reproduced to help clarify the concept.

As can be seen from exhibit 3.2, some seem to use the concept more broadly while others tend to apparently narrow down its meaning to pertain only to employment (opportunities). If we use the concept of affirmative action in a broader sense, we can argue that the deep and widespread inequalities which rend our society require very comprehensive affirmative action measures across many different dimensions, and not just through creating employment opportunities. However, because historically and legislation-wise, affirmative action as a concept has become associated more with the context of employment opportunities, we would like to use a different concept when we refer to the broader implications and context, namely that of 'empowerment'.

As such we regard empowerment to include affirmative action in an employment sense – but it goes beyond that. It includes conforming to employment equity legislation, but it places the emphasis on embracing the diversity of our people and capitalising

> **EXHIBIT 3.2: The concept of affirmative action**

- "Affirmative action refers to specific steps, beyond ending discriminatory practices, that are taken to promote equal opportunity and to ensure that discrimination will not recur. The goal of affirmative action is to eliminate nonlegal barriers to equal employment opportunity, including intentional discriminatory practices and unintentional (structural or systemic) discrimination ... [I]t is best to be clear that affirmative action involves some degree of preferential treatment, because not to do so is to beg the question – it is to force the most crucial issue into the background: the issue of whether preferential treatment for women and nonwhites can ever be morally justifiable." (Taylor 1991: 14)

- "... [A]ffirmative action is generally designed with three goals in mind: To eliminate existing discrimination against minorities and women; to remedy the lingering effect of past discrimination against these groups; and to prevent future discrimination against these groups." (Starks 1992: 940)

- "Affirmative action in the South African context has extremely broad connotations, touching, as apartheid did and still does, on every area of life ... affirmative action covers all purposive activity designed to eliminate the effects of apartheid and to create a society where everyone has the same chance to get on in life. In terms of the ANC draft Bill of Rights, all anti-discrimination measures, as well as all anti-poverty ones, may be regarded as constituting a form of affirmative action." (Sachs 1991: 14)

- "Affirmative action is thus a temporary intervention designed to achieve equal employment opportunity without lowering standards and without unduly trammelling the career aspirations or expectations of current organisational members who are competent in their jobs." (Human 1993: 3)

on that in order to enhance performance. Empowerment thus specifically includes the development of our people and this includes the development of their abilities to engage in entrepreneurial endeavour to enable them even to become self-employed. We elaborate on this later. Let us first briefly reflect on different perspectives or schools of thought on the affirmative action agenda.

Liberal, libertarian and egalitarian perspectives of the concept 'affirmative action'

In the debate surrounding affirmative action, the participants are frequently labelled as falling into certain camps or schools of thought. Since some of these perspectives and relevant terminology are also used in this book, it may be expedient to provide a brief clarification of some of these terms.

An *egalitarian* is someone who holds that the distribution of goods in a just society shall be according to the principle of equal shares, irrespective of differences among individuals in their respective contributions to the creation of a society's wealth (one could associate this view with communism or extreme forms of socialism).

A *libertarian* is someone who contends that the distribution of social goods should be strictly according to merit and that the state's primary task is to protect the individual's freedom to pursue his or her own goals in life (capitalists, free marketers and individualists may be some labels associated with this school of thought).

Liberals are those who hold that, while individuals should be free to pursue their divergent ends, it should be recognised that an individual owes a debt to society and consequently that it is society's duty to distribute wealth more equally (thus wealth creation is protected but the distribution of wealth is not left entirely to the individual – social democrats or capitalists with a human face could be appropriate labels for this group).

Modalities of affirmative action

Inside organisations, affirmative action can take many forms. From a managerial perspective it is thus important to determine the type of affirmative action contemplated as this should be reflected in the organisation's affirmative action policy, for instance. Not all types of affirmative action programmes would be equally immune to challenges from persons who may feel aggrieved by such programmes or the actions that go along with them. The test of fairness of any form of preferential treatment (in cases of promotion, for instance) will have to be found in the organisation's policies and objectives. This makes these modalities important to consider.

Three modalities or forms of affirmative action can be distinguished: a *strong*, an *intermediate/moderate* and a *weak* form. In the strong variant, a person qualifies for preferential treatment solely on the grounds that he or she possesses an immutable characteristic (for example, an employee is promoted because she is a female, without satisfying the job specifications). In the *intermediate/moderate variant* of affirmative action, the person meets the minimum standards/qualification for the job and is given preference over another candidate who is better qualified because of some immutable characteristic which he or she possesses but which the better qualified person does not (for example, the job specifies matric as a minimum qualification but preferably a bachelor's degree, and a black matriculant is promoted rather than the white male graduate candidate). In the *weak variant* of affirmative action, the stance would be that a black/female/handicapped/etc employee will only promoted in preference to an able-bodied white male, for instance, if both candidates are equally qualified for the job. While many South African employers would like to see that only the *weak* modality of affirmative action be adopted or mandated, it should be clear that such a policy will most likely not be the most popular – at least not in the short run.

3.3.1.3 Equality of opportunity, equitable equality and affirmative action as bridge

For our purposes the notion of *equality of opportunity* or *equal opportunity* is used to refer to that ideal state where everyone has an equal chance to compete with his or her peers for access to social goods. We know, however, that such a utopian state is generally not aligned with reality. In chapter 1 we stressed the fact that people differ – and all do not have the same experience, education or innate abilities, for instance. From a purely semantic point of view we reckon that 'equal opportunity' does not exist anywhere (see also exhibit 3.3). We think what is needed ultimately in our country is a state of *equitable equality*.

EXHIBIT 3.3: Equality – three quotes as food for thought

"All animals are equal, but some animals are more equal than others." George Orwell

"Real equality is not to be decreed by law. It cannot be given and it cannot be forced." Raymond Moley

"It's only in the cemetery that all men are equal." Anonymous

Source: Barker (2007: 233–244)

The notion of 'equality' is generally central to the notion of 'justice'. The concept of *equality* has since the earliest times been used in a variety of ways and normally in a context that implies that it is a fundamental element of justice. While justice has many manifestations, we are concerned with distributive justice when analysing the concept of equality. Unfortunately there seems to be little agreement as to what is meant by the concepts of equality and justice. One way of dealing with this is to keep things simple. In this regard, one of the earliest definitions of justice holds that *to treat equals equally, and unequals differently, encapsulates the essence of justice*. We prefer to keep things relatively simple and combine the two terms of *equity* (fairness) and *equality* (sameness or being similar at least).

Equitable equality as concept thus consists of these two terms to give a specific meaning. *Equitable* is derived from the term *equity* – which means fairness or being 'just'. *Equality* is derived from the term *equal*, which literally means being the same in things like value, status, size and so forth – a term derived from Latin *aequalis*, from *aequus*, ('even', 'level' or 'equal'). An ultimate situation of 'equitable equality' would thus mean that all with similar abilities (close to 'the same') will have equally fair chances of sharing in whatever opportunities there might be – such as work and other social goods. To get to a situation of equitable equality in our country we need to first make affirmative action work.

Affirmative action refers to those discriminatory interventions necessitated as a bridge between past unfair discrimination in the distribution of the social goods of our country, and a future of *equitable equality*.

From this formulation it should be clear that we live in a crossover phase of our history during which discrimination and its very badges (such as gender and race) have to be employed to get past the unfair discrimination of the past – there is no other way. This is the essential paradox inherent in affirmative action: to get past (unfair or invidious) discrimination we have to discriminate, albeit 'fairly' (unfair discrimination in the name of a good cause still remains just that, unfair, and exposes affirmative action to the often-heard charge of 'reverse discrimination'). The progress from 'inequitable inequality' to 'equitable equality' is depicted in figure 3.2.

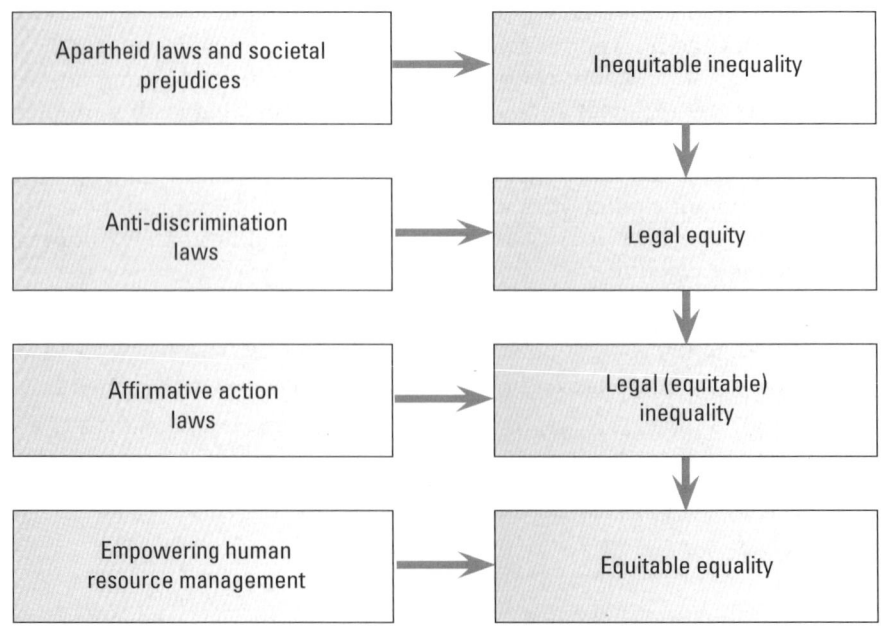

Figure 3.2: Towards equitable equality

From figure 3.2 it can be seen that anti-discrimination laws are not enough. Although they do remove legal barriers to discrimination, they do not eradicate the inequalities brought about by past discriminatory legislation. Anti-discrimination legislation thus brings about legal or formal equality. Affirmative action laws are brought in so that the effects of past discriminatory practices can be addressed and so that we can level the playing fields, so to speak. We have to accept that while we do that (conform to legislation like the EEA and BBBEEA), we are discriminating, but we regard that as 'fair' because we are trying to give everyone the same advantages and opportunities. For example, the EEA causes organisations to hire and promote historically disadvantaged people rather than white men because the latter have been on the receiving end relative to black Africans, coloureds, Asians and females in the past. We thus are left with a situation of legislated 'fair' inequality during this crossover phase. The laws, however, cannot in themselves remove non-legal or societal barriers arising from peoples' attitudes – for this a concerted HRM effort is needed. True equitable equality is difficult to achieve in that it requires a fundamental and honest change of heart among all relevant parties. We first have to empower all the people who have traditionally been disadvantaged – and then we can do away with any form of discriminatory practices. As such we must regard this as a form of 'fair discrimination' necessary in order to move towards a situation where all will genuinely be treated on the basis of 'equitable equality'. We need a situation, ultimately, whereby all of our people, irrespective of their gender, cultural, ethnic or language group, have equally fair opportunities to access all social goods and be productive contributors to South Africa's socio-economic dispensation. In this regard we see HRM as being central to achieving that 'end state'. Moving in that direction requires a different agenda for HRM – one that we like to term an 'empowerment agenda'.

3.3.1.4 Empowerment

We believe that a holistic approach is required, also to the notion and practice of empowerment. As such it is perhaps best to start off by taking a basic look at the meaning of the word *empowerment*.

Empowerment as a concept is derived from the term 'power'. From a semantic perspective it may thus be useful to look at what a dictionary says about the meaning of the word. *Reader's Digest Word Power Dictionary* (1999: 758) says that power is about "… the ability to do something … the capacity to influence other people or the course of events … political authority or control … physical strength … a country viewed in terms of its international influence and its military strength … the capacity or performance of an engine or other device … energy that is produced". This should give a good idea of what power is about. Another way to look at the meaning is to simply ask what it means when someone is without power or 'powerless'. The same source says to be powerless means to be "without ability, influence, or power". To empower would thus mean to make people the opposite of powerless – giving them the ability to do certain things and the capacity to influence other people and events. The same dictionary makes it clear that empowerment is "to give strength and confidence to" (*Reader's Digest Word Power Dictionary* 1999: 313). In essence then, to empower would mean to enhance the capacity to perform.

We see empowerment in South Africa (and in Africa) as including the challenge to give people what is necessary so that they have a greater ability and capacity to perform and influence things for themselves and for society. As such we need to mobilise all the energy and capabilities so that the people can be better at 'producing' or 'delivering' – and thereby actively contribute to our socio-economic system, making South Africa a better place for all. It is one thing to have legislation that says people should not be discriminated against unfairly when they seek employment to devote their energy to a job, yet it is quite another when so many people do not have the ability to identify or exploit such opportunities properly. We must empower people to be able to *positively influence* the work of organisations, their own lives (and that of others) – and our country as a whole.

We even think about empowerment in a much broader sense – one which starts with valuing the inherent worth of all people. All of our people have their own talent, potential, and hopes and aspirations – for work but also way beyond that – for their own lives and for those dear to them. Taking a more holistic approach to the concept then means that we should also acknowledge that people not only have hopes, but they also have fears. Some fear because they do not know how to make ends meet because they do not have a job, others have fears and uncertainties about whether the new environment still has room for them, and yet most also have fears about their own safety and security in a country where violent crime is rife (as covered in the previous chapter). All of these hopes and fears, all of the talents and potential, must be acknowledged and mobilised for the good of our people and our country. We like Johnson and Redman's (1998: xv) views about what empowerment also entails, namely that "[e]mpowerment is also about values. It is about treating people in a different way. It involves seeing people as whole human beings ... Empowered people are treated with respect. Their views are heeded. Their talents are used. They are treated fairly ... They are prepared to work wholeheartedly with others ...".

From chapter 2 we know that millions of South Africa's people still suffer today as a result of a history of disempowerment. We may have about 17 million people who make up our country's economic active population, but almost seven million of these are 'unemployed' (according to the broad definition). As such there are millions of people who are socio-economically 'powerless' in a sense. We also witness how thousands of highly skilled and qualified people are fleeing the country due to feelings of being powerless – that they have no power any longer to escape violent crime, or perhaps to keep options open for career development in an environment of affirmative action. This means that we have to empower *all* people to be able to make meaningful contributions and hence to constructively influence our country's socio-economic development. Our country has a very richness in the diversity of its people, but much of what this offers can only be unlocked if we deliberately devise strategies, policies and practices that empower *all* of our country's people. While affirmative action is thus very important, we view it as merely the baseline – and just one piece of the puzzle of empowerment.

3.3.2 Addressing the affirmative action challenge: conformance and progress

Earlier in section 3.2.8 you were introduced to the rationale, scope and application of the country's Employment Equity Act (EEA). You may want to return to that section to refresh your memory. In this section we are concerned with the implementation of affirmative action by and in organisations. While some progress has been made with this in South African organisations, much still has to be achieved (see table 3.3 and below). During 2006, some legislative amendments were made, driven by the lack of progress up to that time. The amendments placed greater emphasis on the requirements for organisations to report their progress with regard to transformation. Responsibility has to now also be assigned to one or more senior managers in relation to the implementation requirements of the EEA. Consultation on all matters regarding employment equity has also been amplified. The most important amendments are summarised and reflected in exhibit 3.4.

Table 3.3: Comparative race and gender changes on management level from 2001 to 2005

	Top management			Senior management			Professionally qualified		
	2001	2005	% change	2001	2005	% change	2001	2005	% change
Race									
Blacks	25,1%	27,2%	2,1%	19,1%	27,5%	8,4%	50,2%	38,7%	−11,5%
Whites	74,9%	72,6%	−2,3%	80,9%	72,4%	−8,5%	49,9%	61,3%	11,4%
Africans	8,0%	17,9%	9,9%	9,8%	14,5%	4,7%	39,7%	21,5%	−18,2%
Coloureds	13,2%	3,7%	−9,5%	4,6%	6,0%	1,4%	6,0%	9,3%	3,1%
Indians	3,9%	5,6%	1,7%	4,7%	7,0%	2,3%	4,4%	7,9%	3,5%
Gender									
Females	11,9%	16,5%	4,6%	17,7%	23,6%	5,9%	38,2%	38,4%	0,2%
Males	88,1%	83,3%	−4,8%	82,3%	76,3%	−6,0%	61,9%	61,3%	−0,6%
Race & gender									
African females	1,6%	4,7%	3,1%	2,1%	4,2%	2,1%	19,1%	18,0%	−1,1%
Coloured females	0,6%	1,0%	0,4%	1,1%	1,7%	0,6%	3,1%	2,3%	−0,8%
Indian females	0,5%	0,9%	0,4%	0,9%	1,6%	0,7%	1,2%	1,9%	0,7%
White females	9,2%	9,9%	0,7%	13,6%	16,1%	2,5%	4,8%	16,2%	1,4%
African males	6,4%	13,2%	6,8%	7,7%	10,3%	2,6%	20,6%	20,8%	0,2%
Coloured males	12,6%	2,7%	−9,9%	3,5%	4,3%	0,8%	3,0%	4,2%	1,2%
Indian males	3,4%	4,7%	1,3%	3,8%	5,4%	1,6%	3,2%	4,0%	0,8%
White males	65,7%	62,7%	−2,6%	65,7%	56,3%	−9,4%	35,1%	61,3%	26,2%

Source: Booysen (2007: 49), as compiled and adapted from Commission for EE (2006: 56–58)

It is clear that the amendments make reporting more onerous and even though an even greater administrative burden is the result, it was felt that this was indeed necessary given the poor progress with actual implementation of the affirmative action measures by companies. The Commission for Employment Equity (CEE) (2007), for instance, reported a drop of about 47% in the number of employment equity reports that were submitted over the period 2000 to 2006 – clearly a reason for serious concern. It does not seem as though these amendments were sufficient, according to the CEE (2007).

EXHIBIT 3.4: Some affirmative action legislation amendments

■ A senior manager (or managers) in permanent employment of the organisation has to be assigned to deal with employment equity. The person must have executive authority, report to the CEO on employment equity matters and have a budget, and timeframes must be allocated in this regard. These duties must be incorporated in their performance contracts.

■ The new expanded definition of 'designated groups' includes black people (Africans, coloureds and Indians), women and people with disabilities who are natural persons. Natural persons are defined in the Act. This amendment specifically excludes citizens of other countries who lay claim to equity benefits because they are black.

■ An extended method of reporting has been incorporated in the regulations.

■ Employers' duty to consult has been elevated and expanded. For this purpose a forum must be established for equity-related matters, or an existing forum such as a workplace forum must be utilised. Representation should include employees from designated and non-designated groups, as well as at least one senior manager.

■ Provision is also made regarding designated employers whose operations extend across different geographical areas or workplaces – for consolidated as well as separate reporting for each entity. These reports must be made available at each relevant workplace for employee (and trade union) access to information and documentation.

The CEE, in its *Annual Report* 2006–2007 (CEE 2007), for instance, said the following (see also table 3.3):

> The progress towards the achievement of employment equity continues to be woefully slow ... Figures ... show that Black representation at the Top Management level increased accumulatively by a meagre 9.5% from 12.7% in 2000 to 22.2% in 2006 ... The increase in the number of Africans at this level is even worse ... At the Senior Management level the increase rate of Black representation is at a slower rate ... from 18.5% in 2000 to 26.9% in 2006 ... at the Professionally Qualified and Middle Management level ... [I]nstead of making any progress we are actually regressing ... Black representation decreased by 7.6% from 44.1% in 2000 to 36.5% in 2006 ... African representation decreased by 12.6% ... The decrease of people with disabilities from 1% over the years to 0.7% does not bode well for our country ... White females are now over-represented at all management levels and this raises the question whether this group should remain designated ... No economic empowerment that is broad based for Black people, particularly females, can take place without employment equity ... employers must now adopt the following principle when implementing employment equity, 'Less noise, more work and more action' ... The self-imposed moratorium imposed by most employers on employment equity should now be lifted, even if it means introducing forceful measures.

It is little wonder, therefore, that during 2007 the CEE (2007) was recommending a serious and urgent review of the Employment Equity Act, including finding ways of strengthening the enforcement and compliance mechanisms as provided for in the EEA. Implementation thus remains a key challenge, and we believe that most of this has to do with the mindsets of the people who manage our organisations. As Booysen (2007: 48) says, "while legislation is integral to addressing unfair workplace discrimination, it is not enough ... culture change also has to take place ... transformation must be systemic and compliance with legislation is merely the beginning of the change ... EE implementation needs to be supported by coherent employment ... strategies focusing on human capital development, inclusive practices and organisational culture change".

In the rest of this section we deal with the implementation challenges of Chapter II of the EEA. One of the first things to clarify is who is covered by the affirmative action provisions of the EEA. This is reflected in exhibit 3.5.

Very broadly speaking, the EEA requires of the employer to first conduct an audit of its workforce composition in terms of race, gender and disabilities as well as employment practices and policies that may hinder the employment and/or advancement of people from designated groups. Once it has these data on the current situation, the employer must formulate an employment equity plan which is a blueprint of how the organisation is going to promote the employment prospects of people from designated groups. This plan must include progressive targets for achieving employment equity in the organisation. Lastly, the employer must submit annual reports (if it employs 150 or more employees) or biannual reports (if it employs fewer than 150 employees) to the Director-General of Labour to show, with reference to its employment equity plan, what progress the employer has made in achieving the targets. These three steps must all be done in consultation with the workforce and/or its representatives.

3.3.2.1 Duties of designated employers

The Act places the following duties on a designated employer:

- The employer must consult with its employees over the conduct of the employment equity analysis and its employment equity plan as well as the progress reports that the employer must compile and submit to the Director-General.
- The employer must conduct an analysis of its employment policies, practices, procedures and the work environment in order to identify employment barriers which adversely affect people from designated groups, and must include a profile of its workforce within each occupational category and level in order to determine the degree of under-representation of people from designated groups in various occupational categories and levels.
- The employer must prepare an employment equity plan (see exhibit 3.6).
- The employer must report to the Director-General on progress made in implementing its employment equity plan.

For purposes of the EEA, a person may be suitably qualified for a job as a result of any one, or any combination, of that person's formal qualifications, prior learning, relevant experience or capacity to acquire, within a reasonable time, the ability to do the job.

3.3.2.2 Aspects of monitoring and enforcement

General monitoring of an employer's conformance with the EEA is left primarily to employees, shop stewards, trade unions, workplace forums, labour inspectors and the Director-General of Labour. A labour inspector must request and obtain a written undertaking from an employer if he or she has reasonable grounds to believe that a designated employer has failed to comply with his or her affirmative action duties.

A labour inspector may issue a compliance order to a designated employer if that employer has refused to give a written undertaking when requested to do so, or failed to comply with a written undertaking given by him or her. A compliance order must set out, among other things:

- those provisions of Chapter III which the employer has not complied with and details of the conduct constituting non-compliance;

EXHIBIT 3.5: Who is covered by the affirmative action provisions of the Employment Act?

Employers

- a person who employs 50 or more employees;
- an employer who employs fewer that 50 employees, but has a total annual turnover that is equal to or above the applicable annual turnover of a small business (see below);
- a municipality;
- an organ of state;
- an employer bound by a collective agreement in terms of the Labour Relations Act, which appoints it as a designated employer in terms of this Act, to the extent provided for in the agreement;
- an employer, who is not a designated employer, but who voluntarily notifies the Director-General that it intends to comply with Chapter III of the Act as if it is a designated employer; and
- an employer, who is not a designated employer, but who, upon having been found guilty of unfair discrimination, is ordered by the Labour Court to comply with Chapter III of the Act.

  Employees (including job applicants)
- Blacks, Indians, coloureds, women (of all races) and people with disabilities (of all races) are to be the beneficiaries of affirmative action in terms of the Act.

Turnover threshold for designated employers with fewer than 50 employees

Sector or subsectors in accordance with the Industrial Classification	Total annual standard turnover
Agriculture	R2,00m
Mining and quarrying	R7.50m R7,50m
Manufacturing	R10.00m R10,00m
Electricity, gas and water	R10,00m R10,00m
Construction	R5.00m R5,00m
Retail and motor trade and repair services	R15,00m R15,00m
Wholesale trade, commercial agents and allied services	R25,00m R25,00m
Catering, accommodation and other trade	R5,00m R5,00m
Transport, storage and communications	R10,00m
Finance and business services	R10,00m R10,00m R10,00m
Community, social and personal services	R5,00m R5,00m

EXHIBIT 3.6: Prescribed contents of an employment equity plan

An employment equity plan should include:

- the objectives to be achieved for each year of the plan;
- the affirmative action measures to be implemented;
- where under-representation of people from designated groups has been identified by the analysis, the numerical goals to achieve the equitable representation of suitably qualified people from designated groups within each occupational category and level in the workforce, the timetable within which this is to be achieved, and the strategies intended to achieve those goals;
- the timetable for each year of the plan for the achievement of goals and objectives other than numerical goals;
- the duration of the plan, which may not be shorter than one year or longer than five years;
- the procedures that will be used to monitor and evaluate the implementation of the plan and whether reasonable progress is being made towards implementing employment equity;
- the internal procedures to resolve any dispute about the interpretation or implementation of the plan; and
- the persons in the workforce, including senior managers, responsible for monitoring and implementing the plan;
- measures designed to further diversity in the workplace based on equal dignity and respect of all people;
- making reasonable accommodation for people from designated groups in order to ensure that they enjoy equal opportunities and are equitably represented in the workforce of a designated employer;
- measures to ensure the equitable representation of suitably qualified people from designated groups in all occupational categories and levels in the work-force; and
- measures to retain and develop people from designated groups and to implement appropriate training measures, including measures in terms of the Skills Development Act.

- any written undertaking given by the employer and any failure by the employer to comply with the written undertaking;
- any steps that the employer must take and the period within which those steps must be taken; and
- the maximum fine, if any, that may be imposed on the employer for failing to comply with the order.

A designated employer must conform to the compliance order within the time period stated in it, unless the employer lodges an objection to that with the Director-General within 21 days after receiving that order. If the employer is unhappy with the Director-General's decision, the employer can appeal against it to the Labour Court. If a designated employer does not comply with an order within the period stated in it, or does not object to that order, the Director-General may apply to the Labour Court to make the compliance order an order of the Labour Court.

In determining whether a designated employer is implementing employment equity in compliance with the EEA, the Director-General must take into account all of the factors listed in exhibit 3.7. Based on the Director-General's assessment of an employer's employment equity plan or the employer's non-compliance with the Act, the Director-General may make a recommendation to the employer. Should the employer fail to comply with the Director-General's recommendation, the Director-General may refer the employer's non-compliance to the Labour Court for adjudication.

EXHIBIT 3.7: Assessment of employment equity compliance

The following factors will be taken into account:

■ the extent to which suitably qualified people from and amongst the different designated groups are equitably represented within each occupational category and level in that employer's workforce in relation to the:
  - demographic profile of the national and regional economically active population;
  - pool of suitably qualified people from designated groups from which the employer may reasonably be expected to promote or appoint employees;
  - economic and financial factors relevant to the sector in which the employer operates;
  - present and anticipated economic and financial circumstances of the employer; and the number of present and planned vacancies that exist in the various categories and levels, and the employer's labour turnover;

■ progress made in implementing employment equity by other designated employers operating under comparable circumstances and within the same sector;

■ reasonable efforts made by a designated employer to implement its employment equity plan; and

■ the extent to which the designated employer has made progress in eliminating employment barriers that adversely affect people from designated groups.

3.3.2.3 State contracts

Many organisations are wholly or largely dependent on the procurement of state tenders and contracts to remain in business. This gives the state a very powerful economic weapon to ensure compliance by private organisations with the provisions of the Act. In terms of the EEA, every employer that makes an offer to conclude an agreement with any organ of state for the furnishing of supplies or services to that organ of state or for the hiring or letting of anything, must:

■ if it is a designated employer, comply with Chapters II (anti-discrimination provisions) and III (affirmative action provisions) of the Act;

■ if it is not a designated employer, comply with Chapters II and III (affirmative action provisions) of the Act;

■ if it is not designated employer, comply with Chapter II of the Act; and

■ attach to that offer either a certificate which is conclusive evidence that the employer complies with the relevant chapters of the Act; or a declaration by the employer that it complies with the relevant chapters of the Act, which, when verified by the Director-General, is conclusive evidence of compliance.

A certificate of compliance is valid for 12 months from the date of issue or until the next date on which the employer is obliged to submit an employment equity progress report, whichever period is the longer. A failure to comply with the relevant provisions of the EEA is sufficient grounds for rejection of any offer to conclude an agreement or for cancellation of the agreement.

There are certain maximum permissible fines that may be imposed for contravention of the EEA and these are specified in the Act. From an empowerment perspective we are less concerned about these issues of 'non-conformance', seeing that we work from the proposition that affirmative action plans and concomitant interventions are proactively engaged in so that diversity can be embraced in order to enhance performance.

3.3.3 Developing and implementing affirmative action interventions

The challenge facing South African organisations is to develop and implement affirmative action interventions that will enhance capacity to perform and compete through greater diversity of their working people. As a consequence, hopefully growth will mean even more opportunities and hence enhancing further employment equity efforts and achievements. In many African countries measures to redistribute wealth and impose organisational control have been implemented with scant regard for economic growth. The consequences of this approach have been disastrous for the national economies of these countries and have resulted in the impoverishment of all. We should learn from such cases and focus on growth through diversification of our workforces.

In this section we discuss how an organisation can go about developing and implementing affirmative action interventions that actually leverage diversity and turn that into better performance and hence more competitive organisations. It should be stressed that the aim is not, and cannot be, to provide a universally applicable blueprint. Affirmative action interventions should be tailored to the peculiar circumstances of each organisation, taking into account, inter alia, its present human resource base and future needs based on the longer-term direction of the organisation, and its overall resource and competitive position, and so forth. There is thus the need to align and integrate affirmative action plans and targets with the overall organisational strategies and directions, as well as its more general human resource strategies and policies (we turn to these in Part 2 of the book).

Figure 3.2 shows how a government, through legislation, can prohibit discriminatory practices and can promote affirmative action. However, the reach of the law is limited; without organisational culture change and the transformation of individual attitudes, affirmative action cannot succeed. This is so for a number of reasons. If an employer regards affirmative action as a necessary evil, he or she will embark on measures to get the numbers right at what he or she considers to be the least cost to the organisation. This in turn can lead to window-dressing and to a low investment in human resource development. Power will thus remain firmly in the hands of white managers, and black appointees will be 'tolerated' (rather than utilised fully as valuable resources and source of competitive advantage). The appointment of blacks will then tend to be clustered in the lower hierarchical levels, and those blacks who are 'lucky enough' to be appointed to managerial positions will probably find themselves in positions of no real authority and will thus soon leave in frustration. All this will lead to a reinforcement of racial stereotypes and to the entrenchment of the view that affirmative action measures lead to increased costs, a lowering of standards and a dropping of productivity. Just as no law can ensure that a marriage will be successful and compel a couple to be happily married (although the law can (and does) provide the legal framework for the institution of marriage), no statute can force an employer and an employee to make a general success of their employment relationship and of affirmative action in particular. This is why the human factor in broad terms is the key, not numbers – quality, more so than quantity. Interventions that improve and change attitudes for the better and styles of management that unlock the potential and empower people are the important ingredients of successful affirmative action approaches. What is therefore required is an approach which fully integrates and aligns affirmative action with all other areas of HRM, as well as general management strategies and practices. If this is not done, the chances of making affirmative action a success story of empowerment are vastly diminished and it will be doomed to fail. More importantly, it may even lead to complete organisational failure.

Affirmative action, as part of the broader empowerment agenda, thus forms an integral part and key focus area of HRM in South Africa in general. As such it should be treated as a strategic business and HRM priority and managed accordingly. Although 'strategic HRM' issues are addressed in the next two chapters, it is important to emphasise here the necessity of also dealing specifically with affirmative action in a strategic way.

It will be recalled that the EEA requires all designated employers to perform an organisational audit to identify existing barriers to change and to obtain a profile of the existing workforce. This organisational audit can provide a picture of the present and thus form the basis of the aforementioned strategic approach to affirmative action that is required. This is considered in conjunction with the desired state of things – the gap is identified and the appropriate path is crafted. From this we develop the employment equity plans and appropriate implementation interventions – with action plans, budgets, responsible people and so forth – to drive down the path plotted. These things should thus all be done from a strategic change and business perspective, and commitment from all stakeholders will be essential. In particular it is vital to deal with all of this as part and parcel of the empowerment agenda of HRM more broadly. The emphasis must be on development and the unlocking of people's untapped potential. The importance of designing and implementing support interventions that can help all parties cope with the demands and effects of such a strategically driven effort, and that can enhance the competitiveness and success of an organisation, cannot be overestimated.

A key challenge facing an organisation in implementing affirmative action programmes is the need to identify the various stakeholders and to address most of their fears and aspirations. There must be very broad consultation, and all stakeholders must be engaged. This means staff across all levels and categories of work. The most important of the stakeholders are: the intended beneficiaries of the programme; the previously advantaged members of staff; the shareholders; and the community within which the organisation is situated. Only by addressing most of these (often divergent) groups' reasonable fears and legitimate aspirations can an organisation hope to succeed in changing the hearts and minds of its employees – an essential ingredient for employment equity really to succeed. In order to do this it must firstly be appreciated that the objectives of affirmative action do not stand in opposition to the goals of the organisation – that is, affirmative action, when implemented correctly, is not only supportive but indeed essential for the future of the organisation. In diversity, if embraced appropriately, lies power. Our challenge is to unlock that power.

Furthermore, although the economic circumstances of masses of blacks must be improved, this is just part of the puzzle. The need for psychological growth is a universal human attribute that cannot be satisfied simply by giving people impressive titles and inflated remuneration packages. People need to be given the opportunity to develop and this can only be done by placing them in positions of real authority and responsibility (naturally this includes providing training support where necessary and creating well-developed career paths so as not to set them up for failure). We have unfortunately witnessed the phenomenon whereby qualified blacks continually change jobs in pursuit of ever-higher remuneration packages (job-hopping). This may well be symptomatic of managements' failure to appreciate the real challenges we have at hand. The cause of the high turnover among qualified black employees may well be to do with supply and demand issues, but their frustration of being placed in sinecures and at being miscast should not be overlooked or underestimated: it may very well not as much be the quest for better material rewards, but rather perhaps more the search for meaningful employment (meaning authority and responsibility) that may be causing the job-hopping.

Turning to the interests of the historically advantaged group, it must be appreciated that their fears (real or imagined) cannot simply be disregarded. Firstly, it is an unfortunate fact that much needed skills are currently concentrated in the hands of the white minority and that organisations can ill afford to lose their expertise. Secondly, the willingness of this group to impart their skills to other employees is indispensable for the success of affirmative action. Thirdly, depending on the modality of affirmative action adopted in the organisation, it may well be that at least some of their fears are well founded. While it may be persuasive on a macro or theoretical level to point to the moral correctness of affirmative action and to stress the social, economic and political forces that render affirmative action imperative, these arguments will not sound convincing to a 40-something middle manager who has been told (a) that he has to train his (black/female) successor; and (b) that he should not expect to progress any further within the organisation. It is well known that many existing white employees fear for their own career prospects as affirmative action programmes are rolled out in organisations. These fears, whether imaginary or not, must be addressed. Although some reject what has been called 'undue pandering to white fears', it is also true that perceptions are reality for the perceivers and that few organisations at present can afford immediately to replace all their white staff with blacks.

A further challenge relates to the fact that thousands of young white people entering the labour market today never had anything to do with South Africa's historical path of unfairly discriminating against black people. University graduates aged 21 years or so were children aged seven or so when democratic South Africa was born. Instituting affirmative action programmes in ways that exclude them from competing for the opportunities to work in the fields of their qualifications also does not make sense from their perspective. Neither does it from the point of view of losing such qualified people to other countries (as is currently the case). Developing and implementing affirmative action programmes in organisations thus poses a number of very serious challenges, not least of which relates to the delicate balancing act involved in enhancing the opportunities of some while not making the non-beneficiaries completely despondent.

It is thus important that the issue of affirmative action must be placed on the public agenda within the organisation – right from the start. Focus groups where fears and aspirations may be freely identified and aired (and unjustified fears and misperceptions removed) could go a long way in proactively addressing issues. Secondly, management must be honest with all its employees: the management's intentions and the affirmative action measures which are under consideration must be clearly communicated to its entire staff. Thirdly, management should stress that, although previously disadvantaged groups will be given preference, appointments and promotions will be on merit (thereby reassuring present incumbents that they will still be afforded opportunities for advancement within the organisation). Keeping staff informed on a continual basis, running workshops on issues such as the organisation's new recruitment and promotion policies and practices and on attitudinal change, to name but a few, can all be strongly recommended. Lastly, it should be made clear to all staff that unfair discrimination will not be tolerated, and employees who are not prepared to accept the envisaged transformation of the organisation will have to reconsider their continued presence within it. Addressing legitimate concerns and removing imaginary misperceptions and fears is absolutely necessary; however, pandering to the demands of people who do not accept that change is both essential and desirable is not a feasible option. An integrated and strategic approach is therefore required to bring about the required transformation.

3.3.3.1 Managing EE: an integrated strategic approach[2]

Selby and Sutherland (2006: 58–60) provide a model for managing employment equity in an integrated way and we include that here (see figure 3.3 as well as their explanation thereof).

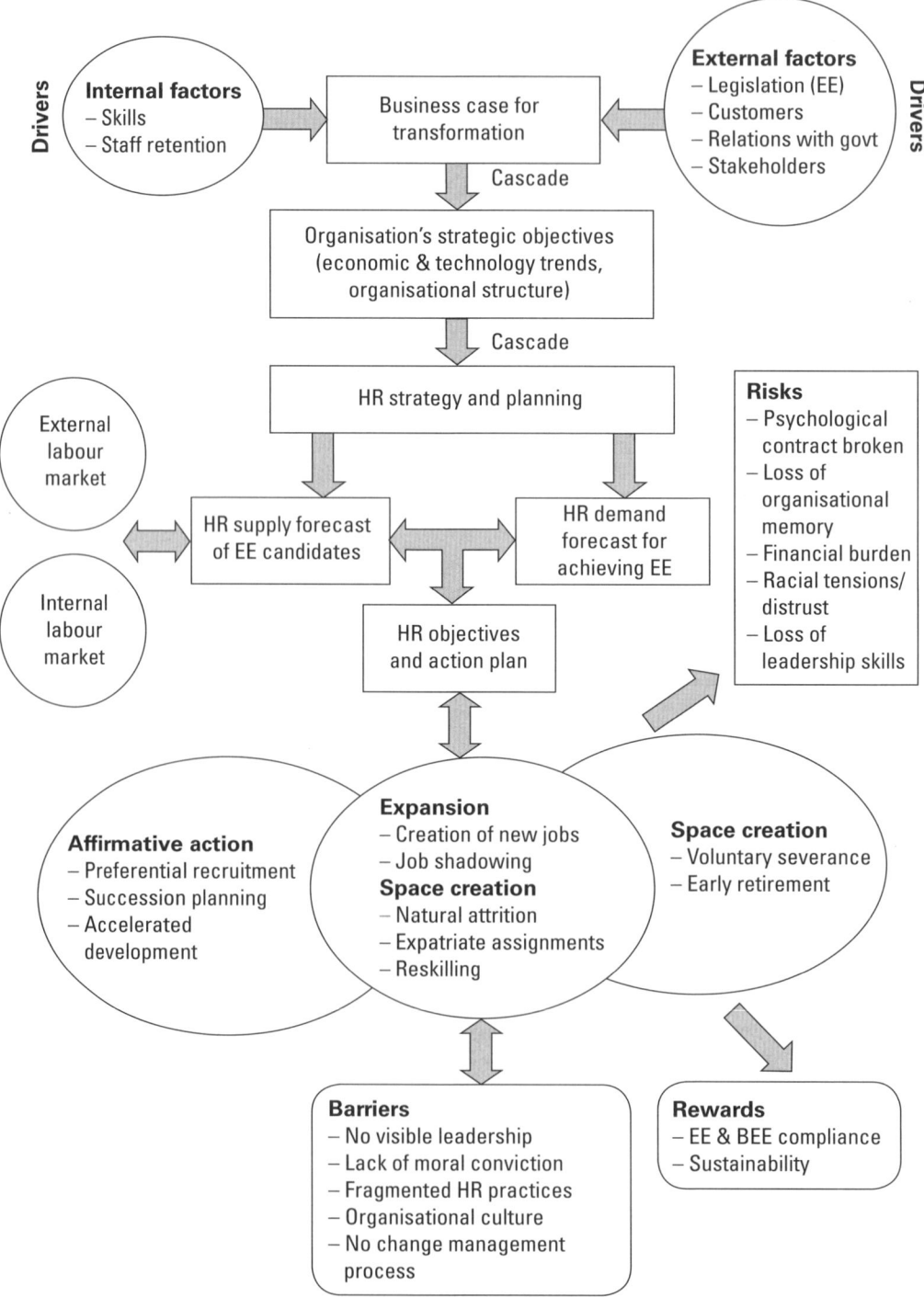

Figure 3.3: An integrated model for managing employment equity in South African organisations
Source: Slightly adapted from Selby & Sutherland (2006: 59)

First and foremost, a strong and clearly articulated business case for employment equity is developed, which takes cognisance of the factors external and internal to the organisation which drive employment equity.

The business case for transformation should then cascade down and be incorporated into the organisation's strategic objectives alongside customer service, cost effectiveness, quality, etc.

Once the transformation objective has been articulated, it cascades down into the company's human resource strategy and human resource planning activities.

The first step in human resource planning is to forecast the human resource demand required to achieve the organisation's employment equity goals.

This is followed by an assessment of the supply of employment equity candidates from within and external to the organisation (i.e. the internal and external labour market).

By comparing the labour demand and supply forecasts, the organisation then draws up action plans to address the shortages and/or surpluses of employees according to their race and gender targets in all occupation categories and levels within the organisation.

Organisations then select from among a number of strategies to achieve their transformation objectives. These include:

- Traditional affirmative action measures such as preferential recruitment and selection, succession planning and accelerated development.
- A combination of affirmative action and 'space creation' strategies such as the creation of new positions, natural attrition, job shadowing, expatriate assignments and retraining, which work to minimise some of the negative consequences of change.
- Interventionist 'space creation' strategies such as voluntary severance and the use of early retirement incentives. If organisations choose these more aggressive strategies, they need to take cognisance of the risks and rewards associated with these strategies and take action to mitigate the negative consequences. Risks take the form of breaking the psychological contracts in place, loss of organisational memory, financial consequences, inter-racial distrust and tensions and loss of leadership skills. Rewards come from all the benefits of EE and BEE compliance which should lead to competitive advantage and medium-term sustainability.

Finally, whatever strategies organisations choose to achieve their employment equity targets, they need to take cognisance of typical barriers to employment equity and put measures in place to overcome these.

In respect of the barriers Selby and Sutherland (2006) refer to in their last point above, we refer you to exhibit 3.8, which reflects what research has shown out to be relevant.

Booysen (2007: 65–69) also makes the following recommendations, which we believe ought to be seriously considered:[3]

Work towards an inclusive organisational culture in which diversity is valued

Organisational cultures that are still 'white elitist' and that are resistant to transformation must be changed. Ongoing diversity education and training, and open discussion forums and dialogue are seen as important in order to change the culture towards an inclusive one that values diversity, where the importance of the correct and speedy implementation of EE is seen as a strategic imperative and not merely a legislative necessity.

EXHIBIT 3.8: Affirmative action failure issues

Booysen (2007: 64–65) has found the following: "In summary, the following were found ... to be the reasons for lack of progress in EE implementation and retention of blacks ...

- Slow EE progress at management level and inconsistent progress across different departments in organisations
- Low commitment to EE from top management, with lip service by leadership about the need for EE
- Ineffective consultation and communication around EE progress and implementation
- A lack of cultural sensitivity where new recruits are expected to assimilate into the current organisational culture
- A lack of cultural awareness programmes and of an organisational culture that values diversity
- A white male-dominant organisational culture that continues to exclude black recruits (formally or informally through exclusionary network practices)
- Black people are perceived as tokens and not fully integrated into companies because of little delegation of real responsibility or decision-making authority, owing to persistent stereotypes
- Black staff are not systematically developed and trained – no effective talent management
- Lack of black mentors and role models".

Work towards a shared understanding of EE

A shared understanding of the necessity of EE should be developed through the following:

- Re-stating the business case, by using all possible communication media, as well as open discussion forums that will also give people who feel threatened an opportunity to express and deal with their fears;
- Training workshops, geared at understanding the business imperative, EE legislation and Charter resolutions;
- Organisation-wide diversity training;
- Ensuring that black employees are fully integrated, and have real responsibility and authority; and
- Celebrating the positives – building on wins and positive developments, and capitalising on initiatives that are going well; making sure that existing initiatives are actually inclusive; linking initiatives that are going well with positive EE outcomes; publicising EE success stories; and creating role models. Lastly, it is important to ensure that the internal communication media cover and represent all groups.

There must be increased, visible management commitment

There should be demonstrated commitment to EE by management at all levels of the organisation, starting at the top. Executive and top management commitment to EE needs to be demonstrated by example. This could be done through leadership changes, and moves towards more representivity and inclusion. Leadership also needs to set the example and promote role model behaviour.

Ensure effective and consistent EE implementation

Specific focus should be on the effective coordination, integration, prioritising and management of the consistent implementation of the EE strategies and action plans. In order to achieve this, the following should be put in place:

- Specific accountability and responsibility need to be monitored and measured.

- Consequences need to be clarified and applied for cases of non-compliance and inconsistencies in compliance.
- Compliance should be built into managers' key performance areas, recognition and rewards should be offered to those who comply consistently. Non-compliance and inconsistencies should carry perceived real consequences or penalties.

Address white male fears

White male fears should be specifically managed in order not to alienate or demotivate this valuable pool of talent, through the following:
- Create a separate parallel stream for white males with talent.
- Make them feel valued, seen and heard again.
- Give them direction, clarify their role in the organisation – even if the news is not particularly good.
- Help them to understand their role in transformation, through training and coaching.
- Give them incentives to train, develop and mentor previously disadvantaged individuals.
- Develop white males for careers outside their present organisations.
- Establish support groups for white males.
- Provide psychological support for white males to help them to deal with their predicament.
  (The above can also be instituted for white females if and when necessary.)

Effectively manage supportive HRM practices

HRM practices that support EE implementation and retention of blacks should be effectively implemented, executed and managed.

Work towards an integrated attraction, development and retention strategy

As a general overarching suggestion it is recommended that existing policies and strategies regarding attraction, recruitment, development and retention should be reviewed and aligned with the EE drive and with one another. Develop an EE consultation forum and get the members intimately involved in the development of these strategies. The relevant HR practitioners should also play a more integral and strategic part in executing the above strategies.

Make the integrated and aligned strategy and specific action plans known explicitly throughout the organisation. Demonstrate commitment to transformation by appointing black males and females at senior management and executive level to act as coaches, mentors and role models. Target specific black institutions for talent, and put black recruiters in the field. Put black staff in front-line positions to attract black talent. Lastly, allocate a dedicated pool of money to attract and retain black talent, since talented blacks are in high demand and are expensive.

Manage talent effectively

Develop, institute and manage a well-planned talent management strategy and policies. Managers should be made responsible for talent management. Specific career paths, training and development plans, succession planning and personal growth opportunities must be in place for each individual. Talent management should further be formalised through coaching and mentoring, and support.

To summarise: Affirmative action will only work if we follow an integrated and strategic approach as part of the broader empowerment agenda of HRM. All the stakeholders and specifically the groups of working people affected by the affirmative action must be involved, and their interests and concerns genuinely addressed and balanced. All must ultimately take ownership of the challenge. Without putting the human element at the core, or following an integrated approach, affirmative action will be little more than a costly and self-defeating attempt at window-dressing, head-counting and a short-term response to a much bigger and longer-term challenge.

3.3.4 Towards real performance: empowering for entrepreneurial endeavour

Employment equity legislation gives a platform and framework to get more of our designated (traditionally disadvantaged) people to take part in the management of existing organisations. We thus need to empower people towards a state of ultimately having an equitable representation of all groups across all occupational categories and levels of our workforces. The BBBEE legislative platform includes this aspect of affirmative action, but it also challenges us to empower more and more black people (African, coloured and Asian – as those who have historically not been empowered) to be able to set up and develop their own business enterprises (and other organisations, such as worker cooperatives, for instance). The aim is therefore to not only diversify the people who can manage, but also those who actually own the productive resources in our society.

Given these huge challenges we face in South Africa, our proposition is that we need to broaden the agenda of HRM to one driven by an empowerment mindset. We believe such an approach will have a better chance to move this country towards a better life for all. From the earlier descriptions of what empowerment entails (section 3.3.1.4) and what the BBBEE definition is (as contained in Act 53 of 2003 – see section 3.2.10), it must be clear that at the very core of our country's empowerment drive is the human resource factor. Human resource development, as mentioned, is pertinently included as central to BBBEE. Clearly the whole issue of work is also at the very core of this empowerment imperative – work as managers, but also work as owners of enterprises. Not only does the inclusion of employment equity (and thus affirmative action) signal the importance of transforming the work roles of black employees in our organisations (to be more part of the managerial and professional cadres), but the expansion of our people's opportunities to 'own' and 'control' and 'manage' productive resources (or assets) in our economy gives the platform for enhancing entrepreneurial capabilities and opportunities.

It thus becomes part of our human resource development mandate to educate and train our people to help them become entrepreneurs. Apart from that, we also regard this agenda to include developing an approach to managing that would make our existing organisations more entrepreneurial. The notion of *corporate entrepreneurship* or 'intrapreneurship' thus comes to the fore. As such, making our organisations more entrepreneurial includes changes in how we structure them, what leadership styles we use and develop, and what cultures we develop in our organisations. All of these become people-related challenges – and thus form part of the broadened HRM agenda now. That is why you will find that we cover these themes and issues in various chapters throughout this book.

3.3.4.1 Developing intrapreneurship

Intrapreneurship, also known as corporate entrepreneurship, is essentially entrepreneurship in the context of established, especially larger, organisations (Morris, Kuratko & Covin 2008). These authors explain that the basics "of entrepreneurship is universal", and that their preferred definition of entrepreneurship which says that the focus is "on a process of value creation through unique resource combinations for the purpose of exploiting opportunity", is a phenomenon that "can occur in ... small firms, mid-sized companies, large conglomerates, non-profit organizations, and even public sector agencies" (Morris et al 2008: 33). They do point out, though, that even while there are similarities between entrepreneurship and intrapreneurship, there are naturally also differences (such as related to risk and ownership). For our purposes these are not so important. What is important is to establish how organisations can become more entrepreneurial and what role HRM plays in that.

The key probably lies in the potential interplay between creativity, innovation and entrepreneurship. All people, generally, possess creative abilities. The challenge is how to unlock them and tap into them for the benefit of the organisation and all its stakeholders, including for the working people themselves. Morris et al (2008: 167) explain that they believe "that each and every employee within an organization is rich in entrepreneurial potential ..." and that our challenge thus becomes that of developing a work environment that "expects or permits employees to demonstrate individual initiative, experiment, try new things ... and related entrepreneurial behaviors". This is therefore clearly a challenge directly aligned with the broadened HRM agenda that is geared towards empowering our people.

If we want to develop more entrepreneurial organisations (and we will have to make strategic decisions about this – see chapter 4), we will have to make sure that our policy frameworks and our organisation design and other structural variables are specifically geared towards that. The same holds for various systems and the culture of the organisation. The whole spectrum of HRM work has to be aligned towards achieving that. Christiansen (2000: 141), for example, shares research findings that showed that organisations that want to be creative and innovative "focus on finding and hiring creative people ...", and "... have a preference for people with a variety of backgrounds". The same author (Christiansen 2000: 143) explains: "Innovative companies not only try to hire creative people. They also develop them in ways which will increase their creative output." Morris et al (2008: 172) go along with this and say that training will probably have to include "an attitudinal component, wherein acceptance of change, a willingness to take risks and assume responsibility, and the value of teamwork ..." will be included.

Similarly such organisations will typically opt for work design (see chapter 5) which is more 'free and open', and jobs and work will thus have to be less restricted by things like rules and regulations, and 'dos and dont's'. MacKenzie (2004: 140–142) says that organisational structures will have to become more flat, that "an innovative enterprise is, above all else, a cultural issue", and that "leadership is the single most important issue in developing an innovative corporate culture". Giugni (2004: 72) argues that the appropriate organisational culture for creativity and imaginative and innovative work can only be achieved if four key components are present, namely "freedom, encouragement, recognition and the desire to achieve". Careers will thus also have to be more flexible so that people can move around and develop the variety of experiences enabling them to develop different perspectives and so forth – and to advance their career prospects and opportunities to achieve. Likewise, the ways in which we manage work performance and reward achievement will have to encourage things like proper risk orientations, and not be punitive when there are failures. MacKenzie (2004: 143) adds: "Rewarding staff appropriately is also important ... If you expect staff to contribute innovative ideas that could dramatically improve the organisation's profit, shouldn't they share the gains?"

It is therefore clear that the whole spectrum of HRM work needs to be reconsidered and engaged in order to empower working people to help make the organisation more entrepreneurial. Naturally, by developing these opportunities and capabilities of staff we will also be achieving the by-product of having working employees who will be able to add value way beyond their careers with us. In this way we thus send former employees into society who have been empowered to perhaps even run their own businesses. In fact, corporate entrepreneurship might specifically include such an aim. We now turn to that in a little more detail.

3.3.4.2 Developing entrepreneurs and entrepreneurial ventures: towards self-employment

Corporate entrepreneurship can take on different forms, including what is known as corporate venturing. Corporate venturing is basically when organisations get involved in actually developing and setting up new businesses. These can range from internal corporate venturing where another business is created from within the organisation and is kept inside the existing corporate structure (thus owned by the parent company), to external venturing (investing in other businesses outside the organisation, such as buying an existing organisation). It may also be that initially the internal corporate venturing route is taken and later the new venture may be 'farmed out' (known also as 'spin-out' companies or ventures). When we engage in these kinds of things it may very well have to be our own human resources who will be developing these and/or be deployed within other structures to launch, establish and/or run or manage those new ventures. We then thus effectively develop entrepreneurs inside our organisations, and empower them to actually step outside and go on their own. Such ventures can sometimes go together with the outsourcing of some of the organisation's work and business. While these may sound a bit extreme, these things happen and are extremely valuable forms of empowerment, as can be seen from 'A case at hand' and the 'Elsewhere in Africa' examples below. People are thus specifically trained and developed in order to be able to become successful entrepreneurs.

A CASE AT HAND

From SAB to SABMiller – empowerment and growth in South Africa and beyond

SABMiller is a multinational company with a true 'global footprint', consisting of a portfolio of businesses and operations spanning a range of countries and continents. Starting off as SAB Ltd (South African Breweries), a growth strategy that included aggressive expansion into international markets with a particular emphasis on emerging economies has now developed this organisation into one of the world's largest brewers, with brewing interests and distribution agreements in over 60 countries across six continents. SABMiller's brands include premium international beers such as Miller Genuine Draft, as well as a range of market-leading local brands such as Carling Black Label in South Africa. Six of the brands are in the world's top 50 beer brands. SABMiller is also one of the largest bottlers of Coca-Cola products in the world.

Graham Mackay, SABMiller's chief executive recently said: "The key to our success is the consistent, disciplined application of our strategic priorities and the knowledge, deeply embedded in our culture, that we must constantly improve every element of our business. As we move forward, we'll continue executing our strategy with the same rigour and determination while constantly analysing the global marketplace to ensure that our strategic priorities remain appropriate."

The central role of knowledge and culture shows that people are at the very core of SABMiller's success. In a case study written up by the International Labour Office (ILO) in 2002 about South African Breweries, the following is stated, again showing that people are at the core:

>>

The high profile and subsequent impact of SAB on the South African economy makes it essential that environmental factors are dealt with in an extremely professional manner. This requires collaboration with key stakeholders, including other businesses, government, communities, labour, etc. SAB's impact on South Africa can be seen in the following ways:

- In terms of excise and company taxation, SAB is the largest single contributor to the fiscus, exceeding the contribution of the mining industry as a whole.
- Conservatively, the up- and downstream impact of SAB's operations translates into the creation of approximately 400 000 jobs, the majority of these being in black-owned retail and on-premise outlets, known as 'shebeens' and 'taverns'.

For this success to be sustainable, it is founded on key success factors in which the company invests, ie growth, people and corporate reputation (image).

One of these investments is the innovative establishment of 'owner-driver' schemes through which employees are empowered to become entrepreneurs. More than a decade ago already (in 1995), South African Breweries (SAB) started outsourcing the driving of distribution trucks to its employees, making them 'x-employees'. Through a structured process, some employees (drivers) buy the trucks and as part of the arrangement they enter into contracts with SAB as one of its customers – hence, the term 'owner-driver'. According to the ILO case study report, this scheme, in short, entails the following:

- employee drivers are selected against communicated criteria and standards to become owner-drivers;
- owner-drivers enter into contracts with SAB, spelling out minimum service requirements and price and payment details;
- SAB facilitates alternative funding options to enable the persons to buy the trucks; and
- SAB puts in place support processes to help these owner-drivers to succeed, for example entrepreneurial skills, financial management skills, etc.

As can be seen in the 'Elsewhere in Africa' box below, SABMiller is spreading this innovative HRM and business practice into Africa through Botswana's Kgalagadi Breweries – empowering more people on our continent to become successful entrepreneurs.

Source: Extracted/adapted and based on sources such as the ILO's project and online book 'Supporting workplace learning for high performance working' (2002) and SABMiller's website www.sabmiller.com

---

Elsewhere in Africa

Kgalagadi Breweries Limited launches driver-empowerment scheme in Botswana

In a bid to enhance service delivery, empower Botswana, and improve efficiencies and productivity, Kgalagadi Breweries Limited (KBL) has announced the launching of Phase 1 of the privatisation of its delivery service, targeting Gaborone and surrounding areas.

According to the company's Director of Corporate Affairs, Percy Raditladi, the initiative – known as the Owner-Driver Programme (OD) – is a product distribution and delivery programme that seeks to support KBL's strategic imperatives of efficiency and service delivery.

Raditladi says the programme started with the internal recruitment of potential owner-drivers among employees and existing third-party distributors known as 'runners'.

The owner-drivers will each employ two to three assistants, creating up to 15 additional jobs between themselves.

Source: Adapted from 'Kgalagadi Breweries Limited launches driver-empowerment scheme'

3.3.5 Towards equitable equality: a last note

The challenges we face in moving towards a situation where we will have a fully inclusive societal fabric are vast. We have ample examples of how to meet these challenges, though – and we should learn from them, and develop and adapt our own ways in the unique circumstances our organisations, and all of us, face. In doing all of this we should never forget that we must aim to become a society where we have equity and fairness regarding all concerned. We do not yet have equitable equality in our country and as we work towards getting to that ideal end state, there are lots of dynamics we must incorporate in all of our efforts and ideas. Through interventions like affirmative action programmes and developing entrepreneurs to whom we can outsource some of our business and work, we will thus be contributing to developing a much more inclusive society. As such we will also be diversifying the role players and stakeholders, and the roles they play both inside and outside our organisations. This is a future state to which we aspire and have to work towards. As we engage in this challenging work, one other key challenge relates to the actual management of diversity. Importantly, diversity also means that not all people have necessarily yet bought into the idea that we must embrace diversity or empower some of our people more so than others. Naturally there are also some people who have negative views and feelings – perhaps because they experience some perceived unfairness in all of these efforts. These all form part of the diversity challenge we face.

An example of people who may feel negatively affected may be some of the younger people who form part of the population group that has traditionally been advantaged at the cost of the others. There is ample anecdotal evidence of relatively young, well-qualified white males (and females) who feel that they are at the losing end in that they do not get the same opportunities from their point of view, even though they themselves had absolutely nothing to do with the discriminatory practices of the apartheid years. From chapter 2 we know that these people also form a major proportion of the skilled human resources that leave our country, people who hope to find greener pastures for themselves elsewhere.

Many feel that due to the fact that the emphasis must now be on black economic empowerment, there is a creeping systemic disempowerment of young (and older) whites – especially males. The opportunities created for others (traditionally disadvantaged people), so the perceptions and arguments go, means fewer opportunities for them. These people thus tend to be more prone to leave the country, taking their capabilities to contribute to building a better South Africa with them. South Africa with its skills shortage cannot afford this. We must not turn a blind eye to these kinds (and other) of views, but rather take them on board as part of our diversity management agenda, as Booysen (2007) has also pointed out (see section 3.3.3 above). Managing diversity is just what it says: it is about managing actively in and towards an environment where we seek to extract, leverage and enhance the best in and out of all the variety of abilities, potential, and so forth, which our different peoples of South Africa have to offer – and these include the views, feelings and ideas of people. This, we often hear, is easier said than done, though.

3.4 EMBRACING AND MANAGING DIVERSITY

There can be little doubt that diversity management requires a concerted and persistent effort. The topic is so vast and deep that covering it within the context of a section of a chapter in a book like this can be no more than a very brief and superficial introduction. In fact, this may well be at the risk of doing an injustice to this all-important theme.

We thus suggest that our readers engage in an extensive separate journey of reading and learning about this topic – there are plenty of books devoted to diversity and the management thereof, as well as lots of other material.

3.4.1 The concept of diversity management

Diversity essentially refers to the fact that no two people are exactly the same. It thus accentuates the idea that there are wide varieties of differences between people that stem from things like genetics and also the environment in which they were born, raised, educated and so forth. We can think of things like gender, race, ethnic group, language, culture, sexual orientation, religious beliefs and worldviews – and also things like personality, knowledge, perceptions, emotions and feelings, and personal values. We must also add things like the different perspectives people may have and the ranges of different opinions and views about matters – these even include views about politics and how to govern countries – and also about how to manage people and organisations. The lists can go on and on. While people might therefore be similar in some ways, they simultaneously differ in other respects. This is what we have to embrace. This is what we have to manage.

The examples we mentioned earlier about the perceptions and negative feelings experienced by some white males about the potential impact that affirmative action and black economic empowerment might have on them and their opportunities in our country must be 'heard' and addressed. This is not a matter of who is correct or who is wrong – in the spirit of what diversity is, we must acknowledged these different perspectives and perceptions, and we must actively manage these as constructively as possible.

Adele Thomas (1996: 10), in her book *Beyond Affirmative Action – Managing Diversity for Competitive Advantage in South Africa*, defines the management of diversity as follows: "A planned and comprehensive managerial process for developing an organisational environment in which all employees, with their similarities and differences, can contribute to the strategic and competitive advantage of the organisation, and where no-one is excluded on the basis of factors unrelated to their productivity."

From this perspective we might, for instance, ask how we can re-engage those white people who might feel that they are now being marginalised. We must hear those voices and try to understand the feelings also of the non-beneficiaries of the current dispensation. More importantly, though, we must empower them as well and channel the energies towards turning perceived threats into opportunities. We must thus seek alternatives. Let us take an example related to something like affirmative action targets. If we want to accelerate the process of making our senior and middle management cadres more representative, and hence we need to appoint more black Africans, coloureds and Indians, then a possibility might be to engage the existing white males who dominate those cadres and offer them alternative roles and opportunities. This might well entail some earlier 'separations' ('space creation' in Selby and Sutherland's (2006) terms) – but initially only partially perhaps, and even maybe gradually. We can help these people (financially and otherwise) to set up their own consulting businesses, and train and coach them to become mentors and coaches themselves perhaps, and otherwise engage in management and leadership development work. The new, much less experienced managers from designated groups can then be twinning or 'buddying' with these senior people who might initially just remain part-time employees for, say, ten or so hours per week. Alternatively, they can immediately enter into some consulting role from outside the organisation and engage in the same coaching work but charge differently. In such a way we might be able to tap into a wider and deeper range of experience, harness the diversity, and develop and exploit opportunities to add value on various fronts.

If we follow these kinds of approaches, it is less likely that we will find people thinking and saying things like 'diversity management is just another disguised concept for reverse discrimination that benefits some but is detrimental to others'. A holistic managerial approach will mean that we do whatever we can to harness as much as possible of what we have in terms of diversity of people and concomitant capabilities – and channel everything towards making our people, our organisations and our country more competitive.

3.4.2 Issues related to the diversity management challenge

A model like the one presented earlier can serve as a useful framework to plan our own way of managing diversity – especially if we want to follow a systematic and strategic approach. The one component refers to the fact that we have to develop action plans to address issues that might have been identified through the climate and culture assessments. The issues can obviously cover a very broad range – from things like apathy by some, lack of appreciation by others, to downright resistance. We devote a separate chapter to change management, and any comprehensive diversity management intervention aimed at establishing a new culture (one in which diversity is valued and lived) will have to deal with factors like resistance to change (RTC). In this section we just want to briefly touch on some relevant issues that are typically at play in organisations when it comes to the challenge of embracing diversity.

3.4.2.1 Hopes and fears: a balancing act

We have already made mention of the issue pertaining to the hopes and aspirations that some might have, as opposed to the uncertainties, concerns and even deep-seated fears that others might have. Culture change is not easy – and it cannot happen overnight. When we talk culture change we are dealing with feelings, emotions, values, perceptions and so on – things that are complex and typically deeply rooted in the very being of the people involved. We have had white-male-dominated organisations with concomitant organisational cultures for many years. As we try to turn that culture around we will have to eradicate certain deep-seated beliefs and replace certain ways of thinking and seeing, and feelings and what people value and have come to enjoy – with different mindsets. These things can create a sense of fear with many of those on who will be affected.

There is thus a need to balance the aspirations and excitement of some with these deep-seated concerns, issues and fears of others. These may require some very professional interventions – even those that deal with the very well-being of people. It can be traumatic for people to let go of mindsets and worldviews that have developed over many years, and to adopt new ones (see exhibit 3.9 below for some research findings in South Africa). Some of these deep-seated issues relate to things like stereotyping.

3.4.2.2 Bias, prejudices, stereotypes and assimilation

Having a stereotype is basically to have some distorted idea or image that generalises about people in terms of certain dimensions. These can be in terms of things like sex or race – or it can be about any other groupings of people, such as managers or politicians. Have you ever heard people saying something like, 'Oh well – but what did you expect? He is a politician.'? This is usually something based on some widely

EXHIBIT 3.9: Some research findings about diversity dynamics in South Africa

Research findings suggest that cognisance be taken of the following: that South African diversity dynamics are here to stay, that they are highly dynamic and constantly evolving, that organisations are experiencing enormous and increasing psychological splits around the many differences inherent in diversity dynamics, especially in relation to the primary dimensions of race, gender and age, and that the splits are filled with high-intensity feelings of frustration, hostility, resentment, non-tolerance and suspicion, even to the point of explosion into violent behaviour.

In order to understand, manage and contain diversity dynamics in organisations, it was suggested that all diversity management endeavours to implement the following:

- Constant monitoring of the level and intensity of diversity dynamics through observation of the levels of feelings in the organisation in general, as well as in all types of meetings, workshops, official and unofficial correspondence. It helps to see no behaviour or event as happening in isolation or by chance (in terms of behavioural dynamics there are no coincidences). The challenge is to see the part and relate it to the whole.

- Typical behaviour to look out for includes defences such as having strong and negative stereotypes about 'the others', and blaming, generalisations and projections of own frustration, anger and incompetence onto and into the other race, gender or generation.

- Where the intensity becomes high and potentially explosive, the individual carrying the projection must be psychologically cared for, for example through coaching or counselling.

- The group must also be psychologically cared for, for example through arranging a focus group where the participants can vent and offload their feelings.

- All one-on-one and group interventions must be conducted by trained officials who understand the system's psychodynamic manifestations of diversity dynamics and who can contain any potentially explosive situation. It is suggested that the consultants/moderators be representative of the primary diverse dimensions of race and gender (and not as in this study where two white people worked together in a diverse scenario).

- All informal or formal findings around diversity dynamics must be taken seriously and compared over time to establish trends and shifts in its manifestations in a type of diversity dynamic audit.

- The above monitoring and auditing can be linked to the employee wellness programme to establish what the total organisational system is experiencing and what the different subsystems are carrying on behalf of the total system.

Source: Cilliers & Smit (2006: 15)

shared view – even though not based on any evidence or true experience in reality. That is when prejudice kicks in – when some people simply have these preconceived ideas about things, like 'trade unions are bad', especially when they have never been members of a trade union themselves. The bias that typically comes along with these will then mean that some things, issues or people are simply favoured at the cost of others without having any objective rationale for that. In the past, with the male-dominated organisations we have had (not only in South Africa – but all over the world), it simply became a vicious circle of self-enforcement to keep it that way – masculine leadership styles were the order of the day, and males were appointed to the managerial positions. These come from age-old ideas like 'the woman's place is in the home'. While genetically women may be best programmed to raise children, this does not mean that they belong outside of organisations and management.

Bias forms the basis for assimilation. Grobler et al (2006: 78) say that assimilation assumes "that the dominant group's performance and style" is superior, adding that in some organisations there is this belief that "they have been successful because the homogeneous ideal made them succeed because of their tough, no-compromise, macho approach …". The same authors issue a warning when they say that pushing assimilation "reinforces the bias that spawns this approach and it perpetuates stereotyping and prejudice … Companies whose workforces cannot adapt to the new century will not survive" (Grobler et al 2006: 78). In this day and age we must break with our past ways and be bold enough to acknowledge that the old ways no longer work, and will not pull us through this age of transformation.

If we are to do that we will be more capable of developing something that is not one colour, but colourful, blending our people into rainbow-like workforces. We thus have to actively engage with all our people to address these deep-seated issues appropriately if we want to embrace diversity and develop an organisational culture that reflects that we truly value diversity. It is not always easy to break stereotypes and personal biases (we all favour some things over others, and we all have different ways of seeing things), but we must work hard at that. These efforts (like training) often start to yield some initial benefits at least of making people aware of their own biases, stereotypes and the like. If we can create the awareness and challenge people to test and test again to see whether there are any objective grounds, then in that way we will be able to gradually turn these things around. These sorts of changes sometimes may need individualised counselling interventions, but a good starting point is collective-based training types of interventions.

3.4.3 Diversity-related training and development

Organisations that are serious about developing a culture in which diversity is valued and embraced must throw resources at it. Time, expertise, energy, money and so forth will be required – and a lot must go into relevant change and human resource development interventions.

The training and development we are talking about here do not relate to training people about what the legislation requires us to do. While that cannot be left out, the issue is really that we need to develop mindsets which value people – full stop. Our earlier descriptions about what we regard as empowerment made that point. We have to put our people through training in which we let them know that we truly value them. The whole issue of top management commitment we spoke of earlier thus comes right to the fore again. Our organisation's value system together with the relevant mission and vision statement must reflect that indeed we put our people right at the core of our business. That is where the diversity awareness starts.

We cannot accept that people are aware of things. We must publish and develop posters and otherwise communicate with all staff that we value people a lot – that they are our most important source of competitive advantage, and that much of this is locked up precisely in the diversity of our people and the talents they have. Obviously, deeds speak louder than words – and the ways in which we actually treat our people – as managers right from the top down to the first-line supervisors – will show what we really value. But as we make people aware we must 'practice what we preach' and show that we tolerate conflict, encourage healthy debate, accept divergent viewpoints – and above all, that we value the diverse inputs.

People may not even be aware of the power locked up in the differences we all have. Some may not even really be acutely aware of the fact that we differ so much. We must do some basic training on 'work psychology' issues to show how different people think and see things – how personalities and personal styles of work can differ, and so forth. A key challenge is that we must have a fair idea of what people know and how they think. The assessment aspect we mentioned earlier is thus important as an input into how we design and develop these relevant training interventions.

When we do the climate and culture assessments these can typically be followed up or combined with more detailed training needs assessments. The content as well as the processes of delivery must be matched as closely as possible with what our needs assessments show to be the important issues. The content can include generic issues, but where appropriate we have to also address certain specific issues. In some parts of the organisation the training might perhaps have to be adapted to be different somehow from other parts. Not all people are equally ready, or resistant for that matter.

It goes without saying that we will have to make sure that the people who design and develop these interventions must be experts at what they do. It is therefore often advised that such people be engaged from outside the organisation if we do not have enough capacity inside. It might be better to do so anyway, given that we can expect existing staff to be part of an existing culture of not valuing diversity as much as we would like. Similarly, those who deliver these sessions or facilitate the sessions should be top class in what they do. If we mess up these interventions, we have a big problem at hand. Needless to say, those involved in designing, developing and delivering these training interventions must reflect diversity as well.

Lastly, we must make sure that our training interventions actually work – and pay off. We must thus do proper evaluations and take the feedback to improve. We must make sure that there is actual impact beyond 'this was an interesting and enjoyable session'. There must be changes in the way people think and behave – we must track and monitor whether these things take hold in our organisations.

In later chapters we elaborate more on aspects pertaining to training and development, and organisational change and transformation. These will obviously hold numerous interface points with what we have covered briefly in this section. At the end of the day we must be able to take everything we have in our 'arsenal' to fight this 'war' – and win it – and become an organisation, and country, that truly embraces diversity and empowers all our people. We must assess and improve – continuously. The results should ultimately reflect in the long-term success of the organisation. The case mentioned earlier of SABMiller (and SA Breweries) is definitely something to consider benchmarking against.

3.5 CONCLUSION

In this chapter we have tried to develop an argument that we must empower our people. HRM, as we have said, should broaden its agenda and be driven by a people-empowerment mindset. This is necessary both in South Africa and elsewhere in Africa. There is no other way in which we will be able to make this country and continent successful in a sustainable way. While the legislative framework that governs and guides HRM is very important from a primarily 'risk-and-compliance' perspective, our real challenge goes way beyond that. We have to empower to embrace diversity and make sure that we have organisations and people in our country who truly value the rainbow in our nation and on our continent.

With this we conclude the first part of this book which is meant to put South African HRM in the appropriate context. We are convinced that only with such a contextualised HRM approach will we be able to face the challenges of our time. We must continuously incorporate the relevant contextual issues into our daily thinking and practices related to the management of our organisations and our people. Being acutely aware, all the time, about the bigger picture and what we need in our country and on our continent should inform our decisions and also our instinctive reactions or responses when we manage and lead people on a daily basis. It should permeate all of our HRM.

In the next part we now focus on the organisational level – starting with the view from the top when we consider strategic perspectives of HRM.

SELF-EVALUATION QUESTIONS

1 What is meant by the 'HRM conformance challenge'?
2 What are the common-law duties of employers and employees?
3 Name and briefly describe any five laws that interplay with the management of human resources.
4 Explain the following concepts:
   ■ affirmative action;
   ■ empowerment;
   ■ equality of opportunity.
5 How can organisations develop and implement affirmative action interventions?
6 Write an essay on the following topic: 'Towards real performance: broadening the HRM agenda to empower people for entrepreneurial endeavour'.
7 Analyse and critically discuss the following statement: 'We need organisational cultures that embrace and value diversity. This requires good diversity management – which is quite a challenging task.'

ENDNOTE

1 Parts of this section are extracted and/or slightly adapted from the comprehensive loose-leaf Juta publication quoted in the text of this section: 'Black Economic Empowerment: Commentary, Legislation & Charters' (Cheadle Thompson & Haysom Inc 2005), Revision Service 2 (2007).
2 The model in this section is taken from Selby and Sutherland (2006).
3 A slightly adapted extract from Booysen's (2007: 65–69) article is reproduced here.

PART TWO
PREPARATORY HRM WORK: STRATEGISING, DESIGNING AND PLANNING

4 HRM STRATEGIES AND POLICIES: FRAMEWORKS FOR MANAGING HUMAN RESOURCES

LEARNING OUTCOMES

After studying this chapter, you should be able to:

- make a short presentation on the nature of strategy;
- demonstrate insight into a strategic approach to HRM;
- apply basic process elements to formulate a strategy for HRM;
- use a diagnostic grid to assist in making integrated decisions about strategies for HRM in organisations; and
- integrate HRM issues and considerations in general strategic business planning.

4.1 INTRODUCTION

You know by now that we regard HRM as an integral and in a sense the most critical part of modern-day South African management and organisational life. It has been stressed all along that the work and people must be managed in an organisationally and societally integrated way. We thus favour a strategic approach to HRM. As Mello (2006: 158) explains, by following such an approach, people management becomes "the most important priority in the organization" and HRM then becomes integrated "within the framework of the company's strategy". Similarly, Salaman, Storey and Billsberry (2005: 1) argue that the rise in significance of strategic HRM is due to the realisation among business organisations that "the way in which people are managed could be one of, if not *the* most crucial factor in the whole array of competitiveness-inducing variables". The management of human resources is thus of strategic significance for organisations.

As such, strategy should form the framework for managerial practice. In this chapter we focus on the strategy–HRM nexus and lay foundations for exploring HRM issues through a strategic lens. We do this because a strategic approach to the management of human resources is a recurrent theme throughout the book. Our aim in this chapter is to introduce you to relevant concepts and issues, and also to specifically explore what some of the main strategy-type HRM decisions or choices entail. We devote attention to the development of HRM strategies before we go on to reflect briefly on translating these into policies. Essentially, HRM strategies are bundles or clusters of processes, practices, functions and so forth pertaining to the management of human resources – as aligned with overall organisational strategy.

First of all we clarify key concepts and look at what strategic management entails more generally. We then shift our focus to human resource strategy issues and choices. We cover both process and content issues pertaining to HRM strategy. We then also look at the development of HRM policies as a foundation for developing appropriate

HRM systems, and show how strategic choice in HRM sets the scene for all other HRM practices, processes and the like.

4.2 STRATEGY AND STRATEGIC MANAGEMENT

Even though our main concern in this chapter is HRM strategy, the key term that focuses our attention is 'strategy'. We therefore first have to explore the meaning of this term, and what strategy in organisations entails.

4.2.1 Strategy: from the military to the business world

Many authoritative writers on strategy in the organisational and business context agree that it is not easy to come up with a definition of the concept that is universally accepted. De Wit and Meyer (2005) point out that in fact there are differing and conflicting opinions and viewpoints on what strategy means and entails.

Boxall and Purcell (2008: 33) also agree: "As many writers have pointed out, the notion of strategy is subject to a confusing variety of interpretations."

From the perspective of clarity and simplicity it would thus have been wonderful if we could have simply provided you with *the* definition of strategy. Seeing that this is not possible, and also aligned with the fact that we would like to encourage you as readers to apply analytical thinking as you go, we may be better off starting with the roots of the concept of strategy.

It should be noted that the notion of *strategy* is relatively new to the field of management, and even more so in relation to HRM. Strategy actually has its roots in military literature. The term derives from the Greek word *strategia,* meaning 'generalship'. In this sense, strategy can almost be thought of as 'the art and task of the general' in a military context.

Already in 500BC, the Chinese military strategist Sun Tzu's classic *The Art of War* covered the topic of strategy (Grant 1998: 14). We all know that, in a military context, war is about winning. Strategy in the military is only concerned about any particular campaigns or battles insofar as these fit into the bigger picture of how to win the war. That was (is), typically, the task and responsibility of the 'general'. Most dictionaries will show that the term 'strategy' denotes something about an overall plan to achieve a long-term aim. In a business and management context, strategy should thus also preferably denote something similar. Strategy, when used in the realm of business and organisational life, should thus also focus on the big picture and the longer term: *who* the organisation is (defining its scope/domain in a specific context and setting); *what* it is trying to achieve; *where* it is aiming to go; and *how* it intends to achieve this in the context of the organisation's resources and capabilities, and its competitive and general external environment.

The focus of strategy is the organisation as a whole, and the ultimate object is the purpose or 'mission' of the organisation. Per definition then, strategy is future geared. As such, and following this line of argument, it must be the primary concern (though not exclusively) of the upper-most leader cadres of organisations. These people are responsible for the success of the organisation as a whole. In the private sector they are the boards of directors and top management teams. Whereas lower-level managers (below top management and governance structures) are responsible for managing and achieving things *in* organisations, these upper-echelon people are responsible for the direction and success *of* organisations. Similarly, in a military context there is a difference between lower-level commanding officers' responsibilities for developments while they are engaged *in* the war, whereas the strategist's (general's) concern is the winning *of* the war. Just like military generals are concerned with the war as a whole and with winding up military campaigns, and just as they use terminology such as utilising 'military intelligence' and 'capturing the territory' of the enemy, the most senior leaders of organisations should focus on the competitive environment and make the overall 'game plans' on how to beat the competition. It is, for instance, not uncommon to hear the use of phrases in the business world such as 'it's a war out there', 'use market intelligence', 'plan new marketing campaigns', or 'let's (re)capture territory from the competition'. We believe that sticking to the roots of the meaning of a concept may help to alleviate some of the confusion and uncertainty about the term 'strategy' and its use in a field such management, and then HRM. This is not to say that we are proposing slavishly transferring the concept from one sphere (like the military) to another without any analytical scrutiny. Quite the contrary, we believe it is essential to keep reminding ourselves about different perspectives, but at the same time we should not lose sight of the original meaning of the concept as we continue on the exploratory journey pertaining to the semantic debate that abounds. For our purposes here, though, rather than giving a single or precise definition, we believe it may be more valuable to identify the key features, dimensions or characteristics of strategy. In this way we can then be guided as to what 'strategic' is and what 'strategic management' would mean or entail.

Drawing on the work prominent strategy scholars such as Johnson, Scholes and Whittington (2008), Pearce and Robinson (2005), and Boxall and Purcell (2008) we can say that strategy and strategic decisions and issues have the characteristics or dimensions as reflected in exhibit 4.1.

EXHIBIT 4.1: Dimensions or characteristics of strategy and strategic issues or decisions

The dimensions or characteristics of strategy and strategic issues or decisions are the following:
- they are future oriented;
- they are purpose driven;
- they are long term;
- they require top-level attention and decision;
- they determine the scope and domain of operations/work/business;
- they pertain to sustained overall competitiveness, and thus are success seeking (remaining viable – survive first, thrive later);
- they reflect expectations and values of multiple stakeholders and role players;
- they involve significant resource commitments;
- they are multidimensional and complex, with associated uncertainties and risks;
- they are holistic and integrating;
- they are focused on aligning internal environments (resources and capabilities) with external environments;
- they are concerned with seeking and setting direction;
- they balance tensions and paradoxes, such as change and continuity; and
- they carry significant consequences for the organisation as a whole.

Johnson et al (2008: 3) summarise strategy as follows: "Strategy is the *direction* and *scope* of an organisation over the *long term*, which achieves *advantage* in a changing *environment* through its configuration of *resources* and *competences* with the aim of fulfilling *stakeholder* expectations." Thompson, Strickland and Gamble (2007: 4) say that strategy consists of the competitive moves and business approaches used to "grow the business, attract and please customers, compete successfully, conduct operations, and achieve targeted levels of organizational performance".

Louw and Venter (2006: 12) go on to differentiate between strategy and tactics, which could also be useful to try to grasp what strategy is (and is not) about: "A *tactic* is a plan for specific action, while *strategy* is the overall scheme for leveraging resources to obtain competitive advantage". Tactics would thus be shorter term and less comprehensive in focus/scope. Importantly, though, tactics and strategy must be linked. Put differently, tactics must be aligned with and geared towards strategy as the bigger picture. Likewise, as Johnson et al (2008: 5–6) explain, the operational decisions, actions and practices must be aligned with strategy because if not, "no matter how well considered the strategy is, it will not succeed".

We find in the literature on organisational strategy, different types of strategy, or strategies with a different focus. Some authors also refer to different levels of strategy. We now look at some of these.

4.2.1.1 Corporate and grand strategies

Corporate strategy essentially revolves around the overall purpose and range of businesses of an organisation. It is about determining the type(s) or line(s) of business (the diversity of it) in which an organisation is engaged (or wishes to be engaged in). According to Johnson et al (2008: 7), corporate strategy is concerned with "the overall purpose and scope of an organisation and how value will be added to the different parts (business units) of the organisation". In some organisations there is a preference to be involved in one type or line of business only, while others prefer to engage in different types or lines. Decisions relating to corporate strategy therefore basically entail deciding on the enterprise's 'business mix' and which industries to be in.

Grand strategies are in a sense related to corporate strategies. Pearce and Robinson (2005: 200) define a grand strategy as "a comprehensive general approach that guides a firm's major actions", and they identify 15 such grand strategy options: market development, product development, concentrated growth, innovation, vertical integration, horizontal integration, concentric diversification, conglomerate diversification, joint ventures, strategic alliances, consortia, turnaround, divestiture, liquidation and bankruptcy. In our view the last two are not really worth being categorised as strategies because they essentially revolve around failure and acknowledgement of non-viability. *Divestiture* revolves around selling off parts of the organisation while *turnaround* strategies typically entail scaling down for a period (cost and/or asset reduction typically) in order to recover and rebuild. The rest are all growth strategies with *concentrated growth* meaning to grow by increasing the sale/use of existing products/services in existing markets, *market development* being the sale/use of existing products/services to new markets, and *product development* strategies being growth through developing new products/ services for present markets. *Innovation* as a grand strategy basically entails growing by being first into the market with new or vastly improved products/services. *Joint ventures*, *strategic alliances* and *consortia* are strategies for growth through various corporate combination approaches. More aggressive and transformational corporate combination approaches entail the takeover of other firms through acquisitions and mergers. These can be done as part of *vertical integration* (acquiring firms that supply the organisation with inputs or which are customers for its outputs) or *horizontal integration* (acquiring organisations operating in the same or similar spot of the supply chain). Diversification strategies essentially mean growing through adding new businesses to the current portfolio of businesses, but in different areas (industries/sectors/etc). *Concentric diversification* means adding where there are synergies, while *conglomerate diversification* means that businesses are acquired irrespective of whether there are any synergies between the lines of business.

4.2.1.2 Business, generic or competitive strategies

Business strategy can be described as the overall approach adopted for a single business organisation in order to compete. Essentially, business strategies "determine how the firm will compete in the selected product-market arena" (Pearce & Robinson 2005: 7).

Michael Porter referred to these as "generic" strategies that capture "competitive orientation in the marketplace" (Pearce & Robinson 2005: 14). This relates to the core idea or philosophy about how to compete. Louw and Venter (2006: 247) refer to these as "generic strategic options". Johnson et al (2008: 224) refer to "competitive strategy" and say that this is "concerned with the basis on which a business unit might achieve competitive advantage". The three fundamental options here are *low cost* (or *cost leadership*), *differentiation* and/or *focus*. The latter essentially entails focusing on either product/service differentiation or overall cost leadership as the dominant competitive orientation, depending on the particular market segment. In the case of overall cost leadership strategies, organisations try to beat the competition by cutting the prices of their products/services through cheaper operational processes (such as production). Organisations that choose product/service differentiation as a generic, business or competitive strategy try to beat the competition by creating a perception in the marketplace that their services/products are unique and offer added value in terms of features such as quality or after-sales service.

4.2.1.3 Functional strategies

Functional strategies relate to those used in areas such as technology, manufacturing or service operations, public relations, marketing and finance. Because from the point of view of business management – and hence strategic business management – the primary objective is to become and remain successful in a competitive environment, these functional strategies are in a sense secondary or 'downstream' to corporate and business strategy. They do, however, form an integrated part of the overall organisational strategy and strategic management. All the different types of strategy are closely linked and interdependent. Because of this reciprocal interdependence, decisions about these different types of strategy have to be taken in a fully integrated way. This, to a large extent, forms the major challenge of strategic management.

4.2.2 Strategic management

In chapter 1 we highlighted the fact that management as a process essentially entails functions such as planning, organising, leading or directing and controlling the resources of an organisation. Strategic management is thus the application of this management process at the top level of the organisation. At this level the focus is on the resources, capabilities and core or distinctive competencies of the organisation as a whole and on the ways to achieve success as a total organisation (either from a business unit or corporate level perspective) over the long term, within the context of changing and competitive environments. Johnson et al (2008: 11–12) explain that strategies "do not happen just by themselves. Strategy involves people, especially the managers who decide and implement ... this book uses strategic management to emphasise the human element of strategy ... Strategic management can be thought of as having three main elements ...understanding the *strategic position* of an organisation, making *strategic choices* for the future and managing *strategy in action*". They go on to explain that strategic position is about matching, balancing and integrating the organisation's strategic capabilities (resources and competences) with the external environment and the influence and expectations of its stakeholders. Strategic choices relate to options and decisions for steering the organisation in particular directions through the use of particular methods. "Strategy into action", according to these authors, is "concerned with ensuring that strategies are working in practice" (Johnson et al 2008: 15). From the foregoing we can conclude that strategic management essentially entails two tasks: strategy making, and making strategy work.

Strategy making involves strategic thinking and strategic planning aimed at making certain choices or decisions with significant long-term consequences for the organisation, in light of alternatives or options and against a backdrop of fluid and often vague environmental issues and dynamics. To make strategy work involves the rolling out of appropriate processes, systems, practices and the active management of the crafted strategies as they are implemented over time, in a changing, complex, uncertain and dynamic environment.

This whole process of strategic management is therefore often described as consisting of strategy *formulation* and strategy *implementation*. Although it is self-evident that the distinction between the two is not watertight and that they are interdependent, we have to understand that in essence the one task and set of activities revolves around finding the path, and the other has to do with taking, following or walking the path. We must acknowledge, though, that in practice things are not always as neat and straightforward, and oftentimes we will find that we have to make paths as we go (especially when we unexpectedly hit roadblocks or traffic jams, so to speak).

For conceptual purposes it remains useful to look separately at these two broad sets of tasks or activities. As we do so, different components of the strategic management process are shown. Please keep reminding yourself, however, that in reality these do not happen as separate things or as a series of discrete steps in a linear process. In practice they are often performed simultaneously or in a different order, making it an iterative and dynamic process by nature.

Most authors distinguish between components like looking at the internal and external environments of the organisation, setting strategic direction through vision and mission formulation, choosing certain strategies about positioning the organisation, formulating these (putting them in writing), and communicating all of them, and making sure that all resources are mobilised towards successful execution. Keep in mind that, typically, these components are identified and stressed by the rational school of thought. This perspective holds that strategic management entails a rational and systematic process. Others, and an increasingly prominent school of thought, say that the real world is much too messy for such an approach. They claim that strategies often emerge as we muddle through almost chaotic circumstances. We believe that it is not a case of either/or, but rather one of both/and – both the generative perspective and the rational perspective hold truths and reflect some realities about the art and science of strategic management. For conceptual purposes it is useful to start off with the more concrete or rational-analytical side, and briefly reflect on the key components or building blocks of strategic management.

Environmental scanning and analysis entails a thorough study of all the strategy-related factors or variables both external and internal to the organisation. The ultimate aim is to create a good match or fit between the two but because of change this is an ongoing and dynamic process. This often takes on the form of a SWOT analysis, and involves the process of analysing and synchronising the organisation's internal strengths and weaknesses, and the opportunities and threats coming from the external environment. This process is aimed at understanding the strategic position of the organisation.

Developing a *vision and mission* statement is an important facet of strategy making. This overarching long-term direction-setting task will reflect the organisation's purpose and reason for being, and what it would like to become and/or be known for one day. It will set the tone of the overall strategic intent. The vision is supposed to be a "BHAG" (big hairy audacious goal – pronounced BEEHAG) and should excite and unite people, according to Collins and Porras. (1996: 73). It is thus almost some kind of a 'dream end state' towards which all would strive in what they do, stretching way beyond the current state of affairs (including resources and capabilities). Johnson et al (2008: 164) say that vision is a statement of what the organisation aspires to be. The mission makes it clear why the organisation exists and it will set the landscape of what business(es) the organisation is in. From that one should know what needs of society it tries to satisfy, what market(s) it serves and who will be the customers (stakeholders, more broadly, should also be detectable). Developing the vision and mission will certainly have to entail a good dose of creative thinking as well, because of the 'dream' component resting in the vision aspect. It is important that in the process of formulating the mission and vision statement, the organisational purpose and perspectives of all stakeholders be duly considered. What also often goes along with the process of mission and vision development is deciding on the core values that will (or should) steer and guide the behaviour and conduct of all organisational members and stakeholders. Johnson et al (2008: 163) say that increasingly "organisations have been keen to develop and communicate a set of corporate values that define the way the organisation operates". Clearly, then, such espoused organisational or corporate core values are at the very heart of the management of human resources.

Certain *strategic choices* are also to be made as various alternatives and options are considered in terms of where to go and how to get there. Another component or task is thus the formulation of long-term objectives relating to, for example, market share, profitability and competitive market positioning. A key component of the strategy-making process logically also includes decisions about which types of strategy to use. In this regard, choices and decisions are made about appropriate generic or business strategies, corporate and grand strategies as well as functional strategies as discussed above. In terms of the various corporate strategy options, choices and decisions are made about aspects such as whether (or not) to grow and how to grow. All of these options and alternatives have different human resource implications. The type of business and industry will be central to the type of labour or human resources (for example skilled/unskilled) to be used, for instance. Labour costs as part of total overall cost structures vary between industries (or sectors), for instance. The unionisation levels also often vary between industries/sectors. Human resource issues and considerations should therefore be integrated with the making of such strategic choices and decisions.

In respect of the various business strategy options, we have already referred to the three generic strategy alternatives and to some competitive strategy options. Another set of alternatives is embedded in the Miles and Snow (1984) typology. This typology provides a conceptual framework with three strategy alternatives and a fourth no-strategy alternative. The latter is called the 'reactor'-type strategy. We believe that, per definition, this is not really a strategy at all, but it certainly is an option. In such a case there is no clear strategy and the organisation opts to just drift along, reacting to changes in its internal and/or external environments. The three real strategy options are the "prospector", "defender" and "analyser" strategy types. An organisation choosing the *prospector* strategy will try to compete and grow through constantly being highly innovative and seeking out new opportunities and new market possibilities. Typical elements of such a strategy include flexibility, decentralised decision making and the encouragement of creativity and risk taking. Those organisations opting for a *defender* strategy will protect their existing markets and do all they can to retain their current customers. They will seek to establish and maintain stable growth. Elements such as stability and efficiency will typically be prominent. The third strategy type, the *analyser*, combines elements of defender and prospector strategies. These organisations will therefore encourage moderate levels of innovation, and seek a proper balance between stability and flexibility. Again, clearly, each of these strategy types will have different HRM-related implications. We will return to this matter a little later in this chapter.

The formal strategy-making process typically culminates in the drafting of strategy documents, such as vision and mission statements, strategic and business plans (containing clear signposts and measurables such as objectives to guide strategic direction), and often also relevant policy documents to facilitate the process of strategy implementation.

The *implementation or execution of strategy* entails creating the necessary 'architectural' configurations, including structures, systems, processes and policies, and building an appropriate culture and climate conducive to all resources' mobilisation towards mission accomplishment. The key challenge here thus relates to the people side of the organisation. In this context, Huselid, Becker and Beatty (2005: 12) explain the role of human capital in strategy implementation: "The term *human capital* implies an asset with a flow of benefits that are greater than the costs ... From the perspective of the firm, human capital will have the greatest value when those benefits take the form of workforce behaviors that execute strategy ... *their strategic value is based on the role they play in your firm's strategy execution.*"

Throughout the strategic management process it is important to monitor and evaluate the extent to which strategic decisions match or fit the changing circumstances, as well as the extent to which they are actually being executed as intended. Naturally, as the processes unfold, changes come into play and as such strategy development and execution form an ongoing, iterative process. We want to stress again that strategic management should not be regarded simply as a neatly packaged set of rational decisions and related behaviour. The role of the socio-organisational side (the 'political' or 'softer' side of management) has become increasingly important. Aspects such as the ideologies of managers, the motivations and attitudes they have, their perceptions and the role of so-called 'cognitive maps' or 'mental models' all play a very significant part in the process of strategic management, as we explain further in the next section.

4.2.3 Strategising: processes in strategy development

It is one thing to say that we should analyse the environment by using SWOT analysis tools or scenarios, formulate mission and vision statements, and make choices about alternative strategies. It is quite another how all of this actually happens in practice. In this subsection we briefly reflect on some of the dynamics related to how strategy development takes place. Behind any strategy development process is some form of strategic thinking, hopefully. We start off with this.

4.2.3.1 Strategic thinking

Hughes and Beatty (2005: 44) describe strategic thinking as follows: "Strategic thinking refers to cognitive processes required for the collection, interpretation, generation, and evaluation of information and ideas that shape an organization's sustainable competitive advantage."

If you think about it (which is what you should be doing as you read this), the very fact that it is human cognition that drives strategy and hence strategic management (and management in general, for that matter) makes strategy and strategic management an exclusive and profoundly human process. Boxall and Purcell (2008: 33) say that "strategic management is a human process beset with all the pitfalls that characterise human attempts to make decisions in conditions of uncertainty, rivalry and limited resources". We have what is known as 'bounded rationality' – the fact that we only 'see and know partly' simply because we do not have all information required as we grapple with the challenges our organisations face. As strategists we thus think about these things (as described in the previous section) even though we know there are no perfect solutions in whatever paths we choose or craft. The importance of *strategic thinking* has thus been on the increase as people realise more and more that things are complex and uncertain – which is what makes strategy and strategic management arguably the most challenging work in and of organisations. This aspect of strategy development has become so important that authors like De Wit and Meyer (2005) regard strategic thinking as one of the three components of the strategy process, and in their book they devote a whole chapter to this theme. Nadler, Behan and Nadler (2006) regard strategic thinking as one of the four key sets of strategic activities of organisations, the others being strategic planning, strategic decision making and strategy execution.

Liedtka (1998) developed a model for strategic thinking, and extracts elements thereof, which Graetz (2002) recognises, but she labels these as 'attributes' of strategic thinking. Drawing on these, as well as the perspectives of Hughes and Beatty (2005), Johnson et al (2008) and De Wit and Meyer (2005), among others, help to develop an impression about the nature of strategic thinking, as reflected in exhibit 4.2. Clearly, strategic thinking encompasses inherent tensions and paradoxes.

As can be gathered from exhibit 4.2, strategic thinking is not simple or straightforward. That is also why the whole process of strategy making and execution is complex and difficult – strategic thinking happens throughout. Even when strategic options emerge unasked for, or unplanned, that would mean considering these developments and the implications for the overall strategic direction of the organisation. This brings us to two different yet complementary processes of strategy development in organisations: deliberate and emergent.

4.2.3.2 Deliberate and emergent processes in strategy development: brief notes

While strategic thinking and intent may be at the very core of strategy development, with concomitant rational thinking as strategic choices or decisions are being made, not all in the process is as straightforward. As we have said before, we have bounded rationality, and as we engage with others to do some collective strategic thinking, all sorts of things can happen. Because strategy development is very much a human-driven process, the social aspects should never be underestimated.

Engaging in the process of strategy development in a deliberate way may well entail formal strategic planning, but the dynamics within that formal process should be well acknowledged as being very powerful. There may hence be some systemised approach where steps are followed in a more or less chronological and coordinated way to develop organisational strategies – which would reflect formal strategic

EXHIBIT 4.2: Strategic thinking: a balancing act – paradoxes and tensions

Strategic thinking is:

- *Holistic as well as about details:* It is about considering the organisation as a whole, but it is also about how some of the details relate to the whole, how parts of an organisation fit together and influence each other and their environments (systems perspective).

- *Intent driven but also in a sense serendipitous:* It concerns itself with the intent and focus of the organisation, with the desired direction or destiny, but it also entails some intelligent opportunism. Within the intent-driven focus, new options may emerge that lead to further searching and consideration of things not thought of before.

- *Analysis as well as synthesis:* It entails dissecting and breaking things into parts and also putting pieces of the puzzle of competitive dynamics and organisational success together into a complex whole. It is about hypothesis generation when we ask the question "What if ...?" and it is about hypothesis testing when we say "If this ..., then ...".

- *Linear as well as nonlinear:* It involves looking for cause-and-effect relationships and sequential processes, issues and challenges, but it also factors in potentially disruptive and chaos-related eventualities that might pose threats or opportunities.

- *Implicit as well as explicit:* Sometimes ideas are just stewing away in the mind of the strategist, mingled up with feelings and intuition (gut feel), and at other times it entails writing these things up for others to read or talking about them as part of collective thinking.

- *Visual as well as verbal:* Having a vision may be about 'seeing' some desired future state – imagining things – but thinking often also happens as we speak during our strategy conversations.

- *About the head, but also the heart:* It entails being rational and reasoning about things in one's own mind, but it often also entails having feelings about things, being passionate about them and thus adding the emotive element.

- *About the future, but also the past:* The present situation is the result of the past and as strategists contemplate 'where to', they tend to implicitly keep in mind what has been learned from past strategic experiences or moves.

- *About using logic as well as creativity:* It entails being logical in questioning things like assumptions and the validity of some things, but it also requires getting a free flow of ideas and drawing on imaginative abilities unhampered by the 'rules of logical thinking'.

- *About change as well as stability:* It entails considering what works well and might be important not to tamper with but it also involves searching for ways to change and improve things.

- *Inside-out as well as outside-in:* It is about considering the resources and capabilities of the organisation and how these lend themselves to exploiting opportunities in the environment, but it is also about looking at the external environment and considering potential threats that might be looming.

- *Individual as well as collective:* Strategic thinking occurs in the mind of the single strategist such as the CEO, but it also happens within a group context when the CEO and his or her top management team all think of strategic things simultaneously. As such, individual and shared mental models are at work when strategic thinking happens.

- *Formal as well as informal:* It takes place in the context of formal strategic planning sessions such as strategy workshops or retreats, but it also happens informally while enjoying a cup of coffee or browsing through the daily newspaper. Sometimes it happens knowingly while being engaged in formal processes, and at times the strategist may not even be aware as the subconscious mind ticks away on strategy-related things.

planning. These may include a range of things, including arranging some strategic planning workshops or retreats, putting out strategy position papers as documents to stimulate debate, engaging external process facilitators or consultants, commissioning some specific strategic projects that would feed information into the process, and so on. There will thus typically (in larger organisations at least) be a lot of human interaction. This will be primarily at the top management level – but also beyond, when boards of directors are engaged. It might very well also include the engagement of lower levels of management as well as other stakeholders from time to time. In all of this one can just imagine that different people (and groups of people) may well have different perspectives and agendas.

While the formal strategic planning will thus entail a lot of analytical and rational thinking, and deliberate consideration of issues and options, often openly discussed and debated with an open, yet critical, mindset, there will also be a lot of unsaid things, or things aired and considered just by some, and even behind closed doors in many cases. This is where things like 'power' and 'organisational politics' also come into the strategy development equation. There may be different groups within groups (there may be factions within a top-management team or within a board of directors), and there may be powerful coalitions who lobby for certain strategic changes while others may be in disagreement with them and lobby against all or some of them. These dynamics are pretty common when relatively significant strategic change is at hand. As such there might well be a certain intent coming from one side, but quite a different strategic direction might result due to the power of informal processes at play, and the fact that people and stakeholders might not always share the same perspectives. Johnson et al (2008: 414) say that powerful "individuals and groups may also strongly influence the identification of key issues and the strategies eventually selected". The same authors thus refer to the important role played by what they call "strategic issue selling" when strategies are developed, describing this as follows (Johnson et al 2008: 570-571): "Organisations typically face many strategic issues at any point in time … in complex organisations these issues may not be appreciated to the same extent by all … [S]enior managers will rarely have sufficient time and resources to deal with all the issues … Managers therefore have to 'sell' their particular strategic issues … They cannot assume that issues get automatic attention, or that they will necessarily win support, however important they might be …".

From this we can say that, in a sense, strategy and strategic decisions 'emerge' more than anything else. There is, however, an even stronger emergence perspective of strategy development when it comes to looking at it over a longer period of time (after a number of years, for instance). Johnson et al (2008: 407) put it thus: "Research on historical patterns of strategy development in organisations shows a pattern of what has become known as incremental strategy development. Strategies do not typically change in major shifts … They typically change by building on and amending what has gone before … [A]pparently coherent strategy of an organisation may develop on the basis of a series of strategic moves …". Some refer to this as logical incrementalism in strategy development because it is almost a process by which the strategy and strategic choices and decisions evolve over time, most of them purposefully, but some of them more as a consequence of something else. We thus get different versions of the organisation's strategy over time, as unexpected things happen and changes have to be made to earlier versions of the strategies in order to accommodate these (thus rather reactively), but also often to proactively create or seize opportunities or/and leverage newly identified strengths in resources and capabilities (Thompson et al 2007).

The processes and dynamics involved in strategy development are thus complex, and present challenges to those engaged in them. The fact that it is now commonly accepted that human resources hold strategic value for organisations makes it almost inevitable to take a strategic approach to HRM. In addition, Boxall and Purcell (2008: 85) point out the following:

> [S]trategic management is a human process, dependent on human strengths, but also affected by our cognitive weaknesses and political agendas. This means that, at the very least, key choices about whom to place in leadership roles and how to build strategy-making processes are critical to the success of firms.

All of this points to a natural nexus between strategic management in general, and HRM. This is in line with the latest and increasingly more prominent 'inside-out' perspective of strategy and strategic management that is based on the resource-based view (RBV) for the firm. Boxall and Purcell (2008: 87) point out that the traditional 'outside-in' perspective or school of thought on strategic management (looking at the outside environment first to see what opportunities and threats there might be) was/ is rather deficient in that it works from improper assumptions: "These models place greatest emphasis on critical choices associated with competitive strategy – primarily choices about ... industry ... and which competitive position to seek ... [T]hey assume that the firm already has a clever leadership team which can make these sort of choices effectively."

From the resource-based view of organisations, the internal organisational environment is the departure point. This will offer the base of resources and capabilities from which to consider strategy options and develop strategic direction. From this perspective at least, then, strategic HRM – or a strategic approach to the management of human resources – thus really becomes a non-negotiable.

4.3 HRM STRATEGY DEVELOPMENT: OPTIONS, ISSUES, CHOICES AND PROCESSES

In this section we devote our attention to some general issues pertaining to a strategic approach to HRM as well as to some more specific issues, choices and challenges related thereto.

4.3.1 Clarifying some concepts and issues of scope and focus

When we mention 'HRM strategy' and 'strategic HRM', we refer to the long-term, top-level and overarching management decisions, choices and actions regarding the organisation's HRM architecture. The latter was initially referred to by Becker, Huselid and Ulrich (2001: 1) as "the sum of the HR function, the broader HR system, and the resulting employee behaviors". In subsequent work (Huselid, Becker & Beatty 2005) the focus was altered and the scope more comprehensive to specifically include how line managers manage and lead their workers. The new concept used became that of "workforce" management. As you are aware, we have made it clear right from the outset that our approach is holistic and that to us HRM indeed includes the role of all involved in the management of the work and working people of and in organisations. When we thus say the 'HRM architecture', we mean the totality of the human resource subsystem (referring back to chapter 1) of the organisation and how this is designed, developed and put to use. It includes the people or human resources (the workforce, including non-employees), the HRM strategies, policies and systems, as well as all the human resource-related functions, practices and processes that are performed by specialist HR practitioners as well as line managers. Our concern is the work of those in HR departments – but going way beyond that to include all HRM practices, processes and so forth pertaining to the work and people doing that work of an organisation. When we talk strategy and 'strategic' in relation to the HRM architecture, we regard these as being fully integrated with the overall and more general strategic management of organisations. It concerns making the strategic choices about the organisation's HRM architecture as an integral part of developing the overall strategic direction of the organisation. This brings us to the concept of strategic HRM.

We do not view strategic HRM as something separate from or subordinate to the development and/or execution of corporate, grand or business (generic or competitive) strategy. It is also not seen as something which is limited to strategy execution. While the work of Huselid et al (2005) seems to emphasise the strategy execution role and the value of workforce management in this, our view is broader and more aligned with the perspective offered by Boxall and Purcell (2008). By strategic HRM we mean it to be an integral part of general strategic management. Aspects connected with the management of human resources permeate all facets of organisational strategy formation and execution. Neither corporate nor business strategy can be developed or implemented without incorporating the relevant human resource-related issues.

If, for instance, the top management of an organisation decides to diversify (diversification strategy) into different markets, industries or lines of business, the human resource related implications that will have to be considered include peculiar labour market conditions in those sectors or lines of business (for example supply/demand of labour, skills needed, wage levels/labour costs, trade union activity/strategies, etc). Similarly, the human resource related requirements will be quite different in an organisation that is following a strategy of growth, from one where a turnaround strategy is to be followed. In the case of the latter, the emphasis will be on cost and/or asset reduction. If, for example, an organisation experiences a phase of decline (for instance because of an economic recession), it may decide to embark on such a strategy with the hope of recovering later. In such a case emphasis will be on strategies to reduce the size of the workforce by natural attrition and/or by means of retrenchment/redundancy interventions. Should people still be required in certain critical areas because of voluntary separations in those areas, the emphasis might be on short-term employment relationships or alternative work arrangements.

On the other hand, if the strategy is one of growth through innovation (prospector strategy type), the organisation's aim will be to beat the competition by concentrating on being creative and flexible, and constantly bringing new or improved products/services to market. By doing so, product life cycles will be shortened, the new/better products/services making the older ones obsolete. This strategy can, however, only be considered if there is the will to employ, train for and facilitate worker creativity and flexibility.

Thus, although many textbooks on general strategic management deal with the human side of things only when strategy implementation is discussed (focusing on aspects such as leadership, culture and reward), we are of the opinion that human resource issues should also be dealt with as an integral part of the general strategy development process. When the top management of an organisation defines the vision/mission statement of the organisation, it should be borne in mind that such a statement is not only important for the investors, the public and the market environment, but in particular also for the employees and other people who help the organisation to be successful. This type of statement can go a long way in getting employees to identify with the organisation and be committed to supporting it in all its mission-driven endeavours. An organisation's vision, mission and value statement should not only outline the typical product-market orientation of the organisation, but it should also specifically serve as something that binds together the sense of direction and the notion of 'what and how we do things here'. The example cited below (see 'A case at hand') of MTN shows clearly how central the people dimension is in the value statements of organisations.

A CASE AT HAND

MTN's five shared values

The MTN Group is a multinational company operating in a wide range of countries and cultures. The Group has, at its core, five shared values that address our business principles, conduct and interaction with all our stakeholders:

LEADERSHIP
Ingredients – Foresight, Commitment, Guidance
- Building a future for our people and the customers we serve.
- Leading the way in connectivity enablement.

INTEGRITY
Ingredients – Solid principles, Trusted, Togetherness
- We are, because of you, our customer.
- We are, because of you, our employee.
- With your trust and belief we will always succeed.

CAN-DO
Ingredients – Optimism, Future focus, Passionate, Happening
- Creating brighter futures, for everyone whose life we touch.
- Empowering people, communities and countries.
- Creating possibility

INNOVATION
Ingredients – Simplicity, Imagination, Insight, Creativity
- Doing things differently.
- Making unlikely connections.
- The unexpected exceeds expectations.

RELATIONSHIPS
Ingredients – Teamwork, Friendly, Personal, Warm & Caring
- Connecting with people on 'their level'.
- Having empathy for their unique situations.
- Building relationships with our customers (internal & external).

Source: http://www.mtn.com/mtn.group.web/explore/profile/brand_values.asp

Furthermore, when doing SWOT analysis as part of deliberate strategy development, it is often found that many of the internal strengths/weaknesses (or perhaps external threats/opportunities) are actually related to human resources. As we have indicated before, the resource-based view of the firm puts the resources and capabilities (much of which relates directly to the people) at the core of organisational strategy generally.

Similarly, the design of organisational structures essentially relates to how the work of the organisation is organised – and this is clearly a people-related issue. The same holds true for strategy execution issues like developing appropriate cultures and leadership to mobilise the working people and all their work efforts towards mission accomplishment. Rewarding high performance means aligning work behaviour with strategy.

Having said all of this, and even though human resource related issues and decisions are dispersed throughout the process of general strategic management, the actual process of strategic HRM can also be conceptualised as consisting of strategy development and execution.

4.3.2 The process of strategic HRM: an overview and reflecting on some dynamics

The process of developing HRM strategy is no different to the processes involved in general strategy development, not least because it is supposed to be an integral part thereof. It involves top-management-level strategic thinking (and engaging others, of course), looking for options, analysing situations and alternatives, 'politicking', strategic issue selling, and making certain pertinent choices and decisions. The basic idea is that appropriate strategies for the management of human resources that will drive sustainable competitive advantage must be found. This happens within the context of the organisation's changing and often very uncertain internal and external environments. Certain strategic choices must thus be made within the context of environmental constraints, opportunities and threats, and the necessary fit between the general strategic direction of the organisation and its HRM architecture is the issue at hand.

There must thus be integration and fit, vertically (between the organisation's strategic direction and general strategies, and the HRM strategies) as well as horizontally (between different functional strategies as well as between different sub-functional HRM strategies). The latter thus specifically means that we need to devise the overall organisational HR subsystem in a way that ensures a good alignment between aspects like how we organise the work of the organisation, how and where do we source our working talent, and also how we nurture, develop and reward our working people. It also specifically includes how we are actually going to enable the people who manage other working people to do so in a way that is aligned with our strategic HRM choices and decisions – in other word getting the HRM strategy execution right. Throughout this whole process of developing and executing HRM strategy, there are important dynamics at play when decisions are made.

There are many who say that, in essence, management is about decision making. In the literature on general management a great deal of emphasis is therefore usually placed on decision making. South African textbooks on general management typically devote separate chapters to the topic of decision making (such as Smit, Cronje, Brevis & Vrba 2007).

For the most part, however, the emphasis seems to fall on rational decision-making theory, with generally little focus on aspects related to the behavioural dynamics. Smit et al (2007: 143), for instance, explain as follows: "A decision implies that managers are faced with a threat, a problem or an opportunity. Various courses of action are proposed and analysed, and a choice is made that is likely to move the organisation in the direction of its mission and goals."

This really makes decision making sound pretty simple and tidy, and that is precisely what the rational perspective of decision making seems to reflect. According to this school of thought, decision makers deliberately, systematically and rationally examine and weigh up various variables and factors and then make appropriate choices that could maximise the benefits to the organisation while minimising the costs. This theory emphasises the process of problem identification, situational analysis by means of gathering relevant information, the generation of possible alternative solutions, the evaluation of the various alternatives and ultimately making the choice of the 'best' alternative(s). In this framework there is little room for the 'softer', less tangible side of decision making.

Because organisations are social entities (in other words they are made up of people), decisions are rarely, in reality, made in such a clear-cut, rational way. Aspects such as gut feeling, emotions, values, intuition, mental models and the perceptions of people all play a significant role. As we have explained, relevant cognitive and political processes are very much at work when decisions have to be made. This is particularly also the case when it comes to making strategic decisions about the management of the human resources of organisations. The beliefs, value systems and even 'ideologies' of people influence how managers think about what may be the most appropriate ways of utilising what working people have to offer the organisation. To be quite frank, whereas some managers work from the basis that people are the most important assets of organisations, others believe that most of their managerial problems come from the people side of things, often contributing to their shying away from devoting proper attention to HRM. At top-management level, where the responsibility for strategic issues rests, the same holds true. Top-management teams consist of people with diverse backgrounds and not all regard HRM as an integral and key part of general management.

It is understandable that people with financial backgrounds (such as accountants), for instance, will tend to focus primarily on the financial perspective of things – such as the cost of getting work executed. The top-level 'technical' or operations managers (directly responsible for things like production in a manufacturing environment) can be qualified in something like engineering (metallurgical and mining engineers in the relevant mining sectors, for instance) and they in turn tend to focus primarily on these relevant technocratic dimensions. In this way, typically, the top-level managers who engage in the strategic thinking, planning and decision making look at the same things (such as developing strategy), but each does so through a different lens. Thus, the views of some are more aligned than those of others. There can hence be conflicting views even on whether something is really of strategic importance, and on strategic priorities and the appropriateness of certain strategic options or courses of action to take. The issues mentioned earlier, like politics, power and concomitant human dynamics, are thus very much at play when HRM strategy is developed. It has, for instance, for quite long been rather common to find that HRM does not really feature on the strategy radar screen of organisations. Many have thus argued for the need to have the top-level HR managers serve on the top-management teams of organisations. While we cannot agree more, we are of the opinion that, irrespective hereof, it is more important that the top-management team is united in one thing, namely that the human resource is critical to the strategic direction of organisations and hence deserves to be on their agenda on an ongoing basis, just like finance would be. Similarly it should feature prominently on the agendas of boards of directors. The reality is that this is not always the case and this makes strategic issue selling especially relevant when it comes to human resources. The very notion of having to engage in some decision making about human resource strategy may be a moot point at top-management level, requiring convincing argument in some cases. Fortunately, due to the increasing prominence of the resource-based perspective of organisations, as the upper echelons of organisational leadership engage in deliberate strategy development, they find that human resources, as the key aspect of resources and capabilities, come to the fore. The education and development of top- and senior-level managerial leaders (such as through MBA programmes) fortunately tend to increasingly reflect this shift. This is a bit of a generalisation, of course, and we are of the view that much more should be done. Similar arguments hold for general management and strategic management textbooks used in relevant management development and education programmes.

4.3.3 Scanning the environment

We know that an important part of deliberate strategy development is to assess one's situation in terms of resources and capabilities to search for possible leverage points for competitive positioning of the organisation. Environmental scanning is thus done. From a systems perspective we know that the human resource subsystem is in interaction with the other internal organisational subsystems (such as the operational, marketing and financial subsystems). It is also influenced by variables or factors in the external environment, as mentioned in earlier chapters. In actual fact, there is a strong interconnectedness between all these systems, and all of these have to be aligned with each other as well as with the overall mission and general strategic direction of the organisation.

HRM strategies thus do not get crafted only to offensively or defensively mediate between the perceived environmental threats, opportunities and constraints. Environmental influences need not be accepted passively. Really proactive managers who are zoomed in on bringing about strategic change will attempt to influence or shape their environments as far as possible – even though such an approach will not necessarily make them immune to forces in the external environment.

Please note that 'external' environment here does not only refer to factors or forces external to the organisation but also to those internal to the organisation, but external to the organisation's human resources subsystem. This means that when environmental scanning is done from the perspective of HRM strategy formation, not only are the relevant factors in the PESTEC environment (political, economic, social, technological, ecological and competitive) explored, but also those related to organisationally internal variables. The alignment and integration of the organisation's general business strategies with the HRM strategies makes it essential to consider HRM strategies as part thereof. As the business strategies are being formulated and the market environment of the business and other PESTEC factors are scanned, particular attention should be paid to the relevant human resource related implications. Incorporating full consideration of ecology-related factors interplay directly with the sustainability of our planet – shared as 'living space' by all human beings and other species. Similarly, as decisions related to the pure financial side of the organisation are made within the context of certain environmental trends that are analysed, the relevant human implications have to be actively searched for. The reverse is also true. The potential financial and business strategy implications of particular human resource related factors have to be seriously considered when top management does environmental analyses for the purpose of deliberate business and corporate strategy formation. In order for the whole organisational system to be successful, all of the parts or subsystems must work together. This is why it is so important to execute an integrated environmental scanning process.

At this stage you may wonder which particular factors need to be analysed. To draw up a complete list in this regard is neither possible nor feasible. Each organisation is different and the environmental makeup differs from one organisation to another. In this regard you are specifically referred to the relevant earlier sections/chapters. In chapter 2 in particular we explored the macro-external context of HRM in South Africa, and in chapter 3 we specifically covered relevant legal aspects and notably the challenges posed by the country's drive towards equitable equality and societal inclusiveness through broad-based black economic empowerment.

In the process of analysing all such environmental factors, different methodologies can be used, including interviews with experts, developing scenarios, the Delphi technique, the nominal group technique, focus groups and document reviews. Typically, the aim would thus be not only to identify the variables but also to analyse and consider how these factors may impact on the organisation, the work that is to be done, the employees and other people who have to do the work and especially the managerial employees who have to manage the work and people. The environmental scanning sets the scene for considering the fundamental goals of HRM in the organisation.

4.3.4 Considering the mission or ultimate goal in respect of HRM

As explained before, typically an organisation's mission statement will contain the scope of its operations in product and market terms. The mission and vision will spell out the 'who, why, what and where-to' of the organisation. As alluded to earlier, adding a statement of core organisational values makes more explicit the 'how we operate as an organisation', and as such these will be particularly relevant to the people management domain.

Formulating the organisation's objectives with regard to its human resources system also requires some explicit statement outlining the intent of the organisation in relation to the management of the relationship between the organisation and its working people as key stakeholders. Ideally this should be reflected in the vision, mission and value statement of the organisation. Going further, consideration should be given to the mission or purpose of the HR specialists and department in the organisation. Some refer to this as developing an HR value proposition – in other words what value the HR department/section would be adding. To us it is more important to consider what value is to be added by HRM in total, simply because the deliverables of an HR department are only one input into the HR system as a whole, with the role of line managers being more pervasive. As Huselid et al (2005: 5) say, although the "HR professionals and the HR management system lay the foundation for building the workforce into a strategic asset, the responsibility for workforce success increasingly falls to line managers", as they are the people who manage the work and working people of and in organisations. We thus believe that a mission statement regarding HRM in the organisation would serve a critical purpose. Any value proposition for an HR section (the HR specialists or practitioners) would then flow from this.

According to Boxall and Purcell (2008), there are basically two sets of overarching HRM goals. They refer to the economic and the socio-political goals (see exhibit 4.3).

As can be gathered from exhibit 4.3, the overall purpose (or mission) with HRM must therefore balance the conformance and performance dimensions as well as the external and internal dimensions. In the end, HRM must add value – to the organisation's strive for success, to the working people and their quality of life, and to society more broadly.

4.3.5 Making some HRM strategy choices

As part of strategy development, various HRM issues and options have to be considered, and certain decisions that will have long-term consequences and directly interplay with the strategic direction of the organisation must be made. These strategic HRM options and choices relate to the work of the organisation, the people or human resources to do the work, as well as to the actual way that HRM will be approached

EXHIBIT 4.3: Boxall & Purcell's overarching goals of HRM

ECONOMIC

- *Cost effectiveness*: This essentially refers to labour efficiency or workforce productivity, ensuring that work and working people management systems add positively to the bottom line, and this is a very industry/sector-specific challenge.

- Organisational *flexibility* and *short-run responsiveness*: This relates to the challenge of fitting and adjusting work-related costs (labour costs) with changing business revenue conditions, and includes numerical flexibility (headcount) according to business cycles (troughs and peaks in work or labour demand). It also includes functional flexibility, where something like multiskilling facilitates lower overall headcount if the workforce is capable of coping with marginal changes in products or processes.

- *Long-run agility*: This also relates to flexibility, but through capacity within the existing workforce to cope and thrive even when conditions change dramatically. "Does the firm have the capacity to create ... long-run changes in products, costs and technologies? Can it adapt better than its major rivals?" (Boxall & Purcell 2008: 15).

- *Competitive advantage*: Human resource advantage can be broken down into human capital advantage (getting smarter people to do the work) and organisational process advantage (developing superior ways of working together). Some refer to the latter as 'social capital', and specifically emphasise such things as the connections, trust, shared values, mutual respect and understanding that drive the relationships and cooperative work-related behaviour.

SOCIO-POLITICAL

- *Social legitimacy*: The human resources are not owned by the organisation, and the value the working people offer is related to investments made in them, and also by the state and themselves (education and training). As citizens of a country, the people are protected by legislation, thus the compliance or conformance goal of HRM is very important. This goes beyond that, though, and pertains to the fact that organisations are embedded in society and as such they should deal with working people in a responsible way (social responsibility).

- *Managerial power*: "All firms can be seen as political systems in which management holds authority but one in which management decisions are subject to legal and moral challenge" (Boxall & Purcell 2008: 19). There are all sorts of pressures that might drive managers to exercise their power and control that may be to the detriment of the people (think of short-term pressures coming from annual reporting obligations to shareholders). In a sense, then, HRM must fulfil some sort of watchdog role in terms of power distribution and fairness in organisations.

Source: Adapted and summarised from Boxall & Purcell (2008: 10–20)

generally. In line with the resource-based view of organisations according to which we first look at our resources and capabilities as we develop strategy, we now focus on the key resource from a general strategy development perspective.

In section 4.2.1.2 we explained that business (or generic or competitive) strategy refers to the overall approach of how the organisation wants to compete in the marketplace and that this relates to some core idea or philosophy as the basis for developing competitive advantage. An integral part hereof relates to the overall approach, core idea or philosophy about managing the work and human resources of an organisation. This is thus the focus of this section (and this chapter, with aspects hereof also explored in the next two chapters). Before we discuss in some detail the nature of particular strategic options and choices in this regard, it is important first to reflect briefly on the complexity of decision making in this context.

4.3.5.1 Generic HRM strategy options: synchronised clustering

Boxall and Purcell (2008: 58–60) explain that "strategic HRM is concerned with the strategic choices associated with the organisation of work and the use of labour … think of HR strategy as a cluster of HR systems … ". They refer to different sets of 'HR systems' and these basically resemble what we call HRM strategies – but they argue for using different strategies for different segments of work and working people.

The fact of the matter is that generally not all the work of any particular organisation will be the same. Some work is more central to the core business and competitive advantage possibilities of organisations. Similarly we thus find different groups of 'labour' – or people and their competencies – to do the different types of work. Huselid et al (2005: 2) explain that "strategic success for the organization requires that both line managers and HR professionals adopt a *different perspective* on managing workforce success … A central theme in this new perspective is the need for greater differentiation – of employees, of jobs, and of the way that firms manage workforce performance". Similarly, Boxall and Purcell (2008) also argue for a 'variegated' approach. We must therefore appreciate that there are different segments of work and working people in organisations. Some of it is really core to the business and strategic direction of the organisation and some would be more peripheral. Our overall approach to HRM strategy might thus very well include building in this form of differentiation when we make decisions to purposefully develop the HRM strategy or strategies.

In chapter 5 we will introduce you to a conceptual tool to aid in strategic thinking and decision making based on some form of differentiation when we design the work of organisations. We thus again have to stress that the chapters are merely separate for purposes of clustering themes and topics in the book. In practice the issues covered and decisions to be made are very much intertwined. Making decisions about how to design the work of organisations are clearly also strategic by nature. In this chapter our focus is on what different types of HRM strategy options are possible. Strategy by its very nature is about getting some integration and coherency. There is thus also the need to synchronise and have some coherence in the strategies we choose and craft – even if for different types of work and workers. So, for example, it could be argued that for the core work and core employees there should be some coherent approach overall. We would like to go even further and say that there will be many shared elements across different strategies even though there might also be some key differences – we thus have integration as well as segmentation possibilities simultaneously. We now turn to the integrative perspective of clustering different HRM strategies.

As explained in section 4.2.1.1, a grand strategy, from a general strategic management perspective, is essentially a comprehensive general approach that guides and directs all other decisions, practices and efforts toward mission accomplishment. An overall or general approach to competitive positioning, as we have explained, ought to be based on a certain core idea about how to compete.

In quite a similar way we can think about the strategies on how to manage the human resources of organisations. There must be some comprehensive general approach to managing the work and the working people of the organisation – in particular the employees (those for whom there is an ongoing need). This choice will also be based on a certain core idea or philosophy of what will work best within the context of the specific organisation's internal and external environments. We wish to stress again here that there might well be a need for some differentiation. In South Africa it is, for example, pretty common to differentiate on the basis of whether employees are unionised or not. The collective dimension of the employment relationship, as manifested in the form of worker representation primarily via trade unions, is thus very important in South African organisations generally. In such cases the role of the trade unions in how we manage our working people and the type of relationship we want to build with the unions thus become of strategic importance as well. The core ideas about how we manage our employees and our trade union relationships thus come into play when these strategic choices have to be made.

Empirical research (Swanepoel 1995) has proved a strong interconnectedness between the way managers (and human resource practitioners/specialists) think about the individual and collective dimensions of employment relationships. With regard to human resource specialists in particular, it has been established that their mindsets (or core ideas) about the collective dimension (trade unions) are almost just as strongly correlated with the type of HRM strategies they prefer, as are their mindsets about the individual dimension (people as individual employees). In general, a strong correlation has also been found between the types of HRM strategies preferred by managers and their tendency to prefer pluralist-based labour relations (collective dimension) strategies. People who favour pro-union strategies tend to favour more progressive HRM strategies. It has thus been empirically established that it is especially the South African managers' core ideas about trade unions that influence their strategic management choices regarding the management of human resources. This is probably the case because trade unions play such an important role in South Africa, which is not the case in all countries.

In the light hereof it can be useful to conceptualise strategic options in this field on a two-dimensional grid, as depicted in figure 4.1. Purcell (1987) initially made use of a two-dimensional grid like this. The empirical research (Swanepoel 1995) later allowed us to refine and adapt this for the South African context in particular.

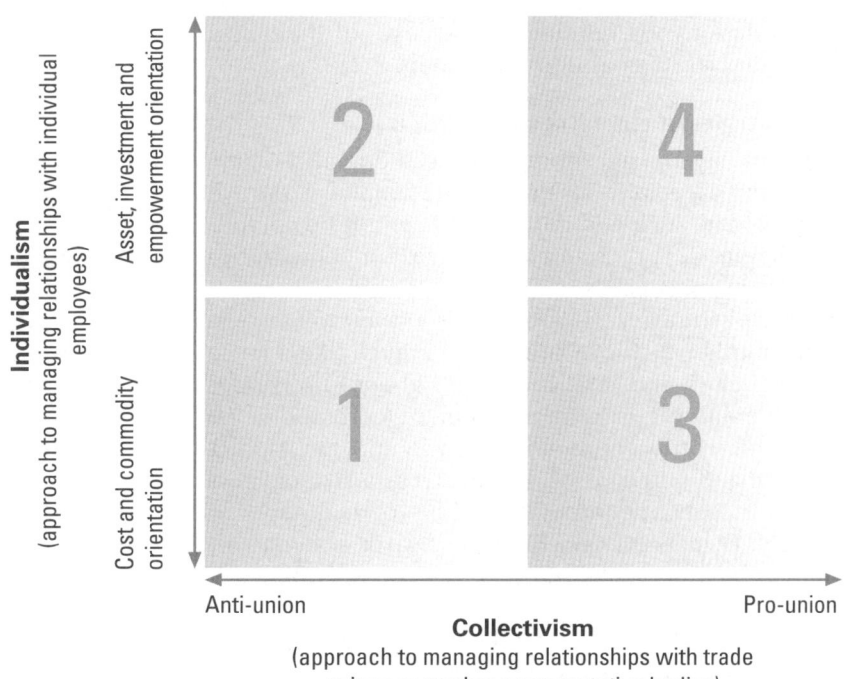

Figure 4.1: Core ideas on managing employment relations: four generic strategy options

The four generic strategy options for managing employment relations within South African organisations can thus be summarised as follows:

1 *Low individualism/low collectivism.* This involves a relatively negative (or non-positive) attitude towards trade unions and a relatively low positive (or perhaps even negative) view of the nature and potential value of the individual worker in general.

2 *High individualism/low collectivism.* Although trade unions are still viewed in a negative light, the attitude towards individual employees is generally much more positive, with a definite belief in each one's inherent value, potential and will to contribute.

3 *High collectivism/low individualism.* Here trade unions and the role that they can play are relatively highly regarded – that is, there is a generally positive attitude towards trade unions. The mindset regarding individual workers is, however, less positive, the view being rather that employees should at best be cared for and maintained. It should be noted, however, that it is not so much a negative mindset, but rather one lacking strong positive features.

4 *High collectivism/high individualism.* The core idea in this instance is that trade unions are good social institutions that may well be capable of making a constructive and positive contribution, and that each individual worker has the inherent nature and potential to contribute a great deal to the organisation – provided that he or she is managed appropriately.

4.3.5.2 HRM grand strategy options: some further clustering

On the basis of the four core ideas or generic strategies spelt out above, decisions can be made at top-management level regarding an integrated, comprehensive general approach to the management of the individual and collective dimensions of employment relations. By refining the two axes of the matrix or grid we can identify eight HRM grand strategy options (see figure 4.2).

Two grand strategies of employee exploitation

Although in this day and age strategies based on anti-human attitudes will in practice be very unlikely, especially in light of the emphasis on a human rights culture for modern-day society, such possibilities still cannot be completely excluded. Strategies 1 and 2 (see figure 4.2) are examples – at least on a theoretical level – of such extreme low individualism approaches to HRM.

In both these strategies each worker is viewed (and preferably dealt with) as if he or she is just another factor of production, much like a machine or money. Concerns about human dignity and the needs and rights of individuals are thus virtually non-existent. Each employee is treated as a mere 'commodity' (labour), and the aim is to get the most out of this commodity even by means of practices like coercion and a system of command and control. Because it is a strategy based on extreme efforts to minimise labour costs, the intention will be to keep pay levels at the absolute lowest possible levels. It may even include piecework systems, and the option of making use of contract labour (via labour brokers, for example) will be seriously considered and generally be regarded as a good one. So too would mechanisation be a seriously considered option – even to the degree of limiting ongoing employment relationships as far as possible. Alternatively jobs will be designed pretty rigidly and with high degrees of standardisation that requires working people to 'conform'. The emphasis would be on a very disciplined workforce (or segment thereof, at least). This will be in line with the core belief that these working people inherently dislike work and

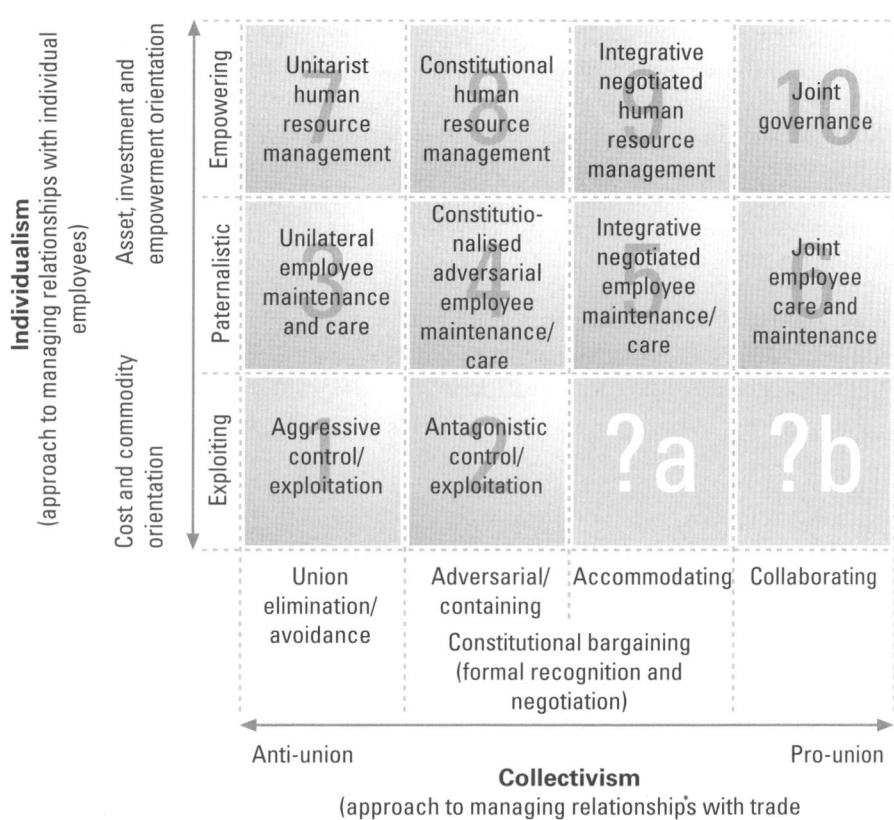

Figure 4.2: Grand strategy options in HRM

do not even really want to work, and are doing so purely for the money. Because labour is regarded a basic commodity that can easily be replaced, hiring and firing will be regarded almost as part of everyday management. Management would prefer to avoid any issues pertaining to worker dissatisfaction – those who are not happy will know that they are free to go. Complaining workers will be frowned upon more than anything else. All of this is combined with one of two options regarding management's broad approach to dealing with trade unions that might want to get involved, especially because of the abusive, exploitative cultures and practices.

In the case of *aggressive control and exploitation*, unions are ruthlessly opposed, undermined and resisted – or at least avoided as far as possible. There will be deliberate plans to keep unions out as far as possible. Such extreme low collectivism is built around the idea that there is absolutely no need for trade unions and that they are actually just a nuisance. If at all possible, campaigns will even be planned to eliminate any form of unionisation. Management will thus devise ways and means (even using underhand tactics and foul play) to keep these 'unnecessary, trouble-making third parties' out at all costs.

In the case of *antagonistic control and exploitation*, the abusive/exploitative features of the handling/treatment of individual employees are combined with a broad, general approach aimed at limiting or containing the involvement of trade unions. Unions are accepted very reluctantly only because there is little else to do (due to legislation, for instance). Management will typically try to define very rigidly the union's scope of involvement – limiting it to collective bargaining about remuneration and working conditions only. Management will take a very adversarial stance when it comes to bargaining, defending managerial prerogative and signalling quite clearly that the unions are actually 'unwelcome intruders'. Management will also want to codify strictly, by means of detailed agreements, the nature of the relationship with the trade union. Management's approach to bargaining will be very distributive, aimed at winning the most and losing the least.

Four grand strategies built around paternalism

The comprehensive general approach towards managing the relationships between individual employees and the organisation in all four of these strategic options (boxes 3–6 in figure 4.2) is to create an atmosphere of general employee care and well-being within a secure environment. Management practices are supposed to reflect a caring image that caters for the social needs of employees. The aim will thus be to devise ways of making all employees feel at home and create the idea that they are members of one big happy family in which everybody knows what is expected and what to expect. Typical elements of these strategies are respect for seniority (as in the family) and hierarchical structures, numerous job classifications and levels, and a focus on order and stability in exchange for reasonable, sufficient and fair pay, while still emphasising the containment of labour costs. There is security in the work environment because jobs are narrowly defined in said job descriptions, with little (if any) scope for worker creativity and participation. Employees feel secure because they know that, as long as they do as they are told, their jobs will be quite safe. In times of economic hardship, however, workers may (in extreme cases) be required to face up to the reality of layoffs or retrenchments unless they are prepared to make sacrifices in terms of pay and benefits, as these are viewed as major cost factors to the organisation. A great deal of emphasis is placed on the distinction between management (at different levels) and labour (as the workers). Competency for the current narrowly defined job is an important driving force and not development for higher-order, future work. Strict adherence to procedures and due processes (such as discipline and grievance handling) also forms part of establishing an environment where all know what is expected. Training is mostly done on the job and is aimed at only the minimum requirements of current jobs. Communication is mostly downward, but employees may air their opinions as and when management allows it. Management will only share limited information, and only on those aspects which they feel the workers will understand.

The differences between these four grand strategies lie in the way in which trade unions are handled or dealt with. In the case of strategies 3 and 4 (see figure 4.2), management follows a similar broad approach towards the collective dimension (trade union interaction) as those adopted in strategies 1 and 2. In the case of *unilateral employee maintenance and care*, unions are actively and aggressively avoided and kept out. However, chances are that unions will not get involved as easily as is the case with strategy 1, simply because workers are not treated as badly. In the case of *constitutionalised adversarial employee maintenance and care* (strategy 4), trade unions are dealt with reluctantly and in a very antagonistic, adversarial manner on the minimum of issues mentioned in strategy 2, in particular pay and working conditions. Once again, because the emphasis is on cost containment, and unions have to be dealt with simply because they cannot be wished away or avoided, the dealings with unions will preferably be built around win–lose, distributive-style negotiations. However, in this instance management's approach will rather be to show the unions that they are not needed because the 'employees are well cared for' and members of a 'happy family'. In this way it is hoped that the workers really will not have any need for unions and that the unions will start to feel unwelcome.

However, when a switch is made to a true pluralist stance that is really more pro-union, the approach will be to engage the worker representatives constructively in certain areas. In the case of *integrative negotiated employee care and maintenance*, management's approach to interaction with the unions shifts from a pure conflict/adversarial stance to a more friendly, accommodating attitude, aimed at broadening the scope of issues over which management will engage in discussions, deliberations and consultation with the unions. The style of interaction will thus be of a more integrative nature, especially when it comes to issues such as job descriptions, job evaluation, employee well-being programmes, etc. Issues such as wages will often be dealt with at a different, higher level, such as a bargaining council, where distributive bargaining will obviously still be prominent. Thus, because trade unions may have been recognised for quite some time and because collective relationships will have matured, management will accept that more constructive relationships in general can actually help to create a happier workforce. The reluctance to deal with the unions has now generally fallen away, and management will now negotiate rather than fight. Such a strategy is viewed as a more mature means of containing costs and keeping control over employment relationships. As is the case with constitutional employee maintenance and care, however, a great deal of emphasis is placed on highly codified agreements which defend areas of managerial prerogative. It is believed that, in this way, stability, order and conflict are best institutionalised. Accordingly, it is hoped that both the unions and the employees will be less antagonistic.

Joint employee care and maintenance takes it one step further. The approach is still to create an image of an organisation which is orientated towards the general well-being of its employees, but there is an even greater shift towards pro-unionism. Trade unions are in fact welcomed as co-equals with management in the effort to create a caring environment. Trade unions are valued as true partners in the process of caring for employees and in the creation of a secure, safe working environment. Structures for union-management cooperation on all the issues related to such an environment (as spelt out earlier) are set up, and an approach of extensive information sharing is followed. Similarly, joint problem solving takes place in areas such as narrowly defined job descriptions, job evaluations, career paths, promotion systems, grievance and disciplinary systems, skills training and even remuneration and working conditions. Integrative (win–win) negotiation is viewed as absolutely essential and, because this is the case, decentralised joint decision making on all these paternalistic-type issues takes place. Shop stewards thus typically undergo joint training with supervisors to equip them in this new task of collaborative employee care. Constructive and fully cooperative interaction is thus preferred, and trust is viewed as the cornerstone of the employment relations. Because trust is emphasised to such an extreme extent, management will, over time, move away from formalised, highly codified agreements. The emphasis, it must be remembered, remains on creating an environment of employee care and well-being to promote loyalty, while at the same time the aim is to limit or contain costs. For this reason the unionists are also trained in the interpretation of cost accounting and other financial information. In this way management tries to ensure that the parties who cooperate actually talk the same language all the time.

Four strategies of employee empowerment

In all four of these grand strategies (boxes 7–10 in figure 4.2), the underlying theme is management's belief in their employees' inherent potential, value and ability to contribute towards organisational goal accomplishment. Employees are viewed as the most valuable assets of the organisation; investment in employees is seen as a means of engendering commitment and empowering workers, which is preferred to an approach of only containing labour costs and merely imbuing loyalty. The assumptions on which these strategies are based are essentially in line with Schein's "self-actualisation man" and McGregor's "theory-Y" (see chapter 9). In terms of these theories, individual employees are generally seen to possess a great deal of creative and imaginative energy, and ingenuity, and to want to take on more responsibility, and as ambitious and committed to organisational goal accomplishment – as long as they can satisfy their self-actualisation needs in the process.

With this in mind, a great deal of professional effort goes into the employee procurement process. In order to attract and employ the right people, sophisticated recruitment and selection techniques are adopted to attract high performers. At the same time, however, work design is broad based. Jobs are broadly defined with a variety of tasks requiring multiskilling to master complexity through innovation and creativity. Hierarchical lines become blurred with few job classifications and few organisational layers. Management prefers teamwork and flexibility in the internal labour market. Because in such a system management believes that employees will easily be bored if they are not given enough freedom and leeway to do things their own way and to experience variety and the challenge to develop themselves fully, holistic work design (where conception is linked with task execution) is preferred. The idea is that, if the right environment is created, employees will stay with the organisation rather than leave as soon as a new external challenge comes up. Management will also prefer elements like job rotation, job enrichment and broad (rather than narrow) career paths.

Management's approach to employee development will thus be driven by future needs and by general multiskilling. Training in areas such as communication and problem solving will be important. A great deal of money will be invested in the development of all employees; this will be linked to a performance management system that has strong group and individual elements, and is driven by results rather than by behaviour. In all of these aspects the long term rather than short term, and flexibility rather than rigidity, are important principles. Individual employees partake fully in decision making at various levels and, because the creative ideas and other positive values of employees are recognised, meaningful two-way communication and extensive information sharing with employees occurs. Although the traditional systems employed to handle discipline and grievances will not be abandoned, the emphasis shifts from paternalism and conformance maximisation to openness and commitment maximisation. In this context management will be prepared to opt for above-average basic pay, typically in the upper quartile – extensive benefits, flexibility and increased individual and (especially) group-based incentive schemes, and even aspects like employee ownership plans and gain sharing.

Because in all four of these strategies the broad approach is to create an open and free environment in which high-potential employees can excel, make contributions and suggestions, take part in problem solving at all levels, and cooperate and commit themselves towards total quality, there is often a need to have more stereotyped work done by subcontractors or part-timers. This will not generally, however, apply to the organisation's core business functions.

These four grand strategies also differ mainly in the manner in which trade unions are dealt with. In this regard the same four options applicable to the four paternalistic-based strategies also apply here. Either unions are vigorously kept out, or they are in constant conflict with management, or they are accommodated and accepted as legitimate stakeholders in the process of creating such a high empowerment environment. In the case of the grand strategy of *joint governance*, there is maximum empowerment on both the individual and collective dimensions. Trade unions and other employee representative bodies are viewed as co-equals with management in steering the organisation as a whole towards mission accomplishment. Managerial prerogative is something of the past and it is not only issues related to the employment relationship that are dealt with on a joint problem-solving basis (as is mostly the case with integrative negotiated HRM), but the organisation as a whole is jointly managed. Parallel structures coexisting with ordinary organisational structures, and consisting of worker-representative committees at all levels throughout the organisation (which are, in any event, fewer than is the case with the paternalistic strategies), will be a natural consequence. Because some trade unions may fear that such developments may be regarded as co-option or as a sell-out by the rank and file, checks and balances will have to be built into the system to ensure that the trade union remains the focal point in the full-blown empowerment process. Typically, aspects like closed shop and agency shop agreements (see chapters 18 and 19) will therefore be preferred. In such a fully integrated organisation there is little (if any) need for old-style distributive collective bargaining over the distribution of wealth generated by the organisation. Because the approach is so inclusive and transparent, all will know that they are getting their fair share. However, this does not mean that there will be no conflict. Disputes may still arise and appropriate dispute resolution processes will thus still form part of the joint governance strategy.

The grid of grand strategy options: some general remarks

In the real world few things (if any) are exact and fixed. It must therefore not be assumed that any of the HRM grand strategies can be rigidly applied; the dotted lines exemplify fluidity and some potential overlap. It would be wishful thinking to believe that these strategy options exist in watertight compartments and that hard-and-fast rules can be applied. In the 'real world' things are not that simple. The grid has been developed from a combination of empirical evidence, theoretical argument development and practical experience. The various grand strategy options for the management of employment relations as reflected here should be regarded as a conceptual tool that can guide our strategic thinking and decision-making processes. This matrix (and an accompanying methodology) has indeed been used to facilitate management decision making and as such its value as a practical tool to detect an organisation's current practices ('emerged strategies') and desired or intended strategies has been experienced. The key is that the way in which we use this should be flexible and pragmatic.

It is important also to guard against the tendency to over-generalise. Obviously, in practice not all organisations stand to potentially benefit from using such a tool. In addition, as we have stressed before, not all the work or even employees are the same. The different segments of the work and working people must thus be factored in. In fact, we must accept that people are complex human beings and that diversity is a fact of life. Although one will tend to use some generalisations in order to formulate a comprehensive general approach to guide and direct all other major HRM decisions and practices, sufficient room will have to be left to manoeuvre and deviate when certain elements just do not fit. It is not reasonable to think that all employees throughout an entire organisation will or must be managed in exactly the same way. This is not about programming management styles, but much rather about establishing a sense of strategic direction and coherence while explicitly factoring in room needed for differentiation.

A further word of caution relates to the progression principle that is inherent in this matrix. As one moves to the right on the horizontal axis, there is a progression in the degree of the pro-union stance taken. There is no exact midpoint, but at some point there will be a shift over from a more unitarist to a more pluralist strategy. In practice organisations may move on this axis (either to the left or to the right) incrementally or gradually, without necessarily having any intention of doing so – purely as a natural response to developments internal and/or external to the organisation. At other times, deliberate decisions might have to be taken in this regard. A similar argument holds for the vertical axis, representing the individual dimension.

As has already been mentioned, it is almost inconceivable in this day and age that a manager could want to pursue any strategy based on pure theory-X principles, even though we cannot rule out any possibilities of its use or existence. In practice, there will be progression from a lower to a higher mode of individualism. In the switch from the former mode to the latter (again, finding an exact midpoint would be an oversimplification), the major difference lies in whether employees are treated well for loyalty and compliance while containing costs, or whether they are invested in and empowered so that they can contribute and maximise their commitment. This shift can occur unintentionally and gradually, or as a deliberate strategic effort towards change. Also, we may deliberately consider different options for different segments of the work and workers (including employees and/or non-employees). When it comes to our employees, it might well be important to develop some distinctiveness in our approach, and this must be aligned with whether it is core work or support work staff (we return to this in the next chapter).

By now you may have wondered about the two grey boxes '?a' and '?b' in figure 4.2. All that can be said here is that it is extremely unlikely that individual employees would be exploited and abused, while management is at the same time working together with trade unions. Should any such situation be identified in practice, serious questions would have to be asked about the trade union's bona fides.

Another aspect which needs some clarification concerns the common characteristics shared by the three 'adversarial containment' strategies (numbers 2, 4 and 8) and the two 'accommodating' strategies (numbers 5 and 9). Although these two differ in terms of the broad way in which trade unions are dealt with, in all these cases there is a great deal of emphasis on true collective bargaining and highly codified collective agreements which create an environment of strict contract administration in order to enhance control, stability and the formal institutionalisation of conflict. This is, in other words, where trade unions (or other worker-representative bodies) are formally recognised and bargained with – in some cases from a more distributive adversarial stance (in the cases of boxes 2, 4 and 8) and in other cases (boxes 5 and 9) from a more accommodating, integrative stance. A move beyond this constitutional bargaining will require maturity in the collective relationship, where trust is at the optimal level and where there is a definite shared vision.

Lastly, the interconnectedness between the two axes must be pointed out. Progression along the two axes will typically show some correlation. As one moves to the right on the horizontal (collectivism) axis, there may be a corresponding (though less) move upwards on the vertical axis. This means, for instance, that even though all four paternalistic strategies share the same essential ingredients, as one moves from 'unilateral employee maintenance and care' towards 'joint employee care and maintenance', the degree and quality of the individualism will progress towards the higher end of the vertical axis. In other words, not only will the quality of employee care improve but more elements of employee empowerment may also start to creep in. Although the correlation is not as evident in the reverse situation – that is, if one moves up towards the higher end of the vertical axis there will also be a corresponding move to the right on the horizontal axis – such a correlation has also in fact been empirically proven to exist (Swanepoel 1995). It is important to note that there is indeed a very complex interrelationship between these two dimensions – and this is why it is proposed that the two dimensions be treated in a fully integrated manner at the strategic level.

A CASE AT HAND

Human resource management strategy at SABMiller

"Unquestionably, SABMiller believes in the value of people as a core element of its business success. We assume that people want to accept accountability and influence outcomes that shape the organisation. Furthermore, we believe that employees want to practice self-management in an empowering organisation that is diverse and unashamedly performance driven.

"Today, SABMiller competes successfully in the global beer industry and is proud to acknowledge that one of our key points of differentiation is our Human Resource Proposition. We believe that the quality of our people is a singular business advantage. We understand the importance of training and development, and of creating a culture of communication and collaboration. As a global organisation, transferability of skills is important to us, and we look to build strong teams of smart educated, motivated people at every level who are capable of working throughout the company, throughout the world. It's about knowledge sharing – the passing of learning from one area of the business to another – and it's about a shared approach – a can-do attitude that comes from a real passion for what we do. Our efforts are founded on the value that a diverse workforce brings to the organisation, we endeavour to create an inclusive culture where all employees feel appreciated for their uniqueness and that contributions are respected. This proposition has established our reputation for attracting talented and diverse individuals. With our HR proposition taking the lead, talented individuals recognise the attraction of working with a global leader that prides itself on:

- Established and aspiring brands
- Highly effective systems and processes
- Challenging job opportunities
- Encouragement to develop and advance
- A uniquely talented workforce
- Consistent business success and growth

"We deliberately recruit smart, ambitious and enthusiastic people who thrive in the company of excellence."

Source: http://www.sabmiller.com/sabmiller.com/en_gb/Careers/Celebrating+culture+and+diversity/

Our talent strategy

Our people are our source of sustainable competitive advantage. Our talent strategy is simple:

Attract, retain and develop the right talent.

SABMiller recognises that successfully managing our people resource is key to achieving our business objectives. With this in mind we invest in putting formal processes and tools in place that ensure the development of the knowledge and skills of our employees. We successfully engage our employees so that they want to remain with us, and build a career within our global organisation.

>>

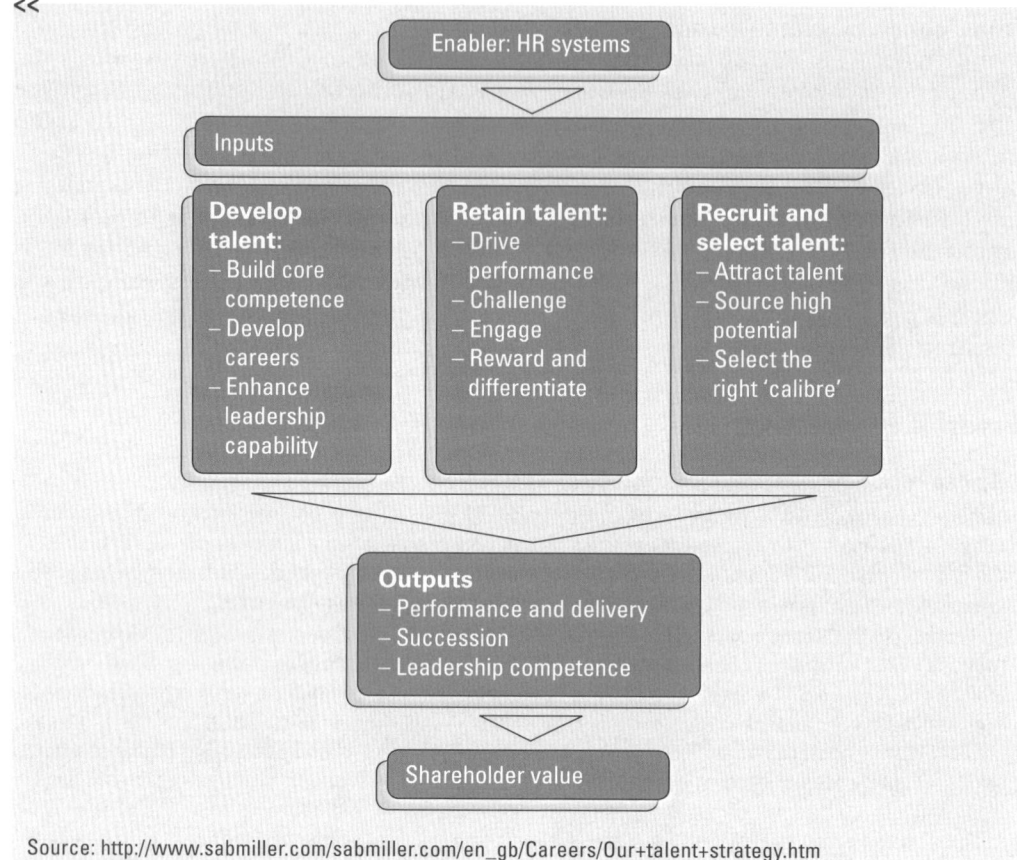

Source: http://www.sabmiller.com/sabmiller.com/en_gb/Careers/Our+talent+strategy.htm

4.4 ESTABLISHING AN HRM POLICY FRAMEWORK

The strategies, if put to paper, are the long-term documents that will steer the way forward in broad and general terms. Even if not formally put to paper, they are meant to be the long-term 'way we will do things' in broad terms. They will set the scene for developing the whole system for HRM of the organisation. This system will in turn consist of subsystems covering the whole spectrum of HRM functions, practices and processes. In order to form the basis for active HRM by all involved in it, something more than the strategies are needed. Establishing a comprehensive HRM policy framework is usually the way of going beyond considering, devising or crafting the HRM strategies. The foundation of the HRM systems typically resides in the HRM policies of the organisation.

4.4.1 General

Pearce and Robinson (2005: 288), in referring to the organisation's general business and grand strategies, say that these are crucial but for these to "become a reality ... the people in an organization that actually 'do the work' of the business need guidance in exactly what needs to be done ... to make those long-term strategies become reality". It is in this context that policies become so important. As Pearce and Robinson (2005: 288) explain:

Policies are empowerment tools that simplify decision making by empowering operating managers and their subordinates. Policies can empower the 'doers' in an organization by reducing the time required to decide and act.

Louw and Venter (2006: 427) follow a similar approach but, like Thomson et al (2007), they go further than policies to include the relevant procedures as important building blocks of the organisational architecture, "designed to guide and align organization's members in their activities and behaviours ... they can be seen to facilitate strategic alignment and implementation ...". In terms of HRM, the same holds – policies (and procedures) are important in laying some foundations for daily HRM practice by those who have to ultimately execute strategy.

4.4.2 What HRM policies are and why to have them

The overriding goal for developing HRM policies is to assist management and other employees and role players (like trade unions) to align HRM practice with the strategic intent and choices made regarding the management of work and the working people in the organisation. This is done through establishing an ordered framework of guiding principles in relation to HRM. The policies are meant to set some baseline boundaries for behaviour and HRM practice in order to help facilitate strategy execution and to promote equitable HRM throughout the organisation. It is meant to reduce uncertainty, promote some consistency in the way 'people and work' are being managed, and to generally enhance fairness in the workplace. It thus helps to set a framework for required performance standards in relation to HRM in the organisation. Policies are used to effectively delegate authority and, as such, HRM policies facilitate the devolvement of HRM practice from the specialists to the line managers. The idea is that the policies should promote some optimal level of uniformity in terms of basic principles underpinning practice, but it is crucial to avoid making things too rigid so as not to stifle flexibility and freedom to be creative in how work and working people are managed. As Louw and Venter (2006: 427) say, "... too many policies and procedures are likely to create a bureaucratic quagmire, simply because they will likely block activity and stifle ingenuity".

The set of HRM policies should form a coherent whole, and it is quite common for larger organisations to ultimately put the whole set of policies into something like an 'HRM Policy Handbook'. This will be what is known as the 'espoused policy'. In the published, official HRM policy documents (the 'espoused HRM policies') it would be appropriate to spell out the principles of the HRM generic or grand strategy in respect of both the individual and collective dimensions of employment relations. This will set the tone for the rest of the policies in relation to employees, and other working people, as well as the handling of matters pertaining to trade unions. The policies in the different areas must be aligned, as mentioned earlier. It is furthermore important to also make sure these policies are aligned with the policies in other relevant areas of the organisation (like finance, logistics, public relations and so forth). From a BBBEE perspective it will, for instance, be crucial to make sure that the general procurement policies (part of the logistics subsystem of the organisation) are in alignment with HRM policies generally, and with affirmative action and black economic empowerment policies in particular.

Horwitz (1991: 220–221) spelt out a number of ideal characteristics of such policies. According to him, such policies should express general principles rather than specific rules for specific situations; they should be long term; and although they are usually developed at top-management level, other levels should be included in their formulation. Furthermore, they should have the approval and support of the highest authority in the enterprise; they should be in writing and available to all parties involved; and they should be subject to regular revision and possible changes. Because policy should be the culmination of the basic strategy-planning process, the continuous task of environmental scanning results in management continually being sensitive to environmental changes. One of the key areas here relates to changing legislation with concomitant changes in the conformance aspect of HRM. It goes way beyond this, though, in that it helps to ensure that any changes in strategy or strategic direction are reflected in the policy changes, thus helping to align practice with the changing environment. Having said this, in practice it can be quite a challenge to keep on ensuring that all things are so well aligned. There is even the often underestimated challenge of aligning the espoused policy with what is commonly referred to as 'operational policy'.

In practice, the espoused policies are often not 'internalised' by managerial staff throughout the hierarchy and hence we tend to find that supervisors who are managing the people working with them do not really implement the policies appropriately, because their superiors do not do it either. The behaviour and day-to-day practices of managerial staff in terms of how they manage the work and the people doing the work, then, really becomes what is known as 'operational' or 'non-official policy'. This starts right at the top.

Lower-level management will typically behave in ways that align with senior management's highest priorities. If top management reflects high priorities in the areas of, say, production and quality, and lower levels of staff actually experience that these areas are strictly monitored for performance purposes, but the same does not happen in respect of HRM, then lower-level managers are likely to behave accordingly. They might then neglect aspects of HRM at the expense of other priorities. The way that the actual performance of managerial staff is managed across the different areas (like finance, production and people management) will thus play a very important role in terms of whether espoused and operational policies are aligned. Aspects like reward, punishment and control exercised by higher-level management thus play an important role in that it sets the example for lower-level managers in terms of how to live out HRM in the organisation. Execution, or rather the lack thereof, then sets the tone for 'how we manage people and work around here' – rather than the actual policy documents. This is what we like to refer to as the policy implementation dilemma – when operational policy (non-official) and espoused policy (official) are not aligned.

Ideally there should be no difference between the organisation's official and operational HRM policies. We do not live in an ideal world, though, and perfect alignment is probably therefore not realistic. In a sense it is also not what one would really expect. That does not deter us, however, from striving towards as close as possible an alignment as we can get. We wish to reiterate that this alignment challenge starts with the actual behaviour of top and senior management because, as also reflected in exhibit 4.4, we know that action speaks louder than words.

4.4.3 HRM policy: reflecting on scope and introducing some content

The content of HRM policy can really cover anything from a general set of introductory principles outlining the philosophy to HRM (thus akin to some form of a generic strategy), to a wide range of key policy areas covering the whole spectrum of HRM. The rationale behind establishing the HRM policy can be a sensible opening point. Stating some overarching goals will be important, specifically also when starting off by making explicit linkages to the organisation's overall 'vision, mission and value

EXHIBIT 4.4: The CIPD on HRM policy

Organisations have HRM policies for different reasons. These can include the need:

- to comply with existing or new legislation, including case law;
- to develop a more formal and consistent approach to meet needs like growth and development, for example, through policies on flexible working;
- to support general management strategy;
- to follow the latest developments in effective people management;
- to deal with internal or external change;
- for business units to conform to relevant head office/parent-company policies;
- to keep up with competitors; for example policies may be reviewed in order to attract or retain talent, particularly in a tight labour market conditions.

Each organisation will need policies that suit their own purpose and strategic direction and that fit with their sector, culture and structure.

Introducing HRM policy at any point in time doesn't indicate that the organisation previously had no provisions in place. It reflects a desire to formalise arrangements in certain areas of people management for the reasons suggested.

Our research has shown that by adopting bundles of HR practices, employers are likely to improve business performance. Employees should have substantial discretion as to how to do their work. It is more likely that they will use their discretion positively if they feel that they are being fairly treated – which is a key reason for having policies. The research found that adopting positive HRM polices alone was not enough – the policies needed to be translated into practice to influence employees' behaviour. This translation and implementation by line managers is critical to the way in which employees respond to go the extra mile; for example staying late to finish a project or going out of their way to deal with a customer problem.

Source: Adapted from CIPD Factsheet 'HR policies and procedures: Why introduce them?'. Originally issued October 2004; latest revision July 2007. http://www.cipd.co.uk/subjects/hrpract/general/hrpolproc-why. htm?IsSrchRes=

statement'. The general and overarching goals may relate to things like respecting human rights, our country's Constitution and respect of the laws of South Africa – as the minimum baseline for all principles of policy and practice. It may go on to make a statement regarding things like the value placed on people and what they have to offer the organisation, and the importance of treating everybody with dignity and establishing relationships based on trust, integrity and fairness. It may include an overriding aim of achieving cooperation and having an environment of mutual commitment and loyalty between employees and the organisation generally. The idea that the policies are there to help all relevant parties to work together as harmoniously as possible towards making the organisation successful should be made crystal-clear. It may also be valuable to point out the differences and interdependence between the policies pertaining more to the individual dimension of the employment relationship, and those pertaining more to the collective dimension, as manifested in trade union-management relations. A statement on the importance attached to the principle of freedom of association will thus be appropriate.

Spelling out general standards in relation to the policy as such and to the implementation thereof (such as the universal application and the inviolability thereof) can add further value. The nuts and bolts of the policy documentation will, however, relate to the actual spectrum of the content covered. The exact nature of this will differ widely from one organisation to the next. Apart from it being an outflow of the basic strategic direction of the organisation, as translated into HRM strategies and thus very much having to be aligned with industry/sector-specific challenges and issues, the stage of the organisation's life cycle will typically be quite a determining factor regarding scope and content of the policies. Typically, the smaller and younger organisations will tend to have less sophistication in respect of HRM policy. As organisations grow and have more people working in and for them, the need to have more comprehensive and sophisticated sets of policies typically also increases. However, we wish to reiterate that care should be taken that the policies do not become counterproductive. Quite the opposite – the policy framework and all the concomitant policies should facilitate the execution of organisational strategy to enhance competitive advantage, while simultaneously enhancing the quality of work life of the working people and also life beyond the workplace in a sustainability sense. We now turn to look at some examples of specific HRM policies and some of their potential content.

Naturally the scope of this book does not allow us to provide a comprehensive coverage of all HRM policies. Instead we here merely touch on what the spectrum of such policies might entail, and introduce some potential content aspects and examples. In various other chapters to follow you will find relevant policy issues and examples, too. For now we really just want to give you some flavour of what HRM policies might look like. As an example we can have an 'HRM Policy Manual' with different policy sub-domain sections structured into a file (hard and/or electronic) of documents as per exhibit 4.5 (please note that this is merely illustrative of a possible spectrum and not intended to claim completeness or otherwise):

EXHIBIT 4.5: HRM Policy Manual for Company XYZ: an outline

■ HRM strategy and goals
  – Company vision, mission and value statement
  – HRM strategy
    • Generic strategy and key principles
■ HRM policy formation and change
■ Employment equity policy
  – Affirmative action policy
■ Workforce planning policy
  – Job analysis and role description policy
  – Annual workforce planning policy
    • Workforce change policy
  – Five-year workforce planning policy
■ Organisation and work design policy
  – Organisation structure policy
    • Organisational restructuring policy
  – Job design and redesign policy
    • Job enrichment policy
■ Human resource procurement policy
  – Recruitment policy
    • Requests for recruitment policy
    • Job advertising policy
    • Job application policy
  – Selection policy
    • Assessment centre policy
    • Interviewing policy
    • Psychological testing policy

    • Reference checking policy
  – Staff appointment policy
    • Outsourcing, temporary employment agencies and independent contractors' policy
■ Remuneration policy
  – Job evaluation and reclassification policy
  – Pay administration policy
  – Performance reward policy
    • Performance bonuses policy
  – Employee share ownership policy
■ Performance management policy
  – Performance planning policy
  – Performance observation and feedback policy
  – Performance assessment policy
  – Performance development policy
    • Substandard work performance policy
  – Performance recognition and reward policy
■ Human resource development policy
  – In-house training and development policy
    • Technical training and learnerships policy
    • Frontline supervisor training policy

>>

- Management development policy
- Leadership development policy
- Corporate entrepreneurship training policy
  - External training and development policy
  - Further study assistance policy
  - Bursaries for school-leavers policy
- ■ Career development and management policy
  - Promotion policy
  - Transfers policy
  - Secondment policy
  - Geographic relocation policy
    - Household removal assistance policy
  - Job rotation policy
    - Multiskilling policy
  - Succession management policy
  - Entrepreneurial development policy
- ■ Communication policy
  - Internal communication policy
    - Transparency and communication policy
    - Briefing group policy
    - Electronic communication and intranet policy
  - Communicating externally policy
  - Whistle-blowing policy
  - Privacy and right to access of information policy
- ■ Leadership and employee involvement policy
  - Leadership roles policy
  - Preferred leadership styles policy
  - Direct participation and preferred leadership styles policy
    - Freedom of speech policy
    - Suggestion policy
  - Indirect participation policy
  - Staff consultation policy
- ■ Staff wellness policy
  - Health policy
    - HIV/Aids policy
    - Tuberculosis policy
    - General illness policy
    - Fitness and recreation policy
    - Nutrition policy
    - Smoking policy
    - Medical assistance policy

- Safety policy
  - Safety management policy
  - Emergencies policy
- Work-life balance policy
- Bullying and harassment policy
- Absenteeism policy
- Employee assistance policy
- ■ Social responsibility and sustainability policy
  - Staff volunteering and elder-care policy
  - Child-care policy
  - Corporate social investment policy
    - School education policy
    - Community upliftment policy
    - Entrepreneurship assistance policy
  - Environmental care policy
- ■ Leave policy
  - Annual vacation leave policy
  - Sick leave policy
  - Compassionate leave policy
  - Maternity and paternity leave policy
  - Study leave policy
  - Sabbatical leave policy
  - Long service leave policy
  - Unpaid leave policy
- ■ Labour and employee relations policy
  - Freedom of association policy
    - Unionisation and trade union recognition policy
    - Closed shops policy
    - Shop stewards' and trade union officials' leave policy
    - Collective bargaining policy
    - Workplace forums policy
  - Discipline policy
  - Staff complaints policy
  - Grievances policy
  - Employment termination policy
    - Resignation policy
    - Retirement policy
    - Dismissal for misconduct policy
    - Dismissal for poor performance policy
    - Redundancy and retrenchment policy
    - Restraint of trade policy
    - Organisation exit policy
    - Re-employment policy

As can be gathered from exhibit 4.5, the spectrum of issues that can be covered in such an HRM policy document can be very comprehensive. There are thus policies within policies as the domains and sub-domain areas of different human resource policy areas are codified into policy. Also note that policies can have accompanying procedures. The extent to which we detail aspects of HRM work into policies and procedures signals the *standardisation* tendency of an organisation. As we have said, it is crucial to make sure that policies help rather than hinder the efforts to gain and sustain competitive advantage. Generally, the more highly codified things are, the less freedom we leave for discretion, which is often an important prerequisite for flexibility. On the other hand, the more open ended we leave things, the greater the uncertainty as to 'how do we go about doing certain things here'. The challenge thus lies in striking a fine balance.

The format in which a policy is formulated can vary. We believe it is important, however, that at least a consistent format is used throughout for all policy areas and sub-domains. A suggested format might be to have an introductory section, a clear statement of purpose and aims or objectives, a scope section that spells out which people are covered by the policy, some fundamentals or principles, and an outline of what the particular policy is intended to provide guidance on. It normally is useful also to have a section (or an appendix) that highlights linkages with other relevant policies of the organisation. A performance management policy can then, for instance, have an introduction section that goes something along the following lines (obviously all of these things really depend on the actual strategic choices made by the organisation):

Company XYZ regards performance management as central to the achievement of its vision and mission and the execution of its business strategy. We thus believe that performance management must become part of our everyday life at XYZ. This policy sets the framework for XYZ's performance management system. It is therefore meant to guide all involved in the work of XYZ to use the system in an integrated and institutionalised way and on an ongoing basis for managing the work and concomitant performance of all staff, and *not* as a periodic event.

Aligned with the foregoing, the purpose and objectives section of the policy might contain statements like the following (please note again that we are merely giving some illustrative examples here – the real purpose and objectives must be decided upon in accordance with the HRM strategic choices):

The framework set by something like the foregoing could then be augmented by a statement that clearly shows which employee groups fall within the ambit of the policy, a set of principles or 'fundamentals' and most importantly then, the 'flesh' that will revolve around guidance as to how implementation is to be effected. The latter could include pertinent statements about what will be required in order to enable parties to make the performance management system a 'living' enabler of strategy execution and spell out the essential approach, steps, methods and techniques to be used in implementing the policy and system.

In all the HRM policies a crucial issue will be the role differentiation between the line managers and the HR practitioners or specialists. The exact nature hereof will ultimately depend on other strategic decisions about structuring the HRM work of the organisation. We deal with these in the next chapter. As mentioned, connections are mostly also made in the policy documentation, with relevant standard operating procedures (SOPs) that accompany and further facilitate policy implementation. In respect of a policy on discipline and grievance handling, these procedures will be absolutely critical (we return to some of these in later chapters). Again, the issue of standardisation and codification versus the need to retain room for flexibility is important.

The purpose of the performance management policy is to guide all relevant parties on how to implement XYZ's performance management system which is geared towards making and keeping the company a high-performance mining/financial/(whatever sector and market environment is relevant) company, capable of competing well with the best in the world. This is to be achieved through a performance management system which:

- is balanced – developing competence and performance to the advantage of staff, and XYZ and its key stakeholders like customers, shareholders and society at large;
- puts a premium on and rewards superior work performance;
- is based on fair process and ethical practice that deals fairly and transparently, yet firmly, with persistent substandard work performance;
- empowers all employees to develop and deploy their potential optimally in the XYZ environment;
- is output driven, where these outputs and concomitant performance goals of all staff can be linked to the 'mission, vision and values statement' of XYZ;
- is appropriately aligned with other policies and systems of the organisation;
- is supported by other relevant policies and procedures, and a high-performance culture spearheaded by leadership that empowers fellow working people as leaders in their own right;
- is suitably resourced so as to facilitate alignment of mission accomplishment, business goals and strategies, and annual budget frameworks;
- focuses on ongoing improvement through employee engagement and empowerment, and the optimal leverage of each person's creative capacity;
- values and encourages teamwork, team performance and team reward; and
- recognises and actively addresses the sustainability challenge of our time.

We can go on to illustrate similar aspects for the other policy areas and sub-domains, but the scope of this book does not allow for this (perhaps a complete and separate book may do justice to such a subject). What must be stressed is the great importance of building a coherent HRM system for the organisation, based on the strategic choices, and as manifested and founded on the relevant HRM policy/ies. You will find some relevant references to policy perspectives in later chapters. All of this merely serves to sensitise you to the spectrum of policy-related issues involved in HRM. In fact, most of what we cover in the book can serve as input for HRM policy development. So, do not underestimate this 'policy-making challenge'. Also, though, keep in mind that the policy and conformance challenge is only one side of the coin of HRM. The greater challenge probably lies in getting the systems and policies working for the organisation, driving added value through high performance as aligned with the organisation's strategic direction. This requires involvement and dedicated effort by numerous role players, most notably line managers and HR practitioners, but also trade unions and their representatives, for instance.

The strategies and policies (as well as the procedures) are relatively long-term documents aimed at facilitating some consistency, predictability and stability over the longer term. The policy framework thus gives some certainty to the role players in respect of what they are expected to do over a longer period of time. Every day has its challenges, though, and the shorter-term operational activities, although intended to be aligned with the overall strategy and policy framework, will inevitably be influenced by tactical issues. Also, budgets are typically based on annual cycles, as are performance measurement systems (like employee performance appraisals). These are all shorter-term frameworks that influence daily HRM practice. In addition we get business plans that are more medium term, aimed at achieving certain targets over periods of, say, three to five years. In this regard it is often also necessary to prepare HRM business plans in order to further facilitate HRM strategy execution – particularly as aligned with budgetary cycles and the oft-needed strategic change interventions. Before we get to that we would like to briefly cover some HRM policy development process issues.

4.4.4 HRM policy development: a few notes

The processes involved in actually developing and producing these HRM policies (and others, for that matter) can be quite challenging, not least because it really involves and stems from the strategy development processes. Generally we can thus distinguish between policy initiators, the actual policy *drafters*, those who are primarily the *implementers* of policy, those who are mainly *facilitators* of policy, the policy *custodians*, and last but not the least, those who are the *signatories* of policy. Policy can be initiated by anyone, really, but generally speaking the HR practitioners or specialists should be proactive and initiate policy development. Because the top-level HR practitioners should ideally be intimately involved in strategy making, it follows logically that relevant policy implications will be clearest to them whenever strategy changes are in motion. They could then thus organise policy-making workshops whereby some other senior HR staff and key line managers can be engaged. It could be wise also to involve the trade union (depending on the guidance as set by the generic/grand strategy and relevant policy, of course) through shop stewards, for instance. These people, as a team and led by any senior person of the team, will then work on writing the policy (or the policy change, perhaps).

At times it may be wise to engage the services of an independent facilitator. This person will focus on the process rather than the actual content. It may also be necessary for such a person to come from outside the organisation. During the earlier years following new legislation on labour relations and employment equity, for instance, there were many 'experts' specialising in the field and assisting organisations to change or develop and write new relevant policies. These people can all be seen as facilitators of policy making. Throughout the whole process we advise as broad as possible involvement of employees and their representatives (if applicable). This serves a dual purpose: Firstly it brings input into the process (and thus hopefully policy content) from those who will actually have to live with it and make it work from day to day and month to month (the implementers) – thus making these policies as implement friendly as possible. Related hereto, it gives the implementers a sense of ownership in the new or changed policies, which enhances strategy and policy execution. Naturally such an approach can be more time consuming, but in our experience the engagement of a representative cross-section of employees (managerial as well as non-managerial) together with shop stewards can go a long way towards saving time and energy when it comes to implementation.

The policy custodians will be those charged with the responsibility for making sure policies are implemented and adhered to appropriately. This is typically the HR practitioners' role. In cases where there are no HR specialists (as in small companies), this will also be line management's task. In the end, the accountability will be that of the CEO and his or her team who are answerable to the board of directors (or similar governance structure in the public service or in non-profit-seeking organisations). Typically, thus, the responsibilities may be delegated to others (perhaps the right and responsibility for signing off on policy may be delegated to the top-level HR manager) – but accountability cannot be delegated. Generally, boards will retain the authority to sign off on many policy frameworks, but one cannot expect that to be the case with all such comprehensive policies as contained in the different policy areas and sub-domains. The key is that policies must be signed off by those duly authorised to do so. Sadly, however, when going into organisations we find that some policies have not been looked at for maybe a decade, having been signed off by people who have long ago left the company and during times when different legislation applied. It is important to keep policies current, and policy reviews should thus happen regularly and timeously.

It should again be noted also that the socio-political realities of organisations create real-world dynamics of policy making that will be similarly fraught with aspects like debate, divergent viewpoints, even conflict at times, 'politicking' and a lot of negotiation and issue selling. Generally, these might be less than in the case of strategy development, though, simply because the strategy framework would already have been decided upon – setting the direction for the policy content. One can never underestimate the challenges posed by details – as the saying goes, the devil lies in the detail. The actual practical implications of who will have to do what and how when it comes to policy implementation, and as realised as the policies are written, can, however, create all sorts of anxieties as people work through the process of writing up the policies. From experience it has been found that, especially in cases where strategic choices have not been formally communicated, such anxieties can revolve around the different roles to be played by line managers and HR practitioners. In many organisations where HRM is still regarded as mainly the job of 'HR' (meaning the HR section or department), line managers tend to shy away from their role in different HRM policy implementation matters, pushing rather for greater roles to be played by the HR practitioners of the organisation. Unfortunately we have found that often the specialists themselves are all too keen to hang onto the expanded role of doing HRM work at the operational level. In drafting the policies, these sorts of things can thus create dynamics that might speed up or delay the policy-making process.

As we have said before, policies are long-term guides – but that does not mean that these documents are static. HRM policies should be kept current, and that would be the role of the policy custodians and initiators. The annual business-planning cycles of organisations (there often are medium-term cycles too, such a three years) also play an important role, as do certain unplanned for eventualities.

4.5 HRM BUSINESS PLANNING

In essence, business plans are documents detailing more medium-term plans and objectives. Such business plans can be for one year, or they can cover three- to five-year periods, and then redrafted annually within the context of formal strategic planning updates. Strategic planning in a formal sense should happen annually as well in order to ensure the necessary fit between internal and external environments. Strategic thinking may be happening on a continuous basis, but the formal planning sessions should typically each year be scheduled well in advance of the organisation's next annual budgetary cycle. This is required so that resource allocations can be aligned with the strategic direction of the organisation. The business plans will thus focus in more detail on various functional areas and on what ought to be done in these areas in the period to come, by whom and how, in order to get strategy implemented. These business plans then typically form the basis for short-term, annual action plans. One action plan might, for instance, relate to the initiation of a new policy that has to be drafted, or a review of some or all of the HRM policy documents. Such action plans must thus be in sync with the annual budgets, and integrated to allow for appropriate resource allocation. In other words, resources (such as money, people, time) are allocated so that action plans and business plans can be carried out, which in turn facilitates execution of the business plan, finally leading to strategy implementation and mission accomplishment. Again, we wish to stress that all of this may sound very neat and simple when in actual fact things are much more messy in the real world.

As you now know, business strategy essentially revolves around how best a particular business organisation can compete in a specific marketplace. You were also informed of Michael Porter's three strategic options of overall cost leadership, differentiation and focus (Porter 1980) as well as the typology used by Miles and Snow (1984) with the concomitant strategy types of prospector, defender and analyser.

When drafting the HRM business plans, the concept of 'fit' is of crucial importance. Not only must the HR business plan fit the HRM strategy but it must also fit the internal and external environmental factors – most notably the organisation's general strategic direction and business plans.

In the process of drafting a business plan for HRM it is thus necessary not only to ensure that the business plan fits the HRM grand strategy but also that the HRM grand strategy's fit with the business strategy will be facilitated by the execution of the HRM business plan. It must also fit the overall HRM policy framework, and it is not uncommon for organisations to have business planning policy as such. Key, though, is that the HRM business plan's purpose should basically be to operationalise or bring about the concept of fit between general business strategy and HRM grand strategy, and it should break up the strategic plans into measurable chunks over shorter time periods. Although the selection/choice of an appropriate HRM grand strategy must itself ensure that there is an alignment between business and HRM strategy, the various elements of the business plan must now clarify how the necessary fit will be achieved.

If, for instance, the organisation's business strategy is one of overall cost leadership (in Porter's terms), or the defender strategy (Miles and Snow's typology), the basic approach will in general in all likelihood entail seeking cost minimisation through the construction of large-scale facilities, through strict control of overhead and fixed costs, including costs linked to marketing/sales and distribution. The focus will also be on product design that facilitates cost containment and, as result, less money may be spent on something like research and development and after-sales service. The emphasis will therefore be on quantity of products/services rather than on outstanding quality. In such circumstances tight management control is more likely to be of paramount importance, often requiring more strict supervisory practices and organisational structures that are hierarchically based along authority lines of demand-and-control. The environment may be relatively more risk averse, with a strong concern for stability and order, which can facilitate efficient operational/production processes. In line with this, the focus may be on relatively more mechanistically designed jobs, work demarcation and more narrowly defined job descriptions and specifications. More emphasis may be placed on detailed work and operating procedures, and employees' training may centre more on compliance and improved hard skills to do their jobs more efficiently. Where there are group processes (such as, for example, quality circles), the focus may be on improving the efficiency of the organisation's delivery systems (for example production). Because control is so central, performance appraisals may focus more on behavioural norms, using this as some form of control mechanism by rewarding behaviour that conforms to the norm. Pay may also be work based rather than output based. In other words, aspects such as job evaluation may be of greater importance. If there is going to be a shift in business strategy, concomitant shifts in HRM strategy will be required, which will mean changes in HRM policy as well as various interventions to change the different HRM subsystems. These must all be built into the HRM business plans (and cascaded down into relevant action plans).

Should an organisation, for instance, shift to follow a business strategy of differentiation (in Porter's terms) or the innovative strategy (in Miles and Snow's terms), aspects such as creativity, innovation, top-class quality, uniqueness of products/ services, and customer care will then have to be emphasised. The focus will typically shift to research and development to ensure that the organisation becomes a leader in its field, and also on excellent marketing strategies, including after-sales service to ensure outstanding quality. In such circumstances, because the emphasis is not so much on cost containment anymore, the HRM strategy emphasis will as a general rule also not be on paternalistic or exploitative strategies (see figure 4.2). Employee creativity, innovation and commitment will now be sought rather than compliance and employee control. Policies will have to be changed to reflect that. Even more so, rigid job descriptions will typically be much less important with more broad-based work classifications and role profiles, rather, as well as broader career paths. These will require system interventions for change (including policy changes) – all of which must be built into business (and action) plans. Flexibility and team-based work design will also be more common, and training will be more focused on developing the person as a whole and on eliciting better thinking abilities for creativity, innovation, excellence and the achievement of self-actualisation. In such a strategy context, the making of errors (within limits, of course) will be tolerated much more because of an environment typified by ambiguity, innovation and greater risk taking. Policy frameworks will have to be changed to reflect that, and these changes to policies and work systems must be contained in business plans for roll-out in the years coming. The ability to work with others and to do different jobs will be more important in such a strategy, and work design or redesign might hence be applicable. An employee's remuneration will now typically be influenced by performance in terms of outputs or results, and performance appraisals as such will typically be used as instruments to facilitate development and change. Group incentives will also be more common because of a greater emphasis on the team concept. However, because new blood will from time to time be needed in order to ensure that the organisation remains at the cutting edge of innovations in product/service engineering, external equity in the sense of good pay will also be important. Changing from one strategy to another will thus have policy-change implications, but effecting the actual change will require resources and people taking responsibility. Business planning helps to accomplish this.

The above should serve to clarify some links between business strategy and HRM strategy, and between strategic planning, change, and policy making and business planning. When drafting HRM business plans, the challenge lies in identifying the key areas or strategic priorities that require attention over the medium term in order to facilitate grand strategy implementation. It may, for instance, be necessary to redesign the work (see chapter 5), to rewrite job descriptions, to recruit new employees with different characteristics, to design a new performance management system and/or to redesign the organisation's remuneration system. The emphasis thus shifts to different functional aspects of HRM, selecting the required strategic change interventions in each area and assigning responsibilities, allocating timelines in respect of each intervention, and aligning all of this with resource allocation processes (such as budgeting). In this way, appropriate targets and objectives must be formulated in order to monitor progress over time. This is thus where strategy making and execution meet, and where the more operational HRM issues kick in. While most of this book covers operational aspects, it is important to make the strategy–policy–operations connections all along. In the end, strategies and policies are only as good as the actual operations that turn the plans into reality.

4.6 CONCLUSION

In this chapter the focus was on, inter alia, the nature of strategy and strategic management, and on how HRM can be integrated with the general strategic management of organisations. The emphasis was on options, choices and decision making in the formulation of HRM strategies that have to match or fit the internal and external environmental conditions of the organisation. Attention was devoted to different HRM strategy options and the necessity of streamlining the organisation's HRM strategies with its general business and grand strategies. In this regard the role of HRM policy has been covered and some examples provided.

We have argued for vertical integration (that is, aligning general business management strategies with those relating to the HR dimension of organisations) and horizontal integration (in other words between all aspects of HR and labour relations management) as prerequisites if any approach is to be strategic – especially in South Africa. The integration of the management of the individual and collective dimensions of employment relationships in South Africa is very important because of the prominence and important role played by trade unions. In other African countries this may be less important, and other strategic choice frameworks may be more applicable.

In this chapter our focus was thus on strategic options and choices regarding HRM. There are some further related issues that must be decided that are also strategic by nature. These relate more to the structural dimensions that play a key role in strategy implementation. These decisions form the focal point of the next chapter.

SUSTAINABILITY CONNECTION?

The strategies of our organisations determine our long-term direction. In this era that we live in, no organisation can think long term and strategise without fully incorporating the whole issue of sustainability. Not only is sustainable competitiveness essential for organisational survival, but organisations must also remain competitive in order to provide the work and income earning potential for our people. Strategies are ultimately about winning – but not winning at all costs. We must strategise in ways that make us a winning nation and a winning continent – and not at the cost of our planet but in direct support of its state of well-being. We can only hope to achieve this if our strategies place our people at the core of our business and competitive manoeuvres. If we put a premium on our people in all of our strategic thinking and decisions and planning, we will develop and empower them to help us execute our strategies. This should not only be the backbone of our efforts to compete but also the foundation for a better life for all of our working people, our customers and also all other stakeholders. Our strategies should be founded on solid values, and built around the idea of adding lasting value to all stakeholders as well as to the sustainability of Earth and all its forms of life.

SELF-EVALUATION QUESTIONS

1 Explain what is meant by the concept 'strategy' by illustrating how it has been transplanted from the military to the management context.
2 Describe and differentiate between the following concepts:
   - corporate strategy;
   - grand strategy;
   - business and generic strategy; and
   - functional strategy.
3 Discuss briefly what 'strategic management' entails.
4 Explain the nature and meaning of 'strategic human resource management'.
5 'Making decisions about HRM strategies is a purely rational process.' Critically discuss the above statement.
6 From a strategic management perspective, what can be done to integrate decisions about the management of workers and their trade unions?
7 What is meant by 'low collectivism and high individualism'?
8 Explain any three grand strategies for HRM that are built around paternalism.
9 'The time has come for empowerment. We have to empower the people employed by organisations!' In the context of this above statement, discuss the nature and potential value of the four employee empowerment strategies explained in this chapter.
10 Write an essay about the need for, role and nature of HRM policy in organisations.
11 What is 'HRM business planning'?

5 DESIGNING WORK, ORGANISATIONS AND HRM WORK

LEARNING OUTCOMES

After studying this chapter, you should be able to:

- explain how strategy and structural issues relate;
- make meaningful contributions to decision making about approaches to work and job design/redesign;
- engage in constructive dialogue about the nature and importance of the notions of organisational and work design for flexibility and high-performance systems in South African organisations;
- make a short presentation about the key variables and principles relating to the design of work and organisations;
- debate issues and trends pertaining to different organisation design options, specifically with reference to implications for the management of human resources; and
- explore different ways of designing HRM work in organisations, among others through using different models or typologies.

5.1 INTRODUCTION

Structure and strategy are closely intertwined. It is often said that structure follows strategy but that is not always the case. As we have explained before, the real world is much too complex to make rigid categorisations in linear, step-by-step fashion. As strategy options and choices are considered, concomitant structural alternatives typically also surface, and vice versa.

Decisions and options about structural configurations revolve largely around the general management task of 'organising', and these may indeed range from strategic to more operational. Irrespective of whether the issue is more strategic or more operational, to a large extent the focal point when it comes to 'organising' is the work of the organisation. The key focus is how the work is to be structured so that people can actually execute it as effectively and efficiently as possible – and, importantly, with the best chances of these people also benefiting optimally from their work experiences.

From the previous chapter the interconnection between different strategy alternatives and the manner in which work is organised should already have been clear. What we cover in this chapter includes some further strategic options and decisions. There are many ways in which work activities, tasks and work roles can be structured, and how the relationships between them and the working people, and the relevant work technologies can be organised. Structuring all of this and the relationships between roles and the flow of work, as well as how these interact with the technical systems involved in work execution, is very important. How working people interact as part of their work roles and the order, structure and flow of work thus form part of the vital building blocks of organisations and their design. Individual work roles and 'jobs' (or positions) cannot therefore be viewed in isolation, because these all work together to make up 'the organisation'. Each working person is supposed to perform certain activities to achieve something (work outputs), and everybody's work is ultimately connected in some way. The work involves the people as well as their relations and also the interaction with the technology. All of these must be coordinated into a coherent work system channelled towards goal accomplishment. The overall flow of the work must be organised in a way that delivers the goods as efficiently and effectively as possible so as to satisfy (or even exceed) customer expectations. In this sense the totality of work has its origin in the requirements of those who want to buy or use the organisation's outputs (products/services) – in other words, the 'customers'.

The way in which this totality of work is organised entails different dimensions and aspects, including the work of individuals, groups, and the organisation as a whole. We look at all of these in this chapter, as well as, specifically, how HRM work can be organised.

5.2 WORK DESIGN

Actually this whole chapter revolves around options and decisions about designing or organising the work of organisations. As we have said – there are different aspects and dimensions involved. Our approach is aligned with that of Hodge, Anthony and Gales (2003: 31), who say that "design is an umbrella concept that includes both process and structural issues".

Johnson et al (2008: 434) refer to this as the strategic task of "organising for success", explaining that "the most important resource of an organisation is its *people* ... the structural roles people play, the processes through which they interact and the relationships that they build are crucial to the success of strategy". Organising is referred to by Hitt, Black, Porter and Hanson (2007: 23) as systematically putting together all organisational resources, and they add that the key to this entails "paying attention to the structure of relationships between positions and the people occupying them, and linking structure to the overall strategic direction of the organisation ... the purpose ... can be thought of as the attempt to bring order to the organisation". Cordery and Parker (2007: 188) use the concept of "work organization", which they define as "the way tasks are organized and coordinated within the context of an overarching work system". They then describe a work system as "a particular configuration of interacting subsystems including work content, technology, employee capabilities, leadership style, and management policies and practices" (Cordery & Parker 2007: 188–189).

Overall there is the organisation as a whole and how it should be structured – and this is referred to as *organisation design*. We also have to consider more micro-level aspects and organise the work to be done by the working people like employees – as individuals and also as structured into different groups (like sections, departments, teams, etc). In this regard the concern is how the 'work systems' of organisations are designed. Included in this will obviously be the way HRM work is designed, or how we organise and structure the work in relation to the management of the human resources of organisations.

5.2.1 What work design generally involves and related terminology

Work design, broadly speaking and from a strategic perspective, revolves around decisions about organising the work systems of organisations. It refers to the way work activities are grouped and structured or organised into the different work categories, roles, tasks, responsibilities and so forth – organising everything that is required to get the work of the organisation done. In this regard, Boxall and Purcell (2008: 112) say that decisions about work systems "involve choices about what work needs to be done, about who will do it, and about where and how they will do it". This boils down to grouping work and work roles into clusters like positions, and other work units such as teams and sections or departments. It thus covers the actual work content, the relations between different work roles and the flow of work as well as the technologies involved in the work and the competencies or capabilities required of those who must do the work.

A fundamental work design decision relates to which work is regarded as being at the core of the business of the organisation, and which is really more support work or even perhaps more peripheral (as also mentioned in the previous chapter). For the core work of the organisation in particular, the work roles are typically structured into positions or jobs. These can range from full-time permanent (or ongoing) positions, to part-time and fixed, short-term positions. Designing such positions is also referred to as *job design*. As we explained in the previous chapter, important HRM strategy decisions also connect directly with the core and non-core work of organisations. As such, the work design decisions are intertwined with the more overarching HRM strategy decisions.

When it is decided that certain areas or aspects of the work of an organisation are not part of its core work, it is likely that job design will generally not be important for these. The required outputs of the work and the concomitant potential arrangements for making use of alternatives like outsourcing and labour brokers will be more important. The providers of the labour service will then have to design the jobs of the people who will have to perform the work. In organisations the core work is, however, typically subject to further job-design decisions.

Job design is how one puts together a particular work role in terms of a particular position – what work or tasks are to be performed, how these are to be performed, the work technology involved, what authority and responsibilities go along with the position and what types of people (with what competencies – knowledge, skills, abilities and other attributes) will be required to execute such a work role (occupy such position).

If the point of departure is the requirement that the organisation must perform well (be efficient and effective), the aim of job design is to cluster work activities, tasks and responsibilities and so forth in ways that could facilitate appropriate on-the-job performance by job incumbents (or jobholders). Although the basis of job design is an analysis of what work needs to be done, the important consideration is how the work could be best organised to facilitate optimal work performance by job incumbents.

Job analysis (which is discussed in greater detail in chapter 6) is the systematic process of collecting information about primarily existing jobs or positions, and exploring the activities of particular jobs. When jobs or positions are being redesigned, job analysis thus becomes particularly relevant.

Whereas work and job design decisions are more longer term and strategic by nature, job analysis can be also be more operational and shorter term. From time to time it may be necessary to do job analysis on some positions, especially when there might have been some incremental shifts or changes in the work over a period due to, for instance, technology changes. Job design decisions are supposed to be aligned with certain strategic options decided on (as per chapter 4) and hence the intentions are long term. On the basis of the core ideas or the particular HRM strategies, the type or form of job design adopted will be decided upon. Again we must stress that a 'variegated' approach is very relevant because not all work and all jobs are driven by the same strategies. While some of the jobs, in particular those related to the core work of the organisation, could be designed in ways that align with the asset, investment and empowerment orientation (higher individualism – see chapter 4), it may well be that for some of the support work the jobs may be designed to be more aligned with a paternalistic HRM strategy, for instance. It should thus be clear that work design decisions and the HRM strategy decisions are intertwined. One of the key strategic issues and decisions (referred to already in chapter 4) relates to the differentiation between different categories of work.

A POLICY PERSPECTIVE

Our work organisation policy aims to optimise structures and processes of work and the workplace that can integrate the people and technical processes of the business as effectively and efficiently as possible.

The purpose of this policy is to support the design and implementation of appropriate work roles, practices, processes and structures so as to optimally align our overall strategic direction, business unit requirements, and the work potential and aspirations of our people. The overall aim is to support and facilitate superior performance and our company's long-term viability.

5.2.2 A fundamental work design decision: core and non-core work differentiation

In chapter 4 as well as above we emphasised the fact that there will generally be different segments or categories of work and working people in organisations.

In figure 5.1 we provide a matrix based on two dimensions, and as such reflecting four strategic design options of the overall work system of organisations, based on differentiating between different kinds of work-related needs of the organisation. These two dimensions reflect the strategic importance (core business work versus non-core work) of the work on the one hand, and the ongoing (or otherwise) need for such work on the other. Others use different dimensions for differentiation and categorisation. The idea is once again to use this as a conceptual guide for our thinking and decisions about longer-term work design in organisations.

According to such a categorisation we thus find that the *core work* of the organisation would be of strategic importance, and the need for such work would be ongoing. The high value of this work thus lies in the fact that it is at the very core of the organisation's business or competitive strategy. There must hence be some 'work design strategy' or approach for such core work, which we would like to favour as an *empowerment strategy*. This will thus be directly aligned with high individualism and the four empowering HRM strategy options, as covered in the previous chapter. The overall way of managing employees in this segment might thus be to empower them so that they can excel and yield superior work performance and outputs that add direct and real value to the organisation's strategic direction and competitive advantage. In a large consulting firm like KPMG this would typically be the work of the professionally qualified consultants. Note that here we are talking about employees, because, as reflected in figure 5.1, we integrate these people into the organisation

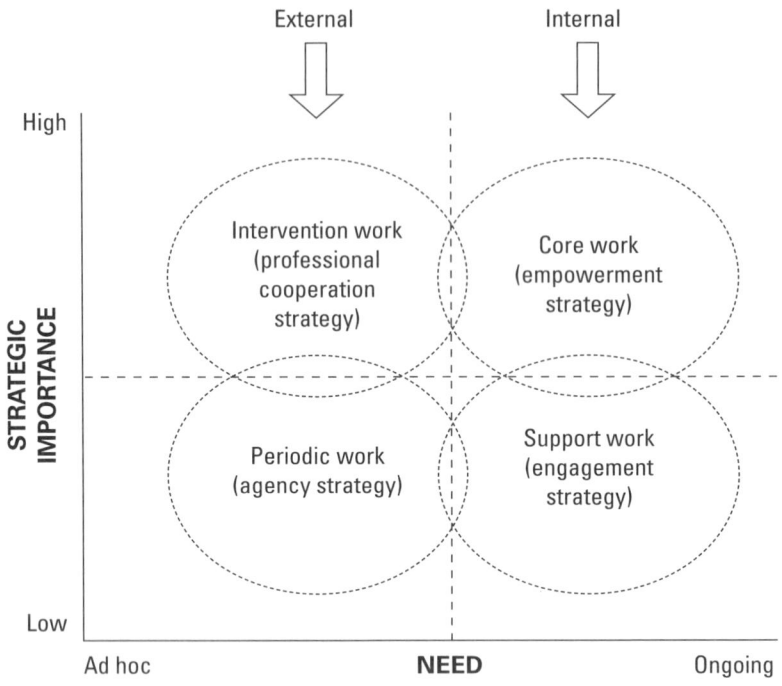

Figure 5.1: Strategic work design options: work and workforce differentiation

through establishing employment relationships that are intended to be long term and ongoing.

For work needs that are equally ongoing by nature even though not of such strategic significance (not direct, core business-type work, or just not making such high-value contributions to the core business operations), we still need to establish employment relationships and hence we refer to this as an *engagement strategy* for our *support work*. At KPMG we can think of the administrative and secretarial support staff in this regard. While we typically engage people to do this work as effectively and efficiently as possible on an ongoing basis, the actual design principles for this work segment will typically be less driven by principles of high individualism and empowerment. It might well reflect some of these elements, but there will be more ingredients of paternalistic 'HRM recipes' (again, refer to chapter 4).

Sometimes we may need to have some work done that really is of great importance and hence strategically significant, but we only need it for a certain fixed period of time at some stage. The need for such work is hence typically not ongoing. We may, for instance, need some market intelligence in order to help us make strategic decisions like repositioning the business or perhaps entering overseas markets which we have not done before. That might be when we seek some external party to come and work with us and help with making that decision – typically engaging a consulting firm that provides expert services in respect of, for example, market research and intelligence. The people working for these firms thus intervene and give strategically significant input, and in that way work with us to enhance our competitiveness – and then they leave. We call this *intervention work* and making use of a *professional cooperation strategy*.

It may also be that from time to time we need work to be performed that is not of such a high-impact nature. We can then thus make use of external agents who can provide us with such people to do the work on a temporary basis (here we think of labour brokers or temporary employment services organisations, for instance). We call this *periodic work* and an *agency strategy*.

This is one way of conceptualising strategic choice for differentiation when it comes to work design. Note that the framework reflects overlap and some fluidity rather than rigid or fixed boxes. It is meant to be a conceptual tool to aid in our strategic thinking and decision making based on some form of differentiation. There is also the need, however, and as explained in chapter 4, to synchronise and have appropriate coherence in terms of the HRM strategies we develop – even if only per different work segment. It is furthermore likely that there will be shared elements across different strategies and work categories even though there may also be key differences. Note also that the fluidity includes exchange possibilities, such as using an agency strategy for some support work.

5.2.3 Variables and principles of work and organisation design

Different structural variables come into play in the process of designing the work of organisations, including the overall design of the organisation (see section 5.4 below). Following are examples of such variables that deserve consideration.

- *Differentiation, division of work and specialisation* refer to the extent to which specific functions and tasks are identified, differentiated, grouped and earmarked for specific individuals or groups to execute. Hitt et al (2007: 228) say that the "main benefit of differentiation is greater specialisation of knowledge and skills". Smit et al (2007: 191) explain that with the division of work "employees have specialised jobs" and that related positions "can then be grouped together … in a functional area such as accounting, administration, marketing …". While these principles of work design thus hold potential benefits, they also bring along with them the need to pull all of these specialised work activities, functions and tasks together.
- *Coordination and integration* are therefore further key principles underpinning the design of work and of organisations. The various work areas, functions and activities are not independent but interdependent rather, requiring measures to bring all of the work in synchronisation. Coordination thus means that the interplay between various work facets must be facilitated and all the work of the organisation (and/or parts thereof) must be integrated and channelled towards organisational goal achievement.
- *Formalisation and standardisation* concern the extent to which work processes and decision-making are formalised and required to be executed in uniform ways, enforcing the use of, for example, official rules, regulations, policies, standard operating procedures, highly detailed written job or position descriptions and similar official documentation. Smit et al (2007: 191) explain that the purpose of standardisation "is to develop a certain level of conformity", which can hence be regarded as a way of intermediating with the uncertainties confronted in any work environment. Through some appropriate measures of standardisation and formalisation, more certainty can be created in terms of certain decisions and work processes, but it should likewise be noted that standardisation can reduce, for example, discretion and initiative in work and organisations. Take note also that it is not only through formalisation that standardisation is brought about, but also through various informal practices that, over time, create custom in the work environment. This is where things like 'unspoken rules' may come in.
- *Managerial configuration* concerns the nature and form of the 'management work system' of an organisation. It relates to how the managerial work within

the organisation is structured and revolves around aspects such as authority, responsibility and accountability, as well as lines of reporting and delegation. It thus also involves the nature of managerial hierarchy in the organisation and as such we find that issues such as the number of levels in the hierarchy, the chain of command and the horizontal and vertical span of control of different levels of managerial positions come into play. A key aspect is thus also the degree of centralisation or decentralisation – the extent to which the power and authority to make decisions is delegated throughout the various levels of the organisational structure.

As can be gathered, these variables hold important implications for how we design the work of individuals as well as groups, and also how we structure the organisation overall. Job design decisions certainly will be influenced by variables such as these, and we now turn to some more detailed aspects pertaining to job design.

5.2.4 Job design: dimensions, approaches and issues

When it comes to job design decisions, a number of job dimensions or characteristics have to be considered within the context of the relevant strategy. In terms of the job characteristics model of Hackman and Oldham (1975), these include, for example, job depth, task range and relationships.

- *Job depth* refers to the extent to which the holder of a particular job or position will be granted the necessary discretion to influence the activities and outcomes of that job. It relates to the level of built-in complexity in the particular job or position.
- *Task range* has to do with the number of different tasks that make up a particular job or position. This relates more to the breadth of the variety of tasks involved in a particular job or position.
- *Job relationships* in this context, refer to the social and socio-technical aspects of a job in terms of relationship requirements and opportunities linked to a particular position: interpersonal work-related relationships, as well as relationships between the technical side of the job (the technology) and the jobholder.

The greater the job depth, the more autonomy the jobholder will have; the greater the job range, the wider the range of activities, tasks or decisions a jobholder will be expected to perform – that is, the greater the variety. Closely related is the job characteristics model of Hackman and Oldham (1975) who developed the "Job Diagnostic Survey". This contains measures of core job characteristics or dimensions, linked to the critical psychological states of workers, which in turn are linked to certain personal and work outcomes. The model recognises that the relationships between the core job characteristics and the psychological states of individuals are moderated by each individual worker's "growth-need strength" – in other words, each person's need for accomplishment, to learn, grow, develop and be challenged by work content.

The core job characteristics are skill variety, task identity, task significance, autonomy and feedback (see exhibit 5.1).

The three critical psychological states are *experienced meaningfulness*, *responsibility* and *knowledge of results*. The first state has to do with the degree to which the jobholder experiences the work as worthwhile, important and valuable. Responsibility is the extent to which jobholders feel responsible and accountable for the outcomes of their work. The last psychological state refers to the extent to which the jobholder knows and understands how well he or she is performing the job on a regular basis.

EXHIBIT 5.1: The core job characteristics

■ *Skill variety* refers to the extent to which a job requires the jobholder to possess a number of different skills, talents, abilities, competencies, etc.

■ *Task significance* refers to the extent to which a job can be viewed as important and as having an impact on others within as well as outside the organisational environment.

■ *Task identity* refers to the extent to which a job requires the jobholder to complete a whole piece of work from beginning to end with a visible outcome.

■ *Autonomy* is essentially the extent to which a job allows or requires the jobholder to control his or her own work. Discretion and freedom to make decisions independently with regard to the way work is to be carried out thus form a part of this characteristic.

■ *Feedback* is the extent to which a job itself provides the jobholder with clear, unambiguous information about work performance and its outcomes.

According to this model, a job which is designed in such a way as to allow the jobholder to experience all three of the critical psychological states will generally lead to higher internal work motivation, higher work satisfaction, higher-quality work, and lower absenteeism and turnover – but only if there is also adequate satisfaction with the work environment (for example working conditions and supervision), and if the job characteristics and the jobholder's abilities and needs are matched.

5.2.4.1 The traditional mechanistic approach to job design: simplification and specialisation

Decisions about job design have long been profoundly influenced by the principles of scientific management, laying the foundation for a very mechanistic form of work design. The key figure in this movement was Frederick W Taylor. Taylor believed that mental and manual work ought to be separated. He also believed in work specialisation. Management, according to him, should specialise in the planning, organisation and control of the work, while workers should actually do the work. He also proposed that complex jobs performed by individual workers should be broken down and fragmented into their most simple component parts. He argued that, in this way, workers would become more efficient and productive in their performance of a limited range of simple, repetitive and, routinised task activities – if they knew exactly what to do, how to do it ('one best way'), if the workplace/shop floor and the tools and equipment layout were such that unnecessary movements were minimised, and if they were given above-average rewards for their performance.

A clear-cut division of labour and the fragmentation and simplification of jobs were thus proposed. A split between conception and execution of work was advocated, with management monopolising the conception work and with the emphasis falling on simplifying the execution part that is left to the workers.

This form of work organisation can be contextualised in the rise of the era of mass production and so-called Fordism. Taylorist narrow job descriptions and the division of labour are often associated with Fordist mass-production setups characterised by assembly lines, short-cycle jobs and standardised products. Taylorism (or scientific management principles) and Fordism (or mass-production systems) are thus often seen to go hand in hand. In these mass-production systems, an important requirement is consistent disciplined performance by workers in the execution of their repetitive and simple tasks. The work efforts and behaviour of individual employees are thus closely monitored. Management clearly specifies work performance requirements, leaving little scope for workers to make decisions related to their work; because the tasks are simple and repetitive, little skill and discretion are required. The main emphasis is on the monitoring activities of managers or supervisors, with centralisation and concentration of authority and decision making, leaving very little scope for job flexibility.

Although such forms of work design may be appropriate from certain perspectives in certain circumstances (such as when large numbers of standardised products are manufactured), a great deal of criticism has been levelled against this type of work design over the years. Specialisation facilitates faster work and requires fewer skilled people to do the work. This means that fewer resources have to be devoted to expensive and time-consuming training, which results in lower-paid work and greater ease in replacing workers. In the case of assembly work, specialisation may reduce work in progress and transformation time, it may require less space and it can simplify control over the production process. All of this may facilitate cost savings and greater profitability – especially over the short term. From the perspective of the employee, however, (and, over the longer term, probably also the organisation), many potentially negative aspects can be identified. Work can become pretty meaningless, boring and monotonous. This can lead to feelings of apathy, carelessness and overall dissatisfaction. Extreme fragmentation and simplification of work may lead to deskilling and to the so-called degradation and dehumanisation of work. Work alienation may follow – an experience of estrangement from one's work or job – which, in the long run, may mean uncommitted, disloyal and uninterested workers. This may impact adversely on labour productivity, with symptoms such as tardiness, poor timekeeping, and high absenteeism and labour turnover rates. Instead of eliciting commitment, all sorts of measures to ensure that workers comply with the requirements of the job and to regulate and control the labour process may thus become necessary.

These and other criticisms have caused management and behavioural scientists to experiment and search for new, more modern approaches to job design, often referred to in general terms as 'work redesign'.

5.2.4.2 Work redesign: horizontal work restructuring

The concept of work redesign can be interpreted from a general or specific perspective. Generally speaking it refers to the trend towards new forms of work organisation. In this regard, reference is often made to the so-called post-Fordist era or new-Fordism in the manufacturing world.

In specific terms, *work redesign* may be taken to refer to those instances where management reconsiders the way in which (aspects of) the labour process is organised or structured in an organisation. This is also often referred to (especially in trade union circles) as 'work restructuring'.

Work redesign does not simply mean altering a job description: it may involve a large-scale, fundamental re-engineering of the overall labour process, or of a substantial component of it. Whereas job design in the true sense of the word refers to the first instance when a job is created by management, work redesign means the reshaping of the way people (including, in particular, employees) have to work. In this sense, work redesign can be thought of as changing job design patterns – often on a large scale. From the perspective of strategic decision making (see previous chapter), the switch from one HRM strategy to another may in all probability require concomitant decisions about the redesign of work.

One form of work restructuring revolves around the actual jobs or positions in organisations, and is aimed at broadening the range of the tasks undertaken by jobholders, while not tampering with the complexity and level of difficulty of the activities involved in these jobs. In this way the requisite activities relating to a particular job are increased, with a concomitant increase in the range of skills required by jobholders. Two of these forms of work redesign are job rotation and job enlargement, both essentially aimed at reducing, for example, monotony and boredom. Both these approaches entail some form of multiskilling in the sense that jobholders will require an increasing number of different skills, although not higher-level skills.

Job rotation

This is the practice of rotating workers from job to job without disturbing workflow, while the different jobs are still narrowly defined. Since the jobs include different tasks and activities, jobholders are exposed to a greater variety of job content, which should lead to a reduction in boredom, fatigue and errors, thus improving job satisfaction and, hopefully, productivity. Rather than redesigning a particular job's content, work is restructured in such a way that workers move from job to job. This is why some critics of this form of work restructuring refer to job rotation as little more than the performance of several monotonous and boring jobs instead of only one, calling it 'pseudo job redesign'.

Job enlargement

Another form of work reorganisation (where task depth remains unchanged but with an increase in task range) is to increase the number of different tasks and duties but to retain the same level of task complexity. This is, in effect, almost the opposite of dividing work or fragmenting it. The number of tasks, activities and duties is increased, and it can thus be seen as a form of de-specialisation in the sense that a job that used to consist of, say, six tasks is redesigned by adding five more tasks (which were previously grouped with other jobs) at the same level of depth. Job enlargement is often equated to multitasking.

5.2.4.3 Increasing job depth through job enrichment: vertical job redesign

Much of the traditional criticism against scientific management was born out of the human relations movement. It was alleged that mass-production techniques and associated efforts towards job fragmentation did not pay enough attention to the socio-psychological needs of workers. Scientific management was deemed to lack the human focus in that it was said to be focused solely on the technicalities of production systems with the aim of creating efficient ways of working. The human relationists alerted management scientists to the fact that the focus should be shifted to human needs, to the employee, employee behaviour and human relations in the work environment. Focusing only on money and sufficient rest was deemed not to be enough. It was argued that work had become meaningless for those who had to execute it and that the humanisation of work was necessary. This required, inter alia, a focus on the worker as a social being.

Elton Mayo was probably one of the first of the leading figures in the human relations movement to draw attention towards workers' social needs. In his view it was important for those who designed work to pay thorough attention to the individual worker's need to experience a sense of belonging, to be able to interact meaningfully with others and to engage in social processes of worthwhile information exchange. It was regarded as important to show employees that management cares by listening to their personal problems and by emphasising the importance of each individual employee in the organisational community or family.

What followed was an era in which the focus of management science research shifted to the needs of human beings and how they could be motivated in the work situation by designing work environments to address their needs. One prominent researcher in this field was the American psychologist, Abraham Maslow, who came up with his hierarchy of human needs. Another prominent figure was Fred Herzberg who devised the so-called two-factor theory of motivation. According to Herzberg (see chapter 9 for more details in this regard), one had to distinguish between hygiene and motivational factors. The former, if attended to in work design, prevent the worker from being unhappy, whereas the motivators, if present, actually enhance satisfaction, better work performance, etc. This led to the conclusion that work had to be redesigned in such a way that 'motivators' were built into jobs, and this meant that jobs had to be enriched.

Job enrichment thus focuses on increasing job depth by giving employees more discretion, autonomy, responsibility and control over their work.

The foundation of this form of work redesign is the individual's need for development and personal growth, taking into account aspects (such as challenging work) that can facilitate a sense of achievement in the worker. This could be facilitated by redesigning jobs so that tasks and task elements (which had previously been fragmented) could be combined into whole and meaningful pieces of work. Enriched jobs will usually require incumbents to be retrained. In this way, the employee would not only improve and receive direct feedback regarding his or her work performance through the work itself, but job enrichment would normally also lead to greater job satisfaction, a better utilisation of potential and talent, and ideally also to better earnings.

5.2.5 Ergonomic issues in work design: some brief notes

De Cieri et al (2005: 190) explain that the 'biological approach' to job design comes from the sciences of occupational medicine, biomechanics (the study of body movements) and work physiology.

Ergonomics concern the interface between an individual jobholder's physiological and psychological features and the physical work environment. As Muchinsky et al (2005: 4) explain, ergonomics are about designing the "work environment to be compatible with human skills and talents", and some also refer to this as 'engineering psychology' or 'human factors psychology'. The basic idea is to structure the physical work environment around the way in which human bodies function.

Ergonomic principles are especially useful in the process of (re)designing aspects of work like physical work space, furniture, equipment, machinery and other technological features. In short, it can be said that principles of ergonomics can be used to design and redesign the physical work environment on the basis of the human characteristics that employees possess. It is an important component of work design and can have quite an impact on the health and well-being of working people, including their levels of fatigue, energy and productivity. In the light of the current drive towards all sorts of organisational flexibility (see section 5.2.6 below), work design may well also include aspects pertaining to the elements of flexibility in, for example, furnishings and adaptability of work space. Designing office chairs and desks, for instance, to be adjustable in terms of height and reach, and to suit different body postures all form part of the ergonomic principles involved in work design.

5.2.6 Some contemporary work design challenges: flexibility, outsourcing and work systems for 'high performance'

The first real large scale efforts to restructure work, as we have mentioned, were founded in classic, industrial-engineering thinking. Frederick W. Taylor was instrumental in this, and he was concerned with production or operational efficiency – the aim was to make work as simple as possible so that people could be trained quickly and easily to perform it 'the one best way' (to maximise operational efficiency). This 'way' was engineered by making use of time and motion studies to determine the most efficient worker movements and actions in the process of work execution. The focus was on the 'mechanistic' and 'technocratic' side of things. Boxall and Purcell (2008: 113–115) explain the essence hereof and how Taylor, together with Henry Ford I, were the fathers of this wave of work reorganisation:

> [W]ith its analysis of the massive efficiency gains to be achieved by the detailed division of labour, factory owners … were taking advantage of new mechanised processes … to create radically new forms of work organisation … The mental models of the early factory owners about the way work should be organised became the standard or 'default' model for the design of work … [M]anagers did the thinking and directing while workers were required to obey instructions and mind the machines … What Taylor advocated and Ford put into practice was the application of more rigorous work measurement processes and the ruthless division of responsibility between management and labour …

The next efforts to reorganise work started to develop from research-informed arguments that Fordist mass production and Taylorist work techniques did not take into account changes in the environment since the era of 'mass production', and that too little attention was paid to the human side of work. As Boxall and Purcell (2008: 117–118) aptly explain: "New ideas did emerge on how to boost productivity through enhancing worker autonomy and job scope and thus reducing boredom and repetitive tasks … [I]n the 1950s, theory developed on 'socio-technical work systems' … psychologists laid increasing emphasis on ways of enhancing employee discretion and increasing responsibility through 'job enrichment' … seen to improve satisfaction with the work itself and thus employee commitment."

Increased environmental turbulence and volatility, globalisation and intensified competition, the information technology revolution and shifting customer expectations were, however, increasingly being put forward as key reasons for the move to a post-industrial/post-Fordist (also referred to by some as the post-bureaucratic) paradigm of work organisation. It is worth quoting the same authors explaining that it was only in the 1970s that the mental models of management about the organisation of work

> … really started to change … the impetus for sustained changes to work systems had much more of its origin in serious *competitive* challenges … Japanese manufacturing firms began to show they had mastered a new form … which delivered better quality … at lower prices … [and] adopted ways … that reduced wasteful stock levels and involved workers (and not simply managers) in enhancing production quality … [I]t created higher levels of skill and identification with company goals … [M]ethods of 'lean manufacturing' … and 'total quality management' … began to take their toll … by the way in which quality improvements could reduce waste and costs … Unchanged, the old forms of work organisation could become a source of competitive disadvantage … transformed to focus more on quality and on more flexibility [and they] had the potential to contribute to competitive advantage in a way unimaginable in the 1960s (Boxall & Purcell 2008: 118–119).

The focus has thus now shifted to flexibility, and a key issue is the employee as a human being who has much more to offer than being programmed in a robot-like fashion as an extension of the machine. The shift, also referred to by some as one of moving from the 'machine age' to the 'information' and 'knowledge age', is seeing increasing emphasis on the human capabilities related to knowledge, learning and improvement of competencies. Naturally, therefore, aspects like the capabilities, needs and behavioural aspects pertaining to human resources now become more prominent drivers in the way work and organisations are being designed.

In the light of external pressures on organisations to become more adaptive, flexible and agile – quick to respond to the world of global business and competition – the trend today is again towards blending the human and the technical-operational side of organisations. The idea is to try to develop a good fit between flexibility in the technology sphere and the flexible utilisation and development of work systems and human capabilities. Whereas in the past the framework was typified by, for example, stability, formal planning, command and control in steep hierarchical and formal structured design types, this is now increasingly changing to features such as instability/chaos, spontaneity/incrementalism, participation/engagement and empowerment in de-layered and more loosely formed network structures that are more informal and flexible. All of this brought to the fore the move towards 'the flexible-firm'. As you will see, differentiation and specialisation principles again play an important part.

Atkinson (1984) came up with the classic, and until today probably the most widely adopted analytical framework of 'the flexible firm'. Figure 5.2 reflects this model which Atkinson and the Institute of Manpower Studies (IMS) developed. This can rather easily be conceptualised in conjunction with section 5.2.2 and figure 5.1 to develop a better sense of the impact of the drive towards flexibilisation of work design and the different ways to configure the workforce of 'flexible' organisations.

The notion of the flexible organisation thus brings along the idea that organisations should 'stick to their knitting' and develop competitive advantage by focusing on their core business, or at least on selected aspects thereof. Non-core business and work, and even some aspects of core work, can then typically be outsourced or subcontracted. As Johnson et al (2008: 459) explain, outsourcing "occurs where organisations decide to buy in services or products that were previously produced in-house". Aligned herewith, Storey (Salaman et al 2005: 197) explains that outsourcing is basically "the externalizing of production and services ... a manifestation of the classic 'make or buy' decision", and that since relatively recently "it has been one of the more popular ways to cut costs and to refocus on core competencies". Interestingly it is added, though, that outsourcing as a phenomenon in work organisation has "as yet, generally found little recognition in the human resource management textbooks" (Storey in Salaman et al 2005: 197).

Making decisions about this form of work organisation means that serious questions must be asked about what the core business of an organisation really is and what core work needs to focused on internally. This in itself can become quite an issue to resolve, as Storey (Salaman, Storey & Billsberry 2005: 197–198) explains, clarifying "just what is core can, however, be problematical. For example, Nike outsources all of its manufacturing; Apple Computers outsources 70 per cent of its components, while GM has outsourced its car body painting activities".

It thus goes beyond a decision as to what is core business/work and what is not. It may well be that some of the core work may be contracted out (blurring boundaries in figure 5.1, for instance) on a periodic or even an ongoing basis (the latter not being captured in the conceptual framework of figure 5.1). Whereas a lot of such outsourcing

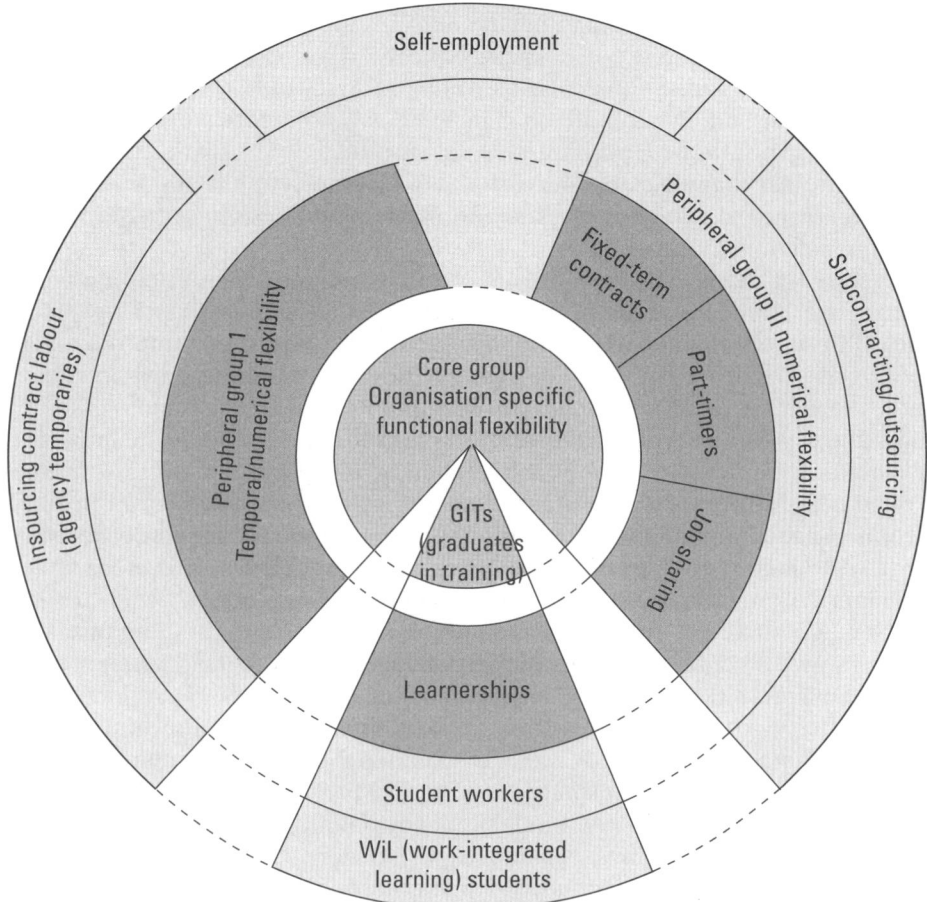

Figure 5.2: The workforce of flexible organisations
Source: Adapted from Magnum & Magnum (1986: 14) in Thompson & McHugh (2002); and Atkinson (1984, 1985)

develops from value chain analyses (see chapter 1) that identify those work activities that do not add direct value to the products/services delivered by the organisation, it can go beyond this to new business models and organisational forms (such as joint venturing and strategic alliances) even. We return to this in section 5.4.

A few decades ago aspects like fleet management, cleaning services, security, facilities maintenance services and food-related services became the initial targets for outsourcing. Later, professional areas of work related to, for example, accounting, legal services and information technology also started to be outsourced, the idea being that those aspects that could be handled more effectively and efficiently by specialists in the fields were better off being subcontracted to these vendors or service providers. Today, as you can understand, some form of externalisation of some core work may thus even be a strategic option in designing the work of an organisation.

We thus find that there has been a mushrooming of organisations that deliver specialised services to client organisations as part of outsourcing (subcontracting) work arrangements, including large accounting firms, legal practices, cleaning companies, security companies, and even marketing and advertising companies. It goes further, though, and, as mentioned, new business models and organisational forms have gained prominence, even encompassing the outsourcing and subcontracting of aspects of the core work of organisations. These typically develop around notions such as forms of network organisations such as joint ventures and strategic alliances (see section 5.4 below) and even entails that in some ways the core work may be shared by different organisations. Hodson and Sullivan (2002: 395) explain that sometimes "the subcontractor manufactures parts that will be incorporated into a final product made by the principal company ... common in the manufacturing of equipment and machinery, including automobiles".

Many of these changes in work organisation mean that careful attention has to be paid to the workflow processes in the value chain and this is where things like just-in-time (JIT) supply chain systems and 'lean manufacturing' come into the equation, as mentioned earlier. Before we elaborate on these, it should be stressed again that it is not uncommon today for organisations, notably in industries such as footwear, clothing and various manufacturing sectors (including automobile, computer and other electronic equipment as well as toy manufacturing), to outsource – frequently even offshore (shifting these to different countries) – entire processes of production work. Shifting such areas of work to other countries is mostly based on decisions to leverage lower labour costs in those countries where labour supply is more abundant and cheaper. As mentioned, these developments in work organisation are largely driven by competitive dynamics. These same pressures have caused organisations to seek other ways of reorganising work internally as well, so that performance can be improved. Several initiatives are relevant in this regard.

Work systems with built-in features of flexibility, collaboration and teamwork, quality improvement and innovation to facilitate high performance and lean production have become increasingly prominent. Much of these can be traced back to the diffusion of practices across international boundaries as markets opened up and multinational corporations became exposed more to different ways of work organisation across national boundaries. Most notably, the West started to learn from Japanese manufacturing companies, mainly in the automobile sector, about superior forms of work design, built around notions such as employee involvement and empowerment, flexibility, and customer and quality orientations (Boxall & Purcell 2008; Salamon et al 2005). Well-known examples include, for example, total quality, lean production and so forth.

Anstey (1995) points out the differences between lean production and mass production. The production focus has shifted from "producer-pushed" to "consumer-pulled" and "customer-choice", to low waste, zero defect, continuous improvement, reduced inventories and other buffers, speed in production and rapid product development. All of this requires new ways of work organisation of which flexibility makes up a core factor.

Cappelli and Rogovsky (1996: 2) summarise the work design implications hereof, as shown in exhibit 5.2.

The approach of lean production is, therefore, not without its critics – especially as far as trade unions in South Africa are concerned. Reference is often made to 'best practice' in this regard (as well as in relation to other aspects), but we believe that context is crucial. Lloyd's work (1994) is a case in point, the issue being that what works in Japanese or other Asian contextual settings may not work as well in South Africa – or elsewhere in Africa, for that matter. Cappelli and Rogovsky admit that these high-performance systems are aimed at 'speed-ups', and Lloyd (1994: 7), like some other critics, refers to it as "management by stress". Lloyd (1994: 7) goes on

EXHIBIT 5.2: Work design implications of high-performance work systems

"The contemporary debate in the US began by identifying 'high-performance' work systems in the context of new production systems. 'Lean' or high-performance production systems were identified and the work systems demanded by them were identified – by definition – as high-performance work.

These production systems are most clearly seen with Japanese manufacturing, and include techniques such as statistical process control, just-in-time inventory systems, continuous improvement and total quality management.

The models of lean production basically argue that increased quality, productivity and flexibility can be obtained by making better use of employees. In particular, responsibility and decision making are transferred from administrative structures directly to employees or to their teams.

These arrangements demand significantly more from employees than do work systems associated with scientific management, where tasks are narrowed and virtually all decision making is in the hands of management.

But it appears that they may demand less than the work systems associated with the behavioural models of work reform. Lean production work systems appear to demand more from workers in the way of stress and effort/work pace than do the behavioural models. They also offer workers substantially less autonomy.

Employee decision making, when it occurs, happens in an aggregated, inter-team setting. The highly regimented tasks of lean production limit individual autonomy, and while they may offer more variety than do work systems governed by scientific management, it is substantially less than that associated with behaviourally based models."

Source: Cappelli & Rogovsky (1996: 2)

to say that those who are proponents of such work systems cannot claim that their organisations are fundamentally better places to work at.

Aligned herewith, Desai (1997) and Hirschohn (1998) refer to how work reorganisation – and in particular into the lean management mode of work – has had an impact on people and work in the South African motor industry. Desai (1997: 41), for example, explains as follows:

> Post-apartheid South Africa's increased exposure to the global economy, facilitated by the lowering of tariffs, has raised the spectre of international competition. This challenge to South Africa's economy has witnessed employers being preoccupied with work reorganisation in a bid to increase productivity. Particular attention has been focussed on the notion of lean production ....

He goes on to illustrate that in numerous cases (in Europe, North America and the UK, for instance), part of the general trend towards 'lean production' has included: "... to totally eradicate, or at least curtail, the influence of trade unions .... Allied to this strategy is the siting of plants where labour is abundant and job opportunities limited ... thereby enabling such organisations to exploit workers" (Desai 1997: 44).

If we take a look at these developments through more analytical and even some critical-thinking lenses, we might very well therefore have to regard, for example, lean management, and accompanying systems and processes like JIT and concomitant aspects of work design like outsourcing and offshoring, with a healthy dose of circumspection. It is our view that any organisation – in South Africa at least – should not consider adopting a lean management or other flexible approach which alienates the labour force and/or their trade unions. The ways in which such work reorganisation issues should be considered ought to be aligned with HRM grand strategies that are more towards the high-collectivism dimension – especially where trade unions are present/involved (see chapter 4). We also specifically encourage an open mind when these design options are considered, always being prepared to see things from a different angle. We cannot stress it enough that context is crucial – and we live and work in Africa. It may thus be useful to consider the views of some who are more critical of some of these developments. In this regard Godard and Delaney (2000: 482–485), for example, address the drive towards high-performance work systems, and explain as follows:

> According to this paradigm, new work and human resource management practices have replaced unions and collective bargaining . . . [with] more cooperative labor-management relations . . . among other things . . . competitive pressures induced managers to rethink their IR/HRM values and beliefs. This led to the adoption of new policies and strategies aimed at enhancing competitiveness by supplanting the adversarial 'job control' model of unionism . . . with a more co-operative and participative one. As it has evolved, the new model of management contains many work and HRM innovations, including flexible work assignments, cross-training, team work sustained by performance-based pay, formal worker participation ... [T]he new paradigm ... views management as the primary actor in the employment relationship ... [T]he new paradigm also generally supports labor law reforms that ensure union participation in the adoption of new work and HRM practices ... [T]hey tend to downplay the role that collective bargaining has traditionally had ... focusing instead on alternative forms of work organization ... In effect, new work and HRM practices are viewed as best practice ... and collective bargaining is seen as second-best.

They go on to critically analyse the implications and point out that, even from a purely theoretical angle, slavishly following any such approaches and accepting these as normative models of best practice without any form of critical assessment may be less than what is required. We concur with this, especially from a South African (and African) perspective, and we favour a more balanced and pragmatic approach. In this regard we again wish to stress that it will be important to integrate these work-design decisions into an overall HRM strategy decision framework – such as the one provided in chapter 4. All strategic decisions are, fundamentally, supposed to be rooted in contingency thinking. In a country like South Africa where trade unions generally are so prominent, work redesign towards systems akin to the lean production, high-performance and flexible models will in all likelihood be better explored as part of an approach whereby trade unions are fully engaged and on board.

In the redesign of work, a host of factors must thus be taken into account. One crucial consideration, as mentioned a number of times already, relates to the notion of work and workforce flexibility, aimed at enhancing organisational agility in an era of hyper-competition. Flexibility within the context of work can take on various forms, including functional, temporal and numerical flexibility.

Functional flexibility refers to multi-tasking and multiskilling so that workers can be more mobile and adaptable in order to undertake a much broader range of tasks. Thompson and McHugh (2002: 158–159) explain as follows:

> Core workers gain greater job security for managers' right to redeploy them between activities and tasks as ... production requires ... [A]ny increased focus on a core workforce is likely to enhance the need for training and retraining ... Surveys reveal that senior managers believe that there has been a significant in-

crease in these kinds of functional flexibility … The most extreme, such as those at Nissan and at Sony, specify complete flexibility, even to the point of managers and clerical staff working on the production line if necessary … mostly directed towards removing 'barriers' between grades and categories … by merging production grades or ensuring job rotation … [A] crucial goal of 'multiskilling' has been the erosion of distinctions between production and other categories such as indirect, maintenance and even craft work … creating flexible craftsmen or 'crafticians' by focusing on the interfaces between crafts, non-crafts, craft assistants, supervisors, and other trades … [G]rowth of teamworking has facilitated functional flexibility …

Temporal flexibility has to do with various patterns of work hours – how the time of working people is being arranged and utilised. Work can be structured in such a way that employees are required to work shifts, for instance. Provision can also be made to allow for part-time work, temporary work, job sharing or even home-working (see 'A case at hand' about Vodacom's approach).

A CASE AT HAND

Flexible work design as differentiating strategy? Towards homeworking at Vodacom

"What truly differentiates Vodacom as an employer … is its focus on work/life balance. Vodacom is currently designing a programme to allow employees to work from home."

Source: Corporate Research Foundation (CRF South Africa 2007: 28)

Temporal flexibility also typically includes, for example, flexitime working (varying the hours when working any day/week/month). Bartol et al (2008: 413) explain that flexitime "specifies core hours when people must be on the job, with flexible starting and finishing times as long as required total hours are worked". This goes along with what is referred to also as 'alternative work schedules', "setting schedules that favour workforce flexibility by balancing work and personal life … help[ing] workers juggle work and family responsibilities … Flexitime, compressed work weeks and job sharing are three major alternative work schedules … Flexitime results in improved employee morale, working parents' needs being accommodated, and reduced lateness and traffic congestion as some workers avoid peak times" (Bartol et al 2008: 413). Exhibit 5.3 reflects an example of such a policy.

Numerical flexibility concerns allowing for variety with regard to the size and structure of the workforce. Making use of temporary staff or subcontracting or outsourcing work are forms of numerical flexibility. Thompson and McHugh (2002: 160) explain quite strikingly: "This is the capacity to vary the headcount according to changes in the level of demand so that there is an exact match between the numbers needed and employment; or as one senior manager bluntly put it, 'A workforce that can be picked up and put down whenever I need them' …".

The extent to which workplace flexibility has been implemented in 626 mostly manufacturing organisations in South Africa was investigated more than a decade ago by Horwitz and Franklin (1996). They found that at the time, flexibility in South African organisations was occurring most commonly in the numerical category. Other elements of numerical flexibility practised include the use of temporary agencies, contractors and consultants. Most organisations have increased their use of contractors

Policy: Flexitime policy
Section: Section AC3
Manual: HRM Policies Manual

Aim

This policy provides a framework for the implementation and maintenance of flexible working arrangements for designated employees, as set out in (1) below, and as such it is aimed at simultaneously facilitating greater balance in work/personal life of staff and at meeting the work needs of XYZ in a more flexible manner.

1 SCOPE AND APPLICATION

This policy document describes the flexitime system to be utilised by Company XYZ and it applies to all employees employed on a full-time, permanent basis that are not required to work in the call centre or warehouse, or are not responsible for the opening and closing of retail outlets. Customer service sites are specifically excluded from working flexitime, as are staff rostered to work on a shift basis.

2 DEFINITIONS

2.1 Flexitime – employees work during a common core time period each day, but have discretion in forming their own workday from a flexible set of hours outside the core time.

2.2 Core time – time period each day during which all employees must work.

2.3 Eligible employees – all employees employed on a full-time, permanent basis that are not required to work in the call centre or warehouse, or are not responsible for the opening and closing of retail outlets. Customer service sites are specifically excluded from working flexitime requirements.

3 PRINCIPLES

3.1 The onus is on each team to self-manage implementation to ensure a balanced distribution of time/resources.

3.2 Flexible working arrangements are allowed subject to the satisfactory execution of assigned work, ie individuals are expected to put in the time necessary to execute the requirements of their posts.

3.3 The Company retains the right to, at any time, reasonably require any employee to work during flexible hours.

3.4 If an employee fails to maintain a satisfactory pattern of attendance or abuses the flexitime system, he or she may be directed to work standard office hours. It is also possible that disciplinary action may be taken.

3.5 Eligible employees who work to a flexitime system are reminded that first priority is the maintenance of effective service to the Company, the community and the public. During flexible time periods, sufficient employees must be available to keep offices open during standard office hours of 08:00 to 17:30. Therefore there must be cooperation between staff, as well as sound administrative supervision.

4 RESPONSIBILITIES

4.1 The human resources manager has overall responsibility for the implementation and maintenance of the flexitime system.

4.2 The senior administrator is responsible for the capture and compilation of records required by this procedure.

4.3 Designated team coordinators are responsible for coordinating and controlling system implementation and maintenance at operational level.

>>

5 PROCEDURE

5.1 The workday shall be structured as follows:

Flexible hours	Core time	Flexible hours
07:30 – 09:30	09:30 – 14:30	14:30 – 17:30

5.2 Each employee must work a minimum of 45 hours per week, during which the employee must at least work during core times each day.

   5.2.1 **NOTE:** This schedule excludes lunch periods.

5.3 The flexitime system shall run on a two-week cycle basis, that is, over a fortnight an employee must be at work for a minimum of 90 hours.

   5.3.1 **NOTE:** No carry-over of hours into the next cycle, either positive or negative, is allowed. There will be no salary payment for excess time worked.

   5.3.2 Employees must not work more than five consecutive hours without a meal break of at least 30 minutes.

5.4 Any employee who fails to work the required hours during the fortnight shall be required to do so during the next cycle, and shall potentially be subject to disciplinary action/withdrawal of flexitime privileges, depending on the individual circumstances of each case.

For instances of authorised work absence (eg annual/sick leave/public holidays), the required working hours for the cycle period shall be credited on a pro-rata basis.

   5.4.1 Notification of ill health on any working day must be given before the start of core time, at the latest.

5.5 For control and monitoring purposes, all eligible employees shall be issued with a clock card and use the new clocking system to record starting and finishing times of works and any breaks each day.

5.6 Should eligible employees be required to perform off-premises work which shall not allow them to clock in the usual manner, an approved timesheet shall be submitted for the hours worked and the time clock record amended accordingly.

5.7 Any requirement to work outside the core and flexible hours or over weekends/public holidays shall be subject to prior approval, and double time is to be included in the employee's total hours for the period. In such instances, time off equivalent to twice the period worked may be taken during core time in consultation and agreement with all parties concerned.

6 RECORDS

The human resource administration section shall maintain a central database, summarising total hours worked for each employee during the current cycle period. This record shall be updated on a daily basis.

Source: Adapted from Workinfo: http://www.workinfo.us/Sub/Sub_for_hr/HR/Manual/Section%204%203.doc

and consultants, and it was reported that the use of subcontractors in South Africa showed a steady expansion of about 20% over two decades since the mid-1970s. This trend has in all likelihood continued, following global trends. The next most common type of flexibility was found to be the temporal category, specifically in the use of shifts, and part-time and temporary staff. The use of functional flexibility was found to be evident in methods to save labour costs, such as training, new technologies and concomitant efforts aimed at work reorganisation to facilitate multitasking/skilling.

5.2.7 Criteria for good work systems

Cordery and Parker (2007: 193–194) draw on a number of other sources to come up with six main criteria against which to assess how well we are doing in terms of designing the work systems of organisations. According to them, we need to check:

- the capacity of our work system to generate high levels of work performance and goal achievement of those working within it and the organisation;

- the extent to which the work system develops and delivers the goods efficiently and effectively;
- the degree to which the work system is capable of sustaining and building on human capital and performance capabilities;
- the capability of the work system to successfully adapt to changes in the organisation's strategic direction (eg cost leadership versus differentiation based on innovation) and operating environments (eg economic and labour market changes);
- the extent to which the work system is aligned with the rewards (intrinsic and extrinsic) for those who operate it; and
- the sustainability of the organisation's work system, "in terms of its impact on the physical and psychological health of employees, the degree to which it builds positive social relationships, and effects a healthy work-life balance".

We should keep in mind that how we design the overall work system of an organisation will directly impact on how successful an organisation is going to be. The work system is the heart of the operations of any organisation. Through the work executed by all the working people, value is supposed to be added at each point in the work-flow process. Work is thus structured into a complex system of interconnected value-creating nodes in a chain of work aimed at customer needs satisfaction and serving a purpose in society, while also addressing all other stakeholder needs and interests appropriately. It is important to create the necessary fit at various levels – a fit between the technology and the work, between working people and the work (such as the employees and the positions they come to occupy), between the different work roles, between different groups of work roles and positions (like sections, departments, teams, etc), between the organisation and the outside world, and so forth. The aim is a work system conducive to efficient and effective work execution that facilitates the achievement of the organisation's goals, including customer satisfaction and with due consideration for the impact of all of this on the environment and the value added overall.

5.3 FROM GROUP-BASED WORK TO TEAMWORK AS INCREASINGLY POPULAR WORK DESIGN OPTION

5.3.1 General

As has been indicated already, teams and teamwork form important features of modern approaches to work design and they facilitate numerous potential benefits we can associate with, for example, empowerment and multiskilling, and also flexibility in the work environment. In the process of organising work, consideration must thus also be given to the possibility of creating structures where groups of employees can work as teams.

The modern trend to focus on teams was largely inspired by Japanese forms of work organisation. Very early efforts to structure work along group lines can, however, be traced back to experiential work undertaken by the Tavistock Institute for Human Relations in London, UK, during the late 1940s and early 1950s. This Institute's researchers found that, by emphasising social interaction and communication through the clustering of jobs into work groups, rather than through traditional functional divisions of labour, better work results were achieved. The research that led to these conclusions was conducted in the coal mining, electronics and textile industries. The initial focus was thus on group work.

In reality very little work in organisations is executed outside any group context. Very rarely do individuals perform their work activities in complete isolation. The fact is that work mostly happens in some form of group – be that as part of certain sections, departments, divisions or teams. Rothwell (2007: 32–33) explains that groups are more than a mere collection of individuals, which is more useful to be thought of as an aggregation – because the notion of a group reflects that two or more people interact and influence each other in the process of trying to achieve some common goal. While work in a group context has thus been receiving attention for a long time, the notion of team-based work design is more recent. Not all groups are teams and not all work executed in group context can be typified as teamwork. As Rothwell (2007: 179) explains, while all teams are, per definition, groups, not all groups are teams.

The following four characteristics are offered as distinguishing teams from groups (Rothwell 2007: 179–182):

- Teams are more reliant on members with different but complementary capabilities than what is generally found in standard groups.
- Teams are more reliant on members working together closely and cooperating, due to the principle of collaborative interdependence between all members.
- Teams typically have a stronger group identity than ordinary groups and they operate more as one unit – team goals are fully shared and the driving force.
- While groups generally tend to not focus on the longer term, teams typically have a longer-term shared mental model that requires time and resource commitments of substantial magnitude.

Groups go through various stages in their development and merely clustering certain work roles and activities together does not mean that the group-based work will be successful. During the *forming* stage, different work roles and people who execute them are put together. Sometimes, as in the case when certain work processes are being restructured, and different work roles and people are put together, people may not even appreciate the fact that they are now part of a (new) group. There may even be resistance to becoming part of a certain newly formed group (such as when two sections or departments merge, for instance). It is thus one thing to design work in ways which bring certain people and work roles together, and it is quite another to make groups operate like teams. During the *storming* stage, one can typically find disagreements and conflict between group members, and tensions and emotions often run high. The next phase is commonly known as the *norming* stage and this is when group members become more sensitive towards each other and diverse expectations and viewpoints, realising that balancing these and overarching group objectives is important. There are thus signs of cautious integration. This then typically develops into the *performing* stage, when groups reach much greater levels of maturity. The focus becomes increasingly the common goals and the need to support each other in striving to achieve them. Rothwell (2007) reckons that whenever groups develop and take on all four of the characteristics mentioned earlier, we can say that they really have become teams. The final phase of group development is known as the *adjourning* stage – when groups really disband and cease to exist.

From the perspective of sport we know how crucial teams and teamwork are. The potential value in teams has now also been realised in the world of business, organisations and work. Internationally, teams are now regarded as a form of work structuring that can facilitate greater task flexibility, cooperation, job satisfaction and enhanced work performance, leading to better quality and customer satisfaction. Teams as a work design option do, however, involve a cost factor as well, and in

South Africa in particular, care should be taken as to how this option should be used.

Team-based work design means that making choices about who should be team members become an even greater challenge than when we are recruiting and selecting people for more individually driven job designs. Issues like diversity and complementary profiles become more accentuated – and this relates to hard issues like competencies as well as softer ones pertaining to, for example, cultural diversity and language. Much more effort and resources will have to be devoted to, for instance, communication and developing shared mindsets or mental models about the team goals and norms. A great deal of emphasis must also be put on training and retraining, not only in technical skills pertaining to work but also in social skills revolving around working and functioning as a team. This in itself may be good, especially if fits with an appropriate HRM strategy that is investment and empowerment orientated. It should, however, be realised that training costs money and trained people who leave the company may have to be replaced, which may also prove costly.

The challenges pertaining to team dynamics when new members join should also be recognised. Furthermore, team-based work organisation cannot be executed in isolation: it has implications for broader organisational structuring decisions (see section 5.5 below). Traditional hierarchical structures cannot easily accommodate work structuring along team lines. It is commonly accepted that the jobs of supervisors will be eliminated, or at least redefined to those of team leaders, in cases of team-based work organisation. The retraining of supervisors to fulfil the role of facilitators rather than overseers will thus also be required. It also means that issues such as career, performance, and remuneration and reward management will have to be adapted. It is, for instance, quite unthinkable that a move to a fully-fledged team-based form of work design will work unless there will also be concomitant changes to bring about some forms of team-based remuneration and reward. Dyer, Dyer and Dyer (2007: 6–7) say that "reward systems that provide strong individual incentives often create strong disincentives to engage in cooperative behaviour within a work team … [M]any organizations, while paying lip service to the importance of teamwork, do little to encourage and support those who work in teams … they do not foster a culture in which teams can succeed".

The benefits of a team-based approach, however, (as it is asserted by proponents of this approach) seem to far outweigh the costs. Stott and Walker (1995: 55), and Smit et al (2007: 331) discuss the potential benefits of teams. If correctly used, such an approach may provide both the organisation and the individuals involved with benefits such as the following (there is some potential interplay and overlap):

- reduced duplication of effort;
- reduced costs;
- increased cooperation;
- enhanced innovation;
- better, wiser and more complete decisions;
- more motivated colleagues;
- improved product and service quality;
- higher standards of performance;
- more speed in terms of delivery;
- increased productivity and profits;
- added flexibility to allow easier adaptation to changing circumstances;
- increased commitment to implementation;
- reduced destructive conflict; and
- improved interpersonal and inter-unit relations and communication.

A CASE AT HAND

Teamwork and customer satisfaction at BESTmed

"BESTmed is centred on people, with a high degree of employee participation in decision-making. Teamwork is paramount and is reflected in the high levels of customer satisfaction obtained from participating members."

Source: Corporate Research Foundation (CRF South Africa 2007: 93)

Although it can clearly be seen from the discussion and examples cited that teamwork as a form of work organisation holds the potential to yield many benefits, a decision to restructure work along these lines cannot be taken haphazardly. It is naturally another decision that has to be fully integrated with general strategic decision making. A decision to restructure work along the principles of team-based work design clearly falls within the HRM strategic direction towards high individualism and a grand strategy with an empowerment orientation (see chapter 4). Other very important questions, especially in South Africa, relate to where this leaves management's approach towards the trade unions, and how the trade unions view such forms of work structuring. Because of the important role played by trade unions in South African organisations in general, it is, for instance, hard to imagine how unionised organisations can succeed with restructuring towards teamwork without getting a full buy-in from the worker representatives – most notably trade unions (where relevant). In fact, we believe that where trade unions are involved in organisations in South Africa, teamwork is likely to fail unless it forms part of either an integrative negotiated HRM or a joint governance grand strategy, in most instances.

Exhibit 5.3 gives a clear indication what some of the unions' requirements and concerns are in respect of teamwork.

Before we proceed with a brief overview of different types of teams that can be found in the workplace, it is important to clarify what we mean by 'work team'.

Rothwell (2007: 182) defines a team as "small number of people with complementary skills who act as an interdependent unit, are equally committed to a common mission, subscribe to a cooperative approach to accomplish that mission, and hold themselves accountable for team performance". From this we can now make a slight adaptation to define what we regard as a work team.

A *work team* can be regarded as a group of two or more working people with different but complementary competencies who act as an interdependent work unit, who are equally committed to a common set of work-related goals, who subscribe to an approach of working cooperatively to accomplish these goals, and who hold themselves accountable for their work performance.

As is clear, it is not easy to provide a non-debatable definition of a work team. Part of the underlying reason for this is probably the fact that many different types of teams can be structured within organisations.

5.3.2 Some different types of work teams and groups in organisations

There are different ways of categorising different types of groups or teams. One can, for instance, focus on levels in the organisational structure to distinguish between top management teams, middle-management teams and worker teams (if these are indeed teams and not mere groups). Dyer et al (2007: 21–24) distinguish between three generic types of teams, namely decision teams, task teams and self-directed teams.

Decision teams exist mainly to make decisions about a wide range of possible

EXHIBIT 5.3: Numsa's stance on teamwork

Teamwork is acceptable only if:

■ the union and workers have the right to negotiate production targets, production schedules and line speed;
■ participation in teams is voluntary;
■ management offers no material incentive or preferential treatment to employees who decide to participate in teams;
■ there is no unfair treatment of those workers who refuse to go into teams;
■ team leaders are to be elected on a rotational basis;
■ there is no additional pay or incentive for team leaders;
■ team leaders have no right to discipline workers;
■ there is an entrenched right of the union to represent workers including team leaders on production-related issues;
■ to each team, an absentee-cover or floater is attached – a role that can be played by the team leader;
■ there is no obligation to meet targets if team members are absent;
■ there is full pay for overtime and team meetings;
■ the skills profile of teams combines common and specialised skills; and
■ bona fide negotiations take place with the union on:
  – areas of work for the team
  – team size
  – responsibility of teams
  – the rights and obligations of team members in relation to first-line management.

Source: Jarvis (1998: 32)

issues, including goals, strategies, allocating resources, developing plans and so forth. *Task teams*, although they also make decisions, are there to execute and perform work aimed at accomplishing end results that are aligned with the decisions taken by others (the decision teams) – these are thus, in essence, implementers in a sense. *Self-directed teams* are teams of working people that are left to get on with it without any interference from others, and are also known as autonomous and/or semi-autonomous teams. These teams thus have more authority to decide what to do and to then actually do whatever they deem appropriate in the circumstances. Often, these teams either have no designated team leaders – and so they may rotate this role or they select their own leader/s.

There obviously are other typologies for categorising teams too, and many may overlap. In organisations it is pretty common, for example, to find project teams, task forces and certain standing committees – some of which may show characteristics of any one or more of the three types of teams mentioned above. Problem-solving teams and quality-improvement teams can be seen as types of special-purpose teams which aim to improve the quality of production or operations. We now briefly elaborate on three types of work teams or groups.

Self-directed work teams (SDWTs), also known as self-managed work teams, are usually relatively small groups (6–18) of well-trained workers that are fully responsible for achieving complex goals such as producing entire products.

The SDWT functions autonomously, and the team members themselves decide over control issues like production planning, setting priorities, and assigning work and rest breaks. The members thus share responsibility for setting and attaining the standards of work performance of these teams.

Within SDWTs, role rotation is usually very common. Because members of SDWTs are required to perform a variety of cross-functional tasks, multiskilling is usually a prerequisite. The team members normally all take part in all decision making and there is a very high degree of information exchange. Interpersonal dynamics are intended to be very open and, in cases of team member problems (such as the poor performance of an individual team member, or excessive absenteeism or poor timekeeping), the rest of the team ensures that the behaviour of an individual team member does not deviate from agreed-upon norms.

Problem-solving teams are typically made up of working people who meet frequently for a couple of hours or so each week to search for and explore ways of improving work processes and outputs, including, for example, efficiency, productivity and quality. At City Lodge Hotels, the kitchen staff, for instance, meet on a weekly basis to consider customer complaints, better ways of preparing breakfasts and other meals, the layout of the dining areas, and so forth (Smit et al 2007: 331). In some sense it is debatable whether these can really be typified as teams because often these groups lack the authority to make final decisions about implementing solutions to problems before taking these to management.

Virtual teams or work groups comprise working people who are dispersed (organisationally and/or geographically) and using advanced communication technologies (for example teleconferencing, videoconferencing, computer nets and e-mail groups) to interact and work together to accomplish their shared work-related goals. Taking Rothwell's (2007) criteria or characteristics that typify teams, it is again doubtful that these forms of work design can really qualify to be named teams in the true sense of the word. These working people typically have far less and often no face-to-face interaction and as such cooperation and especially strong identification with the group can be quite daunting. The cooperative aspect of the work can also be challenging especially from the angle of the need to enhance the social dimension of the work. Developing close relations can be left behind due to that lack of personal touch. It may thus well be more appropriate to refer to these as virtual work groups. A potential benefit of these forms of work organisation includes moving "beyond the organisation's traditional boundaries" to build these virtual work groups with members who "can come from other organisations; for example an outsourced supplier" (Bartol et al 2008: 563). While we agree with this perspective, we do not believe that this potential benefit rests exclusively with virtual work groups.

5.3.3 Team-based work design goes way beyond teams as such

As we have emphasised all along, work design is not about decisions regarding the work of some people in isolation. The bigger context is critically important and as such any decisions to go for team-based work design will inevitably have to go way beyond establishing certain teams. Dyer et al (2007) regard this contextual setting as a crucial determinant for the success of designing work along the lines of teams. In particular they refer to the important role of organisational *culture*, *systems* and *structure* in this regard. They explain:

> An organization's culture represents the basic shared values and assumptions held by most people in the organization ... It is critical ... that the shared culture emphasizes that teamwork is essential and that people at all levels get into trouble if they do not collaborate with others and respond readily as members of

the total team. If the culture is either openly or passively resistant to the importance of teamwork, any attempts to foster collaboration, participation or involvement will be seen as either a temporary action or a management manipulation (Dyer et al 2007: 24–25).

About systems, the same authors (Dyer et al 2007: 26) say that

> [P]ay systems, evaluation and promotion systems, decision-making systems, and management information systems are all examples ... It is critical that the systemic aspects of the organization support team development. People encounter major problems in a company that is attempting to build teamwork into an organization when the pay system is based entirely on individual performance, or if the information is given only to individual senior managers rather than all team members.

Structure, according to Dyer et al (2007: 25), refers to "the basic design of the organization", and they explain that "the formal organization structure can encourage and support teamwork, or it can make it much more difficult for teams to form and function effectively". In the next section we now turn to the whole issue of organisational design and structure.

A CASE AT HAND

Work teams at SABMiller plc

South African Breweries is one of the world's lowest-cost brewery facilities and a key component of its strategy to achieve this revolves around the design and development of "world-class manufacturing teams". This included the introduction of new performance measures, the redesign of shop floors, the establishment of work teams and concomitant work practices, the development of new problem-solving skills and the streamlining of supply and distribution work. The work teams at SAB are cross-functional and geared towards resolving problems close to the source and very quickly. There is a strong emphasis on training in technical as well as team problem-solving skills, with a focus on waste elimination and great emphasis on team goal setting. The underlying drive is said to be a drive towards improved quality and manufacturing excellence.

Source: Adapted from Smit et al (2007: 332)

5.4 ORGANISATION DESIGN: TRENDS, ISSUES AND CONSIDERATIONS

Structuring the flow of work throughout the organisation overall will also ultimately mean that decisions must be made about how the organisation as a whole is structured. This is commonly referred to as organisation design. It entails more than structure because processes and systems are also involved – such as in relation to reporting relationships and systems of authority and control. Organisation design ought to be done in a way that aligns the organisational structure and concomitant work processes with the strategic direction of the organisation. Although it still concerns how the work of the organisation is organised, it is in a sense quite removed from the jobs of the working people as such, since it revolves around the way the organisation as a whole is designed. This holds specific implications for relationships between working people because it will, for instance, dictate who will work together and who will form part of what sections of the organisation. As such these decisions are also intertwined with the management of the human resources of organisations. Although a comprehensive discussion of organisation structure and design is beyond the scope of this book, a brief overview of some relevant issues is essential.

5.4.1 Factors that influence organisation design

Designing organisations is a complex matter, not least because so many variables interplay with this task. These include aspects like the type of organisation or the sector in which it operates and exists. The environment is naturally key because the type of industry or sector will have certain characteristics that may not be shared across other sectors or industries. The retail environment is obviously rather different than a police or military context, or a mining environment. The technology is also a key variable, as Bartol et al (2008: 365) explain: "Different organisations need different structures partly due to technology – the knowledge, tools, equipment and work techniques used to deliver a product or service." Naturally, the general nature of the organisational environment pertaining to, for example, stability and uncertainty also play an important part. The more volatile and uncertain, the greater will be the need for more flexible and adaptive structural configurations, in all likelihood.

One can thus expect aspects such as competitive forces and the type of product/ service and the general market environment (including the customer base) to play a key role. Hence it is quite expected that private-sector design will have to factor in issues that might not be the same than in the public sector, for instance. Other aspects include the size of an organisation and also an organisation's stage in its life cycle (for example, whether it is a newly established start-up company, in a growth phase, or in a decline phase, perhaps).

The key thing is that strategy and structure are intertwined. Generally, the factors and variables that can impact on the strategies and strategic choices of organisations, can impact on the organisation design options and choices. There is a broad range of organisation design types, options and choices. Perhaps this may be a bit of an overstatement, but Bolman and Deal (2003: 46) give us something to think about by saying the following: "The alternative design possibilities are infinite, limited only by human preferences and capacities."

5.4.2 Different types of organisation structure and design

There are many ways of categorising different types of organisation design types and structures. Some differentiate design types that revolve around outputs such as the products, services or markets served, versus those that are developed around functions or inputs. We do not follow any particular categorisation approach here, but rather briefly cover some examples of different types of organisation structure and design. Keep in mind that there is scope for overlap, and hybrid design types are quite common.

The *simple design* entails a structure where there is a "low degree of departmentalisation, wide spans of control, authority centralised in a single person ... little formalisation ... [I]t usually has only two or three vertical levels, a loose body of employees, and one individual in whom the decision-making authority is centralised ... most widely practised in small business in which the manager and the owner is one and the same" (Robbins, Judge, Millett & Waters-Marsh 2008: 549). As one can deduct from this, it is a design type that has application in a limited sphere, namely primarily where organisations are small enough. As soon as organisations get bigger and employ more people, and the work demands become more complex, the single decision maker, typically the owner-manager, cannot handle all the complexities and as a result information overload can be a problem. Because there is no managerial delegation, it can be experienced as very disempowering by the people working in such organisations, depending on the style of the manager. It also carries the risk that comes with such extreme form of centralised authority: if the owner-manager becomes very ill suddenly, the work will basically come to a standstill, unless some contingency plans are in place.

Functionally designed organisation structures group positions and roles together according to the traditional managerial functions of organisations. Here, as Bartol et al (2008: 350) say, things are clustered together "on the basis of similarity of expertise, skill and work activity". Similarly, Hodge et al (2003: 197) explain that here the working people "are grouped together on the basis of the functions they perform ... such as production, marketing, finance ...". This is, therefore, a design option that is driven by specialisation and as such it brings with it challenges related to coordination and integration. It can actually quite easily lead to too narrow a focus of organisational units on their respective functions with a lack of cross-functional and organisation-wide perspectives often coming along with that (often referred to as 'silo mentality'). Bartol et al (2008: 351) mention that this type of structure can also often lead to limiting the development of the working people like managers "as they operate within one function and have little knowledge of others". As mentioned earlier, organisations can also be designed around the *products/services* delivered and/or the *customers* and/or *markets* served. The latter might typically include geographical structures such as having organisational units responsible for all the work related to serving specific regions. This is also where the *divisional* organisation design types can come in (this is discussed below). It is quite common to find combinations where organisations are designed with aspects of functional as well as product/customer/market dimensions, especially in divisionally designed organisations. *Matrix* design types also combine these aspects, as do *project-based design* types.

Divisional organisation design leads to structures "characterised by a set of self-contained, autonomous units coordinated by a central headquarters" (Robbins & Barnwell 2002: 116) . In organisations designed this way we thus find, as mentioned, combinations of other design types. The autonomous units are often referred to as strategic business units (SBUs), with each having its own focus, such as a particular market segment (for example a certain geographical area, like a region or even perhaps a country in the case of a multinational company) or a product line perhaps. Each separate business unit might then have its own structural configuration, for instance, including perhaps functions (such as finance, sales and marketing, logistics and human resources). These organisational units are then typically not autonomous, but semi-autonomous rather, because of their relationship with headquarters. Eskom, for example, has its headquarters at Megawatt Park, with a divisional designed structure that includes functional as well as regional aspects. Divisions include, for instance, Transmission, Generation and Enterprises – and there are specialist functional groups like human resources and finance. Within the Generation division there will be different power stations, and each might typically have departments or sections that specialise in their different work areas like finance and human resources, purchasing and logistics, and perhaps mechanical and electrical maintenance. Within the Transmission division there may be a structural configuration based on geographical areas, and there may also be similar functional substructures. Simultaneously there may be such functional areas structured as part of the organisation's headquarters. Clearly, then, these types of structures are complex rather than simple in their design

– and all of this is intertwined with how the organisation's work and human resources are managed. These types of organisation design and structure can often go hand in hand with what is known as organisational bureaucracy.

Bureaucratic organisation structures result from what is known as the *mechanistic* approach to organisation design. Some even refer to these as mechanistic structures (Robbins & Barnwell 2002). This type of organisation design can be largely attributed to the prominent German sociologist, Max Weber (1864–1920) (the father of scientific management, and Frederick W. Taylor (1856–1915)). Robbins et al (2008: 550) describe this design type as "characterised by highly routine operating tasks achieved through specialisation, very formalised rules and regulations, tasks that are grouped into functional departments, centralised authority, narrow spans of control, and decision-making that follows the chain of command". Typically this will lead to a tall pyramid-shaped structure with a hierarchy of many different levels. As a strictly rule-driven and well-defined hierarchical design type, this organisational form typically leads to or goes along with top-down command-and-control, almost military-like management. The great deal of emphasis placed on departmentalisation and work specialisation often lead to work being structured into rigid jobs and functional work units, with definite boundaries between jobs, sections and other work units. These types of design can hence clearly lead to excessive specialisation with lack of integration and cross-fertilisation of different work areas, often going along with communication and information-flow problems, and what is commonly known as 'red tape'. The latter relates to the slowness of decision-making processes, primarily linked to many managerial levels and too much formalisation in terms of such things as procedures, rules and regulations. Figure 5.3 reflects such a typical tall, bureaucratic organisation structure.

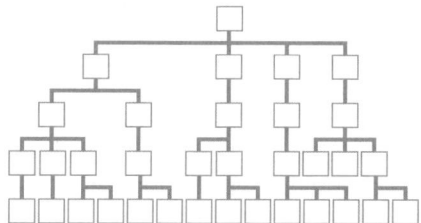

Figure 5.3: Bureaucratic organisation structure

The *organic design* approach typically leads to more fluid and flatter organisation structures. According to Gibson, Ivancevich and Donnelly (1994), this design type emphasises aspects such as the importance of high levels of adaptiveness, responsiveness, development through limiting the use of rules, regulations and procedures, and with an emphasis on decentralisation of authority and lower degrees of specialisation. As a result, one typically finds fewer layers of management, and cross-functional teams are also often part of these organic design types that tend to be organised around different customers, services or products, rather than functions. Robbins and Barnwell (2002: 243) say that these organic structural configurations are "flexible and adaptive, with emphasis on lateral rather than vertical communication, influence based on expertise and knowledge rather than authority of position, loosely defined responsibilities rather than rigid job definitions, and emphasis on exchanging information rather than giving instructions". Figure 5.4 is an example of a flat structure that fits the organic design approach, and the case of Nedcor (cited below) reflects an example of a South African organisation that has changed to flat structures.

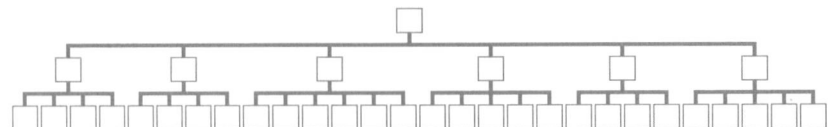

Figure 5.4: Flat organisation structure

A CASE AT HAND

From bureaucratic to flat structures at Nedcor

Nedcor delayered its organisational structure to reduce the number of employee levels and streamline reporting lines. The old hierarchical system of layers within layers is universally regarded as a ladder too steep to climb for energetic, ambitious staff.

Source: Corporate Research Foundation (1998: 184)

Apart from these types of organisation design and structures, there are other designs (such as project and matrix design as mentioned) that also build on cross-fertilisation principles because cross-functional work arrangements tend to apply. Some more modern design types that are also emerging and extending these more flexible and loose, cross-boundary approaches include network designs, even virtual organisations, as well as what is referred to as 'boundaryless' organisations.

A few remarks about these modern design types are necessary because, as Storey (Salaman et al 2005) indicates, the HRM implications and connections have been under-explored, and warrant serious consideration.

The idea of *boundaryless* organisation design was introduced by Jack Welch, former top executive of General Electric when he argued for the removal of four types of boundaries that, according to him, were stifling organisations. These are vertical, horizontal, external and geographic boundaries, and by breaking these down the restrictions which formal structures can impose on working people are removed, the flow of information and other resources across and even beyond single organisations can be facilitated, hierarchies are flattened, functional silos are broken down, and the interface and interaction between different organisational stakeholders and role players across the world are opened up and improved (Robbins et 2008; Bartol et al 2008). This form of organisation design thus typically shares with flat organisation structures the idea that boundaries between organisational units ought to be broken down. However, they go a step further in that boundaries between organisations and their customers, suppliers and potential competitors are also broken down to an extent. In this way relationships are formed that allow these organisations to pool and share resources such as employees, information and distribution channels. Typically, in cases of joint ventures, cross-organisational teams are set up so that they can work together. This type of design is very much related to network design types.

With regard to the *network* design type, Smit et al (2007) and Bartol et al (2008) explain that these organisations arrange themselves, through agreements and commercial contracts, into relationships like strategic alliances or/and joint ventures. Aspects such as outsourcing and contracting out of some work and hence collaborating on various fronts with various other organisations or outside people, are common features of network design types. Some also refer to this as the *modular* form of organisation design. Storey (Salaman et al 2005: 192) says that in this "shift from hierarchy to 'modular' forms in order to increase flexibility ... [t]hese semi-independent units require coordination through a mix of contractual-like deals and the design of mutually beneficial relations". According to Tapscott and Caston (1993: 75), such organisations are "based on cooperative, multidisciplinary teams and businesses networked together across the enterprise. Rather than a rigid structure, it is a modular organizational architecture in which business teams operate as a network of what we call client and server functions". Likewise, Smit et al (2007: 444) explain that in these cases each "member of the network performs some portion of the activities necessary to deliver products and services to the network as a whole", with one core organisation in the network typically performing certain key areas of the work and coordinating "the activities of the network members". They go on to show that "network designs can facilitate the management of highly diverse and complex organisations" and that the focus is on sharing resources, responsibilities and these organisations cooperate and the networks operate almost as "mutually interdependent departments and managerial processes" (Smit et al 2007: 444).There is often the need for 'stable networks', and Smit et al (2007: 444) say that a "stable network is a network structure that utilises external alliances selectively as a mechanism for gaining strategic flexibility ... Although these suppliers are independent of the central organisation, they are typically highly committed to the core organisation".

A CASE AT HAND

BMW: stable network design?

The way in which BMW is designed resembles quite a bit of the network type, in particular the stable network. BMW outsource between 55 and 75% of their production to outside organisations. Although the suppliers are independent of BMW, they are highly committed to BMW and in certain cases, they supply solely to BMW. BMW maintains stable long-term relationships with its suppliers and may even make financial investments in them where appropriate.

Source: Adapted from Smit et al (2007: 245) based on www.bmw.com

Some refer to the *virtual organisation* as an altogether different type of design – but in essence it seems to be a version of the network design type. Warner and Witzel (2004: 1) explain that the virtual organisation "is the newest and potentially most important form ... to have emerged for decades ... [D]riven by new information and communications technologies, most importantly the Internet, the virtual organization model offers ... a chance to reduce costs, become more flexible and extend their market reach all at once". The virtual organisation design type is thus built around extensive use of information communication technology where the different people doing work in the network of collaborating individuals, groups and organisations share information and knowledge regardless of things like place, time, and organisational boundaries.

As can be gathered from the foregoing, the trends and changes in organisation design and redesign are intertwined with trends in the more micro-level redesign of work and jobs, as covered earlier. These are also all connected with the different HRM strategies we covered in the previous chapter. The key point is that all of these developments are intertwined with how we manage our human resources. So, for example, the decision to outsource some aspects of the organisation's work may lead to the loss of important competencies and capabilities. Forming strategic alliances may mean that competencies and capabilities are dispersed across a network of different organisations, bringing along with them uncertainties about how to identify, harness and develop appropriate combinations and synergies of cross-organisational competencies and capabilities. Key challenges also specifically relate to the actual processes and managerial practices involved in changing to flatter structural configurations – which almost always involves not only de-layering, but also downsizing. Organisational restructuring efforts (changing the design and often becoming more flexible) almost always lead to de-layering and the elimination of some management levels. It is well known that the waves of restructuring that we have seen increasingly over the past few decades particularly have been branded as the 'RE'-fallacy – **re**structure, **re**-engineer, **re**design, **re**organise but, ultimately, mostly ending in **re**trenchments. These often mean uncertainties and loss of trust from the side of employees, and resistance by trade unions. For all of these reasons and others – HRM and broader aspects of organisation design should be regarded as being two sides of a coin.

5.5 ORGANISING HRM WORK

Just as decisions have to be made regarding the structuring of the work of organisations in general, they must also be made about how to organise the work pertaining to managing the human resources of organisations. Questions must be answered about who must do what in relation to managing workers and their work. This will include decisions regarding the extent to which this area of management in an organisation is left to the HR specialists (specialisation) or given to the actual managers of the workers and their work (devolving HRM to line management). Furthermore, it will have to be decided at what organisational level certain HRM decisions will be taken – that is, whether HRM decisions and work will be centralised or decentralised. In addition, in line with general trends regarding new organisation design types, decisions must be made about the 'make or buy' of various aspects of HRM work. This refers to outsourcing of HRM work. These types of structural design decisions and issues regarding HRM thus require careful consideration.

5.5.1 Specialisation and/or devolution of HRM work

Probably the most fundamental decision when it comes to organising HRM work relates to the question of who plays what role. We have been emphasising right from the start of this book that the management of human resources can never be the domain of select group of specialist HR practitioners alone. Per definition, all managers must manage human resources. In fact, although the devolution of HRM to line managers has been on the increase for quite some time, the evidence is increasingly mounting (Larsen & Brewster 2003) that these trends are becoming pretty widespread. Devolving HRM more and more to managers seems to happen more because it is realised that the impact of these people on the workers they manage is crucial. Based on rigorous empirical research by Purcell and Hutchinson (2007: 3), they say that evidence shows that the "HR practices perceived or experienced by employees will, to a growing extent, be those delivered or enacted by line managers", and that is what will shape the attitudes and work behaviour of these working people. Half a decade ago already, it seems Renwick (2003: 262) detected and pointed out that the very concept of HRM gives line managers a "centre stage" role in it.

Having said this, the issue here becomes rather more one of determining what exactly the role is and by whom it should be played. In small organisations with, say, only 10 or 15 workers, this may be a straightforward issue: all aspects pertaining to managing the workers and their work will typically be executed by the line manager, and it may even well be the one and only 'owner-manager' of the organisation. However, in large organisations with thousands of people working as employees, contractors, consultants and so forth – and where there might typically also be specialist staff and sections dealing with HRM-related issues – the decision involves much more.

Brewster and Larsen (1992) conceptualise the issue pertaining to the role of the human resource department/specialists vis-à-vis that of line management on a matrix involving two dimensions. The horizontal axis depicts the extent of devolution, described as the degree to which the line managers, rather than human resource specialists, are involved in and responsible for HRM. On the vertical axis, the second dimension, referred to as integration, represents the degree to which HRM issues are regarded as an integral part of the general management and in particular the business strategy of the organisation.

From the matrix, four HRM models are identified (see figure 5.5).

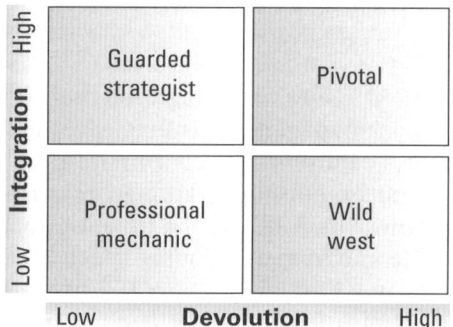

Figure 5.5: Brewster and Larsen's models of HRM
Source: Adapted from Brewster & Larsen (1992: 414)

These models allow us to analyse the role of the human resource specialists or department, and also the nature of HRM as a general management function.

The 'professional mechanics'

The bottom left-hand corner of the matrix depicts a model of HRM where the integration of human resource issues with business strategy is low, and little devolvement of HRM to line management takes place. In this case the human resource specialist is termed the *professional mechanic* and is viewed as a 'professional' in almost the same way as in other professions (such as engineers or lawyers). Here, the human resource specialists see themselves as having higher imperatives, beyond those of organisations. They believe that many or most areas of HRM are beyond the grasp or mastery of other managers. As a result, the interests of an HR department diverge more and more from the strategic interests of the business, and there is an increasing concern with the technical details of the human resource profession. The consequence of this is "an ever-greater isolation from other members of the management team" (Brewster & Larsen 1992: 414).

The 'wild wests'

In the wild west model, the integration of human resource issues with the business aspects of the organisation is still low, but HRM is substantially devolved to line managers. Managers are thus almost free to develop their own ways of managing human resources. They sometimes even have the power to reward, and to hire and fire employees as they deem fit. In this model, inconsistency, incoherence and even strong employee reaction could quite easily result, according to these authors.

The 'guarded strategists'

In the guarded strategist model, HRM is highly integrated with business strategy, the human resource department retains authority and the human resource specialists are viewed as very powerful people in the organisation. They work with senior management when corporate strategy is formulated. The human resource departments are influential and control the number of employees, who is employed and developed, and how they are rewarded – all in line with the business objectives. For line management this can create a situation of considerable frustration. They often find that most aspects of their relationships with their subordinate employees are practically "abrogated by the personnel function: the weaker managers will welcome the chance to slough off their responsibilities, while simultaneously having someone else to blame for all failures; the better managers will be frustrated" (Brewster & Larsen 1992: 416).

The 'pivotals'

In the pivotal model all HRM issues are integrated with business strategy, and the devolvement of HRM to line management is extensive. Here the senior personnel specialists act as facilitators, catalysts and coordinators of all the human resource issues at the top level of the organisation. Human resource departments are thus small, but competent and powerful, fulfilling the functions of monitoring and advising on HRM-related issues. Line and human resource specialists are often exchangeable. Furthermore, as Brewster and Larsen (1992: 415) point out: "the concentration on the development and monitoring of policy is correlated with the devolution of responsibility and authority to carry out the policy to line management." In these organisations difficulties can arise in staffing the human resource department with competent human resource specialists of a high quality, who can understand the business of the organisation and who can also train and develop line managers to perform operational level HRM successfully.

A CASE AT HAND

Devolution of HRM at Momentum

There is no traditional human resource department at Momentum – it is seen as a potential stumbling block to efficient hands-on people management. There is a human resources consultant in each business unit to assist with recruitment, communication and other people management issues. Line management ultimately retains responsibility for these functions.

Source: Corporate Research Foundation (1998: 153)

A framework or model like this is thus helpful conceptually and can guide the thinking behind decisions about how to organise the HRM work of organisations. There are other things to decide as well, such as the degree to which HRM work should be centralised or decentralised. This will naturally be closely linked to other more general organisation design issues, as discussed before. It will also be closely linked to the actual role to be played by the HR specialists or practitioners in any organisation, which is something we will now focus on in greater detail.

5.5.2 Designing the work of the HR practitioners: different role options

The work of Tyson and Fell (1986), Tyson (1987) and Sisson (1989) had led to the development of three different possible roles to be played by HR practitioners and departments in organisations.

The 'clerks of works' role

Here the key role of the HR practitioners is that of administrative support. The emphasis falls on the routine tasks of correspondence and record keeping about absenteeism and staff turnover. The HR department may also sometimes fulfil a supportive role in staffing functions (such as employment interviews), as well as a welfare role (for example in visiting the sick). The staff of these HR departments will have little specialised training, there will be a lack of sophisticated HRM systems and the specialists will not have any real clout.

The 'contracts managers' role

In this role the emphasis falls on meeting all events with systems (Tyson 1987: 526). The key role of this type of human resource department is thus most likely to be "the making and interpretation of procedures and agreements ... [to] resolve day-to-day problems" (Sisson 1989: 12). The HR departments playing this role will thus typically have to be staffed with highly skilled and experienced labour relations specialists in particular, whose role will be primarily reactive by nature. However, these practitioners may possess considerable power and authority due to their ability to solve personnel and labour relations-related problems.

The 'architects' role

This role type calls for the HR practitioners to play a constructive role in the organisation's strive towards success in a competitive business environment. Their role is thus comprehensive, and extends beyond pure personnel issues in that these specialists often view themselves as "'business managers' first and 'personnel managers' second" (Sisson 1989: 12). The head of the HR department is typically a member of the top management team and he or she fulfils a strategic role in helping the organisation to achieve business success, for example through the design of organisational structures and the formulation of policies which seek to give effect to corporate and/or business plans. Right from top management level downwards, there is an integrated system of cooperation between line managers and HR specialists, the latter as a rule being highly qualified, trained and competent in their specialist areas while simultaneously having a broad-based business and general management background. It is therefore almost an internal consultant type of role which is highly valued by all of those involved in HRM in general.

Like in the previous section, it may be useful to take a look at various typologies or models that have been devised about the possible roles to be played by the HR practitioners or departments of organisations.

5.5.2.1 Model/typology 1

Storey's research (1992: 166–185) led him to a typology of the role which HR practitioners and departments can play in organisations. Two dimensions are utilised to form a matrix with four alternatives (see figure 5.6).

The 'advisers'

In terms of the advisers role, the HR practitioners act as internal consultants or advisers upon request from line management (being quite reactive or non-interventionary). Devolution is thus high and the HR department leaves HRM largely over to the other managers, although, when it comes to strategic (or policy) issues (even broader business/strategic), the small group of competent HR specialists are often approached for their advice.

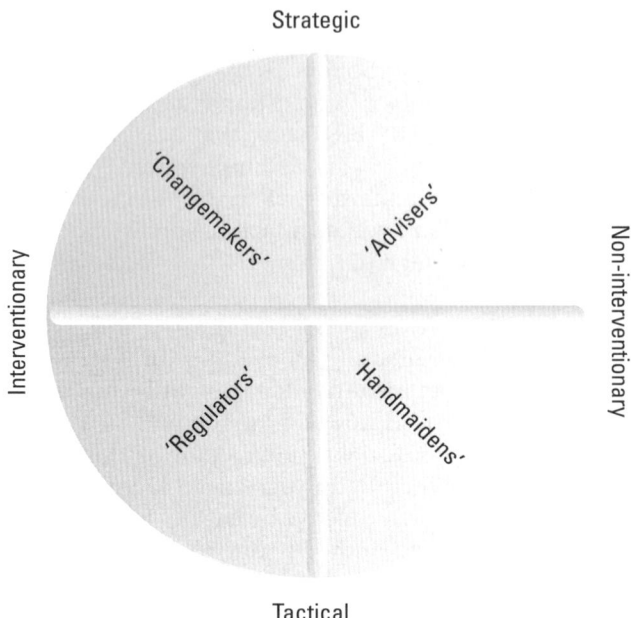

Figure 5.6: Storey's types of personnel management
Source: Adapted from Storey (1992: 168)

The 'handmaidens'

In the handmaidens model, the HR department's role is also relatively non-interventionary or reactive (acting when approached), but their role is actually limited to pure HR issues such as looking after the welfare of employees and performing clerical functions such as record keeping, collating information on the payroll, monitoring absenteeism statistics, headcounts, and so on. Furthermore, in terms of this role type, the HR department's function is to help line managers in the area of labour relations when such assistance is requested. The term *handmaiden* is used precisely to signal a type of attendant, subservient relationship between the HR specialists and line management with regard to HRM. Storey (1992: 75) notes that the major difference between this role and the advisers' one is that "the service offered was of a more routine administrative, or at best tactical kind, rather than being in the nature of strategic advice". Devolution is thus still high, while the specialists are mostly engaged in servicing line's routine requirements upon request.

The 'regulators'

The HR departments which fall into the role type of *regulators* are referred to as "managers of discontent" who seek order and stability, inter alia through temporary, tactical truces with organised labour (trade unions) and the formulation, promulgation and enforcement of employment rules (including union-management agreements and personnel procedure manuals). In this case, although the role of the specialists is interventionary (proactive) by nature, the specialists very rarely engage in wider business strategy issues.

The 'changemakers'

In the changemakers model, the HR department plays an interventionary and strategic role by initiating new forms of people management in line with the needs of the business and aimed at eliciting employee commitment and the willingness to "go the extra mile". Storey (1992: 180) says of this role that:

> the orientation is away from bargaining, away from ad hocery, and away from 'humble advice' ... The dual forms of integration ... (integration of the different aspects of resourcing, planning, appraising, rewarding and developing; and the further integration of all of this into the business plan) are characteristics of this type ...

Furthermore, Storey indicates that within this role type there are two further variations – the hard and soft roles. In the former the emphasis falls on the business language of numbers and hence the quantification of input/output ratios. An extreme profit orientation is thus emphasised where the HR department and specialists constantly concentrate on the value they add to the bottom line of the organisation. The HR specialists thus become business thinkers – to the extent that they are eventually not even typified as specialists any longer, and line and personnel managers often exchange roles. In the soft role type, the focus is on the distinctive nature of the specialist's inputs to the management of the organisation in inventing and displaying unique techniques to tap the creativity and commitment of resourceful humans.

From the above it should be clear that the nature of HRM – and particularly the role of HR departments in this regard – can vary from situation to situation, especially as far as the role differentiation in HRM between the HR department/specialists vis-à-vis the general/line managers is concerned.

5.5.2.2 Model/typology 2

Dave Ulrich's work (1997, 1998) provides another typology by which to diagnose the role of HR practitioners in organisations. The two-dimensional grid in figure 5.7 reflects an adapted version of Ulrich's (1997) framework for categorising the roles of HR practitioners in organisations.

Figure 5.7: Ulrich's multiple-role model for HR professionals
Source: Adapted from Ulrich (1997, 1998)

According to Ulrich (1997, 1998), HR practitioners and departments should undertake multiple roles to add value at various points in the organisational system. Their focus could/should be strategic (to a greater/lesser degree) *and* it could/should be operational (to a greater/lesser degree). In addition, the activities of HR specialists (professionals) could/should be related to the people (the human resources as such) and to the processes (systems, tools, policies, etc) – in both respects to a lesser or greater degree.

The *strategic partner role* requires the HR department/professionals to be active members of the business and strategic team/s of the organisation. The key deliverable will be that general organisational and business strategies will incorporate and be fully integrated with HRM dynamics to ensure strategy execution. HR strategies will be aligned to business strategies. The *change leader* role will essentially entail that the HR professionals/departments will team up (or partner) with line managers to act as change agents or champions of change. They will co-lead the processes related to organisational change, development and transformation. The key deliverables will be renewed organisations, through processes, practices and system changes (such as organisation redesign, process redesign/re-engineering, etc). The role as *administrative expert* relates to providing efficient and quality support services. Operational support will thus be delivered in areas such as recruitment and selection, remuneration and HR information. The deliverables will be related to a smooth-running HR function and system to cater for the day-to-day personnel administrative needs of the organisation. The *employee champion* role is directly related to the commitment, capability and performance of employees. The overall deliverable will be a competent, committed and high-performing workforce. This role will include taking care of employees' personal needs and interests, promoting HR development (including leadership development, coaching, etc), facilitating employee opinion surveys and managing the performance and behaviour of employees.

Ulrich (1997, 1998) propagates a move away from an 'either/or' paradigm, towards a multiple-role one. This means that decisions have to be made as to whether the HR practitioners and department/s will be strong and/or weak (or average) on each of these four role categories.

The actual role to be played by the HR practitioners of an organisation is thus clearly a matter of choice, and this will ultimately drive the way in which the HRM work of an organisation is organised. Structuring all HRM-related work in organisations thus entails making important strategic decisions in conjunction with decisions on generic and grand strategy (see chapter 4).

Another dimension in this regard relates to the *centralisation/decentralisation* of the HR work in organisations, and along with it comes the actual structuring of the organisation's HR department or section – should there be a separate one. A more basic consideration thus relates to first deciding which HRM work can or should be done from inside the organisation and which should perhaps be done by outsiders. This is also referred to as a 'make or buy' decision.

5.5.3 Specialised HRM work: different role players and alternative design options

Earlier we mentioned that an option in designing the work systems of organisations may be to outsource aspects of its work. While this trend started off primarily in respect of the non-core work of organisations, we have mentioned that organisations even outsource some of its core work and that these network design types have become more prominent relatively recently. The same trends and issues apply to HRM work as such. This means that all specialised HRM work need not be performed inside the organisation and that there is always the option of outsourcing some of it to specialised service providers or vendors in the field.

5.5.3.1 Outsourcing HRM work

The outsourcing of HRM work basically entails shifting some aspects of the work to an external HR service provider. The actual HRM work that can be outsourced is basically anything except that which is the role of the line manager in managing the workers and their work. Included in this are the strategic HRM decisions that have to be made by the upper echelons of the organisation's managerial leadership cadre. While these cannot be outsourced as such, even these may include buying in some advisory services of others from outside the organisation, such as HRM consultants who may be well-known experts in the field. The decision to outsource HRM work rather than doing it all internally is basically one which ought to be driven by a consideration of what would add the most value to the organisation, its working people (managers and non-managerial workers as well as non-employee workers) and the work of the organisation as such. The spectrum of HRM work that can be outsourced is thus broad, but guidance regarding what to ultimately 'buy' and in what form, and what to 'make' inside, can be sought also in relation to the different roles, as discussed in the previous section. The 'clerks of works' and 'administrative expert' roles are possibly good candidates for outsourcing, for instance. In this regard Mello (2006: 259) says that a key potential benefit for outsourcing some HRM work "is that the assignment of transactional and administrative work, such as payroll and benefits administration, can free up HR staff to focus on more strategic issues".

Information technology and services generally would probably be among some of the most common areas of work for which organisations make use of outside service providers. As part of the information technology revolution, large IT service providers, mostly international ones, have stepped in and were able to help organisations establish and maintain superior IT infrastructures by the late 20th century. This trend gained momentum especially into the 1980s and as part hereof, or as a spin-off in a sense – organisations also increasingly outsourced some of the technology-driven HR work, in particular payroll systems. Large IT service providers generally have better capacity to process large payrolls, and small and medium-sized organisations especially thus stand to benefit from the economies of scale offered by these IT companies. It is not only an issue pertaining to the size of the organisation, though. Even large organisations may decide to do so as part of decisions to outsource some technology-driven HRM work. As we have said, it is actually a basic 'make or buy' decision. Greer et al (in Mello 2006: 279) explain: "Innovations in HR information technology also influence outsourcing practices ... outside vendors are installing integrated or enterprise software, such as PeopleSoft or SAP, with human resource information system (HRIS) components."

Another aspect of HRM work that has for quite a long time been popular to outsource, relates to the legalities of HRM. Law in general and labour law in particular are quite complex and specialised fields, and as such it is very common for organisations to develop ongoing relationships and make contractual arrangements with organisations that specialise in labour relations and law. It should be noted, though, that it is not necessarily an issue of 'make or buy' – but it can be both. This is, of course, not limited to something like labour-related legal work, but can apply to any area of specialised HRM work. All of the roles we have discussed earlier are possible candidates for making use of the services of outside vendors like consultancy firms or other HR service providers. It is quite common, for instance, to also make use of such external service providers when it comes to organisational change work. While an organisation might have specialised HR staff who help with change management processes, external change management consultants' services may also be brought into the organisation. Similarly, an organisation may, for instance, have a position which includes legal advisory services pertaining to labour relations work, and still it may have an external service provider in this field as well. Sometimes when organisations go through restructuring processes (or business process re-engineering) they buy in the temporary services of change management consultants. Because such cases can often involve the elimination of some jobs (such as middle manager roles typically when organisations change to flatter structural configurations), the issue of HR risk management may require external advice also on relevant labour law issues pertaining to redundancies and retrenchments (aspects that we also cover in Chapter 20).

From another perspective we can add that organisational restructuring efforts often also include cutting back on internal HR practitioner positions and thus downsizing HR departments or sections as such. This may specifically include moving to a model of making more use of external HR service providers, rather than having a large contingent of HR practitioners as employees. This may entail outsourcing only a few areas of HRM work – or even all of it in extreme cases. While the latter may be rare, it is not completely impossible and there are such cases (according to the Chartered Institute of Personnel and Development (CIPD) in the UK). The CIPD makes it quite clear that there are some good and prominent examples of primarily global organisations that have outsourced significant aspects of their operational HRM work (support functions of specialists/practitioners), often through contracts covering relatively long periods (like five to ten years). They go on to report that some organisations even go so far as to shift some of their HRM work to other countries, and they, like Mello (2006: 258), thus refer to *offshoring* such work. The CIPD has found, however, that the offshoring of HRM work is still relatively uncommon.

As mentioned, the decision to outsource some HRM work must ultimately be driven by the right reasons – and these must be linked to the value added to the organisation's strive to be successful in the broad sense of the word and as judged from a multiple stakeholder perspective. If, for instance, outsourcing means better quality and quantity of HRM-related services to line managers (with resultant positive implications for the workers as well) and these also lead to more cost effectiveness, it will be hard to argue against it.

In this regard it is also rather common, for instance, for organisations to outsource some of their work related to finding the right talent. Recruitment is thus an aspect of HRM that commonly makes extensive use of the services of external recruitment agency companies. These recruitment companies typically have access to a much better pool of potential candidates with appropriate talent. We will return to this aspect specifically again in chapter 7, which deals with the challenges related to finding people who can do the work of the organisation.

It can thus be seen that the range of areas of HRM work that can be considered to be outsourced (in part or in total) is broad. It is, as we have said, a matter of strategic choice, but, as also stressed before, it is essential to not take such decisions without due consideration of all issues and factors because of the implications. It should only follow on from a proper process in which all the potential benefits and risk factors are carefully weighed up (see exhibit 5.4 in this regard).

EXHIBIT 5.4: CIPD advice on outsourcing HRM work

Potential benefits

When organisations put forward a business case for HR outsourcing, there are a number of potential benefits that many cite. In practice, these benefits are not necessarily mutually exclusive and a number of them could be achieved through some alternative solution rather than via outsourcing. Commonly mentioned benefits include:

■ reduced cost;

■ increased efficiency;

■ access to improved HR IT systems;

■ improved people management information (including human capital metrics);

■ access to HR expertise not available internally;

■ increased flexibility and speed of response to HR problems;

■ part of an overall strategy (for example the organisation is outsourcing a number of its support functions, of which HR is just one part);

■ reduced risk to free HR resources to operate more strategically.

Potential challenges

From a practical point of view, there are also a number of potential pitfalls that it is useful to bear in mind when considering outsourcing. Some of the main ones are:

■ Don't outsource what you don't understand. The outsource provider will only have to subsequently solve the problem (at a cost) and the provider's solution might not be most suitable from your organisation's perspective.

■ Outsourcing does not absolve the organisation of good people management practices nor of overall responsibility for the provision of HR services.

■ Increasingly, outsourcing arrangements are often long term (five to ten year contracts are not unusual). An understanding of the organisation's current and future business strategy and potential changing business (and hence risk) profile by the outsourcing provider is important before entering into any contractual arrangement. This helps to avoid being tied into unfavourable contractual arrangements.

■ Loss of local knowledge and processes which instead reside with the outsource provider.

■ Standardisation of processes in line with outsource provider not organisational preferences.

■ Fragmentation of the service provided means that day to day operations are split from strategy and policy direction.

■ The need to constantly review the success of the outsourcing arrangement against specified metrics.

■ The need for outsourcing services may change as the business environment changes, and there are instances of services being brought back in-house.

Source: CIPD: http://www.cipd.co.uk/subjects/corpstrtgy/general/hroutsourcng.htm

5.5.3.2 Centralising HRM work and the case for shared HR service centres

As we have explained before, some more complex organisations can be designed along the lines of divisional structural configurations. These typically include that there will be headquarters and multiple other divisions that may be structured along geographic lines and/or around markets or customers, and/or products/services. When this is the case, the issue of centralisation versus decentralisation becomes an important design decision. This also relates to HRM work.

The extent to which the HRM support work (of and by HR practitioners) is to be performed more centrally at headquarters, or more decentralised, say, at the level of separate organisational units (like SBUs), is something to be considered in the context of all the relevant strategic and organisation design variables. In some organisations, greater decentralisation may be the case and indeed be more appropriate, whereas in others more centralisation of HRM decisions may be the better way to go. Two such diverging examples are reflected below.

A CASE AT HAND

To centralise or decentralise HRM: Telkom vis-à-vis Unilever SA

According to De Witt (1998: 28), decentralisation of HRM was the chosen Telkom option: "In Telkom human resources was decentralised into business units with only a small component remaining at head office for overall policy, transformation and direction."

In contrast, Unilever SA tends to have decided on the route of centralisation: "There is also a strong central focus on human resources (at the corporate office), particularly as Unilever treats management as an international resource. Much of the recruitment, development and training is treated centrally."

Naturally the decision about the extent to which the specialised HRM work will be centralised will be part and parcel of the general decision about centralisation and/or decentralisation in the organisation. If financial decisions are very tightly centralised, for instance, it is rather unthinkable how some HRM decisions can be decentralised – such as pay levels and increases. On the other hand, an organisation with a multi-business corporate strategy may have a headquarters for corporate affairs while some semi-autonomous business units may operate as profit centres responsible for all their own costs and revenues, including all HR-related costs. In such cases the parent organisation may decentralise all of the HRM decisions and work to these business entities as well.

In such cases of decentralisation, the organisation may, for instance, maintain a small human resource section, or perhaps just one position at senior- or top-management level, with HR departments or sections based at the decentralised level of separate business units. The actual structure of HR sections or departments can thus vary considerably in terms of aspects such as size (number of HR practitioner staff) and functions performed or services rendered. Much of this will depend on the decisions about the HR department's specific type of role within the organisation. These will be influenced by factors such as the kind of industry, organisational strategy, size, structure and life-cycle stage, as well as top management's basic philosophy or ideology (or core idea – see chapter 4) regarding the management of human resources.

In the case of a relatively small or medium-sized manufacturing organisation with only one establishment that has a functionally designed structure and, say, about 300 employees, an HR department may, for example, be one of the usual functional areas, such as the finance department, the production department and the marketing department (see figure 5.8.)

In such a case, the HR department, headed by an HR manager, can, for example, be structured as per figure 5.8, with different sections responsible for certain activities and functions. The structure of such a department will therefore also be strongly influenced by the relative importance of the various functions or tasks to be performed by the HR department as well as, for example, the extent to which aspects of HRM is being devolved to line management.

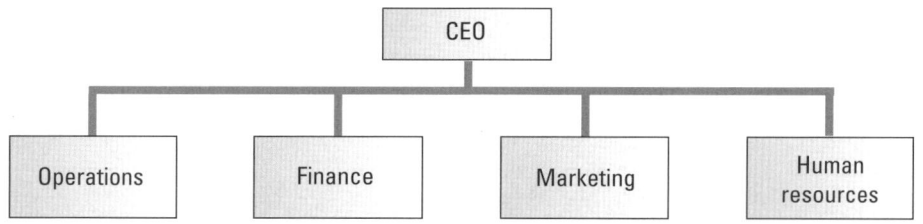

Figure 5.8: Placing the HR department within the functionally designed organisation structure

In the case of large and more complex multidivisional organisations with various organisational units dispersed geographically, there might be a decision to centralise some HRM support work and decentralise some others. A relatively more recent trend has been the establishment and use of shared HR services centres (SHRSCs) at a centralised level. Such centres then typically provide a standard range of HR support services across the whole organisation, including to corporate headquarters staff and also to managerial staff and non-managerial workers based at different business units or establishments. Such centres might even typically, in the case of network design-type organisations, provide HR support services to other organisations that form part of the network configuration, such as alliance partners or supplier organisations.

Establishing such SHRSCs often forms part of more comprehensive organisation redesign efforts – such as when an organisation goes into joint ventures or other forms of business partnering, or when decisions are made to centralise some aspects of HRM work and to devolve more HRM work to line managers. It can thus easily also form part of new arrangements, which might include, for example, outsourcing, and in the case of multinational companies, even offshoring. There is no reason why consideration cannot be given to establishing SHRSCs which combine some internal service provisioning by HR staff at headquarters with some outsourced services to outside vendors. In addition, it is not uncommon to find that these reconfigurations include greater use of information communication technology. These may include establishing employee and management self-service portals on the intranet systems of organisations, as well as HR call centres. These kinds of innovations in the design of HRM work systems tend to be more common in large (and often multinational) organisations that operate in different countries. The SHRSC might then be located in one country, while even delivering services in the form of HR support work to people working in different countries.

As is the case with the outsourcing option, the range or types of HRM support work that may be considered to form part of the shared service centre is a matter of choice. It may include the routine transaction and administrative-type work and also more professional services such as labour legislative services, health services (including occupational safety, support to HIV/Aids infected workers, etc) and also training- and development-related services. The key driver is again that it should only be considered if this will mean improvement in the ways in which human resources will be managed in the organisation.

The emphasis falls on service delivery, and the users of these services, such as line managers dispersed throughout the organisation or even beyond, and other workers, or even perhaps contract workers, are all regarded as the true 'customers' of these service centres. Service standards are thus typically specified and performance in accordance with them is of paramount importance.

There are quite a number of South African organisations that make use of shared services centres for the delivery of HRM-related services, including Standard Bank, Sasol, De Beers, Kumba Resources and Eskom. Exhibit 5.5 reflects some information about an SHRSC at Eskom, called an HR Shared Services Unit (HR SSU), and established during November 2004.

EXHIBIT 5.5: HR shared services unit at Eskom

November 2004 saw the launch of the Eskom HR Shared Service Unit (HR SSU for Corporate Divisions). Since the launch, HR SSU services have been extended to Transmission Division, Enterprises Division, and currently Generation Division.

HR Shared Services is about:
- Bringing together high-volume transactions that are often duplicated and inconsistent across different business units;
- Allowing line HR to focus on more advisory and strategic issues in the Divisions;
- Reducing the costs of administration through greater economies of scale;
- Providing standard and consistent information to the employees; and
- Carefully tailoring services to individual Business Units as customers.

The HR SSU has been designed to serve as a central point of contact for all customers, ensuring that processes are standardised and that customers receive consistent, professional and world-class service.

The benefits for Eskom are reduced costs and increased efficiency as HR activities and programmes are aligned with the strategic direction and business needs of the organisation.

HR SSU provides the following services to its customers, namely: Salary & Benefits Administration, Learning Administration, and Recruitment. The HR SSU Centre of Expertise (COE) provides professional expert advice in the various HR disciplines like Resourcing & Transition, Performance & Talent Management, Learning, Remuneration & Benefits, Industrial Relations, HR Management Information, International Assignment & Secondments, and Psychometric Assessments.

HR SSU amongst the best

During May 2006 the HR SSU, as new as it is, was nominated for the annual *Business Times* Careers Awards for 2005 and walked away with two of these prestigious awards under two different categories, namely
- Best Black and White Advertisement in the category for Trade/Technical/Artisan; and
- Best Blank and White Advertisement in the category for Engineering.

Winning these two awards provided considerable motivation to the rest of the SSU staff.

HR SSU in numbers

To ensure that the unit gives the best possible service to its customers – as it is a customer-centric environment – Service Level Agreements were developed to guarantee efficient and effective service delivery. Below are some interesting facts about HR SSU:
- 312 602 calls were received between 1 November 2004 and 31 August 2007.
- 420 246 requests were lodged between 1 November 2004 and 31 August 2007.
- The 100 000th request was logged on 6 January 2006.
- 952 positions were advertised internally, attracting 31 258 applications – that is, 75 applications per position from January to October 2006.

By implementing online job applications, SSU has saved 576 870 A4 pages of CVs from January to October 2006.

Source: Letlape (2007: 13)

Because the emphasis is on quality service delivery with these structural configurations of HRM support work, these units are ideally positioned to be developed into centres of excellence. In this way, pools of expertise and capabilities are thus developed. One should not even exclude the option to consider making such SHRSCs profit centres that may even make their services available to third parties. As such, these structures can then become vendors for other organisations where outsourcing might be considered. Those brave enough may even venture into the realms of exporting such services to other countries ultimately – or even setting up decentralised structures in other countries, perhaps through some form of partnering with locals. One can just imagine how the richness of expertise and capabilities developed in South Africa – for instance in shared service centres like Eskom's – might possibly be transferred into neighbouring countries like Botswana, Namibia and so forth. Fortunately, technology makes it easier to even contemplate setting up some of these with network structures that contain elements of virtual organisations, teaming up with HR specialists in those countries to bring on board the contextual and institutional depth and breadth peculiar to different countries. It certainly is not unconceivable for such innovative designs of HRM support work to crystallise as we move deeper into the 21st century.

5.6 CONCLUSION

In this chapter we focused on HRM decisions that relate to structure and design. These are all decisions with long-term implications and should be regarded and treated as strategic. We covered design options and issues at the level of individual jobs, from a group-level perspective as well as from the perspective of workflow in the organisation as a whole. We have shown that work design at these levels is interconnected. Job design and organisation design are connected – and both of these are, in turn, connected with strategic decisions, as covered in chapter 4. We have also placed particular emphasis on options and issues pertaining to the design of HRM work as such, including HRM support work performed by HR practitioners or specialists. All decisions regarding these aspects are long term, hold serious resource implications and require top-management attention.

SUSTAINABILITY CONNECTION?
The ways in which we design our organisations, including how we organise the work – will directly interplay with how well we can perform as an organisation and also with the quality of work life of our working people. If we can design work and organisations in ways that enhance their performance, that will help these organisations to remain competitive and hence to survive and hopefully thrive in competitive global market environments. This will mean people have jobs and if these are well designed, they will thus be able to use their work to improve the quality of their lives, as well as those dear to them. If we do not, organisations will cease to exist and people will lose their work and income, which can have dire consequences for families and communities – and in fact all of society. The work of organisations should always be designed in ways that can lead to optimal contributions to the general well-being of the people who will do the work and also the general state of our planet. How we design work must be based on values that clearly put our people and our planet first. The outcomes of our work should add value to the organisation and all its stakeholders, and contribute to the sustainability of the Earth and all life on it.

SELF-EVALUATION QUESTIONS

1 Differentiate between the concepts of 'work design' and 'job design'. Where does 'job analysis' fit in?
2 Differentiate between horizontal and vertical job redesign.
3 'Flexibility within the context of work and organisations can take on various forms.' Explain the meaning of this statement and discuss its application in South Africa.
4 Explain and critically discuss teamwork as a work design option.
5 Write an essay about the following: 'Organisation design – recent trends and issues.'
6 'Devolving HRM work to line managers is very dangerous and should be avoided at all costs." Analyse and critically discuss this statement.
7 Make use of 'models' or 'typologies' to describe the different roles that HR practitioners or specialists might play in organisations.
8 What does 'outsourcing of HRM work' mean and entail – and 'shared HR services centres'?

6 WORKFORCE PLANNING

LEARNING OUTCOMES

After studying this chapter, you should be able to:

- define the concept of job analysis and explain the stages in the job analysis process;
- list the different uses of job analysis and apply the different job analysis methods;
- demonstrate, with the aid of an example, the principles of job analysis;
- explain how to write a job description and a job specification;
- outline some implications of the Employment Equity Act for workforce planning;
- explain the concept of workforce planning and who is responsible for it;
- explain the purpose and importance of workforce planning, as well as describe the workforce planning process; and
- list and explain the various phases in step 1 of the workforce planning process.

6.1 INTRODUCTION

In the previous chapter our focus was on options and decisions pertaining to the design of the work of organisations. We covered the way in which the work of an organisation is structured into work units such as individual positions and teams, and also how organisations can be designed more generally. When an organisation has been operating for some time, the work to be performed by the people would already have been structured. At times we thus have to consider whether the ways in which we have organised the work are really the most appropriate for where the organisation is heading. That is when we engage in some work redesign considerations, and these may cover certain parts of the organisation, the whole organisation, or perhaps just a few jobs or positions.

However, most of the time, hopefully, we do not have to consider making big changes in terms of work design. Even if work is not redesigned, it is still important to plan what work needs to be done and who will be best to do it. As explained in chapter 5, it is necessary to decide, first of all, which work we regard as part of the core of the organisation's operations, and hence to be more likely to be performed by employees, and which we regard as being more peripheral that might rather be executed by other means, like subcontracting. We thus need to plan what kinds of positions we will need, what types and numbers of people with what kinds of competencies will be required to ensure the successful operation of the organisation, and which of these will or will not become part of our organisation's staff establishment.

When we consider these types of issues we have basically already embarked on the management process known as workforce planning, Some refer to this as human resource planning. We prefer the concept *workforce planning* because in this way we can differentiate it from strategic planning, and decisions pertaining to HRM strategy (as covered in chapter 4). We might as well have also used the concept used mostly, namely human resource planning, but we prefer not to for conceptual reasons more than anything else. In practice all of these preparatory decisions and issues are intertwined. For example, as we have to engage in making strategic decisions about how we would like to manage our human resources generically speaking, we have to consider design issues such as core versus non-core work. As mentioned before, we might have a different approach to the core employees compared to non-core workers. When it comes to planning the workforce requirements, naturally the same issues are relevant: what constitutes our core workforce of employees? As will soon be apparent, the issues covered in this chapter are very closely related to aspects covered in the previous two chapters.

We regard *workforce planning* as a systematic, yet dynamic process of estimating the future demand for and supply of employees to execute the organisation's work in ways that will best support its strategic direction, and deciding how to align and match them.

We thus work from the assumption here, purely for conceptual purposes, that we have already decided about what the core workforce of the organisation will be – our core work and staff/employees as well as the support work and groups of employees who will be engaged for that purpose. The focus in workforce planning is on the employees we might need. Practically speaking, things are not so clear-cut and neatly boxed. As we plan what work needs to be covered by our staff, it might well turn out that we decide some of the work demand or needs may be more temporary or less strategically valuable – and hence we might shift to consider alternative ways of trying to match the demand and supply. The starting point is to purposefully consider what work is required to be done in order to move the organisation in the strategic direction decided upon, and the relevant work and organisation design.

Workforce planning thus uses information and knowledge about the work needs of the organisation as translated from the business needs. For organisations in operation this means that the work must actually be analysed and because jobs are the basic units of analysis, *job analysis* as such is central to the process. In order to get the right people to do the work, we need to understand and know what the work entails, what jobs or positions are involved and what kinds of competencies and people we need to execute the work. Apart from the work to be outsourced or executed by means of some subcontracting arrangement, we now plan for the work to be kept inside the organisation and to be performed by employees. We thus plan about what kinds of employees we might need by when, and for which job categories, and how we are going to secure them.

Such jobs will be subject to *job analysis* to make sure we ultimately employ people whose profiles are aligned with the actual work they need to perform. Effective HRM in an organisation cannot take place without proper workforce planning, and job analysis in turn is quite central to all of this. The first part of this chapter is devoted to job analysis and the second to the actual process of workforce planning.

6.2 JOB ANALYSIS

The most basic component of an organisation's structure is (as we pointed out in the previous chapter) the work and the different work units. The most basic units of work are the positions created. Most of the work of organisations is typically carried out by employees who are appointed in specific roles, positions or jobs. While we do not necessarily have to engage in the analysis of all jobs on an ongoing basis, we must make absolutely sure that our knowledge and information about the positions are current. In this context, job analysis can be defined as follows:

> *Job analysis* is a systematic analysis of the tasks, duties and responsibilities of a job as well as the necessary knowledge, skills and abilities a person needs to perform the job adequately (Hartel, Fujimoto, Strybosch & Fitzpatrick 2007: 272).

The information gathered from a job analysis generates two outcomes, namely job descriptions and job specifications (see figure 6.1).

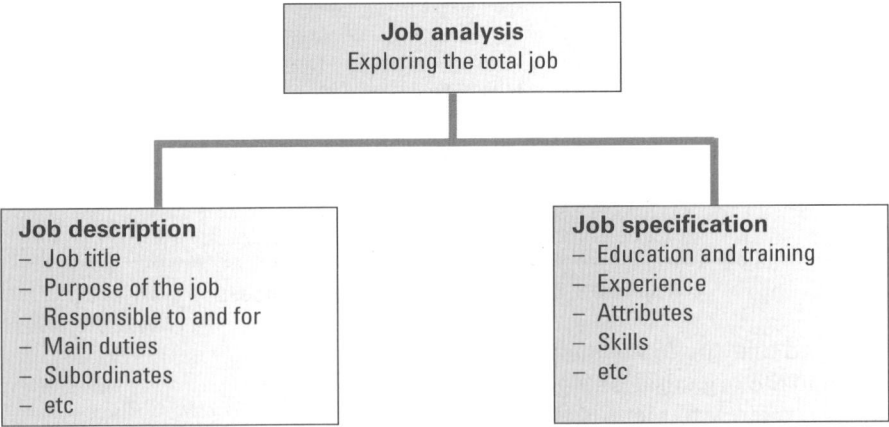

Figure 6.1: Job analysis

Job descriptions (also known as position descriptions) must capture the purpose of a role, define the nature of the job content, identify the immediate work environment, and spell out certain conditions under which work is to be carried out. It is supposed to be a written statement of the content of a job which is derived from the job analysis. It typically states the job title, the purpose of the role and position, what the position holder or occupant will have to do (tasks and duties), to some extent also how it might have to be done in some cases and under what conditions, and also relevant authority lines and responsibilities.

Job specifications (also known as person specifications) stipulate the minimum required knowledge, skills and abilities jobholders must have in order to be able to do the job. These may include some general attributes (like being well presented and friendly, and being able to develop good interpersonal relations), specific skills and qualifications, and also prior experience.

In a sense the job description says what work is required to be done and the job specification says what type of person will be needed to do it. One of the key aspects to develop from these will be the actual criteria pertaining to good performance of the work role. These become essential, particularly when it comes to making some decisions like selecting people to become employees, or when deciding on promoting people or transferring them to different positions and work roles.

6.2.1 Stages in the job analysis process

The job analysis process can follow various stages (see figure 6.2).

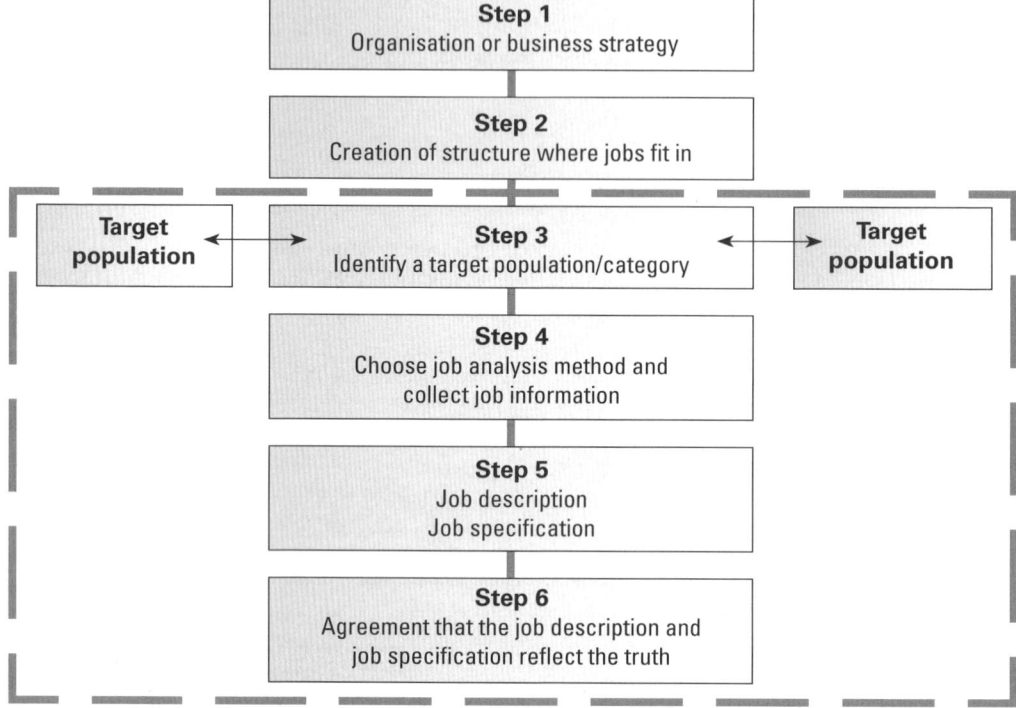

Figure 6.2: Stages in the job analysis process

It is suggested that the following procedure be adopted:
- determine the organisation's general business strategy;
- create a structure to identify the various jobs;
- identify a target population to be analysed;
- decide on a job analysis method to collect and verify job information;
- compile the job descriptions and job specifications; and
- ensure that the group agrees that the job descriptions and job specifications accurately reflect the jobs concerned.

6.2.2 What job analysis can be used for

Job analysis can be used for a number of purposes (Cushway 1994: 41):
- *Workforce planning* helps to ensure that the right number of employees, with the right skills, knowledge and abilities, are available in the right places at the right time in an organisation. Objectives are set based on the business strategy, whereafter a plan must be devised to acquire the human resources necessary to meet the stated objectives. Organisational outputs required are derived from the objectives, and decisions must then be made on how many jobs are required to achieve the various outputs. The implications of this may be that certain jobs should remain as they are, or that certain jobs should be slightly changed, or that completely new jobs should be designed. Workforce planning cannot be accurately undertaken without information about the different jobs (see section 6.3).
- *Selection* can take place only if the job requirements have been clearly identified. With a job description and a job specification available it will be clear what

qualifications, experience and personal attributes a potential candidate must possess. The key issue is the job performance criteria and these can only come from proper processes and practices pertaining to job analysis.

- *Training and development inputs* based on a proper training-needs analysis can only take place once the job standards have been determined and the individual's performance has been measured against the set standards. With accurate job information available, discrepancies in individual performance can easily be detected.
- *Job redesign* requires job analysis. With organisations changing rapidly to realign themselves as a result of increased competition and other external forces, responsibilities and duties must often be reallocated. This makes accurate job analysis information essential.
- *Performance management* cannot take place without proper job information. To measure job performance it is necessary to compare the incumbent's performance with the standards set by the job. Without clear job objectives and job performance criteria, proper performance management cannot take place.
- *Organisational restructuring* can only take place with accurate information about the various jobs available. Duplication of responsibilities can be eliminated to ensure more smooth operations through better work flow processes.
- *Labour relations* may improve if every individual in an organisation knows as far as possible what his or her responsibilities and reporting lines are. Proper job analysis helps to ensure that the chances of communication gaps are minimised.
- *Job evaluations* and remuneration decisions require job-related information that stems from the job analysis process.

6.2.3 Information to be obtained through a job analysis

- One of the first tasks in the process of job analysis is to identify the job clearly – the job title, where it fits into the organisational structure (for example in which section or department) and the number of employees that will be required to perform the same type of work role.
- The reporting relationships must be identified. It is essential to provide the title of the job immediately superior to the job in question and to understand the relationships and coordination links between different jobs and job categories.
- The job content must be well understood; this includes the purpose of the job, the boundaries of the role, and the tasks and activities to be undertaken.
- The required performance standards and how these are to be measured must be determined. The key performance areas (KPAs) or outputs of the job must be established and the standard to which they should be performed must be clear, as well as the relevant accountabilities.
- The connections between "required employee behaviors that drive job performance outcomes" are critical to identify (Hunt 2007: 125). These refer to determining the job performance criteria.
- Any constraints must be identified: the scope and limits of authority and decision making must be established.
- The responsibilities that go along with the job (such as budget, equipment, material) must be determined.
- The working conditions under which incumbents must execute the work must be established.
- The required competencies and attributes of potential jobholders that will drive the required work-related behaviours must be identified. This includes the

knowledge, skills and abilities required of the incumbent to meet the relevant
work-related performance requirements.

■ Any other relevant information (for example training requirements or aspects of a
temporary nature) must be included.

6.2.4 Job analysis methods

The following methods can be used to obtain the necessary job information (De Cenzo
& Robbins 1994: 135):

6.2.4.1 Individual interviews

Jobholders are identified and interviewed with the purpose of determining what the
job entails. This will usually result in the preparation of a job description which will
be confirmed by the supervisor. This is a time-consuming but effective method and is
commonly used. An important drawback of this method is that people can inflate the
importance of their jobs. It is also important that the interviewer prepares him- or
herself properly for the interview.

6.2.4.2 Group interviews

Some similar principles that apply to individual interviews apply to group interviews, the difference being that in the latter a number of jobholders are interviewed
simultaneously. Group dynamics may increase or decrease the effectiveness of this
method. Job assessments may be more accurate and time effective but one has to be
able to manage and use the group process properly.

6.2.4.3 Observation

Observation involves watching employees while they perform their duties. This can
be done by means of direct observation or through videos. A negative aspect of this
method may be that employees do not perform as they normally do while knowing that
they are being observed. A further problem is that certain aspects of jobs cannot always
be observed all the time, for example in the case of certain categories of managers and
salespeople.

6.2.4.4 Structured questionnaires

One of the methods most widely used to obtain information about jobs is the
questionnaire. Employees are given a structured questionnaire on which they check
or rate duties which they perform in the course of their work. This method is less
time consuming and less costly than interviews, but exceptions may be overlooked and
follow-up questions may not be asked or vague points clarified. The most common
systems used are the Position Analysis Questionnaire (PAQ) and the Saville and
Holdsworth Work Profiling System, which is a consulting service. The details of these
methods, which are used worldwide as well as in South Africa, fall beyond the scope
of this book.

6.2.4.5 Self-reports

In the case of self-reports, jobholders are required to write their own job descriptions. It is, however, essential to provide the required training beforehand. Without
the necessary guidance, the quality of the information received may be of no use. The
success of this method also depends on the report-writing skills of the jobholder.

6.2.4.6 Conference method

In this method, the information about a job is obtained from the jobholder's supervisor. The supervisor acts as expert and one of the aspects which may be overlooked is the jobholder's own perceptions of what he or she actually does on the job. Subject-matter experts can also be drawn from other organisations. This method is also very useful if a new job is to be created, for example when a new operator is appointed after a computer network has been installed.

6.2.4.7 Diaries and logs

Jobholders must record their daily activities in a diary or a log. This can be very time consuming and must take place over a long period to ensure that all the activities are recorded. This method is better suited to higher managerial levels.

6.2.4.8 Critical incident methods

Jobholders are required to recall critical incidents that have occurred in the course of their work. This process has as its ultimate aim the identification of critical aspects of the job that are related to failure or success. The incumbent is required to write down all relevant issues; this could, however, result in the omission of important mundane aspects of the job.

6.2.4.9 Hierarchical task analysis

This method requires that the job be broken down into a hierarchical set of tasks and subtasks. Clearly identified objectives are defined as well as their means of execution. The standards which must be achieved and the conditions applicable to the job must be identified.

6.2.4.10 Checklists

This method requires that a checklist of items that might be applicable to the job be drawn up. The jobholder and supervisor must then indicate which items are applicable to the job or to part of the job. Checklists are quick to complete and make it easy to obtain information about a large number of jobs. The items or tasks must, however, be carefully formulated, and all relevant items or tasks must be included. This method is especially useful in determining the less well-defined aspects of a job, for example the labour relations responsibilities of a certain level of managers.

6.2.4.11 Specific job analysis methodologies

There are quite a number of commercially available 'tool sets' that organisations can make use of to do job analysis. Many of these are consultant administered.

- *Management Position Description Questionnaire (MPDQ)*. This method analyses managerial job activities in terms of responsibilities, instructions, activities and demands.
- *Positional Analysis Questionnaire (PAQ)*. This analyses jobs in terms of information input, mental processes, work output, relationship with others, job context in both physical and social terms.
- *Job Element Inventory (JEI)*. This is an adaptation of the PAQ, but presented at a much lower reading level.
- *Occupational Analysis Inventory (OAI)*. This provides vocational guidance and occupational exploration.

6.2.4.12 Competency profiling

To an extent it is debatable whether this is indeed a form of job analysis. It focuses on the people performing work roles more so than the actual job content.

Taylor (2005: 156–157) regards competency frameworks as an alternative to job analysis: "A competency approach is person-based rather than job-based. The starting point is thus not an analysis of jobs ... but an analysis of people and what attributes account for their effective work performance". The following steps are involved:

- The performance effectiveness criteria (for example profits and customer satisfaction) must be defined.
- A sample of superior performers must be defined (for example the top five or 10 performers achieving targets).
- Using expert panels or focus groups, information must be collected regarding the competencies of both the superior and the average jobholder. Competencies can also be obtained from the 360-degree performance ratings (jobholders, peers, supervisors and clients are involved in such ratings).
- Once the competencies of an average and an above-average performer have been identified, the last step is to validate the predictive validity of the competency model using a second sample of jobholders.

There are variations in terms of the use of competencies as part of job analysis (and also workforce planning and other aspects of HRM). Some make use of rather generic competency frameworks, for instance, while others use such frameworks in conjunction with job analysis to identify and match appropriate competencies to different jobs or positions. Some of the most commonly found generic competencies include (Taylor 2005: 158) communication, teamwork, customer orientation, results orientation, leadership, adaptability, problem solving, analytical thinking and interpersonal relations. See exhibit 6.1 for an example of a list of competencies for senior manager roles in South Africa – and note the overlap with these generic competencies mentioned.

EXHIBIT 6.1: Competencies for senior managers

Competencies for senior managers at a large engineering firm in South Africa:
- business acumen;
- participative approach to human resources;
- client service;
- teamwork;
- leadership;
- managerial skills;
- resilience;
- drive and flexibility; and
- communication.

6.2.5 Principles of job analysis

The following principles are applicable to job analysis (Cushway 1994: 43).

6.2.5.1 Analyse the job, not the person

The focus area is the job and not the job incumbent (note our remarks above about competency profiling). The requirements of the job in terms of skills, knowledge and experience are analysed. The incumbent's skills, knowledge and experience may, in fact, be far different from what the job requires. The job content may also be affected by a variety of aspects such as superiors' expectations, individual abilities, other jobs, colleagues, attitudes of managers and organisational structure.

6.2.5.2 Analyse the full ambit of the job

An analysis of the job is not simply a list of tasks; the job should be broken down into its different components. All the aspects of the job should be fully described to give a complete picture of what the job entails. An indication of how the job is linked with other jobs and what the complexities and the challenges of the job are should be clearly spelt out. Lastly, what the job contributes to the ultimate success of the organisation must be clearly stated.

6.2.5.3 Do not be judgemental

Consideration should be given only to the job content. How appropriate and how logical the job content is, is not relevant.

6.2.5.4 Focus more on the present status of the job

The job must be analysed as it is presently structured and the focus should be on the job content. Possible future changes should generally not be the focus, unless the purpose includes job redesign (as covered in the previous chapter). From a workforce planning perspective it is important to be aware, however, if there are pending changes. In such cases the focus is more on 'job families' than on individual jobs.

6.2.6 Writing job descriptions

When writing a job description, it must always be borne in mind why it is being written. The content of a job description will depend on the nature of the job, the organisation and the environment. Job descriptions (also see the example of a job description in exihibit 6.3) should contain information such as the following (when it includes job specification information):

- job title;
- job identification details;
- name of the current jobholder;
- reporting lines;
- main purpose of the job;
- tasks and responsibilities (key performance areas);
- context (optional);
- relation to other positions;
- subordinate positions;
- financial and statistical data required to do the job;
- working conditions;
- experience required;
- competencies required;
- other relevant information; and
- signature and date.

6.2.7 Job specifications

The information necessary to compile a job specification is normally obtained during the process of job analysis and is often described as part of the job description document (see section 6.2.3).

Job specifications are used primarily to facilitate the recruitment and selection

EXHIBIT 6.2: Job or role descriptions

Flexible working hours, flexible pay, wide payment bands and a small number of generic job descriptions fit well together. With general or non-specific job descriptions the emphasis is on the description of the job – what is done, not how it is done or what it is done to. Thus, for example, in any given organisation the functions of secretaries are usually substantially the same irrespective of the department or office in which the work is done. So separate job descriptions are not needed for finance clerks, personnel clerks, purchasing clerks, sales clerks and so on, because close scrutiny will show that what they do is much the same: what is different is what they do it to and where they do it. Often in job evaluation it is found that in reality some of the differences between jobs are small. For example:

- the same job description apart from changes of words such as 'simple' to 'complex' and 'several' to 'numerous';
- duties, responsibilities and skills are substantially similar but it is the point of application that is different; and
- differences in job titles may also reflect differences in the competence, contribution, or experience of the job holder rather than in the job content itself. Examples of this might be the use of words such as senior, principal or chief before a job title.

A large number of job titles is not conducive to job flexibility or simplified job evaluation and grading. Often opportunities exist to merge individual job descriptions into more generic roles. There may also be opportunities to produce generic job descriptions for jobs at the same level but being performed in different departments. The maintenance of large numbers of job descriptions has several disadvantages:

- it is administratively burdensome;
- it encourages employees to emphasise differences in their jobs that in reality are small and have no impact on grading; and
- the introduction of broad salary grades, which facilitate flexibility, makes the emphasis on small differences between jobs unnecessary.

Why have job descriptions at all? A potential employee relations difficulty resulting from job descriptions is that if the task is not on the document the employee may be reluctant to do what is being asked, even if it is well within his or her capability; or the employee might ask for extra money. Certainly there has been a move, albeit only slight, to dispense with job descriptions, particularly in the context of a small number of wide payment bands.

A difference of opinion that exists in management texts is whether the content of job descriptions should describe what actually happens or what should happen. Many say that it should be the former. This surely is nonsense, since it has the effect of confirming the status quo, be that good, bad or indifferent. If, for example, an organisation has performance-related pay, what is the employee in a singleton post to be judged against if a job description has been written to describe the job as it is currently being performed? In these cases the description must be written to capture what should happen.

A solution in some circumstances is to have role descriptions, that, in effect, describe both the job and the people. Role descriptions cover the 'hows' of a job as well as the 'whats' by incorporating the technical expertise required, behaviours that must be displayed, tasks that must be undertaken and the essential outcomes of the role. One way of visualising the difference in approach is to consider a part in a play, as it is described by the playwright in the written text, as the equivalent of a job description. How different directors and actors might bring to the play their own individual expertise and interpretation of the text, whilst still delivering what the playwright wanted, is the equivalent of a role description.

Source: Massey (2000)

process. Without a job specification, the characteristics of the ideal job incumbent are unknown and comparisons between job applicants cannot be made. The job specification should be directly built on the actual job requirements and must be consistent with the particular activities and duties of the job. It forms the reference point and should thus contain the job performance criteria.

When a qualification is attached to a job, utmost care must be taken to determine whether that qualification is indeed necessary. Job specifications should be constantly monitored to determine whether the specifications are not too high or too low, or whether the incumbent possesses the right profile. Cognisance must be taken of the possibility of indirect discrimination in job specifications due to preconceived and entrenched attitudes, prejudices and assumptions (see also chapter 4).

All the information that flows from job analysis efforts is eventually used for the purposes of workforce planning, recruitment and selection, training, and so forth. The first area, however, is workforce planning. Before we look more closely at workforce planning, it is important to reflect on the connection between the EEA and job descriptions and specifications.

6.2.8 Employment Equity Act: possible implications

As you already know, the Employment Equity Act prohibits unfair discrimination (Chapter II of the Act) against an employee (also an applicant for employment) and in any employment policy or practice, unless it is for affirmative action purposes or on the basis of relevant inherent requirements of the job. In the case of affirmative action, any differential treatment which is based on an affirmative action policy or plan to address past discrimination practices will in itself not be considered unfair discrimination.

Fair discrimination will therefore have to be based on inherent requirements of the job. Job analyses and descriptions address the core of what is required in a job, and managers should therefore realise how important a task the professional execution of job analysis and description is. Job analyses and descriptions form an inherent part of how an organisation's work is designed and organised, and to a large extent also impact on organisational structures. It will thus play a fundamental role in recruitment and selection policies and practices, as well as training and promotion decisions. All of these decisions and practices are ultimately supposed to be linked to job analysis and description, and all of these have to be done in such a way that they are free of any form of unfair discrimination.

Employers should, when job descriptions and specifications are drawn up and decided upon, ensure that the inherent requirements of the job are very clearly spelt out.

Active steps must also be taken here to ensure the promotion of affirmative action. An aspect high on the list in this respect is work redesign. It may be necessary to reorganise work in such a way that the opportunities for women or disabled people as designated groups can be enhanced. In this regard one may, for instance, consider work reorganisation in respect of more flexibility relating to time and place. Examples may be job sharing, part-time work or even working from home. Rewriting job descriptions and specifications along such lines may help organisations to achieve their employment equity targets.

We now turn to workforce planning.

EXHIBIT 6.3: Sample job description summary

JOB TITLE	WORK TEAM LEADER? yes/no	DIVISION/DEPARTMENT	
LOCATION	part-time: __ hours full-time	DATE WRITTEN	

REPORTS TO

Name:	Title:

SALARY GRADE	SALARY RANGE		SHIFT

PURPOSE (Include primary accomplishments, products and services, and who benefits from them and how.)

GENERAL DESCRIPTION (How would you describe this job to someone who has never done it?)

PRINCIPAL DUTIES AND RESPONSIBILITIES (What do you have to be able to achieve the desired results of your job? Include management and leadership responsibilities for work team leaders.)

KNOWLEDGE, SKILLS AND ABILITIES REQUIRED

MINIMUM REQUIREMENTS (What is required to perform the essential duties?)

WORKING CONDITIONS

I have reviewed and determined that this job description accurately reflects the position.

------------------------------------- ---------   ------------------------------------- ----------

Work team leader signature   Date   Employee signature   Date

FOR STAFFING USE ONLY

Posting #   Posting date _____/_____/_____

EE Act Job Group Male ☐ Female ☐ Black ☐ White ☐

The above declarations are not intended to be an all-inclusive list of the duties and responsibilities of the job described, nor are they intended to be such a listing of the skills and abilities required to do the job. Rather, they are intended only to describe the general nature of the job.

Source: workinfo: http://www.workinfo.us/Sub/Sub_for_hr/HR/Manual/Section%202%2019.doc

6.3 THE NATURE OF THE WORKFORCE PLANNING PROCESS

Workforce planning must be directly linked to the strategic and business planning for an organisation – it addresses the major objectives of the organisation in that it spells out what types of people will in future be needed to execute the work in order to accomplish the organisation's business goals. In this sense it is thus directly linked to and flows from other strategic HRM decisions (see chapters 4 and 5).

To ensure effective workforce planning, the starting point is the organisation's mission statement and the strategic plan. As mentioned before, part of strategic planning is the formulation of strategies, goals and objectives (goals being long-term broad purposes or aims, and objectives being short term and much more detailed). Because strategic planning and strategy development are typically an ongoing process, workforce planning is also to be an ongoing process.

This has the implication that the structure of the organisation, the particular jobs to be performed, the financial and technological resources needed, and the types and numbers of people employed must always reflect the general organisational strategies and goals, the design types and also the HRM strategies and concomitant work design.

Hercus (1993: 405) summarises workforce planning by stating that it is a management process involving the following elements:

■ forecasting workforce requirements for an organisation to execute its business plan;
■ forecasting human resources available for meeting these needs and doing a scan of the internal and external environments of the organisation;
■ identifying the gaps between what will be needed and what will be available, and developing the necessary action plans; and
■ implementing and monitoring these action plans.

The following are typical issues that a workforce planning section will have to address (O'Doherty 1995: 119):

■ How many employees does the organisation employ?
■ Where are these employees to be found?
■ What is the age profile of employees by department?
■ What skills do these employees possess?
■ Which are the biggest departments?
■ How many employees leave the organisation per year and in which job categories?
■ In which departments are we likely to lose more employees?

Proper workforce planning ought to play the dominant role in answering questions such as these.

6.3.1 The purpose and importance of workforce planning

As stated earlier, the main purpose of workforce planning is to identify future human resource requirements and to develop action plans to eliminate any discrepancies between the demand and supply of labour that may be foreseen. Excessive turnover and absenteeism, low labour productivity and ineffective training programmes can be reduced and expenses lowered if workforce planning is executed properly. According to Dolan and Schuler (1987: 42), the purposes of workforce planning are more specifically to:

- reduce labour costs by helping management to anticipate shortages or surpluses of human resources, and to correct these imbalances before they become unmanageable and expensive;
- provide a basis for planning employee development that makes optimum use of workers' aptitudes;
- improve the overall business planning process;
- provide more opportunities for minority groups in future and to identify the specific skills available (affirmative action);
- promote greater awareness of the importance of sound HRM throughout all levels of the organisation; and
- provide an instrument for evaluating the effect of alternative human resource planning activities and policies.

With the aid of computer technology, all these aims are now more easily attainable than ever before. Computers allow for vast numbers of job-related records to be maintained on each job and employee, thereby creating a human resource information system. Records could include information on employees' job preferences, qualifications, work experience, performance evaluations, individual job history in an organisation, and a complete set of information on the jobs or positions held in the organisation and/or elsewhere. This can be used to facilitate workforce planning in the interests of the individual as well as the organisation.

Workforce planning is thus important to organisations for reasons like the following:
- labour costs can make up a great proportion of overall cost structures of organisations and better planning allows greater financial control;
- business planning is central to organisational success, and financial, marketing and corporate planning without proper workforce planning will be inadequate;
- the labour supply is neither constant nor flexible, and people's social aspirations must be considered;
- environmental changes (technological, political, social and economic) mean that HRM is becoming more complex and challenging, which makes planning essential; and
- changing product demands have social implications for labour (ranging from redundancy to retraining), and planning can help to accommodate these demands.

6.3.2 The responsibility for workforce planning

The responsibility for workforce planning will depend to a large extent on variables such as the size of the organisation (in terms of resources – in particular human resources – numbers of people required to do the work), the maturity of management thinking about HRM, and the extent to which HRM is handled by specialists or has been devolved to other levels of management (see chapter 5). For example, in very large organisations, overall workforce planning might typically be spearheaded by a specialist section in the HR department, with the necessary inputs from line management, while in smaller organisations it may be carried out largely by the line managers of the particular organisation.

Very large multi-business corporate organisations that are centralised with little devolution of HRM might have separate sections staffed by workforce planning specialists, at a centralised point such as headquarters (if multidivisional) who focus on the process of reconciling the number of available employees with the present and future demand for employees. This may indeed include consideration of options to bring down the actual headcount in terms of employees – and maybe finding alternative options for getting the work of the organisation done. These people will typically have a futuristic mindset – thinking about where the organisation is heading strategically, what the environmental dynamics might entail, the implications hereof for the work of the organisation, and the people required to do it. Naturally such people will have to work hand in hand with the line managers who are responsible for their areas of work operations. The line managers will know best about the work and concomitant staffing requirements pertaining to their operations, including what work may be more prone to being outsourced, for instance. In the end, the workforce planning staff may provide ideas and table options – but the line managers will have to be comfortable that whatever is planned will most likely work best for what they are responsible for achieving.

One of the most fundamental issues when it comes to workforce planning thus relates to making sure that the organisation is ready for engaging in such a process and then putting together the right team of people to drive the process. Experience has shown that while HR support staff may be indispensable members of such planning teams, they ought not to be the official team leaders. Making line management responsible for the process creates the required 'ownership', after all, the planning is about the workforce they will need to get the work executed for which they are responsible. The key role for the relevant HR support staff will be to coordinate everything and make sure the relevant issues are tabled and all processes are productive and streamlined, as they are supposed to be the process experts and also the people most acutely aware and knowledgeable about the environmental challenges, risks, opportunities and constraints.

A general approach to workforce planning would be to include all affected by the process. In the South African context, for example, it might even be better to include employee representatives in this process. This could prove to be invaluable when the organisation is in a process of 're-engineering', or restructuring, which can often lead to plans to downsize the workforce. Because South African organisations are facing increasing international competition, organisations are forced to do more with less, and this can include a smaller core workforce to yield more flexibility and responsiveness to help make organisations more competitive. Proper workforce planning will not only assist in the smooth running of any such necessary downsizing, but the inclusion of employee representatives in the workforce-planning process could also assist in planning for, for example, retrenchments and perhaps even affirmative action implications (see also chapter 4). The requirement that the staff composition of organisations should reflect our demographics is an important aspect that should be addressed as an integral part of proper workforce-planning efforts (as explained before).

The role that the line manager plays in the workforce planning process is, as mentioned, crucial. It is accepted that the business plan and long-term strategic goals determine the direction of the organisation. As explained in chapter 5 as well, the nature of the market and the product or service to be delivered will influence the organisation design and structure. It is therefore the line manager who must manage the work, and the employees who will be required to do it. The manager will know best how the strategic direction of the organisation translates into workload requirements for his or her area of responsibility. It is ultimately on the shop floor that the plan must come together, where the success or otherwise of the plan will be demonstrated. The active participation of line managers in the workforce-planning process is therefore essential, as they can provide information on issues such as:

- whether there are enough and appropriate jobs to ensure delivery of the work output;
- whether there are enough and appropriate job categories;
- whether the incumbents are performing in accordance with accepted standards;
- whether there is a high or low turnover of employees;
- whether more or different product output will necessitate more or different jobs; and
- whether a change in product technology will change the job content with a concomitant change in training or recruitment requirements.

We believe, therefore, that although workforce planning specialists in large organisations may be responsible for initiating and coordinating the overall process, these people should work hand in hand with line managers (and perhaps the employee representatives) to develop workforce plans that are pragmatic tools to help all to make the organisation run more smoothly. These plans should in the end be aids in reconciling the ideals and aspirations of the line managers, and the realities of the resource constraints of the organisation.

One important issue to be considered in this process of reconciliation is the budget requirements of the organisation concerned. The organisation's budgeting process will be intertwined with the centralised or decentralised nature of workforce planning. In large and complex organisations it may be common practice to monitor the workforce-planning process (once it has been designed by all the stakeholders) according to an approved strategic and concomitant overall business and financial plan for the organisation. This may help ensure that head office keeps control over activities and that the organisation as a whole continues to move towards stated goals. Different business units and departments can then carry out the necessary workforce planning, using the standard methods of deploying the workforce (for example introducing flexible working hours, and engaging contract employees and seasonal workers) to ensure the optimal utilisation of employees. In smaller organisations, a centralised process of workforce planning is recommended due to the number of employees. The workforce-planning process could be decentralised should centralisation prove to be unsuccessful. Another important issue is the fact that engaging in proper workforce planning can in itself be quite a costly exercise. Before embarking on such processes, it is essential to make sure to secure top-management buy-in and support not only at the level of strategic thinking, but also in particular at the point of committing the necessary resources to actually execute a decent process of workforce planning.

6.4 THE WORKFORCE PLANNING PROCESS[1]

The workforce planning process cannot actually be kick-started unless we know that we have the necessary top-level support for it, both at strategic thinking level, as well as in terms of committing the resources to it. Once this has been secured – often only after serious efforts of strategic issue selling (see chapter 4), especially where HRM maturity is low – we can try to get going with the actual active process of planning the workforce profile and so forth. Another issue relates to the model or process used when embarking on the workforce planning process, especially when this is happening for the first time in an organisation. There are many different models of how to go about workforce planning. Likewise there are different experts and consultants who are keen to provide specialised support, using their own models. Decisions about these things obviously are important for especially the first-time workforce planning organisations. In the rest of this section we merely provide a general conceptual process framework to guide thinking when it comes to workforce planning. In practice it may be quite beneficial to shop around for specific models, most of which might well include very sophisticated computerised elements and standardised templates to guide the planning process.

As stressed before, the first and most fundamental task in the process of planning for the future workforce requirements of the organisation is to ensure that there is a clear link between the organisation's general strategic plans, the formulated HRM strategies and structures, and the workforce plans as such. Cognisance must thus be taken of the organisational goals and, more particularly, of the human resource implications hereof. Once the external and internal factors have been considered, the supply and demand of current and new employees can be analysed.

The external factors include issues such as labour market conditions, government policies and educational trends, while the internal factors refer to issues such as the number of employees leaving the organisation who will have to be replaced, the number of employees retiring in the future and the career progression of employees remaining in the organisation (see figure 6.3). An important aspect to mention here is the impact of the Employment Equity Act (see also chapter 3). Affirmative action target setting will have to be an integral part and major driving force behind workforce planning. Other factors to consider include organisational reward systems, current work practices, the labour relations climate, the technology, turnover targets, production processes and profit targets. All of these issues are identified and analysed with the purpose of drafting a plan that can best utilise the implications these factors may have for the organisation. In other words, these factors must be incorporated into the workforce plan to ensure that their influence on the organisation is properly managed as the programme or plan is implemented.

6.4.1 Step 1: Gathering, analysing, and forecasting workforce supply and demand data

Step 1 outlines the various important phases to be followed and methods and techniques to be used to ensure the successful implementation of workforce planning and programming.

6.4.1.1 Phase 1: Forecasting

When personnel forecasting is undertaken, the workforce planner attempts to ascertain estimates of the supply and demand of various types of personnel in terms of the key performance areas that flow from business plans. The primary goal is to predict areas in the organisation where there may be labour surpluses or shortages. Forecasting on both the demand and supply side can be done by judgemental and/or statistical methods (see phases 3 and 5 below). Statistical methods are used mainly to capture historic trends in an organisation's demand for labour and can, given the right conditions, provide much more accurate predictions than judgemental processes. In other circumstances the judgemental approach is more appropriate, for example in the absence of historical data regarding events occurring in the marketplace or in an organisation. To achieve an appropriate and balanced result, workforce planners should ideally combine statistical and judgemental approaches when forecasting. Although many sophisticated forecasting techniques have been developed, forecasting is often informal and judgemental. Forecasting in stable organisations is more accurate than those in volatile environments. The value of

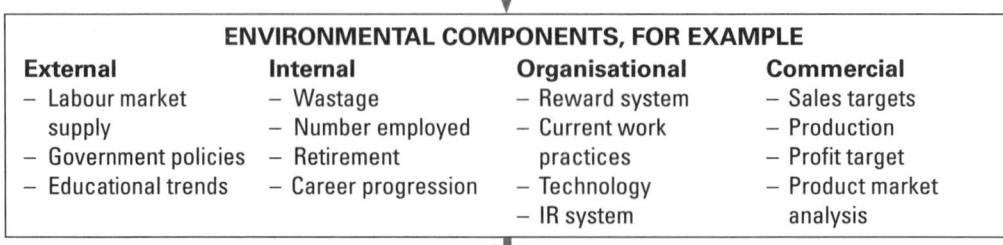

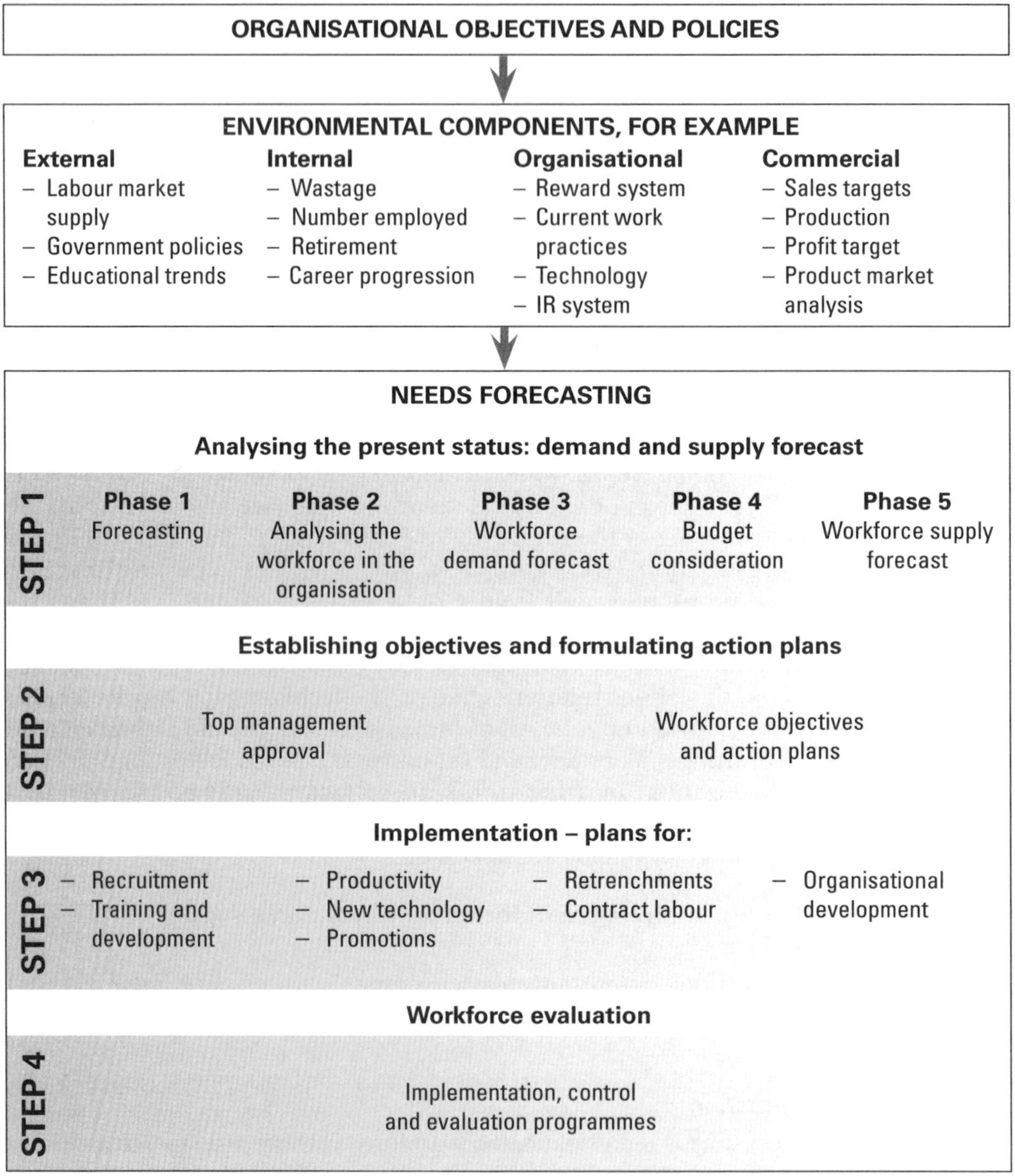

ORGANISATIONAL OBJECTIVES AND POLICIES

↓

ENVIRONMENTAL COMPONENTS, FOR EXAMPLE

External	**Internal**	**Organisational**	**Commercial**
– Labour market supply	– Wastage	– Reward system	– Sales targets
– Government policies	– Number employed	– Current work practices	– Production
– Educational trends	– Retirement	– Technology	– Profit target
	– Career progression	– IR system	– Product market analysis

↓

NEEDS FORECASTING

Analysing the present status: demand and supply forecast

STEP 1

Phase 1	**Phase 2**	**Phase 3**	**Phase 4**	**Phase 5**
Forecasting	Analysing the workforce in the organisation	Workforce demand forecast	Budget consideration	Workforce supply forecast

Establishing objectives and formulating action plans

STEP 2

Top management approval   Workforce objectives and action plans

Implementation – plans for:

STEP 3

– Recruitment	– Productivity	– Retrenchments	– Organisational development
– Training and development	– New technology	– Contract labour	
	– Promotions		

Workforce evaluation

STEP 4

Implementation, control and evaluation programmes

Figure 6.3: The workforce planning and programming process
Sources: Adapted from Dolan & Schuler (1987: 47) and French (1994: 132)

a forecast should, however, be judged not so much on its accuracy but on the extent to which it forced managers to think and consider alternatives.

6.4.1.2 Phase 2: Analysing the existing workforce in the organisation

This phase begins with an analysis of the inventory of the current workforce and the current jobs in the organisation. Questions that need to be asked include: Who are our employees? What skills do they have? How good are they? How are they developed? These are but a few of the questions that need to be answered. To know what the skills, abilities, interests and preferences of the current workforce are forms only one part of the inventory. It is also important to determine the characteristics of present jobs, how they are organised and structured, and the skills required to fill them. Organisational charts could, for example, be useful in this regard. Proper job analysis facilitates this part of the inventory. Much of the information in larger organisations can be stored, adapted and retrieved from a human resource information system (see chapter 22).The importance of having updated records of all the jobs in an organisation cannot be overemphasised. Lately there seems to be some trend to regard rigid job descriptions and job specifications as outdated methods of determining the required skill levels in organisations. The important issue, however, is not the method used but that the competency requirements at all levels in the organisation should be known and determined by the requirements of the jobs and not by the characteristics of current incumbents. Many organisations fail to produce credible workforce plans because of the lack of accurate information on job requirements – in other words, job descriptions and specifications.

An analysis of the flows or patterns of employees through the organisation is important because it not only provides supply data but also identifies any changes in human resource flow patterns. Such an analysis illustrates the availability of employees who are ready to advance to new jobs, and it identifies those ready to retire as well as the average rate at which employees progress through jobs (McBeath 1992: 31).

Another key aspect to be considered when workforce planning is done is the probable future national composition of the labour force. Data from the external analysis on labour force composition, current demographic and economic data are used to make labour-force projections, which are most often very general in nature. They do, however, provide an organisation with information for its workforce plans, particularly regarding its long-term needs. In this regard, as explained in chapter 4, affirmative action is currently of paramount importance in the process of workforce planning in South Africa. (See chapter 3 where the Employment Equity Act is discussed, as well as exhibit 6.4 below.)

Another aspect to analyse is organisational labour productivity and how it will change in the future. Projected employee turnover, absenteeism and retrenchments, for example, influence the productivity of an organisation's workforce and its future workforce needs. These issues must be analysed so that plans can be developed to address them. It is suggested that a one-off productivity improvement approach be avoided and that an attempt be made to develop long-term productivity plans for the organisation (Sibson 1992: 60).

Another aspect of this phase is the examination and projection of an organisational structure for the organisation. The probable size of the top, middle and lower levels of the organisation, including both managers and non-managers, must be determined. Information about changes in the organisation's workforce needs and about specific activities or functional areas is crucial to the workforce-planning process. Determining the type of organisational structure which will be required in the future is obviously essential to forecast workforce needs (see chapter 5).

6.4.1.3 Phase 3: Workforce demand forecast

The demand for employees can be determined by a number of forecasting methods. It should, however, always be borne in mind that, at best, forecasting results in approximations. The accuracy of forecasts depends on the information available and on the predictability of events. In the short term, events are more predictable and information will usually be more accurate. Dolan and Schuler (1987: 50) distinguish

EXHIBIT 6.4: Some employment equity implications for conducting workforce analyses

Organisational variables

Every organisation is unique in terms of the way it is structured and will have to report to the director general (DG) of the Department of Labour about its existing structures, possible future changes to the existing structures and any new methodologies to structure job classifications, etc. The following aspects are relevant in the context of conducting workforce analyses that will form input for the Employment Equity Plan:

- organisational structures;
- job evaluation system(s);
- job categories broken down per discipline/department or division; and
- number of positions per job category/occupational family.

Occupational analysis

It will also be important to analyse the situation with regard to the critical competencies and job entry requirement. Without appropriate information the DG will make certain assumptions with regard to the plans/targets the organisation sets for itself – which may not be correct and which could lead to further justifications being requested.

The occupational analysis requires, among others:

- job skills/competencies/qualifications/experience required per job category;
- identification of job categories/occupations, which are critical to the overall success of the business;
- summary of education/training and development institutions responsible for the development of the skills/competencies identified as being of critical importance;
- average cost estimates to acquire the required (critical) skills/competencies etc (based on actual/historial training and development costs);
- average remuneration analysis and breakdown of benefits; and
- average cost of employment to the organisation (per job category and total).

Employee statistical analysis

This section is obviously very important as it will provide the DG with an overall picture of the race, gender and people with disabilities distribution within the company. The following aspects are included here:

- employee complement versus strength per occupational level;
- employee strength by race and gender per occupation level;
- employee strength – disabled employees per occupational level (male/female);
- comparative statistics: representatives per occupational group versus industry demographics, regional demographics, national demographics or economically active population; and
- statistics of suitably qualified persons available – internally and externally.

Financial and economic factors

This section is important both with regard to the above, ie acquisition of skills and section 27 of the Act and also in terms of section 18 of the Act:

- analysis of the total wage costs of the organisation;
- analysis of overheads associated with employment;
- costs associated with recruitment, selection and placement;
- costs associated with training and development;
- economic and financial factors relevant to the organisation, sector or industry
- present and anticipated economic and financial circumstances of the organisation; and
- short/medium/long-term financial forecasts.

between two classes of forecasting technique to project an organisation's demand for employees, namely judgemental forecasts and conventional statistical projections; these are briefly discussed below.

Judgemental forecasts

- The *Delphi technique* is most commonly used in judgemental forecasts. This technique requires a large number of experts to take turns presenting forecast statements and assumptions (Schuler, Dowling, Smart & Huber 1993: 64). Each expert makes forecasts, which are routed to the other experts, who then revise their own forecasts until a viable composite forecast emerges. Specific projections or a range of projections may be developed, depending on the positions and experience levels of the experts.

  This technique has produced better short-term forecasts than linear regression analysis, but problems are sometimes experienced, for example in integrating the opinions of experts. This technique is, however, very useful for generating ideas about unstructured or relatively less-developed subject areas, such as workforce planning.

- The *nominal group technique* also entails using multiple inputs from several persons. The information can be obtained in a structured format and it is a structured variation of small-group discussion methods (Newstrom & Scannel 1980: 107). People sit around a conference table and independently list their ideas regarding the forecast on a sheet of paper. After a period of time they take turns expressing their ideas to the group. Each member's ideas are recorded so that everyone can see all of the ideas and refer to them later on in the session. For example, a group of managers from different departments may get together with the purpose of determining the number of employees who will be required in two years' time due to a change from the traditional, labour-intensive production method to a semi-automated approach. Each manager will have the opportunity to state his or her case. This process prevents the domination of discussion by a single person, and encourages the more passive persons to participate. Eventually all the ideas of the managers are prioritised and integrated.

- The *managerial judgement technique* involves managers deciding, possibly in consultation with other staff, what their future activities are likely to be and what types of staff they will need to ensure success. This approach can be top down or bottom up (lower-level managers who make estimates and pass them up), or a combination of the two. The biggest problem with this technique is that it is judgemental in nature and is focused on the managers' experience only. It is, however, straightforward and can be implemented easily (Cushway 1994).

Statistical techniques

- *Linear regression analysis* can best be explained by the case of a perfect linear association between two variables, for example production and employment (Babbie 1995). If a relationship can be established between the level of production and the level of employment, predictions of future production can be used to make predictions of future employment. Although there may be a relationship between production and employment, however, the relationship is often influenced by a number of factors. For example, if production doubles it does not mean that employment must be doubled – it could be achieved by better productivity arrangements.

- *Multiple linear regression analysis* is used to analyse those situations where a given dependent variable is affected simultaneously by several independent ones. For example, instead of using only production to predict employment demand, productivity data and equipment-use data also may be used. The reason why this method is used is because it incorporates several variables related to employment, and may produce more accurate demand forecasts than linear regression analysis. It seems that only relatively large organisations use multiple regression analysis (Schuler et al 1993: 65).
- The *unit demand forecasting* technique is a method by which departmental or functional managers provide certain labour estimates because they know what business activity will be performed by their units/departments in the future. When the estimates for all departments are added up, they form an overall forecast for the organisation; this often differs from the organisation forecasted demands (as prepared by the workforce specialist). An example of this is where an organisation finds that 10 salespeople will retire in 24 months and that a radical product expansion will probably exacerbate the shortage. By anticipating the problem, a plan can be drafted for new salespeople to be recruited. This will make department managers more aware of the skills, abilities and desires of their employees, and may reveal a discrepancy in respect of the aggregate organisational forecast. The broad organisational forecast may not, for example, take into account certain losses of personnel due to a lack of intimate knowledge about employees' performance. A compromise will then have to be reached to establish the real organisational demand. This exercise will probably produce a higher-quality forecast. An obvious advantage is that the unit/department manager knows how many new positions will be needed to achieve output and is therefore the right person to participate. A disadvantage is, however, the fact that a large group of people have to be organised and that they could work on different assumptions.

Other statistical methods

According to Schuler et al (1993: 66), other statistical methods may be helpful too:
- *Productivity ratios*
  Historical data are used to examine past levels of a productivity index (P). Where constant or systematic relationships are found, human resource requirements can be computed by dividing predicted workloads by P.
- *Personnel ratios*
  Past personnel data are examined to determine historical relationships among the employees in various jobs or job categories. Regression analysis or productivity ratios are then used to project either total or key group human resource requirements, and ratios are used to allocate total requirements to various job categories or to estimate requirements for non-key groups.
- *Time series analysis*
  Past staffing levels (instead of workload indicators) are used to project future human resource requirements. Past staffing levels are examined to isolate seasonal and cyclical variations, long-term trends and random movement. Long-term trends are then extrapolated or projected using a moving average, exponential smoothing or regression techniques.
- *Stochastic analysis*
  The likelihood of landing a series of contracts is combined with the personnel requirements of each contract to estimate expected staffing requirements. This has potential application in government contracts and construction industries.

6.4.1.4 Phase 4: Budget agreement

A budget is a plan for controlling the use of funds over a period of time (Jarrell 1993: 86). By reconciling workforce planning and budgeting, the whole exercise is placed into a financial perspective. Managers have to indicate the need for additional personnel to fill posts in the future. This whole process is based on managers making accurate estimates. This forecasting method is highly judgemental, varying from a bottom-up approach (where the manager determines his or her own needs) to a top-down approach where top managers place constraints either in terms of budget allocations or numbers of employees. Unit/department managers are then required to plan these objectives within this framework (Cherrington 1995: 160). The workforce forecast must be expressed in rand terms, and must be compatible with the organisation's monetary objectives and overall budget limitations. The budget reconciliation process may also indicate that the budget has to be adjusted to accommodate the workforce plan. This step provides the opportunity to align the objectives regarding the personnel of the organisation with those of the organisation as a whole.

6.4.1.5 Phase 5: Forecasting workforce supply

Forecasting supply can be derived from internal and external sources. The internal source is generally most important and readily available. There are basically two categories of techniques to help forecast internal labour supply, namely judgemental and statistical.

Judgemental techniques
- *Replacement planning* is a shorter-term technique which uses replacement charts to show the names of the current incumbents of positions in the organisation together with the names of likely replacements. Replacement charts make it clear where potential vacancies may occur, based on the performance levels of the employees in the current jobs. It is important to note that aspects such as gender, race and age should be omitted from these replacement charts to prevent these criteria from being used in making promotion decisions. This will avoid possible violations of the Labour Relations Act of 1995.
- *Succession planning* is a longer-term, more flexible method, which focuses on the development of managers or leaders (see figure 6.4). This technique is widely practised, especially in large organisations like Eskom and Absa. There is a tendency to emphasise the characteristics of the managers themselves and to downplay the characteristics of the job to which employees may eventually be promoted. This approach is flawed as both aspects have to be emphasised.

The following differences between succession planning and replacement planning can be identified.
- Replacement planning covers a short time span (for example up to 12 months) and the best candidate is chosen, while succession planning is more long term and the candidate with the best potential development is chosen.
- Replacement planning is very flexible but can be limited by the structure of the plan, while succession planning is perceived as being flexible but is intended to promote development and thinking about alternative candidates.
- In the case of replacement planning, the experience base of those managers to be considered is based on the judgement and observation of candidates, and this forms the basis of the plan. In the case of succession planning, the results of the plan are based on inputs and discussion involving a number of other managers, and is thus a group effort.

Management succession plan				
Organisation: .... Date:				
Probability of vacancy: A = within 1 year B = after 1–3 years C = beyond 3 years				

Position incumbent	Readiness			Contingency plan
	A Now	B 1–3 years	C 3 years +	
J Cocker				

Figure 6.4: Succession planning
Source: Adapted from French (1994: 133)

■ The development planning for managers in replacement planning is normally informal, while for succession planning it is more formal and extensive. Specific long-term personal development plans for individuals are developed as part of succession planning.

■ With replacement planning the identified candidate will fill a vacant post, while with succession planning all candidates are considered to fill the post because a pool of candidates has been identified.

Statistical techniques

When statistical techniques are not widely used, it is usually because of inadequate databases, lack of software computer programs and a shortage of trained professionals.

The following are examples of a few statistical methods (Schuler et al 1993: 69).

■ *Markov analysis.* This type of analysis projects future flows to obtain availability estimates through a straightforward application of historical transition rates. Historical transition rates are derived from analyses of personnel data concerning losses, promotions, transfers, demotions and, perhaps, recruitment.

■ *Simulation* (based on Markov analysis). Alternative (rather than historical) flows are examined for effects of future human resource availabilities. Alternative flows reflect the anticipated results of policy or programme changes relating to voluntary and involuntary turnover, retirement, promotion, etc.

■ *Renewal analysis.* Renewal analysis estimates future flows and availabilities by calculating vacancies as created by organisational growth, personnel losses and internal movements, and the results of decision rules governing the filling of vacancies. Alternative models may assess the effects of changes in growth estimates, turnover, promotions or decision rules.

■ *Goal programming.* This type of programming focuses on optimising goals. Desired staffing patterns are established, given a set of constraints concerning such things as the upper limits on staff flows, the percentage of new recruits and total salary budgets.

The last stage in Step 1 focuses on the process of reconciliation necessitated by the mismatch between the quantitative and qualitative demand for employees based on the future plans of the organisation and on current projections of employee availability – that is, the supply of employees. At first this imbalance will be portrayed by a numerical shortfall or surplus in employees that is likely to occur in the future. Shortfalls in the organisation may result in departments running at overcapacity due to employee shortages, resulting in overtime work with concomitant long-term problems. Surpluses of employees may, on the other hand, lead to low productivity, financial losses and, if employees are not transferred or retrenched, to the eventual closing of the organisation. Proper workforce planning is thus essential to maintain a proper balance in the number of employees required by the organisation and to avoid the ill effects of employee problems or organisational readjustments. The supply forecast, once complete, can be compared with the workforce demand forecast to help determine action programming necessary to identify workforce talent, and to balance the supply and demand forecast. It must, however, be borne in mind that most current forecasting of labour supply and demand is short range and used for the purpose of budgeting and cost control.

6.4.2 Step 2: Establishing objectives and formulating plans

As we have stressed many times, workforce objectives are directly related to general organisational objectives and strategies. The impact of the organisation's strategies, goals, policies and plans on workforce planning is crucial – that is really the crux of proper workforce planning. However, not too many organisations achieve a sufficient link between their general strategic and business planning, and their workforce planning. Step 2 focuses on the desired end result and on providing a target to measure the achievement of success in addressing the labour surplus or shortages in the organisation. Definite objectives (including a timetable for their achievement) should be set to measure effectiveness (for example that the number of miners in a particular mine should be increased by 35% within the next year).

Once the objectives have been set, action plans must be formulated to facilitate their achievement. Responsibilities must also be assigned to different persons for the execution of the action plans. There are a number of options that can be considered to reduce an expected labour surplus in an organisation, for example retrenchments, demotions and transfers. Such decisions can be put into effect quickly, but the possible consequences and impact on employees can be harsh. Other options which are slow to take effect but which can still be considered are normal retirement, resignations and the retraining of staff.

A possible labour shortage can be quickly remedied by, for example, taking on temporary employees, subcontracting and working overtime. Other possible options are to reduce resignations, to retrain employees for new jobs and to recruit new employees. This is, however, a slow process.

6.4.3 Step 3: Implementing and adapting the workforce plan

In reality this is not part of planning for the workforce, but actually the execution of the workforce plan. Once the goals have been set, individuals must be held accountable for the planned actions, and the necessary resources must be made available. Plans relating to recruitment, training and development, increasing labour productivity, retirements and so forth must be executed with the necessary professionalism. For example, a retrenchment decision must follow the specified procedures. The important thing is that a plan is just that – a plan. Things change, and unexpected things might force us to reassess our workforce plan. As we thus execute, we must monitor and adapt our workforce plans. Especially important will be the integration of affirmative action or employment equity plans or programmes with our workforce planning. It may well be that targets may be reached and we adjust our workforce plans only to find that resignations of designated staff bedevil them and we have to change them again. It is thus an iterative process because monitoring and evaluation of how well our plans roll out will be necessary as we execute them.

6.4.4 Step 4: Assessing or evaluating workforce planning

From time to time it is important to determine how well our workforce planning processes are working. This we can do through thorough evaluation of the plans and programmes and how things developed when we ultimately implemented.

Possible criteria or standards for evaluating workforce planning include the measurement of:

- actual staffing levels against established staffing requirements;
- productivity levels against established goals;
- actual personnel flow rates against desired rates;
- programmes implemented against action plans;
- programme results against expected outcomes (for example improved applicant flows, reduced quit rates, improved replacement ratios);
- labour and programme costs against budgets; and
- ratios of programme results (benefits) to programme costs.

The information we collect through such evaluations may the serve as a basis for fine-tuning and improving our workforce planning.

6.5 CONCLUSION

In this chapter we covered workforce planning, and explained that job analysis is, in some sense, foundational to the process. It was again stressed that work and organisation design and the development of organisational strategies and HRM strategies are also all linked with workforce planning. The centrality of employment equity and affirmative action targets and planning to the process of workforce planning in South Africa has also again been highlighted.

We explained what workforce planning entails and showed its purpose and importance. We stressed that workforce planning must be a process which engages line managers as well as relevant HR support staff such as workforce planning specialists.

Workforce planning is essentially the last aspect of the preparatory work of HRM. The active aspects of actually putting into action all that has been planned for, prepared and so forth starts next. This is obviously an over-simplified view of HRM as a sequential process, but merely given here to help you conceptualise the full spectrum of work involved in HRM. In the next chapter we now turn to the challenge of searching to find the right people to do the work of the organisation.

SUSTAINABILITY CONNECTION?
Without the right quality and quantities of people to do the work of the organisation, there can be no hope of achieving sustainable competitive advantage. With too may people, the costs will be too high to maintain the operations efficiently and effectively. With not enough people there will be too much strain on those who

---

must do the work, and that cannot be sustained either. It is therefore essential to plan as accurately as possible what work needs to be done if we are to execute our strategies and business plans effectively and efficiently, and what talent we will need and how we will get that timeously. In this way workforce planning based on a good understanding of the work (through work and job analysis processes) of the organisation can help us to direct our HRM efforts towards building a sustainable organisation. There is no way in which we can ensure perfect workforce plans all the time, but the more aligned we can make our plans with our actual work requirements, the better are the chances of making positive contributions to the organisation and all the people working in and for it. The more we can make such contributions, the better the chances of organisational success and hence survival. Poor planning or the absence thereof exposes our organisations to too much risk, and that can lead to poor performance, lack of competitiveness and even perhaps complete failure/closure, with concomitant job losses. All of these things can only have a negative impact on all people involved – even the families and communities served through these organisations and their working people.

SELF-EVALUATION QUESTIONS

1 What is workforce planning and how does it relate to developing HRM strategy? How does it relate to work design?
2 'Job analysis, workforce planning and work design are interconnected.' Discuss this statement.
3 Differentiate between a job description and a job specification. How are they connected and how do they relate to job analysis?
4 Describe different job-analysis methods. What method would you recommend if approached to analyse (a) the jobs of accountants who work in all the major cities in South Africa; and (b) 10 computer analysts working in Johannesburg? Why?
5 How does workforce planning relate to affirmative action?
6 Who should play what role in respect of workforce planning in an organisation? Explain and give reasons for your point of view.
7 Suppose you were to present a lecture to a group of engineering students enrolled in a course known as 'Managing your engineering business enterprise' and the topic for your lecture is the following: 'The value and nature of the workforce planning process.' What would your presentation entail?
8 Explain possible options to address shortages and surpluses of employees in an organisation.
9 What are the possible areas of direct and indirect discrimination which must be addressed in the process of doing job analysis, developing and writing up job descriptions and job specifications, and compiling workforce plans (you will have to integrate work from previous chapters, most notably chapter 3).

ENDNOTE

1 This section is based partly on Dolan & Schuler (1987: 45–58); French (1994: 132–137); Schuler, Dowling, Smart & Huber (1993: 60–66); and O'Doherty (1995: 134–136).

PART THREE

SOURCING WORK TALENT

7 SEARCHING FOR THE RIGHT PEOPLE TO DO THE WORK

LEARNING OUTCOMES

After studying this chapter, you should be able to:

- define recruitment and explain what a recruitment policy and procedure entails;
- debate the internal and external factors influencing recruitment;
- describe the aspects that play a role in job choice;
- list and explain the different recruitment sources and methods;
- explain the factors involved in drawing up a recruitment advertisement;
- explain the recruitment process; and
- engage in meaningful dialogue about issues related to finding workers through temporary employment services organisations, rather than as employees.

7.1 INTRODUCTION

The workforce plans are useful in that these help us prepare for how we intend to meet the future work requirements of the organisation, and/or parts thereof, with matching the supply and demand for employees. Whereas the job design (perhaps even redesign) and job analysis-related information will be essential to know what kinds of employees we will need, and the workforce plans will identify how we intend to bring about the match – reality can often turn out differently. The workforce plans assist to develop more comprehensive 'pictures' of where we are heading, and what our needs might be and how we plan to address them. These are essential from a financial planning perspective. We know, however, that plans are no more than that – these are just 'best estimates' of what we expect to happen in the future.

We might plan the work – but we must work the plan. We must make sure that we actually have the people to do the work as designed and described in the position or job description. That means we must actively do something to try to secure the appropriate people to come and help further our organisation's strive to be successful. We must actively solicit potential suitable employees to apply for jobs at the organisation. Once again, we must now actually make sure that we not only attract the required applicants for jobs from which selection (dealt with in the next chapter) will take place, but we must find the other people who might be needed to perform the work for which we do not have actual positions. We must thus engage in recruiting potential job candidates, but we must also source other workers who may never become part of our organisation as employees, such as for work that we might outsource to labour brokers.

Recruitment can be described as those HRM activities that are undertaken in order to solicit job applications from people who have the necessary potential, knowledge, skills and abilities (competencies), to fill positions as employees who will assist the organisation in achieving its objectives.

The recruitment process may be set in motion by the workforce planning process – as we actually execute what we have planned for. However, it also happens that vacancies just arise spontaneously from movements (such as resignations, promotions or transfers) never factored into our plans. From time to time the organisation has to attract job candidates with the required competencies for the jobs or positions that have been created. The response of potential employees depends on their attitude towards both the work to be performed and the organisation, as well as their perception of whether the necessary fit can possibly be established between them and the organisation trying to employ them. We must also find organisations that can help us get the work done which does not form part of our position establishment.

This chapter deals with recruitment as well as alternative methods of finding the appropriate people to help get the work of the organisation done. Because most work will typically be executed as part of jobs and hence by employees, that is also where we put the emphasis in this chapter. We thus first cover recruitment as a crucially important part of HRM work. We take a brief look at policy and procedure regarding this task before we cover the issue of work choice that any potential employee has to make. We also cover the sources and methods of recruitment, and the recruitment process in general. Lastly, we cover some relevant issues pertaining to alternative ways of getting people to help execute the work of the organisation, without becoming employees of the organisation.

7.2 RECRUITMENT POLICY AND PROCEDURES

The recruitment policy stipulates broad guidelines on how an organisation intends to deal with recruitment. The answers to the following questions may be of assistance when formalising a recruitment policy:

- What legal prescriptions regarding fairness and discrimination should be taken into account (for example the Labour Relations Act of 1995, the Employment Equity Act of 1998 and the Bill of Rights in our Constitution)?
- Which clauses in collective agreements with trade unions are applicable (for example recognition agreements and bargaining council agreements)?
- How can recruitment be carried out within budget limitations?
- How urgently should vacancies be filled?
- What are the prescriptions of the workforce planning and succession planning documents? For example:
  - Will promotions from within the organisation take preference?
  - May relatives of existing employees be employed?
  - Will handicapped persons be employed?
  - May part-time employees be employed?
  - May minors be employed?
  - Which department or person (designated title) will be responsible for the execution of the policy and procedure?

A recruitment policy is developed largely to provide broad guidelines in terms of how recruitment is done in an organisation. The procedures provide more detailed guidelines to assist in executing a recruitment process aimed at attracting suitable job candidates as cost and time effectively as possible. These are aids in helping and guiding managers to be effective and efficient in recruitment. A recruitment policy and procedure document will normally allow managers to use a variety of recruitment sources and methods which should facilitate the avoidance of discriminatory recruitment practices (see section 7.4) that may be unfair.

Various factors influence recruitment policy and practice. These may be divided into external and internal factors – those variables outside the organisation, such as labour market conditions, government and trade union influences, and those inside the organisation, such as plans, policies and procedures.

7.2.1 External factors influencing recruitment

7.2.1.1 The economy and labour market conditions

The state of a country's economy plays a crucial role in terms of the state of the labour market. In a strong and growing economy there is normally a concomitant growth in and ample demand for suitably qualified job candidates. If there is an abundance of qualified candidates who meet the job specification requirements, a small recruiting effort may generate many applications. If the job market is tight, more creative and expensive efforts might be necessary. Skills shortages will require larger compensation packages to attract the right candidates. The Department of Labour has statistics available for different sectors of the labour market. Human resource specialists should remain abreast of current trends in the labour market to employ the right recruitment policy.

7.2.1.2 Government policy and legislation

Government policy will in future play an increasingly important role in the determination of recruitment practice. As explained in chapter 3, South Africa has a comprehensive legislative framework governing HRM-related matters, including, for example, affirmative action and unfair discrimination.

The following instances may be viewed as guidelines of where possible unfair discriminatory recruitment practices may take place:

- Discrimination against a potential employee on the grounds of pregnancy, intended pregnancy, or any reason related to pregnancy.
- Discrimination against a potential employee, directly or indirectly, on any arbitrary grounds such as race, gender, ethnic or social origin, colour, sexual orientation, age, disability, religion, conscience, belief, political opinion, culture, language, marital status or family responsibility.
- As you already know, our legislation provides protection of the rights of persons seeking employment. The Labour Relations Act (LRA) 66 of 1995 expressly prohibits an employer from advantaging, or promising to advantage a person seeking employment in exchange for that person's undertaking not to exercise any right conferred by the LRA (for example joining a trade union, participating in protected strike action, participating in workplace forums or in other procedures provided for in the LRA).

This means that the Labour Relations Act 66 of 1995, in addition to the Employment Equity Act 55 of 1998, places certain important prohibitions on unfair discrimination in any employment policy or practice, also specifically including applicants for employment. This obviously holds direct implications for recruitment policy and practice.

As you would already know, the Employment Equity Act states very clearly that no person may unfairly discriminate, directly or indirectly, against an employee on any of the various grounds. Organisations will thus have to change their recruitment policies, procedures and practices to ensure that no unfair discrimination takes place and to promote affirmative action. According to Pons and Deale (1998: 18–28), advertisements for available positions should in no way indicate an intention to unfairly discriminate against members of a particular group. Some examples include the following:

■ Subconscious discriminatory language, for example the word 'she' is used when advertising secretarial positions and 'he' when advertising the post of a production manager.
■ Inherent requirements of the job must be clearly spelt out to ensure that prerequisites or qualifications attached to the job are justifiable. For example, when a job of a typist is advertised, the requirements would be for a person who can type and not for a person who has a certificate in typing. By requiring a certificate in typing, a group of people may be excluded from potential applicants.
■ When using advertising media it is suggested that advertisements should be placed where people from a particular race group are not excluded or disproportionately reduced.

7.2.1.3 Trade unions

This may be related to the trade union movement in general, as well as to the actual trade unions representing employees in a particular organisation. As such this is not necessarily an outside or external variable or factor. Generally speaking, though, the state of the union movement in any country does hold implications for recruitment. In some countries, trade unions may be rather inactive whereas in others the opposite might apply. In cases where trade union activity is too disruptive, organisations may simply pack up and leave, shifting their operations to another country. In South Africa, the role of trade unions must be factored in simply because these are such important stakeholders in our society and our organisations.

Many unions seek to persuade managers of organisations to enter into agreements stipulating that only union members will be employed by the enterprise concerned. Unions may also seek participation in recruitment processes to make sure there is no irregularity. The particular sources used for recruitment are of interest, for example, as are the selection criteria that may go into the recruitment drive. Management should take cognisance of the influence of unions and adopt recruitment practices which are acceptable to all the stakeholders.

7.2.1.4 The outside image of an organisation: 'brand' as employer

Organisations spend huge amounts of money to develop brand identity in relation to their products/services so that they can get customers to be loyal to the brand they offer and stand for. Just as organisations are competing for customers, they are also competing for talent. Our brand as employer is therefore just as important. If the people out there do not have a positive image about what type of organisation we are, the best among them will not be keen to be associated with us. It is therefore very important to build a reputation that gives us a good name as an employer. While we are thus here referring to this as an external factor (because we are talking about the image that people outside the organisation have of us), our brand as employer is built from the inside. It develops through what our own staff think and say about us in terms of what they experience while working for our organisation. According to research (Sartain 2005: 182), we can use "branding to pinpoint, distinguish, and tout the unique values", culture and hence work environment our organisation offers to prospective employees. Importantly, though, this branding will also serve to bind together our existing staff and employees, who may also be keen to apply for positions advertised (if we do not advertise internally first – as discussed below). We thus actually build an image inside the organisation, which is projected to the outside as our brand as employer. Gibbon (2004: 39) explains: "But the employer brand goes far beyond the intangible concept of image. It is also derived from the very real facets of the relationship such as compensation, the location of our facilities, advancement opportunities, development programs, and internal communications. It is strongest if your internal policies and procedures directly support your external branding and sales efforts."

If we have a great brand as employer we will be better at attracting the top-class talent, but if the brand is not good the highly talented people outside in the labour market will rather not make themselves available. As such, it is crucial for recruitment efforts.

7.2.2 Internal factors influencing recruitment

7.2.2.1 Strategy

Recruitment must not be seen as an isolated activity. The organisation's plans are the basis for the workforce plans on which many recruitment efforts are based. The recruitment of potential and talent is thus in a very real sense our early efforts to get the right people to help with executing our strategies and business plans. Organisations need high-calibre working people to get the work done towards mission accomplishment. Our brand as employer, as explained above, will be very important in attracting the most appropriate talent. We should therefore align our product/service branding with the branding of our organisation as employer, as mentioned above. Our HRM strategies must thus include how we want to brand ourselves as employers. Likewise, our recruitment policies must be developed in line with the HR strategy decided upon (see chapter 4), which, as we have stressed all along, should be part and parcel of broader organisational strategy.

7.2.2.2 Policy

The organisation's recruitment policy must be clarified as soon as possible. If preference is given, for example, to affirmative action candidates or to promotion from within or employment of the handicapped, the policy must state this clearly, and certain procedures must be implemented to ensure the execution of the policy. It is, however, recommended that all the stakeholders in the organisation be included in the process of determining the organisational recruitment policy.

A POLICY PERSPECTIVE

Our recruitment policy aims to attract job applications from as many as possible of the potentially most suitable candidates. Attracting top-class talent should provide a pool of candidates from whom we can then select the most suitable one/s. Because we value our people, we endeavour, as far as we reasonably can, to first recruit from inside the organisation through internal advertisement. Because we value diversity, our recruitment campaigns are to be particularly geared towards workforce diversification.

The purpose of this policy is to support the design and implementation of appropriate recruitment practices, processes and methods – and targeting appropriate sources of recruitment. The overall aim is to attract job applications from people who will fit well with the strategic direction of the organisation and, if any of these people turn out to be selected, we ought to be reasonably confident that they will help us on our way towards superior performance.

7.2.2.3 Recruitment criteria

Abnormally stringent criteria will hamper recruitment efforts. Accurate job descriptions and specifications will help to set realistic job performance criteria, which could help facilitate more effective recruitment. Criteria must also be drawn up to avoid any unfair discriminatory practices. People will apply if they think their own profiles match the criteria which are put out as part of the recruitment campaign.

7.2.2.4 Costs

Smaller organisations do not always have the resources to allow for expensive recruitment drives, and often substandard compensation packages are offered. In larger organisations the HR department will probably have a recruitment budget based on forecast employee losses and future personnel requirements (see chapter 6, which deals with workforce planning). In larger organisations, budgets play an important role in determining the number of people to be recruited. In many organisations, however, there is a trend to minimise appointments to ensure organisational survival rather than to appoint personnel simply because a vacancy has arisen.

7.3 THE POTENTIAL EMPLOYEE

Both the employer and the person considering employment have a lot at stake in the employment process. The applicant can be viewed as a person seeking a position that will provide him or her with both material and psychological rewards. As explained in chapter 1, potential employees have different perceptions, expectations, needs, etc, and managers trying to employ a person are expected to take note of these differences. For most people, the process of job choice begins long before they become aware of any recruitment efforts by organisations. Recruiters must be aware of the factors influencing job choice, as this will enable them to give better advice and to make better choices when recruiting candidates. Job choice for most people consists of three components, namely occupational choice, job search and organisational commitment.

7.3.1 Occupational choice

During early childhood, an individual starts thinking about work and occupation. This process continues through adolescence and adulthood, and involves a number of decisions until an initial choice is made. During this process, psychological, economic and sociological factors influence the occupational interests of the individual. As occupational interests become more focused, the individual begins to seek employment that will best satisfy his or her particular interests.

7.3.2 Job search

When designing a specific recruitment programme, one must consider the most preferred methods of job seeking used by candidates. There are both informal and formal methods, an example of the latter being the use of employment agencies. However, many candidates may prefer more informal recruitment methods, such as asking friends or responding to newspaper advertisements.

With this in mind, management should design the recruitment drive around these preferred methods. One word of caution, however: should an employer decide to encourage existing employees to refer friends and family, this could be seen as nepotism. This may influence other plans to redress the current cultural mix within an organisation and hence it may lead to unfair discrimination.

7.3.3 Organisational commitment

The recruiter plays a major role in gaining the prospective employee's commitment to the organisation right from the outset. Recruitment can play an important role in marrying the candidate's vocational and job-related needs with the organisation's ability to satisfy them. Greenhaus (1987: 127) suggests that the recruiter should display the following desirable qualities in the initial interaction between candidates and the organisation:

- ensure that you are perceived as both knowledgeable and well prepared;
- ask relevant questions;
- discuss career paths;
- produce positive responses from candidates; and
- display warmth, enthusiasm and perceptiveness.

The recruiter must not be afraid of providing realistic information, both positive and negative, as this will enhance commitment. Realistic information serves to:

- prevent the formation of unrealistic expectations;
- facilitate balanced and improved decisions regarding careers; and
- allow individuals to feel that they have greater freedom of choice.

The following basic questions may be asked by job seekers before making a final decision on a particular position (Ivancevich & Glueck 1983: 163). Since questions of this type are almost unlimited, the following should be viewed simply as examples:

- How hard do I like to work?
- Do I like to be my own boss or would I rather work for someone else?
- Do I like to work in a group or on my own?
- Do I like to work at an even pace or with bursts of energy?
- Do I like to work near home?
- How much money do I want? Would I prefer a more interesting job for less money?
- Do I like to work in one place or many? Indoors or outdoors?
- How much variety do I want in work?
- Does the organisation have a good future?
- Do I want to work in a small or large organisation?

7.4 RECRUITMENT SOURCES

Once it has been decided that additional employees are needed, the recruiter is faced with the decision of where to search for applicants. Two basic sources of applicants can be used: internal (current employees) and external (those not presently in the employ of the enterprise). As you wll see, the sources and methods are closely linked.

7.4.1 Internal sources

Existing employees are a potentially rich source of finding suitable candidates when vacancies arise. There are different ways of soliciting applications from existing staff:

- *Skills inventories and career development systems.* If the employee shortage is for higher-level employees, a skills inventory system may be used to search for appropriate candidates, or employees may be identified from a careers development system. A skills inventory is simply a record system listing employees with specific skills (Singer 1990: 166). This is normally a fast way of identifying potential candidates but it is also in some cases limited to objective and factual data.
- *Job postings.* Vacancies within the organisation are placed on notice boards, in information bulletins and in company newsletters, and most commonly nowadays on the intranet sites of organisations. Details of the job are provided and only existing employees may apply. This method enhances the possibility that the best candidate can apply for a job, but it may also have the effect that the position may not be filled for a long period and employees may hop from job to job.
- *Inside moonlighting or contracting.* In the case of a short-term need or a small job which does not involve a great deal of additional work, the organisation could offer to pay bonuses of various types to people in the same organisation. Employees who perform well could be identified and this could also increase multiskilling.
- *Supervisor recommendations.* Supervisors know their people and can nominate employees for a specific job. Supervisors are normally in a good position to know the strengths and weaknesses of employees, but it could be that the supervisor's opinion is subjective and thus susceptible to bias and discrimination.

In using current employees as a source, one must be very careful not to engage in any form of favouritism or other form of potentially unfair discriminatory practices.

7.4.2 External sources

- *Employment agencies.* These organisations usually build up pools of potential job candidates over time. People register with them, and we might thus approach them to see if they have any likely candidates whose profiles might be aligned with our needs. These agencies might also advertise or use their placement database (the database of the curriculum vitae (CV) of jobseekers which the agency is trying to place). There are some relatively general employment agencies and also some that are more specialised. The latter might, for instance, specialise in managerial recruitment, or in, say, the recruitment of professionals such as engineers or medical staff.
- *Walk-ins.* Often, prospective employees will apply directly to the organisation in the hope that a vacancy exists, or will complete an application form and send it to the enterprise concerned. One-third of employees obtain their first jobs in this manner (Singer 1990: 168).
- *Referrals.* This is a word-of-mouth technique in which present employees refer candidates from outside the organisation. It is an inexpensive technique which is effective in finding candidates with specific skills quickly.
- *Professional bodies.* Accounting, engineering and scientific institutes look after the interests of their members by allowing vacancy advertisements in their publications. Opportunities for networking are also afforded through conventions.
- *Executive searchers or headhunters.* Top-level executives and professionals are often sourced through specialised headhunters who basically act as consultants in

the field. The persons are approached personally with an offer to apply for specific vacancies.

■ *Educational institutions.* Schools, colleges, technikons and universities provide grassroots-level opportunities for recruiters to pick the cream of the crop. This is especially important in areas of skills shortages and professional appointments. The recruiter normally makes a presentation to final-year students and invites desirable candidates to visit the company concerned. Once again, however, care should be taken not to approach only the traditionally 'white' universities. Specific efforts to recruit from tertiary institutions that traditionally cater more for people from designated groups may even form part of an organisation's affirmative action drive.

All applicants' personal details are treated confidentially and accepted professional recruitment procedures should be followed at all times. Professional bodies (such as the South African Board for Personnel Practice (SABPP)) may take disciplinary action if breaches occur among consultants/professionals. To ensure client protection, a contract should be established with the consultancy firm. The client should also determine whether the consultant is experienced and is an expert in recruiting for a particular vacancy.

7.5 METHODS OF RECRUITMENT

Various recruitment methods can be used, and some of the more important ones are discussed in this section. Note that these methods are closely linked to the sources to be tapped into, as just covered above.

7.5.1 Advertising

The most popular method of recruitment is the advertisement. Advertising can be used internally as well as externally. Our focus here is on advertising to attract candidates from outside, thus tapping into external sources. Whether in the daily newspaper, weekend job supplement or periodicals, organisations often advertise their vacancies in a carefully worded manner to attract as many as possible of the right applicants. Other media used are billboards, radio, the Internet and television. Professional publications are also used effectively to attract those in their respective professional fields.

Advertising has one basic underlying principle and that is communication. The purpose of an advertisement is to gain the right person's interest and attention, which must then lead to action. The AIDA (Attention, Interest, Desire, Action) formula may be used to structure an advertisement.

Remember that, in terms of the Employment Equity Act, the employer's advertisements should reach a broad spectrum of people and especially members of the designated groups. Therefore, to advertise in a newspaper which is read mostly by one population group may not be the best option available. On the other hand, to require all employers to advertise any vacancy, irrespective of its seniority, in newspapers which have a national circulation (such as the Sunday newspapers) would be to place too onerous a burden on them. It is suggested that the fairness of an employer's advertising policy and practice should be determined by reference to its size, its financial resources, its geographic spread (regional or national) and, lastly, the seniority of the vacancy in question (that is, a junior-level job need not be advertised in a very expensive medium, whereas this may be appropriate for a more senior vacancy).

7.5.1.1 Attention

An advertisement must attract attention. The following aspects are important for this purpose.

Headings

A meaningful heading can describe a potential job by making use of specific subject areas or by naming particular posts. Headings should be large and readable, and should also describe what is expected by the employer. Headings should be specific, not ambiguous or misleading.

Visual layout

The visual layout should have immediate impact on a potential applicant. The size and form of the advertisement may influence the extent of the reaction which it evokes. Where the advertisement is positioned on a page is also important.

Variety

Potential applicants may be attracted by various factors which make the advertisement stand out.

- *Background differences.* The use of a dark background can serve to draw readers' attention.
- *Colour.* Because of the high costs involved, only some newspapers make use of colour in recruitment advertisements. Research should be conducted to determine the influence of colour in attracting attention to advertisements.
- *Outline.* Outlining is used to make an advertisement more prominent. The use of outlining may draw attention to an advertisement by emphasising it and contrasting it with competing advertisements. Neatness and unity are also emphasised.
- *Imagery.* The use of imagery can serve to attract attention. Images may consist of people and faces, enlarged emblems, background images and work situations.
- *Typeface or font.* Different typefaces or fonts may be used to make an advertisement easier to read and to differentiate it from other advertisements. Eye-catchers are especially black, broad typefaces. The position being advertised is usually clear and large. Smaller typefaces are usually used in subheadings and in the general content areas.

7.5.1.2 Interest

One of the most important elements of the interest factor is the organisation itself. Information about the organisation may include a short description of its line of business, its activities and goals, its growth potential and its expectations for the future.

Information about the position being offered is also important and should be short, describing the responsibilities involved and what is expected of the successful applicant.

Lastly, the relevant requirements of candidates should also be included, limited only to information such as educational qualifications, experience and other job-relevant attributes.

7.5.1.3 Desire/urge

In this context, 'desire' refers to the wish of the reader of an advertisement to work for a particular organisation, but is not limited to a formal request for a post. The proposed salary may or may not be named; it may, however, serve as an important screening device. Something that can really be detrimental to recruitment campaigns relates to setting unrealistic job performance criteria. As mentioned before – these must be realistic and reflect the true requirements of the job.

Advantages of mentioning a salary

If a salary is very attractive and competitive, this will be in the organisation's favour. Possible candidates may desire such financial advantages and may thus be more eager to apply for the post.

Disadvantages of mentioning a salary

Some potential applicants may resist applying for a post because they are receiving a lower salary at present. This will mean that the organisation will not come into contact with such potentially successful candidates. Another disadvantage of advertising the salary being offered is that other organisations may raise their current salary levels in order to remain competitive. Employees may also feel dissatisfied if they are being paid less than the advertised salary.

7.5.1.4 Action

Advertisements are only successful if applications from many 'right' types of candidates for the job roll in. Potential applicants should know what to do next, in response to the advertisement. In other words, the advertisement should be clear about the action to be taken by interested people – be that to go online and complete an application form, to mail or fax a CV, or to make an initial phone-call.

Sometimes applicants are required to fill in coupons or short job request forms so that basic details can be obtained and a larger number of responses elicited by the advertisement. Whatever the method chosen, the objective is to encouraged people to respond, take action and show their interest in the job.

7.5.2 Special-event recruiting

Some companies stage open houses and visits to headquarters, and even son-and-daughter days. Others address specific groups of students on campuses when they visit schools and universities, and so on. Career exhibitions can be organised, which often go hand in hand with other appropriate events such as conferences. The key of any such recruitment events is thorough preparation and ensuring the event is well planned and executed.

7.5.3 Vacation work and work-integrated learning schemes

Many full-time university students seek work during their vacations and this provides a potential source of external candidates. Organisations can thus employ such students for short-term periods. This might help the organisation to get specialised piecework completed and simultaneously to identify prospective permanent employees. Universities also increasingly make use of courses or modules that are offered as work-integrated learning options for students. Students are thus required to achieve certain learning objectives through practical learning about certain tasks in the work environment. In these ways students are afforded an opportunity to experience working life, thereby eliminating unrealistic expectations. Sometimes students take up a great deal of supervisory time and the work done is not always of the highest standard, mainly due to lack of experience. On the other hand, students often tend to have unrealistic expectations as well for such limited exposure periods or assignments. Students may thus even become disillusioned when their initial expectations are not met. Upon return to their educational institutions, they may then actually become reverse recruiters, having a negative effect on the company's recruitment drive.

7.5.4 Technology-driven recruitment

Information communication technology is causing what some say is nothing short of a revolution in recruitment. The rapidly growing use of the Internet for recruiting purposes makes this method a very popular way to reach potentially interested people as part of an external source. Electronic recruiting, also known as e-recruiting or Internet recruiting, is becoming increasingly popular as a cost-effective, easy and very fast means of reaching thousands of potentially suitable candidates.

Lee (2004: 80–82) confirms the potential of this method, but a warning is added when it is said that "studies show that Internet recruiting is difficult to master ... Instead of using the Internet to simply automate traditional recruiting, an Internet recruiting campaign must be well planned and executed ... [I]f done so effectively, its potential could be staggering ... The future of Internet recruiting is bright. It will be an integral part of standard candidate searches, and will continue to save companies time, effort, and ..." money.

Smith (2007: 33) reports that also in South Africa people are increasingly "realising the importance of utilising online as part of their candidate sourcing mix. Online recruitment has not only widened access to the labour pool ... but it [also] offers a wide range of tools to enhance the services offered ... Nielsen/NetRatings recently reported that internet usage in South Africa had grown at the rate of 50% per year over the last two years and, with this medium becoming more accessible and affordable, penetration is set to continue growing". See also exhibit 7.1 in this regard.

Many organisations have developed their own websites, which are used to advertise vacancies as they arise, to promote the organisation as an 'employer of choice', and to receive and process online applications. Applicants can complete application forms online and submit them, often with CVs attached, with simply a few clicks of the mouse. Systems are typically designed to generate automatic, standard-response e-mails to the applicants. Recruitment agencies can follow similar approaches.

Various general and specified online sites are used for national and international recruitment purposes. Examples of these include www.careerjunction.co.za, www.mycareer.co.za, www.kelly.co.za and www.renwicktalent.co.za, and websites of newspapers (such as www.sundaytimes.co.za/careers), journals/magazines and relevant associations (such as www.ipm.co.za).

Elsewhere in Africa

Among the recruitment sources in Zambia are mass media which include radio (Zambia National Broadcasting Services, Radio Chikuni, Radio Mazabuka, Radio Maria), television (Zambia National Broadcasting Services), and newspapers (*Times of Zambia, Zambia Daily Mail, The Post* and *The Monitor*). Companies recruit from colleges and the country's two universities (the University of Zambia in Lusaka and the Copperbelt University in Kitwe) ... Electronic recruiting is also now possible ... organizations can now use the internet provider ZAMNET (http://www.zamnet.zm) to advertise positions.

Source: Muuka & Mwenda (2005: 40–41)

EXHIBIT 7.1: Companies should have online recruitment policies

Companies and recruitment agencies should not be wondering whether to use online recruitment but rather formulating unique e-recruitment policies, says Kris Jarzebowski, MD of Internet job site CareerJunction. Different e-recruitment models exist and clients can choose to subscribe to a particular site or place ad hoc advertisements, to handle the responses themselves, or to outsource different aspects of the process.

Especially when backed up by print advertising, an online search casts a wide net. Thanks to new technology, web-based job applications can be easily and quickly screened. Jarzebowski says e-recruitment is growing exponentially. "Two to three years ago, 1% of placements were made off the Internet. Today it is 20%."

Shaun Peacock, founder member of placement agency Kinetic Solutions, says it is a powerful tool for recruiting in areas of high specialisation such as clerical and financial services, as well as middle management and information technology (IT).

"The percentage for IT is higher than for the others. With e-recruitment you are reaching the younger set – the skilled, mobile 20- to 30-year-olds." Peacock says he uses only one website as most applicants post their curricula vitae (CVs) on all of them. "It doesn't make sense to pay more than one subscription to get the same candidates."

CareerJunction is a large generalist site, advertising a range of jobs from administration to managerial level. Then there are small niche sites such as CareerWeb, which cater for the IT industry and financial services sectors. Both serve agencies and have some corporate clients.

While online recruitment holds benefits for all users, 'power users' who exploit the technology and use the tool to its maximum stand to reap huge rewards. Peacock is a power user, running an average of 11 positions on CareerJunction at any time. At age 35, and part of the Internet generation, Peacock says: "In the past two years 65% to 70% of our placements have come from CVs posted on the net."

The agency advertises in daily newspapers too. Highly specialised positions, for example in insurance, are also advertised in specialist and trade publications. Peacock says the turnaround time on e-recruitment is unbeatable, and the ability to update the online information continuously is convenient for applicants and recruiters alike.

An advantage for job applicants is that they decide when to display and when to withdraw their CVs, and CVs can be stored and reactivated at any time. Privacy is guaranteed through tools such as Truste, a US-based online auditor.

Peacock says screening candidates is quicker and easier online than on the telephone. "Our in-house computer system helps with screening ... We insist on a covering letter and can usually see from this whether the candidate is suitable. Our advertisements are extensive and indepth, enabling us to ensure there are no mismatches." Marketing and advertising co-ordinator of recruitment agency The Oval Office, Hannelie du Toit, says you can put more information into a web advertisement than a print ad.

"Because it is online you can manage it more easily and a spin-off is that you can build a database. We place all our advertising on the net, and 40% of it goes into print as well." Du Toit sees e-recruitment as the way forward. However, she admits that the volume of responses is high and suggests companies employ a full-time staff member to deal with them.

Jarzebowski says clients should factor e-recruitment into their budgets as they can cut their recruitment advertising bills significantly by going online. A monthly subscription fee allows clients to place an unlimited number of advertisements on CareerJunction, and services are free to job seekers. Fees for other services depend on how much of the recruitment function is outsourced. Clients can request reference, credit and criminal record checking as well as preliminary interviewing.

They can outsource response handling to agencies such as Admark and Altolevel, which forward suitable applications to the client and send regret messages to unsuccessful candidates. CareerJunction recently linked up with Totaljobs – one of the largest online job sites in Britain giving South African applicants access to jobs in that country.

Source: Gering, (2002). *Business Day,* 12 August

7.5.5 Outsourcing recruitment work

When we covered different recruitment sources we made mention of employment agencies, headhunters and consultants. A basic decision thus relates to whether we are going to run our own recruitment campaigns, or to what extent we are rather going to outsource the task of recruiting potential suitable job applicants or rent the services of specialist recruiters in what is known as 'contract recruiting'.

Wentworth (2004: 108) explains that contract recruiting is basically when "a company hires or rents a recruiter to sit inside their offices and recruit. The person can be paid in a variety of ways: by the hour, by retainer plus a per-hire bonus".

Alternatively, we can decide to outsource aspects of or the whole recruitment effort to an employment agency or consultant, or headhunters. In such cases, especially when we outsource most or all of our recruitment work to outside service providers, it is absolutely essential that we build very good relationships with them and make sure they are fully informed about our organisation's staffing needs. We also believe that while recruitment up to the point of preliminary shortlists may be outsourced with good measures of success (if we avoid pitfalls), beyond that it becomes too much of a risk to outsource selection processes. This is, however, where things can get quite tricky because in practice, as you will learn, the recruitment and selection process should actually develop almost seamlessly.

7.6 THE RECRUITMENT PROCESS

The following components of the recruitment process (see figure 7.1) are quite generic and can be a guide as an approach to recruitment. Note, however, that organisations and their circumstances differ and so do recruitment processes. While we refer to 'steps', we must accept that such linear depictions of recruitment are more for conceptual purposes.

Step 1: Determine the exact need

Consider the circumstances under which the need for recruitment arose. Make sure that the decision can be substantiated with facts obtained from objective measurements or available valid management information. The need for recruitment would often be an outflow of the workforce planning process but as we have said before, it is also very common to happen in an ad hoc fashion as vacancies arise. It is important that line managers be full partners in the process because they are the people who have the need for employees in their areas of responsibility. Typically they initiate the recruitment process.

Step 2: Consult the recruitment policy and procedure

The recruitment policy and procedure document will contain specific guidelines for recruitment, and should be consulted in the interest of consistency and to ensure effective and efficient roll-out of the recruitment process. The policy and procedures document will give guidance as to who will play what role in this process, and also which sources and methods of recruitment may be applicable under which circumstances.

Step 3: Obtain approval to recruit

Recruitment can be rather costly. The budget of the organisation for recruitment should thus always be considered. Approval must be obtained from the appropriate managerial staff authorised to do so. This may entail completing some paperwork – such as filling out a staff requisition form that will be signed off by managerial staff

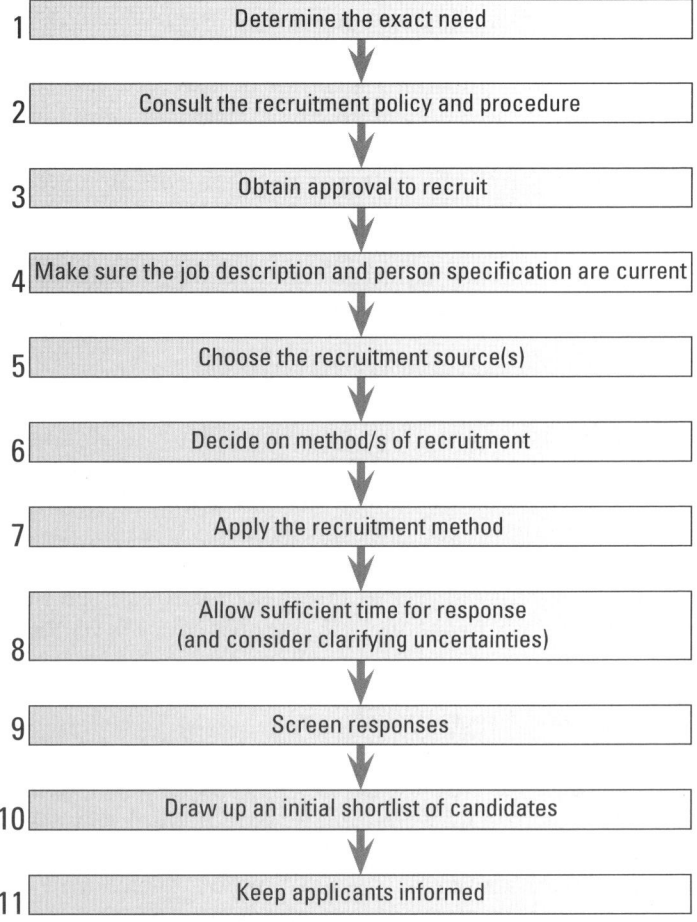

1	Determine the exact need
2	Consult the recruitment policy and procedure
3	Obtain approval to recruit
4	Make sure the job description and person specification are current
5	Choose the recruitment source(s)
6	Decide on method/s of recruitment
7	Apply the recruitment method
8	Allow sufficient time for response (and consider clarifying uncertainties)
9	Screen responses
10	Draw up an initial shortlist of candidates
11	Keep applicants informed

Figure 7.1: The recruitment process

to whom this authority has been delegated. This will ensure that the recruitment is compatible with broader organisational and workforce plans and budgets. This also creates the opportunity to reconsider the overall recruitment approach as well as alternatives to recruitment, for example overtime and/or outsourcing. The most basic question will thus be: is it essential to fill this vacancy?

Step 4: Make sure the job description and person specification are current

We have already explained the role and nature of job descriptions and person or job specifications. These form the point of departure for all recruitment activities; it is thus essential that these documents are up to date, and accurately reflect what the job entails and requires. Problems arise when job descriptions and job specifications are not current. These documents must reflect the key performance areas of the particular job. A key issue thus relates to the actual job performance criteria. These should not only be as accurately described as possible, but ideally the advertisement must ultimately reflect these as clearly articulated selection criteria. Prospective possibly interested applicants must be able to spot whether their own profiles suit these selection (and job performance) criteria. This can thus have a serious impact on who might decide to lodge an application – and who not. We do not want to scare away possibly suitable prospective candidates, but we also do not want to be inundated with hundreds of applications of people who turn out to be unsuitable.

Keep in mind that job specifications may not be used to block the appointment of members of previously disadvantaged groups ('designated employees' in terms of the Employment Equity Act). When we embark on a recruitment effort we must thus make very sure that the required minimum job requirements are indeed correct and a fair reflection of current realities. For example, it may be risky to assume that certain jobs are suitable only for males (for example a fireman or a prison guard in a high-security prison). These documents should normally accompany the 'request to recruit' that may be submitted with the aid of the mentioned requisition form.

Step 5: Choose the recruitment source(s)

When we know what types of people we wish to solicit applications from, we can consider the most appropriate recruitment source/s. Historical data on the success rate of certain sources could be very useful in this regard. As mentioned in step 2, the recruitment policy may give an indication of whether the person(s) should be recruited internally or externally, and once this has been ascertained, the recruiter will make a choice of one or more sources (depending on the group or person required). It is generally good policy to try to recruit internally first of all and then, if a suitable candidate cannot be identified, to channel the recruitment effort externally. In certain cases recruitment will have to be done externally.

Step 6: Decide on method/s of recruitment

Recruitment methods which have traditionally proved successful will normally be a good first guide to make this decision. If, for example, newspaper advertisements (which are very common) have proven to work well it will be hard to think why other methods will be preferred at some point in time. Naturally there is also scope to experiment with alternative methods to seek more effectiveness and/or efficiency in our recruitment campaigns. The most suitable method or methods for recruitment should be well documented with facts and figures that back things up. It is very important to guard against being accused of discrimination through using one particular recruitment method to the exclusion of others. This could be the totally unintentional result of a traditional practice in the organisation – for example advertising in only one newspaper which is circulated in only one particular area and in the process excluding potential employees from other areas in which the newspaper is not circulated.

Step 7: Apply the recruitment method

In the case of a newspaper advertisement, the planned advertisement must be screened to prevent embarrassment to the organisation and to potential employees. When a recruitment agency is used, clear parameters of what is expected must be communicated well in advance. Advertisements, for example, must provide a clear indication of the tasks to be performed and the job specifications required. Other aspects to be specified are the location, pay, allowances, application procedures, deadlines, telephone numbers, and contact fax numbers. Steps must be taken not to allow any discrimination other than those issues inherent in the job requirements and in affirmative action appointments.

Step 8: Allow sufficient time for response (and consider clarifying uncertainties)

The method used will dictate the time that should be allowed for responses. Set clear deadlines, but remain flexible to ensure the maximum number of responses.

Step 9: Screen responses

Potential employees will respond to the recruitment method used and the majority of the applicants will not be successful. Initial sifting is done by working the applications which would typically entail the completed application forms and also the accompanying CVs. In cases where things may not be so clear-cut, further information may be collected for screening purposes by means of telephonically contacting such candidates.

The applicants' particulars must at this stage be compared with what has been stipulated in the job description and specification. The unsuccessful candidates must be separated from those who may be considered for possible appointment. Screening should take place according to the initial criteria set for the job. Recruiters should guard against prejudice and subjective opinions that could lead to discrimination against applicants. Sometimes initial screening will lead to only some people receiving application forms. During this step the recruiter may also screen applicants on the grounds of already-completed application forms and/or CVs.

Step 10: Draw up an initial shortlist of candidates

This is already in a sense the start of the selection process. As part of this component we try to draw up a shortlist of possible suitable candidates. Also here telephonic screening can be helpful to obtain important information which can further help to distinguish between suitable and clearly unsuitable applicants. Much of this work can be done by the HR support staff (if there are such people). The shortlist of potentially suitable applicants as well as perhaps some borderline cases must be discussed with the relevant line managers before proceeding into the full-on selection process.

Step 11: Keep applicants informed

It may be a good idea to acknowledge that you have received an application (see exhibit 7.5 for a standard letter format in this regard).

It is also good practice to advise applicants as soon as possible of the outcome of their applications – should these people be screened out early on in the process. There is more than one way to do this. Great care must be taken to ensure that the reputation of the organisation remains unblemished. One should be realistic in terms of cost implications, though, and often one finds that literally hundreds of people might apply, many of whom do not remotely meet the stipulated criteria. It is not uncommon to state in an advertisement, for example, that only successful candidates who will be invited for interviews will be contacted. One could then stipulate something to the effect of the following: 'Should you NOT receive any further correspondence from us within four weeks of the closing date for this recruitment campaign, please accept that you have not been successful on this occasion and that we appreciate your interest in our company.'

7.6.1 Additional steps/issues

Proceed to selection

Shortlisted applicants must be invited to take part in the rest of the selection process. This discussed in more detail in chapter 8.

EXHIBIT 7.5: Example of a letter of acknowledgement

[Organisation's name]
[Address]
[Date]

[Applicant]
[Address]

Dear [Applicant]:

[Title of job and reference number of advertisement]

We refer to recently received correspondence indicating your interest in the abovementioned position at [*organisation's name*]. Thank you for your interest and effort to compile and submit your application. Be assured that we will consider your application in a fair and careful way.

If your profile matches our needs in this case, you will be contacted by phone, mail or e-mail to schedule further arrangements. This can be expected within about three weeks of the closing date for applications as per the advertisement.

Should no such contact be received within four weeks of the closing date, please accept that your application has not been successful at this occasion.

Please refrain from contacting our offices if we do not establish contact with you as we can assure you that we follow up diligently in all meritorious cases warranting further consideration or processing. We follow this process simply due to labour market conditions and the administrative workload that accompany the multitude of applications we receive in response to our advertisements for vacancies as a recognised 'employer of choice'.

We wish you the very best in your career.

Yours faithfully

[Name of manager or HR officer]
[Title/position]

Evaluate the recruitment effort

Recruitment is aimed at soliciting as many as possible applications from people who are potentially suitable for the job. The number of such applications received is thus an important measure of whether we have used the appropriate methods and sources, and whether we have generally executed the recruitment process well. The reality is that if this produces a good pool of potentially suitable candidates, and we can sift through them to finish with a shortlist of a number of candidates who really seem to be very well suited (on paper, at this stage), and if we managed to achieve this in a cost-effective way, we are probably doing rather well in terms of our recruitment drive. Several methods can be used for evaluating the effectiveness of recruitment and selection efforts (see section 7.7 below and chapter 22).

7.7 ASPECTS OF QUALITY CONTROL IN RECRUITMENT

The last issue as discussed above is actually already part of the effort of exercising some form of quality control in respect of recruitment. It should be borne in mind that recruitment is a costly process that includes things such as the advertising costs, the time and hence the salary of all involved in recruitment work, including the proportional remuneration of the HR staff helping with the process. Other costs may be the fees charged by any recruitment agency that may be used to assist in the process. There can be a range of other direct and indirect costs. It is therefore essential to make sure the recruitment work of any organisation provides 'value for money' overall.

It is crucial to evaluate the cost/benefit ratio of each recruitment method or a combination of recruitment methods employed – and in relation to various types of work/jobs/vacancies. When weighing up their cost effectiveness, factors such as external conditions in the labour market, the numbers of suitable applications in comparison with non-suitable ones received, time taken to move through the recruitment process, and the vacancy and the nature of the job must all be taken into consideration. Some sources or methods may work well for some types of work or jobs while others might be more effective and efficient for other types of work.

It is naturally also very important that an assessment be made of the equal-opportunity situation. The different applicants can, for example, be categorised in terms of their race, gender, religion and disability status. A further list can be compiled in terms of the number of applicants for a particular position, and the number who were not unsuccessful and the number who were, including the reasons for their success.

It is very important to keep accurate records of each facet of the recruitment work of an organisation, including the relevant documents. This will enable the organisation to answer any possible questions which interested parties may have at any time during the selection process.

7.8 FINDING NON-EMPLOYEE WORKERS TO GET WORK DONE: TEMPORARY EMPLOYMENT SERVICES

The decision to make use of contract labour to get some of an organisation's work done means that the recruitment task now becomes one of finding an appropriate labour broker. There are many organisations that specialise in the leasing out of their employees to do certain work for and at other organisations.

In terms of South African legislation, we refer to labour broker firms as 'temporary employment services' organisations. As independent contractors, they hire out labour or work-related services to client organisations. The service provider enters into a commercial contract for the delivery of a service in the form of people who will do a certain set of work. The temporary employment service is the employer and the people that will thus come and work on our premises, if we engage the services of such a labour broker firm, are the employees of that firm, and not of our organisation. We are thus not leasing employees, but the services provided by the temporary employment services organisation (which happen to be 'labour') to get some of our work done. The important thing in this regard is to find the right organisation because if we contract them and they contravene a binding collective agreement, provisions of the Basic Conditions of Employment Act (BCEA) or an arbitration award or wage determination, we as the client organisation (or principal) as well as the labour broker are rendered jointly and severally liable (Grogan 2007: 28). An employee of such temporary employment services organisation who might seek redress in such situations will then thus have the choice of suing them and/or us as the client organisation (or principal).

It therefore becomes a matter of seeking widely and carefully to try to find reputable labour brokers or temporary employment services organisations – organisations well known in the specific type of work for which labour is sought. We might advertise and invite expressions of interest (EoI's) from any such organisations as the early stages and we may then later opt for the route of inviting some of these specifically to take part in a formal tendering process. In the early stages we can work through the EoI's received and engage in some form of sifting process to make a shortlist of possible service providers.

The track records of such service providers should be a key variable to consider and if this is what we need to do, we must be rigorous in assessing evidence of their performance and delivery to other clients. There must be a record of having successfully delivered in terms of similar outsourced labour services to such other client organisations. It is probably best to set up appointments and meet with representative managers of such other client organisations to discuss the experiences they have had with the temporary employment services organisations under consideration.

Next we can approach those labour brokers whom we feel reasonably comfortable with and alert them when we launch a specific tendering invitation process (if we use a tendering process). These processes then logically lead us into the realm of actually selecting which labour brokers or temporary employment services organisation to make use of – a theme which we continue in the next chapter.

7.9 CONCLUSION

No plans are sufficient to get the work of the organisation done. We actually need people to become employees to do it, apart from the work which we choose to outsource. We must thus find suitable employees and to do this we engage in recruitment.

Recruitment is thus a very important aspect of HRM in South Africa, and also, naturally, in the case of other countries in Africa. Recruiting should ideally be guided by a recruitment policy. We must be aware of various external and internal factors that can impact on recruitment, and can use various sources and methods for finding prospective employees. We covered these as well as the typical recruitment process, and also the evaluation of our recruitment efforts.

We highlighted the fact that we may opt for outsourcing our recruitment work and ended this chapter with a brief note on the challenge of finding temporary employment services organisations or labour brokers, to consider possible other arrangements to get work done (through other means than standard employment). In the next chapter we shift our focus to actually making the decisions about whom to employ and use as service providers.

SUSTAINABILITY CONNECTION?
Without using the best possible avenues (for example sources, methods and techniques) to find the best possible pools of talent, we might have to choose from among people less capable to perform well at work while other more capable people are not even making themselves available. We must have the right brand as an organisations and 'employer of choice' so that we can attract top-class talented people who are keen to work with us – as employees or through other arrangements. If we are known to be an organisation that does not care for the environment and/ or does not value our people, we will not be able to attract the right talent. Without this we jeopardise our chances of being successful and hence also the chances of contributing to making our country a better place for all to live in.

SELF-EVALUATION QUESTIONS

1 Why is it important to have some policy on recruitment in an organisation?
2 What factors can impact on recruitment efforts?
3 Draw up a recruitment advertisement for an HR officer specialising in recruitment for a platinum mining company.
4 Compare the recruitment process discussed in this chapter with the one followed in an organisation of your choice. What are your observations?
5 Discuss briefly how you would go about addressing your organisation's needs in relation to finding temporary employment services organisations or labour brokers.

8 ESTABLISHING EMPLOYMENT RELATIONSHIPS AND OTHER WORK ARRANGEMENTS

LEARNING OUTCOMES

After studying this chapter, you should be able to:

- describe what is meant by 'personnel selection';
- distinguish between 'criteria' and 'predictors', provide examples and explain their role in personnel selection;
- define 'reliability' and 'validity' and describe the different types of both;
- engage in meaningful dialogue about the selection process, showing analytical and critical thinking abilities;
- distinguish between different types of selection tests;
- explain the nature and importance of the employment interview, and give guidelines in this regard;
- discuss the assessment centre as a method of personnel selection;
- describe the nature and importance of fairness in selection decisions within the South African context;
- discuss the process of appointing and socialising new employees; and
- write notes about engaging non-employee work services.

8.1 INTRODUCTION

The purpose of recruitment is to gather together a large pool of good-quality applicants from whom to select and appoint the most suitable. The focus of this chapter is mainly on making the decisions about whom to select for the relevant position/s. We also look at orientating newly appointed employees. Because non-employees can also be engaged to do work for us, we also briefly cover relevant aspects pertaining to deciding on whom to choose as labour brokers or temporary employment services providers.

As said in the previous chapter, it is not always possible to draw a distinct line between the steps of the recruitment and the selection process. This is the case because selection flows naturally from the recruitment process. Similarly, as we try to find possible service providers that can help with our needs pertaining to non-employee workers, we find that the process also naturally evolves into a process of choosing from among various potential vendors.

Because the bulk of the work of most organisations is typically carried out by employees, our focus in this chapter is primarily on what is commonly known as 'personnel selection' decisions. Making such decisions is a process based on individual differences between human beings – that is, on the fact that attributes differ from one person to another, with each potentially suitable job candidate offering unique traits and competencies (knowledge, skills and abilities).

Selection is essentially the process of determining which individuals will most likely make the best employees to match particular job requirements of the organisation, taking into account individual differences, the job or role as such, and also the organisation more generally, including its internal and external environments. This is also referred as 'personnel selection' (Muchinsky, Kriek & Schreuder 2005: 137), probably because in essence we decide about either making someone part of the organisation's personnel or about placing existing personnel in other positions (such as in the case of promotion). The same authors provide a simple definition of personnel selection as being "the process of identifying from the pool of recruited applicants those to whom a job will be offered ... the process of separating the chosen from the rejected applicants" (Muchinsky et al 2005: 137–138).

Essentially, therefore, selection tends to rest on some efforts to try to predict the likelihood of future work performance in relation to individual differences. We try to appoint people who, we believe, would have the best chances of performing very well and hence contribute to organisational success. We base the selection decision on information we collect about the candidates and matching this with information about the job/role's work requirements and also of the organisation more generally. The key will be the knowledge, skills and abilities of the candidates as matched with the work in terms of the job/role requirements. Selection decisions therefore require one to know how such knowledge, skills and abilities can be assessed – and this makes the proper use of 'predictors' in selection very important.

The bulk of this chapter focuses on differences between predictors (selection instruments or tools) and criteria, the requirements of good predictors, the selection process, the value of the different selection devices, assessment centres and on the importance of fairness in selection decisions. We also offer a brief overview of the process of orientating newly appointed employees. The final section of this chapter covers some issues involved in choosing which labour broker or temporary employment services provider (or consultants, for instance) to use, and how to enter into an appropriately structured relationship with such entities.

8.2 PREDICTORS AND CRITERIA

Personnel selection decisions must stand the test of fairness. In order to make a valid selection decision, the decision maker should know what distinguishes successful performance from unsuccessful performance in a specific job. In this regard, the relevance of job analysis (see chapter 6) must again be emphasised. Job analysis provides the necessary information to develop relevant job performance criteria and these are essential to make good personnel selection decisions. Muchinsky et al (2005: 51) explain that we need to identify these "criteria for effective job performance", because these would "become the basis for hiring people (choosing them according to their ability to meet the criteria of job performance)".

A *predictor* is a selection instrument or tool that is used to assist managers in making selection decisions, the 'classic trio' (Taylor 2005) of these being the application form (also known traditionally as application blank), the selection interview and the checking of references of candidates. A *criterion* is a standard to be attained, for example job performance in relation to communication. If we set as one selection criterion for a particular job as, for instance, superior interpersonal skills, we mean that a person must be able interact well with other individuals. A predictor is thus any method that can be used to forecast a criterion. We might use examples of past behaviour as an indicator of whether a person can indeed develop good interpersonal relations with other people. We might observe behaviour of a person, and in the case of criteria such as verbal communication or interpersonal interaction abilities, we might even use an interview situation as part of the methodology (the predictor) to try to assess whether superior abilities are displayed by any candidate/s.

The information needed to select meaningful predictors is supposed to be reflected in the job specification, which should be directly based on the job analysis and hence directly linked to the job description. The job analysis facilitates the development of criteria for job success, and the position description should make clear the connection among tasks, responsibilities, the work environment and so forth – and the job performance criteria. The job or person specification should clearly articulate the type of competencies and person that will be required to be able to meet the job performance criteria. It is common that job descriptions include job specifications.

Choosing a criterion measure is not always easy, as it could be influenced, for example, by a supervisor who might have a certain style and/or who might be biased. Criteria can come from the use of objective sources for objective criteria like delivery data (for example items produced, sales volume) and personal data (qualifications, training, timekeeping, absenteeism, promotions), or more subjective sources like superiors' ratings of candidates in past performance appraisals.

As you already know, the Employment Equity Act 55 of 1998 stipulates that criteria to be used for determining whether a person is 'suitably qualified' for a particular job should include any one or a combination of formal qualifications, prior learning, relevant experience or potential (capacity to acquire the ability to do the job).

Some predictors and criteria are used more frequently than others. Taylor (2005: 199) says that most people applying for a job "expect to fill in an application form, attend one or more interviews and then receive an offer of employment subject to satisfactory references being provided by referees ... the 'classic trio' are the most straightforward and least expensive of the range of selection methods available to employers".

8.3 ASSESSING THE QUALITY OF PREDICTORS

The Employment Equity Act 55 of 1998 requires selection instruments (psychological testing and other similar assessments) to be scientifically shown to be valid and reliable. Reliability and validity of predictors are thus prerequisites for fairness in selection. The success of a predictor can therefore be judged by its reliability and validity.

Note once again that an important consideration in assessing the suitability of selection instruments is the provisions of the Employment Equity Act. Section 8 of the Act prohibits psychological testing, and other similar assessments of an employee are prohibited, unless the test or assessment being used has been scientifically shown to be valid and reliable, can be applied fairly to all employees, and is not biased against any employee or group. In a multicultural society such as South Africa, a selection instrument may fall foul of this provision in any number of ways, such as: (a) the test is valid (or more or less valid) for one group but not for another; (b) the test's reliability varies from group to group; or (c) it under-predicts the success of some groups. The Act places the onus on the employer to show that the selection instruments comply with section 8, which may prove to be a very expensive exercise. Employers must therefore use selection instruments with care.

8.3.1 Reliability

Reliability can be defined as the consistency of a measure. Consistent results must be obtained at various times to ensure that a specific predictor (selection instrument) can be confidently applied. Widely diverging results achieved by the same candidate on different days under the same conditions would serve as an indication to the employer that the test being applied is not reliable. This renders the test in question useless to the employer.

Various methods may be used to assess the reliability of a measure. One of these is the *test-retest method* in terms of which subjects are required to take the same test twice, at different times. The results are correlated and the degree of correlation between the two sets of scores indicates the reliability of the test.

Another approach to assessing the reliability of a test is the *parallel forms method*. Two versions of the same test are compiled and both tests are taken by the same group of people. The correlation between the two scores achieved indicates the reliability of the test. It is assumed that both tests measure the same qualities.

The *split-half method* is a third way of assessing the reliability of a test. The test is divided into two equal parts, with a score being calculated for each. The correlation between the two sets of scores serves as an indicator of reliability.

A final approach used to determine reliability is *internal consistency*. This is the degree to which a score obtained from one item in a test can be generalised to those obtained from the other items in the same test. The more homogeneous the items in a test, the higher the reliability with which one score on a test item may be generalised to scores on the rest of the test items. Internal consistency could therefore be regarded as an aspect of test reliability.

8.3.2 Validity

A selection instrument does not need to be just reliable; it also has to measure certain attributes that are essential for success in a job. Where reliability refers to consistency and stability, *validity* refers to accuracy. A valid measure is one that yields correct estimates of what is being assessed.

Various approaches may be used to assess the validity of a measure. The criterion-related validity method compares the test score achieved by an individual with a measure of job performance. Criterion-related validity may be divided into predictive and concurrent validity.

- *Predictive validity* is the preferred measure used in personnel selection. The relationship between a predictor (test score) and the criterion (job performance) is established. The test is given to all applicants, but is not used as a selection instrument. Data on job performance are subsequently collected and the original test scores are then compared to the actual job performance. If they correlate well, the test can be used for purposes of personnel selection in future.
- *Concurrent validity* is determined by giving the test to current employees as opposed to job applicants. The job performance data are therefore collected at the same time as the test scores. The degree of the relationship between the predictor (test) and the criterion (job performance) determines the validity of the predictor (test). This method is also known as the 'present-employee' method.

In addition to the criterion-related validity method, the methods of content validity and construct validity may be used.

- *Content validity* raises the question of whether a predictor (test) is a fair representation of the entire job content or at least of the most important tasks involved.

The ability of the applicants to perform actual job tasks is evaluated. A definition of content validity would thus be the degree to which the tasks included in the test are representative of the total set of tasks or job goals.

■ *Construct validity* refers primarily to the degree to which a specific test measures the construct that it is designed to measure. Furthermore, it must be established to what extent the construct corresponds to the job requirements. Job analysis can be used to prove the relevance of the construct to the job. It is difficult to determine the construct validity because theoretical constructs may be abstract.

8.4 COMPONENTS IN A SELECTION PROCESS

The selection process can consist of several components, which can vary from organisation to organisation and situation to situation. Some of the components that could at least be considered include those indicated in figure 8.1. These can almost be thought of as steps or phases in the overall process, and this may be regarded as a broad guide for most personnel selection processes and decision making. After each step or phase, applicants can be rejected (or accepted). As can be seen, there may – in practice – be an overlap between the recruitment and selection processes. Already, especially during the latter phases or steps of the recruiting process, selection starts to take place, specifically when screening takes place (see chapter 7).

8.4.1 Preliminary interviews

The selection process can start with some preliminary interview, which may be swift and concise. The main purpose is some pre-selection, eliminating applicants who are obviously not suitable for the job in question. Straightforward questions around areas such as qualifications, experience, and salary can be asked. This is normally done when people just walk in or phone in, or when job applications are submitted without being clearly linked, perhaps, to a specific job/position advertised. Sometimes people respond over-hastily to recruitment efforts, or they submit applications to a multitude of organisations for a multitude of possible positions, some directly to organisations and some to employment agencies, for instance. When we receive such applications we generally have to do some further screening. Keep in mind that merely disregarding such applications may possibly lead to eliminating a high-potential candidate – someone who might actually have the potential to become a very valuable employee. These processes can typically happen telephonically and in a certain sense may also be viewed as part of the recruitment process (see chapter 7 again for the preliminary screening of applicants).

8.4.2 Written applications

The first real step in the selection process would be to look at the written applications as submitted by the applicants. Those people who might have been screened out by preliminary interviews when they walked or phoned in, and who still submitted written applications may be looked at again, just to make sure some high potential candidates have not been eliminated based on some misunderstanding or oversight.

Advertisements will typically state that interested persons should submit their written applications by a specified closing date. Such written applications may have to include a completed application form, an up-to-date CV, and also perhaps a statement in relation to job-specific selection criteria as stipulated in the job advertisement.

An *application form* is a document completed by the applicant providing information such as education, work history, some personal data, medical history, hobbies,

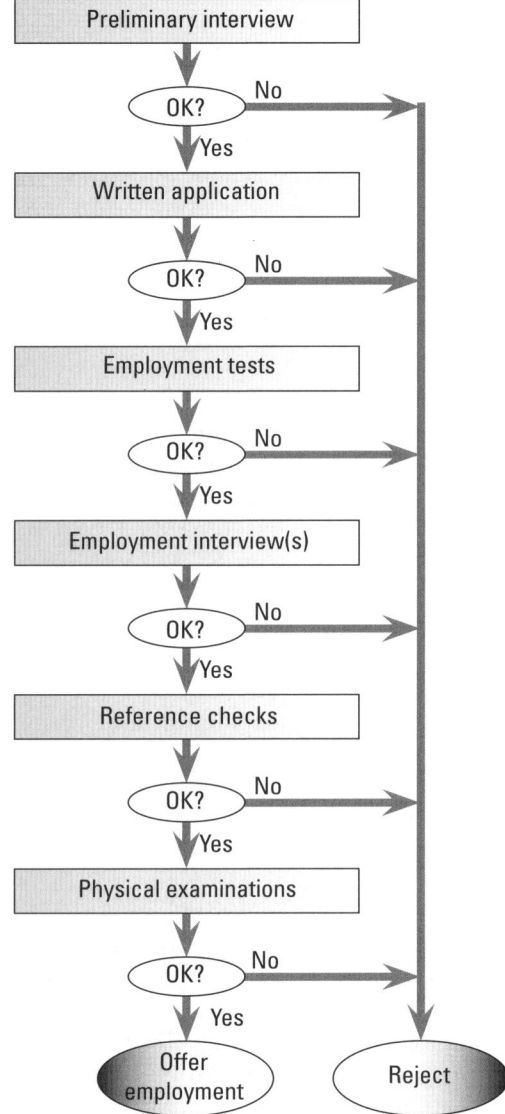

Figure 8.1: The selection process

etc. This information gives an indication of an applicant's suitability for a job. The use of past behaviour to predict future performance continues to form part of the selection process and, as a result of research, application blanks have become more scientific and, to some extent, more predictive because of the refinements.

The accuracy of the information is, however, often a problem. To improve accuracy, reference checking, which will be discussed later, can be used to verify some of the information. Another way of ensuring the accuracy of the information is to require the applicant to sign a statement in which he or she certifies that the information given is true and correct. An example of an application blank for Vodacom is provided in the appendix to this chapter.

A significant advance in the use of biographical data for selection has been the development of the weighted application blank (WAB). The WAB is used to determine whether there is a relationship between responses on specific questions and job performance defined in terms of predetermined criteria, for example job tenure (Cascio 1998).

For instance, an organisation may find that its successful salesmen were very active in social activities at school and technikon, but average in academic performance. These items are given a definite score when applicants are evaluated. To develop weighted application forms is very time consuming and should be restricted only to the key positions in an organisation.

Written applications, as mentioned, should ideally include more than the application blank or form. A suggested approach may be to also state, as part of the advertisement, some specific *selection criteria* (derived directly from the job performance criteria and job or person specification) associated directly with the vacant position in question. Candidates could then be requested to submit, together with their application form, a written document that systematically addresses each of these selection criteria, demonstrating why they believe that they actually have evidence to show how well they meet each of these criteria. A useful way of building this into the process is to suggest to applicants to address each criterion based on the STAR acronym:

S (Situation)
T (Task)
A (Action)
R (Results)

Applicants should thus be required to explain, in their written application, why they are of the view that they meet each of the criteria by briefly explaining a relevant *situation* (such as at a specific organisation where they have worked before) which involved a particular *task* that was at hand (such as a project or a specific challenge that was faced), how they *approached* it and hence what *actions* they took (what they actually did), and what *results* were achieved (what was the actual outcome of it all). The idea is that as we work through the written application we can try to assess the potential of someone based on his or her description of relevant past experience and actual work-related behaviour that may have direct relevance to required competencies (knowledge, skills and abilities) associated with the vacant position in question.

In the context of employment equity and affirmative action, managers will also have to scrutinise their organisations' application forms to ensure that these do not lead to unfair discrimination claims. For example, items relating to age, sex, race, religion, health, disability and an applicant's criminal record will have to be handled with circumspection. Only if one is confident that information is really relevant in order to select a suitable person for the job in question, should these be retained. For example, should the application form require an applicant to disclose that he or she is HIV positive but the vacancy carries no risks in this way for other people, this may form the basis of alleged unfair discrimination. This will place the organisation in a difficult position, because the onus will be on the employer to show that the information was not used to disqualify an HIV-positive candidate. It would therefore be in the interests of the organisation to delete such items on application forms.

On the other hand, it may indeed be justifiable to include items relating to sex and race on the application form, for instance to assist in the initial screening process with the aim of working towards affirmative action goals or targets. If an organisation has set certain targets for the active promotion of women, it will, for instance, be very difficult to actively pursue this route without knowing from the completed application forms which applicants are male and which are female.

The important point is that one will have to ensure that the information elicited by all items on the application form are aligned with requirements relating to the prevention of unfair discrimination and the promotion of affirmative action.

8.4.3 Employment tests

Once the applicants have been screened by means of the application form, candidates may undergo employment tests. An *employment test* is an instrument which is used to obtain information about personal characteristics. Constructs such as ability, aptitude, interest and personality are usually measured. The purpose of selection tests is mainly to predict job success among a number of applicants.

Psychological tests are used in different walks of life. In schools, intelligence, aptitude and interest tests can be used to assist learners in making subject and career choices. In other organisations, tests are used to help select employees at various levels. They are also administered to current employees to identify personnel with the potential for promotion. Psychometric assessment can play a key role in placing people in the right kinds of careers and ensuring that they receive the right kind of training. Different types of tests measure different things. We now briefly look at some of these.

8.4.3.1 Types of test

Cognitive ability (intelligence)

The measurement of intelligence has always been a popular ability test for selection. An intelligence test gives an indication of general intelligence by means of a single score.

The following intelligence tests are used in South Africa:

- the South African Wechsler Individual Intelligence Scale for Adults;
- the Mental Alertness Scale of the National Institute for Personnel Research (NIPR); and
- the New South African Group test.

Aptitude tests

Aptitude measurement is used, inter alia, for the selection of job applicants. Most aptitude tests, such as the High Level Scales and the Senior Aptitude Test (SAT), are based on Thurstone's primary group factors such as verbal ability, word fluency, memory, deductive reasoning, inductive reasoning, numerical ability, perceptual speed, form perception, spatial aptitude and coordination.

Personality tests

Most experts agree that personality has an influence on work performance. The aim of personality questionnaires is to identify personality traits. People are then more aware of their behaviour and are able to make valid assessments. The Occupational Personality Questionnaire (OPQ) is widely used in South Africa. Muchinsky et al (2005: 94) say that research in South Africa has confirmed "the usefulness of personality in predicting work performance across cultures and across different jobs".

Performance tests

The purpose of performance tests is to assess the applicant's performance on specific tasks that are representative of the actual job. As performance tests are designed for a specific job, there are many different versions. Examples would be a typing test (for typists), mechanic tool identification, editing skills, etc.

Performance tests appear to be good predictors of job success, and studies have revealed that these tests are more valid than written tests (Scarpello & Ledvinka 1995).

Interest tests

Interest is regarded as an important determinant in choosing an occupation. Interest is related to an individual's motivation and satisfaction. The basic premise in measuring interest is that people will be happy in a job if they like the activities involved. The following are examples of such tests:

- Strong Vocational Interest Blank;
- Kuder interest questionnaires; and
- Field interest inventory.

8.4.3.2 Psychological testing in South Africa: dead or alive?

Again it should be noted that section 8 of the Employment Equity Act prohibits psychological testing and other similar assessments of an employee unless the test or assessment has been scientifically proven to be valid and reliable, can be applied fairly to all employees and is not biased against any employee or group. The use of psychological tests therefore has to be validated for every culture and situation, and managers should ensure that the tests and assessments used in their organisations adhere to the requirements of the Employment Equity Act.

Since the introduction of employment equity legislation in South Africa, there has been quite a debate surrounding the status and value of psychometric testing in our country. Erasmus and Arumugam (1998: 39–41), for instance, claim that "psychometric testing is dead". They maintain that the "conventional approach to the standardisation of psychometric tests and the ways in which validity and reliability are traditionally established, render it totally impossible to develop tests that are really fair to all in a diverse society. The existing approach to the standardisation of psychometric tests is more than a century old" (Erasmus & Arumugam 1998: 40–41). They further point out that apart "from the conventional approach to 'standardisation', one also needs to establish standards that apply to the specific company ... to each job type within the company – and to 'weigh' a particular individual's results against standards applying to a particular designated group, where and when required. The quest is clearly for a state-of-the-art situation-specific approach ...".

In reaction to the Erasmus and Arumugam article, Kemp (1999) wrote that "psychometric testing is not dead". He argues that psychometric testing in South Africa is controlled by the Test Commission of the Republic of South Africa (TCRSA), and that only professionally qualified and registered as such persons (such as psychologists and psychometrists who are registered with the Health Professions Council of South Africa) are allowed to administer psychometric tests. Kemp (1999: 17), however, goes on to say that it

> ... would be wrong to deny that many of the existing psychometric instruments need improvement and upgrading. But to generalise and criticise all tests ... is wrong ... The claim that there is no place for psychometric tests must be seriously challenged ... Tests are an aid in the selection process and if used properly, supply invaluable information which is not easily gleaned in interviews ... The Equity Act does not prohibit the use of psychological tests. All it calls for is the correct use of tests, something psychologists do in any case. Psychologists will

welcome the Act. It is the unqualified who are trying to pass as psychologists who will have a problem with the Act.

From this it is clear that, as we progress further into the new millennium, the use of psychological tests and similar assessments will have to be scrutinised and improved. The quality of all our assessment tools will indeed need to be sharpened. Muchinsky et al (2005: 99) conclude as follows: "what we have learned about psychological tests … is that some tests are useful in forecasting job success and others are not. As an entire class of predictors, psychological tests have been modestly predictive of job performance."

8.4.4 Employment interviews

One of the commonest tools used for personnel selection decisions is the employment interview. In practice, managers are very keen on using the selection interview, and huge costs are often incurred to fly candidates in and provide them with accommodation, and so forth. Yet, as Taylor (2005), Cooper, Robertson and Tinline (2003), and Smith, Gregg and Andrews (1989) report, the predictive power of interviews do not seem to be so good from a research and academic point of view. We briefly return to this again a little later.

The aim of the interview includes to meet and interact with the top-rated applicants from the pool of received applications, and specifically also to clarify and explore issues in order to try to assess further the likelihood of suitability for the job. The idea is still to be matching information gained from the interview situation about the applicant to the role requirements of the job in question. Applicants may be interviewed by a number of different people, most important of which being the line manager who is responsible for the work that forms the immediate context of the role and job in question. The rest may include some combination of other line manager/s, like, perhaps, the one more senior to the immediate line manager (such as the supervisor's superior), worker representatives (such as shop stewards), special affirmative action committee members and also, if relevant, specialist HRM support staff. Selection interviews are social situations and hence the importance of trying one's best to make the interview situation and experience as positive and useful to all as possible.

8.4.4.1 Types of interview

Interviews usually range from being unstructured to structured. The *unstructured interview* refers to the coincidental, loosely organised type of interview where there is a lack of coherence in the attempt to explore specific areas for information. In personnel selection these are generally not recommended because the specific purpose of an interview is to collect information about the applicant which is directly related to the job for which the person is applying. With unstructured interviews it may thus happen that the interviewer and/or interviewee may raise topics and/or issues not considered to be all that relevant or important. This increases the risk of being seen to be unfair in the selection process. (Keep in mind that one need not be unfair as such to be challenged by a party who has developed a perception that there might have been an unfair process – and such legal cases can take up a lot of time and money.) Although it is not necessarily detrimental to concede such freedom to an interviewer, this method can give rise to a lack of validity if the interviewer has no training in conducting interviews. In the hands of an untrained and incompetent person, this method might not differentiate accurately between applicants with either a high or low potential.

Structured interviews are so named because these social interactions are planned.

They are generally (and hopefully) characterised by two key features: careful, systematic planning of the interview, and use of people skilled in the process of interviewing. It is to be expected that a systematic approach to any problem would normally produce better results than coincidental, random procedures. Naturally an interview is planned according to the requirements of the job for which the selection is taking place. The reason for conducting the interview is therefore to obtain precise job-related information about the applicant.

A systematic analysis leads to clear statements of objectives, a plan for obtaining the necessary information and procedures according to which this information can be assessed. A structured interview provides for a more organised approach and a more stable basis for assessment of the different candidates. The procedure of the structured interview provides guidelines for the general framework of the questions. The specific questions that will be asked remain the responsibility of the interviewer, and develop from the interview situation. In organisations you will find that most interviews fall between structured and unstructured – and we can hence refer to these as *patterned interviews*. Patterned interviews are structured to fit a particular pattern and flow, but even though there is a framework for this and the procedure is guided accordingly, there is room for deviating and thus some flexibility.

8.4.4.2 Problems with the employment interview

Research has shown, however, that an interview may not be the most suitable selection instrument after all. It has been found that interviews may be an unreliable and even an invalid method of selection because interviewers tend to compare applicants with their own perception of the ideal employee. In addition, interviewers often base their decisions on first impressions rather than on the information gleaned during the interview, or even make up their minds about applicants during the first few minutes of the interview. It has also been shown that females are often rated lower than males and that traditional sex roles tend to predominate. Most interviewers also do not improve with training because their inborn social prejudices distort any new insight that they may have gained (Smither 1988).

Despite all these problems, there is still a need to meet the applicant face to face to ensure that he or she will fit in with the organisation. The interview is therefore here to stay, and the onus is on the manager to improve the success of it. No organisation can really afford to appoint the wrong people. In spite of this, very few interviewers are really capable of obtaining adequate information to ensure a proper fit between the worker and the work. The value of the interview can be increased by ensuring interviewers are well trained and skilled. Below are some guidelines that can be used to improve the skills of the interviewers.

8.4.4.3 Guidelines for interviewing

Preparing for an interview

One of the major reasons for ineffective interviewing is the fact that the interviewer is often unprepared. The following may help to prepare better for a selection interview:
- Be very sure about the job requirements. Compton, Morrissey and Nankervis (2006: 79) say one of the key issues relates to getting right the focus of the interview and in this regard the main challenge is "to establish valid selection criteria" and that "the person/s making the final selection sets out those essential and desirable factors" that are associated with successful job performance. These thus relate primarily to the competencies of the candidates – their knowledge,

skills and abilities – but also to, for example, relevant personal attributes pertaining to the job. The position or job descriptions and job specifications must thus, again, be very important in this part of the preparation.

- Study the written application very carefully, including material such as the completed application form, the résumé or CV, any personal statements that address the selection criteria, and also any testimonials that may have been attached.
- Make notes about any gaps, contradictions or incomplete information in the documentation, and what questions need to be asked in respect of these.
- Formulate preliminary ideas about issues for further exploration in the interview. Make sure that all issues are relevant to the job/role, and eliminate any potentially unfairly discriminatory questions.
- Remain aware about your own possible prejudices and guard against using yourself as a model. Think about the job requirements and try to evaluate the person's strengths and weaknesses as objectively as possible.
- Plan the areas that you want to cover, for example background, education, work history, etc, in a logical manner. Plan to avoid going into issues for which sufficient information is already available. Before you go into an interview, make sure you know what information has already been provided.
- Questions should preferably be about topics that directly relate to the selection criteria as such. These can relate to generic competencies such as problem-solving abilities, team work and interpersonal skills, communication and so forth. The job-specific competencies may include knowledge, skills and abilities that may be rather unique to the position in question – for example a position for a manager of an electrical engineering section may include specific criteria, such as knowledge pertaining to the latest developments in this specific field. Similarly, questions can be asked about latest developments in the field of recruitment and selection if the position is for an HR specialist practitioner in this field.
- If the interview is going to involve more than one interviewer – as in the case of a panel interview – those involved should get together to plan who is going to ask questions about what, and also in what order. This is especially the case with structured interviews. Naturally there should be some flexibility, and in preparing one must build in potential for follow-up questions whereby different people may be allowed to engage with questions about relevant issues as the interview unfolds.
- It is very important to make sure that all the necessary prior arrangements are well organised way in advance. This may include setting the date, place and time of the interview, and informing all relevant parties hereof, including the panel members (if applicable). It is important to make sure about appropriate contact details so that in the event of unplanned problems (such as illness or an emergency situation), applicants can contact the organisation (or vice versa, perhaps). The actual venue and set-up where the interview is to take place must also be well prepared, including, for example, reception, the furniture in the actual room (and the required ergonomic-related issues such as temperature and lighting), and in particular also the seating arrangements. Ensure that there will be no interruptions, and that everything is geared towards comfort and projecting a professional image.

Opening the interview

If a panel interview is used, the introduction should include the name and job title or role of each member of the interview panel. A nameplate could also be put in front of each of the interviewers. The interviewer should also give an idea of the degree of formality expected by using (or not using) first names.

- *Establishing rapport*

  The atmosphere must be friendly and relaxed. Most people experience the employment interview as stressful. The interviewer is primarily responsible for putting the applicant at ease, which is called establishing rapport. This can be seen as the process of creating a harmonious relationship between the interviewer and the applicant so as to develop the applicant's confidence in the interviewer to such an extent that he or she begins to talk spontaneously.

- *Purpose of the interview*

  Once rapport has been established, the purpose of the interview should be explained. In this regard, the applicant should be told that the purpose is to find out more about his or her previous experience, training, background, interests, goals and values. The applicant, in turn, will be told more about the job in question and the organisation, and should also be invited to ask questions.

Obtaining information

The main purpose of the employment interview is to obtain the required job-related information in order to enable the interviewer to make a decision. The following guidelines with regard to questioning can be followed (Fear & Chiron 1990: 57–68):

- Making use of questions phrased in an open-ended way is generally preferred. This will enable the applicant to talk freely. Use phrases such as 'tell us about' and 'share with us your experience when' to make questions open ended.

- Questions must be work related – and in particular, it is also suggested, specifically related to the selection criteria that have been identified as being important to the job or position. To avoid issues which may be regarded as unfairly discriminatory, interviewers must ensure that the questions that they ask are job related. Try to obtain only the necessary information required to determine whether or not the applicant will be successful on the job.

- Make use of follow-up questions in order to clarify any aspects regarding the extent to which an applicant might, or might not, meet the critical job requirements (the selection criteria).

- The interviewer should clarify the true meaning of the applicant's casual remarks. Where the interviewer is concerned about an applicant's remarks, for example his or her dislikes, the interviewer should establish the extent of these dislikes by means of further questioning – if these relate to the job and selection criteria.

- The interviewer must search for evidence which substantiates hypotheses established earlier. Interviewers often observe clues to an applicant's behaviour early on in the discussion, and an hypothesis is then established. Further questions should be asked to determine whether or not there is support for such a conclusion.

- Emphasise the present abilities rather than the distant past, and concentrate on real job experiences relatively recently. While experience and examples of 20 years ago may not be irrelevant, the question to be asked would be to what extent the relevant competencies are 'current'.

- The interviewer should also be careful not to lose rapport. Careful observation (also of body language, perhaps) and concentration will thus be important. It is generally good to make and maintain appropriate eye contact.

In order to avoid accusations of unfair discrimination, the interviewer should bear in mind that many variables come in to play. Care should, for instance, be taken that interviewers are aware of culturally related issues during the interview situation. Interviewers must understand that cues such as body language (for example eye contact), assertiveness (women often tend to phrase their responses less assertively), differences in verbal fluency, the choice of words and intonation may be job irrelevant if viewed from a cultural diversity point of view. Such factors should not be taken into account unless they can be shown to be job related. Certain specific guidelines also need to be followed when questions are asked during the interview. The following are some of them:

- Ask all the candidates the same basic opening questions (follow-up questions naturally differ).
- Avoid asking questions out of curiosity.
- Avoid asking females questions such as their plans for marriage, children, etc.
- Do not ask questions that can be seen as unfairly discriminatory against older people, the disabled, etc.
- Avoid asking questions such as the following, generally:
  - How old are you?
  - Are you living with anyone?
  - Do you have any plans for marriage?
  - Have you been married in the past?
  - How long have you been single?
  - Are you considering having any/more children in the future?
  - What is your religion?
  - How can you be sure that you will be reliable given the fact that you have small children?
  - Which sport do you play?
  - Which country clubs do you belong to?
  - Have you ever been a member of a trade union?
  - Will you be joining the union active in the company should you be successful in your application?

Closing the interview

Interviewers must remember that the applicant will also have to ask certain questions in order to make sure that this is the right job for him or her. The interviewer should at least give the applicant enough information to make an informed decision. The applicant should also be given an indication of when to expect a response regarding the outcome of the application.

8.4.4.4 Other ways of improving the effectiveness of the interview

As indicated earlier, the interview is not rated highly as a selection instrument because of its low validity. Recent research findings have, however, revealed a more optimistic view of the predictive capability of the interview. Two studies found average validities in the 0,40 to 0,50 range (Landy, Shankster-Cawley & Moran 1995). Schmidt and Rader (1999) reported research that indicated that selection interviews had higher validity for predicting job performance than previously believed and that validity could be generalised.

It appears that structured and panel interviews make a significant difference (Smith et al 1989: 46). The validity of structured interviews can reach the same level as that of ability tests. Two types of structured interview, namely the situational interview and the patterned behavioural description interview (PBDI), will be referred to. The situational interview deals with samples of work behaviour. The applicant's response to situations which are typical of the job and crucial to the successful performance of the job is tested. It has been found that the predictive validity of the situational interview is around 0,30 and 0,46 (Singer 1993: 26).

In the PBDI, the applicant is expected to recall an incident similar to the situation described and to relate his or her reaction to it. The predictive validity of the PBDI is around 0,45 and 0,72 (Singer 1993: 26).

The panel interview gives more people the chance to assess the applicant. The fact that more people are involved in the selection process leads to a fairer assessment. Not too many interviewers should be involved, however. Usually only a chairperson, the line manager and the HR practitioner, for instance, are necessary.

To summarise, the effectiveness of the interview can be improved by doing the following:

- training interviewers in the skill of interviewing;
- changing to more structured and situational interviews;
- using job-related questions; and
- using the panel interview.

8.4.5 Assessment centres

An increasingly popular approach is to use a very comprehensive, integrating selection method (actually a combination of numerous methods) known as an assessment centre (referred to as an AC by some). This approach is not captured in figure 8.1 but if used it can replace the third component (employment tests). Cooper et al (2003: 115) explain assessment centres as follows:

> In essence, the AC approach utilizes all the main selection methods (eg work-sample tests, structured interviews, and 'paper and pencil' tests of mental abilities, aptitudes and personality) in a comprehensive and integrated manner, culminating in a written report for each candidate that usually provides an overall assessment rating (OAR). In combination, multiple methods are thought to lead to more accurate predictions about a candidate's future job performance ... Candidates are generally assessed in groups of six to eight, by groups of senior managers and/or psychologists over two to three days, although sometime it may be as little as one day, or as long as a week.

The assessors must be professionally trained to assess the applicants. Assessment centres are most often used in the selection of more senior managers. The idea is that some good objectivity is built in, hopefully, that the multiple-method approach yields more 'rich' information, and that the comprehensiveness somehow lessens the possibilities for 'bluffing' or 'conning' one's way into a job.

The foundation is, once again, the information coming from the job analysis, and hence the actual criteria. The process is thus to take these, find appropriate combinations of predictors and the subjecting the shortlisted candidates to the assessment itself. As Cascio points out, "By ... pooling the judgment of multiple assessors in rating each candidate's behaviour, it is felt that the likelihood of successfully predicting future performance is enhanced considerably" (Cascio 1998: 328).

The assessment centre is regarded as a valid indicator of job suitability, a finding which has been confirmed by research conducted in South Africa (Kriek 1991: 34–37). Research has shown that the assessment centre can be used as a valid predictor of supervisory performance across all groups (Kriek, Hurst & Charoux 1994). In the US the courts have found the assessment centre to be superior to other traditional selection instruments. Cascio (1998) reported that recent research on the predictive validity of the assessment centre is so impressive that the operational use of the method has spread rapidly. Particularly in South Africa, where organisations are under pressure to introduce fair HRM practices, assessment centres appear to be an option for the future. In a recent study on the use of assessment centres, almost half of all respondents were found to be making use of them already (Kriek & Von der Ohe 1996).

In cases of using ACs, the employment interview as such may take on quite a different form and be conducted for a different purpose – more to clarify issues, perhaps, and especially to meet the person face to face. In such situations the idea would not really be to get information in order to assess the person as a potential employee, and it would typically be one-on-one interviews between the candidate and the prospective supervisor. It may involve a higher-level superior as well in some cases.

8.4.6 Reference checks

Reference checks are conducted after the employment interview to find out more about an applicant's employment record, education and training, and behavioural patterns. These details are used to predict the expected competence of a particular applicant for the job in question. An example of a reference check form is shown in exhibit 8.1.

Reference checking is important for the following reasons (Kieffer 1991):
- input is obtained from a number of people;
- there is useful feedback on the strengths and weaknesses, achievements and failures of individuals; and
- the organisation receives a verbal report on an individual's performance.

8.4.6.1 Guidelines for checking references

A popular way of checking references is by telephone. Candidates are required to furnish the names and contact numbers of previous employers and other people that may be contacted for this purpose. References are useful if they satisfy the following four requirements:
- The person providing the reference must have observed the candidate in a relevant situation (for example during work).
- The person providing the reference must be capable of assessing the candidate's performance.

EXHIBIT 8.1: Reference check form

Name of applicant: .... (Vacancy: ....)

Reference: .... Date: ....

Relationship to applicant: ....

1 Period of employment: ....

2 Positions and duties held: ....

3 Reason for resignation: ....

4 Would the candidate be re-employed?..

5 Job performance: ....

6 Relevant selection criteria (eg.): ....
- Managerial ability: ....
- Communication skills: ....
- etc. ....

7 General comments: ....

- The person must be prepared to express his or her forthright opinion.
- The person must express him- or herself without any possibility of misinterpretation.

Although all of the abovementioned points are of importance, the honesty with which an opinion is expressed is probably the point on which most references fail, as people are often reluctant to state a negative opinion.

The person following up references may also ask about the candidate's job title, employment period and salary, and whether his or her previous company would consider rehiring him or her. As a general guideline, only the references of serious candidates are worth checking. The validity of the information provided must be checked, the candidate should be informed that the references he or she provided will be checked, and the questions to be asked should be formulated in such a way that information about the candidate's qualifications, skills, work habits, sense of judgement and performance level will be obtained. In view of recent reports of widespread fraud in respect of educational qualifications, such as 'fake' degrees from certain institutions, it is even more important to check that all educational particulars are verified as valid.

8.4.7 Physical examination

Before the successful applicant is appointed, he or she may be required to undergo a physical examination. The purpose is to determine the applicant's physical suitability for the position for which he or she has been selected. Organisations must also be careful when specifying a physical qualification to ensure that it is job related and that the employee would not otherwise be able to do the job properly.

The Employment Equity Act stipulates in section 7 that medical testing of an employee is prohibited unless legislation permits or requires it or unless it is justifiable in the light of medical facts, employment conditions, social policy, the fair distribution of employee benefits or the inherent requirements of the job. The Employment Equity Act states that the testing of an employee to determine his or her HIV status is prohibited unless the testing is justifiable by the Labour Court. Medical testing is further defined in the Act as "any test, question, inquiry or other means designed to ascertain, or which has the effect of enabling the employer to ascertain whether an employee has any medical condition". When a medical test is required by law, such as in the case of certain sectors of the food industry, it may not be prohibited. It is, however, more vague in the case where justifiable testing is required based on the inherent requirements of the job. One would have to prove, for instance, that certain medical conditions will hamper the execution of a particular job. A flight controller may, for instance, be tested for blackouts or lapses because it may be a requirement of the job for a flight controller to be alert at all times. Also, it is important to note that testing for HIV would not be permissible unless one can show that having HIV would affect the employee's or co-employees' performance or well-being (see also chapter 17).

8.5 THE PREDICTIVE POWER OF SELECTION METHODS: A BRIEF NOTE ON WHAT SOME RESEARCH REVEALS

Taylor (2005) cites the work of various rigorous research studies into the scientifically proven value of different selection methods as predictors of success on the job. The statistical measure that would typically be used in such research is the correlation coefficient, measuring "how closely scores at the selection stage correlate with those awarded for later" performance in the job or work situation (Taylor 2005: 200). If there is a perfect correlation, the coefficient will show out as 1, and this will mean that the predictive power is 100% accurate. On the other hand, a correlation coefficient of 0 would mean that the predictive power is zero and that the selection method thus has no accuracy at all. Table 8.1 shows the results of meta-analyses about the accuracy or predictive power of various selection methods based on the work of Smith et al (1989). Taylor (2005: 200–201) concludes that the results of these meta-analyses have "apparently confirmed ... that traditional methods of selection such as interviews are markedly poorer at accurately predicting job performance than more sophisticated techniques such as personality tests and assessment centres ... More recent meta-analytic studies have given a rather better press to structured interviews ... However, what is particularly interesting ... is the response of employers when asked to reflect on which selection techniques they found most useful ... a very clear majority stated that the interview was the most important tool for them in making selection decisions ... thus a great gulf between the considered views of academics and practitioners about the relative usefulness and value of different selection methods ...".

Table 8.1: Predictive power of some selection methods according to research based on meta-analyses

1,0	Perfect prediction
0,9	
0,8	
0,7	
	Assessment centres (promotion)
0,6	
	Work sample tests; ability tests
0,5	
	ACs (performance); personality tests (combination)
0,4	
	Bio data; structured interviews
0,3	
0,2	
	Typical interviews; references
0,1	
0,0	Astrology; graphology

Source: Adapted from Taylor (2005: 201), based on Smith et al (1989)

8.6 MAKING THE SELECTION DECISION: FAIRNESS IS KEY

Fairness in personnel-selection decisions is an important issue generally. In South Africa the notion of fairness will take on a peculiar meaning due to relevant legislation aimed at redressing the unfair discrimination against non-white people that we have had under the almost five decades of apartheid. It is interesting to note, however, that also in other countries in Africa, fairness in personnel decisions has its own challenges and peculiarities (see the box below). It will remain quite a dream to build a just and inclusive society in any country (and on our own continent, Africa) if such things as favouritism and nepotism are at the order of the day.

Elsewhere in Africa

In Ivory Coast, job applicants often complain about the lack of fairness in the hiring process. Critics of the hiring process contend that employers prefer to hire people they know or who have political connections ... Under these conditions, getting hired depends more on who you know rather than what you know ... [A]necdotal evidence suggests that most of the time employees tend to be of the same ethnic group as those who hold powerful positions within organizations ... [M]anagers may consider having a moral obligation to help their less fortunate relatives or tribesmen ... by recruiting ... fellow tribesmen, managers may build a power base within their respective organizations.

Source: Extracted and slightly adapted from Beugré (2004: 140)

Based on all the information collected, a decision has to be made as to who will be offered the job. One thing is to decide who seems most likely to be the most suitable person for the job. This is not necessarily the same, however, as the decision on whom to actually offer the job and whom to reject. A key issue becomes employment equity, and the balancing hereof with the more straightforward process of identifying and/or ranking all the shortlisted candidates from most to least suitable. A decision according to a strictly libertarian approach would simply mean rejecting all but the 'best' applicants. However, such an approach (see section 3.3.1.2) would obviously not always facilitate the achievement of affirmative action targets. This is why many other factors have to be considered before the final selection decision is made. Special attention should, for instance, be paid to what the Employment Equity Act stipulates as being relevant criteria to consider, such as appropriate experience and prior (also informal) learning, as well as the potential to acquire the ability to do the job within a reasonable period.

Such an approach need not result in a lowering of standards, work performance or productivity, provided that the organisation does not indulge in window-dressing by appointing incompetent people in a misguided attempt to get its workforce profile right. Without going into complex models of the selection process, it will suffice to say that the best candidate is not necessarily the person who obtained the highest composite score on a battery of selection devices used by the organisation.

However, when making a selection decision, one must ensure that all the information used:

- is objective, that is, related to relevant prior learning, experience, qualifications and competencies, and not coloured by the beliefs and prejudices of the person who collects or interprets it;
- is based on the inherent requirements of the job;
- has the same meaning to members of different groups;
- is actually used in a standardised way for a specific purpose;
- is preferably quantified or classified in distinct unambiguous categories; and
- is unquestionably relevant to the selection decision being made.

Also, when it is decided to turn down a candidate, the following are important, especially from an equity point of view:

- Keep written records indicating why each applicant was rejected. In the event of a claim of unfair discrimination, such records will be necessary to prove that no unfair discrimination took place. Normally, reasons need not be provided when a person is informed that his or her application has been unsuccessful.
- However, should a candidate ask for reasons for having been turned down, the major reason (or two) should be provided, and particular care should be taken to ensure that the reason(s) given are based on objective criteria only. Such reason(s) should preferably be given in writing (even in the case of internal applicants to whom verbal explanation had already been given at the time of the request) in a succinct business-orientated manner to avoid any possible future disputes. Normally, reasons should not be given verbally to outside job applicants.

In summary, managers of South African organisations will in future be increasingly expected to prove the scientific basis and/or fairness of their selection decisions. It is important to realise that selection decisions are more likely to be regarded as fair if the links between the requirements of the job and the personal characteristics required to do it can be proved and specified. Once these links have been established, selection tools to help identify these personal characteristics can be considered. This emphasises, once again, the need for proper job analysis.

Managers of South African organisations must therefore realise the need for proper job analysis processes as well as the potential usefulness of valid predictors of job performance. They have to ensure that they are in a position to defend all such decisions with scientific proof. Selection techniques and decisions must be proved to be job related if they are to be considered fair, and a more scientific approach to selection is therefore essential.

A POLICY PERSPECTIVE

Our selection policy aims to assist decision makers to make an informed choice about whom to make an offer of employment to, from a pool of job applicants. Attracting top-class talent is important but making the selection decision will determine whom we want to make a member of our organisation.

The purpose of this policy is to support the design and application of appropriate selection methods, processes and practices that can help ensure we make fair and equitable placement decisions about whom would probably be most suitable for employment. The overall aim is to appoint people who are most likely to fit well with the strategic direction of the organisation and about whom we are the most confident that they will demonstrate superior work performance and find fulfilment through becoming a member of our organisation.

8.7 APPOINTING AND ORIENTATING NEW EMPLOYEES

As soon as the selection process has been completed and a final decision has been made, it is usual practice to discuss a provisional offer with the prospective employee. We usually do not yet advise the other shortlisted candidates of not having been successful. Keep in mind that more than one and often all the shortlisted candidates may have been found to be suitable, but not in an equally ranked fashion. If we have found some candidates to not be 'appointable' (hence found to be not 'suitable' for employment for that job), we may advise the person of not having been successful at this occasion.

It may happen that our first choice of candidate does not accept what we can offer. It may also be that he or she simply withdraws for reasons beyond our control at any point in the process that point (he or she may simply not have liked what was experienced during the recruitment and selection process). We might then go back to the candidate that was ranked second and explore the possibility of making him or her an offer. As soon as agreement is reached verbally or informally with a candidate, we proceed with the formal process of employing the person. A letter of appointment can then be provided to the successful candidate. If appropriate, this is done by the HR department or section. Sometimes the person is contacted telephonically and requested to come to the organisation in order to finalise the offer and hand over the letter of appointment. It is thus generally advisable, especially in the case of more senior-level appointments, that the person should accept the job offer in principle (and conditions of service) and preferably in the presence of witnesses, before a letter of appointment is provided. The reason for this is that we only give the letter of offer to serious candidates. In practice some people use such letters purely as tools to negotiate promotions or better offers at existing employers.

As soon as the person has accepted the offer in writing, all the other suitable applicants must be informed in writing, and in a courteous way, that their applications have been unsuccessful. Such a letter must thus be of a high standard and must always be politely worded. After all, this is the beginning of another recruitment process, as it is yet another way of portraying the image of the organisation externally.

Once the employment relationship has been formally established, the new employee's first few days and weeks in his or her new working environment form the next important facet of HRM.

'First impressions last!' This statement has been proven countless times in practice. If people are negatively disposed towards an organisation during their first days or weeks in its employ, this may have a lasting influence on their orientation and attitude towards the organisation in the long term. The opposite is equally true. For this reason it is essential that newly appointed employees be positively disposed towards the organisation, towards the section in which they are working, towards their jobs and towards other employees.

The organisation's socialisation programme (induction or orientation programme) is thus a formal attempt at changing this potential threat into an opportunity for better human resource utilisation. The socialisation or orientation programme is aimed at gradually (but as soon as possible) introducing new employees to the organisation, the work unit in which they will be working, the particular work and the people and things with which they have to work.

It is basically a structured process involving welcoming, receiving and introducing the newly appointed employees, providing them with the necessary information, and making them feel at ease so that they can settle down as soon as possible. This helps to ensure that they will be happy and become productive at work.

The process is aimed at making the newcomer feel at ease and involves aspects like the following:
- reducing anxiety/tension;
- creating a feeling of security as soon as possible;

- creating realistic expectations on the part of the employee;
- creating a foundation for the integration of personal and organisational objectives (creating the match or fit); and
- making the employee productive as soon as possible.

One aspect of orientation involves introducing the employee to the organisation itself. This entails providing the employee with information about aspects such as the following:

- a brief overview of the company – its history, market, industry, products, organisation structure and the top management team;
- conditions of employment and benefits – such as normal hours of work, holidays, medical and pension schemes, group life insurance;
- remuneration policy, pay scales, when paid and how, payroll administration;
- work rules and standard procedures;
- human resource and labour relations management policy;
- disciplinary code and procedure;
- grievance procedure;
- relationships with employer organisations;
- trade union-related arrangements (for example which unions, recognition agreements, consultative structures);
- training and development policy and facilities;
- employee wellness policy;
- medical and first-aid infrastructure;
- restaurant facilities;
- social responsibility policy;
- community involvement policy;
- procedures for internal and external telephone system and correspondence;
- procedures relating to travelling and subsistence expenses; and
- issues relating to confidentiality of certain company information.

The other important component relates to actual work orientation, and to the immediate work environment (such as the relevant section or department). In this case the focus is on the work in the department or work unit overall of which new employees will be part, and in particular also on the people with whom they will have to work. In the process newly appointed employees will obtain a brief introductory overview of the workflow process, the nature of their specific work role and on how their department and job fits in with the rest of the organisation.

The initial socialisation or induction of an employee is thus a shared responsibility. The human resource specialists or department will be primarily responsible for the general organisation-level orientation, while line management takes primary responsibility for introducing the employees to their more immediate work environment. These role players should liaise and work together to help new employees to feel at ease and to become productive as soon as possible. Exhibit 8.2 may help as some checklist.

EMPLOYEE ORIENTATION CHECKLIST

Use these guidelines to conduct a simple yet effective employee orientation, ensuring that all important employment practices are communicated to employees. It is also a good workplace practice to regularly re-orientate employees annually or when changing employment practices in your *Employee Handbook* or *Human Resources Manual*.

Keep this orientation checklist on an employee's file for later use, for example to demonstrate to the CCMA or Labour Court that employment practices have been communicated to a particular employee.

NAME	ID #
JOB TITLE	WORK UNIT
START DATE	RATE OF PAY
SUPERVISOR'S NAME	TELEPHONE NUMBERS (W) (H)
REVIEW DATE	CELL NUMBER

Department structure and functions	
■ Overview of department ■ Department orientation ■ Customer orientation ■ Organisational chart ■ Function of work unit ■ Work duties of others in the work unit ■ Review of specific departmental procedures ■ Mission statement and operational objectives ■ Job duties and responsibilities ■ Performance standard for the job ■ Probation period ■ Issue an *Employee Handbook* ■ Where to get department help and information ■ _____ ■ _____ ■ _____	**Notes**

Physical surroundings and equipment	
■ Work area ■ How to use the telephone ■ Location of supplies ■ Care of equipment ■ Parking ■ Keys and key control ■ Housekeeping and safety	**Notes**

>>

- After-hours access
- Staff ID card
- Fire extinguishers and exits
- Smoking rules
- Review of specific policies pertinent to department
- _____
- _____
- _____

Pay for time worked

- Pay cheques
- Pay dates
- Check distribution
- Problem with pay cheque, see supervisor
- Changes in personal/income tax status (name, address)
- _____
- _____
- _____

Notes

Hours of work

- Work week and hours of work
- Meal breaks – when and how long
- Work schedule changes
- Break periods – when and how long
- Punctuality
- Attendance
- Review of relevant *Human Resource Manual* procedures
- Required overtime, Sunday work, night work or work on public holidays
- _____
- _____
- _____

Notes

Leaves and absences

- Holidays
- Vacation leave request
- Vacation leave accrual
- Use of leave and approval after six months of service
- Sick leave request
- Medical release may be required
- Sick leave accrual rate
- Sick leave w/o pay
- Compassionate/bereavement leave
- Family responsibility leave

Notes

- Department procedures on leave reporting
- Leaving during working hours
- _____
- _____
- _____

Rights and responsibilities

- Conduct and dress code
- Effective work relationships
- Professional ethics
- Telephone – how to answer
- Personal calls
- Rules outlining the use of equipment/resources for personal use
- Employee assistance programme
- Job injury reported to supervisor
- Confidential Information
- Complaint and appeal procedures
- Disciplinary process
- _____
- _____
- _____

Notes

Other employment practices communicated

- _____
- _____
- _____
- _____
- _____
- _____
- _____
- _____

Notes

Original retained by supervisor on employee file

Date for follow-up/re-orientation of employment practices: _____

Copy to employee:

I, the undersigned, hereby confirm that the above-mentioned policies and procedures have been communicated to me.

_____   _____

EMPLOYEE SIGNATURE   DATE

I, the undersigned, hereby confirm that the above-mentioned policies and procedures have been communicated to the above-mentioned employee.

_____   _____

SUPERVISOR'S SIGNATURE   DATE

Source: workinfo.com: http://www.workinfo.us/Sub/Sub_for_hr/HR/Manual/Section%202%2013.doc

8.8 SELECTING AND CONTRACTING A VENDOR FOR PROVIDING WORK AND WORKER-RELATED SERVICES[1]

In cases where we want to make use of the services of an outside provider of, say, contract labour or consultancy services, it is just as important to make sure that we do our best to choose the right one and to structure the relationship as well as we can. We should keep in mind that labour brokers or temporary employment services organisations engage in commercial contracts with the principal that make them independent contractors. They thus provide us with labour for a specific purpose and will typically use their own equipment and have their own supervisory staff on our premises, managing the work related to this contract, as well as their workers. As mentioned before, these workers are the employees of the organisation that is the independent contractor (the labour broker firm/temporary employment services provider).

There are many such vendors who make it their business to provide contract labour to organisations that outsource some of its work. Often, such workers come on site and mingle and work with some of our employees. They then typically use our organisation's amenities like restaurants and change-rooms. The key is that we want such working people to add optimum value to our organisation's work requirements. If they do not, we must seek alternatives, which may include reverting to some work redesign and bringing back some of the work into the control sphere of our organisation. It is thus essential, if we have decided on this option, to find the right vendors, to establish contractually sound relationships, and to also develop good commercial and general working relationships. The starting point for this, as already mentioned in chapter 7, is to search for as many potential labour brokering firms or vendors as possible. Exactly the same principles apply if we want to engage the services of consultancy firms, for instance. We must 'shop around' and ultimately make a decision as to which firm to bring on board to help with certain work.

Using a tendering process is generally advisable when it comes to these kinds of work-related needs. When we place advertisements that call for tenders to be submitted we must make sure that all our systems and processes are in place to manage the tendering and concomitant decision-making process. Key in this regard is the design of the relevant tendering documentation, which should provide for uniform submissions. We must be able to 'compare apples with apples'. We must thus clearly stipulate the exact needs for work to be contracted out, what the scope of work entails, what the expected performance standards will be, and what the relevant terms and conditions will entail – and also in particular exactly what the tender submission process entails and what the closure date is. We must preferably have clearly stipulated weighted 'performance criteria' so that tendering vendors know what we will look at and what is important to us in our assessment of each tender received. Obviously, some of these will include such things as the proven capability to get the work done, based typically on past performance of similar contracts for other principal organisations. Tendering vendors must generally submit, as part of their tender, details of relevant companies who might be approached to provide testimonials. We need to know that these service providers are properly registered and are in good standing in relation to, for example, government taxes and levies (evidence to be enclosed in the submitted tender documentation), and have good track records generally, and that it would generally be preferred if they have prior experience in the same industry or sector as our own organisation. The managerial and financial capacity and expertise, and the length of time of being in operation may also be important. Naturally, the costing and fee structure will also be very important variables.

Once we have assessed all the tenders that we have received and made our decision, we engage in processes to finalise the contracting side of affairs as we contact the successful vendor. The scope of the contract should be no surprise because of the tendering process, but it is nevertheless essential that the contract be 100% clear on the scope of services that are being contracted. If, for instance, we outsource some HRM work we must be very clear as to what is included for the purposes of this contract and what not. Let us say it is to outsource 'employment services'. We will have to be unequivocally clear on what the responsibilities will be. If the services are to be rendered away from our business premises, where will we meet to discuss shortlisting, for instance? If we would like to have interviews conducted at our premises so that prospective candidates can see the place of work when being interviewed, this must be stipulated. We will also have to stipulate things, in such an example, like who will play what role. Who will provide advice and who will make the selection decision? What weighting factor, for instance, will apply to what the employment agency says and to what we say?

The contracts (see exhibit 8.3 for an example of such a contract) should also be very clear on terms and conditions, and on performance criteria. The terms and conditions involve, for example, the following: contract duration; start and end dates/ times; confidentiality principles; invoicing, and payment procedures and cycles; technology, and work-space and facilities issues; implications related to unforeseen changes in such things as work volumes, government regulations, interest rates and exchange rates; and breach and termination of contracts. The performance criteria can be formulated along the lines of service level agreements (SLAs) that stipulate how delivery standards will be measured in terms of, for example, quality, quantity, timelines, and efficiencies or relevant productivity measures. In the case of outsourcing certain types of work, aspects such as intellectual property may be very relevant, as well as contract severance. The latter refers to practical ways of exiting from a contractual relationship, such as when there is failure to deliver on the part of the vendor, but there may also be some intellectual property issues involved.

Establishing a relationship with another organisation to help us get some of our organisation's work done can thus become 'tricky business'. Given that it is becoming an increasingly popular way of designing the work systems of some organisations (as covered in earlier chapters), we must take utmost care in how we choose the vendor and how we set up the relationship. This goes way beyond the extremely important legal side of things though. If we enter in these kinds of arrangements to get work done, there usually is a longer-term intention of doing so (even if an initial contract period may not be that long – say for only two years or so). There are vested interests on both sides. The relationship side of things is crucial and as the saying goes, well begun is half won. Right from the outset it is essential to develop appropriate communication channels and to start working on, for example, trust and respect. Celebrating the start of such a relationship with a little social event that brings together key role players from our organisation as well as the vendor might not be such a bad idea.

Lastly, once the work actually starts it may also be wise to have a good two-way communication session that involves the people who will actually be doing the work or the workers or labourers in the case of temporary employment services for work such as cleaning or catering services.

AGREEMENT

between

ABC (PTY) LIMITED

("the client")

and

XYZ CC t/a

LABOUR MANAGEMENT CONSULTANTS

("the contractor")

1. **DEFINITIONS**

   1.1 "Day(s)": Calendar days
       "Effective date": ....
   1.2 "Employment Legislation": The Basic Conditions of Employment Act 75 of 1995; any applicable Bargaining Council agreement, any applicable Wage Determination or their successors in title.
   1.3 "Personnel": Suitably qualified employees in the employment of the contractor or persons who have the skills necessary to carry out the assignments as per schedule "A".
   1.4 "The client": ABC (PTY) LIMITED
   1.5 "The Contractor": XYZ CC t/a Labour Management Consultants
   1.6 "Schedule": A schedule forwarded to the client by the contractor recording all invoices for assignments carried out by personnel during a particular week.

2. **INTRODUCTION**
   The contractor acknowledges that the fundamental basis for the agreement is that the contractor will supply personnel to the client from time to time in accordance with the terms of this agreement.

3. **COMMENCEMENT & DURATION OF CONTRACT**
   The contract shall commence on the effective date and shall be valid for the duration of one (1) year. Each individual's assignment shall be for the duration of the contract subject to clause 6.

4. **CLIENT'S RESPONSIBILITIES**
   The client shall be responsible for:
   4.1 the provision of all equipment and materials required to carry out the assignment;
   4.2 common-law liability insurance for all personnel on any of the client's sites.

5. **CONTRACTOR'S RESPONSIBILITIES**
   The contractor shall be responsible for:

>>

5.1 the mobilisation and demobilisation of personnel to and from site. The contractor shall supply a member of personnel to the client not later than one (1) week after receipt of the written order from the client. Should the contractor not comply with the request within one week, the client may directly contract with other contractors on a once-off basis.

5.2 the payment of all salaries, bonuses, PAYE deductions, personal accident insurance, relocation, movement allowances and all other remuneration and benefits in terms of the prevailing employment legislation.

5.3 the supply of the personnel specified by the client from time to time in accordance with the provisions of this contract.

5.4 public and employers liability insurance cover for all personnel engaged under this contract.

6. **TERMINATION OF ASSIGNMENT BY PERSONNEL**

6.1 During the probationary period

6.1.1 During the personnel's probationary period the client may with immediate effect terminate the services of any member of the personnel during their first thirty (30) calendar days of service with the client for unsatisfactory performance by giving written notice to the contractor by telefax or e-mail. Any notice pay due to personnel in such circumstances shall be paid by the client.

6.2 Outside of the personnel's probationary period

6.2.1 The client may terminate the services of any member of the personnel by giving two (2) weeks' notice, and such notice shall commence running upon receipt thereof by the contractor in writing by telefax, or any other hard copy.

6.2.2 If the contractor's personnel resigns from their employment, a two-week notice period will apply starting from the day of receipt by the client of written confirmation of termination from the contractor.

6.2.3 The client may terminate the services of any member of the personnel with immediate effect if that member is guilty of an act of serious misconduct. The client shall be liable to pay for the services of any such member of the personnel only for the period up to and including the date upon which the contractor receives written notification by facsimile or any hard copy of the termination of the services of a member of personnel.

6.2.4 In the event where the client terminates the services of any member of personnel for misconduct, the client shall assist the contractor in the preparation and execution of a disciplinary enquiry and undertakes to do all such things necessary and incidental to the contractor's obligations to comply with fair dismissal procedures as required by the Labour Relations Act of 1995.

6.3 Any notice pay due to a member of personnel shall be paid by the client.

7. **REPLACEMENT OF TERMINATED PERSONNEL**

In the event of a termination under clause 6, the client may request the contractor to provide a suitable replacement as soon as possible. However, the client is under no obligation to take a replacement and need only do so at its discretion.

8. **PAYMENT BY THE CLIENT**

The contractor will submit invoices for the services of the personnel on a weekly basis. The client shall pay the contractor the amount shown on the invoices within thirty (30) days of the date on the invoices by direct transfer or such other method as the contractor shall direct. If payment is not made within the thirty-day period then the contractor may suspend the services provided by the personnel.

9. CALCULATION

9.1 The client shall pay the contractor the basic rate stipulated in the order for each member of the personnel. The rate applicable to the personnel will be for all hours worked.

9.2 This contract is divisible. The work performed in each week during the currency of this contract shall be invoiced separately. Each invoice for work performed in any week shall be payable by the client in full, in accordance with the terms of payment provided for herein, without reference to and notwithstanding any defect or default in the work performed or to be performed in any other month.

10. FAILURE OF CLIENT TO PROVIDE WORK

If for any reason beyond the contractor's control any of the personnel cannot work or are prevented from working, the client shall pay to the contractor the basic rate stipulated in the schedule (subject to variation in accordance with these contract conditions) for each such member of the personnel provided they have presented themselves for work at the client's premises and have tendered to work normally.

11. VARIATION OF RATES

If the cost to the contractor of supplying the personnel increases during the term of the contract by reason of an increase in tax or other public or local government-imposed levies or any other statutory cost, then the rates in the schedule shall be increased so that the contractor shall be compensated in full for any such additional expenses. Subject to the provisions of this clause, the rates in the schedule shall not be changed during the period of the contract.

12. EXPENSES

The client shall reimburse the travelling and other expenses incurred by the personnel in pursuance of the work subject to such expenses being first approved by the client in writing. Such approval may not be unreasonably withheld. [Optional]

13. WARRANTIES & INDEMNITIES

13.1 The contractor warrants, guarantees and undertakes in favour of the client the following:

13.1.1 Personnel supplied to the client shall be the contractor's employees as defined in terms of section 213 of the Labour Relations Act 66 of 1995.

13.1.2 For the full duration of the contract, the contractor shall fully comply with all its obligations as employer of the personnel howsoever arising or connected to the provisions of the prevailing employment legislation and its contracts with the personnel.

13.1.3 The contractor shall indemnify and hold the client harmless against any claims instituted by its personnel against the client whatsoever and howsoever arising from or connected to any breach of a failure to comply with the prevailing employment legislation.

13.1.4 The contractor warrants and confirms that it is registered as a labour broker in terms of the Income Tax Act as well as a VAT vendor.

14. HEALTH AND SAFETY

The client shall be responsible for all obligations regarding the safety, health and protection from injury of the personnel while on the client's premises. The client shall at all times indemnify and hold the contractor harmless against all actions, claims, losses, damages, costs and expenses incurred by the contractor as a result of any failure by the client to comply with these obligations.

15. MOTOR VEHICLES

The client accepts responsibility for all actions, claims, losses, damages, costs and expenses resulting from the use by any member of the personnel of any motor vehicle belonging to or under the control of the client, and will indemnify the contractor in respect thereof.

16. ADDITIONAL PAYMENTS BY CLIENT

Subject to the provisions of clause 5.1, if the client should knowingly engage the services of any of the personnel either directly or indirectly to carry out work for the client within the period of this contract or for a period of three (3) months subsequent to its termination and notwithstanding that the client may have terminated the services of a member of personnel under clause 6.2.3, then the client shall be liable to pay to the contractor a fee equivalent to the rate for such member of the personnel for a period of three (3) months.

17. RELATIONSHIP BETWEEN PARTIES

Nothing in this contract shall create the relationship of employer and employee or partnership between the client and the contractor or between the client and the personnel.

18. TAXATION

18.1 The contractor shall ensure that it is registered as a labour broker with the Receiver of Revenue and shall furnish a certificate to the client in the absence of which the client shall deduct tax from payments made to the contractor.

18.2 The contractor shall register as a value-added vendor and shall furnish the client with a copy of its VAT certificate

18.3 The contractor is responsible for all deductions in respect of PAYE, SITE and the like from the personnel, and indemnifies and holds the client harmless against any claims from the South African Revenue Service (SARS) in this regard.

19. CONFIDENTIALITY

All documents, data, drawings, specifications and other information prepared specifically for use on the contract shall become the property of the client. Any information acquired by the contractor's personnel whether relating to the specified duties or not shall be regarded as confidential and shall not be disclosed to any third party without the prior permission of the client.

20. PATENTS AND COPYRIGHTS

The contractor shall assign the rights to any inventions arising from the specified duties of the personnel assigned under this contract to the client, and shall, at the client's expense, execute any documents to enable the client to seek the granting of patent for such inventions. Furthermore, the contractor shall assign to the client the copyright and design right of all documents and drawings prepared by the contractor's personnel assigned under this contract. The client shall have the right to make use as the client sees fit of such documents and drawings without further payment to the contractor.

21. EXCLUSION OF LIABILITY

The contractor shall not be liable to the client in any manner whatsoever for any claim, loss, damage, cost, expense, or action arising from any act, omission or neglect on the part of the personnel in the course of the carrying out the assignment (or otherwise while under the control of the client) and the client shall indemnify and hold the contractor harmless against such claims.

22. MATERIAL TERMS

22.1 The contractor acknowledges and agrees that clauses 2 and 13 are material terms of this agreement. In the event that the contractor is in breach of these clauses and notwithstanding the provisions of clause 3, the client shall be entitled to cancel this agreement by giving the contractor ten (10) days' notice in writing. In such an event, the client may withhold any payment due in terms of clause 8 of this contract and shall be entitled to pay directly to the personnel any remuneration and benefits due to them by virtue of their contracts of employment with the contractor and/or arising out of the provisions of the prevailing employment legislation. Nothing in this clause shall limit the right of the client to recover from the contractor any amount of money paid to any of the contractor's personnel by the client as a result of the contractor's breach of its obligations in respect of its personnel's contracts of employment or the provisions of the prevailing employment legislation.

23. DISCLOSURE

23.1 The contractor shall give the client reasonable access to its books of account or such other documentation as may be reasonably necessary to ensure that the contractor complies with its obligations to its personnel by virtue of the provisions of prevailing employment legislation.

23.2 The contractor shall furnish the client with a pro-forma contract of employment of its personnel and shall advise the client should the terms thereof change in any material respect and furnish the client with an updated copy.

23.3 The contractor shall furnish the client with a copy of its equity plan within fourteen (14) days after having received such a request. The contractor shall allow reasonable access to the client to inspect is books of account and such other documentation as may be necessary to verify the contents of the contractor's equity plan.

24. CONDUCT

The personnel supplied to the client shall at all times conform and comply with the client's vision and ethos of its business. Personnel shall at all times present themselves in a proper uniform at the client's premises or such other attire as the client may determine from time to time.

25. CESSION AND ASSIGNMENT

The contractor shall not cede any of its rights or delegate any of its obligations hereunder without the prior written consent of the client. The contractor warrants that the interest/ shareholding reflected on annexure "A" is correct and will advise the client in writing of any proposed change. Any change in shareholding shall entitle the client to cancel this agreement by giving ten (10) days' written notice.

26. VARIATION NOT EFFECTIVE UNLESS IN WRITING

26.1 No variation, modification or waiver of any provision of this agreement, or consent to any departure therefrom, shall in any way be of any force or effect unless reduced to writing and signed by the parties, and then such variation, modification, waiver or consent shall be effective only in the specific instance and for the purpose and to that extent for which made or given.

27. PARTIES NOT AFFECTED BY WAIVER OF BREACHES

27.1 The waiver (whether express or implied) by any party of any breach of the terms or conditions of this agreement by the other party shall not prejudice any remedy of the waiving party in respect of any continuing or other breach of the terms and conditions hereof.

27.2 No favour, delay, relaxation or indulgence on the part of any party in exercising any power or right conferred on such party in terms of this agreement shall operate as a waiver of such power or right, nor shall any single or partial exercise of any such power or right preclude any other or further exercises thereof or the exercise of any other power or right under this agreement.

28. SOLE AGREEMENT

This agreement constitutes the sole agreement between the parties, and no representation not contained herein shall be of any force or effect between the parties.

29. DOMICILIUM

29.1 The parties hereto choose domicilia citandi et executandi for all purposes of and in connection with this agreement as follows:

29.1.1 The client ....

29.1.2 The contractor ....

30. ARBITRATION

30.1 Any dispute between the parties in regard to:

30.1.1 the interpretation of;

      30.1.2   the effect of;

      30.1.3   the parties respective rights and obligations under;

      30.1.4   a breach of;

      30.1.5   any matter arising out of;

      this agreement shall be decided by arbitration in the manner set out in this clause.

30.2   The said arbitration shall be held subject to the provisions of this clause:

      30.2.1   at Johannesburg;

      30.2.2   informally;

      30.2.3   otherwise in accordance with the provisions of the Arbitration Act 42 of 1965, as amended; it being the intention that if possible it shall be held and concluded within twenty-one (21) working days after it has been demanded.

30.3   The arbitrator shall be if the question in issue is:

      30.3.1   primarily an accounting matter an independent accountant agreed upon between the parties;

      30.3.2   primarily a legal matter, a practising advocate or attorney with no less than ten (10) years standing agreed upon between the parties;

      30.3.3   any other matter an independent person agreed upon between the parties.

30.4   If the parties cannot agree upon a particular arbitrator in terms of clause 30.3 above within seven (7) working days after the arbitration has been demanded, the nomination in terms of clause 30.3.1, clause 30.3.2 and clause 30.3.3, as the case may be, shall be made by the President for the time being of The Law Society of Gauteng (or its successor in title) within seven (7) days after the parties have so failed to agree.

30.5   The parties irrevocably agree that the decision in these arbitration proceedings:

      30.5.1   shall be binding on them;

      30.5.2   shall be carried into effect;

      30.5.3   may be made an order of any court of competent jurisdiction.

31. OPERATIVE LAW

The contract shall be governed by and construed in accordance with the laws of South Africa.

AMENDMENTS

SIGNED ON BEHALF OF

AUTHORISED SIGNATORY _____

DATE _____

WITNESS _____

AND ON BEHALF OF XYZ CC t/a LABOUR MANAGEMENT CONSULTANTS

DIRECTOR _____

DATE _____

WITNESS _____

Source: Workinfo.com: http://www.workinfo.us/Sub/Sub_for_hr/HR/topic/TempEmployAgree.doc

8.9 CONCLUSION

In this chapter the focus has been on making decisions about who will actually be engaged to do the work. Selection is the process of making decisions about the matching of individuals to jobs, taking into account individual differences and the requirements of the job. The selection process consists of different steps, and the success of the whole process can be improved by continuously improving each one. There are a lot of different methods and techniques involved in making personnel selection decisions. Some may only be used by professionally trained experts while in most of the selection work the key people are the ultimate decision makers – the managers. When the selection process has been completed and a final decision has been made, a provisional offer is discussed with the prospective employee and, once an agreement is reached, the successful candidate is appointed. When successful employees start with the organisation, they are supposed to be orientated, during which period they are introduced to the work environment and the organisation. The idea of socialisation is to ensure that new employees are as happy and productive as possible, as soon as possible.

In the case of having to choose and contract an appropriate provider of independent contract work, there are different processes and challenges involved – but all perhaps equally challenging and important. At the end of the day, this route is just another means of getting the work of the organisation done and it is thus just as crucial to get these decisions as accurate as possible and to start the relationships with outside vendors on the right foot – and to keep it there (which we will look at in later chapters again).

SUSTAINABILITY CONNECTION?
Creating a sense of fulfilment requires a good fit between the working people and the work for which they are employed. Furthermore, work performance is the backbone of organisational performance and we can only hope for superior work performance in our organisations if we engage people who are capable of working superiorly and if we create an environment that facilitates that. We might however create the most appropriate work environment through things like work and organisational design – but if we don't select and appoint the right people, the organisation is very likely to perform sub-optimally. Sub-optimal performance cannot lead to sustainable competitive advantage and hence organisations can go astray – posing risks related to continued existence. We must therefore make sure that we get the right talented people to work for and with us, or else we might seriously jeopardise our chances of being successful and helping to create a better life for all.

SELF-EVALUATION QUESTIONS

1 What is personnel selection?
2 Who is involved in making personnel selection decisions? Explain how it may differ between a small and a large organisation.
3 Distinguish between a predictor and a criterion. Give examples of each.
4 Which method to determine validity is preferred in personnel selection? Explain the method.
5 What is an application form? What else can form part of a written job application?

6   Distinguish between ability, aptitude and personality tests.
7   What is a reference check? What is the underlying principle of a reference check? Should it be used for all jobs? Substantiate your answer.
8   What is an assessment centre (AC)? What are your views about the potential value of ACs?
9   Write notes about the following topic: 'Fairness of personnel selection decisions.' How fair are these decisions in your organisation? Why do you say that?
10 How would you go about appointing and socialising a new employee after a selection decision has been made?
11 Write a short essay on the following topic: 'Issues to consider when having to search, find, choose and contract a temporary employment services provider.'

ENDNOTE

1   This section is guided by the work of Lane (2004) in 'Australian Master Human Resources Guide', published by CCH.

PART FOUR
THE PEOPLE EMPOWERMENT CHALLENGE

9 MOTIVATION AND WORK

LEARNING OUTCOMES

After studying this chapter, you should be able to:

- discuss fully the implications of the different assumptions about the nature of 'organisational man', for HRM in general and motivation in particular;
- describe in detail the basic motivational process and its relationship to anxiety and performance;
- list and explain the different motivational theories classified as content theories, process theories and reinforcement theories respectively; and
- compare and critically analyse the different motivational theories in terms of their relative strengths and weaknesses.

9.1 INTRODUCTION

Once a person is at work, motivation plays a very important role. We might have recruited a great pool of potential workers, we might have made good selection decisions, or we might have established a relationship with a labour broker firm that has a very good reputation, but none of this guarantees that the working people will perform as we would have hoped for. A person might have all the skills, knowledge and abilities to be able to perform well, but if the work motivation is not right, work performance will be suboptimal. Work motivation is thus the underlying theme of this chapter. Levy (2006: 252) defines work motivation as a "force that drives people to behave in a way that energizes, directs and sustains their work behavior".

The rest of this chapter is based on the assumption that our concern is about the work-related motivational challenges we face when we have to manage people in the course of their employment. Note that the focus now shifts to 'being in employment'. Even if some people are helping to do some of our work as employees of another organisation, such as a temporary employment services provider, the work motivational issues are just as relevant – but perhaps more so for the labour broker firm and its supervisory staff. We do not make the distinction in the rest of this chapter – we merely focus on motivating people in a work context. Naturally we must understand that work motivation forms one sub-part of a much broader theme pertaining to human motivation.

We have to start off by issuing a warning: people are extremely complex beings; the complexities involved in human motivation are vast and deep.

Given the complexity of work itself, the different shades of meaning that can be attached to work in modern life, as well as the inherent complexity of the human psyche, the links between managerial efforts to motivate employees to want to perform better at work and the actual work performance realised is highly complex and can at best only be partially understood.

Compounding this complexity in the South African situation is our socio-political heritage, the great disparities in living standards and, of course, our great cultural and ethnic diversity. These uniquely South African aspects of the problem of developing, utilising and maintaining a high-performance workforce make it risky to import concepts and theories from other countries without trying to place these in the South African context.

Nevertheless, given the dearth of basic research on the topic of motivation in South Africa, we are forced to start our enquiry with the traditional (Western) literature. Thus, given that it is the whole individual (bringing along his or her cultural and psychological makeup to the workplace) who reports for work (and not just that dehumanised fraction of the person as a factor of production), it is impossible even to begin to do justice to this topic in the course of a book chapter like this. For this we would have to explore the realms of disciplines like psychology and anthropology, to name just two.

9.2 HUMAN MOTIVATION AND SOME ASSUMPTIONS

If good management includes the ability to motivate people so that they are actually inspired to perform well at work and help to achieve organisational goals, managers must develop the ability to create work environments in which people are motivated to do so. When we consider ways of motivating workers, we must remember that each of us also brings to the work situation our own unique complexities, including what motivates us and our own assumptions about what motivates others.

Schein (1972: 55–79) has formulated a useful classification of managerial assumptions about people. The four sets of assumptions about the nature of "man" – and "organisational man"[*] in particular – are the following: (i) rational-economic man; (ii) social man; (iii) self-actualising man; and (iv) complex man. Please note that "man" here refers to 'human'. These four sets of assumptions find expression in specific managerial practices and thus have a very real impact on how businesses are run and on HRM practice. Schein's historical classification of management's assumptions about people is still one of the most useful ways of introducing you to motivation as it provides an overview of theories of motivation (and their concomitant managerial implications). Before dealing with the different theories of motivation in more detail (and with leadership in the next chapter), we thus start with Schein's classification by way of an overview.

9.2.1 The rational-economic man view
The assumptions underlying the rational-economic man theory is the proposition that people are motivated by the avoidance of unpleasantness and attraction towards that which gives pleasure. The rational-economic man can be described as a rational computer programmed to maximise self-gratification and interest. In terms of this hedonistic view of man, combined with McGregor's Theory X assumptions (see section 9.3.10), the characteristics of employees are those listed in exhibit 9.1.

---

[*] We use the term 'man' as it was used in the literature. It is intended to include women.

- Employees are motivated primarily by money and will always do that which will result in the greatest material gain.
- Since economic incentives are under managerial control, employees are passive pawns to be manipulated, moved and controlled by management.
- Employees' feelings are irrational and must be prevented from interfering with their pursuit of self-interest. This can be achieved through appropriate organisational design and managerial control mechanisms.
- Employees are inherently lazy and must thus be motivated by external incentives.
- Employees' natural objectives run counter to organisational objectives; employees must thus be subjected to external controls to ensure that they work towards (and not against) organisational objectives.
- Because of their irrational feelings, employees are inherently incapable of self-discipline and self-control.

Not surprisingly, this denigrating view of employees presupposes that there are other human beings who possess superior attributes: the managers! Managers are people who are self-motivated, self-controlled and less of a victim to their feelings. Schein (1972: 56) summarises this as follows:

> Ultimately, then, the doctrine of rational-economic man classified human beings into two groups – the untrustworthy, money-motivated, calculative mass, and the trustworthy, more broadly motivated, moral elite who must organize and manage the mass. As we shall see, the main problem with this theory is not that it fits no one, but rather that it overgeneralizes grossly and oversimplifies ...

9.2.1.1 What this means for managing people at work

Given South Africa's apartheid legacy, there is an uncomfortable parallel between Schein's summary and some of the assumptions which underpinned grand apartheid (think of the Verwoerdian notion of black as opposed to white education). Unfortunately, the structural and social inequities resulting from apartheid were also tainted with the self-fulfilling prophecy that if a group of people are continually told that they are inferior and cannot aspire to anything but the lowest of stations in life, many of them may come to believe it. Therefore, one could plausibly hypothesise that in South African business, some of the victims as well as the beneficiaries of apartheid hold views that approximate those of the rational-economic man model; both groups are thus in need of re-education.

If a manager holds the assumptions associated with the rational-economic man model, his or her managerial style might very well be grounded upon elements like the following:

- Since workers are motivated by money and are inherently irresponsible, management should take a paternalistic attitude towards them and strictly control them. There should be minimal delegation of authority, a very formal hierarchy of power must be enforced, and people must be rewarded extrinsically. Management must be task orientated, and the emotional aspect of people (managers and employees alike) must be suppressed.
- If work performance is unsatisfactory, the solution lies in the redesign of jobs and organisational structure, as well as in restructuring the reward system and

controls. One could typify this as a 'scientific management' approach to the management of people.

■ The onus for organisational performance rests exclusively with management. Workers are expected to do no more than that which the reward and control systems encourage and permit.

As Schein correctly points out, the great danger for an organisation operating under these assumptions "… is that they tend to be self-fulfilling. If employees are expected to be indifferent, hostile, motivated only by economic incentives, and the like, the managerial strategies used to deal with them are very likely to train them to behave in precisely this fashion" (Schein 1972: 57). Another way of putting this is that, if management treats its workforce like irresponsible children, the workforce will quickly conform to this notion and live up to managerial expectations. It could plausibly be conjectured that in the early post-industrialised world this paternalistic approach to the management of employees led to the rise of trade unions, and that, while the assembly line mode of production proved its efficiency as work became more complex, management found that workers as mindless automatons were not up to the task demanded by modern production methods. A different type of worker was thus needed: one who wanted to exercise his or her own discretion and judgement, and who was motivated by non-financial incentives.

An economy based on simple products and production methods could run on the lines proposed by the rational-economic model (pay human robots for doing simple, repetitive tasks). However, an economy based on the provision of complex services and production methods cannot. For this type of economy a more autonomous and self-directed workforce is needed: one that is not satisfied by mere money and that will not tolerate the external and formal strictures placed upon it by a paternalistic management intent on keeping tight control. As jobs became more demanding (and hence management's expectations of their employees became more exacting) so the expectations of employees grew in terms of what they wanted to get out of the employment relationship (see figures 9.1 and 9.2).

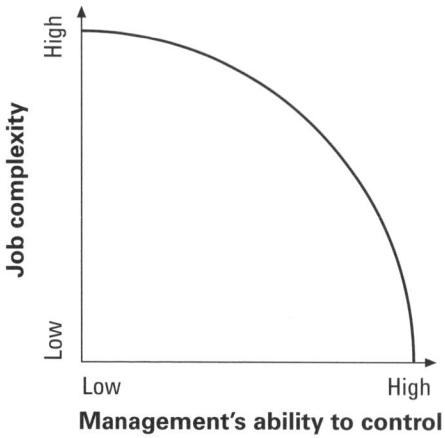

Figure 9.1: Relationship between job complexity and ability to manage by means of external controls

Figure 9.2: Relationship between job complexity and employee's expectation

9.2.2 The social-man view

The second stage in the development of our understanding of the human side of organisations is identified by Schein as being that of the 'social-man model' (1972: 58–65). The notion that workers are at least, if not more, motivated by social factors present in their work environment rather than by monetary rewards, can be traced to the seminal research done in the 1920s at the Hawthorne Plant in the US. The 'Hawthorne Studies', as they came to be called, dramatically drew attention to the fact that people's need to be accepted by co-workers is at least as important as monetary incentives in determining their performance. On the basis of his Hawthorne studies, Elton Mayo developed assumptions about the nature of man in the context of the world of work that are diametrically opposed to the assumptions derived from the rational-economic model of man. These are summarised in exhibit 9.2.

EXHIBIT 9.2: Employees – the social-man view

- Employees are fundamentally motivated by social needs and develop their self-identity through relationships with others.
- The Industrial Revolution and the consequent fragmentation of work removed the meaning from the work itself, and meaning must therefore be sought in the social relationships at work.
- Employees are more responsive to their peer group than to the incentives and controls of management.
- Employees are responsive to management to the extent that management can meet their social needs and needs for acceptance.

Source: Adapted from Schein (1972: 59)

9.2.2.1 What this means for managing people at work

As observed above, the assumptions underlying the social-man model are almost the direct opposite of those identified as belonging to the rational-economic man model. Likewise, a manager operating under the social-man set of assumptions will be a totally different type of manager from his or her more 'scientific' counterpart. More specifically, the 'social-man manager' will tend to be associated with the following characteristics:

- The manager will not concern him- or herself exclusively with the task at hand – the needs of the people who must perform the task will also be taken into account.
- Instead of focusing on motivating (by manipulating external incentives) and controlling subordinates, the manager will pay much more attention to subordinates' feelings (especially those relating to the need for acceptance and identity).
- Since employees want to belong, the manager will accept the reality of informal groups within the organisation and thus concentrate on group incentives rather than on individual incentives.
- The manager's role shifts from the traditional generic managerial functions (planning, controlling, etc) to becoming a conduit between his or her subordinates and higher levels of management, and being sensitive to their needs and feelings.
- The burden for organisational performance shifts from the manager to all employees. As Schein puts it (1972: 59): "The manager instead of being the creator of work, the motivator, and the controller, becomes the facilitator and sympathetic supporter".
- The manager still sets goals for the group, but leaves them much discretion in deciding how they will accomplish these goals.

The expected payoff of this type of employment relationship is that more loyal and committed employees will result (because of their greater identification with the organisation through their greater need satisfaction – this goes beyond the mere instrumental value of getting money to embrace more fundamental needs such as the need for affiliation and a positive self-identity). In terms of this model, the great danger resulting from management's failure to look after the social needs of its workforce lies in the fact that employees will nevertheless seek to satisfy these needs by creating and joining informal groups whose objectives will run counter to those of the formal organisation. For instance, employees may join a trade union to satisfy their social needs and channel their frustration at the formal organisation's failure to satisfy these needs into industrial action 'to punish management'.

Although it is tempting to view the 'social-man manager' as the 'good guy' and to cast the opposite, the 'rational-economic-man manager', into the role of the 'bad guy', this would be incorrect, for the simple reason that both amount to unjustified over-generalisation and, perhaps more fundamentally, because people differ in their needs structure (the latter being a function of a multitude of factors).

9.2.3 The self-actualising man view

According to this view, modern work has become meaningless; this meaninglessness, however, is related not so much to people's social needs as to man's inherent need to fully develop and utilise all his potential. Job specialisation, job fragmentation and the resultant deskilling of jobs have caused work to become unchallenging and alienating in the sense that employees are no longer permitted to use and develop their abilities to the full or to see a clear connection between their activities and the total organisational goals. For instance, workers in a cottage industry busy themselves with a wide range of activities that are intimately involved with the ultimate goal of their endeavours. Think, for example, of a family unit who all work together to produce clothing to sell on the local market – tending the sheep, shearing, spinning yarn, making garments and finally taking them to the market to sell. All of these activities are clearly and meaningfully related to the ultimate goal of the family as an economic unit, thereby giving meaning to each family member's activities. Compare this with a modern production worker whose job may involve the monotonous repetition of the same movement (the author once worked 12-hour shifts on an assembly line fastening the left-hand front wheel of a relentless procession of lawnmowers). It is difficult to see this activity as meaningful or to relate it to any organisational objectives!

Maslow's hierarchy of needs is probably the best-known version of the self-actualising-man model of human behaviour as a function of motivational states. An application of Maslow's model in the employment relationship is depicted in exhibit 9.3.

9.2.3.1 What this means for managing people at work

There are similarities but also differences between the way in which the self-actualising-man manager and the social-man manager will approach the task of managing subordinates.

■ The manager will place less emphasis on showing consideration for employees' feelings and more emphasis on making the job intrinsically more challenging and meaningful. Employees will be given the scope and freedom in their jobs to achieve and obtain a sense of pride and self-esteem. Take note that, should the manager assess an employee's level of need-fulfilment to be at the level of social needs, he or she will respond appropriately (see the next point).

EXHIBIT 9.3: Employees – the self-actualising model

- Employees' needs (which can act as motivators) fall into five sequential classes. These are (from the bottom to the top) – basic needs for survival, safety and security; social needs; self-esteem needs; autonomy and independence needs; and self-actualisation needs.
- Employees want to grow in their jobs (which implies that they expect some autonomy and independence); to adopt a long-term perspective; to develop their skills; and to have some flexibility in adapting to work circumstances.
- Employees are primarily self-motivated and self-controlled; external controls are seen as threats to their need to grow to maturity in their jobs.
- There is no inherent disparity between organisational goals and the self-actualising goals of the individual employee; given the opportunity, an employee will integrate his or her own life goals with those of the organisation.

Source: Adapted from Schein (1972: 66)

- The manager will have to be an accomplished diagnostician to determine which of the five levels of needs a particular employee will respond to in order to delegate responsibility to employees in accordance with their differing levels of need-fulfilment.
- Relating to the manager's role as diagnostician, the manager also will have to be flexible enough to adapt his or her managerial style to match the different need levels of each of his or her subordinates.
- Most importantly, the basis of motivation shifts from being extrinsic (that is, control that lies outside the job content) to being intrinsic, in the sense that management must provide the opportunity (through job design, job enrichment, delegation of authority, etc) for the employee's innate motivation (aroused by the ultimate need for self-actualisation) to be unleashed by jobs characterised by challenge, autonomy and scope for growth towards maturity.
- In order to allow for greater subordinate autonomy, the manager will be prepared to divest him- or herself of much of the traditional managerial power or managerial prerogative; the organisation will thus be characterised by greater delegation of authority to lower levels and a more equal distribution of power throughout all levels of the organisation.

To summarise: the self-actualising model of man holds that people have inherent needs and are thus self-motivated, provided that they are given the opportunity to strive towards whatever will result in fulfilling that level of need that is hierarchically above the need(s) that has already been satisfied (for a more complete discussion of this topic, see the section below). In the words of Schein (1972: 69):

> ... the assumptions underlying the concept of self-actualizing man place emphasis on higher-order needs for autonomy, challenge, and self-actualization, and imply that such needs exist in all men and become active as lower-order security and social needs come to be satisfied. There is clear evidence that such needs are important in the higher levels of organizational members like managers and professionals on the staff. It is not clear how characteristic these needs are of the lower-level employee, although many of the problems which were interpreted to be examples of thwarted social needs could as easily be reinterpreted to be instances of thwarted needs for challenge and meaning.

Perhaps this quote from Schein is a bit slanted towards the higher-level needs, which only come to the fore once the lower-level needs have been substantially satisfied. The challenge for the manager is to determine what will be need-fulfilling and thus act as a powerful motivator of a specific individual at a specific time. For the masses of poor and unskilled workers in South Africa it may well be their security and safety needs (such as job security and a reasonable income). In the South African context it could also be argued that, due to the greater prevalence of the extended family and involvement in community issues (as compared with the situation in Western developed countries), as well as the existence of powerful trade unions, social, independence and autonomy needs are at this stage satisfied to some extent by other social institutions (the family, the community and the trade union), so that the work context is relied upon primarily to satisfy the need for material well-being.

9.2.4 The complex-man view

After reviewing the preceding models of man, Schein (1972: 69) comes to the conclusion that these models all contain elements of truth, but that they suffer from the defect of being generalisations which do not reflect the complexities of reality. He comes to the conclusion that:

> Man is a more complex individual than rational-economic, social, or self-actual-izing man. Not only is he more complex within himself, being possessed of many needs and potentials, but he is also likely to differ from his neighbour in the patterns of his own complexity. It has always been difficult to generalize about man, and it is becoming more difficult as society and organisations within society are themselves becoming more complex and differentiated (Schein 1972: 69–70).

Schein (1972: 70–76) suggests that the assumptions summarised in exhibit 9.4 will do justice to this complexity.

EXHIBIT 9.4: Employees – the complex-man perspective

Employees are not only complex but also very variable; many motives operate at different levels of importance to the employee, with this hierarchy of needs and motives changing from time to time, and from situation to situation.

Employees learn new needs and motives through their organisational experiences. Motivational patterns are thus partly a function of the interaction between initial needs and organisational experiences.

An employee's needs and motives may differ, depending on the type of organisation in which he or she is employed or on the sub-organisation within the larger organisation. A person who is in an alienating formal position may find fulfilment of his or her social and self-actualising needs in the informal organisation, social groups, or even the trade union. If the job itself is complex and challenging, some aspects may fulfil some needs while other aspects will fulfil others, with much less reliance on factors external to the job for need fulfilment.

Organisational effectiveness is also dependent on factors other than motivation; for instance, a highly skilled but unmotivated employee's contribution to organisational performance may equal that of a very unskilled but highly motivated employee.

There is no one managerial approach based on one set of assumptions about the nature of man that will be appropriate for all employees at all times under all circumstances.

Source: Adapted from Schein (1972: 70)

9.2.4.1 What this means for managing people at work

The complex-man model presents managers with the following two challenges:

■ managers must be a good diagnostician in that they must be able to determine what motivates different individuals under different circumstances; and

■ managers must value difference and possess the personal flexibility and range of skills to vary the approach appropriately, depending on their assessment of the differential needs of each of their subordinates.

These two core competencies, namely diagnostic ability and the ability to adopt a flexible leadership style, are specifically apposite for a multicultural society characterised by great disparities in the development of its human resources. For the South African manager who must acquire the skills to manage a diverse workforce effectively, the complex-man model probably provides a more realistic representation of reality than the other models discussed, and is particularly instructive in that it brings to the fore the daunting tasks facing management as our country approaches the 21st century.

Having examined Schein's perspectives on the nature of 'organisational man' and what motivates him, we now turn to an overview of the best-known motivation theories.

9.3 MOTIVATION: THEORIES ABOUT HOW IT WORKS

What is motivation? Why do people act in the way that they do? Why do others refrain from doing certain things? And can we in a predictable and systematic way influence people to act in the way we want them to? At best we have partial answers to these questions. In this section we introduce some of the theories developed to answer the above questions in the organisational context. Without attempting to answer the first question (there are a multitude of potential answers), the following working definition of motivation will suffice: "Motivation is generally defined as an internal state that induces a person to engage in particular behaviors ... it has to do with the direction, intensity, and persistence of behavior over time" (Spector 2006: 194).

The basic motivational process is shown in figure 9.3.

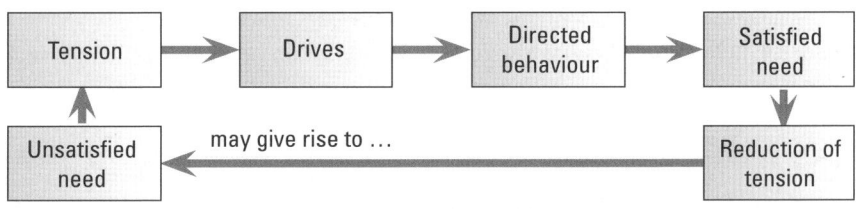

Figure 9.3: The basic motivational process

Another preliminary aspect of motivated behaviour that needs some clarification is the role of anxiety in the effectiveness of behaviour. In terms of our basic motivational process model, we see that needs give rise to tension, which in turn spurs behaviour directed at a specific goal which is perceived as being desirable in that it will lead to need fulfilment. However, what figure 9.3 does not show is the possibility that anxiety as a by-product of the tension, or arising from some other source (for example due to some form of psychopathology), may impact negatively on the person's performance. The correlation between anxiety levels and effectiveness of performance is illustrated in figure 9.4.

Recognition of the role of anxiety in effective work performance may lead to the following implication for management (Korman 1977: 40–41): in the case of employees who perform relatively simple jobs it may be effective to use anxiety as a means of stimulating more effective performance; for subordinates who perform complex tasks the reverse will apply.

A popular taxonomy of motivational theories divides the various theories into *content*, *process*, and *reinforcement theories*. *Content theories* focus on factors that allegedly motivate people, for example 'needs' (they try to answer the question: what motivates people?). *Process theories*, on the other hand, try to analyse the process or manner in which people get motivated (they focus on the question: how are people motivated?). *Reinforcement theories* focus on how people can be conditioned to exhibit the desired behaviour (these try to answer the question: how do people learn to exhibit desirable behaviour?). The content theories discussed in this book are Maslow's needs hierarchy, Alderfer's ERG theory, Herzberg's two-factor motivation theory, McClelland's achievement motivation theory and Locke's goal-setting theory. The process theories which are examined include cognitive dissonance theory, Stacey Adams' equity theory and Vroom's expectancy theory. Reinforcement theory and McGregor's theory X and theory Y are also briefly discussed.

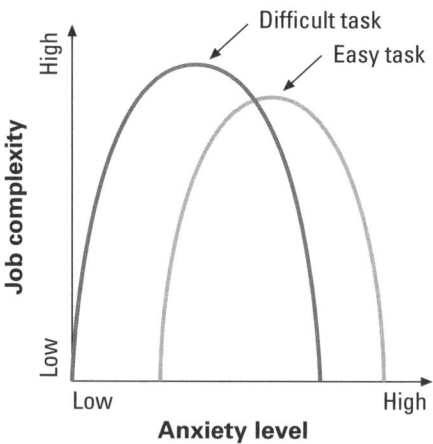

Figure 9.4: Relationship between anxiety and performance: easy versus difficult task

EXHIBIT 9.5: Anxiety and performance

■ Anxiety facilitates performance on easy tasks.

■ Anxiety debilitates performance on difficult or demanding tasks.

■ For any task, an upside-down bell curve can be plotted that will show that, up to a certain point, anxiety will increase effectiveness of performance, but beyond that point, increased anxiety will decrease it.

■ For easy tasks, the level of anxiety can be increased considerably before it will become debilitating. For more difficult tasks only a slight increase in the absolute level of anxiety may prove to be debilitating.

9.3.1 Maslow's hierarchy of needs theory

It can safely be stated that probably the best-known theory of motivation is Abraham Maslow's hierarchy of needs. Maslow's theory, which postulates that within every person there exists a hierarchy of five need levels, is depicted in figure 9.5 (see also section 9.2.3).

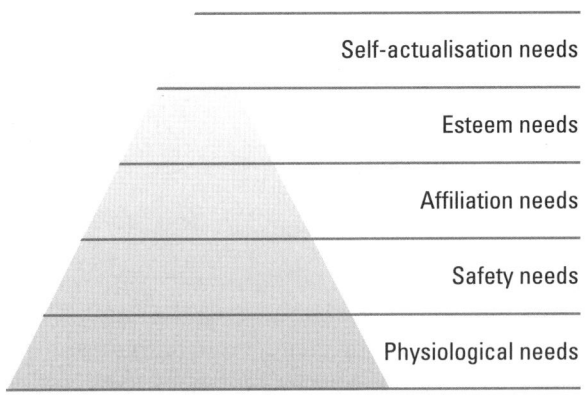

Figure 9.5: Maslow's hierarchy of needs

The self-actualisation model (of which Maslow's hierarchy is the best-known example) is based on the work of existential philosophers who postulate that man has the innate drive to achieve his full potential, but that it is the conditions of everyday life that place constraints on this 'instinct for self-actualisation' and cause him to perform suboptimally. Maslow's five levels of 'needs' (or 'motives', which are simply the other side of the coin, as can be seen from figure 9.5) are:

- *Physiological:* These include hunger, thirst, shelter, sex and other physiological needs associated with the biological survival of the individual and the species.
- *Safety:* These include security and protection from physical and emotional harm.
- *Social:* These include the needs to belong, to be liked and for friendship.
- *Self-esteem:* These include internal mental states such as self-liking, autonomy, achievement, as well as external factors such as needs relating to status, recognition and attention.
- *Self-actualisation:* This concerns the need to become what one is capable of becoming and includes needs relating to growth and development, achieving one's potential and self-fulfilment.

The key to an understanding of Maslow's schemata is the concept of 'prepotency'. This simply means that as lower-level needs become substantially fulfilled, the next higher-order needs increase in strength, and thus become powerful motivators. People fighting for their very survival (that is, those whose safety needs are unfulfilled) will not be motivated by opportunities to fulfil their status needs, because safety as a lower-order need must first be satisfied before the higher-order esteem needs. However, once their physiological, safety and social needs have substantially been met, they will become aware of their esteem needs. People who are barely able to provide for their own sustenance would not be motivated, for example, by the chance to acquire a better office, while people who earn an above average wage would be motivated by status symbols such as a better type of carpet or a bigger desk in their office. Companies do in fact pay a great deal of attention to the motivational value of status symbols at different levels within the organisational hierarchy (see table 9.1).

Although Maslow's theory enjoys wide support, this in all probability is due more to its intuitive appeal than to its empirical validation. Possibly the greatest

Table 9.1: How status symbols vary at different levels of the organisational hierarchy

Visible appurtenances	Top dogs	VIP	Brass	No 2s	Eager beavers	Hoi polloi
Briefcases	None – they ask the questions	Use backs of envelopes	Someone goes along to carry theirs	Carry their own – empty	Daily – carry their own – filled with work	Too poor to own one
Desks, office	Custom made (to order)	Executive style (to order)	Type A (Director)	Type B (Manager)	Castoffs from No 2s	Yellow oak – or castoffs from eager beavers
Tables, office	Coffee tables	End tables or decorative tables	Matching tables, type A own desk	Matching tables, type B	Plain work table	None – lucky to have wall
Carpeting	Nylon – one inch pile	Nylon – one inch pile	Wool-twist (twist pad)	Wool-twist (without pad)	Used wool pieces – sewed	Asphalt tile
Plant stands	Several – kept filled with strange, exotic plants	Several – kept filled with strange, exotic plants	Two – repotted whenever they take a trip	One medium-sized – repotted annually during vacation	Small – repotted when plant dies	May have one in the department or bring their own from home
Vacuum water bottles	Silver	Silver	Chromium	Plain painted	Coke machine	Water fountain
Library	Private collection	Autographed or complimentary books and reports	Selected references	Impressive titles on covers	Books everywhere	Dictionary
Parking space	Private – in front of office	In plant garage	In company garage – if enough seniority	In company properties – somewhere	On the parking lot	Anywhere they can find a space – if they can afford a car

Source: Certo (1994: 419)

practical virtue of the theory lies in the fact that it draws attention to the fact that people have different needs and are therefore motivated by different things: what acts as a motivator for one person may be totally ineffectual for another, or what is an effective motivator for a person at one time may not be effective on another occasion.

9.3.2 Alderfer's ERG theory

Alderfer adapted Maslow's need hierarchy on the basis of empirical research (Robbins 1996: 218–219). According to Alderfer, there are three core needs, namely 'existence', 'relatedness' and 'growth' – hence the name ERG theory. These are summarised in exhibit 9.6.

EXHIBIT 9.6: ERG hierarchy of needs

- **Existence needs**: These needs relate to our basic material existence needs (similar to Maslow's physiological and safety needs).
- **Relatedness needs**: These needs relate to our desire for interpersonal relationships and interaction (similar to Maslow's affiliation/social needs and the external aspect of Maslow's esteem needs).
- **Growth needs**: This grouping of needs relates to our inherent desire for personal development (this includes the internal aspects of Maslow's esteem needs and his self-actualisation needs category).

Apart from conflating Maslow's five-level hierarchy of needs into three levels, ERG theory represents a refinement of Maslow's theory in that it more closely relates to our everyday observations about people and is thus regarded as a more valid version of the needs theory of motivation. Alderfer's ERG theory differs from Maslow's hierarchy of needs theory in the following important respects:
- ERG theory does not postulate a rigid hierarchy of needs where a higher-order need only becomes operative once a lower-order need has been satisfied substantially; therefore, in terms of ERG theory, two or even all three needs categories can influence behaviour simultaneously; and
- ERG theory also suggests that, should one level of needs remain unsatisfied for a period, the person may regress to a lower-order needs category. Whereas Maslow held that a person will remain fixed on a particular need level until that need has been satisfied, ERG theory postulates that continued frustration of a need may cause an exaggerated desire to have a lower-order need satisfied. For example, a person who does not experience personal growth in his or her job (frustration of the growth needs) may develop an inordinate need to earn a lot of money (an existence need).

Two important inferences can be derived from ERG theory. First, an exaggerated need for something may indicate that the employee is experiencing frustration in satisfying a higher-order need. The implication of this would be that to provide that individual with more of what he or she professes to want may not be enough, since the higher-order need that gave rise to the regression and exaggerated perceived lower-order need will remain unsatisfied. For example, workers' demands for higher salaries may in truth be caused by unsatisfied needs for recognition and/or growth in their jobs. Secondly, needs fulfilment is not a one-dimensional process as more than one level of needs can be operative in the same person at the same time. Managers should therefore attend to different levels of needs simultaneously. In other words, needs do not present themselves in a neat, linear, chronological order from lower to higher levels.

9.3.3 Herzberg's two-factor theory

Frederick Herzberg investigated the question: 'What do people want from their jobs?' From his research he concluded that all variables that make people feel either good

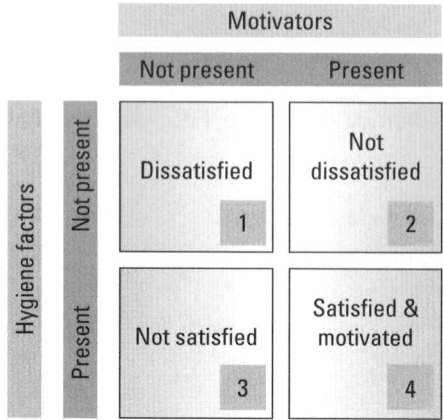

Table 9.2: Herzberg's two-factor theory of motivation
Source: Herzberg (1968)

or bad about their jobs can be grouped into one of two factors or categories (hence the appellation 'Herzberg's two-factor theory of motivation'). The more intrinsic factors, such as achievement, recognition, the work itself, responsibility, growth and advancement, seem to be related to job satisfaction. Extrinsic factors, such as status; security; company policy; administration; remuneration; supervision; interpersonal relations with subordinates, peers and supervisors; and working conditions, on the other hand, tend to be associated with job dissatisfaction. Herzberg suggests that the opposite of satisfaction is not dissatisfaction.

Removing dissatisfying aspects (the hygiene factors) from a job does not necessarily make it satisfying. According to Herzberg, job satisfaction is a function of challenging, stimulating activities or work content (these variables he calls 'motivators'). On the other hand, dissatisfaction is a function of the environment, supervision, co-workers and general job context (these he calls 'hygiene factors'). The presence of hygiene factors will not lead to a state of job satisfaction but simply to a state of what he calls 'no dissatisfaction'. This in itself is, however, not sufficient to motivate employees; in order to do that, the motivators must also be present. Conversely, for motivators to operate as motivators, the hygiene factors must be present. In other words, hygiene factors are a necessary but insufficient prerequisite for a motivated workforce.

It is only in the fourth quadrant that both hygiene factors and motivators are present, leading to a state of satisfaction and motivation. In the third quadrant, the presence of hygiene factors leads to a state of 'no dissatisfaction', which, in the absence of motivators, is in itself insufficient to produce a motivated workforce.

Unfortunately, Herzberg's theory has received scant empirical support, and, most damning of all, other researchers have failed to replicate his results in follow-up studies, leading to the conclusion that the original research results are suspect and/ or that the research design was flawed (see Blum & Naylor 1968: 376–378; Korman 1977: 140–143).

9.3.4 McClelland's theory of needs

David McClelland (Robbins et al 2008: 186–188) proposes that the following three basic needs are operative in the workplace:

■ *The need for achievement (nAch):* This is the desire to exceed some standard of behaviour; the need to excel; the need to be successful.

- *The need for power (nPow):* The need to make others behave in a way in which they would not otherwise have behaved; the need to control others; to be influential.
- *The need for affiliation (nAff):* The need for warm and close interpersonal relationships; to be liked and accepted by others.

If the above-listed needs constitute the totality of needs, it remains for the manager to determine his or her subordinates' dominant need and to offer opportunities whereby the individual's needs and the organisation's goals can simultaneously be met. For example, a person with a high nAff can be placed in a job situation where the need for affiliation can be satisfied. Remember: a good rule of thumb definition of a motivated employee is a person who realises that his or her personal or life goals can be achieved by promoting organisational goals! McClelland's theory holds some interesting implications for the selection of personnel.

Research undertaken by McClelland and other researchers has revealed the following factors which tend to support his theory:

People with a high nAch prefer the following work situations and will work harder in them than individuals with a low nAch:

- *Situations of moderate risk:* In situations of low or high risk, feelings of achievement are absent.
- *Situations where knowledge of results is provided:* People with a high nAch want to know whether they have achieved or not – they want feedback.
- *Situations where individual responsibility is provided:* The high nAch person wants to take personal responsibility for achieving (and also wants to take the credit, of course!).

Therefore, a person with a high nAch prefers jobs with moderate risk, feedback and personal responsibility. Under these conditions high achievers will be strongly motivated. Since these types of situations are typically present in entrepreneurial roles, it is not surprising that people with a high need to achieve are successful entrepreneurs.

Interestingly, individuals with a high nAch generally do not make good managers, especially in large organisations. For instance, the hyper-enthusiastic salesperson does not generally make a good sales manager.

The best managers are people with a *high need for power* (nPow) and a *low need for affiliation* (nAff).

One can think of some jobs which pose interesting contradictions in terms of McClelland's taxonomy of needs. For instance, think of the work of a life insurance representative. To be successful in this job one needs to have a high need to achieve, but in order to be successful one will have to project a caring attitude, which is typically a high nAff attribute! This may explain why retired sport stars are frequently very successful insurance (and other types of) representatives. In order to achieve in sport one presumably needs a high nAch but, especially in team sports, the person's ability to be part of a team (nAff) should be highly developed – exactly the attributes one is looking for in a sales representative!

9.3.5 Locke's goal-setting theory

Edwin Locke suggests that, all other things being equal, people will perform better if they strive towards a definite goal than if they are expected to perform without a specific objective in mind (Robbins et al 2008: 189–191). Therefore, the crux of this theory is that specific goals operate as powerful motivators in that they tell the individual what needs to be done and how much effort is likely to be required in the process. For example, to give a person an amorphous goal such as 'to work harder' is much less likely to motivate the individual than to have him or her work towards a specific goal such as a '20% increase in units produced next month'. All things being equal (such as ability and acceptance of goals,) goal-setting theory postulates that the more difficult the goal, the higher the level of performance, provided that the person believes that he or she is capable of achieving that goal. Other important contingency factors associated with goal-setting theory are the following.

- Persons will perform better when they receive continuous feedback on how well they are progressing towards the goal, because feedback provides information regarding gaps between what they have done so far and what they wish to achieve.
- At present there is little unambiguous, empirical evidence to suggest that goals that have been set by the individual him- or herself enjoy any inherent superiority over those that have been set by someone else. It has been found, however, that goal-setting by the individual for him- or herself, or jointly by the individual and the supervisor, will increase the likelihood that the individual will accept the goals as legitimate and be committed to achieving them. In the South African context, the latter consideration may be of decisive importance in opting for participative goal setting rather than unilaterally imposed goals, given our general low levels of trust between management and workers. The failure to gain legitimacy and acceptance of goals by workers may render the fact that workers are capable of achieving these goals irrelevant.
- Goal-setting theory presupposes that the person is committed to the goal. Research suggests that commitment is most likely to be present if goals are made public, if the person has an internal locus of control, and when the goals are self-set rather than unilaterally assigned.

9.3.6 Cognitive dissonance theory

A discussion of this theory is included for two reasons: first, it provides explanations for results which cannot be explained by expectancy-value theories (discussed later), and secondly, the theory of Stacey Adams (discussed in section 9.3.7) is an important derivative of the more general cognitive dissonance theory. The general theory of cognitive dissonance was first proposed by Festinger (Korman 1977: 59–63), and is summarised in exhibit 9.7.

Cognitive dissonance theory presumes that, if people do poorly a number of times in a task, they will do poorly again, even if they can do better, in order to be consistent with their cognitions (self-perception) of incompetence developed in the preceding tasks. Employees with low self-esteem will forfeit the opportunity to achieve in order to be consistent with their self-perceptions. This surprising result is difficult to explain in terms of an expectancy model of motivation. In the words of Korman (1977: 61–66), "if individuals have negative self-cognitions, they need, according to the consistency model, negative outcomes in order to achieve a consistent result, and this is what happens in a good many cases".

9.3.7 Adams' equity theory

Stacey Adams' equity theory (Robbins et al 2008: 195–200) is very important and has its roots in cognitive dissonance theory. Its importance is particularly relevant in South Africa with its huge inequities and skew distribution of wealth. People do not

- An individual's cognitions (ideas, attitudes, opinions, etc) may have the following three types of relations to one another.

  Consonant: When cognition A follows from cognition B. For instance, if a person works for an organisation and says (and feels) that it is a good place to work (the cognition of liking the company is consonant with the cognition gained from experience).

  Dissonant: When cognition A does not follow from cognition B. For instance, if the same person says that he or she dislikes working for that organisation.

  Irrelevant: If cognition A has no relation to cognition B. For example, the same person decides to buy him- or herself a cat.

From the above-listed possible cognitive relations it is postulated that a dissonant set of cognitions constitutes a negative motivational state that the person finds unpleasant and is motivated to reduce. The way in which this negative motivational state can be eliminated is by changing one's cognitions and/or the behaviour leading to these cognitions so that they become consonant.

- When a person is paid by piecework, his or her productivity will be greater when the piecework rate is perceived as being deserved than when it is regarded as undeserved.

- Women with high self-esteem who want to go to college are more likely to engage in behaviours designed to achieve this goal than women with low self-esteem who want to go to college.

- People who, on the basis of past experience, expect that they will have to do something unpleasant, and choose to do it, even when they could perform a more pleasant one.

- People who, on the basis of past experience, perceive that they are getting a higher piece rate than they deserve, decrease their performance, whereas people who are getting less than they perceive they deserve increase their performance.

One can summarise cognitive dissonance theory by the old saying that 'nothing succeeds like success' (and add that 'nothing fails like failure'). One obvious managerial implication of the theory is that, if a manager always finds fault with a subordinate's work and accordingly corrects it, this will result in the subordinate's seeking failure since this will be the only outcome consonant with his or her self-perception. In other words, for this individual, success will create cognitive dissonance which he or she will be motivated to reduce, and this can be done by failing. Therefore, even if the boss can improve marginally on the subordinate's report for the board, the manager should have the wisdom to allow the report to be submitted to the board, minor warts and all (provided, of course, that it is of an acceptable standard).

work in a vacuum: they work alongside others and they make comparisons between their perceived efforts and concomitant rewards, and the exertions of others and their rewards. Equity theory asserts that the employee compares his or her input:outcome ratio with the input:outcome ratio of relevant others. If these ratios are equal, a state of equity is said to exist. Since the employee perceives the situation to be fair, he or she will not be motivated to change anything. On the other hand, if the input:outcome ratio comparison yields an unequal equation, inequity is said to exist and the individual perceives this to be unfair and is thus motivated to do something to equalise the equation. Inputs, according to Adams, are anything that the person may invest in a task, such as effort, education, time, money. Outcomes are anything he or she might receive, such as money, praise, recognition, etc. The motivational hypothesis is that unequal ratios lead to negative motivational states which the person tries to reduce.

The equity model can be expressed by the equation in exhibit 9.8.

$$\frac{\text{Perception of own inputs}}{\text{Perception of own outcomes}} = \frac{\text{Perception of others' inputs}}{\text{Perception of others' outcomes}}$$

If the depicted equality is not obtained (because the left-hand ratio is either bigger or smaller than the right-hand one), inequity and unfairness exist, and the person is motivated to restore the equilibrium by either one or more of the following means:

■ distorting the perception of one's own or the other's inputs and/or outcomes;
■ withdrawing from the situation (for example by resigning from one's job);
■ behaving in a certain way so as to cause others to change their inputs and/or outcomes;
■ changing one's own actual inputs and/or outcomes; and/or
■ changing the comparator (that is, selecting a different person with whom to compare oneself).

There is an impressive body of research that supports predictions of work behaviour based on equity theory. Some of these predictions, which have been verified by research, are summarised in exhibit 9.9.

These are indeed interesting findings that suggest that in certain situations the following reward systems could be appropriate.

■ *If quantity of output is more important than the quality:* Pay per unit produced (that is, piece-rate reward system) and slightly underpay employees.
■ *If quality is more important than quantity:* Employees could be paid either on a piece rate or an hourly basis, but should be slightly overpaid.

Of course, in reality, things are not quite as simple as the above propositions would suggest. First, remember that outcome can consist of things other than monetary rewards (for example recognition and/or status); secondly, there is the problem of whom the employee chooses as comparator. With regard to the latter, one must also bear in mind the fact that the person may pick him- or herself as the comparator, in which case the individual's present situation will be compared with situations in which he or she had been in the past. This would suggest, inter alia, that it would not be wise to offer job applicants a smaller salary to do the same work that they did in the past (in their previous employment), even if they are desperate to have the job and insist that they are prepared to work for less. Inequity would soon come into play when they compare their present input-outcome ratio with previous ones. (For instance, during a recession one may be able to employ a highly qualified and experienced retrenched manager for a fraction of what he or she had earned before.) Other things being equal, equity theory would seem to suggest that this course of action would not be prudent because the person would in time perceive the situation to be unfair and might reduce the inequity by reducing output.

One last word about equity theory. Despite the research findings which support this model, most people will recognise intuitively that the absolute value of rewards for performance is pretty meaningless unless one has a standard with which to compare it and that most people tend to seek a comparator. You may be quite happy to do task X for Ry until you hear that I am paying another person Ry + Rz for doing the same work. Your unhappiness upon hearing this cannot derive from any reduction in your rewards (there is no question of reducing your income). It can only result from your feeling that, compared with the other person, you are being treated unfairly.

EXHIBIT 9.9: Predictions based on equity theory

■ Overpaid employees who are paid for hours worked will produce more than equitably paid employees (salaried/hourly paid employees will maintain a high quality and/or quantity of production in order to increase the input side of their ratio and so bring about equity).

■ Overpaid employees who are paid on a piece-rate basis (that is, per unit produced), will produce fewer but higher-quality units than equitably paid employees (employees paid on a piece-rate basis will increase their effort to achieve equity by increasing the quality of their inputs, but they will not increase the number of units produced since this will only increase the inequity; therefore effort is expended in increasing quality rather than quantity).

■ Underpaid hourly employees will produce less or their output will be of a poorer quality (inputs will be decreased, which will cause fewer units to be produced or production of a lower quantity, in an effort to decrease the inequitable ratios).

■ Underpaid piece-rate employees will increase the quantity of their production, even if this results in the production of a large number of low-quality units (the employees reduce the inequity by producing more units and by trading off quantity of output for quality; the increase in their rewards is achieved at little increased effort on their part).

9.3.8 Vroom's expectancy theory

Vroom's expectancy theory of motivation holds that the tendency to act in a certain way depends on the strength of the expectation that the act will be followed by a given outcome, and on the degree to which the person desires that outcome. The expectancy theory is illustrated in exhibit 9.10.

EXHIBIT 9.10: The expectancy theory formula

Motivation strength	=	Perceived value of the result of performed behaviour	×	Perceived probability that the result will materialise

Motivational strength is therefore dependent on the following three variables.

■ *Attractiveness:* The importance that the person attaches to the rewards that can be achieved by performing a task.

■ *Performance-reward link:* The degree to which the person believes that performance at a given level will result in the desired outcome.

■ *Effort-performance link:* The degree to which the person believes that his or her efforts will lead to the performance necessary to achieve the desired result.

For example, certain employees may greatly desire a promotion, but may still not be motivated to work hard for any one or more of the following reasons:

■ they may believe that, however hard they are capable of working, they will never be able to perform at the level necessary to get the promotion (absence of the individual effort-performance linkage); and

■ they may believe that they are capable of performing at the required level, but may nevertheless be of the opinion that in the company they work for, promotions are based on whom you know and that they would not be promoted (absence of performance-rewards linkage).

It could, of course, also be that some employees may have a life goal to start up their own business and that they do not value the organisational reward (that is, promotion) because they does not think that it will bring them any nearer to achieving their ultimate goal of being self-employed.

Once again, the expectancy theory holds some important implications for management, some of which are listed below.

■ Set attainable performance standards for employees and provide the necessary support (for example training) to assist them in achieving these standards.
■ Ensure that rewards are clearly linked to set performance standards (for example merit increases directly linked to objectively assessed performance).
■ Try to ascertain the personal goals of subordinates and to link these to organisational rewards. For instance, one may expect that a young workforce would more easily perceive monetary rewards as contributing to personal goals, whereas in the case of an older workforce, security or status needs may be more prominent (the implication being that rewards should be structured to satisfy these needs).

With regard to points 1 and 2 above, it is important to remember that it is not the actual attainability (or the manager's perception of this) that determines employees' motivation to exert themselves: it is the subordinate's perceptions that are important. Therefore, it is crucial that management should ascertain whether workers believe that the performance standards are attainable and that rewards will follow upon performance.

9.3.9 Reinforcement theory

In contrast with goal-setting theory, which is a cognitive theory (it postulates that people direct their conduct wilfully and in a purposeful manner towards the achievement of a goal that has been explicitly identified), reinforcement theory is a behavioural approach. Behavioural theories of personality hold that the mental processes that determine behaviour are unfathomable – the human mind is a 'black box' in which certain inputs are made which in turn cause certain reactions.

We can study the relationship between inputs and outputs in an effort to predict and manipulate behaviour, but the mediating processes between these two events (that is, the internal cognitive processes) are not capable of being studied scientifically (and indeed we do not need to concern ourselves with these). In its simplest form, reinforcement theory holds that consequences shape subsequent behaviour. This principle is also known as operant conditioning and is most closely associated with the work of B F Skinner. For example, if a worker who has exhibited certain behaviour is rewarded for it, the probability that this behaviour will be repeated increases (the behaviour is 'reinforced'). Conversely, behaviour that is not rewarded or that is punished leads to a decrease in the likelihood that this behaviour will be repeated in future (the behaviour is 'extinguished'). Without going into any detail it should be noted that withholding rewards for behaviour is not the same as punishing behaviour and that these two types of 'negative reinforcement' have different behavioural implications. Suffice it to say that as a general rule it is better to employ strategies that amount to the withholding of rewards than those that amount to punishment. In the work environment, performance bonuses can serve as an example of the application of reinforcement theory: if workers exhibit certain behaviour that results in desirable outcomes, that behaviour is rewarded by the payment of monetary rewards. On the other hand, undesirable behaviour is extinguished by withholding the reinforcement (bonuses are not paid). Giving a worker a warning for behaviour that constitutes misconduct could be an example of punishment following behaviour that management wishes to extinguish in the workplace.

Reinforcement or conditioning is undoubtedly an important variable in determining behaviour and can be used to great effect both in and outside the workplace. Space unfortunately prohibits us from going into this fascinating subject in any further detail, save to say that reinforcement and extinguishing of behaviour exert an influence on all of us from the day we are born (and even in the prenatal phase of development), and that the ubiquitous nature of these influences on our subsequent behaviour is frequently the result of unintended responses from those who stand in a relationship of authority to us (such as parents, teachers and supervisors). Thus, it may be useful for managers who are confronted with behavioural problems exhibited by subordinates to reflect on their reactions to these. They may discover that they are themselves partially responsible for this undesirable state of affairs in that they are quite unintentionally reinforcing the inappropriate behaviour!

9.3.10 McGregor's theory X and theory Y

Although McGregor's theory is typically regarded as a theory of leadership and is thus also discussed in the next chapter, his theory is included in this chapter because, as was shown in section 9.2, our assumptions about people fundamentally influence our motivational strategies. In fact, it influences our approaches to managing people – as we have also clearly shown in chapter 4.

Douglas McGregor's greatest contribution to the study of working people is precisely his focus on the importance of underlying assumptions about people in dealing with our co-workers, peers and especially subordinates. McGregor, in his seminal work, *The Human Side of Enterprise* (1960), proposed that managers hold one of two diametrically opposed views of the nature of man and that these implicit philosophies are determinative of managerial style: "Behind every managerial decision or action are assumptions about human nature and human behaviour. A few of these are remarkably pervasive" (McGregor 1960: 33).

These two theories are designated as theory X and theory Y, and are also discussed in chapter 10 because they are actually related directly to leadership styles.

Relating McGregor's theory to that of Maslow, it should be apparent that theory X assumes that lower-order needs dominate individuals, whereas theory Y assumes that higher-order needs are prevalently dominant in persons. McGregor himself argued for the adoption of theory Y and therefore proposed ideas such as participative management, responsible and challenging jobs, and good group relations as strategies that would optimise employees' motivational levels. Once again, as is the case with Maslow's theory, there is little empirical validation of McGregor's theory, but its singular virtue is that it draws our attention to the fact that our implicit (and frequently unconscious) assumptions of our fellow man direct our behaviour towards others. The following example should be familiar to students. When given the choice between doing an assignment together with another student (and thus sharing the mark for their collective efforts) and submitting an individual assignment, students frequently prefer the latter option. When questioned on their choice they frequently say that they are worried that a partner will not do his or her fair share and that they therefore prefer to rely on their own efforts rather than on those of others, even if only to a limited extent. When it is pointed out that this is a very good example of theory X reasoning, this comes as a complete surprise!

9.4 MANAGERIAL IMPLICATIONS: A CONSOLIDATED PERSPECTIVE

Figure 9.6 provides a graphic summary in which the theories of Maslow, Herzberg, McGregor and Alderfer are compared, and with intrinsic versus extrinsic needs. A few managerial implications are also provided.

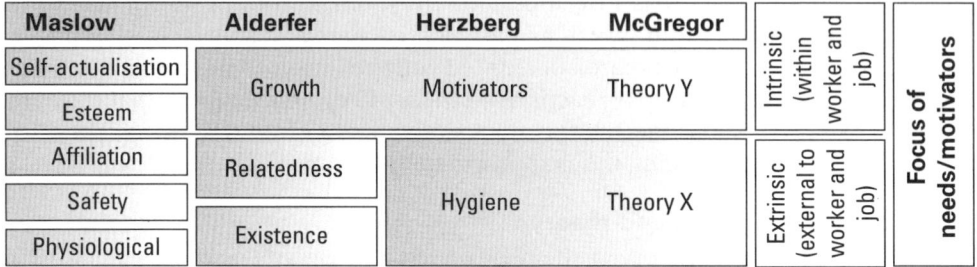

Figure 9.6: Comparison of the theories of Maslow, Herzberg, McGregor and Alderfer

In this chapter some of the best-known and important theories of motivation were discussed and compared. But what are some of the general overall implications for managers? Some implications associated with specific theories have already been pointed out. Without discussing this in any further detail, the following pointers for managing working people can be inferred:

- recognise individual differences in employees;
- place people in jobs that suit their profiles;
- work with employees to set specific goals for them that they perceive as attainable;
- provide employees with feedback on how they are performing;
- link rewards clearly to performance, and recognise that different people may value different rewards;
- ensure that the principle of internal equity is honoured in the company's reward system.

Although the modern trend is to place great emphasis on 'intrinsic motivators', one should not forget the fact that most people work for money and that one's system of monetary rewards therefore remains of great importance. Also remember that motivation is influenced by personal values and that we acquire values within particular cultural contexts. Motivation is thus connected with culture.

Especially in South Africa, with our great cultural and ethnic diversity, managers from one group will assume at their own risk that what they regard as self-evident motivators also hold for their subordinates, especially if they are from another cultural or ethnic group. Many of these theories assume the presence of universal variables, such as the so-called Protestant Work Ethic and the individualistic concept of man that is so prevalent in Western society. For example, Morris (1996: 235–236) points out that in Japan, Greece and Mexico, security needs would be placed at the top of Maslow's hierarchy of needs. In the current South African environment with its extremely high levels of violent crime (see chapter 2) it may well be that security needs are much more prominent – even in our business and other organisations (see exhibit 9.11).

EXHIBIT 9.11: Crime and its effects on organisations/people – employees and customers

Crime is the one factor that is affecting business organisations – the staff and the customers – over which they feel they have no control. The South African community, including business, has been "seriously affected by the unacceptable, sustained, high rates of crime" – and this ranges "most seriously from the debilitating, demoralising effects of violent, personalised attacks on employees and customers of all socio-economic and demographic groups on the streets, in their cars and homes, to the organised and random theft of billions of rands ... of the assets of organisations." Organisations had to "deal with trauma and skills depletion from death, injury or emigration as a result, and have to invest abnormally in protecting people ..."

The titles of two articles capture the impact of these dynamics, in a sense quite peculiar to South Africa, on motivation and what organisations and their managers have to do: 'Fear hits bottom line: Businesses are paying the price in lost staff and increased security costs'; and 'Protecting your people'.

When the latter heading hits space in *People Dynamics*, the publication of South Africa's Institute of People Management (IPM), red lights flash in terms of the interplay between the environment, people's needs, fears and motivation, and managing these in our places of work.

Sources: Adapted and extracted from Newmarch (2008: 2); and 'Protecting your people' (2007: 25)

Motivation theories and the practical implications are thus very much linked to time and place. The needs of people may change over time – depending on circumstances and context more generally. In a general sense it may well be that in the African context, socialisation needs might occupy a different position from that proposed by Maslow. These uncertainties regarding the applicability of foreign theories of motivation in South Africa once again underscore the need for local scientific research to develop and validate theories of motivation applicable to our national culture and circumstances. This is, of course, not to imply that there are not any cross-cultural consistencies; the point is that we, as South African managers, simply do not know!

9.5 CONCLUSION

In conclusion, research has revealed some interesting comparisons between the ability of various motivational theories to explain and predict the impact on, for example, work performance and concomitant variables such as productivity and job satisfaction. Theories and research are important to consider when we think about what can and must be done to develop work environments and circumstances that are more conducive to high motivation to work superiorly.

It is therefore essential to have knowledge of various theoretical perspectives concerning the motivation of people in the context of the work environment. It is not advisable to regard any single theory as most or least correct. Rather, one should study all theories and learn by trial and error in practice. The fact that all of us, managers included, tend to adopt that theory that is most congenial to our own personalities also indicates the necessity of preferring an eclectic approach, rather than promoting one specific theory of motivation.

SUSTAINABILITY CONNECTION?

Part and parcel of sustainability is the challenge to create work environments that make working people want to be there and perform well. At the core of an approach that promotes sustainability is that we value people as the single most important part of our organisations. We can only empower people if we truly believe in their inherent capabilities and hence we must build our approach to managing our core workers around the idea of creating workplaces that are motivating. If we do not do that, we stand not only to lose our highly talented staff, but also those who remain will in all likelihood not be motivated to perform as well as they can. If they do not, we risk the very future of our organisation because we need superior performance to enable us to become and remain competitive. We must create work environments that are conducive to eliciting the best from our workforce in order to survive in highly competitive global environments.

SELF-EVALUATION QUESTIONS

1 Explain how our assumptions about people and motivation can hold implications for the ways in which we manage workers.
2 Differentiate between the basic assumptions underlying Edgar Schein's rational-economic man and social-man theories. What are the implication differences for how we manage people in organisations?
3 Briefly describe Herzberg's two-factor theory of motivation, as discussed in this chapter.
4 What does the hierarchy of needs theory tell us about human motivation? How relevant do you think this might be for us in South Africa today? Do certain basic needs, such as those related to security, have any relevance in today's organisations and how we manage our people, for instance employees and customers?
5 Explain equity theory and its potential implications for managing workers, specifically keeping in mind South Africa's challenges with regard to affirmative action.
6 Write an essay on the following topic: 'Motivating employees in South African organisations: an evaluation of the nature, relevance and value of different motivational theories.'

10 LEADING PEOPLE AT WORK

LEARNING OUTCOMES

After studying this chapter, you should be able to:

- describe the general nature of leadership in organisations;
- explain different leadership theory paradigms and concomitant theories;
- identify and explain contemporary issues in leadership; and
- debate 'the South African leadership challenge' in terms of transformation and diversity.

10.1 INTRODUCTION

Leadership and motivation go hand in hand, as you would have already picked up in the previous chapter. From a managerial perspective we would like to see workers who are motivated to do well at the work they engage in. While people may be motivated to do well, it is quite possible that certain things in the work environment may not be very helpful in channelling the behaviour and work performance in the right direction. This calls for leadership.

Leadership is something that we often hear and read about, yet the notion of leadership is often used rather loosely. While our focus in this chapter is on leadership, the angle from which we look at it is not generic. We therefore have to clarify, right away, that our focus is managerial leadership. While there may be many generic principles involved that can be transferred to leadership in other spheres of life (as in sport, politics or religion), our concern here must be primarily about the challenges pertaining to leading people at the workplace. Naturally we can draw ideas and lessons from leadership more generically, and we also do that in this chapter.

Over time, the concept of leadership has been attributed with a variety of meanings. More than 50 years ago Hemphill and Coons (1957: 7) described leadership as "the behavior of an individual ... directing the activities of a group toward a shared goal". Half a century later and well into the new millennium, Waddell, Devine, Jones and George (2007: 193) define leadership as "the process by which an individual exerts influence over other people and inspires, motivates and directs their activities to help achieve group or organisational goals". Although a little more detailed, the contemporary definition offered by Waddell et al (2007) is not much different to the one offered about 50 years ago. Perhaps the one thing that is accentuated in the more contemporary definitions (and this is quite generally accepted) is the centrality of the *influencing role* of the leader in relation to the other people. Leadership thus entails influencing the behaviour of others in the direction of goal achievement. Given this, and our definition of HRM, the close interconnectedness between leadership and HRM must be clear – in fact, we believe these are two sides of a coin, as argued also elsewhere (Swanepoel 2005).

Increasingly, there are arguments (also developed as based on empirical research evidence) for putting together HRM and leadership. Some propose that this requires using a new concept, namely 'people management' (Purcell & Hutchinson 2007), specifically because of the role of line managers in terms of leadership (as well as in terms of what more traditional views are of what HRM is about). Purcell and Kinnie (2007: 545) explain that what the employees experience at the place of work is really a conflation of how they are being led and "how their managers apply" HRM practices, and "since the line manager is the dominant influence in both, it is likely to be hard for employees to distinguish between them in any meaningful way". Similarly the rigorous research of Purcell and Hutchinson (2007: 16) has led to the finding that in practice there is "an interactive and dynamic relationship between the leadership behaviour" of line managers and the impact of their "HR practices". While we devote only one chapter to leadership in this book, this should by no means be taken to mean that it plays only a small part in how we manage human resources. In fact, quite the contrary is true. As Purcell and Kinnie (2007: 545) explain, research has shown that "leadership is the strongest factor associated with organisational commitment and work satisfaction as well as with other attitudinal factors such as loyalty to consumers". They add, however, that it is not just the quality of the relationship between the line manager (as the leader) and the (subordinate) employees that is important, "but also the extent to which line managers are perceived to be the providers of effective HR practices" (Purcell & Kinnie 2007: 545). While we thus focus on leadership in the rest of this chapter, keep in mind that it is not something that stands alone. It is just another, yet extremely important, piece of the 'HRM puzzle'.

Over the past nine decades, numerous studies concerning leadership have been conducted and many theories have been developed. While none of these is definitive, there is solid empirical evidence in support of each of them, as we present in this chapter. Note, however, that most of these research findings and theories are only partly helpful in developing the leadership capabilities of (potential) leaders of diverse ethnic groups, or of international organisations, or for those who will be interacting with individuals from nations and cultures other than the US. This is because we have relatively little knowledge of the diverse demands placed on leaders in cultures other than the North American one. By far the majority of the prevailing theories of leadership and the empirical evidence available are distinctly North American in character: individualistic rather than collectivistic; emphasising assumptions of rationality rather than ascetics, religion or superstition; stressing follower responsibilities rather than rights; assuming hedonistic rather than altruistic motivation; and assuming centrality of work and democratic value orientation.

Given the increased globalisation of markets, and the increased interdependence of nations over the past two decades, there is a significant need for a better understanding of cultural influences on leader behaviour and effectiveness. This chapter therefore not only focuses on traditional leadership research and theory, but also on more contemporary issues such as diversity's influence on leadership.

House (1993) has analysed a number of American textbook leadership definitions and has come to the conclusion that if leadership is defined in such a varied way within the US culture, it will surely be defined in different ways across cultures. He then lists some interesting examples of how different cultures see leadership, including the following:

■ The Dutch culture places emphasis on an egalitarian society and is sceptical about the value of leadership. Terms such as 'leader' and 'manager' carry a stigma. If a father is employed as a manager, Dutch children will not admit it to their schoolmates.

- The Arabs worship their leaders – as long as they are in power!
- The Iranians seek power and strength in their leaders.
- The Oriental leader is expected to behave in a manner that is humble, modest and dignified, and to speak infrequently and only on critical occasions.

Given that there is no consensual definition of leadership, and given that cultural-semantic and evaluative interpretations of leadership vary widely, leadership can probably be defined somewhat differently according to the culture studied, and the type of preferred leadership can vary across culture and over time and within different contexts. The GLOBE project (House et al 2004) is an international study of leadership covering more than 60 different cultures across the world. Its focus is to do cross-cultural analyses, and some of the preliminary results pertaining to beliefs about effective leader behaviours and attributes indicate that, whereas some attributes (behaviours, skills and traits) are viewed as relevant across all the cultures, others show great variation. Aspects such as having integrity, being decisive, having visionary abilities, and being inspirational and diplomatic seem to be rated highly relevant in general. However, some attributes were found to vary widely in relevance across cultures: ambitious, cautious, compassionate, domineering, formal, independent, indirect, intuitive, logical, orderly, risk taking, self-effacing, self-sacrificing, sensitive, status conscious and wilful (Yukl 2006: 434).

In this chapter we now proceed to provide a brief overview of evolving paradigms in leadership theory, after which we also take a look at some relatively more recent emerging trends and contemporary issues in leadership from a South African, and African, perspective. We also look specifically at leadership and diversity.

10.2 LEADERSHIP THEORIES OF THE INDUSTRIAL ERA

Lussier and Achua (2004: 15) argue that we can identify four leadership theory paradigms, each of which is basically "a shared mindset that represents a fundamental way of thinking about, perceiving, studying, researching, and understanding leadership". These are the *trait theory paradigm*, the *behavioural leadership theory paradigm*, the *contingency leadership theory paradigm* and the *integrative leadership theory paradigm*. The first three form part of the industrial era.

10.2.1 The 'trait theory paradigm'
Some of the very earliest leadership research found that great leaders possess a unique set of qualities or traits that distinguish effective leaders from non-leaders. These were the trait theories. Until the late 1940s, theorists concentrated on identifying the traits associated with leadership in an effort to develop a universal set of characteristics common to all leaders.

Rost and Smith (1992) assert that conceptions of leadership based purely on individual differences began to fall out of vogue in the late 1940s and 1950s, primarily as a result of two major reviews of the leader trait literature by Stogdill (1948) and Mann (1959). These researchers concluded that no single trait, or constellation of traits, clearly and consistently differentiates leaders from non-leaders. Robbins (1996) argues that the main reasons why this approach did not prove to be successful in explaining leadership are the following:
- it overlooks the needs of the followers;
- it generally fails to clarify the relative importance of various traits,

- it does not separate cause from effect (for example, are leaders self-confident or does success as a leader build self-confidence?); and
- it is difficult to specify traits without taking situational factors into account.

In recent years there has been a distinct re-emergence of interest in individual differences research, most significantly as it applies to understanding leaders' performance. Researchers are now attempting to identify the set of traits that people implicitly refer to when they characterise someone as a leader. Robbins (1996) argues that this line of thinking proposes that leadership is as much style – projecting the appearance of being a leader – as it is substance. Table 10.1 provides a summary of some of the research findings in this field.

Table 10.1: Leadership traits and skills

Personality	Abilities and intelligence
■ Adaptable	■ Able to enlist cooperation, and to cooperate
■ Alert	
■ Ambitious	■ Interpersonally skilled
■ Independent	■ Diplomatic and tactful
■ Assertive	■ Socially skilled
■ Responsible	■ Fluent in speech
■ Persuasive	■ Has good judgement and concept formation
■ Organised	■ Creative
■ Dependable	■ Decisive
■ Energetic	■ Knowledgeable
■ Persistent	■ Courageous
■ Self-confident	■ Competent
■ Tolerant of stress	
■ Emotionally stable	
■ Honest and principled	

Sources: Adapted from Darling (1992); Kreitner & Kinicki (1993); Greenberg & Baron (1993); and Robbins (1996)

10.2.2 The behavioural leadership theory paradigm

Several alternative approaches to leadership emerged in line with the behavioural movement in the late 1950s. The first of these approaches was the move to delineate characteristic patterns or styles of leadership behaviour such as Lewin's *Three Classic Styles of Leader Behaviour*, the *Michigan and Ohio State Studies*, and the managerial grid of Blake and Mouton (1964).

Table 10.2 summarises Lewin's three classical styles of leader behaviour.

The Michigan studies defined job-centred and employee-centred leadership as opposite ends of a single leadership continuum. A leader could exhibit either one of these two behaviours, but not both.

The Ohio State leadership studies defined consideration and initiating structure behaviours as independent dimensions of leadership, for example low or high consideration behaviour, and low or high initiating structure behaviour. These dimensions are set out in figure 10.1.

The managerial/leadership grid was developed by Blake and Mouton, and evaluates leader behaviour along two dimensions, namely concern for production and concern for people, which essentially represent the Ohio State dimensions of consideration and initiating structure, or the Michigan dimensions of employee centred and job

Table 10.2: Lewin's three classical styles of leadership

	Authoritarian	Democratic	Laissez-faire
Nature	■ Leader retains all authority and responsibility ■ Leader assigns people to clearly defined tasks ■ Primarily a downward flow of communication	■ Leader delegates a great deal of authority, while retaining ultimate responsibility ■ Work is divided and assigned on the basis of participatory decision making ■ Active two-way flow of upward and downward communication	■ Leader denies responsibility and abdicates authority to group ■ Group members are told to work things out themselves and to do the best they can ■ Primarily horizontal communication among peers
Primary strength	■ Stresses prompt, orderly and predictable performance	■ Enhances personal commitment through participation	■ Permits self-starters to do things as they see fit without leader interference
Primary weakness	■ Approach tends to stifle individual initiative	■ Democratic process is time consuming	■ Group may drift aimlessly in the absence of direction from leader

Source: Kreitner & Kinicki (1993)

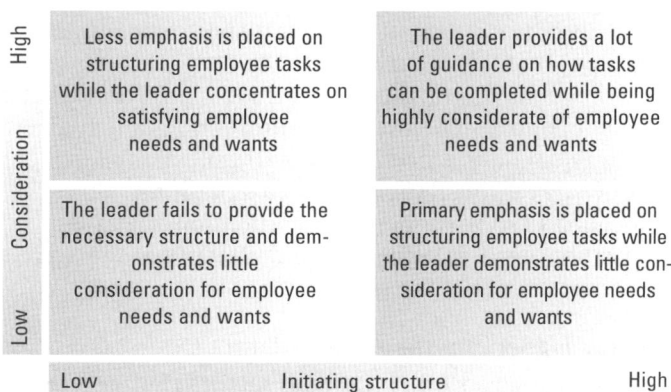

Figure 10.1: Four leadership styles derived from the Ohio State studies
Source: Kreitner & Kinicki (1993)

centred. It also suggests that effective leadership styles include high levels of both behaviours (see figure 10.2).

The grid has nine possible positions along each axis, creating 81 different positions in which the leader's style may fall. Based on the findings of Blake and Mouton,

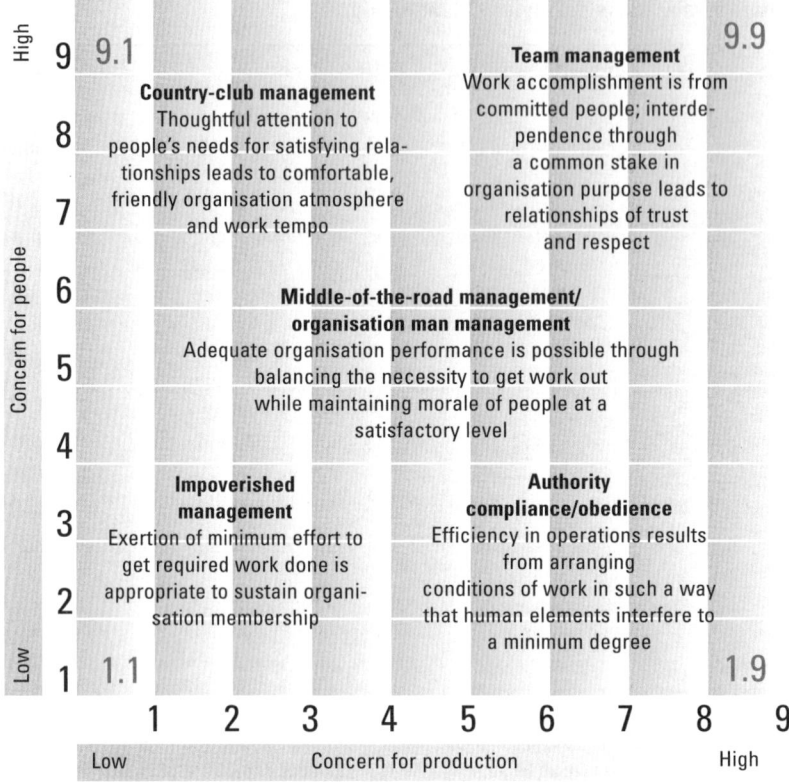

Figure 10.2: The leadership grid
Sources: Adapted from Kreitner & Kinicki (1993); and Robbins (1996)

managers were found to perform best under a 9,9 style, as contrasted, for example with a 9,1 (authority type) or 1,9 (country club) style.

The grid, like the other behavioural theories of leadership, offers a better framework for conceptualising leadership styles rather than presenting tangible new information to clarify the leadership quandary, since there is little substantial evidence to support the conclusion that one style is most effective in all situations.

Hersey and Blanchard (1982) support the contention that there is no one best leadership style, and point out that successful and effective leaders are able to adapt their style to fit the requirements of the situation.

10.2.3 The contingency leadership theory paradigm

A third school of thought focuses on situational factors that determine the pattern of leadership. This approach assumes that effective leadership depends on the particular situation and involves a fit between personality, task, power, attitudes and perceptions. Effective managers diagnose the situation, identify the leadership style that will be most effective, and then determine whether they can implement the required style. Gordon (1993) argues that early situational research suggested that subordinate, supervisor and task considerations affect the appropriate leadership style in a given situation. Variants of this approach emphasised situational contingencies that constrained or heightened the operations of particular individual qualities and leadership styles.

10.2.3.1 McGregor's theory X and theory Y

You have already encountered this theory in the previous chapter. As explained, according to theory X and theory Y, leadership styles are based on the individual's assumptions about other individuals, together with characteristics of the individual, the task, the organisation and the environment. McGregor compiled two sets of assumptions which leaders may have concerning employees and which may affect the leader's behaviour towards subordinates. These two sets of assumptions are summarised in table 10.3.

Table 10.3: Theory X and theory Y assumptions

Theory X assumptions	Theory Y assumptions
■ People are inherently lazy, and will avoid work if possible	■ People are not inherently lazy, and mental or physical effort associated with work is as natural as relaxation
■ People are extrinsically motivated and rate security above any other need	■ People are intrinsically motivated and seek self-actualisation
■ People are incapable of self-discipline and self-control, prefer to be controlled and avoid responsibility, and have little ambition	■ People exert self-control and seek responsibility
■ Most people have limited creativity when solving organisational problems	■ Creativity in the solving of organisational problems is a general phenomenon

Source: Adapted from Robbins (1996)

10.2.3.2 Fiedler's contingency model

Fiedler's theory proposes that effective group performance depends on the proper match between the leader's style of interacting with his or her subordinates and the favourableness of the situation or, in other words, the degree to which situations give control and influence to the leader. Fiedler suggests that leaders have a natural tendency towards either a task- or a relationship-oriented leadership style. He developed a measuring instrument called "least preferred coworker", which purports to measure whether a person is task or relationship oriented. He argues further that, because of this natural tendency towards a specific style, an individual leader's style is rather inflexible and difficult to change, but that organisations must put individuals in situations that fit with their style. From this assumption it also follows that if a given situation requires a task-oriented leader and the person in the leadership position is relationship oriented, either the situation has to be modified or the leader must be removed and replaced if optimum effectiveness is to be achieved.

Fiedler also identified three situational factors or contingency dimensions in the organisation that influence the favourableness of the situation, which in turn influences the effectiveness of the leader, namely leader–member relations, task structure and position power.

- The leader–member relationship can be either good or poor, and depends on factors such as the degree of confidence, trust and respect subordinates have in their leader.
- Task structure can be either high or low, and depends on whether the task is relatively structured or unstructured.
- Position power can be either strong or weak, and depends on the degree of

influence the leader has over rewards (such as promotion and salary increases) or punishments (such as disciplinary steps).

After a person's leadership style and the favourableness of situations have been identified, it is necessary to match the leader with the situation to achieve maximum leadership effectiveness.

Robbins (1996) has examined Fiedler's research on 1 200 groups in which he compared relationship- versus task-oriented leadership styles in each of the eight situational categories. Fiedler concluded that task-oriented leaders tend to perform better in situations that are very favourable to them and in situations that are very unfavourable to them. Relationship-oriented leaders, however, perform better in moderately favourable situations. Fiedler's research findings are summarised in figure 10.3.

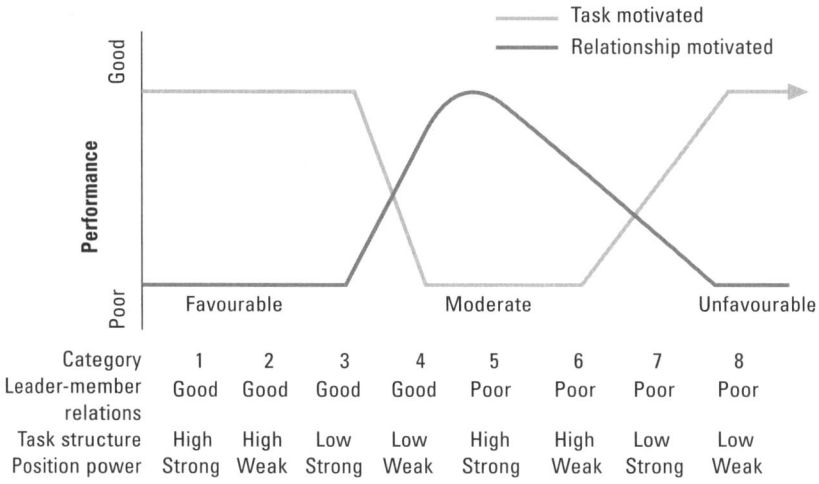

Figure 10.3: Findings from Fiedler
Sources: Robbins (1996: 423); Cherrington (1994: 64)

Fiedler's model in essence concerns the fit between leader and situation, but because he sees leadership style as fixed, there are only two ways to fit the leader and the situation – either by selecting the right leader for a given situation or by changing the situation to fit the leader. Cherrington (1994) points out that, rather than changing the leader to fit the situation, Fiedler recommends changing the situation to fit the leader through what he calls job engineering. Job engineering consists of changing one or more of the situational factors to increase or decrease the favourability of the situation.

10.2.3.3 The revised Vroom-Jetton-Jago leadership-participation model

The leadership-participation model of Vroom-Jetton-Jago is both a decision-making model and a theory of leadership. It provides a set of rules to determine the form and amount of participative decision making in different situations. To be able to handle different situations, the model identifies five leadership or decision-making styles on a continuum from autocratic, through consultative, to group decision making, along with a series of diagnostic questions on contingency variables, which are answered on a five-point scale, to determine which style is most appropriate. The five leadership/ decision-making styles can be described as follows.

- The leader decides alone without soliciting any input from members.
- The leader decides alone after obtaining the necessary information from members.
- The leader makes the decision after consulting with group members individually. The leader shares the problem with them and obtains information, ideas, suggested alternatives and evaluation.
- The leader makes the decision after meeting with the members as a group to collect their information, ideas, suggested alternatives and evaluation.
- The leader and members arrive at a group decision through consensus decision making. The leader may chair the group, but is simply one of the group and does not try to influence it to adopt a particular solution.

This model assumes that leadership behaviour is flexible, that no single leadership style is appropriate for all situations and furthermore that leader behaviour must adjust to reflect the task structure. Robbins (1996: 431) argues that, according to this model, it probably makes more sense to refer to autocratic and participative situations than to autocratic and participative leaders.

10.2.3.4 Hersey and Blanchard's situational theory

Hersey and Blanchard's (1982) situational theory focuses on the follower. It proposes that effective leader behaviour depends on the readiness or maturity level of the leader's followers. Readiness is defined as the extent to which a follower possesses the ability and willingness to complete a task. The emphasis on the followers in this leadership theory reflects the reality that it is they who either accept or reject the leader. Regardless of what the leader does, effectiveness depends on the actions of his or her followers. Robbins points out that this is an important dimension that has been overlooked or underemphasised in most earlier leadership theories.

Situational leadership uses the same two leadership dimensions that Fiedler identified: task and relationship behaviours. However, Hersey and Blanchard go a step further by considering each as either high or low, and then combining them into the following four specific leader behaviours.

- *Telling* (high task–low relationship). The leader defines roles and tells people what, how, when, and where to do various tasks. Directive behaviour is emphasised.
- *Selling* (high task–high relationship). The leader provides both directive and supportive behaviour.
- *Participating* (low task–high relationship). The leader and follower share in decision making, with the main role of the leader being facilitating and communicating.
- *Delegating* (low task–low relationship). The leader provides little direction or support.

The final component in Hersey and Blanchard's theory is defining four stages of follower readiness.

- People are both unable and unwilling to take responsibility to do something. They are neither competent nor confident.
- People are unable but willing to do the necessary job tasks. They are motivated, but currently lack the appropriate skills.
- People are able but unwilling to do what the leader wants.
- People are both able and willing to do what is asked of them.

The situational theory of leadership is summarised in figure 10.4.

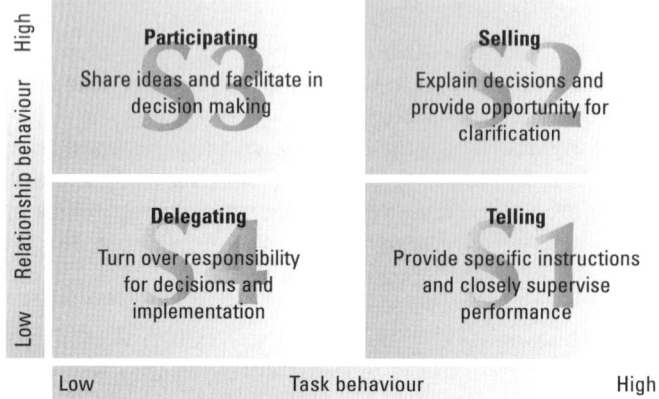

Figure 10.4: Situational leadership behaviour
Sources: Kreitner & Kinicki (1993); and Robbins (1996)

Figure 10.4 integrates the various components and suggests that as the followers mature, they may require different styles of leadership from their managers. Inexperienced subordinates may require a high level of structuring by their leaders. Those who are moderately mature may require a high level of social and emotional support (showing consideration). However, those who are fully mature may require low levels of both types of behaviour on the part of their leaders.

Actually there is a high similarity between Hersey and Blanchard's four leadership styles and the four extreme corners in Blake and Mouton's managerial grid. The telling style equates to the 9,1 leader, selling equals 9,9, participating is equivalent to 1,9 and delegating is the same as the 1,1 leader. Hersey and Blanchard (1982), however, claim that the grid emphasises concern for production and people, which are attitudinal dimensions, whereas situational leadership, in contrast, emphasises task and relationship behaviour. Robbins argues that, despite Hersey and Blanchard's claim, it is a pretty small difference, and the question can very well be asked whether situational leadership is then not merely the managerial grid with one major difference – the replacement of the 9,9 contention (one style for all occasions) with the recommendation that the 'right' style should align with the readiness of the followers.

10.2.3.5 The path-goal theory of House

The path-goal theory is a situational theory developed by Robert House (Robbins 1996). This theory extracts key elements from the Ohio State leadership research on initiating structure and consideration, and the expectancy theory of motivation. The theory explains how leaders can facilitate task performance by showing subordinates how their performance can be instrumental in achieving desired rewards or goals.

Essentially this theory explains what leaders should do to:
- influence the perceptions of subordinates about their work, through coaching, guidance, support or rewards;
- identify important personal goals for subordinates; and
- clarify the various paths to goal attainment.

It claims that leader behaviour is motivating and satisfying or accepted to the extent that it clarifies the paths to the goals and increases goal attainment. House has identified two basic leader behaviours, namely path clarification and gatekeeper of rewards, (that is, increasing the number of rewards available to subordinates by being supportive and looking after their needs).

House has identified four distinct leadership styles that enable leaders to perform these two functions:

- directive leadership tells subordinates what is expected of them and provides specific guidance, standards, and schedules of work;
- supportive leadership treats subordinates as equals and shows concern for their well-being, status, and personal needs, and seeks to develop pleasant interpersonal relationships among group members;
- achievement-oriented leadership sets challenging goals, expects subordinates to perform at their highest level, and continually seeks improvement in performance; and
- participative leadership means consulting with subordinates and using their suggestions and ideas in decision making.

Unlike Fiedler's model, which implies that leadership style is resistant to change, the path-goal theory maintains that the four styles of leadership can be displayed by one manager at different times in different situations; for example, if a directive leader discovers that the situation has changed and now requires a participative style, it is possible to change.

Cherrington (1994) points out that a fifth leadership style, the punitive leader, ought to be added to this theory. He argues that the path-goal model focuses almost exclusively on the leader's ability to administer positive reinforcement and ignores the powerful impact of carefully administered punishment.

Although the path-goal theory does not explain how to identify the appropriate leadership style, the theory does identify two types of situational factors: *subordinate contingency factors*, which include locus of control, authoritarianism and abilities; and *environmental contingency factors*, which include the nature of the task, the formal authority system within the organisation, and the group norms and dynamics that need to be considered.

10.3 EMERGENCE OF AN INTEGRATIVE LEADERSHIP THEORY PARADIGM

Rost and Smith (1992) propose that in order to understand the concept of leadership, leadership theory must move away from the industrial school of leadership, which is noted for emphasising only some aspects, and even some which might well be rather more peripheral to the nature and content of leadership today. These aspects include traits, personality characteristics, goal attainment, contingencies, situations, style and so forth. What we have thus found is, as Lussier and Achua (2004: 16) explain, that from "the mid-to-late 1970s, the paradigm began to shift to the integrative, or neo-charismatic" which is an "attempt to combine aspects of the trait, behavioral, and contingency theories". In this section we thus focus on the more modern theories that fit this paradigm.

10.3.1 Charismatic leadership

The charismatic leadership theory emerged in the late 1980s and is an extension of the attribution theory. Like the trait theories, it assumes that charisma is an individual characteristic of the leader. Although traits may well play a role in charismatic leadership, there is a growing belief that it makes more sense to view such leadership as involving a special type of relationship with followers.

Several studies have been conducted to identify the personal characteristics of the charismatic leader, one very comprehensive analysis in this regard being the study undertaken by Conger and Kanungo (1988). They propose that charismatic leaders possess the characteristics as set out in exhibit 10.1.

Charismatic leadership may not always be needed to achieve high levels of employee performance. It may be most appropriate when the follower's task has an ideological component. That is why charismatic leaders are most likely to emerge when an organisation is introducing a radically new product or facing a life-threatening crisis – in other words, in times of dramatic change.

Gordon (1993) points out that there will, however, also be a dark side to charismatic leadership, if the leader overemphasises devotion to him- or herself, makes personal needs paramount or uses highly effective communication skills to mislead or manipulate others. Such leaders may be so driven to achieve their own vision that they ignore the costly implications of their goals.

EXHIBIT 10.1: Key characteristics of charismatic leaders

Charismatic leaders:
- have an idealised goal or vision that they want to achieve;
- have a strong personal commitment to their goal;
- are perceived as unconventional;
- are assertive and self-confident; and
- are perceived as agents of radical change, rather than as managers of the status quo.

The charismatic leader has the following relationship with his or her followers:
- The leader has a strong need to influence his or her followers. The leader communicates high expectations about follower performance.
- The leader expresses confidence in followers. The followers trust the correctness of the leader's beliefs. The followers' beliefs are similar to the leader's. The followers accept the leader unquestioningly. The followers feel affection for the leader. The followers obey the leader willingly; in other words, they are motivated.
- The followers have an emotional involvement in the organisation's mission.
- The followers have heightened performance goals.
- The followers believe that they can contribute to the success of the group's mission.

Source: Conger & Kanungo (1988)

10.3.2 Transformational leadership

Transformational leadership emerged in the 1990s and is closely related to charismatic leadership. Transformational leadership is the set of abilities that allows the leader to recognise the need for change, to create a vision to guide that change, and to execute the change effectively. This type of leader can influence in every direction – downward with subordinates, laterally with colleagues, upward with superiors, and outward with clients and customers. Thus, transformational leaders can change the culture of the organisation.

Transformational leaders are also charismatic and possess all the above-mentioned characteristics associated with charismatic leaders, but they have more than charisma. Avolio and Bass (in Robbins 1993) describe the difference between these two leaders as follows:

The charismatic leader may want followers to adopt the charismatic's world view and go no further; the transformational leader will attempt to instil in followers the ability to question not only established views but eventually those established by the leader.

From this it follows that the transformational leader empowers followers. Charismatic leadership, which results in compliance, keeps followers dependent on the leader. Transformational leadership is aimed at creating follower independence.

Apart from being charismatic, transformational leaders also have the following characteristics:

■ they identify themselves as change agents;
■ they are value driven;
■ they believe in people;
■ they take risks and are courageous individuals;
■ they have the ability to deal with:
  – complexity;
  – ambiguity; and
  – uncertainty;
■ they are lifelong learners;
■ they engage in impression management, using tactics and techniques designed to enhance their attractiveness and appeal to others; and
■ they are visionaries, and engage in framing , defining their vision or purpose in a way that gives meaning and purpose to whatever actions they are requesting from followers.

It is clear from the above characteristics that their influence does not stem from the possession of semi-magical traits, but is rather a logical result of a complex cluster of behaviours and techniques.

Exhibit 10.2 lists the differences between transactional and transformational leadership.

The industrial and post-industrial (or modern) leadership views should not, however, be seen as opposing approaches to getting things done. Transformational leadership is built on top of transactional leadership, and it is not a case of saying we can do away with any transactional dimensions. We still need to design work, set goals, negotiate pay, reward performance and take corrective measures as and when appropriate. It is precisely here where we find the nexus between the more traditional (and, according to us, more limited view of) HRM aspects and leadership challenges of our time. As we have said before, these become two sides of a same coin, almost in the same way that Herzberg's two-factor theory of motivation does.

While some thus argue that 'the one is in and the other is out', we cannot agree with that, given the practical realities of organisations, work and people who must do the work.

10.4 SOUTH AFRICAN LEADERSHIP: SOME PERSPECTIVES REFLECTING ELEMENTS OF TRANSFORMATION

Charlton (1996) points out that studies conducted in South Africa have shown that leaders' ability to manage themselves is very important. This involves diagnosing inappropriate or ineffective behaviour, and assuming personal responsibility for learning, productive growth and change. A decade later this is still supported by

EXHIBIT 10.2: Transactional and transformational leaders – a comparison

Transactional leader

- Establishes goals and objectives
- Designs workflow and delegates task assignments
- Negotiates exchange of rewards for effort
- Rewards performance and recognises accomplishments
- Searches for deviations from standards and takes corrective actions
- *Contingent reward:* Contracts exchange of rewards for effort, promises rewards for good performance, recognises accomplishments
- *Management by exception (active):* Watches and searches for deviations from rules and standards, takes corrective action
- *Management by exception (passive):* Intervenes only if standards are not met
- *Laissez-faire:* Abdicates responsibilities, avoids making decisions

Transformational leader

- *Charismatic:* Provides vision and a sense of mission, gains respect and trust, instils pride
- *Individualised consideration:* Gives personal attention, and treats each person individually, coaches
- *Intellectually stimulating:* Promotes learning, encourages rationality, uses careful problem solving
- *Inspirational:* Communicates high performance expectations, uses symbols to focus efforts, distils essential purposes

Source: Adapted from Cherrington (1994) and Robbins (1996)

Pretorius (2007). Charlton also argues that a leader needs to create an empowering environment where followers are motivated, able and allowed, (that is, have the responsibility and authority) to perform to their potential. Charlton (1996) concludes by saying that "empowerment is both a consequence (indication) and competence of effective leadership". Likewise, Pretorius (2007: 8) argues for empowerment:

> Every team member must feel that his or her work has special meaning and that the individual contribution is valuable. Syndicated leadership is the solution in our new, more complex world. Today's leadership challenges cannot be solved by the lone, heroic leader ... Develop, train and invest in people, they have huge untapped ability. Effect people-driven growth ... Create a learning culture ... It is the responsibility of leaders to optimise their organisation's return on human capital. Employees should be treated as an investment, not an expense.

Research undertaken by Booysen and Van Wyk (Booysen 1994) on the preferred leadership style of effective leaders in South Africa has found that outstanding leaders in our country are perceived to show a strong and direct, yet democratic and participative leadership style. They are perceived as agents of change, visionaries and individualists. This indicates a preference for a transformational leadership style. Although they are seen as being moderately charismatic, they are also seen as responsible, not as agitators.

The research also indicated that South African leaders are perceived as being sensitive to followers' needs and are expected to reflect followers' ideas, to satisfy their needs and to be respectful and understanding. South African leaders are expected to be pragmatic and creative; by utilising their interpersonal skills and knowledge they must act reactively as well as proactively, depending on their analysis of a situation.

Brand Pretorius, CEO of McCarthy Motor Holdings, speaking at a business update conference of South Africa's Institute of Company Directors, shared some strong sentiments about the type of leadership we need in order to be successful at transforming our country towards one characterised by sustainable growth:

> Leadership, with its prime function to give direction and energy, is the most critical success factor which will determine our future ... [I]t ... shapes destinies, it can build or it can destroy. It sparks energy and enthusiasm for change. It drives passion, it lights inner fires, it ignites emotions, purpose, goals, shared values and beliefs ... turns weakness into strength, obstacles into stepping stones, despondence into hope ... Total leadership is critical ... Total leadership is about both personal development and team development. It starts with leadership of self ... (Pretorius 2007: 6).

Clearly, these sentiments reflect the need for transformational leadership in our country, as also echoed by Dr Reuel Khoza, president of South Africa's Institute of Directors (IoD), saying that

> [No] country, region or continent can elude the need to seriously reflect on itself in the light of globalisation, global warming and, against that background, reskill its people ... redesign its processes and redirect its resources ... Transformational leadership is an imperative for every enterprise as much as for every nation, every continent ... Only those who can imagine and pre-emptively create the future will be around to enjoy it (Khoza 2007a:10).

In a recent Juta publication, *Trailblazers: South Africa's Champions of Change* (2007), the focus is on the lives of South Africa's most influential black business leaders and what we can learn from them. According to the findings from having interviewed these 50 most influential black South African business leaders, these 'trailblazers':
- respect and honour their roots;
- learned independence at a young age;
- know that education is vital;
- embrace lifelong learning and self-development as a lifestyle;
- strive for excellence in all they do;
- are not afraid of taking risks;
- know adversity is part of the journey to victory and thus bounce back;
- know their own strengths and use them to shine;
- have a clear vision;
- embrace change and do not fear it;
- believe in work–life balance;
- are compassionate leaders;
- show remarkable commitment to a collective cause;
- put integrity above all else; and
- regard transformation as part of their role.

Khoza (2007b: 24) argues that South African leadership should be situated squarely in the Africa context, explaining that "African leadership is dominated by values ...", and that the Africa leadership paradigm ought to thus be "Afrocentric", which means the following: "Afrocentricity is about Africans putting Africa at the centre of their existence and consciousness. It is about Africans anchoring themselves in their own continent; its history, traditions, cultures, mythology, creative motif, ethos and value systems exemplifying the African will."

As such we are faced with challenges of transforming our own leadership paradigms in a sense – or at least do some very serious introspection about whether our ways of leadership are appropriate for the challenges we face in our country and on our continent.

We return to this issue in section 10.5.2, but for the moment we want to concur with Van Rensburg's (2007) arguments that we ought to be careful with how we frame who is 'African', because our country has a rich diversity, also in terms of the wide range of ethnic groups we have. Van Rensburg (2007: 47) quotes Gueye from his book, *African Renaissance as an Historical Challenge*, saying the following:

> This concept of African-ness is a factor of continuous enrichment, in that it offers scope for cultural diversity and to ethnic or racial minorities that were brought by history to become part of Africa. It allows them opportunity to assert themselves and contribute to the 'rainbow-identity' which has become one of the trump cards of the continent in its meeting the challenges of globalisation.

The South African leadership challenge is thus multidimensional and very complex because although we are part of Africa, we are also part of the global village in which competitiveness is key, and diversity a reality. If we want to develop our own brand of leadership, we have to tap into the richness offered by that diversity. Transformation in South Africa has been and will be achieved only if we cast the net wide to capture leadership lessons from people who really lead the way in transforming across various spheres of life. We cannot, for example, ignore the leadership of a person like F W de Klerk, who as political leader, showed the will and tenacity to lead our country into an era of political transformation. More importantly, we believe that one important piece of the leadership puzzle in South Africa must be addressed in any discussion about leadership: our country's iconic visionary and transformational leader, Nelson Mandela, or rather Madiba (his clan name).

Even though reflecting on Mandela as leader does not have organisational leadership as a focus, the key is to search for possible transferable aspects. As we have mentioned earlier, many aspects of leadership cut across different spheres, from political to religious to sport. In the July 2008 edition of *TIME* magazine, Richard Stengel has put together what the cover of that publication called 'The secrets of leadership: Eight lessons from one of history's icons', to coincide with Mandela's 90th birthday celebrations. Exhibit 10.3 reflects these lessons, as distilled by Stengel (2008: 17–22).

While these 'lessons' reflected in exhibit 10.3 are the interpreted perspectives of Stengel (2008) of our country's iconic political leader, they surely hold important potential food for thought for the leaders of and in our organisations – in South Africa, but also beyond. In our organisations we need to show the courage and inspire our people to join hands in transforming how we do business and how we work together to build a successful country through globally competitive and successful organisations that actively work towards a sustainable world. We should adopt patterns of *shared* or *distributed leadership* that empower all our people, not just some. If we must follow the notion of nothing being 'black or white', we should develop our own unique leadership brands that reflect the 'rainbow' which symbolises life in all its colour and beauty in our country and on our continent. This therefore brings into the realm of leadership the whole issue of diversity.

EXHIBIT 10.3: The eight leadership lessons of Nelson Mandela – according to Richard Stengel

Stengel explains: "I wanted to make what might be a final visit and have my sons meet him one more time. I also wanted to talk to him about leadership. Mandela is the closest thing the world has to a secular saint, but he would be the first to admit that he is something far more pedestrian: a politician ... I've always thought of what you are about to read as Madiba's Rules ... and they have been cobbled together from our conversations old and new and from observing him up close and from afar. They are mostly practical. Many of them stem directly from his personal experience. All of them are calibrated to cause the best kind of trouble: the trouble that forces us to ask how we can make the world a better place."

Stengel formulates the eight lessons as follows:

- Courage is not the absence of fear – it is inspiring others to move beyond it.
- Lead from the front – but don't leave your base behind.
- Lead from the back – and let others believe they are in front.
- Know your enemy – and learn about his favourite sport.
- Keep your friends close – and your rivals even closer.
- Appearances matter – and remember to smile.
- Nothing is black or white.
- Quitting is leading too.

10.5 DIVERSITY AND LEADERSHIP

Prior to the 1960s, the study of leadership was limited largely to the study of white men occupying leadership positions in business organisations. In the 1970s and 1980s, there was a surge of interest in the US in the experiences of women and minority men in management (Berry & Houston 1993). Moss-Kanter and Corn (1994) point out that as economies globalise and organisations increasingly form cross-border relationships, there is a resurgence of interest in the management problems caused by national cultural differences – in values, ideologies, organisational assumptions, work practices and behavioural styles – spawning research into cross-cultural leadership.

The idea of the world as a global village is already a reality. Communication networks such as teleconferences, interactive visual links and the Internet have made it possible to transact business as quickly between Johannesburg and New York as between two organisations in Johannesburg. The increasing multinationalism and multiculturalism pose significant challenges for any leader or manager. In South Africa we do not only experience the influences of globalisation and internationalisation, but internally, in our own country, we are faced with numerous diversity issues, such as cultural diversity, diverse languages and religion, and race and gender inequities. Not only are more women, blacks, coloured and Indian people entering the labour market but they are also entering more management/leadership positions. In order for South African organisations to survive, it is of utmost importance to understand and manage diversity effectively.

In the following sections, gender and cultural issues in leadership are discussed.

10.5.1 Gender-related issues and leadership

Betters-Reed and Moore (1995) argue that, although the (US) workforce is becoming increasingly diverse, the predominant paradigm for educating and managing this new labour force has remained rooted in an exclusively Anglo-American male mindset. Even management development programmes designed to focus on females have suffered from the tendency to encourage women to 'think manager, think male'. They assert that the implicit (and sometimes explicit) assumption has been that women will succeed if they adopt the characteristics of effective white male managers. The constantly reinforced message is that women can succeed only if they become more assertive and competitive, 'dress for success' and are more politically and socially astute. This is unfortunately also the case in South Africa. Importantly, the male-dominated managerial leadership approach is also very much to be found in other countries of Africa, as confirmed by authors such as Webster and Wood (2005), and Horwitz, Kamoche and Chew (2002) who draw on the research publications of others (also see the *Elsewhere in Africa* box below, where we share some research reported on the serious challenges in this regard in Zimbabwe, for instance). Because of the above-mentioned assumptions and because they were breaking new ground, the first female executives adhered to many of the rules of conduct that spelt success for men.

Elsewhere in Africa

There continues to be numerical gender inequalities in organisational leadership in Zimbabwe. The breadth and depth of the gender gap in organisational leadership and the influences therein have been studied ... Women perform the vital function of producing society's producers and yet this role is made to appear private, marginal and without economic value. There are structures that keep men and women in separate spheres and ensure that the sphere of men is dominant and that of women subordinate ... A very recent shocking experience with gender bias in Zimbabwe was with the Department of the Registrar General where a mother could not consent for a child under the age of 18 years to take a birth certificate ... She could only do that with the evidence that the father was deceased by producing a death certificate ... Ours is a strong patriarchal society to the core ... Women are the social custodians of the family welfare ... These same women have no legal guardianship over their children. In Zimbabwe if a child is not well behaved, society blames the mother; however, when a child is successful and well behaved it is because of the father ... Some women in Zimbabwe choose to ignore these gender injustices. In Zimbabwe it is 'cultural' for women to be subordinate to men. (Booysen 2007: 78–79)

Rosener (1990) points out that a second wave of women is making their way into top management, not by adopting the style and habits that have proved successful for men but by drawing on the skills and attitudes that they have developed from their shared experience as women. She adds:

> These second generation of managerial women are drawing on what is unique to their socialisation as women and creating a different path to the top. They are seeking and finding opportunities in fast-changing and growing organisations to show that they can achieve results – in a different way. They are succeeding because of – not in spite of – certain characteristics generally considered to be 'feminine' and inappropriate in leaders.

This second wave of women leaders is equipped with a leadership style that is more based on consensus building, more open and inclusive (power and information sharing), more likely to encourage participation by others, to enhance the self-worth of others and to energise them, and that tends to be more caring than the style adopted by many of their male counterparts. Rosener (1990) refers to this approach to management as an interactive leadership style.

Betters-Reed and Moore (1995) argue that as a result of competitive pressures and strategic rethinking which has brought about flatter organisational structures and more decentralised authority and decision making, the trend is towards more collaborative styles of management – working across organisational departments to create an environment where teamwork encourages innovation and creative problem solving. They point out that Senge (1990), in Betters-Reed and Moore (1995), has spurred interest in the importance of understanding open models of communication among all employees for the purpose of improved learning and performance, and that total quality management also demands that these principles be adopted. It is clear from the above that these trends are in line with what Betters-Reed and Moore (1995) refer to as a feminist or women-centred approach.

Robbins (1993) points out that the research suggests two conclusions regarding gender and leadership. First, the similarities between women and men tend to outweigh the differences; and secondly, the differences suggest that male managers feel more comfortable with a directive style, whereas female managers prefer a more democratic style. Appelbaum and Shapiro (1993) argue that since men have occupied most executive positions, their leadership style is defined as traditional – and thus, because the female leadership style contradicts the traditional, it is seen as non-traditional. Table 10.4 compares the feminine leadership model with the traditional masculine model.

From table 10.4 it is evident that, generally, women tend to follow a more transformational leadership style with the emphasis on the followers, consensus, and the use of charisma, personal reference and personal contact to enhance interpersonal relations and to influence followers. Men in general, on the other hand, tend to follow a more directive style where job performance is seen as a series of transactions with subordinates, where rewards are exchanged for services and punishments for inadequate performance – that is, more of a transactional approach. Men seem to be more inclined to use formal position, power and authority to control people.

It is, however, very important to emphasise that the above are generalisations and that many men possess certain attributes that are linked mainly to the female model as set out in table 10.4, and vice versa.

In conclusion, even though men have historically held the great majority of senior positions in organisations, and some people therefore still think that the noted differences between men and women will automatically work in favour of men, this is no longer the case. In today's flatter organisations, flexibility, networking, teamwork, trust, information sharing, empowerment and self-leadership are replacing rigid and hierarchical structures, competitive individualism, control and secrecy. The better managers listen, motivate, empower and provide support to their people. We need a new brand of managers who can develop and use feminine skills and attitudes in conjunction with the skills used by traditional managers.

> Optimally, what would emerge from this transformation is neither a masculine nor a 'feminine' model of leadership, but a synergistic model that enables people to work together to maximize their collective strengths and avoid their individual weaknesses (Smith & Smits 1994).

Table 10.4: Comparison of masculine and feminine leadership styles

Variables	Masculine	Feminine
Operative style	■ Competitive	■ Cooperative
Organisational structure	■ Vertical and hierarchical	■ Horizontal, network, egalitarian
Objective	■ Winning	■ Quality
Problem-solving approach	■ Rational and objective	■ Intuitive and subjective
Key characteristics	■ High control ■ Cling to power ■ Strategic ■ Unemotional ■ Analytical	■ Low control ■ Power sharing/empowerment ■ Empathetic ■ Collaborative ■ High performance
Perceived power base	■ Organisational position and formal authority concentrated at the top	■ Personal charateristics shared within a group
Perspective on leadership	■ Social change in terms of transactions	■ Follower–leader commitment relationship

Sources: Appelbaum & Shapiro (1993); Govender & Bayat (1993); Smith & Smits (1994); and Rosener (1990)

10.5.2 Cultural issues: Afrocentric leadership and/or ethnic diversity?

> Europeans would be crazy to behave as though they were not European; Americans and Japanese would come across as both funny and phoney if they tried to be anything other than American and Japanese respectively. Similarly Africans, in our particular case, South Africans, had better stop behaving as though they were an outpost of Europe or somebody else (or a state of America). We have to get to know ourselves and begin to use our existential reality as a departure point (Khoza 1994).

In previous sections we primarily looked at Euro-American approaches to and theories of leadership. The aim of this section is not to discuss the merits and demerits of the Euro- and Afrocentric leadership or management approaches, nor is the aim to discuss Afrocentric leadership in detail, but simply to explore some of the implications of Afrocentric views on leadership.

Khoza (1994) argues that it is a fallacy to believe that a business culture can be imposed on people, and that it can work perfectly, without taking into account the cultural archetypes of the people in question. Yet, he adds, corporate South Africa is guilty of just this: "Corporate culture as experienced in South Africa is very Eurocentric. Business practice as currently conceptualized in most South African corporations is generally cast in a Eurocentric mould, in fact, worse, an Anglo-Saxon mould."

Exhibit 10.4 reflects Khoza's (2007b: 24–27) views on the particular values that underpin Afrocentric leadership.

A constellation of values should and does characterise the African leadership paradigm. These include:

Valuing humanity

Sound African leadership, drawing from deep-seated African cultural archetypes, values humanity, essentially unconditionally, except for those who factor themselves out through extreme forms of barbaric behaviour. This value is captured through such expressions as:

- *Umuntu mgumuntu ngabantu* – a human being finds genuine human expression in humane relationships with other humans. (I am because you are, you are because we are.)
- *Motho ke montho ga ana bosetihane* – a person is a person regardless of structure or stature. (Human life is of equal value.)

This contrasts sharply with the Western world view, predicated on the Darwinian philosophy of 'survival of the fittest' which asserts that 'self-preservation is the first law of life'.

But this is a fallacious premise. I would say other preservation is equally important. Equally important precisely because we cannot preserve self without being concerned about preserving other selves.

The universe is so structured that things go awry if people are not diligent in their cultivation of the other regarding dimensions. The self cannot be self without selves. Self-concern without other concern is like a tributary that has no outward flow to the ocean; stagnant, still and stale; it lacks both life and freshness.

In a real sense all life is interrelated. The agony of the poor impoverishes the rich; the betterment of the poor enriches the rich. The leader's success at leading depends on the co-operation of the led. We are inevitably our brother's keeper because in the broader scheme of things we are our brother's brother.

Whatever affects one directly affects all indirectly. *Inkosi yinkosi ngahalandeli bayo* – a king is king because of his followers.

Consultation as a value orientation

African traditional leadership processes rely heavily on consultation particularly where vexing problems need to be solved. The king-in-council relies on the outcome of intensive debate and discussion by his councillors.

Typically there is no voting. Issues are deliberated upon until consensus or sufficient consensus emerges.

The king then sums up and gives direction, guided by the collective wisdom of his councillors.

In a real sense this was the precursor to the world-renowned durable solution from CODESA and the World Trade Center deliberations that begot South Africa's democracy.

Interdependence as a superior value to independence

Western culture generally extols independence and individual excellence to a degree seen as excessive in an African context.

The African proclivity by contrast would tend to value interdependence over independence as borne out by the following idiomatic expressions: *Rintiho rin 'we a ri nusi hove Xitsonga* (one finger cannot pick up a grain – or you achieve more through co-operation and synergy).

Akukho qili linoku zikhoth' emh lane (isiXhosa – no genius is so clever that he can lick his own back). Even the most able among us needs to be supplemented.

Individualism versus collectivism and the African inclination

The lone ranger syndrome where a single individual rocks up and saves an entire community or organisation, providing instant leadership, is commonplace in the Western milieu. In the African context, even though heroes and heroines are adored, rabid individualism is abhorred.

>>

>>

A leader who lives by the tenets of consultation and persuasion is preferred. Leadership collectivism that pursues group survival and defends group claims is upheld.

It is this architecture that holds the leadership centre intact, enabling it to manage the reconciling of conflicts that may from time to time arise as a result of ethnic, language and religious differences.

It is this inclination that gives imprimatur to the trade union slogan: 'An injury to one is an injury to all', a pillar of trade union solidarity. At the international level, this tendency informs preference for multilateralism over unilateralism.

Far be it for the putative accusation of African suffering from a herding instinct.

Source: Khoza (2007b: 24–27)

Avolio (1995) points out that in South Africa there appears to be both an individualistic and communalistic orientation, depending on whether the group is white, black, Asian or coloured. Koopman (1994) espouses the view that whites have primarily designed exclusive institutions which give primacy to the individual, and his or her development and self-fulfilment, which serve to foster liberal democracy. He further says that blacks, on the other hand, believe that man is very much part of the societal fabric and see the need for individuals to find their place in a societal structure, to play their particular role in it and, to a large extent, to subordinate themselves to the societal needs – which leads to inclusive organisations.

As explained in chapter 3 as well, we believe that South Africans have to come to terms with each others' differences, acknowledge them and put them in perspective. We must discover the strengths and weaknesses in different ideologies and take the best from it all as we embrace and value diversity to create the best prospects of unity through diversity. In particular, for too long have we neglected Afrocentric leadership perspectives.

As reflected also in exhibit 10.4, *ubuntu* is central to Afrocentric management. *Ubuntu* is not a management style or a business technique, but an epistemology, a humanistic philosophy – African humanism – which focuses on people and puts down some guidelines for leadership style and management practices. *Ubuntu*, literally translated, means: "I am because we are", an expression of our collective personhood and collective morality. Simply put, it implies encouraging individuals to express themselves through the group through group support and commitment, acceptance and respect, cooperation and consensus, caring and sharing, and solidarity. Khoza (1994) points out that *ubuntu* is opposed to individualism and insensitive competitiveness, but is not comfortable with the kind of collectivism that stresses the importance of the social unit to the point of depersonalising the individual.

Ubuntu places a great emphasis on concern for people, as well as being good and working for the common good (Khoza 1994; Mbigi 1995a, 1995b, 1995c). Mbigi (1995b) argues that "the heart and soul of *ubuntu* is the solidarity principle, group conformity and care in the face of survival challenges, based on unconditional group compassion, respect, dignity, trust, openness and cooperation".

Avolio (1995) argues that African humanism or *ubuntu* is much more closely tied to *transformational leadership*. Specifically, transformational leaders typically work to create a climate and culture where the people and the group can achieve their visions, including reaching full potential. In doing so, transformational leaders can facilitate the Africanisation of South African organisations and hopefully lead us towards the reality, and not merely the dream of an African Renaissance.

The implications of an *ubuntu*-oriented leadership style do not only include teamwork down to grassroots level but also the encouragement of the team members or followers to sacrifice their personal gains/goals for the gains/goals of the group. This style includes creative cooperation, open communication, teamwork and reciprocal moral obligations (Khoza 1994; Avolio 1995, Mbigi 1995b). Table 10.5 shows some potential aspects of *ubuntu* that can be capitalised on to help us develop competitive advantage in South Africa (and elsewhere in Africa), and exhibit 10.5 reflects Mangaliso's (2001: 32) advice regarding the managerial leadership implications of *ubuntu*.

Table 10.5: Competitive advantages from *ubuntu*

Assumptions about	*Ubuntu*	Competitive advantages
Relationships with others	Relationships are reciprocal vs instrumental. Treat others as brothers/sisters. Individual predicated on belonging to collective. 'I belong, therefore I am.' Extended family is important	People are intrinsically motivated to contribute more when they are valued members. Mutual respect and empathy are *ubuntu* advantages
Language and communication	Oral tradition. To name is to create. Meaning of words is strongly related to context. Poetic expression and ability to play with words are signs of wisdom	Shared understanding of deeper meanings supports complex consensus. *Ubuntu* communication means concerted action that is adaptable
Decision making	Decisions by consensus. Dissenters are compensated for. The process is circular. Polyocular vision. Dispute resolution to restore harmony	*Ubuntu* might be slow to action, but greater commitment to goals means more long-run effectiveness and efficiency
Time	Not a finite commodity; it is the healer; allow enough of it for important issues before arriving at a decision	Punctuality is a virtue, but time's healing dimension is a hidden competitive advantage for *ubuntu*
Age and leadership	Age is an ongoing process of maturing and acquiring wisdom. Older people are respected. Grey hair is a sign of wisdom	Older workers bring experience, wisdom, connections, informal networks. Competitive advantage from *ubuntu*
Belief systems	Belief in the Creator, *uNkulunkula*, and the existence of the mesocosmos. The mediating role of the *isangoma*. Christianity is also prevalent	Spirituality brings out the best qualities in humans. *Ubuntu* has the edge

Source: Slightly adapted from Mangaliso (2001: 25), as taken from Hampden-Turner & Trompenaars (1993)

EXHIBIT 10.5: Guidelines for implementing *ubuntu*

Several South African companies have begun to embrace the guidelines of *ubuntu* and to introduce them in their corporate practice with notable successes ... [M]ore writings are coming forth from authors giving advice ranging from corporate governance to marketing ... [G]uidelines for helping managers in the process of incorporating the philosophy of *ubuntu* in their organizations are given below. Though not exhaustive, the guidelines are meant to provide a good starting point for managers wishing to incorporate the principles of *ubuntu* in their organizations.

Treat others with dignity and respect. This is a cardinal point of *ubuntu*. Everything hinges on this canon, including an emphasis on humility, harmony and valuing diversity. Helpfulness towards others creates an environment of collegiality based on caring and sharing. After all, who would not like to be appreciated, valued and respected for their contributions for what they bring to the workplace?

Be willing to negotiate in good faith. Take time to listen with empathy, especially in conflict resolution. Being listened to is tantamount to being acknowledged. In *ubuntu*, being acknowledged is a very important first step toward agreement and cooperation. Transparency and trust replace suspicion and hostility.

Provide opportunities for self-expression. Honouring achievement, self-fulfilment and affirmation of values are all important aspects of creating goodwill among employees. Periodic celebrations to punctuate achievement are one way to fulfil this need.

Understand the beliefs and practices of indigenous people. Carefully incorporate into standard corporate policies the indigenous practices and beliefs discussed above. If employing people who are relatives has been successful, use it. Learn more about the belief systems that employees subscribe to. Engaging them in their own belief system will go a long way toward ensuring employee self-fulfilment and thus smooth-running operations.

Honour seniority, especially in leadership choices. All things being equal, seniority adds value through experience, connections and the wisdom that older employees have from their record of past experience.

Promote equity in the workplace. Fairness is a value that is upheld in most cultures, but it takes a special significance in countries such as South Africa, where there has been a history of socio-political inequities. Recruiting and promoting qualified individuals from previously disadvantaged groups, ie blacks and women, into senior management ranks is essential.

Be flexible and accommodative. Applying the recommendations above will require a careful balancing act by management between the imperatives of *ubuntu* and other tried-and-tested management principles. A carefully balanced blending, with flexibility and accommodation, holds the promise of greater value added to corporate performance.

Effective management in South Africa and elsewhere will hinge on the successful harnessing and harmonising of both indigenous and traditional corporate cultures. For managers, the challenge is to become familiar with these values, incorporate them into their policies, or run the risk of being outperformed by rivals who do.

Incorporating *ubuntu* principles in management holds the promise of superior approaches to managing organisations. Organisations infused with humaneness, a pervasive spirit of caring and community, harmony and hospitality, respect and responsiveness will enjoy more sustainable competitive advantage.

Source: Slightly adapted extract from Mangaliso (2001: 32)

It is our view that managers in this country need to extract the best management tools from camps representing a variety of cultural management orientations both within and outside South Africa, and that managers who understand and value the cultural diversity of the South African workforce, and who are flexible in using what works from a cultural perspective, will more likely have the competitive edge.

Just more than a decade ago Professor David Beaty (1996) offered some insights regarding the debate on 'Afrocentric versus Eurocentric' management styles, and we quote (also see the appendix to this chapter):

> I believe that managers do not, and should not, choose between Eurocentric and Afrocentric management approaches in South Africa. What's more, placing these two approaches on two ends of a continuum is not the current reality facing most managers in South Africa. South African managers don't face a 'melting pot' of people from one or two cultures. In fact, the South African workplace reflects many diverse cultures – including European, African, Asian, Indian, Middle Eastern and others. What's more, people from the same culture in South Africa frequently differ along regional and ethnic lines and reflect a workplace that I describe as a cultural 'fruit cocktail'.

Similarly, Horwitz et al (2002: 1032) provide further very insightful analyses, arguing that the managerial leadership styles in various "African countries reflect both Western values ..." and also aspects of authoritarianism that are typically "rooted in high masculinity cultures" which can specifically also be found in Africa. In addition they (Horwitz et al 2002: 1034) add: "[O]ur analysis of the southern African-Asian HRM context underlines the need to strengthen analysis beyond descriptive cross-cultural adoption to within-cultural variables, such as the degree of homogeneity or diversity within the culture ...".

We believe that these perspectives hold true today in South Africa and can allow for a healthy approach of embracing diversity to its full extent. We thus attach the article by Professor Beaty as an appendix to this chapter, agreeing that we also believe it is important to acknowledge the realities of subculture, such as even within any particular country or society.

Particularly relevant also in this regard in South Africa, but also beyond our country elsewhere on the Africa continent, is the issue of ethnic groups and 'ethnicity'. Dr Stephen Nyambegerra from Kenya (Daystar University) offers views in this regard (see exhibit 10.5).

If, in South Africa, and in Africa as a whole, we must get to the point where we can say we have 'unity in diversity', we will have to make very sure that we embrace diversity in all of its multidimensionality. Only diverse leadership teams that include the full spectrum of variables regarding diversity, such as both feminine and masculine as well as proponents of Afrocentric, Eurocentric and also Asia-centric leadership strengths, will be strong and flexible enough to help South African organisations to compete in today's highly competitive, global marketplace. This is aligned also with the preferences that Nelson Mandela had for the actual leadership cadre of the ANC as political party, according to Gumede (2007: 56) in his book about the 'battle for the soul of the ANC':

> Mandela ... strongly favoured a non-Xhosa as his deputy, and made it clear during consultations ... he was anxious not to repeat the pattern of other African liberation movements dominated by a single ethnic group and went so far as to appoint a commission, chaired by Sisulu, to look at how the NEC could best be restructured to represent a cross-section of South Africa's population.

We believe that we should try to learn from this, and in our organisations we should actively embrace diversity, also in our leadership and management approaches – as also discussed in chapter 3.

> **EXHIBIT 10.5: Nyambegera on ethnic groups, 'ethnicity' and power distribution in sub-Saharan Africa: political leadership and HRM connections – some food for thought**
>
> Although ethnicity constitutes a primary dimension of diversity because of the sense of identity that it engenders, there is a dearth of research on diversity management in sub-Saharan Africa ... A few decades ago it was believed that ethnicity as an element of culture would gradually disappear as an organizational form ... However it is now evident that ethnic groupings are affirming themselves more and more ... It is therefore recognized that ethnicity arises when ethnic groups are competitive rather than co-operative ... When people join organizations from whichever ethnic group, they carry a baggage of values inherent in their identity that is later reflected in their work behaviours ... The ethnic diversity found in African organizations has played a major role in excluding talented and capable people ... Those in positions of authority are usually under intense pressure to provide jobs for their relatives ... This is intensified mainly by Africa's cultural values that are group oriented and paternalistic in nature ... After independence many African leaders started projects to homogenize their states, which became problematic due to several factors such as authoritarianism, socio-economic crises and inequities embedded in the distribution of power in a multi-ethnic context ... This led to a feeling that only when a particular ethnic group has its own kind in political or organizational power can they benefit from the nation's or organization's resources, hence increasing the phenomenon of ethnic identity ... Clearly, ethnicity has been the organizing principle of African politics before, as well as after, independence ... Those in power have tended to manipulate ethnicity in order to establish control ... The fact that some ethnic groups were exposed to more resources that gave them power through education and wealth due to an advantaged position of having their kind in the government system might have heightened ethnic identity among people in many African countries. This, in essence ... leaves the majority of people of certain ethnic groups continually without access to society's opportunities and rewards. High-level corruption, embezzlement and the granting of favours have created a wealthy elite in most African countries ...
>
> Source: Nyambegera (2002: 1077–1080)

10.6 CONCLUSION

Throughout this chapter it has been emphasised that leadership is important, and that the styles, actions, attributes, orientations and approaches of leaders all have a major effect on workers and ultimately on the success of organisations. In South Africa we have our own issues and challenges regarding leadership and organisational success.

The increasing multinationalism and multiculturalism of workforces pose significant challenges for leaders in South African organisations. Some argue that there is still a value system of old conventions and traditions to be challenged – that of the traditional white South African male manager. While the resistance and negative attitudes towards old-style managerial leadership by many workers must be taken into account on the one hand, the uncertainties and fears of others must also be acknowledged. These are among the critical HRM issues that the managerial leaders of South African organisations must confront.

SUSTAINABILITY CONNECTION?
Leadership can make or break organisations' capabilities to perform and compete. Probably one of our biggest challenges has to do with developing the leadership capacity of our organisations. People do not have to be managers to be leaders. The more people we help equip with leadership competencies and capabilities – and the more we allow people to take charge, to take the lead with whatever they engage in at work – the more we will have empowered people. This type of shared or distributed leadership that revolves around empowering our working people can help organisations improve their performance, if it goes with skills development and appropriate culture change. The better we are at achieving this, the better are the chances of making a success of our country over the long term.

SELF-EVALUATION QUESTIONS

1 Define leadership. How is it relevant to human resource management?
2 Differentiate between the 'trait theory paradigm' and the 'behavioural theory paradigm' of leadership and explain two theories of each.
3 What do you understand by transformational leadership?
4 Explain what charismatic leadership entails.
5 Briefly describe what you know about 'South African perspectives of leadership'.
6 Analyse and critically discuss the following statement: 'South Africa needs its own unique way of leadership because none of the Western theories of leadership has any applicability or potential value for our country.'

APPENDIX: EUROCENTRIC OR AFROCENTRIC MANAGEMENT – DO SOUTH AFRICAN MANAGERS HAVE TO CHOOSE?

By Professor David Beaty
University of South Africa Graduate School of Business Leadership

South African managers face a dilemma that concerns two different management approaches in this country. On the one hand, some people argue that 'Eurocentric Management' (unlike 'Afrocentric Management') has proven value in improving organisational performance worldwide. And they assert that this management approach has made significant positive contributions to South African work and organisation.

On the other hand, supporters of 'Afrocentric Management' (using terms that include '*Ubuntu*' and '*Nhorowondo*') argue that for managers to be relevant in South Africa, they must accept concepts embodied in such terms as 'solidarity', 'conformity' and 'relationships'. They argue with their critics by claiming that those in opposition do not understand Afrocentric Management and suggest that critics misrepresent the approach as just another 'oversimplified' and 'bastardised' business technique.

This article is not written to explore the merits and demerits of both management approaches. Indeed, a number of recent books, articles, speeches, media reports, and even television programmes have devoted adequate time and space to this issue. And each camp has marshalled what each believes are the 'right' facts to support their conclusions. Both sides argue for understanding and acceptance of their opinions by managers in a new South Africa.

It's no wonder that managers listening and watching this debate are confused about 'who's right' and 'who's wrong'. Anyone? Everyone? Indeed, each camp presents a list of logical points in hopes of persuading the opposition (and any observers) to their point of view. However, while academically intriguing, the debate has become divisive. In fact, emotional temperatures have risen as supporters from both camps rally around their viewpoints. What's more, the real problems facing South Africa of low productivity and poor international competitiveness have become obscured in the desire to prove who's right and who's wrong.

This article is written to offer a different perspective on the debate. I believe that managers do not, and should not, choose between Eurocentric and Afrocentric management approaches in South Africa. What's more, placing these two approaches on two ends of a continuum is not the current reality facing most managers in South Africa. South African managers don't face a 'melting pot' of people from one or two cultures. In fact, the South African workplace reflects many diverse cultures – including European, African, Asian, Indian, Middle Eastern and others. What's more, people from the same culture in South Africa frequently differ along regional and ethnic lines and reflect a workplace that I describe as a cultural 'fruit cocktail'.

So the debate between supporters of Eurocentric and Afrocentric management is, I contend, mined with pitfalls and not unlike to common practice of business firms presenting elaborate marketing and strategic plans without listening to real live customers and staying reality-based. Bandying around survey data, business techniques, models, opinions from political, literary and trade union leaders – like supporters in both Eurocentric and Afrocentric camps do – is no substitute for 'on the ground' – eye-ball to eye-ball – contact with people from diverse cultures. In fact, I believe that managers in this country need to extract the best management tools from camps representing a variety of cultural management orientations within and outside of South Africa. Managers in this country need to use 'whatever works' to improve management and worker performance.

How will South African managers know 'what works'? The answer – simple in concept but requiring great diligence to carry out – is found, I believe, in 'naive listening'.

Naive listening is just what its name implies: active, nonjudgemental listening to a target person(s) with no rebuttals, arguments, or debates. The concept grew from the discovery that senior managers are frequently out of touch with customers' and employees' needs and desires because they don't regularly interact with them. Getting out of the office regularly (not 'whenever I have some time'), daily (not my 'once-a-quarter visit to the troops'), informally (not the typical adversarial negotiating sessions or the occasional regal visit with employees) for the purposes of listening and learning as well as for monitoring and educating will be a significant step in the direction of addressing the productivity and competitive dilemmas facing managers in this country.

People who have succeeded in international business emphasise the importance of knowing the language, culture and norms of those in the host country in order to conduct naive listening. This advice is sound within South Africa itself, since this is a rainbow nation of multiple languages and cultures. For managers, it pays to know the language and culture of the different peoples from which one's labour force and customers are drawn. For example, when Sony opened a plant in San Diego, an American city near the Mexican border, one of the first things that the new plant manager (a Japanese) did was to learn Spanish, since the majority of his workforce was Mexican and Chicane.

The following true case example is given to illustrate the need to use 'what works' in South Africa, and to avoid being constrained by one or two 'cultural' management approaches.

A firm, with operations in a medium-size Eastern Transvaal city, had major problems in the theft of goods from one of its plants. In fact, the Managing Director suspected that the culprits were employees (including managers and workers). So he implemented a system in which a sum of R50 000,00 was deposited into a bank account. Then, all employees were informed that whenever an item was stolen, the value of that item would be deducted from the money deposited. At the end of a six-month period, the outstanding amount left in the kitty would be divided equally among all employees. The MD's objective was to get employees to police themselves since all stood to gain by having the full amount available at the end of the period. This, he believed, would lead to a decrease in company theft.

Two months into the scheme, the theft of goods continued unabated. What's more, a company bakkie had been stolen and the MD suspected it was an inside job. So he brought in the police to question and fingerprint all employees. Nothing turned up. Frustrated, the MD considered what some might find to be a strange strategy in identifying the culprit and locating the bakkie.

The MD called in a Sangoma and all employees were told by the Sangoma that whoever had stolen the bakkie would be given 24 hours to confess the crime. If the culprit did not confess, the individual(s) would die from a spell that had been cast on all employees. The result – within eight hours the Managing Director received a knock on the door of his home and an employee confessed to having stolen the bakkie as well as other items in the plant.

This case is not written to suggest that Sangomas are the only solution to workplace theft. Rather, the case is used to illustrate how a variety of different management approaches were used to solve a business problem. These strategies reflected different cultural values. For example, peer-based control systems reflected practices consistent with Asiancentric management; police investigations and fingerprinting reflected Eurocentric practices; and calling on the services of a Sangoma reflected African cultural practices.

South African managers who understand and value the cultural diversity of all South Africans and are flexible in using 'what works' from a cultural perspective will have a competitive edge over their foreign counterparts. As Clive Barker said in a newspaper interview while discussing the remarkable victory of Bafana Bafana in the Africa Nations Cup, 'I keep saying to the players: If we play like Germany we'll never beat Germany; if we play like the Dutch we'll never beat them either. But if we play like South Africa, there are no limits.'

What lessons can managers learn from this article? First, managers in South Africa should have a healthy scepticism of so-called gurus who preach one (or even two) management solutions to South Africa's productivity malaise. Second, managers need to use 'what works' in solving work performance problems. Knowledge of many culturally diverse management approaches combined with a heavy dose of naive listening to those we say we are trying to lead, is an important step forward in improving organisational performance. Finally, South African managers are beginning to explore a 'home-grown' management recipe. But our need to learn from the rest of the world and adopt a best-practices approach to management must be central in our drive for world class competitiveness.

Source: *Business Day*. 1996. Mastering Management Supplement, Part 2, 11 March, 15.

11 ASSESSING AND ENHANCING WORK PERFORMANCE

LEARNING OUTCOMES

After studying this chapter, you should be able to:

- discuss why performance appraisal is important and what various purposes it can serve in your organisation;
- explain the difference between performance appraisal and performance management;
- design and evaluate appraisal systems according to the basic requirements for effectiveness;
- formulate solutions to the typical problems that may be experienced with performance appraisal;
- apply the basic steps in the development of an appraisal system;
- advise your manager on the most appropriate appraisal techniques in your organisational context, and motivate the advantages and limitations of each;
- analyse the need for self-appraisal and multi-rater appraisal in South African companies; and
- advise line managers on how to conduct an effective appraisal interview.

11.1 INTRODUCTION

In previous chapters it was emphasised that measuring and assessing is an activity that finds application in virtually all the human resource management functions. Naturally, therefore, individual performance as the outcome of work activities must also be subject to measurement. In the course of their daily managerial activities, supervisors and managers ought to continuously assess on an informal basis how well their subordinates are doing their work. Such informal assessment enables the individual manager to make the necessary decisions regarding the most effective utilisation of staff, motivating those who perform well and rectifying substandard performance. Performance appraisal is a separate but central subset of overall performance management (see 11.2.2). It is simply the process of formally evaluating work performance, making decisions on the effective utilisation, rewarding and motivating of staff, rectifying substandard performance, and providing feedback to individual employees. Depending on the size and nature of a business, performance appraisal can be very basic, such as having an informal discussion with subordinates and ranking them in order of merit, or it can be part of a sophisticated and integrated system of organisational performance measurement, such as a balanced scorecard with multi-rater 360-degree assessment (see section 11.6).

Informal appraisal, which usually results in an overall impression of worker efficiency and effectiveness, often operates satisfactorily in small organisations where the management knows and interacts with all employees. However, even though it may be argued that effective supervisors continually provide informal feedback to their subordinates, the information generated through an unsystematic, informal evaluation has limited value for making valid and justifiable HRM decisions in a large organisational context. Furthermore, since human memory for specific instances of employee performance tends to deteriorate over time, supervisors need to have a mechanism for accurately recalling employee behaviour (Kinicki & Kreitner 2006: 99). In large organisations we thus require accurate performance data obtained through standard processes for activities related to, for example, workforce planning, training and development, compensation, career development and succession planning. It is in the areas of the development, implementation, maintenance and use of such systems that the human resource specialist has to play a leading role.

In this chapter we shall explore this role together with the current HRM technology available for providing organisations with meaningful formal appraisal systems.

11.2 DEFINITION AND ROLE OF PERFORMANCE APPRAISAL IN HRM

Performance appraisal may be defined as a formal and systematic process by means of which the job-relevant strengths and weaknesses of employees are identified, observed, measured, recorded and developed.

The above definition captures the essential components of what the process of performance appraisal should ideally entail (Gómez-Mejía, Balkin & Cardy 2001: 225):

- *identification* refers to the rational and legally defensible determination of the performance dimensions to be examined;
- *observation* indicates that all appraisal aspects should be observed sufficiently for accurate and fair judgments to be made;
- *measurement* refers to the appraiser's translation of the observations into value judgements about how 'good' or 'bad' the employee's performance was;
- *recording* concerns the documentation of the performance appraisal process outcomes; and
- the *development component* indicates that appraisal is not simply an assessment of the past but that it should also focus on the future and on the improvement of individual performance.

It may be stated that performance appraisal finds its true definition only by its application, or the purpose it serves in the attainment of organisational goals. This contention will be further expanded upon in later sections of this chapter.

In establishing the role of performance appraisal within HRM, we need to consider the typical purposes for which appraisals can be used and the relationships that may exist between the appraisal system and other HRM functions in an organisation.

11.2.1 Purposes of performance appraisal

The overall purpose of appraisal, naturally, is to provide information about work performance. However, we can trace this back to a number of different uses for such information (see exhibit 11.1 for reasons for performance appraisal in South Africa).

EXHIBIT 11.1: Reasons for performance appraisal in South Africa

Reason	Survey of the most common reasons (35 large companies)	Survey of prevalence of use (551 companies)
Identify training and development needs	20,2%	85,2%
Compensation levels/incentive pay	16,3%/10,1%	68,5%
Performance feedback to employees	14,7%	–
Planning future performance/determining organisational HR development needs	14,0%	69,5%
Communicating organisational goals/organisation of work	12,4%	55,8%
Motivating employees to perform better	11,6%	–
Career planning and development	0,8%	83,8%
Determining promotion potential	–	83,0%

Source: Based on Deloitte & Touche (2002) (used with kind permission of Deloitte & Touche Human Capital Corporation Pty Ltd); and Grobler (2001: 30–33)

The information we collect when we do performance appraisals can thus serve a variety of purposes, which generally can be categorised under the two main headings of 'administrative purposes' and 'developmental purposes' (Cascio 2006: 333).

Administrative purposes concern the use of performance data as bases for personnel decision making, including:

■ human resource planning, for example compiling skills inventories, obtaining information regarding new positions to be created, and developing succession plans;
■ reward decisions, including salary and wage increases (or withholding them), merit bonuses, etc;
■ placement decisions such as promotions, transfers, dismissals and retrenchments; and
■ personnel research, for example validating selection procedures by using appraisals as criteria, or evaluating the effectiveness of training programmes.

Developmental purposes of performance appraisal can focus on developmental functions on the individual as well as the organisational level. Appraisals can serve individual development purposes by:

■ providing employees with feedback on their strengths and weaknesses and on how to improve future performance;
■ aiding career planning and development; and
■ providing inputs for personal remedial interventions, for example referral to an employee assistance programme (performance impairments may be due to factors outside the work environment).

Organisational development purposes may include:

■ facilitating organisational diagnosis and development by specifying performance levels and suggesting overall training needs;

- providing essential information for affirmative action programmes, job redesign efforts, multiskilling programmes, etc; and
- promoting effective communication within the organisation through ongoing interaction between superiors and subordinates.

Figure 11.1 illustrates diagrammatically the centrality of performance within some of the different functional human resource areas and the role of appraisal in an integrated human resource cycle.

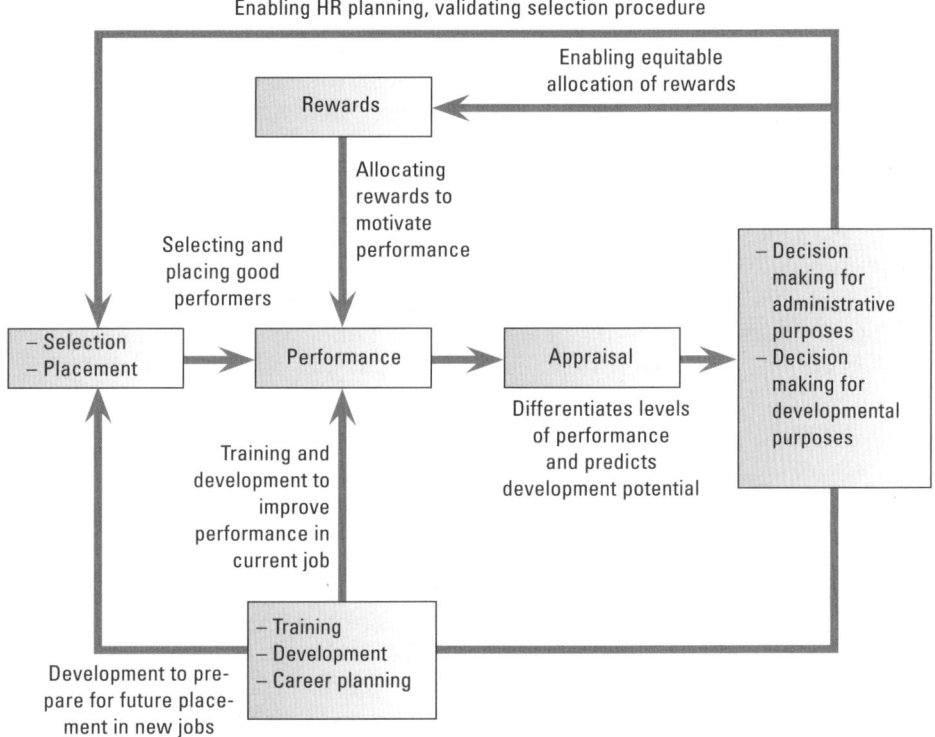

Figure 11.1: Performance appraisal in the HRM cycle
Source: Adapted from Fombrun, Devanna & Tichy (1988: 252)

11.2.2 Performance appraisal versus performance management

Since it is the performance of individual employees that primarily determines the attainment of the goals and objectives of an organisation, the measurement or appraisal of performance rightfully deserves a central position in any HRM programme (refer to figure 11.1).

Performance appraisal (also referred to as performance evaluation, merit rating, staff assessment, performance review, etc) is also the human resource function most often criticised and whose systems carry the greatest risk of either failing, falling into disuse or degenerating towards a meaningless, paperwork exercise.

The typical problems associated with performance appraisal will be explored in greater depth in a later section. At this stage suffice it to say that increasingly competitive business environments; criticism of traditional approaches to performance appraisal; the perception of appraisal as a negative, disliked activity; and the concept of total quality management have led to a shift in emphasis from performance appraisal to performance management.

Performance management can be defined as: "A process which contributes to the effective management of individuals and teams in order to achieve high levels of organisational performance. As such, it establishes shared understanding about what is to be achieved and an approach to leading and developing people which will ensure that it is achieved" (CIPD 2007).

Performance appraisal is a part of performance management, which is focused on organisational performance improvement through a number of HR processes, including performance appraisal. Appraisal is a formal time-specific assessment or 'dipstick'-snapshot of individual employees' performance, whereas performance management entails a cyclical and ongoing endeavour.

As such, performance management can be regarded as a non-time specific ongoing process that involves the planning, managing, reviewing, rewarding and development of individual and group performance (Härtel, Fujimoto, Strybosch & Fitzpatrick 2007: 342).

While performance appraisal systems are often no more than a system of measurement (that is, a specific form together with certain written rules and procedures controlling its use), the concept of performance management signifies an attempt to entrench performance appraisal as a legitimate and integral part of a manager's job of getting subordinates effectively to achieve the results and goals expected of them.

Houldsworth (2004: 81) offers quite a comprehensive explanation when saying that in its full extent,

> performance management may be seen to be related to the appraisal of old, but it is very much the strategic, 'grown-up cousin'. State-of-the-art performance management is now typically described as an ongoing process of good management practice throughout the year. Manager and individual are now increasingly involved in a joint review that places emphasis on both the objectives ('what' of performance) and also the behaviours associated with success ('how' of performance). A development plan will usually be produced and although ratings still occur at most annual review meetings, they are not given the emphasis of old and the link to pay is usually less direct ...

The theoretical foundations of the performance management approach may be operationalised within an integrated cycle of separate but related managerial processes, as illustrated in figure 11.2.

11.3 PERFORMANCE APPRAISAL SYSTEMS: SOME FUNDAMENTAL REQUIREMENTS

Specific requirements for an appraisal system as a criterion for judging the work performance of individuals are: relevance, reliability, discriminability or sensitivity, freedom from contamination, practicality, acceptability and legal compliance.

Relevance

The requirement of relevance refers to the question: 'What is really important for success in this job and this organisation?' The appraisal system must therefore be directly related to the objectives of the job and the goals of the organisation. Cascio (2006: 334) suggests three necessary processes to ensure relevance: (i) establishing

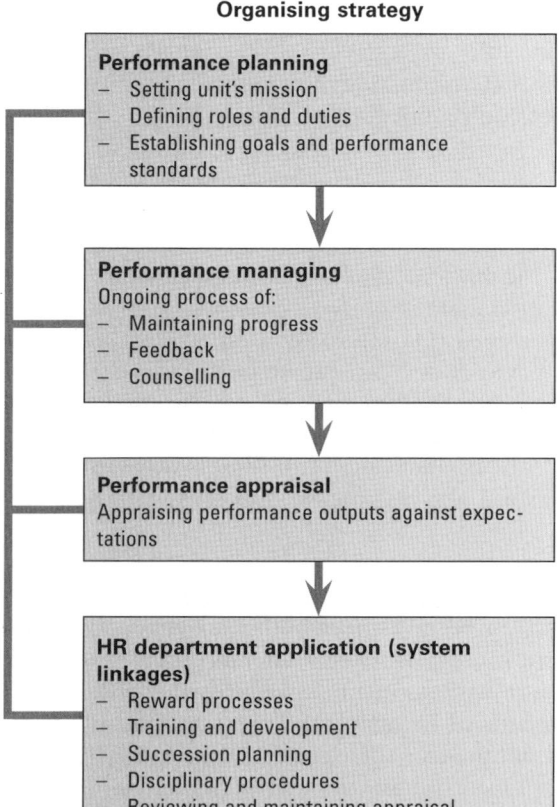

Organising strategy

Performance planning
- Setting unit's mission
- Defining roles and duties
- Establishing goals and performance standards

Performance managing
Ongoing process of:
- Maintaining progress
- Feedback
- Counselling

Performance appraisal
Appraising performance outputs against expectations

HR department application (system linkages)
- Reward processes
- Training and development
- Succession planning
- Disciplinary procedures
- Reviewing and maintaining appraisal system and process

Figure 11.2: An integrated performance management cycle
Source: Adapted from Fombrun, Devanna & Tichy (1988:252) In *The Strategic Human Resource Management Sourcebook*, eds. LS Baird, CE Schneier & RM Beatty, Amherst, Mass: HRD Press.

clear links between the performance standards of all jobs and the organisational goals; (ii) establishing clear links between the critical job elements of each job (as determined through job analysis) and the performance dimensions to be rated on the appraisal form; and (iii) ensuring the regular maintenance and updating of job descriptions, performance standards and appraisal systems.

Reliability

The system must produce evaluations or ratings that are consistent and repeatable. The requirement of reliability does not only refer to the psychometric properties of the measuring instrument itself, but also to the need for judges who carry out the rating process both competently and consistently, and who have the opportunity to observe the behaviour that is to be rated.

Discriminability/sensitivity

Despite being highly relevant and reliable, a system will still be of no use if it is unable to distinguish between good and poor performers. If the system gives rise to similar ratings for both effective and ineffective employees through either design deficiencies (for example insufficient performance categories) or rating errors (for example central tendency), results cannot be used for developmental or administrative decisions.

Freedom from contamination

The system should be able to measure individual performance without being contaminated by factors that are outside the employee's control, for example material shortages, inappropriate equipment or procedures.

Practicality

This requirement implies that an appraisal system should be easy to understand and to use by managers and subordinates alike. It should therefore be user friendly and manageable in terms of the amount of administration (time and paperwork) it requires and in terms of its cost effectiveness.

In making design decisions relating to the practicality and utility of an envisaged system, the practitioner may have to make some compromises, since an increase in practicality usually comes at the expense of measurement precision. Conversely, technically advanced systems, such as behaviourally anchored rating scales (BARS), may perhaps be superior in meeting requirements of relevance, reliability and discriminability, but they are also complex and expensive to develop and implement.

Acceptability

The acceptability of a system is an extremely important prerequisite, since the support and perceived legitimacy a system receives from both managers and employees will probably carry more weight in determining its success than its inherent technical soundness.

In order to establish a positive attitude towards the system, it would be prudent to utilise all possible means of involving the eventual end-users in its development, implementation and maintenance; they must also be made to feel that they are the actual owners of the appraisal system.

Legal compliance

Since work performance data is being used for management decisions on promotions, dismissals, employment equity and rewards, lodging of grievances and legal challenges of such decisions are often a workplace reality. The performance appraisal system should therefore be tested for compliance with the requirements of relevant labour legislation. Examples of areas in the system to be checked are possible unlawful discrimination in terms of section 6(1) of the Employment Equity Act, and soundness of documented performance appraisal data to meet criteria of substantive and procedural fairness in dismissals on grounds of poor work performance.

A POLICY PERSPECTIVE

Our performance management policy aims to enhance the work performance of all employees, as individuals and as teams throughout our organisation – based on aligning the work-related goals of our people with the goals and strategic direction of the organisation. It is only through superior work performance that we can become and remain competitive and therefore it is essential to develop an organisational culture which puts a premium on enhancing performance in an ongoing way.

The purpose of this policy is to support the design and institutionalisation of systems, processes and practices that will enable all our staff – as individuals and as groups/teams – to add measurable value to our organisational goals and strategic direction. The overall aim is to have a workforce that is performing superiorly so that we can have an organisation that performs superiorly.

11.4 SOME GENERAL PERFORMANCE APPRAISAL PROBLEMS AND POSSIBLE REMEDIES

In a previous section, reference was made to the so-called inherent problematic nature of performance appraisal. Since McGregor first took an "uneasy look at performance appraisal" in his famous 1957 article, a vast amount of research has focused on identifying the shortcomings of the performance appraisal process and on finding possible solutions to these problems. The literature abounds with lists of reasons why appraisal systems fail, and in practice many problems are experienced. The results of a recent study in the US, Canada, the UK and Australia entitled *Reviewing the Performance of Performance Management* led one commentator (Davis 2007: 26) to voice exasperation as follows: "I can think of no other aspect of business where so much is invested in something so important for such little return year after year." Let us thus explore some of the fundamental reasons for appraisal systems consistently failing to live up to the expected results.

South African research indicates that problems in performance appraisal typically stem from:

- technical issues in the system itself (for example choice of format and administrative procedures; purposes for which it is designed, linking it to other systems such as reward system); and
- human issues related to perceptions and the interaction process between supervisor and subordinate (for example employee mistrust of the real goals of performance review; feedback not being regular or meaningful enough for improving performance; relationships among employees seen as more important than performance; supervisors being prejudiced in their ratings). (See, for example, Rademan & Vos 2001; Viedge 2004).

11.4.1 System design issues

It would be safe to state that there is not a single method or format of performance appraisal that is not subject to some limitations. Indeed, the very fact that there are so many different formats of varying complexity from which to choose is a direct result of trying to overcome deficiencies of previously conceived formats. Such deficiencies in the design of performance appraisal instruments are mostly related to concerns regarding their reliability and validity as basic psychometric requirements for any measuring instrument.

Reliability in assessment refers to the consistency and stability of the measurement process. Typically, four approaches may be used for improving reliability in performance measures:

- increasing the number of items in the rating instrument that measure the same performance dimension;
- using more than one evaluator in order to obtain multiple observations;
- increasing the frequency of observations; and
- standardising the administration of the appraisal process.

The question of validity addresses the 'what' and 'how well' an instrument measures and whether it really measures what it is supposed to measure.

In terms of format design, the use of irrelevant performance criteria or reliance on personality trait measures may compromise validity, while certain rater biases may detract from validity during the evaluation process. (The commonest of these biases or errors are discussed separately in section 11.4.3.)

With research pointing towards the limited impact a specific format may have on the accuracy of actual ratings (Gómez-Mejía et al 2001: 35), human resource practitioners must bear in mind that the technical soundness of an appraisal system alone does not ensure its success.

In practice, frustrations resulting from the imperfect nature of appraisal systems often prompt organisations to modify or totally redevelop their current systems. A South African survey found the average length of time that current systems had been in use to be a mere four years (Deloitte & Touche 2002). Naturally, the development of a 'new tool' is more often than not a futile exercise that does little for establishing the credibility of the appraisal process or convincing line management of its essential purposes. Consequently, human resource practitioners faced with demands for more effective appraisal should not approach the dilemma purely by adopting more technically advanced and complex techniques, but by focusing on the proper implementation and improvement of the process as such, that is, by taking a performance management perspective.

11.4.2 Conflicting purposes and roles

If we refer to the many possible purposes that performance appraisal may serve (see section 11.2.1), it should be clear that no single general method can be appropriate for all of them. Within the two general categories of purposes which were distinguished (namely administrative (or judgemental) and developmental), the basic objectives are in direct conflict.

Administrative objectives focus on the evaluation of the past performance of employees to enable managers to make decisions regarding the differential award of pay increases, candidates for promotion, etc. To allow supervisors to make comparisons between employees, an appropriate system will have to utilise some relative rating format such as ranking procedures (that is, listing employees in some order of merit). However, the nature of such employee-to-employee comparison methods does not only make the process of appraisal feedback difficult but also provides little information for the identification of individual performance deficiencies and how to address them in terms of training and development interventions.

To address the developmental objective, an appraisal system needs to focus on absolute rating formats where each individual is evaluated against several specified performance standards, for example rating scales, or against specific objectives, for example management by objectives (MBO). Since these formats require the rater to evaluate the employee without direct reference to other employees, valid comparisons across individuals or groups are not possible, and administrative purposes cannot thus be effectively served.

The two general purposes also force managers into fulfilling conflicting roles during appraisal interviews – that is, simultaneously serving as both judge and counsellor. Naturally, managers feel uncomfortable about first criticising an employee (and possibly having to justify an unpopular decision about salary increases or other employee expectations that have not been met) and then trying to set a positive tone for constructively discussing future improvement and setting new performance goals. It is generally accepted that single interviews attempting to serve both purposes of informing and justifying administrative decisions and then providing feedback and counselling are less effective than interviews addressing these purposes separately. In keeping with the philosophy of the performance management approach, the best way to resolve the judgement-versus-development dilemma would probably be the emphasis on developing effective and ongoing supervisor–subordinate interaction.

If a supervisor manages performance on a daily basis, all subordinates will have a reasonable idea of where they have succeeded and where they have failed, and no formal appraisal session will hold unexpected surprises. Therefore any formal annual appraisal interview should essentially be a summary of previous formal and informal discussions.

11.4.3 Rating errors/judgemental biases

Performance appraisal requires the supervisor or manager to observe and judge behaviour as objectively as possible. Since both these processes are conducted by human beings, and managers may not be experts in all the operational fields in their department, the appraisal process is necessarily prone to distortions and biases (Mullins 2002: 707).

In order to evaluate the effectiveness of an employee's behaviour, the supervisor must first have observed such behaviour. Unless the rater is able to observe his or her subordinates continuously and to provide regular evaluative feedback, annual appraisal judgements will have to be based on a limited sample of observed performance events (those which the supervisor still remembers). Since many managers may simply not have the time or the inclination to practice 'management by walking around' and observing their subordinates at work, sampling errors such as the recency effect and infrequent observations may lead to invalid and subjective evaluations.

- The recency effect refers to the tendency to emphasise recent behaviours rather than the individual's performance over the entire review period. Good performers who may have slacked towards the end of the rating period may thus be penalised unfairly.
- The error of infrequent observations usually manifests itself in ratings based on non-representative samples of behaviour and unsubstantiated inferences.

Apart from the obvious advantages that continuous performance management may hold in this regard, the utilisation of multiple raters may alleviate the problem somewhat.

Some commonly encountered judgemental biases or so-called rater errors are outlined below:

- *Leniency and strictness error.* This is the tendency of some evaluators to assign either mostly favourable ratings or mostly very harsh ratings to all employees.
- *Central tendency.* This is the tendency to assign all ratings towards the centre of all scales, thus evaluating all workers as 'average'.
- *Halo error.* This is the tendency to allow the rating assigned to one performance dimension to excessively influence, either positively or negatively, the ratings on all subsequent dimensions.
- *Same-as-me and different-from-me error.* This refers to the tendency to assign more favourable ratings to employees who are perceived by the rater to be similar to or to behave in a similar way to the rater or, alternatively, to rate less favourably those workers who demonstrate traits or behaviours different from those of the rater.
- *Contrast error.* This is the tendency to allow the rating of an individual to be positively or negatively influenced by the relative evaluation of the preceding ratee. Thus an average performer may receive a poorer rating than would otherwise have been the case if his or her appraisal follows that of the company's star performer.

EXHIBIT 11.2: Illustration of rating errors

Leniency error

Dimension	John					Sipho					Mary				
Volume of work	1	2	3	4	5✓	1	2	3	4	5✓	1	2	3	4	5✓
Knowledge	1	2	3	4	5✓	1	2	3	4	5✓	1	2	3	4	5✓
Accuracy	1	2	3	4	5✓	1	2	3	4	5✓	1	2	3	4	5✓

Strictness error

Dimension	John					Sipho					Mary				
Volume of work	1✓	2	3	4	5	1✓	2	3	4	5	1✓	2	3	4	5
Knowledge	1✓	2	3	4	5	1✓	2	3	4	5	1✓	2	3	4	5
Accuracy	1✓	2	3	4	5	1✓	2	3	4	5	1✓	2	3	4	5

Central tendency

Dimension	John					Sipho					Mary				
Volume of work	1	2	3✓	4	5	1	2	3✓	4	5	1	2	3✓	4	5
Knowledge	1	2	3✓	4	5	1	2	3✓	4	5	1	2	3✓	4	5
Accuracy	1	2	3✓	4	5	1	2	3✓	4	5	1	2	3✓	4	5

Halo error

Dimension	John					Sipho					Mary				
Volume of work	1	2	3	4	5✓	1	2✓	3	4	5	1	2	3	4✓	5
Knowledge	1	2	3	4	5✓	1	2✓	3	4	5	1	2	3	4✓	5
Accuracy	1	2	3	4	5✓	1	2✓	3	4	5	1	2	3	4✓	5

11.4.3.1 Overcoming rating errors

Three basic approaches can typically be followed in trying to combat rating errors:

- The first strategy focuses on the statistical correction of ratings by, for instance, converting all ratings to some type of standard score or by using a forced distribution of ratings in terms of the requirements of a normal curve. In the latter case, the assumption of a normal distribution of employee performance ratings (that is, that there are certain percentages of excellent, average and poor employees in every group) may be a fallacy, since star performers and underperformers may already have been promoted or fired from the group. Similarly, a group may, for example, consist entirely of top performers due to excellent selection and training.
- The second approach follows the traditional route of addressing appraisal problems, namely that of developing new, more sophisticated techniques and formats that incorporate design features and procedures aimed at minimising the risk of subjectivity.
- Finally, the third approach comprises the training of raters in three important areas:
  - training aimed at eliminating or at least lessening rating errors and biases;
  - training aimed at promoting better observational skills among raters; and
  - training aimed at improved interpersonal and communication skills during appraisal interviews.

Reviews of the effects of rater training generally support the effectiveness of this approach (Cascio 2006: 355; Muchinsky, Kriek & Schreuder 2002: 213).

11.4.4 Human interaction issues

The very notion of evaluation – as well as the appraisal process itself – may often be a highly emotional issue for both raters and ratees alike.

Raters who feel uncomfortable about any confrontation with subordinates may, for instance, assign average ratings where poor ratings would have been appropriate; ratees facing even the most accurate and objective criticism may resist or trivialise findings if they perceive the assessment as a blow to their self-esteem.

In addition, many situational factors (such as stress, defensiveness, sexual and racial biases, leadership style, etc) have been implicated in contaminating accurate and valid ratings (Nelson & Quick 2006: 194).

Kinicki and Kreitner (2006: 209) cite six common issues:
- feedback being used to embarrass or punish employees;
- recipients of feedback seeing it as irrelevant to their work;
- providing feedback too late for it to do any good;
- recipients of feedback believing it relates to matters beyond their control;
- too much time devoted to collecting and recording feedback data; and
- feedback being complex or too difficult to understand.

Clearly, not even the most advanced and complex technique could possibly hope to control all such possible interactional problems. However, interventions such as training in coaching and mentoring skills, deliberate focus on changeable behaviours rather than personality-based attributes and advance planning and organising of performance feedback sessions may go a long way towards constructive face-to-face engagements. The importance of fostering effective supervisor–employee relations in the daily performance management process cannot be overemphasised.

11.5 DEVELOPING A PERFORMANCE MANAGEMENT SYSTEM

While the foremost requirement for any effective performance management system would be a tailor-made design and process that fits the specific needs, business environment, culture, etc of the organisation, there are a number of basic components common to developing such systems. It is very important that such a system be developed, not as an isolated project but well aligned to the other HRM systems. In chapter 4 we stressed the fact that a coherent HRM policy framework, based on the relevant strategic choices made, is the appropriate way to go. We also, in the same chapter, provide some example of what such a performance management policy might include. Typical issues or questions to be addressed to ensure an appropriate customised performance management system are highlighted in the subsections that follow.

11.5.1 Pre-design considerations

An effective performance management system should enable and empower line management to implement the strategy and objectives of the organisation successfully. If an organisation, for example, changes the emphasis of its strategy from cost containment to innovation, the focus of its existing work and performance management systems and concomitant criteria should be changed accordingly. Whereas the emphasis might have been on cost effectiveness and the containment of wastage and errors, and risk avoidance through standardised work routines, the shift might be to the encouragement, development, reinforcement and reward of those behaviours that contribute to experimenting through creative work and the search for new ways of improving what we do and how we do things to outperform the competition.

The pertinent questions to be addressed during the early stages relate to the typical problems and fundamental system requirements mentioned previously, for example:

- What is the purpose of the performance management system?
- How do we cascade the organisation's strategic goals down to those of work units like sections, teams and individual employees?
- How do we align the work systems and other aspects of the structural and systemic configurations of the organisation with the way in which we want to manage work performance?
- Who will drive and take part in developing the system?
- What is to be assessed (behaviour, quantitative outputs, traits, etc)?
- Who will be involved in actual performance appraisals (direct supervisor, peers, etc)?
- Will it be purely individual based, or perhaps with group or team elements, or perhaps only based on the level of group performance?
- How will the process and information coming from performance assessment be used?
- What organisational factors need to be taken into account (size, dispersion of branch offices, prevalent culture or management style, etc)?

Probably one of the most crucial aspects during the very early stages of planning the introduction of systematic performance management would be the very question of whether we want to have such a formal system for managing work performance. While specialist HR practitioners might well see the value and have relevant expertise, the key is that the top management team must be keen to have it. If it can be demonstrated that such a system is fundamental to the actual process of strategy execution, it should be pretty straightforward. Naturally such things as the organisation's size, complexity and stage in the organisational life cycle will be quite determining. The overriding argument is that organisational strategy and goals must be translated into the work and concomitant performance requirements. This forms the foundation of performance management systems.

The saying of 'put your money where your mouth is' becomes relevant as soon as there is buy-in by the key decision makers that we need to have such a system. From a budget perspective, the relevant required resources must be committed to go forward and get the system developed.

11.5.2 Designing the system

Once the decision has been made, we must actively engage in developing the system. Here we usually need the input of specialists – from inside and/or from outside the organisation. Probably the most important issue is that we engage the people (or a good representative group of them) who will be using the system. There are plenty 'off-the-shelf' systems available commercially and there are many consultants who can help. Most importantly – any system must be adapted and custom-made to fit the actual organisation and its work and environment. The strategy framework of the organisation is therefore to be used as point of departure.

The following essential activities must be performed to actually develop the system:

Obtaining basic job information

Job design and analysis, which form the cornerstone of gathering job-related information. The written job descriptions, as we have discussed in chapter 6, should thus be very important. The nature of the work and typical job duties and responsibilities should guide how the systems should look and work.

Establishing performance standards and performance criteria

Performance standards describe the conditions for desired work performance. The system should probably be designed such that the work performance standards are mutually agreed upon by those who must do the work and those to whom they report. These standards should provide details as to:

- the worker action or output that will be assessed;
- the criteria to be used for the assessment; and
- how performance will be measured.

Setting appropriate criteria that meet the requirements is a crucial component of the entire system and a key determinant of its success. Criteria are the measures of what a person has to do to be successful at performing his or her job, and may be obvious in certain jobs (for example the number of arrests and number of cases solved for policemen).

(Note that these criteria may not be appropriate if the strategic emphasis of the policeman's job is on community relations and involvement.)

Choosing the format and the sources of appraisal information

Decisions on the format of the appraisal instrument and the sources that should generate the ratings (that is, the direct supervisor, peers, subordinates, consultants, etc) must again be the outcome of thorough deliberation on many factors such as the overall objectives, potential advantages and disadvantages, organisation-specific circumstances, etc.

Preparing documentation

The relevant policy documents should form the framework for the processes and procedures that detail more finely who should be doing what and when in terms of planning and managing work performance. The actual performance appraisal forms are very important because they will form the basis for discussions as well as where we will be able to access relevant work performance-related information. It normally is quite important to develop user guides together with the policies and procedures manual for managers. Particularly important in this regard will be the guidelines in relation to the actual processes of assessing and discussing matters related to work performance.

Reviews of literature (Posthuma & Campion 2008: 48–49) on good practices in designing performance assessment systems suggest the following essential elements:

- The content of the performance appraisal should be based on job analysis or shown to be job related.
- Subject-matter experts such as current job incumbents should have input on factors to be evaluated.
- The appraisal should be specific rather than generic, and should be based on observable job behaviours rather than on traits.
- Appraisals need to be reliable and appropriate standardisation of administrative procedures and forms is required.

11.5.3 Introducing and 'operationalising' the system

Processes related to the implementation phase focus mainly on various training sessions and introductory exercises. The contents of such training may be determined by the level of involvement of users during the development phase, the complexity of the specific system and the existing competence in performance management of the supervisors.

Although familiarisation and rater training may take on many forms, ranging from mere information provision to 'dry-run' conferences and intensive workshops, a few basic aspects need to be covered to ensure its success. The following are some of the important components of effective rater training:

- a training format which allows for the active involvement of raters in the training process, for example modelling, role play, group discussions;
- thorough familiarisation with the measurement instrument and scales;
- developing rater consensus regarding the interpretation of performance standards and relative levels of behaviour effectiveness (for example how does 'superior' effort differ from 'good' effort?);
- encouraging the recording of specific examples of behaviour;
- allowing for experiential exercises and practice;
- providing raters with feedback regarding their own rating behaviour (for example comparison with expert ratings); and
- reinforcing desirable rater behaviour through periodic follow-up training.

11.5.4 Maintaining the system

The maintenance of an appraisal system entails activities such as:

- monitoring the consistent application of performance ratings;
- reviewing satisfaction levels of managerial as well as non-managerial staff who are using the system and finding out about what can be done to improve the system;
- devising and arranging training and development interventions indicated by review results;
- monitoring the internal and external environment for changing circumstances that may necessitate a review or adjustment of current practices; and
- auditing and evaluating the effectiveness of the system comprehensively from time to time.

11.6 TECHNIQUES FOR PERFORMANCE APPRAISAL

Performance-appraisal techniques may be categorised according to the type of criteria use, namely:

- trait-oriented methods (for example trait scales);
- behaviour-oriented methods (for example critical incidents, BARS); and
- results-oriented methods (for example MBO).

Alternatively, techniques may be classified according to the main purpose that the procedure serves, namely:

- comparative purposes (relative standards); and
- developmental purposes (absolute standards).

In keeping with our contention that the specific objectives of an appraisal system should determine the choice of format, the second classification approach will be used for distinguishing various appraisal methods.

11.6.1 Relative rating techniques

11.6.1.1 Ranking

Straight ranking entails simply the rank ordering of individuals, according to overall merit or according to other performance factors, from the best through to the worst performer.

Clearly this is a very basic evaluation procedure and it is suggested that its use should be limited to cases where:
- only small numbers of individuals are to be rated;
- only the 'better than' is important and not the 'how much better than';
- employees will not be compared across groups; and
- the evaluation is not aimed at feedback to employees.

11.6.1.2 Paired comparisons

This procedure requires the evaluator to compare each worker separately with each of the other workers. The eventual ranking of an individual is then determined by the number of times he or she was judged to be better than the other worker. The number of comparisons required may be calculated by the formula $\frac{N(N-1)}{2}$, where N refers to the number of individuals to be ranked. The more workers to be ranked, the more unwieldy the method becomes. Limitations are similar to those identified for ranking (see exhibit 11.3).

Exhibit 11.3: Example of paired comparisons

1 Employees to be rated: John, Sipho, Mary, Portia, Peter
2 Paired comparisons: indicate the better performer in each pair

John✓	Sipho
John✓	Mary
John✓	Portia
John✓	Peter
Sipho✓	Mary
Sipho✓	Portia
Sipho✓	Peter
Mary	Portia✓
Mary✓	Peter
Portia✓	Peter

Scoring:

Employee	Number of times chosen	Rank
John	4	1
Sipho	3	2
Mary	1	4
Portia	2	3
Peter	0	5

11.6.1.3 Forced distribution

When using this technique, the evaluator is required to assign certain portions of his or her workers to each of a number of specified categories on each performance factor. The forced distribution chosen can specify any percentage per category and need not necessarily comply with the requirements of a normal curve. Whilst this format controls rating errors such as leniency and central tendency, the forced distribution chosen may differ substantially from the performance characteristics of the ratees as a group (see figure 11.3)

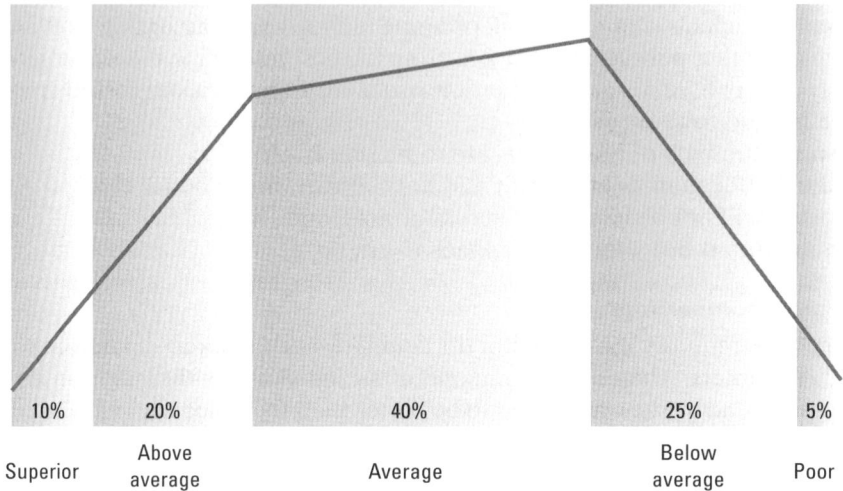

| 10% | 20% | 40% | 25% | 5% |
| Superior | Above average | Average | Below average | Poor |

Figure 11.3: Example of a forced distribution

11.6.2 Absolute rating techniques

11.6.2.1 Essay method

The rater is required to write a report on each employee, describing individual strengths and weaknesses. The format of the report may be left entirely to the discretion of the rater, or certain specific points of discussion may have to be addressed. This is generally a time-consuming method, the success of which is very much dependent on the writing skills of the raters. If done well, however, it may prove valuable as a feedback tool for the ratees.

11.6.2.2 Critical incidents

This technique requires the supervisor to record continuously actual job behaviours that are typical of success or failure as they occur. While this method focuses on behaviour rather than on traits as a basis of appraisal and thus has the potential for meaningful feedback, the recording of incidents is both time consuming and burdensome for supervisors. This obstacle may often lead supervisors to try to recall and document incidents only towards the end of the review period, thus confounding objectivity and opportunities for timely feedback.

11.6.2.3 Behavioural checklists

This format provides the rater with a list of descriptions of job-related behaviours which have to be marked if they are descriptive of the individual being rated. In a variant of this format, the summated ratings method, the behavioural statements are followed by a Likert-type scale of response categories, each of which is weighted, for example 'strongly agree' = 5 to 'strongly disagree' = 1. The weights of the checked response for each item are then summed and represent the overall performance score of the individual.

Although this format does not really lend itself to diagnostic feedback, it has the advantage of being behaviourally rather than trait based and has acceptable reliability and controls for some rating errors, for example the halo error.

EXHIBIT 11.4: Example of a portion of a summated rating scale*

Knowledge	Strongly agree	Agree	Neutral	Disagree	Strongly disagree
Makes effective use of developments in his or her field of specialisation					
Interprets user's requirements accurately					
Can explain specialist knowledge to non-specialists					
Obtains all relevant information before making decisions					
Keeps abreast of latest developments in his or her field					

*Adapted extract from a Nedbank format

11.6.2.4 Graphic rating scales

As this is a very popular format, many variations of graphic rating scales can be found. Basically, a scale for a specific trait or characteristic consists of a continuum between two poles on which the rater indicates to what degree the ratee possesses that characteristic. The variations on this basic format stem from:

- the dimensions on which individuals are to be rated;
- the degree to which the dimensions are defined; and
- the degree to which the points on the scale are defined.

The popularity of graphic rating scales is due to advantages such as the fact that they are easy to understand, they allow for comparisons across individuals because they are standardised, they are acceptable to users and they are less time consuming to develop and administer than some other formats.

11.6.2.5 Behaviourally anchored rating scales (BARS)

In essence, BARS are a variation of graphic rating scales with the difference that performance dimensions are defined in behavioural terms and the various levels of performance are anchored by examples of critical incidents. Behaviourally anchored rating scales are job specific and require a high level of participation from supervisors. The development of BARS is a complex process, the details of which are beyond the scope of this chapter. Only rudimentary details regarding the different steps in the construction of BARS are provided.

Steps in the development of BARS:

- behavioural statements/incidents describing effective, average and ineffective behaviour are gathered from job knowledgeable employees and supervisors;
- supervisors classify the statements in terms of performance dimensions (for example motivation, know-how) and reject those that are ambiguous;
- a different group of judges then retranslates each statement by rating it on a scale ranging from outstanding to poor performance; and

- specific statements are then chosen as anchors on the final scale, with the calculated average of the judges' ratings determining where on the scale the statement will feature.

Research indicates that these scales have the advantage of clarifying which behaviours represent good performance and which do not, they are job relevant, they reduce rating errors and they have a high level of user participation. On the other hand, the complex development procedure makes it a relatively time-consuming and expensive method. In addition, their job-relatedness does not allow them to be used across dissimilar jobs and, if job requirements should change, new BARS have to be constructed (Muchinsky et al 2002: 212; DeCenzo & Robbins 2007: 264).

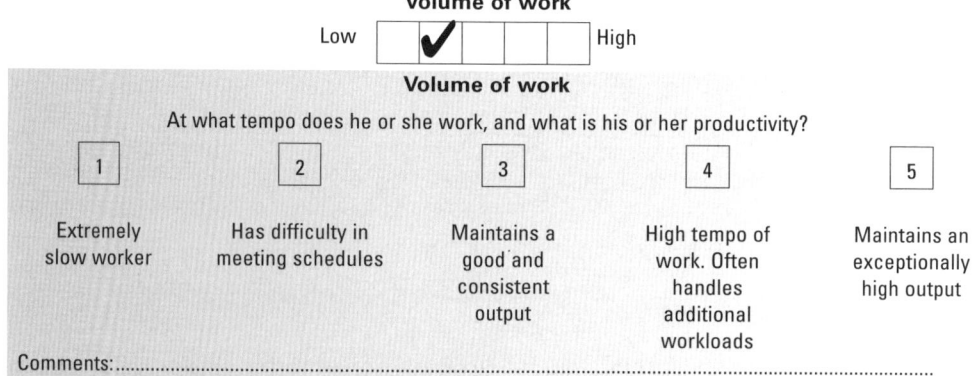

Figure 11.4a: Examples of graphic rating scales

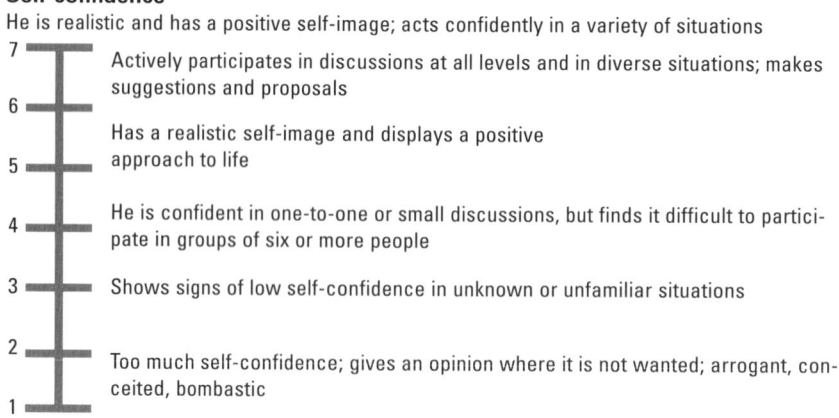

Figure 11.4b: Example of a behaviourally anchored rating scale
Source: Adapted from Spangenberg et al (1989: 23)

11.6.3 Other appraisal methods

There are other performance appraisal methods also. Two appraisal methods referred to in this section – management by objectives (MBO) and assessment centres – did not originate as appraisal techniques, although they may be used as such. Finally, the implications of the growing use of team-based work processes on performance management practices are explored briefly.

11.6.3.1 Management by objectives

Management by objectives (MBO) is a system of management that focuses on setting and integrating individual and organisational goals, but due to its process can also be used for evaluating performance. Harvey and Brown (2001: 345) describe MBO as a technique to identify organisational goals at all levels and to encourage participation in setting the standards for evaluating subordinates performance. Participation in the goal-setting process allows managers to control and monitor performance by measuring results against the objectives employees helped to set. This method typically entails:

- supervisors and employees mutually establishing and discussing specific goals and formulating action plans;
- supervisors aiding and coaching their employees to reach their set goals; and
- each supervisor and employee reviewing at a preset time the extent to which objectives have been attained.

As a results-based method of appraisal, MBO typically does not address the 'how' of performance and is therefore unable to appraise whether achievements are really the outcome of individual excellence or of external factors.

MBO has been around for the past 30 years and although its popularity has severely declined due to mixed results and unrealistic expectations (see, for example, Viedge 2004: 208), similar goal-setting programmes are still often found in stable industrial settings and where incentives are associated with goal achievement (Nelson & Quick 2002: 171–172). The elements of emphasis on mutual goal setting, opportunities for participation, periodic reviews and regular supervisor–employee interaction are valuable components that are applied in many contemporary performance management systems.

11.6.3.2 Assessment centres

An assessment centre is a procedure originally adopted to assess managerial potential. It is an assessment method that consists of a standardised evaluation of behaviour based on multiple raters and multiple measures such as in-basket exercises, paper-and-pencil ability tests, leaderless group discussions, simulations and personality questionnaires.

Strictly speaking, an assessment centre is designed to appraise individuals' current managerial ability, rather than their past performance. This future orientation would therefore make the method quite suitable for developmental purposes. This realisation has led to the evolution of assessment centre technology ranging from early selection orientation to the current developmental centres which focus on diagnosing development needs, making development recommendations and providing participants with comprehensive feedback.

In the South African context, assessment centres enjoy a relatively high level of popularity, and well-known companies that are using assessment centre technology include Clover, Frito-Lay, Liberty Life, SABC, Santam, Stellenbosch Farmers' Winery and Vodacom.

The application of the technology is monitored through an assessment centre study group in terms of professional guidelines adapted from international standards (Spangenberg 1991: 29–32), and already a substantial body of evidence has been amassed to confirm the value and utility of the technique (Kriek 1991: 34–37).

Despite its potential advantages, the assessment centre has fundamental shortcomings as a practical performance appraisal technique for all levels of employees.

Such limitations emanate from the inherently costly nature of the procedure, its overwhelming emphasis on managerial jobs and its exclusive future orientation.

11.6.3.3 Self-appraisal

Inclusion of self-appraisal in the formal performance management process has been found to be highly prevalent in South African companies (Grobler 2001). Using self-evaluations in performance feedback is reported to lead to more constructive evaluation interviews, less defensiveness during the appraisal process and an even higher level of commitment to organisational goals (Nelson & Quick 2002: 176).

Owing to limitations regarding low levels of agreement with supervisory evaluations and employees often rating themselves too leniently, the application of self-appraisal is found to be more appropriate for personal growth and developmental purposes (for example Newstrom & Davis 2002: 142; Robbins 2001: 488).

11.6.3.4 360-degree appraisals

Another approach that has gained increasing popularity is the so-called 360-degree performance appraisal technique. The format derives its name from the fact that appraisal feedback is provided from all directions, namely from the top (that is, the direct supervisor), the sides (that is, colleagues and co-workers), the bottom (that is, subordinates), and sometimes even from customers. Essentially this is therefore a multiple rater/multiple source approach to the assessment of an individual's work performance. While benchmarking data in the US suggests a high prevalence of 360-degree feedback use (for example 52% of ASTD Benchmarking Forum companies in 2001), South African reports indicate a still limited but growing implementation of multi-rater assessment systems (for example Theron 2000; Grobler 2001).

The essence of the process revolves around gathering and processing performance assessments on individual employees involving persons such as customers (both internal and external to the organisation), suppliers, peers and team members, superiors and subordinates, as well as the person assessed. The data collection process normally includes aspects such as formal and structured interviews as well as informal discussions, surveys and observations. The assessment information is used as feedback to the employee, and serves as important inputs for career and management and training development. Because of the use of multiple sources, a broader perspective can be developed of an individual's strengths and weaknesses. This enhances self-insight in the process of developing to one's full potential.

This approach fits more comfortably with the latest trends in leadership thinking (see chapter 10) and with strategies emphasising aspects such as empowerment, self-responsibility and teamwork. Using multiple data sources can also go a long way in helping to make performance appraisal fairer, simply because elements of subjectivity are lessened, and a more balanced view of a person's actual work performance can be created. This can also lead to more accurate training-needs analyses and to drafting more realistic personal development plans (PDPs). It also provides a rich source on which to base one-to-one developmental processes such as mentoring and coaching. It furthermore serves the purpose of opening up communication and information flows in the organisation, and in this way it supports more transparent and democratic management. Because it involves customers, it is also a valuable means of demonstrating to the customers that the organisation is really customer focused. Despite the good face validity of 360-degree programmes, rigorous research of their effectiveness has not kept pace with the practice of implementation of these programmes (Ivancevich & Matteson 2002: 192). Generally, however, research seems to indicate that 360-degree formats do provide positive results regarding more accurate feedback, reduced subjectivity in evaluations, empowering employees and developing leadership in an organisation (DeCenzo & Robbins 2007: 274).

A good example in South Africa is found at the Liberty Group, which operates an e-HR gateway system that includes an e-performance component, allowing individuals to develop their own job profiles from a series of approved generic profiles and to set up an online automated 360-degree performance feedback system.

In the broader African context, the implementation of 360-degree formats present specific challenges regarding the upward rating process, since generally employees rarely rate their managers in African organisations (Beugré 2004: 346). In general it seems as though performance appraisals pose some challenges in some other countries in Africa (see the box below).

Elsewhere in Africa

Kenya

Performance evaluation in Kenyan organisations is not a uniform process, and appraisals differ in aims and procedures. The exercise is complicated by cultural and social issues, and concerns about job security. Ethnicity and kinship affiliation play a role in favourable appraisals and worker selection for redundancies, which places politics and good interpersonal relationships above organisational goal-oriented performance.

High unemployment and job insecurity have further politicised performance appraisal, and while 'best practices' from overseas headquarters are brought in by multinational companies, the socio-cultural and economic contexts are such that many managers are under pressure to give favours while at the same time projecting an image of objectivity.

Source: Extracted and adapted from Kamoche, Nyambegera & Mulinge (2004: 92)

Libya

Performance appraisal problems in Libya are common to all enterprises in general, and industrial enterprises in particular. Since Libyan organisations profess the Islamic faith, performance appraisals focus primarily on personal characteristics rather than on job performance. Cultural factors render subordinate and peer ratings uncommon, and it is culturally acceptable for people in positions of power to treat subordinates kindly as if they are their brothers and sisters. Employees prefer not to report anything negative about their peers, since it would affect their future within the organisation.

Source: Extracted and adapted from Almhdie & Nyambegera (2004: 177)

11.6.3.5 Performance management and teams

As explained in chapter 5, a particular trend in the 1990s that has had a major influence on jobs has been the introduction of teams in the workplace. Some commentators ascribe an almost fad-like status to this movement (for example Ancona et al 1999), and best practices benchmarking studies in the South African context appear to indicate that team-based structuring is set to remain a key element of the 'organisation of the future' (for example Veldsman 1999).

EXHIBIT 11.5: Best practices for multi-rater 360-degree appraisals

Reviews of literature on and practices of 360-degree appraisal systems indicate the following recommended best practices:

- appraisal instruments must be reliable and validated;
- the purpose and process of the multi-rater feedback must be clear and well communicated;
- appraisal feedback should be used for developmental rather than evaluative purposes;
- assessing readiness and training of all parties involved is crucial for successful implementation;
- commitment by top management to the practice is essential;
- participation of the raters should be voluntary;
- interdependencies and connections within groups and across boundaries must be acknowledged in evaluating individual contributions;
- only observable aspects of a ratee's job must be focused on;
- employees should be helped to interpret and react to ratings, perhaps even with the help of a personal coach;
- an automated, computerised system is necessary for the magnitude of questionnaire processing, collating and scoring workloads; and
- the system should be pilot tested in one part of the organisation.

Sources: Atwater & Waldman (1999); Peiperl (2001); and Cascio (2006)

Common purpose and approach and mutual accountability are typical elements distinguishing team orientations from traditional individually oriented effectiveness criteria. Naturally, such a shift in desired new outputs and behaviours needs to be appropriately reflected in the design of performance evaluation and reward systems. Robbins (2001: 269–271) highlights the problem of individual resistance in this process, since an employee's success is no longer defined in terms of individual performance. Good performance as a team member may rather include aspects such as the ability to communicate openly and honestly, the ability to confront differences and resolve conflicts, the capacity to sublimate personal goals for the good of the team, and emphasising cooperation rather than competition. Härtel et al (2007: 337) point out that performance in teams is often dependent on aspects such as a shared purpose, group norms, member roles, communication, group cohesion and available resources. Since well-functioning teams are expected to meet both the social and task needs of the group in the accomplishment of a goal, it is important that such needs be linked to the performance dimension to be measured and rewarded.

Performance dimensions to be reflected in appraisal instruments focused on teams may therefore be deduced from the conceptualisation of team effectiveness as proposed by Sundstrom and McIntyre (in Ancona et al 1999: M-37). According to them, team effectiveness comprises four components:

- performance – how well team members produce output, measured in terms of quality, quantity, timeliness, efficiency and innovation;
- member satisfaction – how well team members create a positive experience through commitment, trust and meeting individual needs;
- team learning – how well team members acquire new skills, perspectives and behaviours as needed by changing circumstances; and
- outsider satisfaction – how well team members meet the needs of outside stakeholders such as suppliers and customers.

The appropriate structuring of rewards for team-based work is discussed in chapter 16.

11.6.3.6 Balanced scorecard format

The balanced scorecard was conceptualised by Robert Kaplan and David Norton of Harvard University as a management system that would track organisational performance, not only from the traditional reliance on short-term financial measures, but would also combine hard and soft measures together with short- and long-term ones. The focus is not purely on management accountancy bottom-line measures, but incorporates performance measures from four balanced perspectives, that is, financial, customer, internal business processes, and employee learning and growth (see exhibit 11.6).

Designing the individualised balanced scorecard for an organisation and deciding what metrics to use starts off with a clarification of the organisation's strategy by top management and linking it to the vision and mission. The central question of each of the four quadrants would need to be examined and in response to these questions, critical objectives are set and appropriate measures are determined. For each measure, targets are then set and initiatives are devised that will result in their achievement. Once this process of designing the organisation's balanced scorecard is completed, the measures need to be cascaded down to departmental level. Using the strategy that has been articulated, the individual departments would need to discuss their respective purpose and how they contribute to the envisaged overall results. Their appropriate key measures that are aligned to the strategy are then determined. This ensures that departments are empowered to design measures themselves, rather then being dictated to by a top-down approach. Departmental performance and initiatives are thus ideally aligned to the strategic intent of the organisation, and once all their measures are in place, the next step of developing individual scorecards by means of performance contracts can follow (see exhibit 11.7 for an example of a part of a individual performance contract).

Viedge (2004: 215) rightfully points out, however, that the mere fact of having in place a well-constructed and strategically aligned performance contract for each

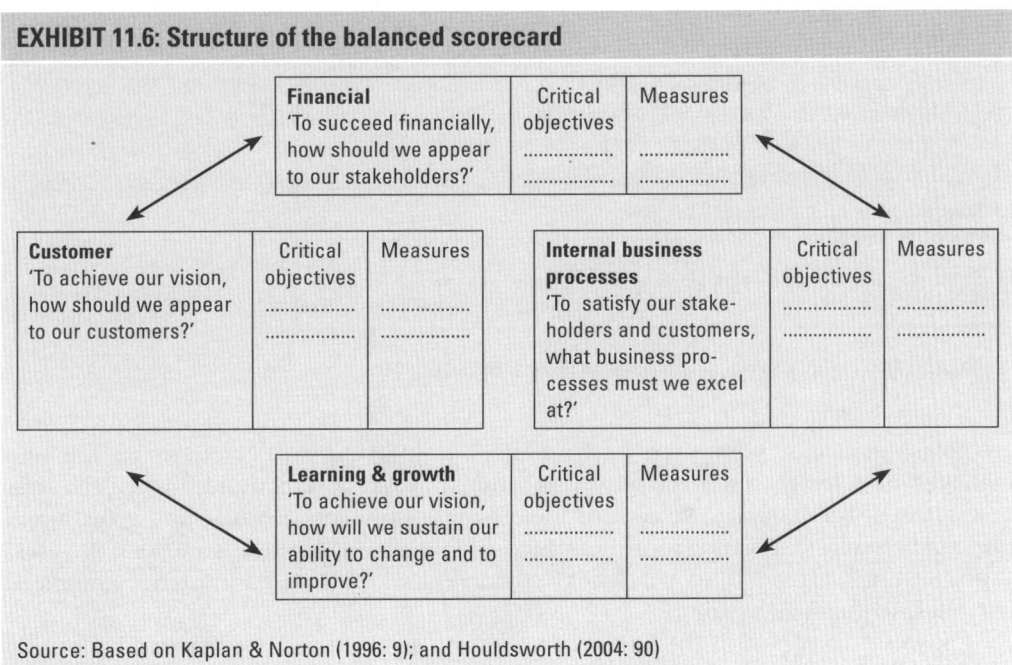

EXHIBIT 11.6: Structure of the balanced scorecard

Financial
'To succeed financially, how should we appear to our stakeholders?' — Critical objectives / Measures

Customer
'To achieve our vision, how should we appear to our customers?' — Critical objectives / Measures

Internal business processes
'To satisfy our stakeholders and customers, what business processes must we excel at?' — Critical objectives / Measures

Learning & growth
'To achieve our vision, how will we sustain our ability to change and to improve?' — Critical objectives / Measures

Source: Based on Kaplan & Norton (1996: 9); and Houldsworth (2004: 90)

PERFORMANCE AGREEMENT				A
REVIEW PERIOD: FROM: July 2007			**TO:** June 2008	
NAME OF JOB HOLDER: xxxxx			**JOB TITLE:** Head of internal audit	

OUTPUT	Internal audit balanced scorecard	**CUSTOMER/S**	CEO	**RATING OF 1, 2, 3 OR 4**
WEIGHT %	5%	**DUE DATE/S**	Annual	

STANDARD OF DELIVERY REQUIRED, PERFORMANCE INDICATORS AND MEASUREMENT:	**REASON FOR RATING:**
Contribute to all other internal audit BSC items which fall under the responsibility of the incumbent. Measurement: Based on quarterly BSC reviews 1 = less than 69% of number of items achieved 2 = 70% to less than 79,9% of number of items achieved 3 = 80% to less than 92,49% of number of items achieved 4 = 92,5% and more of number of items achieved	

OUTPUT	Personal development	**CUSTOMER/S**	CEO	**RATING OF 1, 2, 3 OR 4**
WEIGHT %	5%	**DUE DATE/S**	Annual	

STANDARD OF DELIVERY REQUIRED, PERFORMANCE INDICATORS AND MEASUREMENT:	**REASON FOR RATING:**
Participation in the following training activities: 1 IIA Conference and/or relevant audit training course 2 Annual Forensic Conference and/or relevant forensic training course (ACFE) **Measurement:** Assessment by CEO Successful conference participation and/or completion of training courses – as well as application of the new knowledge in the job	

Source: Extract reprinted by kind permission of Munich Re (SA) (2007)

employee does not guarantee performance. Employees still need to be led and managed effectively to deliver on the specific strategy. Interaction between the four quadrants of the balanced scorecard means that employee learning and growth and the competence that flows from them feeds into the organisation's internal business processes, which feeds into customer satisfaction which in turn influences financial bottom-line financial results.

The intuitive appeal of the balanced scorecard has ensured a widespread adoption of the model also in South Africa. Some practitioners do, however, report that cascading down to the individual level is often not executed effectively, and caution that extensive training is needed to ensure that line managers and employees fully understand what is needed to make the balanced scorecard work (Human Capital Management 2006: 133).

11.7 THE APPRAISAL INTERVIEW

Although a continuous or at least regular interaction process is advocated by the performance management process, the formal appraisal interview at the end of a review period remains a prominent feature of most performance-appraisal systems. Irrespective of the appraisal techniques or methods used, appraisal results need to be communicated to employees in a constructive way in order to achieve the aims of providing feedback, motivating and counselling the individuals, and also rectifying poor performance.

Despite the fact that the interviews are the responsibility of line management, it will most probably be the HR practitioner's job to ensure the effectiveness of this process by training supervisors how to plan and conduct appraisal interviews properly.

Three types of appraisal interview are usually distinguished: tell and sell, tell and listen, and problem solving.

- *Tell and sell approach*: The supervisor acts as judge and jury, and needs to persuade the ratee to change his or her behaviour in a prescribed way.
- *Tell and listen approach:* During the first part of the interview, the employee's strong and weak areas of performance are addressed; during the second part the focus falls on the employee's feelings about the appraisal.
- *Problem-solving approach:* The supervisor acts as helper and facilitator, and discusses the problems, needs, innovations and dissatisfactions, etc that the employee may have experienced since the last performance interview. The main focus is on growth and development.

Job- and employee-specific factors may exert a moderating influence on the effectiveness of the interview process, thus implying that there cannot be one single 'best approach' for conducting all appraisal interviews. The supervisor should be knowledgeable about such variables and be trained in the necessary skills for a flexible and situational approach towards appraisal interviews.

It should also be noted that the skills and requirements for effective appraisal interviews correspond with those applicable to other types of interview, and general aspects such as pre-interview preparations, active listening, questioning and feedback techniques should therefore not be excluded from rater training programmes.

In the South African context, with its still-characteristic racial imbalance in managerial positions, it may also be prudent to focus training efforts on intercultural aspects of communication and interaction.

11.8 PERFORMANCE ISSUES REGARDING NON-EMPLOYEE WORK

When we decide to rather establish other arrangements to get some of the work of the organisation done, it is also very important to make sure that the work that gets done in this way is executed as well as possible. If we have engaged the services of a temporary employment services provider (labour broker firm) it will be in the interests of us as the client organisation as well as the vendor that we build a longer-term relationship. This can only be the case if the labour broker firm or vendor delivers in terms of the agreement (as we have said in chapter 8 – these can be referred to as service level agreements or SLAs). The key thing is again the relationship between the organisations.

If there are any performance issues surfacing it will be very important to provide clear and honest feedback timely. We must make sure that we have contact with the appropriate senior-level managers of the vendor. It usually is important for both organisations to appoint contract managers who can serve as the first points of contact and communication. The idea must be to have ongoing open communication as the time goes by into the contract period. It might also be a good idea to build into the agreements that we will have periodic sessions to discuss and assess performance in terms of what had been agreed upon. We must remember that any such a relationship can almost be thought of as some kind of a partnership arrangement, because the vendor is helping the client organisation to be successful, and if that happens, hopefully the benefits will be mutual. There will thus be mutual interests in making a success of the arrangement.

Just like with managing the performance of our staff, we should keep in mind that such things as praise in cases when we are really happy with the work-related services provided by the vendor is good practice. We may even have built into the agreement some targets regarding performance standards. If these are exceeded, we must acknowledge that and there might even perhaps be some financial incentives linked to that. On the other hand, it may also happen that the arrangements fail. For such circumstances we will have to act in accordance to whatever exit clauses we may have included in the agreement/contract between us and the service provider. Should we encounter such situations, we must obviously also be ready in that we must have some form of back-up plan (such as how to do the work ourselves in-house again, or perhaps a second-choice service provider that we might have on hold). Importantly, if we do encounter such failing arrangements we must do some review of what went wrong and why, and how we can learn from that to prevent future reoccurrence.

11.9 CONCLUSION

Managing the work performance of staff is crucial to achieve organisational goals. It is equally important for employees because that is part and parcel of the process of enhancing their own capabilities to deliver better work results, add more value and develop their own careers. If line managers are held responsible for strategy execution and to achieve objectives as cascaded down from the organisation's mission, strategy and business plans, the alignment of the work performance objectives and outcomes of their staff is essential. This is the reason why most organisations insist on a formal and systematic process whereby work performance can be assessed, managed and enhanced.

While in the South African context this seems to be realised pretty well, especially in larger organisations, this is not always the case in other African countries, it seems. In our country, the value of performance management in improving both individual and organisational performance is recognised (Whitford & Coetsee 2006), with a 2006 'best company to work for' benchmark study reporting that, on average, our companies conduct 2,4 performance reviews, that is, individual feedback sessions per employee, annually.

In this chapter we have thus shown why performance management is so important, and we have covered aspects like performance appraisals and concomitant interviews, suggestions for designing and implementing these systems, some common challenges or problems associated with performance appraisals, as well as various performance appraisal techniques and methods. While specialist HR practitioners are instrumental in designing and rolling out these systems, line managers are the crucial link, because they actually implement and use the system. This is also why the development of these systems should be a process that fully involves them as the ultimate users thereof. Getting performance management right is important for the organisation as well as the employee, because ultimately it is linked directly with people's careers. In the next chapter we specifically turn to career management.

SUSTAINABILITY CONNECTION?

Superior work performance is central to high-performance organisations and to becoming/remaining competitive. Without being competitive, the survival of any organisation is threatened. If we cannot, on the whole, perform well as an organisation, we will cease to exist. If people do not excel in terms of their own work performance, our organisations therefore will not perform adequately to survive. If our organisations fail to survive, all will suffer – customers, employees, suppliers, owners, and all other stakeholders. That clearly will not be in the interests of developing a sustainable country or continent.

SELF-EVALUATION QUESTIONS

1 Explain the nature (definition), role and value of performance appraisal in HRM.
2 What is the difference between performance appraisal and performance management?
3 'There are certain fundamental requirements underlying successful performance appraisal systems.' Discuss this statement.
4 What are some of the common problems related to designing performance appraisal systems?
5 Explain the problems of 'rating errors/judgemental biases' within the context of performance appraisal. How can these be overcome?
6 Write an essay detailing the process of developing, implementing and maintaining a successful performance appraisal and management system.
7 Discuss the merits and problems of self-appraisal and multi-rater appraisal in the performance management process.
8 Can MBO still contribute to contemporary performance management? Motivate your answer.
9 What guidelines can you provide regarding the successful conduct of a performance appraisal interview?
10 Explain how the balanced scorecard concept of organisational performance measurement can be applied to individual performance appraisal.

12 MANAGING AND DEVELOPING CAREERS

LEARNING OUTCOMES

After studying this chapter, you should be able to:

- define various career related concepts and explain how change impacts on careers;
- explain the career choice theories of Holland and Super;
- explain two career management models;
- define the concept 'career anchor', apply this to yourself and explain the different anchors and how these relate to you and your possible career plans;
- describe and debate various other important career-related issues;
- explain different ways in which organisations can provide career development support to employees; and
- write an essay about mentoring and the roles of mentors and mentees.

12.1 INTRODUCTION

As we engage with our staff to help enhance their work performance, we naturally should also discuss and consider their longer-term career intentions and prospects, and how to develop them accordingly. The whole idea is to unlock and develop the full potential of people if our approach is to empower. Managing the performance of employees and helping them manage their own careers thus go hand in hand. There are, however, some longer-term trends and dynamics that are having implications for how we go about developing the careers of people, including our own. We take a brief look at some of these before we clarify some concepts and explore some theories and issues pertaining to career choice. The rest of the chapter is then devoted mainly to covering a range of career-related issues such as career anchors, patterns and movements. We end off the chapter with a brief overview of some methods that the management of organisations can use to help with the career development of employees. While the focus of this chapter is thus specifically on employees, we must stress again that increasingly, due to all sorts of changes happening in labour markets and organisations, career development is the primary responsibility of each person. That is not to say, though, that as managers we should not be supportive of helping employees with this.

12.2 A CHANGING WORLD OF WORK MEANS CHANGING CAREER DYNAMICS

As we have stressed a number of times, organisations across the world are experiencing some serious change. We find that they are changing in terms of design and structure, workforce composition and size, and in technological makeup. The global economy and technological revolution bring new international competition, which imposes new demands on organisations. Organisations are under pressure to do more with less and to be more flexible – and organisations respond by, among other things, flattening structures, organising around processes rather than functions, using work teams, putting less emphasis on 'command and control' and narrowly defined jobs, and by reconfiguring themselves in network configurations together with other organisations. At the same time we are living in an era when there can be people from four or even five generations working side by side, who often do not share the same kinds of worldviews or have the same interests or motivations, including why they work and what they would like to get out of it.

All of these forces and changes pose wide-ranging challenges for careers and how we manage them. Schreuder and Coetzee (2006: 35–37) provide a succinct view on the implications of this changing environment for people's careers and how these are managed (see exhibit 12.1).

EXHIBIT 12.1: Careers in changing times

The realities of a changing world, and a changing world of organisations and work, mean that the traditional working relationship where the employee offered loyalty, conformity and commitment to the organisation in return for employment security and promotional prospects is making way for something different: a working relationship that emphasises individual responsibility and a broader range of skills, with flexibility being key. The characteristics of the contemporary working relationship include, for example, less certainty and security, self-responsibility for career development, a flexible employment and work scenario, less trust in employment relationships, and reward for performance.

The potential career implications are summarised in the table below.

Changing organisations and career implications for careers in the 21st century, as per Schreuder and Coetzee (2006: 36–37)

Protean career	A career shaped and managed by the individual. It consists of all the person's varied experiences in education, training and work in several organisations, and changes in occupational field, and is characterised by a high degree of mobility, self-reliance and internal career thinking
Boundaryless career	A career characterised by flexibility, mobility, and movement between different global-organisational contexts
Composite career	Having more than one working role or holding more than one form of employment

>>

Entrepreneurial career	Choosing self-employment as a career option, which could include establishing and managing one's own business
Career progress and success	Career progress refers to individuals' experiences of career growth, which may include moving upward, increasing competence and expertise, and gaining broader experience across multidirectional career movements Career success refers to the objective and subjective (psychological) sense of achievement individuals experience regarding their careers
Continuous learning	The process by which one acquires knowledge, skills and abilities throughout one's career in reaction to, and in anticipation of, changing performance criteria
Career resilience	The ability to adapt to changing circumstances by welcoming job and organisational changes, looking forward to working with new and different people, having self-confidence and being willing to take risks
New knowledge and skills required	A more complex and differentiated organisation results in the employment of more specialists and knowledge workers
New employment relationships	Changes in the workplace are characterised by a change in employment relationships, which includes long- and short-term insiders, and long- and short-term outsiders
Employability	A person's value in terms of future employment opportunities, which is determined by the accumulation of knowledge, skills, experience, and reputation, which can be invested in new employment opportunities as they arise
Changing work and family values	The multicultural, multigenerational workforce and shift to non-traditional family structures gives rise to diverse employee needs
The psychological contract	The mutual expectations and satisfaction of needs arising from the relationship between individual employees and their organisations. The contemporary psychological contract is a partnership relationship characterised by conditional attachment arrangements

In light of these developments and changes, each individual person is expected to take control of and actively manage his or her own career. The organisation typically plays more of a supportive role in this largely self-managed process.

12.3 SOME CAREER RELATED CONCEPTS

An indication of the changes currently taking place in organisations is that, according to Hall and Mervis (1995), careers should become more protean. The term *protean* is taken from the name of the Greek god Proteus, who could change shape at will (Hall & Mervis 1995: 322). We now look at some relevant concepts.

- A *career* can be defined as any sequence of employment and related work experiences, including upward and lateral movements and as such it can be multidirectional, cut across various organisations and span multiple roles in one's work life.
- *Career development* can be defined as an "ongoing process by which individuals progress through a series of stages, each of which is characterised by a relatively unique set of issues, themes or tasks" (Greenhaus, Callanan & Godshalk 2000: 13).
- *Career exploration* is when people collect and analyse information regarding career-related issues, becoming more aware of how they might fit into the world of work (Greenhaus et al 2000).
- *Career planning* can be described as a process by which people engage in career exploration, obtaining information and becoming knowledgeable about themselves (for example their interests, preferences, abilities, aptitudes, personalities, etc) and about the world of work and employment, and then making active plans on how to achieve a proper match (adapted from Schreuder & Theron 2001: 21).
- *Career paths* are "objective descriptions of sequential work experiences" (Schreuder & Coetzee 2006: 59) and how these develop or evolve over time.
- *Career management* entails a number of things: it is an ongoing process whereby people gain self-insight in relation to the world of work and employment; they plan accordingly about matching their own interests, talents, values, preferences and so on with alternative work-roles like jobs and occupations; they consider alternatives to implement their career development plans (such as joining organisations or starting a business); they take charge of executing the paths chosen and developing their careers; they keep actively monitoring and adjusting what they do and how their career paths unfold as they obtain feedback; and so they try to make the most of their lives through meaningful work and careers.

12.4 CAREER CHOICE

Career choice "involves the individual's career preferences, orientations and decisions, and can be studied in terms of development over the life span and in terms of the match between individual characteristics and aspects of work" (Muchinsky et al 2005: 297), and it happens in the context of and is influenced by, for example, socio-economic conditions and factors such as family and education (Schreuder & Theron 2001: 37).

Over the last 50 years, many different theories of career choice have been formulated to explain how individuals choose careers. These can be divided into the so-called content theories, which describe career choice in terms of specific factors, such as individual characteristics or the psychological phenomena that are involved in choice, and the so-called process theories, which describe career choice as a dynamic process that evolves over stages of development (Schreuder & Theron 2001). Career choice is now described in terms of a process theory (Super) and a content theory (Holland).

12.4.1 Super's theory

According to Super, career choice refers to a whole series of related decisions which are made during a development process covering five life stages from childhood to old age. The following career stages are identified (Super 1992).

1 *Growth* (from birth until the beginning of puberty, from about 0 to 14 years)
Although during childhood careers have not yet become a relevant factor, it is now generally believed that the instinct of curiosity makes children explore their environment, all the while gathering information, particularly through contact with adults whom they adopt as role models. During this time, they ought to develop certain concepts of their future roles as adults, their autonomy, self-esteem, a perspective on the future and a feeling of being in charge of their lives. Once they have developed interests through fantasy, experience and feedback, they are able to plan for the future. As they gradually become aware of the opportunities that life offers them, their interests become more closely linked to reality.

2 *Exploration* (adolescence, from about 14 to 25 years)
While the only type of systematic exploration during this stage is provided by schools and other organisations, an adolescent's social exploration is stimulated by his or her parents and/or peer group. This may lead to the first tentative attempts at career exploration, which later become more focused. If, however, an adult has set an adolescent career goal, his or her career exploration may be too focused, which may lead to unhappiness and frustration later in life.

3 *Establishment* (early adulthood, from about 25 to 45 years)
As early adulthood is reached, some individuals stabilise as far as their career exploration is concerned, while others continue to change careers, their field of activity and their level of employment throughout their lives. It was found, however, that children of well-educated parents tend to be well educated themselves and to be employed at higher levels than the children of those with a low level of education. Young adults also tend to pass through a stage of trying out various careers in their late 20s, followed by stabilisation in their 30s and early 40s. This is in turn followed by a period of consolidation and advancement, without which the individual usually becomes frustrated, causing him or her either to stagnate in a career or to change careers.

4 *Maintenance* (middle age, from about 45 to 65 years)
Those adults who had previously stabilised in a career now attempt to maintain their position in the workplace in the face of competition from younger people, whose more up-to-date training may pose a threat to the career advancement of their older counterparts. Those who fail to advance tend to stagnate and become disillusioned. They now avoid opportunities to learn new skills and develop a passive approach to their work instead of actively acquiring and applying new knowledge. The more motivated keep up to date in their career fields, while the innovators are constantly exploring new avenues.

5 *Decline* (old age, from about 65 years onwards)
As people age, they often grow to resent their physical and mental decline and the implications that this has for their future. In fact, the process of decline already begins around the age of 25. This is particularly apparent in physically-oriented careers, such as in sports. As older people become aware of their declining powers, they tend to slow down, sometimes disengaging themselves from some areas of life. Others continue to work long past retirement age. Indeed, for many people, retirement is a negative experience, while for some it means a wealth of new opportunities, a feeling of being wanted and the excitement of returning to the explorative stage.

12.4.2 Holland's theory

One of the most widely used approaches to guide career choices is the theory of John L Holland. According to Holland (1985), personality (including values, driving forces and needs) is an important determinant of career choice. Holland (1985) says that the choice of career is, in fact, an expression of personality. He states that there is an interaction between personality and the environment, so that individuals are drawn towards environments which correlate with their personal orientation. Holland found it necessary to categorise people according to their personality types, and to associate these personality types with specific environmental models. He identified six basic personality types and, according to him, each person shows a degree of similarity to one of these types. The greater the degree of similarity, the more an individual will exhibit behaviour patterns typical of a certain personality type. With regard to the environmental models, he distinguishes between six similar types, and by integrating the individual and the environment, conclusions can be made regarding career choice, career stability, career performance, personal capabilities and social behaviour. Holland (1973) based his theory on four primary points of departure:

- In our culture, most people can be categorised as one of six types – realistic, investigative, social, conventional, enterprising and artistic. Each type is established through a unique interaction between various socio-cultural, personal and physical environmental factors. Each individual belongs primarily to one of these personality types, but may also exhibit characteristics of the other types. In this way a profile is derived which could indicate that individual's personality pattern.
- There are six similar environmental types: realistic, investigative, social, conventional, enterprising and artistic. In each environment there are individuals of similar personality types. Each environment also has certain limitations, and individuals of the same personality type group together according to the same environmental models.
- People seek out environments which will allow them to practise their capabilities and abilities, to express their attitudes and values, and to accept problems and roles. This pursuit takes place in various ways, and has the result that a realistic person will, for example, find the biggest potential for self-expression in a realistic environment, and the social person in a social environment.
- A person's behaviour is determined by the interaction between a personality and an environment. Being aware of an individual's personality pattern and the type of environment he or she prefers could facilitate a prediction with regard to career choice, career stability and career performance, as well as educational and social behaviour.

12.4.2.1 Personality types

Holland (1973: 14–17) describes the characteristics of the personality types as follows.

- The preferences of the *realistic personality type* include the clear and orderly manipulation of aspects such as tools, machinery and animals, through which, among others, mechanical, electrical, technical and manual skills could be acquired. This personality type prefers realistic careers, such as those of a craftsman, a farmer, and so forth, and avoids socially-oriented careers such as barman, social worker, etc. This person values concrete things such as money, and personal characteristics such as status and power.
- The *investigative personality type* develops a preference for the observation and creative investigation of physical, biological and cultural phenomena, with the aim of understanding and controlling these phenomena. This personality type

prefers investigative careers in fields such as economics, engineering, psychology, veterinary science, computer programming, tool making, and so forth, and avoids situations of an enterprising nature. This person regards him- or herself as learned and has a high regard for scientific knowledge.

■ The *social personality type* develops a pattern of behaviour preferences which includes the manipulation of people by means of activities such as training and assistance. This type of person usually prefers socially oriented careers, such as social work, teaching, and so forth, and avoids realistic careers, such as mechanical engineering, plumbing, etc. Such people regard themselves as being well equipped to help other people, and to understand and educate them, and they also place a high priority on social and ethical matters.

■ The *conventional personality type* displays a pattern of preference for orderly, systematic jobs, such as keeping records, filing, and so forth, through which clerical and accountancy skills, for example, are acquired. This type of person prefers conventional careers such as record keeping and typing, and avoids careers in the arts such as photography, music, etc. Such individuals see themselves as conforming and orderly, and as having clerical and numerical skills, and have a high regard for business and economic achievements.

■ The *enterprising personality type* develops a pattern of preference for activities which entail the manipulation of people in the pursuit of organisational objectives or economic advantages, through which leadership and interpersonal and persuasive skills are acquired. This type of person prefers careers and situations which demand an enterprising nature, such as those of the banker, estate agent, and so forth, and avoids careers requiring analytical skills such as those of an economist, an actuary, etc. Such personality types regard themselves as aggressive, popular, full of self-confidence and blessed with leadership and communicative skills, and have a high regard for economic achievements.

■ The *artistic personality type* develops a pattern of preference for free, unsystematic activities which involve the manipulation of human, physical and verbal material, and the acquisition of skills in the fields of language, art, music, drama and writing. This type of person prefers a career in the arts such as that of a language teacher, dramatist, etc, and avoids conventional activities such as typing, accountancy, and so forth. Such individuals regard themselves as creative, non-conforming, independent, organised and blessed with artistic and verbal skills such as writing, communicating, acting and having a high regard for the aesthetic.

12.4.2.2 Environmental types

Holland (1973: 29–33) describes the characteristics of the six corresponding environmental types as follows:

■ The *realistic environment* is characterised by the domination of environmental demands and opportunities, involving the orderly and systematic use of tools, machinery and animals, and is also marked by a population consisting mainly of realistic personality types.

■ The *investigative environment* has dominant characteristics such as the observation and symbolical, systematic and creative investigation of physical, biological or cultural phenomena.

■ The *social environment* is distinguished by a population consisting mainly of social personality types.

- The *conventional environment* is characterised by the dominance of environmental demands and opportunities involving the orderly and systematic manipulation of data, such as record keeping, filing, reproducing documents, compiling data according to a prescribed plan, and working with business machines and data processors. This environment is dominated mainly by conventional personality types.
- The *enterprising environment* is characterised by demands and opportunities from the environment regarding the manipulation of other persons in order to achieve personal and/or organisational goals, and is also marked by the presence of especially enterprising personality types.
- The *artistic environment* is dominated by demands and opportunities which include ambiguous, free and unsystematic activities and skills for the creation of art and art products, and consists mainly of a population of artistic personality types.

When an individual is faced with a career choice, his or her characteristics are compared with the above-mentioned types, with the aim of determining with which type he or she displays the most similarities. A person's personality type is the primary determinant of career choice in that an enterprising type would thus most probably select an enterprising career. The first and second sub-personality types will determine the individual's second and third choices. The vocational guidance tutor who works according to this approach will concentrate on determining the individual's personality style and on the selection of a suitable career environment.

12.4.3 Environmental influences on career choice

Thus far we have only discussed individual differences which influence career choice. There are, however, also a number of environmental influences which play a role in career choice. These are described as non-psychological factors (Crites 1969: 79).

The family undoubtedly plays an important role in career choice, as even at an early age children identify with their parents and often prefer the careers which their parents hold in high esteem. It is often believed that the family, through its economic interests, affiliations and values, determine the careers of family members. Hall (1976: 22) asserts that the background and attitudes of the parents have a greater influence than those of friends, teachers and other influential people in society.

According to Crites (1969: 88), the school, second to the family, exerts the biggest influence on career choice.

Sometimes individuals find themselves in a career which they did not purposefully pursue, but are appointed in a position due to coincidence, or unplanned and unforeseeable circumstances. These are normally referred to as the 'chance factors' which influence a person's career choice.

The role of these chance factors can often be underestimated – especially in the context of some countries in Africa. Various researchers have found that issues pertaining to aspects such as nepotism, tribalism and even bribery and corruption can play a key role in how people can, for instance, get jobs and promotion opportunities in organisations in Nigeria, for example (Anakwe 2002; Beugré 2002; Okpara & Wynn 2008). Naturally these sorts of things have real implications, not only for career choice, but also for how individuals may have choice in developing their careers (see also section 12.6.5, and specifically the *Elsewhere in Africa* box in that section).

12.5 TWO MODELS OF CAREER MANAGEMENT[1]

Schreuder and Coetzee (2006: 67–69) differentiate between traditional and more modern career management models. The former is said to have emphasised the 'plan-and-implement' aspects related to career management (Ibarra 2003). It reflects "career management as a linear process in which dissatisfaction with the status quo leads to setting a goal, from which flows an implementation plan" (Schreuder & Coetzee 2006: 67). It is thus basically viewed as a step-by-step process planned, organised and executed rationally and sequentially. In this traditional context we can now look at various steps in career management according to Greenhaus et al (2000).

Career exploration (*step one*) is the collection and analysis of information to enable individuals to become aware of themselves (values, interests, talents) and their environment (occupations, jobs, organisations). This information will create an *awareness of self and of the environment* (*step two*) so that more informed decisions can be made. Because of this greater awareness, *a career goal* (*step three*), that is what individuals decide they want to *accomplish* (*step four*) can then be formulated. Once the career goal has been decided on, a *career strategy*, which will enable individuals to attain their career goal, can then be *developed* (*step five*) and *implemented* (*step six*). Once a strategy has been implemented, *progress toward the career goal* (*step seven*) can be made and useful *feedback* (*step eight*) can also be provided to the individuals. The feedback will enable them to do a *career appraisal* (*step nine*), which is the process that enables them to determine whether their goals and strategies are still relevant. The information obtained from the career appraisal can be used for *career exploration* (*step one*), and so the career management cycle is continued.

The modern career management model is argued to be a consequence of all the changes that organisations and the world of work are going through with the concomitant development of boundaryless careers and multidirectional career paths – and as such it is said to be 'circular' in nature (Schreuder & Coetzee 2006: 67). They go on to explain as follows:

> Career planning and management is a process in which iterative rounds of *action and reflection* lead to updating personal career goals and possibilities. The emphasis is on change that accompanies frequent *career transitions* with the ideal of improving individuals' ability to formulate and test hypotheses about *future possibilities* and *multiple work roles* or *identities* they could explore along their life journey. This process is inductive in nature, with progress by iteration with leaps of insight or 'ahas'. Individuals require implicit knowledge which is continuously created throughout the career planning and management process (for example, exploring and testing what is feasible and what is appealing to them).

The traditional and modern career management models are compared by Schreuder and Coetzee (2006: 68–69) as reflected in table 12.1.

In the same book, Coetzee's (2005) *career invention model* is presented and we also offer it here, as taken (and slightly adapted) from Schreuder and Coetzee (2006: 81–85).

The career-invention model is based on the principle that the 21st century career is circular and that individuals have the power to change the nature of their career

Table 12.1: Characteristics of the traditional plan-and-implement career models and the modern test-and-learn career models

Plan-and-implement career models	Test-and-learn career models
Use a **linear process** in setting career goals, from which flows an implementation plan	Use a **circular process** in which iterative rounds of action and reflection lead to updating goals and possibilities
The end goal is usually **fixed** with the ideal of identifying it as clearly as possible at the outset	Career goals are continuously **changing** with the ideal of improving one's ability to formulate and test hypotheses about future possibilities along the way
Career planning and management process is **deductive**, with progress in stages, each building on the preceding step. The starting point is **analysis and reflection**: individuals use **introspection** to find an inner truth that can help identify the desired end goal. An action plan is devised and implemented to get to that goal	Career planning and management process are **inductive**, with progress by iteration with leaps of insight. The emphasis is on **taking action** and **experimenting** with various future **possibilities.** Individuals learn from **direct experience** to recombine old and new skills, interests, and ways of thinking about themselves, and to create opportunities that correspond to the evolving self-concept
Individuals require **explicit knowledge** which is used as an input to the career-management process: eg what jobs exist, what skills they like to use, what areas interest them, what their personality is, etc	Individuals require **implicit knowledge** which is continuously created through the career-management process: eg what is feasible, what is appealing
Useful in facilitating **career competency, career self-efficacy** and **career maturity** in particular in young adults or **new entrants** to the world of work	Useful in facilitating **career adjustment** and **career resilience** in adults dealing with **career transitions**

Source: Schreuder & Coetzee (2006: 68–69)

paths. Individuals are not dependent on the environment or organisation to make jobs available to them – they are the ones co-creating new alternative forms of work or employment through their creativity and talents. The periods when people are not employed are often used for deep self-reflection on past experiences. It is also a time in which individuals review their own development and the competencies they have gained. This process of deep self-reflection helps individuals to remember the dreams and desires they have not yet explored. Individuals can also fruitfully use the 'between-jobs' periods to figure out what they truly want and how their needs, desires and dreams are linked to their overall life purpose (Ibarra 2003).

As people become more skilled in inventing or co-creating their lives and careers, changing career paths proactively may become the norm and they might well start to take the initiative to decide on how long they want to stay with any particular organisation before exploring other career possibilities elsewhere. As such, people can become 'competence traders' – they negotiate the conditions for their work roles and careers based on their knowledge, skills, abilities and personal attributes which they believe can be used to add value to the cause of various organisations.

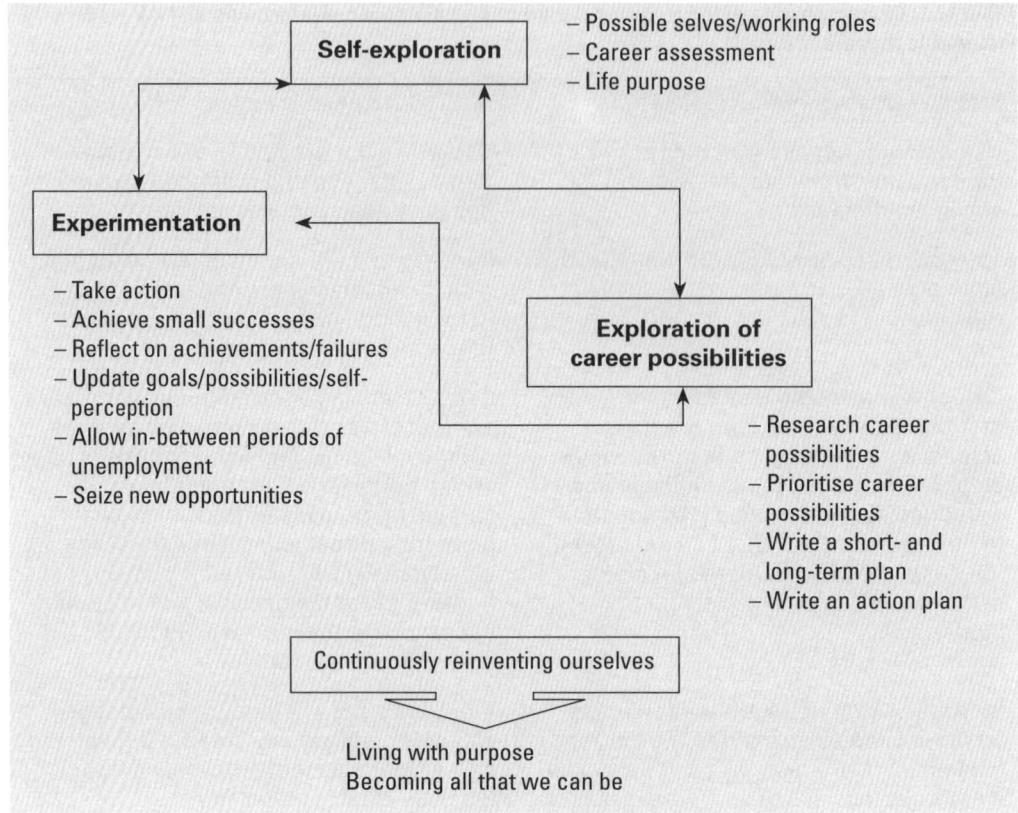

Figure 12.1: Coetzee's (2005b) career-invention model
Source: Schreuder & Coetzee (2006: 85)

The career-invention model is depicted in figure 12.1.

The cycle of career invention constitutes three components (called 'steps' by Coetzee), namely *self-exploration, exploration* of *career possibilities*, and *experimentation* with various career possibilities. The following is a mere overview of these three components ('steps'):

Component 1: Self-exploration
1 Identifying one's possible selves or working roles;
2 Assessing one's career interests, career orientation, career values, skills, knowledge, talents and abilities, career personality preferences, career assessment;
3 Figuring out what one really wants, one's dreams, desires and life purpose.

Component 2: Exploration
1 Researching career possibilities and alternatives that match one's career-assessment and general self-exploration activity outcomes;
2 Prioritising the identical career possibilities;
3 Writing a short- and long-term career plan;
4 Writing a plan of action to explore and experiment with the identified career options.

Component 3: Experimentation

1 Taking action – finding the job or form of work/employment;
2 Achieving small successes;
3 Reflecting on achievements and failures, and learning from them;
4 Updating goals, possibilities and self-conceptions about one's skills, abilities, possible selves;
5 Allowing 'in-between' periods of unemployment;
6 Seizing new opportunities by taking action (*engage in components 1 to 3 continuously*).

According to Schreuder and Coetzee (2006: 85), the career-invention model is self-developmental in nature as it emphasises career self-management and the idea of subjective career success: "In order for individuals to be successful in the pursuit of their careers within the context of the 21st century world of work, they must develop a set key of characteristics." Figure 12.2 gives an overview of these characteristics.

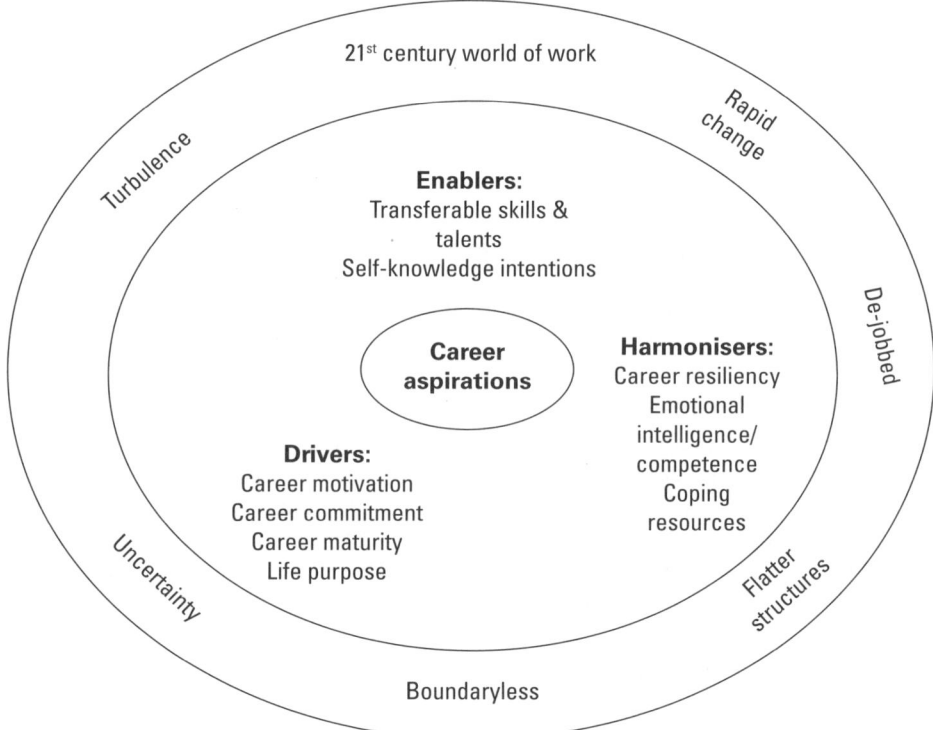

Figure 12.2: Coetzee's characteristics of a successful career
Source: Schreuder & Coetzee (2006: 85)

12.6 IMPORTANT CAREER–RELATED ISSUES

12.6.1 Career anchors

Career anchors are developed during the early stages of an individual's career, that is, during the establishment and achievement stages, although it is quite possible for an individual only to become aware of his or her career anchors much later.

12.6.1.1 Definition of career anchor

Although new employees may be appointed to a position for which they have been trained, this does not mean that they will be able to meet the present and future requirements of their job and potential career. New employees will not know whether they will like the new work or whether their values will fit those of the organisation. During the initial period of employment, the organisation and new employees get to know each other. This allows them to acquire more information about the career they have embarked on. New employees gradually gain more knowledge about themselves and develops a clearer self-concept. This self-concept comprises the following three components, which, according to Schein (1978), together form employees' career anchor.

Schein (1978: 125) describes a career anchor as follows:

- self-perceived talents and abilities based on actual successes in a variety of work settings;
- self-perceived motives based on opportunities for self-testing and self-diagnoses in real situations and on feedback from others; and
- self-perceived values based on actual encounters between self and the norms and values of the employing organisation and work setting.

According to Schein (1978, 1990), a career anchor consists of individuals' talents, motives and values, as perceived by themselves, which they use to delimit motives and stabilise their career. If employees are not aware of their career anchor, they could land up in a work situation in which they lack job satisfaction. As individuals are likely to make job selections that are consistent with their self-image, career anchors can serve as a basis for career choices (Schein 1990).

12.6.1.2 Types of career anchor

Schein (1990: 58–60) identified the following career anchors:

Technical/functional competence

Employees for whom technical/functional competence is a career anchor attempt to find ways in which they can use skills to improve their competence. They are self-confident and enjoy challenges. Such employees are usually competent leaders in their own fields of specialisation, but tend to avoid general management because this usually involves leaving their field of expertise. As the working environment becomes increasingly technologically complex, the need for technical/functional expertise will grow. However, the rapid advances in technological development means that such experts must constantly keep up to date and abreast of the progress being made in their particular fields (Schein 1996: 83).

Managerial competence

Employees for whom general managerial competence is a career anchor like to coordinate the activities of other employees and want to be seen to be making a positive contribution to the success of the organisation or department for which they work. A person with this type of anchor 'needs' to be a manager as he or she must give expression to interpersonal skills (influencing and controlling people), analytical skills (identifying and solving problems in uncertain situations), and emotional stability (stimulation by emotional and interpersonal crises, rather than experiencing them as tiresome). Schein (1996) foresees that the need for general management will increase and permeate the lower levels of organisations. Greater coordination and integration at lower levels will be required as work becomes more technically complex.

Autonomy/independence

Employees for whom autonomy/independence is a career anchor like to carry out their work in their own way. They enjoy variety and flexibility, but are unsuited to strictly regulated jobs or jobs that require them to exercise control over others. If forced into such position, they may well decide to start a business of their own. As the working environment is changing rapidly, such employees often find the world an easier place to negotiate. Schein (1996: 82) puts it as follows: "The autonomy anchor is aligned, at least for the present, with most organisational policies of promising only employability." Self-reliance, which is important for future career survival, is already part of these employees, and they may become the role models of others in future (Schein 1996).

Security/stability

Employees for whom security/stability is a career anchor consider both financial and job security to be important. They like to settle at a company, and are prepared to employ their skills in any manner required of them. If such employees change from one organisation to another, they always choose a similar type of organisation and a similar type of work. At present these employees are experiencing the most severe problems due to the current shift from 'employment security' to 'employability security' which is taking place in organisations. This means that employees can only expect from employers the opportunity to learn and they should become dependent on themselves (Schein 1996).

Entrepreneurial creativity

Employees for whom entrepreneurial creativity is a career anchor would jump at the opportunity of creating a business of their own. They want to show the world that they can create a business that is the result of their own efforts. These people often work for a company initially to gain the experience that they need to go out on their own. Current developments in the working environment are convincing more and more people that they can develop their own business. The opportunities for people who are anchored in entrepreneurial creativity will probably greatly increase in future.

Lifestyle

Employees for whom lifestyle is a career anchor like to find a compromise between their personal and family needs, and the requirements of their career. Schein (1990: 60) explains this as follows: "You want to make all of the major sectors of your life work together toward an integrated whole, and you therefore need a career situation that provides enough flexibility to achieve such integration." Sometimes such employees have to sacrifice certain aspects of their career (for example, they are often reluctant to accept a transfer to another city or country). They define success in broader terms than simply career success, and their identity is dependent more on how they live their total life. Schein (1996: 82) states that, since his original research of the 1960s and 1970s, this anchor has shown the most change. As social values are moving towards more autonomy and concern for self, people are becoming more preoccupied with lifestyle. Just as in the US, the current trend in South Africa is for executives to shift away from the technical/functional or general management category or career anchor.

Sense of service/dedication to a cause

Employees for whom service/dedication is a career anchor are always prepared to do something to improve life in general, whether to upgrade the state of the environment or to promote peace, etc. These employees may even change employers in order to carry on doing this kind of job and do not accept any promotion unless the new position meets the requirements of their value system. Schein (1996: 85) reports that the number of people with this anchor is increasing. He states that not only young people but people of middle age are expressing this need to do something meaningful in a larger context.

Challenge

Employees for whom pure challenge is a career anchor enjoy undertaking difficult tasks and solving complex problems. They never choose the easy way out of a problem and like to achieve the impossible. They tend to grow bored quickly when the job holds no challenge for them. Schein (1996: 85) is of the opinion that the number of people with this career anchor is growing. However, he is uncertain whether this is the result of more people with this predisposition entering the labour market or the result of an adaptation to the present-day changing and challenging working environment.

Recent research about career anchors in South Africa has yielded some interesting findings, as reflected in exhibit 12.2 below.

EXHIBIT 12.2: Career anchors, gender and race: some recent research findings in South Africa

Overall, the black participants and both male and female participants showed a higher preference for the values-based anchors (*service/dedication to a cause* and *pure challenge*) and the needs-based *lifestyle* career anchor than for the talent-based career anchors. In terms of the needs-based career anchors, the white participants in general showed a preference for the *lifestyle* career anchor, while black and white male participants showed a preference for the *autonomy* career anchor ... The findings indicate that the race and gender groups differ significantly regarding their career anchors ... The male participants appears to be especially committed to the organisation that provides them with the autonomy to do their job in an independent fashion, while the female and white participants seemingly tend to be especially committed to the organisation that respects personal and family concerns. The black participants appear to be more committed to an organisation that provides them with the opportunity to express their sense of service to the people component of the business. Generally these findings suggest that the participants would most probably be more committed to the organisation that provides them with the opportunity to move into challenging positions where they can gain recognition for their contributions to the greater good of the organisation and society as a whole, and that allows them to integrate their personal, family and career needs (Coetzee, Schreuder & Tladinyane 2007: 81–82)

12.6.2 Career patterns

Just as career success and advancement can indicate whether or not an individual's career is oriented around a specific career anchor (Schein 1993), so too can these factors be indicative of the career patterns that individuals follow (Brousseau 1990).

For some, success may mean promotion, for others, recognition in a field of expertise, while others seek to live a life of social contribution or to move frequently from one challenge to another. Driver (1979) has developed a model that suggests that individuals possess unique views about how their careers should develop. This model can be used to identify an individual's preferred career pattern and also to provide a basis for career decisions. The following four career patterns describe different types of careers, and are ways of describing the ideal career. Each career pattern is based on underlying motives (Brousseau 1990).

The linear career pattern

Employees who prefer a linear career pattern like to progress within the organisational hierarchy and be rewarded with promotion and instant recognition, as well as financial rewards such as high salaries, perks and incentives schemes. They are usually in managerial positions and hold power, achievement, status and money in high regard.

The expert career pattern

These employees work within their chosen career field for their entire career. They identify themselves with their fields of expertise, and aspects such as expertise, security and stability are strongly correlated with this pattern. Their emphasis is on the acquisition of special skills. Examples of this career pattern are medical practitioners, engineers and lawyers. These people prefer to be rewarded by speciality assignments and skills training. They prefer recognition for their expertise in a specific field.

The spiral career pattern

Employees who prefer a spiral career pattern tend to change their career field periodically. These changes are major and entail a change from one field to another, thus allowing them to acquire new skills and capabilities while using their previous experience. Motives such as self-development and creativity are highly regarded by the spiral career person.

The transitory career pattern

Employees with a transitory career pattern tend to change career fields as often as every two to four years. This pattern has been referred to as a 'consistent pattern of inconsistency'. They are independent and like variety in life. Their most favoured rewards are immediate financial rewards, flexible working hours, job rotation and autonomy.

12.6.3 Career plateaus

Career plateauing happens to just about everyone in the course of a career. It is "the point in a person's career when there is no longer any opportunity to progress in the organisational hierarchy" (Leibowitz, Kaye & Farren 1990: 28).

A distinction can be made between structural and content plateauing. Structural plateauing refers to a situation in which opportunities for promotion are restricted by the structure (pyramid) of the organisation. Only a few employees can make it to the top. Content plateauing occurs when an employee knows the job too well and no challenges are left. The challenge for managers is at least to address the problems of content plateauing, as it is the easier one to avoid (Leibowitz et al 1990: 28).

12.6.3.1 Plateaued performers

Four kinds of plateaued performers are identified by Leibowitz et al (1990: 30), namely productively plateaued, partially plateaued, pleasantly plateaued and passively plateaued.

Kinds of plateaued performers

1 Productively plateaued
These employees experience job satisfaction because they feel that they have achieved their ambitions. They are loyal to the organisation because they feel that it supports

them in achieving their personal goals and recognises their contributions. They are productive high performers, but occasionally require motivation.

2 Partially plateaued

Employees who are partially plateaued feel that the organisation does not do much for them, but they usually have an interest that maintains their involvement in the job. These people are usually a specialist in a certain field, but feel that their job lacks excitement and that their organisation does not support them enough in acquiring new skills. They value any opportunity to acquire new skills.

3 Pleasantly plateaued

The employees who are pleasantly plateaued do not aim for promotion and change, but prefer to remain where they are. They are unlikely to be innovative and usually stay with one organisation.

4 Passively plateaued

Employees who are passively plateaued feel that they have been in their jobs for too long and know them too well. They lack challenge and display no interest in additional training in their fields. However, they also feel unable to change their situations.

12.6.3.2 Dealing with plateauing

Certain steps can be followed to address the problem of plateauing.

The following are possible solutions (Alien, Poteet, Russel & Dobbins 1995: 15-18; Leibowitz et al 1990: 32):

- change the structure of the organisation;
- pay for performance;
- set up job rotation programmes to create lateral movement and broaden skills;
- give candid feedback;
- establish a career plan and goals;
- provide individual career planning opportunities (for example career planning workshops, self-assessment of skills);
- encourage career exploration; and
- encourage further education.

12.6.4 Obsolescence

Obsolescence refers to the extent to which employees lack the up-to-date competencies necessary to maintain successful performance in either their current or future work roles. This simply means that an individual is becoming outmoded and outdated.

12.6.4.1 Dealing with worker obsolescence

Worker obsolescence illustrates the continuous process in which the balance between the employee and the job is upset, either by technological factors such as computerisation or by organisational factors such as restructuring, or even by an action on the part of the employee. Once the balance has been upset, symptoms such as frustration, hostility or resistance to change may result. Once the symptoms have been identified, treatment in the form of training courses, organisational changes or career counselling may follow to restore the balance between the worker and the job, until the cycle is repeated (Bracker & Pearson 1986).

Managers can take certain actions to prevent worker obsolescence and to reduce feelings of obsolescence. These include the following:

- providing training and education;
- encouraging continuous learning;
- providing challenging initial work;
- encouraging people to attend conferences and to subscribe to professional journals;
- stimulating employees to stay up to date with new techniques; and
- creating a culture of growth and development.

12.6.5 Career movements

Careers are by their very nature not static. As mentioned in section 12.2, protean career in particular refers to the changing inherent nature of careers. There can be various reasons for career moves by individuals, both within and outside a particular organisation. Employee dissatisfaction may cause a career move, and such dissatisfaction may be the outflow of various factors such as technological and work design changes; changing employee values, attitudes or objectives; career plateaus; or behavioural (such as interpersonal dynamics between employees) or work performance-related problems.

Career movements within organisations usually take on the form of lateral, vertical or even diagonal moves within the organisational structures. Typical lateral movements are transfers. When an employee is transferred, it is a horizontal move from one job to another, at a similar job level with similar level duties, responsibilities, status and remuneration. Transfers are often accompanied by aspects such as reskilling (when an employee's new job is in a different field that requires some different competencies) and/or geographical relocation (especially in the case of large organisations with geographically dispersed units). With organisational structures becoming flatter it is becoming more and more common for employees to make such lateral career moves.

Vertical career moves within an organisation usually take on the form of demotion or promotion. Moving into a job of a higher level is known as promotion. Promotions typically entail aspects such as higher-level responsibilities, more complex work, greater competency demands and better remuneration. In South Africa, promotion has and will become an increasingly contentious issue, due to aspects such as employment equity, affirmative action and the concept of merit. Because promotion decisions are traditionally based on aspects such as work performance history and 'meritorious work-related grounds', and because flattening organisational structures are limiting promotion opportunities, it is to be expected that promotion decisions will lead to a lot of debate and even unhappiness. Promotion and fair opportunities in other African countries also show some interesting challenges that may be faced (see '*Elsewhere in Africa*' box).

In the context of employment equity and affirmative action in South Africa, the following should be kept in mind in the case of promotional decisions within organisations:
- all employees should be provided with information regarding promotional opportunities;
- the standards that will apply in promotions must be clearly communicated to all employees;
- unsuccessful candidates must be provided with feedback regarding the reasons for their failure to be promoted. Furthermore, suggestions must be made regarding ways in which they can supplement deficiencies in their competency profiles (for example suggesting particular training courses);

- employees from designated groups must be groomed for promotion;
- all employees must be provided with career paths and supplementary training, experience and skills necessary at each stage in their career paths in order to be considered for promotion;
- promotion decisions must be made on the basis of aspects such as competencies, not merely on paper qualifications, also taking into consideration prior learning and relevant experience;
- job specifications must be reassessed to determine whether these are really in line with essential and inherent requirements of the job;
- the use of promotion selection panels that are representative of all important stakeholders (for example trade union representatives, and current and prospective supervisors) must be considered for making promotional decisions, rather than leaving it in the exclusive domain of managerial prerogative;
- psychometric testing must be used carefully and only in line with the Employment Equity Act (see also chapters 3 and 8). This will involve not basing one's decision exclusively on psychometric results but viewing such valid and reliable test results only as one source of information in the decision-making process. Such tests must also have cross-cultural validity and reliability, and preference should be given to tests that measure potential and competencies rather than constructs that may be unduly influenced by differences in candidates' formal education; and
- the organisation's affirmative action programme and goals must be taken into account in the final decision on whom to promote from the list of candidates who satisfy the minimum job specifications.

Elsewhere in Africa

Nepotism in Africa? Research findings show not all countries provide same, fair career advancement opportunities

In Nigeria, research findings "indicate that promotions ... are based on favouritism, nepotism and tribalism. Promotions ... based on favouritism and similar factors lead to incompetence ... Managers should develop a system where promotions ... are granted because of ... job-related factors and not ... non-work-related factors" (Okpara & Wynn 2008: 72).

In contrast, research in Eritrea, Africa's newest independent country, has led to findings such as the following by Ghebregiorgis and Karsten (2007: 730) : "Normally, in Eritrea ... current employees shall be given priority over external candidates ... [I]t gives them a feeling that management cares about the advancement of its employees whenever an opportunity is created and there are chances of career development ... [P]romotion opportunities within the firm bind workers and employers ...".

As regards the last point, it is suggested that the following guidelines be considered to be adopted as policy regarding promotional issues:
- in 'same merit' situations, 'designated' employees may be promoted over other equally qualified* employees
- unqualified 'designated' employees may not be promoted over qualified white male employees; and

---

*The term 'qualified' here refers to meeting the minimum job specifications and being suitably qualified as spelt out in the Employment Equity Act.

■ if 'designated' employees are qualified, they may be promoted over better qualified white male employees.

It is important that such decisions not be made on an ad hoc basis. All such policy guidelines should be formalised and all employees should be well informed of them.

Lastly, we have to stress that a reassessment of the importance of relevant past experience as a consideration in making promotional decisions is necessary. If in-organisation experience in a particular job is included in an employer's merit or performance evaluation system, this may taint promotions with discrimination. This form of discrimination is called 'the present effects of past discrimination', and it does not matter that the actual discriminatory practices which precluded protected group members from acquiring the requisite experience took place prior to the enactment of discriminatory legislation. Now that prospective employees are protected against discrimination by our legislation, organisations that have experience requirements may be exposing themselves to unfair labour practice (discriminatory promotional) claims. For instance, employees who were previously barred from certain jobs by job reservation or organisational policy or who have been appointed as temporary employees for indefinite periods for which they have received no seniority recognition, may claim that they are being unfairly discriminated against and file a dispute. The employer's defence in such cases will have to be based on the 'inherent requirements of the job' rationale (that is, that the prescribed experience is absolutely essential for the job in question).

Demotion is basically a downward career move within an organisation. This is typically when an employee is put into a lower-level job, with fewer responsibilities, lower status and fewer competency requirements. It is indeed very rare that an employee would prefer and initiate a demotion. This could happen when an employee has realistic career views and realises that he or she was possibly promoted to a level beyond his or her capability or potential to acquire the ability (known as the Peter Principle). However, demotion may, under certain circumstances, be the only real option to an employee, and usually this comes about by an employer-focused decision. For instance, it may be that due to organisational restructuring, a certain position becomes redundant and that no positions at a similar level are vacant within the organisation. The employee may then be afforded the opportunity to choose between being laid off (retrenched – see also chapter 20) or accepting a lower-level position within the organisation. With the scarcity of work in the form of formal job opportunities in South Africa, chances are that opting for a demotion may be more viable than normally expected. Alternatively, a situation may arise due to employee misconduct or poor work performance, when the only option short of dismissal may be for the employee to agree to be demoted. It is of importance to note, however, that an employee may in general not be demoted by a unilateral decision from the employer's side. Demotion has to be a voluntary acceptance by the employee in question. Also, it should be noted that demotion need not always be accompanied by an immediate reduction in employee remuneration and benefits. It is in particular advisable that should demotion become the only alternative to a no-fault termination of the employment relationship (such as in the case of retrenchment), an attempt be made that the remuneration and benefits be kept at existing levels for as long as is practically possible. It should also, in any event, be remembered that any downward career move, and in particular if it is caused by no fault on the employee's part, involves certain delicate dynamics (such as psychological adjustment) that have to be managed properly.

Diagonal career movement refers to when employees move up or down the career ladder but also across disciplines. Such may for instance be the case when an employee that used to be an operations/production manager, is promoted to a senior financial manager position within the organisation.

Outward career movements generally refer to situations when persons' career changes entail moving outside of a particular organisation. This generally entails employee separation – in other words, when the paths of an employee and his or her employing organisation depart. This may, for instance, be the case when an employee decides to resign or go on early retirement. This may also, however, happen involuntarily, such as in the case of job loss.

Job loss can be defined as any involuntary separation from an organisation's workforce. It can occur at any career stage, but if it happens during the later stages it could be more traumatic.

It is well known that an individual's emotional well-being can be extremely adversely affected by the loss of a job. It is even more traumatic if any of the following conditions are present (McKnight 1991):
- if it appears unlikely that the individual will find alternative employment;
- if the individual lacks multiple skills;
- if the individual has worked for only one employer; and
- if the employee perceives him- or herself to be unemployable.

As can be gathered, job loss can be caused by a multitude of factors, including organisational restructuring efforts such as downsizing, rightsizing, re-engineering and the outsourcing of certain organisational functions. As Stevenson (1998: 40) says: "Not a week goes by without one of the national newspapers reporting on South African companies downsizing, restructuring or laying off staff. Reasons put forward include re-emergence of international competition, affirmative action, the lack of growth in the economy or, as more frequently appears to be the case, mergers, acquisitions and buy-outs." He then goes on to illustrate the importance of aspects such as career transition counselling and outplacement when job loss occurs, and says that although "an employer's responsibility is primarily to those who remain, it would be wrong of them to ignore those who must go. It is most definitely in the employer's interest to help the leavers retain their self-esteem and dignity, and to assist them in establishing themselves on a new career path" (Stevenson 1998: 43).

Such an approach will fit in nicely with the more holistic approach to career development proposed by Boden (1998: 24–25): "The recent economic decline has contributed to a renaissance of career support activities by employers ... Instead of creating loyalty which, by association, implies longevity in the partnership between employer and employee, staff need to become more entrepreneurial, committed to lifelong learning ... Career development is about work and life balance and therefore life management."

From the foregoing it should be quite clear that due to all the changes in organisational environments, career movements and the management and development of careers require a much more holistic and flexible approach where employability rather than employment becomes the focus and anchor.

Managers can thus take a number of steps, such as the following, to assist people who have lost their jobs due to reasons beyond their control:
- introduce training programmes which teach workers who have been laid off how to manage stress and take control of the future;
- help people to overcome the initial shock of job loss, and provide advice on career moves (professionals can be used in this regard); and
- give them entrepreneurial and small/own business management skills.

12.6.6 Working couples and work–family conflict

A *working couple* can be defined as "any two people in an ongoing, committed relationship, where both partners work, where there may or may not be children, and where decisions (family and work) are influenced by the working situation of each partner" (Guterman 1991: 169).

Working couples are more likely to experience work–family conflict than couples in which only one partner works. *Work–family conflict* can be defined as "a form of interrole conflict in which the role pressures from the work and family domains are mutually incompatible in some respect" (Greenhaus & Beutell 1985: 77).

Three types of work–family conflict have been identified (Greenhaus & Beutell 1985: 88):

■ *Time-based conflict* develops when time that is devoted to one role cannot be devoted to another. Time-based conflict would occur when time pressures in one role make it impossible to satisfy the expectations of the other role. Inflexible work schedules, excessive overtime and work involvement can be related to work–family conflict.
■ *Strain-based conflict* occurs when performance in one role is adversely affected by the stress that is experienced in another. For example, a crisis in the family can cause fatigue, which results in poor performance at work.
■ *Behaviour-based conflict* occurs when certain patterns of role behaviour are in conflict with expectations of behaviour in other roles. For example, a male manager is expected to be self-reliant, emotionally stable and somewhat aggressive, whereas the manager's family expects him to be warm and caring.

Conflict between work and family roles can, for instance, be created by the following work-related factors:

■ number of hours worked;
■ lack of control over the decision to work overtime;
■ an inflexible work schedule;
■ irregular starting time; and
■ psychologically demanding work.

On the basis of current research, Schreuder and Theron (2001: 186) suggest, inter alia, the following action to balance family and work needs:

■ more organisational sensitivity for home life;
■ the introduction of flexible benefits to assist employees with family needs such as child care and the care of sick children;
■ the introduction of flexible work hours and work-at-home programmes;
■ the revision of relocation policies to make provision for the needs of the modern worker; and
■ the introduction of alternative career paths – not all employees want to climb the corporate ladder.

The diversity of today's workforce underscores the need for flexible policies to accommodate the personal responsibilities, aspirations and needs of employees.

12.7 CAREER DEVELOPMENT SUPPORT METHODS

While employees are primarily responsible for their own career planning, the organisation's management can do a great deal to support them in managing their careers and in making more realistic career decisions. Schreuder and Coetzee (2006: 313) say that "formalised career management practices can avoid employee turnover ... Taking an interest in employees' careers can also improve morale, increase productivity, and help the organisation become" more successful. They go on, adding that a formal "organisational career-management system can also help create a positive career-development culture, which can help address a range of issues, such as productivity and competitiveness, employment equity, succession planning and workforce forecasting, talent retention, management-potential selection and development" and so forth. The potential impact can thus be very positive.

A POLICY PERSPECTIVE

Our people are the most important assets of our organisation and our country. This career management policy therefore aims to assist with the development of the careers of our employees. While each person must take responsibility for his or her own career and the development thereof, we believe in providing appropriate support for our people in the management of their own careers.

The purpose of this policy is therefore to support the design and implementation of a system that is aligned with our performance management and other HRM systems, and that will be available to all our staff to help them manage their own careers. The overall aim is to contribute to the development of our people so that they can have fulfilled lives that also have some good alignment with the strategic direction of our organisation.

In this section we merely reflect rather briefly on some of the things that organisations can do to try and assist with the career management of staff. Please keep in mind the importance of integration of organisational systems. The same holds for HRM systems. Aligning the performance management system and the career management system is,

A CASE AT HAND

At Liberty, in the highly competitive financial services sector in South Africa, the career management system (or 'human capital management' model) reflects the work and workforce differentiated issue as discussed in earlier chapters. It is thus recognised that at different levels in the organisation there are different worlds of work.

For the executive and senior management positions a 'high touch, personalised' approach is followed, which includes:
- succession planning for 110 key positions and which is reviewed twice a year
- executive development programmes in partnership with local and international Business Schools
- incentive programmes focused on retaining scarce skills.

A Group Development Committee under the chairmanship of the CEO, oversees these processes.

At the team leader and more junior employee levels, where large numbers of employees are involved, that is approximately 3 000, the career management processes focus mainly on high-tech empowerment tools and systems to foster and support a culture of self-management. The cornerstone of this empowering system for team leaders and their staff is a unique e-HR intranet website called e-Careers that provides access to information on career streams, work profiles, available training opportunities, available positions, experts to talk to, a reading room, as well as a facility to record interest in each of Liberty's business and support units. The system also comprises an embedded 360-degree performance feedback component ...

Source: Meyer (2007: 416)

for instance, a prerequisite. It might well be that the two are packaged together as a 'performance and career management system'. Some organisations have relatively advanced career management systems, such as reflected in the case of Liberty below.

The following are some methods that can be used by organisations to support career development and management.

12.7.1 Career planning workshops

Career planning workshops are widely used by organisations as part of their career development systems. In such a workshop people obtain self-knowledge (that is, insight into their strengths and weaknesses) and are introduced to work opportunities. An action plan usually results.

Such workshops should cover the following aspects (Otte & Hutcheson 1992: 19–20):

- individual assessment (information about self);
- environmental assessment (information about work);
- comparison of self-perceptions with those of others (reality testing);
- establishing long- and short-term career goals (goal setting);
- choosing among alternatives (decision making); and
- establishing and implementing plans (action planning).

12.7.2 Career discussions

"A career discussion is a planned discussion between a manager and an employee who are attempting jointly to clarify developmental options in the employee's current job, examine career issues in light of current job performance and goals of the organisation, and/or clarify future career options for that employee" (Otte & Hutcheson 1992: 46).

Conducting career discussions is one of the most important HRM tasks of the manager. In this way managers support career planning. The manager should act as an advisor and facilitate the career development process. While the above description emphasises the formal and planned career discussions, we believe that the general discussions that managers have with their staff, even and particularly the informal ones, should from time to time include some attempts to explore how well they feel things are going in terms of their career. Naturally these should not become regular points of conversation because that might just signal potentially negative messages, because career discussions generally will include possible future issues and the impression may be given that a manager wants the employee to move on if such issues are raised to frequently. Probably the most sound approach would be to include career issues when we engage in work performance reviews, as covered in chapter 11. Some informal follow-up discussions about career issues might then be specifically arranged as well.

12.7.3 Providing career-related education and information, and assistance with formal education

Apart from the career workshops methodology described earlier, organisations can do quite a bit along the lines of feeding information to staff, or at least making career-related information available. With the increasingly accepted notion of the importance of lifelong learning, employees should be challenged to read, think ahead, and even engage in formal education to possibly develop their future career prospects. Career centres may be an option. As Jones (2007: 7) indicates, this may take on the form of "career libraries" and/or "career resource centres" that contain a repository of the relevant material to assist employees in thinking about and perhaps planning their careers. These may include brochures, magazines, books and videos about various types of careers and also processes related to managing careers. In addition there may be computer facilities to allow access to relevant information. In addition, Jones (2007: 7) says that communicating "via the intranet on career self-management, job satisfaction ...", and so on is another possibility. Information can also be provided to inform the employees of possible career opportunities within the organisation – as well as to help avail them of self-knowledge.

Well-designed career workbooks can also be made available for employees to self-educate about career dynamics and challenges. The individual then typically works alone through a series of assessment exercises and thereby obtains valuable self-knowledge. In this way a workbook can achieve some of the objectives of a career planning workshop.

In addition to this career management-related assistance, organisations can help employees financially to further their own formal education. This may include enrolling for further studies at universities, for instance.

12.7.4 Mentoring

Mentoring is becoming a very popular way of helping employees to develop and manage their careers. To support mentoring, organisations can design formal mentoring programmes, ensure that the corporate structure supports mentoring relationships and use the existing pool of managers and top performers effectively.

According to Clutterbuck (2001: 3), mentoring is "offline help by one person to another in making significant transitions in knowledge work or thinking". It thus is a matter of establishing a relationship with an experienced person (the mentor) and as the inexperienced person (the mentee), you basically 'partner' or 'twin' with him or her to learn and receive guidance. The mentor provides the mentee with ongoing support and opportunities to learn and develop.

According to Schreuder and Coetzee (2006: 325–326), mentors

> ... can advise on development and on the way to manage a career plan; they can challenge assumptions, and, where relevant, they can share their own experience. Mentoring has proved to be very effective in transferring tacit knowledge within an organisation, highlighting how effective people think, take decisions, and approach complex issues. Sharing views and ideas builds understanding and trust. The mentor and mentee relationship often evolves into a key friendship, invaluable when difficult decisions arise ...

The same authors offer the following additional information which we have slightly adapted (Schreuder & Coetzee 2006: 326–329).

We can distinguish between informal and formal mentoring. *Informal mentoring* is more of a spontaneous relationship, and *formal mentoring* is typically arranged and overseen by the organisation. These can obviously involve HR practitioners who may initiate and coordinate a mentorship programme, but generally it will be line managers who will become mentors of more junior staff in the case of developing managerial potential and careers. Naturally it is important to support mentors, such as providing them with training to fulfil such roles.

Organisations can further support mentoring that will foster career success by doing things such as the following (Hill & Bahniuk 1998; Klasen & Clutterbuck 2002):

■ Design formal mentoring programmes that correspond with informal mentoring.
■ Ensure that the corporate structure supports mentoring relationships.

- Introduce sessions for potential mentors by focusing on mentoring functions.
- Investigate innovation programmes, such as using an 'electronic mentor'.
- Use the existing pool of managers more creatively.
- Use top performers in the company effectively.
- Consider group mentoring, where one mentor is assigned to a team of four to six protégés that work together on career advancement.
- Consider offering incentives to top managers to encourage the mentoring of diverse groups.

If this is the route an organisation chooses to take, it is important that mentorship relationships be actively promoted and supported by senior management. The individual's career success can be enhanced, and the individual's chances for survival in the organisation are probably also increased. It may well also be enriching for the mentor as it serves as an avenue of adding value to the lives of other, more junior, staff. Table 12.2 reflects information about the roles of mentors and mentees according to Coetzee and Stone (2004), as quoted in Schreuder and Coetzee (2006: 327–329).

Table 12.2: Roles of mentors and mentees

Role of the mentor	Role of the mentee
Advisor: Gives an opinion about what to do or how to handle a specific situation **Counsellor:** A person who is close to the learner, whom the learner trusts, and to whom the learner confides personal issues and concerns on a more confidential level **Encourager:** Recommends actions or gives advice **Subject matter expert:** Gives courage, hope or confidence to another; helps and gives support; celebrates successes **Friend:** Supporter or ally; a person at the other end of the journey **Guardian:** Watches over, protects, cares for and defends **Leader:** Directs or guides **Motivator:** Excites or moves another to action **Role model:** A person in a specific role to be followed or imitated owing to the excellence or worth of that role **Knowledge developer:** Shares knowledge or insight; an instructor; shows or guides another to do something	**Self-knower:** Understands own needs, aspirations, goals, beliefs, values, interests, competencies and skills; is aware of personal style and behaviour and of how these influence the relationship **Owner:** Takes ownership of learning, career, choosing a mentor, preparing for discussion and personal development **Portfolio builder:** Develops a portfolio that includes transferable skills and competencies **Action taker:** Does concrete action planning and takes action; measures progress towards specific goals **Evaluator:** Evaluates mentor–learner relationship, personal needs and aspirations, and initiates new relationships

Source: Schreuder & Coetzee (2006: 327)

For mentoring interventions to add optimal value, the roles of the parties must be clear and well understood by mentors and mentees. The actual career progress review discussion sessions between these two partners are obviously very important. In this regard table 12.3 (taken from Schreuder & Coetzee (2006: 328–329) but originally the work of Coetzee & Stone (2004)) provides some useful information about the kinds of responsibilities and dynamics related to the roles of the mentor and mentee.

Table 12.3: Conducting review discussions: roles of mentor and mentee

Conducting progress-review discussions		
Mentor's role	**Mentee's role**	**Organisational results**
Listen Encourage learner to talk about him- or herself Listen to results of learner's self-assessments and assessors' assessments Ask questions to clarify learner's assessments Give ideas on resources for further exploration	**Communicate** Talk openly about satisfaction/ dissatisfaction Use resources to assess values, interests and skills Communicate results of assessment to mentor Consider own talents and abilities	Clear understanding by mentee and mentor of mentee values, interests and skills
Clarify Establish clear standards and expectations Give feedback with supporting evidence and rationale Add information overlooked by learner Link learning progress/ performance to potential	**Ask for information** Ask for feedback on realism of self-assessments and on formative assessments by assessor Accept feedback without becoming defensive Ask for clarification and specific examples	Mentee gains a clear understanding of mentor's perceptions of his or her skills and development needs
Look ahead Give views about current problems regarding development programme and about career options and challenges Link learner with others who have relevant information Provide awareness and insights regarding changing in industry, sector, organisation and profession	**Explore** Seek advice on organisational realities, employment realities/options, and career implications Follow up on network and alliance building Seek data on changes in industry, sector, organisation, and profession	Organisation's strategic direction linked to career opportunities
Give guidance Relate changes/challenges/ options to learner career/ employment/further education goals Express support or reservation related to learner goals Provide ideas and input regarding opportunities	**Develop strategies** Select multiple career/ employment/further education options Use information to make options realistic, relevant, and specific Communicate goals to mentor	Clearly defined multiple mentee career/employment/further education goals that are realistic and relevant to the organisation and the mentee
Review Review development plan Offer suggestions to strengthen plan Refer to resources that can assist with implementation Schedule reviews Debrief development plan assignments.	**Plan** Analyse development needs Identify development activities and complete a written plan Submit plan for mentor review Move forward to implement plan	A written plan for mentee development leading to constructive action and follow-through.

Source: Schreuder & Coetzee (2006: 328–329)

12.8 CONCLUSION

This chapter examined various factors related to the management of employees' careers and the implications of recent developments taking place in organisations worldwide. We explored relevant concepts. The concept of career was defined from the angle of flexibility and adaptability. "The new career is about experience, skill, flexibility and personal development. It does not involve predefined career paths, routine ticket punching, stability or security" (Hall & Mervis 1995: 330). We shared two different models about career management after taking a good look at the issue of career choice and different theories related to it. Career issues such as plateauing, job loss and working couples are the order of the day, and we made some suggestions regarding what can be done about some of these.

Although career management is primarily the responsibility of the individual, the organisation has a role to play in helping the individual to make better career decisions. This can be achieved when specialised HR practitioners (either inside or outside the organisation) develop and facilitate or provide things like in-house career workshops, career-related information centres and other ways of educating staff such as career workbooks, and/or career counselling. Line managers should also always show interest in the careers of their staff and discuss these with them and, when necessary, advise them to seek additional assistance (such as through in-house HR services). These informal discussions are an option but more formal discussions that link up with performance appraisal sessions are also good alternatives. In addition, we stressed the increasingly prominent role that mentorship can play.

SUSTAINABILITY CONNECTION?
Only people can make the difference between a sustainable and unsustainable world. How people develop will determine the contributions they can make to our organisations and our world more generally. Careers typically span different organisations and work situations, and when we help working people to develop themselves and their careers we are adding value not only to those people, but also to the organisations/societies to which they will be contributing. We owe it to our people, our country and our continent to help develop the capabilities and careers of our workers – even if that means that we are contributing beyond the boundaries of our specific organisation. If we do this, we are contributing to making this world a better place for all over the longer term.

SELF-EVALUATION QUESTIONS

1 Do individuals have a responsibility to manage their own careers? Explain.
2 How would you describe the employer's responsibility in career management?
3 Would you agree that career choice is a single event which usually occurs in the early 20s? Substantiate your answer.
4 What is a career anchor? With which anchor do you associate best and why?
5 How would you use career anchors in career management?
6 Describe briefly what appears to you to be the ideal career.
7 How would you distinguish between structural and content career plateaus?
8 Distinguish between two different models of career management.
9 How can organisations help employees to manage their careers?

10 Write a short essay on mentoring as a way of helping employees with the management of their careers. Pay particular attention to the roles of the mentor and the mentee.

ENDNOTE

1   This section is largely based on Schreuder and Coetzee (2006: 67–69).

13 DEVELOPING HUMAN RESOURCES: THE SOUTH AFRICAN AGENDA AND FRAMEWORK

LEARNING OUTCOMES

After studying this chapter, you should be able to:

- describe the various national training initiatives introduced by government;
- discuss briefly the problems relating to education and training in South Africa;
- discuss the role of the National Qualifications Framework (NQF);
- describe the role and functions of the South African Qualifications Authority (SAQA); and
- briefly discuss the Skills Development Act and the Skills Development Levies Act.

13.1 INTRODUCTION

We have stressed at different occasions throughout this book that South Africa lacks highly skilled human resources. On the other hand we have an abundance of low or poorly skilled people. Illiteracy is a big challenge, for instance. The government is constantly seeking ways to alleviate our illiteracy problem and despite a number of literacy programmes run by government and private-sector groups, literacy levels in our country remain low. It is estimated that about 27% of South Africa's people could be described as illiterate (that is, having little or inadequate formal schooling – an education level lower than Grade 7) (Erasmus, Loedolff, Mda & Nel 2006: 50). About 67% of persons aged 15 years and older are considered functionally literate. This figure compares well with literacy levels in other developing countries like Nigeria (61%), India (55%) and Mozambique (42%), but is lower than in countries like Zimbabwe (87%), Mexico (84%), Malaysia (86%) and Brazil (90%). Compared to some other countries, we really do not do too well (for instance in comparison with the US, the UK and Australia (99%)).

As explained in chapter 2, we have to become a more competitive nation in order to improve standards of living, and to do so we will have to do much better at educating and developing our country's people. Education levels will have to be dramatically improved, and naturally literacy is just the starting point. The less a person is qualified, the less likely it is for him or her to find work in the formal sector of the economy. Erasmus et al (2006: 50) provide interesting statistics: approximately 45% with no education are employed in the formal sector while 85,4% with a Grade 12 and higher qualification are employed in the formal sector.

Tertiary education is naturally also a key challenge, even though we are making progress. In 1995 South Africa had 542 398 new graduates and in 2004 this figure was

1,18 million. This shows good growth, but we should keep in mind that the economy has expanded a lot over the same period and at an even faster rate over the period 2002 to 2007. We therefore need to do even better in terms of growing the number of people who graduate from our universities. Not only that, but we also have to make sure that we target the right fields of study. The largest growth in terms of fields of qualifications has been in the fields of business and management studies while the lowest growth over the same period was in the fields of health studies, and in engineering sciences and technology (Pandor 2005). Not only do we therefore have to increase the output of formal education generally, we also have to make sure that we educate and develop people in the fields that require more qualified people.

Just like we have discussed the need and challenges related to planning for supply and demand of workers when we do workforce planning at the level of the organisation (chapter 6), it is also important to do similar planning at a more macro level. The focus of human resource development at the macro level is crucial for the economic prosperity and general quality of life of all South Africans. Human resource development at the level of the organisation cannot be done without taking due cognisance of the bigger picture in our country. As we have stressed many times before, as we develop and empower our people in our organisations we must keep in mind that even if we lose these people to other organisations (such as when they resign and take up work elsewhere), we are still adding value to the human capital of the country. Ultimately we all share this same continent – and so the more we do to develop our human resources, the more we contribute to making Africa a more successful continent which is capable of sustaining itself for generations to come. It is therefore, we believe, essential to understand the broader national developments in training and development. At least also because these form the parameters within which organisations can train and develop their employees.

While the next chapter focuses on the training and development practices and processes at organisational level, in this chapter we take a look at human resource development from a macro or national perspective.

13.2 NATIONAL TRAINING INITIATIVES

In April 1994 the National Training Board (NTB) published a document entitled *A National Training Strategy Initiative*. This document proposed an integrated approach to education and training for the future, and also emphasised the centrality of training in the quest to ensure international competitiveness.

The national training strategy provided a new vision for education and training, namely that "it must meet South Africa's need for a human resources development system in which there is an integrated approach to education and training which meets the economic and social needs of the country and the development needs of the individual".

The emphasis was that we must no longer think about education and training as separate entities but rather view them as an integrated system. Education and training must therefore be dealt with as a whole, but this does not, however, imply that each aspect cannot be dealt with in its own unique manner. Learning must be considered a lifelong process and this culture must be instilled as soon as possible and maintained for as long as possible.

13.2.1 Principles

Twelve principles formed the basis of the national training strategy (NTB). These are outlined below:

1. Education and training should form part of a system of human resources development which provides for the establishment of an integrated approach to education and training.
2. Such a strategy should be and remain relevant to national development needs.
3. The strategy should have international and national credibility.
4. It should adhere to a coherent framework of principles and certification.
5. It should be expressed in terms of a nationally agreed framework and internationally accepted outcomes standards.
6. The strategy should provide for participation in planning and coordination by all significant stakeholders, and should be legitimate.
7. Access to appropriate levels of education and training should be provided for all prospective learners in a manner which facilitates progression.
8. The national training strategy should provide for learners, on successful completion of accredited prerequisites, to move between components of the delivery system.
9. It should ensure that the framework of qualifications permits individuals to progress through the levels of national qualifications via different appropriate combinations of the components of the delivery system.
10. It should provide for learners to transfer their credits or qualifications from one learning institution and/or employer to another (portability).
11. It should, through assessment, give credit to prior learning.
12. It should provide for the guidance of learners by persons who meet nationally recognised standards for educators and trainers.

Subsequent to the above-mentioned report, various other education and training reports were published, of which the following must be emphasised, namely the *Human Resource Development Strategy for South Africa*, the *State of Skills in South Africa 2005* and the *National Skills Development Strategy 1 April 2005–31 March 2010*. The latter report will be discussed briefly in the next section.

13.2.2 State of skills in South Africa

13.2.2.1 Background

Research conducted by the NTB found that worldwide education and training systems have been developed in countries where a common sense of identity exists in the population, and have often followed unrest which led to or threatened large-scale impoverishment or economic depression. These international systems have nurtured those competencies which are prerequisites for success in industry, small business and the informal sector and which encourage the development of a partnership between business, trade unions and the state in education and training. Strong links and a culture of cooperation have also been developed between the education and training systems and organisations to act as champions for the development of these systems. Those education and training systems which achieved success were seen as credible by all relevant stakeholders. In contrast with the above, the South African education system faced serious problems in 1994, for example:

- large-scale inconsistency in standards;
- the breakdown of the culture of learning;
- imbalances in funding qualifications, the provision of facilities and teacher:pupil ratios;
- the legacy of illiteracy; and

PRESENTATION BY THE DEPUTY PRESIDENT MLAMBO-NGCUKA 2006

Introduction

The core objective of government as set out in 2004 is to halve poverty and unemployment by 2014. We believe that these objectives are feasible – indeed we would hope to surpass those objectives – because of the steady improvement in the performance and job creating capacity of the economy.

Growth averaged about 3% during the first decade of freedom. Since 2004 growth has tended to exceed 4% per year, reaching about 5% in 2005. Good economic policies, positive domestic sentiment, and a favourable international environment have created the opportunity to consolidate our recent gains, and prepare to take our performance to yet a higher level.

With the improvement in the growth rate has come rapidly improving employment creation, though unemployment remains high at over 26%. This is considerably better than the 32% unemployment rate reached a few years ago, but the challenge to reduce unemployment to below 15% and the challenge to halve the poverty rate will not be achieved without effective economic leadership from government and effective partnerships between government and other key stakeholders such as organised labour and business.

In the course of exploring our opportunities, government consulted with a range of stakeholders. Such consultations and discussions will continue during the course of the implementation of AsgiSA. On the basis of these interactions, government believes that South Africa is ready for AsgiSA to be a **national shared growth initiative**, rather than "government's programme".

In government's investigations, supported by some independent research, we found that the rate of growth needed to allow us to achieve our social objectives is around 5% on average between 2004 and 2014. Realistically assessing the capabilities and deficiencies of the economy and the international environment, we have set out a two phase target. In the first phase, between 2005 and 2009, we seek an annual growth rate that averages 4,5% or higher. In the second phase, between 2010 and 2014, we seek an average growth rate of at least 6% of GDP.

Binding constraints

The following constraints have been identified:
- The volatility and level of the currency
- The cost, efficiency and capacity of the national logistics system
- Shortage of suitably skilled labour amplified by the cost effects on labour of apartheid spatial patterns
- Barriers to entry, limits to competition and limited new investment opportunities
- Regulatory environment and the burden on small and medium businesses
- Deficiencies in state organisation, capacity and leadership

Education and skills development

For both the public infrastructure and the private investment programmes, the single greatest impediment is the shortage of skills – including professional skills such as engineers and scientists; managers such as financial, personnel and project managers; and skilled technical employees such as artisans and IT technicians. The shortfall is due to the policies of the apartheid era and the slowness of our education and skills development institutions to catch up with the current acceleration of economic growth.

Key measures to address the skills challenge in the educational sphere are:
- The QUIDS UP programme aimed at achieving high levels of literacy and numeracy in the lowest grades;
- The Maths and Science (Dinaledi) programme for 529 high schools to double maths and science high-school graduates to 50 000 by 2008;

>>

<<

■ An upgraded career guidance programme; and

■ A huge upgrading of the Further Education and Training colleges. In addition, the Adult Basic and Education Training programme is to be ramped up, based on a model developed in Cuba and New Zealand.

Other key interventions in the skills sphere include the development of an Employment Services System (to close the gap between potential employers and employees), and Phase 2 of the National Skills Development Strategy. A short-term project is the development of a scarce skills database based directly on the expected needs of the over **100 individual projects** included in AsgiSA.

Other key skills projects include the **deployment of experienced professionals and managers** to local governments to improve project development implementation and maintenance capabilities. The project managed by the Development Bank of Southern Africa will deploy an estimated total of 150 expert staff, with the first 30 to be deployed in April 2006. The project will also include skills transfer to **new graduates. The DBSA is compiling a database of 'retired experts'** for this and further possible deployments.

The Umsobomvu Youth Trust is driving a number of initiatives, many of which entail youth volunteers, to support a range of skills development programmes.

A new institution is the **Joint Initiative for Priority Skills Acquisition (JIPSA).** This is a structure led by a committee of key ministers, business leaders, trade unionists and education and training providers or experts. Its job will be to identify urgent skills needs and quick and effective solutions. Solutions may include special training programmes, bringing back retirees or South Africans and Africans working out of Africa, and drawing in new immigrants where necessary. It may also include mentoring and overseas placement of trainees to fast track their development. JIPSA will have an initial timetable of 18 months, starting in March 2006, after which its future will be reviewed.

Source: Mlambo-Ngcuka (2006)

■ too few graduates in mathematics and science to sustain economic growth in a modern, technologically advanced economy.

There is thus no doubt that an integrated system for training and development needs to be created and that various lessons can be learnt from international systems.

According to the NTB (1994) report, technical and skills training has historically never been a priority in South Africa and there is a lack of coordination between the different components of the training system. For example, in the workplace many forms of technical training take place but, apart from artisan training, these are not recognised. There are many other causes for concern:

■ in the education and training field the basic assumption is that teachers and trainers should be more highly qualified than their students before being allowed to teach or to train. These requirements are increasingly being met within the education system, but such requirements do not apply when trainers are appointed to train in organisations;

■ the unemployment training programmes lack legitimacy because they do not deliver;

■ educators and trainers are not developed to meet South Africa's needs;

■ there is only limited provision for formal and informal organisational links between education, training, business, labour and the state. An example of this is the fact that school-leavers cannot find jobs;

■ there is no nationally recognised framework of qualifications;

■ the existing career counselling system is inadequate. The limited range of occupations for which education and training currently caters does not provide for progression within recognised career paths; and

- the methods used to provide access and the recognition of prior learning do not cater for the effects on individuals of the inadequacies of existing education and training programmes.

At present the following are considered to be education and training problems in South Africa, and compared with 1994, it is very similar:
- Poor standard of primary and secondary education in certain areas
- Poor record of mathematics and science education, and poor pass rates
- Skills shortages in technical skills for example artisan and high level technical skills
- Low education and training levels among in the SA community
- Impact of unemployment and HIV/Aids

13.2.2.3 Human Resource Development Strategy for South Africa

The Human Resource Development Strategy (HRDS) has its origins in the Reconstruction and Development Programme (RDP), which identified the people of South Africa as its most important resource and attempts to meet the needs of the economy (Erasmus et al 2006: 61).

VISION, MISSION AND GOALS

The vision for the HRD strategy is as follows:
- A nation at work for a better life for all.

The mission for the HRD strategy is:
- To maximise the potential of the people of South Africa, through the acquisition of knowledge and skills, to work productively and competitively in order to achieve a rising quality of life for all, and to set in place an operational plan, together with the necessary institutional arrangements, to achieve this.

The three broad goals are:
- To improve South Africa's position on the Human Development Index (measure quality of life aspects such as life expectancy);
- To improve South Africa's rating on the Gini Coefficient (reduce disparities in wealth and poverty and develop a more inclusive society);
- To improve South Africa's position in the International Competitiveness League in absolute terms

Source: Department of Labour 2005: National Skills Development Strategy

---

13.2.2.4 State of Skills in South Africa 2005

In 2005 a report was published by the Department of Labour addressing the State of Skills in South Africa. This report, inter alia, provided a sketch of the economic and employment context; the emerging socio-economic programmes which government is developing to fight poverty, joblessness and slow growth; and a comprehensiveness overview of the current state of skills. The report concludes will the launch of a 'National Skills Development Strategy' which endeavours to align skills development practices with broader socio-economic development policies.

Elsewhere in Africa

Development of adequate and appropriate human resources is necessary for Tanzania to achieve its economic and development objectives. Unfortunately, Tanzania witnessed a decline in HRD during the economic crisis period in the 1980s and early 1990s ... HRD was in crisis in Tanzania and the failure of the Tanzanian government to invest in human capital partly explained the backwardness of their economy ... [T]here still are critical shortages of skills at almost all levels ... [T]his fact has been recognized by the government and it is making attempts to tackle them.

Source: Extracted and slightly adapted from Debrah (2004: 77–78)

13.3 NATIONAL SKILLS DEVELOPMENT STRATEGY

Nation Skills Development Strategy (NSDS) for 2005 to 2010 was developed with a vision, mission, principles and objectives (Department of Labour 2005). The vision is "Skills for sustainable growth, development and equity". The NSDS mission is stated as "The NSDS contributes to sustainable development of skills growth; development and equity of skills development institutions by aligning their work and resources to the skills needs for effective delivery and implementation". The principles of the NSDS are:

1 Support economic growth for employment creation and poverty eradication.
2 Promote productive citizenship for all by aligning skills development with national strategies for growth and development.
3 Accelerate Broad-based Black Economic Empowerment and Employment Equity (85% black, 54% women and 4% people with disabilities, including youth in all categories). Learners with disabilities are to be provided with reasonable accommodation such as assistive devices and access to learning and training material to enable them to have access to and participate in skills development.
4 Support, monitor and evaluate the delivery and quality assurance systems necessary for the implementation of the NSDS.
5 Advance the culture of excellence in skills development and lifelong learning.

Five objectives are stated with success indicators and are as follows:
Objective 1: Prioritising and communicating critical skills, for sustainable growth, development and equity
Objective 2: Promoting and accelerating quality training for all in the workplace
Objective 3: Promoting employability and sustainability livelihoods through skills development.
Objective 4: Assisting designated groups, including new entrants, to participate in accredited work, integrated learning and work-based programmes to acquire critical skills to even the labour market and the self-employed.
Objective 5: Improving the quality and relevance of provision.

The Skills Development Strategy was part of various initiatives launched by the Department of Labour. The others were the enactment of the Labour Relations Act in 1995, the South African Qualifications Authority Act in 1995 (soon to be replaced by the National Qualifications Framework Act, see paragraph 13.4) and the Employment Equity Act in 1998. The Skills Development Strategy interacts with all the abovementioned Acts and supports the main principles of the skills development strategy for South Africa (Meyer et al 2007: 25).

13.4 THE SOUTH AFRICAN NATIONAL QUALIFICATIONS FRAMEWORK

13.4.1 General

The South African Qualifications Authority (SAQA) Act 58 of 1995 was passed in September 1995 and its purpose is to "provide for the development and implementation of a National Qualifications Framework (NQF) and the establishment of the South African Qualifications Authority". This Act forms the legal baseline for further development of an integrated approach to education and training in our country.

The Department of Education published on 11 February 2008 a General Notice (256 of 2008) where a call for comment was requested on the following Bills:

- National Qualifications Framework Bill, 1995
- Higher Education Amendment Act, 2008
- General and Further Education and Training Quality Assurance Act Amendment Bill, 2008

The introduction of the new National Qualifications Framework Bill is important for this section because it might repeal the South African Qualifications Authority Act, 1995.

In the explanatory memorandum (2008) on the NQF Bill, it is explained that the ministers of Education and Labour have published a joint policy statement on "Enhancing the Efficacy and Efficiency of the National Qualifications Framework (NQF)", and the new Bill gives legislative effect to the new policy. The new policy is the result of a study concluded by international and local specialists on the NQF and its implementation. The Ministers of Education and Labour indicated that in little more than 10 years the NQF, which was developed by SAQA, has become an essential frame of reference for all education and training institutions and workplaces alike.

The main features of the Bill (National Qualifications Bill, explanatory memorandums, 2008: 23–25) are:

- *The NQF.* The SAQA Act did not describe the NQF. The NQF Bill, 2008 contains such a description and in so doing clarifies the concept of an NQF and the way it is organised. The change of name of 'SAQA Act' to 'NQF Bill' reflects the new focus.
- *Ministerial authority.* The SAQA Act requires the ministers of Education and Labour to achieve agreement on many matters in consultation with one another. Such provisions reflect the wide scope of the NQF, which covers all education and training, but they have proved cumbersome in practice. The NQF Bill requires the two ministers to act collaboratively, but prescribes clear spheres of ministerial responsibility.
- *SAQA's role.* The SAQA Act gave SAQA the responsibility of conceptualising the NQF and leading its implementation. The NQF Bill secures an apex role for SAQA as custodian of the values of the NQF, research organisation, learning database manager and advisor on the entire NQF system to the government (among other responsibilities). The Bill gives executive responsibility for NQF implementation to three sectoral Quality Councils which will act in close liaison with each other and with SAQA.
- *A fit-for-purpose approach.* The NQF Bill will foster a variety of fit-for-purpose approaches to standard setting and quality assurance.
- *Simplification.* The SAQA Act empowered SAQA to establish or recognise substructures to carry out the design of standards and qualifications, and to

undertake quality assurance. SAQA did this by way of regulations. Many Acts added new statutory quality-assurance bodies that were required to work within the SAQA system. NQF processes were thus complicated by the proliferation of substructures with overlapping mandates. By naming Quality Councils for General and Further Education and Training, Higher Education, and Trades and Occupations respectively, the NQF Bill provides a radically simplified sectoral architecture with clear lines of accountability and explicit requirements for collaboration and dispute resolution.

■ *Sectors not bands*. The regulations under the SAQA Act formalised the concepts of NQF bands as an organising principle: the General Education and Training (GET) band (level 1), the Further Education and Training (FET) band (levels 2–4), the Higher Education and Training (HET) band (levels 5–8). This horizontal organisation was meant to give expression to the integration of all forms of learning within a band, no matter how or where it was provided. The Bill, by contrast, is based on the idea of education and training sectors: the General and Further Education and Training sector, the Higher Education sector, the Trades and Occupations sector. The first two sectors comprise formal education institutions (schools, adult education centres, FET colleges, higher education institutions) and fall under the Minister of Education. The third comprises education and training in and for the workplace, and falls under the Minister of Labour.

The NQF Bill will therefore be accompanied by Bills to amend the General and Further Education and Training Quality Assurance Act, 2001, the Higher Education Act, 1997, and the Skills Development Act, 1998.

The National Qualifications Framework Bill (2008) consists of the following chapters:
■ Chapter 1: Interpretation, object and application
■ Chapter 2: National Qualifications Framework (NQF)
■ Chapter 3: Responsibilities of Ministers
■ Chapter 4: South African Qualification Authority
■ Chapter 5: Quality Councils (QC)
■ Chapter 6: Professional Bodies
■ Chapter 7: Miscellaneous

The rest of this section will focus on the important sections of the NQF Bill, 2008 and sections of the present SAQA Act which will be retained in the new NQF Act.

13.4.2 A national qualifications framework

The National Qualifications Framework (NQF) (see table 13.1) is a comprehensive system for the classification, registration, publication and articulation of quality assured national qualifications (Chapter two of the NQF Bill).

The NQF is organised as a series of levels of learning achievement in ascending order from one to eight (new proposal up to level 10). Each level on the NQF is described by a statement of learning achievement known as a level descriptor. A level descriptor provides a broad indication of learning achievements or outcomes that alter appropriate to a qualification at that level. Level descriptors are developed and determined for each sector, which are for Trades and Occupations, for General and Further Education and Training, and for Higher Education. SAQA will assign a qualification to a particular level on the NQF.

As illustrated in table 13.1, the NQF could provide the integrating factor for education and training. The various levels defined in table 13.1 are the following.

- *Level 1*. Two ways of reaching level 1 are possible. The Adult Basic Education and Training (ABET) levels 1, 2, 3 and 4 comprise the one route to the Trades and Occupations sector and the other is the compulsory nine to 10 years of schooling.
- *Levels 2 to 4*. National and higher certificates of schooling (General and Further Education and Training sector) could be acquired in any number of ways, ranging from education at senior secondary schools, technical community colleges, private providers, etc.
- *Levels 5 to 8*. At tertiary and research levels study would lead to national diplomas and degrees (Higher Education and Training sector).
- The suggested new levels are from 5 to 10 – refer to table 13.1.

Table 13.1 contains both the levels 1 to 8 and the new levels 1 to 10. Please consult with SAQA to obtain the latest explanation on levels 1 to 10.

13.4.3 Objectives of the NQF

In terms of the Act the objectives of the NQF are as follows:
- to create an integrated national framework for learning achievements;
- to facilitate access to and mobility and progression within education, training and career paths;
- to enhance the quality of education and training;
- to accelerate the reparation of past unfair discrimination in education, training and employment opportunities; and
- to contribute to the full personal development of each learner, and the social and economic development of the nation at large.

13.4.4 South African Qualifications Authority (SAQA)

Chapter IV of the new Bill provides for the continuation of SAQA as a juristic person. The Authority is governed by a board and members are appointed by the Minister. The chief executive officer (CEO) of SAQA and the CEO of each QC is a member by virtue of their offices and the board may establishes committees.

13.4.5 Functions of SAQA

The main functions of SAQA are to:
- oversee the development of the NQF;
- recommend level descriptions;
- recommend a policy framework with respect to qualifications quality assurance, recognising professional bodies.

13.4.6 Quality Councils (QC)

The NQF Bill proposes three QCs, namely: QC for General and Further Education and Training where Umalusi will be QC; QC for Higher Education where the Council on Higher Education is the QC for Higher Education; and QC for Trades and Occupations where the QC for Trades and Occupations (QCTO) (see also section 13.5.8) will perform various functions (chapter five of the NQF Bill).

The main functions of QCs are
- to advise the relevant minister on matters relating to its sub-framework in terms of Act
- develop and manage the sub-framework in accordance with a multiyear rolling strategic plan, budget and implementation framework.

Table 13.1: National Qualifications Framework (old and new)

NQF level		Sectors	Types of qualifications and certificates	Locations of learning for units and qualifications		
10*	8	Higher Education and Training sector	Doctoral degrees	Universities		
9	8		Master's degrees	Universities		
8	7		Honours/post-graduate diplomas	Universities		
7	6		First degrees/advanced diplomas	Universities		
6	6		Diploma/higher certificates	Universities		
5	5		Occupational certificates	Universities		
General and Further Education and Training sector						
4		Further Education and Training sector	School/college/adult training centres Mix of units from all	Formal high schools/ private/state schools	Technical/ community/ police/nursing/ private colleges	RDP and labour market schemes/ SETAs/union/ workplace
3						
2			School/college/training/ certificates Mix of units from all			
			School/college/training certificates Mix of units from all			
Trades and Occupation sector						
1			Senior phase — ABET level 4	Formal schools (urban/rural/ farm/special)	Occupation/work-based training/ RDP/labour market schemes/ upliftment programmes/ community programmes	NGOs/churches/ night schools/ ABET programmes/ private providers/ industry training boards/unions/ workplace, etc
			Intermediate phase — ABET level 3			
			Foundation phase — ABET level 2			
			Pre-school — ABET level 1			

*Proposed new framework – not yet approved at time of going to print.

- with respect to levels on its sub-framework –
  - (i) propose level descriptors to SAQA for consideration and recommendation to the Minister; and
  - (ii) keep level descriptors under review in order to ensure that they remain current and appropriate.
- with respect to qualifications for its sub-framework –
  - (i) propose a policy framework to SAQA for the development, registration and publication of qualifications, after consultations within the sector;
  - (ii) propose a policy framework to SAQA for assessment, recognition of prior learning, and credit accumulation and transfer, after consultations within the sector;
  - (iii) ensure the development of such qualifications as are necessary for the sector, which may include appropriate measures for the assessment of learning achievement; and
  - (iv) recommend qualifications to SAQA for registration.

- with respect to quality assurance within its sub-framework –
  - (i) propose a policy framework to SAQA for quality assurance, after consultations within the sector;
  - (ii) ensure the integrity and credibility of quality assurance;
  - (iii) make provision for the delegation of powers to undertake quality assurance;
  - (iv) ensure that such quality assurance as is necessary for the sector is undertaken; and
  - (v) publish reports on the outcomes of quality assurance processes.
- with respect to information matters –
  - (i) maintain a database of learner achievements and related matters for purposes of this Act; and
  - (ii) submit such data in a format determined in consultation with SAQA for recording on the national learners' records database contemplated at section 14.

13.4.7 Professional bodies

According to the NQF Bill (Chapter six), professional bodies (statutory or non-statutory body of expert practitioners in an occupational field) must apply to SAQA to be recognised as a professional body. It further stipulates that a professional body must cooperate with the relevant QCs in respect of qualifications and Quality Assurance in its occupational field, and that a professional body must apply to SAQA to register a professional designation on the NQF. A professional body must, in consultation with SAQA, maintain a database for purposes of this Act and submit such data in an agreed format for recording on the national learners' records database.

13.5 THE SKILLS DEVELOPMENT ACT (SDA)

The Skills Development Act 97 of 1998 was signed by the President of the Republic of South Africa on 20 October 1998 and repealed the following laws:
- The Manpower Training Act 56 of 1981
- The Guidance and Placement Act 62 of 1981
- The Local Government Training Act 41 of 1985)
- Sections 78 to 87 of the Telecommunications Act 106 of 1996)

The SDA (1998) has been amended by the Skills Development Amendment Bill, 2008. An importance change suggested by the Amendment Bill is the inclusion of a definition of a 'learning programme', which means a programme of occupationally directed learning which includes a learnership, an apprenticeship, an internship, a skills programme, a programme of foundational learning and any other prescribed learning programme which includes a structured work experience component.

Proposed amendments are included in the discussion below, which highlights the most important sections of the SDA.

13.5.1 Purposes of the Act

Section 2 of the Act set out the various purposes of the Act, which are:
- to develop the skills of the South African workforce;
- to increase the levels of investment in education and training in the labour market, and to improve the return on investment;
- to use the workplace as an active learning environment to provide employees with opportunities to acquire new skills, and to provide opportunities for new entrants to the labour market to gain work experience;

- to employ persons who find it difficult to be employed; to encourage workers to participate in learning programmes;
- to improve the employment prospects of persons previously disadvantaged by unfair discrimination and to redress those disadvantages through training and education;
- to ensure the quality of learning in and for the workplace;
- to assist work-seekers to find work, retrenched workers to re-enter the labour market and employers to find qualified employees; and
- to provide and regulate employment services.

The following institutions are established by the Act, namely the National Skills Authority; the National Skills Fund; a skills development levy-financing scheme as stipulated in the Skills Development Levies Act; Sector Educational and Training Authorities (SETAs); Labour Centres; Department of Labour provincial offices; Artisan Development and/or Institutes of Sectoral Occupational Excellence; Quality Council for Trades and Occupations (QCTO); Skills Development forums in each province, and a national artisan moderation body.

13.5.2 National Skills Authority

The main functions of the National Skills Authority are as follows (section 5 of the Act):
- to advise the Minister of Labour on a national skills development policy and strategy; guidelines on the implementation of the National Skills Development Strategy; and any regulations to be made;
- to liaise with SETAs and the national skills development policy, and the National Skills Development Strategy;
- to report to the Minister on the progress made in the implementation of the National Skills Development Strategy;
- to conduct investigations on any matter arising out of the application of the SDA: and
- to liaise with QCTO on occupation standards and qualifications.

13.5.3 Sector education and training authorities (SETAs)

Establishment of SETAs is described in Chapter III of the Act and the Minister of Labour may establish a SETA with a constitution for any national economic sector.
   The Minister of Labour must, however, take the following into account:
- the education and training needs of employers and employees;
- technologies;
- the potential of the proposed sector for coherent occupational structures and career pathing; and
- the scope of any national strategies for economic growth and development; the organisational structures of the trade unions, employer organisations and government in closely related sectors; any consensus that there may be between organised labour, organised employers and relevant government departments as to the definition of any sector; and the financial and organisational ability of the proposed sector to support a SETA.

SETAs have various functions, of which the most important are to:
- develop a sector skills plan within the framework of the National Skills Development Strategy;
- implement its sector skills plan by establishing learning programmes; approving

workplace skills plans and annual training reports; allocating grants in the prescribed manner to employers, education and training providers, and workers; and monitoring education and training in the sector as prescribed by the QCTO;

- promote learning programmes by identifying workplaces for practical work experience;
- support the development of learning materials; improve the facilitation of learning; and assist in the conclusion of agreements for learning programmes to the extent that is required;
- register learnership agreements within a week from its establishment; and
- liaise with the National Skills Authority on:
  - the national skills development policy;
  - the national skills development strategy; and
  - its sector skills plan.

A SETA may consist only of members representing organised labour; organised employers, including small business; relevant government departments; any interested professional body; and any bargaining council with jurisdiction in the sector.

- A SETA may establish chambers in its sector and must have a constitution.
- A SETA is financed from the skills development levies collected in its sector; the monies paid to it from the National Skills Fund; grants, donations and bequests made to it; income earned on surplus monies deposited or invested; income earned on services rendered in the prescribed manner; and money received from any other source. The money received by a SETA must be paid into a banking account at any registered bank and may be invested.

13.5.4 Learnerships

Learnerships are described in Chapter IV of the Act, and a SETA may establish a learnership if firstly, the learnership includes a structured learning component; secondly, it includes a structured work experience component; thirdly, it would lead to a qualification registered by the South African Qualifications Authority associated with a trade or an occupation; and lastly, the intended learnership is registered with the Director-General in the prescribed manner. It is further noted that any reference to 'learnership' in this Act includes an apprenticeship and any reference to a learner includes an apprentice.

Learnership agreements are agreements entered into for a specified period between a learner, an employer or a group of employers, and a training provider accredited by QCTO. The employer has the responsibility:

- to employ the learner for the period specified in the agreement; to provide specified practical work experience; and
- to release the learner to attend the education and training specified in the agreement.

The learner has the responsibility to work for the employer and to attend the specified education and training; and the training provider must provide the education and training and the learner support specified in the agreement.

13.5.5 Contract of employment with learner

If a learner was in the employ of the employer party to the learnership agreement concerned when the agreement was concluded, the learner's contract of employment is not affected by the agreement. But if the learner was not in the employ of the employer party to the leadership agreement concerned when the agreement was concluded, the employer and learner must enter into a contract of employment. Disputes about learnerships must be referred to the Commission for Conciliation, Mediation and Arbitration (CCMA). For further information on learnership, the Skills Development Act, 1998, Learnership Regulation, 2007 (No. R 519 of 29 June 2007) should be consulted.

13.5.6 Administration of the Act by the Department of Labour and Labour Centres

The Act (section 22) makes provision for various functions of the Department in terms of the Act. The main functions are to research and analyse the labour market in order to determine skills development needs and to assist in the formulation of the National Skills Development Strategy and sector skills development plans.

Labour Centres are the other institutions established by the Act. The main functions of these centres in respect of employment services are to provide information to workers, employers and training providers, including improvement of such services to rural communities; to register work-seekers; and to register vacancies and work opportunities.

13.5.7 Artisan development

An artisan moderation body will be established to coordinate artisan development, and the Minister of Labour will list any occupation in the 'Framework of Occupation' as a trade for which an artisan qualification is required. A national register of artisans must be maintained, and no person may be registered as an artisan unless they have passed a trade test.

13.5.8 Quality Council for Trades and Occupations (QCTO)

An QCTO will be established which is managed by the provisions of the Public Finance Management Act. The QCTO consists of 16 members appointed by the Minister with main functions to advise the Minister on all matters of policy concerning occupational standards and qualifications; quality assurance; establishing and maintaining standards; and liaising with the National Skills Authority and South African Qualifications Authority.

13.5.9 Financing skills development

The National Skills Fund (Chapter VII of the Act) must be credited with, firstly, 20% of the skills development levies as stipulated in the Skills Development Levies Act; secondly, the skills development levies collected and transferred to the fund; thirdly, money appropriated by parliament for the fund; fourthly, donations to the fund; and lastly, money received from any other source.

The money in the fund may be used only for the projects identified in the National Skills Development Strategy as national priorities or for such other projects related to the achievement of the purposes of this Act as the Director-General determines.

13.6 THE SKILLS DEVELOPMENT LEVIES ACT

The purpose of the Skills Development Levies Act 9 of 1999 is to provide for the imposition of a skills development levy. The most important aspects of the Act will be outlined in this section.

13.6.1 Levy to be paid

According to section 3 of the Act, every employer must pay a skills development levy and the South African Revenue Service (SARS) will be the national collection agency.

Every employer must pay a levy from 1 April 2000 at a rate of 0,5% and from 1 April 2001 at a rate of 1% of an employee's total remuneration. Pensions, super-annuations or retiring allowance are, for example, excluded according to section 2(5) of the Act.

13.6.2 Exemptions from the Act

The following categories of employers are exempted:
- any public service employer in the national or provincial government;
- any employer whose remuneration to all its employees during the following 12-month period will not exceed R250 000 and who is not required to apply for registration in terms of the Fourth Schedule to the Income Tax Act;
- any religious or charitable institution which is exempted from income tax; and
- any national or provincial public entity that receives 80% or more of its funds from parliament.

13.6.3 Registration for payment of levy

Employers who are liable to pay the levy must apply to the Commissioner of SARS to be registered, and indicate the jurisdiction of the SETA within which they belong. The employer must also register with the SETA.

13.6.4 Payment of levy to Commissioner and refund

An employer must pay the levy to the Commissioner of Inland Revenue Services not later than seven days after the end of each month. A statement reflecting the amount of the levy due by that employer and other information as the Commissioner may require must accompany the payment. Instead of paying levies to the Commissioner of Inland Revenue, the Minister of Labour may, in consultation with the Minister of Finance and by notice in the *Government Gazette*, decide that employers should pay levies to the SETA, subject to certain criteria. This payment must also be done not later than seven days after the end of each month.

Late payments are penalised by interest that is imposed at a rate equivalent to that in the Income Tax Act Penalties. The levies, interest and penalties collected by the Commissioner, after deduction of refunds, must be paid into the National Revenue Fund (section 8 of the Act).

The National Skills Fund will receive 20% of the levy, and organisations will be able to claim for financing for up to 80% of the levy less the set-up and running costs of the SETA.

An employer has certain responsibilities towards a SETA (Chapter II of the Act), of which paying the said levies at due dates is the most important in terms of the Act.

A labour inspector appointed in terms of section 63 of the Basic Conditions of Employment Act 75 of 1997 is regarded as an inspector for the purposes of this Act, for collection of levies by a SETA or its approved body (section 15).

An inspector may, without warrant or notice, at any reasonable time enter any workplace or any other place – which is not a home – where an employer carries on business or keeps any records, to enforce compliance with this Act. An inspector may enter a home with the consent of the owner or occupier or with an authorised warrant.

EXHIBIT 13.2: Training and developing employees: macro-level perspectives

SOUTH AFRICA MUST CREATE JOBS

Johannesburg – South Africa's economy will have to create between 510 000 and 740 000 jobs a year to meet its accelerated and shared growth initiative for SA (AsgiSA) target of halving unemployment by 2014, according to Merrill Lynch.

The first figure is based on South Africa's official unemployment rate of 25 percent. The definition excludes "so called" discouraged job seekers. The second figure is based on the broader definition which shows that up to 40 percent of the labour force is unemployed.

The economy has grown by more than 4 percent a year over the past three years and Statistics SA figures show this has added only about 500 000 jobs each year.

Merrill Lynch said, despite the improvement in employment growth, the economy still fell "well short of the required rate to achieve the AsgiSA target".

The economy's employment intensity – the number of formal jobs (excluding agriculture) per R1 million worth of production – has declined from about 16 in 1967 to less than eight in 2006.

Unless this trend stabilises, the economy will have to grow its GDP by an average rate of 7 percent to meet the AsgiSA employment target, the investment bank warned.

South Africa will have to create 510 000 jobs a year, a job growth rate of 3,5 percent.

Employment has grown by an average of 2,7 percent each year for the past five years.

The Merrill Lynch report said that, if the job growth and labour participation rates remained unchanged, this would lead to the creation of 380 000 jobs a year, well short of the AsgiSA target. The government's target of 6 percent economic growth, which would apply for the period between 2010 and 2014, would be too late.

Goolam Ballim, group economist at Standard Bank, said targeting a 7 percent growth rate would be "ambitious" and would require a "fervent growth dynamic" and a robust export strategy. He said the economy could give up chasing higher growth rates if employment intensity improved.

But Dave Mohr, chief economist at Citadel, said the current economic and employment growth rates point to a need for higher growth, beyond the 6 percent targeted under AsgiSA.

There would have to be a switch to export-led growth, and to do so the rand/dollar exchange rate would have to weaken to between R8 and R9. The economy could achieve the AsgiSA employment target with GDP growth rates of 6 percent if a bulk of this growth was from labour intensive sectors.

The Merrill Lynch report said construction, the most labour-intensive sector of the economy, had experienced employment growth of 10 percent a year over the past two years.

The government's multibillion infrastructure upgrade programme would help buffer employment growth.

The government sector, which has the third highest labour intensity, accounts for about 13 percent of all formal sector employment.

But the report said greater job creation would have to come from low-skill sectors such as mining and manufacturing.

Source: Mafu (2007)

13.6.5 Offences in terms of the Act

Section 20 of the Act clearly states that any person who fails to apply for registration for purposes of the levy; fails to pay any levy on the date determined for payment thereof; furnishes any false information in a statement or other document; fails to submit or deliver any statement or other document; fails to disclose any information; or hinders or obstructs any person in carrying out functions; commits an offence and is liable on conviction to a fine or imprisonment for a period not exceeding one year.

13.7 MANAGERIAL IMPLICATIONS OF THE LEGISLATION

The South African Qualifications Authority Act (National Qualifications Framework Act), Skills Development Act and the Skills Development Levies Act brings about further challenges for employers to manage the training and development of employees in organisations. These challenges are to:

■ ensure that all stakeholders in the organisation are aware of the different acts and the employer's responsibilities;
■ participate in the bodies as set out by the various training legislation, for example SETA learnerships;
■ align the organisation's human resource strategy, and in particular Education and Training strategy, with the overall business strategy;
■ make finances and personnel available to involve themselves in the NQF alignment process as well as for paying levies;
■ appoint a skills development facilitator; and
■ take note of the interrelatedness of the other labour legislation, for example the Employment Equity Act, Labour Relations Act and the National Skills Development Strategy as well as its impact on organisation strategy and development initiatives.

Mindset changes are required for all managerial staff in organisations to focus on education and training initiatives based on needs analysis, to uplift the skills based especially for designated groups.

13.8 ADULT BASIC EDUCATION (ABE)

Research has shown that some 9,4 million adults with less than nine years of schooling have received no education at all. Millions more have received little formal education, and what they have received has been of low quality (Erasmus et al 2006).

The challenges of addressing low literacy have been part of South Africa's history for many years. But since the new democracy in 1994, renewed attention has been given to ABET as a national dilemma.

The NTB (1994) report recommended that the following important aspects should be addressed:

■ The development of a culture of learning and skills development should commence at primary-school level. Programmes to assist in this development should be multifaceted and, wherever possible, have short-term effects.
■ An organisation or coordinating body should be formed to facilitate linkages between formal and micro-enterprise sectors, to act as an organised voice for the micro-enterprise sector and to facilitate the obtaining of capital.
■ The development of targeted programmes for different categories of the unemployed, such as unemployed youth, women, etc, through appropriate agencies.
■ The state should encourage and support the development of service/commerce/ industry plans for industries undergoing a process of restructuring so that retrenched people can be accommodated.
■ The state should ensure the development of an integrated approach to education and training to allow school leavers more structured access.
■ The state should develop funding programmes to provide incentives to employers to support practical training.

- Provision must be made for the training needs of small business, and they must be encouraged to identify the outcomes that they require and for which they can provide training within the structure of the National Qualifications Framework.
- Affirmative action policies should be an integral part of development programmes.
- A large number of career guidance and placement centres should be established, and these should aim at becoming high-profile services within the communities they serve. They should be responsible for the development of their own databases reflecting vacancies and the range of available education and training courses. The centres should be linked to both the regional and national databases.

Since the NTB report, various initiatives have been launched by government and private organisations to provide ABET to those seeking further development. The Department of Education published a policy document on Adult Basic Education and Training during 2003, which provided guidelines to improve illiteracy levels. Recently (in 2008) a literacy campaign, the *Kha ri Gude* Mass literacy campaign, was launched (see exhibit 13.3).

EXHIBIT 13.3: The *Kha ri Gude* mass literacy campaign

The South African Literacy Campaign launched by Minister Naledi Pandor is intended to enable 4,7 million adults to become literate between the 14 April 2008 and the end of 2012. It is through this campaign that the developmental state welcomes new learners to the portals of learning.

Kha ri Gude, Tshivenda for 'let us learn', invites those adults who missed out on their schooling and who cannot read or write, to join one of about 20 000 literacy classes that will be held all over South Africa and which will start opening their doors on the 14 April.

The *Kha ri Gude* literacy campaign was developed in response to the call by Minister of Education, Naledi Pandor, for a national campaign to end illiteracy among South African adults. As a programme of government, and as one of the Apex programmes announced by President Mbeki in his 2008 State of the Nation address, the Campaign can be seen as one of the important ways in which the developmental state prioritises the needs of the poor and addresses the right of all citizens to basic education in the official language/s of their choice.

The campaign resulted from the recommendations of the Ministerial Committee on Literacy and is intended to provide the opportunity for 4,7 South Africans to become literate. Achieving this target would also mean that South Africa will have fulfilled its 2000 Dakar commitment – that of reducing illiteracy by 50% by 2015.

In order for a national programme of this magnitude to reach its target, the campaign requires voluntary support from a wide range of people and organisations drawn from all sectors of society and across all provinces, who will assist in establishing learning sites around the country, help to recruit literacy volunteer educators and work with them to recruit learners.

Source: www.doe.co.za

13.9 CONCLUSION

In this chapter the focus was on some national-level trends regarding the development and training of employees. The background to the development of the National Training Strategy and the problems related to training and development in South Africa were briefly discussed. The National Qualifications Framework and the various structures associated with it were described. A discussion was provided on the Skills Development Act and the Skills Development Levies Act and their implications for management. It was clearly stated that the SAQA Act will probably be replaced by a new Act, the National Qualifications Framework Act, and that various amendments to the SDA is suggested by the Skills Development Amendment Act, 2008. Readers are advised to contact the state printer or the government website (www.gov.co.za) for the latest news on these amendments and changes. The last part of the chapter focused on adult basic education. In the next chapter we focus on organisational-level aspects of the training and development of employees.

SUSTAINABILITY CONNECTION?

The single most important contributing factor to making our country and continent a success over the longer term would relate directly to the challenge of developing our people. This makes human resource development, which includes education and all other forms of training and development, probably the key factor which will impact on our future. It is, for example, only through the appropriate development of our people that the collective will can be harnessed to care for each other and for our planet.

SELF-EVALUATION QUESTIONS

1 Discuss the problems associated with the training and development of human resources in South Africa.
2 Describe how the knowledge and experience of the international community can assist in the development of a National Training Strategy.
3 Explain the main elements of the proposed National Training Strategy. Discuss the elements involved and the role that the NQF will play.
4 Explain how the NQF will impact on training and development in your organisation.
5 Discuss the influence of a coordinated and well-developed National Training Strategy on the competitiveness of South African organisations.
6 Analyse the role of ABE in your organisation, and discuss the role that it can play in the improvement of knowledge and skills in South Africa.
7 Explain the importance and appropriateness of the structures created by the South African Qualification Authority Act (the new National Qualifications Framework Act) to meet South Africa's training and development needs.
8 Discuss the impact of the Skills Development Act and the Skills Development Levies Act on the management of training and development in organisations.
9 List the steps management has to implement to ensure adherence to the Act, but also to attain organisational goals.

14 TRAINING AND DEVELOPING EMPLOYEES: ORGANISATIONAL-LEVEL PERSPECTIVES

LEARNING OUTCOMES

After studying this chapter, you should be able to:

- explain the concept human resource development;
- distinguish between 'training', 'education' and 'development';
- list the reasons for human resource development in organisations;
- illustrate the training process with the aid of a sketch;
- discuss the training needs assessment phase and training phase; and
- explain how the effectiveness of training will be evaluated.

14.1 INTRODUCTION

All organisations engage employees to execute certain activities in order to achieve their goals and objectives. It has been emphasised a number of times that, irrespective of the nature of these goals and objectives, organisations must have competent employees to perform the tasks and to accomplish them. Although well-thought-out strategies and efficient human resource planning, recruitment and selection initially provide an organisation with the required employees, additional training is normally necessary to provide them with job-specific skills which enable them to survive over time.

Compared with other developing countries, South Africa usually ranks among the last in the people category in international competitive ratings. Aspects such as literacy and education are critical in this regard. For a very long time organisations in South Africa have neglected to invest in their employees to equip them for the challenges of our modern, globally competitive world. According to the annual South African ASTD report (2007), South African organisations spend 3,4% of payroll on training – more than the US, which is on 2,52%. Investment in human resource development should play a prominent role in South African organisations today and in the future.

In this chapter the focus is on training and development efforts within the organisation. The training process starts with assessing training needs and formulating objectives for training programmes. The next step is to design and deliver the necessary training programmes using those methods and procedures most likely to ensure that they achieve their desired ends. The training programmes are then evaluated to ensure that objectives are met. Sustainable long-term growth for the organisation essential, and employee motivation and training and development are key features to this end.

14.2 HUMAN RESOURCE DEVELOPMENT: CONCEPTS AND IMPORTANCE

The importance of human resource development (HRD) as a means of ensuring that organisations maintain their competitiveness in an ever-changing environment cannot be overemphasised. The country's history, technological innovations, competitive pressures, restructuring and downsizing, the low level of literacy and numeracy and the increasing diversity of the workforce are some of the important issues which force organisations to retrain employees and to provide basic literacy training, thus ensuring that employees are ready to face present challenges and to prepare themselves for the future.

14.2.1 What is HRD?

Human resource development can be defined as a learning experience organised mainly by an employer, usually within a specified period of time, to bring about the possibility of performance improvement and/or personal growth (Nadler & Nadler 1989: 6; Analoui 2007).

The main focus of HRD is learning, and its principal aim is to attain the objectives of both the organisation and the individual. HRD takes place over time and concerns itself with the provision of learning, development and training opportunities to improve individual, team and organisational performance. HRD is a long-term investment which will ensure the sustainability of the organisation by ensuring a planned way that employees possess the capabilities to achieve strategic goals.

Generally, learning can be viewed as a relatively permanent change in behaviour, and HRD focuses on intentional rather than incidental learning. The learner focuses on a learning experience with the express purpose of learning something.

Although a person can learn something incidentally by watching TV, reading the newspaper or having a discussion with friends, the main purpose of such activities is not to learn. Intentional learning can be formal or informal. Broadly speaking, formal learning refers to the situation where an employee is taken out of the normal working environment to attend a course or lecture or to do a practical course. Informal learning, on the other hand, includes non-structured on-the-job training which is provided by the supervisor or by a person designated to do the training.

14.2.2 Employee 'training', 'education', 'development' and 'outcomes-based education and training': clarifying concepts

- Employee training is job-related learning that is provided by employers for their employees. The main aim is the improvement of employees' skills, knowledge and attitudes so that they can perform their duties according to set standards.
- Employee education in the organisational context concerns the preparation of an individual for a job different from the one he or she currently holds. In this case, the outcome of performance is clearly defined.

  Employee education usually refers to the preparation of managers for higher-level jobs or for possible changes in the future. In many organisations it is also termed 'management development'. Education in the general sense refers to the broad educational process covering pre-school, primary, secondary and tertiary education. This usually occurs outside the organisation (except for adult literacy, life skills and numeracy training, which normally occur within the organisational context).
- In contrast to training (which is job related) and education (which is the preparation of an employee for a different job), employee development is a broad

term which relates to training, education and other intentional or unintentional learning, and which refers to general growth through learning.

It is important to note that 'outcomes-based education' has only recently been introduced in South Africa. Its primary focus is on the desired end result, or outcome, of each learning process, which must be demonstrated. The secondary focus is on the instructive and learning process that will assist learners through the process – in other words, it is learner centred (Van der Horst & McDonald, 1997: 13; Erasmus, Loedolff, Mda & Nel 2006: 159). It is further important to note that 'training', 'education' and 'development' do not form part of a continuum. Employee development can also take place through the process of training and education. It must, however, be emphasised that, in this case, it does not refer to the job context but that its activities vary widely and are not constrained by the relationship to a present or future job.

According to Killen (2002), outcomes-based education (OBE) is an approach to planning, delivering and evaluating instruction that focuses on the *desired results of education*, results that are referred to as 'outcomes'. In addition to the idea that outcomes should describe long-term significant learning, OBE is underpinned by four essential principles (Killen 2002):

■ The first principle is clarity of focus. This means that everything educators do must be clearly focused on what they want learners ultimately to be able to do successfully.
■ The second principle is often referred to as designing back and it is inextricably linked to the first principle. It means that the starting point for all curriculum design must be a clear definition of the significant learning that learners are to achieve by the end of their formal education.
■ The third basic principle of OBE is that educators should have high expectations for all learners. There is ample evidence that educators must establish high, challenging standards of performance in order to encourage learners to engage deeply with the issues about which they are learning.
■ The fourth principle of OBE is that educators must strive to provide expanded opportunities for all learners. Fundamental to this idea is that not all learners can learn the same thing in the same way or in the same time.

OBE has been accepted by SAQA as the system for education and training programmes which require accreditation in terms of the NQF.

14.2.3 Importance of HRD

The following are a few of the many reasons why organisations train and educate employees:

■ to improve the performance of employees who do not meet the required standards of performance, once their training needs have been identified;
■ to prepare employees for future positions;
■ to prepare employees for forthcoming organisational restructuring or for changes in technology;
■ to ensure competitiveness in the marketplace by retraining employees;
■ to increase the literacy levels of employees;
■ to benefit the individual employee; for example, HRD helps the individual to make better decisions and increases job satisfaction, which in turn should benefit the organisation; and
■ to improve interpersonal skills and to make the organisation a better place to work.

It is of utmost importance that HRD should be tailored to fit the organisation's strategy and structure. No organisation in South Africa, or elsewhere on the continent for that matter, can afford to 'look away' from our HRD challenges and all should hence help to train and develop our people.

Elsewhere in Africa

In Zambia's new post-privatisation dispensation, there is unfortunately no government-mandated policy on training, at least not of the type that existed among parastatal companies earlier ... Training dynamics have changed dramatically in the private sector. Although companies still send employees for training at home and abroad ... most companies, due to the high incidence of HIV and Aids, no longer do so with the same keenness as they used to before. Part of the reason ... is that these companies are not sure that the employees that are being trained will live long enough to share their new knowledge and skills.

Source: Extracted and slightly adapted from Muuka & Mwenda (2004: 41–42)

14.2.4 The relationship of HRD to other HRM functions

HRD is, as we conceive of it in this book, one of the central pillars of HRM. Because the slant we take is to manage our human resources in ways that can add value to the organisation and beyond, specifically to sustainability, HRD is a key leverage to achieve this. We only really empower people when we develop their capabilities. When we strategise and do work design, we factor in to what extent we follow an empowerment mode and this should then be translated into the extent that we will invest in educating, training and developing our working people. When we do workforce planning, we identify the quality and quantity of employees required by the organisation, and training and development, as you have learned, may well be a key to help bring about a match of supply and demand in the future. When we recruit and employ people, we do so with the idea that they have further potential to be developed, which will require training.

Performance assessments and career planning are also directly linked with HRD. Performance assessments allow for the identification of possible training requirements and possible career opportunities in an organisation – or beyond, perhaps. Likewise, remuneration and reward should also have a clear connection with the levels and

---

A POLICY PERSPECTIVE

Because we regard our people as the most important assets of our organisation and our country, we believe in investing in their development. This HRD policy therefore aims to assist with the education, training and development of our employees. The idea is that each employee will have adequate opportunities not only to be trained for existing work roles, but also to unlock their potential to become more of what they are capable of being.

The purpose of this policy is therefore to support the design and implementation of an HRD system that is aligned with our other HRM systems (such as career and performance management), and that will facilitate the education, training and development of all our employees. This should serve our organisation's needs to have a continuous and consistent flow of competent working people at all levels and in all areas of our operations. The overall aim is to contribute to the development of our people to help them to build better-quality lives and to align this with the strategic direction of our organisation.

---

kinds of competencies of staff. All HRM functions and practices can somehow be connected with HRD. That is also why it is essential to have an appropriately formulated policy on HRD in an organisation – as part of the overall HRM policy framework.

14.3 A MODEL FOR SYSTEMATIC TRAINING

One of the main reasons why training fails in an organisation is the lack of a systematically developed training model. The principal aim of training is to contribute to an organisation's overall objectives; however, in many instances such objectives have not been clearly formulated, training programmes are never evaluated and it seems that behaviour changes do not form part of the HRD effort. A systematic approach to the development of training is essential. In figure 14.1 a systematic approach to training is outlined. Three phases are shown in this model, namely the needs assessment phase, the training phase and the training evaluation phase. Table 14.1 provides an example of a typical training cycle in an organisation. The rest of the chapter is devoted mainly to a discussion of each of these phases of the training model as explained in figure 14.1.

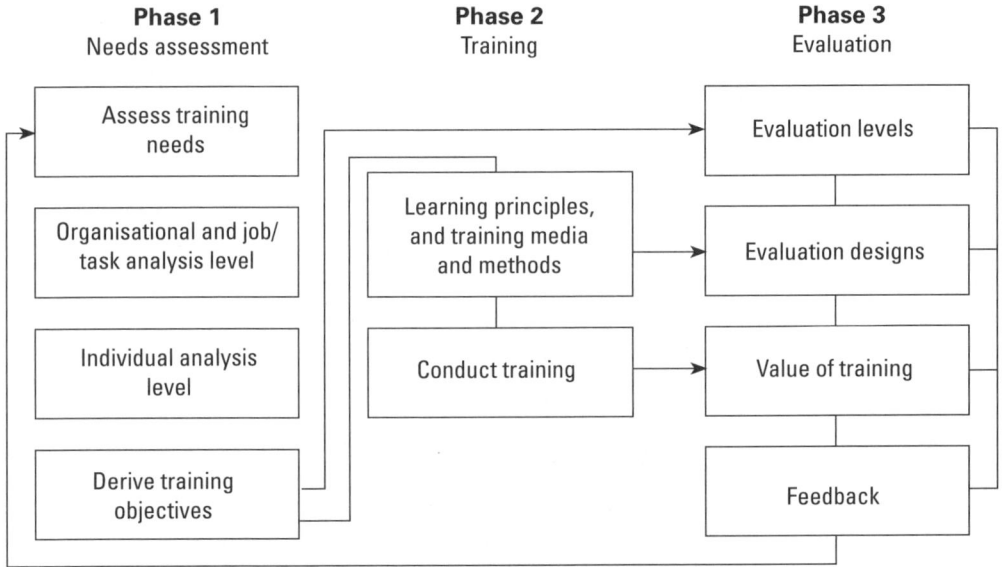

Figure 14.1: General model for training
Source: Adapted from Cascio & Aguinis (2005: 385)

14.3.1 The training needs assessment phase

Successful training begins with a needs assessment to determine which employees need to be trained and what they need to be trained to do. The training needs analysis phase culminates in the formulation of a set of objectives which clearly state the purpose of the training and the competencies required of trainees once they have completed the programme.

Needs analysis requires time, money and expertise. Unfortunately, many organisations undertake training without making this essential preliminary investment. Often there is no systematic plan to predict future training needs or to determine whether perceived needs and problems can be addressed by training. Training which is undertaken without a careful analysis of requirements is likely to be ineffective and to reduce the motivation of employees to attend future programmes.

Table 14.1: Example of the training cycle in an organisation

Steps	Management actions	Training department actions
Management goals	Management decides that it wants to reach specified target markets using radio marketing techniques	No decision making. Should actively pursue up-to-date knowledge of management direction and key goals
Training needs identified	Makes a decision that a segment of the new agent orientation programme should cover target markets and how to use radio marketing techniques to reach those markets	Suggests and recommends ways that training might best be used. May identify areas that could best be learned on the job. Recommends ways for line managers to support desired performance
Audience and training content determined	Hires new agents. Determines training schedule. Provides key people for training departments to interview to determine training content	Conducts a content analysis using interview and observation data. Recommends training content. Makes suggestions on prerequisite skills
Training designed and delivered	Communicates expectations to trainees prior to programme, including on-the-job application of skills to be learned	Provides advice on how to conduct pre-course discussions with trainees. Designs and delivers a programme that enables students to use radio-marketing techniques to reach certain target markets
Skills applied on the job	Gives specific assignments for new agents to use radio-marketing techniques to reach certain target markets. Gives rewards for effort and results in this area	Provides suggestions on how to follow through and support the skills learned in the programme
Training outcomes evaluated	Determines if new agents are using the radio-marketing techniques and if their performance shows that the techniques are helping them reach target markets	Gathers specific data on the application of new skills. Provides feedback to management on revisions to training content, audience, pre-course preparation and/or supervision for application on the job

Source: Adapted from Fisher, Schoenfeldt & Shaw (1993: 371)

14.3.1.1 What is training needs assessment?

Training needs assessment is an investigation which is undertaken to determine the nature of performance problems in order to establish the underlying causes and how these can be addressed by training. A training gap is usually defined as the difference between the required standard of the job (normally specified in a job description) and the performance of the incumbent. The ultimate aim of needs analysis is to determine:

- what needs actually exist;
- whether they are important;
- how they became apparent;
- how they were identified;

- how they may best be addressed; and
- what the priorities are.

There are several sources of information which can be used for needs analysis and many ways of gathering such information. The choice of methods and sources depends partly on the nature of the problem and the purpose of the training. If the purpose is to improve an employee's present job performance, the trainer must start by identifying performance deficiencies or areas where improvement is necessary.

Information on performance deficiencies can be obtained, inter alia, through supervisors' and clients' complaints, performance appraisal feedback, measures of output and/or quality, and performance tests given to employees to establish their current knowledge and level of skills (Fisher et al 1993: 372; Millward 2005: 88). Specialists in HRD can also collect critical incidents of poor job performance and obtain reports to identify skill or knowledge problem areas.

The following are examples of methods of gathering data for training needs analysis:
- searching existing records by studying performance appraisals, performance records, productivity records and training records;
- individual interviews with job incumbents, supervisors and clients;
- group interviews;
- assessment centres;
- the Delphi technique;
- observation;
- nominal group technique;
- collection of critical incidents;
- questionnaires;
- job analysis; and
- performance tests.

Once the performance deficiency or training needs have been identified, the next step is to determine whether the deficiency or need should be addressed by training. Sometimes employee motivation, organisational constraints, or poor task design may cause the deficiency and, in these situations, training in job skills will not solve the performance problem.

14.3.1.2 Levels of needs analysis

Any thorough needs assessment effort must address three key areas: the *organisation*, the *job* and the *individual*.

In the first place, organisational assessment (Truelove 2007: 5) considers the proposed training within the context of the rest of the organisation. The following questions may be asked in the organisational analysis portion of the needs assessment to highlight problem areas (Fisher et al 1993: 376).
- What are the training implications of the organisation's strategy?
- What will the result be if we do not train?
- How does this training programme fit in with the organisation's future plans and goals?
- Where in the organisation is training needed?
- How are various departments performing in relation to expectations or goals?
- In which departments is training most likely to succeed?
- Which departments should be trained first?

- Can the organisation afford this training?
- Which training programmes should have priority?
- Will this training adversely affect untrained people or departments?
- Is this training consistent with the organisation's culture?
- Will this training be accepted and reinforced by others in the organisation, such as the trainees' superiors, subordinates and clients?

An important consideration, however, is whether or not the proposed training will be compatible with the organisation's mission, strategy, goals and culture. Corporate culture compatibility is of utmost importance for training and management education in an organisation. Possible factors that can create a need for future training are:
- product changes – an increase or decrease in demand as a result of population shifts;
- economic changes – availability of credit and loan facilities which could jeopardise small business;
- political changes – examples are affirmative action and the creation of new regional structures in South Africa with the integration of the former homelands;
- sociological changes – demographic changes, such as high urbanisation; and
- technological changes – more efficient machinery and methods.

The impact that the training of one department has on others must also be considered in an organisational assessment.

The second crucial aspect is the job and task responsibilities (Truelove 2007: 25). This step is called *task analysis* and different methods are used, for example the critical incident method and the Delphi technique. A training practitioner can use any or a combination of methods. Once the duties or tasks in which training is needed are identified, the detailed analysis of each task may begin. The purpose of this step is to find out if the task is important and if training is essential and to determine the procedures that should be taught. Subject-matter experts such as superiors and high-performing employees could be used to generate this information. Examples of questions to be asked by the experts are the following (Fisher et al 1993: 376):
- How difficult is this task?
- Should it be taught in training or can it be learned on the job?
- How important is it that incumbents should be able to do the task from the very first day on the job?
- What knowledge, skills, information, equipment, materials and work aids are needed to do this task?
- What signals the need to perform this task?
- What are the steps in performing this task?
- Can the incumbent explain if the task has been performed correctly?

The final level of analysis focuses on the *individuals to be trained* (Truelove 2007: 6). Here it must be determined which employees should receive training and what their current levels of skill and knowledge are. Individuals may be nominated on the basis of their past performance, or an entire work group may be identified or all incumbents with a specific job title. The trainer should assess, or at least estimate, the skill and knowledge levels of the chosen trainees so that the training fits their needs.

If individual assessment indicates that a wide range of skills and knowledge is required, it is advisable to group employees together into basic and advanced groups. Alternatively, a training method that allows for self-paced learning or individualised

---
EXHIBIT 14.1: The biggest supporter of Vodacom staff

Margaret Harris speaks to Matimba Mbungela, managing executive: RM Management Services at Vodacom Group.

How is seamless succession planning ensured?

We have a number of initiatives in place to build our leadership strength – and this has been the case for a number of years, so we are able to fill most positions through internal appointments. We have an integrated talent management approach focusing on identifying potential, building capabilities and retaining our key staff in the business.

How do Vodacom's employees qualify for an overseas posting?

You need to be a driven and self-sufficient person and to have already proved that you have leadership skills. The people posted overseas are going there to lead a team, so they must have those skills.

What do you look for when recruiting employees for Vodacom?

They must be able to fit into the environment through the attitude they bring to the company; Vodacom is a very driven and challenging environment. Change is the order of the day – we don't want clock watchers. Each and every member of staff has to meet their particular goals.

What technical skills should employees have?

They must have a good understanding of the industry; many need engineering/IT skills. We also look for service-type skills for our call centres; almost half of our South African staff work in call centres.

Is there room for Vodacom for graduates who lack experience?

We have a number of graduate programmes. For example, one is a gender-biased programme to attract female BSc graduates with no experience who have the potential to grow into telecoms specialists. At the moment there are 50 highly inspired, sought-after participants on this programme.

How much training and development do Vodacom employees receive?

We take this very seriously. In the past financial year we spent almost 4% of payroll of people development. There are a number of interventions: call-centre staff need to be equipped to deal with customer queries, some of which can be very technical. Our technical staff are also given training on our latest technology platforms as we are in a very innovative environment. We also provide management and executive training. Employees are picked by the CEO for some of our executive programmes.

Source: *Sunday Times*: Business Times Careers (22 June 2008)

---

instruction should be developed. This kind of flexibility should be planned for before the training commences to ensure that all learners can have a satisfying learning experience and contribute to organisational goals.

14.3.1.3 The Workplace Skills Plan

In chapter 13 the functions of SETAs were discussed. One of the important functions is to approve workplace skills plans (WPSPs), which are submitted by organisations based on the training needs to achieve strategic objectives. According to Coetzee (2002: 95), the WPSP refers to the strategic human resource training and development aim of developing the workforce skills capacity and thereby achieving the business goals contained in the business plan. This section is discussed here to highlight the importance of the needs analysis phase in the WPSP and the importance of a skills audit.

According to the 'Regulations for the period 01 April 2000 to 31 March 2001 regarding the Funding and Related Issues' as published in the *Government Gazette* No. 6729, linked with the Skills Development Levies Act (1999), the following information should be contained in the WPSP:

- number of persons in each occupational group who received training during the year ended as specified in the regulations;
- strategic skills development priorities for the levy grant for the period as mentioned in the regulations;
- qualitative information relevant to skills planning (referring to the recruitment and filling procedure);
- training skills needs for the period required referred to in the regulations; and
- issues relating to quality assurance with reference to staff education, training and development.

Developing a WPSP is a systematic process which entails the following:

- proper workplace planning;
- proper job analyses as an input to the workforce planning process;
- identifying and defining the skills requirements of the organisation as derived from the workforce planning process;
- a skills audit to determine the actual skills of the current workforce;
- defining skills training priorities as derived from the skills audit;
- identifying skills programmes to address the skills training needs;
- implementing the WPSP;
- monitoring, evaluating and reporting of the WPSP; and
- establishing a quality assurance system to ensure effective and value-added skills training and development.

A *skills audit* is an investigation which is undertaken to determine the actual skills of the current workforce in order to define the skills gaps and real skills requirements of the organisation (Coetzee 2002; Meyer et al 2007). This activity will usually be the responsibility of the internal education, training and development practitioner or HRD team. The ultimate aims of a skills audit are to establish (Coetzee 2002).

- what skills actually exist within the organisation;
- how these compare with the organisational skills requirements as determined through the workforce planning and job analyses process;
- what the skills development priorities are (per occupational group, levels and demographic profile);
- how the skills development priorities may best be addressed through a systematic plan and when;
- what the key success indicators/measures of the workplace skills plan will be;
- how to implement, track and monitor progress; and
- what to report to management and the relevant SETA.

A skills audit requires time, money and expertise. Unfortunately, many organisations undertake training without making this essential preliminary investment. Often there is no systematic plan to predict future skills development needs in order to determine whether perceived skills development requirements can be addressed by training.

14.3.1.4 Identifying training objectives

The last step in the assessment phase of training is to translate the needs identified by the organisational, task and individual analyses into measurable objectives that can guide the training process. Behavioural training objectives state what the person will be able to do, under what conditions, and how well it will be done.

Training objectives should focus on a behaviour component, which describes in clear terms what a learner has to do to demonstrate that he or she has in fact learned. Words which are open to few interpretations should be used such as 'compare', 'construct' and 'identify'. Avoid vague words such as 'to know' and 'to understand'. The conditions or limitations under which performance should take place must also be clearly stated. The tools or equipment needed to perform the task must also be specified, for example: 'without help', 'using a calculator', 'given a list of'. A criterion component which provides the standard of performance, for example how well the learner has to perform to be considered successful, must also be included. The standard can focus, for example, on speed (within 10 minutes), accuracy, sequence and quality.

EXHIBIT 14.2: Example: learning objective

With the aid of a pair of scissors, cut from a sheet of paper the shape of a tree within five minutes.
- with the aid of a pair of scissors – condition
- cut out – behaviour
- within five minutes – criterion

Writing training objectives is more difficult than it may appear. The following guidelines must be considered:
- write objectives as concisely as possible and avoid being long-winded;
- do not use vague language;
- avoid using descriptions that are linked to instructor satisfaction, for example 'to perform to the satisfaction of the instructor'; and
- when describing the condition required for learning, avoid producing a long list of necessary equipment.

Once the training objectives have been identified, training practitioners can begin to plan both the *training* and *evaluation* phases of the training cycle (Fisher et al 1993: 379).

It is, however, important to note the differences between objectives and outcomes. The differences between objectives and outcomes are as follows:
- objectives focus on what the teacher does, whereas outcomes focus on what the learner will do;
- objectives describe the intent of teaching, and outcomes describe the results of learning;
- objectives focus on the opportunities provided for learning, and outcomes emphasise how learning is used and can be applied in new areas;
- objectives estimate how much can be learned in a given period of time, and outcomes require flexible allocation of time; and
- objectives are viewed as input driven, whereas outcomes are viewed as output driven.

Arguments against the use of objectives are that objectives are knowledge driven, giving rise to a static form of learning and thus promoting rote learning. The outcomes approach encourages the use of an end result which is a product of a learning process in which knowledge is obtained through participation and transparency (Erasmus & Van Dyk 2003: 174).

An outcome statement should:
- describe the learner's performance in terms of observable, demonstrable and assessable performance;
- contain action verbs, and be clear and unambiguous;
- involve more than mere isolated tasks or skills; and
- refer to knowledge, skills and attitudes/values (abilities).

An outcome must indicate:
- who is to perform;
- what task is to be performed;
- what conditions apply (if any); and
- what the minimum response is that will indicate mastery of the task (Erasmus et al 2006: 159).

14.3.2 The training phase
Once the training needs have been determined and behavioural objectives stated, a training programme can be developed to achieve the stated objectives. In order to ensure the success of the training programme, appropriate training methods must be selected and suitable training materials developed to convey the required knowledge and skills identified in the training objectives. The necessity of understanding how people learn in order to design an effective training programme cannot be overemphasised. This aspect will be dealt with first.

14.3.2.1 Learning principles
A number of principles which can facilitate the learning process have been identified, and will be discussed briefly. However, attention must first be devoted to the preconditions for learning, which are in themselves also learning principles.

Preconditions
There are two preconditions for learning: readiness and motivation.

Trainee readiness concerns the situation where trainees possess the background skills and knowledge necessary to master the material that will be presented to them in the new training programme. For example, a basic knowledge of mathematics is a prerequisite for learning statistical quality control techniques. Trainee motivation requires trainees to experience a need to learn new skills and therefore to understand the need for training. Learning that takes place without motivation is not as successful as learning with motivation. Learner motivation can be improved by (Anderson 1994: 125):
- learners who attend courses voluntarily;
- learners who are involved in needs analysis;
- learners who are given a short summary of the benefits of the training and how it will influence their careers;
- learners who set their own ideas on how they will approach the training; and
- enhancement of self-efficacy by persuasion (telling the learners that they can do it), by modelling (showing the learners others like themselves who have succeeded) or by enactive mastery (allowing the learners to experience success in the early stages of training).

In addition to the preconditions for learning, other relevant learning principles include:

- conditions for practice;
- knowledge of results;
- overcoming interference;
- transfer of training; and
- adult learning principles.

Conditions for practice

Actively practising the skill or task being learned can increase learning. An important condition in designing training is to decide whether to have the whole task learned and practised as one unit or whether to break it down into separately learned and practised parts. A second condition of practice is to determine whether the practice should be divided into spaced segments or scheduled in one long session. A last condition of practice is to decide how much practice is enough. Overlearning is practising beyond the point at which the trainee has mastered and performed the task correctly. Overlearning should be used in those circumstances where the trainee is learning a task which demands that the first reactions be absolutely correct. It is important because it increases retention over time, makes the behaviour more automatic, increases the quality of performance under stress and helps trainees to transfer what they have learned to the job setting.

Knowledge of results

Effective learning requires that trainees receive feedback, or knowledge of results, on how they are performing. Feedback is critical for both learning and motivation and, if it is not provided, trainees may learn a technique incorrectly or lose the motivation to learn. Feedback maximises trainees' willingness to learn and is also necessary if goals for maintaining or improving performance have been set (see also the preconditions for learning).

Overcoming interference

A trainee experiences interference when habits and/or learning acquired before the start of training make it difficult for the trainee to absorb new material. High interference occurs when the trainee has learned a strong stimulus–response connection in the past and now has to learn a totally different response to the same or similar stimulus. To overcome interference, the trainer should teach the principles underlying the new response, and provide support and sufficient practice to increase the strength of the new stimulus–response connection.

Transfer of training

If learning that has taken place during training is not transferred to the job situation, the training programme has been ineffective.

Learning theorists recommend the following traditional ways of maximising the transfer of training:
- maximise the similarity between the training situation and the job situation;
- provide as much experience as possible with the task being taught;
- provide a variety of examples when teaching concepts of skills;
- label or identify important features of the task;
- make sure that general principles are understood before expecting any transfer;
- make certain that the training behaviours and ideas are rewarded in the job situation;
- design the training content so that the trainees can see its applicability;

- emphasise the usefulness of the new material during the training, drawing on illustrations from the work environment; and
- ask trainees to set specific and measurable goals for performing the new behaviours back on the job.

After the training, trainees should be encouraged to assess themselves against these personal goals on a regular basis. Trainers should also plan as carefully for the transfer of training as for the classroom presentation. If the above suggestions are implemented in a training programme, it is more likely that positive transfer to the job will take place and that job satisfaction will result.

Learning principles for adults

Most employees in organisations are adults. The science of teaching adults is known as *andragogy* while the science of teaching children is termed *pedagogy*. There are several differences that adult educators consider important, for example:
- adults already possess a great deal of knowledge and experience on which they can rely;
- adults normally take responsibility for themselves and their learning; and
- adults focus on present problems and want to learn things that have immediate use.

Andragogy is based on the premise that learning should be active and learner centred, that training should focus on real-world problems and on applying techniques such as case studies and role playing, and that the experience and knowledge of adults can be used productively.

When a trainer assumes that adults know very little and that their experience is irrelevant, thus treating them as children, adults do not learn effectively. Particularly in South Africa, where a large majority of adults need to be trained, this could have disastrous consequences.

14.3.2.2 Teaching style

The way in which training practitioners approach teaching may influence the effectiveness of learning. Training practitioners must take particular note of the following characteristics that may affect optimal teaching style:
- instrumentality is the extent to which the trainee is concerned with the immediate applicability of the concepts and skills being taught;
- scepticism is the extent to which the trainee exhibits a questioning attitude and demands logic, evidence, and examples;
- resistance to change refers to the extent to which trainees fear the process of moving in to the unknown, or the effect which that process may have on them;
- attention span is the length of time for which the trainee can focus attention before substantial attentiveness diminishes;
- expectation level is the quality and quantity of training that the trainee requires from the trainer;
- absorption level is the pace at which the trainee expects and can accept new information;
- topical interest is the degree to which the trainee can be expected to have personal (job-relevant) interest in the topic;
- self-confidence is the degree to which trainees independently and positively view themselves; this determines their need for feedback, reinforcement and success experiences; and

- locus of control is the degree to which the trainee perceives that he or she can implement the training successfully back on the job with or without organisational support.

14.3.2.3 Training methods for non-managerial employees

The term 'training' has historically been used to describe technical or job skill training for non-managerial employees. 'Development', on the other hand, is the term which has traditionally been used for the education of managers. In some cases, because of the different learning content, different methods have been used. As we move into the 21st century, the distinction between training managerial and non-managerial employees is becoming less clear. Organisational structures are changing rapidly and more emphasis is being placed on self-managed work teams, while the fact that first-line supervisors should also be trained in managerial skills such as planning, organising, leading and controlling is being increasingly acknowledged.

However, the distinction between the training of non-managerial and managerial employees is still made. This section discusses the training methods more commonly used for technical training, while the next section focuses on methods used for developing management skills.

Once clearly defined training objectives have been formulated and cognisance has been taken of the learning principles, the appropriate training method can be chosen. Some of the methods can be used on the job, while others can be more appropriately used off the job.

On-the-job training

On-the-job training (OJT) is conducted at the work site and focuses on the actual job. The advantages of OJT are as follows (Byars & Rue 2006: 167):
- the transfer of training to the job is maximised;
- a full-time trainer and separate training facilities are avoided;
- trainee motivation remains high because what employees are learning is relevant to the job and provides a sense of satisfaction; and
- the employee is assimilated more quickly into the organisation.

An OJT programme should be planned as carefully as any other training programme (see figure 14.2). OJT should be designed to form part of the total training effort in an organisation. Classroom training normally forms an important part of OJT as it will cover the orientation part of the training programme. In the classroom, trainees will be informed of the equipment involved and the function each performs, and the total production process will be explained. This will be followed by a tour of the department. Knowledge gained in the classroom can now be transferred to the job and the procedure explained in figure 14.2 would then be of value. Avoid the following when conducting OJT programmes:
- frequent interruptions as the trainer or trainee is called away to perform other duties;
- abandoning employees busy with OJT and expecting them to pick up necessary skills when they can;
- not informing employees about important but infrequent events; and
- allowing co-workers to teach them bad habits.

Off-the-job training

Training offered at locations away from the job is designated off-the-job training (for

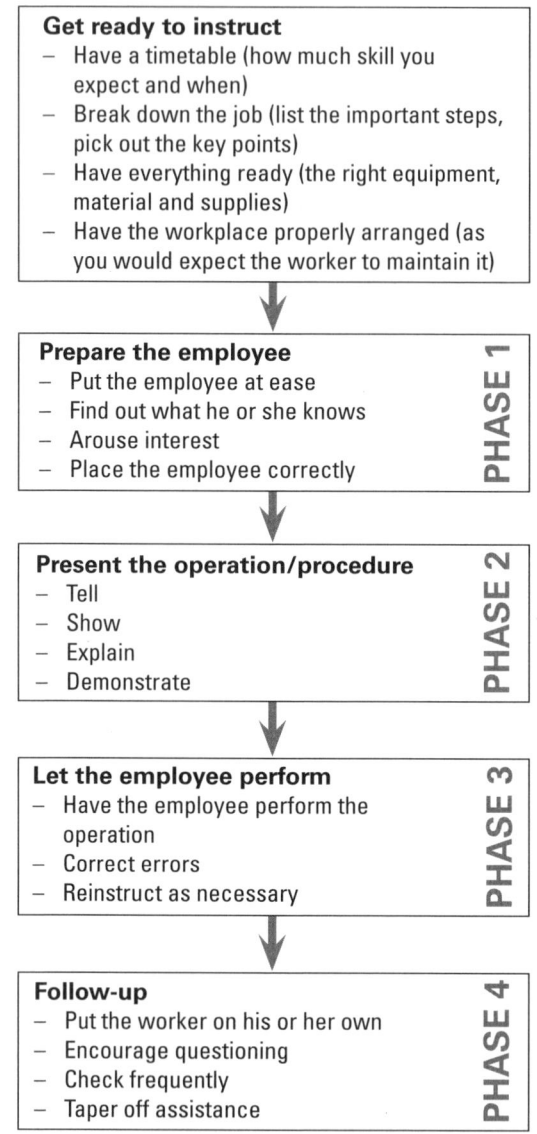

Get ready to instruct
- Have a timetable (how much skill you expect and when)
- Break down the job (list the important steps, pick out the key points)
- Have everything ready (the right equipment, material and supplies)
- Have the workplace properly arranged (as you would expect the worker to maintain it)

Prepare the employee — PHASE 1
- Put the employee at ease
- Find out what he or she knows
- Arouse interest
- Place the employee correctly

Present the operation/procedure — PHASE 2
- Tell
- Show
- Explain
- Demonstrate

Let the employee perform — PHASE 3
- Have the employee perform the operation
- Correct errors
- Reinstruct as necessary

Follow-up — PHASE 4
- Put the worker on his or her own
- Encourage questioning
- Check frequently
- Taper off assistance

Figure 14.2: A job instruction procedure which could be of value for OJT

Source: Adapted from Fisher et al (1993: 387)

example locations near the workplace or away from work, at a special training centre or at a resort). Training which is conducted away from the workplace minimises distractions and allows employees to devote their full attention to the training offered.

Methods and materials often used are lectures, group discussions, role playing, assigned reading, case studies, videotapes and vestibule training. Vestibule training requires trainees to do the whole job with the same tools and machines that are required on the job.

14.3.2.4 Training with the aid of information communication technology

This section deals with the various training approaches which use information communication technology (ICT) (mainly computers) as a tool. (This section is based on Hart 1987: 470–485; Fisher et al 1993: 387–391; Wills 1993: 91-95; and Erasmus et al 2006: 97.)

- *Computer-based training (CBT)*
  CBT as concept usually means that the use of the computer is central to the training effort. As such, training that is designed, developed and delivered with computers being the cornerstone may only be suitable in places where computer technology is readily available and accessible. In general we can say that comprehensive or 'complete' CBT packages might have good potential but we believe they should rather not be used in organisations as stand-alone HRD interventions. This brings us to the fact that CBT includes computer-assisted instruction (CAI) and computer-managed instruction (CMI), which we briefly reflect on next.

- *Computer-assisted instruction*
  Computer-assisted instruction (CAI) uses the computer almost as a fully self-contained 'teaching machine' that presents 'lessons'. The trainee is requested to respond to some questions and, if the answers are correct, the computer indicates that the trainee can proceed to the next level of information. These instructional units thus typically supplement more traditional classroom activities and include aspects such as drill and practices, tutorials, simulations and games, and problem-solving exercises.

- *Computer-managed instruction*
  Here the computer determines the employee's initial level of competence and then provides a customised set of learning modules and exercises. Computer-managed instruction (CMI) uses the computer to organise instruction and to track student records and progress. The instruction does not have to be delivered via computer, but very often CAI is combined with CMI. Performance is assessed frequently, and the content is modified continuously to suit the learner.

- *Computer-mediated education*
  Computer-mediated education (CME) describes computer applications that facilitate the delivery of instruction, for example e-mail, computer conferencing and 'e-learning' (where the Internet is used).

- *Computer-based multimedia*
  The aim with computer-based multimedia (CBM) is to integrate various voice, video and computer technologies in a single accessible system. An example of CBM is CD-ROM. CBM will allow the instructional designer to focus on content requirements, and students need a relatively constraint-free technological environment. Interactive video training is really a form of CBM.

- *Interactive video training (IVT) using DVD*
  Interactive video training (IVT) involves training with the use of video clips (or full-length movies), usually using DVDs played through the computer and screened on a monitor. It is especially useful for people who tend to be more 'visual' learners.

Which method should the trainer select? Aspects that the organisation must consider are the cost of the method, the number of individuals to be trained, their location, the availability of skilled trainers and, most important, the fact that the method must be consistent with the training content.

MANAGERS MUST TAKE RESPONSIBILITY FOR TRAINING AND
DEVELOPMENT

All managers should accept personal responsibility for the training and development
of their staff. Managers ultimately take the responsibility of the human resources
under their control and/or in their teams. They do not only motivate, reward,
discipline and manage their performance. They must also ensure that they are
trained and developed to acquire the skills and knowledge to perform.

Think about this...
1   'Without the manager's input in determining training needs of employees,
    training will be a disaster.' What is your view?
2   Should managers motivate staff to be trained?
3   'Return on investment from a training and development perspective is very
    difficult to measure.' What is your view?
4   Are your organisation's training and development initiatives aligned with your
    organisational strategic objectives?

Advantages and disadvantages of using computers as training tools

The following advantages and disadvantages are applicable when using computers:

Advantages
- Self-pace learning is facilitated and immediate feedback and reinforcement are
  provided.
- Computers are interactive, which makes learning very flexible and allows for
  learner control.
- Computer-assisted instruction can be conducted at remote sites on all shifts. It
  can be fitted into lulls in the work schedule that would otherwise be unproductive.
- Managers and supervisors can be trained in their offices so that they are available
  to deal with job-related problems if necessary.
- Transportation and lodging costs for trainees are non-existent, and overall training
  costs can be reduced once the system has been developed.
- There is consistent quality of instruction over time and from group to group, and
  subjectivity is eliminated.
- Disruptions during instruction due to unexpected trainer problems (for example
  illness) are excluded.
- Updates and changes can be made to all points very quickly.
- Retention of learning content is at least as good as with other instructional methods.
- Slow learners have a greater chance of success than with classroom training.
- Customised instruction according to each learner's needs can be developed.

Disadvantages
- computers require motivated learners and students must be au fait with computer
  operations before they can learn;
- systems are costly to develop;
- computer technology is changing rapidly and an effort will have to be made to
  keep abreast with the latest changes; and
- there is still widespread computer illiteracy and an effort has to be made to help
  employees overcome blocks.

EXHIBIT 14.3: e-Learning

e-Learning is not new. It has been around in some form or other for the past 10 years. However, interest is rapidly growing. A quarter of all learning is expected to take place electronically in five years' time.

e-Learning involves the delivery and administration of learning opportunities and support via computer, networked and web-based technology to help individual performance and development.

In its broadest form, e-learning encompasses:

- the provision of information via information or communication technologies in a very accessible and immediate way that can enable individuals to refresh or extend their knowledge and improve their performance;
- the provision of interactive learning materials and packages designed to facilitate skills or wider personal development. The actual courses currently provided via e-learning focus mainly on IT skills and, to a lesser extent, on softer skills (people-to-people training) such as general management skills, or more specific aspects of management such as interviewing, negotiation, conducting meetings, etc;
- at the third level, e-learning is multidimensional and embraces both the first two levels into a wider performance support framework. This is coupled with processes to administer and monitor learning provision and outcomes, and to provide learners with various forms of support from experts and peers. On administration, e-learning can provide access to learning resources, including previews, registration and tracking of use. This can be done to a greater or lesser extent either through passive portals or more learning management systems.

Sources: Pollard & Hillage (2001); and Erasmus et al (2006: 203)

14.3.2.5 Management development and education methods

This section deals with management education, and focuses on the different methods used to educate employees. Because managerial work is important, complex and challenging, many organisations provide regular management training. In South Africa where there is a critical shortage of high-level management expertise it is essential that organisations should identify potential candidates and educate them accordingly.

On-the-job methods

Managerial education normally takes place off the job but a great deal of learning takes place on the job. According to Fisher et al (1993: 395), there have been several studies of managerial learning and skill development in the US as a result of on-the-job experience. This research suggests that managers learn the most from assignments that are very difficult and challenging. A programme of management education should include assignments and job-rotation plans that stretch managers to their limits. The general on-the-job management education methods will be discussed briefly.

- *Coaching*

  In coaching, experienced managers guide the actions of less-experienced managers to help them develop their delivery. The advantage of coaching is that it provides immediate feedback on performance. A possible disadvantage is that it maintains the present values since the less-experienced manager may adopt the same values and approaches as the coach (Byars & Rue 2006: 185).

- *Committee assignments*

  Junior executives are assigned to committees where they can observe more experienced managers in action because a lot of organisational work takes place in committees. The purpose of this method is to use normal committees as training instruments, one which will also help inexperienced managers to participate. The major reason for their presence is, however, to observe the proceedings, for example the interpersonal processes, agreements and disagreements, decision-making processes, negotiations, and successes and failures of the committee.

■ *Job rotation*
This method entails moving from one job assignment to another within the same organisation, and can take four to six months. The inexperienced manager will gain insight and broad understanding of the organisation and allow specialists to turn to generalists. This is true for senior management who must obtain an overall perspective of the organisation especially, and who must spend more and more of their time managing the total organisation and less and less time managing on the micro level. Job rotation is a method for broadening individuals' exposure to company operations, reducing boredom and stimulating new ideas. A further advantage of job rotation is that people are prepared to assume greater responsibility in the higher levels. A disadvantage, however, is that it can demotivate intelligent and aggressive employees who seek specific responsibilities and can eventually produce a number of employees with limited job knowledge (DeCenzo & Robbins 1994: 272). (See also chapter 6.)

■ *Understudy assignments*
A person who acts as an assistant to someone else may be termed an understudy. Understudying is similar to coaching, but this method is a full-time mentor-understudy arrangement where coaching is only periodic. The understudy works with the mentor on a daily basis to learn how the job is done. In the manager's absence, the understudy performs the role of the manager on non-critical activities, and develops valuable managerial skills. A disadvantage of this method is that managers may feel threatened by understudies and may not assist them as they should.

Off-the-job methods

Managerial education programmes often occur off the job and away from the place of work. An important reason for the off-site location is to remove the manager from the daily environment of the organisation and thereby minimise interruptions and distractions. Organisations conduct their own management education programmes or send managers to universities or consulting firms. Commonly used off-the-job methods are discussed below.

■ *Sensitivity training*
Sensitivity training includes techniques such as laboratory, T-group training communication workshops and outward board trips (Ronen 1989: 438). The purpose of sensitivity training is to make employees more aware of their own behaviour and how it is perceived by others. It also increases the participants' awareness and acceptance of the differences between them. Small groups of eight to 14 individuals who are strangers to each other are normally grouped together and assisted by a trainer. During the discussion, employees discuss themselves, their feelings and the group process.

The most frequent changes derived from this training include a more favourable self-perception, reduced prejudice, improved scores on tests of interpersonal relations, and changed interpersonal behaviour as observed by others, all of which are particularly relevant in South Africa.

■ *Team building*
Team building focuses on intact work groups, and strives to develop the ability of managers to work together with them on the types of tasks they face each day. Team building is also an important organisational development technique.

The first phase is normally a data-collection phase, followed by questionnaires or interviews with team members. Information about how the group works together, what problems exist and what norms are followed is sought.

Typical activities in a team-building exercise include goal setting, development of interpersonal relations, and role analysis to clarify roles and responsibilities. A summarised version of the information is fed back to the group so that an objective look can be taken at their functioning. The facilitator helps the team understand the feedback and develop action plans for improving group processes. Team building attempts to use high interaction among group members to increase trust and openness.

■ *Behavioural-modelling training*

Behavioural-modelling training holds that most human behaviour is learned by observing others and then modelling their behaviour when appropriate. Learning from others reduces the need for failure.

A fixed sequence of steps is normally followed (Latham 1989: 269–273). Firstly, the trainer introduces a single interpersonal skill. Secondly, trainees view a videotape of a supervisor performing the skill correctly. During this process, the learning points should be highlighted. Thirdly, trainees practise the skill by role playing with other trainees. Lastly, trainees get feedback on the effectiveness of their role-playing behaviour.

■ *Case study*

With a case study, a trainee is presented with a written description of an actual or hypothetical problem in an organisational setting. The trainee is required to read the case, identify and discuss the problem, and recommend possible solutions.

The purposes of a case study is to:
- show learners that there is usually no easy solution to complex organisational problems.
- show learners that different perspectives and solutions to the same case may be equally valid; and
- help managerial trainees develop their problem-solving skills.

The case study provides stimulating discussion and opportunities for individuals to defend their analytical and problem-solving abilities. It is an effective method of improving decision-making abilities within the given contexts (Byars & Rue 2006: 186).

■ *Simulation methods*

By using simulation methods, the work setting in which the trainee will have to perform is replicated for the trainee to try out different behaviours or strategies. The objective is for trainees to learn from their own actions, and from the group discussion that follows the simulation. Various forms of simulation are used, for example:
- in-basket exercises;
- role plays;
- leaderless group discussions;
- large-scale behavioural simulations; and
- computerised business decision-making games.

The aim of the *in-basket exercise* simulation is to provide practice in aspects such as setting priorities, making decisions, managing time and delegating. Participants individually play the role of a manager who has a certain period of time to deal with certain items in the in-basket within set conditions and constraints (Pfeiffer 1994: 58).

Role playing allows the participants an opportunity to practise new behaviours in a controlled environment. They can be coached and receive feedback on interpersonal skills such as active listening, problem solving, communication and information sharing.

In two-person role playing, trainees, and at times trainers, assume the roles of characters and act a simulated situation. The success of this method depends largely on the trainees' willingness to adopt the roles and to react as if they are really in the work environment.

The *leaderless group discussion*, also used in assessment centres, is a larger-group simulation consisting of four to eight trainees working together to solve a problem. Group members are assigned different roles to play in the simulation, and given information unique to that role.

Large-scale behavioural simulations can become complex and involve simulated organisations of up to 20 people in different roles, lasting from six hours to several days. Simulations at this level of complexity are used with executives rather than lower-level supervisors.

Computerised business decision-making games may be defined as sequential decision-making exercises structured on a model of a business operation, in which the trainee assumes the role of managing the simulated operation (Pfeiffer 1994: 58).

One of the objectives of the business games is to teach general management skills such as decision making, setting priorities, long-range planning, and the effective use of time, personnel, and equipment. Trainees also develop an appreciation of the complexity of organisations and the many factors that must be considered before making a decision.

Action learning

One of the best ways to educate managers is to give them challenging jobs with support systems to help them learn. Action learning is the study of real-life problems and then solutions within a real-life environment (Reid, Barrington & Kenney 1992: 119). This approach provides challenges and demands the transformation of problems into opportunities for managers.

Table 14.2: Comparing action learning with traditional learning

Traditional learning	Action learning
■ Individual based	■ Group based
■ Knowledge emphasis	■ Skills emphasis
■ Input orientated	■ Output orientated
■ Classroom based	■ Work based
■ Passive	■ Active
■ Memory tested	■ Competence tested
■ Focus on past	■ Focus on present and future
■ Standard cases	■ Real cases
■ One way	■ Interactive
■ Teacher lead	■ Student lead

Source: Margerison (1991: 40)

Action learning revolves around principles such as the following:

■ management development must be based on real work projects;
■ identified projects must be owned and defined by senior managers as having significant impact on the future success of the company;
■ managers must aim to make a real return on investment;
■ managers must work in a team and learn from each other; crossing departmental and functional boundaries;
■ real action and change must be the end result;
■ the content (knowledge) and the process (questions and methods) of change must be studied; and
■ managers must publicly commit themselves to action and report on outcomes.

14.3.2.6 Conduct the training

An important aspect which needs to be finalised before training can be conducted is a proper analysis of the learner group. This could entail an analysis of their past experience, qualifications, job titles, reason for training, and supervisors' reasons for nominating the trainee.

The choice of a training method to a large extent also determines how the training should be conducted. Apart from the above, a curriculum should be planned and the course content should be set out in a logical order. Part of the introduction would include the purpose of the lesson, the time duration, other sources to facilitate the learning process, learning objectives, possible problem areas which might be experienced by the trainer, and possible questions to stimulate discussion if required.

EXHIBIT 14.4: Key findings of the state of the South African Training Industry Report: 2007

In this study, 328 respondents participated and represent human and resource training managers. The key findings were:

■ South African organisations spend 3,43% of payroll on training (3,11% in 2006) which is more than the 1% required by the Development Levies Act, and more than the percentage reported in the US State of the Training Industry Study (2,33%).
■ 87% of organisations have human resource information systems (HRIS) in place.
■ Questionnaires (80%), interviews (65%) and performance management data (76%) are the major training needs analysis methods. Significantly, the use of performance management data increased by 10% on the previous year.
■ Over the past couple of years there has been a decrease in outsourcing, with 38% of all training programmes being outsource in terms of the delivery of training programmes, compared with 28% in the US.
■ Despite the growth in e-learning, classroom training is still the most popular method of training – its prevalence increased from 58% in 2003 to 63% in 2004, and has since grown to 80%. The use of e-learning increased from 17% in 2003 to 26% in 2006, and grew to 30% in 2007 (28% in the US).
■ While only 9% of organisations measured the financial ROI of training programmes in 2004, this figure has increased substantially to 33%.
■ Interestingly, 70% of South African organisations use mentoring and coaching (in comparison to 63% in the UK), and 55% of them said that it is either 'effective' or 'very effective'.
■ As regards the prevalence of talent management, 46% of companies have talent management strategies in place, and 54% of them view its implementation as 'effective' or 'very effective'.
■ Contrary to media reports, 67% of respondents are satisfied with the service they receive from SETAs.

Source: Fifth Annual ASTD State of the South African Training Industry Report (2007)

Apart from the fact that the appropriate facility must be chosen and that pre-course material must be available, the trainer must be fully prepared to present the content. Although this phase of the training process represents only the tip of the iceberg, it is essential that it is executed successfully.

14.4 THE EVALUATION PHASE

The last phase in the training process is the evaluation phase. The purpose of this phase is to determine the extent to which the training activities have met the stated objectives. Evaluation of training is often done poorly or not at all. One reason for this is that there is a general assumption that training will work and that a fear exists by those who initiated the training that an objective evaluation of the effectiveness of the training will prove otherwise.

The basic approach to evaluation should be to determine the extent to which the training programme has met the learning objectives identified prior to the training. Planning for the evaluation should commence at the same time that planning for the training programme begins.

14.4.1 Evaluation levels and measures

Kirkpatrick suggests four levels of evaluation (Erasmus et al 2006: 224).

14.4.1.1 Level 1: Reaction

The first level is the reaction level, or the participants' feelings about the programme. If trainees enjoyed a programme it does not imply that the programme was useful to the organisation, but unpopular programmes may be cancelled due to a lack of interest. A questionnaire is normally used to obtain the information during or immediately after the programme. Typical questions to be answered are: 'Are you satisfied with the programme arrangements?' and 'Are the learning objectives clear to you?'.

14.4.1.2 Level 2: Learning

Learning measures the degree to which trainees have mastered the concepts, information and skills that the training intended to impart. Learning is assessed continually, for example during and/or at the end of the training programme with paper-and-pencil tests, performance tests and examinations.

14.4.1.3 Level 3: Behaviour

Once the training has been completed, on-the-job training can be assessed by any of the performance evaluation techniques discussed in chapter 11. Behaviour ratings can be collected from the superiors, peers, subordinates or clients of the trained employees. The training practitioner should visit the worksite, for example, two to three months after the training has be completed and objectively assess the change in behaviour (Truelove 2007: 193).

14.4.1.4 Level 4: Results

The impact of the training programme on the work group or organisation as a whole is assessed objectively. The appropriate objective measures to use depend on the content and objectives of the training, and include cost savings, profit, productivity, quality, accidents, turnover and employee attitudes. A cost/benefit analysis could be executed to determine the benefit derived from training from a cost point of view. It should be remembered that all three levels should be considered to assess the overall effectiveness of the training programme.

Table 14.3: Evaluation matrix

Degree	I	II	III	IV
What we want to know	Are the trainees happy? If not, why not?	Do the materials teach the concepts? If not, why not?	Are the concepts used? If not, why not?	Does application of the concepts positively affect the organisation? If not, why not?
What might be measured	Trainee reaction during workshop	Trainee performance during workshop	Trainee performance at end of workshop	Assignments. Ongoing management support
Measurement dimensions	Relevance. Ease of learning	Perceived "worth"	Understanding. Application	Analysis. Results
Sources of data	Trainee comments. Questions about exercises. Questions about concepts	Learning time. Performance on exercises. Presentation. Use of tools on exercises	Results. Discussions	Results. Discussions
Data gathering methodology	Observation. Interview. Questionnaire	Observation. Review. Questionnaire	Questionnaire (critical incid.). Interview	Interview. Questionnaire (critical incid.)

So how can we evaluate training? Well, we can apply the evaluation model shown below in table 14.3.

14.4.2 Evaluation designs

Apart from Kirkpatrick's four levels of evaluating training, other complex and effective designs for evaluating training also exist. These designs focus mainly on the effectiveness of the training phase, and a few of the commonly used ones will be discussed below (Fisher et al 1993: 409).

14.4.2.1 One-off post-test design

This evaluation design is not planned prior to training but only half-way through it. The trainer decides to collect data but because there is no pre-training measure and no untrained group to compare the results with, this exercise could prove to be worthless. This ad hoc approach, if not done for a specific reason, should be avoided.

14.4.2.2 One-group pre-test/post-test design

This is a simple evaluation design. A group of trainees is assessed both before and after the training. This design allows the trainer to identify a change in behaviour due to training but it cannot necessarily be concluded that the change was due to the training input. The reason why the change in behaviour cannot directly be attributed to training is that a number of factors might influence behaviour by chance during or after the training period. It nevertheless remains a useful indicator to establish whether knowledge has been gained.

14.4.2.3 Multiple-baseline design

Certain shortcomings of the above designs are overcome by the multiple-baseline design. The training group is measured several times both before and after the training. The trainer probably should not use an obtrusive measure, such as a questionnaire or learning test. Trainees could improve over time because they are gaining practice with the measure. Objective measures of behaviour or results are less obtrusive, and they are easy to collect repeatedly.

This design allows the trainer to observe trends in performance and to see if there is a change in the trend immediately after the training.

14.4.2.4 Pre-test/post-test control-group design

This design uses a control group of employees who are very similar to the training group except that they do not receive the training. Here both the group to receive the training and the control group are measured at least once before and once after the training. This allows the trainer to draw quite firm conclusions about whether any change has occurred and if it has, whether it is as a result of the training and will benefit the organisation in the short and long term.

14.4.3 The value of training in monetary terms

The value of training in this context is determined by the net rand gain realised by an organisation as a result of adopting a given HRD approach. (Also see level 4 of Kirkpatrick's approach in section 14.4.1.)

Calculating the value requires both assessing the cost of the training and putting a rand value on the benefits of the training. Some cost categories associated with training are:

- one-off costs;
- needs assessment;
- salaries of training developers, consultants and instructional designers;
- evaluation of the programme when first offered;
- presentation costs;
- salaries, travel, and lodging costs of trainers;
- facilities rental;
- purchase of training equipment and materials;
- trainee costs;
- transportation and lodging for trainees during training;
- trainee wages or salary during training; and
- training materials and handouts.

By determining the value of training in rand terms, an employer can build a solid justification for a training programme on purely economic grounds. It must, however, be emphasised that the evaluation of training is a complex process and that a change in human behaviour and its benefits to an organisation cannot only be expressed in rand terms and it is therefore suggested that all the results from the evaluation exercise be considered before definite conclusions are drawn. Finally, feedback should be given throughout the process.

14.5 CONCLUSION

In this chapter HRD as a concept was discussed. Attention was given to the concepts of training, education and development. The complete training process, from the assessment of training needs to the training phase and the evaluation phase, were discussed. It is apparent that the importance of HRD in South Africa and the complexity of the process of HRD make this aspect of South African HRM an immense challenge.

SUSTAINABILITY CONNECTION?

Engaging in the education, training and development of our employees is an investment in the future – of the organisation, of the people, of other organisations for whom they may work, and as such in our country and continent. Without making the investments in training and developing (and educating) our working people, there is no hope for a better life for all over the longer term in this country. Developing our human resources is probably the crux of the sustainability challenge because only through enhanced human development can we enhance the very sustainability of our planet. Each time we invest in human development in our organisations, we contribute to improving lives and prospects for our country and continent.

SELF-EVALUATION QUESTIONS

1 What is the relationship between the HRD and other HRM functions?
2 What are addressed at the organisational analysis phase of training needs assessment?
3 What are the purposes of the individual analysis phase of training needs assessment?
4 Write a behavioural objective for your learning from this chapter.
5 Explain three preconditions for learning.
6 What is overlearning?
7 How can a trainer facilitate transfer of training?
8 Explain why adult learners may need to be treated differently from child learners.
9 What are the advantages and disadvantages of on-the-job training?
10 Do computers play a role in training? Discuss.
11 Explain the levels at which training can be evaluated.
12 Describe the most useful designs for evaluating training, and substantiate your reasons.
13 You are to develop a training programme to teach reading and writing to adults with no more than a Grade 5 education. The objective of the training programme is to teach the trainees how to master reading and writing skills at basic level (grammar, vocabulary, handwriting, etc). The trainees must learn the skills to be able to write a basic letter and read one page of simple language.
   ■ How will your training programme incorporate or deal with each of the following learning principles or conditions? Are there any that will not concern you?
     – Readiness
     – Motivation
     – Interference
     – Feedback
     – Overlearning
     – Distributed versus massed practice
     – Whole versus part learning
     – Transfer of training
   ■ Which training methods will you use? In what order?
   ■ How will the success of your programme be evaluated?

PART FIVE
THE REWARD AND CARE CHALLENGE

15 REMUNERATING EMPLOYEES

LEARNING OUTCOMES

After studying this chapter, you should be able to:

- define remuneration and distinguish between different types of organisational rewards;
- explain the objectives of remuneration systems;
- distinguish between the external and internal factors influencing the design of remuneration systems;
- establish a job-based remuneration system that is internally consistent and linked to the labour market;
- advise your manager on appropriate quantitative and non-quantitative methods of job evaluation;
- demonstrate your understanding of the fundamental mechanics of the major job evaluation systems in use in South Africa;
- design a basic pay structure; and
- analyse the relevance of skills-based remuneration systems in different organisational environments.

15.1 INTRODUCTION

As we have explained right from the outset, HRM revolves around managing the work and people who perform the work in the context of its being a socio-economic activity. The economic aspect refers thereto that our concern is about people who work in return for some form of return. Remuneration has therefore always stood at the heart of the employment relationship. As explained, in its simplest form the employment relationship is usually based on an economic motivated process where certain inputs (physical and mental work behaviour) are exchanged for something else that are considered to be desirable in satisfying individual needs or goals. Thus, in this exchange relationship the employer provides a mix of rewards valued by employees and in return the employees provide their time, talent and efforts towards achieving organisational goals. The utilisation of rewards can therefore be a very important and powerful tool for shaping and determining work behaviour aimed at attaining the strategic objectives of an organisation.

Rewards such as pay and benefits which people gain from an employment relationship are highly important to individuals since they can meet many needs. Satisfaction of needs can range from the most basic human needs for food and shelter to those signs of achievement, status and power (for example luxury cars, overseas vacations, etc) that may be bought if sufficiently high levels of remuneration are received. Self-esteem needs may also be addressed, because levels of pay usually indicate an individual's worth to the organisation.

From the organisation's perspective, remuneration is of equally critical importance, since employee remuneration is often the single largest cost item to an organisation. The total cost of the overall remuneration and reward system can have a decisive bearing on an organisation's competitive position; effective management of the cost, nature and distribution of rewards therefore demands careful attention.

A multitude of possible rewards can be included in an overall reward system, and various categories exist according to which these rewards may be classified.

Common categories include extrinsic versus intrinsic rewards, financial versus non-financial rewards, and performance- versus membership-related rewards. Naturally, rewards may be classified in other ways and certain rewards can fit equally well in more than one category.

15.1.1 Remuneration defined

The extrinsic-intrinsic typology used in figure 15.1 is especially useful for defining the domain of remuneration management.

Intrinsic rewards are self-administered rewards that are associated with the job itself, such as the opportunity to perform meaningful work, experience variety and receive feedback on work results.

Although certain HRM-related decisions may focus on intrinsic rewards (for example flexible working schedules, job enrichment and job rotation), the fact is that these rewards will not help much if employees do not get paid. Herzberg's two-factor theory of motivation thus has relevance until today. Employees can decide how much effort they put into their work above the absolute minimum required to retain their jobs; this is sometimes called discretionary effort. To secure the extra effort from their employees that will really make a difference to their business, organisations must identify the triggers that will encourage this discretionary effort, and design rewards that will reinforce the continuation of such efforts.

Extrinsic rewards include all those rewards an employee gets from sources other than the job itself. An organisation has a large degree of control over the nature and monetary cost of the extrinsic rewards with which it intends to compensate the efforts of its employees and can therefore manipulate the use of these external rewards to affect employee behaviour.

In light of the above, *remuneration* may therefore be defined as the financial and non-financial extrinsic rewards provided by an employer for the time, skills and effort made available by the employee in fulfilling job requirements aimed at achieving organisational objectives.

Concepts that are sometimes used as more or less equivalent to remuneration management are reward management, compensation management, or salary and wage or pay administration. Take note, however, that the administration aspect used to be emphasised more in the past. While pay-related administration is still essential, remuneration management (or remuneration or reward management) is usually taken to be a more comprehensive concept.

15.1.2 Remuneration management: an overview

Remuneration management has become a complex and specialised HRM function and it must be emphasised from the outset that there is no one best reward system that will work for every organisation. Because it is such a specialised function, this is also

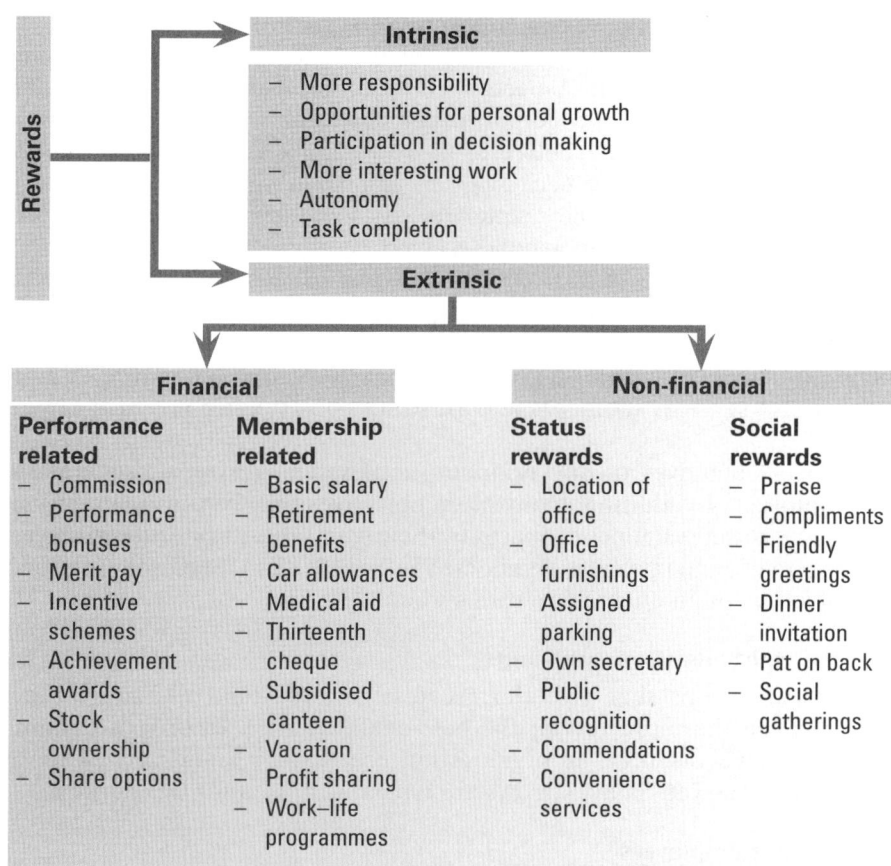

Figure 15.1: Types and structure of rewards
Sources: Adapted and expanded from DeCenzo & Robbins (2007: 287); and Luthans (2002: 550)

probably the one aspect of HRM in which the line manager's role is relatively minor – especially on an ongoing basis.

For designing an appropriate remuneration system, two challenges typically have to be met to link the remuneration strategy to the organisation's overall business strategy (Gómez-Mejía, Balkin & Cardy 2001: 325):

- the system must enable the organisation to achieve its strategic objectives; and
- it must be shaped to fit the organisation's unique characteristics and environment.

In choosing between the large variety of available design options, the remuneration manager therefore has continuously to keep in mind the overall reward strategy in order to ensure that design features are congruent and fit well with other human resource practices and with the organisation's business strategy.

The following three issues have to be addressed in this design planning process.

- What should be the overall objectives of the system?
- What external and internal influences exist, and what impact may they have on specific design decisions?
- What policies should govern the system?

The consideration of these issues constitutes the first part of the chapter.

The second set of design issues focuses on the essential elements, or nuts and bolts, of a remuneration system. Aspects such as job evaluation, pay surveys and pay structure are examined in the second part of the chapter.

As Steers and Porter (1991: 487) note, even the best-designed reward systems can go awry in producing their intended results because of the manner in which they are implemented. In view of this, the final part of the chapter reviews some important implementation or process issues such as communication policies and decision-making practices.

15.2 REMUNERATION OBJECTIVES

Remuneration objectives are those guidelines that determine the nature of a reward system. They also serve as standards against which the effectiveness of the system is evaluated.

The classical objectives of any remuneration system are to attract, retain and motivate employees. In addition, many more objectives may be formulated to ensure that the remuneration system contributes to the organisation's overall objectives (the evolving concept of total reward is highlighted in exhibit 15.1). The following are some common objectives of an effective reward system.

Attracting the right quality of applicants

Generally, organisations that give the greatest rewards tend to attract the most applicants and can therefore recruit the best-qualified staff. In order to maintain a competitive pay-level strategy, an organisation needs some knowledge of the going rate in the labour market. Salary surveys are typically utilised for this purpose.

Retaining suitable employees

To encourage valuable staff members to remain, the remuneration system must provide sufficient rewards for these employees to feel satisfied when they compare their rewards with those received by individuals performing similar jobs in other organisations.

Maintaining equity among employees

In the context of remuneration the concept of equity relates to perceptions of fairness in the distribution of rewards. It is generally considered to be one of the most important objectives of any remuneration system.

Different types of equity can be distinguished: external, internal and individual.
- *External equity* concerns comparisons of rewards across similar jobs in the labour market. Pay surveys are usually used for information regarding external equity.
- *Internal equity* deals with comparisons of rewards across different jobs within the same organisation. It addresses the issue of the relative worth of, for example, an engineer versus an accountant working for the same employer. The techniques of job evaluation and pay structuring are to establish internal equity. The whole issue of 'income differentials' (in terms of the Employment Equity Act) is thus very relevant here.
- *Individual (or procedural) equity* is concerned with the extent to which an employee's remuneration is reflective of his or her contribution and the fairness with which pay changes such as increases are made. Changes may be based, for example, on individual performance, on competencies, or according to fixed increments or seniority.

EXHIBIT 15.1: 'Total rewards' as the new era of linking reward to strategy

The concept of 'total rewards' has emerged over the past ten years and is gaining increasing popularity as an approach towards an integrated and holistic management of extrinsic and intrinsic rewards linked to business strategy. Various definitions and models of *total rewards* exist, but in essence the concept refers to a strategically focused reward strategy that seeks to integrate the components of financial rewards and benefits with non-financial elements of reward that in combination will leverage employee engagement and satisfaction as well as business performance and results.

As remuneration guru, Michael Armstrong puts it: "It is about all the ways in which people are rewarded when they come to work – pay, benefits and the other non-financial rewards – put together to make a coherent and integrated whole."

Following a comprehensive review, the remuneration association WorldatWork introduced their conceptual model of total rewards in 2006. The model recognises the impact of external influences, and that total rewards operate in the context of overall business and HR strategies, and organisational culture. It comprises five elements of total rewards, each of which includes programmes and practices that collectively define an organisation's strategy to attract, motivate and retain talent. These elements represent the overall reward 'toolkit' from which the organisation chooses to offer and align a value proposition that creates value for both the employees and the organisation. The outcomes of an effective total rewards strategy are productive, satisfied and engaged employees who in turn then create business performance and results.

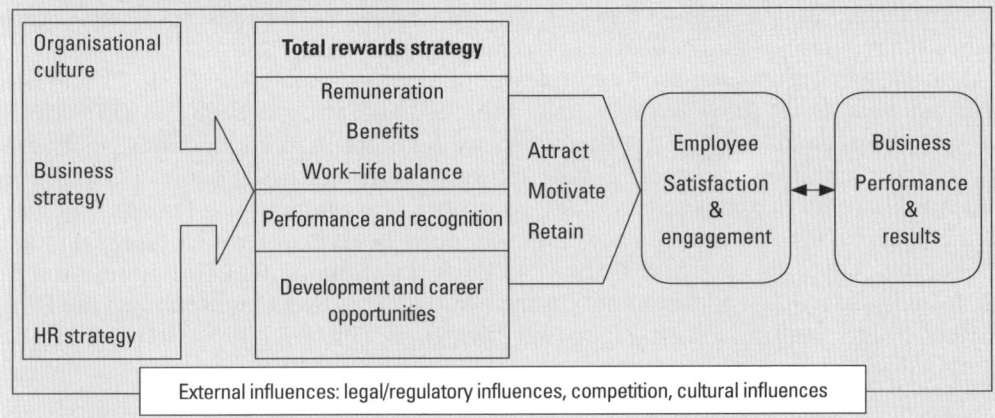

Source: Adapted from *WorldatWork Total Rewards Model: A Framework for Strategies to Attract, Motivate and Retain Employees*

Rewarding good performance and providing incentives for desired behaviour

An organisation can structure its reward system to encourage employee behaviour directed towards improving corporate performance and achieving specific aims. (See the case studies below.)

Maintaining cost-effectiveness

The remuneration system often constitutes the single largest operating cost of an organisation and should therefore be designed and assessed from a cost/benefit perspective. A systematic pay structure is therefore needed to prevent undue expense and possible over- or underpayment of employees.

CASES AT HAND

Edcon links increases to reaching HR targets

In support of a corporate strategic objective of staff attraction and retention, Edgars Consolidated Stores (Edcon) designed a scheme by which 50% of the performance review of each manager or supervisor is linked to a human resources index that measures progress in employment equity, training, perception survey results, performance management and leadership. If managers do not deliver on people-related issues, they suffer the consequences of not getting a good performance review. It is this review that determines the level of salary increases.

Metrobus designs scheme for artisans project

Johannesburg Metrobus designed a reward scheme in support of a particular project. Initially the incentive scheme was designed to support a project of increasing artisan efficiency in the mechanical workshops. It failed to produce the intended results of quicker turnaround times and was subsequently revised towards an objective of reducing the number of buses out of commission at peak passenger times. With the introduction of additional measures, the scheme succeeded to such extent that the purchase of new buses could be delayed for a number of years.

Sources: Corporate Research Foundation (2005); and Honnet (2006)

Complying with legal requirements

Remuneration design faces certain legal constraints and needs to comply with legislative regulations and collectively bargained agreements.

Labour legislation such as the Employment Equity Act and the Basic Conditions of Employment Act have a direct impact on remuneration design and collectively bargained agreements reached with unions also restrict the freedom of design choices for the remuneration manager. Furthermore, the structuring of salary packages to maximise take-home pay needs to conform to the provisions of the Fourth Schedule of the Income Tax Act and the Seventh Schedule, in terms of which employers are obliged to deduct Pay As You Earn (PAYE) from all amounts of remuneration in the form of cash or specific benefits. In the area of executive remuneration, the King II Report on corporate governance also provides specific guidelines that need to be complied with.

Providing for flexibility and administrative efficiency

Design should be flexible enough to prevent bureaucratic rigidity and allow for dealing with alterations in relative market rates and individual differences in terms of merit. In addition, it should be simple enough to explain, understand and operate.

General objectives of total reward models

Major consultancy firms such as Towers Perrin, Watson Wyatt and Hay Group, have developed proprietary total reward models, but consistent themes identified by CIPD in all such models include:

- Holistic focus on staffing and retention through using an array of extrinsic and intrinsic rewards.
- Best-fit approach tailored to the organisation's unique culture, objectives, structure and processes.
- Integration of rewards with other HR policies and practices.
- People centredness through focusing on finding out what employees really value in the work environment.

- Customisation by offering choices in a flexible mix of rewards designed to meet different lifestyle and life-stage needs.
- Distinctiveness through creating an 'employer brand' that differentiates the organisation from rivals.
- Evolutionary, long term approach based on incremental changes.

Sources: (CIPD 2007; Hay Group 2005; Watson Wyatt 2005; and Wilkinson 2007)

15.3 REMUNERATION POLICIES

Remuneration policies are formalised guidelines for remuneration-related decision making by management. Such policies indicate to management what behaviour is expected in given circumstances when reward issues are to be dealt with.

A CASE AT HAND

Sasol Group remuneration philosophy

Recognising that the group is operating in an international environment, the Sasol remuneration philosophy:
- plays an integral part in supporting the implementation of Sasol's international business strategies;
- motivates and reinforces individual and team performance;
- integrates financial and non-financial rewards and benefits; and
- is applied equitably, fairly and consistently in relation to job responsibility, the employment market and personal performance.

Sasol's application of remuneration practices in all business and functions in South Africa and internationally:
- aims to be market competitive in the specific labour markets in which people are employed;
- determines the value proposition of the various positions within job families or functions;
- ensures that performance management forms an integral part of remuneration, thereby influencing the remuneration components of base pay and incentives; and
- applies good governance to remuneration practices within approved structures.

The alignment of these remuneration principles aims to meet the strategic objectives of:
- attracting, retaining and motivating key and talented people;
- competing in the marketplace with the intention of being a preferred employer;
- rewarding individual, team and business performance; and
- supporting Sasol's core values of customer focus, winning with people, excellence in all we do, continuous improvement, integrity and safety.

Source: Sasol Remuneration report in Annual Report (2007)

15.3.1 Remuneration policy areas

The areas in which remuneration policies need to be formulated, include (Armstrong & Stephens 2005):
- *Pay level:* This area concerns external competitiveness and is expanded upon in section 15.3.2. The policy questions will be: should the level of pay be above, below or at the prevailing market rate? What government regulations, union influences and market pressures need to be considered?

- *Equity:* To what degree is the organisation going to strive for internal equity and by what means are internal relativities between jobs to be established?
- *Performance-related rewards:* How should achievement be rewarded and what role should incentive and bonus schemes play?
- *Market rate policy:* To what extent should market rate pressures (for example scarce, highly regarded skills) be allowed to affect or possibly distort the salary structure and sacrifice internal equity?
- *Salary structure:* Is a formal structure required and, if so, what type of structure is necessary to ensure consistent and equitable, yet flexible administration of salaries? (See section 15.10 for a definition and discussion of this aspect.)
- *Control:* What is the amount of freedom given to individual line managers to influence the salaries of their staff?
- *Total package:* What is the best reward mix of basic pay, benefits and incentives for the different categories of employees?
- *Communication:* How much information about the remuneration system should be made freely available to employees and/or their representatives, and what degree of pay secrecy should be enforced?

A further important design decision concerns the relative emphasis that is to be placed on the different policy areas. For example, the aims of pursuing internal equity may be compromised if external competitiveness takes precedence in certain cases where job offers exceed the pay ranges stipulated by the organisation's internal pay structure. This could lead to a problem of compression, that is, the reduction of pay differentials between jobs or levels of jobs due to, for instance, the pay rate for jobs filled from outside the organisation increasing faster than the pay rate for job incumbents within it.

(There may be other causes for pay rate compression, but the problem typically occurs when employees in a particular job grade perceive that there is not a sufficient difference between their level of remuneration and that of the employees in the next lower job grade.)

15.3.2 Pay level policy

Essentially, an organisation's pay level policy refers to how its average pay rate for a specific group of jobs compares to that of its competitors. This policy is of particular importance since it has a direct impact on an organisation's ability to attract and retain appropriately qualified and competent employees and its competitive position in its market – that is, the level of external equity it maintains.

In positioning itself in its prevailing external labour market, the organisation can choose between three broad pay level policy options:
- lead policy;
- match policy; and
- lag policy.

A lead policy implies that the employer pays at a higher rate than his or her competitors for comparable jobs, a match policy means paying at the average market rate, and a lag policy obviously means paying below the market average.

Many of the influencing factors identified in the next section will have a bearing on the organisation's pay level policy, and the optimum policy is dependent on the employer's unique set of circumstances. For example, an employer who wishes to attract only the best candidates, pursues an image of prestige and tries to limit labour turnover would probably need to consider a lead policy.

A match policy is the most common and in practice this would mean that the employer pays at the market median or 50th percentile, that is, that salary value where 50% of the market sample earns more than this salary and 50% earns less. Implementing a lead policy could, for example, be achieved by either redrawing the market line at a higher level or paying at the 75th percentile or higher.

15.4 INFLUENCES ON REMUNERATION POLICIES

There are various interacting factors that have an impact on the design of the remuneration system. Some of these are external forces, while others are a function of the internal conditions of the organisation.

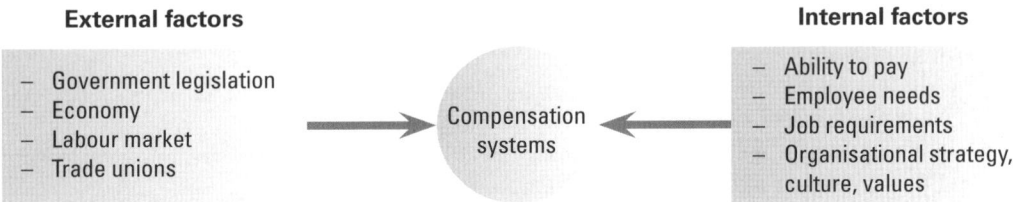

External factors
- Government legislation
- Economy
- Labour market
- Trade unions

Compensation systems

Internal factors
- Ability to pay
- Employee needs
- Job requirements
- Organisational strategy, culture, values

Figure 15.2: Major influences on remuneration systems

15.4.1 External factors

Government legislation

South African legislation impacting on remuneration policies includes:
- the Labour Relations Act 66 of 1995
- the Basic Conditions of Employment Act 75 of 1997
- the Employment Equity Act 55 of 1998
- the Skills Development Act 97 of 1998
- the Skills Development Levies Act 9 of 1999
- the Unemployment Insurance Act 63 of 2001
- the Income Tax Act 58 of 1962, as amended – in particular also Schedule 7 of this Act which pertains to fringe benefit taxation and 8c regarding share schemes.

Economy

Broad economic conditions such as high levels of inflation, recessionary periods, differences in the cost of living in different parts of the country, general level of employment and competitiveness in the local or international product market can greatly affect the general level of remuneration.

Labour market

Remuneration levels may often vary according to the forces of supply and demand in terms of general labour or specific skills.

Unions

Organised labour can have a significant impact on the determination of wage levels and benefits by means of collective bargaining and other mechanisms.

EXHIBIT 15.2: Trends in the South African remuneration field

The following trends have been highlighted in various recent surveys in the South African environment:

In the area of executive pay, the following trends are found:

- a move towards a total package approach to pay;
- customising packages and offering flexibility regarding benefits and lifestyle choices;
- moving from fixed pay to variable pay, with emphasis on rewarding output and results rather than simply activity;
- business performance measures such as shareholder value and economic value-added (EVA) measures are used to determine rewards;
- increase in levels of variable pay relative to guaranteed pay due to increasing difficulties to justify top executive remuneration levels and due to corporate governance (King II) recommendations for emphasis on performance-related elements of remuneration; and
- payment of 'attraction' premiums and financial inducements to secure scarce executive talent and equity candidates.

Trends at all levels:

- provision of retirement benefits, medical care and housing is provided for the majority of public sector workers, compared to 40% in the private sector;
- skills shortages at specialist and managerial level, particularly from previously disadvantaged groups, create pay pressures in these areas;
- the concept of total reward as opposed to remuneration in isolation is finding favour, and increasingly non-financial benefits are being offered to retain key staff;
- retention of critical skills drives remuneration policy in private enterprises towards combinations of measures of share schemes, aggressive bonus schemes and upper-quartile market positions for scarce job families;
- increasing movements towards the total cost to company remuneration approach and differentiation of reward practices according to different needs and wants of generations (veterans, baby boomers, generations X and Y) – future mass customisation of rewards is foreseen;
- flexibility and work–life balance become more valued than pay increases; and
- South African companies follow global trend to 'pamper' employees by providing a range of services including gyms, crèches, massage therapy, wellness centres and full concierge services.

Sources: Paycon (2006); Bussin (2007); P-E Corporate Services (2006); and Piliso (2007)

15.4.2 Internal factors

Ability to pay

An organisation's ability to pay has a big impact on its general level of remuneration. The level of productivity, its profitability, its size and its competitors are all determinants of its ability to generate revenues for paying its human resources (Mondy & Noe 2005: 288).

Employee needs

Employees differ in terms of what they prefer to receive as remuneration. Younger employees may have a higher cash need than older ones, highly compensated executives' needs differ from those of general workers, etc. There may thus be a need to build choices into the system.

Job requirements

Requirements regarding the average skill level of employees may impact on the pay level that the organisation can set and still be able to obtain sufficient numbers of qualified employees.

Strategy, culture and values

As previously emphasised, pay policies should be supportive of the organisation's strategic objectives. In addition, organisational values such as decision-making style, openness regarding communication and social responsibility may have a bearing on remuneration policies. (For example, organisations valuing a competitive, achievement-driven climate will probably opt for performance-related rather than fixed increment pay increases; companies that are sensitive to the needs of female employees may adopt policies of fully paid extended maternity leave, etc.)

15.5 PAY SYSTEM DESIGN

The traditional and predominant pay system design is job-based remuneration.

This means we pay jobs, or, put differently, an employee who holds a job just happens to get the salary that is assigned to that position. The amount paid to each job is based on an assessment of its internal and external importance and worth. Because not all jobs are equally important to the company, the remuneration system's primary objective is to allocate pay in a systematic manner to ensure that the most important jobs pay the most (Gómez-Mejía et al 2001: 335). Internal worth is established through the use of job evaluation systems, and external worth is through market surveys. A pay structure is established to set boundaries on pay, based on the results of the job evaluation and market survey. Movement takes place within the pay structure based on time spent by the individual in the job category (seniority), or by merit.

The emerging alternative to the job-based pay system is an employee-based system such as skills-based pay.

Skills-based pay (also termed knowledge-based or competency-based pay) is an unconventional remuneration scheme in which employees are paid at a rate based on their range, depth and types of skills in which they demonstrate capability, irrespective of the job they are assigned to (Newstrom & Davis 2002: 154).

Three types of skill are usually identified in skills-based pay (Heneman, Ledford & Gresham 2000: 212):

- *depth of skill*, indicating increased knowledge of one technical speciality. An example would be apprenticeship systems for workers in the skilled trades;
- *breadth of skill*, meaning increased knowledge of a variety of tasks or jobs. For example, factory workers may be rewarded for learning all jobs in their work team; and
- *vertical skill*, which refers to self-management skills. For example, team members may all get an increase when they prove they can operate without direct supervision.

In this approach, organisations create various skill steps that are aligned with the specific process requirements of their organisation. Pay is then related directly to the total number of skills steps for which an individual has demonstrated capability. The basic assumptions behind linking base pay to skills acquisition are that employees become more efficient and capable as their competency profile broadens, and that a group of multiskilled employees can perform greater quantities of work in a more flexible manner.

Endorsement of the approach is mixed, and despite advantages such as flexibility, reduction of competition between workers, broadbanding possibilities and decrease in supervisor cost, disadvantages such as high development and maintenance costs, continued payment for skills that are no longer used routinely or are no longer associated with required processes, and time-consuming training make skill-based pay a potentially high-risk endeavour (Armstrong & Stephens 2005: 249).

Gómez-Mejía et al (2002: 330) suggest that skill-based remuneration systems may be suitable in organisational environments where:

- employee participation and teamwork are applicable;
- opportunities for upward mobility are limited;
- opportunities exist for learning new skills;
- the technology and organisational structure change frequently;
- a relatively educated workforce exists with both the willingness and ability to learn different jobs; and
- cost of turnover and absenteeism in terms of lost production are high.

The commonest job-based pay methodology is the time-based system, where the individual is paid in accordance with the amount of time he or she spends on the job; that is, hours worked for hourly-paid jobs, or a monthly fraction of an annual rate of pay for salaried staff. Since such job-based pay systems dominate the South African remuneration scene and are still supported most widely in terms of job evaluation and salary survey services, the sections that follow are aligned to the job-based approach.

15.6 ESSENTIAL ELEMENTS OF A TRADITIONAL REMUNERATION SYSTEM

Having planned and established the overall objectives, desired design features and guiding policies of the remuneration system, remuneration specialists can now set out to put the plans into practice and construct the system. To achieve this aim, four basic tools of the job-based remuneration system design should be used:

- job analysis;
- job evaluation;
- pay surveys; and
- pay structuring.

Owing to the complexity of some of these elements, each will be discussed in a separate section (that is, in sections 15.7 to 15.9 below).

15.7 JOB ANALYSIS

As with so many other HRM functions, the process of job analysis and the resulting job descriptions constitute the basic building blocks for remuneration system design. Job analysis was discussed fully in chapter 6. In the context of remuneration system design, its purpose is twofold (Cascio 2006: 425):

- to identify the important characteristics of each job so that job evaluation can be carried out; and
- to identify, define and weigh the compensable factors; that is, all those shared characteristics of jobs that provide a basis for judging job value. These factors are

typically linked to the specific job evaluation plan, for example decision making (Paterson) or know-how, problem solving and accountability (Hay) (see section 15.8.2).

15.8 JOB EVALUATION

Job evaluation may be defined as a systematic process of determining the value of each job in relation to others in the organisation.

The purpose of this process is to rank jobs within a hierarchy that reflects the relative importance or worth of each job within the organisation.

Job evaluation is concerned with the relative worth of jobs as such and not with the worth of the job incumbents. The latter issue is addressed by performance appraisal, which has already been discussed in chapter 11.

Job evaluation is essentially a process of comparisons (comparisons with other jobs, comparisons against defined standards, or comparisons of the extent to which common factors are present in different jobs) and it is these different comparisons which form the foundation of the different job-evaluation methods (Aamodt 1999: 91–93; Kleiman 2000: 245–248).

15.8.1 Job evaluation methods

15.8.1.1 Job ranking

The job ranking method is the simplest but least used job evaluation method. It involves judging each job as a whole and determining its place in the job hierarchy by comparing it with all other jobs and arranging them in order of importance. While its simplicity and inexpensiveness may be attractive characteristics, the method has major drawbacks that make it an unsuitable option for all but the smallest of organisations. Disadvantages are:

- cumbersomeness and unreliability with increasing numbers of jobs;
- a lack of specific criteria for the ranking process; and
- an inability to indicate the extent of differences between job levels.

15.8.1.2 Job classification

The job classification method entails the placing of groups of jobs into a number of job grades or classes. The job grades and grade descriptions are established first and then individual jobs are fitted into the grade with the most appropriate description. Grade definitions are based on discernable differences regarding certain criteria such as the level of decision making (for example the Paterson method).

Jobs are allotted grades by comparing the whole job description with the grade definition. Job classification methods have the advantage of being quite simple to understand and operate, and relatively expedient and inexpensive to implement. However, major criticisms have been expressed regarding the oversimplification of using single job factors to establish remuneration differentials (Biesheuvel 1985: 64), higher levels of subjectivity than for the points method, and the inability to cope with complex jobs which will not fit neatly into one grade.

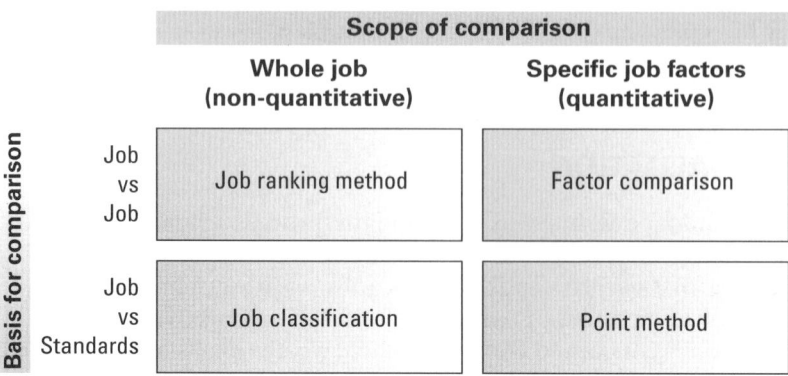

Figure 15.3: Basic job evaluation methods
Source: Adapted from Sherman & Bohlander (1992: 315)

15.8.1.3 Factor comparison

The factor comparison method is a complex ranking method where jobs are ranked against a number of compensable factors. Four basic steps are used in developing and using a factor comparison scale.

- Step 1: Selecting and ranking a number of key jobs/benchmark jobs (important jobs that are widely known and have a relatively stable job content).
- Step 2: Allocating monetary values to the compensable factors for each key job.
- Step 3: Setting up the factor comparison scale where the results from step 2 are displayed.
- Step 4: Evaluating non-key jobs against the key jobs.

This method is very cumbersome, difficult to explain to employees and lacks flexibility. As with any other jobs, key jobs change over time and each time that this occurs the whole exercise will have to be repeated.

15.8.1.4 Point method

The point method is the most frequently used system in job evaluation plans. Although many variations exist, point systems essentially comprise a mathematical (quantitative) method whereby point values are assigned to the degree to which certain identified compensable factors are required for a particular job. The following are the typical steps followed by point systems. (The boxed portions provide a step-by-step practical illustration of the point method.)

Step 1: Selecting compensable job factors
A number of factors which are considered to be common to all jobs in the organisation are selected and clearly defined.

Example: Skills required, responsibility, degree of effort, working conditions

---

Step 2: Dividing factors into degrees

The chosen factors are divided into different degrees that describe the extent to which the factor exists in a given job.

Each degree has to be defined clearly.

Example: working conditions
- Degree 1: Job performed in air-conditioned private office from 09:00 to 16:30; no overtime or weekend work requirements
- Degree 4: Shift-work with unstable, long working hours; stressful, noisy conditions; weekend work required

Step 3: Allocating weights (points) to factors and degrees

The total number of points that can be allocated (for example 1 000) and the percentage of this total that will be assigned to each factor has to be decided upon. The more important the factor, the higher its point total will be. Points are assigned to each degree within the factors to provide a system of weighting each factor within the point system.

Example

Factor	Degrees				Factor weights %
	1st	2nd	3rd	4th	
Skill	90	175	260	350	35%
Responsibility	60	125	180	250	25%
Effort	75	150	225	300	30%
Working conditions	25	50	75	100	10%
				1 000	100%

In our example, the assumption was made that skill requirements are the most important and working conditions the least important compensable factors. A relative weight allocation of 35%, 25%, 30% and 10% between the respective factors was decided upon. The points allocation to each degree represents a proportionally equal progression up to the maximum points total for each factor. Note therefore that the maximum points for each factor add up to the maximum points total for the system, that is, 1 000.

Step 4: Rating jobs on each factor and totalling points

Jobs are evaluated by an evaluation committee which determines for each factor the degree that best defines the level required for the job. Once each factor has been rated, points are added to give the total points value of the job.

Example

A general labourer's job evaluated in terms of our example at the 1st degree of skill and responsibility, 2nd degree of effort and 3rd degree of working conditions, will be worth a total of 90 + 60 + 150 + 75 = 375 points.

The conversion of points to pay is a separate exercise that is independent of the evaluation process.

While the point method has the major disadvantage of being complex and time consuming to develop and maintain, it does provide a higher level of objectivity and face validity than especially the non-quantitative methods. Another advantage is its ability to assess relative differences between jobs. Organisations often avoid the difficulties involved in the development of a tailor-made, point-based system by subscribing to ready-made plans such as the Peromnes, Task and Castellion systems.

15.8.2 Major job evaluation systems in use in South Africa

A large variety of job evaluation systems based on some of the methods discussed are currently in use in South Africa. Many companies and industries utilise in-house systems that have been developed as tailor-made systems taking into account the specific situation and requirements of these organisations. On the other hand, extensive use is also made of standardised, ready-made systems that have been developed locally or abroad. The most dominant systems in this category are the Paterson Decision Band Method, the Peromnes system and the Hay Guide-Chart profile system. Despite lacking perhaps the tailor-made nature of in-house systems, these systems have the important advantage that they are all supported by major consultancies and provide their users with access to the data of regular and comprehensive salary surveys. The underlying principles of the dominant systems are outlined below.

15.8.2.1 Paterson Decision Band method

The Paterson Decision Band method (which is often called the Paterson plan) is a job evaluation system that is essentially based on the job classification method. It was developed by Professor TT Paterson in Scotland, primarily as an alternative to time-consuming point systems which were at that time using a large number of factors. His research led him to the conclusion that a single factor, 'decision making', was present in all jobs and could be used on its own to measure job level.

Six bands of decision making are defined in terms of the level of complexity of decisions required from job incumbents. The levels range from the completely defined decisions at band A to policymaking decisions at band F. Each of the bands (except band A) is divided into an upper and a lower grade, with the upper grade coordinating or supervising the work performed at the lower grade.

There are thus 11 grades which can be further divided into subgrades according to the specific needs of the company. Typically 28 subgrades are utilised, with upper and lower grades having two and three subgrades respectively. Table 15.1 provides an outline of the Paterson plan.

When the Paterson plan is applied, jobs are first classified under the specific band (A to F) with the definition that agrees most closely with the job requirements. Jobs are then sorted into the lower and upper grades in terms of the coordinating principle – that is, where a job includes coordination of other jobs in the same band, it is placed in the upper grade.

Subgrading is generally done according to the principle that in any one grade those jobs which require more decisions of that grade are deemed to be more important and difficult, and are therefore placed in a higher subgrade (Anglo American Corporation 1984).

The Paterson system is used in various European countries, Canada, Australia, India and southern Africa.

The Paterson method is simple and easy to understand and implement, inter-nationally recognised and cost effective. Its major disadvantages are, however, its reliance on a single factor to measure all jobs, lack of uniformity regarding subgrading

Table 15.1: Paterson's decision and grading structure

Band	Type of decision	Skill level	Title	Grade and typical subgrade		Characteristics of decision
F	Policy making	Top management	President Managing director Vice president Executive director	Upper F (Coord) Lower F	F5 F4 F3 F1	Creating the policy affecting the whole enterprise in terms of parameters which are limited only by legislation, by labour practices and by economic considerations
E	Programming	Senior management	General manager Works manager	Upper E (Coord) Lower E	E5 E4 E3 E1	Programming the policy laid down by the board. Concerned with long-term planning in major functions such as production, sales, finance, human resources
D	Interpretive	Middle management	Dept manager Superintendent Section manager	Upper D (Coord) Lower D	D5 D4 D3 D1	Making the rules and establishing the precedents that enable employees in bands C, B and A to produce. Interpreting the programmes laid down by senior management by applying material and human resources to achieve the objectives outlined in the programme and specific to a minor organisational function
C	Routine	Skilled	General foreman Artisan	Upper C (Coord) Lower C	C5 C4 C3 C1	Decisions are based upon a knowledge of theory and systems. Choosing the appropriate routine from a limited array of routines or rules. Working within rules or standards laid down (eg mechanic)
B	Automatic	Semiskilled	Chargehand Apprentice Machine operator	Upper B (Coord) Lower B	B5 B4 B3 B1	To become competent in the job, workers need to be trained and be given practice or experience in the work. They have to be trained to make decisions of a more general routine nature from which they can make a specific judgement to meet new situations not yet encountered (eg driver)
A	Defined	Unskilled	Labourer	Lower A	A3 A1	Workers can be taught the complete job in a short time. The job is quite specific and defined. No decisions additional to those taught to the worker are required to perform the job (eg cleaner)

Source: Adapted and expanded from IPM Fact Sheet 172, *IPM Journal* (July 1988)

procedures and difficulties in grading complex management hierarchies (for example in a conglomerate where the corporate structure is made up of a large number of separate companies).

A Paterson plan derivative, the TASK (tuned assessment of skills and knowledge) system, that uses a point system with a number of factors for subgrading (skill level, knowledge, complexity, influence, pressure), was developed by FSA-Contact consultancy in the early 1980s to address the problem of subgrading.

15.8.2.2 Peromnes system

The Peromnes system has its roots in the Castellion Job Evaluation method that was developed for South African Breweries by Professor Simon Biesheuvel (the latter system derives its name from the SAB's Castle and (now defunct) Lion products). The Peromnes system is essentially a simplification of the Castellion method, which uses 11 factors and subfactors. Since the late 1960s when the Peromnes system was developed, it has been adopted by over 600 organisations and it is currently solely marketed and supported by Deloitte & Touche Human Capital Corporation (Pty) Ltd, who are the copyright holders. The Peromnes system (the Latin words *per omnes* mean 'for all') is based on the point method and evaluates jobs on the basis of eight factors, of which the first six are job content factors and the remaining two job requirement factors. The eight factors are listed in exhibit 15.3.

During the evaluation process, each factor is evaluated according to comprehensive definitions on a progressive scale of complexity. The evaluation committee examines these definitions to arrive at the one which most satisfactorily describes the highest level of activity or the highest requirements of the job on the given factor. Each definition has certain point values which are added up for each factor to provide a total point value for the job. By means of a conversion table, the job is then graded into one of 21 grades, varying from 1 (the highest possible) to 19 (the lowest possible). The grades correspond approximately to the job levels listed in table 15.2.

EXHIBIT 15.3: The eight factors on which the Peromnes system is based

1 **Problem solving:** The nature and complexity of decision processes (including those required in formulating recommendations).

2 **Consequences of judgement (limits of discretion):** The consequences of firm decisions on the organisation or any of its parts, taking account of controls and checks that may exist to prevent the implementation of judgements, especially those which are adverse.

3 **Pressure of work (division of attention):** The pressure inherent in a job, as reflected in the variety and type of work to be achieved in the available time, the need to set effective priorities, and the interruptions and distractions due to interaction with other jobs.

4 **Knowledge:** The level of knowledge required, in operational (NOT formal) qualification terms, to perform the job competently.

5 **Job impact:** The extent of influence that the job has on other activities, both within and outside the organisation.

6 **Comprehension:** The level of understanding of written and spoken communications expected continuously in the regular course of the job.

7 **Educational qualifications required in the post:** The minimum essential requirements are considered, NOT the merely desirable ones.

8 **Subsequent training/experience required:** The period necessary to achieve competence in the job by the shortest possible reasonable route.

Source: Reproduced by the kind permission of Deloitte & Touche Human Capital Corporation Pty (Ltd)

Table 15.2: Peromnes grades and approximate job levels

Example of job level	Job grades
Top management and most senior specialists and professionals	1+ + –3
Senior management and specialists	4–6
Middle management, superintendents and lower-level specialists	7–9
Junior management, supervisors and higher-level skilled and clerical positions	10–12
Skilled and semiskilled workers and clerical personnel	13–16
Low-skilled and unskilled workers	17–19

The popularity of the Peromnes system may largely be attributed to advantages such as:
- its application value regarding all types and levels of posts in any type of organisation;
- its relative simplicity of terminology and application (not requiring any complex calculations or the use of any formal job description); and
- the direct comparability of the job grades between different organisations.

The system's non-dependency on formal written job analyses may, however, compromise the quality of the description of job content to be evaluated. The system has also been criticised because of its choice of factors and its assignment of the same weight to all the factors (Biesheuvel 1985: 55); because the same elements may be evaluated more than once under different headings; and because, in assigning the same points range (35) for all factors, it does not allow for differences in their relative importance as determinants of job performance.

15.8.2.3 Hay Guide Chart method

The Hay Guide Chart method was developed by the Hay Group in the early 1950s and introduced into the South African market during 1978. The system is used extensively overseas (more than 5 000 users in 30 countries). It is probably the most widely used evaluation system, and is marketed and supported in South Africa by Hay Management Consultants. While the roots of the system are in the factor comparison methods, the current form of the Hay system also has strong elements of the point method.

The Hay system measures three common factors along eight dimensions (see exhibit 15.4).

Each of the three factors is measured as a matrix and the evaluation of the involvement of these factors in a particular job is done according to a rather complex quantitative system, the details of which are subject to copyright.

Essentially, point scores for each factor are derived from the guide charts and a profile for the job is drawn up, which indicates its level and nature. The total point score places the job in an organisation-specific evaluation hierarchy ranging between 0 and 4 000 points. The point score for each job is used to obtain a monetary value for the job by means of the regular Hay market surveys from which the number of rand paid per Hay point may be ascertained. Guide charts are adapted to specific client company circumstances and jobs are typically not divided into grades, thus making salary survey comparisons with other evaluation systems impracticable.

While the conceptual merits of the system and the thoroughness and reliability of the evaluation process are well established, these very same advantages also make the system complex and time consuming to implement.

EXHIBIT 15.4: The Hay system

Know-how

This is the sum total of all expertise needed for acceptable job performance, for example knowledge, experience, training, education and intellectual ability. Know-how is measured against the dimensions of:

- depth according to skill, education and training requirements;
- breadth of management know-how; and
- human relations skills.

Problem solving

This entails the thinking challenge required by the job for problem solving (for example analysing, evaluating, reasoning and drawing conclusions). Mental processes involved in problem solving are considered to be based on existing knowledge of facts and principles, and therefore problem solving is treated as a percentage utilisation of 'know-how'. Two dimensions are measured:

- the environment in which the thinking takes place; and
- the challenge presented by the required thinking.

Accountability

Accountability for action and the resultant consequences of action underlies this factor. Three dimensions are distinguished:

- the freedom to act;
- the impact on end results; and
- the magnitude of impact (usually in financial terms).

Table 15.3 provides an approximate correlation between some of the major job evaluation systems mentioned in the preceding section.

15.8.3 Job evaluation in a changing environment

Traditional job evaluation systems as described in the previous section have, over the past few years, been subject to a debate about their continued relevance in a changing business and employment environment. The essence of the criticism lies in the argument that the traditional methodology for evaluating the relative worth of the workforce has its roots in the Taylorist/Fordist production methods flowing from the scientific management movement. Smith (2000: 36) raises a further concern that job evaluation's lack of focus on the ability of the employee assigned to the job may cause poor performers to be overpaid for the worth they can deliver to their employer whereas high performers may often be insufficiently rewarded. A movement from bureaucratic, hierarchical organisational structures to flatter, more flexible organisations employing a more knowledge-oriented workforce together with fundamental changes in job design will also necessitate more flexible job evaluation and remuneration schemes (Heneman et al 2000: 204).

In the South African context, for example, Cosatu has formulated a policy stipulating job grading mechanisms that should provide for team-based production runs and skills-based career paths and succession opportunities.

Concepts such as broadbanding and knowledge- or skills-based remuneration are often utilised as attempts to increase skills flexibility, flatten organisational structures and achieve greater workforce mobility in an increasingly competitive business environment. (The concept of broadbanding is explained in section 15.10.2.) Competency or skills-based pay has been referred to in section 15.2, but needs to be highlighted again since the concept is becoming more common in remuneration practice.

Table 15.3: Approximate relationships among some major job evaluation systems

Job level	Paterson		TASK	Peromnes	Hay
	Band	Subgrade	grades	grades	(typical application)
Unskilled	A	A1	1	19/18	
Paterson (defined)		A2	2	17	63–72
TASK (basic)		A3	3	16	73–84
Semiskilled	B	B1	4	15	85–97
Paterson (automatic)		B2	5		98–113
TASK (discretionary)		B3	6	14	114–134
		B4	7	13	135–160
		B5	8	12	161–191
Skilled	C	C1	9	11	192–227
Paterson (routine)		C2	10	8	228–268
TASK (specialised)		C3	11	10	269–313
		C4	12	9	314–370
		C5	13	8	
Lower/middle management	D	D1	14	7	371–438
Paterson (interpretive)		D2	15		439–518
TASK (tactical)		D3	16	6	519–613
		D4	17		614–734
		D5	18	5	
Senior management	E	E1	19	4	735–879
Paterson (programming)		E2	20		880–1 055
TASK (tact./strategic)		E3	21	3	1 056–1 260
		E4	22		1 261–1 507
		E5	23	2	1 508–1 808
Top management	F	F1	24	2	1 801–2 140
Paterson (policy making)		F2	25		2 141–2 550
TASK (strategic)	F3	26	1	1	
		F4	27	1+	2 551–3 020
		F5	28	1++	3 021–3 580

Source: Adapted from TASK Remuneration Survey, FSA-Contact Pty (Ltd) (Deloitte & Touche); and update on grading structures and trends, 21st Century Pay Solutions

Whereas traditional job evaluation-based remuneration uses the job as the basis for level of pay, in the case of the competency- or skills-based pay system the person provides the basis for pay. The controversy surrounding the distinction between jobs versus people as the unit of analysis for remuneration is likely to continue, and Heneman et al (2000: 205) suggest that the mix of job and people requirements should be balanced according to the unique strategy, structure, processes and people in the specific organisation. Despite the above trends, both local and international analysts appear to agree that present job evaluation systems will remain an essential element of remuneration practices for some time to come (Bussin 2006; CIPD 2007).

15.9 PAY SURVEYS

Once jobs have been graded by means of job evaluation, the next step in the development of a remuneration system is the determination of a pay rate for the grades. The remuneration tool used to set the monetary worth of jobs or grades of jobs is the pay/remuneration survey. A pay survey provides information on how other employers compensate similar jobs and skills in an organisation's labour market. The labour market for a specific job category may be defined as that area where employees are drawn from or lost to. Having identified the appropriate labour markets in which he or she is competing for human resources, the survey user can determine the relative position of his or her own pay rates against those of competitors. Pay surveys therefore enable an organisation to maintain external equity.

An organisation can obtain pay survey data by conducting or commissioning its own pay survey that is designed according to its specific informational needs, or it can subscribe to any of various comprehensive external surveys that are conducted on a regular basis by large consultancies such as Deloitte & Touche Human Capital Corporation, P-E Remuneration Services, International Remuneration or Hay Management Consultants. Access to the data of these surveys is usually limited to subscribing companies who pay a fee and are obliged to submit input details for the surveys in order to receive the resulting survey reports.

15.10 PAY STRUCTURING

Pay structuring refers to the process whereby the information obtained from the job evaluation exercise (that is, the relative worth of jobs within the organisation) is combined with the information obtained from the pay surveys (that is, market values of jobs) to establish a pay structure.

A pay structure consists of an organisation's pay scales relating to single jobs, groups of jobs or grades. Among the various types of salary structures (see, for example, Armstrong & Stephens 2005: 208–222), the graded salary structures are probably the most common and will be used as an example to illustrate the process of pay structuring. The development of a pay structure is determined by considerations of the organisation's pay slope, the number of pay grades, the range of each pay grade and the degree of overlap between them. The meanings of these terms are illustrated in figure 15.4, which represents a simple salary structure.

In terms of section 27 of the Employment Equity Act, every designated employer must include in its annual affirmative action report a statement on the remuneration and benefits received in each occupational category and level of that employer's workforce. Where disproportionate income differentials are reflected, a designated employer must take measures to progressively reduce them.

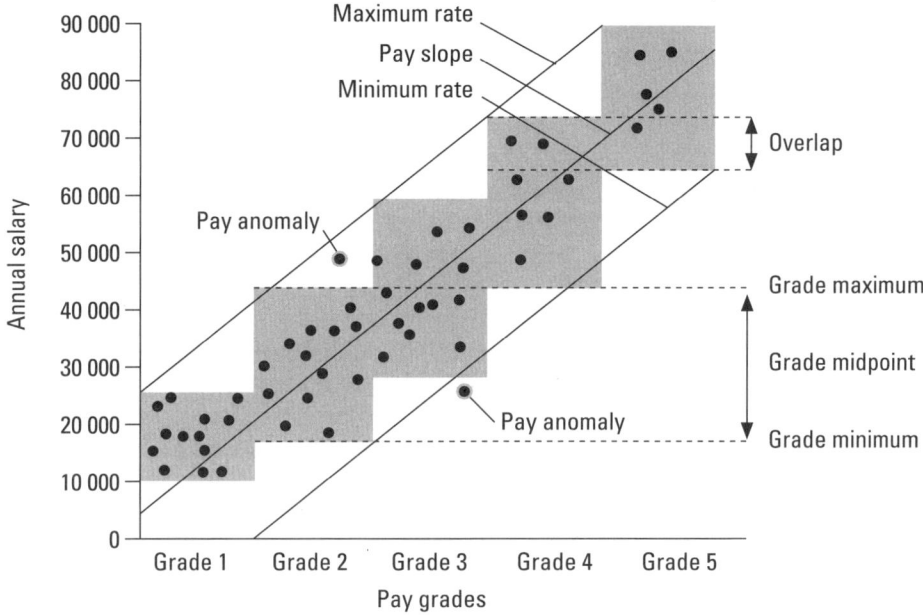

Figure 15.4: A basic pay structure

15.10.1 Pay slope

The pay slope refers to the angle or steepness of the pay curve. The pay curve (which is a curve due to pay being exponential) can be straightened by transforming the pay data (that is, the dispersion of job salaries in all the pay grades) into logarithmic form. The pay slope can be expressed quantitatively in ratio form, as indicated in figure 15.4.

The pay slope percentage between two grades may be calculated by the following formula:

$$\frac{\text{Pay rate for grade 2} - \text{Pay rate for grade 1}}{\text{Pay rate for grade 1}} \times 100$$

While the percentage size of the pay slope is dependent on variables such as the number of grades and economic factors, a pay slope of 15–20% between pay grades is generally appropriate for most circumstances.

15.10.2 Number of pay grades

The various jobs in an organisation are usually classified into pay grades with all jobs falling within a given pay grade receiving the same pay rate (with individual differences based on factors such as seniority or merit). A pay structure based on the Paterson job evaluation plan will have 11 pay grades, and one based on the Peromnes system will have 21.

As can be seen from figure 15.5, the fewer pay grades a structure has, the steeper the pay slope will have to be, and vice versa. Too few pay grades (with a resulting very steep pay slope) may create internal inequity and employee morale problems because jobs with significantly different job content and responsibilities may be paid the same pay rate.

On the other hand, an excessive number of pay grades will result in very similar pay differentials among different jobs. Reduced numbers of pay grades may result from changes in organisational design, such as the recent trend to de-layer organisational hierarchies to yield flatter structures.

The latter problem (that is, too many grades) may arise, for example, from practices such as multiskilling and skill-based remuneration systems where the assigning of subgrades for each group of skills would result in severe difficulties in differentiating between the many categories and maintaining internal equity.

A method of remuneration administration that has emerged as a tool for determining the optimum numbers of grades in changing organisational circumstances is the concept of broadbanding. Essentially, this is a process aimed at decreasing the number of job grades by collapsing the number of original grades into broader bands, but without compromising accurate job measurements within these broad bands. The concept is illustrated in figure 15.6.

The three 'bands' (that is, the large boxes) in a broadbanded pay structure replace four or more traditional salary grades. Another example of broadbanding would be to place all managers into one band, all technicians into a second band, all clerical employees into a third band and all part-time employees into a fourth band (Ivancevich & Matteson 2002: 208).

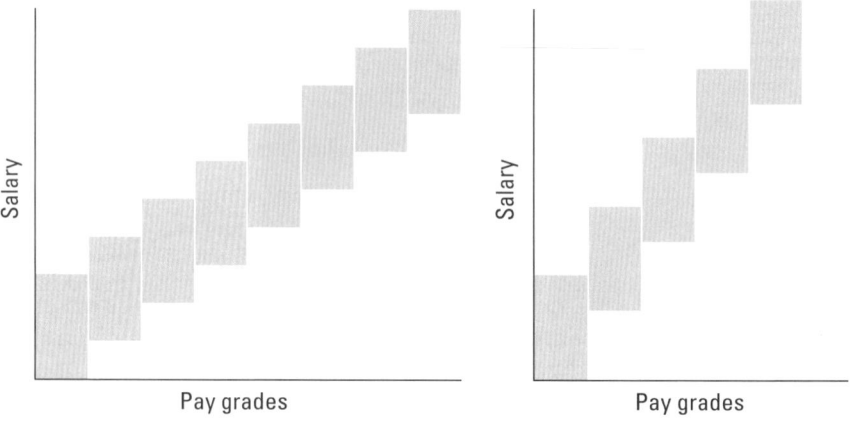

Figure 15.5: Pay structures with different numbers of grades

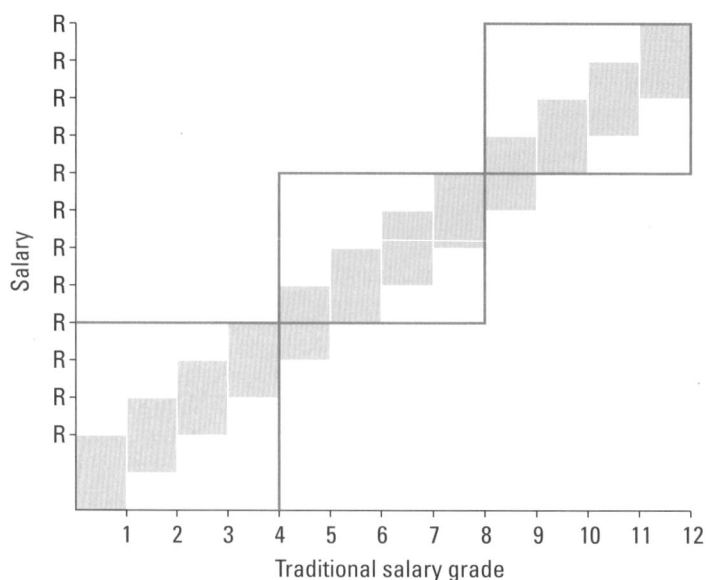

Figure 15.6: A broadbanded salary structure

15.10.3 Pay ranges

The pay range refers to the difference between the minimum and maximum for each pay grade. It therefore reflects the width of a pay scale. In determining the optimum width of a pay range, two factors need to be considered:
- the relative emphasis to be placed on promotion and performance; and
- the nature of the jobs within a particular grade.

A narrow pay range is appropriate if the company wishes to encourage employees to seek promotion. In order to increase his or her basic pay, an employee is obliged to vie for promotion to the next grade.

A wide pay range, on the other hand, is appropriate if performance is to be encouraged within the context of the employee's current job. A wide range allows for the accommodation of greater variations in employee performance.

Narrow pay ranges are more susceptible to the problem of 'topping out', where a person at the top of a pay grade can only receive a pay increase if there is either an across-the-board adjustment or if the job is re-evaluated and placed in a higher grade (Mondy & Noe 2005).

The width of a pay range is also determined by the nature of jobs; that is, the length of the learning phase before a job can be performed at an acceptable standard and the extent of variation in individual performance.

For instance, for routine, well-defined jobs that can be mastered in a short period of time and have little flexibility regarding how the job is done, a narrower pay range is justified. Similarly, for managerial jobs where the learning phase is longer due to the many tasks to be mastered and the wide variations that can exist between good and poor performance, a wider pay range would be appropriate.

15.10.4 Grade overlap

Grade overlap refers to the extent to which the minimum pay of the higher pay grade is overlapped by the maximum pay of the lower grade.

Such overlap acknowledges the fact that an inexperienced newcomer to the higher job grade may initially be of lesser value to the organisation than an experienced, well-performing employee in the next lower job grade.

Once the pay structure has been fully developed, only a small number of implementation considerations or process issues need to be addressed before we have our fully operational remuneration system in place (apart from the benefits component, which is discussed in the next chapter).

15.11 PROCESS ISSUES IN REMUNERATION ADMINISTRATION

The processes by which remuneration systems are implemented and administered in organisations is often considered to be just as important as the technical soundness of the design itself (Henderson 2000: 597–603).

Process issues are often closely linked to the perceptions that employees have about a remuneration plan. Irrespective of whether these perceptions are justified or not, they may have a powerful influence on the effectiveness of the pay system.

Some of the more important process issues that will be discussed briefly are:
- performance appraisal and its link to reward administration;
- decision-making practices; and
- communication policies.

15.11.1 Performance appraisal

If a remuneration system is designed to distribute rewards in relation to differences in performance, it is absolutely essential that the organisation has an effective system in place for assessing the relative quality and quantity of employee performance. If such an appraisal system is unreliable or is perceived to lack validity, it is unlikely that the rewards distributed on the basis of that system will have any positive effect on levels of performance and productivity.

The profound influence exerted by this issue is illustrated by the research of Spangenberg (1994) into South African performance management practices, which led the researcher to question the expediency of actually linking performance appraisal results to the reward system. Spangenberg states that it is not advisable to establish such a direct linkage, unless a strong supportive culture, good job designs and adequate manager–employee relationships exist in the organisation (Spangenberg 1994: 233). This contention is supported by many commentators and Price (2004) cites a common view as: "Pay for performance is the holy grail of modern remuneration administration – widely sought but hard to actually achieve." In the following chapter the design of effective pay-for-performance systems is explored in more detail.

15.11.2 Decision-making practices

Traditionally, remuneration design and administration decisions have been made in a top-down manner with no input from line management or other employees. No doubt this approach is still valid for organisations where the management style suits the hierarchical decision-making process, but it would appear that higher levels of employee participation in remuneration design and administration can result in significant benefits for organisations that have a culture of open communication and employee involvement (Lawler 1990: 221–242).

Such participation can include aspects such as co-determining compensatable factors and choosing their own mix of benefits in a flexible remuneration system.

The advent of the 'total rewards' approach is likely to ensure that the design of reward systems will be a far more inclusive process between remuneration managers, top management and staff than what has been the practice in the past.

15.11.3 Communication policy

The question of how much information about the remuneration system should be communicated to employees is not an easy matter to resolve. While the practice of pay secrecy is probably more the rule than the exception, it is generally a matter of degree of how open pay policies are. The organisation may, for instance, provide full disclosure of how pay rates are set, but divulge no information on individual pay levels. Relevant stipulations in labour legislation regarding information disclosure are obviously very important in this regard. In the South African context the King Report on corporate governance, for example, strongly recommends that companies provide full disclosure of director remuneration on an individual basis, giving details of earnings, share options and all other benefits.

Ivancevich and Matteson (2002: 200) point out that research on the pay secrecy issue has produced mixed findings and outline the following factors that appear to be necessary for an open system to succeed:

- measures of performance must be objective and available for all important aspects of a job;
- the pay–performance link must be apparent to employees;
- there must be a low amount of interdependence among employees; and

- there should be no blatant pay inconsistencies between employees with comparable jobs.

15.11.4 Remuneration management and information technology

While the advances in computer technology and software applications have for some time provided indispensable tools for payroll administration, salary package modelling, scenario planning during wage negotiations, etc, many new applications are continuously being developed as aids to professional remuneration management.

Dessler (1997: 440) highlights the streamlining of the often-cumbersome manual job evaluation process by means of computer-aided job evaluation (CAJE). Such CAJE systems typically feature electronic data entry, computerised checking of questionnaire responses and automated outputs of job evaluation. These are seen rather as an enhancement than a replacement of the traditional job evaluation system, which is usually still needed for initial analysis of benchmark jobs. A computerised version of the popular Peromnes system has already been introduced into the South African job evaluation market.

For participation in salary surveys and utilising survey data, information technology provides useful tools for remuneration specialists and managers. Not only can survey information be submitted electronically, but packages such as RemNet, which is operated by FSA-Contact (now Deloitte & Touche Human Capital Corporation), allows subscribers access to a database of survey data and to manipulate and project such data, produce graphs, etc.

Self-service by employees is becoming a growing trend in the application of IT. Intranet-based self-serve human resource systems typically replace paper documents with electronic transactions, and free human resource staff from routine information request and benefits related transactions. At British American Tobacco South Africa (BAT SA), for example, the objective of their employee self-service system is to enable employees to directly update certain personal details on the human resource database, electronically file administrative documentation (for example leave forms), and view and print personal details on company records, including pay slips (Ciucci 2001).

The World Wide Web also provides various sites for access to useful remuneration and salary survey information. Useful sites are those of the South African Reward Association (SARA), www.sara.co.za, WorldatWork, previously the American Remuneration Association, http://www.worldatwork.org, and the Society for Human Resource Management, http://www.shrm.org or http://jobsmart.org/tools/salary/. Websites of major consultancies often also provide information on recent research and trends, eg Towers Perrin, www.towers.com/towers, Hay Group, www.haygroup.com, Watson Wyatt, www.watsonwyatt.com and 21st Century Pay Solutions, www.21century.co.za.

Elsewhere in Africa

Tanzania

Following a period in the 1990s where public sector pay was characterised by extensive pay inequity and pay levels which were of such low levels that public servants were virtually forced to resort to extensive moonlighting and other activities to supplement their incomes, government introduced a reform programme in public sector reward practice. Long-term goals of this initiative will be to raise minimum basic salaries to the minimum living wage and to raise the salaries and other benefits of its top public servants to levels consistent with the feasibility to recruit and retain top talent into the public service. Benchmarking against progressive practices of the private sector and the implementation of performance-related reward systems are also planned.
Source: Extracted and adapted from Debrah (2004: 76)

Ghana

Wage and salary determination in Ghana comprises basic wages, benefits and allowances. The Ghanaian Tripartite Committee on Salary and Wages determines a national minimum wage. Most medium to large organisations maintain a salary structure and, given the general absence of performance-related pay, annual increases are seniority rather than merit based. Although the nature of Ghanaian society is male dominated, there are no gender-based differences in earnings. Owing to declining real wages, the primary mechanisms for extrinsic motivation are benefits and allowances.
Source: Extracted and adapted from Aryee (2004: 128)

15.12 CONCLUSION

Sound remuneration programmes are of critical importance to organisations because the way they are designed and administered can have a significant influence on employee behaviour and on their commitment to achieving organisational objectives. Of the many types of rewards available to an organisation for compensating the productive efforts of its employees, pay remains to be the most important extrinsic reward. Therefore, the effective utilisation of monetary resources for rewarding and motivating workers constitutes a major part of the manager's role to manage his or her people.

Remuneration systems can be designed in many ways, and the challenge for the organisation lies in the development of a system that is best suited to its own particular objectives with regard to factors such as cost effectiveness, motivational ability, equitable distribution of rewards and administrative efficiency. This chapter identified the various external and internal influences that may impact on the design options and policies an organisation may wish to implement.

The remuneration system mechanics of job analysis, job evaluation, pay surveys and pay structuring were explored in some detail with the aim of systematically leading up to a fully operational pay structure. Finally, performance appraisal linkages, communication policies and decision-making practices were briefly addressed as important considerations in the implementation and administration of pay systems.

Remuneration management involves some complex topics, not all of which could be adequately explored within the scope of this chapter. Two important aspects that form an integral part of a comprehensive remuneration system are benefits administration and incentive remuneration practices. These topics are discussed in the next chapter.

SUSTAINABILITY CONNECTION?

Without proper remuneration, no employee can be expected to remain with an employer or organisation. We have to make sure that we remunerate our working people adequately and fairly. That will help us retain talent and it will also help our people to be more content and be able to have good lives and also help those dear to them to have good lives. No individual or family can enjoy a good life without adequate income. While we have huge unemployment challenges in our country, we should remind ourselves that those who do have work need adequate and fair remuneration because they support many of the jobless people who have no income. A just society is essential for a sustainable future and through proper remuneration management systems and practices we can contribute to bringing about greater fairness in our country and even beyond.

SELF-EVALUATION QUESTIONS

1 'Remuneration has always stood at the heart of any employment relationship.' Discuss this statement critically.
2 By making use of a diagram, differentiate between different types of rewards.
3 What are the important objectives of remuneration management systems?
4 Write brief notes on remuneration policies and aspects that influence them.
5 Describe the basic elements of a remuneration system.
6 Write an essay on the topic of job evaluation. Pay particular attention to major job evaluation systems used in South Africa. What are some recent trends regarding job evaluation within the context of new approaches to work design?
7 Explain what 'pay structuring' entails.
8 Describe the role of the following process issues in remuneration administration:
   - performance appraisal;
   - decision-making processes; and
   - communication and information disclosure.
9 Contrast the benefits and limitations of job-based and person-based remuneration systems.
10 Explain your views on the merits of the total rewards approach in contemporary remuneration management practice.

16 PROVIDING INCENTIVES AND BENEFITS

LEARNING OUTCOMES

After studying this chapter, you should be able to:

- explain why it is often difficult to relate pay to performance;
- develop an effective incentive remuneration plan by using appropriate design principles;
- advise line managers on different types of individual-based and team-based incentive schemes appropriate to different organisational environments;
- design different sales commissions plans and discuss their relative merits;
- explain the importance of benefits in the overall remuneration system;
- devise an appropriate benefit arrangement strategy and explain the principles guiding the choice of strategy; and
- discuss the importance of the elements of choice, flexibility and administrative delivery for successful benefits programmes.

16.1 INTRODUCTION

A total remuneration package includes the three components of base remuneration, comprising the regular fixed pay received as salary or wages; pay incentives that are designed to reward employees for good performance; and benefits or indirect remuneration. In the previous chapter we explored the development of a base remuneration system; the focus of this chapter falls on the incentive and benefits components of total remuneration.

Incentive remuneration differs from other forms of remuneration in that it constitutes an additional reward for outstanding efforts aimed at achieving organisational goals. It is usually financially based and its widespread use stems from the general belief that pay is able to motivate individuals or groups of employees to exceed minimum performance requirements and increase organisational effectiveness.

Benefits, on the other hand, are linked to employment rather than to performance and may be described as an indirect form of remuneration that is mainly intended to improve the quality of work life for an organisation's employees. A wide array of possible benefits may be incorporated in a total remuneration package. While the provision of some of these benefits (such as a retirement plan, and accident and death insurance) are required by law, the possible range of employer-provided benefits is bound only by the limits of the creativity of remuneration specialists (and the scrutiny of the South African Revenue Service).

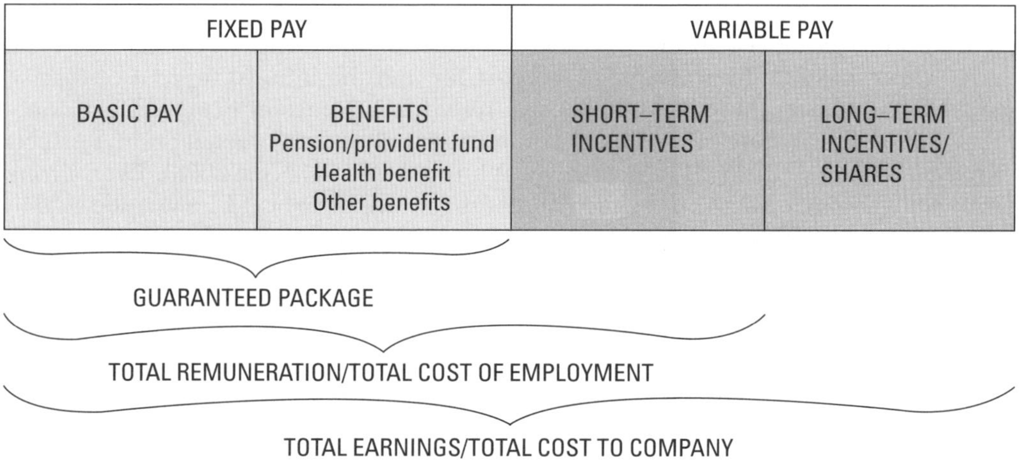

FIXED PAY		VARIABLE PAY	
BASIC PAY	BENEFITS Pension/provident fund Health benefit Other benefits	SHORT–TERM INCENTIVES	LONG–TERM INCENTIVES/ SHARES

GUARANTEED PACKAGE

TOTAL REMUNERATION/TOTAL COST OF EMPLOYMENT

TOTAL EARNINGS/TOTAL COST TO COMPANY

Figure 16.1 The full remuneration picture
Source: Adapted from Bussin (2008)

16.2 INCENTIVE REMUNERATION

Although the basic salary structure discussed in the previous chapter can motivate and reward superior work effort by increasing an individual's pay within the salary range or by promoting the individual into a higher pay grade, such rewards are usually provided on an annual basis. Owing to the delay effect, the recipients of such rewards may not link these directly with performance.

Incentive remuneration schemes are devised essentially as an attempt to link rewards to superior performance in a direct and prompt way. They usually function in addition to basic pay and are specifically aimed at the achievement of specified results, outputs or productivity targets.

Reasons for introducing incentive remuneration plans typically are:

■ to increase the organisation's competitiveness in the labour market for attracting and retaining talent;
■ to stimulate individual, team or organisational performance by making incentive rewards dependent on agreed targets or work outcomes;
■ to recognise and reward better performance;
■ to encourage employee identification with the organisation's objectives and values; and
■ to control fixed remuneration costs by putting a portion of pay at risk if certain agreed objectives are not achieved (Armstrong & Stephens 2005: 233; Muchinsky, Kriek & Schreuder 2002: 268).

In this section we explore the nature, requirements, types and applications of incentive remuneration schemes within the South African context.

16.2.1 Linking pay to performance

Over the past few years South African remuneration specialists have consistently reported a trend towards relating rewards to performance. This 'paying for performance' trend has also been confirmed by national surveys of South African remuneration practices (21st Century Pay Solution Group 2008; P-E Corporate Services 2006). From such surveys it would appear that many South African organisations are designing reward systems that reduce the guaranteed component of pay packages and increase the portion of pay at risk by means of the introduction of incentive systems.

However, despite the widespread support for and the intuitive appeal of linking pay to performance, there is also extensive research evidence of many performance-related pay systems more often than not failing to produce the expected positive effects (Kreitner & Kinicki 2006: 213; McNabb & Whitfield 2007; Hansen 2008). Even strong proponents of performance-related remuneration such as Edward Lawler agree that the design of an effective pay-for-performance programme is a difficult undertaking that should be approached with circumspection (Lawler 1990: 70–131). Such cautious introduction of performance-related pay is due to the complexity and sensitivity thereof in the context of employee relations. Usually it is introduced gradually, as an add-on to normal pay, and typically commences with senior managers as an employee group that is more likely to be committed to the principle of reaching demanding performance objectives (Price 2004: 543).

16.2.1.1 Problems with pay for performance

In chapter 11, the challenges pertaining to performance management were covered. This very same set of issues can generally be said to represent many of the underlying challenges in effectively relating pay to performance. The often subjective nature of performance assessment and the difficulties in eradicating the resulting inconsistencies create the risk of pay differences that cannot be justified.

The following common problems are often responsible for the failure of performance-related pay systems:

- the lack of objective, quantitative performance measures for many jobs and the resulting reliance on subjective performance ratings by managers;
- poorly perceived link between performance and pay, usually due to systems ignoring the principle of immediate reinforcement by linking performance to the reward only at the end of the year;
- aspects of performance that are rewarded are not related to the overall strategic performance objectives, thus encouraging 'wrong' kinds of behaviour (for example, a production bonus scheme that rewards according to levels of output could encourage workers to take short cuts with quality assurance procedures);
- inadequate communication about the objectives, procedures and benefits of the scheme;
- the level of the performance-based portion of pay not being perceived as being sufficiently large enough to be motivational for the additional efforts required; and
- union resistance to performance-based schemes and resistance to change in general (DeCenzo & Robbins 2007: 297; Price 2004: 550).

16.2.2 Requirements for effective incentive remuneration plans

However, although there is no single recipe for selecting the most appropriate design and implementation procedure for a successful incentive scheme, there are a number of generally accepted guiding principles that are relevant to all schemes (see, for example, Armstrong & Stephens 2005: 313; Gupta & Shaw 2000: 147–152; Wilson 2003: 189–220).

While the literature on remuneration management is replete with lists of 'success criteria' for incentive systems, it should be borne in mind that each organisation considering the implementation of pay-for-performance plans will be faced with a unique set of issues and problems for which it will have to find its own specific solutions.

16.2.2.1 Establish a pay-for-performance work culture

The effectiveness of remuneration systems is linked to the extent to which such systems are appropriately matched to their organisational context. In order for an incentive scheme to achieve its desired results, the organisational culture must therefore be generally conducive to the principles of individual merit and performance. Given that so many South African attempts at comprehensive performance management are thwarted by a lack of a work culture of productivity and quality, this requirement probably poses the biggest challenge to South African managers and remuneration specialists.

Two considerations are of importance in creating an appropriate performance-oriented work culture, namely the measurement of performance and establishing determinants of performance.

The first consideration entails the development of performance evaluation systems that are regarded as meaningful and equitable by both management and employees (see chapter 11 for guidelines). Spangenberg (1994: 233) cautions that the link between a newly designed performance appraisal system and the pay system should not be established until such time as employees and managers have developed the trust needed to conduct participative performance discussions. The second consideration entails the establishment of an environment or climate that is conducive to the following worker-related determinants of performance:

- employees' views regarding the value of money relative to other rewards;
- employees must be able to control the rate of performance;
- employees must be capable of increasing their performance;
- employees must believe that increased performance will be rewarded; and
- employees must perceive the size of the reward as sufficient to warrant increased effort.

16.2.2.2 Ensure employee acceptance

Employees and their representatives such as trade unions must accept the incentive scheme, and it should be welcomed by all those employees covered by it. Employee acceptance may be fostered by means of effectively communicating the benefits of the scheme, establishing a highly visible and clear connection between employees' incentive payments and their performance, and by encouraging employees to participate in administering the scheme.

16.2.2.3 Ensure a clear line of sight

The concept of line of sight refers to the degree to which employees can see a clear connection between their behaviour and the payout from an incentive system. For example, rewards for corporate performance (profit sharing or share options) may have a weak line of sight. Employees at lower levels of a large organisation may find it difficult to believe that they can influence the incentive payouts because they do not see how they can affect overall company performance. By contrast, individual- or team-based incentives such as sales commissions or production bonuses have a clear line of sight and therefore often stronger motivational effects.

16.2.2.4 Set high but attainable standards of performance

Performance targets should be attainable, but not too easily. They should become progressively more difficult to achieve as the levels of potential reward increase. Incentive payments should never be permitted to be seen as virtually guaranteed.

16.2.2.5 Establish clearly defined and accepted performance standards

Performance standards or output targets should be based on objective, preferably quantified, measures, and should be agreed upon with each individual or group.

16.2.2.6 Ensure a simple and understandable design

The incentive scheme should be sufficiently simple to enable all employees to understand its operation so that they can easily calculate what their rewards will be.

16.2.2.7 Provide for flexibility and review

Schemes should be sufficiently flexible to allow for adjustments that may be called for by changes in the business environment. The effectiveness of the scheme should be monitored on an ongoing basis. Typical areas that need regular review are:
- whether the performance factors that determine the level of payments still reflect the organisation's operational realities and are still relevant to the strategic business objectives;
- whether the scheme is losing motivational value due to employees taking the incentive payments for granted; and
- whether the scheme needs re-communicating and repackaging to revitalise interest and improve performance.

16.2.2.8 Ensure effective administration

The ongoing success of an incentive scheme is often determined by the efficiency of the administrative support structures and procedures associated with the scheme. Some vital administrative issues are:
- effective ongoing communication and procedures for addressing questions and complaints;
- consistent and fair application of the rules within each group and across groups;
- sufficient budget provision, and full and timeous payment in accordance with the rules; and
- congruence with the overall remuneration system, for example incentive schemes should not be used to make up for deficiencies in the basic salary structure.

16.2.3 Types of incentive schemes

Incentive schemes are usually categorised according to whether the system is applied on an individual, group or organisation-wide level. Further distinctions are sometimes made according to the category of employees involved, for example sales personnel, non-managerial workers and executives.

In general the choice between individual or group-based incentive plans is dictated by whether performance is a function of individualised or collective effort and whether the organisation can readily evaluate individual versus group performance. It is, however, not uncommon for the same employee or group of employees to be covered by various types of incentive schemes at any given time. For example, a miner at an Anglo American gold mine may, for instance, currently receive a drilling bonus based on individual performance and also be covered by organisation-wide profit-sharing and employee share ownership schemes.

16.2.3.1 Individual incentive schemes

Individual incentive schemes can take several forms, but they all share one primary advantage – employees can distinctly see the relationship between what and how much they do and what they get.

EXHIBIT 16.1: Types of incentive schemes

Individual schemes:
Production/amount of output
- Piece-rate plans
- Standard-hour systems
- Individual bonuses
- Suggestion systems

Sales
- Commission plans
- Merit awards
- Merchandise and travel incentives

Management
- Bonuses based on work unit performance
- Deferred compensation
- Share options
- Supplementary benefits

Group/organisational schemes:
- Bonuses based on group performance
- Gain-sharing, for example Scanlon & Rucker plans
- Profit sharing
- ESOPs (employee share ownership plans)
- Skill-based pay
- Suggestion systems

Source: Adapted and expanded from Gómez-Mejía, Balkin & Cardy (2001: 366); and Härtel, Fujimoto, Strybosch & Fitzpatrick (2007: 381–382)

This advantage is, however, often the cause of some unwanted effects (Luthans 2002: 548–549). For example, an organisation may 'only get what it pays for', since employees will be likely to concentrate their efforts only on those activities of their total job outcome that are being measured and rewarded (for example, a commission system that is only based on sales volumes may encourage employees to neglect the customer care aspect of their jobs). Furthermore, the increased competition among employees may become dysfunctional due to workers becoming reluctant to share knowledge or ideas that can lead to overall improved productivity, or due to work groups imposing informal ceilings on outputs, and enforcing these less-than-optimal productivity levels by means of peer pressure.

Popular individual incentive approaches include piece-rate plans, standard-hour plans, commission plans and individual bonuses.

Piece-rate plans

Under piece-rate plans individual pay is directly linked to the number of units produced.

Straight piece-rate plans usually pay an employee a set wage (for example minimum wage) for an expected minimum level of output (the standard) and a piece-rate incentive for all production above the standard. This standard is determined by job analysis and workstudy techniques, and is often adjusted by collective bargaining.

Differential piece-rate plans are a common variation, according to which the employer pays a smaller piece-rate up to the standard and a higher piece-rate for production above the standard.

Standard-hour plans

Standard-hour plans are similar to piece-rate plans, with the exception that the productivity standard is not measured in terms of output units, but is set in terms of time units needed to complete a particular task. Employees who complete such tasks in less than the standard time qualify for incentive payments on the basis of the time saved.

By way of illustration, suppose that at Louis Motors an oil change has been calculated as requiring 30 minutes to complete (standard time). A mechanic earning R100 an hour will earn R50 to complete the job, irrespective of whether he used more or less time than the allotted 30 minutes (0,5 standard hour R100). Should he manage to complete three oil changes within one hour, he would consequently be paid R150 (1,5 × R100) under a time-bonus system where the full benefit of the time saved goes to the employee.

Commission plans

The competitive and largely independent nature of sales work demands a sustained high level of motivation and enthusiasm from salespersons, and makes financial incentives therefore well suited to this category of employees. Most salespersons are usually rewarded according to some form of commission plan based at least partially on their sales volume.

Types of plans range from a straight commission to various combinations of salary, plus commission and/or sales bonuses. Under a straight commission plan, pay is entirely determined by volume of sales, whereas under combination plans, the salesperson is paid a guaranteed basic salary plus a (usually smaller) commission on sales. In addition to or sometimes instead of commission, companies often also pay sales bonuses for sales that exceed a specific predetermined quota. Another variant is the draw plan, which is often implemented to counter the negative effect of fluctuating earnings caused by periodic changes in business climate and typically associated with straight commission plans. Essentially this involves the payment of a basic salary which is deducted from future commissions.

Individual bonuses

A bonus is an additional one-off reward for high performance. It is a discretionary payment – that is, it is not guaranteed and it does not become part of the recipient's basic salary as in the case of a merit pay increase. Bonuses may be based on a variety of performance measures, for example the achievement of specific objectives, performance ratings or, in the case of executives, a percentage of total profits or return on shareholders' investments.

Care should be taken not to allow a bonus to become a virtual extension of basic salary due to the payment thereof becoming practically guaranteed, as has happened in the case of the typical South African annual bonus (13th cheque).

In the case of executives, a bonus payment may sometimes take the form of

	Straight commission plan	Salary plus commission
Formula	1% of total monthly sales	R300 per week + 0,7% of total monthly sales
		4 × R300 = R1 200
Pay	1% × R400 000 = R4 000	0,7% × R400 000 = R2 800
		= R4 000

	Draw plan	Salary plus bonus
Formula	1% of total monthly sales less R400 weekly draw-in	R300 per week + 2% of sales excess of quota of 2 600 units
Pay	Total draw already advanced: R1 600	4 × R300 = R1 200
	commission still owing:[1] R2 400	2% × R140 000[2] = R2 800
	R4 000	R4 000

[1] R4 000 – R1 600

[2] 1 400 excess units @ R100   *Based on sales of 4 000 units at R100 each.

shares or options to buy shares in the organisation. A bonus payment may also be deferred until a set future date (for example retirement) in order to realise income tax savings. Deferred bonus payments may also serve as 'golden handcuffs' with which an organisation may attempt to retain the services of valuable senior personnel and sustain managerial performance (see section 16.3.1 for executive remuneration).

16.2.3.2 Group and organisation-wide incentive schemes

Group or team-based incentive schemes provide incentive pay to all group members, based on the performance of the entire group. Such schemes are most applicable in situations where:

■ work tasks are so intertwined that it is difficult to single out individual contributions (for example research teams in R&D laboratories);
■ jobs are interdependent (for example assembly lines);
■ cooperation is needed to complete a task or project;
■ the measurement of individual output is difficult; and
■ the objective is to foster entrepreneurship in self-managed work groups (Cascio 2006: 443).

Another determining factor is the value that is placed on individualism. Dominant collectivist cultures place greater emphasis on the individual as an element of the team than typical Western orientations towards individualism, and the prevalence of such orientations in an organisation will have an influence on the ease of implementing team-based incentive systems (Nelson & Quick 2002: 178).

In the South African context, indications are that at the operational level team-based incentive schemes are more applicable than individual-based ones. However, a benchmarking study on team management and measurement conducted by the Saratoga Institute in 1997 found that there was no consensus regarding recognition or rewards for teams, and that the issue of individual versus team rewards was equally undecided. The recommendation is made that rewards and recognition should align with and co-implement the cultural norms of the organisation, unless, of course, there is a conscious desire to change the culture (Saratoga Institute 1998: 19). Trade union positions on pay linked to productivity and collective bargaining agreements no doubt also exert tremendous influence in this regard.

Incentives for teams typically need to take cognisance of the effects of peer pressure, which is bound to be present when people working together aim for a common objective. The dynamics of the same people competing as a team will be different than for them competing as individuals. Think, for example, about the salespeople in a car dealership competing for the salesperson of the year bonus and as a combined team competing in the sales team of the year award for the entire group of dealerships. Fisher (2006: 63) suggests four approaches to deal with the payment of team rewards.

■ *Paying for total team performance.* The team is treated as a single entity and all members receive an equal share irrespective of the level of input or seniority.
■ *Using a points pool.* The reward is divided up according to the measurable contribution of each member. Objective measures against clear standards of performance are needed for such a strategy.
■ *Paying personal bonuses.* This is a combination strategy of the previous two approaches. A group standard is achieved for a specific team award, with some members receiving additional bonuses for individual achievements.
■ *Using rank order.* The team reward is divided in rank order of the members' individual performance.

Organisation-wide incentive schemes are generally aimed at involving employees in a common effort to achieve overall organisational effectiveness. Specific objectives of such schemes may be:
■ to encourage economic or financial participation of employees;
■ to foster improved productivity or reduced production costs;
■ to increase worker commitment;
■ to enhance employees' security and identification with the company; and
■ to attract and retain workers more easily (Cascio 2006: 444)

The most common organisation-wide schemes are gain-sharing and profit-sharing schemes, employee share ownership plans (ESOPs) and suggestion systems.

Gain-sharing plans

Gain-sharing plans are organisational systems for sharing the benefit (gains) of cost reductions or improved productivity and quality in the form of cash awards. They are generally based on the assumption that better cooperation between workers and management and among workers themselves will result in greater effectiveness. Unlike profit-sharing plans that use profit as an organisation-level performance measure, gain-sharing plans use performance measures that are likely to be seen as more controllable by the efforts of employees. Also, distribution of payouts is not deferred (such as receiving your bonus in March 2008 for company profits of 2007) and are more frequent than in the case of profit-sharing schemes.

Well-known examples of such plans are the Scanlon, Rucker and Improshare plans, which find wide application in the North American context. Key features of gain-sharing plans are (Bernardin & Russell 1993: 488; Noe, Hollenbeck, Gerhart & Wright 2003: 511):
■ a philosophy of participatory management;
■ rewarding groups for suggestions by individuals in the group;

- joint worker/management committees administering the plan and evaluating suggestions; and
- reward allocations to all participants according to some formula determining the contributions of specific groups of employees in defined areas of performance.

Profit-sharing plans

Profit-sharing plans essentially allow employees to share in the financial success of an organisation by distributing a portion of the profits back to the employees. The underlying assumption of such schemes is that they increase commitment and identification with the organisation and its profit goal, and consequently lead to increased productivity and cost savings.

A CASE AT HAND

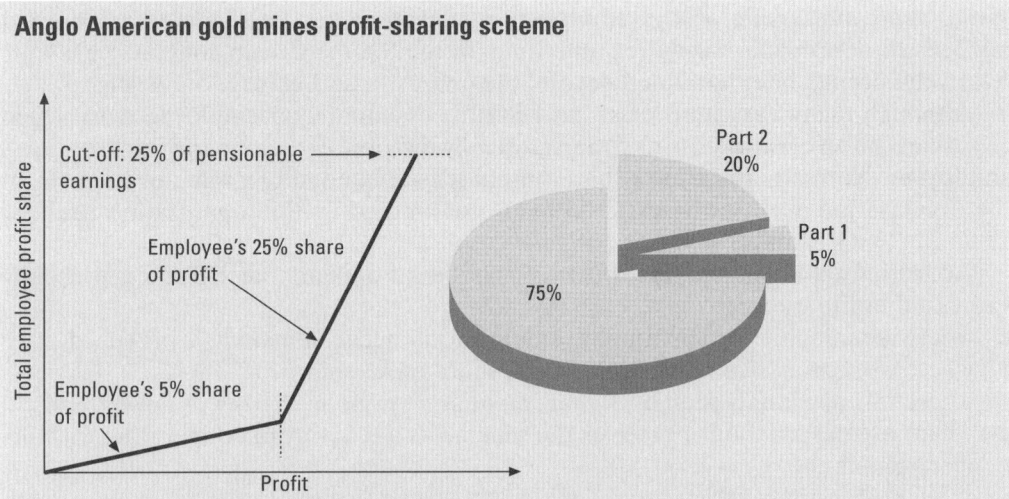

Anglo American gold mines profit-sharing scheme

- Every three months the mines calculate their total profit and deduct capital expenditure.
- The rest is divided into two parts:
  - Part 1 is money up to a trigger profit level. Five per cent of all profits below the trigger level are put into the employees profit-sharing pool.
  - Part 2 is money in excess of the trigger profit level. Twenty per cent of these extra profits are put into the profit-sharing pool.
- The trigger profit target is based on the mine's average quarterly profit for the previous year and differs from mine to mine.
- The employees' profit-sharing pool has a maximum size of 25% of the pensionable earnings of all employees of the mine.
- Profit-sharing bonuses are paid out each quarter in two portions. The first portion is divided equally among all employees and the rest is paid as a percentage of salary (subsequent refinements and changes to the system have been negotiated with the unions).

An added advantage, especially to companies and industries with unstable markets and proportionately high labour costs (for example the South African gold mining industry), is that wage or salary supplements can be provided that do not add to the fixed cost element and therefore need not be perpetuated for years to come when adverse business conditions may prevail.

The downside for employees, however, is that they have to share in both the good times and the bad times, and therefore their total income is often prone to fluctuations.

It is also often difficult for employees to see the link between their own individual effort and its result on the overall performance of the organisation. In addition, external factors outside the control of the employees (for example economic conditions) may have a far greater impact on the organisation's profitability than any actions of the employees themselves (DeCenzo & Robbins 2007: 279). In the South African context, profit-sharing schemes have become fairly well entrenched.

The Anglo American gold mines profit-sharing scheme, which covered about 150 000 employees at its inception, is briefly illustrated above as a typical South African example (this reflects the original version and not subsequent modifications).

Employee share ownership plans (ESOPs)

While share ownership in the employer organisation has been a well-established remuneration principle for quite some time, in the South African context it has only relatively recently been extended beyond the executive and managerial levels.

Although many variations exist, an ESOP is essentially an employee trust which buys shares in an organisation and then gradually distributes them to the organisation's employees. Normally the trust's share purchases are funded by grants or loans from the organisation itself, or by external loans guaranteed by the organisation (Bekker 1995: 22–23; Greenblo 1989: 4).

According to Innes (Boyens 1991: 26), it would appear that ESOPs are usually successful in situations:

- where meaningful participation by employees in decision making is practised;
- where workers derive real benefits from share ownership;
- where it is not simply seen by management as a symbolic sharing of power; and
- where organised labour perceives the scheme as a real way of cooperating with management.

In the recent South African context, ESOPs are also closely associated with Black Economic Empowerment (BEE) codes of good practice and allow companies an increase in the ownership score on the BEE scorecard (Hlope 2007). The following example has been reported and illustrates this development (Wray 2008: 19):

> Sasol's 14 534 black workers and their 10 037 white counterparts would each receive shares worth about R350 000 in the petrochemical giant in South Africa's biggest empowerment deal to date, the company said yesterday. The company's 235 black managers will get shares worth between R2 million and R10 million, depending on their seniority, and on top of their share options. The shares will vest in 10 years ... The deal will transfer 10 percent of the company's shares to staff (4 percent), the newly created Sasol Inzalo Foundation (1.5 percent), retailers and suppliers already associated with the company (1.5 percent) and the black public (3 percent). Sasol will fund the shares that will go to staff in its entirety. It will partially fund the balance, depending on circumstances. This means Sasol will take a R7.1 billion knock on its bottom line over the next 10 years ... about R3 billion would be expensed this year ... This equates to 2.8 percent of the company's market capitalisation, a figure not out of sync with other empowerment deals.

A CASE AT HAND

What happened to ESOPs?

When Anglo American and a number of other blue-chip companies implemented ESOPs for their workers during the late 1980s, it was hoped that a new era of productivity and worker participation had been ushered in. Since then ESOPs have unfortunately not met all such expectations. It appears as if they now have run aground on the twin rocks of union opposition and taxes.

ESOPs have been classified as attempts by management to co-opt workers and thus were rejected. While many companies operate a variety of stock ownership schemes for their management, the perception exists among workers that such schemes do not really empower them and that there is no real commitment towards worker participation.

It is, however, especially the tax dispensation that discourages companies from implementing ESOPs. The Katz Commission has also recommended that the current dispensation should remain and that the prerequisites of ESOPs should continue to be taxable.

Nevertheless, there is a resurging interest in ESOPs as a mechanism to effect particularly black empowerment via black-controlled enterprises. Cosatu and Nactu, for instance, have significant share holdings in New African Investments (Nail) and Real African Investments (Rail). Bussin (2001), and Bussin and Thomson (2000) report a resurgence in the popularity of share option schemes with a more open approach to eligibility at junior levels. Recent survey data of 551 companies indicated an offering of share options to clerical and manual job categories respectively at 10% and 8% (Grobler 2001).

Within the Income Tax Act (section 8B), government introduced legislation in 2004 to attempt to address historical inequality by encouraging the broad-based empowerment of employees through the receipt of shares at less than market value without adverse tax consequences. Restrictive provisions have, however, caused a limited usage of the plan, leading to an announcement in the 2007 Budget that such an incentive is to be reconsidered by the government (Kruger 2007).

Source: Extracted from 'Wat het van ESOPs geword?' *Finansies en Tegniek*, 19 April 1996; Bussin & Thomson (2000); Kruger (2007)

Suggestion systems

A suggestion system is an incentive scheme under which employees receive rewards (usually cash) for useful ideas on reducing costs, improving safety or product quality, or generally increasing organisational effectiveness. Typically, such systems utilise forms that employees can use to write out their suggestions and deposit them in conveniently placed boxes for submission and evaluation by management or a special committee.

Marx (1992: 3) cautions against the informality of suggestion boxes and sets the following criteria for a formal suggestion scheme:

- accepted suggestions must relate to specific or potential problems or opportunities to improve processes or situations;
- a suggestion must provide a solution or possible strategy; complaints do not qualify;
- suggestions should be in writing and must be signed by the employee;
- written suggestions must be received and registered by the suggestion office; and
- the scheme must be recognised and accepted by top management.

Although employees value the reward linked to suggestion systems, it also has a communication benefit, and probably the most important aspect of a sustainable and effective system is for employees to witness management action (DeCenzo & Robbins 2007: 113)

EXHIBIT 16.3: Incentive remuneration in South Africa

In a survey on human resource practices covering 551 companies, Grobler (2001) found variable pay and performance-related pay as the most common option in place for managers in 71% of the companies. Group bonuses being offered ranged from 49% of the companies offering them at managerial level to 42% at manual worker level. Profit-sharing had also a wide coverage, with 43% of companies offering this option to managerial staff and 14% to manual workers.

An analysis of the stated remuneration practices of the Top Ten companies of the *2005 Best Companies to Work for in South Africa* survey indicated that all companies had, as part of their overall remuneration strategy, some performance-related remuneration programme and performance-driven incentives. Indeed, of all 42 participants in the survey, only five companies did not explicitly report the use of performance bonuses for at least some of their employee categories. Some specific incentive practices among the top companies include:

- Pick n Pay (2nd): The 'dare to dream' reward scheme was designed to foster service excellence and lets achievers visit the Disney Institute at Disneyworld in Orlando, Florida to learn about service excellence. Since the introduction of the scheme in 1997, more than 1 000 mostly shop-floor employees have attended the Disney Institute. Furthermore, Pick n Pay operates a share incentive scheme that has enabled more than 10 000 of its 30 000 employees to own shares or share options in the company.

- Sasol (6th): Within each business unit, a team incentive scheme is provided. The company also provides a share saving scheme with a compounding effect, allowing staff to buy portions of shares. If these shares are kept for a period of one year, Sasol adds 20% to whatever the employee has acquired, subject to a cap.

- Edcon: All of Edcon's employees are guaranteed a 13th cheque, and 14th and 15th cheques may be paid based on performance.

Sources: Grobler (2001); Corporate Research Foundation (2005)

16.3 REWARDING SPECIAL GROUPS OF EMPLOYEES

In a changing world of work where lifelong employment and traditional career paths are no longer the norm, where non-permanent employment contracts are becoming increasingly common and multinational corporations operate on a truly global scale, remuneration specialists have to cater for special needs of employee groups that have emerged as important sectors of the total workforce of many organisations. In remuneration practice, five such employee groups are commonly identified and deserve some special focus: executive management, expatriate employees, contingency workers, sales employees and 'engine room' staff.

16.3.1 Directors and senior executives

Few areas of HR management generate as much scrutiny, heated debate and news coverage as that of executive remuneration. Common perceptions of linking executive remuneration to news headlines of 'fat cat excesses' and 'snouts in troughs' have been fuelled by many reports of huge executive bonuses despite mediocre company performance, excessive severance packages for failed business leaders, and survey data that the 'wage gap' ratio of the package of typical CEOs compared to the lowest paid employee in their companies is 500:1 in the US and may be 100:1 in some South African companies (Naidu 2003: 30)

Such trends together with Enron-type corporate failures have led to legislative interventions and introduction of corporate governance guidelines such as the King Report, published in March 2002. Nowhere is the war for talent as fierce as at executive level, and the market forces of supply and demand are reflected in the seemingly exorbitant packages and incentives paid by companies to lure and retain scarce top-management skills. In the South African context, the long-acknowledged severe shortages of management and senior professional skills, increasing international mobility of top local talent, and pressures to meet economic growth targets and development plans related to infrastructure development and service delivery (including the 2010 Soccer World Cup building programme), are all factors that will ensure that the executive talent war will rage on. Irrespective of the controversies surrounding executive pay, the question relevant to our chapter is twofold: firstly, as a special group, what different considerations affect the rewards of directors and senior executives and, secondly, what arsenal of remuneration tools is available and effective for attracting and retaining executive talent.

Scarce skills, corporate governance and heightened public scrutiny have been alluded to as drivers of current practices in executive remuneration. For example, in August 2007 the South African Department of Public Enterprises introduced remuneration guidelines for state-owned enterprises (SOEs) for guiding remuneration committees in determining remuneration levels of chairpersons and non-executive directors according to a model of categorising SOEs in four bands of SOE size, based on asset bases and revenue (RSA 2007).

Further driving factors are greater international mobility of executives, emphasis on entrepreneurial skills, the importance of intellectual capital in the 'knowledge' industries, employment equity compliance and implementation of affirmative action and empowerment strategies.

Common trends in executive remuneration reported in recent reviews (Bussin 2006; Naidu 2003; P-E Corporate Services 2006) include

- The trend of rising levels of variable pay; that is, smaller proportions of total remuneration being made up of base pay, and increasingly greater proportions made up of variable and incentive rewards linked to performance. This trend is typically linked to three considerations:
  - the assumption that the more successful the company is, the more those managers responsible for the success should be personally rewarded;
  - legislative support of long-term incentive plans such as offering share options;
  - efforts by employers to manage their fixed pay costs more effectively by shifting some of the cost burden to the employees; that is, variable pay is in theory a less-risky strategy than base pay because such rewards are only paid to such employees if they perform effectively (Cotton 2007: 4).
- Increasing use of a Remuneration Committee of the Board being responsible for deciding executive remuneration policy in compliance of corporate governance principles set out in the King Report.
- The payment of financial inducements or 'attraction' premiums to secure the services of specific executive talent and sought-after 'affirmative action' candidates.
- Increasing use of flexible remuneration planning. In such flexible arrangements, common policies are either negotiated at a single cost to company packages, with executives selecting their desired benefits and the rest representing the cash component of the package, or often also a flexible selection of benefits and any additional desired benefits beyond the defined range being paid on a salary sacrifice basis.
- Growth in the popularity of performance-related pay as part of the package. Such performance-related incentives include, firstly, short-term incentives such as performance and/or profit-share bonuses with a performance horizon of one year that are designed to encourage achievement of financial and performance targets,

and, secondly, long-term incentives such as share-option schemes that are used as retention strategies.

16.3.2 Expatriate employees

Globalisation of businesses and international mergers and acquisitions require many employees to be globally mobile and work abroad as expatriates. Such international assignments could range from short-term providing of expertise to long-term secondments or contract appointments lasting several years. Designing equitable and motivating remuneration packages for expatriates is complex, and policies need to address questions such as:

- how to compensate for the disruption of, for example, home life and spouse's career, and possible hardship for locations deemed challenging to live in;
- how to ensure that working abroad does not result in the expatriates being either better or worse off;
- how to compensate competitively and maintain home-country living standards for expatriates;
- how to maintain equity in remuneration between expatriates coming from different countries; and
- how to deal with problems arising from expatriates being paid more than the nationals of the host country working in similar jobs.

The most common approach to expatriate remuneration seems to be the balance-sheet approach or home-based method (Armstrong & Stephens 2005: 302; DeCenzo & Robbins, 2007: 303). In this approach, the remuneration is 'built up' into a package that demonstrates that individuals will not lose by going abroad by considering the elements of base pay, differentials, incentives and allowances or assistance programmes.

The basic steps involve:

- determining the after-tax salary that would be paid for the expatriate's job in the home country;
- calculating the net disposable income which represents the portion of income used for day-to-day living expenses at home;
- applying the relevant differential (cost of living index) to the net disposable income in the host country to ensure the equivalent buying power in the host country; and
- adding additional allowances and incentives to make the assignment attractive and compensate for disruption.

Less-often-used approaches include the:

- host country/local basis, which utilises the host-country remuneration structure; that is, paying the expatriate the market rate for the job in the host country and adding allowances for living abroad;
- selected country or headquarters-based system, where the remuneration structure of the country where the headquarters of the company is sited is used as base and then built up further according to the home-based method; and
- better of home or host method, where expatriates get paid the higher of the home or host country system.

Recent trend survey results indicate a predominance of 76% use of the balance sheet approach, 11% use of headquarters-based approaches and the remaining 13% made up by alternative approaches (Williams 2007).

Typical allowances and benefits that multinational businesses provide to expatriates include:

- hardship allowances, to compensate for discomfort in the host country such as climate, risk, isolation, language difficulties or poor amenities;
- separation allowances if expatriates cannot take their spouses or family abroad;
- relocation and housing allowances to cover costs of moving households, storage of household goods and additional accommodation costs; and
- education costs for children, travel and annual home leave allowances, shipment of pets, security allowances and club memberships.

Expatriate remuneration with its associated high cost and intensive administration remains a challenge in international HR. In the light of the globalisation of the marketplace and mobility of the workforce, trend surveys confirm that international moves will require special handling until some distant future when harmonisation of salary, tax and pension programmes across international borders will render expatriate assignments no more complex than a simple domestic transfer (Gould 2007: 5).

16.3.3 Sales and professional services employees

This category of employees covers all jobs in industries ranging from retail to professional services (eg estate agents, management consultants) where targets based on sales, billings or business brought in determines the judgement of individual employee performance.

In this type of environment, incentives can also have a negative effect by causing self-oriented behaviour among employees that can be detrimental to long-term business goals. Examples are:

- territorial behaviour, where sales representatives or consultants guard their territory or client base from others in their company to meet own targets, even if that client base is too large for only one consultant to effectively exploit for their firm.
- a single-minded focus on quantity of sales or business and a resultant lack of focus on quality and customer service.

Long-term business sustainability in such environments requires a balance between rewarding behaviour geared towards short-term business success and also emphasising building customer relationships and high-quality work. One common approach to this challenge is to structure rewards that encourage both individual performance and team-oriented behaviour. For example, the employees' bonus could be paid only partly in cash and the remainder paid in shares in the company they work for, with such shares held in trust for a specified period whereafter ownership is transferred to the employees (Härtel et al 2007: 391).

Various commission plans were discussed in the previous section and exhibit 16.2. It needs to be further noted that sales employees often receive other non-cash rewards that incentivise performance. These include:

- gifts, vouchers, merchandise and catalogue prizes, which are often linked to specified targets. Care should be taken, however, not to exclude the dependable 'solid' sales persons by focusing exclusively on the 'super' sales reps.
- competitions where prizes are awarded to individuals or teams with notable sales achievements. Travel to exotic locations is a widely used incentive in this category.
- social and symbolic recognition, such as 'sales rep of the month' certificates, dinner for two, flower arrangement from the CEO, public applause or a private 'thank you' at staff gatherings.

Non-cash rewards usually supplement other reward programmes and to be effective, care must be taken that they are indeed valued by the recipients.

16.3.4 'Engine room' staff

This category of staff includes those employees in manufacturing, retail, public service delivery or call centres where the inherent nature of the job makes it unlikely that they will be promoted more than a level or two over their working life. Sustaining motivational levels and retaining such staff over the long term requires creative and imaginative use of extrinsic and intrinsic rewards. This could include 'chill-out rooms' with good sound systems for young call-centre staff, company social events involving family, or team charity fundraising competitions which provide community involvement and recognition (Murlis 2004).

A CASE AT HAND

RCI's Olympic Champions programme

RCI Southern Africa, part of the global holiday exchange company, has at the heart of its business the call centre that handles on a daily basis between 4 000 and 6 000 inbound and outbound calls for local and international holiday exchanges. In 2004 the company launched its Champions programme based on the Olympics theme. In keeping with the five rings of the Olympic logo, staff are measured on a monthly basis on key performance areas that have been termed 'quintiles'. Staff are categorised as gold, silver and bronze medallists, with the obvious focus being on striving for gold medallist status. Three winners from each area of the business receive acknowledgement by means of a gift voucher, surprise breakfast served at their desk and a medal. Categories that are recognised are top performer, most improved performer and best attitude. Employees achieving this status for three or more times per year get to choose from a variety of lifestyle experiences. RCI also provides free massages on Wednesdays and an EAP° toll-free helpline where employees can at any time receive free emotional, legal and practical help and advice.

Source: Corporate Research Foundation: *Best companies to work for in South Africa* (2005)

16.3.5 Non-employee workers

These people are typically paid by the labour-broking firm that is the 'vendor'. The principal or host organisation enters into service level agreements (SLAs) with the labour broker (the temporary employment services provider). From a performance and reward management perspective, a challenge may relate to the attitudinal and motivational aspects at the place of work. Workers who are actually employed by the temporary employment services firm (the labour broker) often identify and have a stronger emotional affiliation with the host/client organisation, firm in which they are deployed than with their real employer. This is especially common in cases where deployment is for an extended period of time. Tensions between employees and non-employee workers might arise from perceived different treatment in the workplace, and these may obviously interplay with levels of commitment and work performance. Research conducted by Manpower Inc. (2006) identified the following expressed needs of these types of working people that might drive levels of engagement:
- being treated with respect;
- having a clear understanding of what is expected;
- having a sense of belonging;
- being treated equally;
- access to tools, resources and information to perform;

- receiving the training that is needed to perform in the role;
- open and honest two-way feedback; and
- receiving recognition;

16.4 EMPLOYEE BENEFITS

16.4.1 Introduction

Benefits are indirect forms of remuneration that, like direct remuneration, are intended to aid the achievement of the human resource objective of attracting, retaining and motivating employees.

Both locally in South Africa and abroad, benefits form a very substantial portion of total remuneration expenditure. In the first place this section examines the major reasons behind the existence of benefits, as opposed to direct cash remuneration. Then a benefits classification is provided and the most common benefits offered by South African organisations are detailed in terms of this classification.

The degree to which the benefit arrangement offered by an organisation aids the achievement of the human resource objectives of attracting, retaining and motivating employees is largely determined by the benefit arrangement strategy followed by the organisation. This section, therefore, also deals with different benefit arrangement strategies, and the merits of providing the elements of choice and flexibility within such strategies.

Well-structured and appropriate benefits are, however, not enough to ensure the success of an organisation's benefit programme. This section therefore concludes by detailing a number of important considerations aimed at ensuring the successful administrative delivery of benefits to an organisation's employees.

16.4.2 Reasons for providing employee benefits

Although the providing of benefits has strong 'welfare' roots, meaning that they are provided based on organisations' acknowledgement of a responsibility to their employees to support their health, safety, security and general well-being needs, modern benefits practices recognise their importance as an integral part of an effectively working total-reward strategy. Benefits play an important role in attracting and retaining good employees, but due to the fact that they are generally membership based and thus offered to all employees irrespective of their individual performance, they have little direct impact on this performance. Ironically, however, the lack of adequate benefits is found to be linked to employee dissatisfaction, and increased absenteeism and turnover (DeCenzo & Robbins 2007: 314). This suggests that a major reason for providing such extensive and expensive benefits (typically costing 30–40% of payroll cost) is preventative and reactive by nature. This should, however, not detract from the value that well-designed and administered benefits programmes create for employees.

The extent and nature of the benefits commonly offered by organisations within a particular country are largely determined by the country's specific circumstances and laws. In South Africa, for example, the need to travel long distances together with the lack of adequate public transport has contributed significantly to the fact that company cars and travel allowances are sought-after and commonly provided benefits for certain classes of employees.

A country's laws also exert a profound influence. (For example, Zambian labour legislation stipulates a compulsory funeral benefit, comprising the provision of a coffin, transport to the cemetery and a quantity of mielie meal.)

A number of the benefits offered by South African organisations are mandated by law (see also chapter 3).

Some of these mandatory benefits are:

- minimum leave provisions stipulated by the Basic Conditions of Employment Act 75 of 1997, for example:
  - annual leave (21 consecutive days' annual leave);
  - sick leave (six weeks' paid sick leave in every cycle of 36 months);
  - maternity leave (four consecutive months); and
  - family responsibility leave (three days during each annual leave cycle);
- paid public holidays as stipulated by the Public Holidays Act 36 of 1994;
- unemployment insurance benefits as stipulated by the Unemployment Insurance Act 63 of 2001; and
- remuneration for injuries or diseases contracted while working, as stipulated by the Remuneration for Occupational Injuries and Diseases Act 130 of 1993.

In addition, it may be expected that the Employment Equity Act will also gradually lead to organisations considering the provision of benefits that may otherwise not have been provided. The case of an organisation employing a significant number of working mothers may, for instance, lead to the provision of child-care facilities.

The tax laws of a country, in particular, contribute very significantly to the extent and nature of benefits commonly offered. In a country like the US, where the marginal tax rates are relatively low, most of the remuneration package is given directly as cash. In South Africa, on the other hand, marginal tax rates are relatively high, and benefits, despite the introduction of benefit taxation, are still generally conservatively taxed. This results in a significant portion of remuneration packages being given indirectly in the form of benefits. This practice is particularly common at managerial levels in South Africa.

16.4.3 Types of benefits

South African organisations, like many organisations elsewhere in the world, provide a truly amazing range of benefits. They are available to employees while on the job (for example shift allowances, tea breaks) as well as off the job (for example private use of company cars, vacation payments). In addition, benefits are also provided to the families and/or dependants of employees (for example medical aid, life insurance).

Benefits can be categorised in a number of ways. A popular one is to categorise benefits into cash and non-cash benefits. Non-cash benefits are then typically further subdivided into current benefits (that is, those enjoyed immediately) and deferred benefits (that is, those enjoyed at some future date). A list of the most common benefits offered in South Africa is provided in terms of this benefit classification.

The nature and range of benefits employers offer often reflect the changing trends of the contemporary labour force (DeCenzo & Robbins 2007: 316; Luthans 2002: 162). For example, an organisation employing a significant number of working mothers may be obliged to provide on-site child-care facilities to retain the services of this sector of its staff complement. Realities such as the nature of modern urban life, the emergence of dual-career families and globalisation, etc have led to innovative new benefits and so-called wellness and work-family benefits (De Vries 2008):

- on-site child-care facilities or elder-care facilities or transportation to such centres;
- convenience benefits, such as on-site dry-cleaning services, ATMs, postal service, etc;
- health promotion benefits (or wellness programmes) such as on-site or subsidised membership to commercial fitness centres, company-provided flu shots or stress management programmes;

- comprehensive relocation and extended settling-in programmes;
- leave/time-off policies and pay-back for unused days off;
- alternative work schedules and telecommuting;
- sick-child care and back-up child care; and
- legal and financial planning, tuition reimbursements and casual day programmes.

The exact nature and range of benefits provided (such as those listed in exhibit 16.4) will be influenced by the changing labour market trends, legislative changes and the benefit arrangement strategy followed by a particular organisation.

For example, the nature of car benefit schemes for the past number of years showed a growing popularity of the car allowance schemes at the expense of company car schemes. This was reflective of the trend of employee desire for flexibility and freedom of choice, and a tax regime that made the allowance option more tax efficient. Recent

CASES AT HAND

Pampering employees in SA companies

In line with the trend of greater employee emphasis on valuing wellness, convenience and work–life balance, South African companies increasingly provide an array of benefits that aim to cater for such needs and also cut down on the hours staff spend outside the office to attend to personal and family issues.

Liberty Life's wellness and lifestyle benefits include
- an on-site wellness centre with medical services ranging from doctor and dentist to podiatrist and reflexologist;
- health management benefits ranging from subsidised medical aid and HIV/Aids programmes to gyms, and sports and social clubs;
- counselling and financial services, including life management (debt/money management, legal), GLA, disability benefit, 'My Banking' and free financial advice;
- work–life balance benefits, including flexible leave policy, canteen, crèche, on-site banking and shopping, dry-cleaners and Blue4U lifestyle services/concierge programme helping staff with the practicalities of daily living, for example finding products, planning holidays, helping children with homework.

Microsoft SA includes in its wide range of benefits free coffee/tea and soft drinks throughout the day, massage therapist visits twice a month, on-site gym with consultant for individual fitness programmes, on-site carwash, and annual children's Christmas party.

Other interesting examples are as follows:
Old Mutual is building at their headquarters in Cape Town a R97 million private shopping centre that in 2008 will contain, among other stores, food outlets, a beauty salon, a hairdresser, an optician, a clothing store and a postal service.

Santam launched its 'Yell for Yellow' concierge service that offers everything from fetching dry-cleaning, paying fines, renewing licences and watering plants, to organising weekend getaways, planning events and moving house.

Nedbank offers a 'survival' course for mothers returning to work after maternity leave, and runs two crèches at its Sandton offices.

Hollard Insurance not only has a games room with a climbing wall but also a gym with a full-time biokineticist.

Eli Lilly pharmaceuticals offers a 'Parents in a Pickle' benefit whereby the company pays for an au pair to look after children of employees who are away on business.

Sources: *Sunday Times* (2007: 8); Corporate Research Foundation (2005); Liberty Group Limited sustainability report (2005)

EXHIBIT 16.4: Classification of common benefits in South Africa

CASH BENEFITS

Bonuses

- Fixed annual bonus
- Incentive/performance bonus

Allowances

- Entertainment allowance
- Acting allowance
- Car allowance
- Abnormal working conditions allowance
- Shift allowance
- Tool allowance
- Stand-by allowance

Other

- Overtime pay
- Payment for time not worked (leave)
- Commission

NON-CASH BENEFITS

Current

Transport/travel

- Company car
- Overseas travel
- Second company car
- Free or subsidised parking
- Free or subsidised transport to and from work
- Free or subsidised rail/bus/sea/air fares

Accommodation

- Housing subsidy
- Holiday accommodation
- Housing loan
- Free or low-rental accommodation

Deferred

- Pension fund
- Share options
- Disability cover
- Group life cover
- Deferred compensation
- Accumulated leave
- Accident insurance
- Provident fund

Other

- Interest-free or low interest loan
- Club fees/professional fees
- Medical aid/health care benefits
- Cellular phones
- Free or cheap services
- Meals and refreshments
- Encashable leave
- Computer and faxes at home
- Free or cheap company products
- Newspapers and periodicals
- Incentive award
- Share purchase
- Educational assistance
- Telephone account payment
- Long-service award

tax legislation changes according to which SARS now taxes mileage claims far more rigorously and imposes a 30% residual value on the cost of a car at the end of a five-year period, are compelling employers to review their car benefit strategy to remain tax efficient as well as allowing for customised individual flexibility.

ELSEWHERE IN AFRICA

Augmenting base pay with benefits and incentives: perspectives from Kenya

> Legislation ... plays a role through annually adjusted minimum monthly wage, which in 2002 was set at the equivalent of US$46 for the two main urban centers, Nairobi and Mombasa, and US$27 elsewhere. However, in some sectors like the agricultural sector and some Asian-owned firms, labor laws, including minimum wage legislation, are often flouted due to the abundance of cheap labour. In addition to direct financial rewards, firms typically offer a house allowance or a house and transport.

> The pressure to cut costs has resulted in many organizations eliminating perks that were previously seen as an entitlement, such as chauffeurs that come with company cars for executives. Pensions are administered through the National Social Security Fund (NSSF), and increasingly many firms maintain a provident fund ... Private firms normally have separate medical and life insurance cover ... some organizations (especially banking) provide a number of discretionary benefits such as loans to build or buy a house and education allowances ... As the society shifts from a collectivist to individualistic ethos, especially for urban dwellers ... many employees are now expecting rewards based on individual performance ... young professionals believe it offers them some sort of safeguard against the more subjective approaches that are prone to ethnic and political manipulation.

Source: Kamoche, Nyambegera, & Mulinge (2004: 92)

16.4.4 Benefit arrangement strategies

16.4.4.1 Strategy alternatives

In return for their services, South African organisations typically offer their employees a basic salary to which a number of benefits are added. Eligibility for such benefits generally tends to be based on an employee's length of service and/or job level. There is also a tendency for the value of such benefits to increase with increase in length of service and/or job level.

Typically these benefits are also managed and reviewed in relative isolation to each other (and basic salary) and the employee is tied to a cash/benefit mix as defined by the organisation. This relatively isolated management of benefits very often results in employees not being aware of their total earnings, inclusive of the organisation's expenditure on benefits.

The benefit arrangement strategy described above is often referred to as the add-on benefit arrangement strategy. The term 'add-on' refers to the nature of the employment agreement between employer and employee which, as described above, offers the employee a basic salary to which a number of benefits are added.

The local opposite of the add-on benefit arrangement strategy is the pure flexible benefit arrangement strategy, which is often called the cafeteria-style programme.

Instead of a basic salary plus benefits, employees receive a total package value in return for their services. Each employee's remuneration is managed and reviewed in terms of a single entity, namely total package value, as opposed to the relatively isolated management and review of basic salary and individual benefits.

Under the pure flexible benefit arrangement strategy, individual employees also have full discretion over the cash/benefit mix of their own total package value.

Essentially, an organisation will determine the total package cost it is prepared to spend in employing each of its different employees. It will then compile a list of types of benefit that it is prepared to offer an employee. From this 'menu' of benefits employees can choose those which best suit their individual needs. The cost to the organisation of providing the particular mix of benefits is then added up and is deducted from the total package value in order to calculate the net cash salary of the employee.

Although the pure flexible benefit arrangement strategy serves a very useful purpose as a theoretical opposite to the add-on benefit arrangement strategy, it is seldom implemented in its pure form. The most important reason for this is that organisations wish to safeguard themselves from possible adverse consequences arising from particular employee choices. An example would be where the organisation has to inform the widow of an employee that no funds will be payable to her as her late husband opted out of group life cover and pension benefits, and converted these into improved company car benefits.

One can obviously argue that employees and their families have to live with the consequences of their own decisions. Many, if not the majority of organisations, would, however, prefer to design their benefit arrangements in a way that precludes the possibility of events similar to the above example. This is achieved through a flexible benefit arrangement that includes so-called core benefits. As opposed to the other benefits under a flexible benefit arrangement strategy, which are optional, employee participation in so-called core benefits is compulsory. In practice employees are obliged to channel specified minimum portions of the total packages offered to them into these defined core benefits. The range of core benefits should ideally include basic retirement, death, disability and major medical expense benefits (for example surgery, hospitalisation).

The most common advantages and disadvantages of flexible benefit arrangements are summarised below.

Advantages of flexible benefit arrangements

- Flexible benefits promote a clearer understanding for employers and employees of the real costs associated with benefits and how they contribute to the total package values.
- Employers have improved control over the predictability of remuneration expenditure, since package values are not driven by changing external factors or fluctuations in employee utilisation of specific benefits (for example medical aid).
- Fairness and internal equity are enhanced, since differences in total package values typically only result from differences in performance and job complexity, and not from differences in personal circumstances. (For example, under a non-flexible system, two employees with the same entitlement regarding a housing subsidy benefit and a fully maintained company car benefit may end up with substantial differences in the value of the benefits if one of them rents a flat and lives close to work, while the other has a large bond on his house and travels a long distance between work and home.)
- Employees are permitted to choose benefits most suited to their individual needs and also to structure their package in the most tax-efficient way.

Disadvantages of flexible benefit arrangements

- Flexible systems are more complex to set up and to administer. Despite the availability of computer software that can address the complexities of the payroll administration and the financial modelling of optimum package mixes, additional resources are usually needed for providing individual advisory and counselling services for each employee in the system.

- The problem of adverse choice may sometimes be encountered (Gómez-Mejía, Balkin & Cardy 2001: 420). This relates to the situation where those employees who have a specific and immediate need for a particular benefit select that option more often than the average employee, thus causing an inordinate rise in the cost of such benefit. (For example, employees close to retirement may attempt to buy as many additional retirement benefits as possible, or an employee with a serious medical condition as much medical and group life insurance as possible.) The inclusion of compulsory core benefits can, however, often address this problem.
- Unions may sometimes offer resistance to flexible benefit schemes if previously negotiated benefit improvements or the loss of control over a benefit programme is at stake.

16.4.4.2 Choosing a suitable benefit arrangement

The choice between particular arrangement strategies should take account of certain fundamental remuneration principles in order to ensure a benefits system that not only addresses particular organisational needs and circumstances, but will also be in line with the objectives of the overall remuneration strategy. These principles are detailed in exhibit 16.5.

Generally, it would appear that a flexible benefit arrangement strategy has a greater potential for satisfying the fundamental remuneration principles mentioned above, and it is therefore not surprising to find an ever-increasing number of South African organisations of all sizes following the international trend towards greater flexibility in benefit agreements.

Successful delivery of benefit arrangements

Well-structured and appropriate benefits are not enough to ensure the success of an organisation's benefit programme. The administrative delivery of the benefits to the organisation's employees must also be on time and as contracted before it can be regarded as a success. Of particular importance in this regard is the integration of effort across functional lines within the organisation and the issue of benefit programme communication.

EXHIBIT 16.5: Remuneration principles

The following remuneration principles should be considered when choosing a benefit arrangement strategy:

- *Cost control.* Limit the exposure of remuneration packages to unpredictable cost factors over which the organisation has very little or no control.
- *External equity.* The positioning of remuneration levels inside the organisation relative to comparable remuneration levels in the broader labour market should be done on the basis of total package values.
- *Internal equity.* Differences in the total package values of individual employees should only be due to differences in job complexity (as measured by the job evaluation process), skill premiums payable to certain occupational groupings (as measured by remuneration surveys) and differences in job performance (as measured by a performance appraisal system).
- *Flexibility.* Individual employees should be given the opportunity to select a cash/benefit mix that satisfies their personal needs without adding to the total remuneration expenditure of the organisation.
- *Simplicity.* Benefit arrangements should be simple to administer and easily understood by the employees to whom they apply.

16.4.4.3 Integration of effort

The administrative delivery of a benefits programme seldom involves only one functional area within the organisation. Responsibility for this delivery often spans the human resources, financial and information technology functions. Given the diversity of these functions, a significant potential exists for important responsibilities to 'get lost' between these areas.

Where more than one functional area is responsible for the administrative delivery of a benefits programme (which is almost always the case), it is advisable for these areas to clarify and document their respective responsibilities. A coordination committee with representation from all the functional areas responsible for the administrative delivery of the benefit programme is also advisable. Benefit arrangements are seldom if ever static, and such a body can play a very important role in realigning the administrative infrastructure whenever changes are made to the organisation's benefit arrangement.

16.4.4.4 Benefit programme communication

Remuneration affects employees directly and personally. It is therefore imperative that they fully understand the processes and personal responsibilities associated with the organisation's benefit programme. The proper communication of this is of the utmost importance. Inadequate communication could quite easily result in employer and employee having different perceptions as to what has been contracted.

Under a flexible benefit arrangement strategy, benefit programme communication becomes even more vital. A flexible benefit arrangement always means transferring at least some responsibility for the structuring of individual remuneration packages from the employer to the employee. The employee has to know and accept this responsibility.

Booklets, presentations, workshops and videos are among the most popular means for ensuring understanding and acceptance of the processes and personal responsibilities of the organisation's benefit programme.

16.5 CONCLUSION

Incentive systems and benefit programmes usually form an integral part of an overall remuneration system. A wide variety of financial incentive plans are used in an effort to link the pay of employees more closely to their performance. This link is not always easily established, since the success of an incentive system not only depends on the sound mechanics of the plan but also on a variety of determinants such as the organisational climate, employee acceptance, effective administration and suitability to particular organisational needs and circumstances.

In achieving the common goal of fostering increased performance or output, incentive schemes use a variety of approaches in terms of the class of employees to be covered, the measures of performance utilised, the types of behaviour or areas of performance to be encouraged, the organisational level of performance to be rewarded and the nature of the rewards themselves. These differences in options must be carefully considered when deciding what type of incentive plan will be the most appropriate in addressing the particular needs and remuneration objectives of an organisation.

Benefits usually comprise a substantial component of employees' total remuneration. Other than incentive payments, however, benefits are not normally linked to performance, but are mostly regarded as entitlements; that is, they are seen as part of the conditions of employment. While some benefits are mandated by labour legislation, most of the wide array of possible benefits are provided by employers in an attempt to attract and retain employees and thus remain competitive in the labour market. In devising a suitable benefits programme, various benefit arrangement strategies may be utilised, the most common of which are the add-on and the flexible benefit strategy. The latter has become increasingly popular in the South African context in line with a trend towards greater choice and flexibility in accommodating differing employee needs.

Efficient administration plays a major role in ensuring the success of a benefits programme.

Incentive remuneration and benefits programmes, together with the basic salary structure, are equally important components of an overall remuneration system. The challenge for effective reward management lies in finding the optimal balance between these components and their congruence with the strategic objectives of the organisation, and in particular also the HRM strategies decided upon. Wilson (2003: 343) summarises the essence of the total remuneration system discussed in the two chapters well:

> Organisations can create conditions in which people find a wide variety of re-wards in the work they do. Some of these rewards come from the work itself, some from peers, some from customers, and some from managers or supervisors. Reward systems should be designed with the central purpose of providing people to share in the achievements of their contributions. The process does not imply that people are not already performing at a fully competent level. Rather, it is aimed at continually improving performance at a rate that is faster than that of competitors. Sincerity is key to effective use of consequences. If reward systems are established as a way to manipulate people, they are likely to fail. If, on the other hand, they are established to reinforce progress, achievement, and service to the customers, they are likely to succeed.

SUSTAINABILITY CONNECTION?

Incentives and benefits form part of remuneration systems that aim to attract and retain talent and reward superior performance. Through providing benefits and rewards for superior work performance we also encourage and help people to improve the quality of their lives. Crucially important also, benefits and incentives are essential ingredients to help sustain superior organisational performance (through attracting and retaining high-performing working people and encouraging superior work performance). It is only through sustained superior organisational performance, driven by superior work performance of our people, that organisations can hope to survive in an increasingly competitive world. If our organisations do not survive, our people and our country and continent will suffer.

SELF-EVALUATION QUESTIONS

1 Discuss what is meant by 'incentive remuneration' and 'pay for performance'.
2 Motivate why it is important to have incentive schemes in a total rewards system.
3 Discuss the important principles that underlie the process of establishing incentive systems.
4 Distinguish between different sales commission plans.

5 Differentiate between and compare the merits of individual- and organisation-based incentive systems.
6 Discuss the nature and potential of ESOPs and gain-sharing plans in countries that have a collectivist cultural orientation.
7 Explain the rationale for and different types of benefits that can be provided to employees.
8 Briefly explain the remuneration principles to be considered when a benefit arrangement strategy has to be chosen.
9 How would you go about successfully delivering different benefit arrangements?
10 What specific considerations apply in the remuneration of executive managers and expatriate employees?

17 WELL-BEING AT WORK – AND BEYOND

LEARNING OUTCOMES

After studying this chapter, you should be able to:

- argue a case for moving from a narrow health and safety compliance focus to a holistic approach of 'well-being at work – and beyond', and describe the role of different role players and stakeholders in this regard;
- give a brief overview of the statutory regulations governing occupational health and safety in South Africa;
- explain and debate a range of specific issues pertaining to the well-being of people in the work context;
- write an essay about the HIV/Aids challenge; and
- write concise notes about the notions of corporate citizenship and socially responsible management.

17.1 INTRODUCTION

If we value our people, then their well-being will be important to us. By well-being we simply mean a state of optimal social, physical and mental health. We can also use the word 'wellness'. We favour a holistic approach to looking after the physical, psychological and social state of well-being of the people who work in and for our organisations – most notably the employees. The starting point is to ensure legal compliance and to have a working environment that is safe and meets basic health standards.

Although some types of work are generally more dangerous than others, a common-law duty rests on all employers to provide their employees with safe working conditions. South African courts have often endorsed the common-law principle that requires employers to take reasonable care of the health and safety of their employees. Apart from the common-law requirements, there is specific legislation in South Africa which focuses on the health and safety of employees (see chapter 3 and below).

This chapter begins with a brief introduction to some of the important aspects relating to health and safety legislation in South Africa. It should be noted that there are developments under way to bring about changes to the existing legislation.

We believe, however, that taking good care of our working people goes far beyond simply meeting the requirements of the relevant occupational health and safety legislation. We propose a proactive and holistic approach that even reflects a concern beyond the well-being of employees at work. To achieve optimal states of wellness (or well-being) that are beneficial to our employees, our organisations and our country, we also need to show and take action to enhance the well-being of the communities from which we draw our human resources. This chapter therefore reflects elements of such a holistic approach.

17.2 THE LEGISLATIVE FRAMEWORK GOVERNING HEALTH AND SAFETY AT WORK

17.2.1 General

Apart from the common law and the Bill of Rights (in the Constitution), there are two pieces of legislation with refined legal requirements regarding employee health and safety, namely the Occupational Health and Safety Act (OHSA) 85 of 1993 and the Mine Health and Safety Act 29 of 1996.

The overall aim of the OHSA (also see chapter 3) is to provide for the health and safety of employees at work (including aspects such as health and safety hazards, and the safety of plant machinery and equipment). Certain employers and employees are, however, specifically excluded from the ambit of the OHSA. These include parties covered by the Merchant Shipping Act and people employed in mines, mining areas or any works as defined in the Mine Health and Safety Act 29 of 1996.

17.2.2 The Mine Health and Safety Act: a few comments

Historically in South Africa, the concern for the health and safety of workers arose from the dangers inherent in mining. This is not surprising if we consider the statistics revealed in the following quote (Lewis & Jeebhay 1996: 431 (footnotes and references omitted)):

> As a result of this legal and political system, 69 000 mineworkers died in the first 93 years of this century, and more than a million were seriously injured. In 1993 the government mining engineer's statistics showed that there were 1,54 mineworkers killed and 25,8 seriously injured for every 1 000 workers exposed to underground risk in all sectors of the industry. The vast majority of injuries and deaths occurred at or in underground mines (99%). Of these, the gold mines were the most dangerous, accounting in 1993 for 85,6% of all reported injuries and 72,7% of all reported fatalities. 61,7% of gold mining fatalities (263 lives in 1993) were due to underground rockbursts or rockfalls. The next most dangerous subsector in 1993, the coal industry, was responsible for 15,4% of all mining fatalities.

Today safety remains a huge challenge in our mining industry:

> Despite the South African mining industry's aim to improve safety statistics by 20% each year between 2003 and 2013, there was actually an increase in fatalities between 2006 and 2007, with the number of those killed on the mines rising from 199 to 221. According to many in the industry, the problem is a typically South African disregard for risk – and the solution a difficult proposition: a change of culture (Peacock 2008: 17).

Apart from the common-law right to work in a safe environment, safety in the mining industry was regulated by industry-specific statutes, the earliest of which was the Mines and Works Act of 1911. The latest statute in this regard is the Mine Health and Safety Act 29 of 1996. The objectives of the Act are summarised in exhibit 17.1.

EXHIBIT 17.1: Objectives of the Mine Health and Safety Act*

The objectives of this Act are:

- to protect the health and safety of persons at mines;
- to require employers and employees to identify and eliminate hazards, and to control and minimise the risks relating to health and safety at mines;
- to give effect to the public international law obligations of the Republic that concern health and safety at mines;
- to provide for employee participation in matters of health and safety through health and safety representatives and the health and safety committees at mines;
- to provide for effective monitoring of health and safety conditions at mines;
- to provide for enforcement of health and safety measures at mines;
- to provide for investigations and inquiries to improve health and safety at mines; and
- to promote: (i) a culture of health and safety in the mining industry; (ii) training in health and safety in the mining industry; and (iii) cooperation and consultation on health and safety between the state, employers, employees and their representatives.

*Section 1 of Act 29 of 1996

Apart from placing appropriately onerous duties on the owners and managers of mines to provide for health and safety, the Act also grants employees wide-ranging powers to be involved in health and safety issues and decisions. The pre-eminent body established in terms of the Act to regulate health and safety issues in the mining industry is a tripartite body, called the Mine Health and Safety Council, which must advise the Minister of Mineral and Energy Affairs on health and safety at mines. The Council consists of five members representing owners in the mining industry; five members representing employees in the mining industry; four members representing departments of the state; and the Chief Inspector, who must chair the Council.

As is the case with the Occupational Health and Safety Act (OHSA) (see below), the Mine Health and Safety Act provides for the reporting of incidents and accidents, and for the appointment of health and safety representatives and committees. Considerations of space do not allow further discussion of this Act, but it is important to note that in the mining industry the Occupational Health and Safety Act 85 of 1993 is not applicable to any matter in respect of which any provision of the former Act is applicable (this means, in effect, that only in a case where the Mine Health and Safety Act is silent on any specific issue would one turn to the Occupational Health and Safety Act for statutory guidance).

Employees in the mining industry who are injured in the performance of their duties or who suffer from occupational diseases are compensated in terms of the Occupational Diseases in Mines and Works Act (ODMWA) in a similar manner to which workers in other industries are compensated for occupational diseases or work-related injuries in terms of the Compensation for Occupational Injuries and Diseases Act (COIDA).

17.2.3 Some important aspects of the OHSA

17.2.3.1 General

As we indicated earlier, the Occupational Health and Safety Act 85 of 1993 (OHSA) forms the legislative framework in respect of health and safety issues in most South African organisations. The overall aim of the OHSA was spelt out in chapter 3.

The OHSA makes the following provisions for the achievement of its objectives:

- The establishment of an Advisory Council for Occupational Health and Safety.
- Every employer must provide and maintain, as far as is reasonably practicable, a working environment that is safe and without risk to the health of his or her employees, as well as other people affected by the operations of the business.
- Every supplier or manufacturer of items used in a workplace must ensure that such items do not pose a safety or health risk.
- Every employer must inform his or her workforce (and the appointed health and safety representatives) of hazards at the workplace.
- All employees must:
  - take reasonable care for the health and safety of themselves and of other persons who may be affected by their acts or omissions;
  - carry out any lawful order given to them, and obey the health and safety rules and procedures laid down by their employer;
  - report any unsafe or unhealthy situation which comes to their attention; and
  - report any incident which may affect their health or which has caused an injury to themselves.
- The appointment of health and safety representatives. The Act provides that every employer who employs more than 20 employees at any workplace must appoint health and safety representatives. The functions of health and safety representatives are summarised in exhibit 17.2.
- The establishment of one or more health and safety committees in respect of each workplace where two or more health and safety representatives have been designated. The functions of health and safety committees are summarised in exhibit 17.3.
- Certain incidents must be reported to an inspector (see exhibit 17.4).
- Occupational diseases must be reported to the chief inspector.
- Wide powers of inspection, entry, enquiry and seizure are conferred on inspectors.
- A wide range of acts of omission and commission are declared offences and can incur criminal penalties.

17.2.3.2 Health and safety representatives and committees

(See exhibit 17.2 for the functions of health and safety representatives, and exhibit 17.3 for the functions of health and safety committees.) An employer must provide the agreed-upon facilities, assistance and training that the health and safety representative reasonably requires for the performance of his or her functions. Health and safety representatives shall not incur any civil liability by reason of the fact only that they failed to do anything which they may do or are required to do in terms of the Act.

17.2.3.3 Reporting duties

In the event of an incident in which a person dies, or was injured to such an extent that he or she is likely to die, or suffered the loss of a limb or part of a limb, no person may, without the consent of an inspector, disturb the site at which the incident occurred or remove any article or substance involved in the incident. This provision, as well as the provisions relating to the reporting of incidents, does not apply in respect of a traffic accident on a public road, an incident occurring in a private household (provided that the householder reports the incident to the South African Police), or an aviation accident.

A health and safety representative may perform the following functions in respect of the workplace or section of the workplace for which he or she has been designated:

- review the effectiveness of health and safety measures;
- identify potential hazards and potential major incidents at the workplace;
- in collaboration with his or her employer, examine the causes of incidents at the workplace;
- investigate complaints by any employee relating to that employee's health or safety at work;
- make representations to the employer or a health and safety committee on matters arising from his or her performance of the preceding functions;
- make representations to the employer on general matters affecting the health or safety of the employees at the workplace;
- inspect the workplace with a view to the health and safety of employees, at such intervals as may be agreed upon with the employer;
- participate in consultations with inspectors at the workplace and accompany inspectors on inspections of the workplace;
- receive certain information from inspectors; and
- in his or her capacity as a health and safety representative attend meetings of the health and safety committee of which he or she is a member, in connection with any of the above functions.

In order to perform the above functions, a health and safety representative is entitled to, in respect of the workplace or section of the workplace for which he or she has been designated:

- visit the site of an incident at all reasonable times and attend any inspection *in loco*;
- attend any investigation or formal inquiry held in terms of this Act;
- in so far as it is reasonably necessary for performing his or her functions, inspect any document which the employer is required to keep in terms of this Act;
- accompany an inspector on any inspection;
- with the approval of the employer (which approval shall not be unreasonably withheld), be accompanied by a technical adviser on any inspection; and
- participate in any internal health or safety audit.

EXHIBIT 17.3: Functions of health and safety committees

A health and safety committee:

- may make recommendations to the employer or, where the recommendations fail to resolve the matter, to an inspector, regarding health or safety matters;
- shall discuss any incident at the workplace in which any person was injured, became ill or died, and may in writing report on the incident to an inspector; and
- shall perform such other functions as may be prescribed.

17.3 PROMOTING AND MAINTAINING EMPLOYEE WELLNESS: A PROACTIVE AND HOLISTIC APPROACH TO THE MANAGEMENT OF HEALTH AND SAFETY

17.3.1 General

Traditionally, management has not always been proactively altruistic: if it is anticipated that there is no real benefit to be derived from a particular investment of resources (in other words, to offset the outlay), the investment may well be made elsewhere.

EXHIBIT 17.4: Reporting of certain incidents to an inspector

The following must be reported to an inspector: each work-related incident or incident in connection with the use of plant or machinery, in which, or in consequence of which:

- any person dies, becomes unconscious, suffers the loss of a limb or part of a limb or is otherwise injured or becomes ill to such a degree that he or she is likely either to die or to suffer a permanent physical defect or likely to be unable for a period of at least 14 days either to work or to continue with the activity for which he or she was employed or is usually employed;
- a major incident occurred; or
- the health or safety of any person was endangered and where a dangerous substance was spilled, the uncontrolled release of any substance under pressure took place, machinery or any part thereof fractured or failed, resulting in flying, falling or uncontrolled moving objects; or
- machinery ran out of control.

Management has thus tended to adopt a follow-the-rule-book policy in matters of health and safety.

The spiralling costs of medical care and the growing realisation that absenteeism has a very negative impact on productivity and can thus cost organisations a lot have led management of some organisations to consider alternatives that may yield results superior to the reactive, minimalist approach of legal compliance. Taylor (2005: 317) for instance explains as follows: "If the absence rate is running at 5 per cent a year, it is necessary to employ 5 per cent more staff than would otherwise be the case ... In a large organisation employing thousands of people, the total cost is therefore considerable indeed." Obviously, not all absenteeism cases are related to poor physical health – some are also attitudinal, relating to the social, psychological or mental well-being of a person.

It is therefore important for managers to consider the potential benefits of a system focused on proactively promoting and maintaining the socio-psychological and physical well-being of employees rather than dealing with health and safety problems as they occur. Such an approach has various characteristics.

17.3.2 A strategic and holistic focus

It has already been stated that a holistic approach requires that care be taken of the whole person or employee. This means that the focus is not only on safety or on the provision of medical aid assistance but also on the acknowledgement that any person coming to work comes there as a whole person. One cannot detach the worker from the human being. It can almost be said that what needs to be taken care of proactively is thus 'body, mind and soul'. This means that even the broader social and domestic dynamics of employees, such as those related to personal and family lives, must be taken into account. In this respect attention must, for instance, be paid to a well-balanced work and family life.

In addition, and linked to such a holistic approach, is the strategic focus that is required. Part of a strategic approach to managing human resources will include a comprehensive wellness plan and programme. A wellness policy should therefore ideally form the framework, spelling out at least what the organisation's philosophy is in respect of promoting and maintaining the general well-being of its human resources. Developing such a strategic framework should ideally also be an inclusive process in which all the stakeholders are engaged.

A POLICY PERSPECTIVE
Our employee wellness policy aims to establish the foundation of a holistic system of promoting the general well-being of all our employees. We believe that employees who are well work better and can have a better quality of life. The starting point for all of this is to create a work environment that is safe and free from anything that can negatively affect the health and general well-being of our staff. The progressive aspects relate to preventative care.

The purpose of this policy is to support the design and implementation of a comprehensive employee wellness system at our company which is to be to the benefit of all our personnel. The overall aim is to be proactive and promote the health, safety and total wellness of our employees, and to put in place systems, practices, processes and facilities that employees can make use of in order to improve their general well-being. We care about the well-being of all our employees and we know they care about how well we are doing as an organisation.

17.3.3 Aspects of managing for employee wellness

The old adage that prevention is better than cure can be taken one step further in the context of employee wellness: it has been proven that not only is prevention better than cure, it is also cheaper than cure. A preventative approach entails a number of factors to be incorporated in the strategies, policies and action plans or programmes.

17.3.3.1 Ergonomics and workplace design

Ergonomics, as you should already know, have to do with matching the physical work environment to the workers. Nankervis, Compton and Baird (2008: 443) say that ergonomics "focuses on the physical features of the work environment (e.g. workstations, work processes and machinery) ....".

The idea is thus that care should be taken right from the outset at the point of workplace design – including relevant equipment, the design of buildings and infrastructure, and the actual workstations of people. This is where the use of ergonomics expertise can add good value. Nankervis et al (2008: 443), for instance, explain in this regard that "the best recent example of the contributions of ergonomics ... is its approach to occupational overuse syndrome (or repetitive strain injury) ... [E]rgonomists were often employed to prevent the rising incidence of OOS/RSI by designing workstations to minimise the repetitive strain on workers in selected occupations ... [with, for example,] [m]ore comfortable chairs, [and] modified keyboards ... to reduce the physical and postural strains ...".

17.3.3.2 Health screening and safety auditing

Traditionally, health screening was often viewed as a perk earmarked for senior management and especially executive employees. This situation is, however, gradually changing, with some organisations offering such a service to all levels of employees. Health screening or assessment tests are basically medical investigations that do not arise from an employee's request to be assessed with regard to a specific health-related complaint. It is a proactive intervention to make an early identification of any diseases from which an employee may be suffering and to diagnose an employee's general state of health.

By conducting such assessments, health-related problems can be detected at early stages, and a health status baseline can be developed; from this a programme of lifestyle improvement can be designed. Comprehensive health-screening interventions may furthermore go beyond assessing concrete health measures (such as coronary heart disease, respiratory disease, blood pressure, cholesterol levels, etc). Aspects such as habits, knowledge and attitudes may also be screened in such comprehensive health-screening interventions. Other tests may include stress-level, hearing and vision, urine, blood and fitness tests. Nutritional assessments can also be conducted to collect information on aspects such as food intake and eating patterns to detect how healthy an employee's lifestyle is. Determining the nutritional status of employees should be an important component of holistic health assessment interventions in South African organisations.

Safety audits, on the other hand, are aimed at establishing the quality of an organisation's safety policies, programmes, procedures and practices. This may include conducting safety attitude surveys to determine the extent to which workers are sensitive and knowledgeable about a safety-driven environment.

These assessments and audits are necessary to identify and detect timeously potential threats to the establishment of an environment conducive to employee wellness. These evaluations therefore have to be conducted on a regular basis.

17.3.3.3 Sensitisation and education

If an organisation wishes to establish a work environment of employee wellness, it is essential to launch aggressive campaigns to promote the philosophy that employee health, safety and general well-being are important and beneficial to both the employee and the organisation.

This begins with a process of awareness creation by means of methods such as posters, leaflets, talks, competitions, videos, demonstrations, or advertisements in internal/in-company newspapers. The idea is, however, not only to sensitise employees or to create an awareness. At the end of the day, the efforts to promote such an environment require employees to be proactive and to do something about their own health and safety. The idea is to impart information to explain the importance of health and safety, and to persuade employees to become more serious about these aspects in their day-to-day lives and in the workplace. Such efforts should thus include workshops where employees can learn from others (co-employees preferably) how to go about being more safety conscious and leading a more healthy lifestyle. An important component of a healthier lifestyle is looking after fitness and relaxation.

17.3.3.4 Fitness programmes and recreation facilities

Research has shown that proper physical exercise and general fitness can not only enhance a person's quality of life but also prolong it. Promoting exercise and the improvement of the fitness of employees is therefore an important component of a holistic, proactive approach to the establishment of employee wellness. Being fit is important for the healthy functioning of the cardiovascular system, the endocrine system, as well as the musculoskeletal system. It helps to control weight and to reduce stress, thereby making a positive contribution to a person's general feeling of well-being – and thus to his or her state of mental health. Fit employees are generally regarded as being more energetic and as better workers. Such employees will usually be happier and more productive, and absenteeism will, in all likelihood, decrease.

There are various ways of promoting exercise and fitness. Sport as a recreational activity often forms part of the lifestyle of fit people. Sport can serve as an effective release valve for stress that people might have. Many people get their exercise from participating in different types of sport, and so sport as a recreational activity in a work context can form an important component of a comprehensive organisational wellness system.

Organised recreational activities such as sports events can have the additional benefit of enhancing the social dimension of the work environment. Some informal gatherings lead to constructive interaction and communication, which can create a sense of togetherness and team spirit among employees.

Improving physical fitness through organised recreation and sports events (such as soccer, cricket, volleyball, golf, etc) can thus improve morale and cooperation among employees. Apart from team sports, there are also outdoor activities such as hiking, backpacking, sightseeing and fishing, and cultural activities such as attending art and music festivals. Obviously not all of these contribute positively to physical fitness, but they do have the potential to act as stress release valves. Exercise can take various forms, such as gymnasium work, aerobics, jogging, cycling, squash, swimming, tennis, walking, etc.

It is up to the management of an organisation to decide what premium they put on the physical fitness of their employees. If fitness is seen as beneficial, free fitness assessments may be offered and it may be decided to provide recreation and exercising facilities on the organisation's own premises.

17.3.3.5 Work and family life interactions

Research has shown that conflicts between family and working life are related to aspects such as increased health risks for parents, poor morale, depression, reduced life satisfaction, absenteeism, poorer work performance and decreased productivity.

Work–family conflict is becoming an increasingly important issue within the context of HRM. Because our workforces are becoming more and more diverse, with the female:male ratio increasing and with a rising number of two-career couples, the chances of employing individuals who experience job–family conflict are greater. This phenomenon is, however, not limited to female employees. Any employee who experiences the dual pressure of having to comply with the competing requirements and expectations of work and family life may suffer from the conflict.

Various options are available to organisations to prevent job–family conflict levels which are so high that they impact adversely on employee mindset, and on performance and productivity. These range from providing child and elder (parent) care facilities, to more flexibility in terms of time, workplace and leave, and the involvement of spouses and children in certain recreational, fitness and other social activities and facilities of the organisation. An organisation may even, as part of their management development initiatives, for instance, occasionally involve the spouse of the employee in the development programme. Part of the performance incentive scheme of an organisation may be to award 'family breakaway vouchers' for high achievers.

It seems that one of a popular and feasible option is flexibility. This may include different possibilities like work-schedule adaptations, flexitime, job sharing, flexi-place and telecommuting. Such arrangements may provide employees with the necessary scope and flexibility to attend to family-related issues such as caring for sick children or attending school activities such as sport (for example an athletics meeting, or a rugby or soccer match).

Another important aspect is the need for employers to show concern about childcare. Options in this area are also quite diverse. One option is that of providing resource and referral services. An official is appointed or an agency is contracted to provide employees with consultation on childcare and to make lists available regarding childcare options. The employer may even establish an on-site day-care facility or it may purchase slots in existing community facilities which are then reserved for the children of the organisation's employees. Other options are to enter into some joint venture with other nearby organisations or to appoint an official of the organisation to organise and supervise a day-care network of caregivers in the neighbourhood.

Irrespective of the way in which organisations go about dealing with potential work–family conflict, it is essential that they be fully aware of the importance and potential value of this aspect of HRM. Organisations that show they appreciate that blood is thicker than water will demonstrate, through policies and practice, that they really care, and that can have positive spin-offs related to the morale and motivation levels of the working people.

17.3.3.6 Nutrition programmes

An essential component of a healthy lifestyle is a good balanced diet. Unfortunately, we live in an era in which junk food is extremely popular. Many of the health problems plaguing our society, such as cancer and cardiovascular disorders, can possibly be linked to unhealthy lifestyles and poor eating habits. Many people today are overweight, which can sometimes be a threat to a person's health and can also be linked to diet deficiencies and poor eating habits. Nutrition programmes are basically aimed at improving the eating habits of individuals and at encouraging them to follow a more balanced diet.

Some workplace nutrition programmes are very basic and aim simply at informing employees about the potential disadvantages and risks associated with poor nutritional habits and the potential benefits of following a good diet. This may include increasing staff awareness by means of leaflets, booklets and posters, or even group sessions involving short presentations using visual aids such as videos or films. Other programmes are much more interventionary by nature and aim at preventing or even treating diet-related health problems through weight control and diet modification. Such interventions will normally form part of a holistic wellness programme that includes fitness exercises (see above), stress-control elements and anti-smoking programmes (see below). In such nutrition programmes which involve behaviour change, assessments will be done to identify employees' eating habits and the quality of their diet. This may include physical examinations (for example weight, height, blood pressure) and screening the usual intake of fats, carbohydrates, protein, vitamins, minerals, sugar, etc. It may also include an investigation into the perceptions and attitudes of the employee regarding eating and nutrition. After determining the employee's dietary habits and particular needs, an individualised programme is worked out that may include food-choice combinations and meal plans, as well as guidelines regarding meal preparation and general eating habits. These programmes will typically also be longer term, including some kind of ongoing monitoring, feedback and support systems.

Although such comprehensive interventionary workplace nutrition programmes may be very expensive and not entirely appropriate for many smaller South African organisations, larger organisations may well find them worth considering as part of their promotion of holistic employee wellness.

17.3.3.7 Smoking policies

It is common knowledge today that smoking causes health problems. These problems can basically be categorised into two groups:

■ the health implications for the employee who smokes; and
■ the health and other implications for non-smoking employees who become passive smokers as a result of their colleagues' smoking habits.

The health risks associated with smoking are generally well known. Smoking is, for instance, a major contributing factor in chronic respiratory diseases and coronary heart disease.

The implications of smoking for organisations are thus abundantly clear. Apart from the implications for the smoker, there are also major implications for non-smoking employees and for the organisation as a whole. The breathed-out smoke contains the same harmful ingredients (such as carbon monoxide and recognised carcinogens – in other words, chemicals that cause cancer) to which the smoker is exposed. In addition, smoking often bothers non-smokers, causing conflict, hostility, negative feelings and deteriorating interpersonal relations, all of which may impact negatively on workforce morale and productivity. It is therefore essential for organisations to tackle the issue of smoking in the workplace, including striking some balance regarding the interests of smokers and non-smokers.

Smoking thus imposes certain costs on an organisation, such as those linked to absenteeism and productivity, as well as cleaning costs and medical retirements. The control of smoking in the workplace through a professional process of formulating and implementing an appropriate non-smoking policy will enhance the health and general well-being of both smoking and non-smoking workers. This, in turn, can result in major positive benefits for the organisation. It may even be possible for the organisation to negotiate an improved benefit premium deal with its medical aid company.

THE STATUTORY REGULATION OF SMOKING IN SOUTH AFRICA

In 1999 the Tobacco Products Control Act (Act 83 of 1993) was amended (by Act 12 of 1999) to prohibit or restrict smoking in public places and to regulate the sale and advertising of tobacco products. In terms of the Act a 'public place' means any indoor or enclosed area which is open to the public or any part of the public and includes a workplace and a public conveyance; and a 'workplace' means any indoor or enclosed area in which employees perform the duties of their employment (this includes any corridor, lobby, stairwell, elevator, cafeteria, washroom or other common area frequented by employees during the course of their employment but excludes an area specifically designated by the employer as a smoking area and which complies with the prescribed requirements). Therefore, the South African lawmaker recognises the dangers inherent in smoking and employers have little option but to prohibit smoking in the workplace or to make special arrangements where smokers may smoke without exposing co-workers to the risks attendant on passive smoking.

17.3.3.8 Being prepared for emergencies

Part of a proactive approach to managing employee health and safety at work is to draw up contingency plans and to have the necessary infrastructure to deal with any emergencies. There are many types of emergency situations that can arise in the work situation and that can threaten the life, safety or general wellbeing of employees. A distinction can be made between natural and man-made disasters. The former refer to situations such as floods, storms, earthquakes and epidemics, while the latter include riots and serious labour unrest, bomb threats and fires.

Apart from constantly ensuring that all the necessary emergency equipment such as fire appliances and equipment (fire extinguishers and fire alarms) are in the right places and in working order, it is important to ensure that adequate emergency escape routes exist and that these are easily visible and clearly marked. Although all employees should be trained to observe the housekeeping rules so that emergency situations such as fire outbreaks can be prevented, emergency procedures covering all kinds of eventuality should be well established, and all employees should be thoroughly drilled in how to deal with any kind of emergency situation.

The emergency infrastructure should include the necessary first-aid facilities such as a first-aid room, equipment and material. Certain employees, who are specifically designated as first-aiders, should receive special training in first aid. Often these employees are trained by outside experts, especially if the organisation does not have the necessary internal expertise. Furthermore, all employees should receive at least some very basic, introductory first-aid training.

As already mentioned, one of the most important elements of a proactive attitude towards employee safety and health is to establish adequate contingency or emergency plans and procedures that can cater for a variety of eventualities such as fires, bomb scares or explosions. Obviously, contingency plans will depend largely on the nature of the workplace. The evacuation process would, for instance, differ radically in a gold mine, an open-core coal mine, a chemical factory or an Edgars or other retail store. Regardless of the exact nature of these infrastructural elements, plans and procedures, it is essential not to neglect these aspects, as they form an essential component of also proving to employees that the organisation's management values employee safety and health.

Part of any such emergency plan is to appoint a person who will be the emergency controller. This person will have the responsibility of drafting the emergency plan and organising the emergency training. In order to do this, he or she will require the following (Acutt 1992: 168–169):

- a plan of the whole site together with a floor plan of the buildings indicating all entrances and the different areas, which must include:
  - the position all main electricity boards, hazardous substances, inflammable materials, gas cylinders, etc;
  - the position of all fire extinguishers, first-aid boxes and emergency equipment, including rescue equipment;
- updated lists of names, addresses and telephone numbers of all emergency personnel, senior management and local emergency services;
- an effective communication system;
- an identification system for emergency personnel;
- an emergency transport system; and
- an efficient evacuation system.

Other aspects to be catered for relate to security; an emergency command centre; the structuring and framing of rescue, fire control and first-aid teams; transport; and detailed plans to protect buildings, material, plant, equipment, stock and especially the employees of the organisation.

17.3.4 Some specific workplace health and safety issues

17.3.4.1 Occupational mental health

Occupational mental health (OMH) as an applied field of clinical and abnormal psychology deals with the maladjustment or adjustment of employees in the work or organisational context. This is an extremely specialised topic, to the extent that it is a separate branch of industrial/organisational psychology as field of study. For the purposes of this chapter, a brief introduction to some of the issues (and topics) which fall within the field of OMH will suffice.

The first question one may wish to ask relates to what constitutes an adjusted or maladjusted employee. In other words, what criteria are used to evaluate psychological adjustment (or maladjustment) in the work environment? In this regard there are many relevant criteria and these can be classified in many different ways. It must be emphasised, however, that a person's behaviour at work, and the meaning of that behaviour, must always be compared with certain criteria in the context of his or her actions. Some of the general categories of criteria, within which more specific criteria can be set, include the following:

- attitudes towards and observations of one's own personality (self), which include accurate observation of one's self-image, attitudes towards one's own personality (self), and an understanding of one's identity;
- growth, development and self-actualisation, where the level of development and the person's usefulness in a role are evaluated;
- integration, which refers to the individual's ability to assimilate and handle influences from the environment;
- autonomy, which implies the ability to act effectively by means of internal powers (needs, etc) without the unnecessary domination of external influences;
- the observation of reality, which implies the accurate assessment of the external environment in terms of internal psychological needs;
- interpersonal efficiency, which refers to the establishment of interpersonal relationships;
- affective conditions, which include emotional manifestations such as manic-depression, anxiety, fear, etc;
- specific pathological conditions, both physical and psychological, for instance schizophrenia, neuroses, brain syndromes, etc; and
- adjustment and adaptability – in other words, the person's ability to meet the demands of the environment in terms of his or her personal capabilities.

A complex web of potential factors may separately or in various combinations influence the state of OMH of an employee either positively or negatively. Before we briefly look at these, it is important to take note of certain types of psychological work-adjustment problems that may be encountered by employees in organisations.

Some psychopathological conditions relate to stress-based disorders; others to anxiety; some to personality disorders or to psychosomatic, narcotic and organic conditions; and still others to mental retardation.

Stress-related adjustment problems can, for instance, occur immediately or some time after a very traumatic experience such as a disaster, for example after an explosion in a factory or a rock slide in a mine. Emotional disorders such as fear, anger or depression may follow, which may in turn lead to poor concentration or absenteeism. On the other hand, neurotic conditions are characterised by internal emotional states such as anxiety, which can directly have a negative effect on work behaviour. As far as personality problems are concerned, it is important to note that some experts believe that general personality disorders need not affect the work personality (the work personality is the personality of a person in the work or production situation). Some people, for instance, have a negative perception of work and of their roles as employees – possibly because they were brought up in an environment where work was overemphasised to the extent that it could be equated to something akin to slavery. For some, work may arouse feelings of fear, discomfort or tenseness – for instance if they doubt their abilities or are handicapped.

Psychosomatic disorders refer to cases where physical symptoms and psychological states are closely interlinked. So, for instance, negative emotions such as anger, worry and anxiety can contribute to the formation of stomach ulcers. As soon as the physical symptoms are identified, the person begins to worry all over again.

Organic conditions refer to the negative emotional, intellectual and behavioural implications that brain damage can cause. When there is mental retardation due to underdeveloped intellectual functioning, behavioural problems may also arise in the workplace.

All these types of disorders may have effects that lead to problems such as absenteeism, accidents, underachievement, poor productivity and staff turnover. There are also other psychological work adjustment problems such as 'workaholism', burnout and work alienation.

Work alienation occurs when an employee has a feeling of being detached from his or her work, which seems to have lost its meaning and value. 'Workaholism', on the other hand, is a kind of addiction to work. The person's workload does not decrease at all and there is a compulsion to work continuously. Some may suffer from these symptoms because they have an intense need to be successful, while others may do so to withdraw from unpleasant domestic situations such as an unhappy marriage relationship. Burnout refers to the situation where a person eventually becomes listless, ineffective, inefficient and unproductive due to a prolonged period of work overload which has negatively impacted on the physical and mental health of the employee. Such an incapacity at work can in turn lead to stress, and behaviour such as an increased use of alcohol and increasing conflict with co-employees.

The potential spectrum of causes is wide, varied, complex and often interlinked. Some factors are unique to the individual (such as personality type, intellectual ability, needs, values, attitudes, self-image, occupational concepts and psychiatric problems such as psychotic or neurotic conditions). Sometimes the causes may form part of the work environment itself, for example certain managerial processes and practices (such as retrenchments or job design along the lines of Fordism and Taylorism) and physical factors (such as workload, toxic substances, working hours, temperatures, noise and physical dangers in the workplace). (Think, for example, of mines, and refer to the quotation earlier in this chapter.) Other factors that may play a role in psychological work adjustment can be categorised as being external to the employee or the organisation. These include aspects such as family life, traumatic external events such as war or major political change, ecological factors such as housing and pollution, and economic conditions such as a depression.

Irrespective of the actual problems or their underlying causes, it is essential for organisations to be aware of the importance of OMH. Organisations must strive continually to create a situation where the employees experience, as far as is possible, optimal states of OMH.

17.3.4.2 Stress and work

A topic that has been receiving increasing attention in the area of occupational health over time is that of work-related stress. As the world around us – and especially the world of work and business – has become increasingly subject to fast-changing forces (such as increased competition, the pressure for quality, innovation, and an increase in the pace of doing business), the demands on working people have grown equally dramatically. This creates stress within the people who must work smarter and harder, for longer hours and so forth.

Recent research in South Africa has found that stress and related psychological issues such as depression are increasingly contributing to work absenteeism. Johnny Johnson of CAM Solutions, a company doing research on workplace absenteeism, has said that in 2006 3,9% of all absenteeism cases were due to stress, depression and anxiety, and in 2007 these were the cause of 4,8% of all absenteeism cases (Ueckermann 2008: 1).

Stress and related issues are not only caused by the work itself, but also by aspects related to the peak-time traffic challenges experienced by many who travel to and from work in metropolitan areas that have traffic congestion problems (Ueckermann 2008). Other sources of stress may relate to personal factors such as relationships with others and the use of free time.

But what is stress?

Stress can be defined as the arousal of mind and body in response to an environmental demand (the stressors).

What is a stressor to one person may not be regarded as such by another, simply because people differ in the amount of arousal they need to act and the amount that they can take before the situation becomes personally distressing. Arousal patterns therefore differ from person to person. As human beings we require additional energy as soon as we have to face up to a particularly difficult and stressful situation (the stressor). Thus, as we think of all the things that we have to do (as we worry and plan), energy is released; sometimes, however, it becomes bound within us, building up in areas of the body, for example the neck and shoulders, and then we develop tension headaches and tensed shoulders. This can become even worse, leading to physical problems like ulcers, a lowering of the immune system and even heart problems. It is therefore essential to develop ways of managing stress. Smit and Venter (1996) propose a process approach to the management of stress. The first step is to identify the sources or causes of the stress by tracing whether any symptoms of stress are present. Exhibit 17.5 lists various symptoms of stress that one can use as a checklist to determine whether one suffers from stress.

EXHIBIT 17.5: Symptoms of stress

Mental symptoms	**Physical symptoms**
■ Feeling wound-up; anxious	■ Headaches
■ Worrying a lot	■ Spastic colon
■ Irritability	■ Indigestion
■ Easily frustrated	■ Ulcers
■ Aggressive outbursts	■ High blood pressure
■ Poor concentration	■ Palpitations
■ Forgetfulness	■ Hyperventilation
■ Depression	■ Asthma
■ Lack of fun in life	■ Stiff, sore muscles
■ Poor motivation	■ Trouble with sleeping
■ Wanting to be alone always	■ Change in appetite
■ Poor self-esteem	■ Change in sexual drive
■ Feeling out of control	■ Decreased immunity (easily ill)

Other symptoms
- ■ Increased smoking
- ■ Increased alcohol intake to try to cope better
- ■ Increased intake of medication to try to relieve stress-related symptoms

Source: Smit & Venter (1996: 11)

The next step is to assess whether the stress justifies the end result and whether one's health can sustain the stress. If it justifies the end result and one can sustain it, there is no need to change anything. If the response to either of these two is negative, then one needs to do something about it by working on eliminating the sources, and doing things deliberately to relieve the symptoms. This may include relaxation techniques, hobbies, shrugging off things that you cannot change or cope with, regular exercise, getting sufficient sleep and possibly eliciting help from outside, for example a psychologist, occupational therapist or an addiction clinic (in the case of substance dependence).

One aspect that has been proven to be closely related to stress levels is the personality type of an individual. Type A and type B personalities are relevant in this regard. Type A people have an intense drive to achieve, an eagerness to compete, the need to accelerate the execution of all physical and mental activities, an extraordinary mental and physical alertness and a persistent need for recognition, and are constantly involved in many things with deadlines. These people are prone to higher stress levels than type B people, who are basically the opposite.

Although stress management remains, at the end of the day, the responsibility of each individual employee, it is important for organisations to provide the necessary assistance and support.

17.3.4.3 Substance abuse and employee assistance

Employee assistance (EA) essentially concerns social services offered to troubled employees who need professional treatment for varying kinds of personal problems with which they cannot cope and which may have a potentially negative impact on their work performance and personal lives.

Historically, employee assistance has been linked to alcohol dependency. Other chemical dependencies today fall in the same category. It is well known that a chemically dependent employee can cost an organisation a lot of money, not to mention the negative effect it has on family and personal life. According to Fisher (1999: 10), a chemically dependent employee costs an organisation approximately 25% of his or her salary, in terms of aspects such as absenteeism and poor productivity. (Exhibit 17.6 reflects some research results about substance abuse in South African organisations.)

EXHIBIT 17.6: Drug trafficking, substance abuse and the South African workplace

According to a recent report, a byproduct of South Africa's transition from an apartheid to post-apartheid society has been an increased exposure to drug trafficking and its concomitant problems. (This is partly ascribed to aspects such as the reintroduction of the country into the world economy and an increase in tourism.) South Africa now, for instance, boasts a population of more than half a million cocaine addicts and has become a major trafficking centre for mandrax, heroin, LSD and cocaine. Marijuana and alcohol are the drugs of choice in the South African workplace. It has been found that up to 89% males and up to 77% females in South Africa drink alcoholic beverages, that 20% of psychiatric admissions to mine-based hospitals were for chemical dependency and that 72% of mine employees drink alcohol – with 44,5% of these indicating that they had lost the ability to control their drinking.

The high rate of alcohol consumption on South African mines also contributes to other health and psychosocial problems among mineworkers, such as enuresis and sexually transmitted diseases.

Source: Maiden (1999: 41–51)

As mentioned, employee assistance programmes (EAPs), as a health management intervention, have specific historical links with alcoholism rehabilitation. The scope of such programmes is, however, much broader nowadays. It covers treatment for all sorts of substance dependence, abuse or addiction, as well as therapy and counselling for personal problems such as marital problems, stress and depression, and financial problems.

Substance abuse and dependence can have ripple effects that impact negatively on various areas of people's lives. Alcoholism, for instance, causes a person to neglect his or her diet and in this way the nutritional value of food intake deteriorates, which can in turn destroy stress-coping skills, leading to more drinking. This eventually results in more stress and a deterioration of cognitive processes, emotional problems like depression, lack of motivation and aggression, a deterioration in personal affairs (for example family life), poor work performance and absence from work. Finally serious physical health problems and even death can result. It is generally widely recognised that alcoholism is a disease that needs professional treatment rather than condemnation. Employee assistance programmes specifically include alcoholism rehabilitation interventions.

As mentioned, however, EAPs are supposed to play a much more comprehensive role. Harper (1999: 1–2), however, says that "many South African companies have been reviewing and considering the role of Employee Assistance Programs... Although many programs have been implemented in South Africa, the essential success components have been varied ... [M]any companies appear to be unaware of the scope and role employee assistance programs ... can and should be playing in their organizations." Exhibit 17.7 reflects some research results on EAPs in South Africa.

EXHIBIT 17.7: EAPs in the top 100 South African companies

Harper (1999) researched the prevalence and scope of EAPs in South Africa's 'Top 100 Public Companies', across sectors such as mining, transport, engineering, retail, and food and beverage. Just over half (51 out of 93) of the responding companies do not have EAPs in any of their operations, with 42 having an EAP in at least one of their operations. Only 14 of these companies have EAPs in all their group's operations. The key focus seems to be on physical disease management through lifestyle change support programmes such as cholesterol control, smoking cessation and weight management. Says Harper (1999: 3):

> The low incidence of EAPs across the operations of the eligible top 100 companies reflects the lack of priority South African companies have given and are giving to mental, biopsycho-social health and psycho-social determinants of productivity and health utilization.

Source: Harper (1999: 1–3)

Managers should thus be very sensitive in respect of substance abuse by their subordinates. They are in an ideal position to play a proactive role in this regard. When there is any doubt, relevant experts should be approached, such as specialist EA staff, but great care must be taken regarding aspects pertaining to confidentiality and privacy.

An even more proactive approach to working towards employee wellness would be the inclusion in EA programmes of elements that are aimed at the not-so-troubled employees – those who abuse chemical substances such as alcohol from time to time but not to the extent that it may overtly impact negatively on work behaviour and performance. If such people are not helped in time, the situation may well become more serious. In this regard, educational interventions run by experts from inside or outside the organisation can be very helpful. In general, health awareness campaigns should also include substance abuse warnings.

Although EA programmes may require substantial amounts of money, this should be viewed as an investment with longer-term returns. However, from a management point of view it is important regularly to evaluate the quality of such programmes and to undertake cost-benefit analyses.

One aspect that requires consideration is whether to opt for the internal or external models of EA programmes. The internal model involves the employment of EA professional staff in the organisation. This may be more cost effective, but poses the problem of confidentiality, especially in the eyes of those who need to make use of the service, often causing them to shy away from using it. In the external model, use is made of professionals from outside the organisation. This may be more expensive, but aspects like credibility and confidentiality may be viewed more positively. Other factors which must be considered when a choice has to be made in this regard include things such as availability of expertise and the views or preferences of employees and unions. Naturally we must ensure that all of these services and programmes are monitored from a quality and value-adding perspective.

Regardless of which model is chosen, it is important – if one wants to create a caring environment – to provide one or another form of employee assistance. Management should make a policy decision in this regard and when the policy is formulated it is important to acknowledge that, at the end of the day, employees must also be willing to help themselves.

17.3.4.4 Occupational diseases, hazards, accidents and injuries

In practice it is often very difficult to distinguish between so-called occupational and non-occupational diseases. This is because the causal relationships between any person's ill health and hazards in his or her work or private life are very complex and interconnected. When we refer to an 'occupational disease', we essentially mean one that is caused purely or mainly by factors that are peculiar to the work environment and thus develop because of the work environment, even though the actual manifestation of the disease may arise some time after one has stopped working in that environment. In the Compensation for Occupational Injuries and Diseases Act 130 of 1993 (COIDA) it is stated that an occupational disease is any disease mentioned in the first column of schedule 3 of the Act, arising out of and contracted in the course of an employee's employment. Schedule 3 of the Act lists the relevant diseases in the first column and the work which gives rise to those diseases in the second one. It is specifically stated that, if a worker has performed any work involving the handling of or exposure to any of the listed substances in use in the workplace, and he or she contracts the corresponding occupational disease, it is presumed that the disease arose out of and in the course of that workers' employment – unless the contrary is proved.

Various occupational diseases can be identified, such as anthrax, occupational dermatitis, occupational asthma, tuberculosis of the lung, and hearing impairment. What is thus more important is to focus on the occupational hazards that may lead to occupational diseases.

Occupational hazards can cause harmful effects to employees in various ways, such as when certain hazardous substances are inhaled, swallowed or even absorbed through the skin. One can distinguish between various categories of occupational hazards, including chemical, mechanical, biological, physical and psychological hazards.

Chemical hazards include gases, vapours, fumes and dust. Mechanical hazards relate mainly to the overexposure of an employee to machine-related vibrations (for example turbines and pressure drills). Employees who work with other people and with animals can be exposed to biological hazards such as viral, bacterial or fungal infections. Physical hazards include exposure to radiation, sound and noise, lighting, extreme temperatures and abnormal atmospheric pressures. Psychological hazards relate directly to OMH, and may include aspects such as the risks and dangers involved in a particular job and the way in which work is designed (meaningfulness versus alienation, work overload and other factors that can cause work stress).

A CASE AT HAND

A Swiss-based company agreed to compensate several thousand people who became ill because of exposure to asbestos dust and fibres in Danielskuil and Kuruman in the Northern Cape. The Becan Group had no previous presence in South Africa, but it is liable to compensate the victims because it acquired Eternit, a company that had an indirect interest – through one of its subsidiaries – in the two towns' asbestos mines. The size of the grants payable to qualifying applicants would take into account loss of earnings, pain and suffering, and medical costs incurred or likely to be incurred by a victim.

Source: *Business Report*, 8 March 2006 (in Smit et al 2007)

Accidents and injuries

Workplace safety revolves around creating a work environment in which the chances for and effects of accidents and injuries are minimised and personal security maximised. Hattingh (1992: 33) defines an accident as "a sudden, uncontrollable, unplanned, undesirable happening which disrupts the normal functions of persons and causes or has the potential to produce or cause unintended injury, death or property damage and/or business interruption".

There are different types of accidents and injuries. Injuries that result from accidents occurring during the course of work can be minor (requiring only some first-aid treatment) or more serious (causing temporary total disablement). In extreme cases permanent disablement that may be partial, total or fatal may occur. Accidents can be officially classified as follows (Hattingh 1992: 34–35):

- being struck by falling objects;
- being caught in, on or between objects;
- stepping on, striking against or being struck by objects;
- falls from a different level (for example from a ladder);
- falls on the same level (for example slipping on a wet floor);
- electrical exposure or contact;
- strain, over-exertion or strenuous movements (pushing, pulling, picking up);
- exposure to or contact with harmful substances through inhalation, ingestion or absorption.

Accidents may be caused by various factors that revolve around unsafe conditions and/or unsafe behaviour or acts. Unsafe conditions can be caused by equipment deficiencies or inadequacies or by unsafe working environments. Unsafe behaviour and acts result from the human-error factor. Factors that can play a role include employee fatigue and boredom, employees' levels of experience, as well as certain social, psychological and physiological factors. Poor eyesight or hearing may lead to accidents, and so can certain attitudinal and emotional conditions. On the social side, alcohol usage is often linked to accidents and injuries. Measures to prevent unsafe acts, behaviour and conditions include:

- creating a safety infrastructure with control mechanisms and processes;
- establishing safety standards;
- planning and designing the work and workplace with safety in mind;
- installing safety committees and representatives;
- carrying out regular inspections to ensure that safety standards are adhered to;
- establishing who is accountable and responsible;
- training all employees to be safety conscious;
- ensuring that employees are aware of and alert to safety issues; and
- developing and running accident-prevention programmes.

To ensure the success of accident-prevention programmes, management must lead by example, creating safe, healthy working environments and conditions, and inculcating a culture of safe working habits and practices. This calls for management commitment (particularly in terms of resources) right from the top down to the lowest supervisory levels. It also requires the maintenance of day-to-day discipline, as well as a system of rewards and recognition for those who live by the policy of safety first.

17.3.4.5 Workplace bullying and sexual harassment

Stone (2002: 660) says that workplace bullying "includes persecuting or ganging up on an individual, making unreasonable demands or setting impossible work targets, making restrictive and petty work rules, constant intrusive surveillance, shouting, abusive language, physical assault and open or implied threats of dismissal or demotion". Nankervis et al (2008: 469) say that the most recent interpretations include "less favourable treatment of a person by another or others ... which may be considered unreasonable and inappropriate ... ranging from physical violence to degrading or humiliating language or actions". Workplace bullying can thus manifest in various situations and even develop into claims of constructive dismissal or unfair labour practice.

Sexual harassment, on the other hand, may include unwanted physical contact; indecent sexual comments, language or references; making unwelcome sexual advances to fellow employees; and even the display of sexual material. Sexual harassment is unlawful in South Africa, and the Employment Equity Act deals with the topic. Nel et al (2008: 319) say that in "recent years, various court cases have declared sexual harassment a serious workplace problem. In one such case, the employee was awarded R82 000 ... for ... medical expenses, pain, suffering and impairment of her dignity". It is important that organisations have policies that clearly prohibit any such negative behaviour and should there be any case reported, it should be dealt with promptly and firmly.

17.3.4.6 People with disabilities

In terms of the Employment Equity Act, 'people with disabilities' means those who have a long-term or recurring physical or mental impairment which substantially limits their prospects of entry into, or advancement in, employment. The Act places a duty on designated employers to provide reasonable accommodation for people with disabilities, such as modifying or adjusting a job or the working environment that will enable them to have access to, participate in or advance in employment, in order to ensure that they enjoy equal opportunities and are equitably represented in the workforce of a designated employer. What is 'reasonable accommodation' will be determined by the size and resources of the employer, the nature of the job, and the nature and degree of the disability in question.

17.3.4.7 Working time and well-being

The arrangement of working time may have a direct impact on the health and safety of employees. This is especially true in the case of night work and shift work. In recognition of this fact, a code of good practice on the arrangement of working time has been issued under the Basic Conditions of Employment Act. The objective of this code is to provide information and guidelines to employers and employees concerning the arrangement of working time and its impact on the health, safety and family responsibilities of employees.

In some of South Africa's metropolitan areas, like particularly the greater Johannesburg and Pretoria surroundings, traffic congestion during peak hours (mornings and late afternoons), creates serious travel-related challenges (which can cause a lot of stress, as mentioned). This can be addressed, for instance, by allowing for some flexitime arrangements (Ueckermann 2008). In addition, more-flexible working time might allow working people to manage their personal lives better, perhaps including better possibilities for spending quality time with family around the breakfast table or perhaps for devoting time to health and fitness such as going to the gym before work in the mornings.

17.3.4.8 Pregnant and post-natal employees

Keeping in mind that there is a duty on employers not to discriminate against women on the basis of pregnancy (which includes intended pregnancy, termination of pregnancy and any medical circumstances related to pregnancy) as well as a duty to provide a safe working environment, a code of good practice on the protection of employees during pregnancy and after the birth of a child was issued under the Basic Conditions of Employment Act. The objective of this code is to provide guidelines for employers and employees concerning the protection of the health of women against potential hazards in their work environment during pregnancy, after the birth of a child and while breastfeeding.

17.3.4.9 Tuberculosis

Tuberculosis is a big problem internationally, with about two million people dying from the disease every year. Caelers (2008: 1) says that if "TB is not yet top priority, getting started on interventions is definitely overdue, considering the disease is a heavy burden on business, disrupting workflow, reducing productivity, and pushing up both direct and indirect costs ... According to our Health Department, a TB patient here can lose an average three to four months of work time". The disease can thus have serious implications – but these naturally extend way beyond the place of work, and a genuine attitude of care will thus lead to showing concern for social implications as well. Certain parts of the community tend to show higher prevalence rates and, due to social disruption and loss of income, these can place a heavy burden even on whole communities. As Caelers (2008: 1) explains: "In high-prevalence settings – and the Western Cape is certainly one – TB is a major contributor to ill health and poverty in communities which are in turn a source of workers, services, contractors and business."

Organisations can and should thus engage actively and help to manage the TB problem proactively. Carol O'Brien, vice-president of the Global Business Coalition on HIV/Aids, TB and Malaria says that "no one should die from TB, which is both preventable and treatable", and she adds that we should actually "increase our efforts hundredfold to educate and empower people on how to prevent infection, and teach those who are infected with TB how to manage it" (Caelers 2008: 1).

In South Africa where HIV/AIDS is so rife it may be a good idea to link HIV programmes and TB interventions because these two diseases are linked. We now turn to HIV/AIDS as an issue that deserves separate discussion.

17.4 THE HIV/AIDS CHALLENGE

It has been estimated that globally there were about 33 million people living with HIV in 2007, about two-thirds of whom were living in sub-Saharan Africa (UNAIDS 2008). The same region accounted for about 72% of all the Aids-related deaths in the world (UNAIDS 2008). South Africa has about 5,7 million people living with HIV, and it is predicted that this will grow to more than six million by 2015, by which time we would have had about five and a half million South African people died of Aids (see section 17.4.1 below).

Initially former President Thabo Mbeki questioned the link between HIV and AIDS, arguing that a syndrome cannot be caused by a virus. He also questioned HIV infection and Aids-related mortality statistics, referring to some racist thinking (about aspects like black African sexuality and rape) possibly being behind notions about the Aids epidemic. After considerable pressure, Cabinet ultimately agreed in 2002 to make antiretroviral (ARV) therapy available to rape survivors, and by late 2003 it was announced that a comprehensive Aids treatment plan (that would include free ARV therapy) would be rolled out in the country. The government now has a strategic plan to address HIV/Aids and STDs (sexually transmitted diseases) in our country, and it includes a focus on work to prevent, treat and provide care and support for people affected by HIV/Aids, as well as research and monitoring work together with work on addressing the human-rights implications of the disease.

Sadly, the general population's perception of HIV/Aids still seems to be informed by prejudice, stigmatisation and ignorance, rather than scientific fact and sober reflection. The social reality presented by the disease is almost as intractable as the disease itself and places a heavy burden on our managers first to inform themselves and then to educate our other workers about the disease.

HIV/Aids is a disease that goes through different stages, ultimately destroying the human body's ability to defend itself against the daily onslaught from illnesses of which a healthy individual is largely unaware. These illnesses, which are caused by the body's inability to defend itself against germs and viral infections, are also referred to as Aids-related complexes (ARCs). A carrier of HIV may look healthy until an illness (which other people can generally fight off) suddenly causes them to fall fatally ill. This is due to the fact that HIV gradually disables the immune system, resulting in the infected person becoming increasingly vulnerable to almost any infection by another virus, bacterium, fungus or parasite. These opportunistic infections mainly tend to occur in the skin, the lungs, the digestive system, the nervous system and the brain. The final stage of the disease is what is referred to as 'full-blown Aids'. At this stage, major life-threatening infections invade the body, and sufferers are likely to experience various Aids-related diseases, which will vary from patient to patient. Some might experience pneumonia caused by a parasitic *pneumocystis carinii*; others might experience a cancer affecting the skin called *kaposi sarcoma*; yet others might experience diarrhoea, also referred to as the 'slim disease', which causes the sufferer to become extremely thin and grossly fatigued. At the final stage the patient would typically suffer multiple infections such as shingles, thrush, herpes and tuberculosis. Full-blown Aids is always fatal, and sufferers tend to live no longer than three or four years after having been diagnosed.

17.4.1 Magnitude of the HIV/Aids problem

Although the focus of this chapter is mainly on what organisations can do to enhance the well-being of people at work, the fact of the matter is that any country that has people living with HIV (and/or full-blown Aids) naturally has a supply of human resources that can bring the implications of the disease into the place of work. In any event, as you know by now, it is our view that the call for 'corporate citizenship' requires all organisations to look beyond the 'labour' they need, and add value to society more generally (beyond the 'goods' they deliver). Because HIV/Aids is such a huge challenge in South Africa (and in Africa), we believe organisations should help to tackle it – as many already do.

Aids and HIV infection is a major problem in Africa and especially in sub-Saharan Africa (see Table 17.1). An estimated 22 million adults and children were living with HIV in sub-Saharan Africa at the end of 2007, a year during which an estimated 1,5 million Africans would have died from the disease (UNAIDS 2008). The HIV/Aids epidemic has thus far orphaned more than 11,5 million African children.

Table 17.1 reflects some statistics about individual countries in sub-Saharan Africa at the end of 2007 – such as the estimated number of adults (and children) living with HIV/Aids, the number of deaths from Aids, and the number of orphans due to Aids.

Rob Noble investigated various research studies about HIV/Aids in South Africa and comes to the conclusions as reflected in exhibit 17.8, saying that what "is clear from every study is that there is an exceptionally severe epidemic of HIV/Aids in South Africa".

EXHIBIT 17.8: Conclusions about various research studies on HIV/Aids in South Africa

In such a large and diverse country as South Africa, no-one can know exactly what the true figures are. What is essential is that the limitations of each study are acknowledged whenever their results are interpreted ... UNAIDS and WHO recommend that antenatal and population-based studies should both be conducted at regular intervals. In countries with generalised epidemics, antenatal clinic attendees are thought to represent the adult population with good accuracy. Moreover, when conducted regularly such surveys can reveal long-term trends in prevalence. On the other hand, household surveys tell us more about the nature of the epidemic by providing prevalence data according to gender, race, wealth and other characteristics. Such information informs better interpretation of antenatal data ... Based on a wide range of data, including the household and antenatal studies, UNAIDS/WHO in July 2008 published an estimate of 18.1% prevalence in those aged 15–49 years old at the end of 2007. Their high and low estimates are 15.4% and 20.9% respectively. According to their own estimate of total population ... this implies that around 5.7 million South Africans were living with HIV at the end of 2007, including 280 000 children under 15 years old ... The ASSA 2003 model produces a similar estimate of 5.4 million people living with HIV in mid-2006 ... It predicts that the number will exceed 6 million by 2015, by which time around 5.4 million South Africans will have died of AIDS ... What is clear from every study is that there is an exceptionally severe epidemic of HIV/AIDS in South Africa. This epidemic affects all parts of the population, though women are more likely to be infected than men. Many tens of thousands of people are dying. For South Africa there are tremendous challenges remaining in the fields of HIV education, prevention and care.

Source: Noble (http://www.avert.org/safricastats.htm)

Table 17.1: Some HIV/aids statistics in individual countries in sub-Saharan Africa at the end of 2007

Country	People living with HIV/Aids	Adult (15–49) rate %	Women with HIV/ Aids	Children with HIV/ Aids	Aids deaths	Orphans due to Aids
Angola	190 000	2,1	110 000	17 000	11 000	50 000
Benin	64 000	1,2	37 000	5 400	3 300	29 000
Botswana	300 000	23,9	170 000	15 000	11 000	95 000
Burkina Faso	130 000	1,6	61 000	10 000	9 200	100 000
Burundi	110 000	2,0	53 000	15 000	11 000	120 000
Cameroon	540 000	5,1	300 000	45 000	39 000	300 000
Central African Republic	160 000	6,3	91 000	14 000	11 000	72 000
Chad	200 000	3,5	110 000	19 000	14 000	85 000
Comoros	<200	<0,1	<100	<100	<100	<100
Congo	120 000	3,5	43 000	6 600	6 400	69 000
Côte d'Ivoire	480 000	3,9	250 000	52 000	38 000	420 000
Dem. Republic of Congo	400 000- 500 000	1,2–1,5	210 000– 270 000	37 000– 52 000	24 000– 34 000	270 000– 380 000
Djibouti	16 000	3,1	8 700	1 100	1 100	5 200
Equatorial Guinea	11 000	3,4	5 900	<1 000	<1 000	4 800
Eritrea	38 000	1,3	21 000	3 100	2 600	18 000
Ethiopia	980 000	2,1	530 000	92 000	67 000	650 000
Gabon	49 000	5,9	27 000	2 300	2 300	18 000
Gambia	8 200	0,9	4 500	<1 000	<1 000	2 700
Ghana	260 000	1,9	150 000	17 000	21 000	160 000
Guinea	87 000	1,6	48 000	6 300	4 500	25 000
Guinea-Bissau	16 000	1,8	8 700	1 500	1 100	6 200
Kenya	1 500 000– 2 000 000	7,1–8,5	800 000– 1 100 000	130 000– 180 000	85 000– 130 000	990 000– 1 400 000
Lesotho	270 000	23,2	150 000	12 000	18 000	110 000
Liberia	35 000	1,7	19 000	3 100	2 300	15 000
Madagascar	14 000	0,1	3 400	<500	<1 000	3 400
Malawi	930 000	11,9	490 000	91 000	68 000	560 000

>>

Mali	100 000	1,5	56 000	9 400	5 800	44 000
Mauritania	14 000	0,8	3 900	<500	<1 000	3 000
Mauritius	13 000	1,7	3 800	<100	<1 000	<500
Mozambique	1 500 000	12,5	810 000	100 000	81 000	400 000
Namibia	200 000	15,3	110 000	14 000	5 100	66 000
Niger	60 000	0,8	17 000	3 200	4 000	25 000
Nigeria	2 600 000	3,1	1 400 000	220 000	170 000	1 200 000
Rwanda	150 000	2,8	78 000	19 000	7 800	220 000
Senegal	67 000	1,0	38 000	3 100	1 800	8 400
Sierra Leone	55 000	1,7	30 000	4 000	3 300	16 000
Somalia	24 000	0,5	6 700	<1 000	1 600	8 800
South Africa	5 700 000	18,1	3 200 000	280 000	350 000	1 400 000
Swaziland	190 000	26,1	100 000	15 000	10 000	56 000
Togo	130 000	3,3	69 000	10 000	9 100	68 000
Uganda	1 000 000	6,7	520 000	110 000	91 000	1 000 000
United Rep. Of Tanzania	940 000	5,4	480 000	130 000	77 000	1 200 000
Zambia	1 100 000	15,2	560 000	95 000	56 000	600 000
Zimbabwe	1 300 000	15,3	680 000	120 000	140 000	1 000 000
Total sub-Saharan Africa	22 000 000	5,0	12 000 000	1 800 000	1 500 000	11 600 000

Notes: Adults in this table are defined as men and women aged over 15, unless specified otherwise. Children are defined as people under the age of 15, whilst orphans are people aged under 18 who have lost one or both parents to AIDS.
Source: UNAIDS (2008)

17.4.2 Countering the threat of Aids

No cure or vaccination has been developed for HIV. The most promising treatment regime so far is a cocktail of drugs that attacks the virus on multiple fronts. Experimentation with this approach was first made public in 1996 and holds out the promise that, although it is not a cure, it can arrest the increase of the virus in the body, thereby raising the T-cell count to acceptable levels. This treatment changes the status of the disease from being a fatal to a chronic disease. Over the past decade, the costs of antiretroviral drugs have fallen dramatically but even these are beyond the means of many South Africans, and Africans beyond our borders even more so. Given the absence of a cure or a vaccination or affordable medication to arrest the fatal progression of the disease, as well as the nature of the disease and the lack of understanding and knowledge about it among the general population, educating people about the disease is, in the absence of a medical breakthrough, the best way of containing it. Since the major cause of transmission of the disease is through voluntary conduct, behaviour modification on a large scale, if this could be achieved, would be very efficient in reducing the threat of Aids. For example, abstaining from casual sex or taking precautions when engaging in sexual encounters (by insisting on the use of a condom) or by distributing free needles to drug users or assisting drug users to rehabilitate, could go a long way in countering the spread of the disease. In this, employers can play an important role by sponsoring Aids-awareness programmes, by training employees how to avoid becoming infected and by emphasising the low risk of contracting the disease from a co-worker. Resources expended in this manner would be justified not only by altruistic motives, but, given the speed with which the disease spreads, enlightened employers could also save themselves huge amounts in increased medical aid contributions and the costs associated with replacing experienced employees. It should be remembered that the people most at risk are those who are in the most productive phase of their lives.

17.4.3 South African organisations' reaction to the HIV/Aids challenge

The impact of the disease in organisations manifest in many ways, including a loss of productivity as a result of employees absenting themselves from work for treatment. There are increases in the cost of medical aid and pension schemes as well. Employers thus have to engage in managing this challenge actively, as many already do (see MTN example in "A case at hand" below). According to the AIDS Foundation South Africa (2005):

> The business sector, particularly the mining industry, started to recognise the potential impact of HIV/AIDS on profits and the wider economy from the mid-1980s. Since HIV/AIDS was striking the economically active age group, companies started seeing reduced productivity, absenteeism, sickness and then deaths among the workforce. Many employers initiated workplace awareness and education programmes to help prevent the spread of HIV. However, as the infection rate increased and employee sickness and death affected profits coming in and benefits being paid out, companies started to look at how they could minimise their losses and meet the needs of infected workers. The larger corporates, such as Anglo American, soon recognised that, in addition to humanitarian and human rights considerations, it made economic sense to invest in maintaining the health and productivity of infected workers rather than waiting until they became too sick to work and then paying out death benefits, and recruiting and training new staff as more and more employees died without access to treatment. So more and more large companies have started workplace treatment programmes. Since 2002, Anglo American, for example, has incorporated into its HIV/AIDS programme free ARV treatment for all employees who need it, and sees this as an important incentive for workers to find out their HIV status. All employees who test positive are enrolled into a wellness programme to ensure ongoing support and monitoring. The company had nearly 2 500 employees on treatment by the end of 2004 and reported that 94% of them were able to carry out normal work. That year, it was costing the company more than R16 000 per patient per year to keep employees on treatment (including all the drug, laboratory, infrastructure, training and support costs). This is seen as a sound investment compared to the financial and human cost of employees becoming sick and dying. Anglo American has identified several areas where it wants to improve the effectiveness of the programme but, along with other major employers, its experience is starting to provide important

models for workplace treatment and for public/private/community partnerships in the fight against AIDS.

A CASE AT HAND

MTN and HIV/Aids

MTN South Africa continues to sponsor the national television programme, *Beat It*, launched in association with the SABC in 2005. The programme deals primarily with HIV/AIDS-related themes. Estimated viewership has increased from 350 000 in 2005 to 11,5 million in 2006.

Source: http://www.mtn.com/mtn.group.web/sustainability/social.asp

17.4.4 Discrimination against HIV/Aids sufferers

Despite the steps being taken to protect HIV/Aids-infected employees, research has shown that, in the face of pressure from co-workers, a third of the organisations will discriminate against the infected employee. The problem is exacerbated by the fact that no distinction is drawn between those employees who have tested HIV positive and those who have full-blown Aids. The difference is based on the fact that the former could still be alive and well for the next five to 15 years. Discrimination against infected employees, whether it be because of HIV or Aids, places them at a disadvantage. The significance of this has been highlighted in various articles written on the subject, both in South Africa and US.

Discrimination against employees who are HIV/Aids infected can take various forms, for example:

- compulsory medical screening at pre-employment level and of employees at any stage of employment;
- denial of employment to potential employees who admit to being HIV positive;
- disciplining of employees who inform their employers that they have Aids;
- demotion or transfer of employees who test HIV positive or who admit to having Aids;
- workers forcing their employer to have an employee tested because he or she is suspected of suffering from Aids;
- the testing of foreigners who enter the country to seek employment;
- suspension with salary of HIV-infected employees;
- variation of the conditions of employment (for example changing the area of work); and
- dismissal.

Exhibit 17.9 contains an example of a case involving South African Airways and the 'Elsewhere in Africa' box reflects a Namibian example. In both these cases, job applicants successfully challenged the prospective employer's refusal to offer them employment because of their HIV status.

Except in a few situations in which discrimination may be justified (for example an HIV-positive healthcare worker), there can be no justification for discrimination in the workplace. Many eminent writers on the subject have condemned the practice of discrimination in the workplace because, at present, medical consensus is that HIV is transmissible essentially through body fluids: that is, blood or semen. The prime risk is for the virus to be transmitted from an HIV-positive person to another person during

This case is about the right of persons living with HIV/AIDS not to be discriminated against when applying for employment. The case is particularly important because of the high incidence of HIV/AIDS on the African continent. It is reported that sub-Saharan Africa accounts for over 70% of the world-wide incidence of HIV/AIDS.

With the potential problems of dealing with workers living with HIV/AIDS in terms of chronic illness resulting in absenteeism and low productivity, it is not surprising that employers should be reluctant to employ HIV-positive applicants and tend to exclude such applicants through pre-employment testing for HIV/AIDS. This case, however, emphasises that access to employment for HIV-positive persons is a matter of human rights, in particular the right not to be discriminated against unfairly and the right to human dignity. It should be instructive for other jurisdictions in Africa and elsewhere.

Hoffmann applied for a position with South African Airways (SAA) as a cabin attendant. He was one of 173 applicants. He successfully went through a four-stage selection process and found himself among 12 applicants found suitable for employment. The decision on suitability was, however, subject to a pre-employment medical examination, including a blood test for HIV/AIDS. The medical examination found him fit and therefore suitable for employment. However, the blood test indicated that Hoffmann was HIV-positive. The medical report was then altered to say that he was HIV positive and therefore "unsuitable" for employment. He was informed that he could not be employed as a cabin attendant as he was HIV positive.

Hoffman challenged the decision not to employ him in the High Court on the ground that the refusal was unconstitutional as it constituted unfair discrimination and infringed his rights to equality, human dignity and fair labour practices. He sought an order directing SAA to employ him as a flight attendant. SAA defended its decision on medical, safety and operational grounds. It claimed that its flight crew had to be fit for world-wide duty and had to be vaccinated against yellow fever as they may be required to fly in yellow-fever endemic countries. It argued that HIV-positive persons may react negatively to the vaccination and therefore may not be vaccinated. Without such vaccination, however, they run the risk of contracting yellow-fever and spreading it to fellow crew and to passengers. HIV-positive persons would also be prone to contracting opportunistic diseases such as tuberculosis and chronic diarrhoea and could spread them to other flight crew and passengers.

Moreover, flight attendants suffering from opportunistic diseases would not perform their duties properly, especially in emergencies. SAA also offered an economic reason for exclusion. The life expectancy of HIV-positive persons was too short to justify the costs of training them. SAA further justified its action on the basis that other major airlines had similar employment practices.

The High Court agreed with SAA's arguments and dismissed the application. It held that the exclusion was based on "medical, safety and operational grounds" and was "aimed at achieving a worthy and important societal goal". It further held that "it is an inherent requirement for a flight attendant, at least for the moment, to be HIV-negative". The High Court concluded that the practice of denying employment to HIV-positive applicants did not amount to unfair discrimination.

Hoffmann appealed to the Constitutional Court. The court found medical evidence, including that tendered by SAA's expert, to be at variance with SAA's claim that Hoffmann would be a medical and safety risk. The evidence showed that only HIV-positive persons whose immune system had deteriorated to the immunosuppressed stage and whose CD4 + count had dropped to below 350 per microlitre of blood would not be safely vaccinated against yellow fever.

Further, HIV-positive persons who had not reached that stage were not susceptible to secondary infections. The evidence also showed that modern medical treatment dramatically altered the progression of the HIV infection and that the treatment was capable of completely suppressing the replication of the virus and the person's immune system could recover. At a meeting of a number of experts, including the SAA expert, it was agreed that "with the advent of the [HAART] treatment, individuals are capable of living normal lives and they can perform any employment tasks for which they are otherwise qualified". The medical experts concluded: "on medical grounds alone exclusion of an HIV-positive individual from employment solely on the basis of HIV positivity cannot be justified".

>>

<<
The Constitutional Court held on the basis of its previous decisions that SAA's conduct amounted to unfair discrimination contrary to section 9 of the Constitution. Although section 9(3) does not list HIV/AIDS status as a prohibited ground of discrimination, it is now recognised as a ground analogous to those listed. The determining factor for finding conduct to be unfair discrimination is its impact on the victim. The conduct should adversely impact on the victim's dignity or affect him/her in a comparably serious manner. Ngcobo J, for a unanimous court, held that the denial of employment to Hoffmann because he was HIV positive had impaired his dignity and constituted unfair discrimination and violated his right to equality. The court observed that the discrimination was not based on a legitimate purpose but rather on prejudice against persons living with HIV. Although legitimate commercial requirements were an important consideration in determining whether to employ a person, "we must guard against allowing stereotyping and prejudice to creep in under the guise of commercial interest. The greater interests of society require the recognition of the inherent dignity of every human being and the elimination of all forms of discrimination". Justice Ngcobo further admonished: "People who are living with HIV must be treated with compassion and understanding. We must show ubuntu towards them. They must not be condemned to (economic death) by the denial of equal opportunity in employment".

Having found that Hoffmann had been unfairly discriminated against, the court reversed the decision of the High Court and ordered SAA to employ him with effect from the date of the judgement of the Constitutional Court.

The lesson of this case is that the decision to employ or not to employ a person living with HIV should depend on the medical condition of the particular applicant. No consideration should be given to the perceptions and prejudices of members of the public regarding persons with HIV.

Source: Excerpted from Rugege (2001: 237–241)

either homosexual or heterosexual intercourse, or when an abrasion or excoriation occurs with resultant exposure of capillaries or cells, involving also the factor of mucosal spread. Blood transfusions pose a threat if the blood or equipment used for the transfusion is contaminated.

Based on the above, none of the ways in which infection takes place is directly connected with most work situations as such, or with the social and occupational contact which employees ordinarily have with each other in the workplace. In exceptional cases there may be a relatively minor risk of infection in the work situation. One such situation is in the operating theatre if a doctor fails to take the necessary precaution of wearing surgical gloves, and accidentally cuts himself with a scalpel while operating on an HIV-infected individual. Consequently, the spread of HIV at the workplace is very unlikely. This, however, will not guarantee an Aids-free workplace, since, judging from the statistics, one or more employees will be infected sooner or later, forcing management to face the question of how to deal with HIV-positive employees.

Elsewhere in Africa

A case in Namibia also involved the denial of employment to a person who was HIV positive. The applicant in this case, a former SWAPO combatant in the struggle for the liberation of Namibia applied to be enlisted in the Namibian Defence Force (NDF). As part of the application process, he was required to undergo a medical examination, including a blood test to test for HIV. The NDF doctor who examined the applicant found him to be HIV positive and informed him that because he was HIV positive he would not be accepted by the NDF.

About one month after he tested HIV positive, the applicant underwent a medical examination (described by the court as a "thorough clinical examination") by a medical officer of the state, who found him to be in good and sound health. The medical report included a question to the doctor whether he considered the applicant to be in good health and free from any physical or mental defect, disease or infirmity which was likely to interfere with the proper performance of duty as a government official in any part of Namibia. The medical officer replied in the affirmative.

The applicant approached the Namibian Labour Court alleging that he was refused enlistment into the NDF on the sole ground that he was HIV positive, which, he argued, constituted unfair discrimination as envisaged in section 107 of the Labour Act 6 of 1992. Alternatively, he averred that he was discriminated against on the impermissible ground of disability in conflict with section 107 of the Labour Act 6 of 1992.

He sought an order directing the respondent to discontinue discriminating against him and directing the respondent to process the applicant's application for enlistment in the NDF.

On the basis of the medical report, the court held that the applicant was, at the time of his application, in good health and fit to carry out any duties assigned to him and that the sole and only reason for refusing to enlist him into the NDF was his HIV status.

The court proceeded to inquire whether the respondent was justified in refusing to enlist the applicant in the NDF. It referred to section 107 (1) of the Labour Act, which provided for a remedy where "any person has been discriminated or is about to discriminate in an unfair manner or so discriminating against him on the grounds of his ... disability, in relation to his employment".

The court relied on the evidence of medical experts of both litigants and found that a person who is HIV positive is not necessarily either ill or unable to perform the normal functions required in the Defence Force. The experts agreed that in order for such a person to be susceptible to opportunistic infections or to be unable to perform normal duties, his or her CD4 + count (indicating the number of defensive white blood cells per cubic millilitre of blood) had to have fallen below 200 and the presence of the virus in the body (the viral load) had to be above 100 000. In the case of applicant, no tests had been done to determine the CD4 + count or the viral load. Moreover, it was admitted by the respondent's employees that there were people living with HIV/AIDS in the Namibian Defence Force and that facilities existed for their treatment and mechanisms existed for redeploying them to less demanding departments within the NDF when the need arose.

The court came to the conclusion that the exclusion of the applicant from the military, solely because he was HIV positive, constituted, at the time of his application for enlistment, discrimination in an unfair manner in breach of section 107 of the Labour Act. However, because the tests had been made four years before the hearing, the court felt it was not proper to order immediate enlistment since the applicant's condition could have deteriorated in the four years. On the other hand, medical evidence had shown that a person who is found to be HIV positive could be fit and healthy for several years. The court decided that the appropriate remedy was to order enlistment subject to applicant undergoing a CD4 + test and a viral load test. Consequently, the court ordered the respondent to enlist the applicant in the NDF should the applicant reapply for enlistment, provided his CD4 + count was not below 200 and his viral load not above 100 000. As a general practice, the court ordered that medical examinations which applicants into the NDF are required to undergo should include an HIV test together with a CD4 + count test and a viral load test and that no applicant should be denied enlistment solely on the basis of the person's HIV status unless his/her CD4 + count is below 200 and viral load above 100 000.

It should be noted that, unlike Hoffmann, the applicant did not rely on the equality clause in the Constitution to have the discrimination declared unconstitutional. Article 10 of the Namibian constitution is narrower than its South African counterpart. It states that "(1) All Persons shall be equal before the law; (2) No person may be discriminated against on the grounds of sex, race, colour, ethnic origin, religion, creed or social or economic status". Although HIV status is not mentioned in section 9 of the South African Constitution, HIV has now been recognised by the constitutional court via Hoffmann as a prohibited ground of discrimination analogous to the listed grounds.

Source: Excerpted from Rugege (2001: 237–241)

MTN and HIV/Aids in Nigeria

In Nigeria, MTN formally launched the first of its six targeted HIV/AIDS voluntary counseling and testing (VCT) centres in April 2006. Situated in Kogi State, the VCT centre was built, equipped and donated as part of the MTN foundation's focus on healthcare related community programmes. The centre offers pre- and post-test HIV counseling, care and support. More than 500 in-school youth have received training as peer educators in the programme. The centre aims to provide education and services to pregnant women relating to prevention of mother-to-child transmission. More than 250 people have received counseling since the opening of the first VCT centre.

Source: http://www.mtn.com/mtn.group.web/sustainability/social.asp

17.4.5 Protection of employees who are HIV positive

In terms of section 6 of the Employment Equity Act (also see chapter 3), unfair discrimination against an employee or the harassment of that employee due to his or her HIV status is explicitly prohibited. Should such an employee be dismissed because of his or her HIV status or be forced to resign because of being HIV positive (the so-called 'constructive dismissal' scenario – see chapter 20), such a dismissal would also automatically be an unfair dismissal in terms of the Labour Relations Act. Likewise, the unfair treatment of an employee or job applicant because of his or her HIV status would in all likelihood be categorised as unfair.

In addition, as you already know, medical testing is made subject to very stringent requirements in the Employment Equity Act, which will make it more difficult for an employer to justify the testing of employees or job applicants for their HIV status. As usual, in cases where the nature of the job is such that an unacceptable risk will ensue if the job incumbent were to be HIV positive, the escape clause could be used by an employer to show that the discrimination against an HIV-positive person amounted to fair discrimination.

17.4.6 Dismissal of employees due to their HIV/AIDS status

Although dismissal is dealt with in detail in chapter 20, a brief explanation of those aspects relevant to HIV/Aids is essential here. All employees have the right not to be unfairly dismissed (section 185 of the Labour Relations Act of 1995). This principle does not allow for any exceptions and is equally applicable to the individual who has Aids or who is HIV positive.

As will be seen in chapter 20, one may terminate the services of an employee only if it can be justified on the basis of the employee's conduct or capacity, or for reasons relating to the operational requirements of the organisation. Failure on the part of the employer to justify the dismissal in terms of one of these grounds will render it unfair. Furthermore, should the dismissal be regarded as discriminatory, it will amount to an "automatically unfair dismissal" in terms of section 187 of the Labour Relations Act. The same principles apply in the case of the employee who suffers from Aids or who is HIV positive. In dismissal cases it is especially important for employers to distinguish between the case of the employee who is in the latter stages of the disease (that is, who is suffering from full-blown Aids) and the employee who is HIV positive (that is, who is a carrier of the disease but who does not present any symptoms). In the former case dismissal may be justifiable on the basis of the person's inability to perform his or her duties (as is the case with any employees suffering from a debilitating disease rendering them incapable of doing their job). In the latter case it may be more difficult to justify the dismissal and to evade the charge of unfair discrimination, since the employee would normally then still be perfectly capable of performing his or her duties. In the following paragraphs, the dismissal of infected employees on the basis of one of the three grounds that may be offered as justification is examined in greater detail.

1 (Mis)conduct

This justification would in most instances not be available to the employer. The mere fact of having contracted the disease would obviously not constitute misconduct. Conceivably, an infected employee who knowingly and wilfully exposes a co-worker or customer of the employer to infection could fall under this category.

2 (In)capacity

An investigation into the employee's alleged incapacity is required, and should be done by conducting a fair hearing. During this investigation, certain factors may be taken into account, such as the experience of an employee or the type of work concerned. However, when it is evident that an employee has become incapable of doing the work properly, his or her long-service record as such will be to no avail. It should also be established whether the employee's particular disability, such as poor eyesight, could create a dangerous situation for co-workers (or, for that matter, for anybody else) (Brassey, Cameron, Cheadle & Olivier 1987: 445). The fact that Aids is communicable is irrelevant, because, according to the current knowledge of the aetiology of the disease, there is virtually no risk of communication of the disease in the work situation. What would clearly be decisive would be the degree to which the disease itself, or a secondary condition caused by it, makes the employee unfit to do the required job (which may be manifested by factors such as absenteeism, debility, lack of concentration, confusion and general unproductiveness). When the employee's incapability has indeed been proved (or admitted), alternative employment (and not dismissal) should be considered, and the employer should consult with the employee in this regard (Brassey et al 1987: 446). Because the condition of a person with Aids may deteriorate rapidly (in the last stage the body's defences collapse, and bacterial and viral infections which are normally harmless become life threatening), it would seem that the possibility of alternative employment may often not be feasible.

3 Operational reasons

Under this heading the so-called commercial rationale for dismissal may be put forward. What this justification amounts to is that the employee's continued presence in the employer's workforce frustrates the employer's legitimate objective of being in business to make a profit. A dismissal for being HIV positive may be fair, provided that it can be shown that the news of an employee's HIV-positive status is the direct and only cause of an appreciable decline in business, and all alternatives to the dismissal of the employee have been exhausted (Cameron 1992: 3). It should be cautioned, however, that the commercial rationale as a justification for dismissal is a very tenuous one and may well be found to be unfair, unless the employer has done whatever could reasonably be expected to remedy the situation, short of resorting to the dismissal of the employee. The same applies where co-workers of an infected individual refuse to work with him or her. To dismiss the infected person would most definitely be unfair, unless it is resorted to as a measure of absolute last resort.

17.4.7 HIV/Aids and pre-employment testing

As justification for testing, organisations have argued that an organisation requires a healthy workforce which will be productive and not result in a high labour turnover.

HIV-infected people have been seen as a high risk. This argument is irrelevant, since organisations do not test for any other life-threatening diseases in particular. Furthermore, available statistics clearly show that more and more people could become infected with the disease while being employed, making an HIV/Aids-free work environment virtually impossible.

Another reason why pre-employment testing is unjustifiable is that the way in which the disease is identified does not clearly indicate whether a person is HIV positive or HIV negative when he or she is tested, first because the disease can be dormant for a long time in the person's system, and, secondly, because as a result of human error a person who is HIV negative could be diagnosed as HIV positive, thereby disqualifying the person unfairly from possible employment opportunities.

Pre-employment testing could result in serious social problems. Tests carried out on a wide scale are expensive, and thousands of people will be unemployed where they are capable of being employed. This means that all these skills (if they are skilled employees) would be lost to the economy.

Managers need to be aware of the impact of tests on employees, and should carry the responsibility of their testing policy by providing necessary support and counselling to those tested. The rejection of an employee solely because he/or she tested HIV positive is unwarranted, since statistics have shown that in South Africa the period between testing positive and developing full-blown Aids is from five to 10 years. During this period those who tested HIV positive could fulfil most of their responsibilities in a position. To reject employees with HIV/Aids has an impact not only in the workplace but also on society, since while an employee with HIV/Aids continues to work, that person is a productive member of society and does not have to rely on the state for support. Realistically, the employee contributes to the economy and saves the state money because it will not have to make special provision for the employee.

Our labour legislation extends the right to fair treatment and the protection against unfair discrimination to prospective employees. This means that the rejection of a job applicant because he or she was shown to be HIV positive by the pre-employment test will amount to unfair discrimination unless the employer can show that the job in question requires a person not to be a carrier of the infection and that no reasonable precautionary measures could be taken to adjust the work content or process to accommodate the person. For instance, a medical doctor who is HIV positive may still be gainfully employed provided that he or she wears protective clothing and is prohibited from doing certain duties. It should be noted that employers may find themselves in a difficult position because by law they are required to provide employees with a safe working environment and they could furthermore be held vicariously liable should a member of the public be infected by an employee during the course of his or her duties. However, these risks should be rare in the case of HIV, and should it not be reasonably possible to safeguard co-workers or members of the public due to the nature of the job, an employer will not be guilty of unfair discrimination in refusing to employ an infected job applicant.

A code of good practice was published on 1 December 2000, containing useful guidelines and legal requirements for employers, trade unions and employees who grapple with the HIV/Aids pandemic.

In exhibit 17.10 an example is given of an employer who, in his effort to come to grips with HIV/Aids in his workforce, received approval from the Labour Court to conduct the necessary testing.

EXHIBIT 17.10: An employer and its workforce get it right in their fight against HIV/Aids

Joy Mining Machinery, a manufacturer, supplier and service provider in respect of machinery to the mining industry employed about 800 employees. Joy Mining, with the support of the representative union and most non-union "D" employees, wished to test its employees for HIV in order to determine the incidence of the disease amongst its staff so as to be better able to deal with the pandemic. It proposed that the testing be voluntary, anonymous and that the ELISA saliva test be used. It applied to the Labour Court for an order granting it permission to carry out a HIV status test in terms of s 7(2) of the Employment Equity Act 55 of 1998 (EEA).

The Labour Court noted that it was required to determine whether the proposed testing for HIV-status is justifiable. The court considered that it would seem that whether something is justifiable must be tested against certain norms and values, eg the standard of reasonableness, legality, ie the applicable legal rules or moral standards etc. In the context of the EEA "justifiability" will be informed by the statute including the objects of the Act and guidelines for interpreting the Act and the Code of Good Practice: Key Aspects of HIV/AIDS and Employment, which was published on 1 December 2000.

The court was of the opinion that in deciding whether a HIV test is justifiable it is appropriate also to take into account the more general test for medical testing set out in section 7(1)(b) of the EEA. The court held that in determining whether the testing of employees for their HIV status is justifiable, it will take the following considerations into account, in so far as they are applicable to the factual circumstances of the case: the prohibition on unfair discrimination, the need for HIV testing, the purpose of the test, the medical facts, employment conditions, social policy, the fair distribution of employee benefits, the inherent requirements of the job, and the category or categories of jobs or employees concerned.

The court will also wish to be informed about the following which do not go to justifiability but which are also relevant to arriving at a proper decision: the attitude of the employees, whether the test is intended to be voluntary/compulsory, the financing of the test, preparations for the test, ie whether the employees are able to give their informed consent, pre-test counselling, the nature of the proposed test and procedure, and post-testing counselling.

Source: *Joy Mining Machinery, a Division of Harnischfeger (SA) (Pty) Ltd v National Union of Metalworkers of SA & others (2002) 23 ILJ 391 (LC)*

17.5 ROLE PLAYERS IN OCCUPATIONAL HEALTH AND SAFETY

As we have stressed throughout this chapter, the promotion and maintenance of health and safety is important for the well-being of the individual, for the success of organisations and for the country. Individual employees and their representatives like trade unions thus form one stakeholder group, and employers (and managers as their representatives in the workplace) form another group with a vested interest in employee health and safety. The state or government is, however, also an important stakeholder in the sense that healthy and safe working environments and employees who enjoy a general state of well-being make up crucial building blocks of any society striving for stability and prosperity. Each of these stakeholder groups thus has a certain role to play.

The government's principal role lies in the realm of promulgating and enforcing legislation such as those Acts which were briefly discussed early on in this chapter. The general duty imposed on employers by the OHSA (section 8(1)) is to provide and maintain, as far as is reasonably practicable, a working environment that is safe and without risk to the health of employees. Furthermore, the OHSA (section 14) imposes the general duty on all employees at work to take reasonable care of the health and safety of themselves and of other employees who stand to be affected by their behaviour. In general the OHSA encourages the parties (employers/employees) to regulate and promote health and safety in the workplace themselves and to cooperate in this regard. To this end the roles and duties of safety representatives and committees are spelt out in detail in the OHSA (sections 18 and 20).

The OHSA furthermore facilitates the policing of the enforcement of the Act's provisions by means of the creation of an inspectorate, which is part of the Department of Labour. The inspectorate is headed by a chief inspector (appointed by the Minister of Labour) who is in charge of other inspectors, all of whom are charged with the administration of the OHSA's provisions and regulations. The inspectorate has to monitor continuously compliance with the OHSA's provisions and regulations. The Department of Labour also has a chief directorate of Occupational Health and Safety. This directorate has, in addition, a number of different directors, each charged with the administration of certain delimited areas/aspects of health and safety. Each of the Department of Labour's regional and satellite offices in the country also has a deputy director responsible for matters of occupational health and safety, who is in charge of controlling inspectors who in turn have authority over the ordinary inspectors. The Act also contains provisions for investigations and inquiries that have to be conducted when accidents occur at work.

Another important role player is NOSA (the National Occupational Safety Association), a not-for-gain incorporated association that is partially funded by the State Accident Fund. The National Occupational Safety Association was established in 1951 as a joint venture of the then workmen's compensation commissioner and employers through their employer organisations.

The overall purpose of NOSA is basically to provide occupational health, safety and environmental services. NOSA's aims are as follows (NOSA 1995):

- to promote the prevention of occupational accidents and diseases and to endeavour to eliminate their causes and results in industry and commerce;
- to act as a national body encouraging and promoting health and safety, and to carry out occupational health and safety publicity;
- to deal with all matters and questions pertaining to occupational health and safety; and
- to act as a general advisory body on all occupational health and safety matters.

Although the state and NOSA are important role players, the bulk of the responsibility for promoting and maintaining health and safety at work lies with the primary role-playing parties: employers and employees.

As explained already, the OHSA spells out a number of duties and prohibitions imposed on employers. These stipulate how the employer must treat employees in order to promote health and safety at work. The CEO of an organisation is made responsible for ensuring, as far as is reasonably practicable, that there is compliance with the employer's duties imposed by the Act. An officer who delegates responsibility, as he or she is well entitled to do, is not absolved (either that CEO him- or herself or the employer) from the ultimate responsibility of ensuring compliance with the duties of employers in terms of the OHSA.

Thus, although the CEO may make it part of the job of lower-level line management to manage aspects of health and safety, in the eyes of the law he or she will remain responsible at the end of the day.

It is thus clearly evident how important health and safety matters in the workplace are for the government and for employers in general. Each and every manager responsible for other employees under his or her authority should thus have a key performance area dealing with aspects of health and safety promotion and maintenance. Because of the importance of this aspect, however, senior or top management will most likely also want to employ specialists to help ensure that health and safety matters are attended to in a very professional way.

Because health and safety have to do with the human dimension of organisations, it is largely the responsibility of the HR department to initiate and finally draft and oversee, in collaboration with line management, the implementation of the organisation's health and safety policy, procedures, programmes, etc. Obviously, as stated before, this process ought ideally to be an inclusive one, involving all other role players and stakeholders – especially all other employees (management and non-management) and their representatives such as trade unions.

The horizons of occupational health and safety have broadened to such an extent today, however, that in most cases it is no longer possible or feasible for one individual to be responsible for the whole spectrum of employee wellness promotion and maintenance. The need for various specialist skills has thus developed gradually over time. The overall role of the HR specialist in this regard is summarised by Saunders (1992: 63) in exhibit 17.11.

EXHIBIT 17.11: General role of HR specialists in health and safety

Task	Specific activity
■ Accident investigator	To carry out investigations into all accidents and dangerous occurrences in order to establish contributory factors.
■ Advocate	Establish health and safety as a priority within the organisation and secure its recognition at board level. Secure sufficient resources.
■ Auditor	Carry out regular examinations of current health and safety policy, procedures, practice and programmes to ensure satisfaction.
■ Leader	Know and understand the workforce and lead by example. Motivate workers and develop schemes and plans to change attitudes and behaviour.
■ Planner	Plan, implement, monitor and evaluate remedial measures designed to reduce or prevent accidents from happening.
■ Provider	Issue protective clothing and/or equipment. A knowledge of the legal requirements is necessary. Expert help is sought where necessary.
■ Trainer	Provide on-the-job training, safe systems of working, indoctrination, workplace rules and regulations, and employee responsibilities.

Source: Saunders (1992: 63)

As mentioned previously, various other specialist role players may be involved in the promotion and maintenance of employee wellness in the organisation. These may include medical doctors, occupational nurses, dentists, physiotherapists, psychologists, social workers, ergonomists and safety officers.

17.6 PROMOTING WELL-BEING BEYOND ORGANISATIONAL BOUNDARIES[1]

As we explained in chapter 1, organisations are embedded in society and the world is today very much 'organisation driven'. Owing to the central role that organisations play in modern-day society, it is our belief that the well-being of society and its members generally should be a key issue for managers. Our focus here is now mainly on the profit-seeking business organisations and the managers working in and for them and, as we have said all along, the pressure is really on for these organisations and their managers to contribute actively to making our world more sustainable.

Because all business organisations are intertwined with society, we argue that the managers of these organisations must make socially responsible decisions and manage accordingly more broadly. Smit et al (2007) say that corporate social responsibility basically implies that managers, in the process of serving their business interests, are obliged to protect and enhance society's interests generally in order to improve quality of life in the broadest possible sense. They mention, however, that not everybody would agree with this view and that there are different perspectives.

17.6.1 Levels or degrees of social responsibility

There are different views about what 'levels' or degrees of corporate social responsibility organisations and their managers ought to engage in (Smit et al 2007).

Level 1: Social obligation

Here the view is essentially that because organisations exist within any particular society to serve the needs/interests of those who use their products/services, organisations owe nothing else than to make profits from the products/services they sell. According to the social obligation perspective, the generation of profits within society's legal framework represents socially responsible behaviour. Thus, the view is that socially responsible management consists of looking after economic interests and meeting legal obligations. Economic interests relate to, for example, the provision of products and services at market relevant prices, the creation of work opportunities where relevant, and the making of profits in return for the business enterprise undertaken.

Legal responsibilities refer to the organisation's obligation to comply with all the relevant laws of society. In recent years, consumer and environmental movements in our country have made quite a bit of progress in convincing our government to introduce laws that require business to protect the environment and care for consumer safety. Dunphy et al (2008: 15) refer to the 'compliance' stance where a company puts the emphasis on "being a 'decent employer and corporate citizen' by ensuring a safe, healthy workplace and avoiding environmental abuses that could lead to litigation or strong community action directed towards the firm".

Level 2: Social reaction

This perspective maintains that organisations owe society more than the mere provision of products and/or services and can at least be held accountable for the ecological, environmental and social costs resulting from their decisions and business operations. Within this school of thought some would argue that organisations might even respond to some of society's problems beyond those that the organisations are directly responsible for. Here, socially responsible management would therefore be regarded as including voluntary actions to support 'worthy causes' in helping to address some of society's problems. The approach might still be rather reactive in that much might only happen when civic groups approach these organisations, asking for donations for such things as anti-drug campaigns or sponsorships of sports teams.

Level 3: Social responsiveness

At this level, socially responsible management is regarded as an approach whereby we actively seek to find solutions to societal challenges – current as well as those we foresee in the more distant future. It may hence well include supporting or opposing public issues and communicating, liaising and collaborating with the government and other organisations to enhance the general state of affairs in communities and in the world more broadly speaking.

Dunphy et al (2008: 15–18) seem to identify at least two sub-stages at this level, namely 'strategic proactivity' and the most advanced stage which they call 'the sustaining corporation'. In the case of the former, the company's "strategic elite views sustainability as providing a potential competitive advantage ... [T]hey try to position the organization as a leader in sustainable business practices: with advanced human resource strategies that help make the organization an 'employer of choice', with 'corporate citizenship' initiatives that build stakeholder support and with innovative, quality products that are environmentally safe and healthy ... [C]ommitment to sustainability, however, is strongly embedded in the quest for maximising longer term corporate profitability ..." (Dunphy et al 2008: 15–16). The same authors say the following about 'the sustaining corporation' (Dunphy et al 2008: 16): "The *sustaining corporation* ... is one where the strategic elite has strongly internalized the ideology of working for a sustainable world ... Its fundamental commitment is to facilitate the emergence of a society that supports the ecological viability of the planet and its species and contributes to just, equitable social practices and human fulfilment."

MTN is an example of a South African company which seems to be leaning towards becoming this 'third wave'-type of organisation of Dunphy et al (2008), as can be seen from the box below. The approach of another South African company, Murray & Roberts, is also reflected in the same box. We cite some further examples in chapter 21.

A CASE AT HAND

MTN and Murray & Roberts

To succeed, MTN must bring sustainable development to the core of our company practice. As with any business practice that requires measurable indicators, such as return on investment, rigour is demanded in determining the business case for sustainable development.

Increasingly, investors and creditors are realising that issues relating to sustainable development can reduce the potential for social risk and reduce future liabilities. As a result, a number of investors and creditors are attaching conditions in this regard.

MTN acknowledges that this presents a strategic business imperative and will provide the necessary information to communicate to investors that we conduct our business along sustainable development principles.

Source: www.mtn.com

Our business activities have a profound impact on the communities in which we operate and we are committed to managing this impact responsibly. Murray & Roberts focuses its Corporate Social Investment (CSI) activity on development projects aligned with its business strategy, supporting mathematics, science and technology education, numerical education in early childhood development, and environmental education. We spent almost R10 million on scheduled CSA projects during the year. Our key investments were the Murray & Roberts Building Africa Exhibition at the new Sci-Bono Discovery Centre in Newtown, extension of the Technology Olympiad to remote rural schools in KwaZulu-Natal and Limpopo provinces, the Murray & Roberts Chair of Environmental Educations at Rhodes University, and establishment of the Chair of Manufacturing at the University of the Witwatersrand.

Source: www.murrob.com

South African society as a whole thus stands to benefit from corporate social involvement efforts that support the constructive development of our people and communities way beyond the actual organisational boundaries. These may therefore include support of educational programmes like helping illiterates to learn to read and write; financial support for schools and other forms of education and training; promoting arts, culture and the sciences; helping the poor and needy people by engaging in welfare projects; and even engaging in uplifting communities internationally – on our African continent and even beyond.

According to Smit et al (2007), the political reforms in South Africa served as a stimulus for enhanced corporate social investment, and they mention the following factors which have been playing a role:

- Organisations have been decentralising some of their corporate social investment projects to regional operations where management and other workers better understand local challenges and issues.
- They are publishing more information about their spending and are networking with one another to share resources on projects and to link up in particular regions or areas.
- Foreign organisations are also contributing to redevelopment in South Africa.

Today, many social investment programmes are financed and managed by corporate South Africa and although organisations often cooperate to enhance the well-being of communities and society more generally, there are sometimes also signs of some less cooperative and more competitive stances taken – for the good of society too (see the Mondi Kraft example below).

A CASE AT HAND

Concerns raised by Mondi Kraft, the paper manufacturer with a plant in Richards Bay, had caused Tata Iron & Steel Co (Tisco) to find an alternative site for their ferrochrome smelter. This has resulted in the company postponing its construction of the plant at Richards Bay until the completion of another environmental impact study to assess the environmental impact of the smelter on the new site.

The smelter project is estimated to be costing Tisco around R650 million. Mondi Kraft, a neighbouring paper manufacturing company in Richards Bay where Tisco had originally proposed to set up its plant, raised a major concern, stating that their customer's perception of the safety of Mondi Kraft's products (mainly in the food-packaging industry) would be affected adversely if a ferrochrome plant were set up next to it. Based on detailed interactions with Mondi Kraft and understanding the gravity of their problem, Tata Steel had agreed to shift to an alternative location.

Source: www.tatasteel.com

17.6.2 Sustainability reporting

It is pretty common in business circles for people to refer to a company's economic performance as 'the bottom line' because profit is usually the last item on the income statement. The drive for more socially responsible corporate behaviour has led to the notion of the 'triple bottom line', something which the King 2002 Report on Corporate Governance (King II) advocates. This is also known as sustainability reporting. One of the challenges in accounting on sustainability reporting is that it is difficult to measure the financial implications of environmental aspects (the effect on the environment of the product or services produced by the company) and social activities (values, ethics and the reciprocal relationships with all stakeholders).

In South Africa, sustainability reporting is becoming routine practice. According to Smit et al (2007), a recent KPMG survey found that more than 80% of the top 100 JSE-listed companies reported on sustainability issues during their most recent fiscal year. In many cases, this reporting is in response to the guidelines contained in integrated sustainability reporting.

If you were to visit the websites of some of South Africa's leading corporations (see exhibit 17.12 below as well) you will find their reports on sustainable development.

International and local indexes measure the performance of companies in terms of recognised corporate responsibility standards.

The FTSE4Good Index, developed in the UK, measures the performance of companies that meet globally recognised corporate responsibility standards. Investors use the FTSE4Good Index to guide them in investment decisions regarding socially responsible companies. SABMiller has, for instance, been included in the index since its inception (see exhibit 17.12 below).

The JSE launched the Socially Responsible Investment Index (SRI) in 2007. It is the first of its kind in an emerging market. The index represents a departure from the FTSE4Good methodology in that it focuses primarily on sustainable development performance and does not exclude outright particular sectors, such as tobacco companies.

The JSE's Socially Responsible Investment Index (SRI)

In its 2005/2006 annual review, the JSE announced the Socially Responsible Investment Index top performers of the year in three categories:

- *High environmental impact:* A tie between Anglo American plc and Anglo American Platinum Corporation Limited
- *Medium environmental impact:* Woolworths Holdings Limited
- *Low environmental impact:* Nedbank Group Limited

Source: www.jse.co.za

EXHIBIT 17.12: The SABMiller sustainable development framework

In 2006 we introduced our sustainable development framework based on the 10 sustainable development priorities most material to our business. Having a clear framework has provided a consistent approach for all operations under our day-to-day management control of SABMiller companies. At the same time it has given operations a degree of freedom to focus on the particular issues most relevant to them. Whilst all operations focus on responsible drinking as a top priority, other priorities such as HIV/Aids, water quality and availability, CSI and human rights will have different levels of relevance for different operations.

More information on our 10 sustainable development priorities is given in our Sustainable Development Report 2007 which can be found on www.sabmiller.com/sabmiller.com/en_gb/Our+responsibility.

Given our experience in emerging markets, we are in a strong position to contribute to the debate regarding sustainable development issues. We work in partnership with governments, non-government organisations and other partners to share knowledge and best practice on these issues.

>>

<<

Sustainable development review

Our ability to be successful and profitable is inextricably linked to the health and prosperity of the communities in which we operate.

Key achievements

- Introduction, group-wide, of a self-assessment management performance system across all 10 sustainable development priorities
- Reduction in carbon dioxide emissions ratio from 14.44 kg/hl to 12.74 kg/hl in 2006
- Energy use in our operations reduced from 163 mj/hl in 2006 to 146 mj/hl
- US$26 million, representing 0.9% of profit before tax, invested in corporate social investment programmes
- Water consumption ratio in brewery production reduced from 4.60 hectolitres to one hectolitre of beer in 2006 to 4.56 hl/hl, representing a notional cost saving of US$2 million
- Environmental management systems, based on the principles underlying ISO 14001 standard or similar, established for 84 sites
- KickStart, a programme encouraging entrepreneurship, launched in a third market, Colombia
- Signatory to the UN Global Compact in January 2007

We have continued to make progress this year on sustainability, particularly as a result of our focus on our 10 sustainable development priorities and the development of a group-wide method of collating performance data. Our 2007 Sustainable Development Report provides more detail on our social and environmental performance, but it is mainly our economic success which continues to make a real improvement in how people live in our communities.

A study by the Bureau for Economic Research, conducted for SAB Ltd, detailed the company's contribution to the South African economy, including the direct impact of our operations and the relevant economic multiplier effects. At the time of the study, SAB Ltd employed 8 600 workers directly, 73% of whom were from previously disadvantaged groups. The study found that our operations supported an estimated 46 000 jobs at first round suppliers and more than five times that number in the wider economy. In all, 362 000 full-time jobs (or 3% of total employment in South Africa) can be directly or indirectly traced back to the production and sale of SAB Ltd's products.

Our business success has resulted in a contribution of US$4,529 million in taxes and excise duties this year to local and national governments and authorities in the countries in which we operate. In addition, US$26 million has been invested in corporate social investment (CSI) programmes, over and above our funding of responsible drinking programmes. An important part of our CSI programmes is the effort to build wealth through encouraging entrepreneurs and supporting local businesses. Many of our operations run enterprise development programmes which create local employment and, in some cases, extend our supply chain. Overall, this wealth creation is important for the communities in which we operate, but it also enhances the market for sales of our products.

As well as our economic impact, we focus on the material opportunities and risks that arise from our environmental and social impacts. The growing consensus around climate change, the accessibility of sufficient quantities of safe and clean water, the social impacts of irresponsible drinking, poverty and HIV/Aids are all crucial considerations for how we run our business.

Sustainable development framework

The 10 sustainable development priorities identified by the strategic review of our approach to corporate accountability are shown below and overleaf.

Priority	Future	Actions	Objective
The need to discourage irresponsible drinking	Promote responsibility in the use of beverage alcohol, as part of a healthy lifestyle, while at the same time endeavouring to prevent alcohol misuse and abuse, through targeted interventions aimed at underage drinking, drink driving and unhealthy patterns of consumption Ensure that our commitment to responsible consumption is seamless across the company, while at the same time acknowledging cultural differences in different markets	Focusing on educational campaigns, self-regulation in marketing, consumer information initiatives and supply chain programmes The SABMiller Alcohol Manifesto and Code of Commercial Communications guide our marketing communications Liaising with governments and relevant bodies regarding the alcohol debate	Evolve the Alcohol Manifesto Upgrade the fluency of targeted employees on alcohol matters
The need to make more beer but using less water	Manage our water footprint, particularly in areas of water stress, to include: Watershed mapping Managing internal water consumption efficiencies Engaging with suppliers Direct CSI to improve access to water within local communities	Operations in the USA, South Africa, India and Uganda are collating information on water availability and quality in the context of future requirements Continuing to improve operational efficiencies within our facilities Working with farmers to use water more efficiently in the production of raw materials Operations in India, Tanzania and South Africa support CSI projects to provide water to local communities	Develop a watershed mapping tool in conjunction with our Europe region to evaluate the risks and opportunities associated with community water requirements, water availability and water quality issues Become more water efficient whilst identifying new ways to deal with waste water which benefit our breweries and the local community Work with suppliers to understand and improve their water footprint Direct CSI to improve access to reliable water supplies in communities where we have facilities

>>

The need to reduce our energy and carbon footprint	**Reduce energy consumption** **Reduce carbon dioxide emissions** **Explore opportunities for renewable energy, including the use of biogas**	Assessing fuel types used and their impact on CO_2 emissions Evaluating boiler efficiencies Encouraging operations to use renewable energy, for example by extending biogas production. India is already using coconut and rice husks and Honduras uses sugar cane off-cuts as fuel	Develop a carbon footprint methodology with Miller Brands UK to facilitate understanding and management of emissions throughout the value chain Further evaluate renewable energy options to offset traditional energy sources, particularly through an expanded roll-out of biogas recovery Improve measurement of greenhouse gas emissions, including transport emissions
The need to have a vibrant packaging reuse and recycling economy	**Reduce, recycle and re-use packaging to cut environmental impacts (for example, landfill and litter) and costs (packaging, landfill and regulatory)**	Lightweighting packaging materials where possible - examples in many operations such as in South Africa, Italy and Angola Using recycled materials, for example nearly all Miller's aluminium cans are made from recycled materials	Evaluate where packaging materials can be substituted with improved alternatives. Our global packaging team will conduct trials on new materials such as biodegradable shrink film in Poland Map and compare the lifecycle environmental footprints of different packaging materials
The need to work towards zero waste operations	**Reduce environmental impact and cost of waste disposal by focusing on five areas:** **Waste generation and disposal** **Waste segregation and classification** **Waste disposal duty of care** **Upstream waste minimisation** **Emissions**	Re-using organic wastes such as spent grain, trub and yeast – eg sold to farmers, used to produce biogas Recycling glass cullet, paper and board, plastics and metals Installing new CFC-free fridges Introducing joint waste management agreements with suppliers	Review best re-use and recycling options for selected brewery waste streams, initially with Miller in the USA Explore the feasibility of achieving a zero-waste to landfill brewery

			Incorporate Responsible Sourcing Principles into supplier contracts
The need to have supply chains that reflect our own values and commitment	Encourage understanding, ownership and improved performance on sustainable development issues throughout the value chain	Conducting supplier workshops External study which assessed the economic impact of SAB Ltd in South Africa Working with small-scale farmers in Uganda, Zambia, Zimbabwe, Tanzania and India	Extend the coverage of our supplier engagement workshops to at least two other regions Field test our good practice agriculture principles with SAB Ltd in South Africa and SABMiller Africa and Asia Involve suppliers in carbon and water footprinting initiatives
The need to have respect for human rights	Respect the diverse national cultures and differences in laws and traditions in countries where we operate At the same time seek to abide by the values of the international community, notably the United Nations Universal Declaration of Human Rights	Embedding our human rights principles within our global operations Incorporating the human rights principles within our work with suppliers	Ensure that all group companies have embedded the human rights principles in their local human resources policies
The need to bring benefit to the communities we serve	To improve the quality of life in the communities in which we operate, with a particular emphasis on enterprise development, water and HIV/Aids	KickStart programme launched in a third market – Colombia Other enterprise development programmes in the Czech Republic, Hungary, the USA and Africa, including South Africa Community-led water programmes in South Africa, India and Tanzania, and HIV/Aids community programmes in Uganda and Zambia	Ensure every operation has a formal CSI strategy including management, monitoring and measurement Improve the measurement and recording of indirect community investment of our operations SAB Ltd in South Africa to increase employee involvement in community volunteering through its Outreach programme to 65%

>>

The need to contribute to the reduction of HIV/Aids within our sphere of influence	**Focus on operations with a prevalence rate of more than 5%** **Undertake aware-ness and educational campaigns in potential 'at risk' operations with lower prevalence rates**	Existing infections managed through voluntary counselling and testing, early diagnosis and managed healthcare, including free anti-retrovirals Aim to reduce and prevent new infections through effective education programmes, incorporating a behavioural change component In operations with a prevalence rate greater than 5%, running programmes which cover employees and their families, the local community and suppliers	Improve the percentage of spouses and dependents on treatment Introduce awareness initiatives in two further operations outside Africa Run education workshops for community organisations and suppliers in Tanzania and Zimbabwe
The need to be transparent in reporting our progress on these sustain-able develop-ment priorities	**Aim to improve our reporting in response to stakeholder needs, consistent with leading benchmarking criteria**	Communicating through our Sustainable Development Report and updates on 'Our responsibility' pages of www.sabmiller.com Working with relevant stakeholders across the globe on our sustainable development priorities Individual reports on sustainability issues by our South African, Czech Republic, US, Colombian and Canary Islands operations Producing group level reports on individual priorities – water and HIV/Aids	Increase frequency of internal reporting by operations to every six months Encourage the production of local sustainable development reports which inform progress against the 10 priorities

Source: http://www.sabmiller.com/Annval_Report_2007/8_sustainable/sustaindevreport.html

17.7 CONCLUSION

In this chapter we have shown what we believe to form part of a proactive and holistic approach to the well-being of our people at work, and also beyond organisational boundaries. It was argued that a reactive approach to employee health and safety is no longer sufficient and that we should show that we genuinely care for our people and our communities. This means that we must not only ensure legal compliance and basic risk management, but we should also find ways of actually adding value to the well-being of our working people and the communities where they come from. Socially responsible management is therefore the way to go if we want to work towards a more sustainable world in South Africa and on our continent.

SELF-EVALUATION QUESTIONS

1 'The best we can do in our organisations, when it comes to health and safety, is to ensure that we comply with the law.' Critically discuss this statement.
2 Write concise notes on the nature and managerial implications of the following: the Mine Health and Safety Act; the Occupational Health and Safety Act.
3 Describe the role of health and safety representatives in terms of the OHSA.
4 'Ergonomics and work design hold no implications for employee wellness.' Do you agree? Why/why not?
5 Write brief notes on the nature and importance of being prepared for emergencies in organisations.
6 What does 'occupational mental health' entail? How does this relate such things as stress, anxiety and depression? What are the managerial implications of these things?
7 Differentiate between and cite examples of occupational diseases and hazards.
8 Write an essay about the following: 'The HIV/Aids pandemic and the implications hereof for organisations and managers in South Africa.' Make reference to the sub-Saharan Africa context.
9 Analyse and critically discuss the following statement: 'South African business organisations must become much more socially responsible "corporate citizens" and actually strive towards being 'sustaining corporations' that add value to our country, our continent and our planet.'

ENDNOTES

1 Parts of this section are taken/adapted from Smit et al (2007)

PART SIX
LABOUR AND EMPLOYEE RELATIONS CHALLENGES

18 LABOUR RELATIONS IN SOUTH AFRICA: SOME BASICS

LEARNING OUTCOMES

After studying this chapter, you should be able to:

- write an essay that outlines the essentials of labour relations;
- differentiate between different theoretical approaches to, and perspectives of, labour and industrial relations;
- describe the nature, functioning and role of trade unions in South Africa;
- discuss the meaning and fundamental role that freedom of association and protection against victimisation play in our system of industrial relations;
- explain the different meanings and contexts in which the notion of trade union representativeness is used in the Labour Relations Act (LRA);
- list and explain the organisational rights granted to trade unions in terms of the LRA;
- explain the values and objectives that underpin the LRA;
- describe the role of Nedlac in our system of industrial relations;
- discuss the statutory regulation of collective bargaining;
- discuss the different bodies created to facilitate dispute resolution in terms of the LRA;
- explain and compare arbitration and mediation as dispute resolution processes; and
- write an essay that outlines the most important principles of industrial action.

18.1 INTRODUCTION

From chapter 2 it ought to be quite clear how important a role the organised labour movement has played in the historical development of HRM in South Africa. Especially during the 1980s and early 1990s, trade unions had a tremendous impact on the way management dealt with issues related to their workforces, as well as the transformation of our society more generally. It is therefore essential that any person interested or involved in HRM in South Africa be afforded the opportunity to make a study of issues related more particularly (although not exclusively) to the collective dimension of workers as 'labour' who are represented by their trade unions.

18.2 UNDERSTANDING THE ESSENTIALS OF LABOUR RELATIONS

Before discussing those particular aspects related to the South African system of industrial relations, it is important to clarify some of the general theoretical fundamentals underlying labour relations and collective bargaining.

18.2.1 Clarifying key concepts

Various authors use different terms and concepts when they discuss the collective aspects of the employment relationship. Concepts that are sometimes used interchangeably vary from 'labour relations' and 'industrial relations' to 'employee relations', and even 'employee voice', and 'collective bargaining'. The view taken varies, not only because of differences in the international context, but also because of the fact that this topic (or aspects thereof) can be analysed and discussed from many different angles. These range from the legal, economic or sociological to the organisational (managerial) or psychological.

'Industrial relations' gained status as a separate field of study somewhere during the mid-20th century. Themes, topics and issues related to this field can, however, be studied from the point of view of various other fields of study or disciplines. This makes it multidisciplinary because many disciplines make a study of aspects pertaining to industrial relations. It is essentially an interdisciplinary field of study as well, though, because it borrows elements from many disciplines such as sociology, economics, law and psychology.

An interdisciplinary approach allows for a coherent study of a very distinct set of phenomena in society – phenomena revolving around certain types of relationships between employer(s) (and/or their representative(s)), employee(s) (and/or their representatives) and government(s) within the context(s) of different countries, organisations and industries. As a distinct field of study it is traditionally referred to as 'industrial relations' or, by some, as 'labour relations' ('labor relations' in the US). The term 'industrial' comes from the fact that the field has its origins in the Industrial Revolution which brought about drastic changes in the world of work and the nature of employment relationships. There is an international trend to now refer to this field of study as 'employment relations', partly because in this post-industrial phase the same phenomena exist and these can also be studied in non-industrial settings, but also to denote the broadening of the scope of this field.

Typically when the concept of 'employment relations' is used, it reflects that the traditional field of labour relations (or industrial relations), and HRM, are put together as one body of information. Keep in mind though that when that is the case it is generally not meant to be a subfield or part of management (except when referred to as something like 'employment relations management'), but it is then rather clustered as a separate, stand-alone field of study or body of knowledge. A recent example of such an approach is found in the work of Balnave, Brown, Maconachie and Stone (2007). Balnave et al (2007: 29) explain:

> The concept of employment relations has developed in recent years in response to the changes in the world of work and the inability of industrial relations and/ or HRM to conceptualise these changes and current state of play within the confines of their traditional disciplines. Although the exact nature and boundaries of 'employment relations' are still debatable, it is generally regarded as a legitimate bridging term ...

They go on to provide the following definition then (Balnave et al 2007: 29): "*Employment relations*: a bridging term that both integrates industrial relations and HRM, and broadens the boundaries of both disciplines to encompass a wider range of stakeholders and environmental factors." The following ten chapters then make up the general body of information of the book (the first chapter is introductory and a 12th chapter is just country specific): the government and employment relations; management and employer associations; trade unions; enterprise bargaining and negotiation; employing people; performance management and employment relations; rewarding people; developing people; managing occupational health and safety; and managing dismissals.

As we have said, though, many aspects related to the field of study of industrial relations can be analysed from the point of view of various academic disciplines. With specific reference to the collective dimension, the student of labour economics can, for instance, study collective bargaining between trade union and management representatives from the angle of its economic and labour market implications. Similarly, the student of psychology (most notably industrial and organisational psychology) can, for example, study the human behavioural aspects related to negotiations or conflict dynamics between representatives of labour and the employer. At the same time, the sociology student (in particular the student of industrial sociology) can make a study of trade unionism and the labour movement as phenomena in society. Similarly, the student of law (focusing on justice in society) can make an in-depth study pertaining to the legal aspects regarding people who work in employment contexts when he or she specialises in labour law. The student of business management studies various aspects pertaining to industrial relations from the angle of how these things interplay with organisational success.

Because this book is written from a management perspective, our approach here is as just mentioned and we prefer to use the concept 'labour relations', particularly when we focus on the more collective aspects.

> Labour relations as a topic in management can thus be viewed as being concerned with the relations (primarily collective but also to a lesser extent individual) between employer(s) (and/or manager(s) as the representatives of the employer) and workers (and/or their representatives such as trade unions) which develop from employment relationships and which are essentially concerned with balancing the various interests of, and regulating the levels of cooperation and conflict between, the parties involved. In all of this, the government and its relevant representatives, institutions, structures, systems and laws play an important, though secondary role, and the role of other stakeholders is also important.

From the above it ought to be clear that it is difficult to demarcate precisely the list of issues to be studied under this heading. The reason for this is partly that there is an extremely close interrelationship between labour relations dynamics on the one hand and HRM on the other. Reference to the definition of HRM as a field of study, theory and practice, as outlined in chapter 1, should help to clarify this intrinsic interrelationship further. It is desirable, from a management perspective, to approach these topics in a fully integrated manner. Because the employment relationship and work are central to HRM and labour relations, they should be viewed as two sides of the same coin. The international trend is to integrate these two areas and to call it 'employment relations'.

In this book, labour relations, as part of management, revolve more around the collective aspects of employment relations. They are, however, not exclusively concerned with issues related to labour unions or other forms of employee collectives.

The notion of 'employee relations' is specifically intended to add the dimension of one-on-one, individual relationships at work – the daily human relationships, especially between superiors and subordinates, which form such an important element of our working lives.

> Employee relations as a topic we take to refer predominantly to those aspects related to the conflict, cooperation, involvement and communication in the relationships between managers and non-management employees, irrespective of the type of work or industry concerned and irrespective of the presence or absence of trade unions or worker representatives. In this book we thus prefer to use the notion of 'labour and employee relations'.

Thus, although the emphasis in chapters 18, 19 and 20 falls on aspects such as South Africa's system that regulates workers' organisational rights, dealing with trade unions, bargaining with labour representatives, handling labour-related disputes, and industrial conflict, it is also concerned with issues such as handling grievances and disciplining and dismissing employees (as individuals and/or as groups), involving and communicating with employees, and with other aspects that are fundamental to the enhancement of sound human relations in the workplace.

Collective bargaining forms an essential part of labour relations. Drawing on the work of Bendix (1996: 249–250), collective bargaining can quite comprehensively be described as

> … a process, necessitated by a conflict of needs, interests, goals, values, perceptions and ideologies, but resting on a basic commonality of interest, whereby employees/ employee collectives and employers/employer collectives, by the conduct of continued negotiation and the application of pressure and counterpressure, attempt to achieve some balance between the fulfilment of the needs, goals and interests of management on the one hand and employees on the other – the extent to which either party achieves its objectives depending on the nature of the relationship itself, each party's source and use of power, the power balance between them, the organisational and strategic effectiveness of each party, as well as the type of bargaining structure and the prevalent economic, sociopolitical and other conditions.

18.2.2 The employment relationship as the basis of all labour and employee relations dynamics

From chapter 1 you know that an employment relationship is essentially one of exchange which comes into being when a person is employed by another party to be available to work in exchange for some form of reward.

Without this employment relationship, then, there can be, by definition, no labour, employee or industrial relations. It is an inherently complex relationship exhibiting a simultaneous need for cooperation between non-management and management employees (due to mutual interests) and a natural state of some conflicting interests, perceptions and needs.

This employment relationship is complex partly because of its multidimensional nature.

The *economic dimension* of this relationship derives from the fact that the primary parties are engaged in a relationship of exchange. The employees give their energy, knowledge, skills, abilities and productive time in return for some sort of reward which includes an economic or financial aspect. Money as the exchange medium is thus central to the employment relationship.

The *legal dimension* derives from the fact that the parties enter into a legally binding agreement and that there are specific laws and formal rules which have an official bearing on the relationship between employer and employee. Some legalities pertain to the *individual dimension* of the employment relationship – in other words, to the relationship between an individual employee and his or her employing organisation as a single legal entity. In this regard one can think of the common law (law of contract) which forms the basis of the contract of employment between an employee and employer.

On the other hand, collective labour law ensures that there can be some sort of formality in the relationship on the *collective dimension* – in other words, between labour as a group (including trade unions) with their representatives on one hand, and the employer(s) (and/or their representative organisations) on the other. This would include legislation relating to collective bargaining (including dispute settlement and industrial action). The legal dimension can therefore also be referred to as the formal dimension of the employment relationship because it forms the basis of the formal rights and duties of the parties.

The *social dimension* gives the employment relationship its informal character; it revolves around the interaction and behaviour between people associated with the human activity of employment or work. The social or informal dimension thus refers essentially to human behaviour in organisations within the context of the collective dimension (in a group context which may include labour unions), and/or the individual dimension (in an individual and interpersonal context). Human beings as individuals and as group members all have certain feelings, needs, attitudes, perceptions, etc (see chapter 1), and therefore bring with them to the employment relationship the dynamics which flow from these social and psychological phenomena. This dimension can also be referred to as the soft dimension of the employment relationship.

18.2.3 The parties involved in labour relations and their roles, rights and duties

Any industrial relations system has at least three parties: the two primary parties are employers (and management as their representatives) and labour (and their representatives such as trade unions); the third (secondary) party is the government in its regulatory role (as opposed to its role as an employer).

Sound industrial relations are a prerequisite for the socio-economic stability and prosperity of any country, and the government's primary concern is therefore to provide a suitable statutory framework within which the primary parties can conduct their relationship in an orderly fashion.

The role of the government as third party is thus to create and enforce the legal framework which can regulate the rights and duties of the two primary parties. In this sense it plays the role of master and referee in that it also has to enforce all those laws pertaining to the different dimensions of industrial relations in the country. It does, however, also play the role of servant in that it can proffer the necessary assistance to enable the primary parties to conduct their relations in a sound and mutually acceptable manner. The government can, for example, provide the parties with relevant information and guidance regarding industrial relations procedures, structures, institutions, systems, developments and the like. The government, therefore, as protector of the public interest, has a natural interest in overseeing and guiding the conduct of all the parties in order to ensure that the nature and quality of industrial relations does not have a negative impact on the country's inhabitants. The government is also an employer; in labour relations in the public sector, the government therefore also becomes a primary party.

Employers (including organisations) and management (as their representatives) form one of the primary parties in the tripartite industrial relations system. Management want their organisations to be successful; management must therefore see to it that the right things are done in the right way to ensure the achievement of the organisation's objectives (which may include the financial objective of creating surplus funds or returns on investments). Management's role is traditionally to make the necessary decisions regarding the optimal utilisation of all the organisational resources.

Management's interests in labour and employee relations (and thus in collective bargaining) are therefore quite obvious. Managers are required to engage in collective bargaining and related labour-relations dynamics in such a way that it ultimately serves the interests of the employer – but not without balancing these with the interests of other stakeholders. Once non-management employees (workers) are at work, the concerns of management revolve around getting the workers (as individuals or as group members) to respond in a positive way to the work situation. They seek ways to manage the work process and work-related behaviour and performance so that the objectives of the owners of the organisations can be achieved, but with due cognisance to the objectives of other stakeholders and particularly justice issues. The responsibilities of management thus include:

- protecting and serving the interests of employers;
- determining objectives;
- arranging for the optimal utilisation of the organisation's resources (including the human resources);
- ensuring customer satisfaction;
- ensuring that the necessary standards of product and/or service quality are maintained; and
- ensuring that all operations of the organisation are conducted in a cost effective and efficient manner, which will include the control of labour costs.

It is the particular duty of management to see to it that the quality of labour relations ultimately contributes to the success of the organisation. This will obviously include management's duty to respect and uphold the basic rights of workers.

With regard to the latter, the duties of management include:

- keeping workers in the service of the organisation and not dismissing them arbitrarily;
- paying workers for their work and for services rendered;
- allowing workers to join trade unions;
- negotiating with the workers and/or their representatives;
- providing safe and healthy working conditions; and
- ensuring that all aspects related to the human activity of employment are dealt with within the bounds of the law.

The other primary party in any industrial relations system consists of the workers and their representative bodies (such as trade unions). It is the duty of workers to hire out their labour potential (energy, skills, knowledge, abilities, etc) to perform certain work on behalf of the employer (organisation), under the control of management, and ultimately to further the interests of the employer or owners of the organisation. Workers therefore have a particular role to play, which include duties such as:

- behaving in the required manner at work;
- performing their work as required;
- remaining obedient and loyal to the employer (and management);

- complying with reasonable rules and instructions; and
- exercising the right to associate, bargain and strike in a responsible manner.

The rights of workers in South Africa include the right to work, the right to strike, the right to fair remuneration and service conditions, the right to training, the right to associate and form and belong to trade unions, and the right to protection in the workplace (which includes the right to protection from health and safety hazards, and from unfair employment practices). The primary role of trade unions and/or other bodies which represent workers (such as staff associations) is to protect and further the rights and interests of the workers and to represent them in collective bargaining.

All three parties must always acknowledge the role of other stakeholders, most notably of competitors and customers.

18.2.4 Some fundamental dynamics underlying labour relations

The way in which labour or industrial relations evolve in any particular organisation or country is dependent on a variety of factors. These include the economic situation in the country, the financial situation of organisations, the politics and power relations both in society and in organisations, the country's legal system and demographics, the characteristics of the labour force, labour market conditions, the nature of the labour movement(s), ideologies of the parties, and many more.

However, a number of aspects are pivotal in any given industrial or labour relations situation. These aspects can be said to be fundamental to the dynamics of labour and industrial relations.

As noted earlier, the natural conflict between the employer and employee as parties to the employment relationship forms the basic reason for labour and industrial relations dynamics. The parties have – to some extent at least – conflicting goals, needs, interests and values. The most basic conflict revolves around the economics of the exchange relationship – the economics related to the distribution and sharing of the profits and the value added by the labour process. Owners or shareholders in the private sector want to maximise profits for maximum return on their investments. To this end they have to maximise revenues and minimise costs – most notably, they have to curb labour costs and ensure maximum employee productivity. Conflict therefore develops around issues such as working conditions, remuneration and even matters relating to the organisation of work, the decision-making process and control structures. Conflict in labour relations is natural and the different solutions which are devised to deal with this and to optimise the levels of conflict thus form an essential building block of labour relations.

Another dynamic aspect underlying labour relations (referred to above) is that of control. Due to the conflict, both parties seek to control the situation so as to ensure that they derive maximum benefit from it for themselves. Management seeks to control the process of getting the work done in a way that will best serve the interests of the employer or owners of the organisation. Managers try to control the behaviour and performance of workers in such a way that it adds maximum value to the products and/or services rendered by the organisation. From such a perspective, organisations can be viewed as structures of control. The parties try to control not only the way in which the work processes are to be performed in order to provide the necessary services and/or products, but also especially the way in which the wealth created in the process of delivering the goods/services is distributed among the various stakeholders (such as the shareholders, management and the workers).

Workers have traditionally been under the control of management as representatives of their employers. However, workers and trade unions have for some time challenged this traditional management prerogative to control and to make decisions. Through collective bargaining processes, the primary parties try to conclude agreements about how to institutionalise and jointly control and regulate the conflict inherent in the employment relationship.

Along with these dynamics of conflict and control comes the issue of power. Employees join trade unions particularly because as individuals they lack the power to influence the employer or to control the work process or the rewards related to the work they perform. The more dependent one party is on the other, the more power the latter will possess. If an individual employee is totally dependent on one employer to earn a living (in other words, if there are no other job opportunities), the employer will wield most of the power. On the other hand, if the employer is heavily dependent on a particular group of workers because they cannot easily and speedily be replaced, the power balance will be more even.

This principle is expressed in the trade union credo of 'united we stand, divided we fall'. There is power in standing together and therefore employees form collectives such as trade unions in order to have more power to influence and control issues related to the employment relationship.

However, conflict, control and power form only one side of the labour relations equation. The other side relates to the fact that there is interdependency and an inherent mutual interest and need to cooperate between the two primary parties. Both conflict and cooperation are created simultaneously in the organisation of people and work. Management (and employers) and workers are interdependent: the latter need the former to provide the work opportunities (to be able to earn a living) and to guide and assist them in doing their work; the former needs the latter to perform the work so that the organisation can deliver the needed products/services and so that the owners can earn a satisfactory return on their investments. Workers thus want to earn money by hiring out their labour potential, and management is prepared to pay and reward them for their effort on behalf of the employer.

Both the primary parties, as well as the government as third party, thus have a basic commonality of interest in the continued successful existence of the organisation.

The need to cooperate arises from this mutuality of interests: without the need for cooperation, industrial relations as a field of study and collective bargaining as a process in practice would never have existed. Unfortunately, the literature dealing with industrial and labour relations often underplays the importance of this natural dynamic which underlies all employment relationships.

Owing to the simultaneous existence of elements of mutual and conflicting interests in all employment relationships, there are usually some signs of resistance and some signs of consent on a continuous basis.

18.3 THEORETICAL APPROACHES TO AND PERSPECTIVES OF INDUSTRIAL AND LABOUR RELATIONS

As has been indicated, it is difficult to provide definitive definitions of industrial or labour relations. Different perspectives are taken by different people, partly because they have different frames of reference – due to the fact that the topic can be studied from many different angles.

This also holds true within the context of employing entities or organisations. The particular frame of reference adopted will largely determine the way in which specific labour relations issues and situations are analysed, the way in which the parties are expected to behave, and the means adopted to influence or control their behaviour.

A few of the various theoretical approaches to industrial and labour relations are outlined below.

18.3.1 The unitarist perspective

This approach stresses a so-called natural common goal in all employment organisations and the fact that there is actually no need for divisions in the organisation because all are part of one team. Proponents of this perspective emphasise the fact that generally all members of an organisation have similar needs and values, and that conflict is therefore basically unnecessary, unnatural and irrational. Those who challenge or who are in conflict with management are viewed as transgressors or aberrants. Trade unions are therefore seen largely as unnecessary opposition groupings which actually intrude and try to compete for the loyalty of workers. Trade unions are seen as an external force that creates conflict. Unitarists are of the view that employees are content with what management does and how they manage things. Collective bargaining is basically seen as unnecessary and a waste of time.

18.3.2 The pluralist perspective

Those who adhere to this ideological framework believe that any organisation is basically a coalition of people with a variety of different beliefs, interests, goals and aspirations. Not all employees will share the same goals, and conflict is thus seen as a normal occurrence which must simply be managed in such a way that the different interests and goals are kept in some kind of equilibrium. Conflicting views and objectives are thus acknowledged and would be reconciled in such a way that they ultimately contribute positively to organisational success and the well-being of all the parties. Some limited common purpose (in the form of the continued successful existence of the organisation) is also acknowledged, and the parties who will naturally come into conflict are thus willing to work out ways of ensuring a balance between conflict and cooperation. Trade unions are viewed as the natural consequence of certain individuals who form coalitions because they share certain interests and objectives which differ from those of other individuals or groups. Trade unions are not viewed as a threat or as intruders or troublemakers, but rather as legitimate bodies which can help to restore the power imbalances inherent in all employment relationships and to ensure some form of equilibrium between the natural conflict and common interest between the parties, through a process of collective bargaining.

18.3.3 The radical perspective

This approach is founded on the ideology that no balance of conflict or power can be achieved in any capitalist system and that an alternative, more radical approach has to be taken. This perspective is based on the Marxist thesis that the roots of the conflict and division between the workers who sell their labour and the owners of capital who exploit it as a commodity are not to be found in the employment relationship as such, but rather in the wider society and in the capitalist way in which the production process is organised. The essence of this perspective is the basic power imbalance which results from the fact that the owners of the means of production in a capitalist system occupy the superior position. Proponents of this perspective therefore take the view that there can be no point of common interest and that the whole capitalist system has to be overthrown and replaced by a system of communal control and the abolition of the social constructs of private property and ownership. It is believed that in a capitalist system of production workers will always be exploited, as they are the only ones who can really add value and increase the profits of the owners of the means of production. Industrial conflict is therefore seen as an extension of the broader conflict in society between the working class and the owners of capital. Trade unions and collective bargaining are viewed to be only instrumental in the process of radical change in society.

18.3.4 The societal-corporatist perspective

Although this ideological framework also acknowledges the natural presence of conflict inherent in employment relationships, it places greater emphasis on the need for more cooperation and coordination between the parties involved in labour relations. In this sense it can thus be viewed to incorporate elements of both the unitarist and pluralist perspectives.

While conflict is regarded as natural, it is also believed that it can be best managed if the parties (state, labour and capital) can focus more on their interdependencies and commonalities of interest. In terms of processes the emphasis therefore shifts away from adversarialism and competitive interactions, towards processes of consensus building, and greater collaboration and coordination. Because the focus is more on common goals, the approach is to take more of a holistic perspective and to create structures through which the role players can negotiate agreements that are ultimately more beneficial to all the stakeholders over the long term. The needs of broader society are thus incorporated in such an approach, rather than focusing only on short-term, 'their loss and our gain'-types of negotiation outcomes.

18.4 TRADE UNIONS

As has been pointed out throughout this book (and in particular in chapter 2), trade unions are key stakeholders and role players in South Africa. Not only has the South African labour movement (trade unions and their federations) played an important role in transforming the country from an apartheid society to a democracy, but the labour movement remains a strong force, and trade unions, their federations and their leadership cadres are major stakeholders and role players in the governance of our country. In this part of the book the spotlight falls on the nature of trade unions as organisations in their own right in South Africa – but in the box below we give a glimpse of similar dynamics elsewhere on our continent.

18.4.1 The anatomy of trade unions: a brief overview

In chapter 1 we explained what an 'organisation' is. From that it can be deduced that a trade union is just as much an organisation as any business enterprise. It is a formal social entity that brings together resources for a purpose.

18.4.1.1 What a trade union is

According to the Labour Relations Act 66 of 1995, a trade union is viewed as "an association of employees whose principal purpose is to regulate relations between employees and employers, including employers' organisations". Although collective bargaining as a process can be highlighted as a particular means through which trade unions get involved in representing the interests of their members, there are also other processes that may be used for this purpose. In this regard more cooperative processes such as joint problem solving, indirect participation in decision making through consultation, and even processes of co-determination may form part of how

Elsewhere in Africa

Trade unionism in both the private and public sectors has existed in Ghana since the introduction of wage employment by the colonial government and a labour federation, the Trades Union Congress (TUC), was established in 1945. The early unions operated autonomously and were concerned primarily with issues relating to the employment relationship. However, the co-optation of trade unions into the struggle for independence marked the beginning of an exchange relationship between the government and the labour movement. This exchange relationship entailed the labour movement advancing the interests of their membership through legislation in return for embracing the development objectives of the government. While the 1965 Act sought to conform to International Labour Organization (ILO) regulations, it is fair to suggest that it represents a positive outcome of the political exchange between the labour movement and the Nkrumah government.

The legislation provides for the recognition of a central labour movement, Trade Union Congress (TUC), as the sole representative of the labour movement and the structure and functioning of the labour movement. To address the fragmented state of the labour movement, the 1965 Act structured unions along industrial lines and allowed for the affiliation of 17 national industrial unions to the TUC. A noteworthy feature of the Act, which may be indicative of the political exchange between the labour movement and the government, is the legally mandated check-off of union membership dues. This ensures the financial security of the unions. Although the compulsory check-off is a potential solution to the free rider problem, it has been noted to contravene ILO standards ... The TUC does not, however, participate in the negotiation of collective bargaining agreements on behalf of its affiliates. Instead, it provides advice on issues relating to the employment relationship, coordinates the activities of its affiliates, and represents the interests of workers through its membership of various national bodies ...

Given the close link between socio-economic and political factors and industrial relations, the implementation of the ERP (economic recovery program) continues to impact the practice of industrial relations ... [T]he downsizing in the public sector, the traditional bastion of unionism, has led to a decline in union membership from 635 000 in 1985 to 520 936 in 1996. The economic crisis requires not only a cooperative labour-management relationship but also new strategies to address the challenges of increased productivity, efficiency, and competitiveness.

Source: Slightly adapted extracts from Aryee (2004: 128–130)

trade unions serve the interests of their members within organisations and society at large. Although the primary interest of trade unions relates directly to the employment relationship, they often also seek to serve the interests of their members more indirectly by serving a macro-level role in society. In South Africa, trade unions (mostly through their federations) take part in political processes, such as policy formulation in Nedlac (National Economic Development and Labour Council).

There are many different types of trade unions. Some organise their membership and operations without any emphasis on the specific industry, but with a particular focus on certain occupational groups such as related crafts. Others strive to represent the interests of diverse types of workers, as long as they all work in a particular industry. Some others may, however, prefer to be more general and open, striving to attain the 'utopian' situation where the whole working class is organised into one association. In this case, the emphasis is to a large extent on so-called class consciousness.

18.4.1.2 Why trade unions exist

From what has already been said it should be quite clear why trade unions exist: they are formed to serve the interests of their members, the workers. The question arising from this is why certain employees want to belong to a trade union. In essence we can say that trade unions exist simply because certain groups of employees do not feel satisfied with their employment relationships. With the advent of the Industrial Revolution, the nature of employment relationships changed considerably due to the rise of mass production, factories and capitalism. The focus was on outputs only and the needs of workers were often grossly neglected. Some groups of employees thus experienced (and many still do today) certain discrepancies between what they felt they were actually getting out of their employment relationships relative to others, and what they felt they ought to get (relating to aspects such as job satisfaction, freedom to make decisions for themselves in the workplace, working conditions, remuneration and/or fringe benefits).

Broadly speaking, it is thus the primary purpose of trade unions to restore and maintain some sort of balance or equity in employment relations, as well as in society as a whole. We generally find imbalances in power and inequalities between certain classes of people in society – most notably between the so-called working class and those who own and 'control' the productive resources and concomitant organisations, such as business enterprises and state-owned enterprises (SOEs).

From this one can derive many different generalised objectives of trade unions:

- they try to improve the working conditions of their members as well as their terms of employment;
- they want to ensure that workers are treated fairly at work;
- they strive towards ensuring that workers get a fair share of the wealth generated by organisations;
- they aim at improving social security;
- they want to achieve greater democracy in the governance of individual organisations, industries and society at large by taking part in decision-making processes;
- they aim in particular at getting greater control over the management of employment relationships within organisations; and
- they strive to do away with class structures in societies where some have a great deal while others have very little and many may even not be employed at all.

In order to achieve their objectives, trade unions have to operate efficiently and effectively.

Since about the beginning of 1997, South Africa saw the birth of a new type of 'union' with the specific aim of representing employees at CCMA and bargaining council conciliations and arbitrations. Some consultants registered as trade unions as provided for in the LRA. Consultants saw this as a way of getting around the LRA's not allowing consultants to represent employees at these proceedings. Similarly they formed employers' organisations to represent employers at proceedings. There were instances of a consultant producing a trade union registration certificate at conciliation and a registration certificate of an employers' organisation at another process in the same day. Stricter controls were implemented which later saw the cancellation of the registration of some of these unions. These clearly, therefore, are not really trade unions in the true sense of the word.

18.4.1.3 How trade unions operate: their structures and methods

Just as business organisations have to be managed in order to achieve their objectives, trade unions as organisations in their own right also have to be managed. They have to plan and set objectives, they have to be structured (or organised), leadership is essential, and control has to be exercised. The topic of how to manage a trade union falls beyond the scope of this book. It is, however, necessary to develop a general understanding of how trade unions operate; we thus focus on the overall structuring and methods employed by these organisations.

Although details regarding the structuring of unions may differ in accordance with variables such as type, size, policy and affiliation to a federation, a general structural pattern can be sketched.

The structure of trade unions

In contrast with most business organisations, the power of a trade union is vested in its membership and not so much in its top hierarchy. Trade unions are democratic organisations, and workers usually join them voluntarily. Although top-level leadership, experience and power are important, the real strength of a union lies in its members who form the foundation of any trade union.

The members elect shop stewards to act as the link between the union, the members and the management of organisations, who often form shop steward committees within the organisations in which they act as representatives of the workers. These committees thus make up the next structural layer (on top of the membership base) of the trade union. Typically, the next structural level is formed by the trade union's branch offices, which usually include full-time union officials (full-time employees of the trade union) and members of the shop steward committees (or other shop stewards duly elected by the committees).

Should a trade union's membership be significant, it may be necessary to create regional structures in the form of regional union offices. Full-time union officials and branch level members may also be involved at this level.

At the next level there is the national committee and national executive. This structural level usually consists of a president of the trade union or a chairperson, a vice-chairperson, a general secretary and a treasurer. These officials are appointed or elected, and their roles are determined in accordance with the constitution of each individual trade union. The roles of president and vice-president are normally filled by union members who are shop stewards. Full-time union officials usually take on the roles of treasurer and secretary. Sometimes the members of the national committee and national executive come from the ranks of the local or regional committees; in other cases they may be elected by the general congress. The task of the national committee – and in particular the national executive – is to implement the policies of the trade union and also to act and speak on its behalf. Overall responsibility for the smooth functioning of the trade union rests with these structures.

Unions are democratic organisations. All union policy decisions are made at the level of the national congress. The national congress represents grassroots membership and elects the executive. The overall management of trade unions thus rests with the executives at the different structural levels. These structures consist of elected union members (office bearers) or officials appointed or elected by the union members who are the employees of business or public enterprises. It can thus truly be said that the members manage the union, in line with the credo of government by the people.

Trade unions may thus not accord organisers or officials appointed from outside (such as the general secretary) a vote in committee or executive decisions. As such, union officials become employees of the union. The general management principles spelt out in this book also apply to these employees.

Methods used by trade unions to achieve their goals

Trade unions can make use of various methods in order to achieve their objectives or goals.

In line with the philosophy of trade unionism that unity is power, one of the principal methodologies that they employ is to unite their forces and stand together. This they do by, inter alia, forming networks through which they collaborate (see 'A case at hand' below), and by officially affiliating with trade union federations at a national level – such as Cosatu. These trade union federations can also officially link up with political parties of countries. In South Africa the prime example is the alliance between the ruling ANC party and Cosatu (and the SACP). Trade unions and their federations also often form collaborative networks on an international level (as can also be seen from 'A case at hand' below).

A CASE AT HAND

Trade unions collaborate in South Africa, and also across various African countries and beyond. Ditsela (Development Institute for Training, Support and Education for Labour) is a good example of national level collaboration. It was established in 1996 by the then main Union Federations in South Africa, with offices in Johannesburg and Cape Town. In 2008, Ditsela celebrated the tenth year of running 'DANLEP' (the Ditsela Advanced National Labour Education Programme) and below is its 'vision and mission' statement.

Vision

Ditsela strives to be a responsive, innovative, dynamic and democratic learning organisation that contributes to building a strong labour movement. It conducts relevant and high-quality trade union education and support, as well as education research work with a clear working-class bias in response to the needs of the labour movement. Ditsela's approach recognises the primary role of the trade union movement and the working class in transforming society, and the important role played by trade union education. We acknowledge that we have to learn from the struggles of workers in South Africa and the world.

Mission

We aim to contribute to strengthening the labour movement by:
- Delivering programmes that are at the cutting edge of trade union education, research and support
- Supporting the development of the organisational capacity of trade unions and federations towards delivering their own education programmes and building working class power
- Striving to be a workers' education centre that offers dynamic, vibrant, critical and inspiring education that engages the evolving challenges facing the trade union movement and the broader working class
- Building a comprehensive and responsive programme that can be reproduced, adapted and sustained throughout the labour movement
- Maintaining an open space for critical reflection and engagement
- Embodying and promoting the democratic ethos of worker control
- Providing a dynamic model as a responsive learning organisation
- Encouraging through practice, the commitment amongst participants to plough back their learning to strengthen the labour movement

>>

<<

The 'ALRN' (African Labour Researchers Network) is an example of cross-country collaboration by trade unions in Africa. It was established in 2001 when a group of African trade union-based researchers met in Johannesburg. Initially the network included Ghana, Namibia, Nigeria, South Africa, Zimbabwe and Zambia, and it later grew to include countries like Angola, Kenya, Malawi and Tanzania. One of the ALRN's objectives is to address policy issues that affect African workers and their trade unions by providing relevant research and education materials.

There are projects involving even broader collaboration, such as the ASO (African Social Observatory) project. The ASO is coordinated by NALEDI (the National Labour & Economic Development Institute), on behalf of the ALRN – and it is financially supported by the Finnish Trade Union Solidarity Centre (SASK) and the Netherlands Trade Union Federation (FNV Mondiaal), with support also from the Canadian Labour Congress (CLC) and the Belgian Fund for Development Cooperation (FOS).

Sources: Compiled from African Labour Research Network (ALRN) (2005), Jauch (2007), and the brochure 'Ditsela 2008'

Successful trade unions are founded on two important factors: on their organisation from grassroots level upwards, and on their ability to negotiate and otherwise interact collectively. They also take part in the decision-making processes of various structures, bodies or institutions at a national level. These include, in South Africa, Nedlac, and the Unemployment Board. Sometimes trade unions use power strategies such as organising industrial action in the form of strikes, stayaways (protest action), consumer boycotts, picketing, etc. Trade unions also devote attention to the education and training of shop stewards and officials, especially at the level of the union federation. They also conduct research, and publish reports and opinions, and many unionists make presentations at conferences to market the role and views of trade unions. It is also well known that, should circumstances warrant it, trade unions will engage in costly litigation to further the interests of their members.

18.4.2 Rights relating to trade unionism in South Africa

In South Africa, trade unionism has been entrenched in the country's Constitution, and the rights that stem from this have been defined by the Labour Relations Act (hereafter also referred to as the Act). These rights are founded on the right to freedom of association which every South African enjoys. Because of this right, trade unions can legitimately be formed, and their rights have accordingly also been spelt out in the Act. It should be noted that, although the focus in this section is on trade union rights and duties, most of these also apply to employers' organisations.

18.4.2.1 Freedom of association

Section 4 of the Act grants employees the right to participate in the formation of a trade union or a federation of trade unions and, subject to the union's constitution, to join that trade union. Union members have the following rights:
- to participate in the lawful activities of their union;
- to participate in the election of any of its office bearers, officials or trade union representatives;
- to stand for election and be eligible for appointment as office bearer or official and, if elected or appointed, to hold office; and
- to stand for election and be eligible for appointment as a trade union representative and, if elected or appointed, to carry out the functions of a trade union representative in terms of the Act or in terms of any collective agreement.

Union members have the same rights in respect of a trade union federation of which their union is a member.

Section 5 of the Act further protects freedom of association by prohibiting discrimination, victimisation and so-called yellow-dog contracts of employment. No person may compel or threaten to compel an employee or job applicant to become, to be or not to become a member of a trade union or a workplace forum or to give up membership of a trade union or workplace forum. Furthermore, no person may discriminate against any person on these grounds or prevent a person from exercising any right conferred by the Act or from participating in any proceedings in terms of the Act. No person may prejudice or threaten to prejudice an employee or job applicant because of past, present or anticipated membership of a trade union or a federation of trade unions or workplace forum, or for his or her participation in forming a trade union or federation of trade unions or in establishing a workplace forum, for his or her participation in the lawful activities of a trade union, federation of trade unions or workplace forum, or for his or her failure or refusal to do something that an employer may not lawfully permit or require an employee to do, or for his or her disclosure of information that the employee is lawfully entitled or required to give to another person, or for his or her exercise of any right conferred by the Act, or for his or her participation in any proceedings in terms of the Act. Furthermore, no person may advantage, or promise to advantage, an employee or a job applicant in exchange for that person not exercising any right conferred by the Act or not participating in any proceedings in terms of the Act. A provision in any contract that directly or indirectly contradicts or limits freedom of association is automatically invalid, unless the contractual provision is permitted by the Act. (For example, section 26 of the Labour Relations Act provides for closed-shop agreements, which could, but for this provision, be found to be void since it could be argued that the closed-shop practice contravenes the principle of freedom of association. Note: the closed-shop agreement, which is discussed elsewhere in this book, does allow for safeguards against forced membership.)

It should be noted that sections 6 and 7 of the Act extend the right to freedom of association and the protection against victimisation to employers.

According to section 8 of the Act, a trade union (or employers' organisation) has the right:

- to determine its own constitution and rules;
- to hold elections for its office bearers, officials and representatives;
- to plan and organise its administration and lawful activities;
- to participate in the formation of a federation of trade unions or a federation of employers' organisations;
- to join a federation of trade unions or a federation of employers' organisations, subject to its constitution, and to participate in its lawful activities; and
- to affiliate with, and participate in the affairs of, any international workers' organisation or international employers' organisation or the International Labour Organization, and contribute to, or receive financial assistance from, those organisations.

Disputes arising from any alleged interference with freedom of association or from victimisation may be referred for conciliation to a bargaining council or the Commission for Conciliation, Mediation and Arbitration (CCMA). (Note that, whenever the phrase 'bargaining council or the CCMA' is used in this chapter, it is used in the following context and as shorthand to describe the following process: the Act encourages labour and capital to establish their own structures and procedures; thus if there is a functional bargaining council which has jurisdiction, that council will deal with the dispute. Only in the absence of such a council will the CCMA be required, as the default option, to deal with a matter.) Should the dispute remain unresolved, it may be referred to the Labour Court for adjudication. The process is depicted in figure 18.1.

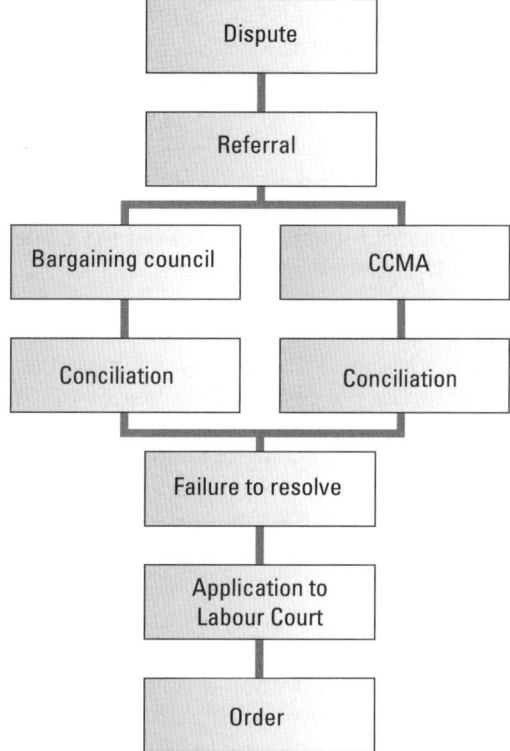

Figure 18.1: Freedom of association disputes

A complainant simply has to prove that he or she has been compelled, threatened, prohibited or detrimentally affected in almost any manner, after which the burden shifts to the defendant to prove that the conduct complained of did not constitute prohibited conduct in terms of this chapter of the Act.

18.4.2.2 Organisational rights of trade unions
The freedom to associate would have had little meaning in practice had the rights of the organisations with whom one may associate not also been catered for in the legislation.

Linkage between level of representativeness and entitlement to organisational rights
Depending on how many workers a union represents – its so-called level of representativeness – it will enjoy certain statutory organisational rights. At this point it may be instructive to note the four different types of trade union representativeness encountered in the Labour Relations Act 66 of 1995 as a whole and their attendant rights.

Sufficiently representative

Only a registered trade union (two or more unions may act jointly in order to establish sufficient representation) which is sufficiently representative of employees at a particular workplace will be afforded certain organisational rights. These rights include the following:
- the right of access to the workplace;
- the right to hold meetings at the employer's premises (outside working hours);
- the right to conduct a ballot at the workplace;
- the right to have trade union subscriptions deducted from members' salaries;
- the right of employees who are office bearers of the trade union to take reasonable leave during working hours for trade union business; and
- for registered unions that are parties to a bargaining council, automatic right of access and the right to stop-order facilities at all workplaces falling within the jurisdiction of the bargaining council, regardless of the trade union's level of representativeness at any particular workplace.

In the domestic sector, the right of access to the premises of the employer does not include the right to enter the home of the employer, unless the employer agrees (that is, without the employer's consent, a union office bearer may not enter the former's home, although he or she will have to be allowed entry to the premises for the purpose of recruiting members, communicating with members, etc).

The Act does not attempt to define 'sufficiently representative', but one can accept that it does mean a significant membership, albeit falling short of an outright majority.

Some clues as to what may affect the evaluation of whether the 'sufficient representativeness' criterion has been met in any specific case are to be found in section 21 of the Act, which instructs the adjudicator of a dispute about whether or not a registered trade union is a representative trade union, to seek to minimise the proliferation of trade union representation in a single workplace and to minimise the financial and administrative burden of requiring an employer to grant organisational rights to more than one registered trade union. In addition, consideration must be given to: (i) the nature of the workplace; (ii) the nature of the organisational rights that the registered trade union seeks to exercise; (iii) the nature of the sector in which the workplace is situated; and (iv) the organisational history at the workplace. From these statutory guidelines it is clear that no numerical value can be set as a threshold for sufficient representativeness – it will have to be determined case by case.

Sufficient representation could be determined by the amount of pressure the union's members could put on the employer if they were to embark on a protected strike.

Majority representation

Only registered trade unions with a majority support (more than 50%) in a particular workplace will be afforded the following organisational rights (as is the case with 'sufficiently representative', two or more unions may act jointly to establish majority representation in a workplace):
- the right to appoint shop stewards;
- the right to demand (subject to certain limitations and conditions) that the employer disclose information to the union should such information be necessary to enable the union or its representatives to fulfil their functions;
- the right to reasonable time off with pay during working hours for shop stewards to perform their functions and to be trained as shop stewards;

- the right to negotiate specific thresholds for certain rights (see the next paragraph); and
- the right to enter into an agency or a closed shop agreement.

Collective agreement thresholds

An employer and a majority trade union (or the employer and employee parties to a bargaining council) may conclude a collective agreement establishing a threshold of representativeness required in respect of the rights associated with the 'sufficient representativeness' criterion (that is, access to the workplace, stop-order facilities and leave for trade union activities for trade union office bearers). These thresholds may not discriminate between trade unions.

Thirty per cent representativeness

The fourth type of representativeness encountered in the Act' is that pertaining to statutory councils. A registered trade union that wishes to establish a statutory council requires a membership of at least 30% in the sector in question. Two or more trade unions may join together for the purpose of meeting the threshold level of representativeness.

The various circumstances under which a trade union may become entitled to organisational rights are listed below:
- when a union enjoys majority support in the workplace;
- when a union is sufficiently representative in the workplace;
- when a non-majority union meets the thresholds as determined for specific organisational rights in a collective agreement between the majority union and the employer;
- when an employer has conferred upon a union certain organisational rights in terms of a collective agreement;
- when a union is a member of a bargaining council or a statutory council: and.
- when a recognition agreement concluded in terms of Act 28 of 1956 that is still in force confers some organisational right on a union.

Disclosure of information

A controversial provision of the Act is the right afforded majority unions to require of an employer to disclose to a shop steward all relevant information that will allow the shop steward to perform his or her functions effectively, and the duty it places on an employer, whenever he or she consults or bargains with a majority trade union, to disclose to that trade union all relevant information that will allow the trade union to engage effectively in consultation or collective bargaining. This is, however, not such a radical innovation to our system as some employers would like us to believe, since there is jurisprudential support for the notion that good-faith collective bargaining requires disclosure of information as envisaged by the Act. Neither is the trade union's right to information, and the employer's concomitant duty to disclose the information, without boundaries that should adequately protect the interests of all stakeholders. Firstly, employers may inform the shop steward or the trade union in writing if any information disclosed is confidential. Should a trade union act in breach of its fiduciary duty not to disclose confidential information, a CCMA commissioner may order that the right to disclosure of information in that workplace be withdrawn for a period specified in his or her arbitration award. Secondly, an employer is not required to disclose information that is legally privileged; that the employer cannot disclose without contravening a prohibition imposed on the employer by any law or order of any court; that is confidential and, if disclosed, may cause substantial harm to an employee or to the employer; or that is private, personal information relating to an employee, unless that employee consents to the disclosure of that information. Any dispute about the disclosure of information must be referred to the CCMA, who must attempt to resolve it through conciliation, failing which the dispute may be arbitrated. The right to the disclosure of information is excluded in the domestic sector (for example, a shop steward may not demand information relating to the financial affairs of the employer of a domestic worker).

Exercising organisational rights

Any registered trade union may notify an employer in writing that it seeks to exercise one or more of the said rights in a workplace. The notice must be accompanied by a certified copy of the trade union's certificate of registration and must specify:
- the workplace in respect of which the trade union seeks to exercise the rights;
- the representativeness of the trade union in that workplace, and the facts relied upon to demonstrate that it is a representative trade union; and
- the rights that the trade union seeks to exercise and the manner in which it seeks to exercise those rights.

Within 30 days of receiving the notice, the employer must meet with the registered trade union and endeavour to conclude a collective agreement regarding the manner in which the trade union will exercise the rights in respect of that workplace. If a collective agreement is not concluded, either the registered trade union or the employer may refer the dispute in writing to the CCMA for resolution. Any dispute concerning the granting or exercise of organisational rights may be referred to the CCMA who must try to resolve it, first through mediation. If that fails, one of the parties may request that the CCMA-appointed commissioner arbitrate the dispute.

18.4.2.3 Trade union registration and relevant statutory requirements

A simplified registration procedure is provided for in the LRA. Of great importance is the fact that, although the process for registration has been made very simple, all rights in terms of the Act are now granted only to registered trade unions. The Act makes no provision for a dual system such as prevailed under the old Act. (It should be noted that all the provisions referred to in the text that relate to the rights and duties of trade unions, except those relating to shop stewards, also apply in essence to employers' organisations.) Unregistered bodies would not be recognised under the Act although in keeping with the principle of voluntarism, there is no direct compulsion to register in terms of the Labour Relations Act. Any trade union may apply for registration (see LRA Form 6.1 below), provided that it has adopted a suitable name, its constitution meets the statutory requirements (see subsection below), it has an address in South Africa, and it is independent. The last requirement is an expression of the legislator's disapproval of the practice of some employers to set up trade unions as their puppets in opposition to 'difficult' or 'radical' trade unions in order to divide the loyalty of the workforce and thus to undermine the undesirable trade union(s). In terms of the Act, a trade union is independent if it is not under the direct or indirect control of any employer or employers' organisation and it is free of any interference or influence of any kind from any employer or employers' organisation. With the exception of the independence requirement, the same provisions apply to employers' organisations that wish to register.

(See LRA Form 6.1 on accompanying CD)

Statutory requirements relating to the constitutions of trade unions

The constitution of a trade union that intends to register must:

- state that the trade union or employers' organisation is an association not for gain;
- prescribe qualifications for, and admission to, membership;
- establish the circumstances in which a member will no longer be entitled to the benefits of membership;
- provide for the termination of membership;
- provide for appeals against loss of the benefits of membership or against termination of membership, prescribe a procedure for those appeals and determine the body to which those appeals may be made;
- provide for membership fees and the method for determining membership fees and other payments by members;
- prescribe rules for the convening and conducting of meetings of members and meetings of representatives of members, including the quorum required for, and the minutes to be kept of, those meetings;
- establish the manner in which decisions are to be made;
- establish the office of secretary and define its functions;
- provide for other office bearers, officials and trade union representatives, and define their respective functions;
- prescribe a procedure for nominating or electing office bearers and trade union representatives;
- prescribe a procedure for appointing, or nominating and electing, officials;
- establish the circumstances and manner in which office bearers, officials and trade union representatives may be removed from office;
- provide for appeals against removal from office of office bearers, officials and trade union representatives, prescribe a procedure for those appeals, and determine the body to which those appeals may be made;
- establish the circumstances and manner in which a ballot must be conducted;
- provide that the trade union, before calling a strike, must conduct a ballot of those of its members in respect of whom it intends to call the strike;
- provide that members of the trade union or employers' organisation may not be disciplined or have their membership terminated for failure or refusal to participate in a strike or lockout if no ballot was held about the strike or lockout, or a ballot was held but a majority of the members who voted did not vote in favour of the strike or lockout;
- provide for banking and investing its money;
- establish the purposes for which its money may be used;
- provide for acquiring and controlling property;
- determine a date for the end of its financial year;
- prescribe a procedure for changing its constitution; and
- prescribe a procedure by which it may resolve to wind up.

In addition, it is specifically provided that the constitution of any trade union which intends to register may not include any provision that discriminates directly or indirectly against any person on the grounds of race or gender.

In terms of the Act, the Registrar of Labour Relations has a very limited discretion in the matter of registration. If the Registrar is satisfied that the applicant meets the requirements of the Act, he or she must register the applicant by entering the applicant's name in the relevant register (register of trade unions or the register of employers' organisations). After registering the applicant, the Registrar must issue a certificate of registration in the applicant's name and send it and a certified copy of the registered constitution to the applicant. If the Registrar is not satisfied that the applicant meets the requirements for registration, the Registrar must send the applicant a written notice of the decision and the reasons for it and, in that notice, inform the applicant that it has 30 days from the date of the notice to meet those requirements. Failure on the part of the applicant to meet the requirements within the 30-day period will result in a notification informing the applicant in writing of the Registrar's refusal to register the applicant.

Any person who is aggrieved by a decision of the Registrar may appeal to the Labour Court against that decision, within 60 days of either the date of the Registrar's decision or, if written reasons for the decision are demanded, the date of those reasons. The Labour Court, on good cause shown, may extend the period within which a person may note an appeal against a decision of the Registrar.

Effect of registration of a trade union

A certificate of registration is sufficient proof that a registered trade union is a body corporate with limited liability. This means that the fact that a person is a member of a registered trade union does not make that person liable for any of the obligations or liabilities of that organisation. A member, office bearer or official of a registered trade union or a shop steward is not personally liable for any loss suffered by any person as a result of an act performed or omitted in good faith by the member, office bearer, official or shop steward while performing their functions for or on behalf of the trade union.

Duties of registered trade unions and their federations

Every registered trade union (take note again that similar principles apply to employers' organisations) is obliged to do the following:
- keep proper books of account, records of its income, expenditure, assets and liabilities;
- within six months after the end of each financial year, prepare financial statements, including at least a statement of income and expenditure for the previous financial year, and a balance sheet showing its assets, liabilities and financial position as at the end of the previous financial year;
- arrange for an auditor to undertake an annual audit of its books, records of account and financial statements; make the financial statements and the auditor's report available to its members for inspection; and submit those statements and the auditor's report to a meeting or meetings of its members or their representatives as provided for in its constitution;
- preserve each of its books of account, supporting vouchers, records of subscriptions or levies paid by its members, income and expenditure statements, balance sheets and auditor's reports for a period of three years from the end of the financial year to which they relate;
- keep a register of its members;
- keep the minutes of its meetings for a period of three years;
- keep ballot papers for a period of three years;
- by 31 March each year, supply the Registrar with a certified membership list as at 31 December of the previous year;
- supply the Registrar, within 30 days of receipt of its auditor's report, with a certified copy of that report and of the financial statements;

- supply the Registrar, within 30 days of receipt of a written request by him or her, with an explanation of anything relating to the membership list, the auditor's report or the financial statements;
- supply the Registrar, within 30 days of any appointment or election of its national office bearers, with the names and work addresses of those office bearers;
- supply the Registrar with notice of change of address 30 days before a new address for service of documents will take effect;
- send the Registrar a certified copy of the resolution should a trade union wish to change its constitution or name; and
- should a registered trade union wish to amalgamate with another trade union, the amalgamating trade unions may apply to the registrar for registration of the amalgamated trade union.

Any federation of trade unions (or any federation of employers' organisations) is obliged to provide the Registrar with the following:
- within three months of its formation, and after that by 31 March each year, the names and addresses of its members and the number of persons each member in the federation represents;
- within three months of its formation, and after that within 30 days of any appointment or election of its national office bearers, the names and work addresses of those office bearers, even if their appointment or election did not result in any changes to its office bearers;
- within three months of its formation, a certified copy of its constitution and an address in the Republic at which it will accept service of any document that is directed to it;
- within 30 days of any change to its constitution, or of the address provided to the Registrar as required, notice of that change; and
- within 14 days after it has resolved to wind up, a copy of that resolution.

18.4.2.4 The state of South African trade unionism: a few remarks

The focus in this section is on the various trade union federations, with some reference also to statistics and trends in the South African trade union movement.

Chapter 2 dealt with how the development of trade unions has over the years influenced South African society generally. Trade union membership figures grew very strongly in South Africa especially during the 1970s, and throughout the 1980s while the struggle to end apartheid had its greatest momentum. There was some growth still into the early 1990s.

According to Nel et al (2008: 54) and Barker (2007: 92–93), about three million South African workers belonged to trade unions by 2005, comprising just less than 40% of all employees working in the formal sector of the economy. This trend of relatively high (and growing) unionisation levels sharply contrasts with trade union membership trends generally across the world over the period. The peculiar development of South African history, and the central role of the labour movement herein, would obviously have been the prominent factor in this regard. It should be noted, however, that trade union membership in South Africa peaked at a figure of close to three and a half million employees by 1993 (Levy & Associates 1996: 12) and the growth rate then plateaued.

According to Department of Labour records, membership figures of registered trade unions actually went into a decline phase from the period 1993 to 1994. Some might argue that this may be linked to the actual stage of South Africa's political history at the time, in that the working people of South Africa might have felt their mobilisation efforts over especially the prior two and a half decades were finally paying off with the dawn of the 'new' South Africa in 1994. We must keep in mind, however, that the economic dynamics (such as structural shifts and growing competition) would have had quite an impact as well. Many organisations, for instance, had to downsize, which meant loss of jobs and hence also union membership, and there were and still are sectoral shifts – away from those which have been characterised by high unionisation density traditionally. According to the statistics used by Levy and Associates (1996), total union membership figures were just below three million by the end of 1996. After the period of more or less ten years that followed, these membership figures remained about same overall, while some fluctuations were recorded from year to year. There can be much speculation about possible future trends in this regard but we will have to wait and see how things develop in our country. The fact of the matter is that trade unionism in South Africa is fully intertwined with the broader political and socio-economic dynamics – as also discussed in chapter 2.

Up until late 2007, South Africa had only three very prominent trade union federations (Cosatu, Fedusa and Nactu) and one smaller, much less prominent one. The latter is Consawu (Confederation of South African Workers Unions) which had about 150 000 members via its affiliated trade unions (Barker 2007: 94).

Cosatu (Congress of South African Trade Unions) is South Africa's largest federation and it also boasts the affiliation of the country's four largest trade unions (apart from other unions, of course). These four are the NUM (National Union of Mineworkers) with almost 300 000 members, Nehawu (National Education, Health and Allied Workers Union) with about 234 000 members, Sadtu (South African Democratic Teachers Union) with about 214 000 members, and Numsa (National Union of Metalworkers of South Africa) (Barker 2007: 94).

Some of the important principles driving Cosatu include non-racialism, one union per industry, cooperation between affiliates and a national level, working-class upliftment and worker control. Today it is very well known that this federation has been instrumental in the turnaround of South African society and is continuing to play a significant role in the country through its official alliance with the ANC as the ruling political party of the country, and the SACP.

Since about 2005, the two other large federations and the smaller one engaged in increasingly more serious discussions about possibilities for collaboration. On 9 November 2007 the South African Confederation of Trade Unions (Sacotu) was launched – about a year later than initially was the target – and without Consawu (Confederation of South African Workers Unions) being a party to it. The membership of this new umbrella federation is limited to Fedusa and Nactu (and automatically the unions affiliated to Fedusa and Nactu). (Also see 'A case at hand' below).

A CASE AT HAND

The country's largest non-politically aligned labour federation was launched on Friday – a full year behind schedule.

The National Council of Trade Unions (Nactu) and the Federation of Unions of South Africa (Fedusa) merged to form the South African Confederation of Trade Unions (Sacotu). With one million paid-up members, Sacotu is the second-largest representative of organised workers, behind the Congress of South African Trade Unions (Cosatu), which has 1.8 million members.

Sacotu is led by Mary Malete, the former president of Fedusa.

>>

Fedusa, Nactu and the Confederation of SA Workers' Unions (Consawu) had planned to launch a super labour federation last October. The target date was moved to sort out issues such as differences in financial practices, staff structures and provincial offices. That process has now left Consawu on the sidelines.

Sacotu's new positioning in the organised labour movement presents challenges to Cosatu.

"We hope that the new confederation will not take a narrow and short-sighted role of trying to be a rival to Cosatu. The real enemy of the labour movement is the employer," said Bheki Ntshalintshali, Cosatu's deputy general secretary, when addressing Sacotu's policy conference on Friday.

The prospect of a single-union federation in the country is nowhere near because of Cosatu's political alignment.

Ntshalintshali said Cosatu had invited Fedusa and Nactu to talks early next year on how to move forward with a possible merger.

However, Joseph Maqhekeni, Nactu's former president and now the deputy president of Sacotu, dispelled any possibility of merging with a trade union that is politically aligned.

"Sacotu is a genuine giant federation that is independent and non-political. Anyone that wants to merge with us must leave the marriage of political parties," he said.

Cosatu is in alliance with the ANC and the SACP.

However, Ntshalintshali argued that the role of the labour movement has to be broader than workers' bread and butter issues.

Although Sacotu believes in social democracy, it is against any political alignment to trade union federations.

Dennis George, former general secretary of Fedusa, said it was a challenge to merge the two trade federations, given their different organisational and long-held cultural traditions.

In the past Fedusa was a conservative bulwark that catered for the needs of white workers. In recent years, the union has transformed dramatically and allowed black participation in all levels within its structures.

Nactu had also subscribed to the ideologies of the Pan African Congress, but the union has a solid record of championing left-wing politics that are aimed at advancing the needs of the workers and the poor. "Both organisations have long histories, but they had organised separately along racial lines. It was difficult merging them, but it was also fun," said George.

He said Sacotu would never allow any political interference in trade unionism.

Cosatu has been drumming up support for ANC deputy president Jacob Zuma in the ruling party's succession battle.

Labour Minister Membathisi Mdladlana challenged Sacotu to mobilise vulnerable workers such as domestics and farm labourers.

The trade federations in the country are failing to organise and mobilise workers, particularly those in the informal sectors of the economy, he said.

Mdladlana said about five million workers are organised into trade unions in South Africa, while over 12 million were not unionised.

It is also estimated that 16% of all employees in South Africa earn less than R500 a month.

Recent studies have shown that workers who are organised earn 20% more than those who do not belong to unions.

"You'll need to leave the comfort of your offices. Workers must know that their leaders are there to protect them. You must deploy more shop stewards on the floor to protect the workers against all forms of exploitation," he said.

Sacotu said it is supportive of the country's economic transformation discourse.

Maqhekeni criticised those who lashed out at the government's affirmative action policies.

"There would be no transformation without affirmative action. We support government's transformation policies."

Source: Mgibisa 2007 (www.news24.com/City_Press/Finance/0,186-246_2218863,00.html)

18.5 STATUTORY PROVISIONS REGARDING STRUCTURES AND PROCESSES FOR COLLECTIVE BARGAINING AND DISPUTE RESOLUTION

18.5.1 General

As mentioned previously, the primary legal source of the rules governing collective bargaining in South Africa is the Labour Relations Act 66 of 1995. At the outset it must be noted that the Labour Relations Act (hereinafter also referred to as "the Act") does not make collective bargaining compulsory in the private sector (with the notable exception of certain issues that are the subject of joint decision making if a workplace forum exists). It is equally important to understand that the Act vigorously encourages collective bargaining. This understandable bias in favour of collective bargaining is evident from the features listed in exhibit 18.1.

EXHIBIT 18.1: Inducements to collective bargaining in the LRA of 1995

- Granting of strong organisational rights
- Agreements are enforced through arbitration
- A refusal to bargain may be referred to advisory arbitration
- Emphasis placed on central bargaining
- Strong right to strike underpins the need to bargain
- Uncertainties of the Act (better to regulate agreement)
- Pre-eminence of agreements over provision of the Act
- Collective agreements are binding irrespective of whether they were concluded at central or plant level
- All agreements must contain a conciliation and arbitration procedure

---

The objects of the Act, as stated in its long title, are summarised in exhibit 18.2.

EXHIBIT 18.2: Objects of the Labour Relations Act 66 of 1995

- to give effect to the constitutional right to fair labour practices;
- to regulate the organisational rights of trade unions;
- to promote and facilitate collective bargaining at the workplace and at sectoral level;
- to regulate the right to strike and the recourse to lock out in conformity with the Constitution;
- to promote employee participation in decision making through the establishment of workplace forums;
- to provide simple procedures for the resolution of labour disputes through statutory conciliation, mediation and arbitration, and through independent alternative dispute resolution services accredited for that purpose;
- to establish the Labour Court and Labour Appeal Court as superior courts;
- to provide for a simplified procedure for the registration of trade unions and employers' organisations, and to provide for their regulation to ensure democratic practices and proper financial control; and
- to give effect to the public international law obligations of the Republic relating to labour relations.

In furtherance of these objectives the Act provides for forums to be established by the parties (bargaining councils, statutory councils and workplace forums) on which employers' representatives and employees' representatives can interact on matters of mutual interest and prevent or resolve disputes which may arise between them. In addition, the Act grants recognition and strong rights to shop stewards (called 'trade union representatives' in the Act). The Act also provides for the establishment of specialist courts (the Labour Court and the Appeal Court) to adjudicate certain labour matters. In addition to the Labour Relations Act, regard must also be taken of the National Economic, Development and Labour Council Act 35 of 1994, which provides for the establishment of a national economic, development and labour council (Nedlac).

In table 18.1, a brief summary is provided of the primary modes of interaction between the parties, the categories of issues, as well as the statutory structures and processes created to deal with them.

Table 18.1: Structures, issues and processes for interaction

Structures	Issues	Processes
Nedlac	National labour market policy (eg labour market flexibility and drafting of labour legislation)	Politics
Bargaining councils	Sectoral and substantive issues (eg wages bargaining and macro-level issues such as industry restructuring)	Politics, conciliation, mediation, advisory arbitration, industrial action
Workplace forums	Workplace issues related to equity and wealth creation	Consultation, joint decision making, conciliation, mediation, arbitration, industrial action
Shop stewards and their committees	Organisational rights at workplace level and all issues related to agreement administration and the policing of workers' rights	Interpersonal (informal) dynamics, representational facilitation, conciliation & mediation
Commission for Conciliation, Mediation and Arbitration (CCMA)	Certain disputes must be referred to the CCMA; also acts as default option in the absence of a (functioning) bargaining council	Conciliation, fact finding, mediation, arbitration, training, advice giving
Labour Court & Labour Appeal Court	Disputes of right	Adjudication

Although the Act promotes collective bargaining, it has to be accepted that from time to time bargaining may break down. This is why one of the objects of the Act is also to facilitate and promote effective and efficient dispute resolution. Disputes often arise in labour relations and it is therefore important to understand what labour disputes entail. In this regard it is necessary to distinguish between a dispute of right and a dispute of interest.

Although the concepts 'dispute of rights' and 'dispute of interest' are nowhere to be found in the Act, the distinction between these two types of dispute are fundamental to the philosophy informing the dispute resolution procedures of the Act.

Dispute of rights

A dispute of right is a dispute about the interpretation of an existing right. The parties are not in disagreement about the existence of the right, only over whether the right has been infringed, or not, by one of the parties. For example, in an alleged unfair dismissal dispute, the employer does not maintain that the employee does not have the right not to be unfairly dismissed; the employer asserts that the employee was fairly dismissed and therefore that his right not to be unfairly dismissed has not been infringed. Employment-related rights may derive from labour statutes, collective agreements, the employment contract or the common law of employment. Rights disputes typically involve dismissal disputes or disputes over the interpretation of a collective agreement. It should be evident that these disputes are of a legal nature and therefore that the best way to resolve them would be to make use of a judicial or quasi-judicial process such as arbitration. To allow industrial action over such disputes would be to endorse the laws of the jungle that legal rules are disposable at the option of the party which is the strongest (a 'might is right' approach). To permit this will undermine the whole edifice of the self-regulation of industrial relationships by way of collective agreements. In order to protect our system from such anarchy and lawlessness, the Act makes it impossible to embark on a protected strike or lockout over rights disputes. For example, a strike over the alleged unfair dismissal of a co-worker will always be an unprotected strike, the fairness or otherwise of a dismissal being a rights issue.

The Act allows only one exception to the general rule that industrial action over rights disputes would be unprotected, and that is in respect of disputes over organisational rights. A trade union may elect to strike over such disputes, in which case the union forfeits its right to refer the same dispute to arbitration for a period of 12 months.

Disputes of interest

Disputes of interest are disputes over issues of mutual interest between employer and employees where neither party has a right to that which it wants. In contrast to disputes of right, a dispute of interest is not over an existing right, but over the creation of a new one. An example would be a wage dispute. The union is not asserting that it has a right which it wishes to enforce (there is no right to a wage increase) but it wishes to create a right to a new (higher) wage. In such disputes it is appropriate that the outcome should be determined by power play, because there is no 'right' or 'wrong' answer in the sense that a third party can interpret an existing agreement or legal provision. Only in cases where the parties agree to refer an interest dispute to arbitration or where policy considerations (for example the social and economic costs to society in general of industrial action in essential services) prohibit recourse to industrial action will disputes of interest be resolved through arbitration. Consequently, the Labour Relations Act provides for disputes of interest, subject to certain limitations, procedural requirements and exclusions, to be determined by collective bargaining underpinned by the threat of industrial action. It is this realisation – that the other party may resort to industrial action if deadlock is reached – that motivates the parties to enter into negotiations and to reach agreement. It follows that industrial action that is functional to collective bargaining over disputes of interest is protected by the Labour Relations Act. Remember that industrial action is collective bargaining continued by other means or, to put it differently, industrial action is part and parcel of the collective bargaining process. We will now focus on the structures for collective bargaining and dispute resolution in South Africa.

18.5.2 The National Economic, Development and Labour Council (Nedlac)

Nedlac is governed by an executive council and consists of four chambers, namely:

- a public finance and monetary policy chamber;
- a trade and industry chamber;
- a labour market chamber; and
- a development chamber.

The membership of Nedlac comprises representatives of organised business, representatives of organised labour, parties who represent organisations of community and development interests, and representatives of the state. The functions of Nedlac are summarised in exhibit 18.3.

EXHIBIT 18.3: The objectives of Nedlac

- to strive to promote the goals of economic growth, participation in economic decision making and social equity;
- to seek to reach consensus and conclude agreements on matters pertaining to social and economic policy;
- to consider all proposed labour legislation relating to labour market policy before it is introduced in parliament;
- to consider all significant changes to social and economic policy before it is implemented or introduced in parliament; and
- to encourage and promote the formulation of coordinated policy on social and economic matters.

In pursuance of these objectives, the Act confers on Nedlac the authority to:

- make such investigations as it may consider necessary;
- continually survey and analyse social and economic affairs;
- continually evaluate the effectiveness of legislation and policy affecting social and economic policy; and
- conduct research into social and economic policy.

EXHIBIT 18.4: Responsibilities conferred on Nedlac by LRA of 1995

- Demarcation of the sector and area in respect of which a bargaining council is to be registered
- Nominating members to the governing body of the CCMA
- Preparing Codes of Good Practice relating to industrial relations at the workplace for publication in the Government Gazette
- Advising the President on the appointment of judges to the labour courts
- Facilitating consultation between the Minister of Labour and the Minister of Public Service and Administration and Nedlac on matters concerning the LRA
- Monitoring of socio-economic issues giving rise to protest action

---

It can be expected that Nedlac will have (and indeed has already had in its short history) a telling influence on the development of economic policy, labour laws and our system of industrial relations. Through the Labour Relations Act 66 of 1995, Nedlac also has a direct role to play in that it is, inter alia, responsible for the issues listed in exhibit 18.4.

18.5.3 Bargaining councils

Bargaining councils must be registered in respect of a specific area and sector. They are established when employers' and employees' organisations come together and decide to create a permanent forum on which to regulate matters jointly in their industry and area. The parties apply for registration of a bargaining council for a specific industry and area to the Registrar who will register the council once he has satisfied himself that the applicants are registered employer and employee organisations, that there is no existing bargaining council which has jurisdiction, and that the parties are sufficiently representative in the area and industry. In assessing the representativeness of a council, the Registrar may regard the parties as representative of the whole area, even if the trade union or employer parties to the council have no members in part of the area. Representativeness must be reviewed annually.

The registration of the council will be in respect of a specific industry and area only (this means that more than one bargaining council can be registered for the same industry, but each will cover different areas or that more than one council will have jurisdiction in the same area, but for different industries). Bargaining councils are permanent bodies and consist of an equal number of representatives from labour and employers respectively. These are, on the employer side, an employer, group of employers, registered employers' organisations, group of registered employers' organisations, or any mixture of these groups; and a registered trade union or group of registered trade unions on the labour side.

Any registered trade union or registered employers' organisation may apply in writing to a council for admission as a party to that council. An applicant must be advised of the council's decision within 90 days of that council having received the application for admission, failing which the council is deemed to have refused the applicant admission. If the council refuses to admit an applicant, it must within 30 days of the date of the refusal advise the applicant in writing of its decision and the reasons therefore it. The applicant may apply to the Labour Court for an order admitting it as a party to the council. The Labour Court may admit the applicant as a party to the council, adapt the constitution of the council and make any other appropriate order.

A bargaining council can be likened to a mini-parliament which has jurisdiction over a particular geographical area and industry (for example the chemical industry in KwaZulu-Natal). All employers and all employees (and their representative bodies) within that area and industry will thus fall under the jurisdiction of the particular bargaining council registered for that area and industry, irrespective of whether the individual employer or employee organisation is actually represented on the council (membership of a bargaining council is voluntary). This implies that, if a dispute were to arise between an individual employer and a trade union, neither of whom are members of a bargaining council, they would still have to refer their dispute to the council, should both or either of them wish to embark on industrial action. A bargaining council regulates matters of mutual interest in its industry and area by way of collective agreements (these are the 'laws' issued by the 'mini-parliament'). This lawmaking process proceeds as follows: a decision voted for by the majority (as prescribed in the constitution of the bargaining council) of the council's members will be regarded as a decision by the council.

In the early 1970s, a dual system of collective bargaining developed in South Africa: established trade unions bargained at centralised level through the industrial council system while some of the so-called emergent trade unions rejected the official system in favour of plant-level bargaining and the conclusion of recognition agreements. Unfortunately, the legal status of recognition agreements has always proved problematic and such a dual system inevitably generated its own friction and conflict. The Act solves this problem by making all collective agreements, whether concluded at centralised or decentralised (individual plant) level, enforceable in terms of the Act. In terms of the transitional arrangements provided for in the Act, existing recognition agreements are regarded as enforceable collective agreements under the Act.

The Act stipulates that a collective agreement binds the parties and their members to the agreement – as well as those employees who are not members of the trade union which is party to the agreement – if those employees fall within the bargaining unit, the agreement is expressly intended to cover them, and the trade union enjoys majority representation in a particular workplace. Collective agreements continue to bind members of the trade union and employers' association to a collective agreement, irrespective of whether those employees/employers remain members of the trade union/employers' association. Individual employment contracts are automatically amended by the provisions of collective agreements. Unless otherwise specified, any party to a collective agreement may terminate the agreement by giving reasonable notice to the other parties to the agreement.

Procedures for the settlement of disputes regarding the interpretation or application of a collective agreement must be provided for in the agreement. The procedure must first provide for mediation and thereafter for arbitration.

Disputes may also be referred to the CCMA for conciliation followed by arbitration if the collective agreement does not contain the required dispute settlement procedure, the procedure is not operative, or a party to the agreement has frustrated the resolution of the dispute in terms of the agreed-upon procedure. In the case of disputes over the interpretation or application of agency or closed shop agreements, these must be referred to the CCMA for conciliation/arbitration.

The parties to a council must attempt to resolve any dispute between them in accordance with the constitution of the council. Any party to a dispute who is not a party to a bargaining council, but who falls within the registered scope of the council, may refer the dispute to the council in writing. The party who refers the dispute to the council must satisfy it that a copy of the referral has been served on all the other parties to the dispute. If a dispute is referred to a council in terms of the Act and any party to that dispute is not a party to that council, the council must attempt to resolve the dispute through conciliation. If the dispute remains unresolved after conciliation, the council must arbitrate the dispute if the Act requires arbitration and if any party to the dispute has requested that it be resolved through arbitration, or if all the parties to the dispute consent to arbitration under the auspices of the council. If one (or more) of the parties to a dispute that has been referred to the council do not fall within the registered scope of that council, it must refer the dispute to the CCMA. Every council must apply to the CCMA for accreditation to perform the conciliation and arbitration functions referred to previously, or appoint an agency accredited by the CCMA to perform those functions on its behalf.

Bargaining councils typically conciliate and arbitrate the following types of disputes:

- dismissal for misconduct;
- dismissal for incapacity;
- constructive dismissal;
- dismissal where the employee does not know the reason for his or her dismissal;
- unfair labour practice disputes; and
- disputes about the interpretation or application of the council's constitution or of collective agreements.

Other disputes are conciliated by the bargaining council, but if conciliation fails, they are referred to the Labour Court for adjudication; for example disputes about dismissal for operational requirements, automatically unfair dismissals, dismissals because of an unprotected strike and an alleged infringement of freedom of association.

Subject to the constitution of the bargaining council, a collective agreement concluded in a bargaining council binds only the parties to the bargaining council who are parties to the collective agreement. However, a bargaining council may ask the Minister in writing to extend a collective agreement concluded in the bargaining council to any non-parties to the collective agreement that are within its registered scope and are identified in the request. This may happen if the employee and employer parties who represent the majority of employees and employers respectively voted in favour of such an extension. A collective agreement may not be extended by notice in the *Government Gazette* unless the Minister is satisfied about the matters listed in exhibit 18.5.

EXHIBIT 18.5: Extension of collective agreements

A collective agreement may not be extended by notice in the *Government Gazette* unless the Minister is satisfied that:

■ the majority of employees employed within the registered scope of the bargaining council are members of the trade unions that are party to the bargaining council;

■ the members of the employers' organisations that are party to the bargaining council employ the majority of the employees employed within the registered scope of the bargaining council;

■ the non-parties specified in the request fall within the bargaining council's registered scope;

■ the terms of the collective agreement do not discriminate against non-parties;

■ the collective agreement establishes or appoints an independent body to grant exemptions to non-parties and to determine the terms of those exemptions from the provisions of the collective agreement as soon as possible; and

■ the collective agreement contains criteria that must be applied by the independent body when it considers applications for exemptions, and that those criteria are fair and promote the primary objects of this Act.

Especially noteworthy are the last two requirements relating to exemptions. These provisions are supposed to safeguard the interests of small and medium-sized enterprises against the predations and monopolistic tendencies of large corporations. Whether these will prove to be an effective shield remains to be seen. Under the previous dispensation, the right to apply for exemption from industrial council agreements was frequently made nugatory by the delays encountered in getting a response to an exemption application.

18.5.3.1 Powers and functions of bargaining councils

The most important functions and powers of bargaining councils are listed in exhibit 18.6.

18.5.3.2 Constitutions of bargaining councils

The constitution of every bargaining council must provide for those matters listed in exhibit 18.6.

Only if the constitution of the bargaining council (see exhibit 18.7) complies with the requirements spelt out in exhibit 18.6 may the Registrar register the bargaining council. Of particular importance is the requirement pertaining to small and medium-sized enterprises (SMEs). It is often charged that the erstwhile industrial councils (the predecessors of the bargaining councils) did not cater for SMEs and indeed inhibited the growth and performance of these very important sources of business innovation and job creation.

EXHIBIT 18.6: Powers and functions of bargaining councils

Bargaining councils are conferred with the following powers and functions:
- to conclude collective agreements;
- to enforce those collective agreements;
- to prevent and resolve labour disputes (mainly through mediation/arbitration);
- to establish and administer a fund to be used for resolving disputes;
- to promote and establish training and education schemes;
- to establish and administer pension, provident, medical aid, sick pay, holiday, unemployment and training schemes or funds; or any similar schemes or funds for the benefit of one or more of the parties to the bargaining council or their members;
- to develop proposals for submission to Nedlac or any other appropriate forum on policy and legislation that may affect the sector and area;
- to determine by collective agreement the matters which may not be an issue in dispute for the purposes of a strike or a lockout at the workplace; and
- to confer on workplace forums additional matters for consultation.

18.5.4 Public service bargaining councils

Prior to the new Act, the Public Service Labour Relations Act and the Education Labour Relations Act established the Public Service Bargaining Council and the Education Labour Relations Council respectively as the bargaining forums for these two public service sectors. These two councils, operating under different laws, covered only certain sectors of the public service. The new Act provides for the creation of a single overarching structure, the Public Service Coordinating Bargaining Council, which should regulate and coordinate collective bargaining across the public service as a whole, as well as for (subordinate) bargaining councils in sectors in the public service. The old Public Service Bargaining Council and the Education Labour Relations Council became bargaining councils for their respective public service sectors in terms of the new Act.

It should be noted that the state may also be an employer party to a bargaining council in the private sector, if it is an employer in a sector and area covered by a private sector bargaining council.

18.5.5 Statutory councils

During the deliberations at Nedlac leading up to the Act, a major bone of contention was the demand by Cosatu-affiliated trade unions for the inclusion in the Act of a provision making centralised bargaining compulsory in all sectors of the economy. The employer parties to Nedlac strongly opposed this demand, and the outcome was a compromise, namely a proto bargaining council designated a statutory council. In terms of the Act, any trade union or employers' organisation which represents at least 30% of employees or employers in a sector and area in respect of which no bargaining council is registered may apply to the Registrar for the establishment of a statutory council. Having satisfied him- or herself that the applicant meets the prerequisites of the Act, the Registrar must then invite all registered trade unions and registered employers' organisations in that sector and area to attend a meeting for the purpose of concluding an agreement regarding the parties to the statutory council and a constitution for that council. This meeting is to be chaired by a CCMA commissioner. If an agreement is reached at that meeting, the Minister must still approve of the registration of the statutory council before it can be registered by the Registrar.

EXHIBIT 18.7: Constitutions of bargaining councils

The constitution of every bargaining council must provide for:

- the appointment of representatives of the parties to the bargaining council, of whom half must be appointed by the trade unions that are party to the bargaining council and the other half by the employers' organisations that are party to the bargaining council, and the appointment of alternates to the representatives;
- the representation of small and medium enterprises;
- the circumstances and manner in which representatives must vacate their seats and the procedure for replacing them;
- rules for the convening and conducting of meetings of representatives, including the quorum required for, and the minutes to be kept of, those meetings;
- the manner in which decision are to be made;
- the appointment or election of office bearers and officials, their functions, and the circumstances and manner in which they may be removed from office;
- the establishment and functioning of committees;
- the determination through arbitration of any dispute arising between the parties to the bargaining council about the interpretation or application of the bargaining council's constitution;
- the procedure to be followed if a dispute arises between the parties to the bargaining council;
- the procedure to be followed if a dispute arises between a registered trade union that is a party to the bargaining council, or its members, or both, on the one hand, and employers who belong to a registered employers' organisation that is a party to the bargaining council, on the other hand;
- the procedure for exemption from collective agreements;
- the banking and investment of its funds;
- the purposes for which its funds may be used;
- the delegation of its powers and functions;
- the admission of additional registered trade unions and registered employers' organisations as parties to the bargaining council;
- a procedure for changing its constitution; and
- a procedure by which it may resolve to wind up.

Should no agreement be reached at the meeting, the CCMA commissioner must facilitate the conclusion of an agreement. However, if this also fails, the Minister must admit any applicant and any other registered trade union or employers' organisation to become a party to the statutory council. In the absence of a registered trade union or a registered employers' organisation to complete the bipartite structure of the council, the Minister must appoint appropriate persons as representatives of employees or employers, as the case may be.

The powers and functions of a statutory council are to prevent and settle labour disputes, to promote and establish training and education schemes, and to establish and administer pension, provident, medical aid, sick pay, holiday, unemployment schemes or funds or any similar schemes or funds for the benefit of one or more of the parties to the statutory council or their members.

Therefore, statutory councils cannot negotiate wages or conditions of employment (that is, substantive issues), except if the parties to the council agreed to negotiate substantive issues; the purpose of a statutory council is to centralise regulations of certain labour matters as a precursor to becoming a fully fledged bargaining council. Statutory councils are mechanisms created in the name of self-regulation but which are essentially undemocratic and counter to the principle of voluntarism in that a basically unrepresentative body can gain power over an area and industry subject only to the approval of the Minister.

18.5.6 Dispute resolution and the Commission for Conciliation, Mediation and Arbitration (CCMA)

18.5.6.1 Establishment and functions of the CCMA

Thus far we have referred several times to the CCMA. The Labour Relations Act provides for the establishment of the CCMA, which is to be independent of the state, any political party, trade union, employer, employers' organisation, federation of trade unions or federation of employers' organisations. The CCMA is governed by a governing body, consisting of a chairperson and nine other members (labour, employers and the state, each represented by three persons), each nominated by Nedlac and appointed by the Minister to hold office for a period of three years, and the director of the Commission. The Commission has jurisdiction in all the provinces of the Republic. The CCMA can easily be described as the centrepiece of the new industrial relations system introduced by the Act. The CCMA has no one predecessor: in certain respects it fulfils the conciliation functions that the former conciliation boards were supposed to perform (but unfortunately failed to fulfil); in other respects it takes over many of the functions of the old Industrial Court. In addition to this, the CCMA is assigned a host of other tasks not previously given to any specific body. Since most disputes must be processed through the conciliation-arbitration route via either a bargaining council or, as the default option, the CCMA, these bodies have their work cut out for them.

The functions of the CCMA can be broadly grouped into four categories. The CCMA must:

- attempt to resolve, through conciliation, any dispute referred to it in terms of the Act;
- if after conciliation a dispute still remains unresolved, arbitrate the dispute if the Act requires arbitration and any party to the dispute has requested that it be resolved through arbitration, or all the parties to a dispute in respect of which the Labour Court has jurisdiction consent to arbitration by the Commission;
- assist in the establishment of workplace forums; and
- compile and publish information and statistics about its activities.

The CCMA must further:

- if asked, advise a party to a dispute about the procedure to follow in terms of the Act;
- assist a party to a dispute to obtain legal advice, assistance or representation;
- offer to resolve a dispute that has not been referred to it;
- accredit councils or private agencies (see below);
- subsidise accredited councils or accredited agencies;
- conduct, oversee or scrutinise any election or ballot of a registered trade union or registered employers' organisation if asked to do so by that trade union or employers' organisation;
- publish guidelines in relation to any matter dealt with in this Act; and
- conduct and publish research into matters relevant to its functions.

The CCMA may provide, on request, employees, employers, registered trade unions, registered employers' organisations, federations of trade unions, federations of employers' organisations or councils with advice or training relating to the main objectives of the Act, such as:

- the establishment of collective bargaining structures:
- the design, establishment and election of workplace forums and the creation of deadlock-breaking mechanisms;
- the functioning of workplace forums;
- the prevention and resolution of disputes and employees' grievances;
- disciplinary procedures;
- procedures in relation to dismissals;
- the process of restructuring the workplace;
- affirmative action and equal opportunity programmes; and
- sexual harassment in the workplace.

In addition, the CCMA must perform any other duties assigned to it by or in terms of the Act and may perform any other function entrusted to it by any other law. The CCMA may appoint commissioners in either a full-time or part-time capacity to perform the functions of commissioners.

The CCMA may accredit and subsidise bargaining councils and private agencies to perform conciliation, mediation and arbitration functions. In essence, provision is made for the privatisation of dispute resolution. Once the CCMA is satisfied that an applicant agency or bargaining council meets the set standards, the CCMA may accredit such body to perform all or some of the aforementioned functions (on application the terms of an accreditation may be amended). An accredited council or accredited agency may charge a fee for performing any of the functions for which it is accredited, provided that the fee is in accordance with the tariff of fees determined by the CCMA.

18.5.6.2 Resolution of disputes under the auspices of the CCMA

Detailed provision is made in the Act for the settlement of different types of disputes through conciliation, mediation and arbitration. In an effort to settle a dispute, a commissioner may try many techniques, such as mediation, conducting a fact-finding exercise or making a recommendation to the parties, which may be in the form of an advisory arbitration award.

Any party to a dispute about a matter of mutual interest may refer it in writing to the CCMA. The party who does so must also send a copy of the referral to all the other parties to the dispute. As should be clear by now, the general route any dispute would follow is first conciliation, failing which arbitration (or, in a few cases, adjudication).

Resolution of disputes through conciliation

When a dispute has been referred to the CCMA, it must appoint a commissioner to attempt to resolve it through conciliation (no provision is made, as is the case in arbitration, for the parties to request a specific commissioner to be appointed to perform the conciliation function). The appointed commissioner must attempt to resolve the dispute through conciliation within 30 days of the date the CCMA received the referral; the parties may, however, agree to extend the 30-day period. In the conciliation proceedings, a party to the dispute may appear in person or be represented only by a co-employee or by a member, an office bearer or official of that party's trade union or employers' organisation and, if the party is a juristic person, by a director or an employee. At the end of the 30-day period, or any further period agreed between the parties, the commissioner must issue a certificate stating whether or not the dispute has been resolved.

Resolution of disputes through arbitration

Disputes may be resolved through arbitration if:

- the Act requires settlement through arbitration;
- a commissioner has issued a certificate stating that the dispute remains unresolved; and
- any party to the dispute has requested that the dispute be resolved through arbitration.

The commissioner tasked with arbitrating the dispute may be the same commissioner who attempted to resolve the dispute through conciliation. However, any party to the dispute may object to the arbitration being conducted by the same commissioner who conciliated the dispute, in which event the CCMA must appoint another one. Although parties to a dispute may request a specific commissioner to deal with their dispute, the CCMA is under no obligation to accede to their request if it is impracticable to do so. Should the parties have a stated preference, this must be put in writing (listing no more than five commissioners) and must state that the request is made with the agreement of all the parties to the dispute; it must be submitted within 48 hours of the date of the certificate stating that the dispute remains unresolved.

Provision is also made for the appointment of a senior commissioner to arbitrate in a matter at the request of any party to the dispute. When considering whether the dispute should be referred to a senior commissioner, the director of the commission must hear the party making the application, any other party to the dispute and the commissioner who conciliated the dispute. The director may appoint a senior commissioner to act as arbitrator, after having considered the nature of the questions of law raised by the dispute, the complexity of the dispute, whether there are conflicting arbitration awards that are relevant to the dispute, and the public interest. The director must notify the parties to the dispute of the decision. The director's decision is final and binding, and may only be taken on review after the dispute has been arbitrated. The Act expressly provides that commissioners must "… determine the dispute fairly and quickly, but must deal with the substantial merits of the dispute *with the minimum of legal formalitie*s [emphasis added]". In addition the Act specifies that, within 14 days of the conclusion of the arbitration proceedings, the commissioner must issue an arbitration award with brief reasons, signed by that commissioner (the director may extend the period within which the arbitration award and the reasons are to be served and filed).

Fairness, speed and procedural simplicity are the objectives stressed in these proceedings. A commissioner is also granted considerable leeway in the manner in which the arbitration proceedings are conducted; for example, if all the parties consent, the arbitration proceedings may be suspended and an attempt to resolve the dispute through conciliation may be made. During the proceedings a party to the dispute may give evidence, call witnesses, question the witnesses of any other party, and address concluding arguments to the commissioner. In any arbitration proceedings, a party to the dispute may appear in person or be represented by a legal practitioner, a co-employee or by a member, office bearer or official of that party's trade union or employers' organisation and, if the party is a juristic person, by a director or an employee. It should be noted that the only outsiders allowed to represent a party at arbitration proceedings are legal practitioners, and even they are excluded in proceedings dealing with misconduct and capacity disputes. A commissioner may make any appropriate arbitration award (including, but not limited to, an award that gives effect to any collective agreement, that gives effect to the provisions and primary objects of the Act, that includes, or is in the form of, a declaratory order). However, a commissioner may not include an order for costs in the arbitration award unless a party, or the person who represented that party in the arbitration proceedings, acted in a frivolous or vexatious manner by proceeding with or defending the dispute in the arbitration proceedings, and/or in its conduct during the arbitration proceedings.

Special provisions for arbitrating certain disputes

The Act makes special provisions for disputes in essential services, disputes about dismissals for misconduct or incompetence, and disputes in respect of which the parties have agreed to waive their right to adjudication by the Labour Court in favour of arbitration by the CCMA.

■ *Arbitrating disputes in essential services*: If a dispute about a matter of mutual interest proceeds to arbitration and any party is engaged in an essential service, then the commissioner has 30 days (or such longer period as the parties may have agreed upon) from the date of the certificate stating that conciliation has failed to settle the dispute, to complete the arbitration and to issue a signed arbitration award providing brief reasons for the award.

■ *Arbitrating disputes about dismissals for reasons relating to conduct or capacity*: If the dispute being arbitrated is about the fairness of a dismissal and a party has alleged that the reason for the dismissal relates to the employee's conduct or capacity, the parties are not entitled to be represented by a legal practitioner in the arbitration proceedings unless the commissioner and all the other parties consent, or the commissioner concludes that it is unreasonable to expect a party to deal with the dispute without legal representation. In coming to this conclusion, consideration should be given to the nature of the questions of law raised by the dispute, the complexity of the dispute, the public interest, and the comparative ability of the opposing parties or their representatives to deal with the arbitration of the dispute. Provision is also made for the commissioner, if he finds that the dismissal is procedurally unfair, to charge the employer an arbitration fee.

■ *Consent to arbitration under the auspices of the CCMA*: In section 141, provision is made for all the parties to agree to arbitration under the auspices of the CCMA of disputes that, but for that agreement, a party would have been entitled to refer to the Labour Court for adjudication. Any party to such arbitration agreement may apply to the Labour Court at any time to vary or set aside that agreement. If any party acts in breach of such an agreement by commencing proceedings in the Labour Court, any party to those proceedings may ask the Court to stay those proceedings and refer the dispute to arbitration, or to continue with the proceedings with the Court acting as arbitrator.

Arbitration awards

An arbitration award is final and binding, and may be made an order of the Labour Court unless it is an advisory arbitration award. An arbitration award may only be amended or rescinded if it was erroneously sought or erroneously made in the absence of any party affected by that award, or if it contains an ambiguity, obvious error or omission, or if it was granted as a result of a mistake common to the parties to the proceedings.

Any party to a dispute may take an arbitration award on review to the Labour Court asking for an order setting aside the award, based on an alleged defect in the arbitration proceedings, such as improper conduct on the part of the commissioner, or a gross irregularity in the conduct of the arbitration proceedings, or the alleged exceeding by the commissioner of his powers, or that an award has been improperly obtained. Review applications must be made to the Labour Court within six weeks of the date that the award was served on the applicant, unless the alleged defect involves corruption, in which event, within six weeks of the date that the applicant discovers the corruption.

Resolution of dismissal disputes by conciliation–arbitration (con-arb)

The Labour Relations Amendment Act of 2002 provides for a joint conciliation and arbitration process of dispute resolution for *dismissal disputes*. The CCMA (or a council with jurisdiction) must enrol the dispute for a hearing within 30 days. The CCMA (or council) must notify the parties that the dispute will be arbitrated immediately if conciliation is unsuccessful.

At the hearing, the CCMA must first attempt to conciliate the dispute. If the matter cannot be resolved, the parties must be advised that further conciliation would serve no purpose. The employee must then be asked whether he or she wishes to have the dispute arbitrated. If the employee requests arbitration, the arbitration hearing must commence immediately, unless the proceedings are postponed on application by either party to the dispute.

Despite the fact that the commissioner may decide to stand down or postpone the arbitration proceedings, the CCMA may decide to refer the dispute to the Labour Court on application by either party. When receiving such an application, the reason for the dismissal, the questions of law raised by the dispute, the complexity of the matter and public interest must be considered. The parties and the conciliating commissioner must be afforded an opportunity to make representations before a decision is made. The parties must be notified of the decision, and the dispute must be referred to the CCMA for arbitration or to the Labour Court for adjudication. The decision of the CCMA is final and binding. No person may apply to any court of law to review the decision until the dispute has been arbitrated or adjudicated, as the case may be.

A party may appear in person in a con-arb or may be represented by a legal practitioner, a candidate attorney, a member or official of a registered trade union or employers' organisation or, if the party is a juristic person, by a director or employee. In the case of a company, a director or employee of the party's holding or subsidiary company or an accredited labour adviser may represent that party. Representation by a union or employers' organisation is possible only if the party to the dispute was a member of that union or organisation prior to the date on which the dispute arose.

18.5.7 Process of 'alternative' dispute resolution

In this context 'alternative' refers to the processes other than adjudication. You have already learned about alternative dispute resolution (ADR) under the auspices of the CCMA, but you have not yet been exposed to the nature and dynamics of these methodologies.

It is therefore necessary now to clarify some concepts and processes from a more general point of view. We must keep in mind that the statutory framework provided by the government does not preclude the possibilities of engaging in alternative dispute resolution processes outside of those provided for by the legislative framework. In this sense then we are now also taking a brief look at 'alternatives' for dispute resolution that exist more generally (and outside of the work of the CCMA and bargaining councils, for instance).

The terms 'conciliation' and 'mediation' are used interchangeably by many writers and dispute-resolution bodies, as does Tokiso, the best known labour dispute resolution body (and recently commercial mediation too). In South Africa, prior to the Labour Relations Act of 1995 it was referred to as 'mediation'. After 1995, because of conciliation as a dispute resolution process in the LRA, 'conciliation' was used.

Often when referring to dispute resolution at the CCMA or bargaining councils it is referred to as 'conciliation' whereas if it is a private, voluntary process many people tend to refer to it as 'mediation'.

Some refer to mediation as a sub-process of conciliation The reason may relate to the fact that in the LRA Section 135(3) under 'resolution of disputes', reference is made to the fact that a commissioner must determine an appropriate process, which may include mediation.

Whether used interchangeably or, as preferred by some, as two different processes, conciliation and mediation are third party-assisted interventions for dispute resolution.

Important elements of mediation or conciliation are that the third party does not have ruling powers. The mediator or conciliator controls the process in assisting the parties to reach an agreement. The parties can be in joint or side meetings with the mediator or conciliator.

It is a process that ensures confidentiality. It is a without-prejudice procedure, and records or minutes are not a feature of the process, which means it is off the record. The resolution agreement, if reached, is usually recorded at the end by way of a settlement agreement.

- *Voluntary mediation*: The basic notion of voluntary mediation is that the parties who find themselves in a polarised position appoint a neutral third person, respected and trusted by both parties, to act as go-between and to try to achieve a settlement by affecting a change in the position of one or both parties so that agreement can become possible.

- *The mediator*: The conflict, communication and people-handling skills of the mediator or conciliator are of paramount importance (rather than legal or technical expertise). The mediator has to be completely impartial, show understanding for the parties' points of view (be empathetic), and treat confidential information as such. The mediator's primary task is to promote constructive communication and to moderate any aggression and personal acrimony between the parties. The mediator should never take credit for an agreement – this must go to the parties. At joint meetings, the mediator should avoid making suggestions and these should rather come from one of the parties. In order to maintain the credibility of the mediation process, mediators should also be honest with themselves and the parties, and withdraw if they see that they cannot help the parties to reach an agreement.

- *The mediation process*: This begins when the parties agree to use mediation. After the mediator has been appointed and a date fixed for the first meeting, the parties compile written submissions about the dispute which are sent to the mediator so that he or she can determine the nature and extent of the dispute. It is better for the parties to meet on neutral territory, such as a hotel, rather than at the employer's factory of the union's offices. The meeting place should preferably have separate rooms where the parties can each caucus in private and can meet with each other (thus at least three rooms). The mediator should first meet with each of the parties separately to determine their (conflicting) views of the dispute and to clarify any obscure points in the written submissions. At this stage the mediator does not make any suggestions – he or she merely encourages the parties to review the matters in dispute calmly, in order to create the right atmosphere for such a review of their respective points of view.

- *Arbitration*: Arbitration involves the appointment of an impartial third party, acceptable to all the disputing parties, to act as final judge in a dispute. The arbitrator gives a final and binding decision regarding the provisions of the settlement. What happens in effect is that the parties renounce their right to further negotiation, request the arbitrator to settle the dispute on their behalf and undertake to be bound by the arbitrator's decision (the arbitration award). The parties usually resort to arbitration when they feel that they cannot possibly settle the dispute themselves but they both have too much to lose by capitulating. Arbitration under the LRA is prescribed mainly for some rights disputes, such as dismissal disputes based on misconduct, incapacity and other rights disputes, such as unfair labour practice.
- *Advisory arbitration*: An advisory arbitration award is a non-binding award and as such can be accepted or rejected by both or one of the parties. The purpose of such an award is to persuade the parties to accept or at least entertain the considered opinion of an outside expert. The new Act requires that an advisory arbitration award be made prior to industrial action over a refusal to bargain.
- *Con-arb*: The idea underlying the con-arb process is that, if the parties do not reach a resolution at the conciliation stage, a third party (the arbitrator) will do so on their behalf through a legal process, and will act as an inducement for the parties to reach a settlement. In addition, the con-arb process itself also obviously expedites the resolution of disputes.

18.5.8 Dispute resolution through adjudication: the Labour Court and Labour Appeal Court

The Act provides for the establishment of the Labour Court as an open court of law with jurisdiction in all the provinces of South Africa. The Labour Court is a court of record and has the same powers and status as a provincial division of the Supreme Court. The Court is presided over by a Judge President, a Deputy Judge President and as many judges as the President may consider necessary, acting on the advice of Nedlac and in consultation with the Minister of Justice and the Judge President of the Labour Court. In order to qualify for appointment as a judge on the Labour Court, a person must have knowledge, experience and expertise in labour law, and either be a judge of the Supreme Court or have been a legal practitioner for a cumulative period of at least 10 years before his or her appointment. The Labour Court has exclusive jurisdiction in respect of all matters that in terms of the Act are to be determined by the Labour Court but does not have jurisdiction to adjudicate an unresolved dispute if the Act requires the dispute to be resolved through arbitration. Interestingly, the Court may refuse to hear a matter, other than an appeal or review, if the Court is not satisfied that an attempt has been made to resolve the dispute through conciliation. The Labour Court may make any appropriate order or fulfil certain functions, including those listed in exhibit 18.8.

In any proceedings before the Labour Court, a party to the proceedings may appear in person or be represented by a legal practitioner, a co-employee or by a member, an office bearer or official of that party's trade union or employers' organisation and, if the party is a juristic person, by a director or an employee. The Labour Court may make an order for the payment of costs, according to the requirements of the law and fairness. When deciding whether or not to order the payment of costs, the

EXHIBIT 18.8: Powers of the Labour Court

The Labour Court has the power to:

- grant urgent interim relief;
- grant an interdict;
- order the performance of any particular act which order, when implemented, will remedy a wrong and give effect to the primary objects of this Act;
- grant a declaratory order;
- award compensation;
- award damages;
- order costs;
- order compliance with any provision of this Act;
- make any arbitration award or any settlement agreement, other than a collective agreement, an order of the Court;
- request the Commission to conduct an investigation to assist the Court and to submit a report to the Court;
- determine a dispute between a registered trade union, a registered employers' organisation, and one of its members about any alleged noncompliance with the constitution of that trade union or employers' organisation;
- condone the late filing of any document with, or the late referral of any dispute to, the Court;
- review the conduct of any person who performed (or failed to perform) a function provided for in the Act;
- review any decision taken or any act performed by the State in its capacity as employer;
- hear any appeals brought under the Occupational Health and Safety Act; and
- deal with all matters necessary or incidental to performing its functions in terms of the Act or any other law.

Labour Court may take into whether the matter referred to the Court ought to have been referred to arbitration in terms of this Act and, if so, the extra costs incurred in referring the matter to the Court as well as the conduct of the parties in proceeding with or defending the matter before the Court and during the proceedings before the Court. The Labour Court may order costs against a party to the dispute or against any person who represented that party in those proceedings before the Court.

A court of appeal in labour matters is instituted by the Act. The Labour Appeal Court is a court of law and equity. The Labour Appeal Court is the final court of appeal in respect of all judgements and orders made by the Labour Court in respect of the matters within its exclusive jurisdiction. In relation to matters under its jurisdiction, the Labour Appeal Court has the same power and status as the Appellate Division. There is no further appeal from the Labour Appeal Court to the Appellate Division. The Labour Appeal Court consists of the Judge President of the Labour Court, the Deputy Judge President and three other judges of the Supreme Court. The Labour Appeal Court is constituted before any three judges whom the Judge President designates from the ranks of the aforementioned judges, provided that no judge of the Labour Appeal Court may sit in the hearing of an appeal against a judgement or an order given in a case that was heard before that judge. The Labour Appeal Court has exclusive jurisdiction to hear and determine all appeals against the final judgements and the final orders of the Labour Court, and to decide any reserved question of law referred to it by the Labour Court.

18.5.9 Industrial action in South Africa

18.5.9.1 General and some reflection on trends

As mentioned already, industrial action is an intrinsic part of collective bargaining and can actually be characterised as 'collective bargaining by other means'. Industrial action is power used by one party to exert the highest degree of pressure on the other. It can take on various forms, such as go-slows, work-to-rule, sympathy strikes, overtime bans and, on the part of the employer, lockouts.

As you learned from chapter 2, South Africa experienced severe episodes and periods of industrial action during the 1980s in particular. Naturally these went hand in hand with the broader political and socio-economic developments in the country. We must remember that industrial action is the expression of unhappiness and the show of collective power to try to change whatever may be the cause of the state of unhappiness of the workers. Exhibit 18.9 contains slightly adapted extracts from the Department of Labour's *Industrial Action 2006 Annual Report*, and figure 18.2 is also taken from the same source. These give us some idea of the latest trends in industrial action in South Africa.

EXHIBIT 18.9: Extracts from the Department of Labour's *Industrial Action 2006 Annual Report*

Between 2002 and 2006, the number of working days lost due to industrial action in South Africa increased by 574,4% (3 536 840). This means it increased from 615 723 working days lost in 2002 to 4 152 563 in 2006. The Department of Labour believes that this is because the country experienced longer national strikes in 2006 than in the previous years. For example, the National Contract Cleaners strike lasted for 49 working days, the Shoprite/Checkers strike lasted 69 working days, the security guard strike lasted 96 days, the Sun International strike lasted 56 days and the Sasko strike lasted 22 working days.

Furthermore, the year 2006 was also characterised by socio-economic protest actions called by the federation Cosatu (18 May 2006) against job losses and privatisation. Worker violence against non-strikers and 'scab' labour was also observed in the same year. In this regard, two strikes involving Satawu and Cleaning Companies, and Satawu and Security Employers were reported to be violent. Two further strikes between Saccawu and Shoprite/Checkers, and Saccawu and Karan Beef were also reported to be violent.

Wage-related issues remain the key reason for industrial action in South Africa. About 3 847 985 working days were lost due to pay-related strike action in 2006. This represents approximately 92,7% of the total working days lost in that year.

Using the number of working days lost per 1 000 employees (time:loss ratio) enables a meaningful comparison of annual work stoppages. Time:loss ratio is a standard measure that is used to convert working days lost into a strike rate that takes into account the size of total employment. After thus controlling for the rise in employee numbers over the years 2002 to 2006 (due to the economy's expansion), the time:loss ratio reveals an overall rising trend from 54 working days lost per 1 000 employees in 2002 to 334 in 2006, as shown by figure 18.2.

>>

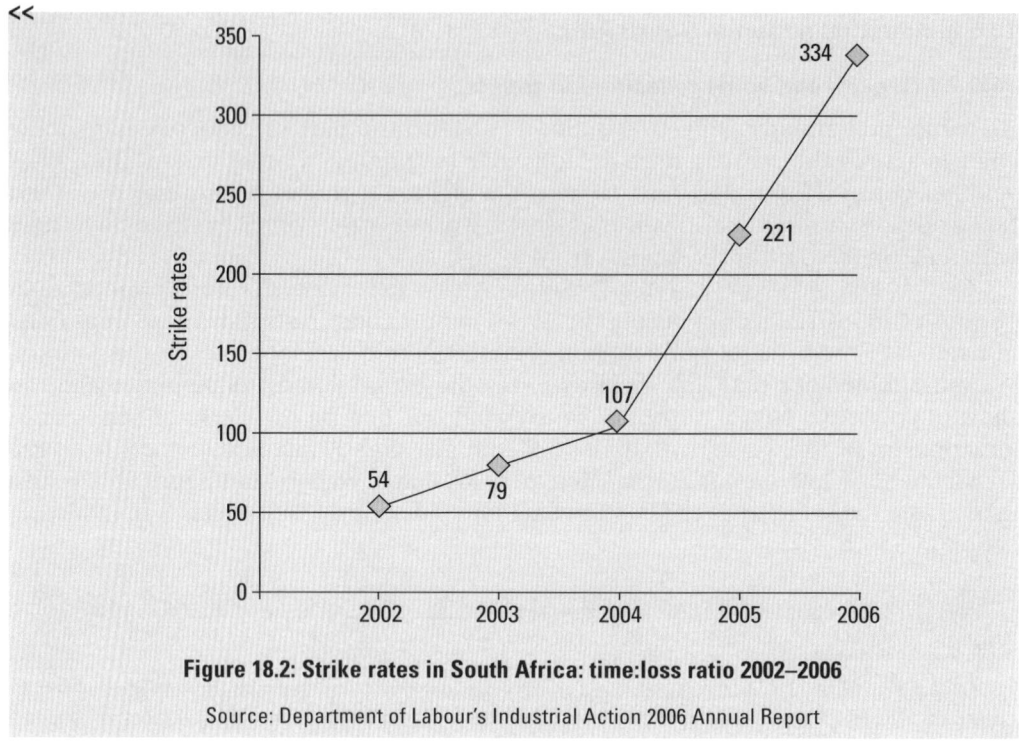

Figure 18.2: Strike rates in South Africa: time:loss ratio 2002–2006

Source: Department of Labour's Industrial Action 2006 Annual Report

18.5.9.2 Defining 'strike' and 'lockout' in South Africa

The Act provides a strong right to strike in that workers engaged in a strike protected by the Act may not be dismissed for striking.

The Act defines a strike as follows:

> ... the partial or complete concerted refusal to work, or the retardation or obstruction of work, by persons who are or have been employed by the same employer or by different employers, for the purpose of remedying a grievance or resolving a dispute in respect of any matter of mutual interest between employer and employee, and every reference to 'work' in this definition includes overtime work, whether it is voluntary or compulsory.

From this definition, the following constituent elements of a strike can be distilled:

- *Concerted action*: This implies, first, that one worker cannot go on a strike (two or more workers are needed), and secondly, that the refusal to work, etc must be the result of some form of collusion or understanding between the workers (two or more workers who refuse independently to work do not constitute a strike as defined).
- *Type of action*: The action constituting a strike may be a refusal to work or the retardation or obstruction of work (thus go-slows and sit-ins could qualify as strikes as defined).
- *Purpose*: This is the crucial and ultimately defining constituent element of a strike. Only strikes in support of a demand in respect of a matter of mutual interest between employer and employee will qualify as strikes in the legal sense.

Only if all three of the above elements of a strike are present can one talk of a strike in the defined sense. Other interesting aspects of the strike definition are the following:

- *Status of workers*: Employees as well as ex-employees employed by the same or different employers may be the participants in a strike.
- *Overtime work*: The positive law position (as developed by the Appellate Division) prior to this Act was far from satisfactory: a concerted refusal to work compulsory overtime in support of a demand was regarded as a strike, whereas the same refusal in respect of voluntary overtime could not be regarded as a strike but could constitute an unfair labour practice. The definition brings much-needed common sense and consistency regarding the refusal to work overtime (see the last part of the strike definition).

The Act defines a lockout as:

> ... the exclusion by an employer of employees from the employer's workplace, for the purpose of compelling the employees to accept a demand in respect of any matter of mutual interest between employer and employee, whether or not the employer breaches those employees' contracts of employment in the course of or for the purpose of that exclusion.

It is important to note that a lockout will only be recognised as such if the conduct and intent satisfy the definition. Two elements need to be present simultaneously for it to be a lockout in terms of the Labour Relations Act are (i) a particular course of action on the part of the employer; and (ii) it must be accompanied by a certain intent. It should further be noted that in order to qualify as a lockout (as in the case of a strike), the demand has to be of a certain type: it must be an economic demand (thus a demand that the employees should refrain from endorsing the policies of a particular political party will be regarded as a political demand and, as such, will, as per the definition, disqualify the conduct as a lockout).

Lockouts can be classified as either offensive or defensive. In the case of the defensive lockout, the employer locks his workforce out in reaction to their industrial action. This could, for instance, be appropriate where the employees are on a go-slow, work-to-rule, partial strike or a sit-in. In these situations, the employer is prevented from employing temporary employees to do the work of the strikers (due to the physical presence of the strikers on the premises). By locking them out, he can overcome this obstacle. In other situations it may make strategic sense for the employer to take the initiative during negotiations by embarking on an offensive or pre-emptive lockout. This will be the case, for instance, where the employer wishes to avoid a strike at a time when he will be at his most vulnerable (for example during periods of peak demand and production). By locking out the employees, management tries to exert pressure on them to accept management's offer, thereby hoping to bring the negotiations to a conclusion.

18.5.9.3 Status of strikes/lockouts in terms of the Act

Statutorily speaking, strikes and lockouts can be categorised as prohibited, protected or unprotected.

Prohibited strikes/lockouts

These are strikes or lockouts that are absolutely prohibited. These usually occur under the following circumstances:

- if a collective agreement is in force that prohibits industrial action in respect of the issue in dispute;
- if the issue in dispute is subject to compulsory arbitration;
- if the issue in dispute is one that a party has the right to refer to arbitration or to the Labour Court in terms of the Act;
- if the employee is employed in an essential service (see below);
- if the employee is designated as a maintenance worker (see below);
- no strike or lockout may occur during the first year of a wage determination made in terms of the Wage Act that regulates the issue in dispute; and
- no strike or lockout may occur when a binding arbitration award or a ministerial determination that regulates the issue in dispute has been made.

Employees participating in a prohibited strike are guilty of misconduct and may be dismissed provided that a fair procedure is followed.

Protected strikes/lockouts

These are strikes or lockouts that conform to the procedural requirements stipulated in the Act. The most important legal consequence of a protected strike is that the strikers may not be dismissed for partaking in it.

Procedure for protected industrial action: Every employee has the right to strike and every employer recourse (not 'right') to lockout, provided that certain procedural requirements are met. In essence, these procedures require a dispute to be referred to a council or, if there is no council with jurisdiction, to the CCMA, which has 30 days to resolve the dispute through conciliation, failing which the trade union or the employer may give 48 hours' written notice of its intention to strike or lockout. After the expiry of the notice period, the strike or lockout will be protected (provided, of course, that the prohibited circumstances are not applicable). The procedure is depicted in figure 18.3.

Deviations from the above general procedure are applicable under the following circumstances:

- *Strike/lockout procedure in a collective agreement*: If there is a collective agreement containing a procedure for strikes and/or lockouts, then a strike or lockout that conforms with that procedure will be protected industrial action. This is another example of how the Act promotes collective bargaining. Under the previous Act, compliance with the procedure prescribed by a collective agreement would have been irrelevant so far as the legality of the strike or lockout would have been concerned – the only way to have achieved legitimacy was to comply with the provisions of the Act. In stark contrast to this legalistic approach, the Act in effect allows the parties to contract out of the provisions of the statutory strike law in favour of their own (self)-regulated agreed procedure.
- *Defensive strike/lockout in reaction to unprocedural industrial action by the other party*: If the strike or lockout is in response (a so-called defensive strike or lockout) to an unprocedural strike or lockout, then the defensive strike or lockout will be protected under the Act.
- *Constitution of a council*: If the parties to the dispute are members of a bargaining council or a statutory council that has dealt with the dispute in terms of its constitution, then the industrial action will be a protected strike or lockout under the Act.

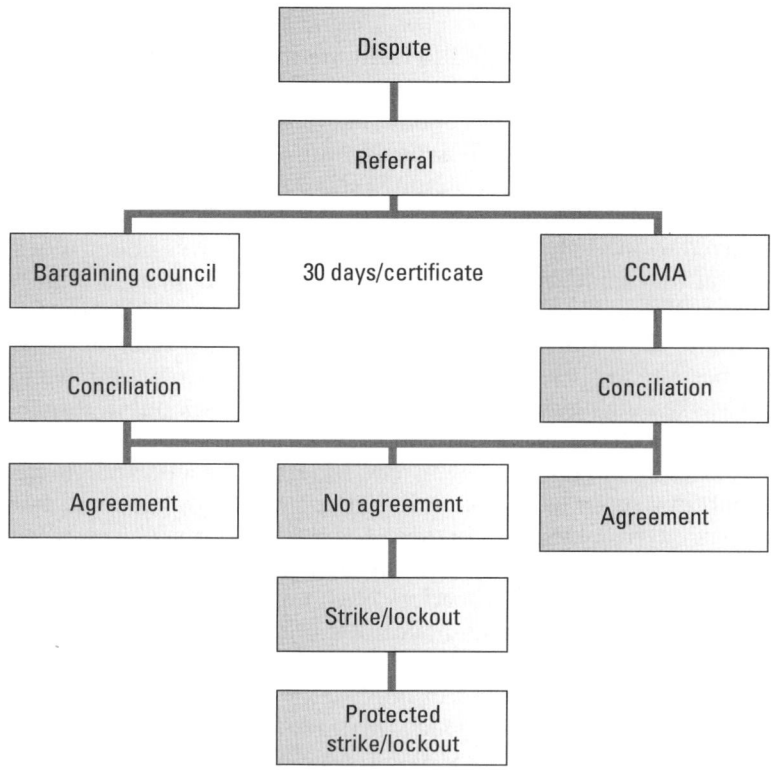

Figure 18.3: Procedure for protected industrial action

- *Unilateral change of employment conditions by the employer*: If the employer unilaterally altered a term or condition of employment or intends to do so, and if the trade union or employee who has referred the dispute to a bargaining council or statutory council or the CCMA at the same time sent a copy of the referral, giving 48 hours' notice to the employer not to proceed or to reverse the unilateral alteration, and the 48-hour period has ended without the employer having retracted the change (whether implemented or intended), then the strike in reaction to this unilateral action will be protected, even though it does not comply with the general procedural requirements set out in figure 18.3.
- *Refusal to bargain*: If the issue in dispute concerns a refusal to bargain, an advisory award must have been made by the CCMA before the 48 hours' notice of the start of the proposed strike/lockout can be given. A refusal to bargain includes a refusal to recognise a trade union as a collective bargaining agent, or to agree to establish a bargaining council; or a withdrawal of recognition of a collective bargaining agent; or a resignation of a party from a bargaining council; or a dispute about appropriate bargaining units, or levels or bargaining subjects.
- *Strikes over retrenchment*: The Labour Relations Amendment Act 12 of 2002 introduced a controversial provision to our collective labour law, namely the right to negotiate (including the right to strike) over retrenchment. An employer may dismiss employees, and a registered trade union or the employees who have received notice of termination may either give notice of a strike or refer a dispute concerning whether there is a fair reason for the dismissal to the Labour Court. This may be done after 60 days have elapsed from the date on which the employer issued a written notice inviting the other counselling party to consult

with it, and the employer discloses in writing all prescribed relevant information. If a third party has been appointed to facilitate the dispute, there is no need to refer it to conciliation; whereas, if a facilitator has not been appointed, the normal requirement to refer the dispute to conciliation applies. A union may not give notice of a strike if it has referred a dispute concerning whether there is a fair reason for that dismissal to the Labour Court. Likewise, if it has given notice of a strike in this regard, the issue (whether there is a fair reason for dismissal) may not be referred to the Labour Court. If a trade union gives notice of a strike, no member of that trade union (and no employee to whom a relevant collective agreement has been extended), may refer a dispute concerning whether there is a fair reason for dismissal to the Labour Court. Any such referral to the Labour Court that has already been made is deemed to have been withdrawn upon a notice of a strike being given. An employer may only lock out in respect of a dispute in which a strike notice has been issued.

- *Essential services and maintenance services*: In terms of section 65, no person may take part in a strike or a lockout if that person is engaged in an essential or a maintenance service. Disputes in these services must first be resolved through conciliation, and should that fail, then through arbitration. The only exception to the no-strike rule in essential services is where the parties to a dispute have previously provided for the maintenance of minimum services in a designated essential service by way of a collective agreement which has been ratified by the Essential Services Committee. For example, a trade union and a hospital may have concluded an agreement in which the trade union undertook to keep certain essential services staffed during a strike. If such an agreement is ratified by the ESC, it would mean that workers may strike in the essential service but that they undertake to continue providing certain agreed-upon minimum services for the duration of the strike. Considering that the right to strike is a constitutionally protected right as well as the fact that there is no real equivalent surrogate for the strike weapon (arbitration remains a very poor second-best option), the introduction of minimum services provisions in our strike law is to be welcomed.

    The Act defines an *essential service* as "a service the interruption of which endangers the life, personal safety or health of the whole or any part of the population, (or), the Parliamentary service, (or) the South African Police Service". The ESC is entrusted with the task of determining whether or not the whole or a part of any service is an essential service, and then deciding whether or not to designate the whole or a part of that service as an essential service; to determine disputes as to whether or not the whole or a part of any service is an essential service; and to determine whether or not the whole or a part of any service is a maintenance service. A service is defined (in section 75(1)) as a maintenance service "if the interruption of that service has the effect of material physical destruction to any working area, plant or machinery". An example of a maintenance service could be the operation of water pumps in a mine shaft. Should the continuous pumping of underground water be interrupted because of a strike, it may well happen that the whole workplace is destroyed by flooding, thereby causing the permanent loss of jobs, something strikers would typically not intend to cause by their strike. If there is no collective agreement relating to the provision of a maintenance service, an employer may apply in writing to the ESC for a determination that the whole or a part of the employer's business is a maintenance service.

- *Scab labour:* An employer may not make use of replacement labour under the following two circumstances: first, to continue or maintain production during a protected strike if the whole or a part of the employer's service has been designated a maintenance service; or secondly, for the purpose of performing the work of any employee who is locked out, unless the lockout is in response to a strike. Replacement labour includes persons engaged through the services of a temporary employment service or an independent contractor.

Unprotected strikes/lockouts

These are strikes or lockouts that fall outside the procedures of the Act. The most important legal consequences are that the Labour Court may interdict such strikes or lockouts and order any just compensation for losses attributable to such strikes or lockouts. In addition, strikers participating in an unprotected strike may be dismissed for striking, provided that their dismissal is procedurally and substantively fair.

As a summary, exhibit 18.10 contains some comparative perspectives regarding the consequences of these different categories of industrial action.

EXHIBIT 18.10: Consequences of industrial action

Protected strike/lockout
- Workers cannot be dismissed for striking (but may be dismissed for misconduct during the strike or for operational reasons).
- Involvement in a protected strike/lockout cannot constitute a delict.
- Employer is not obliged to remunerate strikers except in respect of payment in kind.
- Civil legal proceedings may not be instituted against a person for his/her involvement in a protected strike or lockout (except if the conduct constitutes an offence).
- Conduct in contravention of the Basic Conditions of Employment Act or the Wage Act does not constitute an offence.
- Some limitations apply in respect of the employer's ability to employ replacement workers during a protected strike if a part of his operations had been designated as maintenance services.

Unprotected/prohibited strike/lockout
- The Labour Court may interdict the strike or lockout.
- The Labour Court may award just and equitable compensation for any loss attributable to the strike or lockout, having regard to a number of considerations [s 68(1)(b)]:
  - whether attempts were made to comply with the provisions of the chapter on strike law and the extent of those attempts;
  - whether the strike or lockout was premeditated;
  - whether the strike or lockout was in response to unjustified conduct by another party to the dispute;
  - whether there was compliance with a Labour Court order or interdict restraining any person from participating in industrial action;
  - the interests of orderly collective bargaining;
  - the duration of the strike or lockout; and
  - the financial position of the employer, trade union or employees.
- involvement in an unprotected/prohibited strike may constitute a fair reason for dismissal (it is regarded as misconduct), provided that a fair procedure is followed.

18.5.9.4 Specific types of statutory industrial action

Thus far the focus has been on strikes as a form of industrial action in South Africa. The Act, however, caters for various types of industrial action, including lockouts already referred to.

Secondary strikes

In line with the trade union credo of 'united we stand, divided we fall', employees sometimes wish to support workers of another employer in a dispute those workers are having with their employer. The latter workers and their employer are referred to as the primary strikers and the primary employer to distinguish them from the secondary strikers (that is, those who are not in dispute with their own employer but who wish to embark on industrial action in support of the demands of the primary strikers). Statutory regulation of secondary or sympathy strikes is introduced by the Act, which provides for this type of industrial action provided certain conditions are met. The Labour Relations Act 66 of 1995 defines a secondary strike as

> … a strike, or conduct in contemplation or furtherance of a strike, that is in support of a strike by other employees against their employer but does not include a strike in pursuit of a demand and referred to a council if the striking employees, employed within the registered scope of that council, have a material interest in that demand.

A secondary strike must therefore qualify as a strike as defined and in order to qualify as a protected industrial action, the primary strike must itself be a protected strike (that is, both the secondary and the primary strikes must be in conformity with the Act). The requirements for a secondary strike to qualify as a protected strike are summarised in exhibit 18.11.

EXHIBIT 18.11: Protected secondary strikes

A secondary strike will qualify as a protected strike, provided that:
- the primary strike is a protected strike;
- the secondary strikers gave their own employer at least seven days (14 days if the strike is over dismissals for operational reasons) written notice prior to the start of the secondary strike; and
- the harm caused to the secondary employer is reasonable in relation to the possible effect that the secondary strike will have on the business of the primary employer.

Proportionality test

The nature and extent of the secondary industrial action should not be more harmful to the secondary employer than that which is reasonably required to make an effective impact on the primary employer's business. So, for instance, to embark on a crippling secondary strike in circumstances where neither the secondary employer nor his business relationship with the primary employer is such that the secondary strikers' aim of bringing pressure to bear on the primary employer is likely to materialise, would likely render such a secondary strike unprotected.

Three further points regarding the proportionality test and secondary strikes are worth noting:
- The principle of proportionality may often have the consequence that secondary industrial action will have to be pared down to something less than a full-blown strike, for example picketing may be effective as a pressure tactic but entail less harm to the secondary employer.
- For a secondary strike to be a protected strike it is not a requirement that there should be some form of formal relationship between the primary and the secondary employer (such as, for example, that both employers belong to the same group of companies).

■ Proportionality requires effectiveness of the secondary action (in the sense that it impacts on the primary employer).

Picketing

Picketing may be described as a public expression by workers of their grievances in order to make it known to and elicit support from the general public and other relevant constituencies for their cause. It typically involves some form of public protest directed at the employer and in the near vicinity of the employer's place of business as well as efforts to dissuade the general public and suppliers from normal business dealings with the targeted employer and to persuade other workers to stop working and to join the picket.

The old Act did not make provision for picketing resulting in much uncertainty, with the most important source of law relating to picketing being municipal bylaws regulating traffic flow and public disturbance. Under the Act, picketing is recognised as a legitimate form of industrial action worthy of protection subject to certain conditions (see exhibit 18.12). This is not surprising since the right to picket is a constitutionally protected right.

EXHIBIT 18.12: Protected picketing

Employees who picket enjoy the same protection as workers involved in a protected strike, provided that:
■ they are members of a registered trade union;
■ that trade union has authorised the picket;
■ the picket amounts to a peaceful demonstration;
■ the picket is in support of a protected strike or in opposition to any lockout;
■ the picket takes place in a public place outside the employer's premises (or, with the employer's permission – which permission may not be refused unreasonably – inside the employer's premises); and
■ the agreed upon picketing rules (or in the absence of such agreement, the picketing rules prescribed by the CCMA) are followed.

Protest action

'Protest action' is defined in the Act as "… the partial or complete concerted refusal to work, or the retardation or obstruction of work, for the purpose of promoting or defending the socio-economic interests of workers, but not for a purpose referred to in the definition of strike".

The more common name for protest action is 'stayaway', a phenomenon not unknown to most South Africans.

The purpose element of the definition of a strike ("… for the purpose of remedying a grievance or resolving a dispute in respect of any matter of mutual interest between employer and employee …") and more particularly the mutual interest component thereof, exclude industrial action aimed at broader socio-economic issues. What constitutes socio-economic interests of workers is not amenable to precise definition. For instance, whereas protest action against proposed legislation on labour matters or taxation or against the government's intended privatisation of state assets (insofar as job security may be affected) would clearly fall within the ambit of socio-economic interest of workers, a stayaway for or against the reinstitution of the death penalty or a political party should not be regarded as permissible protest action.

In exhibit 18.13, the requirements for protected protest action are summarised. The Labour Court can interdict protest action that does not comply with the laid-down prerequisites or grant a declaratory order in respect of such action.

EXHIBIT 18.13: Protected protest action

Employees participating in action to promote or defend the socio-economic interests of workers will enjoy the same protection as workers involved in a protected strike, if the following requirements have been met:

- employees must not be engaged in an essential service or maintenance service;
- the protest action has been called/authorised by a registered trade union;
- Nedlac has been given 14 days' notice of the protest action;
- the matter giving rise to the protest action has been considered by Nedlac or some other appropriate (tripartite?) forum; and
- the employees do not act in breach or contempt of an order of the Labour Court relating to the protest action.

Lockouts

Section 27 of the Interim Constitution of the Republic of South Africa (Act 200 of 1993) guaranteed the fundamental right of employers to take recourse to the lockout. Under pressure from Cosatu, the government forced the Constituent Assembly to drop the lockout clause from the draft Final Constitution. It must be understood that apart from the possible negative consequences this may have had on overseas investors' confidence in South Africa, the effect of this omission is zero as long as recourse to lockout is provided for in the Labour Relations Act. The constitutional void will only emerge as of crucial importance should a future government wish to outlaw employers' recourse to lockout (such an amendment to the Labour Relations Act would not have been possible had the lockout provision been retained in the final Constitution). The lockout is the employer's economic weapon during the collective bargaining process to compel workers to accept its offer or proposal. The definition of the lockout contained in the Labour Relations Act 66 of 1995 (see above) read together with other provision of the Act introduced some important changes from the previous regime. These are discussed below.

The definition of 'lockout' contains two elements – firstly, certain action on the employer's part and, secondly, that this action must be in pursuit of a specific objective. From existing case law it can be accepted that both elements must be present simultaneously for the employer's conduct to qualify as a lockout as defined. Apart from this similarity between the old and the new definition, the following important differences should be noted:

- The definition of a lockout is substantially narrower than that which obtained under the Labour Relations Act 28 of 1956 in that only the exclusion of employees from the employer's premises is now recognised as action falling within the definition. For instance, the so-called dismissal lockout would no longer be recognised as a form of lockout.
- Lockout dismissals are, in terms of section 187, regarded as automatically unfair dismissals ("a dismissal is automatically unfair if ... the reason for the dismissal is ... to compel the employee to accept a demand in respect of any matter of mutual

interest between the employer and employee ..."). Thus not only are lockout dismissals not regarded as lockouts any more, it is in fact stringently censured as constituting an "automatically unfair dismissal".

- Employees who go on strike in response to a unilateral change in their conditions of employment will be protected even if they did not comply with the prescribed procedures relating to protected strikes.
- The total or partial discontinuance by the employer of his business is no longer regarded as a form of lockout.

Once it has been established that the action taken by the employer constitutes a lockout, as defined, it remains to be determined whether the lockout conforms to the requirements of the Act. The requirements are, with the necessary changes, the same as those applicable to strike action. Likewise, the consequences of a protected lockout and an unprotected lockout respectively are similar to the consequences that follow upon a protected and unprotected strike respectively.

18.6 CONCLUSION

In this chapter you were introduced to certain theoretical perspectives underpinning industrial and labour relations, and aspects of the South African industrial relations system and dynamics were discussed in broad terms. This now forms the foundation for the next chapter in which we examine certain organisation-level aspects of labour relations.

SUSTAINABILITY CONNECTION?

Organised labour plays a key role in South African society. Apartheid was not a sustainable political dispensation but had it not been for the role in particular of the labour movement in South Africa, it may have taken very much longer to dismantle that system. The labour relations system of South Africa also paved the way for bringing about the transformation – as that is where we learned to negotiate and come to agreements that we can all live with. Labour relations in South Africa, and in particular the organised labour movement as manifested in Cosatu, are still playing a key role in our country's socio-political and economic dispensation.

While irresponsible leadership of the labour movement can hurt any country rather seriously, in our country we need a strong, responsible labour movement to balance interests in society. Trade unions continue to play a very important role in balancing the interests of workers with those of the 'owners of wealth' of the country. Had it not been for trade unions, the gap between the rich and the poor in South Africa would have been even greater, which goes directly against a sustainable situation.

SELF-EVALUATION QUESTIONS

1. Explain the concepts 'labour relations', 'employee relations' and 'industrial relations'. Are there any differences? If so, what do they entail?
2. Who are the parties involved in labour and industrial relations? What are their respective roles, rights and duties?
3. Describe four theoretical perspectives of industrial and labour relations.

4 Explain why and how trade unions exist and operate.
5 Discuss the organisational rights of South African trade unions.
6 Write an essay explaining the structures and processes for collective bargaining and dispute resolution in South Africa in terms of relevant statutory provisions.
7 'Only some striking workers may be dismissed in terms of the Labour Relations Act 66 of 1995.' Explain.
8 Distinguish between 'dispute of right' and 'dispute of interest'.

19 MANAGING LABOUR RELATIONS AT ORGANISATIONAL LEVEL

LEARNING OUTCOMES

After studying this chapter, you should be able to:

- describe the nature and importance of communication in labour relations;
- explain the nature of employee grievances and the value of handling such grievances properly;
- discuss the importance of eliciting greater employee involvement and participation;
- explain how discipline can be successfully maintained in the workplace;
- write concise notes on union–management interactions;
- differentiate between different types of collective agreements;
- explain various broad types or kinds of collective negotiation;
- discuss statutory workplace forums as structures for promoting union–management cooperation; and
- write an essay on the management of strikes.

19.1 INTRODUCTION

In chapter 18 you were introduced to the general theoretical basis of labour relations and the nature of South Africa's industrial relations system. The focus now shifts to those aspects which are more directly related to the management of labour and employee relations at the level of the organisation.

In this chapter, the emphasis is therefore on how managers can deal with certain aspects in the workplace which relate to labour and employee relations. With regard to the collective dimension, the focus is on dealing with union–management interaction at the level of the organisation. As far as the individual dimension is concerned, the primary emphasis is on handling different aspects of employee relations, including communication, discipline and grievance handling. Considering that conflict in relations occurs, which may manifest in industrial action, some attention is also paid to issues involved in the handling of strikes.

19.2 ESTABLISHING SOUND EMPLOYEE RELATIONS

Regardless of whether or not employees belong to trade unions, managers have to see to it that the relations between themselves and their subordinates, between the subordinates themselves, and between the employees and their work are maintained at a standard conducive to a generally more successful organisation. Activities and practices of managing employee relations can therefore be viewed as those aimed at improving cooperation and minimising conflict levels among various categories of employees, irrespective of the presence or absence of trade unions.

19.2.1 Communicating with employees

19.2.1.1 The nature and importance of communication in employee relations

One of the most important tasks all managers have is to communicate with their subordinates. Some experts estimate that up to 80% of the working time of managers is spent on some form of communication-related activity. Without appropriate communication, employees may not know what is expected of them in relation to what work to do, how to do it, how well they are doing it, etc. Just as other relationships depend on some form of communication, the quality of labour and employee relations depends to a considerable extent upon the nature and quality of the communication between all the parties involved. However, it would be an overstatement to say that good communication is the panacea for all the labour-relations problems in the workplace. Although the quality of communication can have an important effect on the quality of labour and employee relations, the causes of labour relations-related problems lie (as mentioned in the previous chapter) in the more deeply rooted differences between the different role players in the employment relationship. Communication is, however, a very necessary medium or means through which the parties can identify and address these differences. Effective communication is a necessary but not sufficient precondition for sound labour relations.

Communication can generally be viewed as the process of conveying and sharing information between interacting people. It is a process of information exchange between receivers and senders. In the context of labour and employee relations, communication can be viewed as the exchange of information related to anything that flows from or can have an impact on the employment relationship. Through the medium of communication, people can relate to one another in the workplace and through communication meaning is given to relationships.

Communication can occur on a one-on-one basis, such as when an individual subordinate informs his or her superior that a particular job has been completed. It can also occur on a one-on-group basis, such as when the head of the salary administration section informs all of his or her subordinates at a joint meeting of the newly acquired computerised payroll system.

Representatives of groups of employees also often communicate. During the process of negotiation there is, for example, a constant flow and exchange of information between the members of the negotiating teams, with the aim of influencing and persuading each other to move closer towards an agreement.

Communication can be non-verbal or verbal, in oral or written form. During negotiations a hard slam on the table by one party can convey to the other party how the former feels about something which came to the fore during the course of the negotiations – that would be an example of a non-verbal form of communication. Worker representatives can request a meeting with a manager by means of a written letter or memorandum or by means of a telephone conversation. An employee who was not given an expected promotion and who gives the boss a note of complaint and later cries in the superior's office as a result of his or her disappointment is communicating in the verbal, written and oral, as well as in the non-verbal form.

Whatever the form of communication, the aim remains the transmission of messages to receivers so that they can understand the intended meanings of the senders' messages. There may, however, be many different obstacles or barriers to successful communication. Before we examine these, it is important to focus briefly on some of the methods used for communication with employees in the workplace.

19.2.1.2 Methods of communicating with employees

It must be remembered that proper communication is a two-way process. Because there are two parties (receiver and sender), there is normally some need for a flow of information between them. This is not to say that one-way communication does not sometimes occur. However, when management devises methods to convey information to employees, it is advisable to incorporate checks to see whether the information has been received correctly and whether the particular communication methods work efficiently and effectively.

Different methods can be used to communicate with employees.

Formal letters or memoranda

Some letters are of a personal nature, such as when an individual is informed that a request for a transfer has been approved. At other times it is necessary for management to inform all or a particular group of employees of something very specific which applies to all concerned. A general letter or memorandum can, for example, be distributed by the personnel department to all the members of the organisation's medical aid scheme when some of the conditions of membership change.

Notice boards

The conventional notice board is still commonly used. Frequently, management wants to make information of a general nature available to those who may be interested, while not bothering those who may not be interested. Notice boards can, for example, be used for notices of vacancies elsewhere in an organisation – for those who may be interested in a career or job change. Notice boards are also often available to trade union representatives (shop stewards) for posting union notices. It is a low-cost method and easy to use, and often has widespread acceptability due to its convenience. It is, however, suitable mainly for brief messages rather than lengthy, complicated information documents.

In-house newspapers/journals

As a general rule such publications are produced and distributed to all employees free of charge. Such a publication is usually published quite regularly (on a monthly or two-weekly basis), and normally contains interesting and important general information about the organisation and its employees. It can, for example, be used to recognise employees' achievements (both in and out of work), to inform the staff of important new appointments or staff movements, to advertise internal vacancies, to inform the readers of business developments, and so forth. Important and interesting newsworthy information can thus be made available to all employees and even to outsiders who may be interested.

Special publications or reports

Sometimes it is wise to publicise something very important in a special way. So, for example, when an organisation undergoes a major change in corporate image or business direction, it may be necessary to publish and distribute a high-quality booklet which spells out the necessary details about the change in direction or new image.

A CASE AT HAND

Communication in Eskom

When Eskom (South Africa's giant electricity utility), for example, realised that a change of culture was needed in its dealing with employees, their representatives and trade unions, the organisation embarked on a new process of union–management interaction. Whereas in the past the approach had often been quite autocratic and paternalistic, Eskom decided to cooperate with organised labour to develop and institute processes to facilitate meaningful input by recognised trade unions over decisions that affected them as key stakeholders. To explain the rationale behind this move and the complexities and benefits involved, a glossy 52-page document entitled *A Vision Unfolding: The Path to Power* was published.

Sometimes organisations also publish glossy employee reports on an annual basis. These written documents (akin to those for the shareholders) are normally specifically aimed at the employees and provide information relating to the performance and level of success of the organisation for a particular financial year (see also chapter 22).

In-house videos and television technology

A method which can be quite expensive, but often well worth the cost, is the production of video briefings. An organisation may sometimes wish to convey complex information where different issues have to be explained in a simple, user-friendly and uniform way to a great number of employees. When an organisation, for example, introduces a new employee share ownership plan, or when a major reorganisation exercise is embarked upon and employees need to be informed about why and how it may affect them, a video can be produced with members of the top management team discussing the relevant issues. Big corporations with many establishments can produce such videos in-house and then distribute them to the various business units or establishments for the employees' information. Other forms of television technology can also be used. Different TV watchpoints can be utilised at the various establishments or plants of an organisation by means of an open line rented from a TV broadcasting organisation, one day per week, for a specific time slot.

E-mail

In the current era of information technology, there are hosts of opportunities to make use of computer technology to transmit information to employees. Important and urgent messages can, for example, be sent to certain managers via an e-mail system. They can then pass the necessary information on to their subordinates if not all the employees have access to the system. If, for example, there is a strike and labour unrest in particular areas of a multi-plant organisation, managers in other areas can constantly be kept informed of developments in order to monitor the chances of the unrest spreading. Intranet is a very common communication medium in today's organisations.

Briefing groups

This is a structured system which can be used on a regular basis by management to cascade down, throughout the organisation or relevant parts thereof, news of particular developments or issues which may be of importance. As a rule, a written document containing the relevant information is distributed from a particular level of management downwards, with each manager or supervisor reading the information to the group of subordinates reporting to him or her. Each level of manager does the same right down to the level where the lowest first-line supervisor reads out the same document to his or her small group of workers. The relevant issues are then normally also discussed in question-and-answer sessions.

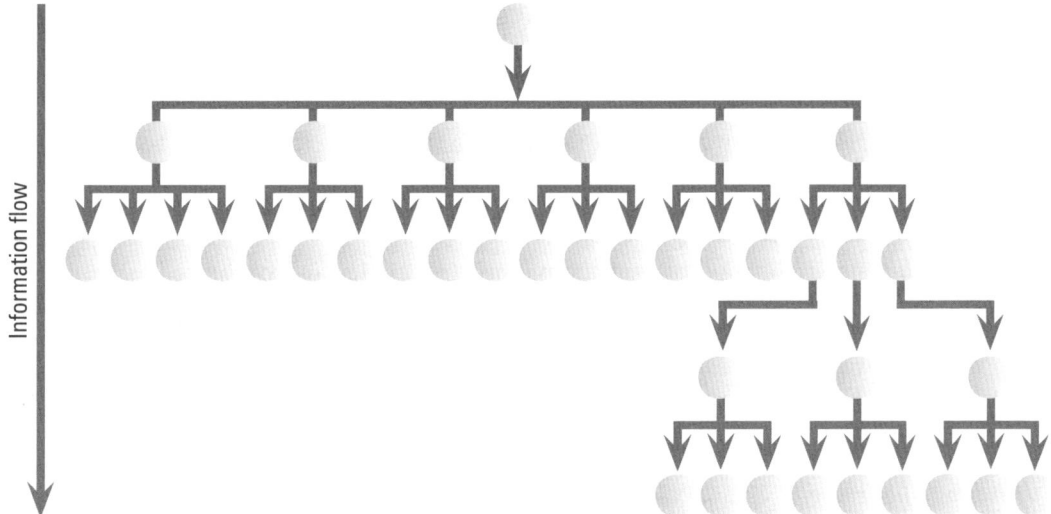

Figure 19.1: Briefing groups

Committees

The establishment of formal committees, where representatives of management and non-management employees (including, but not limited to, union representatives) get together to deal with certain issues in a formalised manner, can be viewed as a method of securing more employee involvement, participation and thus (hopefully) identification with and commitment to the organisation's objectives. Such committees (for example health and safety committees, workplace forums or other consultative committees), can also be regarded as forums where employees can communicate formally about important issues connected to the employment relationship. One of the objectives of a workplace forum is, for example, to facilitate better communication on issues such as transport, accommodation, physical working conditions, rest and meal breaks, general worker problems or complaints, or even possible changes in organisation policy. At safety committee meetings, safety representatives exchange information particularly related to the safety of persons in the workplace, often with the objective of making recommendations to management. Similarly, via safety representatives and committees, management can disseminate important safety-related information to the workforce.

Diverse face-to-face methods

'Open management' is a concept which is used to refer to a style of management which focuses on promoting the upward flow of information. It is often said that a particular manager or organisation policy statement supports an open-door policy. This simply means that as much as possible is being done to enhance opportunities for upward communication from subordinates to superiors.

It is therefore quite an informal method of communication. A particular technique in this regard is sometimes referred to as MBWA (management by walking around). This occurs when a manager is seen walking, talking, listening and observing the job situation. In this way, information which may relate to or influence the employment relationship can be exchanged in an informal way.

Another approach may be to hold get-together sessions. This is not the same as the formal meetings scheduled from time to time so that managers and workers in particular departments, sections or committees can discuss specific issues according to an agenda. Get-together sessions may be more informal and less frequent, and enable the parties to talk out or speak up about things that they may like or dislike in the work situation. Sometimes they can even take the form of after-hours social sessions. Various informal or formal face-to-face interaction opportunities can thus enhance the quality of communication.

Diverse written communication methods

There are many other ways of exchanging information in the workplace. Sometimes it is necessary simply to inform employees or their representatives without requiring any feedback or two-way communication.

Often this is the case with the written word. Management may want to remind workers of something or inform them about something, and then use may be made of *notes in pay packets* or *flash notices*.

At other times it may be really necessary to get the attention of employees, and use may be made of huge, colourful *placards* or *posters* to convey a certain message. Management may also make use of other forms of written communication such as *brochures* or *pocket cards* which may, for example, contain the mission and value statement of the organisation. Other methods include *information bulletins* and *newsletters*.

Policy handbooks and *manuals* represent another form of written communication, albeit a more comprehensive form. There are therefore many different written communication methods which can be used.

Special surveys

Sometimes it is necessary to get very specific information from employees. Attitude surveys are, for example, conducted in many organisations on a one-off or regular basis. Use can be made of questionnaires (and/or interviews, for example) to try to discover the views, opinions, feelings – the attitudes – of employees regarding a variety of aspects which relate to the employment relationship.

Management can, for instance, arrange for an audit to check the quality and nature of communication in the organisation. Similarly, labour relations audits and so-called climate surveys can be undertaken.

The idea is to collect the information, interpret it, draw conclusions and make recommendations regarding the specific area which has been surveyed. It is also very important to ensure that the relevant employees receive the necessary feedback regarding such survey results.

The scientific nature of these methods may make them more expensive and time consuming, but if professionally qualified people are employed to conduct a survey properly, it is generally worth the cost.

Mass-media communication

Some large corporations have their own phone-in slots on radio stations. Employees are encouraged to raise issues and comments on air, which a management representative responds to. In this way it is hoped to reach a large employee audience (as well as society at large).

Sometimes organisations also use full-page newspaper advertisements to communicate management's point of view (on a critical issue of dispute with a trade union, for example) both to its employees (and society at large).

Typically, the mass media are resorted to if the issue is deemed to extend beyond the workplace and employees.

19.2.1.3 Communication barriers

Despite the fact that the importance of communication is widely recognised in organisations, some experts maintain that labour-related problems in the workplace can often be attributed to a failure to communicate properly. Miscellaneous obstacles or barriers are often advanced as the underlying causes of this failure. The objective of this section is simply to draw the reader's attention to this problem, given the limited scope of the book.

Barriers can relate to such things as *differences in frames of reference* (see chapter 3); language or semantic problems (not understanding the meaning of a term, phrase or symbol); selective perception (paying attention only to that which one believes is necessary); lack of attention (due to concentration problems resulting from noise, physical or psychological problems, or information overload); *contextual problems* (such as timing problems, the size of the unit where communication takes place, or the emotional state of any of the parties); the *deliberate creation of obstacles* (such as refusal to listen or to pay attention, switching off, or deliberately providing misleading information); *incompetent communicators* (people often simply lack the necessary communication skills – they do not understand the dynamics of communication, they are not aware of the possible obstacles and/or they do not know how to overcome them).

A conscious effort has to be made to overcome communication obstacles such as those cited above, and thereby to improve information exchange in the workplace.

19.2.1.4 Communication: concluding remarks

The importance of effective communication in the workplace cannot be overemphasised. To many management experts, communication is the lifeblood of the management process. It is omnipresent in all organisations and in life in general. As you read this section, communication is taking place; hopefully the authors' message will be understood as it was originally intended.

There are many other possible forms of communication; these will be highlighted in following sections dealing with establishing sounder employee and labour relations.

19.2.2 Handling employee grievances

As has already been mentioned, sound employee and labour relations are dependent on constant efforts to obtain the best fit in the employment relationship. Both the formal (for example stipulations of the employment contract) and informal (for example expectations in terms of the psychological contract) aspects of the employment relationship can be the root cause of employee dissatisfaction. When an employee is unhappy or dissatisfied with something in the workplace, he or she may ultimately decide to terminate the relationship by resigning if the matter is not resolved. However, before such a drastic final step is taken, there should be an opportunity to address the relevant issue(s) in a formalised manner.

Grievance handling refers to the process whereby management formally deals with the officially presented complaint(s) of workers relating to the employment relationship (excluding disciplinary matters). A grievance must, however, be distinguished from a

A CASE AT HAND

Communication policy at Anglo Platinum

The Company has implemented an employee communication policy. The objectives of this policy are to:

- promote the empowerment of line management, with emphasis on line management taking responsibility for being primary communicators to their employees;
- ensure an understanding of the communication roles and responsibilities of all parties and provide a common approach to communication within Anglo Platinum;
- create a framework to improve employee communication and put support resources in place for line management to achieve sustainable communication success; and
- monitor and audit the effectiveness of employee communication to ensure an understanding of how to improve communication.

The policy also details the structures of communication at various levels of the organisation, for example supervisors having face-to-face meetings with their teams to discuss production and safety issues.

Source: http://www.angloplatinum.com/

worker complaint or problem. A worker may experience a problem that is not work-related, but which may eventually have an influence on the employment relationship – such as personal financial difficulties, family problems or drug addiction problems. These are not grievances because they are not directly related to the employment relationship. On the other hand, a worker may be dissatisfied with something directly related to the employment relationship, but the dissatisfaction may simply be expressed in an informal way – for example by complaining to somebody else. Such a case does not involve a grievance as such because the issue has not been formalised or fed into the official grievance procedure.

Employees' work-related complaints can be formalised as official grievances by means of a grievance procedure. By formally presenting such a complaint to management, the worker communicates to management the fact that there is either a real or a perceived breach of the psychological or employment contract. The grievance procedure can therefore be viewed as a method of (mostly) upward communication in the workplace. The formality of the grievance procedure does not preclude management from proactively dealing with worker dissatisfaction or problems even before these become grievances. Such a procedure does, however, help to prevent managers from dodging difficult-to-deal-with worker complaints and to ensure greater consistency in the process of attending to official work-related complaints.

19.2.2.1 Principles underlying grievance handling

A number of important principles (some of which have already been referred to in the preceding paragraphs) form the basis of grievance handling and related procedures.

- Management must acknowledge the fact that workers may from time to time be dissatisfied with aspects related to the employment relationship.
- Management must accept the responsibility for addressing and settling all legitimate employee grievances in a fair manner.
- It is best to solve grievances as promptly and as close as practically possible to the point of origin.
- All employees who air grievances must enjoy guaranteed protection against any form of discrimination, victimisation or prejudice whatsoever.

- Management must accept the fundamental right of workers to make use of the help of representatives (either union or otherwise) in the process of airing and handling grievances.
- Management is responsible for the smooth operation of the organisation; although grievance handling is extremely important, the utilisation of the grievance procedure should not unnecessarily disrupt (but rather facilitate) the operation of the organisation.
- A number of time-specified and progressive procedural steps should be spelt out and followed, from the lowest to the highest level of management, in order to arrive at the point where a grievance is solved to the optimum satisfaction of all parties concerned.
- The right of employees to pursue channels of dispute resolution beyond the organisation in cases where grievances cannot be solved through the grievance procedure must be recognised.

19.2.2.2 The grievance procedure

The grievance procedure is usually in a document which spells out the stages or steps to be followed when employees (as individuals as well as in a group context) have grievances. The exact nature and sequence of steps will vary from organisation to organisation, depending on variables such as their complexity, size and structure. Nonetheless, certain steps can be outlined by way of example.

Step 1 occurs when the aggrieved person verbally informs the immediate supervisor about the complaint. In this way the grievance is made official and it can therefore be recommended that the event (if solved) be recorded in some way. At this stage it may not yet be necessary for any third-party involvement (for example in the form of a worker representative). However, if the issue involves or relates to the immediate supervisor, the grievance procedure normally stipulates the first step to be the referral of the issue to the next higher level of management. If the issue is not solved within a reasonable time (say 24 hours), step 2 will follow.

Step 2 generally entails putting the grievance in writing (usually in triplicate), involving a third party such as a shop steward (if so wished), and presenting it to a higher level of management (that is, to the superior of the immediate supervisor). One copy is kept by the employee and the other is normally handed to the industrial relations or HR officer. If the grievance is not solved within a reasonable time (say another 24 hours) step 3 will follow.

Step 3, the last stage, will (depending on the organisational characteristics) involve consideration of the issue by an even higher level of manager or a formal grievance investigation led by a grievance committee. As a rule such an impartial committee consists of a labour relations/human resources expert, employee representatives, a senior manager and any other experts who may be of particular value with regard to the specific issue at hand. More time is usually allowed at this stage (approximately another two to six days) because at this point it is realised that the issue at hand is quite serious and difficult to solve. The outcome of the grievance committee's investigation has to be announced in writing to all relevant parties. If the issue is not solved, the process of external dispute resolution may be put in motion.

19.2.2.3 Grievance handling: a final comment

It is of utmost importance for sound labour and employee relations, as well as for organisational success in general, to establish and maintain a formally recognised procedure, acceptable to all parties, that can serve as the channel for upward communication when employees are dissatisfied with aspects relating to the employment relationship. In this way, unnecessary tension can be relieved and an open climate, conducive to a relationship of trust and security, can be created. However, it should be noted that, in South Africa, in contrast to the US for example, the grievance procedure is not used for addressing employee dissatisfaction regarding disciplinary matters. For this purpose, appeal procedures are normally necessary.

19.2.3 Eliciting employee involvement and participation

In chapter 10, various leadership styles were highlighted. The way management leads subordinates can exert a profound influence on the quality of labour and employee relations within the organisation. As indicated in section above, the aim of management with regard to employee relations is to facilitate employee cooperation and to minimise conflict levels. As pointed out in chapter 10, democratic or participative leadership styles often offer the best potential to do just this. According to Kemp (1992: 13), the power struggles and conflict between trade unions and the management of organisations revolve largely around different perceptions of the extent to which employee participation (and thus forms of industrial democracy), as opposed to autocratic management practices, is actually practised.

The concepts 'employee involvement' (EI) and 'employee participation' (EP) are sometimes used interchangeably, and are even viewed by some as having the same meaning as industrial democracy. Without getting involved in the complex semantic debate which surrounds this issue, the approach taken in this book is that EI and EP basically refer to management initiatives to give employees the opportunity to become involved or to take part in the decision-making processes related to their daily work and the operations of the organisation in general. They refer to any form of altering the power relations within the organisation, either directly or indirectly (through representatives), beyond the traditional form of power sharing embedded in the collective bargaining process. Some methods of facilitating better communication within the organisation can thus also be viewed as forms of EI and EP. Relevant examples cited in the previous section include team briefing, meetings and committees.

In line with Nel, Erasmus and Swanepoel's (1993: 50–52) view, EI/EP essentially involve those processes whereby non-management employees are given the opportunity to take part in (and to feel part of) and to influence areas of decision making that have traditionally been labelled 'management prerogatives'. This means, to a certain extent, that management will have to yield control and seek more cooperative people-management styles and methods.

Employee involvement and participation can take on various forms at various levels within the organisation and can be introduced in varying degrees. Also, the focus of EI/EP can differ from situation to situation. The focus may, for example, be purely financial – such as when all employees can join directly in profit-sharing schemes (see also chapter 16), or involve high-level decision making – such as when indirect participation is facilitated by having trade union representatives on the organisation's board.

The form of involvement can thus be either formal or informal, and either direct or indirect. The degree of EI/EP is related to the extent to which employees can exert an influence on the relevant processes, decisions or outcomes. In this regard various techniques of EI/EP can be identified, ranging from simply informing employees, to two-way communication, consultation (where employees' views are sought without any commitment to necessarily incorporate their ideas), negotiation and even co-determination.

In some techniques, such as team briefing, employees are primarily informed, although there can sometimes be two-way communication. With other techniques, such as quality circles, the employees' degree of involvement and participation is greater. The most extreme degree of EI/EP is found in organisations which are fully controlled by the workers or employees. Although not very widespread in South Africa, worker cooperatives fall into the latter category. Recent policy and legislative trends (such as the Co-operatives Act 14 of 2005) create the platform for enhancing the establishment of these types/forms of worker control in South Africa.

Many other ways of eliciting EI/EP can be cited. In the case of suggestion schemes, for example, employees are given the opportunity to put forward ideas for improvements in the organisation's operations; these are normally rewarded if greater success actually results. Sometimes work is redesigned to provide for autonomous work teams or other forms of teamwork (see also chapter 6) in which work tasks are assigned to whole groups rather than to particular individual employees. In the case of quality circles, all the workers who form part of a particular section or department are trained to become competent participants in a continuous process of problem identification and problem solving in order to improve the quality of work processes in their section/department/ area. As can be gathered from the foregoing paragraphs, EI/EP is aimed largely at eliciting greater employee identification with and commitment to the organisation and the work itself by creating opportunities to improve the quality of their working life. The collective dimension of trade unions should, however, never be neglected in a country like South Africa where they play such an important role. Even when direct forms of participation are considered, it is advisable to involve the trade unions right from the start, especially when the relevant trade unions have high representativity and thus a strong power base. In sections 19.3 and 19.5 the notion of union–management cooperation as a form of indirect participation is further explored.

19.2.4 Disciplining employees

The origin of the term *discipline* lies in the term 'disciple', which can be defined as a learner. This means that the ultimate aim of disciplining employees must be to teach them how to behave (and how not to) within the context of getting the work done in an organisation. Discipline should not be viewed negatively as being synonymous with punishment and enforcement.

The aim of discipline is therefore, according to Salamon (1992: 592), to ensure that all employees conform to the performance and behavioural standards and criteria necessary for the successful operation of the organisation. From a positive point of view, discipline is therefore a constructive element of management designed to facilitate learning and opportunities for personal growth, as well as the achievement of organisational objectives.

The process of disciplining employees entails both informal and formal aspects. The informal part of discipline forms an integral part of managing the performance and behaviour of employees on a continuous basis. Just as the creation of opportunities for employee involvement is aimed at eliciting better performance, the ideal of continuously teaching subordinates what is right and what is wrong, and what is acceptable and vunacceptable, lies at the very heart of people management. On an informal basis, employees are supposed to be taught not simply to conform to minimum requirements related to performance and behaviour, but actually to display superior behaviour and work performance. The first stage of disciplining employees is therefore informal by nature.

At times, however, some employees fail to adhere to the basic minimum standards and requirements. It is therefore advisable for organisations to have a system for formally disciplining such employees. Apart from an organisation's formal policy statement regarding discipline, this formal disciplinary system usually consists of a written disciplinary code and procedure which has to be applied by management.

19.2.4.1 The disciplinary code

As a general rule a disciplinary code is drafted to assist management in the identification of offences warranting formal disciplinary measures and to help ensure consistency in disciplinary matters. Such a code therefore usually contains a list of possible offences and the concomitant sanctions to be considered by management. It is mostly used as a guideline rather than a set of hard and fast rules.

In this way employees can be made aware of the rules and requirements related to behaviour and performance (and of the potential consequences of not adhering to them). It is good practice to educate all new employees on the disciplinary code and procedure during the course of induction programmes.

Owing to the fact that the nature of various offences may differ in terms of seriousness (ranging, for instance, from minor to moderate to very serious), some form of progressive discipline is usually built into the disciplinary code's section dealing with the penalty guidelines connected to the various types of offences. The first step in a formal disciplinary process is normally a written warning, which progresses to a final warning and ultimately even to dismissal. The dismissal of employees for misconduct should, however, always be viewed as the last option and not as a penalty in the true sense of the word. Termination should never be imposed over-hastily or in an improper manner. Under normal circumstances, terminating the service of employees in essence means ending the employment relationship. However, if this is not done fairly, it may very well happen that an order is eventually made (by the Labour Court or in terms of an arbitrator's decision) for the employment relationship to continue. Chapter 20 of this book focuses specifically on the termination of employees' services.

It is important to note that, in respect of first-, second- and third-time offences, where the penalties will have to become progressively more severe in order to rectify (or eliminate) undesirable behaviour, time limits will normally have to be applied. Depending on the type of offence, warnings can be taken to cease to apply after a "clean period" of, for instance, three to 12 months. In order to incorporate the principle of progressive discipline, other types of penalties which may be warranted (depending on the relevant circumstances) can include suspension without pay (only if the parties agree to this), or demotion (it may similarly not be imposed unilaterally), before dismissal as a last option may be decided upon.

An example of a disciplinary code of a South African organisation is provided in the appendix to this chapter.

19.2.4.2 Aspects of the disciplinary process and procedure

The disciplinary process should start off in an informal way; once a superior has determined that a violation of rules or of required behavioural standards has occurred, some form of counselling should take place. If this does not help, and rehabilitation does not take place, the transgressor has to be informed of the possible consequences should his or her behaviour not change.

Should an employee be charged with misconduct that could possibly lead to dismissal, management must act in line with the fundamental rights of employees regarding procedural fairness in discipline. As a general rule, these rights may include the following:

- the right to be told the nature of the offence or misconduct with relevant particulars of the charge;
- the right to a timeous hearing;
- the right to be given adequate notice prior to the enquiry;
- the right to some form of representation (the representative can be anyone from the workplace – either a shop steward, workplace forum representative, a colleague or even a supervisor – who can assist the employee and ensure that the disciplinary procedure is fair and equitable);
- the right to call witnesses;
- the right to an interpreter;
- the right to a finding (if found guilty, the employee has the right to be told the full reasons);
- the right to have previous service considered;
- the right to be advised of the penalty imposed (for example verbal warnings, written warnings, termination of employment); and
- the right of appeal, for example to a higher level of management. This is provided for in some organisations but it is not a requirement of the Labour Relations Act.

The process of disciplining an employee should therefore be based on principles of professional and reasonable management. As can be seen from the guidelines spelt out above, it is advisable that a disciplinary hearing normally forms an integral part of this process.

First of all, it is essential to ascertain whether sufficient grounds exist for the holding of a hearing. A form of preliminary investigation is therefore normally necessary before one proceeds with the actual disciplinary hearing.

The disciplinary procedure concerns the detailed steps to be followed in the case of alleged employee misconduct. An example of a disciplinary procedure is provided in figure 19.2.

As can be seen from the above example, a formal disciplinary hearing may form an essential part of the disciplinary procedure and process. Although, in terms of the Act, a formal hearing is not always required, it became the custom during the previous dispensation for such formal hearings to be viewed as prerequisites for any decision to dismiss an employee.

A disciplinary enquiry can be divided into two basic stages. The first is an investigation to resolve the question of whether the employee did in fact commit the act of which he or she is accused (this involves the valid reason requirement, and the employee's personal circumstances may not be discussed or considered here). Should the employee be found guilty of the misconduct as charged, the second stage is entered where a decision has to be taken as to the appropriate disciplinary action. Here the employee's personal circumstances (such as his or her service record, disciplinary record and period of service with the enterprise) are considered. For example, assume that employees X and Y are both found guilty of being under the influence of alcohol at work. Assume that employee X has received two warnings during the past year for the same offence, while employee Y has a clean record and has been working for the enterprise twice as long as employee X. Under these circumstances the employer could possibly be justified in dismissing employee X and not employee Y.

19.2.5 Conducting fair labour practices

Over the last two decades the notion of 'unfair labour practice' has been developed and established. Today it is common knowledge that employees are protected against

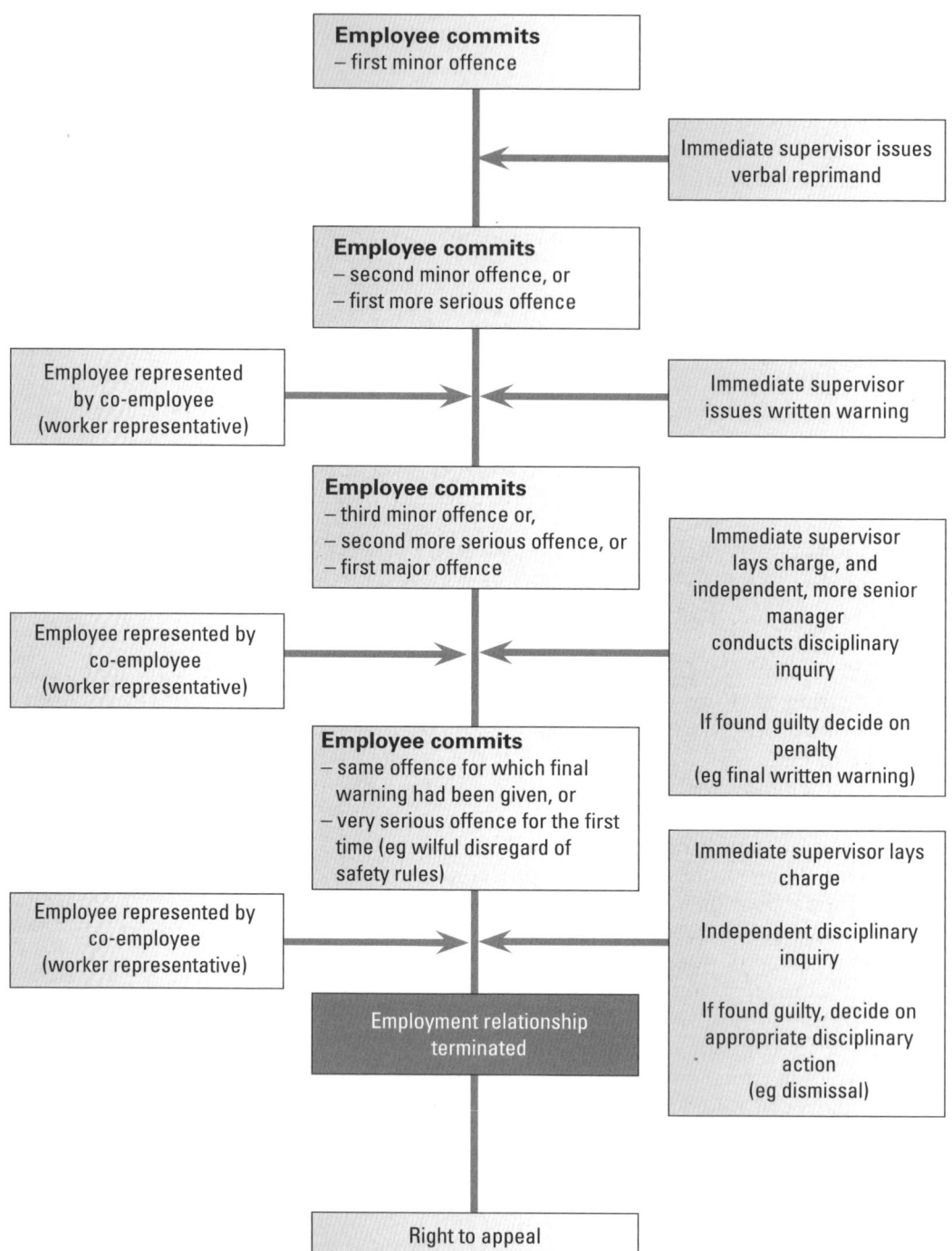

Figure 19.2: Flow diagram of a disciplinary procedure: an example

unfair labour practices. To put it more positively: it is well known that 'fair labour practice' plays an important role in establishing sound labour and employee relations. In order to fully appreciate and understand what fair labour practice entails, it is necessary to grasp the meaning of what not to do in order to avoid conducting any unfair labour practice. Under the old Labour Relations Act 28 of 1956, the industrial court and arbitrators used the general unfair labour practice jurisdiction to develop the scope and nature of the concept. It is now codified into the Labour Relations Act 66 of 1995 by means of what is referred to as 'residual unfair labour practice'.

In Part B of Schedule 7 to the Labour Relations Act provision is made for unfair labour practices. These are defined as:

> … any unfair act or omission that arises between an employer and an employee, involving … the unfair conduct of the employer relating to the promotion, demotion or training of an employee or relating to the provision of benefits to an employee; the unfair suspension of an employee or any other disciplinary action short of dismissal in respect of an employee; or the failure or refusal of an employer to reinstate or re-employ a former employee in terms of any agreement.

From this it is clear that any disciplinary action short of dismissal (such as demotion or suspension, or the entering of a warning on the employee's record) may be challenged on the grounds that it amounts to an unfair labour practice.

Disputes over alleged unfair labour practices may be referred to conciliation, and if the dispute remains unresolved, a party may request that the dispute be resolved through arbitration. The relation between unfair discrimination (including harassment but excluding dismissals) and unfair labour practices are as follows: if the employee alleges that the employer's conduct amounts to unfair discrimination, the dispute has to be dealt with in terms of chapter 2 of the Employment Equity Act (see chapter 3), whereas, if he or she alleges that it amounts to an unfair labour practice not involving unfair discrimination, schedule 7 of the Labour Relations Act will apply.

19.2.6 Sound employee relations: concluding remarks

In the previous paragraphs you were introduced to the complex management task of working towards sound employee relations on primarily the individual dimension. These efforts will, however, all be in vain if insufficient attention is paid to the collective dimension as represented primarily by union–management relations. As we have said before, these dimensions are intertwined and we merely separate them for structural purposes in the book. In practice the quality of the relations on individual and collective fronts are very much one entity.

19.3 TOWARDS SOUND UNION–MANAGEMENT RELATIONS

Because trade unions play such an important role in South African organisations today, it is essential for management to be professional in its dealings and interactions with such employee representative bodies. No matter how much attention is paid to the individual dimension of employee relations – in other words, to ordinary HRM practices and to one-on-one employee relations – negligence in respect of the collective dimensions (particularly as far as trade unions are concerned) can have serious negative consequence for an organisation's quest for success.

From a strategic perspective (see chapter 4), one of the most fundamental management decisions in this regard relates to the organisation's general approach to dealing and interacting with trade unions.

19.3.1 Deciding on a comprehensive general approach

As explained in chapter 4, the frames of reference or mindsets of managers (and of unionists) may have a significant influence on how management/union relationships develop over time. As explained, an organisation's strategies and policies regarding dealings with trade unions are often strongly influenced by the decision makers' mindsets or ideologies. Different mindsets are based on managers' differing beliefs about, perceptions of and reactions to trade unions and their leaders. Obviously these mindsets are formed over time and are therefore often influenced by the attitudes and methods of trade unions in their interactions with management. A country's labour history, trends in collective bargaining, and factors such as the economy and political situation also obviously play a role in shaping the mindsets of managers.

In general it can be said that decision makers will be either relatively positive or predominantly negative towards trade unions. In reality, a continuum ranging from extremely negative to extremely positive can be drawn.

The more negative the mindset, the more of a unitarist the person concerned is (also see chapter 4 and 18). People who fall towards the other end of the continuum are more pluralist in their thinking. The more unitarist a person is, the more adversarial his or her approach towards trade unions will be. If circumstances allow, a top management team whose members share a very strong unitarist frame of reference will in all likelihood prefer to oppose trade unions with every available means because they do not really believe that unions should exist or that they should interfere in any way with the management of employee affairs. This resistance towards (or even fear of) union involvement may then result in strategies to avoid unions and to keep them out as far as possible.

Towards the middle of the continuum, but still towards the negative, lie those who favour a broad approach of union containment. This is still basically an adversarial type of approach towards union–management relations. Management may perhaps realise that the trade unions cannot really be kept out, perhaps because of legislation. Attempts may therefore be made to devise ways and means of restricting trade union involvement. In such cases, interaction with trade unions will be limited to issues such as conditions of employment, remuneration and working conditions (and these aspects will often be rigidly codified into agreements). Slightly more to the right of the neutral point, where pluralism becomes the shared frame of reference, management may realise that a more professional and peaceful relationship with the trade unions must be sought. Unions are thus accepted as part of organisational life and are respected as the legitimate representatives of the workers. Although generally more positive towards trade unions and their role, management may still be critical of certain aspects of trade union involvement, and initially may still generally oppose trade union demands. In general, however, a spirit of accommodation may start to develop: management is prepared to accommodate the union by establishing an ongoing pragmatic working relationship with it. In such a relationship there will thus be scope for real compromise and flexibility in a process dominated by more win–win bargaining.

Managers who fall towards the extreme positive side of the continuum will prefer to establish cooperative relationships with trade unions. Although the accommodation type of approach allows a certain degree of joint or cooperative interactions, it is only where a very strong pluralist stance is taken that trade unions are in essence welcomed as important stakeholders in the organisation. The emphasis in this approach shifts to mutual concerns, common ground, real joint problem solving and integrative, win–win interactions and negotiation. Fundamental to this approach is the belief that, although the parties are distinct groups with different values and objectives, they are dependent upon each other and will be able to achieve their objectives better if they support each other overall. The way in which management deals with trade unions will thus vary, depending on the decision taken at top-management level.

19.3.2 Handling initial trade union contact

Even though an organisation's management may not be involved with a trade union at a particular point in time, it may still be wise to decide beforehand upon a particular broad approach (as spelt out in 19.3.4) regarding dealings with trade unions. At some point a trade union may approach or contact management for the first time. This initial contact may be in the form of a letter or by means of a telephone call. In some instances it may be a direct person-to-person contact between a union official or a person who says that he or she has been elected as shop steward, and a management representative. The issue at hand may be a request for recognition as the ongoing representative of a group of workers or it may entail a once-off representation of an employee regarding an issue such as a grievance, the alleged unfair dismissal of another employee, or the need to negotiate improved wages and/or working conditions for employees.

Whatever the form of the initial contact and irrespective of the reason put forward for it, it is important for management not to lose the initiative or to panic, or to engage over-hastily in interaction with the trade union. The approach should be handled correctly and it is therefore essential to gather the necessary information first. As much as possible should be found out about the trade union and, if the first contact is by telephone, it is advisable to obtain the name of the trade union, its address and telephone numbers, the name of the official and details regarding the issues/requests/demands at hand.

It is also advisable to request the person to fax through a letter confirming the discussion details. At that stage it is normally not wise to make any overhasty commitments other than that the union will be contacted again as soon as possible. If the initial approach is in writing, or when the fax has been received, a prompt written response is professional. Receipt of the letter should be acknowledged and the contents should be studied carefully. The next step should be to set up, as far as is practically possible, a face-to-face meeting with the appropriate official at the earliest possible opportunity.

The purpose of the first meeting should involve getting to know each other better. It is therefore imperative to make it clear that, in order to have a fruitful first meeting, the parties should be willing to exchange certain information.

In this regard it is sound practice for management to request a copy of the union's constitution, as well as its registration certificate in advance. A first meeting could then be arranged at a date, time and venue convenient to both parties. A reasonable time should be set aside for such a meeting, and the time and duration thereof ought to be specified.

The first meeting is normally important for setting the tone or climate for future interactions. The maxim 'first impressions last' is especially true in this regard. If an approach of union–management cooperation is preferred, the first meeting should preferably end on a positive note. However, because of our history of very adversarial union–management relations – especially during the 1980s and early 1990s – it should be borne in mind that a trade union will often not be prepared for a cooperative type of meeting initially. At the first (and later meetings) it is thus largely up to management to keep the initiative in setting up an appropriate climate for the future, long-term collective relationship.

19.3.3 Formalising the union–management relationship

19.3.3.1 General

Formalising the relationship with a trade union usually involves some kind of an agreement between the parties. The process of formalisation will often depend to a large extent on the level of the union's representativeness in the organisation. This means that generally, before such a relationship is formalised, the trade union will be required to present proof of its membership. This normally includes the submission of signed and correctly completed union membership forms that have to be verified.

The next step is then to make known to the trade union, management's approach regarding the type of representativeness required before a trade union will be recognised as an official representative body of the organisation's workers, or of some of them. Furthermore, bargaining units (particular employee interest groups – for instance, per geographic area and occupational interests and job grades) played an important role in this decision during the 1980s to mid-1990s. In the all-comers approach, management was basically prepared to recognise any trade union having membership of some employees in a particular bargaining unit. In the majoritarian approach, management usually only recognised a trade union on a quantitative basis – that is, once the union could prove that it had a membership figure of more than 50% of the employees in a particular bargaining unit. The sufficiently representative approach was often based on a qualitative evaluation of the wisdom of recognising a trade union even if it had less than 50% membership. In the latter case, factors such as the unique skills of certain employees (who are union members) and the ease with which they could be replaced would play a role.

Management will have to be guided by the principles laid down in the LRA 66 of 1995 (see chapter 18). It seems that the LRA has subordinated the importance of bargaining units to the notion of majoritarianism in the workplace. This means that a trade union has now only to provide proof of sufficient or majority representation in order to be able to exercise certain organisational rights, depending on its level of representativeness in the workplace (see chapter 18). Management's discretion in this matter has thus to some extent been curtailed by the labour relations legislation.

As soon as a decision has been made in principle to recognise a trade union and thus to formalise the relationship by means of a collective agreement, the parties start to negotiate the nature of the agreement itself.

In the Labour Relations Act of 1995, a collective agreement is defined as any written agreement regarding conditions and terms of employment or any other matter of mutual interest concluded by one or more registered trade unions on the one hand, and – among others – one or more employers on the other (it could also include one or more registered employers' organisations).

Recognition agreements are procedural agreements which should be distinguished from substantive agreements; while the former spell out the 'how to' of the collective relationship, the latter contain the detail regarding the 'what' of the relationship (for example conditions of service, wage levels, etc).

Formalising the recognition relationship thus essentially entails recognition of the fact that a particular union (or unions) will act as the collective bargaining and representative agent of a specified group of employees. According to Bendix (1996: 289–290), a recognition agreement will confirm that management accepts the union as a bargaining agent and it will also stipulate the parameters of the future relationship and the way in which it will be conducted. The issues and procedures that will be subject to bargaining will be spelt out in the recognition agreement. In this regard it can be said that a recognition agreement is the plant-level equivalent of the constitution of a bargaining council.

Bendix (1996: 289–290) also distinguishes between different types of recognition agreements. A written recognition agreement may take on the form of a skeletal agreement or a full agreement. While the former simply states the broad principles involved, the latter is a comprehensive agreement containing detailed procedures and providing for most eventualities. A full procedural agreement can be advantageous in that it may serve to eliminate some of the uncertainties encountered by the lower-level managers and shop stewards who have to implement and live by the agreement on a day-to-day basis. In such agreements the rights and obligations of all role players are usually also clearly stipulated, facilitating contract administration and any litigation that may be necessary should there be a breach of the agreement at any stage. Full procedural recognition agreements can, however, often be extremely complicated and too legalistic. On the other hand, a skeletal agreement, while allowing for more flexibility, could lead to greater uncertainties. Skeletal agreements naturally presuppose a more mature relationship and greater trust between the parties. The majority of recognition agreements which have been signed in South Africa to date have, however, been full procedural agreements; this is understandable considering the lack of trust which has characterised our labour relations history.

A general pattern has developed over time with regard to the contents of such full procedural recognition agreements. Typically such an agreement will start off with a preamble that sets the tone of the collective relationship. This is usually followed by a section containing definitions and the clarification of terminology used further on in the agreement. The so-called recognition clause, whereby the organisation's management officially commits itself to recognising the trade union(s) as the representative and bargaining agent of a group of employees who are union members, usually follows the definition section.

Other aspects usually covered by the recognition agreement include the regulation of access by trade union officials to the organisation's premises and arrangements regarding stop-order facilities. As a rule, a separate section deals with the election, rights, role and functions of the recognised trade union's shop stewards in the workplace.

Although the number of shop stewards to be appointed is guided by the Act 66 of 1995, the number of shop stewards may still be arranged in accordance with the nature of the workplace. It has become customary to divide eligible employees into constituencies and to allocate specific numbers of shop stewards per constituency. Management may also agree to appoint full-time shop stewards. Typically these people will have special privileges and a special role to play in the workplace.

The rights and duties of different categories of shop stewards are normally stipulated in the recognition agreement, for instance that shop stewards may not leave their places of work without permission from their supervisors. Shop stewards are, however, usually granted reasonable time off and access to their members. The recognition agreement usually also regulates the holding of shop steward meetings within normal working hours, as well as aspects such as time off for the training of shop stewards to enable them to fulfil their functions properly. The Act spells out these functions clearly.

In terms of the Act, shop stewards (designated as 'trade union representatives' in the Act) essentially have the following functions in the workplace:

- assisting and representing workers in grievance and disciplinary proceedings;
- monitoring the employer's compliance with the relevant provisions of the Act;

- reporting any contraventions of workplace-related provisions of the Act to the employer, to the union, or to the responsible authorities (usually the Department of Labour); and
- performing any other functions agreed to between the union and the employer.

The Act also provides that an employee who is a trade union representative or office bearer of a registered majority trade union has the right to take reasonable leave during working hours for the purpose of union activities. The parties may put into the agreement the number of (paid or unpaid) days' leave and the conditions of leave to which the shop stewards or office bearers will be entitled.

Other aspects normally covered by a recognition agreement include a procedure and parameters for further negotiations in the future (for example on substantive issues such as wages/working conditions on an annual basis), procedures for dealing with disputes, stipulations regarding the duration and amendment of the recognition agreement, as well as a section containing the physical addresses of both parties.

19.3.3.2 Two specific types of collective agreements

In terms of the Act, management and a trade union may opt to enter into closed-shop and/or agency shop agreements. Management and a majority trade union may conclude an agreement in terms of which all employees covered by the agreement are compelled to become members of that trade union. This is known as a closed-shop agreement and is controversial because of its compulsory nature and, as some allege, the curtailment of the freedom of association as a basic human right, which makes it somewhat uncertain whether the closed-shop provision would survive a constitutional challenge. It is therefore not surprising that the drafters of Act 66 of 1995 found it necessary to build in various checks and balances (for example, a mandatory ballot must be held in which at least two-thirds of employees who vote must vote in favour of the closed-shop agreement) in an effort to protect the closed shop from possible constitutional challenge. The Act explicitly provides that it would not be unfair to dismiss an employee who is refused membership or who is expelled from a trade union party to a closed-shop agreement (if the refusal/expulsion is in accordance with the trade union's constitution and the reason for the refusal or expulsion is fair, including, but not limited to, conduct that undermines the trade union's collective exercise of its rights), or for refusing to join a trade union party to a closed shop. Only two exceptions to this rule are allowed: the existing employees at the time a closed-shop agreement takes effect may not be dismissed for refusing to join a trade union party to the agreement, and employees may not be dismissed for refusing to join a trade union party to the agreement on grounds of conscientious objection (in both these instances, employees may be required by the closed-shop agreement to pay an agreed agency fee).

An agency shop agreement is an agreement between an employer and a trade union in terms of which the employer is compelled to deduct from the wages of employees within the bargaining unit who are not trade union members an amount equal to or less than (and in lieu of) the membership fees paid by the trade union members. The agency shop was introduced to counter the free-rider complaint of trade unions. This refers to the situation where non-union member employees within the bargaining unit enjoy the benefits of the trade union's efforts and its members' contributions without incurring any of the costs borne by the trade union members. On the other hand, it may be regarded as morally questionable to require of someone to belong to a trade union against his or her wishes (as is the case where a closed-shop agreement prevails). In terms of the Act, an amount equal to or less than the subscription dues may be deducted from non-union members and paid into an account administered by the trade union, to be used to advance the socio-economic interests of employees in general. Note that in both the closed-shop and the agency shop agreement, the union party to the agreement must enjoy majority support in the workplace.

19.3.4 Broad types of collective negotiation

Negotiation can be described as a process of interaction between two or more parties in a situation in which the parties believe they have to be jointly involved so that the resultant agreement can be balanced and acceptable to all parties concerned.

In this process the parties, although they may have certain different needs or objectives, realise that there are common interests and that a mutually acceptable outcome can be arrived at through processes involving information exchange, communication, reasoning and persuasion.

Although some may hold the view that negotiation and bargaining as concepts have different meanings, Pienaar and Spoelstra (1991: 5) argue that these terms can be used in much the same way, implying that they have much the same purpose and meaning, and follow the same methods. This does not mean, however, that collective bargaining and negotiation are synonymous concepts.

Collective bargaining and collective negotiation are, however, used interchangeably in this book. The qualification 'collective' indicates that the negotiations are conducted by representatives on behalf of their constituencies comprising a particular group of people – the group of employees who are union members and the group called management who represents the interests of the employer at the bargaining table.

19.3.4.1 Distributive negotiation

Many people think that this is all that management–trade union bargaining is about. The parties' behaviour during the processes of negotiation is driven primarily by their conflicting and opposing needs, interests, objectives and positions. The parties view the negotiation process as a zero-sum game where the only real outcome of the situation can be one party winning and the other losing. What the one party wins, the other party will have to lose. The size of the pie over which the parties negotiate is viewed as a given, and the purpose of the interaction between the parties is seen as being to fight for a fair share for their constituencies. The parties often display hostile behaviour towards each other, viewing each other as the enemy. In this type of bargaining the parties are generally antagonistic and display little reasonableness in the process. Focusing on positions and using power are seen as central elements of this type of negotiation. Trade unions usually view management as equating the owners of capital who want to exploit all workers and to control fully the labour or work process. Likewise, management often negotiates from the assumption that the trade union is an unnecessary intruder making management's life difficult and serving no real economic purpose as they simply cause labour costs to rise. This type of negotiation is associated with the collective side of employment relations, with the result that the collective bargaining process is traditionally viewed as being of an adversarial, win–lose nature.

The process of distributive negotiation

In distributive collective negotiation management and trade unions make demands, counter-demands and offers so that agreements can be reached. Each negotiation situation is unique. For this reason (and in line with the scope of this book) only broad guidelines regarding distributive collective negotiations can be provided. Three phases or stages of the process of distributive negotiation can be identified, namely the pre-negotiation phase, the interactive phase and the post-negotiation phase.

Phase 1: The pre-negotiation phase

Thorough planning, preparation and organising are vital for successful negotiation. Preparation and planning for initial negotiations start with the first contact between the parties. When an agreement is concluded, the preparation phase for the next round of negotiations has already started. The more comprehensive and complex the topics for negotiation, the more time and energy will have to be spent on the pre-negotiation phase. The topics can vary from procedural aspects such as grievance, disciplinary, staff-reduction or dispute-settling procedures to substantive aspects such as working hours, wages, leave, job evaluations, bonuses, equal opportunities, health and safety, and so on.

Even before the first negotiations commence, decisions have to be made about pre-negotiation aspects such as the levels at which to negotiate and the appropriate scope of issues about which to negotiate. Obviously, the broad negotiations approach must also fit in with the overall strategic posture (see chapter 5).

Furthermore, during this phase of negotiation, the wide range of environmental influences which could have an impact on the negotiations must also be taken into consideration. For instance, the other party's envisaged positions, objectives and tactics must be considered, and the negotiation mandate of the management negotiation team itself must also be clearly established. Intra-organisational negotiations thus typically form an important element of the pre-negotiation phase – that is, negotiation among managers themselves regarding their own priorities, objectives and positions. Furthermore, it is also important to appoint competent negotiation teams during this phase, to train them and to synchronise their efforts.

The pre-negotiation phase thus involves a great deal of time and effort. At this stage the collection of all sorts of information is extremely important. The underlying organisation of the negotiations will also have to take place, with aspects such as dates, times, venues with appropriate facilities for caucusing, tea breaks, meals, secretarial and record-keeping facilities, and media coverage arrangements being attended to.

The methodology used and the quality of these preparations and planning efforts are of cardinal importance in ensuring successful negotiations. An important part of this phase relates to setting objectives and structuring negotiation priorities.

It is very important, before the bargaining team actually enters into the physical or interactive phase of negotiating with the trade union representatives, to analyse and identify exactly what issues are at stake. As far as possible one should divide and subdivide the issues into sub-issues by carefully analysing the range of issues and considering which may be dealt with as stand-alone topics and which need to be combined. As this process progresses, it also becomes necessary to prioritise the negotiation issues. When this is done it is also wise to consider the likely priorities of the other party.

A so-called bargaining range is also established for each issue. The bargaining range determines just how much the parties to the negotiation process can shift their positions. If, for example, the issue at hand is the monthly wage levels of workers and the current level is R1 900 per month, management's bargaining range may be between R1 995 and R2 280. This will mean that the most optimistic outcome for management would be an increase of 5%. On the other hand, the highest increase that management will be prepared to settle for (if trade-offs with other issues can be made) is 20%. This means that the bargaining range of management is between

5% and 20%. Within this range there will be some point of realism – in other words, what management could actually expect the realistic outcome to be. This point or sub-range will, however, only be determined once the likely bargaining range of the other party is also considered and the area of overlap is identified. This overlapping range would give the most likely range of settlement. If, for instance, the bargaining range of the trade union is between 32% and 14%, the realistic settlement range would in all likelihood amount to anything between 14% and 20%.

In this way the negotiating team prepares all the issues by prioritising them in terms of relative importance, establishing opening positions and working out bargaining ranges with ideal and fall-back positions. Planning fall-back positions is extremely important. Anstey's (1991: 134–135) opinion in this regard is clear:

> It is important for an employer to plan fall-backs from the onset of the bargaining process. Usually projections have to be made for labour costs into the future to allow for accurate business planning and budgeting, and competitiveness. Where an employer must tender for business in a highly competitive industry this becomes particularly important. However, many employers do not think through their fall-backs, often carelessly identifying an inflationary increase as the point of no further offers. This is often naive, being based on what they desire rather than what is practicable.

In one negotiation, the union reduced its demand from 25% to 22%, to which the company made a 'final offer' of 12%. A mediator spent considerable time with the management team discussing the implications of this. If a final offer was made too early and too bluntly it would not allow the union side time and room to reconsider its position for purposes of further movement. It would be left with a 'take it or leave it' situation, in this instance, with a large gap to close. If the company stated that this was a final offer, but then moved at the first sign of a strike, it would be saying to the union that its 'finals' could not be trusted and inviting the union to strike every year to test the seriousness of a position. The factory manager stated that 12% was the limit of the mandate, beyond that they had been directed from board level to 'dig the trenches and do whatever fighting was necessary'. The union rejected the offer and indicated to the company that it would be taking a strike ballot. When the factory manager returned to head office that afternoon he advised the directors that deadlock had been reached and that a strike was probable. Looking again at the order book and stock levels, the directors realised that a strike would be very damaging to the business – and immediately raised their offer to 20%! This reflects some wise last-minute shifts, but very bad planning and poor use of the bargaining process – in effect the union called a bluff which the company did not consciously consider making!

Companies might need to plan several fall-back scenarios, based on various business conditions, for example, stock levels, orders, competition, peak periods, etc. A series of 'what-ifs?' need to be considered. A distinction between what would be desirable and what is possible under various conditions is necessary. An employer may actively resist movement from a given point, but whether it would accept a strike for two months at that point, or stand the risk of severing relations with workers is another issue. Points of resistance signal to the other party that a final position may be close, but it is incorrect to state that it is 'final' if it is not! It locks parties into battles of trust and entraps them in principles that might be expensive to live out.

By doing this sort of planning for all the negotiation issues or items, one can start to develop an overall plan regarding aspects such as opening moves, pressure tactics, and when and how concessions may be made on what issues. Obviously, in mapping out this negotiation plan, it is essential to take into consideration the power dynamics in the relationship. In this regard, aspects like the general state of the economy; the strength of the trade union in terms of membership figures and leadership; the organisation's market, financial and logistical/stock situation; and the overall climate in the country/region in terms of industrial action all have to be considered. Only if such variables have been carefully considered within the context of the bigger picture relating to the total bargaining situation and employment relations in general can one really start to work out the different tactics that may be used during the course of the actual interactive phase of negotiation.

Phase 2: The interactive phase of negotiation
In this phase the two parties face each other and systematically try to persuade each other to change points of view regarding the positions of the parties.

During this stage particular negotiating tactics are applied within the context of the broad negotiation approach or strategy. Remember that 'strategy' refers to the overall approach, plan and policy in respect of the negotiation process, while 'tactics' refer to the particular conduct of the parties during the actual negotiations.

Knowledge and particular skills play a major role during this stage. Exhibit 19.1 lists some potentially useful hints to help during this phase of negotiations.

During the course of the interactive phase, the core aspects revolve around communication, persuasion and debate. Getting down to the nitty gritty of the actual conduct of negotiations basically boils down to the various parties discussing and debating the merits of each other's arguments. One must always remember that collective negotiations take place in order to reach agreements and that negotiating for the sake of negotiating can only be to the detriment of all.

The final stage of this interactive phase – that is, agreeing on solutions, recording the agreements and summarising the bargains that have been struck – should be sought on a continuous basis. Finally, all parties should explicitly accept responsibility for communicating and implementing the agreed-upon issues. Make sure, before you depart, that you understand everything and do not rush the final stages of the interactive phase. Remember, how you greet and depart sets the climate for future negotiations and for the spirit in which the parties will go out and implement the agreements.

Phase 3: The post-negotiation phase
The importance of implementing agreements correctly cannot be overemphasised. The interactive phase usually concludes with some sort of agreement (or contract), which is usually put in writing. This means that differences have been settled or that agreements have been reached on particular issues. Negotiations can also, of course, be less successful at times. Further dates must then be set for future negotiations, or the parties must follow the relevant dispute-settling procedures in the event of deadlocks.

Both parties must, however, respect all agreements – even in difficult circumstances – because this builds trust and mutually beneficial long-term relationships. Contract administration is the key concept.

The post-negotiation phase usually refers to the total validity period stated in agreements. During this period the parties make sure that all role players abide by the agreed-upon procedures and substantive issues (such as wages and other conditions

EXHIBIT 19.1: Guidelines for the interactive phase of negotiation

- Keep to the agenda as far as possible.
- Maintain order at all times.
- Stick to the facts and do not discuss people as such (separate problems from people).
- Take note of and use body language and gestures effectively.
- Listen more and talk less (two ears, one mouth) – ask a lot of appropriate questions, in the right way to get the right information.
- Remain alert all the time.
- Regularly confirm when you have understood and get confirmation that others understand.
- When in doubt or uncertain about anything, call for a caucus.
- Take your time and never talk, act or make decisions overhastily.
- Be pleasant, true and decent all the time.
- Treat everyone else with due respect.
- Be sensitive to cultural and language differences.
- Make careful notes and keep looking for alternatives and inaccuracies in information and arguments.
- Offer various possible choices of options to the other party and make sure that everything is understood within the context of the real interests at hand.
- Be emotionally stable – do not become unnerved by militant action or provocation. Let a colleague talk when you are angry.
- Regularly check progress and summarise where the process stands – seek confirmation of common understanding on this.
- Always keep some flexibility in your negotiation positions or stances and always remind others of the interests at hand.
- The negotiator should not only be concerned with what the other party says and does, but must constantly find out the real interests and the reasons underlying these positions or stated problems.
- If something is not well understood, ask for thorough explanations.
- Respect the importance of face-saving for the other party and be graceful. Give other parties the necessary dignity.
- Be constantly alert to the real intents of the other party, not only with respect to objectives and positions but also to priorities and real interests.
- Build a reputation for being fair but firm.
- Make each negotiation decision in relationship to the other decisions – that is, link all interests into a whole.
- Pay close attention to communication, do not interrupt and listen with interest to what is being said and what not. Never hesitate to make sure that you understand things as they are meant to be understood.
- Remember that collective negotiations in the labour area should essentially be a process of compromise. There is no such thing as winning or getting your own way in everything.
- Try to understand the people on the other side of the table, their personalities, fears, interests, perceptions, needs, concern, and so forth – it could bear fruit during negotiations.
- Always consider the impact of the current negotiations on future negotiations – remember that collective bargaining revolves around long-term relationships.
- Remain positive and assertive.
- Sanctions may be used but not misused.
- Pay close attention to the wording of each clause of agreements negotiated. Words and phrases (or expressions) are often the source of valuable information.
- Read agreements carefully before signing and do not ignore the fine print.
- Close the negotiations by summarising key, agreed points and by breaking the eye contact – then get up and shake hands in a pleasant, decent manner.

of service). The role of the grievance and disciplinary procedures applied during this phase is, of course, extremely important.

During this phase the role of the lower-level supervisors and shop stewards is of equally crucial importance. Good communication and day-to-day contact between all the other relevant role players are some of the other key elements of this phase. The supervisors and shop stewards have to ensure that all clauses in the agreements are adequately maintained. Where negotiations are conducted at sectoral level, the inspectors of bargaining councils also have an important part to play.

The whole concept of good-faith bargaining becomes quite watered down if the post-negotiation phase is neglected by any of the parties. All agreements have to be implemented and adhered to in a decent, honest, truthful and sincere manner. This is the phase where the quality of the long-term collective employment relationship can really be developed or undermined.

The interactive phase may very well be the dramatic highlight of collective bargaining, but the actual proof of the pudding lies in contract administration and adherence by both parties. Trade unions are often more interested in the post-negotiation phase – this is why shop stewards and supervisors play such an important role during this phase. These key role players have to ensure that agreements operate smoothly on a day-to-day basis, otherwise the agreements are not worth the paper on which they are written. Any problems which arise in this regard have to be brought to the attention of the trade union and/or management, so that the necessary follow-up meetings and discussions can be arranged.

Competencies and characteristics of successful negotiators

Exhibit 19.2 lists some essential characteristics of successful negotiators, based on the works of Salamon (1992); Kniveron (1974); Bendix (1996); and Alfred (1984).

19.3.4.2 Integrative negotiation

The parties to negotiation sometimes wisely recognise and emphasise the fact that there is indeed common ground between trade unions and management. According to this approach to bargaining, the parties explore the possibilities of creating win–win situations. The parties, although they acknowledge the basic conflict in perceptions, goals and interests, deliberately channel their energies towards enlarging the areas of common concern. They thus concentrate on interacting in such a way that the outcomes of the negotiation process eventually lead to overall mutual gains. The parties are not as adversarial in their behaviour and relationships, and they are prepared to grant concessions in order to move to situations where both parties gain something. More emphasis is placed on trust, openness, information sharing, constant meaningful two-way communication and joint problem solving. The parties emphasise the fact that they have to solve problems jointly in order to reach optimum solutions. Examples include negotiating on measures to reduce absenteeism and labour turnover in order to improve the work processes and the quality of the organisation's products/services, thus saving (and creating) jobs, increasing turnover and revenue, and increasing the size of the pie. Negotiation is thus not viewed as a fixed-sum game.

Another example could be where the parties deal with the health, education and housing problems of workers, which in turn enhance the workers' ability to perform better on the job (because they feel better physically, are not as unhealthy and do not suffer from fatigue as a result of travelling problems). This could in turn help the organisation to be more successful – thus increasing the size of the pie. The parties could then also look at the fair redistribution of the bigger pie – eventually all

EXHIBIT 19.2: Essential characteristics of successful negotiators

- They have to be well trained and knowledgeable in the intricacies of negotiations.
- They have to possess good social interpersonal skills.
- They have to like dealing with people, especially in difficult circumstances.
- They have to be good planners and thus need good information-processing skills.
- Their nature should be positive towards mutual gains and not filled with greed and egocentrism.
- They have to be good communicators, being able to listen sincerely and express themselves clearly.
- They need a lot of persuasive abilities.
- They should be very alert and perceptive to what is happening around them (and what is not).
- They need high-quality discretionary judgement and analytical skills.
- They have to be patient and should possess good stress tolerance.
- They have to be able to control their emotions (keeping cool under heated circumstances).
- They need good conceptual abilities in order to relate aspects and continually to see the bigger picture.
- They have to be long-term orientated.
- Although they have to be goal orientated and persistent, they also have to be flexible, open-minded thinkers.
- They have to be creative in order to come up with counterproposals and alternative arguments.
- They have to be intellectually well developed with a quickness of mind, coupled with the ability not to act overhastily.
- They have to have a good sense of humour.
- They have to be reasonable and prepared to compromise when necessary.
- They have to have the ability sometimes to take a backseat and they should not be overconcerned with defending the self (being modest).
- They have to possess diplomatic abilities and must be sincere, honest people.
- They have to be hard on facts and soft on people.
- High levels of perceived integrity are essential for long-term success in negotiations.

can win! The parties would thus be more positive towards each other and prepared to underplay their differences in order to channel their energies towards common goals. Openness, trust, concessions and mutual support are emphasised rather than opposition, competition, power and adversarial behaviour.

An analysis of the literature (Fisher & Ury (1981); Fisher & Brown (1988); Höck (1991/92); and Power (1991)) reveals that there are certain approaches or styles which can be used to bring about or facilitate more integrative types of collective negotiation. Two such styles are interest bargaining and target-specific bargaining.

Interest bargaining: some principles

One of the key ideas of this approach is that parties who engage in collective bargaining should focus on the interest which motivate the parties and their claims rather than on the claims themselves. For example, if a trade union's claim is a 20% across-the-board wage increase, the question that ought to be asked is: why? Similarly, if an organisation's position is an offer of 2%, the question that ought to be asked is: why? As the parties explore these underlying questions, they will most likely discover that the reasoning behind the claims or bargaining positions represents the interest range of the parties, and that for every interest range there is normally more than one possible settlement position which could satisfy the interest underlying the initial position. In this way they are more likely to identify common ground or interests which are compatible. These interests are explored during pre-bargaining meetings, even before letters of demand are tabled by the union.

The parties thus acknowledge that the real conflict lies not so much in their respective bargaining positions, but that these should rather be viewed as the symptoms of conflicting desires, needs, concerns and interests. In focusing on their respective interests, the parties have to be open and frank, and have to discuss their interests honestly and sincerely. Parties should be flexible and should be prepared to recognise each other's interests, fears and needs; they should look to the future rather than dig up the past; and they should be prepared to list concisely the specific problems and their causes.

In this way the focus of attention is drawn away from the opposing parties' respective positions so that progress is no longer measured in terms of successively relinquishing and adopting a sequence of positions. During the collective bargaining process, the parties do not try to defend their positions by saying 'we have given in here and there, and on these and those aspects', but instead they defend the underlying real needs, concerns and interests of their constituents. The elements of egoism and face-saving thus become less important.

Another important element of interest bargaining is to separate the people from the problems. Thus, although a party may be hard on defending their interests (not their positions as such), they will be soft on the people – that is, the other party's negotiators. To this end it is important, when following the interest bargaining approach, to accept the legitimacy of the other party's negotiators as the representatives of certain real interests which are important to them and to those whom they represent. Parties should thus be prepared to try to understand each other's needs and concerns, the fact that people are people (all with different personalities, emotions, feelings, fears, needs, etc) and that, at the end of the day, the failure to reach workable agreements could be to the detriment of all. Furthermore, the parties must be committed to exchanging the necessary information and to opening up communication in order to understand each other's interest better. Fisher and Brown (1988: 85) suggest that good-quality communication does not necessarily equate with being best friends and that it is almost even more important (and certainly more difficult) to communicate successfully with those with whom one has conflict than with those with whom one has no conflict and whom one likes.

Yet another extremely important principle of interest bargaining that also relates to the human side of the collective bargaining process is that of trust. One aspect that has a major influence on collective bargaining is that of trust. The levels of trust between the parties play a determining role, and more than four decades ago Walton and McKersie (1965: 358) made the following assertion, for instance:

> Trust plays a more central role in integrative bargaining. It does more than circumscribe conflict behaviour of the participants; it enables them to increase their joint gain. The integrative process requires open communication which in turn depends on trust. Moreover, the more trust and other positive attitudes exist in the relationship, the more sincerely motivated each party is to work on the problems of the other, irrespective of anticipated substantive or attitudinal pay-offs.

This quotation underscores the importance of this element when it comes to switching from a distributive approach to an integrative one, when it comes to the restructuring of attitudes and to the adoption of an approach of interest bargaining.

Within this context the importance of integrity, of being honest and sincere, of being reliable and of sticking to agreements and avoiding unlawful or unprocedural actions, cannot be overemphasised. The manner in which negotiations take place is also of fundamental importance. Fisher and Brown (1988: 132) put it as follows: "Just as my ability to negotiate with someone is affected by the quality of our relationship, so the quality of the relationship is affected by the way I negotiate. How we try to influence each other has a significant impact on the ability to deal with future differences." It is thus obvious that less adversarial, hostile types of behaviour will have to be demonstrated. Less reliance will have to be placed on power positions and coercive tactics such as verbally attacking people during the course of negotiations, or threatening to withdraw if a certain demand (or position) is not adhered to. Emphasis will instead have to be placed more on persuasive tactics. Bostrom (1983: 11) describes persuasion as "… communicative behaviour that has as its purpose the changing, modification, or shaping of the responses (attitudes or behaviour) of the receivers".

Persuasive tactics, as a primary means of bringing about attitudinal restructuring, also form an important component in the move from distributive to more integrative types of bargaining. This is the case because the actual collective bargaining process is viewed as only one part of the collective employment relationship. The quality of this relationship can, in terms of this perspective, only be built on principles such as respect, trust, integrity and fairness. In all of this, the softer aspects of mutually beneficial relationship building through, inter alia, interest bargaining are viewed as being more important than the harder aspects of legalism and the actual eventual formal written agreements flowing from the negotiation encounters.

The process of target-specific bargaining

Power (1991: 15–20) provides quite an elaborate discussion of this relatively new approach to collective bargaining. According to him, the results of this approach in the US have "… been extremely encouraging for parties seeking an alternative to pure adversarial bargaining", and he proposes that it "… may represent a creative alternative for South African employers and unions interested in developing sounder relations, based on shared information, and for parties locked into the crises induced by interaction of rising expectations and problems of economic survival and growth" (Power 1991: 20).

This approach is based on the idea of changing the bargaining process to one which is actually productive for both parties, through the use of valid information and with the aim of generating less confrontation. It thus contains similar characteristics and principles as interest bargaining, but it also has, as is illustrated below, certain distinct features – especially as far as the process is concerned. As an approach it is claimed to fall somewhere between win–win and win–lose types of bargaining, and extensive use is made of a mediator. Again, one of the fundamental elements is that of trust. Power (1991: 15) states, for example, that "… trust and information has been characterised in the historic past of adversarial bargaining … Target Specific Bargaining requires the joint identification and organisation of information to solve problems brought forward by labour and management. This gives validity to the information brought forward through a joint process".

Power (1991: 16–20) then proceeds to describe a seven-step process which structures the target-specific bargaining approach.

Step 1 is a problem-seeking process during which both management and the union go back to their members (constituents), where they meet in small groups to record, in a uniform format, all problems and issues, and their symptoms and causes or sources. In this way the factor of trust is reaffirmed because the members identify their problems as well as the real reasons why they exist – thus focusing on the true interests.

Step 2 is a procedural step where each party lists their problems (including the symptoms, reasons, etc) and lodges the list with a central source. This information is kept confidential at this stage.

Step 3 has two stages. Each party goes separately to the mediator with whom they review their list of problems. The mediator asks questions, probes into reasons, points out potential inconsistencies or duplications and helps each party to finalise their list. Up to now the parties have done everything separately. Stage two of this step commences when the management and trade union teams come together to exchange lists and clarify uncertainties. The parties get the information from each other in order to understand the interests better – they are not allowed to criticise each other or to question the legitimacy of any item on the list. The exchange of information is aimed purely at clarifying what each item entails.

Step 4 commences with each party clearly understanding the nature of each problem and its perceived causes. The parties now move to a situation of joint ownership of the problems where they decide jointly what information will be needed to address each specific problem listed by the two sides. The extremely important prerequisite of target-specific bargaining – that is, to disclose fully all information relevant to solving the problems – now comes into play. There is, by now, a joint list of problems, symptoms, possible causes and information needed to address each aspect, all structured in an agreed-upon problem classification system. Use is made of brainstorming techniques to get all the information for this joint bargaining manual. The parties will furthermore decide on how and when joint teams will gather all the necessary data.

Step 5 is the final pre-bargaining meeting where the parties jointly, with the aid of the mediator, set the "bargaining agenda by sequencing the order of discussion by groupings of classifications" (Power 1991: 16).

Step 6 sees the beginning of the actual negotiation process; the joint problem-solving processes are now constructively facilitated by the mediator. As the processes develop, the problem solving becomes more and more complex, in turn requiring various techniques ranging from brainstorming, discussions, constructive debate, analyses and consensus-seeking processes. The mediator focuses especially on dovetailing the interests of the parties and on using consensus processes to arrive at solutions from which all parties will benefit in the interest of those whom they represent. The target-specific bargaining approach requires that agreement be reached on a solution for each listed item (problem or issue).

Step 7 revolves around the ratification and follow-up processes. The parties go back to their members and present them with the agreed-upon solutions. All the parties are jointly trained with regard to the changed situations (contracts) and the parties implement the agreements. Agreement administration is thus also conducted jointly with all parties understanding the new situation. Attitudes are thus more positive and perceptions are streamlined. In this way the possibilities of improved relationships are enhanced, and a move from distributive types of collective bargaining to more integrative styles is thus facilitated.

Elsewhere in Africa

Negotiations for annual salary adjustments in Mauritius are carried out as tripartites, with the state and the employer groups involved, although the union group is generally not an equal player in the game, being unsophisticated and lacking preparedness ... The fragmentation within the union movement makes it extremely difficult for this stakeholder group to exercise much bargaining power ... The fact that wages and conditions remain persistently high on unions' agendas are reflective of an employment situation that is still not quite 'right' with the basics.

Source: Slightly adapted extract from Ramgutty-Wong (2004: 65)

19.4 COOPERATING THROUGH STATUTORY WORKPLACE FORUMS

19.4.1 General

The LRA introduced workplace forums as in-house institutions for employee participation and representation at the workplace. The idea is that, whereas collective bargaining can be used for distributive issues in the time-honoured adversarial fashion, workplace forums should be used to foster cooperative relations through dialogue, information sharing, consultations and joint decision making.

19.4.2 Rationale for and establishment of a workplace forum

For the purpose of workplace forums, the term 'employee' excludes senior managerial employees.

A *senior managerial employee* is defined as a person whose contract of employment or status confers the authority to represent the employer in dealings with workplace forums; or to determine policy and take decisions on behalf of the employer that may be in conflict with the 'representation of employees in the workplace'.

In terms of the Act, the functions of a workplace forum are to strive for the promotion of the interests of all employees in the workplace, whether they are trade union members or not, and to improve efficiency in the workplace. In order to promote these objectives, it has the right to obtain certain information from the employer, to be consulted on certain matters, as well as to participate in joint decision making on other matters (see below).

The general process for the establishment of a workplace forum is depicted in figure 19.3

A workplace forum may be established in any workplace in which an employer employs more than 100 employees. Any representative trade union may apply to the CCMA for the establishment of a workplace forum. The applicant must satisfy the CCMA that a copy of the application has been served on the employer. Once the CCMA receives the application, it has to ascertain whether there are 100 or more employees employed at that workplace, whether the applicant is a representative trade union, and whether there is no functioning workplace forum already established in terms of the Act. Thereafter the CCMA must appoint a commissioner to assist the parties to establish a workplace forum by collective agreement or, failing that, to establish a workplace forum in terms of the Act. The commissioner must convene a meeting with the applicant, the employer and any registered trade union that has members employed in the workplace, in order to facilitate the conclusion of a collective agreement between those parties, or at least between the applicant and the employer.

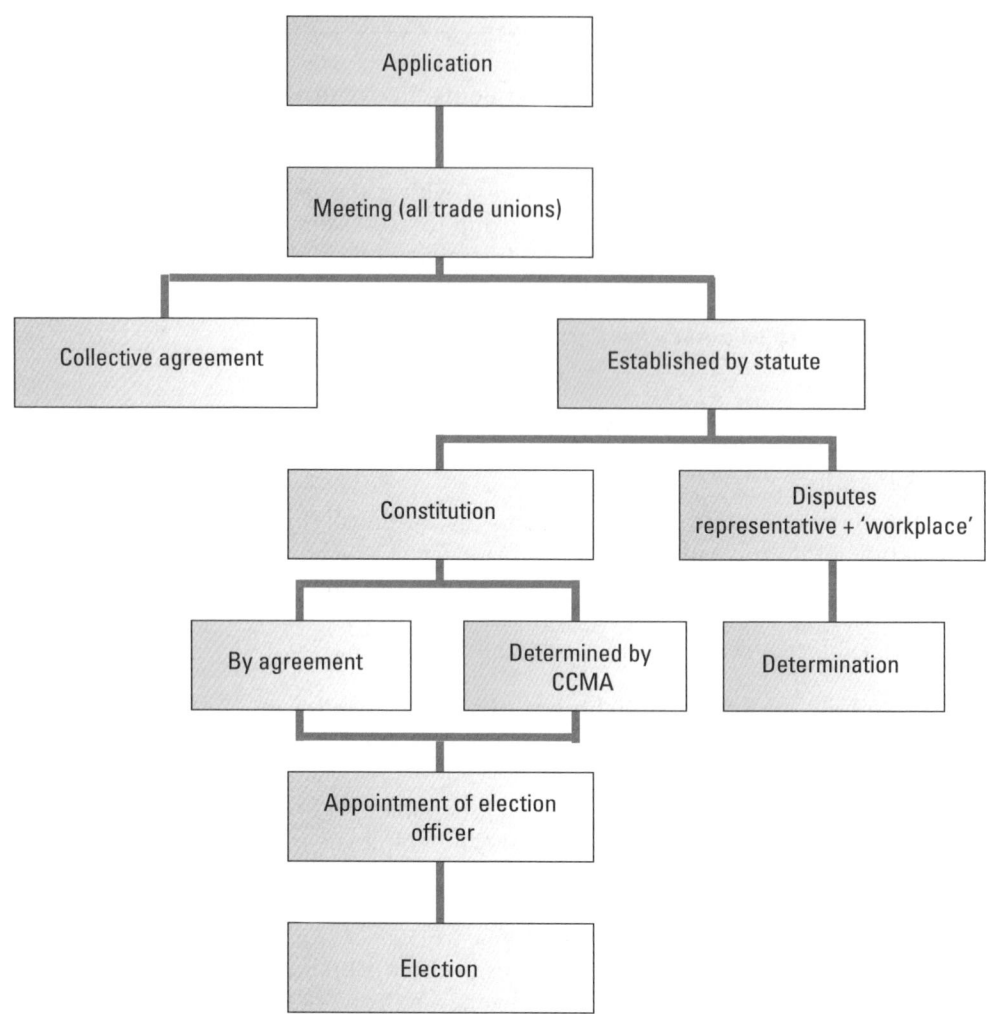

Figure 19.3: General process for the establishment of a workplace forum

If a collective agreement is concluded, the role of the commissioner regarding the establishment of a workplace forum is completed. If a collective agreement is not concluded, the commissioner must once again try to convene a meeting between the relevant stakeholders (or at least between the applicant and the employer), with a view to reaching agreement on a constitution for the workplace forum in accordance with the Act. If agreement is not reached on a constitution, the commissioner must establish a workplace forum and determine the provisions of the constitution in accordance with the Act. After the workplace forum has been established, the commissioner must set a date for the election of the first members of the forum and appoint an election officer to conduct the election.

If a majority trade union enjoys sole bargaining rights in respect of all employees in a particular workplace, that trade union may apply for the establishment of a trade union-based workplace forum. In this case the applicant trade union may choose the members of the workplace forum from among its elected representatives in the workplace. The constitution of the applicant trade union governs the nomination, election and removal from office of elected representatives in the workplace. A trade union-based workplace forum will be dissolved if the collective agreement granting sole bargaining rights to the trade union is terminated or whenever the trade union loses its status as the majority trade union. It should be noted that trade union-based workplace forums will be rare, since, in terms of the Act, the majority tradeunion must represent all employees at a workplace. It is not common in South Africa to have one trade union representing workers as well as supervisors and middle management.

19.4.3 Constitution of a workplace forum

The constitution of every workplace forum must provide for certain matters and may provide for certain other matters.

The constitution of a workplace forum must:

- establish a formula for determining the number of seats in the workplace forum;
- establish a formula for the distribution of seats in the workplace forum so as to reflect the occupational structure of the workplace;
- provide for the direct election of members of the workplace forum by the employees in the workplace;
- provide for the appointment of an employee as an election officer to conduct elections and define that officer's functions and powers;
- provide that an election of members of the workplace forum must be held not later than 24 months after each preceding election;
- provide that, if another registered trade union becomes representative, it may demand a new election at any time within 21 months after each preceding election;
- provide for the procedure and manner in which elections and ballots must be conducted;
- provide that any employee, including any former or current member of the workplace forum, may be nominated as a candidate for election as a member of the workplace forum by any registered trade union with members employed in the workplace, or a petition signed by not less than 20% of the employees in the workplace or 100 employees, whichever number of employees is the smaller;
- provide that in any ballot every employee is entitled to vote by secret ballot and to vote during working hours at the employer's premises;
- provide that in an election for members of the workplace forum every employee is entitled (unless the constitution provides otherwise) to cast a number of votes equal to the number of members to be elected, and to cast one or more of those votes in favour of any candidate;
- establish the terms of office of members of the workplace forum and the circumstances in which a member must vacate that office;
- establish the circumstances and manner in which members of the workplace forum may be removed from office, including the right of any representative trade union that nominated a member for election to remove that member at any time;
- establish the manner in which vacancies in the workplace forum may be filled, including the rules for holding by-elections;
- establish the circumstances and manner in which meetings must be held;
- provide that the employer must allow the election officer reasonable time off with pay during working hours to prepare for and conduct elections;
- provide that the employer must allow each member of the workplace forum reasonable time off with pay during working hours to perform the functions of a member of the workplace forum and to receive training relevant to the performance of those functions;

- require the employer to take any steps that are reasonably necessary to assist the election officer in conducting elections;
- require the employer to provide facilities to enable the workplace forum to perform its functions;
- provide for full-time members of the workplace forum where there are more than 1 000 employees in a workplace;
- provide that the forum may invite any expert to attend meetings of the workplace forum, including meetings with the employer or the employees, and that an expert is entitled to any information to which the workplace forum is entitled, and to inspect and copy any document that members of the workplace forum are entitled to inspect and copy;
- provide that office bearers or officials of the representative trade union may attend meetings of the workplace forum, including meetings with the employer or the employees; and
- provide that the representative trade union and the employer, by agreement, may change the constitution of the workplace forum.

In addition, the constitution of a workplace forum may provide for the following:
- establishing a procedure that provides for the conciliation and arbitration of proposals in respect of which the employer and the workplace forum do not reach consensus;
- establishing a coordinating workplace forum to perform any of the general functions of a workplace forum and one or more subsidiary workplace forums to perform any of the specific functions of a workplace forum; and
- including provisions that depart from those set out in the Act.

19.4.4 Meetings of workplace forums

The Act specifies that there must be regular meetings of the workplace forum. It then proceeds to specify three different types of regular meetings, namely: (i) meetings between the employer and the workplace forum; (ii) meetings between the workplace forum and employees; and (iii) meetings between the employer and employees at a workplace.

1 *Meetings between the employer and the workplace forum:* At these meetings the employer must present a report on its financial and employment situation, its performance since the last report and its anticipated performance in the short and in the long term; and consult the workplace forum on any matter arising from the report that may affect employees in the workplace.
2 *Meetings between the workplace forum and employees*: At these meetings the workplace forum must report on its activities generally, on matters in respect of which it has been consulted by the employer, and on matters in respect of which it has participated in joint decision making with the employer.
3 *Meetings between the employer and employees at a workplace*: Each calendar year, at one of the meetings with the employees, the employer must present an annual report of its financial and employment situation, its performance generally, and its future prospects and plans.

Meetings with employees – (2) and (3) above – must be held during working hours, at a time and place agreed upon by the workplace forum and the employer, without loss of pay on the part of the employees.

19.4.5 Using workplace forums for the purposes of consultation

Consultative decision making may be described as a process in which one party retains the right unilaterally to make and implement a decision, subject to the qualification that he or she must, as part of the decision-making process, allow other stakeholders to make representations. These representations must be seriously considered by the decision maker before making the decision. It should be noted that good-faith consultation requires of the decision maker to suspend the final decision until he or she has elicited and seriously considered the proposals of the other stakeholders. To reach a decision before considering the other parties' proposals would constitute consultation in bad faith, and would therefore not constitute consultation at all. What distinguishes consultative decision making from joint decision making is the fact that the former remains a unilateral process, whereas the latter is a bilateral process (in the sense that the authority to make a decision is shared between two or more parties, which in turn implies that each party has a veto over each of the other parties).

As a unilateral process, consultative decision making does not impose a duty on the decision maker to reach any agreement with the non-decision-making parties to the procedure (accordingly, the Act provides that, after having complied with the statutory duty to consult, employers may implement the proposal, even in the absence of agreement). According to the Act, the purpose of consultation is to reach agreement. Before employers may implement a proposal in relation to any of the listed matters, they must first consult the workplace forum and attempt to reach consensus with it. Employers must allow the workplace forum an opportunity during the consultation to make representations and to advance alternative proposals. They must consider and respond to the representations or alternative proposals made by the workplace forum and, if they do not agree with them, must state their reasons for this. If employers and the workplace forum do not reach consensus, employers must invoke any agreed procedure to resolve any differences before implementing their proposal.

Except where a collective agreement determines otherwise, a workplace forum is entitled to be consulted by the employer about proposals relating to any of the following:
- restructuring the workplace, including the introduction of new technology and new work methods;
- changes in the organisation of work;
- partial or total plant closures;
- mergers and transfers of ownership, in so far as they have an impact on the employees;
- the dismissal of employees for reasons based on operational requirements;
- exemptions from any collective agreement or any law;
- job grading;
- criteria for merit increases or the payment of discretionary bonuses;
- education and training;
- product development plans;
- export promotion; and
- other matters specifically provided for.

The above list could be expanded in the following manner:
- A bargaining council may confer on a workplace forum the right to be consulted about additional matters in workplaces that fall within the registered scope of the bargaining council.

- A representative trade union and an employer may conclude a collective agreement conferring on the workplace forum the right to be consulted about any additional matters in that workplace.
- Any other law may confer on a workplace forum the right to be consulted about additional matters.
- Subject to any applicable occupational health and safety legislation, a representative trade union and an employer may agree:
  - that the employer must consult with the workplace forum with a view to initiating, developing, promoting, monitoring and reviewing measures to ensure health and safety at work;
  - that a meeting between the workplace forum and employer constitutes a meeting of a health and safety committee required to be established in the workplace by that legislation; and
  - that one or more members of the workplace forum are health and safety representatives for the purposes of that legislation.
- A newly established workplace forum may request the employer for a review of existing merit systems, disciplinary codes and procedures, and work-related conduct (see below).

In the case of workplace forums in the public service, matters may be removed from the list of consultative issues, but none may be added.

19.4.6 Joint decision making with workplace forums

Except if a collective agreement determines otherwise, an employer must reach consensus with a workplace forum before implementing any proposal concerning those matters listed in exhibit 19.3. This list of issues may be amended by either a collective agreement between the employer and the majority trade union, or by any other statute that may confer on a workplace forum the right to participate in joint decision making about additional matters.

EXHIBIT 19.3: Matters for joint decision making

Except if a collective agreement determines otherwise, an employer must reach consensus with a workplace forum before implementing any proposal concerning:

- disciplinary codes and procedures;
- rules relating to the proper regulation of the workplace, in so far as they apply to conduct not related to the work performance of employees;
- measures designed to protect and advance persons disadvantaged by unfair discrimination; and
- changes by the employer or by employer-appointed representatives on trusts or boards of employer-controlled schemes, to the rules regulating social benefit schemes.

Should the employer not reach consensus with the workplace forum, the employer may either refer the dispute to arbitration in terms of any agreed procedure or, if there is no agreed procedure, refer it to the CCMA. The employer must satisfy the Commission that a copy of the referral has been served on the chairperson of the workplace forum. The Commission must attempt to resolve the dispute through conciliation. If it remains unresolved, the employer may request that the dispute be resolved through arbitration (see figure 19.4).

19.4.7 Matters for review

Once it has been established, the workplace forum may request a meeting with the employer to review the criteria for merit increases or the payment of discretionary bonuses, disciplinary codes and procedures, and rules relating to the proper regulation of the workplace, in so far as they apply to conduct not related to work performance of employees in the workplace. The employer must submit the necessary criteria, disciplinary codes and procedures, and rules, if any, in writing to the workplace forum for its consideration. A review of the merit increases criteria must be conducted in terms of the prescribed consultative process, whereas a review of the disciplinary codes and procedures, and rules, must be done by way of a collective agreement or conducted in accordance with the procedure depicted in figure 19.4.

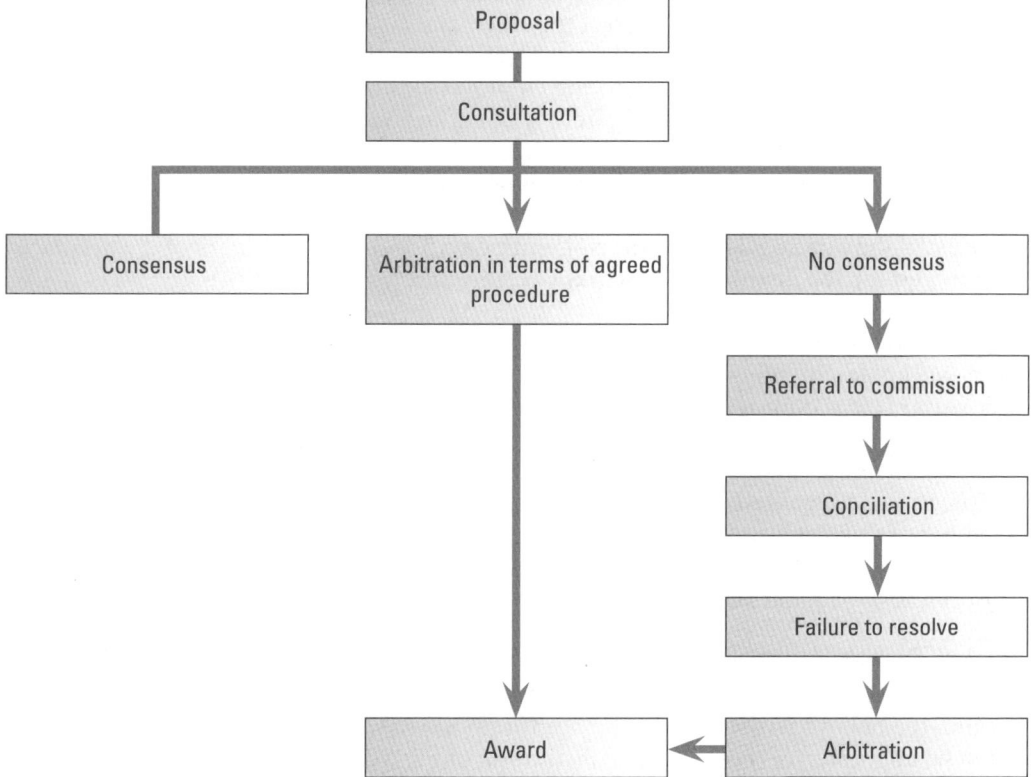

Figure 19.4: Procedure to resolve failure to reach consensus with workplace forums

19.4.8 Disclosure of information

One of the aspects of the Labour Relations Act with which employers are least comfortable concerns those provisions relating to disclosure of information to both shop stewards (see the discussion of organisational rights above) and/or workplace forums. In terms of the Act, an employer must disclose to the workplace forum all relevant information that will allow it to engage effectively in consultation and joint decision making. An employer is not required to disclose information that is legally privileged; that the employer cannot disclose without contravening a prohibition imposed on the employer by any law or order of any court; that is confidential and, if disclosed, may cause substantial harm to an employee or to the employer; or that is private, personal information relating to an employee, unless that employee consents to such disclosure.

If there is a dispute about the disclosure of information, any party to the dispute may refer the dispute in writing to the Commission. The party referring the dispute to the CCMA must satisfy the Commission that a copy of the referral has been served on all the other parties to the dispute. The CCMA must attempt to resolve the dispute through conciliation. If it remains unresolved, any party to the dispute may request that the dispute be resolved through arbitration.

In any dispute about the disclosure of information the commissioner must first decide whether or not the information is relevant. If the commissioner decides that it is relevant, and if it is confidential or private personal information, the commissioner must balance the harm that the disclosure is likely to cause an employee or employer against the harm that the failure to disclose the information is likely to cause the workplace forum in its effective participation in consultation and joint decision making. If the commissioner decides that the balance of harm favours the disclosure of the information, the commissioner may order the disclosure on terms designed to limit the harm likely to be caused to the employee or employer. When making such an order, the commissioner must take into account any past breach of confidentiality at that workplace and may refuse to order the disclosure of the information or any other confidential information that might otherwise be disclosed for a period specified in the arbiwtration award.

Lastly, the Act provides for the appointment of full-time members of a workplace forum and for the dissolution of workplace forums.

19.4.9 Appointment of full-time members

In a workplace in which 1 000 or more employees are employed, the members of the workplace forum may designate from their number one full-time member. The employer must pay a full-time member of the workplace forum the same remuneration that the member would have earned in the position the member held immediately before being designated as a full-time member. When a person ceases to be a full-time member of a workplace forum, the employer must reinstate that person to the position that person held immediately before election or appoint that person to any higher position to which, but for the election, that person would have advanced.

19.4.10 Dissolution of workplace forums

A representative trade union in a workplace may request a ballot to dissolve a workplace forum. If a ballot to dissolve a workplace forum has been requested, an election officer must be appointed in terms of the constitution of the workplace forum. Within 30 days of the request for a ballot to dissolve the workplace forum, the election officer must prepare and conduct the ballot. If more than 50% of the employees who have voted in the ballot support the dissolution of the workplace forum, it must be dissolved.

19.5 PROGRESS WITH THE ESTABLISHMENT OF STRUCTURES FOR WORKPLACE COOPERATION IN SOUTH AFRICA

As mentioned already, management and unions may decide not to opt for the establishment of statutory workplace forums. As a matter of fact, organisations in South Africa that experimented with such union–management cooperation structures long before the Act (66 of 1995) came into operation actually played an important role in spurring on the drafters of the new legislation to build in chapter 5 of the Act (the chapter dealing with statutory workplace forums). Organisations that have gone this route include Nampak, PG Bison, Samancor, Mercedes-Benz, Volkswagen (SA) and Eskom (Webster & Macun 1998), and also, more recently, Anglo Platinum (see 'A case at hand' below).

A CASE AT HAND

Union–management cooperation structures at Anglo Platinum

In terms of the employee relations policy, signed by all recognised unions, associations and management, partnership structures were established at various levels of the Company. The fully functional partnership structures are:

- the central partnership forum (CPF);
- the CPF steering committee; and
- the operating unit partnership forum.

On various matters of mutual interest to the Company and its employees, management regularly consults and communicates with employees belonging to trade unions through the transparent partnership and communication structures enabled by the formation of the central partnership forum (CPF). The convenors of these communication and consultation sessions are required to publish minutes of their meetings. This ensures that all relevant employees are kept informed on issues currently on the union and management agenda.

Source: http://www.angloplatinum.com/

As Anstey (1997: 101) explains: "Statutory workplace forums are merely one form of employee participation available to majority trade union(s) and employers. The parties may collectively agree on the shape of their relationship ...".

While the organisations listed above are a few selected examples of where non-statutory union–management cooperation structures have been established in South Africa, the general trend regarding the establishment of statutory workplace forums is rather disappointing. Van der Walt (1999: 70) reports that

> ... in the time since the LRA came into effect, only 57 applications for the establishment of WPFs had been received by the CCMA. Of these applications 16 were approved, 13 were being processed and 26 were rejected because the applicant trade union(s) did not have majority representation in the organisation concerned. This is a regrettable state of affairs because ideally WPFs should enhance democracy in the workplace through greater worker participation and involvement in decision-making, leading to greater cooperation, labour place and improved productivity and competitiveness.

Not much has changed in this regard over the past decade or so. Barker (2007: 10) confirms that "since the LRA was adopted only a very limited number of workplace forums have been established. Their net effect is thus indeterminable".

This lack of progress may be ascribed to various potential reasons, including trade union fears or a lack of trust (due to historical reasons related to liaison committees, for example) regarding the erosion of their power base and the fact that unions already have structures in place in the workplace (such as shop steward committees). We are of the view, however, that even though workplace forums as such have not taken hold, there have indeed been examples of the establishment of structures for management–union cooperative interaction and that we should learn from these and encourage more such developments. A better balance between the conflict and cooperation dynamics can hopefully serve us well in promoting better-quality labour and employee relations that are so essential in order for our organisations to become more competitive.

A POLICY PERSPECTIVE

Because we regard our people as our most important assets of our organisation and our country, and because many of our people belong to trade unions, we prefer to develop constructive relations with these trade unions with whom we are in formally recognised relationships. This labour and employee relations policy therefore aims to assist with developing good and constructive relations with our people as well as their trade unions.

The purpose of this policy is therefore to support the design and implementation of a labour and employee relations system that is aligned with our general HRM systems and that will help all the parties to develop good and constructive relations. The overall aim is to have a labour and employee relations climate that supports the strategic direction of our organisation and our competitiveness.

19.6 ASPECTS OF STRIKE MANAGEMENT

No matter how much is done by management to improve the quality of employee and labour relations in an organisation, conflict always forms an inherent part of the employment relationship. From time to time this conflict may increase or decrease. The aim of management will, however, always have to be to manage conflict levels to facilitate better chances of the overall success of the organisation. Sometimes this does not happen and it may then even lead to the manifestation of serious forms of organised, collective labour–management conflict such as strikes. Should this occur it is necessary to manage such situations professionally.

19.6.1 General

As already mentioned, strikes are to be regarded as a natural and integral part of the collective bargaining process. It is the ultimate form of power used by labour. The intention of strikers is to suspend the relationship temporarily, not to terminate it. This should always be borne in mind when dealing with strikes.

When dealing with strikes and other forms of work stoppages, it is important to realise that workers may have legitimate grievances related to the employment relationship and that the strike may be a last-resort effort to demonstrate their dissatisfaction and to pressurise management to concede to their demands. Management should deal appropriately with the strike and the striking workers, irrespective of the legality or the exact form of the industrial action as manifestation of conflict.

As is the case with all employment-related issues, managers should always consider how their actions could affect the operations of the organisation, as well as the ongoing relationship with the employees.

19.6.2 Strike management phases

Strike management entails more than strike handling. Strike handling actually refers to the active phase of strike management – the phase when all the plans and preparations are activated and implemented.

The different phases of strike management thus include:
- strike preparation (planning and organising prior to any actual strike action);
- strike handling (the active phase of strike management); and
- post-strike action (evaluation of actions and decisions after the strike has ended).

19.6.2.1 The pre-strike or preparatory phase

Because conflict is naturally inherent in the employment relationship – conflict which, if not dealt with professionally, may eventually grow into serious industrial conflict such as a strike – management has to manage all aspects of the employment relationship in such a way as to minimise the possibilities of disruptive labour actions. It can thus be said that the best way to manage a strike is to engage in management practices that prevent them.

However, no management team can be 100% assured that they will never have to deal with any form of industrial action. It is therefore necessary to take relevant precautionary measures and to be prepared, just in case.

One of the first questions to be answered is: 'In the case of industrial action like a strike, what would the objectives of management be?'. The basic step of the management process, objective setting, thus comes into play.

The primary objective of management must be to handle the situation in such a way that workers become productive again as soon as possible. The idea is to minimise the disruption of operations and to restore order and the normal business processes in the shortest possible time so that financial losses are limited. Obviously this will include the objective of resolving the underlying causes of the conflict. If this is not achieved, labour productivity levels will not be acceptable, even though workers may have returned to work.

It is thus necessary for management to take the required planning and organising steps in order to reach the said objectives. Through preparatory action such as drawing up a strike-handling and contingency plan, management should be more able, when a strike does take place, to identify and address quickly the real causes of the conflict, to relieve unproductive conflict levels, to prevent any form of damage to property or injuries to people, to arrive at mutually acceptable settlements in the shortest possible time, and thus to minimise the disruptions to the normal business processes. The idea is thus to be prepared so that there is little need for impulsive action. By being prepared, management can create a better sense of certainty regarding how such situations should be dealt with. In this way panic can be minimised and uniformity in management thought can be enhanced.

During the preparatory phase, the management of an organisation must thus reassess their objectives and see to it that their strike handling and contingency plans are geared towards the achievement of these objectives.

Even before a strike occurs it is therefore necessary to compile a contingency plan and organise all of those who will have to play an additional role in the event of a strike. Management must appoint a strike-handling team and ensure that all team members are fully informed and sufficiently competent to fulfil their tasks. It is also advisable to ensure continuously that all parties are satisfied with the relevant pre-strike dispute handling procedures and, in addition, plan how to deal with customers in the event of a strike. This will involve, for example, ensuring that contracts with customers contain clauses that will prevent them from having claims against the organisation for damages which may result from strike action.

With regard to the contingency plan and the organising of a strike-handling team, it is always necessary to appoint a strike-handling leader. This person should ideally hold a very senior position in the organisation and must have the responsibility and mandate to make all final decisions regarding the strike situation. He or she should be available at all times during strike action and usually acts as the link between parties such as the negotiating team, the operational team, the consultants, the media and the top-management team.

The members of the negotiating team will as a rule be responsible for negotiating with the representatives of the strikers. Such a team will obviously have to include some of the most competent and experienced negotiators in the organisation. On the other hand, the business operations team will consist of senior persons who have the best knowledge of the core business operations, activities and processes of the organisation (such as the production manager in a manufacturing business), as well as the most important support personnel (such as a plant maintenance engineer who has to ensure the smooth functioning of all technical equipment and production machinery). A group of special consultants (internal and/or external) may also form part of the strike management team. The particular members of this subteam will vary in accordance with the nature of the strike and the strikers' demands. Normally it will include experts in the legal field, language experts, media experts, security specialists and also key personnel who are experts on the administrative and financial implications of any decisions and actions which may be considered during the course of the strike-handling phase. The HR procurement specialist should also be a team member to give the necessary inputs on the procurement of human resources to help ensure continued business operations.

Apart from organising a strike management team, it is also necessary as part of the preparations to train the role players and even to arrange strike-handling exercises. Furthermore, it is necessary to organise the physical infrastructure. This includes aspects such as a strike monitor and control room with the necessary equipment (for example telephones, fax machines, photocopy facilities, radio communication devices, megaphones, etc). Evacuation procedures must also be available should the situation get out of control. Lists with contact details of important parties (for example the police, customers, suppliers, Department of Labour, CCMA, the relevant bargaining council) must also be available. Other facilities may include normal stationery, flip charts (for brainstorming and discussion sessions), and tape recording and video equipment. It is also advisable for management to negotiate (as part of the recognition and procedural agreement) a code of conduct to be applicable in strike situations. This code can spell out the rules of behaviour during strikes.

As can be gathered from the above, the strike preparatory phase involves a multitude of complex planning and organising decisions and actions.

19.6.2.2 The active phase of strike management

As soon as any rumours or suspicions develop that industrial action may be looming, the appropriate member of the strike management team must be informed. This person may then analyse the information and, if necessary, assemble the strike management team.

The strike management team will collect and analyse all the information, discuss possible courses of action, and commence with their functions as stipulated in the strike-handling plan. The negotiating subteam will, for example, get together to analyse relevant information and to prepare their negotiating strategies and tactics.

One of the most important things to be done throughout any strike episode is to record accurately all relevant events which take place during the strike. Use is often made of a so-called strike diary. With the objectives of strike handling in mind, it is obviously extremely important to open up communication with the representatives of those on strike in order to identify the grievances and the real causes of the industrial action. Although a policy of 'no work, no pay' is advisable, management must always try to get the workers productive again as soon as possible, and a deviation from the 'no work, no pay' rule can be used as a trade-off in return for those who resume normal work promptly.

As communication and even negotiations progress, more information will be gathered which has to be analysed in order to identify the relevant facts necessary for appropriate decisions. Whatever the strike-handling team decides to do, however, the need to encourage dialogue and to reach the set objectives must always be facilitated. The sting of a strike is often eased by the spirit in which management deals with the demands, the anger (sometimes the violence) and the people with whom management negotiate. Although strictness and discipline are always important, it is also necessary to show an understanding of the emotions of those involved in the strike. Strikes are usually very traumatic for the strikers themselves, emotions often run high, there is a great deal of uncertainty, and aspects like intimidation and violence can also form part of severe forms of industrial action. It is therefore normally advisable not to address mass meetings of striking workers, but rather to work through their representatives. The most important issue is to settle the relevant issues to the satisfaction of all parties as soon as possible.

Deciding on the dismissal of strikers

It should be borne in mind that strikers in South Africa enjoy constitutional protection (see section 23 of the Constitution). However, this right, like any other fundamental right, cannot be absolute and must therefore be subject to some ascertainable limitations. The Constitution contains a general limitation clause in section 36 detailing the principles to be applied in determining whether a limitation of any constitutional right is constitutional. The question of the limitation of fundamental constitutional rights is one of the most complex issues in constitutional law and certainly falls beyond the scope of this book. Leaving constitutional issues aside, the question still remains whether strikers may be dismissed in terms of the Labour Relations Act.

In the case of protected strikes, strikers may not be dismissed for striking: to do so would amount to an automatically unfair dismissal. However, this does not mean that strikers involved in a protected strike enjoy immunity from dismissal; it only means that they cannot be dismissed because they are legitimately exercising their right to strike. They may still be dismissed for misconduct during the strike (for example because they assaulted non-strikers or damaged company property) or for operational reasons such as plant closure (which may itself be caused by the strike).

In the case of unprotected strikes, different principles apply. In this case workers may be dismissed for striking. This, however, does not mean that an employer may dismiss unprotected strikers with impunity: he or she must still act in accordance with the precepts of fairness as enunciated in the Act. A fair dismissal in the context of an unprotected strike will involve an enquiry into a number of issues, including those summarised in exhibit 19.4.

EXHIBIT 19.4: Questions regarding the fair dismissal of unprotected strikers

- Was a proper ultimatum given?
- Did it reach all the strikers?
- Did it clearly indicate the consequences for the workers if they persist in their strike (ie that they will be dismissed)?
- Did it contain a specific deadline to return to work?
- Were the workers given enough time to consider the ultimatum?
- Did the employer try to contact the trade union?
- What attempts were made to follow the procedures?
- Did the employer provoke the strike?

19.6.2.3 The post-strike phase

After an episode of serious industrial conflict, it is important to take certain steps immediately in order to rebuild the relationship between the parties. These include the following:

- It is essential to ensure that all undertakings (agreements and promises) relating to the negotiations during the strike episode are fulfilled.
- It is necessary to work at restoring relations. During strikes, emotions often run high and trust, respect and communication often suffer. Steps have to be taken to normalise all of these as soon as possible. Without restoring communication between all parties concerned, the quality of the relationships cannot be expected to return to normal.
- It is important to acknowledge that serious conflict and a breakdown in relations has occurred. More important, however, is to acknowledge the real causes and to start focusing on the prevention of a recurrence.
- It is important to ensure that all the normal procedures and processes (such as disciplinary and grievance procedures) are confirmed as operative and applied.
- It is important to adhere to all relevant legal requirements.
- The so-called industrial action post mortem must be attended to. Here the whole incident is reviewed and special attention is paid to the process of strike handling, the effectiveness of the strike-handling and contingency plans, mistakes that were made, the competency of the strike management team members, and the lessons to be learned from the strategies and tactics followed by the parties.
- Appropriate media liaison must take place. Normalising relations with customers, suppliers and the general public can be facilitated by a proper media release on the incident.

19.7 CONCLUSION

In this chapter the focus was on the management of various aspects of labour and employee relations at the organisational level.

Establishing sound labour and employee relations at the level of the workplace is certainly one of the most important challenges facing South African organisations. This is the case largely due to the historical development of this country, with the resultant huge trust gaps existing between labour and management in many organisations. Even though legislation may go a long way towards facilitating more sound and constructive industrial relations in the country, it is ultimately up to the primary parties to work hard at building relationships of trust and cooperation at organisational level.

In this regard we have focused on the important role of communication, grievance handling and especially worker participation and involvement. We have also highlighted how the representatives of labour – most notably trade unions – and those of the employer (that is, management) can interact with each other. In this regard the focus was on collective bargaining and negotiation dynamics. Structures for cooperation and worker participation were also examined. Lastly we also briefly explained the nature and role of strikes in labour relations, and we specifically pointed out some guidelines regarding the management of strikes.

SUSTAINABILITY CONNECTION?
Trade unions are extremely important stakeholders in South African organisations. They are, in fact, key role players in South African society. If we do not develop constructive relations with trade unions, the chances are that aspects such industrial action may do more harm to our society than the purpose such actions serve in the context of the power dynamics and relations between 'organised labour' and 'business'. It is not inconceivable that such industrial action can escalate and evolve into much larger-scale social protests at times – even possibly to the extent of crippling entire economies. We always do whatever we can to develop sound relations that can help us build a better future for all – together.

SELF-EVALUATION QUESTIONS

1 Explain at least 10 methods of communicating with employees.
2 Briefly describe barriers to good communication.
3 List the principles underlying the handling of employee grievances and related procedures.
4 What is meant by 'employee involvement and participation'? How can this be achieved?
5 Differentiate between a disciplinary code and a disciplinary procedure.
6 Explain how one should handle initial contact with a trade union.
7 Describe the issues involved in formalising a relationship with a trade union.
8 Distinguish between a closed-shop agreement and an agency shop agreement. Comment on the merits and demerits of each.
9 Discuss in detail the process of distributive negotiation.
10 List 20 competencies and characteristics required of distributive negotiators.
11 Explain the principles underlying interest bargaining.
12 Describe the seven steps of the process of target-specific bargaining.
13 How can a workplace forum be established?
14 Write concise notes on the constitutions of statutory workplace forums.
15 List the issues earmarked by the Labour Relations Act for consultation and for joint decision making.
16 What has to be done during the planning and preparation phase for strikes?

APPENDIX: DISCIPLINARY CODE OF A SOUTH AFRICAN ORGANISATION

Examples of mandatory offences
Consider dismissal (by formal disciplinary inquiry)
■ Repeated similar misconduct after final written warning within a period of six months.
■ Absent from work without a valid reason within a period of six months after a final written warning for a similar offence.
■ Late for work without a valid reason within a period of three months after a final written warning for a similar offence.
■ Absent from work without a valid reason or notifying the supervisor of the reason for absence for a period of three or more consecutive days. Confirmation of dismissal will be taken on, at the latest, the sixth working day.

- Gambling or unofficial money lending on company premises.
- Causing injury to person(s) or damage to company property by driving any vehicle without a driving permit.
- Assault.
- Serious disrespect, insubordination, impudence or insolence.
- Wilfully clocking another employee's clock card or allowing another employee to clock his or her clock card.
- Possession and/or consuming intoxicating liquor on company premises without permission.
- Fighting on company premises.
- Unauthorised possession of weapons on company premises at any time.
- The making or publishing of false, vicious or malicious statements concerning an employee, supervisor, the company, or its products, the employee council and the union.
- Misuse or removal from the premises of employee data and company records without proper authorisation or the conveying of confidential information of any nature.
- Falsification of personnel or other documents.
- Theft or misappropriation of company property or the property of employees in any manner.
- Disposing of or concealing defective work either directly or as a party to any deception in this regard.
- Wilfully restricting output or attempting to influence other employees to restrict output or stop work except if all existing grievance channels have been used to no avail.
- Refusal to carry out work related instructions or orders from supervisor.
- Permitting a person who is not an employee of the company to use his or her identity card to gain entry to premises.
- Entering or leaving the company premises other than through recognised gates.
- Threatening, intimidating, coercing employees or supervision at any time.
- Tampering with his or her or another employee's clock card in any manner.
- Distribution of written or printed matter of any description or soliciting of any kind without the company's permission.
- Serious immoral conduct or indecency.
- Carelessness or negligence, or committing any act which may result in injury to person or damage to company property, depending on seriousness.
- Posting or removal of notices, signs or writing of any form on notice boards or company property at any time without specific authority of management.
- Tampering with sick certificate.
- Wilful disregard of safety rules and common safety practices.
- Using another employee's identity card or permitting another employee to use his or her identity card to gain entry to company premises.
- Unauthorised driving of any company vehicle.

Examples of non-mandatory offences
Formal verbal warnings (by foremen/immediate supervisor)
- Late for work without a valid reason.
- Leaving own work place or department during working hours without permission from the supervisor.
- Stopping work or making preparation to leave work (such as washing or changing

clothes) before the signal sounds for lunch/tea breaks or before the specified knock off-time.

- Loitering in work area or other departments 15 minutes after having clocked out at end of shift.
- Running in the company premises.
- Failure to use refuse drums – strewing litter on company premises.
- Wearing canvas shoes or sandals on company premises.
- Failure to perform assigned tasks timeously and according to set quantity and quality.
- Overstaying lunch or tea breaks or reporting late at work stations or commencement of shift.
- Wilfully obstructing movement of stock or vehicle in company premises in any manner.

First written warnings (by foreman/immediate supervisors countersigned by general foremen)
- Similar misconduct repeated after formal verbal warning within a period of six months.
- Late for work without a valid reason within a period of two months after having received a formal verbal warning for a similar offence.
- Spitting on the floor or walls in any areas within the company premises.
- Horseplay, ie playing in a manner that distracts others from their jobs or causing confusion that may lead to accidents, injuries or personal friction.
- Absence from work without a valid reason.
- Unauthorised operation of machinery, tools or equipment.
- Consuming any food stuff in other than prescribed eating places or unauthorised sitting in vehicles at any stage of production, or unauthorised switching on of car radios of such vehicles.
- Failure to report for overtime without a valid reason if required to do so.
- Absence from work for a period of up to two consecutive days without notifying supervisor.
- Obstructing movement of stock or vehicles by wrong parking or stacking which may cause injury to person(s) or damage to company property.
- Sleeping while on duty.
- Unauthorised removal of safety guards.

Final written warnings (by departmental superintendent/manager)
- Repeated similar misconduct, after a formal written warning within a period of three months.
- Absent from work without a valid reason within a period of six months after a formal written warning for a similar offence.
- Late for work without a valid reason within a period of two months after a formal written warning for a similar offence.
- Absent from work for a period of up to two consecutive days without a valid reason.
- Smoking in an area which is prohibited due to high fire hazard and/or smoking in vehicles at any stage of production and other nonsmoking areas.
- Poor performance as reflected by a performance appraisal.

20 TERMINATING EMPLOYMENT RELATIONSHIPS

LEARNING OUTCOMES

After studying this chapter, you should be able to:

- explain what counts as dismissal in terms of the LRA;
- list dismissals that will be characterised as automatically unfair dismissals;
- briefly discuss the three grounds of justification for dismissal and explain the fairness standards for dismissal associated with each of these; and
- discuss the statutory remedies for unfair dismissal.

20.1 INTRODUCTION

Despite all HRM efforts to ensure that employment relationships remain sound and add value to organisations' efforts to be successful, the employment relationship between individual employees and the employing organisation will inevitably break down from time to time. The same holds for other kinds of work relationships – such as in the case of making use of independent contractors. In this chapter our concern is about the termination of employment relationships simply because, as you know, this is the dominant type of relationship through which organisations get their work done.

Employment relationships can be terminated by either the employee or the employer. Sometimes employees terminate the relationship by resigning in order to take up a position elsewhere. Naturally all the HRM issues covered in other chapters are all aimed at contributing to retaining good talent for the organisation and not losing it to other organisations. Irrespective of this, we have to accept that voluntary staff turnover cannot be avoided completely. All our HRM work is supposed, as you know, to add value also to the working people like employees and when people resign to work elsewhere the idea is that they will leave our organisation as someone more empowered than when they commenced working for/with us. This is even supposed to be the case also when the termination of the work relationship is initiated by the organisation or employer.

When the initiative to terminate the relationship comes from the employer (represented by management), labour legislation kicks in and we then face some serious 'conformance' challenges. This chapter focuses on these primarily, but we want to stress that from the perspective of sustainability, it is essential for organisations to make sure they always treat employees fairly even, and especially also, when it comes to terminating employment relationships. It thus goes beyond conformance , because the better we are at being fair, the better will be our reputation as being an 'employer of choice', which helps to attract required talent in the future and this in turn helps organisational performance. The point of departure is, however, the law.

Both internationally and in terms of South African law, the services of an employee may be terminated for any one of the following reasons: as a result of misconduct on the part of the employee; for operational reasons; or because of the incapacity (poor worker performance or ill heath or injury) of the employee. In order for a termination of employment to be fair, the employer must comply with the necessary standards of substantive and procedural fairness, and must be able to justify the termination of the employee's services in terms of any one of the above-mentioned three reasons.

Chapter VIII of the Labour Relations Act 66 of 1995 is the primary source of legislation concerning the termination of employment relationships. As mentioned in chapter 19, unfair labour practice excludes unfair dismissal.

20.2 DEFINITION OF 'DISMISSAL'

In the Act, the chapter on unfair dismissal starts by stating in the clearest terms possible that "every employee has the right not to be unfairly dismissed". It then proceeds to spell out in some detail what is meant by 'dismissal'. It should be noted that at this stage the fairness or unfairness of a dismissal is not at issue; the Act simply tells us what conduct will, legally speaking, amount to dismissal. Logically, an enquiry into the fairness of a dismissal should be preceded by asking whether or not there was, in fact, a dismissal in the first place. This is also the sequence followed by the Act. The definition of 'dismissal' in terms of the Act is outlined below.

'Dismissal' is defined as any one of the following:
- an employer has terminated a contract of employment with or without notice;
- an employee reasonably expected an employer to renew a fixed-term contract of employment on the same or similar terms, but the employer offered to renew it on less favourable terms, or did not renew it;
- an employer refused to allow an employee to resume work after she took maternity leave in terms of any law, collective agreement or her contract of employment;
- an employer who dismissed a number of employees for the same or similar reasons has offered to re-employ one or more of them, but has refused to re-employ another;
- an employee terminated a contract of employment with or without notice because the employer made continued employment intolerable for the employee; or
- an employee terminated a contract of employment with or without notice because, after a transfer to a new employer, he or she provided the employee with conditions or circumstances at work that were substantially less favourable to the employee than those provided by the old employer.

These definitions are not an indication that the dismissal is fair or unfair. For the purpose of dispute resolution, an employee who claims to have been unfairly dismissed must prove at the arbitration or labour court that a dismissal has indeed taken place. Thereafter the obligation is on the employer to prove that the dismissal was fair.

Regarding the above possible instances of dismissal enumerated in the Act, note the following:
- Employers who think that fixed-term contracts can be used as a device to cause the termination of the employment relationship without having to adhere to the fairness standards required by the Act are mistaken.
- Women who go on maternity leave enjoy security of employment (although they are not entitled to paid maternity leave).
- An employer who terminated a number of employees' services in a perfectly

legal and fair manner may nevertheless incur liability should he or she afterwards decide to re-employ some (but not all) of the dismissed employees.

The last instance of 'dismissal' is the so-called 'constructive dismissal', when an employee tenders notice, because the employer left the employee with no option but to resign due to the employer's actions.

20.3 THE FAIRNESS OF A DISMISSAL

20.3.1 Automatically unfair dismissals

Employers should be entitled to dismiss employees, given appropriate justification and having followed a fair procedure. Not all dismissals are unfair. Having ascertained that a dismissal, as defined above, has indeed occurred, the next step is to determine whether the dismissal was fair or unfair. The Act introduces an innovation into dismissal law by providing that certain types of dismissals constitute automatically unfair dismissals. One could say that the legislator regards automatically unfair dismissals as more unfair than other unfair dismissals. The reason why these instances of dismissal have been given special treatment is not difficult to ascertain: the listed reasons involve instances of undermining collective bargaining, undermining the authority of the Act and dismissals that amount to unfair discrimination.

Broadly, a dismissal that is not based on the misconduct of the employee, the incapacity of the employee or the operational requirements of the employer is an automatically unfair dismissal.

EXHIBIT 20.1: Automatically unfair dismissals

Dismissing a worker for any of the following reasons will be regarded as automatically unfair:
- victimisation or interference with the freedom of association;
- the employee participated in or supported, or indicated an intention to participate in or to support, a protected strike or protected protest action;
- the employee refused, or indicated an intention to refuse, to do any work normally done by an employee who at the time was taking part in a protected strike or was locked out (unless such work is necessary to prevent the actual endangering of the life, personal safety or health of other persons);
- the employer wanted to compel the employee to accept a demand in respect of any matter of mutual interest between the employer and employee;
- the employee took action, or indicated an intention to take action, against the employer by exercising any right conferred by this Act or by participating in any proceedings in terms of this Act;
- the employee's pregnancy, intended pregnancy, or any reason related to her pregnancy;
- the employer unfairly discriminated against an employee, directly or indirectly, on any arbitrary ground, including (but not limited to) race, gender, sex, ethnic or social origin, colour, sexual orientation, age, disability, religion, conscience, belief, political opinion, culture, language, marital status or family responsibility (despite the preceding, a dismissal may be fair if the reason for dismissal is based on an inherent requirement of the particular job, or, in the case of a dismissal based on age, if the employee has reached the normal or agreed retirement age for persons employed in that capacity); and
- A contravention of the Protected Disclosures Act, 2000, by the employer, on account of an *employee* having made a protected disclosure defined in that Act.

*In terms of the Labour Relations Act

If an employee is dismissed for one of the above reasons, it would be classed as an automatically unfair dismissal.

The Act clarifies that if the reason for the dismissal is based on the inherent requirement of the job, then it is not unfair. A dismissal based on age is fair if the employee has reached retirement age.

A dismissal amounting to discrimination based on arbitrary grounds will be automatically unfair unless it falls within the ambit of the savings clause. A few examples will serve to illustrate how this discrimination clause will work. Assume that a woman has been dismissed for using foul language and she challenges her dismissal on the basis that men using similar language are not even disciplined, let alone dismissed. She, as applicant, will bear the onus of proving the fact of her dismissal, after which the onus will shift to the employer to prove that the dismissal did not amount to discrimination and was therefore not unfair (automatically or otherwise). The employer may discharge him- or herself of this onus either by showing that men who use foul language are similarly disciplined or by showing that the inherent requirements of the job are such that foul-mouthed women cannot be tolerated (it is difficult to think of a justification in this example that would not in itself amount to an impermissible expression of male chauvinism!)

Assume that the minister of a Protestant church is dismissed after he has undergone a change of faith and has converted to Catholicism. The dismissal would have been for religious reasons (one of the listed protected grounds), but the employer would be able to justify it on the basis that the inherent requirements of the particular job (that is, ministering to Protestant members of the congregation) justified his dismissal.

This anti-discrimination provision proscribes direct as well as indirect discrimination. Direct discrimination occurs where the discrimination is explicit, for example when an employer unfairly refuses to employ women. On the other hand, indirect discrimination occurs when an employer follows standards which appear to be neutral on the surface, but which have the effect of unfairly disadvantaging a particular group. An example of indirect discrimination would be the use of selection criteria such as height and weight, which could, although neutral, exclude more women than men. In the case of indirect discrimination, the American term 'disparate impact discrimination' is perhaps more appropriate: the criteria have a disparate impact on one group when compared with the impact on another. It should be borne in mind that after the complainant has proved that direct discrimination or indirect/disparate impact discrimination has taken place (usually by adducing statistical evidence) and the onus has shifted to the respondent (employer), the latter can still show that either the discrimination was not unfair or that the discriminatory dismissal was "based on the inherent requirements of the particular job" (section 187(2)(a)).

It is very important to understand how the provision of unfair discriminatory dismissals in terms of the Labour Relations Act relates to the provisions of Chapter II of the Employment Equity Act (discussed in chapter 3). In terms of section 10(1) of the latter Act, unfair discriminatory dismissals "… must be referred to the appropriate body for conciliation and arbitration or adjudication in terms of Chapter VIII of the Labour Relations Act".

20.3.2 Other unfair dismissals

If a dismissal was not automatically unfair, it must still be determined whether it was fair or not. Employers will have less trouble in acting fairly when dismissing employees if they take note of the points summarised in exhibit 20.3.

A dismissal must be both *substantively* as well as *procedurally* fair: the one element

The Protected Disclosures Act 26 of 2000 affords employees protection against an employer's retaliation for whistle blowing.

The Act was adopted against a background of the necessity to eradicate criminal and other irregular conduct in organs of state and private bodies. The aim is to create a culture which will facilitate the disclosure of information by employees of criminal or other irregular conduct by their employers or fellow employees without fear of reprisal. Comprehensive statutory guidelines are provided to ensure disclosure in a responsible manner and employees are encouraged to disclose information by providing protection in terms of the Act.

The objectives of the Act are:

- to protect an employee, whether in the private or the public sector, from being subjected to an occupational detriment on account of having made a protected disclosure;
- to provide for certain remedies in connection with any occupational detriment suffered on account of having made a protected disclosure; and
- to provide for procedures in terms of which an employee can, in a responsible manner, disclose information regarding improprieties by his or her employer.

The Act applies to any protected disclosure made after the date on which the Act comes into operation, irrespective of whether or not the impropriety concerned has occurred before or after said date.

Disclosure of information entails disclosure of any conduct of an employer or fellow employee by an employee who has reason to believe that the information concerned shows or tends to show one or more of the following:

(a)   that a criminal offence has been committed, is being committed or is likely to be committed;

(b)   that a person has failed, is failing or is likely to fail to comply with any legal obligation to which that person is subject;

(c)   that a miscarriage of justice has occurred, is occurring or is likely to occur;

(d)   that the health or safety of an individual has been, is being or is likely to be endangered;

(e)   that the environment has been, is being or is likely to be damaged;

(f)   unfair discrimination as contemplated in the Promotion of Equality and Prevention of Unfair Discrimination Act 4 of 2000; or

(g)   that any matter referred to in paragraphs (a) to (f) has been, is being or is likely to be deliberately concealed.

An employee who discloses any of the above is protected against reprisal only if the disclosure is a "protected disclosure". A disclosure is protected if it is:

- made to a legal practitioner or to a legal advisor with the object of and in the course of obtaining legal advice;
- made in good faith to an employer. If the employer has not prescribed any procedure for the disclosure of information, any disclosure to him in good faith is protected. If a procedure has been prescribed, the disclosure must be made in accordance with that procedure in order to qualify as a protected disclosure. If the prescribed procedure authorises disclosure to a person other than the employer, disclosure to that person is considered to be disclosure to the employer and is protected;
- made in good faith to a member of Cabinet or of the Executive Council of a province if the employee's employer is an individual appointed in terms of legislation by a member of Cabinet or of the Executive Council of a province; a body, the members of which are appointed in terms of legislation by a member of Cabinet or of the Executive Council of a province or an organ of state;

>>

- made in good faith to the Public Protector or the Auditor-General (or a person or body prescribed for the purposes of this provision) if the relevant impropriety concerns a matter normally dealt with by the Public Protector, etc and if the information and/or allegation is substantially true; and
- made in good faith to any person or body by an employee who reasonably believes that the information is substantially true. A disclosure in these circumstances is protected only if (i) it is made not for personal gain; (ii) if it is reasonable to make the disclosure, having regard to the identity of the person concerned, the seriousness of the impropriety and whether it is likely to continue, whether the disclosure is in breach of a duty of confidentiality, and public interest; and (iii) if the employee has reason to believe that he or she will be subjected to an occupational detriment if the disclosure is made to his or her employer, that evidence relating to the impropriety will be concealed or destroyed if disclosed to the employer, if information that is substantially the same has been disclosed previously and no action was taken within a reasonable period or that the impropriety is of an exceptionally serious nature.

A protected disclosure does not include a disclosure in respect of which the employee commits an offence by making that disclosure or a disclosure made by a legal adviser to whom the information was disclosed in the course of obtaining legal advice.

No employee may be subjected to any occupational detriment by his or her employer on account, or partly on account, of having made a protected disclosure. An "occupational detriment", in relation to the working environment of an employee, means:

(a) being subjected to any disciplinary action;

(b) being dismissed, suspended, demoted, harassed or intimidated;

(c) being transferred against his or her will;

(d) being refused transfer or promotion;

(e) being subjected to a term or condition of employment or retirement which is altered or kept altered to his or her disadvantage;

(f) being refused a reference or being provided with an adverse reference from his or her employer;

(g) being denied appointment to any employment, profession or office;

(h) being threatened with any of the actions referred to in paragraphs (a) to (g) above; or

(i) being otherwise adversely affected in respect of his or her employment, profession or office, including employment opportunities and work security.

If an employee is dismissed because he has made a protected disclosure, the dismissal is considered an automatically unfair dismissal in terms of section 187 of the LRA. The dispute resolution procedures applicable to automatically unfair dismissal must then be followed.

An employee who has been subjected, is subject or may be subjected to an occupational detriment may approach any court, including the Labour Court, for appropriate relief or pursue any other process allowed or prescribed by any law.

An employee who has made a protected disclosure and who reasonably believes that he may be adversely affected as a result, must be transferred to another post or position within the employer's organisation (or to another organ of state if the State is the employer) if that employee applies for such a transfer and if it is reasonably possible or practicable to transfer him/her. Once transferred, the conditions of employment may not, without the employee's written consent, be less favourable than the terms and conditions applicable immediately before the transfer.

Any provision in a contract of employment or other agreement between an employer and an employee is void if it excludes any provision of the Act or if it precludes the institution of any proceedings under this Act.

of fairness cannot substitute for the other. Thus, to dismiss an employee for some extremely gross form of misconduct (for example, a grievous and unprovoked assault on a co-worker) may very well be substantively fair, but it will be procedurally unfair if the dismissed employee is not given an opportunity to state his case; the dismissal as a whole will then be tainted with unfairness.

The Act places the onus on the employer to show:

- that the reason for dismissal is a fair reason (related to the employee's conduct or capacity or based on the employer's operational requirements); and
- that the dismissal has been effected in accordance with a fair procedure.

In addition, the person considering whether or not the reason for dismissal is a fair reason or whether or not it has been effected in accordance with a fair procedure must take into account the *Code of Good Practice* contained in Schedule 8 of the Act. It should be noted that Schedule 8 deals only with dismissals based on misconduct or incapacity; dismissals based on the operational requirements of the employer are dealt with in section 189 of the Act.

We now discuss in more detail each of the three grounds of justification for terminating the services of an employee: namely conduct, capacity and operational reasons.

20.4 DISMISSAL FOR MISCONDUCT

Schedule 8 of the Act contains a Code of Good Practice relating to dismissals based on conduct or capacity. Although it would be technically wrong to state that Schedule 8 represents a codification of our labour law on dismissals, it is in fact largely reflective of the positive law. As the Code itself makes clear, one should, when interpreting and applying the Code, always bear the following key principles in mind.

- The Code is general in nature, therefore departures from the norms established by this Code may be justified in appropriate circumstances.
- The Code is not intended to replace collective agreements, therefore disciplinary codes and procedures which have been agreed to between the parties (either during collective bargaining or as the outcome of joint decision making with a workplace forum), will take precedence over the guidelines provided in the Code of Good Practice.
- There must be mutual respect. The Code states that the: "...key principle in this Code is that employers and employees should treat one another with mutual respect ... [a] premium is placed on both employment justice and the efficient operation of business ... [w]hile employees should be protected from arbitrary action, employers are entitled to satisfactory conduct and work performance from their employees." Therefore, formal compliance with the Act and the guidelines set out in the Code may be seen simply as an operationalisation of this basic norm: employers and employees should treat one another (as well as each other's divergent interests) with respect.

Mindful of the fact that the Code of Good Practice provides guidelines which may be departed from under appropriate circumstances, the Code suggests that the following principles be adhered to with regard to dismissals based on conduct. (Note: The following section has largely been taken from Schedule 8.)

EXHIBIT 20.3: Fairness standards and the three justifications for dismissals

Fair reason for dismissal and fair procedure

There are only THREE justifications (fair reasons) for dismissals:

■ (mis)conduct by the employee;

■ (in)capacity on the part of the employee; or

■ because of the operational requirements of the employer.

The fairness standards differ depending on which of the above reasons is relied upon to justify the dismissal.

Regardless of the reason for the dismissal, a fair procedure must always be followed, which procedure can be summed up by the following two principles:

Nemo judex in sau causa:[1]

■ The person hearing the matter must be unbiased and not have an improper interest in the outcome of the case; and

Audi alteram partem:[2]

■ The employee must be given a proper opportunity to state his or her side of the story.

1 No one may be a judge in his own case.
2 I have heard the other party.

EXHIBIT 20.4: Requirements for a fair dismissal

Fair dismissal = Substantive fairness + Procedural fairness

EXHIBIT 20.5: Shifting onus in dismissal disputes

Proof of dismissal	Proof of fair dismissal
On employee ══════════▶	On employer

20.4.1 Disciplinary procedures prior to dismissal

All employers should adopt disciplinary rules that establish the standard of conduct required of their employees. The form and content of disciplinary rules will obviously vary according to the size and nature of the employer's business. In general, a larger business will require a more formal approach to discipline. An employer's rules must create certainty and consistency in the application of discipline. This requires that the standards of conduct are clear and made available to employees in a manner that is easily understood. Some rules or standards may be so well established and known that it is not necessary to communicate them. The courts have endorsed the concept of corrective or progressive discipline. This approach regards the purpose of discipline as a means for employees to know and understand what standards are required of them. Efforts should be made to correct employees' behaviour through a system of graduated disciplinary measures such as counselling and warnings. Formal procedures do not have to be invoked every time a rule is broken or a standard is not met, informal advice and correction is the best and most effective way for an employer to deal with minor violations of work discipline. Repeated misconduct will warrant warnings, which themselves may be graded according to degrees of severity. More serious infringements or repeated misconduct may call for a final warning, or other action short of dismissal. Dismissal should be reserved for cases of serious misconduct or repeated offences.

20.4.2 Dismissals

Generally, it is not appropriate to dismiss an employee for a first offence, except if the misconduct is serious and of such gravity that it makes a continued employment relationship intolerable. Examples of serious misconduct, subject to the rule that each case should be judged on its merits, are gross dishonesty or wilful damage to the property of the employer; wilful endangering of the safety of others; physical assault on the employer, a fellow employee, client or customer; and gross insubordination. Whatever the merits of the case for dismissal might be, a dismissal will not be fair if it is not done in accordance with a fair procedure. When deciding whether or not to impose the penalty of dismissal, the employer should, in addition to the gravity of the misconduct, consider factors such as the employee's circumstances (including length of service, previous disciplinary record and personal circumstances), the nature of the job and the circumstances of the infringement itself. The employer should apply the penalty of dismissal consistently with the way in which it has been applied to the same and other employees in the past, and consistently between two or more employees who participate in the misconduct under consideration.

20.4.2.1 Fair procedures

Normally, the employer should conduct an investigation to determine whether there are enough grounds for dismissal. This does not need to be a formal enquiry. The employer should notify the employee of the allegations using a form and language that the employee can reasonably understand. The employee should be allowed the opportunity to state a case in response to the allegations, and should be entitled to a reasonable time to prepare the response and to the assistance of a trade union representative or fellow employee. After the enquiry, the employer should communicate the decision taken, and preferably furnish the employee with written notification of that decision. Discipline against a trade union representative or an employee who is an office bearer or official of a trade union should not be instituted without first informing and consulting the trade union. If the employee is dismissed, then he or she should be given the reason for dismissal and reminded of any rights to refer the matter to a council with jurisdiction or to the Commission, or to any dispute-resolution procedures established in terms of a collective agreement. In exceptional circumstances, if the employer cannot reasonably be expected to comply with these guidelines, he or she may dispense with pre-dismissal procedures.

EXHIBIT 20.6: Guidelines in cases of dismissal for misconduct

Any person who is determining whether a dismissal for misconduct is unfair should consider:
- whether or not the employee contravened a rule or standard regulating conduct in, or of relevance to, the workplace; and
- if a rule or standard was contravened, whether or not:
  - it was a valid or reasonable rule or standard; and
  - the employee was aware, or could reasonably be expected to have been aware, of the rule or standard;
- the rule or standard has been consistently applied by the employer; and dismissal was an appropriate sanction for the contravention of the rule or standard.

20.4.2.2 Disciplinary records

Employers should keep records for each employee specifying the nature of any disciplinary transgressions, the actions taken by the employer and the reasons for the actions.

20.4.3 Dismissals and industrial action

Participation in an unprotected strike is misconduct. However, like any other act of misconduct, it does not always deserve dismissal. The substantive fairness of dismissal in these circumstances must be determined in the light of the facts of the case, including the seriousness of the contravention of the Act, whether attempts were made to comply with the Act, and whether or not the strike was in response to unjustified conduct by the employer.

Prior to dismissal the employer should, at the earliest opportunity, contact a trade union official to discuss the course of action it intends to adopt. The employer should issue an ultimatum in clear and unambiguous terms that should state what is required of the employees and what sanction will be imposed if they do not comply with the ultimatum. The employees should be allowed sufficient time to reflect on the ultimatum and respond to it, either by complying with it or rejecting it. If the employer cannot reasonably be expected to extend these steps to the employees in question, the employer may dispense with them.

20.5 DISMISSALS RELATING TO THE EMPLOYEE'S CAPACITY

20.5.1 Case one incapacity: poor work performance

A newly hired employee may be placed on probation for a period that is reasonable, given the circumstances of the job. The period should be determined by the nature of the job and the time that it takes to determine the employee's suitability for continued employment. When appropriate, an employer should give an employee whatever evaluation, instruction, training, guidance or counselling he or she requires to render satisfactory service. Dismissal during the probationary period should be preceded by an opportunity for the employee to state a case in response and to be assisted by a trade union representative or fellow employee. After probation, an employee should not be dismissed for unsatisfactory performance unless the employer has: (i) given the employee appropriate evaluation, instruction, training, guidance or counselling; and (ii) after a reasonable period of time for improvement, the employee continues to perform unsatisfactorily.

The procedure leading to dismissal should include an investigation to establish the reasons for the unsatisfactory performance, and the employer should consider other ways, short of dismissal, to remedy the matter. In the process, the employee should have the right to be heard and to be assisted by a trade union representative or a fellow employee

---

EXHIBIT 20.7: Dismissal for poor work performance – guidelines

Any person determining whether a dismissal for poor work performance is unfair should consider:

- whether or not the employee failed to meet a performance standard; and
- if the employee did not meet a required performance standard, whether or not—
  - the employee was aware, or could reasonably be expected to have been aware, of the required performance standards;
  - the employee was given a fair opportunity to meet the required performance standard; and
  - dismissal was an appropriate sanction for not meeting the required performance standard.

Source: From item 11 in Schedule 8 (Labour Relations Act 66 of 1995)

20.5.2 Case two incapacity: ill health or injury

Incapacity on the grounds of ill health or injury may be temporary or permanent. If an employee is temporarily unable to work in these circumstances, the employer should investigate the extent of the incapacity or the injury. If the employee is likely to be absent for a time that is unreasonably long in the circumstances, the employer should investigate all the possible alternatives short of dismissal.

When alternatives are considered, relevant factors might include the nature of the job, the period of absence, the seriousness of the illness or injury, and the possibility of securing a temporary replacement for the ill or injured employee. In cases of permanent incapacity, the employer should ascertain the possibility of securing alternative employment, or adapting the duties or work circumstances of the employee to accommodate the employee's disability.

In the process of this investigation the employee should be allowed the opportunity to state a case in response and to be assisted by a trade union representative or fellow employee. The degree of incapacity is relevant to the fairness of any dismissal. The cause of the incapacity may also be relevant.

In the case of certain kinds of incapacity, for example alcoholism or drug abuse, counselling and rehabilitation may be appropriate steps for an employer to consider.

Particular consideration should be given to employees who are injured at work or who are incapacitated by work-related illness. The courts have indicated that the duty on the employer to accommodate the incapacity of the employee is more onerous in these circumstances.

20.6 DISMISSALS BASED ON OPERATIONAL REQUIREMENTS

It has been observed that the sequence in which the three grounds of justification for dismissal (namely because of misconduct or incapacity or for operational reasons) are normally listed represents a descending order of fault or guilt that can be attributed to the employee. Whereas an employee is clearly at fault in cases of misconduct, employees who lose their job because of events not of their making and beyond their control, such as economic forces impacting on the employer's business (or because of other reasons such as technological innovation), are blameless. The so-called no-fault dismissals are deemed to be deserving of special treatment. It has been said that losing one's job is economic capital punishment. Losing one's job when one has not even committed the 'murder' (of committing serious misconduct) is doubly unfortunate and cries out for special compassion on the part of the employer. The requirements of a fair dismissal for operational reasons are summarised in exhibit 20.9.

EXHIBIT 20.8: Dismissal arising from ill health or injury – guidelines

Any person determining whether a dismissal arising from ill health or injury is unfair should consider:

- whether or not the employee is capable of performing the work; and
- if the employee is not capable:
    - the extent to which the employee is able to perform the work;
    - the extent to which the employee's work circumstances might be adapted to accommodate disability or, where this is not possible, the extent to which the employee's duties might be adapted; and
    - the availability of any suitable alternative work.

Source: From item 11, Schedule 8 (Labour Relations Act 66 of 1995)

EXHIBIT 20.9: Fair dismissals for operational reasons

Substantive fairness
- A valid and fair reason for the retrenchment

Procedural fairness
- Prior consultation
- Prior consensus over certain matters
- Disclosure of certain information
- Allowing employees to make representations
- Genuine consideration of these representations
- Selection of employees to be retrenched
- Payment of retrenchment package

We shall now look at the above requirements in greater detail.

20.6.1 Substantive fairness

In terms of the Act, a valid and fair reason is based on the employer's economic, technological, structural or similar reasons. In brief, the employer's reason for the dismissal must be a genuine one based on the operational requirements of the business. The factors that necessitate retrenchment can be as diverse as a downswing in the economy, the implementation of new technology, restructuring of the business or the shutting down of a plant or part of the business, or even the closing down of the business as a whole.

If an employer tries to get rid of employees for whatever reason (for example because they had joined a trade union or because of the employer's dissatisfaction with their conduct or capacity) under the guise of operational reasons, such a scheme will indubitably be found to be grossly unfair. If employees' conduct or ability to perform their duties is not to their employer's satisfaction, the fairness standards relating to dismissal for misconduct or incapacity must be complied with; to dismiss the 'undesirable' employee under the pretence of operational reasons (for example because the employer has insufficient proof, wants to save the costs of holding a hearing or does not want to waste time on the employee, or for whatever reason) will always be unfair.

20.6.2 Procedural fairness

The requirements (see above) for a procedurally fair retrenchment will now be discussed.

20.6.2.1 Step 1: Consultation

> When an employer contemplates dismissing one or more employees for reasons based on the employer's operational requirements, the employer must consult … (LRA s 189(1)).

'Consultation' means that the decision maker must seek advice or information from someone else. It does not mean that the decision maker must accept the advice or that he or she is constrained to reach consensus with the other party. A duty to consult is not a duty to reach agreement, it is simply a duty to give another party the opportunity to provide inputs into the decision-making process and to consider these inputs seriously before the decision maker makes a final decision (unilaterally). Secondly, the duty to consult arises before the employer reaches the final conclusion that retrenchments will have to take place. This in effect means that, as soon as the employer considers the possibility of retrenchments, the duty to consult arises. That this must be so is clear from the use of the word 'contemplates' in section 189(1), as well as the meaning of 'consultation', as explained above: the decision maker cannot seriously consider representations made to him or her (for example trade union suggestions on how to avoid retrenchments), if he or she has already reached a final decision on the course of action to be taken (that is, prior to hearing the representations). The primary purpose of consultation is to inform the employees (and their trade union) of the possibility of retrenchments and to invite their inputs on how these may be avoided, and if they are unavoidable, how the impact on the affected employees can be ameliorated as much as possible.

Who must be consulted? In section 189(1), the legislator prescribes a preferential sequence of persons with whom the employer must consult:

- Firstly, if the employer is bound by a collective agreement, and that agreement specifies with whom he or she must consult regarding retrenchments, the employer is obliged to consult with that person or party.
- Secondly, if there is no such collective agreement, the employer must consult with the workplace forum, if such a forum exists, and the registered trade union.
- Thirdly, if there is no workplace forum, the employer must consult with any registered trade union whose members are likely to be affected by the proposed dismissals.
- Fourthly, if there is no such trade union, the employer must consult directly with the employees likely to be affected by the proposed retrenchments, or other representatives nominated for that purpose.

20.6.2.2 Step 2: Attempt to reach consensus on certain matters

The second procedural step is specified in section 189(2) of the Act (see below) and entails an effort on the part of the consulting parties to try to reach consensus on certain matters.

> The consulting parties must attempt to reach consensus on:
> (a) appropriate measures
>   (i)   to avoid the dismissals;
>   (ii) to minimise the number of dismissals;
>   (iii) to change the timing of the dismissals; and
>   (iv) to mitigate the adverse effects of the dismissals;
> (b) the method for selecting the employees to be dismissed; and
> (c) the severance pay for dismissed employees.

The matters specified in section 189(2) over which consultations take place can be summarised in the following words: avoidance, minimise, timing, mitigation, selection and compensation. The process is summarised in figure 20.1.

20.6.2.3 Step 3: Disclosure of information (section 189(3))

The Act (section 189(3) read together with section 16) places an explicit duty on an employer to provide the other party, in writing, with any information relevant to the possible retrenchment. This information is summarised in exhibit 20.10.

EXHIBIT 20.10: Retrenchments: written disclosure of information

The employer must disclose all relevant information, including, but not limited to:
- the reasons for the proposed dismissals;
- the alternatives that the employer considered before proposing the dismissals, and the reasons for rejecting each of those alternatives;
- the number of employees likely to be affected and the job categories in which they are employed;
- the proposed method for selecting which employees to dismiss;
- the time when, or the period during which, the dismissals are likely to take effect;
- the severance pay proposed;
- any assistance that the employer proposes to offer to the employees likely to be dismissed; and
- the possibility of the future re-employment of the employees who are dismissed.

Furthermore, it should be noted that the provisions relating to the disclosure of information in section 16 of the Act also apply to the disclosure of information during retrenchment consultations. This implies, inter alia, that:
- 'all relevant information' would entail all information that would put the other party in a position to consult effectively;
- the employer would not be obliged to disclose information that is legally privileged;
- the employer cannot disclose without contravening a prohibition imposed on the employer by any law or order of any court;
- it is confidential and, if disclosed, may cause substantial harm to an employee or to the employer; or
- it is private personal information relating to an employee, unless that employee consents to the disclosure of that information.

Note that the relevancy of the information that an employer is obliged to disclose is determined, in part, by the reasons advanced by the employer for having to embark on retrenchments. For example, if an employer cites financial difficulties as the reason for retrenchments, the union is entitled to the financial information of the organisation, whereas if the employer advances a non-financial reason (for example a strategic reason), the union has no automatic right to disclosure of financial information.

20.6.2.4 Step 4: The employer must afford the other party an opportunity to make representations (section 189(5))

The employer must allow the other consulting party an opportunity during consultation to make representations about any matter on which they are consulting.

The employer must, in good faith, consult with the trade union about the intended retrenchments. Should the employer not allow the trade union (or other party) to make representations during consultations, the retrenchments will be unfair. Issues on which the other party may make representations include 'any matter' and would presumably include at least those matters mentioned in section 189(2).

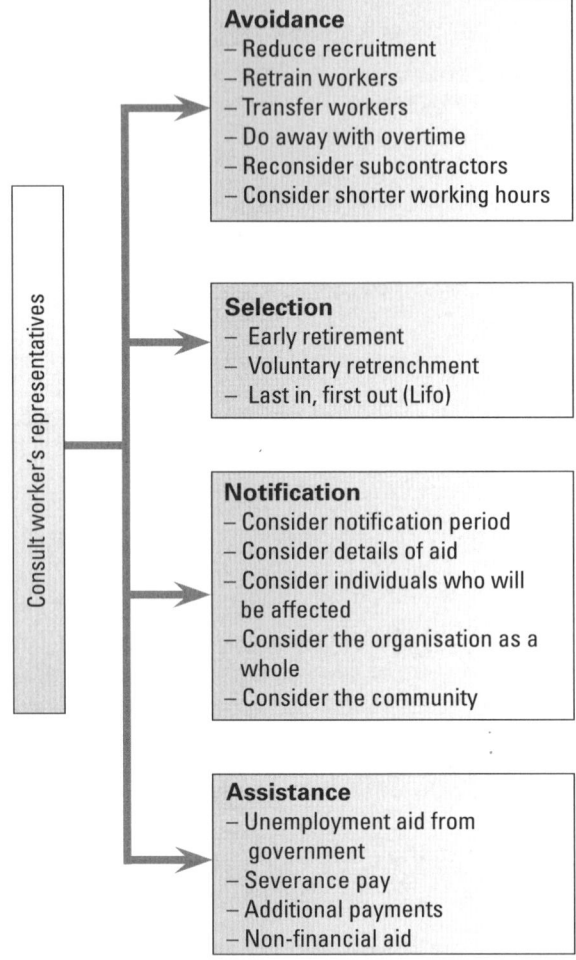

Consult worker's representatives →

Avoidance
- Reduce recruitment
- Retrain workers
- Transfer workers
- Do away with overtime
- Reconsider subcontractors
- Consider shorter working hours

Selection
- Early retirement
- Voluntary retrenchment
- Last in, first out (Lifo)

Notification
- Consider notification period
- Consider details of aid
- Consider individuals who will be affected
- Consider the organisation as a whole
- Consider the community

Assistance
- Unemployment aid from government
- Severance pay
- Additional payments
- Non-financial aid

Figure 20.1: Procedural fairness in dismissals for operational reasons

20.6.2.5 Step 5: The employer must consider and respond to the representations made by the other party (section 189(6))

> The employer must consider and respond to the representations made by the other consulting party and, if the employer does not agree with them, the employer must state the reasons for disagreeing.

Having received the representations of the other party, the employer is under a statutory obligation to consider these proposals in good faith, and to give reasons should he or she not agree with them. Although not explicitly required, it would be best to give this response and reasons in writing to the other party. It is important to note that, although an employer is obliged to consider the representations carefully, he or she is under no obligation to reach agreement on these issues. On the other hand, true consideration of representations implies that at the time these are under consideration the employer must not have already firmly decided upon a course of action: considering representations against the background of a *fait accompli* cannot amount to good-faith consultations. The employer is, of course, not bound to either accept or reject all the representations made as a package; for instance, the employer could reject (with supporting reasons) the proposals made relating to alternatives to retrenchments (for example to work short time), but still accept representations made in respect of certain deserving individuals who were earmarked for retrenchments and who, but for these representations, would have been dismissed.

20.6.2.6 Step 6: The selection of employees for retrenchments (section 189(7))

The employer must select the employees to be dismissed according to selection criteria:
(a) that have been agreed to by the consulting parties; or
(b) if no criteria have been agreed, criteria that are fair and objective.

It will be recalled that the employer must inform the trade union (or whoever is the other consulting party) in writing regarding "the proposed method for selecting which employees to dismiss" (section 189(3)(d)). If the employer and trade union have agreed on the selection criteria, these must be applied; if no agreement was reached, the employer must apply criteria that are fair and objective. "Fairness" in this context would entail a balancing of the interests of the various stakeholders, including, for example, retrenchees, the employer, the workers not to be retrenched, the trade union, shareholders of the organisation, and the public at large. "Objective" would mean criteria that are susceptible to external or third-party verification. Please note that criteria other than the popular last-in-first-out (LIFO) may be used, as long as these are not left to the subjective opinion of any individual. For instance, productivity would be an acceptable criterion if it could be objectively verified by means of production figures, and/or absenteeism figures, and/or accident figures, and/or reject figures. But productivity measurement by asking the subjective opinion of supervisors regarding which of their subordinates they would regard as more or less productive will not do.

20.6.2.7 Step 7: Payment of retrenchment packages (section 196)

Prior to the new Act there was no obligation on an employer to pay a severance package to retrenchees, except under the following circumstances: if the employer had paid packages in the past, or if he or she had promised to pay a package, or if he or she was contractually bound (either in terms of a collective agreement or in accordance with an employment contract) to pay a package.

The payment of retrenchment packages was held to be a substantive issue over which the courts had no jurisdiction (except in the case of any of the three circumstances listed above); it had to be regulated by agreement between the employer and his or her employees. However, although the principle is sound that the courts should not involve themselves in substantive issues, there are some very cogent reasons (if not legal, then at least moral, and as a matter of sound industrial relations) why retrenchment packages should be paid.

Firstly, remember that a retrenchment is an instance of no-fault dismissal (that is, the affected workers lose their livelihood through no fault of their own, as opposed to the case of dismissal for misconduct). Under these circumstances it seems appropriate that the employer should pay employees something in recognition of their loyal service and the hardship of losing their job. Secondly, the obligation to pay retrenchment packages may act as a deterrent or brake on employers who may otherwise too easily resort to retrenchments. Thirdly, in terms of the organisation's wider social responsibility, it may be expected of an employer to tide such employees and their family over for the period that they will be unemployed. Fourthly, keeping in mind the interest that the employer has in a motivated workforce, it may make good business sense to pay retrenchment packages, if only in order to reassure the remaining employees of their employer's good faith and loyalty towards his or her workforce. After a retrenchment exercise, the morale among the survivors is typically low and some show of compassion on the part of their employer may go some way towards addressing the survivors' fears and feelings of job insecurity.

As has been intimated earlier, the new Act contains fairly detailed provisions regarding retrenchment packages, some of the most important of which are summarised in exhibit 20.11. Some aspects warrant special mention.

One can define a *retrenchment package* (or severance pay, as it is also called) as monetary and other benefits which are given to employees in addition to any other benefit to which they may be legally entitled.

From this definition it is clear that the payment of accrued leave, pro-rata bonuses, contractual notice pay, withdrawal benefits in terms of a pension/provident fund, etc, cannot be regarded as part of the retrenchment package. Secondly, should employees be offered a reasonably similar position and they unreasonably refuse to accept the alternative employment, they lose the entitlement to a severance package. Lastly, note that, for the purposes of calculating the monetary value of the package, it is only completed years of service (which service must have been continuous) that are used to calculate the severance package. For example, an employee who worked for an employer for two years, then resigned and was later re-employed by the same employer, for whom he then worked uninterrupted for 10 and a half years prior to retrenchment, will be regarded as having had only 10 years' service for the purpose of calculating the severance package (although in reality the person had had 12 and a half years of service with the employer).

The Labour Relations Amendment Act, Act 12 of 2002, provides for dismissals due to operational requirements by employers who employ 50 or more employees, if the employer contemplates dismissing by reason of the employer's operational requirements, at least:
(i) 10 employees, if the employer employs up to 200 employees;
(ii) 20 employees, if the employer employs more than 200, but not more than 300, employees;
(iii) 30 employees, if the employer employs more than 300, but not more than 400, employees;
(iv) 40 employees, if the employer employs more than 400, but not more than 500, employees; or
(v) 50 employees, if the employer employs more than 500 employees; or the number of employees that the employer contemplates dismissing together with the number of employees that have been dismissed by reason of the employer's operational requirements in the 12 months prior to the employer issuing a notice, is equal to or exceeds the relevant number specified above.

Under these circumstances a facilitator may be appointed to assist the parties in resolving the dispute. If a facilitator is appointed and 60 days have elapsed from the date on which notice was given by the employer that he or she contemplates retrenching employees, the employer may give notice to terminate the contracts of employment in accordance with the Basic Conditions of Employment Act, and a registered trade union or the employees who have received notice of termination may either give notice of a strike or refer a dispute concerning whether there is a fair reason for the dismissal to the Labour Court.

If a facilitator is not appointed, a party may not refer a dispute to a council or the Commission unless a period of 30 days has lapsed from the date on which notice of the impending retrenchments was given. Once this period has lapsed the parties' rights are as explained in the previous paragraph.

If a dispute about a dismissal for operational requirements is referred to the Labour Court, the Court must find that the employee was dismissed for a fair reason if:

(a) the dismissal was to give effect to a requirement based on the employer's economic, technological, structural or similar needs;
(b) the dismissal was operationally justifiable on rational grounds;
(c) there was a proper consideration of alternatives; and
(d) selection criteria were fair and objective.

Before we consider the next topic in this chapter, you are reminded that there are only three grounds of justification for dismissal – each dismissal must be capable of being classified as either a conduct or a capacity or an operational reasons dismissal, and must be justified in terms of the standards of fairness pertaining to those particular grounds of justification.

EXHIBIT 20.11: Prescribed severance pay

Severance pay (section 196)

■ An employer must pay a retrenchment package equal to at least one week's remuneration for each year of continuous service with the employer.

■ Remuneration includes payment in kind.

■ Employers may apply for exemption from the duty to pay retrenchment packages.

■ The payment of a package is in addition to any other amount the worker may be entitled to in terms of law.

■ An employee who unreasonably refuses to accept the employer's offer of alternative employment with that employer or any other employer forfeits the right to a retrenchment package.

20.7 COMMERCIAL RATIONALE

Another type of termination of services that warrants attention is the case where it would be unreasonable to expect an employer to keep an employee in service, even though misconduct in the traditional sense cannot be proven. An employer should be entitled, in a more or less free-market society, to dismiss an employee whose continued presence negatively affects the economic prospects of the business (that is, to dismiss an employee for a valid commercial or economic reason). The following are examples of such situations.

1 *Where the employee does not comply with a request to do something voluntarily, which is necessary for the successful running of the business.*

An example of such a situation could be where the employee refuses to work voluntary overtime and the operations of the organisation are of such a nature that the working of overtime is essential for the continued viability of the business. The Industrial Court in such cases seems prepared to accept that, although the employees are not guilty of misconduct since they are within their rights to refuse to work voluntary overtime, the specific circumstances of the employer's business require employees who can do so to work overtime. The employer may then be entitled to dismiss those employees who could not or would not work overtime. Management must, however, ensure that a dismissal for an economic reason is procedurally fair. This may, for instance, include exploring the possibility of transferring the employee to a job in which overtime is not required or to a location closer to the employee's home. These investigations should take place in consultation with the employee.

2 *Where special circumstances necessitate the employee's dismissal.*
An example of this situation could be where some employees commit industrial sabotage, but it is not possible for the employer to identify the specific culprits in the group or department. In this situation the employer cannot dismiss the whole group on the grounds of misconduct since it would be unfair to dismiss employees for this reason without proving that each individual employee is in fact guilty as charged. It may, however, be fair if management were to terminate the services of all the employees on the basis of commercial rationale.

3 *Where the employee's presence indirectly impairs the profitability or success of the organisation.*
The presence of an employee may indirectly impair the profitability or success of the business where his or her presence prejudices or jeopardises other employees' employment opportunities or work security. This could also be the case where an employee's presence disrupts the business of the employer, or creates or promotes labour unrest, or detrimentally affects the relationship between the employer and the rest of the employees. The courts generally seem to regard the dismissal of such an employee as valid for economic reasons. The court, however, normally requires that the economic reason should be legitimate, that the dismissal should be procedurally fair (the employee must have been consulted about the problems that his or her conduct and presence have been causing), and that management must have considered alternatives to dismissal.

EXHIBIT 20.12: Checklist for fair dismissal: some questions to ask

- Was/is there an employment relationship?
- Was there a dismissal? (Onus on employee)
- Was the dismissal automatically unfair or just unfair? (Onus on employer to show that it was a fair dismissal)
- What are the grounds for justification? (Conduct, capacity or operational reasons?)
- Legality?
- Substantive fairness?
- Valid reason?
- Proportionality of sanction?
- Procedural fairness?
- *Nemo judex in sua causa* (the chairperson must be unbiased and must not have any interest in the outcome of the hearing)
- *Audi alteram partem* (timeousness, reasonable notice, cross-examination, translator, call witnesses, appeal, etc)

20.8 REMEDIES FOR UNFAIR DISMISSAL

20.8.1 Reinstatement, re-employment and/or compensation

The natural remedy for an unfair dismissal is reinstatement or re-employment.

- Reinstatement occurs when employees are placed back in the same position that they held before their putative dismissal.
- Re-employment occurs when an employer is required to accept a dismissed employee back into service, but not necessarily in the same position.

In both instances the order may be from any date between the date of the order and the date of the unfair dismissal.

In terms of the Labour Relations Act, the person adjudicating an alleged unfair dismissal must, upon a finding in favour of the employee, order reinstatement or re-employment, unless (section 193(2)):

- the employee does not wish to be reinstated or re-employed;
- the circumstances surrounding the dismissal are such that a continued employment relationship would be intolerable;
- it is not reasonably practicable for the employer to reinstate or re-employ the employee; or
- the dismissal is unfair only because the employer did not follow a fair procedure.

Of great importance to employers is the provision in the Act which limits the amount of compensation that may be granted to an employee who has been unfairly dismissed.[1] In the past, employers suffered great prejudice when disputes, frequently due to no fault on the part of either party, were resolved after lengthy delays between the date the matter was brought to court and the date of the dismissals. Unfairly dismissed employees should not be disadvantaged by these limits since the Act requires disputes regarding allegedly unfair dismissals to be resolved speedily (hence the absence of any status quo remedies, as provided for under the previous Act, in recognition of the fact that the final determination of dismissal disputes frequently could take very long, resulting in the need for some interim relief). The limits on compensation are summarised in exhibit 20.13.

20.8.2 Urgent interim relief

In terms of section 158(1)(a)(i) of the Act, the Labour Court may grant urgent interim relief. The purpose of granting relief is to come to the speedy assistance of an applicant pending the final resolution of a dispute by the ordinary (and more time-consuming) court procedures. In common law the requirements for the granting of urgent interim relief are as follows:

- the matter must be urgent;
- a prima facie right[2] in respect of which irreparable harm will be suffered if the relief sought is not granted;
- there is no adequate alternative remedy; and
- the damage and inconvenience that the applicant will suffer should the application be refused will be greater than the damage and inconvenience that the respondent will suffer should the application for interim relief be granted.

20.8.3 Agreement for pre-dismissal arbitration

The Labour Relations Amendment Act 12 of 2002 provides for employers to dispense with disciplinary enquiries and replace these with arbitration, under certain circumstances and providing that the employee consents to this. An employer may, with the consent of the employee, request a council, an accredited agency or the CCMA to conduct an arbitration into allegations about the conduct or capacity of that employee. Once again, this amendment is aimed at speeding up the process and to save costs.

EXHIBIT 20.13: Limits on compensation awards for unfair dismissals (section 194)

The compensation awarded to an *employee* whose *dismissal* is found to be unfair either because the employer did not prove that the reason for dismissal was a fair reason relating to the employee's conduct or capacity or the employer's *operational requirements* or the employer did not follow a fair procedure, or both, must be just and equitable in all the circumstances, but may not be more than the equivalent of 12 months' remuneration calculated at the *employee's* rate of *remuneration* on the date of *dismissal.* The compensation awarded to an employee whose dismissal is automatically unfair must be just and equitable in all the circumstances, but not more than the equivalent of 24 months' remuneration calculated at the *employee's* rate of *remuneration* on the date of *dismissal.* The compensation awarded to an employee in respect of an unfair labour practice must be just and equitable in all the circumstances, but not more than the equivalent of 12 months remuneration. An order or award of compensation is in addition to, and not a substitute for, any other amount to which the employee is entitled in terms of any law, collective agreement or contract of employment.

20.9 THE CONDUCT OF PROCEEDINGS BEFORE THE CCMA

In 2002 the CCMA finally published its rules. Because the CCMA plays such a crucial role in dispute resolution, these rules are provided on the accompanying CD.

20.10 CONCLUSION

In this chapter we have focused on the appropriate way to go about terminating employment relationships and other work arrangements. As soon as we have terminated such relationships the need may already again arise for others to continue doing some of the work (except, of course, when a project is completed, for instance, or when we have terminated services for operational requirements). Already then, generally speaking, one will have to thus again start planning and organising around the work to be done and the replacement employee/s required to do it. If employment relationships are not terminated fairly and in the correct way, this could have major negative effects on the organisation. The image and reputation of the organisation as an employer may be damaged to such an extent that it may become difficult to attract, employ and keep the right numbers and quality of employees. Such an approach clearly does not fit in with a strategic approach to the management of human resources, as advocated throughout this book.

SELF-EVALUATION QUESTIONS

1 Define 'dismissal' in the South African context.
2 When will a dismissal be regarded as automatically unfair? Explain.

3   What are the two basic requirements for ensuring that a dismissal is regarded as fair? Explain.
4   Differentiate between fair and unfair dismissal, and discuss fair dismissal in the context of:
   ■ misconduct;
   ■ incapacity;
   ■ operational requirements.
5   Write brief explanatory notes on the idea of terminating employment relationships fairly on the basis of commercial rationale.
6   Explain the different potential remedies for unfair dismissal in South Africa.

ENDNOTES

1   Compensation may, however, not be awarded in respect of any unreasonable period of delay that was caused by the employee in initiating or prosecuting a claim.
2   'Prima facie' means that 'on the face of it' or from the documentation before the court it appears as if the applicant's rights are infringed; no oral evidence is led and the final determination of whether the applicant indeed has a right which has been violated is left for the proper court proceedings that are to follow in due course.

PART SEVEN

ADDITIONAL CHALLENGES, ISSUES AND PERSPECTIVES

21 CHAMPIONING CHANGE

LEARNING OUTCOMES

After studying this chapter you should be able to:

- engage in a debate about the complex and multidimensional nature of organisational change;
- analyse the internal and external forces that may be driving change;
- identify individual and organisational-level factors of resistance to change;
- apply ways to reduce and deal with resistance to change;
- make a presentation about different change options and interventions;
- write brief notes about some contemporary methods of change management; and
- explain the nature and importance of change and transformation in South African organisations.

21.1 INTRODUCTION

As you know all too well by now, the world generally – and the world of work and organisations in particular – is experiencing a wave of serious change. As indicated throughout this book, South Africa especially is experiencing some transformation in various spheres of life. Business and other organisations are not escaping any of that. In fact, these are the very spheres of society where 'deep change' is supposed to be happening. People must effect and drive and see through the change. Technology only changes when people make it happen. Countries only change when people make it happen. Change is people driven and reliant, which is why we argue that becoming change champions is squarely situated in the realm of HRM. In chapter 5 where we reflect on different possible roles for the HR practitioners, we referred to the 'changemaker' role and also, the change leader role. We want to repeat what we say there: the HR practitioners must team up (and hence 'partner') with line managers to become the champions of change in our organisations, taking the lead to make change happen. Managing South African organisations and people, and managing change and transformation should become one. This is easier said than done, though. Getting it right when we change things is complex, not least because there are so many variables at play and so many different types of change.

Different types of change demand different approaches and styles. How we manage – and in particular, rather, lead – change will play a crucial role in how we help our organisations and our country and continent become and remain competitive and successful. We believe that our very survival depends on how well we can champion the required change. Yet the question remains whether South African organisations and their managers and other working people are able to embrace, lead and see through the required change.

Understanding and successfully managing this challenge has become one of the most important issues for South African managers, including human resource managers and specialist practitioners. Waddell, Cummings and Worley (2007: 2) say that "a major challenge facing organisations today is to develop a management style and culture that will enable them to cope with the challenges and opportunities they may face. Irrespective of whether the change has to do with introducing new technology, a reorganisation or new product development, it is important for leaders to have a sound understanding of change issues and theories to help guide" them to make it happen. In this spirit we thus devote this chapter to sharing some ideas about challenges and issues related to change, faced by managers, including specialist HR practitioners.

21.2 THE NATURE OF ORGANISATIONAL CHANGE

From a pure semantic point of view the term 'change', in a concise dictionary-fashioned description, simply means altering something in condition, state, appearance, etc, to make something different than what it is or was. Along these lines Bartol, Tein, Matthews and Sharma (2008: 282) say that change "is an alteration to the status quo". Taking such a basic view may mean that any time a manager employs or dismisses an employee, some change is taking place in the organisation. Whenever any new HR policy or procedure is adopted, there is change. Such an approach can be so broad that almost anything that happens in organisations may then be typified as being part of 'organisational change' and we thus regard it as perhaps too broad and general.

A study of the literature on organisational change will yield that the prevailing view is dominated by the school of thought that organisational change is more than the routine, evolutionary or accidental changes that take place every day in organisations. The focus tends to be more on specific interventions to improve and make things better, thus often going hand in hand with aspects like creativity and innovation. These can still vary from being rather narrow in scope to being very broad (impacting on numerous organisational subsystems), from large- to small-scale change, from slow and very gradual, to fast and very sudden. It may be predictable in some instances, whereas at other times the change may simply and suddenly just 'emerge' without any forewarning.

All of these varieties have to do with the multidimensional nature of change in an organisational context. Because organisations are very complex social entities, blending such complexity with the multidimensional nature of change that might occur in or around an organisation indeed makes organisational change quite an interesting and challenging aspect of managing.

It should therefore come as no surprise that organisational change may mean many different things to different people. As a concept it is certainly open to a wide variety of interpretations, and as a phenomenon and concept it can be analysed and debated from many different angles or perspectives.

In trying to develop a better understanding of organisational change we have to be mindful of its multidimensional nature. There are different kinds or types of change, manifesting at different organisational levels, and in any one or more of the organisational subsystems (and/or the system as a whole). Organisational change situations can vary considerably, it may have many different underlying reasons or causes (referred to by many as 'change drivers') and it may have different implications for the organisation and its staff. In order grasp some of this multidimensional nature of organisational change, we may look at a selection of the varieties of change covered in some of the literature on this topic.

21.2.1 The type of change situation

Drawing on the work of the Open University (1985) and McCalman and Paton (1992), we can distinguish between two broad categories of change situation, namely 'hard' and 'soft'.

In some sense, *hard change situations* are probably the easier ones to identify, specify, describe, demarcate, diagnose and manage. It is usually quite clear what the issues at hand entail (often these have a systems/technical orientation). The role players are likely to share a great deal of common understanding of what the problems and the accompanying solutions (or options) are, and they more or less know what the priorities and objectives (which are usually relatively easily quantifiable) of the change should be. The time scales (typically shorter to medium term) and the resources that will be needed for the change to be effected are also normally quite clearly identified. In the case of *soft change situations* (also referred to as 'messy' types of change situations), time scales are usually very 'fuzzy' (although typically medium to long term in the main), resource implications are very uncertain, and the objectives and priorities are normally uncertain, subjective and 'vague'. The issues at hand are mostly numerous, complexly interrelated and contextually embedded, and the problems are therefore generally ill-defined, highly divergent views on what the potential solutions might be. Typically there is widespread interest in the situation with concomitant conflicts of interest, and diverse attitudes and perspectives. There are usually very few clear-cut 'hard' and objective facts, and it is normally very difficult to disentangle the web of symptoms, causes and effects. Although often ambiguous in terms of detail, the implications are usually very serious and worrying, whereas in the case of 'hard' change situations the implications are typically less serious and more limited to terms of scope.

21.2.2 The scale or degree of the change

According to Dunphy and Stace (1993), there are four different scales of change that can be identified.

Fine tuning is basically an ongoing process of adapting and refining aspects such as processes, policies, procedures and methods in order to ensure that there is an ongoing fit or match between the various organisational subsystems. Examples may include an adjustment in certain recruitment and selection processes and procedures, and implementing a new supervisory training programme considered to be superior to the programme offered traditionally.

Incremental adjustment involves distinct changes to strategies, structures or business processes in response to changes in the external environment – such as establishing a new marketing and sales unit in order to capture market territory, altering some structural configurations within a department to facilitate improved service delivery, or changing certain production technologies to bring about greater efficiencies on a particular production line.

Modular transformation, according to Dunphy and Stace (1993: 917–918), involves a major realignment and/or radical change of large or significant parts (such as departments or divisions) of an organisation. The scope of the change is thus limited to subparts of the organisation, but the 'depth' of the change is dramatic. Examples may include a radical downsizing of the HR department and the subsequent outsourcing of numerous HR-related functions and activities.

Corporate transformation, according to these authors, is revolutionary change that occurs across organisations. Examples include a total change of business direction with a brand new mission, and the formulation and adoption of a whole new set of 'core values'. A concrete example may be the privatisation or even just the commercialisation of institutions that have been state owned. Tushman, Newman and Romanelli (1988), and Senior (2002) refer to this as discontinuous or frame-breaking change.

From the foregoing it is clear that the key variables include the *breadth* (the scope) and the *depth* (or focus) of the change. Organisational change can be applied to the whole organisation, to large or significant parts of it (such as divisions or business units), to certain identifiable subsystems with clear boundaries (such as departments or sections, or even something like the performance management system of the organisation) to smaller organisational units such as workgroups or teams and/or even to individual employees (personal or individual change). Note that it is often not a case of the one or the other, but rather that change will span across more than one of these different 'levels'. The 'depth' or 'focus' of the change has to do with what it is that will be changed. In this regard the key consideration usually goes together with the type of change intervention.

Strategic types of change intervention typically include aspects such as mergers, acquisitions or strategic alliances. Closely intertwined with these are the structural interventions such as organisational restructuring or redesign (see chapter 5, for instance) and hence something like downsizing. There are also interventions aimed at changing systems and technology. These may include process re-engineering, information technology changes and even changes to certain operational policies and procedures. Other interventions focus on the redesign of work (such as employee involvement through teamwork and various forms of job enrichment), whereas there are also numerous change interventions that focus on changing the 'soft' aspects such as values, interpersonal relations and communication or even 'organisational culture'. Again, it should be stressed that it is not unusual to find various combinations of such interventions being implemented in organisations.

21.2.3 The approach to managing the change

There are also different approaches to the handling or management of change in organisations. The literature on change management highlights primarily two broad and distinguishable approaches to organisational change management, namely an *incremental* approach and a *planned* (N-step) approach. We once again do not believe that this is or even should be an 'either/or' issue. While theoretically such a distinction is sound, we believe that in the real world of organisational life, both these approaches have a role to play. There simply is no one best way of approaching, handling, managing or leading organisational change in all situations.

In the *planned* approach, change is seen as a process that is planned and managed through a series of steps or sub-processes to the point of the change having been having been completed. Waddell et al (2007: 24) explain that in this approach the change is "generally initiated and implemented by managers" who often make use of the help of organisational change and development experts "from inside or outside the organisation". The *emergent approach* puts the emphasis on the highly dynamic, evolving, unpredictable and complex nature of organisational change, being open ended and continuous with no real point of starting or completing it. Burnes (1996: 193–194) provides a number of the main tenets of the emergent approach to the management of organisational change, including the following:

- It is an ongoing process of experimenting, adapting and making (mainly) small-scale, incremental changes.
- Managers are not supposed to carefully think through, plan and then manage a process of change implementation, but they should rather play a facilitating role, creating an environment in which continuous experimenting and risk taking, and ongoing development and learning are encouraged.
- Although the above is the case, managers do have to create some common or shared vision and direction to form the road along which the incremental change will be steered over time. Information gathering, communication and learning are seen as the key processes to facilitate change in organisations.

Change management can hence be viewed as an ongoing process, rather than only an event or specifically planned intervention with an end point. Although we may plan some change, the nature of the world generally, and of organisational life, is such that we cannot always anticipate the need for change ahead of time, thus making the management of organisational change an ongoing process. We thus see that there may be three different types of change: (i) planned change, (ii) change that arises spontaneously and that is not initiated and planned, and (iii) change that may be based on opportunities as these arise, not as anticipated, but yet introduced purposefully and intentionally during the change process in response to an unexpected opportunities or threat

The planned approach to managing organisational change follows a more or less linear pattern or model. It involves a rational and logical set of steps with a clear starting point and a number of in-between steps up to an end point or termination of the change intervention. The planned change approach essentially views change interventions as projects involving going into the organisational system, diagnosing the system, making changes, and then terminating the change intervention or project.

One of the earliest models of planned change was Kurt Lewin's (1951) three-step model of 'unfreezing' the status quo, actively changing (or 'moving') the organisation or parts thereof, and 'refreezing' the new organisational state to create a new status quo. In its pure form Lewin's model is obviously quite an oversimplification of how change can be handled in the 'real world'. This model essentially assumes that organisations are relatively static – before the intervention and also after it, when they will return to being static as the new status quo. Today we are more than half a century down the line and we know that organisations and their environments have become far more dynamic. The strength of Lewin's model probably lies in its showing that people within organisations are usually prepared to accept and take part in the change only once they understand why there is a need for such change. This happens during the 'unfreezing' stage, when employees learn not only why change is needed but also that it is indeed possible for things to be done differently and to be improved. This stage therefore entails the essential process of ensuring that there is buy-in by all the relevant organisational members and stakeholders. Without such buy-in the chance of encountering resistance to change is much more likely, simply because the employees will not understand why the change is necessary.

Lewin's model also emphasises the need for reinforcement of change that may take place. It is easy for employees to revert to old ways of doing things after change intervention has been implemented. Refreezing uses aspects such as ongoing support mechanisms and reward to ensure that a new state of organisational equilibrium is achieved.

The action research model is another planned or N-step approach to managing organisational change, but it follows a cyclical pattern and emphasises the role of the change agent or consultant. It stresses that successful change requires a rational, systematic analysis of the situation and problems or challenges at hand (the research and diagnosis part), the feeding back of all information to the organisational system to facilitate learning and action planning, followed by joint action (consultant/change agent together with the relevant organisational role players), and evaluation of the outcomes with the necessary feedback into the system again. This feedback (gathering data about the change action(s)) then again sparks off a further round of joint diagnosis of the situation, making it an iterative process. Action research is therefore a cyclical model in which organisational change is viewed as ongoing.

Lippitt, Watson and Westley (1985) refined Lewin's three phases into the 'planned change model', a seven-phase model of the change process which unfolds as follows:

- Phase 1: The development of a need for change. (This phase corresponds to Lewin's unfreezing phase.)
- Phase 2: The establishment of a change relationship. This is a crucial phase in which a client system in need of help and a change agent from outside the system establish a working relationship with each other.
- Phase 3: Diagnosis of the client system's problem.
- Phase 4: The examination of alternative routes and goals; establishing goals and intended action.
- Phase 5: The transformation of intentions into actual change efforts. (Phases 3, 4 and 5 correspond to Lewin's change phase.)
- Phase 6: The generalisation and stabilisation of change. (This corresponds to Lewin's freezing phase.)
- Phase 7: Achieving a terminal relationship.

An examination of these models of the planned approach to managing organisational change shows a general framework for planned change. This framework provides a basic linear process perspective of change: entry, diagnosis, planning and implementation of change, and evaluation and institutionalisation of change. This model of planned change shows the typical sequence of events that occur in a change process. However, it should be remembered that this is not necessarily the way that organisational change will always take place in the 'real world'. It is a theoretical and conceptual model to guide understanding and learning, and to structure the way that change can be managed. In practice, there are overlaps and there is an interplay between the processes, making change management much more complex than merely rolling out a number of steps in a particular sequence.

Although we therefore recognise the fast-changing, uncertain and dynamic-complex real world of organisational life which makes a neat and tidy N-step approach to organisational change management not always realistic, we also believe that merely treating all change in an incremental way will not be sufficient. As Kotler (1998: 5) puts it: "Building new organizations that will prosper in the new climate requires great change. Incremental adjustments are insufficient ... The key force behind successful transformations is always leadership...". Likewise, Harvey and Brown (2001: 94) say the following: "In a turbulent and changing environment, managers are concerned not only with managing organizations as they exist at the present time, but also with changes to meet future conditions. Change programs do not happen accidentally. Instead, they are initiated with a specific purpose and require some form of leadership to function properly." In section 21.6.3 we return to aspects pertaining to more comprehensive and transformational change.

Irrespective of the particular approach or type of change that may be more appropriate in any given situation, the *content* as well as the *process of leading the change* should be aligned with the type of changing situation faced by the organisation. As has already been stated, not all organisations always face conditions that are equally turbulent, volatile, fast or severely changing. Some situations may be very complex and of tremendous magnitude (requiring a broad scope of change) in terms of the impact they may have on the organisation. Other changing situations may be less serious, with a limited impact and requiring only minor adjustments that are small scale and that can be dealt with incrementally. Likewise, some issues or problems to be dealt with may be 'harder' (more tangible and measurable) and others may be 'messier' or 'softer' (less concrete and more tangible).

We have to stress once again that we do not believe that in the real world of organisational life there is room for an 'either-or' stance to be taken. Organisations may be confronted with both hard and soft change situations simultaneously. In addition, these hard and soft dimensions may be combined with either planned or incremental characteristics. There are no clear-cut rules here, no cast-in-stone boundaries. It is probably within the context of the foregoing that Beer and Nohria (2000) advocate an integration and combination of hard and soft approaches to successfully bring about change in organisations.

21.3 DRIVING FORCES FOR CHANGE

A number of forces, either individually or in combination, can compel organisations to change. One broad set of forces consists of external or environmental forces that are pressures or opportunities that arise from outside the organisation. Most of these in the South African context have been discussed in chapters 2 and 3. Another set of forces is composed of internal organisational forces, relating to aspects like those discussed in chapter 1 (eg strategy, structure, culture).

21.3.1 External drivers

Organisations often have to change as a result of external forces, rather than due to managerial desire to change. As mentioned already, these extra-organisational factors include the major political, economic, social, technological, ecological and competitive forces that leave our organisations with no other option than having to engage in organisational change to be aligned with new realities. The whole issue of sustainability has been emphasised throughout this book – and all over the world this is becoming one of the most crucial drivers for organisational change, or transformation rather. In South Africa we have the additional very important challenges posed by the requirements to remain competitive so as to grow the economy and to establish a just and equitable society – one of socio-economic inclusiveness (as spelt out in earlier chapters, most notably also chapters 2 and 3).

It is a well-known fact that globalised economies are creating increased threats and opportunities, forcing organisations to make dramatic improvements not only to gain a competitive advantage but simply to survive. Kotter (1996: 18) states in this regard that "globalisation, in turn, is being driven by a broad and powerful set of forces associated with technological change, international economic integration, domestic market maturation within the more developed countries, and the collapse of worldwide communism". We know from earlier chapters that South Africa – and also Africa – is experiencing serious and deep issues and challenges to make our 'rainbow nation' and 'Africa Renaissance' dreams a reality. These call for 'second order' change – transformational change. To this topic we return again in section 21.6.6.

21.3.2 Internal drivers

Inside South African organisations, changes are occurring as a result of, inter alia, organisational life cycle evolution, the redesign of core structures and processes, changing expectations of workers and the role of unions in the workplace. Changes in workforce demographics towards a more culturally diverse population, in part because of employment equity programmes, also create a major impetus for the way organisations will need to change.

While both external and internal changes are forcing South African organisations to continuously reassess their strategies and operations, it can generally be said that the methods and timing in which employees all over the world respond to change and transformation differ. Indeed, organisations will have to learn to cope with different responses to change. For organisational transformation and change management to be successful and to help organisations to survive and eventually to prosper through employee buy-in, certain fundamentals will have to be retained.

In the face of organisational change, organisations need to retain some stability in the form of the organisation's ultimate purpose, core technologies and key people. Indeed, embarking on a transformation initiative when an organisation has a cash-crunch crisis, a leadership vacuum, or too much of an adversarial management–union relations climate, should be avoided if at all possible. Such factors should be dealt with first before embarking on any full-scale transformation process.

The principle here, drawn from the field of psychotherapy, is that in order to be able to cope with large-scale and complex change and transformation, people need to have something stable to hold on to. Change must thus be brought about by keeping some aspects the same, by building some stability into the process of change (Nadler 1983). The paradox facing managers in organisations undergoing change and transformation is therefore how much turbulence to expose their employees to, while at the same time retaining some form of continuity and stability in order to obtain their employees' commitment to the transformation process. Indeed, planned change – that is, change designed and implemented in an orderly and timely fashion – is preferable to reactive change – that is, a piecemeal response to problems as they develop (Griffen 1987). While planned change and reactive change are interesting theoretical concepts, the reality facing most South African organisations today is that they no longer have the luxury of always controlling which option to select.

Whichever option is applicable, managers need to understand the dynamics of change if they want to manage it successfully. Much of this relates to the human side of things. In this context, resistance to change is perhaps the greatest impediment to managing change and transformation processes successfully.

21.4 EFFECTING CHANGE: DEALING WITH RESISTANCE

Irrespective of the nature of the change or the driving forces, a key challenge relates to actually making the change as successfully as possible. The following is a simple formula proposed by Gleicher (Beckhard & Harris 1977) to help managers assess the extent to which an organisational change effort is likely to succeed:

$C = (A \times B \times D) \, X$

where:

C = change

A = level of dissatisfaction with the status quo
B = clearly identified desired state
D = practical first steps toward the desired state
X = cost of the change (in terms of energy, emotions, financial costs, etc)

Stoner and Wankel (1986) elaborate on this formula by indicating that change (or transformation) takes place when the cost of the change is not too high. The cost of change will be too high unless dissatisfaction with the status quo (A) is quite strong; unless the desired state (B) is quite evident; and unless practical steps can be taken towards the desired state (D). The multiplication signs indicate that if any of the factors A, B or D is zero, there will be no change. For example, if employees are satisfied with the status quo (A), they are not likely to change even if they can imagine a more desirable state (B) and they can see practical steps to move towards it.

Gleicher (Beckhard & Harris 1977) indicates that in addition to diagnosing how ready the system is for change, and predicting how likely it is that change will take place, the formula can also suggest ways of making the system more ready for change. For example, if dissatisfaction with the current state of affairs is high on everyone's part but there is no concrete notion of how things could be better, a vision of a future ideal state has to be created and communicated.

Some of the best-documented findings in studies of organisational change relate to the existence of individual and organisational sources of resistance to change (RTC) (Robbins 1997; Carrell, Jennings & Hearin 1997; Strebel 1996; Kotter 1995; and Nadler 1983). Inherent congruence in an organisation will make it resistant especially to 'frame-breaking' changes (Nadler & Tushman 1988). According to Robbins (1997), organisations with a history of lengthy periods of success tend to be particularly resistant to change. Furthermore, Dalziel and Schoonover (in Jick 1993a) have found that organisations with historical barriers to change are likely to continue this pattern of resistance. Jick (1993b) argues further that if an organisation has a track record of opposing change, more care should be taken to design a gradual, non-threatening participative implementation process for future changes.

In a classic experiment conducted by Coch and French in the mid-1940s (Coch & French 1948), the researchers noticed that factory workers were resistant to changes in products and production methods. They asked two questions: Why do people resist change? And what can be done to overcome that resistance?

The authors went to an American plant (Harwood Manufacturing) and examined the after-change learning curves of several hundred workers who had been rated as standard or better prior to the job changes. They learned that 38% of those workers achieved the new standard of production shortly after change was introduced, but that "62% either became chronically substandard operators or quit" (Coch & French 1948: 514).

These results showed that relearning was often slower than initially learning the job, and so they designed two experiments to illustrate: (i) the forces creating resistance and (ii) the mechanisms for overcoming them. In the study, they employed two variations of democratic procedures in handling two different groups (all members of both groups participated in the planning and execution of the change). In a third group, they used representatives of the workers in designing job changes. A fourth group, with no participation at all, served as the control group.

After the job changes were complete, the control group did not improve. Frustration was high, some aggression was seen, and 17% of the group resigned. The group with representation improved markedly after the job changes, but the two groups with complete member participation improved even more.

About three months after the initial experiment, the remaining members from the control group (13 workers) were brought together in a job change intervention that involved total participation. With this approach, their performance improved rapidly up to the level of the other groups.

Interestingly, Coch and French's (1948) study was repeated at a Norwegian shoe factory but without producing the same results. The authors speculated on the role played by cultural differences in mediating variables in the results.

As indicated in various chapters, and especially in chapters 2, 3 and 4, the contexts within which organisations operate play a significant role in the way in which one has to manage the human side of organisations. This seems to hold true also for the management of organisation transformation and change as such. Within a South African context, for instance, it would be quite unthinkable for a highly unionised organisation to expect to succeed with any change or transformation intervention if trade union representatives are not viewed as full stakeholders in the process. Union representatives have to be involved in order to avoid eventual collective resistance to change by the workforce. Any form of organisation change or transformation will impact on the employees of the organisation. Although the degree and nature of such impact will vary from organisation to organisation, the representatives of the workforce can be instrumental in dealing with it. The impact experienced by employees (management as well as non-management) collectively is one of the most important factors requiring professional attention during any process of change and transformation.

The general nature of the impact of change and transformation on managers and workers was studied by Richardson (1994), who found the following predictable sequence of responses from employees:

- *Fear*: People become fearful and anxious about the impact of change on themselves (they do not mind change, but resist being changed).
- *New faces*: New faces appear in the organisation, frequently at senior-level positions initially.
- *New questions*: Surveys and studies which are conducted to obtain feedback raise new questions about existing practices and new options.
- *New structures*: Roles and responsibilities, as well as lines of authority, change.
- *New goals and standards*: The organisation creates a new culture, aims and standards in line with the new mission and purpose.

21.4.1 RTC at the level of the individual

Resistance to change may stem from the individual, the organisation, or from both.

Several research studies, as summarised by Robbins (1997), Carrell et al (1997), and Greenberg and Baron (1997: 560–561) have identified the following individual resistance factors to change:

- *Fear of the unknown*: This concerns uncertainty about the causes and effects of change. Employees may resist change because they are worried about how it will affect their work and their lives. Even if they have some appreciable dissatisfaction with their present work, they may still worry that things will be worse when the proposed changes are implemented. When the change is initiated by someone else, they may feel manipulated and wonder about the real intention behind the change.
- *Habit*: To cope with the complexity of work and of life itself, people often rely on habits or programmed responses. Change requires new ways of doing tasks,

and challenges people to develop new competencies. This tendency to respond in accustomed ways may then become a source of resistance.

- *Self-interest*: This relates to the unwillingness to give up existing benefits. Appropriate change should benefit the organisation as a whole, but for some individuals the cost of change in terms of lost power, prestige, salary, quality of work, etc, will often not be viewed as sufficiently offset by the rewards of change.
- *Economic insecurity*: Changes in the organisation often have the potential to threaten employees' job and economic security, either through loss of jobs or reduced pay, and people may therefore resist change.
- *Failure to recognise the need for change*: Employees need to recognise, fully understand and appreciate the reasons for change, otherwise the vested interests that they may have in keeping things the same may result in resistance to the change.
- *General mistrust*: Even though people may understand the arguments in favour of change, they may not trust the motives of those advocating the change. This is especially true in South African organisations where the history of the country has impacted dramatically on people's mindsets.
- *Social disruptions*: Many organisational changes threaten the integrity of friendship groups that provide valuable social rewards; individuals may therefore fear that change will disrupt existing traditions and working relationships.
- *Selective perceptions*: As explained in chapter 3, people have different perceptions and process information selectively. Changes in the organisation may be perceived by some employees as threatening and by others as challenging.

21.4.2 RTC and organisational level impediments

A number of authors have documented various organisational factors that can hinder the implementation of change management processes (Carrell et al 1997; Greenberg & Baron 1997). The following are a few examples of such factors:

- *Structural inertia*: Traditionally, organisations are designed to maintain order and stability. The selection process, induction and organisational socialisation, formalisation of tasks and processes, and bureaucracy are all aimed at creating order and stability. When confronted with change, these forces creating stability often resist change and cause structural inertia.
- *Cultural inertia*: Some organisations have cultures that emphasise stability and tradition. In such cultures, those who advocate change are often seen as being misguided.
- *Work group inertia*: Because of the development of strong group norms that help to guide member behaviour, potent pressures exist to perform jobs in a certain way. Change often disrupts these established normative expectations, leading to formidable resistance.
- *Threats to existing power relationships*: Any redistribution of decision-making authority can threaten long-established power relationships within the organisation. Certain individuals may resist change because they fear the loss of their power base. Changes from autocratic to participative management or self-managed teams are often seen as threatening by supervisors and middle managers.
- *Threats to expertise*: Individuals and groups within the organisation develop certain specialised expertise. Changes in organisational patterns or structures may threaten the expertise of these specialists, causing resistance to change.
- *Threats to resource allocation*: Individuals and groups may believe that change will

threaten future resource allocation. In particular, those groups or individuals who control sizeable resources often see change as a threat.

- *Previously unsuccessful change efforts*: Organisation members who went through previously unsuccessful change efforts may resist change and may be very cautious about accepting any further attempts at introducing change into their system. Individuals may also resist change because they are aware of potential problems that have apparently been overlooked by the change initiators.

21.4.3 Overcoming RTC

Resistance to change on the part of employees could signal to managers that there may be two problems. The first of these could be the proposal for change or transformation itself. Secondly, the problem could lie with mistakes made in the presentation of the proposal. Managers encountering employee resistance need to re-evaluate their strategies after determining the actual causes of resistance, and then remain flexible enough to overcome the resistance in an appropriate manner. Two somewhat different approaches to overcome resistance to change are presented by Kotter and Schlesinger (1969) and Beer, Eisenstat and Spector (1990).

Kotter and Schlesinger (1969) proposed the following six methods to overcome resistance to change:

- *Education and communication*: If the need for and the logic behind the change are explained early – whether individually to subordinates, to groups in meetings, or to entire organisations through elaborate audiovisual education campaigns – the road to successful change may be smoother.
- *Participation and involvement*: According to a classic study undertaken by Coch and French (1948), resistance to change can be reduced or eliminated by having those involved participate in the design of the change. Leavitt (1964) came to a similar conclusion, suggesting that in order to avoid resistance, managers should take into account what he called the social effects of change.
- *Facilitation and support*: Easing the change process and providing support for those caught up in it is another way in which managers can deal with resistance. Retraining programmes, allowing time off after a difficult period, and offering emotional support and understanding may help.
- *Negotiation and agreement*: It is sometimes necessary for managers to negotiate with avowed or potential resisters to change, and even to obtain written letters of understanding from the heads of organisational subunits that would be affected by the change. In South Africa this may include the negotiation of such agreements with representative trade unions.
- *Manipulation and co-option*: Sometimes managers covertly steer individuals or groups away from resistance to change, or they may co-opt an individual, perhaps a key person within a group, by giving him or her a desirable role in designing or carrying out the change process.
- *Explicit and implicit coercion*: Managers may force people to go along with a change by explicit or implicit threats involving loss or transfer of jobs, lack of promotion and the like. Such methods, though not uncommon, risk making it more difficult to gain support for future change efforts.

A particular process approach to overcoming resistance to change and transformation is postulated by Beer et al (1990). According to these authors, the following six steps in overcoming resistance to change should be implemented sequentially:

- *Step one*: Mobilise commitment to change through joint diagnosis of business problems. Help all employees to develop a shared diagnosis of what is wrong in an organisation and what can and must be done about it.

- *Step two*: Develop a shared vision of how to organise for competitiveness. Once commitment is obtained to the analysis of a problem, managers lead employees toward a task-aligned vision of the organisation that defines new roles and responsibilities.
- *Step three*: Foster not only consensus for the new vision, but also the necessary competence to enact it and required cohesion to move it along. Since employee commitment to change is uneven (some are enthusiastic, others are lukewarm, etc) everyone needs to develop competencies to make the changes work, and support mechanisms need to be in place. Managers who cannot adapt to change and transformation issues during this period must be replaced.
- *Step four*: Spread revitalisation to all departments without pushing it from the top. Use teams to break down resistance by enlisting their feedback about how to organise their department and responsibilities.
- *Step five*: Institutionalise revitalisation through formal policies, systems and structures. Enact changes in structures and systems that are consistent with change and transformation during this step (not earlier).
- *Step six*: Monitor and adjust strategies in response to problems in the revitalisation process. Monitoring the change and transformation process needs to be shared by all employees through use of an oversight team – key manager(s), union leaders, secretary, engineer, someone from finance, etc. Regular attitude surveys to monitor behaviour patterns are also essential.

The literature on change management therefore indicates that when organisational change occurs, the climate must be conducive to the change; employee understanding, participation and support are needed; and some of the changes need to be incremental, step by step and congruent with the existing culture in order to maintain some form of stability. Furthermore, any such changes must be implemented with the utmost care and sensitivity. Managers need to balance the opposite ends of the continuum concerned with how to rejuvenate an organisation (change) and yet not demoralise its loyal workforce (stability).

21.5 CHANGE AGENTS AND ROLES

Jick (1993a: 192–193) points out that when implementing change there are three broad action roles in the organisation: (i) change strategists, who are responsible for identifying the need for change, creating a vision of the desired outcome, deciding what changes are feasible, and choosing who should sponsor and defend the changes; (ii) change recipients, the largest group, comprising the employees (management included) who must adopt and adapt to the changes (their adoption of and adaptation to the changes determine whether or not the change is successful); and (iii) the change implementers, who implement the actual day-to-day process of change. They help to shape, enable, orchestrate and facilitate successful progress. They are actually the people in the middle, responding to demands from the change strategists while attempting to win cooperation from the change recipients. This is a challenging role indeed.

There is also a substantial body of literature confirming the nature and importance of the role of the change agent. Various authors (such as Nadler 1983, Kotter 1995; and Jick 1993b) point out that in order for a change agent to bring about effective change, he or she must have the formal authority, position and legitimate power base to put transformation into practice throughout the organisation. Many authors (such as Hart & McMillan 1996; Kotter 1995; and Tushman, Newman & Romanelli 1986) also point out that change can be brought about more effectively by an outside person or group of persons who act as change agent(s).

Change agents are change leaders in that they lead the change effort in an organisation (Leigh 1988). Harvey and Brown (2001: 94–96) clarify the matter by making the following statements in this regard:

> The OD consultant or change leader must deal proactively with these changing competitive forces ... The OD consultant helps the organisation identify differences between where it is and where it would like to be, and then proceeds to design and implement appropriate OD interventions ... The change leader involves all members of an organization ... In every large-scale change program, some person or group is usually designated to lead the change... the change leader, the person leading or guiding the process of change in the organization. The OD consultant may already be a member of the organization or may be a consultant brought in from the outside.

The change agent is not necessarily a single person. The change effort may be led by a project team, a team of consultants from elsewhere in the organisation, or a team of specialists from inside as well as some from outside the organisation. Often an external–internal team of change agents work together to steer organisations through large-scale change initiatives in organisations.

Whether or not an organisation makes use of the services of an external change consultant is contingent upon many factors. The first factor an organisation needs to consider is whether they have the necessary skills within the organisation to use internal specialists to help lead the change effort. An organisation with a relatively large HR (or similar) department may have access to a person who is highly competent in organisational change. Alternatively, a manager from another department may have competency in this area. If either of these two scenarios applies, then the organisation needs to consider the advantages and disadvantages of using that person's skills for the change process.

The advantages of using internal change agents may include (Leigh 1988) being more cost effective, being familiar with the organisation and understanding how the organisation works (including relevant power and political dynamics), and usually being available after completion of the change project to provide ongoing advice and evaluation, and to ensure the initiative is implemented correctly. In addition to these advantages, it may be easier for them to gain the trust of organisational members.

The disadvantages of using internal change agents may include that they may not be objective (they may have their own interests at stake), they may not be trusted or well liked in the organisation (and this may create greater resistance to any changes they advocate) and that they may in some sense be so much a part of the organisation that it may be difficult for them to see deficiencies or ways to overcome them. In addition, it may even be that they may not have adequate time to devote to the change process itself if they are not relieved of their other regular duties.

External change agents come from outside the organisation and they are usually hired on a contractual basis, often through a tendering type of processes. Typically, the change consultant(s) will put together a proposal and in that way a number of parties may be competing for the contract. In some instances change agents are selected on the basis of word of mouth or because they have achieved successful results for the specific organisation (or other known organisation) in the past.

Some of the potential advantages of using external change agents may include that highly competent and experienced change specialist skills may in such a way be bought in on a temporary basis, they may be better able to view and approach the whole process objectively and they may be highly dedicated and focused, being driven by the need to achieve a good result, their reputation being at stake. Potential disadvantages may include that the person(s) may be unfamiliar with the organisation and therefore it may be time consuming to get to a point of fully understanding the organisation and its people, resistance may be generated because they may be unknown to the organisation's members, and some may even feel threatened and hence unwilling to divulge information or take part productively in the change process. Undoubtedly, many would view the external change agent option as being too costly, and it is often said that external change agents tend to rely too heavily on 'off-the-shelf' solutions rather than helping the organisation to diagnose the situation properly, and finding and implementing an intervention that can be a solution specifically suited to the organisation's circumstances. Some consultants also refrain from getting or remaining involved in the change process right to the end of successful completion. There is often no guaranteed satisfactory result.

As can be seen from the foregoing, the decision whether to make use of an internal or external change agent or team of change agents is very much a situational and preference issue (often also a value-laden one). In practice it is very common to have a team of internal and external change agents jointly steering an organisational change process.

Ultimately the most important thing is that the change must be 'owned' by as many as possible people throughout the organisation. We know and must expect that not everybody will buy into it and that resistance to change (RTC) is common. However, irrespective of the team of change agents and how this is composed, we must not go it alone. This means engaging all or most of the relevant working people appropriately. It must thus be line-management driven in the end and commitment is essential, especially across the hierarchy of management. Naturally therefore the change must be clearly necessary and showed to be such, supported by objective reasons (change for the sake of change must be avoided at all costs). This is why we use the notion of becoming 'change champions'. It elevates the role of the senior line and HR managers who must spearhead it all as the key change agents – who must find and craft the worthy path to go onto, and then lead the way forward (even if that means engaging others as fellow change agents).

This may all sound pretty plain sailing, but we can assure you that in practice this is not generally the case. Organisational change is a challenge to get right. Quite a bit depends on the actual type of change intervention at hand – what its focus is and how it is perceived by the working people. Naturally, transformational change – which is 'deep' – can be experienced as more traumatic, especially by people who do not perceive the need. That is why such change must engage 'hearts and minds': the values, feelings, attitudes – as well as the rational, objective, fact-of-the-matter discussions. It is often said that any real change, to take hold, must be coming from within individuals – which often asks for introspection at a very personal level.

21.6 ORGANISATIONAL CHANGE INTERVENTIONS: DIFFERENT TYPES AND FOCI

Until now we have discussed the nature and importance of change and transformation to managers in South Africa, we have looked at some of the roles and processes involved in organisational change management and we have highlighted resistance factors and potential ways of overcoming these. In this section we focus on the types of change intervention that can be applied and we try to answer the questions: What aspects of the organisation can be changed? And what may be the focus of the organisational change intervention?

Robbins (1997: 523–526) proposes five areas of focus which change interventions may target in an organisation: the structural, cultural, technological, people and physical setting areas. Beatty and Ulrich (1993) refer to possible changes in the organisation's hardware (strategy, structure and systems) and software (employee behaviour and mindsets).

21.6.1 Structural interventions

Waddell et al (2007: 210) explain that change interventions "aimed at structural design include moving from more traditional ways of diving the organisation's overall work ... to more integrative and flexible forms".

These include things like 're-engineering' and 'rightsizing' (or as traditionally known, downsizing). Re-engineering "radically redesigns the organisation's core work processes to give tighter linkage and co-ordination among different tasks. This work-flow integration results in faster, more responsive task performance ... process management is often accomplished with new information technology that permits employees to control and co-ordinate work processes more effectively" (Waddell et al 2007: 210).

Rightsizing or downsizing is usually rather a drastic intervention that has severe implications for staff. As Waddell et al (2007: 219) also point out, these interventions often go hand in hand with the trend to look carefully at what work to keep inside the organisation and what to outsource, and it typically includes "decreasing the number of employees through lay-offs, attrition, redeployment or early retirement, or by reducing the number of organisational units or managerial levels through divestitures, outsourcing, reorganisation or delayering". It is important to note also, however, that structural interventions are not always or primarily about scaling down – but also when there is growth and 'upsizing'.

Corporate growth strategies through mergers and acquisitions are relevant in this regard. These have structural as well as cultural implications of a great magnitude. When there is growth though mergers and acquisitions two organisations that were separate entities are brought together – each with an own history, culture and so forth. Often people working for these organisations become pretty nervous and uncertain as to what the future might hold – because there are always possibilities of duplicated work, functions and processes which might require restructuring that can include redundant people. The expectations and feelings of the working people are thus key. Taylor (2005: 21) explains that naturally these strategies are aimed at improving business and competitiveness but that "research into the results of mergers and acquisitions strongly suggests that around half can be described as failures ... [A] number of studies have shown that in many of these cases the failure results from a mishandling of the 'people issues' ... [S]enior managers ... do not make the time to consider the implications for or concerns of staff ... An important task for organisations embarking on a merger or acquisition is the need to manage employee expectations", and as such it thus is essential under such circumstances to assign "sufficient resources to the management of the human dimension".

Similarly, Boxall and Purcell (2008: 270–273) make the case clear:

> Thus, 'human factors' loom large in M&As from the beginning, but become especially acute during the pos-acquisition implementation phase ... A whole range of issues needs to be faced in organisational integration ... [M]ost, if not all, of the HR policies and practices ... will need to be integrated. Since the nature of these policies is a reflection of wider, yet ill-defined, beliefs on organisational culture, the change process can be fraught, especially if the acquired employees refuse to legitimate the new economic and social order ... Culture change programmes are hard at the best of times within existing companies but in acquisitions they are especially fraught.

We return to cultural interventions in section 21.6.5 below.

21.6.2 Technological interventions

The influence of technology on work and motivation has been well documented (Stoner & Wankel 1986). Essentially, these interventions involve designing work – using approaches such as job enrichment and job enlargement (see chapter 5) – that is user friendly to people and technology (for example, designing work that integrates automation and data-processing technologies). In addition, changes that result from introducing new office equipment, information-processing systems, work sequence and work processes, and how these changes impact on performance are also addressed. Techno-structural approaches to change and transformation are a firm's attempt to improve performance by changing both the firm's structure and its technology. For example, small teams are formed around tasks that involve operating new equipment or other technologies.

21.6.3 Organisation development and human resource management interventions

Both technological and structural types of intervention include improving organisational performance by changing aspects of the 'bigger picture', which then impacts on the work situation. The idea would then be to make sure employee behaviour will be aligned herewith to enhance work performance and thus productivity and overall organisational performance and competitiveness. We also, on the other hand, get interventions that focus directly on the working people in order to change the behaviour of employees and enhance their capacity to perform their work better by focusing on their skills, attitudes, perceptions and expectations.

Efforts to change people's behaviour and attitudes can be directed at individuals, groups or at the organisation as a whole. Many (but not all) such efforts are known as organisational development (OD) techniques (we elaborate on this form of planned change again later). Waddell et al (2007: 266) say that "OD practitioners are increasingly attending to the design and implementation of reward systems ... [R]ewards should be congruent with other organisational systems and practices, such as the organisation structure ... and work designs". Other approaches for changing behaviour and working people's performance include leadership development interventions, implementing performance and career management systems, and interventions aimed at work–life balancing. About the latter, Waddell et al (2007: 277) say the following:

This relatively new OD intervention helps employees better integrate and balance work and home life. Restructuring, downsizing and increased global competition have contributed to longer work hours and more stress ... A more balanced work and family life can benefit both employees and the company through increased creativity, morale and effectiveness, and lower turnover.

21.6.4 Physical setting interventions

Robbins (1997: 525) points out that physical settings per se do not have a substantial impact on organisational or individual performance, but that these issues can make certain employee behaviours either easier or more difficult to perform. The layout of work space and of physical settings should therefore not be a random activity, but a thoughtful consideration of work demand, formal interaction requirements and social needs, so that appropriate decisions can be made regarding space configurations, interior design and equipment placement.

21.6.5 Organisational culture interventions

Organisational culture is basically a set of important shared understandings (mostly unstated) between the members of the organisation. These consist of such things as the values, attitudes and mindsets of members in the organisation. It is essentially sharing ideas about 'who we are, what we stand for and how we do things around here'. We must keep in mind that these shared understandings may cut across geographical areas – as wide as a continent or even across different continents (such as organisations that operate in Africa and also on other continents). While different societies might thus have certain cultures, multinational corporations might have their own unique organisational cultures that are based on that shared understanding, irrespective of which society they operate in. On the other hand, any single organisation might have subcultures that may vary in terms of industry and/or sector, or even across departments or other work units. Organisational culture is therefore a very complex facet of change.

Managers wishing to change organisational culture need to acknowledge that cultural change can therefore present numerous challenges and generally take longer. Changing culture is usually more difficult than changing systems and structures because it revolves around deeper issues such as values and mindsets – in particular shared mindsets that develop over long periods. Bringing about a change of culture normally requires multidimensional interventions that cover different foci in organisations – including, for example, structures, systems and technology. Hesselbein (2002: 1–2) says the following: "In times of great change culture gets special attention ... Culture changes when the organization is transformed; the culture reflects the realities of people working together every day."

This brings us to the issue of transformational change.

21.6.6 Transformational change

The complexity and variety of organisations and their environments require change leaders to create organisations that cope successfully with a multitude of problems, challenges and changes – sometimes simultaneously. As change champions we need to be capable of bringing about these larger-scale changes. Waddell et al (2007: 320–321) say: "Successful firms are able to respond to these threats to survival by transforming themselves ... These periods of total system and quantum changes represent abrupt shifts in the organisation's structure, culture and processes."

In South Africa particularly we are at a juncture that requires this 'deep' form of change – or what is also referred to as 'frame bending' (or frame breaking), and transformational change. We need to embrace different mindsets about what we are to do and how. Some organisations have already embarked on that path – most others that need to have not yet even started to contemplate it. There are numerous drivers behind this need to engage in transformational change – in South Africa these include the fact that our society is still in transformation. We discussed various forces and trends in chapters 2 and 3 especially. The essence is that we have to think and act very differently, generally, if we are to develop a sustainable South Africa – which is so crucial for developing a sustainable Africa. This type of change is thus rooted in organisational survival and issues pertaining to sustainability in our increasingly competitive and global (and warming) world.

Dunphy, Griffiths and Benn (2007: 262) say the following, which might equally be applied to South Africa:

> There are many organizations ... that have been or will soon be, subjected to unprecedented and unanticipated public pressure to make radical change. Why? Because some of their current policies or practices are revealed as plundering and polluting the planet, destroying the human capital ... or fracturing community relationships ... respond by initiating radical, transformative change.

They (2007: 265) also add that due to

> ... the magnitude and urgency of the changes needed to bring about sustainability in society, we are confident that over the next few years many organizations will have to undergo corporate transformation ... we know that 'long-living companies', that is, companies that survive for many years, undergo at least one significant period of transformational change and sometimes several ... there is an increasing number of organizations whose basic corporate strategy is continually to transform or 'reinvent' themselves to remain competitive.

Transformational change is thus, in the first place, the task and challenges of the uppermost echelons of organisational leadership, such as the boards of directors and top-management teams. This is the level from where we need to see and experience the inner-organisational drive and commitment to transform – and these transformational issues, as we have said, go way beyond the boundaries of the organisation itself. Even though the championing must be right from the top, we do not view this type of transformational strategic leadership purely through the 'great-person' lens. Transformation is something that must ultimately permeate throughout the organisation, and as such we must subscribe to the 'great-group' approach to leadership – where the change leadership is distributed throughout and shared by all (or then, realistically speaking, most) organisational members. We have to champion transformation by engaging all the people involved in organisations. Transformational change has to be top driven, though, and in particular also in South Africa where we need the corporate will to champion the deep and broad change required to help us and the rest of Africa become a more inclusive and sustainable country and continent respectively. Numerous South African organisations are indeed embracing the type of change that is needed in our society – as also reflected in exhibit 21.1. As can also be seen quite clearly, these efforts and challenges extend way beyond the boundaries of our country – into Africa (and beyond).

Dr Reuel Khoza, President of South Africa's Institute of Directors, says the following:

> No country, region or continent can elude the need to seriously reflect on itself in the light of globalisation and global warming ... The core issue is whether transformation occurs belatedly – in a crisis atmosphere ... The cardinal objective then is a transformation agenda and process that is revolutionary in result, but evolutionary in execution. This is so whether the challenge is universal environmental preservation, regional or world peace and democracy ... fighting crime and corruption, stopping the lunacy of tyranny and oppression; combating the scourge of HIV and AIDS ..." (Khoza 2007: 10).

The challenges for transformational change are thus vast and formidable. Fortunately, many South African organisations are rising to the challenge. Many others, though, still need to.

EXHIBIT 21.1: Anglo Platinum and transformational change challenges

Anglo Platinum Limited is listed on the JSE Ltd and is the sole listed entity for the Group. It has a secondary listing on the London Stock Exchange. International depositary receipts for the Company's shares are listed on the 'Brussels bourse'. It is the world's largest primary producer of platinum delivering about 37% of newly mined production globally, and accounting for half of South Africa's 75% contribution to world primary supplies. It also produces other platinum group metals (PGMs) including palladium, rhodium, ruthenium, iridium and osmium. Nickel, copper, other base metals and gold are by-products.

The Group's main operating mines include Rustenburg Platinum Mines' (RPM) Rustenburg Section, Amandelbult Section and Union Section (85% owned), as well as Potgietersrust Platinums Limited (PPRust) (now Mogalakwena Section), Twickenham and Lebowa Platinum Mines Limited (LPM).

The Group is also in joint ventures and associations with: African Rainbow Minerals Platinum, a historically disadvantaged South African (HDSA) mining company, to operate the Modikwa Platinum Mine; Royal Bafokeng Resources, an HDSA partner, over the combined Bafokeng-Rasimone Platinum Mine (BRPM)/Styldrift properties; the Bakgatla-Ba-Kgafela traditional community who hold a 15% share in Union Mine; Lonmin Platinum and HDSA partners, the Bapo Ba Mogale tribe and Mvelaphanda, over the Pandora PGM reserves; Xstrata to operate the Mototolo Mine and has joint venture agreements with Aquarius Platinum (South Africa), covering the shallow reserves of its Kroondal and Marikana mines contiguous to RPM Rustenburg Section.

The Group's smelting and refining operations are wholly owned through RPM and situated in South Africa. These operations treat concentrates and matte from subsidiaries and from joint ventures.

The Group announced its intention to conclude two major BEE transactions on 4 September 2007 with existing empowerment partners, Mvelaphanda Resources Limited and Anooraq Resources Corporation. The deals when successfully concluded will result in the creation of two major independently HDSA-managed and controlled PGM producers over the Lebowa Platinum Mines, Ga-Phasha, Booysendal and Northam assets.

In Zimbabwe the Group is developing the Unki platinum mine and elsewhere in the world, the Group is involved in exploration in Canada, Russia, Brazil and China. The Group has a representative office in Beijing.

Some 61% of the world's platinum is used in autocatalysts, designed to reduce noxious emissions from vehicles. Demand for autocatalysts rose 2.3% in 2007 as environmental concerns about air quality in many of the world's major cities continue to increase and more stringent vehicle-emission standards are legislated in many countries.

>>

In 2007 Anglo Platinum had a total workforce consisting of just less than 49 000 employees and just over 38 000 contract workers.

It continually works with the relevant host communities to ensure they are not negatively affected by the Group's operations and that they are uplifted through socio-economic development initiatives supported by our operations.

Mining activities have inherently positive and negative social and environmental impacts on the communities which surround operations. Negative impacts are typically mitigated through, and positive impacts enhanced by, social and environmental management programmes. Positive impacts by the Group's operations have included job creation, skills development, education and health investment, business development and infrastructure provision. Negative impacts include:

- social impacts such as proliferation of internal settlements as job seekers move into areas adjacent to the mine;
- complaints of increased prostitution and crime;
- environmental impacts such as noise, dust and boreholes running dry; and
- loss of agricultural land.

It is no longer acceptable to expect communities to be satisfied with just corporate social investment projects in their areas.

Anglo Platinum has established a new dedicated community engagement structure to deal with community issues effectively. The new structure is tasked with managing community issues in an integrated manner that recognises that community development is not a cost but an investment. Clearly, it is important to have a community engagement approach which is proactive and partnership orientated rather than paternalistic and reactive. As a result there have been significant changes in approach and attitude in engagements between communities and Anglo Platinum. The approach with municipalities and other relevant stakeholders has also been transformed from a sporadic one to one that builds relationships that are enduringly beneficial and developmental. The availability and management of data involving communities has also been improved, resulting in swift turnaround in terms of decision making as well as reacting to problems in the communities.

All operations now have established community engagement forums, as part of their broader community plans, which are designed to bring all stakeholders together to deal with community issues more systematically. Anglo Platinum continues to be a key founding participant in various producers' forums and joint development forums in the areas where it operates.

Bafokeng-Rasimone Platinum Mine (BRPM) held an open day in October 2007, which was attended by over 700 community members. The purpose was to bring BRPM closer to the community and to showcase its day-to-day activities.

Exhibition stalls were set up at the Bonwakgogo Primary School hall in Robega village. Various mine departments, including socio-economic development, HIV and AIDS, recruitment, human resources development, environment, safety and procurement had an opportunity to exhibit their products and activities. Community members were also informed about business opportunities available to them at BRPM.

In his opening speech, mine manager Glenn Harris said BRPM was very proud to be opening its doors to the community. He said he was fully aware that the community depended on BRPM for employment and encouraged them to take advantage of the opportunities provided through the mine, including business opportunities.

Empowerment is a high priority for BRPM, and whenever possible the community will be drawn into the mainstream of economic activities and given the necessary support. The community was encouraged to take part in small-, medium- and micro-enterprise development programmes offered by the mine.

A solar cooker was handed over to an NGO at the village. The cooker was manufactured by community members who attended training sponsored by BRPM through ORBIT-FET College. These solar-powered cookers are ideal for use by the NGOs, as they do not receive any funding and sometimes do not have cash to buy wood or electricity.

Fifteen solar cookers will be donated to NGOs in the community. Anglo Platinum is pleased to be associated with projects that contribute to the socio-economic development of surrounding communities.

During the open day, emergency services provided free medical check-ups, tested blood sugar levels and hypertension. Voluntary counselling and testing (VCT) for life-threatening diseases, and eye-testing services, were also provided free.

Anglo Platinum continues to play a meaningful role in community development. Guided by the mining charter, its social and labour plans and corporate citizenship principles, Anglo Platinum invested R126 million in community development projects around its operations in 2007.

The Group's corporate social investment strategy, as a subset of its broader corporate socio-economic development portfolio, is to play a constructive role in enhancing the quality of life of communities surrounding group operations, as well as some regions from which members of the workforce are sourced.

Anglo Platinum continues to focus most of its corporate social investment activities in five areas:

■ Infrastructure: contributing to the sustained improvement of physical infrastructure in underdeveloped areas.

■ Education: supporting the development of quality education centres and improvements in mathematics, science and English-language teaching and learning at primary and secondary schools.

■ Health and welfare: supporting initiatives geared at enhancing government's delivery of primary healthcare and welfare services to the underprivileged sector.

■ Community capacity building: supporting initiatives to improve the skills of community members and their organisations.

■ Small- medium- and micro-enterprise development: supporting programmes intended to promote entrepreneurship in mine communities and labour-sending areas.

It is actively working on projects, plans and programmes to stimulate local economic development in municipalities in which Anglo Platinum has operations. These initiatives are meant to mitigate against the formation of 'ghost' towns after the life of the mine, heavy reliance on the mining operation for employment, and poverty.

In response to the need to stimulate entrepreneurship and facilitate business linkages between local businesses and Anglo Platinum operations, partnerships have been formed with local municipalities to set up these facilities at Tubatse, Fetakgomo, Thabazimbi, Rustenburg and Moses Kotane. Facilities at the Polokwane and Mogalakwena municipalities started operation in 2007.

Anglo Platinum supports forming cooperative-type businesses to broaden participation by local communities in economic development. Emphasis has been on the establishment and promotion of women-owned cooperatives.

Source: http://www.angloplatinum.com/

21.7 PROMINENT PLANNED ORGANISATIONAL CHANGE TYPES

21.7.1 Organisational development

Organisational development (OD) is defined by Waddell et al (2007: 3) as "a systemwide application of behavioural science knowledge to the planned development and reinforcement of organisational strategies, structures and processes for improving an organisation's effectiveness". Harvey and Brown (2001: 4) say that OD

Elsewhere in Africa

Africa focuses on 'triple bottom line'

In a relatively recent article in *Worldlink*, a publication of the WFPMA (the World Federation of Personnel Management Associations), the following was reported.

Late February 2005 saw the African Federation of Human Resource Management Associations hosted the first WFPMA Board meeting since its creation, in Sandton in South Africa. Amongst others, present were AFHRMA's Vice-President, Jowitt Mbongwe, President of the Botswana Institute of HRM, Florence Namatta Mawejje (General Manager, HR for telecommunications company MTN, based in Kampala, Uganda) and Evan Thomas (working for the IPM of Namibia). AFHRMA President, Tiisetso Tsukudu, stressed the need for HR professionals to focus not only on the economic bottom line, but also on the environmental and social bottom lines. The concept of a triple bottom line, identified in South Africa's 2002 King Report on Corporate Governance, highlights the trend towards a more holistic approach to doing business, he said, with the recognition that "if an organisation only strives towards achieving its monetary objectives, it may not succeed in keeping its employees satisfied and productive."

The environmental bottom line refers to the national capital or wealth of nations in terms of both renewable and nonrenewable resources, and HR needed to "help organisations ensure sustainability through responsible use of natural resources and preserving the natural environment." Most important, though, was the issue of the social bottom line. It was HR's role to increase organisational effectiveness by ensuring the development of skills and the education of employees, and also their health and overall well-being.

Also on the social agenda for Africa and among the top issues for AFHRMA members, said Tsukudu, was social responsibility and good corporate citizenship. Organisations were being encouraged to contribute not only to the development of their employees, but also to the communities in which they did business. In many companies employees were involved in fundraising for charities and NGOs that were working with disadvantaged communities, as well as doing voluntary work themselves for community organisations.

Source: Namatta Mawejje (2005: 1)

... is long-range efforts and programmes aimed at improving an organization's ability to survive by changing its problem-solving and renewal processes. OD involves moving towards an adaptive organisation and achieving corporate excellence by integrating the desires of individuals for growth and development with organizational goals ... Organization development efforts, then, are planned, systematic approaches to change. They involve changes to the total organization or to relatively large segments of it ... [A] series of planned behavioral science intervention activities are carried out in collaboration with organization members to help find improved ways of working together toward individual and organizational goals.

OD practitioners employ a variety of techniques to change and transform behaviour. These include survey feedback methods that systematically report results as a basis for change (Carrell et al 1997). Team building is an initiative aimed at improving group effectiveness by improving task performance and relationships between team members. Finally, Grid OD, a six-phase programme based on the concept of the managerial grid (French & Bell 1984), uses a variety of OD activities to bring about a high level of concern for people and production in the firm.

21.7.2 Kotter's seven-step process

Kotter (1995, 1996) examined the multiple approaches to change and transformation that were adopted by more than 100 organisations going through a transformation process and concluded that (i) the change process goes through a series of phases that, in total, require a considerable length of time; and (ii) critical effects in any of these phases can have a devastating impact, slowing momentum and negating hard-won gains. He identified eight errors common to organisational change and their consequences.

These errors include the following:
- underestimating the importance of having a clear vision;
- failing to communicate such a vision;
- allowing obstacles to block a new vision;
- failing to create a sufficiently powerful guiding coalition;
- allowing too much complacency;
- not anchoring changes in the corporate culture;
- not creating enough short-term gains; and
- declaring victory too soon.

As a result of such errors, new strategies may fail to be implemented successfully, downsizing may fail to get costs under control, quality programmes may fail to deliver what was hoped for, and re-engineering efforts may not yield anticipated results.

Kotter (1995, 1996) not only identified common errors but also proposed remedies. He pointed out that the methods used in successful transformation are based on the fundamental understanding that major change will not happen easily for the reasons we have already covered in this chapter. He proposed a multistage process for designing change strategies (Kotter 1996: 20–173). Each stage in the process is associated with solving one of the fundamental errors that undermine transformation efforts.
- Step one in Kotter's (1996) model is to establish a sense of urgency. Nadler and Tushman (1988) argue that energy – which results from this sense of urgency – is necessary to shake up the status quo so that change can be initiated and executed.
- The formation of a powerful guiding coalition is step two in Kotter's model. A group with enough power – in terms of aspects such as titles, information, expertise and reputation – needs to be developed to lead the change effort.
- Creating a shared vision and strategy is step three in Kotter's model. Before change implementation can begin, the change agent must first craft a vision, formulate corporate strategies, transpose these into HR strategies, and then communicate the vision, strategy and core values to the employees continuously (Warren 1992). To build stability into the change process, the past can be incorporated into the vision for the future, as Hurst (1991) observes, the "... purpose is to reinterpret the past and visualise the future, for it is the weaving for the 'texts' or lessons from the past with the expected scenarios or 'contexts' of the future that constitutes the cognitive pattern that we call a 'vision' of the future".

- According to Kotter (1995: 63), the importance of step four – communicating the vision and strategies – cannot be overemphasised. These visionary strategies and their core values must be communicated down to everyone in the organisation, using every possible communication vehicle – memos, meetings, workshops, forums or industrial theatre. Warren (1992: 74) points out that it is crucial to accomplish employee understanding and acceptance of the visionary strategies when bringing about change. He also emphasises that frequent and repetitive communication of a simple message is necessary to do this. Strebel (1996) has identified a common root cause of change problems in organisations that ties in with this step: managers and workers view change differently. Top management sees change as an opportunity to strengthen the business by aligning operations with strategy, as well as an opportunity to take on new professional challenges and risks. However, for many workers, including middle managers, change is both disruptive and intrusive. It is essential, therefore, not only to communicate the vision and strategy to employees at all levels on a continuous basis but also to communicate what is in it for them and how the changes will impact on job descriptions and specifications, personal relationships with colleagues, and on communication with management.

    Hart and McMillan (1996) support Strebel's conclusions by emphasising that for the mission to be aligned with the organisation, it must be communicated to employees in such a way that they see in it a role for themselves that is aligned with their personal ambition. Lynn (1993) details an elaborate communication process that can help to create a (new) mindset in employees, causing them to accept, associate and adapt to change quickly and positively.

- Step five involves "empowering broad-based action", involving the process of getting rid of obstacles, encouraging a culture of risk taking and creativity, and changing structures or systems that undermine the change.

- Step six involves the generation of short-term wins (create performance opportunities and reward them) and the consolidation of gains.

- Step seven entails anchoring the new approaches in the culture of the organisation. In this regard it is very important to articulate the connections between new behaviours and organisational success.

In summary, the value of change and transformation often lies in the process – the journey – and not so much in the actual changes or the end result, because the end result is ever changing in response to internal and external factors facing the organisation. Indeed, organisations need to instil a culture of continuous change for improvement – which may, or may not, involve minor or even radical changes in operations in order to survive and meet competitive challenges. When change is viewed as an ongoing learning process and as a form of continuous organisational innovation and renewal, organisations will have a process that is woven into the fabric of organisational life (Gebert 1996; Robbins 1997).

21.8 SOME SPECIFIC CONTEMPORARY CHANGE AND TRANSFORMATION INTERVENTIONS

Because change and transformation have become such universally important topics, many methods of dealing with them have been proposed. Some are very similar, and buzzwords are frequently used to offer new ideas – which very often are not as new as their tags would indicate. In this regard, concepts often used include 'rightsizing', 'downsizing', 'restructuring', 'reorganisation', 'business process re-engineering', 'redesign', etc. In this section, a brief overview is provided of some of these relatively recently proposed methods of organisational change.

21.8.1 Lean production

Coming from Japan, lean production is often also referred to as the Toyota system. This system is driven by three key elements, namely zero defects, zero waste and zero inventory. Teams of multiskilled employees run a continuous improvement process, known as *kaizen*. They have a constant focus on reducing waste and increasing quality, therefore quite clearly requiring a heavy emphasis on training and development, and high-commitment work practices. These are complemented by a just-in-time (JIT) production and supply chain management system.

21.8.2 Total quality management (TQM)

TQM, unlike lean production, has its origins in the quality movement in the US. It shares many of the lean production principles, however. Goetsch and Davis (1995: 6) define TQM as "an approach to doing business that attempts to maximize competitiveness of an organization through the continual improvement of the quality of its products, services, people, processes and environment". The obsession with achieving ever higher levels of quality is shared by the lean production system. TQM has a very strong customer focus, but the notion of customer is extended beyond the external customer (who uses the end product) to include the 'internal customer' (the next one in line in the value chain, so to speak – fellow employees and sections, teams or departments or organisational units). Quality is defined by the customer, and the aim is to meet or exceed the customer's expectations.

21.8.3 Re-engineering

The process of re-engineering is different from conventional organisational change approaches. Whereas conventional organisational change approaches involve some stability through links with the past and step-by-step incremental changes, re-engineering means radically redesigning the organisation's core processes by starting with a blank sheet of paper and ignoring the way things have been done in the past. The question underlying re-engineering is: If we could start from scratch, how would we do this? Carrell et al (1997: 629) point out that the proponents of re-engineering regard it as neither downsizing nor a programme for bottom-up continuous improvement (although this may be included in the process). Instead, they start from the future and work backward, as if unconstrained by existing methods, people or departments. Indeed, as has already been noted in this chapter, the process of re-engineering is consistent with the notion of organisations undergoing transformation rather than change.

Thus, even though Robbins (1997) concludes that re-engineering is one of the most favoured management tools for implementing radical change, it comes as no surprise to learn that Carrell et al (1997) have found that 50% to 70% of re-engineering efforts fail because of factors such as individual and organisational resistance to change.

21.8.4 The learning organisation

The concept 'learning organisation; refers to an organisation that is continually improving and developing (Senge 1990). Robbins (1997) concludes that this management concept became to the mid-1990s what TQM has been was to the 1980s. Greenberg and Baron (1997: 548) and Robbins (1997: 535) define a learning organisation as follows:

A *learning organisation* is an organisation that has developed the continuous capacity to adapt and change. It is successful at acquiring, cultivating and applying knowledge that can help it to adapt to change.

The importance of change and transformation management in a learning organisation is obvious: in the learning organisation, change is seen as an ongoing process not as an event. Change is woven into the fabric of organisational life as a way of functioning and continuously developing.

21.9 CHANGE AND TRANSFORMATION IN SOUTH AFRICAN ORGANISATIONS: SOME REFLECTIONS

21.9.1 General

Documented findings concerning the attitudes of South African managers to a number of HRM-related issues have revealed a number of priority rankings a decade or so ago (Hofmeyr, Rall & Templer 1995). Then already managers regarded their priority activity as managing organisational change. Managers also indicated that they were having to spend more time dealing with traditional industrial relations issues and training activities instead of handling issues relating to change management at the time.

We believe that we are at a point now that requires attention to all of these, HRD and IR, as well as the management of change and transformation. South African managers will have to understand and accept these realities if they are to help their organisations to compete successfully in the international arena.

External factors – such as political change and tensions, trade union dynamics, the government's direction with social and economic initiatives, such as BBBEE, political turmoil, social responsibility pressures, changes in the economy locally and globally, international competition, the increasing importance of informal business, mergers and acquisitions, crime, etc – all combine to create unusual pressures that require radical shifts in management thinking and practice in South African organisations.

Factors such as affirmative action, especially in management and executive positions, and a major shift in the cultural profile of workforce demographics, are also creating profound adjustments in the organisational culture, management style and practice of South African organisations.

One of the major challenges facing South African organisations is how to transform to really empower the people and communities so as to develop a much more socio-economic inclusive society. This requires new styles of leadership, new HRM systems and approaches and structures, policies and practices that are aligned with the multi-cultural profiles of their workers. After years of isolation in a siege economy, new HRM strategies and practices mean that South African managers will have to grasp the fundamentals of change and transformation management issues and pay particular attention to embracing and managing diversity proactively and constructively. As we have already discussed elsewhere – the pace of change in this regard has arguably been a bit too slow – especially in some circles. Looking back over the past fifteen years or so shows tremendous change in this regard in the public sector for example – but as we've also illustrated before, these changes have unfortunately not translated into greater effectiveness and efficiencies.

Making our organisations more diverse and inclusive is important, but this form of change should happen in ways that enhance the quality and standards of services and products delivered. As we have emphasised throughout this book, what is needed is a form of change that is empowering through development. Changing the profiles of our workforces and the 'colour' of 'ownership and control' of the productive assets of our country can only work if people are developed and empowered to manage these organisations and resources in competitive ways.

21.9.2 Interplay between organisation transformation and change, and labour and employee relations

As has been pointed out before, due to the history of industrial relations in South Africa, a lack of trust is prevalent in many South African organisations. It is often found that labour (non-management employees and their representatives such as unions) and management simply do not trust one another. While there may be a multitude of complexly related factors underlying this trust gap – such as the damage done by the apartheid era, different ideologies and educational backgrounds and especially differences in resources (financially driven) and living standards – the effect thereof is that, whenever organisations embark on change or transformation routes, the rationale is questioned and attacked, and processes are resisted. This is quite understandable, even though many leaders in South African organisations do not appreciate this. Rosenthal and Nolingo (1998) clearly illustrate why such resistance exists (see exhibit 21.2).

From exhibit 21.2 it should be quite clear that change and transformation in any South African workplace should not be embarked upon without having due regard to the workers' interests or without having the relevant worker representatives (the union(s)) as co-equal partners of the change and transformation process. This is what Unilever SA did (see 'A case at hand' below).

EXHIBIT 21.2: Restructuring in the chemical industry and labour and employee relations

Companies in the chemical industry have embarked on an aggressive programme of restructuring. They talk of 'world-class manufacturing', teamwork, flexibility, quality circles and best operating practices. They say they have to restructure in order to become more competitive and to democratise the workplace. While we may dispute the reasons companies give for restructuring, we cannot dispute the end result for workers. Union members lose their jobs, contract work increases and workers who do keep their jobs work harder in less safe conditions. These results are inevitable, unless unions take up the struggle to protect workers' interests. Company restructuring also poses a threat to union organization ... The CWIU has made a commitment to defend, advance and empower our members. The most important thing is to defend our members against job loss ... We must ensure that restructuring improves the living and working conditions of our members ...".

Source: Rosenthal & Nolingo (1998: 63)

A CASE AT HAND

Organisational change and labour relations at Unilever SA

Unilever recognised unions, which represented most of its workforce, in common with its worldwide practice, well before the Wiehahn Commission. It has always believed in developing its workforce and pays shop-floor workers some of the best packages available.

The Value Statement of Lever Ponds, similar to those of other Unilever subsidiaries, commits the company to enhance trust through a shared commitment and responsibility to treat each other with mutual respect, offer equal opportunity through training and development, respect freedom of association and to promote open communication.

One aspect of the value statement that has received considerable attention recently is individual and team empowerment through participation in problem solving and decision making.

Lever Ponds had to draw on a reservoir of goodwill when it decided to close the old Chesebrough-Ponds factory in Wadeville, Gauteng, and to merge it with the old Elida Gibbs factory in a state-of-the-art facility at Durban's Maydon Wharf. The business case for such a merger was overwhelming but it involved reducing the factory complement from 508 to 232.

It undertook an exercise of either redeploying workers within the group or giving them skills for life to enable them to continue earning a living. The company sponsored courses in bricklaying and helped others to get driver's licences. Lever Ponds personal products technical director Flynn Reynolds says that, because the new personal products factory was a greenfields operation, it was able to pick up the most appropriate solutions from Unilever worldwide. The remaining workforce had to be retrained to meet the requirements of the more sophisticated plant. It was a big undertaking because 40% of the workforce had less than two years' schooling.

Unilever SA has set out to create a less hierarchical structure and each factory unit or production line has a team leader chosen by workers. This approach has provided more direct lines of responsibility to facilitate greater clarity of purpose. Lever Ponds MD Doug Baillie says that the benefit has been more added value, accountability for business results, more opportunities for appropriate skills development and more effective teamwork.

At the Maydon Wharf soap factory, Project Ikwesi has reduced the number of layers between top management and the factory floor. This has involved a commitment by the Chemical Workers' Industrial Union to total product maintenance, a local version of the Japanese total product management programme. Machine operators and artisans take responsibility for their work areas by setting objectives and identifying priority areas.

The most comprehensive initiative so far has been the Workplace Change Agreement at Boksburg where both Lever Ponds and Unifoods have their largest production facility.

Charles Zwane, who runs the Lever Ponds plant in Boksburg, says there is a healthy working relationship between unions and management. The last major stoppage was in 1989 after the arrest of local union boss James Mdlalose (who is also president of the Nactu union federation) for political reasons.

One of the foundations of the agreement is a commitment by Unilever to education at three levels – technical, safety and adult basic education (ABET). There has been a move away from the traditional rates of pay for specific tasks towards pay for specific skills.

Production manager Thabo Mabe says the basic objective of the workplace change agreement has been to reduce the cost base and to provide service excellence to consumers with the minimum of dislocation in the workforce. To establish benchmarks for best products in production and remuneration structures, a team from management and the Nactu-affiliated Food & Beverage Workers' Union went to major factories in the Unilever powders group – two in Brazil; in Warrington, England, Cartersville in the US and in Indonesia. The group found that Boksburg had a pay structure at least 20 years out of date and was behind in operations. It was, however, closer to the benchmark when it came to industrial relations.

>>

<<

Union leader Mdlalose says it was essential to address the imbalances of the past but, from the company perspective, the factory still had to be competitive with its peers in the rest of the world. The low literacy levels have been the major obstacle to world-class manufacturing, so basic education has been a union priority. More than 30 people are taken off the shop floor for up to eight months until they have achieved functional literacy.

Unilever has also encouraged workers to become multiskilled so that they run machines, shut them down, carry out maintenance and do quality control. Peter Sykes, human resources manager for Unifoods in Boksburg, says the workplace change agreement has been critical to building common values and creating a more participative structure. It will develop methods of rewarding and recognising whatever contributions are made to turn Boksburg into a world-class facility.

Source: Financial Mail Corporate Report (1998: 49–53)

From the Unilever SA case it should be clear that not only is it a prerequisite for successful change and transformation to have good labour relations, but also that good labour and employee relations, union–management cooperation and organisational change and transformation in South Africa go hand in hand.

Such an integrated approach will almost always be the more appropriate one for South African organisations embarking on the route of transforming towards more productive, competitive and therefore world-class organisations.

At a macro level, the need for this type of transformation has also been accepted. In 1995 a project was launched by Nedlac (National Economic Development and Labour Council), in association the NPI (National Productivity Institute) and the DTI (Department of Trade and Industry), called 'The Workplace Challenge'. It was initiated specifically to help meet the challenge of South Africa's re-entry into the global market and the resulting need for organisations to become more competitive. As Machin (1998: 47) states: "Workplace challenge aims to improve productivity, competitiveness and employment creation by increasing co-operation between management and labour at workplace level."

21.10 CONCLUSION

This chapter introduced you to the nature, the importance of and some challenges relating to leading change in South African organisations. Regardless of the type of change an organisation is having to deal with, change can only be effected by and through people. Employees are thus involved and affected, and the way in which change is managed must hence have the human dimension central to it.

The need to retain some degree of organisational stability while undergoing change was emphasised, and theories that describe the process of change and transformation were highlighted. Resistance to change was also covered, and ways in which this resistance can be dealt with were explained. Finally, several approaches that organisations can use to institute change and transformation processes were described, as were as specific challenges facing us regarding transformation issues and challenges facing us all in South Africa.

We have stressed the increasing importance of going much deeper and wider in our change efforts – to really 'transform' towards an inclusive and sustainable society. Our organisations have an important role to play – and this goes beyond South African borders.

It is thus not only in South Africa where we need to be the champions of change or transformation towards sustainability – it is also particularly important elsewhere into Africa. We have to reach out and collaborate across the continent, as is already happening.

Even though there may be some ongoing debate regarding the current readiness of managers in South Africa (and elsewhere in Africa, perhaps) to successfully manage radical, deep or transformational changes that are needed in our organisations and on this continent, we have to do as much as we can to develop the capacity to do so. A growing body of literature offers insights into the nature and process of change and transformation management, and we have to tap into that and develop programmes of learning and engagement so that we can develop more and more staff to become fellow change champions.

SELF-EVALUATION QUESTIONS

1   Why is it important for South African managers to understand the nature of and the problems involved in the management of change and transformation? Explain in detail.
2   Give a brief overview of the forces underlying change and transformation in organisations today.
3   Write an essay in which you explain the nature of and the challenges posed by resistance to change (RTC). Explain the different ways in which one can deal with resistance to change.
4   Discuss the different approaches to and types of organisational change.
5   What is meant by deep or transformational change? Do we need any of this in South African organisations? Why do you hold these views?
6   Briefly discuss, and illustrate by means of examples, the interplay between change/transformation, and labour and employee relations in South African organisations.

22 MANAGING HRM-RELATED INFORMATION

LEARNING OUTCOMES

After studying this chapter, you should be able to:

- discuss and apply various approaches to 'evaluate' aspects of HRM;
- engage in a debate about the role and nature of record-keeping, aspects of HR information systems and technology in HRM; and
- make a short presentation about the nature and importance of HRM-related reporting and demonstrate how HRM and sustainability reporting can be done.

22.1 INTRODUCTION

Throughout this book we have focused on the nature and importance of managing the human resource architecture of organisations successfully. It has been pointed out on various occasions that the world around and within our organisations has been undergoing (and still is undergoing) substantial change. As the world settles into the information and knowledge age, the need for organisations to develop learning cultures becomes more and more pressing. Facilitating learning and developing knowledge depends to a large extent on information and the appropriate use thereof. All decision making in organisations – and thus also all decisions relating to HRM – must be based on information. Collecting and the appropriate use of such information is therefore of crucial importance. One of the key areas of utilisation of management-related information in general is measurement and evaluation. The old adage of 'what gets measured gets done' holds for HRM just as it holds for management in general.

In this chapter we focus on some of the management implications of this information-driven society. The primary focus is on collecting and utilising information for the purposes of measuring, evaluating and reporting on performance in the HRM field. We start off with a brief perspective on the nature and importance of measuring and evaluating HRM-related aspects. This is followed by a discussion of various approaches to and methods of evaluating and measuring aspects of HRM. The other two sections deal with human resource information systems and the reporting of HRM-related information.

22.2 INFORMATION ABOUT THE QUALITY HRM

We have emphasised right from chapter 1 that HRM is supposed to be at the very core of the organisational value-adding process. The fact of the matter is that people who work in and for organisations can make or break the competitiveness of organisations. Flamholtz (2005: 276) says the following: "As we begin the new millennium, it is increasingly clear that the core strategic asset of enterprises as well as the new foundation of the wealth of nations is human capital. Without the ability to measure these assets, their management is likely to be either rational or optimal."

This is making a clear case for a comprehensive system of measurement pertaining to the totality of the organisation's HR system to answer the question: 'How do we know what contribution is made or what value is added through our HRM in the organisation?' The answer to this type of question will help us come to grips with the quality of HRM in our organisation.

We actually want to establish how valuable the HR architecture of the organisation is – the sum total of the HR subsystem of an organisation. In other words, the human resources (the staff or personnel, as well as the non-core work arrangements) and their behaviours and work-related performance; the HR department (or section – if there is one) and its activities, practices and the work of and role played by the specialist HR practitioners; the HRM systems of the organisation, including the strategies, policies, procedures and infrastructural elements (like structures and processes such as the HR information system); and the HRM practices of line management, including their leadership. The challenge is to be able to generate, find and utilise information that reflects the extent to which this HR architecture of an organisation helps the organisation to survive and compete, and succeed in general.

In the past decade or so there have been increasing trends towards acknowledging the value added by the 'human capital' (an intangible resource) of organisations. The net result of the HR architecture of an organisation should be to improve organisational performance, competitiveness and success through HRM-related outcomes that add value. A logical outflow hereof is therefore to 'measure', 'assess' or 'evaluate' the quality of the organisation's HR architecture. The information in this regard and processes related to gathering, using and presenting of such information form the focus of this section.

22.2.1 The case for measurement and accountability regarding HRM

In making his case for measurement, Dave Ulrich asks readers to imagine a scenario:

> An HR executive is part of a senior management team in a planning setting. The General Manager asks for input on what the plans should be for the business and talks about key financial indicators, including: inventory, margins, product turnover, revenue, expenses, debt, and other financial indicators of success. The marketing Vice President reports the customer requirements of the business and talks about measures of customer service, market share, customer focus groups, customer retention, and other indicators of customer satisfaction. The technology Vice President reports on indicators of emerging technologies, cycle times for product introduction, and research and development budgets and investments. The manufacturing Vice President reports on operating efficiencies, product quality, and volume indicators. What measure does the Vice President of human resources bring to this table? Traditionally, the HR executive could talk abstractly and conceptually about employee morale, turnover, and commitment. To fulfil the business partner role of HR, concepts need to be replaced with evidence, ideas with results, and perception with assessments (Ulrich 1997: 303).

From this it is clear that the focus of measurement and accountability in HRM is traditionally very much on the contributions made by the HR department or section. In the literature it is most common to find people referring to these as the 'HR function' of an organisation. While we know from chapter 1 that our approach in this book is to regard HRM as much broader, we stick to this more narrow notion of the HR function for most of this section as this is where most of the work had been done in relation to measuring or evaluating the quality of HRM. A more comprehensive approach remains "work in progress", as Flamholtz (2005: 273) says – even though we can add that the latest work of Huselid, Becker and Beatty (2005) clearly takes steps towards developing the more comprehensive approach. Huselid et al (2005: xvii) say they "argue that strategy and metrics should focus on the workforce and not just the HR function", and they add that "relevant metrics ought to emphasize the workforce culture, mind-set, competencies, and behaviors that can demonstrate how the workforce executes strategy and impacts the firm's bottom line". We take a look at a more comprehensive approach later. For now the focus is primarily on the HR function in the more narrow sense of the word (thus – the specialist HR practitioners/ sections).

Phillips (1996: 2–4) provides a number of arguments in favour of 'a results-based approach' to the evaluation of the HR function:

■ Human resources often represent a significant cost to organisations, which makes the effectiveness of the HR function an important influence on the overall success of organisations.

■ Several cases are cited of organisational failure that can be directly attributed to poor HRM policies and practices.

■ By contrast, "the success of many outstanding companies today, such as 3M, Proctor & Gamble, Motorola, Federal Express, Merck, and Coca-Cola, can be traced to effective HR policies" (Phillips 1996: 3).

■ Senior executives are also increasingly demanding "an adequate return on their investment in human, as well as other resources"; and they are beginning to question "whether the HR department should continue to expand if there is not a clear connection between its activities and the overall results of the organisation" (Phillips 1996: 4).

■ "An important tenet of continuous process improvement (CPI) is [that] nothing improves until it is measured. The CPI corollary is that when something is measured, it automatically begins to improve" (Phillips 1996: 4).

Phillips (1996: 5–6) also identifies a number of trends that may have an impact on an organisation's financial results and the HR function's role. He (Phillips 1996: 5–6) argues that "these trends enhance or complement the efforts of the HR department to monitor and improve its contribution to organizational performance".

These trends include:

■ An increasing trend towards financial accountability in management generally.

■ A recognition of the increased importance of human resources and the HR function.

■ The proliferation of a variety of organisational change programmmes (see chapter 21). Very often, HR has a significant change agent role to play. Such change and its impact must be measured and evaluated.

■ Increasing pressures for productivity improvement.

■ The trend towards a strategic approach to HRM. The basic tenet of strategic HRM is that it is tied to business success. It must therefore be based on data because business success can only be measured by the data (or information) available.

■ An increasing reliance on HRM partnership relationships. HRM is, as we have mentioned before, viewed more and more as a shared responsibility between line management and HR professionals. Phillips (1996: 20–21) says that a "critical ingredient to a partnership arrangement is that the HR manager must be knowledgeable of the business and contribute to business decisions ... An important part of the partnership relationship is convincing line management of the bottom-line contribution of HR. When line managers see the contribution and understand it, they are less reluctant to enter a partnership relationship".

■ According to Phillips (1996: 21), these trends "have a significant impact on HR's ability to improve organisational performance ... Clearly, the human resources function has taken on new dimensions and has become a valuable business partner in any organization. Still, there is much progress to be made. Increased concern for HR accountability has surfaced, and top management, as well as the other constituencies served by the HR function, are expecting a significant contribution from human resources. It appears that the HR function must meet this demand with new and improved measurement and evaluation strategies".

According to Phillips (1996: 24–25), six major benefits or 'payoffs' will flow from such a results-based measurement and evaluation approach:
■ Evaluation makes good economic sense.
■ Evaluation enables HR staff to show proof of their results.
■ Results from evaluation encourage HR staff to focus on important activities.
■ Data collected for evaluation isolate the causes of problems.
■ Results from measurement and evaluation can lead to additional resources.
■ Evaluation increases personal satisfaction and position.

22.2.2 The case against evaluation and financial accountability regarding HRM

Despite the well-recognised need to evaluate HRM, it appears that many of the models which have been developed to date are quite theoretical in nature and have not been properly tested.

According to Pfeffer (1997: 357), there are numerous problems and pitfalls that need to be taken into consideration if one wants to assess HRM effectively. Pfeffer (1997: 357) says "there is little convincing evidence that existing measurement practices do very well in dealing with these issues and much to suggest they do not".

The following are some of the problems that have been identified:
■ *Perceptual problems*: To some extent the perception exists that the evaluation of HRM will always be subjective. According to McCarthy (1980: 101–105), this subjectivity myth developed from the idea of the intangibility of HRM, and is based on the view that management as such is abstract and difficult to measure. Fitz-enz (1984) has identified the following (not insurmountable) problems which contribute to the subjectivity myth:
 – Specialist human resource staff do not know how to measure their activities.
 – There appears to be a conflict in values; that is, some people regard it as simply impossible or unnecessary to evaluate HRM objectively.
■ HR managers often fear that evaluation might expose their managerial shortcomings and inefficiencies.
■ Top management appears to accept the absence of an HRM evaluation system, which seems to reflect a general lack of interest in it.
■ *Accounting problems*: The evaluation of HRM requires an interdisciplinary approach. Accountancy concepts play an important role in this approach. Unfortunately, the accounting practice has traditionally neglected the value of

human resources. The employee is traditionally regarded largely as an expense or cost factor. The fact that employee-related expenses (such as training) often hold substantial long-term advantages for the organisation is traditionally largely ignored. The most important accounting problem related to the measurement of HRM involves categorising the employee as an asset. According to Flamholtz (1985), it is not humans that should be regarded as assets, but the service expected from them by the organisation; in other words their work performance.

■ *The image of HRM*: Traditionally the HR function does not enjoy the same status as other functions in the organisation such as operations or marketing. As a result, the need for an evaluation system is often underplayed. On the other hand, one can argue that the very fact that the HR function is now trying so hard to 'measure' comes from some sort of inferiority complex. Pfeffer (1997: 359–60) argues that "one indicator of a function's power is the extent to which its role is taken for granted and not assessed using a variety of micro measures".

■ *Lack of time and funds*: The additional work created by the collection of data, compiling the data into the report format, etc, takes time and increases costs.

■ *Time horizon problems*: Whereas accounting and financial reporting practices mostly focus on the short term (typically one year), it is well known that it takes a lot of time to yield results from building the human and social capital of organisations (such as the organisational culture or climate). It is also not always clear exactly when the benefits will accrue and be at a peak.

■ *Lack of a holistic systems focus*: Numerous 'models' or approaches for measuring HRM, as you will see later in the chapter, focus on a plethora of aspects that are measured – mostly without measuring the interconnections and the 'whole'. As Pfeffer (1997: 362) says: "Comprehensive assessment systems that entail multiple measures of multiple indicators are possibly useful for charting the overall productivity or health of a function, but they are almost useless for influencing or directing behaviour." Even this holistic focus seems to be limited to the traditional notion of the HR function, though.

■ *'Political' problems*: Writings on human behaviour in organisations (such as organisational behaviour textbooks) usually cover in detail how complex but important aspects such as power and politics are in organisational life in general. Pfeffer (1997: 363) makes the point that by engaging in the numbers and financial measurement game, HR functions' representatives and leaders are exposing themselves to political games in which they have a distinct disadvantage. This criticism basically boils down to an argument that the HR function and professionals are engaging in power-play games where the rules, tools, techniques and skills give a natural advantage to 'others' (for example the financial managers).

22.3 APPROACHES TO HRM EVALUATION AND MEASUREMENT

A variety of approaches and methods or models for the evaluation of HRM have been published to date. In spite of this, no universally acceptable approach has been developed. Possible reasons for this relate to the problems discussed in the previous section. In this section we will briefly review some of these different approaches and/ or methods.

22.3.1 Human resource accounting (HRA)

The American Accounting Association (1973) defines HRA as the process of identifying and measuring HR data, and the communication of this information to interested parties. The purpose of HRA is to improve the quality of financial decisions regarding the organisation's resources – in this case, its human resources. HRA thus aims at providing a more quantitative framework for HRM decision making. Flamholtz (2005: 269) says that "[h]uman resource accounting can be defined as ... 'accounting for people as organizational resources ... Operationally defined, this means measuring the cost, replacement cost, and economic value of people as organizational resources ... as well as the reporting of human capital in financial statements".

HRA models are divided into two major groups, namely HR cost models and HR value models.

A cost in this sense can be viewed as a sacrifice which is made in order to obtain an anticipated benefit. A cost is normally incurred to obtain tangible benefits. An 'expense' is that part of cost consumed during the current accounting period, while 'asset' refers to that part of cost expected to bring about benefits during future accounting periods. Human resource costs thus comprise costs incurred to acquire, develop or replace employees, and include expense and asset components.

- Two major cost models have been developed, namely the historical cost model and the replacement cost model. These models are outlined in figures 22.1 and 22.2.
- With regard to HR value models, two concepts require definition. Flamholtz (1985: 174) defines value as the current value of future services. HR value is thus the current value of expected future services to be rendered by employees.

The HR value models can be categorised into the three groups, as shown in exhibit 22.1.

EXHIBIT 22.1: HR value models

Non-monetary behavioural models
- social-psychology indicators approach

Monetary approach
- unpurchased goodwill model
- adjusted present value model
- discounted remuneration model
- discounted wage flows model
- current monetary value model
- group model based on Markov-matrix

Combination of non-monetary behavioural aspects and monetary economic value
- human organisation effectiveness model
- dollarised attitudes model
- behavioural economic outcome model
- behavioural cost model
- stochastic rewards valuation model
- certainty-equivalent net benefits model

Source: Sackman, Flamholtz & Bullen 1989

– Trainee time
– Lost productivity during training
– Formal training
– On-the-job training
– Promotion
– Internal appointment
– Recruitment
– Selection
– Socialisation
Indirect cost
Direct cost
Indirect cost
Direct cost
Learning cost
Acquisition cost
Historical HR cost

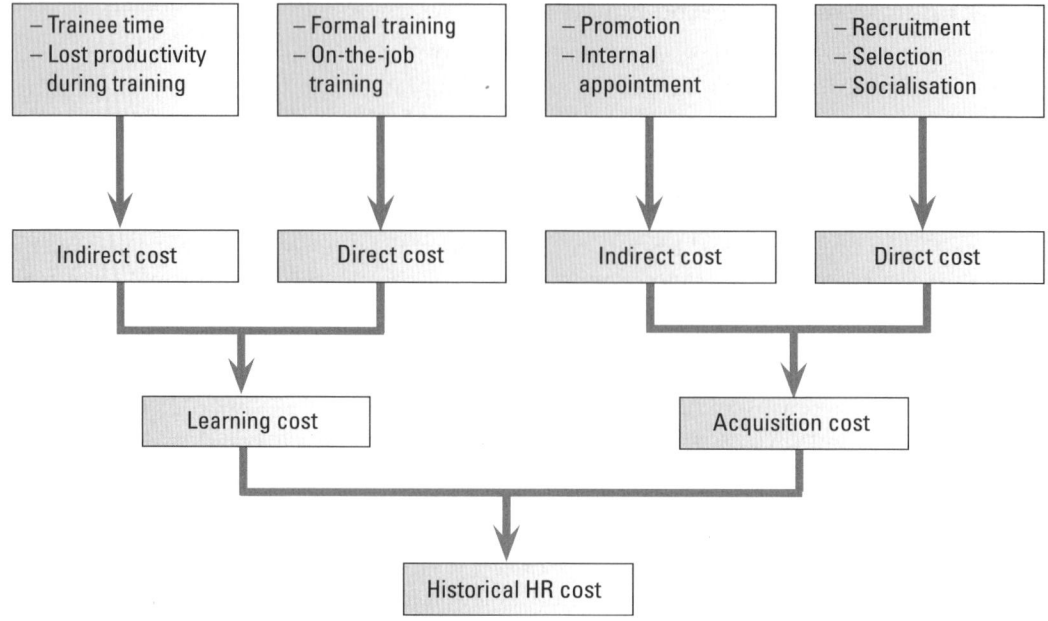

Figure 22.1: Historical cost model

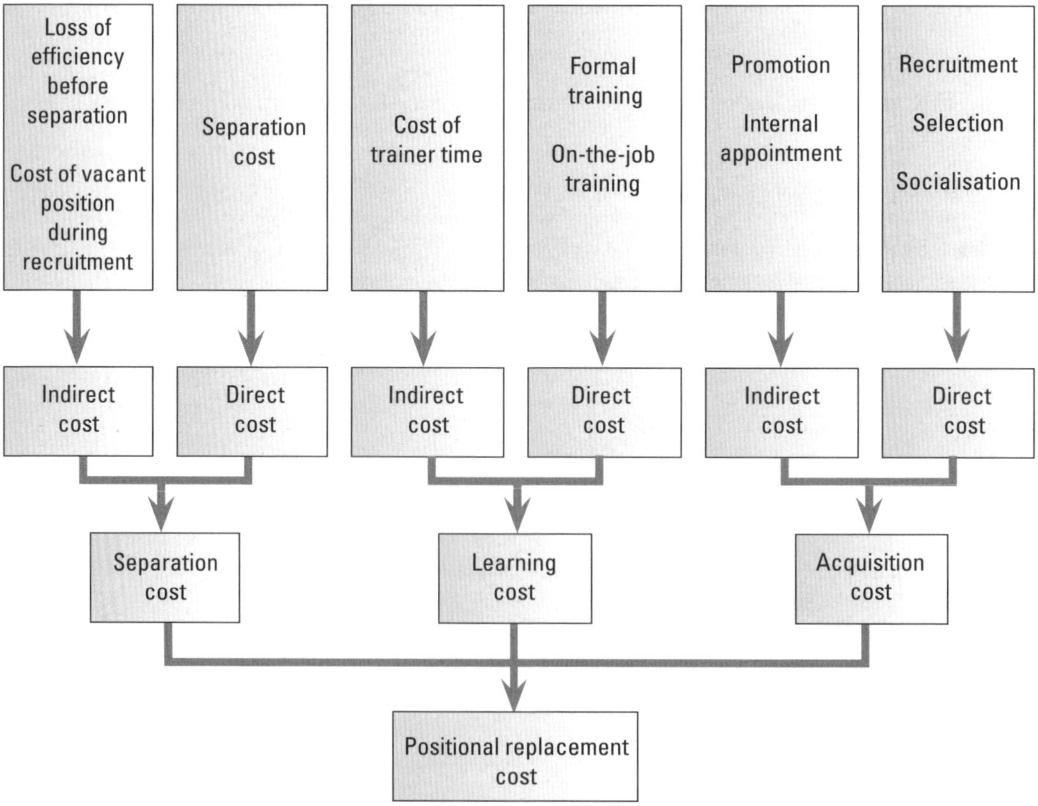

Loss of efficiency before separation
Cost of vacant position during recruitment
Separation cost
Cost of trainer time
Formal training
On-the-job training
Promotion
Internal appointment
Recruitment
Selection
Socialisation
Indirect cost
Direct cost
Indirect cost
Direct cost
Indirect cost
Direct cost
Separation cost
Learning cost
Acquisition cost
Positional replacement cost

Figure 22.2: Replacement cost model

22.3.1.1 Evaluation of the HRA approach

HRA formed the basis for the measurement of HRM, and proponents of this approach played an important role in putting measurement and evaluation on the agenda of HR researchers. It appears, however, that after almost five decades of research, HRA is neither theoretically nor practically operational on a significant level. As Flamholtz (2005: 269–276) acknowledges, HRA has been "in development since the early 1960s ... the development of these measurement methods is a work in progress ... there is a clear and present need to change the perspective of HRM ... This, in turn, will require the further development and application of the measurement tools ... of HRA ... Although the development of HRA is not complete, some progress has been made".

Two general objections can be levelled against HRA:

- The inclusion of human assets, which are regarded as intangible assets, is not provided for in the accounting system. To overcome this problem, an extension of the parameters of accounting is required.
- It seems to be very difficult to establish an operationally acceptable HRA model that conforms to the requirements of validity and reliability.

HRA thus seems to have been unable thus far to become an operational evaluation and measurement approach, but we never know what might happen in the future. A more practical approach at this stage seems to be human resource cost-benefit analysis.

22.3.2 Human resource cost-benefit analysis

Before evaluation can take place, objective measures must be established. Human resource cost-benefit analysis entails developing such measures in order to evaluate HRM costs in terms of time, quantity or quality.

Two factors influence the identification and selection of measures. The first of these is the level of accuracy of measurement required, and the second is the nature of the organisation and thus its specific requirements. The measurements must be of significance and use to the organisation.

A number of important HR activities can thus be highlighted as possibly requiring measurement, including employment costs, costs pertaining to employee development and the costs of labour turnover and absenteeism.

22.3.2.1 Measuring employment costs

A high priority is normally allocated to the employment process, often as a result of legal requirements and the influence of employment on the quality of the workforce. A strong correlation also exists between the quality of employment and the costs related to absenteeism and labour turnover.

The first employment measure analysed here is a cost measure, namely cost per hire (C/H). The cost elements associated herewith are set out in table 22.1.

Determining cost per hire is not as simple as it may appear, and various decisions must be made. As far as source cost is concerned, for example, the cost of one advertisement for one position can easily be allocated to that position. However, when a combination of advertisements is run for more than one position, allocating cost per hire becomes more complex. An advertisement, for instance, may be placed for the positions of supervisor of accounting, senior accountants and bookkeepers. A supervisor, senior accountant and three bookkeepers may be appointed. As it is more complicated to appoint a supervisor than a bookkeeper, the advertisement cost could not simply be divided by five to compute advertisement cost per hire. One way to overcome this problem is to weigh the costs by the salary level of each hire. Then it must be determined whether to use actual salary, entry-level salary or the midpoint of the salary range.

Table 22.1: Cost elements of hiring an employee

Type	Expense
Source cost	Advertising and agency fees paid to generate applicants; hire and/or referral bonuses.
Staff time	Salary, benefits, and standard overhead costs of staff meeting with the manager to discuss sourcing; working with the media and/or agency to commence the search; screening applications, calling applicants in for interviews, interviewing and reference checking; reviewing candidates with the manager and scheduling interviews; making or confirming the offer.
Management time	Salary, benefits, and standard overhead costs of the requesting department relating to planning the sourcing, discussing and interviewing candidates, and making a hiring decision and offer.
Processing cost	Manual or automatic data system cost of opening a new file; cost of medical exams; cost of employment and record verification (mail or telephone), security checks, etc.
Travel and relocation	Travel and lodging costs for staff and candidates; relocation costs.
Miscellaneous	Materials and other special or unplanned expenses. The cost of new employee orientation may be included or considered as part of the training expenses.

No generally accepted method exists for the computation of cost per hire – any of the components included in this table may be excluded or others added according to the needs of the organisation.

According to Fitz-enz (1984: 56), the way the computation is made is not the critical factor. What is important when cost per hire is being calculated over a long period is consistency in the methodology used. Consistency ensures comparable results over time. The basic formula for computing source cost per hire (SCH) is illustrated in exhibit 22.2.

EXHIBIT 22.2: Source cost per hire

Example:

$$\frac{SC}{H} = \frac{AC + AF + RB + NC}{H}$$

$$\frac{SC}{H} = \frac{R28\,000 + R19\,000 + R2\,300 + R0}{119}$$

where:

AC = advertising costs, total monthly expenditure (eg R28 000)

AF = agency fees, total month (eg R19 000)

RB = referral bonuses, total paid (eg R2 300)

NC = no-cost hires, walk-in, non-profit agencies, etc (ie R0)

H = Total hires (eg 119)

Source: Fitz-enz (1984: 61)

Determining the costs of hire for different positions according to the various hiring methods is not sufficient information. What is also important is determining the quality of hires. According to Fitz-enz, a trade-off must be established between the quality of the hire and the time to fill the position. Three measures are important: response time, time to fill and referral factor (see exhibit 22.3).

EXHIBIT 22.3: Determining the quality of hires

Response time

$RT = RD - RR$

Example:

$RT = 22 - 4$
$\quad = 18$ days

where:
RT = response time
RD = date of first qualified candidate referred for interview (eg 22 January)
RR = date the requisition is received (eg 4 January)

Time to fill

$TF = RR - SD$

Example:

$TF = 4$ January $- 10$ March
$\quad = 65$

where:
TF = time to fill the job
RR = date the requisition is received (eg 4 January)
SD = date the new hire starts work (eg 10 March)

Referral factor

$RF = \frac{R}{O}$

Example:

$RF = \frac{76}{22}$
$\quad = 3.5$

where:
RF = referral factor, relationship of candidates to openings
R = number of candidates referred for interview (eg 76)
O = number of openings (eg 22)

Source: Fitz-enz (1984: 70)

In addition to the measurement of the cost and quality of employment, measuring efficiency is also important. A number of efficiency measures are outlined in exhibit 22.4.

Thus far, measures for cost, quality and efficiency of employment have been discussed. It is also important to measure the effectiveness of employment. According to Fitz-enz (1984: 86), a measure of effectiveness is the quality of hire (QH).

Quality of hire:

$$QH = \frac{PR + HP + HS}{N}$$

where:
QH = quality of the people hired
PR = percentage of average job performance ratings of new hires (eg 4 on a 5-point scale = 80%)
HP = percentage of new hires promoted within one year (eg 45%)
HS = percentage of new hires retained after 1 year (eg 90%)
N = number of indicators used (eg 3)

EXHIBIT 22.4: Determining hiring efficiency

Internal hire rate

$$IH = \frac{IA}{H}$$

Example:

$$IH = \frac{49}{76}$$
$$= 64{,}5\%$$

where:
IH = percentage of jobs filled internally
IA = jobs filled by internal applicants (eg 49)
H = total hires (eg 76)

Interview time

$$ALI = \frac{h}{HI}$$

Example:

$$ALI = \frac{6}{5}$$
$$= 1{,}2 \text{ hours}$$

where:
ALI = average length of interviews
h = total hours spent interviewing (eg 6)
HI = total number interviewed (eg 5)

Hit rate

$$HO = \frac{OA}{OE}$$

Example:

$$HO = \frac{42}{50}$$
$$= 84\%$$

where:
HO = percentage of offers which result in a hire
OA = offers accepted (eg 42)
OE = offers extended (eg 50)

Source: Fitz-enz (1984: 75–83)

Example:

$$QH = \frac{80 + 45 + 90}{3}$$
$$= \frac{215}{3}$$
$$= 71{,}7\%$$

The percentage of 71,7 is a relative value. It is up to the person constructing the equation to decide if that number represents high, medium or low quality. The decision can be based on historical comparison, present performance standards or objectives, or management mandates.

22.3.2.2 Measuring training costs

Cascio's (1991) approach is used as an example of the determination of training and development costs. Cascio (1991: 35) identifies three main elements of training costs.

The first is the cost of information/literature (T_1) aimed at formal socialisation and training. This is computed by multiplying the unit cost of information/literature (eg R10) with the number of trainees (eg 300).

$$T_1 = R10 \times 300$$
$$= R3\,000$$

The second is instruction in a formal training programme (T_2). This cost is computed as follows:

$T_2 = (LO \times OV \times AP) + (LV \times CL \times LO)$

where:
LO = length of the training programme (eg 40 hours)
OV = average remuneration rate of trainer(s) (eg R25 per hour)
AP = number of (similar) programmes presented in a year (eg 10)
LV = average remuneration rate per trainee (eg R12 per hour)
CL = number of trainees who participated in the training programmes (eg 300)

Example:
$T_2 = (40 \times R25 \times 10) + (R12 \times 300 \times 40)$
$\quad = R10\ 000 + R144\ 000$
$\quad = R154\ 000$

The third is costs associated with on-the-job training (T_3). Suppose that the trainees (eg 300) are subjected to coaching where two trainees per trained employee are subjected to an on-the-job training period of 60 hours. The remuneration rates of the trainers and trainees are R17 and R12 per hour respectively. While trainers are busy with the on-the-job training, their productivity is lowered by 40%.

$T_3 = 60 \times [(R17 \times 40\% \times 150) + (R12 \times 300)]$
$\quad = 60 \times R1\ 020 + R3\ 600$
$\quad = 60 \times R4\ 620$
$\quad = R277\ 200$

Total training cost (T4) is the summation of the above three elements.
$T_4 = R3\ 000 + R154\ 000 + R277\ 200$
$\quad = R434\ 200$

Two factors must be taken into account in determining training and development costs. The first, according to Cascio (1991: 259), is the differentiation between recurring and non-recurring costs. The development stage of a course prescribed more than once contains cost elements such as equipment (overhead projectors, video machines, etc) and the salaries of course developers, which are incurred only once. The way in which differentiation between costs is made and how the costs are allocated between courses depends on the person doing the accounting. What is important, however, is consistency in determining and allocating recurring and non-recurring training costs.

A second factor to be considered in determining training costs is the computation of the cost of lost productivity time (cost of disruption) while employees involved in the training are away from their jobs. These costs are categorised as opportunity costs, and inclusion thereof in cost models depends on standards of accuracy maintained in cost determination.

Not only the cost but also the benefits of the training and development effort should be measured. Models developed to date for measuring benefits are, however, mostly of a qualitative nature.

As you know, the result or outcome of training can be measured at reaction level, by the change in knowledge, skills, attitudes and work performance (see chapter 15). Information on this may be obtained by means of pre- and post-testing, questionnaires, interviews, observation and performance appraisal.

22.3.2.3 Measuring labour turnover and absenteeism

Three factors must be taken into account when assessing the importance of measuring labour turnover and absenteeism. The first is the impact of labour turnover and absenteeism on HR activities; for example the costs of training and sick leave. Secondly, it is important to note that labour turnover does not only influence the organisation negatively – new employees may also create new ideas and turnover may thus have a cleansing effect on the organisation. A third aspect is that turnover and absenteeism – whether of a voluntary (resignations) or involuntary (dismissals) nature – should be calculated.

Labour turnover

Fitz-enz (1984: 169) proposes two basic measures for labour turnover, namely the accession rate and the separation rate.

Accession and separation rates

$$AR = \frac{H}{E} \qquad\qquad SR = \frac{NT}{E}$$

where:
AR = accession rate
SR = separation rate
H = number hired during the period (eg 725)
NT = number terminated during the period (eg 656)
E = average employee population (eg 3 097)

Example:

$$AR = \frac{725}{3\ 097} \qquad\qquad SR = \frac{656}{3\ 097}$$
$$= 23,4\% \qquad\qquad\qquad = 21,2\%$$

The following are other significant measures for calculating labour turnover.

Stability and instability factors

$$SF = \frac{OS}{E} \qquad\qquad IF = \frac{OL}{E}$$

where:
SF = stability factor of an existing population
OS = original employees who remain for the period, for example 1 year (eg 832)
IF = instability factor of an existing population
OL = original employees who left during the period (eg 80)
E = employee population at the beginning of the period (eg 912)

Example:

$$SF = \frac{832}{912} \qquad\qquad IF = \frac{80}{912}$$
$$= 91,2\% \qquad\qquad\qquad = 8,8\%$$

Obviously, SF and IF are reciprocals. In this case, 91,2% of the employees with 5+ years of service stayed and 8,8% left during the past year. This information can be compared with previous experience, and a value judgement can be made.

The survival or loss rate of new hires is conceptually identical to the stability factor, only here the base population is new hires and not existing employee groups.

Survivor and loss rates

$$SR = \frac{HS}{H} \qquad\qquad LR = \frac{HL}{H}$$

where:
SR = survival rate of new hires
HS = number of new hires from the period who are still employed/stayers (eg 209)
LR = wastage or loss rate
HL = number of new hires who left/leavers (eg 79)
H = total number of new hires during the period (eg 288)

Example:

$$SR = \frac{209}{288} \qquad\qquad LR = \frac{79}{288}$$
$$\quad = 72{,}6\% \qquad\qquad\quad = 27{,}4\%$$

Hall (1981) presents a detailed and practical model for the calculation of labour turnover cost. This is depicted in table 22.2.

The costs attached to labour turnover should never be underestimated. In 1997 it was reported, for instance, that it could cost as much as R4 million to replace a top executive (see exhibit 22.5).

It is therefore often necessary to execute certain measurements relating to labour turnover (and absenteeism).

Absenteeism

For the measurement of absenteeism, two measures are of importance: the absence rate and the labour utilisation levels (Fitz-enz 1984: 164).

Absence rate

$$AR = \frac{WDL}{e \times WD}$$

where:
AR = absence rate
WDL = worker days lost through absence (eg 400)
e = average employee population (eg 550)
WD = number of work days available per employee (eg 22)

Example:

$$AR = \frac{400}{550 \times 22}$$
$$\quad = \frac{400}{12\ 100}$$
$$\quad = 3{,}3\%$$

Table 22.2: Labour turnover cost model

Activity	Cost in rands
1 Recruitment advertising	55 000
2 Agency fees	30 737
3 Internal referrals	14 779
4 Applicant expenses	9 818
5 Relocation expenses	82 132
6 Remuneration of employment personnel	35 200
7 Other employment office expenses	2 300
8 Expenses of recruiters	3 500
9 Direct employment cost (sum of 1–8)	233 466
10 Number of appointments	362
11 Direct cost per appointment (9 ÷ 10)	645
12 Indirect cost per appointment (sum of 18–20)	5 000
13 Total cost per appointment	5 645
14 Number of replacement appointments (labour turnover)	50
15 Total labour turnover costs (13 × 14)1	411 250
16 Target percentage reducement	25%
17 Potential saving (15 × 16)	352 813
18 Cost of management time per appointment	390
19 Training cost per appointment	610
20 Productivity loss (or performance difference)	4 000
21 Total indirect employment cost per appointment	5 000

Source: Hall (1981: 45)

This ratio can be used to find locations where absence levels are relatively high. It can also be applied to job groups to search out types of employees who are often absent. There are two prerequisites that will determine whether or not an absence control programme will work: accurate employee time records and a standard acceptable absence rate.

Effect of absenteeism on labour utilisation

$$U = \frac{Nh}{h}$$

where:
U = labour utilisation percentage
Nh = non-productive hours: absence, breaks, down time, prep time, rework (eg 380 hours)
h = work hours available (eg 10 employees × 40 hours × 4 weeks = 1 600 hours)

EXHIBIT 22.5: Top brass can break the bank

It can cost as much as R4 million to recruit or replace a top executive, according to estimates by Renwick Management Services. The bulk of the cost of recruiting or replacing management is in the cost of training the new employee. The second largest contributor to the cost is the loss of work by the outgoing employee. According to Renwick, it will cost more than R980 000 to replace a technical manager, just over R1 million to replace a marketing or sales manager, around R274 000 to replace an engineering manager, and R328 000 for a financial manager.

Cost estimates of recruiting/replacing management in various disciplines

Cost area	Technical	Market-ing/sales	Engineer-ing	Financial	GM/MD
Writing/production/ placing of one advertisement in the newspaper	R9 000	R9 000	R9 000	R9 000	R9 000
Interviewing applicants	R4 500	R4 500	R4 500	R4 500	R4 500
Response administration	R10 000	R10 000	R10 000	R10 000	R10 000
Testing and checking references	R1 750	R1 750	R1 750	R1 750	R1 750
Loss of work output by departing employee	R105 000[1]	R88 000[1]	R74 000[1]	R93 000[1]	R270 000[1]
Cost of training new employee	R850 000[1]	R930 000[1]	R175 000[1]	R210 000[1]	R3 700 000[1]
TOTAL COST	R980 250	R1 043 250	R274 250	R328 250	R3 995 250

1 Replacement costs calculated on 5% of organisational turnover

Source: *Sunday Times* Business Times, 23 May 1997

Example:

$$U = \frac{380}{1\ 600}$$
$$= 24\% \text{ (utilisation} = 76\%)$$

To show the effect of absenteeism, subtract absent hours (eg 80) from Nh and recompute.

Example:

$$U = \frac{380 - 80}{1\ 600}$$
$$= \frac{300}{1\ 600}$$
$$= 19\% \text{ (utilisation} = 81\%)$$

Utilisation would have been 5% higher if no employees had been absent.

For the calculation of absenteeism cost, a flow diagram devised by Cascio (1991: 61) can also be used. This is presented in figure 22.3.

A number of other areas (for example compensation) can also be subjected to cost-benefit analyses. There are also various other approaches to the evaluation of the organisation's human resource system.

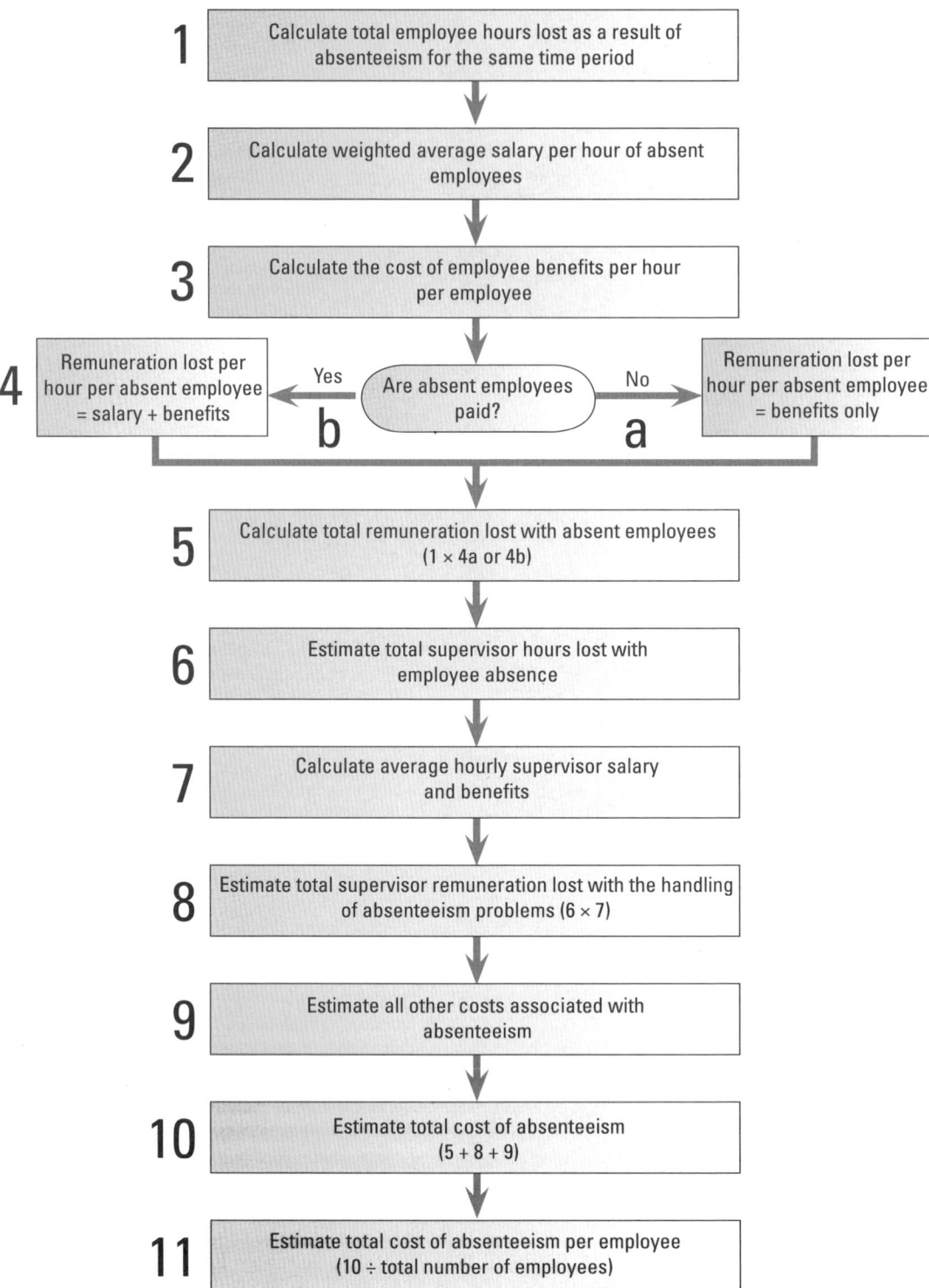

1 Calculate total employee hours lost as a result of absenteeism for the same time period

2 Calculate weighted average salary per hour of absent employees

3 Calculate the cost of employee benefits per hour per employee

4 Remuneration lost per hour per absent employee = salary + benefits **b** ← Yes — Are absent employees paid? — No → **a** Remuneration lost per hour per absent employee = benefits only

5 Calculate total remuneration lost with absent employees (1 × 4a or 4b)

6 Estimate total supervisor hours lost with employee absence

7 Calculate average hourly supervisor salary and benefits

8 Estimate total supervisor remuneration lost with the handling of absenteeism problems (6 × 7)

9 Estimate all other costs associated with absenteeism

10 Estimate total cost of absenteeism (5 + 8 + 9)

11 Estimate total cost of absenteeism per employee (10 ÷ total number of employees)

Figure 22.3: Estimated cost of absenteeism

22.3.3 'Human resource auditing'

Although quite widely used and applied in practice, there is very little agreement in the literature or in the real world about what exactly human resource auditing entails. Likewise there is no agreement as to what exactly it is called. Some refer to an 'HR audit' (for example Stone 2002) and others again to 'auditing HRM' (for example Nankervis, Compton & Baird 2008). Phillips (1996) talks of both 'HR auditing' and the 'human resources audit'. It seems like some use the concept more broadly while there is also a case to be made for using this concept much more specifically.

Pfeffer (1997: 37) takes a broad approach and says the "human resources audit is an investigative, analytical, and comparative process that attempts to reflect the effectiveness of the HR function. It undertakes a systematic search that gathers, compiles, and analyses data in depth for an extended period". According to Stone (2005: 817), an HR audit is "a systematic analysis and evaluation of the efficiency and effectiveness of the HRM function and its contribution to the achievement of the organisation's strategic objectives".

As such, HRA seems to be viewed by some as a comprehensive effort to assess various aspects of the work of the HR function – but as defined narrowly, meaning the work of the group of specialist HR practitioners of the organisation. Typically, HR audits will thus in this sense utilise and yield information on how well the HR department (or section or division) of the organisation performs using different measures. These may include the extent to which the organisation's HRM policies are in compliance with relevant legal requirements and/or the satisfaction and other perceptions in the organisation about the role and quality of the various functions performed by the HR department. From this perspective, the auditing of the HR department might cover all of their work or only selected aspects thereof. It thus seems as though the loose use of the concept 'HR audit' might yield suboptimal results from the perspective of trying to add appropriate value through our evaluation efforts. It should, for example, be noted that Phillips (1996: 38) reaches the following overall conclusion: "In short, it [auditing] is essential and important, yet falls short of a valid approach to measuring the contribution of the [HR] function."

We think the problem may be with terminology in a way. It is important, from our perspective, not to confuse things by using terminology inappropriately. In a recent doctoral study, Andrews (2008: 16) issues a stern warning: "A human resource audit is not a form of management assurance undertaken in relation to the human resource management activities of an organisation. There is a risk that human resource practitioners may claim to be undertaking a human resource 'audit' when they are actually undertaking a 'review'."

From the literature it certainly seems as though this is an accurate 'risk assessment'. Perhaps it would indeed be better to refer to these as 'reviews of HR functions or departments/sections/etc'. As Andrews (2008: 27) says: "Auditing is a distinct activity with a long and distinguished history of independent assurance and auditing activity should not be considered interchangeable with other forms of managerial assurance."

Arens et al (2005: 12) define auditing as "the accumulation and evaluation of evidence about information to determine and report on the degree of correspondence between the information and established criteria. Auditing should be performed by a competent, independent person".

It is our conviction that it would be more appropriate to refer to 'reviews' when the broad and general aspects of assessing aspects (or all) of the HR function (narrowly defined) are at stake. When we use the notion of HR audit, we believe it would be better to stick to the proper meaning of the term 'audit'.

22.3.4 Employee attitude surveys (EAS)

The attitudes, opinions, views, feelings, etc of employees regarding their employment relationships, and issues that may interplay with them, play an important role in determining the behaviour and performance of employees in the work environment. Employee attitude surveys (also referred to in chapter 19) are systematic research-based ways of collecting and analysing information about what employees feel and think about aspects such as their work, their superiors and management, the organisation in general or any other aspect relating to or potentially impacting on their employment relationships. Employee attitude surveys that are professionally conducted can yield information that can be highly beneficial to organisations, such as:

- unknown dissatisfaction and/or grievances;
- suggestions as to areas/aspects of organisational life that may be improved;
- the quality of work–life experiences of employees at different organisational levels and in different parts of the organisation, which can be then determined and compared;
- the state of morale, which may be improved due to staff experiencing that management cares about their views, feelings, opinions, etc (only if they see that such surveys are acted upon); and
- the degree of employee involvement and communication, facilitating accompanying benefits.

Phillips (1996: 34) reports that a study designed to determine the impact of employee surveys on organisations has found that "those organizations responding as more profitable than most of the industry were high users of employee surveys … [T]hose organizations describing themselves as less profitable rarely used surveys".

An employee attitude survey (EAS) can be defined as a systematic, objective investigation into the perceptions, feelings, behaviour, attitudes, opinions, etc of the employees of an organisation.

The rationale underlying such surveys is that, as managers, we have to have knowledge about how satisfied our employees are, about their needs, desires, attitudes, opinions, interests, perceptions and fears. In larger organisations in particular it is not possible to know how your staff feel simply by applying MBWA (management by walking around). In this day and age, when organisations so often assert that their employees are their most valued assets, it becomes increasingly important to pay serious attention to their views, opinions, feelings, ideas, attitudes, etc.

It is unfortunate that some managers tend to shy away from the EAS, especially when everyday indicators such as high absenteeism and staff turnover, generally low morale and motivation levels, and labour productivity problems point to an unhealthy state in organisations. They are generally reluctant to commission this kind of HR research, probably because they fear stirring up more trouble, even though they often instinctively 'know' that they are guilty of neglecting their most valuable assets – the people who work for them. Furthermore, some are reluctant to execute an EAS simply because they really have no idea what such research entails (often thinking that it is some mysterious way of uncovering employees' most secret thoughts and ideas). Some also resist it because they maintain that one cannot precisely measure or accurately use statistics to investigate the human side of the organisation. While there may be some truth in this, we reiterate our contention that quantitative analyses are also important. In EAS, both hard and soft data are usually used (that is, quantitative as well as qualitative).

Although statistical analysis is an important component of employment attitude surveys, information gathered through qualitative processes such as focus groups, unstructured or semi-structured interviews, or brainstorming normally make up a critical part of EAS. In larger organisations with greater numbers of employees it may well be important to have sufficient knowledge of statistics (for example in respect of sampling and measurement scales) in order to execute EAS, but this does not mean that soft data resulting from more unstructured, qualitative research methods must be ignored. On the contrary, in such EASs there is often quite a heavy reliance (in addition to the objective, reliable hard data) on soft data emanating, for instance, from interviews and group processes such as the nominal group technique (NGT).

The hard data is usually collected by means of written questionnaires. It is of crucial importance to design the questionnaire in a professional way, simply because the data thus collected normally constitutes the backbone of the EAS. Before the questionnaire design is finalised, however, a number of other aspects have to be attended to.

First of all it is necessary to be clear what the objectives and underlying reasons for the decision to conduct an EAS are. This will determine the scope of the survey research and thus the specific areas or topics to be investigated. As a rule this requires an initial diagnostic phase which is primarily qualitative. Through group processes and interviews the potential problem areas are detected and the survey population demarcated. The essential purpose is thus to determine the scope and nature of the EAS; the information gathered is used to construct or adapt the questionnaire. During this phase it is very important to make all the stakeholders part of the process by involving all of them. This may include top management, other levels of management and the workers themselves, as well as their representatives. In some instances it may even involve discussions with customers, suppliers or consultants, and subcontractors who may have relevant knowledge. Ownership and commitment from all stakeholders are thus essential ingredients and, right from the very first moment, the participation of all the stakeholders' representatives is of crucial importance.

Once the questionnaire has been finalised (this may be after a pilot study), it is distributed to all relevant employees. If possible the questionnaire should be distributed to all employees. This may not always be feasible, and sampling may sometimes be necessary. Be that as it may, it is important to follow up and to ensure a high rate of return of completed questionnaires. Often it is wise to let relevant employee groups complete the questionnaire at specific time slots so that an expert can assist with the completion of the questionnaires. This very often requires the assistance of an interpreter, especially if the workers are illiterate.

Once the questionnaires have been completed, the data are computerised, processed and interpreted. The findings (results and conclusions) are then normally presented in report format. This may include recommendations; alternatively, all the stakeholders could discuss, debate and brainstorm the findings in order to arrive at decisions regarding subsequent action. The emphasis of this kind of HR research has to be on action. The intelligence generated by the research should lead to the necessary action to improve the human dimension of the organisation.

22.3.5 The 'HR scorecard' and the 'workforce scorecard'

Becker, Huselid and Ulrich (2001: xi – x) say that as HR professionals respond to the challenge of taking a more strategic approach to their role in organisations, "measuring HR's performance and its contribution to the firm's performance emerges as a key theme ... the capacity to design and implement a strategic HR measurement system – what we call ... an *HR Scorecard* – represents an important lever that firms can use to design and deploy an effective HR strategy … [B]eing held accountable for results through measurement can be threatening … The most effective way we know to change the calculus is to develop a measurement system designed to link people, strategy, and performance".

These authors then devote their entire book to the challenges related to designing and implementing such a strategic level measurement and evaluation system. In doing so, they draw on comprehensive and in-depth research and practical experience from actual cases of organisations that have put in the required efforts to design and implement such an evaluation and measurement approach.

The approach of Becker et al (2001) is quite comprehensive, countering some of the criticisms against a case for measuring and evaluating HRM as cited earlier in the chapter – but it still has a narrow focus in the sense of focusing on the 'HR function' as the work of the 'HR professionals', as they call them. They describe a seven-step process to first of all lay a solid foundation for making the HR department/ section a strategic role player and partner in organisations. They then go on to use and apply concepts such as alignment, efficiency and value creation to develop an HR Scorecard.

The HR Scorecard builds on the principles of the balanced scorecard of Kaplan and Norton (1996). As explained in chapter 11, the latter is basically a system for strategic control designed around measures that cover the value-creation process rather than relying only on the financial (accounting-based) results and performance of an organisation. It proposes the measurement of organisational performance on four broad areas, namely financial (for example return on capital employed), the customer (for example customer loyalty), the internal/business processes (for example process quality and process cycle time) and, as they call it, "learning and growth" (for example employee skills). The balanced scorecard also specifically emphasises the importance of focusing on both *lagging* and *leading* indicators. Whereas traditionally, organisational performance/measurement systems have focused almost exclusively on financial measures indicating what has happened in the past (*lagging* performance indicators), the balanced scorecard approach proposes a system that also builds in measures that focus on the future – assessing the key success factors that act as performance drivers in the future (the *leading* performance indicators).

The HR Scorecard is a measurement system that incorporates these same principles. A distinction is made between measuring HRM 'do-ables' (the enablers) and HRM 'deliverables' (the results that drive organisational performance). The process thus includes answering questions such as:

- What are our strategic goals for the organisation?
- How will we achieve these goals – what must the business strategy entail?
- How will we measure our performance (of strategy implementation) as we progress towards goal achievement?
- What type of employee behaviour and performance is required to enable us to implement the strategy successfully?
- What does the HR function need to do in order to enable employees to behave and perform as required (the 'enablers'/'do-ables')?
- What does it currently do in this regard?
- What needs to change?

Questions such as these, say Becker, Huselid and Ulrich (2001: 41), "can generate a wealth of information about how well a firm's HR function is contributing (adding value) to the organisation's strive to being successful". They (2001: 41) go on to suggest "supplementing these discussions with a variety of other information-gathering tools, including questionnaires to test employees' understanding of the HRM's goal surveys to generate additional data about the firm's performance drivers and organisational capabilities". A crucial aspect in this approach is therefore to design the actual measures.

As Becker et al (2001: 48) explain:

> To measure the HR-firm performance relationship with precision you need to develop valid measures of HR deliverables. This task has two dimensions. First, you have to be confident that you have chosen the correct HR performance drivers and enablers. This requires that you clearly comprehend the causal chain for effective strategy information ... Second, you have to choose correct measures for those deliverables.

The HR Scorecard philosophy is to further create a balance between cost control measures (measuring HRM efficiencies – such as source cost per hire and/or hiring efficiency) and value-creation measures. The latter may include measures built around information yielded by HRM reviews, such as the quality of hiring decisions in terms of the number of appeals or CCMA cases lodged (and/or lost). It may also include competency profiling measures, such as the percentage of staff who have the requisite competencies. It may also include a measure such as an employee satisfaction index and the percentage of staff turnover in the organisation.

In essence, then, the HR Scorecard approach entails the development of a rather comprehensive measurement system that can help evaluate the performance of the HR division or department from operational as well as strategic perspectives. It is still, however, an approach that falls short of actually making that connection between the role of the specialist HR practitioners of the organisation and the actual work of the line managers who manage their people.

In an effort to address this perceived shortcoming, Huselid et al (2005) have developed what they term the 'workforce scorecard'. They (Huselid et al 2005: 5) explain that "our experiences with HR professionals and line managers in designing and implementing HR scorecards in a wide variety of firms and industries have made it clear to us that firm success requires an increased emphasis on the role of the workforce and line managers ... While HR professionals ... lay the foundation for building the workforce into a strategic asset, the responsibility for workforce success increasingly falls to line managers".

The four key elements of a workforce scorecard, according to Huselid et al (2005: 70), are the following (and this is where we should build or develop and apply/target our measuring efforts):

1 *The mindset and culture of the workforce*
   The question we need to ask to measure this is: How well does our workforce understand and embrace the organisation's strategy, and to what extent do we have an organisational culture that is conducive to strategy execution?
2 *The competencies of the workforce*
   The question we need to ask to measure this is: Does our workforce, especially our core workforce, possess the competencies and capabilities that we require for strategy execution?
3 *The behaviour of the workforce and the leadership team*
   The essential questions to guide our measuring efforts here are: Do we have a leadership team and rest of the workforce behaving in ways that will lead our

organisation to attaining our strategic goals? Have we nurtured our top talented people in the core workforce to be able to do so?

4 *The success of the workforce*

The final question is: Has our workforce accomplished our organisation's strategic goals and objectives?

These same authors (Huselid et al 2005: 133–146) also spell out five key principles for developing our workforce measurement system, namely:

- The measures must answer an important strategic question.
- Be careful with the feasibility–validity trade-off.
- Think in terms of relationships among metrics before thinking about levels of the metrics.
- Workforce measurement is not just HR's responsibility.
- Focus on the vital few.

The first principle thus essentially says that we should adopt a strategic approach to our measurement and evaluative efforts. The last three principles are pretty self-explanatory but it is the second principle that we wish to stress here. It basically says that we should rather measure (and develop measures) that are feasible (or 'optimal'), than not to measure at all because we cannot really get things measured 'perfectly' yet. Huselid et al (2005: 137) explain:

> The feasibility–strategic validity trade-off is a particular challenge now because some managers and HR professionals don't feel they have the competency to develop measures of workforce success on their own, nor does their firm have the IT capability or software to easily implement the measures. This is gradually changing. The trade-off is slowly becoming less severe as software options improve and knowledge of workforce measurement becomes more widespread. For now, however, developing and implementing a set of workforce measures that truly have value to both the CEO and HR professionals remains a challenge. That's why so few firms do it well.

22.4 HUMAN RESOURCE INFORMATION SYSTEMS, RECORD KEEPING AND INFORMATION TECHNOLOGY

Human resource record and information systems are important in facilitating decision making in all areas related to the management of employment relationships and also in facilitating feedback to other stakeholders regarding HR-related matters.

Although in the past, and in some instances still today (such as in very small organisations), HR records used to be maintained through manual systems. Today such record-keeping systems cannot adequately fulfil the important role being played by HR information. This is especially true in the context of the trend towards more strategic HRM.

With the increasing importance of HR issues in general strategic and business planning and decision making, the capacity of human resource information systems (HRISs) to organise, store, process and manipulate employee-related data has become very important. To be of value to any organisation, the information must, however, be kept up to date and be complete, correct, flexible and accessible. Well-designed, sophisticated and properly utilised and maintained HRISs – especially if they are computerised – can play a major role in aligning HR-related goals and management practices with the business strategies and goals of the organisation as a whole.

22.4.1 The need for HR-related records and information

The overall purpose of any HRIS must surely be to provide the users (that is, all the HR staff as well as top, middle and lower management, and also workers and their representatives) with the relevant information that they need in order to make sound decisions about the management of employment relationships. The point of departure for any organisation is thus to analyse the kinds of HR-related decisions made within the organisation and the types of HR information that such decisions require. After all, as we mentioned at the start of this chapter, good HRM decisions require good HR information.

All HR-related decisions require information. However, this information need not necessarily be complex and comprehensive. Those instances when more detailed information is actually required include forecasts of personnel needs (supply and demand) which are undertaken in the process of workforce planning and the compilation of data about jobs for job specifications (which must always be kept up to date). Similarly, records about each individual employee (for example biographical data, career history, tax details, absenteeism record, pension and medical information) must be maintained. There is also a general need to keep some form of collective database on the workforce as a whole, covering aspects such as numbers, job grades, occupations, labour turnover and absenteeism rates, total wage/salary bill, training records, overtime statistics and demographic characteristics of the staff (for example age, education, race and gender distributions). All of these aspects require a good HRIS.

22.4.2 Definition of a human resource information system

An HRIS is used to systematically collect, organise, store, maintain, retrieve and validate all human resource-related data that may be needed in the process of managing employment relationships.

Such a system need not always be computerised (such as when we have a small firm with, say, five or so employees), but generally in this technology era this is what should rather be used. We can refer to such computerised systems as a 'CHRIS' (**c**omputerised **h**uman **r**esource **i**nformation **s**ystem), but that is not the common jargon used nowadays. Because technology is so freely available, it is almost assumed that when we refer to an HRIS, we mean that it is a computerised system. Nel et al (2008: 574), for instance, say: "A[n] HRIS is a computerised system that collects, stores, analyses, distributes and retrieves information about employees and their jobs."

An HRIS is usually part of the organisation's larger management information system (MIS), which would then also be computerised. These are sometimes also integrated with organisation's internet and intranet facilities.

22.4.3 Value of an HRIS

A number of potential benefits can be derived from the proper utilisation of a well-designed HRIS within an organisation. These include greater speed, the reduction of errors, increases in efficiency and reductions in costs (paperwork will be reduced, forms may be standardised and information is generated and gathered faster). As mentioned already, an HRIS can be used as a tool in strategic planning. Information technology is so advanced nowadays that many functions and operations can be performed which were impossible when manual systems were the only systems available. HRISs can link with other information systems and, in this way, provide valuable information to decision makers and alert them to potential complexities and dynamics. Computerised systems are also much more flexible and can be more easily manipulated to suit the needs of the data users. An HRIS is also much more mobile in the sense that it can allow communication between various organisations or link different parts of an organisation which may be spread across international borders. Generally speaking, the greatest value of an HRIS lies in the fact that it speeds up decision making and saves on administrative costs.

22.4.4 The process of managing an HRIS

Changing to a more computerised HR information system can be a significant intervention requiring careful management. It is imperative that top management supports such a change. The HR department could take overall responsibility for the change intervention, although they will depend a lot on the information technology specialists for technical assistance. In this regard, Krige (1999: 20–21) mentions the importance of the HR and information technology (IT) specialists following a partnership approach in the process of HRIS development and implementation. He, however, makes it clear that

> HR executives need to take charge of HRIS selection, implementation and utili-sation. They need to ensure that systems are configured to support HR strate-gies and not simply to support basic features such as payroll. Also the ongoing maintenance and utilisation of HRIS needs to be built into standard HR pro-cesses in the company ... HR executives have a responsibility to ensure that they and their managers thoroughly understand their computerised human resource information systems (Krige 1999: 21).

In such an intervention a number of important steps must be followed. Kavanagh, Guetal and Tannenbaum (1990) have identified three main phases in this process, namely needs analysis, design and development, and implementation and maintenance.

22.4.4.1 Conducting the needs analysis

This phase is extremely important and involves a number of activities. First of all, one must evaluate the HR information needs of the HR department and of the organisation as a whole. It must be ascertained how well HR operations are being performed and whether an HRIS could bring about improvements. The current state of automation must also be established and it must be ascertained whether similar HR computer applications exist elsewhere in the company. It must always be borne in mind that a new or improved HRIS should support the company's goals, strategies and business, and thus provide better services to the organisation's clients. The next step is to form a project team who will guide the intervention from start to finish. Another important issue is to determine the automation needs. The key here is to identify and prioritise the exact needs. According to the results of the needs analysis, detailed system specifications should be drawn up, specifying the desired outputs, inputs and system processing requirement. It is also necessary to analyse current and future reporting needs by determining what reports are currently being used, what types of reports are needed, and how these will be changing.

All of this will culminate in a request for proposal (RFP) document. This document specifies what the organisation's needs are, and invites vendors to submit proposals regarding how they will meet these needs and what the costs will be. In this way computer packages offered by various vendors are evaluated. It is important not to change the vendor at a later stage, as this may give rise to many problems. After this, a proposal will be submitted to management. The proposal will include an indication of costs and other necessary resources in comparison with the potential benefits expected to be derived from the system.

With the completion of the needs analysis phase, the second phase (that is, the design and development of the system) can be initiated.

22.4.4.2 Designing and developing the system

The design/development phase can be executed with or without the assistance of external vendors. It is, however, important for the relevant HR staff to be involved throughout. Generally speaking, a proper project management approach should be followed which means making use of project teams. As we have said, it is important for relevant specialist HR staff to be members of this project team.

During this phase a detailed project plan is developed, user groups are identified and the hardware is purchased once it has been determined what software will be used to meet the processing and storage requirements of the data. The evaluation of appropriate software packages should be guided by factors such as ease of access, back-up support, guides for users and their general user friendliness.

One very critical step in the process is the establishment of procedures and guidelines to support the system. These must reflect organisational realities and the system's limitations. It is also important to conduct a test run of the system. The necessary data must then be entered into the system. If an organisation, for example, has job codes, each job and its respective code should be entered into a job table on the HRIS.

22.4.4.3 Implementing and maintaining the HRIS

Once it has been established that the system has been set up successfully (in other words, after having conducted pilot or dummy runs), the system has to be made available for use. Certainly the most important aspect of managing an HRIS is to ensure that it is used correctly in order to improve HRM decisions. An important task is thus to provide users with information about the new system and to train them so as to overcome initial resistance. Support to users is important, for example through easy-to-understand manuals, guidelines and procedures, and through providing an easily accessible support system such as a telephone hotline.

An extremely important aspect of system maintenance is to continuously evaluate the system's effectiveness. Techniques that can be used include error analysis, user surveys and audit reports. Evaluating the system over time may lead to a decision to update the HRIS at some stage or to replace it with something else. In such cases the cycle discussed above may thus have to be repeated.

22.4.5 HRM application areas of HRISs

Computerised HR information systems can be used in almost all the areas of HRM, including various personnel administrative matters, workforce planning, employment (recruitment and selection), performance management, training and development, career management, remuneration and labour relations. Only a few areas of application are elaborated upon here.

22.4.5.1 Strategic HRM application areas

Although it is still a largely neglected area (relative to more traditional application areas as spelt out below), there is a huge potential for applying and utilising HRISs for the purposes of various strategic HRM-related issues. Organisational design simulations can, for instance, be facilitated, potential causes and effects that may flow from structural changes such as de-layering and switching to more flexible workforces may also be tracked. Restructuring and reorganisation projects such as downsizing, mergers and re-engineering all have major workforce capacity and concomitant staff deployment implications – in all of which HRISs can fulfil a valuable role if properly utilised. The whole issue of HRM devolution – giving HRM back to line (see chapter 6) – is facilitated by the proper use of computer technology. As Krige (1999: 20) points out: "User-friendly interfaces to HR information via internet screens provide the opportunity to shift the responsibility for many traditional HR functions to line managers".

An aspect such as workforce planning which, as explained in chapter 6, has to be directly linked to general strategic business planning for the organisation, also holds the potential for extensive HRIS applications.

With the help of an HRIS, projections and estimates of future labour supply and demand can be undertaken professionally by extrapolating current staffing levels and skill mixes, turnover, promotions and other staff movements. Part of this process involves skills inventories which answer questions such as whether the organisation will have enough people (also in particular from 'designated' groups) with specific competencies to accomplish production goals and affirmative action targets over a specified period. The core competencies of the organisation can thus be matched with the competency profiles of the workforce, leading to what Krige (1999: 18) refers to as "resourcing for strategic advantage".

Another strategic issue relates to becoming a 'learning organisation' in this knowledge and information-driven era (see section below).

22.4.5.2 Tracking and recruiting job applicants

The HRIS could maintain information on vacancies and candidates for those jobs. In this way applicants can be tracked, and information on their résumés can help match candidates on file to the vacant jobs. Lists of potential candidates can be sent to any manager who has a vacancy. The HRIS can thus carry certain data on individual employees, such as name, address, experience, skills, age, etc. It may also contain data on results of selection tests, reference checks, interview results and any previous job offers.

22.4.5.3 Human resource development and learning

An individual's training and development needs can be compared with the training and development options available within an organisation. On the basis of the personal development plans (PDPs), the subordinates', the peers', the superiors' and others' evaluations of training needs of employees can be put onto the system. The training component of an HRIS can be quite extensive, carrying complete training course information on relevant internal and external courses, training course evaluation data, instructors, costs, room assignments and employees scheduled to participate. Individual records can also be captured, such as educational achievements, further studies and degree certifications, courses taken in-house and outside, results of courses and areas of multiskilling. This and other information can be used as part of the organisation's career management system, as well as for workforce planning purposes.

Krige (1999: 18–19) explains how HRISs can help to encourage a culture of learning in organisations:

> Organisations that can learn faster than their competitors are those that will survive … CHRISs can be powerful enablers in creating this climate. Modules

such as training and organisational design set out career paths that indicate the competencies required … This information not only creates the incentives that staff require to pursue further learning, but also shows them the direction that this learning should take. If this is supported by on-line training reservation systems and access to training material via Internet-type technology, a powerful mechanism for learning can be created via the CHRIS.

22.4.5.4 Remuneration administration

One very common area of application is that of wages, salary and fringe benefit administration. Electronically driven payroll systems are very common and there are numerous software packages that are affordable to even the smallest of companies. HRISs are typically used to administer salary structuring (grades and salary ranges), to track and control various incentive, bonus and commission schemes, and to administer employee share ownership plans (ESOPs).

22.4.5.5 Other application areas

The spectrum of potential application areas is actually almost probably as broad as the field of HRM itself. It stretches from the basics of capturing and managing all our employees' personal data, to capturing and displaying, for example, organograms that reflect organisational structures and reporting lines. We can manage all the information related to our labour relations dynamics (such as trade unions involved, numbers of members per trade union, collective agreements as such) as well as in relation to matters such as occupational health and safety, and general employee wellness issues. Similarly we can have modules that specifically relate to our organisation's career and performance management systems. We can capture, track and monitor relevant statistics related to issues such as absenteeism, time-keeping, and grievance and disciplinary records. As we have said, the scope is really probably almost only limited by the imagination, and IT and concomitant software developments are improving the capacities of these systems on an ongoing basis. This is happening to such an extent that some are whispering ideas about 'electronic HRM'.

22.4.5.6 Towards 'e-HR functions'?

It is becoming an increasingly popular option to design and implement multimodal systems that enable organisations to have numerous traditional functions of the HR department executed electronically. Lawler (2005: 147) says the following: "Organizations can increasingly create electronically enabled HR systems that are largely self-service when it comes to basic HR administration. There is little doubt that a strong Web capability is the cheapest and fastest way to provide HR administration services." Such systems can thus easily help with establishing and running structures like HR shared services centres as discussed in chapter 5. Importantly, a move towards e-HR administration can improve service delivery because various user-friendly employee self-help modules can be directly accessed by staff (such as applying for leave or sick leave or enquiring about leave availability). There can be basic areas accessible to staff that provide, for example, common HRM policy question-and-answer sections. All of these can serve to reduce more routine and administrative HRM work, freeing up the specialist HR practitioners to devote more energy to work that adds more value to the organisation.

Elsewhere in Africa

How technology is affecting the discharge of HRM functions is the final HRM challenge we see emerging in Africa. Large quantities of employee data ... can easily be stored on personal computers and manipulated using user-friendly spreadsheets or statistical software packages ... Although computer usage and connectivity in Africa is not yet at the high levels prevalent in much of the West, the continent's recognition and appreciation of its vital role towards improved work performance is growing. Electronic Human Resource Management (e-HRM) refers to the processing and transmission of digitized information used in HRM ... For example, two Zambian employees of National Breweries (producers of the wildly popular local beer called Chibuku) work in two different parts of Zambia: one is at the company's plant in Mbala, in the Northern Province, while the other is at its Choma plant, some 1,000 kilometres away in the Southern Province. They do not necessarily have to meet at the company's plant in Lusaka, the capital, for them to work together. They can use computers to do this.

Source: Extracted from Muuka & Mwenda (2004: 48–49).

22.5 HUMAN RESOURCE RELATED REPORTING

Through an HR report an organisation can provide various stakeholders with information about the organisation's human resources and issues relating to its HRM system. As a rule such a report will be contained in the organisation's annual report, which serves as the main corporate vehicle for providing information to stakeholders such as shareholders, employees, potentially interested investors and the general public.

In a world dominated by financial and bottom-line concerns, the HR report used to be thought of as the Cinderella in the corporate reporting stakes. One possible reason for the traditional neglect is that a 'standard' for an HR report has not yet been established. However, employment equity legislation does lay down requirements relating to the reporting of human resource-related information. While a frame of reference exists for providing financial information through relevant financial statements (balance sheet, income statement, value-added statement, etc), a similar coherent frame of reference for human resource related information is still lacking.

In this section a brief overview is provided of initiatives to improve corporate accountability on human resources. Reference is made to the King Reports on Corporate Governance and some early research in South Africa, and we also provide a recent example of reporting on HRM and sustainability issues (in the Appendix to this chapter).

22.5.1 Greater accountability in respect of the human resource: background

22.5.1.1 The King Reports

Following the publication of the Cadbury Committee Report on Corporate Governance in England, in December 1992 the Institute of Directors in South Africa established a committee to investigate corporate governance in South African organisations. Mervyn E King, chairman of the Frame Group of companies, served as chairman of this committee, which subsequently became known as the King Committee.

The final version of the first King Committee Report was published in November 1994 following widespread consultation and comment. The recommendations of that King Committee were widely reported on, and enjoyed much acclaim in the business and financial press. One of its major recommendations dealt specifically with the need for transparency and greater accountability on human resources:

> Reports and communication must be made in the context that society now demands transparency and greater accountability from corporations in regard to their nonfinancial affairs, for example, their workers ..." (King Committee 1994: 29).

The first King Report also clearly identified corporate stakeholders as including "shareholders, employees, bankers, suppliers, customers, environmentalists, the community or country in which it operates and the State". It then went on to suggest that the director's reports (annual report) should be directed at all stakeholders and not only shareholders. In this regard the content of a human resource report is likely to be influenced by the information requirements of its particular stakeholders.

The first King Report also gave some indication of the type of issues to be addressed in a report to all stakeholders: "... employment, such as staffing levels, skills levels, new jobs created, retrenchments, affirmative action policy, unionisation, training programmes, etc". The same report further recommended that information be supported by figures. It therefore suggested that the tendency to adopt only a narrative approach in reporting on human resource issues be supported by quantified information. It was recommended that "... a balance between the positive and negative aspects of the activities of the company ..." be attained. This recommendation supports the notion that organisations develop a human resource 'balance sheet' reflecting both the positive (asset) as well as the negative (liability) side of their human resources.

Although the first King Report did not identify all the issues to be addressed in HRM reports, the need for a comprehensive report dealing with HRM issues was clearly indicated.

The second King Report (King II) in 2002 did not show anything to really deviate from this trend. In fact, the King II Report clearly accentuates the human and social aspect though adopting the 'triple bottom line' instead of 'the bottom line' (as per the King I Report). The need for adopting a stakeholder view, and hence a more integrated and inclusive approach to governing South African organisations, emphasises that employees and communities, among others, are very important stakeholders. It therefore becomes essential for organisations to accept this more comprehensive accountability and report on various 'social-' (and hence human-) related aspects, such as pertaining to social responsibility, ethics, fairness, and non-discrimination and transparency. The importance of fair labour practices is pertinently referred to in the King II Report (2002: 10). According to Meyer and Kirsten (2005: 278–279), other aspects related to HRM that can be detected from the King II Report (2002) are linked to aspects such as ensuring that appropriate skills are put in place, that the integrity and values of people should be considered in the processes involved in employing such people and that appropriate organisational cultures and value systems should be developed.

22.5.1.2 The Employment Equity Act

As explained already, the Employment Equity Act (EEA) requires designated employers to submit reports to the Director General (DG) of the Department of Labour (DoL) that will include the organisation's EE plans. Organisations employing more than 150 employees first had to submit their reports by mid-2000, and thereafter submit progress reports annually on the first working day of October. Organisations employing fewer than 150 employees were required to submit their initial or first reports by the end of 2000 and subsequent progress reports once every two years (biennially) on the first working day of October.

These reports should contain detailed information regarding various aspects – including all those that are required to be contained in an EE plan in terms of section 20 of the EEA – such as, apart from general organisational information (for example the name of the organisation, type of business/industry, organisation structures, etc), detailed information about:

■ occupational and job categories;
■ job evaluation systems;
■ number of positions per occupational category;
■ staff composition per occupational category (in terms of variables such as race, gender and disability);
■ job entry requirements (job specifications);
■ comparative industry, regional and national demographics for benchmarking purposes;
■ general economic and financial factors relevant to the industry or sector and the organisation;
■ employment equity objectives, strategies, policies and programmes;
■ relevant targets, timetables and action plans;
■ employee-related costs (remuneration levels and income differentials), recruitment and selection costs, and training and development expenditures; and
■ diversity training.

It should also be noted that a designated public company must include a summarised employment equity report in its annual financial report.

22.5.1.3 Quantifying human resource information

As mentioned already, a narrative approach when reporting on HRM issues has been favoured for quite a long time in previous decades. Such information is often vague. For this reason it may be a good idea to stand up to the 'metrics' challenge also discussed earlier, and to also report appropriate quantified data.

It is suggested that quantifying HRM-related information makes it less vague. Statements such as 'The organisation has spent R5,5 million on training' or '9 900 person-days have been spent on training' are less vague than 'A major contribution, in terms of time and money, is being made towards people development'. Quantified information allows for clear interpretation, ease of analysis and accurate comparison.

Accountability with regard to HRM issues can be greatly improved by quantifying information and expressing it in terms of aspects such as those covered in earlier sections of this chapter.

22.5.1.4 Towards a definition of 'accountability in HRM'

Within the context of the foregoing and the country's drive to devolve democracy to lower levels of society, and in light of the importance of greater overall transparency in this process, we can conceptualise accountability in respect of HRM issues as follows:

The obligation imposed on the management of an organisation to identify, measure, record, and provide relevant information to stakeholders about the organisation's human resources in terms of its responsibility to attract, employ, develop, utilise, reward and care for this resource effectively, efficiently and fairly.

22.5.2 The HRM report vs the employee report

Because of the current practice to produce an employee report in addition to an annual report, it is necessary to distinguish between the two.

The HRM section within an annual report is one which contains comprehensive information about an organisation's human resources. When the King Committee recommended greater transparency and accountability from corporations with regard to their non-financial affairs, it was in fact making a case for the inclusion of, inter alia, a human resource report, a social responsibility report and an environmental report as part of the annual report.

An employee report, on the other hand, can be thought of as a layman-friendly version of the annual report, and can be produced in addition to the annual report. The content of the employee report usually covers the whole spectrum of an organisation's activities with the intention of creating an awareness on the part of all employees of the financial and economic factors affecting the organisation's performance. The employee report addresses the information needs of the employee as a corporate stakeholder. The focus is on providing information in a format that enhances understanding.

22.5.3 Early research in South Africa towards establishing a frame of reference for HRM reporting

Well over a decade ago already, Visser (1995) undertook research to determine how companies portray their human resources in their annual reports. The objective of the research was to establish a frame of reference for HRM reporting based on current practices.

An analysis was made of the 1993 annual reports of 362 companies in South Africa. Most of the companies identified in the *Financial Mail* 1994 Special Survey of Top Companies were included in this analysis. A comparative analysis was also made of the annual reports of 44 selected companies from 17 foreign countries. In the process, valuable perspectives were gained of the HRM reporting practices within the corporate world. Through this research it was also possible to develop a structure and format for an HRM report which can go a long way towards meeting the requirements of comprehensiveness and relevance. The format suggested in the survey is based on Visser's research.

22.5.3.1 Human resource accountability rating

In order to answer the questions 'How accountable are organisations with regard to their human resources?' or 'How well are organisations doing in reporting on their human resources?', it is advisable to adopt a particular standard and to utilise an appropriate evaluation instrument. One such instrument has been developed (refer to table 22.4). Through this instrument a human resource accountability rating has been determined, which is defined as follows:

The *human resource accountability rating* (HRAR) is a numerical value, determined through a given standard or 'mark plan', indicating the extent to which relevant HR information is provided to organisation stakeholders, usually through and included in the annual report, thus reflecting the organisation's accountability regarding their human resources.

By applying this instrument to the 1994 annual reports of 337 companies, most of which are listed on the JSE, it was possible to gain a picture of the extent to which companies provide information about their human resources. This research indicated that only 7% of the companies reviewed had an HRAR of more than 20. A rating of 20 – out of a maximum of 90 – implies that at least some information had been provided about the organisation's human resources. Only three companies had an HRAR of more than 30: Anglo-alpha (45), Adcock Ingram (33) and Sasol (31). Of the companies reviewed, 71% had an HRAR of eight or less, indicating that very little human resource information had been provided. The conclusion reached was that South African companies are not accountable with regard to their human resources.

It has been suggested that part of the reason for this has been the absence of a 'generally accepted human resource practice' (GAHRP), which could provide guidelines to HR practitioners and general managers on how to compile and present human resource information. It is also suggested that an effective HRM report will not only reflect people utilisation within an organisation but will also enhance leadership and HRM in general.

22.5.4 The HRM report: a possible framework

On the basis of the current practices in HRM reporting in annual reports, determined through research, the following basic structure for providing HRM related information could be considered.

22.5.4.1 Supporting information

The value of the HR component of an organisation is underscored by the current practice of providing information on human resources outside the proposed HR report. This practice should be encouraged. Such additional information can be provided in the following sections of the annual report.

Mission statement

It has become common practice to include the mission statement in the annual report. It is assumed that human resources will be clearly reflected in this statement.

Chairperson or chief executive statement

It is likely that the chairperson's statement will address human resources on a strategic level. Issues to be addressed could then include broad strategies in respect of HR and labour relations management; job creation strategies; affirmative action strategies and programmes; strategies to eliminate discrimination in the workplace; staff development; people productivity, etc. Reference could also be made to strategic HR issues on an industry or national level. In this regard the chairperson's statement is likely to reflect a vision or perspective of the future.

Executive management

It is a statutory requirement that the names of directors be included in the annual report. Additional information on the directors is usually also included, for example age, qualifications, date appointed as director, experience and portfolio within the company. The same information is also provided in respect of senior management.

Table 22.4: Human resource accountability: annual report evaluation mark plan

	A	B
Company: Year: Listing category: Number of employees: HR in chairperson's report (1); HR in CE's report (1); Operational report on HR (2); Other location: . . . .(2)(max 4)		
Mission statement (max) HR objectives stated (2) Attitude toward HR statement (2)	4	
Senior management (max) Information provided, eg name, qualifications, age, years service, portfolio	2	
Value-added statement (max) Included plus definition or elaboration (2); VA per employee (1)	3	
Productivity/quality (max) Priority indicated (2); Indicators: re people utilisation (4)	6	
Employee numbers (max) Explanation given on (1); Comparative numbers over ... years (1); Provide per category/division (1); Provided per sex and race (1)	4	
Employee information (max) Retrenchments (1); Employee turnover (1); Service record (1); Qualification distribution (1); Work days lost on industrial action (1); Absenteeism (1); Other . . . .(1)	6	
Employee benefits (max) Remuneration (2); Minimum wages (2); Pension/provident fund (2); Medical aid/health care (2); Housing (2); Education assistance (2); Other . . . .(2)	10	
Safety (max) Issue addressed (2); Relevant information provided (2)	4	
HR development (max) Attitude and commitment to (2); Information on cost, numbers (2); Management development (2); Skills training (2); Technical and apprentice training (2); Education and further studies support (2); Literacy training and ABE (2); Other people development initiatives (2); Training status of industry (2)	12	
Industrial relations (max) Relationship with unions (3); Issues at stake (3); Employee participation strategies (3)	9	
Affirmative action (max) Issue addressed (2); Supporting employee information (2); Programmes/strategies (2)	6	
Other HR issues (max) Recruitment issues (1); HR audits/research (1); The disabled employee (1); AIDS (1); Performance management (1); Job creation (1); Ethics (1); Communication with (1); Harassment (1); Policies (1); Equal opportunities (1); Elimination of discrimination (1); Working environment (1); Address HR issues on a national level (1) Other . . . .(1)	12	
Qualitative evaluation (max) Quantitative support for HR issues (2); Comprehensiveness in HR reporting (2); Layout: use of appropriate headings (2); Style (2)	8	
TOTAL . . . . .%		90

Value added statement

It is becoming increasingly common for companies to include a value-added statement with their year-end financial statements. This statement reflects the relationship between the various stakeholders in the enterprise, giving an indication of their respective contributions. The stakeholders are:

- customers – providing turnover and standards of quality;
- suppliers – providing materials and services;
- employees – providing added value;
- shareholders – providing permanent capital;
- financiers – providing financing and loan capital;
- government – providing a stable, disciplined growth environment; and
- entrepreneurs/leadership – providing increased wealth through retained value.

Productivity/quality

Many annual reports feature a commitment to improved productivity, while recognising the contribution made by the HR component in this regard. Particular productivity indicators are used, for example turnover per employee, assets per employee, value added per employee, etc.

22.5.4.2 Specific HRM-related information

In practice an HRM report usually provides operational information regarding the organisation's HR system. As a rule, the following operational information is included.

Employee numbers

The number of people working in the organisation is indicated. Changes in employee numbers could be explained. Employee profiles in terms of race, gender and disability will be required. A further breakdown of employee numbers in various categories could also be provided.

Employee information

Further information about employees is often provided, including employee turnover, service record, age profile, absenteeism, qualifications profile, literacy levels and language competence.

Remuneration and employee benefits

Information in this regard could include remuneration levels, profit-sharing schemes, minimum wages, retirement benefits, medical aid, housing, education assistance, employee loans, share incentive schemes, reward systems for suggestions, etc.

Health and safety

Information is often provided on efforts to improve health and safety in the work environment and relevant statistics.

HR development

Information on HR development includes aspects such as management development; literacy and numeracy training, and adult basic education; training and development in support of affirmative action; focus of training courses and programmes; reference to training on an industry or national level; technical training; further training schemes; cross-cultural training; multiskills training; etc. Quantitative information is provided.

Labour relations

Information includes the names of participating unions and their membership figures, the status of relations with unions, issues at stake and being addressed, the extent and types of disciplinary and grievance activity, employee participation strategies, etc.

Affirmative action

Information includes the extent to which this issue is being addressed, relevant programmes and strategies in place, and employee profiles (and changes in profiles) in terms of race, gender and disability.

Other HRM and related issues

Other HRM and related information could include reporting on aspects like the following: recruitment issues; any HRM-related surveys, reviews or 'audits', as well as relevant research being conducted (such as regarding HIV/Aids); efforts to accommodate disabled people; performance enhancement strategies; aspects pertaining to ethics; strategies to enhance communication and to involve employees and/or their representatives like trade unions; dealing with harassment; employment policies, specifically in relation such things as equal opportunity, affirmative action and the elimination of discrimination; working environment issues; addressing HRM-related issues on an industry or national level; organisational change and transformation issues, including broad-based black economic empowerment efforts or developments; and even also aspects related to corporate social responsibility and sustainability (including work creation).

The more holistic the approach, the more likely that comprehensive reporting will integrate HRM-related issues with the general other issues about which companies report, especially also in relation to social responsibility and sustainability. If HRM is regarded as a fully integrated and key part of generally managing and governing (see chapter 23) organisations in South Africa, 'other' HRM-related issues will increasingly be interwoven with other aspects of management and governance and concomitant corporate reporting.

Everingham and Kana (2008: 4) state the following:

> The King Report on Corporate Governance recommended that the directors present a balanced and understandable assessment of the enterprise's position to stakeholders. The quality of the information should be based on the guidelines of openness and substance over form and should address material matters of significant interest and concern to all stakeholders … [R]eports and communications should be made in the context of the fact that society now demands greater transparency and accountability from enterprises regarding their non-financial affairs, e.g. employment policies and environmental issues.

22.5.5 Corporate reporting, and HRM and sustainability reporting

In their book, *Corporate Reporting*, Everingham and Kana (2008) devote an entire separate chapter to the 'Annual Report and Corporate Governance' (chapter 5 – one of seven chapters of the book). They provide a comprehensive and rather integrated example of how companies can annually report on performance within a 'triple bottom line' framework. Most of the chapter/example is devoted to aspects pertaining directly to HRM issues. We provide this same example as an appendix at the end of this chapter. Note that aspects such as black economic empowerment, skills development, employment equity, training and development, and health and safety are suggested to be covered by an HRM report, while remuneration is proposed to be dealt with as a separate report (presumably because it is so common for governance structures (boards of directors) to have remuneration committees). Also note how prominent HRM-related issues (HIV/Aids) feature in their proposed 'Sustainability Report'. You might recall we also looked at this issue in Chapter 17, where examples are provided (see section 17.6.2).

22.6 CONCLUSION

It is often said that the world has now moved into the information age. Our organisations are therefore required to become increasingly information driven. Linked to this is the fact that the world is experiencing an era of revolutionary developments in the field of information technology. All of this, coupled with increasing pressure to become more competitive in the global village of business warfare, causes organisations constantly to change and develop through the acquisition of knowledge – the trend towards the so-called learning organisation. Knowledge and information go hand in hand. World-class HRM decisions and practices have to be based on information of the same standard.

In this chapter we have focused on a number of specific areas relating to the management of information related to HRM. We looked briefly at the need to collect and use information in relation to the quality of HRM in organisations, at approaches to the evaluation or measurement of various aspects pertaining to an organisation's HRM system, and also to the nature and value of switching to computerised HR information systems and utilising information technology in the execution of HRM work. The last section was devoted to the nature and importance of HRM and related reporting and accountability, and it was stressed that this issue is becoming increasingly important in an environment where triple bottom line reporting is becoming the accepted norm.

SELF-EVALUATION QUESTIONS

1 What is meant by 'employee attitude surveys'? How should such surveys be executed?
2 Discuss arguments for and against the evaluation or measurement of HRM aspects.
3 Critically discuss the HR accounting model.
4 Explain briefly what a human resource cost-benefit analysis entails.
5 Critically comment on the need for and nature of the measurement of labour turnover and absenteeism.
6 What is an HRIS? Explain the basic components thereof.
7 Discuss the process of managing an HRIS.
8 Explain the HRM application areas of HRISs.
9 Discuss the value and nature of HRM reporting and comment on developments in this regard in South Africa.
10 'Reporting about HRM and sustainability have nothing to do with each other.' Critically discuss this statement.

APPENDIX: UBUNTU LIMITED AND ITS SUBSIDIARIES

HUMAN RESOURCE MANAGEMENT REPORT

Ubuntu's overall objective, as set out in its employment policy, is to ensure that the group's employment practices and remuneration policies motivate and retain talented employees and create an attractive environment for all employees. The employment policy is periodically reviewed to ensure that it remains relevant and practical for the changing needs of current and potential employees.

Our vision

Our vision is to be the employer of choice in our field in every country in which we operate. In countries where specific legislation exists to enhance employment equity and practices, our vision is to be at the top end of compliance by including such requirements into our working practices. To this end, black economic empowerment and employment equity are high on our strategic agenda in South Africa.

Employment equity

The group has employment policies that it believes are appropriate to the business and the market in which it trades. Equal employment opportunities are offered to all employees. In South Africa, specific affirmative action programmes are in place to enhance previously disadvantaged employees. We firmly endorse the four key areas of employment equity identified by the Employment Equity Act:

- elimination of discrimination in decision making;
- promotion of employee diversity;
- reduction of barriers to advancement of the disadvantaged; and
- introduction of measures and procedures for transformation.

Black Economic Empowerment (BEE)

Ubuntu realises that BEE is one of the solutions to realising the full economic potential of the country. To this end, Ubuntu is fully committed to sustainable broad-based BEE initiatives. The group is working towards compliance with the scorecards that are applicable to each of the sectors within the economy where its subsidiaries operate.

The group has developed targets for each of its subsidiaries based on codes relevant to those entities. The targets set are all within the timeframe envisaged by the Department of Trade and Industry. Companies within the group are measured by means of a balanced scorecard as provided by the appropriate industry in which they operate.

The group (and each of the individual companies) have enlisted the aid of consultants to prepare generic scorecards for each South African group company. Once these have been completed, a consolidated score card will be prepared for Ubuntu Limited.

The 5 year targets are as follows:

- Equity Ownership   X% black voting rights
- Management & Control   X% black representation
- Employment Equity   X% black representation – middle to senior management
- Skills Development   X% of payroll expended on training
X% of workforce as 'learners'

- Preferential Procurement   X% of discretionary procurement from black owned and empowered suppliers
- Enterprise Development   X% of NAV invested in black empowerment
  X% non-monetary investment
- Residual   X% of net profit on industry specific initiated to facilitate the inclusion of black people. Includes social development.

The BEE initiatives of the group are discussed in more detail in the BEE section of the company's sustainability report which is available on the company's website.

Building capacity with worldwide skills development practices

Ubuntu is committed to the maintenance of standards by supporting and training staff through its world-class skills development programme. This programme aims to develop both the technical and people skills required for the group to conduct its business on a worldwide basis.

Employment and development policies

Ubuntu has an Employment Equity Forum in each of its offices, which works closely with our human resources infrastructure in each country.

They influence policies and monitor their application. These policies cover:
- induction training;
- mentorship programmes;
- career planning;
- gender issues;
- bursary schemes; and
- recruiting from historically disadvantaged communities.

The group will continue to have its operating decisions made at the appropriate levels of its diverse business. Participative management lies at the heart of this strategy, which relies on the building of employee partnerships at every level to foster mutual trust and to encourage people to think about how they can do things better.

Recognised trade unions

The group recognises the importance of working particularly with trade unions for the purpose of collective bargaining. 70% of our group's employees are members of trade unions.

Recruitment

The company has a large number of interns from previously disadvantaged communities. It has achieved its 20X6 recruitment target of 40% for historically disadvantaged South African (HDSA) candidates in technical positions. For 20X7 and 20X8, these targets have been set at 45% and 50% respectively. Recruitment of people with disabilities is estimated to increase to 6%, and recruitment of HDSA in support functions is set at 100%.

Retention, training, and development

The company strives to retain its top talent in an environment that is competitive and at a time when the demand for HDSA professionals is high. This is achieved by programmes like international secondment and leadership programmes that enable technical staff to acquire international exposure, expertise, and best practice. Training is an ongoing exercise within the group as there is a greater need to keep track of the latest global and local trends and developments in industry. During the year, the group spent RX on formal training. This process is also enhanced by mentorship and coaching. Continuous support and development of staff, especially those from previously disadvantaged communities, is part of our people-management policy globally. The South African company has set targets of 26%, 28%, and 30% for the period 20X7 to 20x9 for the retention of HDSA staff.

Health and occupational safety

The risk management committee is directly responsible for the assessment of Ubuntu's health and occupational safety policies. These are obtainable from Ubuntu's website (www.xxx.co.za). Part of this assessment includes the evaluation of relationships with groups representing workers' interests and the participation of these groups in worker health and safety committees. As at 31 December 20X6 77% of workers were represented in these worker forums. The workers not represented are encouraged to become active in these groups.

Statistics

1. Recruitment and retrenchments

Total employees at beginning of year	X
Recruitments	X
Separations (including 68 redundancies)	(X)
Total employees at end of year	X

2. Skills levels

The following is an analysis of the skills levels of our staff at 31 December 20X6:

Skilled employees	X
Semi-skilled employees	X
Unskilled employees	X
	X

Training per skills level (hours)

Employee type	South Africa		Abroad		Total	
	20X6	**20X5**	**20X6**	**20X5**	**20X6**	**20X5**
Skilled	X	X	X	X	X	X
Semi-skilled	X	X	X	X	X	X
Unskilled	X	X	X	X	X	X
Total	**X**	**X**	**X**	**X**	**X**	**X**

3. Employment statistics

	South Africa	Abroad
Average sales per employee	X	X
Average value added per employee	X	X
Average operating profit per employee	X	X
Average remuneration per employee	X	X
Average net earnings per employee	X	X
Investment in plant per employee	X	X
Average exports per South African employee	X	—
Employee costs as a percentage of sales	X%	X%
Employee costs as a percentage of value added	X%	X%

Labour turnover (number of leavers during year as a percentage of average number employed)

20X6	20X5	20X4
X%	X%	X%

4. Summary of current staff

As at 31 December 20X6, the company employs 1 855 people.

- 40% of the Executive Committee members are from the previously disadvantaged communities.
- HDSA staff constitutes X% of the total staff profile.
- Shareholders constituteX%(X) of the total staff, of whom X are HDSA.
- X% staff members are disabled.
- X% of the total staff are female.
- X% of the total staff are designated, i.e. African, Coloured, Indian, and white females.

Employee type	South Africa		Abroad		Total	
	20X6	20X5	20X6	20X5	20X6	20X5
Permanent staff	X	X	X	X	X	X
Contract based staff	X	X	X	X	X	X
Total	**X**	**X**	**X**	**X**	**X**	**X**

5. Health and Occupational safety

Employee type	South Africa		Abroad		Total	
	20X6	20X5	20X6	20X5	20X6	20X5
Work related fatalities	X	X	X	X	X	X
Lost days and absenteeism due to injury	X	X	X	X	X	X

6. Projections

Based on the recruitment drive, retention policy, and the business growth that is expected, the company plans to have 1 990 HDSA staff by 20X9. We therefore estimate that:

- 50% of the Executive Committee members will be from the previously disadvantaged communities.

- HDSA staff will constitute 45% of the total staff profile.
- 15 disabled staff members will be employed.
- Female staff will constitute 50% of the total.
- Designated staff will constitute 66% of the total staff.

UBUNTU LIMITED

and its subsidiaries

REMUNERATION REPORT

Ubuntu's overall objective, as set out in its Employment and Social Responsibility Policy, is to ensure that through the group's employment practices and remuneration policy it motivates and retains existing staff members and at the same time strives to create an attractive environment for potential employees. The Employment and Social Responsibility Policy is periodically reviewed to ensure that it remains relevant and practical for the changing needs of employees and the communities in which we conduct our business.

1. **Remuneration policy**
   The group believes it is best able to respond to the differing needs of the individual business units with fair and attractive remuneration structures on a timely basis. Remuneration structures comprise:
   - basic salary plus benefits, and, where appropriate,
   - annual performance-related rewards, as well as
   - share incentive schemes.

2. **Salaries and benefits**
   Salaries are reviewed annually, in the context of individual and business unit performance as well as specific industry practices and trends. Reference is made to independent salary surveys on a regular basis. Benefits are largely determined by specific industry practices. All full-time employees are members of defined benefit or defined contribution pension and/or provident fund schemes. The group provides post-retirement medical aid benefits only for existing pensioners. Employees now joining the group do not receive postretirement medical aid benefits.

3. **Annual performance-related awards**
   Where appropriate, annual performance-related payments are made to employees. The level of such payments is dependent upon a number of key measures, including the performance of the individual and the business unit concerned. Reference is also made to key economic drivers, including revenue generation and return on capital.

4. **Share incentive schemes**
   Share options are awarded on both individual and corporate performance. Further details of share options are provided in the notes to the financial statements.

5. **Directors' emoluments**
   Details of directors' emoluments for the year ended 31 December 20X6 are provided in the Directors' Report.

UBUNTU LIMITED

and its subsidiaries

SUSTAINABILITY REPORT

ECONOMIC SUSTAINABILITY

Value-added statement

The value-added statement measures performance in terms of value-added by the group through the collective efforts of management, employees, and the providers of capital. The statement shows how added value has been distributed to those contributing to its creation.

	20X6	%	20X5	%
Sales of goods and services	X		X	
Less: cost of materials and services	X		X	
Value added from trading operations	X	X	X	X
Income from investments	X	X	X	X
Total value added	X	X	X	X

Distributed as follows:

	20X6	%	20X5	%
Management				
Salaries, retirement, and other benefits	X	X	X	X
Employees				
Salaries, retirement, and other benefits	X	X	X	X
Providers of capital				
Dividends to shareholders	X	X	X	X
Interest on borrowings	X	X	X	X
Government				
Taxation	X	X	X	X
Total distributions	X	X	X	X
Retained for reinvestment:				
Depreciation and amortisation	X		X	
Income retained in the business	X		X	
Total reinvested	X	X	X	X
Total distributions (including reinvestment)	X	X	X	X

COMMENTARY

1. Total value added

Total value added increased by 85% due to an increase of 88% in the sale of goods and services, which was offset by an increase of 86% in the cost of materials and services.

2. Total distribution to employees

The proportion of total distributions distributed to employees and management increased by 4%.

3. Taxation paid comprises:

	20X6 R'000	20X5 R'000
SA normal tax and deferred tax	X	X
Share of tax of associates	(X)	X
Secondary tax on companies	X	X
	X	X

4. Income retained in business

Retained income excludes the share of income retained by associates so as not to distort the value added to raw materials, and comprises:

	20X6 R'000	20X5 R'000
Retained profit for the year	X	X
Share of retained deficit/(earnings) of associates	X	X
Outside shareholders' interest in subsidiaries	X	X
	X	X

2006 Value added statement

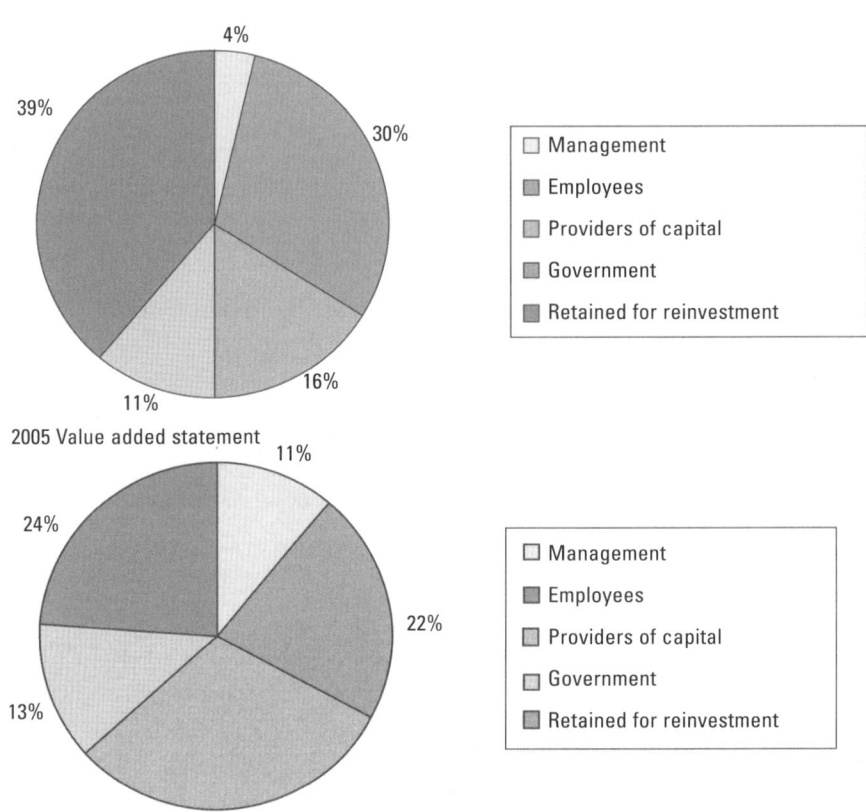

2005 Value added statement

Corporate social investment (CSI)

Ubuntu's Corporate Social Investment Philosophy and function have, over the years, been broadly underpinned by the concept of sustainable development. The policy of the Ubuntu Development Trust (UDT) is to act as facilitator rather than as sole sponsor of social investment projects. In this way, the long-term sustainability of projects is encouraged, additional donors are attracted, and formerly disadvantaged communities are empowered. During 20X6, Ubuntu contributed RX million to the Trust (20X5: RX million). The UDT is a major national initiative through which business and government have joined hands to support the following strategic interventions:

1. **Education**
   Support for education projects spanning the spectrum of needs from pre-school to tertiary study provides the UDT with the opportunity to make a difference in the lives of thousands of young people, expanding their learning skills and helping to build a stronger base for future economic growth.

   Noteworthy contributions during 20X6 were the provision of two classrooms at the Noqekwa Primary School in Charlsworth at a cost of RX and the provision of 50 computers to the James Johnson Secondary School in Landsdonne, at a cost of RX, together with ongoing technical support.

2. **Skills training and job creation**
   One of South Africa's greatest challenges is its high level of unemployment. Ubuntu has become involved in various projects with stakeholder participation, delivering skills development relevant to work opportunities. These projects are aimed at improving the economic livelihoods of people in rural areas, and include training programmes. This is a particularly challenging area of development, but even modest income generation can make a real difference for people on the economic margin.

3. **Small business development**
   The identification of business opportunities and the subsequent establishment of businesses is well on track. Business unit management is actively assisting in identifying business opportunities, which are then made available to individuals from previously disadvantaged communities.

   The group deals with black economic empowerment by implementing various options to allow meaningful equity participation by historically disadvantaged individuals, based on the premise that such participation should be value-enhancing and aligned to the desired long-term positioning and vision of the group. Furthermore, the group is committed to support small entrepreneurs through its own procurement policies. Discretionary procurement is specifically targeted at small companies with particular emphasis on the advancement of empowerment companies.

4. **Environmental**
   In each of its regions, Ubuntu is regulated by a wide range of laws that address, amongst others, issues such as noise, discharges to air and water, and removal of waste. Regulations in all countries in which we operate require that an environmental impact assessment of our project be conducted prior to any planned expansion. Ubuntu proactively engages in these processes to ensure that our current and planned operations meet requirements.

Ubuntu Ltd is not aware of any pending environmental litigation, and no fines or penalties have been imposed during 20X6 for non-compliance with environmental regulations and permits. Any infringements are reported to the relevant regulators and corrective action is taken as soon as practicable in all circumstances.

Ubuntu also contributed toward a number of pilot studies to test the sustainability of environmental projects. These projects include environmental projects at various primary schools in Mpumalanga and the internal housing strategy in Polokwane.

The risk management committee is currently performing an assessment of the group's release of greenhouse gases into the atmosphere as a result of its manufacturing activities. This assessment has been broadened to include a total assessment of the impact of all the group's operations on the environment. Climate changes represent both risks and opportunities for the group. Since Ubuntu Limited is committed to the concept of existing in harmony with the environment in which it operates, future projects will evaluate the possibility of leveraging the group's strong history of environmental responsibility to build plants that are environmentally friendly and that will result in the group obtaining carbon credits. It is not anticipated that future regulation in this field will have a significant impact on the group.

SOCIAL SUSTAINABILITY

Health and safety

Refer to the human resource management report.

HIV/AIDS

The group recognises that one of the biggest challenges facing South Africa is the scourge of HIV/AIDS. The disease affects all facets of the Ubuntu's operations. Employees, suppliers and customers are all affected which leads to a range of challenges which the company must deal with.

The management of HIV/AIDS is an important challenge for Ubuntu. Ubuntu has determined that HIV/AIDS will have an impact on the following risk areas: operations; target market risk; supplier risk; legal risk and health risk. Whilst all these risks are under investigation, Ubuntu has adopted the following core principles as a basis for its HIV/AIDS policy:

- Continuously assess the risks posed by HIV/AIDS on the business;
- Limit the number of new infections among employees;
- Ensure employees living with HIV/AIDS are aware of their rights and that their rights are respected and protected;
- Provide care and support to employees living with HIV/AIDS.

HIV/AIDS structures

In order to achieve the policy objectives, Ubuntu has formed a HIV/AIDS committee (the committee). The committee consists of three experienced independent medical practitioners, four union representatives and five members of senior management. Ubuntu has trained five peer educators who are full-time employees that have shown passion and willingness to assist their fellow HIV positive colleagues, to ensure that HIV positive employees receive care and support in their work environment. Peer educators facilitate peer support groups, which meet once a month during office hours to discuss their issues around living and coping with the disease.

Prevalence rate

To identify the current prevalence rate, the committee, with the cooperation and support of the union conducted two studies: an actuarial study of the group's risk profile and a survey to measure the employees' knowledge, attitudes, practices and beliefs (KAPB) about HIV/AIDS. The results indicate a prevalence rate of 15%. Another study will be performed at the end of the next financial year to assess whether the group's intervention programmes are having any impact.

Actuarial Impact Analysis

The committee employed the services of an actuary to assess the current and future expected costs to the organisation, resulting directly and indirectly from HIV/AIDS. The actuary's conclusions were as follows:

Current costs

	Medical cost Rm	Absenteeism Rm	Operational Rm	Training Rm	Funeral Rm	Total Rm
20X6	X	X	X	X	X	X

Future costs – assuming no further improvement

	Medical cost Rm	Absenteeism Rm	Operational Rm	Training Rm	Funeral Rm	Total Rm
20X6	X	X	X	X	X	X
20X106	X	X	X	X	X	X

Future costs – assuming reduction of new infections by 30%

	Medical cost Rm	Absenteeism Rm	Operational Rm	Training Rm	Funeral Rm	Total Rm
20X6	X	X	X	X	X	X
20X106	X	X	X	X	X	X

Ubuntu recognises the cost involved to both the group and the community of not taking progressive steps in combating the disease and has therefore allocated an additional RX worth of resources from its annual budget to fighting the disease. The HIV/AIDS committee has approved the budget.

Awareness of the disease

The committee has focused its attention on identifying and measuring the extent of the risk of HIV/AIDS to the organisation. In order to identify employees' level of awareness, the committee used the help of three psychologists and a qualified counsellor to anonymously survey all staff members through a KAPB survey. The results of the survey revealed a low level of awareness of the key causes of HIV/AIDS and behaviour to mitigate the risk. As a result, an awareness campaign was launched in partnership with a local NGO, Positive Living. This awareness campaign was carried out over four weeks and all staff, including executive management participated. Each year, twice a year, new employees will attend an awareness session as part of their induction programme. Regular 18-month follow up surveys will be scheduled to identify whether employees' level of awareness has improved.

Education

To build on the awareness programme, an ongoing education programme has been instituted. The first phase of this programme was to train peer educators who will then provide HIV/AIDS education to all staff on an ongoing basis. Peer educators receive training on lay counselling, grief management, company benefits, first aid and treatment of workplace injuries. Peer educators have also formed relationships with community health care centres to refer employees and their family members to for help. In addition, peer educators are trained in condom distribution and demonstration. They are responsible for monitoring condom supply and consumption.

Overall support

It is compulsory for all Ubuntu employees and their immediate family members to be members of a medical aid. The HIV/AIDS committee with the assistance of an actuary is in the process of analysing whether the current medical aid provides adequate cover to employees and their families in respect of HIV/AIDS. From the beginning of the current financial year Ubuntu has employed the services of two doctors and a psychologist to provide free counselling and testing for employees and their immediate family members. The doctors distribute anti-retroviral medication to infected staff members. Counselling and testing treatment facilities are situated off Ubuntu's premises so as to maintain discretion and confidentiality.

Communication

The expected impact of HIV/AIDS on the organisation and procedures to be followed if employees require counselling or testing or want any other information in respect of HIV/AIDS are standard agenda items of the monthly staff meetings. English, Afrikaans, Zulu and Xhosa pamphlets are available to all employees and visitors detailing the rights of employees living with HIV/AIDS. The committee holds bi-annual meetings where all employees, union members and shareholders are invited to attend. The meetings are held to inform interested stakeholders of the goals that have been set and the progress made during the past six months as well as to identify any issues the stakeholders feel are not being addressed.

Key challenges

The committee has identified the following challenges for which plans are currently underway:

■ An increase in the absenteeism rate. The committee is considering extending the current educational programmes to the families of employees and becoming involved in community projects as the majority of employees are drawn from communities where the infection rates are high. The group is in the process of negotiating a fair leave allowance to be granted to employees. Part of this negotiation also includes discussion about additional benefits to be given to HIV positive employees after their death such as family education support and family housing support.

■ A decrease in productivity due to the increased level of absenteeism and mortality rate – consideration is being given to multi-skilling staff members and improving on recruitment and training of staff members.

- An increase in the financial exposure and risk. The committee is analysing the impact HIV/AIDS may have on the group's current suppliers and customers.
- An increase in litigation risk. The group is continually educating its employees on the rights of HIV positive employees. Any employee guilty of discrimination against another as a result of their HIV/AIDS status will be subject to disciplinary action. The group has dedicated training resources to educating all levels of management and particularly, Human Resource staff about the various legislations that govern management of HIV/AIDS in the workplace.

Source: Everingham & Kana (2008)

23 PUSHING BOUNDARIES – GOING BEYOND ...

LEARNING OUTCOMES

After studying this chapter you should be able to:

- describe what is meant by 'pushing boundaries – going beyond ...' in this final chapter of the book;
- write concise notes about issues pertaining to HRM beyond the boundaries of a specific single country like South Africa;
- explain what it means that HRM issues and challenges extend beyond management and into the realms of corporate governance and the work of boards of directors; and
- engage in constructive dialogue about possible scenarios for the future of South Africa, and how HRM connects with these.

23.1 INTRODUCTION

Throughout this book, and in particular in chapter 1, we have shown how HRM as field has been evolving and how there have been shifts. We would like to end with a modest effort to help bring about some shifts in thinking. We thus challenge our readers in this final chapter to think 'beyond'. We keep this chapter very brief – almost as a kind of an epilogue. It is an 'epilogue with a difference', though. As the title of this chapter indicates, we want to stretch the thinking a bit – we want to 'go beyond' and 'push boundaries', and by this we mean more than one thing.

Firstly we think it is necessary that we stretch our thinking beyond HRM in local South African organisations. We have tried, throughout the book, to bring about some sensitivity for the fact that there are HRM dynamics at play way beyond the boundaries of South Africa. We have cited some relevant perspectives pertaining to HRM in other countries in Africa, for instance. In this chapter we want to take this a step further and provide a brief introductory perspective on issues related to managing human resources internationally or globally. We thus 'push boundaries' in the sense that we take a very brief look at some aspects related to HRM when it is practised beyond the boundaries of one country.

Secondly, we also 'push boundaries' because we take a brief look at HRM beyond the actual traditional confines of the field of study of 'management'. In chapter 1 we explained the meaning of management and organisations as the context of this book's focus. Many scholars regard governance or, more specifically, corporate governance, as being beyond management. In this regard we briefly reflect on HR issues in the context of corporate governance – in other words, in the boardroom.

Lastly, we 'push boundaries' by moving way beyond HRM – and even beyond management and organisations – when we share some possible scenarios about the future of South Africa.

23.2 BEYOND A COUNTRY: GOING GLOBAL

Although this book is about South African HRM, we have been sharing glimpses of information about HRM in other countries, especially in Africa, throughout most of the chapters. We now also want to take a brief look at some issues and perspectives pertaining to international or global HRM more generally. We believe this is important because, as explained before, the world has become a global village in the sense that trade, leisure, travel, working and living, etc have become much more internationally integrated over the past three decades or so than ever before. One only needs to take a look at where products come from in our shops to come to an enhanced appreciation of how internationally we are living. Business and the world of organisations, work and management have become much more international or 'global'. Cooke (2007: 489) says that "since 1980 there has been a nearly twelve-fold increase in foreign direct investment and a greater than eight-fold increase in the number of multinational companies (MNCs). As of 2004 there were over 61,000 MNCs with ownership in over 900,000 foreign affiliated operations worldwide. These foreign affiliates alone employed more than 54 million employees …". There can be no doubt that this picture makes HRM, in a multinational or cross-country sense, very important.

In a similar vein, Hough, Neuland and Bothma (2003: 385) say that new "markets opening to South African businesses and new technology in communicating and transport have led to a major expansion of international trade and investment in the early 2000s … If South African companies are to be successful competitors in the global marketplace, they need urgently to be part of the globalization process …". The fact of the matter is, therefore, that we can no longer think about management, organisations, work or HRM in local terms only. We have to think both local and global, making it essential to consider aspects pertaining to HRM through an international or transnational lens, simply because markets have become more global than ever before. International markets that have opened up include not only those for products and services but also in particular, and more than ever before, for labour.

You might recall from chapter 2 that we mentioned how numerous multinational companies set up business operations in countries (especially developing ones) specifically because they find they can be more efficient doing so due to labour cost advantages. With the power of the Internet it becomes pretty easy to research such things as labour costs in various countries. This type of information, which is rather freely available, can inform a whole range of decisions and issues, including strategic decisions regarding where to locate manufacturing operations, for example. Boxall and Purcell (2008) say that it is especially common for organisations in the clothing, toy and footwear manufacturing business, for instance, to move their production operations to lower labour cost countries. They (Boxall & Purcell 2008: 127–130) give another example that illustrates the point:

> For example, steel industry data for labour costs in the production of crude steel show that the unit cost in the USA in 2003 was US $23.8. It was US $26.0 in the UK but as low as US $0.9 in India and US $1.1 in China … Costs in the Ukraine were US $0.8 while in the Czech Republic they were US $6.1 … Offshoring production to countries in which labour costs are markedly lower, and labour regulations are less demanding, has become one of the preferred HR strategies of

multinational companies ... often ... play[ing] one location off against another ... In many cases, established firms have ceased manufacturing altogether in high-wage countries.

This clearly illustrates how the information technology revolution has enhanced our capacity to research markets, in this case labour markets. These things have helped to open markets up and hence business strategy decisions have come to be much more global in scope and focus.

As we have shown throughout this book, many companies from South Africa have already become global players – including organisations such as SABMiller, MTN, BHP Billiton, the Shoprite Group, and many more. We thus have a context which is very different today than, say, four or so decades ago. This whole globalisation trend has been facilitated further by issues such as international economic integration, the development of regional and other trading blocks, and free-trade agreements. Examples include the North American Free Trade Agreement (NAFTA), the South Asian Associations for Regional Cooperation (SAARC) and the Association of South East Asian Nations (ASEAN), possibly one of the most powerful examples being the development of the European Union (EU) with one currency, the Euro. Closer to home we have, for example, the 'African Caribbean and Pacific group' which is made up of 77 member countries, 48 of which are African countries (Hough et al 2003: 72). We also, of course, have the Southern African Development Community (SADC), as well as the Common Market for Eastern and Southern Africa (COMESA) and the Economic Community of Central African States. We mention all of these examples (and there are plenty more) simply to illustrate how things are becoming increasingly interconnected and globalised – and that Africa is also involved. We are, as a country and as a continent, active participants in the global village.

This is the modern-day 'scene' in which organisations operate, including those in South Africa. It seems possible to become more and more the dominant context within which we will have to manage our organisations, the work and our working people. Dowling and Welch (2004) explain that these developments are making HRM (or we can say international HRM or IHRM) even more complex. This greater complexity is attributed to the following six factors, according to Dowling and Welch (2004: 7–12).

- *More HR activities:* To operate internationally, HRM must inevitably include activities not necessary in a domestic environment.
- *The need for a broader perspective:* Managing and leading people internationally means that managers (including HR managers) face the problems for more than one national group of working people.
- *More involvement in employees' personal lives:* When people go and work in other countries (expatriates, for instance), housing arrangements, health care and so forth in other countries must be taken care of.
- *Changes in emphasis as the workforce mix of expatriates and locals varies:* Foreign operations mature and therefore HRM work and challenges change.
- *Risk exposure:* Human and financial consequences of failure in the international arena are more severe than in the case of managing local operations and people.
- *Broader external influences:* The type of government, the state of the economy and the society of the host countries generally, and the accepted policies and procedures there, all impact on HRM in those countries.

These complexities thus mean that we need to carefully consider what the implications are for HRM when organisations actually operate beyond the boundaries of one (their own) country, having to get work done in those other (host) countries through making use of the human (and other) resources of those countries. Before we take a look at some of the variables or factors that play a role in such cases, it is important to briefly consider different ways in which organisations can go global.

The most straightforward way is probably to link up with others in the foreign country who can help with marketing, selling and distributing the organisation's products/services in that country. This can be arranged by means of standard commercial contracts, for instance, or perhaps through licensing arrangements. This is merely going global in terms of the products/services of an organisation without making any real foreign direct investment in that country (such as setting up an infrastructure for manufacturing, for instance). The real management, and particularly also HRM implications, start to surface when we set up operations in the foreign country. This can be done through entering into formal deals with existing organisations in that country – such as through cross-border strategic alliances or international joint ventures (IJVs). Another way may be to buy into existing organisations through some partnering deals. In such cases we might in a sense 'merge' with existing organisations that operate and are based in another country or countries. International mergers and acquisitions (M&As) are becoming increasingly popular ways of going global. This is one way of becoming a multinational company (MNC). Of course, another option could simply be to set up business in another country.

We now turn to take a brief look at some of the variables or factors that can interplay with HRM when we actually do go and invest in foreign countries by setting up some business interests there and hence become an MNC.

23.2.1 Dimensions and variables impacting on IHRM

There obviously are myriad factors that can influence HRM if we have to practise it elsewhere other than in our home country. You will recall that in chapter 2 we took a look at the South African context of HRM. The same kinds of variables will be relevant, but they will be those that manifest in the foreign or host countries where we will have to manage the operations, the work and the people, for example the state of the economy, the political climate and dispensation, and in particular the legal framework. In respect of HRM, it would hence specifically be the relevant labour and related legislation that would be very important.

In more general terms, the nature of that 'society' as a whole will be very relevant. If we want to go and set up operations, work, employ people and manage organisations in a different society, we need to factor in that each society has its own peculiarities. Each society has some unique characteristics regarding its labour markets, for instance (for example education levels). Many regions also share some peculiarities. The comprehensive and truly global research project of House et al (2004), for instance, has led to some clear clustering on regional bases. With regard to African societies generally, Kamoche, Muuka, Horwitz and Debrah (2004: XV), explain that

> ... economic and industrial development in Africa has been hampered by a number of factors ... Among these are the harsh global economic realities which directly impact Africa, economic mismanagement, political ineptitude, and corruption ... Africa is experiencing a serious brain drain as many pursue greener pastures in other countries in Africa or overseas. Factors that drive Africans away from home range from the more extreme life-threatening ones (such as civil wars) to socio-economic concerns such as lack of employment opportunities occasioned by stagnant economies and declining opportunities for personal growth.

These are some generalisations about potential issues and challenges peculiar to African countries. We must remain mindful, though, that there is huge diversity in terms of the societies in Africa. Each country will have its own legal system, for instance, even though culturally there may be some shared aspects (such as *ubuntu* as discussed in chapter 10).

Culture, of course, is one variable or factor that receives a great deal of attention in the literature on international management in general. Edwards and Rees (2006: 28) say:

> National culture is said to impact organizations by selecting and framing the particular sets of organizational values and norms that managers perceive as being consistent with the basic assumptions that are developed within their countries (as a product of national patterns of early childhood, formative experiences and education, language, religion and geography). Differences in national culture affect organizations in many ways ... They create assumptions about: appropriate pay systems and the importance of distributive justice; the importance of centralization and hierarchies ... and attitudes towards job and career mobility.

Regarding social justice (which, as you will know, includes distributive justice) in Africa, Beugré (2002: 1096), for instance, says that the "collectivistic nature of African culture" can be compared to the same collectivistic orientation in Asian cultures and that in these types of cultures, something like inclusionary and exclusionary justice views become important. The latter is when people apply justice principles only to members of the 'in group', which is typical of collectivistic-oriented cultures. Furthermore, the following is said, and we should keep it in mind as we set up operations and work and manage in African countries (Beugré 2002: 1047): "Out-group members in African organizations may also represent employees from other ethnic groups or expatriates."

The same author (Beugré 2002: 1098) explains that in respect of another cultural dimension, African cultures are generally high on 'power distance', and as such,

> ...rarely do subordinates raise direct concerns about the potential weaknesses and/or abuses of the 'chief' ... [M]anagers do not often have to justify their decisions ... Authority lies in the formal position rather than in objective criteria of competence, performance and contribution ... Such an organizational environment may not be conducive to employee productivity and performance ... [and] it may lead to politicking and blind obedience ... In most African countries, distribution of outcomes such as financial rewards ...promotion and the like is still based on 'ethnic distance' (tribal ties) ... One way for employees to gain favours from their managers is to become part of the inner circle ... This tendency may lead to the emergence of a 'yes men' mentality.

It should thus be clear from just these few examples that these sorts of issues or variables that are embedded in societies are important to be mindful of if we have to engage in managing and leading people in organisations in an international context, such as in countries in Africa (or elsewhere). Naturally the range of possible issues is very broad, and we merely mention a few to sensitise our readers to the fact that we really have to think way beyond how things happen in our own country, and how people think and what they value (which all are already reflecting great diversity, as covered in other chapters). When we go global, things become even more complex and variables like these even more uncertain – until we try to learn more about them. The challenge is once again ours – as scholars and practitioners – to actively work towards learning more about these cross-national aspects that interplay with HRM when we go global. We now briefly turn to a few examples of some specific issues we need to learn about and consider as we take on the challenge of IHRM.

23.2.2 Some specific aspects of IHRM

It must be stressed that IHRM has become such an important topic that entire books revolve around it. However, we are going to touch on only a few relevant aspects here.

One of the important aspects obviously relate to the workforce mix in companies that operate in more than one country. The composition will typically include working people from the host country as well as expatriates. A mine of a South African organisation operating in another country like Ghana will typically have employees from Ghana as well as some South Africans. The issue of managing expatriates is a key point of focus in research and other publications in the field of IHRM. In practice, as in theory, this whole issue is very important. Beugré (2002: 1099), for instance, makes an important statement (see also the box below):

> African organizations should also pay particular attention to the difference in treatment between local employees and expatriates. Indeed, most African organizations employ expatriates from Western and Asian countries. These expatriates are often better paid than the locals and hold higher managerial positions. Local African employees tend to consider this situation as unjust. African organizations may reduce this sense of injustice by explaining to local employees the policies and procedures governing these decisions.

Elsewhere in Africa ... a case at hand

In mines in Ghana, a local senior staff member earned only about 14% of the salary paid to an expatriate staff member doing the same or similar work. In other words, the expatriate on the minimum pay scale earned US$3 000 compared to US$422 for his or her local Ghanaian counterpart. This translates into a pay ratio of 7:1 between the expatriate and his or her local staff counterpart who may have higher or a similar qualification.

Source: Slightly adapted from Jauch (2007)

It is not just the management of expatriates as such that is a specific focus area of IHRM. Another key area relates to the whole spectrum of HRM practices, functions and policies that are potentially in dynamic interaction with the broader country context in which the international operations are located. Although remuneration ('total reward') is very important, as mentioned and illustrated above, HRM aspects are actually relevant right from the stage when we contemplate whether to go global or not. The very strategic decision of whether to expand and grow into international markets should include the HRM issues.

Whether we are going to engage in an international strategic alliance or an international joint venture is a business decision but it must factor in the relevant HRM aspects, such as labour market conditions. The latter includes, for example, the supply of well-educated, competent people from where we will have to draw our employees. It is one thing to have access to lower-cost human resources, perhaps, but quite another as to how well people will do the work. In this regard, a whole range of factors play a role, including the competence of the people and also such things as language compatibility. If we set up operations in South America and the expatriate managers cannot speak the language of the majority of the workforce in that country, special efforts to have good and proper communication will be needed. It thus cuts right into aspects that range from workforce planning and recruitment and selection practices, to performance management and especially also leadership. Naturally the education levels also interplay with, for example, training and development, and career management. Similarly, in collectivistic cultures such as in African countries, we will have to seriously reconsider factors such as individual-based rewards for performance.

One basic decision that has to be made at top-management level is whether and to what extent our overall approach or general 'recipe' (or strategy) regarding HRM will be – either to adapt to the host country or to keep things as consistent as possible with how they are in our home country. The question basically revolves around the extent to which we are going to 'think global but act local'. The extent to which we thus centralise control over how we manage human resources is relevant. If the headquarters are based in South Africa and we have operations in, say, Kenya, to what extent do we leave it to the management there to adapt our company's HRM policies and practices to local circumstances? This is an important overarching decision to make, and will have a direct impact on the extent to which there will be a differentiation between the home organisation's preferred HRM policies and practices and those in the host country. It is well known that Western-owned MNCs operating in South Africa have brought with them a lot of their American, British and European ways of managing organisations and people. The same is happening now with South African organisations moving more and more into other African countries.

Newenham (2005) has done research into this theme in Tanzania, involving the South African-owned bank, Stanbic, as well as an American-owned bank, Citibank. It was found that although these two organisations (both being MNCs) have similar HRM policies and systems, "they had distinctive HR/IR practices to suit their business strategies in the host nation" (Newenham 2005: 91). It is further stated that "Stanbic seemed to have gone one step further by … integration (of) HR/IR practices with a localisation emphasis while Citibank did not … Stanbic had a model of work organisation in which employees received support collectively. Team representation and collective bank practices encouraged socialisation and work commitment … [T]he issue of country of origin at Stanbic sheds some light on a possible future direction for South African MNCs operating abroad, particularly in African and other emerging markets in Asia … [D]ivergences between MNCs in Tanzania reflected country-of-origin effect … that of South Africanness and Americanness" (Newenham 2005: 92).

There are thus a number of complexities involved in IHRM – also in particular in Africa. These hold implications for both the theory and the practice of HRM, and scholars and managers should collaborate in pushing the boundaries as we learn and try to improve how we manage organisations and people beyond the borders of South Africa. Our purpose here is merely to put this theme – especially as it relates to South Africa and Africa – on the agenda.

There are many other specific issues that relate to IHRM – also from an African perspective. These include such things as work ethic, ethics more generally, and also leadership dynamics across different cultures (see chapter 10). Other aspects include multicultural manners and how negotiation differs across different countries or regions, and also how we go about with issues related to global staffing. The latter includes challenges pertaining to the management of expatriate assignments and employees, including, for instance, how we plan for these and prepare the people and bring them back to their home countries upon completion of their assignments (repatriation). Lastly, it might be pure comparative perspectives about various HRM practices. The range of potential issues that can and should be covered is therefore broad and, as we have said, actually it is becoming such an important topic in an increasingly global world that perhaps the time is ripe for a separate book to be published about international HRM from the angle of Africa.

23.3 BEYOND MANAGEMENT: HUMAN RESOURCES, THE BOARDROOM AND CORPORATE GOVERNANCE

The people who are at the pinnacle or apex of organisational leadership are really the directors who form, typically (in the case of companies at least), a board of directors. Many scholars and experts in the field of corporate governance do not regard this – the work of boards – to be managerial work. Traditionally, textbooks on HRM would likewise hardly ever include aspects related to boards of directors. We are thus now trying to push some boundaries in this sense.

We would like to argue that directors are also 'human resources' – and we will demonstrate shortly that in fact there are many HRM-type of issues involved when it comes to the work of boards of directors. The mere fact that boards have to do certain work and fulfil certain roles means we are essentially talking about issues of work design (as you should recall from chapter 5).

According to the 'Policy Governance Model' of Carver and Oliver (2002), for example, the role of a board of directors can be regarded as 'governance', and they make the point that governance is not an upward extension of management, but 'ownership one step down'. As such they regard 'governing' as work that is being done on behalf of the owners. The key focus of this role and work is to determine the 'ends' of the business in light of the expectations and interests of its owners. They argue that the 'management' of a company (the top-management team and lower levels of management), on the other hand, is responsible for deciding on 'the means' – the 'how to' – of achieving the 'ends' derived from the interests and expectations of the owners (shareholders), as translated by the board. The task and responsibility of determining and putting to use the 'means' are thus delegated by the board to the CEO and his or her top management team, but within the framework and boundaries as laid down by the board of directors. They argue that if one wants to know what the role of boards is, one has to ask the basic question, 'Why do boards exist?'. Their argument (Carver & Oliver 2002: 3) is that we only have to determine where the board's authority comes from, what the reason is for the board being given that authority, and what the nature of that authority entails. They explain that the source of board authority is the owners (or shareholders) of companies. As they (Carver & Oliver 2002: 5) put it: "... the notion of board authority as a distinct kind of authority occurs only when there is a gap between the ownership of assets and the management of those assets ... The board's position is, therefore, to act as the link between owners and management directing and controlling the company on the owners behalf."

Rather similarly, but not as rigid, perhaps, De Wit and Meyer (2005: 254) explain that "corporate governance, as opposed to corporate management, deals with governing the strategic choices and actions of top management ... [C]orporate governance is about ... building in checks and balances to ensure the senior executives pursue strategies that are in accordance with the corporate mission ... all the tasks and activities that are intended to supervise and steer the behavior of top management". From this it can clearly be seen that actually this is nothing different than designing the work of boards of directors and thus our argument that HRM is beyond management and the boardroom.

De Wit and Meyer (2005: 254), drawing on various other sources, go on to distinguish between the three fundamental 'functions' of corporate governance in the following way:

■ *Forming function.* This function is about influencing the forming of the corporate mission. "The task of corporate governance is to shape, articulate and communicate the fundamental principles that will drive the organization's activities. Determining the purpose of the organization and setting priorities among claimants are part of the forming function. The board of directors can conduct this task by, for example, questioning the basis of strategic choices, influencing the business philosophy, and explicitly weighing the advantages and disadvantages of the firm's strategies for various constituents ...

■ *Performance function.* The second function of corporate governance is to contribute to the strategy process with the intention of improving the future performance of the corporation. The task of corporate governance is to judge strategy initiatives brought forward by top management and/or to actively participate in strategy development. The board of directors can conduct this task by, for example, engaging in strategy discussions, acting as a sounding board for top management, and networking to secure the support of vital stakeholders ...

■ *Conformance function.* The third function of corporate governance is to ensure corporate conformance to the stated mission and strategy. The task of corporate governance is to monitor whether the organization is undertaking activities as promised and whether performance is satisfactory. Where management is found lacking, it is a function of corporate governance to press for changes. The board of directors can conduct this task by, for example, auditing the activities of the corporation, questioning and supervising top management, determining remuneration and incentive packages, and even appointing new managers ...".

The last sentence in particular highlights that HRM work extends right into the realm of corporate governance – because it is about engaging (selecting and appointing) the top-level managers of the organisation as well as managing and rewarding their performance. The book by Kiel, Nicholson and Barclay (2005), *Board, Director and CEO Evaluation*, takes it a step further because this theme is nothing else really than performance management – but applied not only to the most senior manager, the CEO, but even also to the board itself. Keep in mind also that such things as the remuneration and reward of non-executive directors (hence they are not employees) is an issue that clearly engages HRM thinking and decisions, even though it has nothing to do with employees but rather non-managerial directors at board level. Bussin (2007: 18), for instance, looks at the issue of whether non-executive directors should receive performance incentives. In table 23.1 you can see some research results about the reward for non-executive directors of nearly 400 South African organisations across all of the various industries in our country.

We want to return briefly here to some of the views of Carver and Oliver (2002). We do not agree that the work of boards and directors – corporate governance – is based on only the interests and expectations of the shareholders or owners. As we

Table 23.1: Non-executive directors and reward in South Africa

Share purchase scheme for non-executive directors	If yes – average vesting period (years)	Profit-share scheme for non-executive directors	Other benefits paid to non-executive directors	Use of personal resources by non-executive directors to acquire shares in the business
8,1%	3,43%	0,5%	17,4%	33,7%

Source: Bussin (2007: 18)

have said right from the outset in chapter 1, stakeholder perspectives are necessary to broaden the role of organisations in society – and in this regard HRM has a key role to play to move companies to more holistic agendas, even at corporate governance (board of directors) level. We believe that a stakeholder perspective of corporate governance is a much more sustainable approach. Carter and Lorsch (2004) argue that specific attention should be devoted to redesigning the work of boards, and they argue that boards ought to 'go back to the drawing board' and ask certain fundamental questions such as what their role is. They argue that in reality the diversity of shareholders (or 'owners') makes it largely a matter of strategic choice left to the board as to what role it should play. They furthermore alert us thereto that it is not an unassailable fact that the only role of boards is to enhance shareholder value (Carter & Lorsch 2004: 55), saying that, "Boards need to recognise that they have a choice to make in defining the goals of their activities ... Beyond shareholders ... boards do also accept responsibility to other stakeholders ... This broader approach is not necessarily inconsistent with their responsibility to shareholders". We concur with this perspective, and hence it is argued that HRM is right there in the thick of things as these work design choices must be made at boardroom level. As was shown in chapter 22, HRM and sustainability reporting (see also chapter 17 and 21 for examples), should also for instance be part of 'corporate reporting'.

The same authors claim that although there are numerous differences between countries, most of the principles of board work design are generic and appropriate to "all companies in all countries" (Carter & Lorsch 2004: 11). While there may be some truth in that perspective, we do not think that it is 'the whole truth and nothing but the truth'. Countries have different systems of corporate governance. For instance, in countries such as the Netherlands and Germany, two-tier board structures are required. In such systems "there is a formal division of power with a management board made up of the top executives and a distinct supervisory board made up of non-executives, with the task of monitoring and steering the management board" (De Wit & Meyer 2005: 255). It needs to be mentioned also that in Germany, trade unions typically serve on the supervisory boards, elevating aspects of labour relations – which is part and parcel of HRM work too – right to the level of the boardroom and governance of organisations.

A last point in respect of this challenge of thinking about HRM in the context of governance relates to *ethics*. We are all too well aware of various corporate scandals all over the world and the role these have played in enhancing the demands for closer scrutiny and oversight of the performance of boards in relation to governance. This makes the case clear for ethics and accountability right at the top. At the end of the day ethics is a distinctly human aspect. We therefore feel that as part of HRM we should be pushing for bringing ethics not only into the boardroom, but also into top-management echelons and throughout organisations. Ethics in HRM is not merely to be focusing on the ethics role of the HR practitioners – but on HRM as a holistic, organisation and societal pervasive practice. Ethical practices and decisions ought to become a key focus of all governance and managerial work if we really want to develop a sustainable future in South Africa (and in Africa and elsewhere). We now take a look at possible future scenarios for our country.

23.4 THE FUTURE

This section is not so much about the future of HRM as it is about the future *around* HRM – beyond the field of HRM theory and practice. We have stressed throughout this book that the societal embeddedness of HRM is very important. We have stressed right from the outset of chapter 1 that HRM adds value, not only to the organisation and as such to the customers and the owners or shareholders of business organisations, but also to the working people and to societies as a whole. We have also emphasised the complexities that come along with HRM's societal embeddedness – complexities that stem from the interaction between HRM in our organisations and what is happening in the broader environment outside our organisations. In the previous section we thus made the connection between HRM and corporate governance which is, in our view, supposed to be stakeholder driven. Because it is to be stakeholder driven it should have a sustainability connection throughout. Sustainability is about the future – about thinking carefully about what we do now and the implications for the long-term future that will be for the generations we leave behind.

We thus conclude this book with this brief section on what the future of South Africa might hold. There are 'futurologists' and even a field of study such as 'futures studies' – and this section is not meant or claimed to be some prediction of the future. Rather, our approach is to include here some scenarios that have been developed about our country's possible future. We share these with you and then leave it up to all to consider the potential implications, not only for HRM, but also more generally for our organisations and, most importantly for our people – our human resources. Section 23.4.1 contains four scenarios (according to the ANC's planners in 2003) of South Africa through to 2014. Section 23.4.3 reflects the scenarios of Clem Sunter and Chantell Ilbury (2008), while section 23.4.2 contains a recent update of three possible scenarios of the country by 2025 – as produced by the country's presidency during September 2008.

23.4.1 The political economy – the view of the ANC planners[1]

In December 2003 – to very little fanfare – the South African Presidency revealed the results of an 18-month-long scenario-planning exercise to plot what South Africa will look like in 2014.

In the early 1990s the Mont Fleur scenarios, drawn up by, among others, the ANC – then still a government in waiting – were instrumental in shaping the organisation's first years in power and hence the shape of South Africa today.

The ANC's decision to drop nationalisation and adopt a relatively conservative fiscal policy, which focused on stabilising South Africa's macro-economy in its first years in power, can be traced back to these scenarios.

The 2014 scenarios – which also probably influence future policy – suggest that another set of more subtle policy shifts will happen in the next 10 years. Most significant of these is government's re-embracing of the concept of a strong and redistributive state and of the need for fiscal transfer to stimulate the domestic market. The scenarios discount empowerment and global competitiveness as cure-alls.

The economy, in particular with regard to unemployment and the resultant inequalities and social and political tensions between the 'haves' in South Africa's formal economy and the 'have-nots' in the 'second' or informal economy, is the major concern. Government views social instability, brought on by popular dissatisfaction caused by poverty and unemployment, to be the biggest threat to constitutional democracy in South Africa.

It would appear that the government is going to focus on reducing the size of South Africa's unemployed to a more sustainable 12% of the working population, and growing the country's black middle class. It will also move to provide greater social security for those who remain outside the formal economy.

Scenario: 'Life is good'

'Life is good, good, good ...', well at least for the rich and connected, says this scenario. (Encouragingly, its tone illustrates that in some quarters of government, a wheeling-dealing brand of black empowerment that depends on connections and is heavily state assisted is frowned upon.)

This sort of empowerment yields an initial spurt in growth to around 7% in 2008 and then declines to 1% by the decade's end. Joblessness remains high, with opportunities in public works reserved for 'friends and family'. Through the decade, unemployment stays constant.

Primary exports and tourism increase, but competitive strength declines in an economy described as 'stagnant and corrupt'.

This is a scenario that sounds ominously like many post-colonial African societies where an elite takes hold and nothing trickles down to an increasingly alienated and desperate underclass. The rich rely almost entirely on private schools and hospitals, and facilities abroad. Life is good and nice for the elite, but the majority of South Africans feel the pain.

Scenario: 'The beat-up car'

This is also a 'bust' scenario. If South Africa were a car, it would be a much panelbeaten assembly of chop-shop bits and pieces, motoring through an environment where you would not want to get stuck by the side of the road.

Inequality worsens as real government spending tails off midway through the scenario period. In this atmosphere, disunity prevails and images of present-day Zimbabwe loom.

Parliament loses credibility, and the state becomes increasingly intolerant of debate and quickly assumes the character of a weak authoritarian elite, resorting to repressive measures at the slightest opportunity.

Internationally, this is a world in which the 'First World comes first'.

Scenario: 'We're all in this together'

For those of moderate ambition, this scenario is the future within their grasp. It is the social democrat, non-racist dream – a bit of a boom that is not only economic, but also social and political in nature.

Still poor, this is a society that makes room for one more in the taxi. It may be a bit of a struggle to fit everybody in, but the close proximity creates a sense of community solidarity and goodwill.

Growth is moderate at about 2% a year, and unemployment is in a slow but steady decline. Levels of inequality are reduced through the uplifting effects of the larger social wage to the poor, and the high levels of taxation of the rich.

But the large social welfare bill has pushed up both inflation and the budget deficit, raising questions about the sustainability of the system. Ratings agencies keep a beady eye on the country.

Domestic policies are more inspiring as civil society and government find each other. This scenario dreams of a highly involved, politicised society that draws in the young as the deep pockets of social spending begin to yield fruit. Slowly improving education and training standards enable more to find work in the formal economy as matric pass rates improve.

Scenario: 'Shosholoza – on the fast track'

Shosholoza is the boom landscape – its image is that of a sleek train that looks like early artist models of Gauteng's Gautrain, the vaunted high-speed shuttle service linking Johannesburg to the international airport and Pretoria. With grand ambition, the Shosholoza scenario predicts that poverty will be reduced by half in 2014, in line with the UN's Millennium Development Goals.

This scenario is dependent on a strong state, able to run effective health programmes, improve educational standards and cope with natural problems such as periodic drought, and which can insist on, and monitor, an effective system of corporate governance. Growth is more that 5%, while unemployment declines steeply. Outsourcing, communication, tourism, bio-technology, minerals beneficiation and the motor industry thrive.

Social spending continues to increase and has raised local demand, creating a virtuous economic cycle. Inequality is substantially reduced. Clearly the next 10 years are going to be very different from the last 10.

23.4.2 South Africa by 2025?: three possible scenarios as published in 20082

September 2008 saw the publication of "South Africa Scenarios 2025: The future we chose?" by the offices of The Presidency of South Africa. This section reflects the essence of these three scenarios.

Scenario 1 – "Not yet Uhuru"

- In the slipstream of the 2009 elections, the government found itself bombarded by lobbyists urging a new spirit of prudence in the drafting of economic policies.
- They argued the country needed massive foreign investment and foreign skills. As urgently, it needed growth in manufacturing and exports. There was much talk about the need for a 're-seeding and re-blossoming' of its long-stagnant agricultural sector.
- Despite fierce debate and protestations from elements within the tripartite alliance, it was eventually agreed that the fiscal discipline of the pre-2009 era needed to be maintained, especially because of the dark clouds hovering above the world economy.
- The new post-2009 government was clear that it could, at best, create 100 000 jobs a year between growing the public service and public works programmes. The other 400 000 to 500 000 new jobs needed each year simply had to come from the private sector.
- Some direct government intervention in the economy through Eskom and Transnet, and massive investments like Coega and the Pebble Bed Modular Reactor continued, with widespread focus on state leadership in the supplier industries for major infrastructure programmes. But market-led development was [the overarching policy].
- By 2025, more that 15 million South Africans were accommodated in the private healthcare system (double that of 2008) while 20% of learners were in private schools, up from just 2.8% in 2008. Private security guards outnumbered the police four to one, compared with the two-to-one ratio of 2008. And by 2024, private contractors were running all but one prison in South Africa. Tax breaks for private healthcare and retirement provision were extended, and even introduced for the costs of private security and private education. The cost to the government for these

services ballooned. The initial successes of many of these schemes came under pressure as the super-profits of some of the private service providers were exposed. Government regulation and oversight had to be tightened considerably.

- In South Africa, soil degradation, water pollution and wastage, and reliance on coal and coal-to-fuel for the nation's energy needs, impacted heavily on economic growth. With growth rates hovering around 3.5% for much of the second decade of the 21st century, mitigation strategies, which promised to shave off 0.5% to 1% of GDP growth per year, were deemed too expensive. [But] as fuel-cell technology assumed prominence, South Africa's platinum became a blessing.
- World growth averaged about 2.5% a year between 2009 and 2025. Many African nations committed to a trillion-dollar upgrade in infrastructure – particularly roads, trains, ports and telecoms. Unlike the grand infrastructure plans of the past, these were mostly managed better, with deeper efforts to involve citizens and the NGOs, and avoid some of the pitfalls of corruption and debt that plagued the last great investment in infrastructure in the 1980s. This 'counter-cyclical' investment positioned Africa well for the eventual upturn in the world economy in the mid-2010s and greatly improved intercontinental trade.
- [But] there was also massive pressure on wages, as worldwide inflation crept upwards, and the basic necessities of life became more and more expensive. In this context, it was not surprising that the hard work of choosing really new and bold growth paths, and funding the cost of environmental mitigation, was left to another generation to contemplate.
- Politically, the discourse continued to be rancorous.
- South Africa's 'investor-friendly' measures and incentives were not able to match those of more stable, more innovative or more desperate countries. Although some private businesses rose to the challenge posed by the government, by boosting local investment, many businesses were unable to find the kind of innovative mechanisms to create decent jobs and temper excessive profit-taking.
- They were not helped by perceptions that crime and corruption were out of control. This, together with a general Afro-pessimism in the West, pushed international investment to lower than anticipated levels. Sadly, even such mega-projects as the power-generation plants were not exciting enough to stir the global investment community into action.
- The inefficiency of national and provincial investment agencies, from developmental funding institutions to youth development funds, continued to make capital hard to come by for small farmers and entrepreneurs.
- In the private sector senior management remained more than 60% white.
- The free-market-led development strategy was simply too gradual for the vast majority of the poor to feel any substantial progress, particularly in terms of access to well-paying jobs, even by 2025.
- In 2013, disappointed with this trend, a group of leading trade unionists formed a Left party, and it was soon joined by the larger faction of the SACP.
- [Overall, by 2025] six million jobs were created, but in percentage terms, relative to a faster-moving world, the country had been marking time.

Scenario 2 – The Nkalakatha Nation
- Although painted as far more left-leaning than previous administrations, government (in 2009) was in fact pragmatic and shrewd, and worked hard to balance the needs of the people and the conditions for prosperous private enterprise.
- In retrospect, the national dialogue initiated was comparable only to the

negotiations of the 1990–93 period. In convention halls, retreats, summits and on radio and TV, every part of the society got involved in agreeing what they had to give up if South Africa was to prosper in the longer term. Government was able to engender an appreciation among all that short-term sacrifice was needed.

- After a series of summits, fixed investment increased and industrial policy was implemented systematically in the context of an emergent social compact. Rural and agricultural development, too, found a place in the sun, with real resources ploughed into supporting small- and medium-scale farmers.
- In 2012, skilled South Africans had started to return in large numbers, as high economic growth, lower crime rates and a new spirit of solidarity pervaded the nation.
- Emergency educational interventions, primary health and hospital revitalisation programmes, bold public works programmes, and large early childhood development programmes were rolled out.
- Business was clearer than ever that nothing threatened its longer-term accumulation potential more than the growing threat of insurrection and social turmoil brought on by poverty and inequality.
- In the increasingly important area of environmental sustainability, government was initially slow at putting principles into practice, arguing that growth and redistribution came first [but] leadership in this matter soon improved.
- Political instability in oil-producing regions, and a rapid decline in available oil, caused energy prices to spike above $200 per barrel by 2014.
- Having built stronger ties with Asia and Latin America, Africa was able to sustain average growth of 6%, taking advantage of its natural endowments – latterly focusing more and more on agricultural products.
- South Africa also integrated its economy more closely with that of the continent, working hard to create new customs unions and participatory blocs. In phases, GDP growth was roughly 5% (2009–2112); 6% (2013–2019); and 3% (2020–2024).
- Key provincial functions were relocated. More strong mayors worked more directly with central government to ensure that programmes were implemented.
- Government succeeded in doubling the police force by 2020, and funding community police forums around every police station.
- Meanwhile HIV/Aids and TB treatment was rolled out to more than one million people by 2014.
- The state was reluctant to privatise elements of many core services, such as education, health and security. Instead, it took an active part in launching new major industries connected to the massive infrastructure using new and old state-owned enterprises.
- The number of people employed in the civil service grew to 2.5 million. Compared to 2008, about four million more people were receiving some form of social grant by 2017. But fewer people were solely dependent on social grants, as unemployment was reduced to 12% by 2019.
- South Africa was particularly affected by even the small rise in temperatures that marked this decade, with the already declining carrying capacity of the soil being further impacted by dry spells [creating] a food security crisis.
- To the surprise of many, in 2021 government started to talk seriously about removing BEE charters and affirmative action programmes from the workplace. Thirty percent black ownership in land and the JSE was achieved, and 40% of managers and professionals were black.
- Global financial markets crashed in autumn 2018, started with the collapse of the second-biggest bank in the world, headquartered in Mumbai. After much debate,

government bit the bullet and introduced austerity measures, including additional mandatory savings by citizens, and compulsory youth service.

Scenario 3 – "Muvhango"

- After the elections of 2009 and the successful Soccer World Cup in 2010, the annual growth rate breached 5.5%. But despite the favourable conditions, and about four years of excellent growth, substantial current account deficits and daunting levels of cumulative debt steadily weighed down the state.
- By 2012 the paucity of capacity, poor planning and coordination, and bureaucratic inertia, overlaid with startling levels of animosity among politicians, started to filter through to the still strongly performing economy.
- By reducing energy demand substantially by the mid-2010s, the world economy was not as badly affected by high energy prices as feared. The US also recovered well from sub-prime and other credit crunches, and China and India handled their growth well.
- In addition, more concerted multilateralism helped mitigate global environmental degradation, and world growth averaged about 4.5% per annum for the 16-year period to 2025.
- Local growth was stimulated by government infrastructure investment, an accelerated mass-housing programme, and critical shifts to carefully planned areas of investment where SA was internationally competitive. Better terms of trade and more efficient use of technology, along with time-zone advantages, helped South Africa sell more services internationally. These included call-centre operations, customer-relationship management and software development.
- On reflection, notwithstanding the will to succeed in government, it is clear that a core reason for failure were the negligible consequences for inefficiency. Poor performers were shielded by unions and political connections. Excellent hospital managers and excellent school principals, for example, were treated no differently from their more mediocre peers in terms of recognition and reward.
- The key performance agreement system was honoured mostly in the breach and eventually collapsed in 2015. In addition, not enough was done to check public sector corruption, such as tenders going to companies with overt connections to well-positioned individuals and groups within the ruling party, or to curb personal enrichment by people working in government at all levels.
- A major expansion of the public service, with 400 000 new positions filled in less that a decade, helped create jobs and reduce backlogs, but didn't significantly improve the speed and efficiency of delivery. While politics was awash with left-wing rhetoric in the 2010s, the actual lifestyle and conduct of many high-profile leaders sometimes evinced rank corruption.
- Elements in the judiciary and investigating agencies were either cowed or co-opted into what became a permissive era. Despite calls for unity, the divisions in the ANC were accentuated by a number of messy criminal trials in 2009–2011, and the discovery of outbreaks of corruption by individuals both in the old and new guard.
- Trends in elections started to show tactical voting, especially by young people and the middle strata. The ANC majority was drastically reduced, hovering for a while around 50–60% at national level, with three provinces intermittently ruled by coalitions of opposition parties.
- The informal sector was also hobbled by crime and ironically, by the growing efficiency and generosity of the partly outsourced and privatised social welfare system. Inefficiency also increased, and slow turnaround times for basic services stymied economic growth.

- Government throughout the 2010s wanted to do more to protect the environment, and many admirable projects were initiated. These included mega-projects to husband water and soil resources, build wind farms and solar stations, and encourage citizens to save electricity.
- Symbolising the nation's political power struggles, and the slow extinguishing of the Great South African Dream, planned electricity outages became a way of life in the by 2015.
- In the broader economy, inflation stayed in double digits for years, with the differentials between the domestic rate of inflation and those of our trading partners seeing the rand depreciate to R15 per US dollar by 2017.
- While this currency depreciation helped some manufacturing industries, and certainly gave a much-needed boost to agriculture-based output, formal unemployment was not able to dip below 20% of the labour force, even by 2024.
- By 2025 South Africa has sold its major financial services, healthcare, mining and retail companies to foreign multinationals and private equity funds, particularly in the global boom years of the 2010s. Now, a Chinese consortium was offering a 40% premium for 75% control of Sasol.
- Growing on average by 3.5% over the 16-year period, South Africa's proportion of continental GDP declined, so that by 2020 both the Nigerian and Egyptian economies eclipsed South Africa's. As the situation deteriorated, there were many outbreaks of mass anger and impatience: marches, strikes, riots and xenophobia. Despite this, the election in 2014 went relatively well, notwithstanding the factionalism in the ANC. But the ANC majority was reduced – just 55% of voters were prepared to trust the ANC to govern for another five years to 2019.
- A rancorous national conference in 2022 finally produced a revitalisation of the idealism of politics. The ANC, SACP and a breakaway faction of the ANC forged a pact and soon merged into one party.

23.4.3 Scenarios of 'the South African game' – according to Sunter and Ilbury3

South Africa's possibilities within the global context are presented here in accordance with Sunter and Ilbury (2008). These world-renowned scenario makers firstly present four possible global scenarios ('long boom', 'hard times', 'divided world' and 'perfect storm') as the broader international context, based on five 'rules of the game' (the 'global game') and five 'key uncertainties'. The 'rules' of the 'global game' (meaning propositions that are virtually certain to apply under all four scenarios) are the following: China and India (the two most populous nations on earth) are in the throes of an industrial revolution; there is a global shift in the economic centre of gravity away from the Western economies towards the East; China's relationship with Africa is growing; the threat of terrorism will not abate and the war on terror will continue through the 2010s; and environmental concerns are gathering momentum. The key uncertainties (surprises that are lurking in the woods) are the following: a possible US recession; the intensity, extent and nature of acts of terror in the future; the rate and impact of global warming; a possible renewal of the cold war; and the possible arrival and impact of a next global pandemic.

In terms of South Africa, then, they also provide 'rules of the game' and 'key uncertainties' – as below:

The rules of the game

1 Just as a positive team dynamic is what wins you the cup in soccer, social harmony or cohesion is a prerequisite to achieving long-run success in the global economy.
2 To sustain such harmony, the economy must be inclusive, which South Africa's economy

is currently anything but. Its development since 1994 is more akin to a change in the membership of an existing, exclusive club. This brings to mind Karl Marx's rule of the game that if you alienate the masses, you can expect a revolution.

3 In order to achieve a per-annum economic growth of 6% plus, South Africa will need to embrace the characteristics of a winning nation, namely:

(a) A good quality of education at all levels to compete in the knowledge-intensive global game. This particularly applies to maths and science.

(b) A strong work ethic and spirit of entrepreneurship. To give an example of the former, the Chinese built a 7 000-bed hospital in one week when they were threatened by an outbreak of the respiratory disease, SARS.

(c) A high rate of savings because you cannot get around the classic economic equation for a domestic economy – savings equals investment. This implies a low rate of inflation combined with a reasonable after-tax interest rate for savers of capital.

(d) Adequate infrastructure to support a high-growth economy, including road, rail, port and airport systems, electricity grid, water supply and telecommunications.

(e) Being an export-oriented global player that supplies goods and/or services to foreign markets that they cannot get elsewhere. It is about choosing economic spaces that play to South Africa's strengths. For instance, South Africa as a tourist destination is hard to replicate but going head-to-head with the Chinese on any item they produce in bulk would be sheer madness.

(f) A dual-logic economy, which features a symbiotic relationship between a world-class big business sector and a thriving small business one. The best example is Japan where much of the manufacturing process is outsourced by the giants to an enormous network of small businesses, the giant retaining control of the brand and final assembly of the product.

(g) Competitive personal and company tax rates to discourage talented individuals and businesses moving to other countries.

(h) An attractive environment for foreign direct investment that would include the protection of property and a serious intent to create a crime-free society.

(i) Efficient government, especially in terms of service delivery, law and order, macro-economic management and a health system that provides for a universally healthy nation.

4 South Africa is staging the biggest event in the world in 2010 – the FIFA Soccer World Cup. It is a gigantic undertaking and therefore carries with it significant risk. Just as it may provide great opportunities for South Africa to brand itself as a winning nation, the effects could be devastating if things go wrong.

Key uncertainties

As a player on the global game board, South Africa is subject to the external uncertainties that shape the international game. Yet, in addition, there are important uncertainties that are specific to South Africa, and as such could determine the possible outcomes for the country in the 2010s. These include the following:

1 Whether or not South Africa can retain its competitive edge in the global game which itself is becoming increasingly competitive.

2 Whether we continue to be the generally peaceful society we have enjoyed being since 1994 or whether we experience some form of internal conflict as a result of recent political tensions.

3 Whether or not the Constitution remains sacrosanct, and the independence of institutions like the judiciary and the media continues to be observed.

4 Whether or not the issue of land ownership can be resolved peacefully and productively.

5 Whether or not the current inadequacies in the country's infrastructure, particularly relating to electricity supply, can be sorted out in a way that does not hinder economic growth.

6 Whether or not HIV/Aids as the country's worst epidemic and blight on people's lives is ultimately eradicated.

7 Whether or not the crime rate – particularly the violent crime rate – is reduced to an acceptable level.

8 Whether or not we can improve the quality of our education system, bearing in mind the competition from the private sector for skilled people who might otherwise be teachers.

9 Whether or not the critical skills shortages which are developing in parts of the economy can be overcome in the near future.

10 Whether or not Zimbabwe as one of our closest neighbours can climb out of the abyss in which it currently finds itself.

11 Whether or not South Africa can handle the diplomatic balancing act between East and West, especially in a 'hard times', 'divided world' or 'perfect storm' scenario.

The South African scenarios

The aforementioned key uncertainties can be grouped into two pivotal uncertainties that we have chosen to use in formulating different scenarios for South Africa. These are its competitiveness relative to the rest of the world and its cohesiveness as a nation.

We feel that there is no sustainable scenario where we can remain competitive and have internal conflict at the same time. A nation's total energy must be focused on the global game, not dissipated on internal divisions. Nonetheless, one opinion expressed to us is that South Africa has indeed been in that 'space' for some time because the economic imbalances in society have not yet been addressed. We are just lucky that the disharmony which lies under the surface has not manifested itself in open conflict.

We take a different view (like many others to whom we have given this presentation), and that is that South Africa vaulted into the 'premier league' of nations when it became a full-blown democracy in 1994. It has remained there as a result of 14 years of stable government and disciplined macroeconomic policies, all of which took place in the context of the global 'long boom' scenario.

However, as the saying goes, the honeymoon is now over. Staying in the 'premier league' is proving increasingly challenging for South Africa. It demands a more vigorous implementation of the attributes of a winning nation. Greater efficiency in terms of government delivery is key, as well as a dramatic reduction in crime, especially the threat to personal security and private property. Moreover, transformation of the health system and education system is needed. The reality is that other countries have now stepped up to the plate in the global game, and have accepted the conditions and challenges, and are outperforming South Africa. Among them are Sweden, Denmark, Switzerland, Hong Kong and Singapore, as well as developing nations such as China, Russia, India and the Slovak Republic. They have all closed the gap on the US. In fact, South Africa is now facing relegation, having lost ground to the US along with Indonesia, France, Italy, Argentina, Brazil and Mexico.

The proof is forthcoming in three reports released recently that have logged South Africa's decline:

■ The World Economic Forum's (WEF) Global Competitive Index shows a fall for South Africa from 36th position in 2006 to 44th position in 2007.

- In the World Bank's *Doing Business in 2008 Survey* of global ease-of-doing-business rankings, South Africa has slipped from 29th position to 35th. This is the first time the country has fallen out of the top 30 since the survey began five years ago.
- The International Institute for Management Development's *World Competitiveness Yearbook* for 2007 highlights South Africa's 12-place fall from grace. It has descended from 38th to 50th position in a ranking of 55 countries.

So why, according to these surveys, has South Africa slipped almost to the bottom of the 'premier league' – into the so-called 'relegation zone'? Maybe it has to do with the haemorrhaging brain drain and the increasing shortage of skills. Maybe it is our rising cost base. Maybe we have not matched the productivity gains obtained by the countries in the ascendant. Maybe the overseas perception of political risk in South Africa has changed for the worse. Whatever the causes, there is no denying that we are in danger of losing our 'premier league' status along with all the perks that go with it (such as a seat on the UN Security Council, being seen as the leading voice in Africa, and being considered as a partner of choice by China).

So the optimistic scenario is that we do a U-turn and advance our rankings to at least the middle position of the league by the time we get to 2020. This will require the development of new economic spaces, the most obvious one being the principal gateway to Africa. We are the most modern economy on the continent and have all the accoutrements to act as a springboard for any overseas company wishing to launch its bid to gain market share in Africa. And, as the Chinese know, Africa is open for business. Dubai is the gateway to the Middle East; Hong Kong and Singapore to China. It is a very profitable space to occupy, providing you are an excellent service provider. One could interpret the acquisition of a stake in Standard Bank by China's largest bank as a first step towards being acknowledged as a gateway economy. Other deals could follow which cement our relationship with the East.

Losing further ground in the competitiveness stakes will see South Africa knocked out of the 'premier league' into the '2nd division'. The latter is occupied by countries that are euphemistically described as 'poor but peaceful'. It applies to the bulk of the developing world. In this scenario, there is no chance of South Africa living up to the ANC's dictum of a 'better life for all'. The money simply is not there. Furthermore, it is mighty difficult to get back into the 'premier league' after one's position has been filled by another country which, you can be sure, will jealously guard its newfound status. South Africa's opinion on the issues of the day will no longer be sought by the international community, and corruption is likely to spread as no other method is available to escape the trap of poverty.

A greater worry is a scenario where a relapse into the '2nd division' is accompanied by internal disharmony and, eventually, overt conflict. South Africa would very quickly take a sharp turn left and join the likes of Zimbabwe, Myanmar, North Korea and Somalia in the 'failed state' scenario or quadrant. Kenya's (recent) political upheavals and violence demonstrate just how quickly a country can tumble towards this scenario, and just how arbitrary the trigger can be. Pakistan, likewise.

Of course, South Africa is also at the mercy of the global game. If the world moves into a 'hard times' scenario, South Africa's position in the 'relegation zone' could be even more tenuous. It will certainly find it increasingly difficult to maintain its recent trajectory of economic growth or sustain its developmental and welfare policies. All is not lost, though. Should global instability see a shift towards a 'divided world' scenario, South Africa can benefit from the goodwill it has accumulated in the East.

South Africa has definitely lost some footing in the 'premier league' since the ushering in of its Cinderella democracy. Its fall in the rankings has been somewhat disguised by the beneficial effect of the 'long boom' scenario. Complacency, a certain degree of arrogance, a lack of service delivery and some misdirected government policies have taken South Africa's eye off the ball in a game where the demands on the players are unyielding. The country is now in the 'relegation zone' and faces possible ejection into the economic mire of the '2nd division'. And this could happen quicker than we think.

As we all know, the future is never a known. Change happens all the time – often unexpectedly and 'deeply' too. Who would for instance have thought that by September 2008 South Africa would have a new, albeit interim, President? Who would have predicted the extremely negative global financial environment that was developing by the last half/ quarter of 2008? Who would have bet money on the establishment of a new political party in South Africa by the end of 2008? We can be sure – more change is to come! As that happens we must probably re-think our scenarios about the future – for the world, for Africa, and for South Africa. HRM in our organisations do not get practised in isolation of these developments. We must hence be 'wide-awake' at all times – holistic, strategic and driven by a deep yearning to improve people's lives!

23.5 CONCLUSION

This brings this book to a conclusion. We have huge challenges ahead as a country, and it is all about the people of this country – the choices we make about how we deal with what the world holds in store for us as the future unfolds. This makes HRM absolutely central to our future – especially if we are prepared to take up the challenge posed by this book, namely to take a more holistic approach to HRM and to integrate it fully with how we manage and govern our organisations – and our country and continent. What we do with our challenges is up to us – as individuals, as ordinary citizens of this country, as consumers and as working people – as different groups, as trade unions, as business organisations, as political parties and as other kinds of organisations such as charities, churches, schools, universities and public-service organisations at all levels and in all forms – as owners of businesses, as managers, as leaders, as government, and as a country as a whole. Our response to all our challenges will be the key factor in determining which type of scenario will become reality. It is that reality that will have the biggest impact eventually on the quality of life of all of us and our beloved country and its people – and our continent, Africa.

The challenges are ours – the time is now!

SELF-EVALUATION QUESTIONS

1 What makes the difference between practising HRM in South Africa, than when practising it in various other countries in Africa for instance?
2 "HRM, corporate governance and sustainability are not inter-related." Analyse and critically discuss this statement.
3 What are the potential connections between HRM and the way that possible future scenarios of South Africa might unfold?

ENDNOTES

1 Slightly adapted extracts from Henderson (2007: 24–25)
2 Taken from the *Sunday Times* as summarised/reported by Philp (2008: 8) (The full report entitled 'SOUTH AFRICA Scenarios 2025: The future we chose?' was electronically posted at http://www.thepresidency.gov.za/)
3 Slightly adapted extracts from Sunter & Ilbury (2008: 30–33)

BIBLIOGRAPHY

'A breakdown of the South African village'. 2008. <http://www.sagoodnews.co.za/index2.php?option=com_content&task=view&id=1541 ...>

Aamodt, M G. 1999. *Applied Industrial/Organizational Psychology,* 3rd ed. Belmont, CA: Wadsworth.

Acutt, J. 1992. 'Emergencies and disaster planning', in *Occupational Health*, ed Kotzé, A J, 168–169. Cape Town: Juta.

'Africa economic growth still strong'. 2008. <www.sagoodnew.co.za/index2.php>

'Africa economy to remain robust despite global slowdown'. 2008. <www.sagoodnews.co.za/index2.php?option=com_content&task=view&id=1507 ...>

'Africa's economic performance: a promise of things to come?' n.d. <www.sagoodnew.co.za/index.2.php>.

'Africa's progress on development goals linked to growth, environment'. 2008. <http://web.worldbank.org/WBSITE/EXTERNAL/COUNTRIES/AFRICAEXT/0,,contentMDK:21721946~menuPK:258658~pagePK:2865106~piPK:2865128~theSitePK:258644,00.html>.

African Labour Research Network (ALRN) 2005. *Mining Africa. Comprehensive Report and Synthesis Report,* ed Pillay, D. Johannesburg: ALRN.

'Africans optimistic despite challenges'. n.d. <www.sagoodnews.co.za/index2.php>

Alfred, N (ed). 1984. *Bargain, Don't Fight!* Johannesburg: Thompson.

Alien, T D, Poteet, M L, Russel, J E A & Dobbins, G H. 1995. *Influence of Learning and Development Factors on Perceptions of Plateauing.* Paper presented at the Tenth Annual Meeting of the Society for Industrial and Organisational Psychology, Orlando.

Almhdie, A & Nyambegera, S M. 2004. 'HRM in Libya', in *Managing Human Resources in Africa,* eds Kamoche, K, Debrah, Y, Horwitz, F & Muuka, G N. Routledge: London.

Alonso, L E & Lucio, M M. 2006. *Employment Relations in a Changing Society – Assessing the Post-Fordist Paradigm*. Basingstoke, UK: Palgrave Macmillan.

Altbeker, A. 2007. *A Country at War with Itself: South Africa's Crisis of Crime*. Jeppestown: Jonathan Ball Publishers.

Altman, M. 2005. 'The state of employment', in *State of the Nation – South Africa 2004–2005*, eds Daniel, J, Southall, R & Lutchman, J. Pretoria: HSRC.

Ameiss, R P & Williams, D E. 1981. 'Human resource accounting in industry'. *CA Magazine*, August, 113–118.

American Accounting Association. 1973. 'Report of the Committee on Human Resource Accounting'. *The Accounting Review,* XLIX (2), 169–185.

Anakwe, U P. 2002. 'Human resource management practices in Nigeria: challenges and insights'. *The International Journal of Human Resource Management*, 13(7), 1042–1059.

Analoui, F. 2007. *Strategic Human Resource Management*. London: Thomson.

Ancona, D, Kochan, T A, Scully, M, Van Maanen, J & Westney, D E. 1999. *Managing for the Future: Organizational Behavior and Processes*. Cincinnati, Ohio: South-Western.

Anderson, A H. 1994. *Effective Personnel Management: A Skills and Activity-based Approach*. London: Blackwell.

Andrews, C J. 2008. *Developing and Conducting a Human Resource Management Performance Audit: Case Study of an Australian University*. DBA Dissertation. Toowoomba: University of Southern Queensland.

Anglo American Corporation. 1984. *Paterson Job Evaluation Handbook*. Johannesburg: Personnel Systems Department.

Annual Report 2006–2007. *Inspiring a Competitive South Africa*. National Productivity Institute, 1–69.

Annual Report 2007–2008. South African Board for Personnel Practice, Parktown.

Anstey, M (ed). 1990. *Worker Participation*. Cape Town: Juta.

Anstey, M. 1990. 'Worker participation: Concepts and issues', in *Worker Participation*, ed M Anstey. Kenwyn: Juta.

Anstey, M. 1995. 'Can South African industrial relations move beyond adversarialism? Some comparative perspectives on the prospects of workplace forums in South Africa'. *South African Journal of Labour Relations*, 19(4), 13.

Anstey, M. 1997. 'New ball game'. *Productivity SA*, January/February, 7–10.

Anstey, M. 1997. *Employee Participation and Negotiation Forums*. Kenwyn: Juta.

Anthony, R N. 1990. 'The bad and the good of experience'. *Management Accounting*, 71(7), 36–37.

Anthony, W P, Perrewe, P L & Kacmar, K M. 1996. *Strategic Human Resource Management*. Orlando: The Dryden Press.

Anthony, W P, Perrewé, P L & Kacmar, K M. 1999. *Human Resource Management: A Strategic Approach*, 3rd ed. Orlando, Fl: Dryden.

Araujo, J P. 1996. 'The introduction of a no-smoking policy'. *People Dynamics*, 13(12), 39.

Arens, A, Best, P, Shailer, G, Fielder, B, Elder, R, & Beasley, M. 2005. *Auditing and Assurance Services in Australia: An Integrated Approach*, 6th ed. Frenchs Forest, Australia: Pearson.

Armstrong, M & Brown, D. 2006. *Strategic Reward: Making it Happen*. London: Kogan Page.

Armstrong, M & Murlis, H. 1988. *Reward Management*. London: Kogan Page.

Armstrong, M & Stephens, T. 2005. *A Handbook of Employee Reward Management and Practice*. London: Kogan Page.

Arnold, J. 2001. 'The psychology of careers in organisation', in *Organizational Psychology and Development,* eds Cooper, C & Robertson, I. Wiley, 23–50.

Arvey, R D & Faley, R H. 1988. *Fairness in Selecting Employees*. New York: Addison-Wesley Publishing Company.

Aryee, S. 2004. 'HRM in Ghana', in *Managing Human Resources in Africa*, eds Kamoche, K, Debrah, Y, Horwitz, F & Muuka, G N. 2004 London: Routledge.

Atkinson, D. 2007. 'Taking to the streets: has developmental local government failed in South Africa?', in *State of the Nation – South Africa 2007,* eds Buhlungu, S, Daniel, J, Southall, R & Lutchman, J. Cape Town: HSRC Press. 53–77.

Atkinson, J. 1984. 'Manpower strategies for flexible organizations'. *Personnel Management*, August.

Atwater, L & Waldman, D. 1999. 'Accountability in 360-degree feedback'. *HR Magazine*, 43(6), 96–104.

Babbie, E. 1995. *The Practice of Social Research*, 7th ed. Harrisonburg, Virginia: Wadsworth.

Bagwa, W. 1973. 'Welfare facilities for black employees'. *People & Profits*, 1(6), 12–16.

Bakke, E W. 1958. *The Human Resources Function*. New Haven: Labor-Management Center, Yale University.

Baldauf, S. 2006. 'Has Africa finally turned the corner?' <http://www.csmonitor.com/2006/1109/p01s04-woaf.html>

Balnave, N, Brown, J, Maconachie, G & Stone, R. 2007. *Employment Relations in Australia.* Australia: John Wiley & Sons.

Barker, F. 2007. *The South African Labour Market*, 5th ed. Pretoria: Van Schaik.

Barney, J. 1991. 'Firm resources and sustained competitive advantage'. *Journal of Management*, 17(1), 99–120.

Bartol, K, Tein, M, Matthews, G & Sharma, B. 2008. *Management: A Pacific Rim Focus*, 5th ed. Australia: McGraw-Hill.

Bartol, M B & Locke, E A. 2000. 'Remuneration in organizations', in *Current Research and Practice*, eds Rynes, S L & Gerhart, B. San Francisco: Jossey-Bass.

Baue, W. 2005. *Carrots and Sweets: Tying Executive Remuneration to Extra-financial Performance Indicators*. SRI World Group. <www.socialfunds.com/news>

Beach, D S. 1980. *Personnel: The Management of People at Work*, 4th ed. New York: Macmillan.

Beardwell, J & Claydon, T. 2007. *Human Resource Management,* 5th ed. London: Pearson Education.

Beatty, R W & Schneier, C E. 1997. 'New HR roles to impact organizational performance: From "partners" to "players".' *Human Resource Management*, 38(1), 29–37.

Beatty, R W & Schneier, C E. 2005. 'Workforce strategy: A missing link in HR's future success', in *The Future of Human Resource Management – 64 Thought Leaders Explore the Critical HR Issues of Today and Tomorrow,* eds Losey, M, Meisinger, S & Ulrich, D. New Jersey: John Wiley & Sons.

Beatty, R W & Ulrich, D O. 1993. 'Re-energising the mature organisation', in *Managing Change: Cases and Concepts*, ed Jick, T O. Boston: Richard D Irwin, Inc.

Becker, B E, Huselid, M A & Ulrich, D. 2001. *The HR Scorecard: Linking People, Strategy, and Performance*. Boston: Harvard Business School.

Beckhard, R & Harris, R. 1977. *Organisational Transitions: Managing Complex Change*. Reading, Mass: Addison-Wesley.

Beer, M, Eisenstat, R & Spector, B. 1990. 'Why change programs don't produce change'. *Harvard Business Review*, November–December, 158–167.

Beer, M, Spector, B, Lawrence, P, Mills, D & Walton, R. 1985. *Human Resource Management: A General Manager's Perspective.* New York: Free Press.

Beer, M. & Nohria, N. 2000. 'Cracking the code of change'. *Harvard Business Review* (May–June).

Beer, S. 1975. *Brain of the Firm.* New York: Herder & Herder.

Bekker, D. 1995. 'Profit-sharing: Friend or foe?' *HRM,* 11(4), 22–23.

Bellemare, G. 2000. 'End users: Actors in the industrial relations system?' *British Journal of Industrial Relations*, 38(3), 383–405.

Bendix, S. 1992. *Industrial Relations in South Africa*, 2nd ed. Cape Town: Juta.

Bendix, S. 1996. *Industrial Relations in the New South Africa*, 3rd ed. Cape Town: Juta.

Bendix, S. 2000. *Industrial Relations in the New South Africa*, 4th ed. Cape Town: Juta.

Bendix, S. 2001. *Industrial Relations in South Africa*, 4th ed. Cape Town: Juta.

Bennis, W & Mische, M. 1995. *The 21st Century Organisation: Reinventing through Re-engineering*. San Diego: Pfeiffer & Company.

Bergh, Z C. 1992. 'Psychological adjustment of the worker in the work environment'. In *Occupational Health*, ed Kotzé, A J. Cape Town: Juta, 194.

Bernardin, J H & Russell, J E. 1993. *Human Resource Management: An Experiential Approach*. New York: McGraw Hill.

Beugré , C D. 2002. 'Understanding organizational justice and its impact on managing employees: An African perspective'. *International Journal of Human Resource Management*, 13(7), 1091–1104.

Beugré, C D. 2004. 'HRM in Ivory Coast', in *Managing Human Resources in Africa*, eds Kamoche, K, Debrah, Y, Horwitz, F & Muuka, G N. London: Routledge.

Beukes, D. 1987. 'The use of computers in South African human resources management'. *IMP/IPB Joernaal*, 6(2), 30.

Bews, N & Bews, C. 1988. 'Employee assistance programmes: Internal or external model? The options considered'. *IPM Journal,* 7(2), 22.

Biesheuvel, S. 1985. *Work Motivational Remuneration*, vol 2. Johannesburg: McGraw-Hill.

Blair, D & Bernard, J R L. 1998. *Macquarie Pocket Dictionary*. Milton Qld: John Wiley & Sons.

Blum, M L & Naylor, J C. 1968. *Industrial Psychology: Theoretical and Social Foundations*. New York: Harper & Row.

Boden, A. 1998. 'Career development: What works and what doesn't?' *Management Today*, 14(4), 24–26.

Bodibe, O. 2006. *The Extent and Effects of Casualisation in Southern Africa: Analysis of Lesotho, Mozambique, South Africa, Swaziland, Zambia and Zimbabwe*. National Labour & Economic Development Institute.

Bolman, L G & Deal, T E. 2003. *Reframing Organizations: Artistry, Choice, and Leadership*. San Francisco: Jossey-Bass.

Booysen, L. 2007a. 'Barriers to employment equity implementation and retention of blacks in management in South Africa', *South African Journal of Labour Relations*, 31(1) 47–71.

Booysen, L. 2007b. 'Leadership and gender: The Zimbabwean scenario'. *Management Today*, 22(10), 77–80.

Booysen, L, Nkomo, S & Beaty, D. 2003. 'A best practice model for building a valuing diversity culture'. *Management Today*, 19(1), 33–36.

Bosman, E. 2007. 'Integrating wellness initiatives', *People Dynamics*, 25(10), 4–5.

Bostrom, R N. 1983. *Persuasion*. Englewood Cliffs, NJ: Prentice Hall.

Botha, B. 1992. 'Window for opportunity'. *People Dynamics*, 10(12), 7.

Boudreau, J W & Ramstad, P M. 2005. 'Talentship, talent segmentation, and sustainability: A new HR decision science paradigm for a new strategy definition', in *The Future of Human Resource Management: 64 Thought Leaders Explore the Critical HR Issues of Today and Tomorrow,* eds Losey, M, Meisinger, S & Ulrich, D. New Jersey: John Wiley & Sons.

Bown, W. 2007. 'Career development', *People Dynamics*, 25(2), 17.

Boxall, P & Purcell, J. 2003. *Strategy and Human Resource Management*. New York: Palgrave Macmillan.

Boxall, P & Purcell, J. 2008. *Strategy and Human Resource Management*, 2nd ed. New York: Palgrave Macmillan.

Boxall, P, Purcell, J & Wright, P. 2007. *The Oxford Handbook of Human Resource Management*. New York: Oxford University Press.

Boyens, A. 1991. 'Vakbonde verander deuntjie oor ESOPs'. *Finansies & Tegniek*, March, 26.

Boyle, B. 2008. 'While rich get richer, the poor get angry'. *Business Times*, 16 March, 8.

Bracker, J S & Pearson, J N. 1986. 'Worker obsolescence: The human resource dilemma of the 80s'. *Personal Administrator*, 31(12), 113.

Bracks, R & Van Wyk, M W. 1994. *The Position of HIV/Aids Employees in South African Companies: A Legal and Empirical Survey*. Unpublished MBL research report, Graduate School of Business Leadership, Unisa.

Bragg, A. 1990. 'Checking references'. *Sales and Marketing Management*, 142, 68–70.

Brase, N. 1995. 'How safe is safe?'. *People Dynamics*, 13(1), 24.

Brassey, M, Cameron, E, Cheadle, H & Olivier, M. 1987. *The New Labour Law*. Kenwyn: Juta.

Bratton, J & Gold, J. 2003. *Human Resource Management: Theory and Practice*, 3rd ed. Palgrave Macmillan, New York.

Bremen, J M & Coil, M. 1999. 'Comparing alternative base pay methods: Which one meets your organization's need?'. *ACA News*, June, 21–28.

Brewster, C & Larsen H. 1992. 'Human resource management in Europe: Evidence from ten countries'. *The International Journal of Human Resource Management*, 3(3), 409–434.

Brewster, C & Tyson, S. 1991. *International Comparisons in Human Resource Management*. London: Pitman.

Brewster, C, Farndale, E & Van Ommeren, J. 2000. *HR Competencies and Professional Standards*. June, World Federation of Personnel Management Associations.

Brousseau, K R. 1990. 'Career dynamics in the baby boom and baby bust era'. *Journal of Organizational Change Management*, 3(3), 47–58.

Bryant, W. 1990. 'Child care options for employers'. *IPM Journal*, 9(1), 17–21.

Budhwar, P S. 2004. *Managing Human Resources in Asia-Pacific*. Oxon: Routledge.

Buhlungu, S & Webster, E. 2006. 'Work restructuring and the future of labour in South Africa', in *State of the Nation – South Africa 2005–2006*, eds Buhlungu, S, Daniel, J, Southall, R & Lutchman, J (eds). Cape Town: HSRC.

Buhlungu, S, Daniel, J, Southall, R & Lutchman, J. 2007. *State of the Nation: South Africa 2007*. Cape Town: HSRC.

Burgess, L R. 1989. *Remuneration Administration*, 2nd ed. Columbus, Ohio: Merrill.

Burkholder, N C, Edwards, P J & Sartain, L (eds). 2004. *On Staffing: Advice and Perspectives from HR Leaders*. Hoboken, NJ: John Wiley & Sons Inc.

Burnes, B. 1996. *Managing Change: A Strategic Approach to Organizational Dynamics*. London: Pitman.

Bussin, M. 2001. *Determining the Best Total Remuneration Mix*. Paper delivered at the Strategic Compensation PayCon 2001 Conference, Sandton.

Bussin, M. 2004. 'Strategic remuneration trends', in *Building Human Capital: South African Perspectives*, eds Boninelli, I & Meyer, T. Randburg: Knowres.

Bussin, M. 2006. *Strategically Aligning your Remuneration Strategy to Company Objectives*. Unpublished paper delivered at Paycon 2006 Conference, Sandton.

Bussin, M. 2007. 'Yes or no?', *People Dynamics*, 25(4), 18.

Bussin, M. 2008. *Rewards Transformation: Turning Total Rewards from a Cost into an Investment*. Unpublished paper delivered at 2nd Talent Management Summit Conference, Sandton.

Bussin, M & De Beer, B. 2003. 'Executive share options not a candy machine'. *HR Future*, September 2003, 10–13.

Bussin, M & Thomson, D. 2000. 'Wealth sharing for all South Africans'. *People Dynamics*, February.

Butler, A. 2007. 'The state of the African National Congress', in *State of the Nation – South Africa 2007*, eds Buhlungu, S, Daniel, J, Southall, R & Lutchman, J. Cape Town: HSRC Press, 35–52.

Byars, L L & Rue, L W. 1987. *Human Resource Management.* Homewood, Illinois: Irwin.

Byars, L L & Rue, L W. 2006. *Human Resource Management,* 8th ed. Boston: McGraw-Hill.

Caelers, D. 2008. 'Frontline of the TB fight is in the workplace'. *Weekend Argus*, 22 March, 1.

Cameron, E. 1992. 'Comments: Aids and HIV in employment'. *Andrew Levy News*, 1(7).

Campion, M & Thayer, P. 1985. 'Development and field evaluation of an interdisciplinary measure of job design'. *Journal of Applied Psychology*, 70, 29–34.

Cappelli, P & Rogovsky, N. 1996. 'What do new systems demand of employees?' *Business Day* supplement: Mastering Management Series, Part 5, 1 April, 2.

Carter, C B & Lorsch, J W. 2004. *Back to the Drawing Board: Designing Corporate Boards for a Complex World*. Boston: HBS Publishing Corporation.

Carrell, M R, Jennings, D F & Hearin, C. 1997. *Fundamentals of Organisational Behaviour.* New Jersey: Prentice Hall Inc.

Carver, J & Olivier, C. 2002. *Corporate Boards that Create Value: Governing Company Performance from the Boardroom*. San Francisco: Jossey-Boss.

Cascio, W F. 1991. *Costing Human Resources: The Financial Impact of Behavior in Organizations*, 3rd ed. Boston: PWS Kent.

Cascio, W F. 1998. *Applied Psychology in Human Resource Management.* Englewood Cliffs, NJ: Prentice Hall.

Cascio, W F. 2005. 'From business partner to driving business success: The next step in the evolution of HR management', in *The Future of Human Resource Management: 64 Thought Leaders Explore the Critical HR Issues of Today and Tomorrow*, eds Losey, M, Meisinger, S & Ulrich, D. New Jersey: John Wiley & Sons.

Cascio, W F. 2006. *Managing Human Resources: Productivity, Quality of Work Life, Profits*, 7th ed. New York: McGraw-Hill.

Cascio, W F & Aquinis, H. 2005. *Applied Psychology in Human Resource Management*, 6th ed. New Jersey: Pearson.

Castle, J. 1995. 'Affirmative action in three developing countries: Lessons from Zimbabwe, Namibia and Malaysia'. *South African Journal of Labour Relations*, 19(1), Autumn, 6–33.

Certo, S C. 1994. *Modern Management: Diversity, Quality, Ethics and the Global Environment*, 6th ed. Boston: Allyn & Bacon.

Chapple, E & Sayles, L R. 1961. *The Measure of Management*. New York: Macmillan.

Charlton, G D & Van Niekerk, N. 1994. *Affirming Action – Beyond 1994*. Kenwyn: Juta.

Chartered Institute of Personnel and Development: Professional Standards. London: CIPD.

Cheadle Thomson & Haysom Inc. 2005. *Black Economic Empowerment: Commentary, Legislation & Charters.* Cape Town: Juta.

Cherrington, D J. 1983. *Personnel Management: The Management of Human Resources.* Dubuque, Iowa: WMC Brown.

Cherrington, D J. 1995. *The Management of Human Resources*, 4th ed. New Jersey: Prentice Hall.

Childs, J T. 2005. 'Workforce diversity: A global HR topic that has arrived', in *The Future of Human Resource Management: 64 Thought Leaders Explore the Critical HR Issues of Today and Tomorrow,* eds Losey, M, Meisinger, S & Ulrich, D. New Jersey: John Wiley & Sons.

Christiansen, J A. 2000. *Building the Innovative Organization.* London: Macmillan.

Cilliers, F & Smit, B. 2006. 'A psychodynamic interpretation of South African diversity dynamics. A comparative study'. *South African Journal of Labour Relations*, 30(2), 5–18.

CIPD. 2007. 'Performance management: an overview'. London: Chartered Institute of Personnel and Development, <www.cipd.co.uk> (accessed on 10 July 2007).

CIPD. 2007. 'Total Reward Factsheet', <www.cipd.co.uk>

CIPD. 2008. 'HR shared service centres'. <www.cipd.co.uk/subjects/hrpract/general/hrshrscen?cssversion=printable>

Ciucci, P. 2001. e-*Remuneration: Dawning Reality or Myth? A BAT Case Study.* Paper delivered at Paycon 2001 Conference, Sandton.

Clegg, S, Kornberger, M & Pitsis, T. 2005. *Managing and Organizations: An Introduction to Theory and Practice.* London: Sage.

Clutterbuck, D. 2001. *Everyone Needs a Mentor: Fostering Talent at Work.* London: Cromwell Press.

Coch, L & French, J R. 1948. 'Overcoming resistance to change'. *Human Relations*, August, 512–532.

Coetzee, J A G. 1976. *Industrial Relations in South Africa.* Cape Town: Juta.

Coetzee, M. 2002. *Getting and Keeping your Accreditation.* Van Schaik: Pretoria.

Coetzee, M. 2005. *Career Planning in the 21st Century: Strategies for Inventing a Successful Career in a Workplace without Jobs.* Unpublished manuscript, Department of Industrial and Organisational Psychology, Pretoria: Unisa.

Coetzee, M, Schreuder, D & Tladinyane, R. 2007. 'Organisational commitment and its relation to career anchors'. *Southern African Business Review*, 11(1), 65–85.

Coetzee, M & Stone, K. 2004. *Learner Support: Toward Learning and Development.* Randburg: Knowres.

Cogill, C. 1988. 'The Paterson way: Does it pay?'. *HRM*, September, 32–34.

Cole, K. 2007. *Workplace Relations in Australia: A Practical Guide to Work Choices.* Australia: Pearson Education.

Collins, J C & Porras, J I. 1996. 'Building your company's vision'. *Harvard Business Review,* September/October.

Commission for Employment Equity, Annual Report 2006–2007, Department of Labour, Pretoria, 1–54.

Compton, R L, Morrissey, W J & Nankervis, A R. 2002. *Effective Recruitment & Selection Practices*, 3rd ed. Australia: CCH.

Compton, R L, Morrissey, W J & Nankervis, A R. 2006. *Effective Recruitment & Selection Practices*, 4th ed. Sydney: CCH.

Conger, J A & Kanungo, R N. 1987. 'Towards a behavioural theory of charismatic leadership in organisational settings'. *Academy of Management Review*, 12, 637–647.

Connerley, M L & Pedersen, P B. 2005. *Leadership in a Diverse and Multicultural Environment: Developing Awareness, Knowledge, and Skills.* California: Sage.

Cooke, R. 1988. 'Human resource management: A case for reference checking'. *Credit Union Management*, 11(10), 28–29.

Cooke, W N. 2007. 'Multinational companies and global human resource strategy', in *The Oxford Handbook of Human Resource Management*, eds Boxall, P, Purcell, J & Wright, P. New York: Oxford University Press, 489–508.

Cooper, D, Robertson, I & Tinline, G. 2003. *Recruitment and Selection: A Framework for Success.* London: Thomson.

Cooper, W W & Leavitt, H J (eds). 1964. *New Perspectives in Organisation Research.* New York: Wiley.

Cordery, J & Parker, S K. 2007. 'Work organization', in *The Oxford Handbook of Human Resource Management,* eds Boxall, P, Purcell, J & Wright, P. New York: Oxford University Press, 187–209.

Corporate Research Foundation. 1998. *The 49 Best Companies to Work for in South Africa.* Halfway House: Zebra.

Corporate Research Foundation. 2005. 'Best Companies to Work for: 2005'. <www.microsoft. com/southafrica/careers>

Corporate Research Foundation. 2005. *The Best Companies to Work for in South Africa: 2005.* Cape Town: CRF.

Corporate Research Foundation. 2007. *Best Employers in South Africa*. Cape Town: CRF.

Corporate Research Foundation. 2007. *Best Employers South Africa*. Cape Town: CRF.

Cotton, C. 2007. 'Executive remuneration and the lot of the HR professional'. <www.worldlink.com> (accessed July 2007).

Country Reports. 2008. *The Africa Report,* 9, 110–193.

Covin, T J & Brush, C C. 1993. 'Attitudes toward work–family issues: The human resources professional perspective'. *Review of Business,* 15 (2), 25–29

Cowling, A & James, P. 1994. *The Essence of Personnel Management and Industrial Relations.* London: Prentice Hall.

Craven, P. 2008. 'Southern African unions speak out for democracy in Zimbabwe', <www.unionaidabroad.org.au/projects/africa/news/1207713051_12918.html>

Crites, J O. 1969. *Vocational Psychology.* New York: McGraw-Hill.

Cronbach, L J. 1970. *Essentials of Psychological Testing*. New York: Harper & Row.

Cronje, F. 2006. *Fast Facts – When your Number's up*. South African Institute of Race Relations, no. 10.

Croome, B. 2001. *Structuring your Remuneration Packages.* Unpublished paper presented at PayCon 2001 Conference, 26 September, Sandton.

Crous, M J. 1990. 'Decision making', in *General Management*, ed Kroon, J. Pretoria: Haum.

Crous, W. 1990. "n Nuwe Suid-Afrika op die horison – implikasies vir die menslike hulpbronbestuurder'. *IPM Journal*, 8(8), 3.

Cuming, M W. 1989. *The Theory and Practice of Personnel Management*, 6th ed. Oxford: Heinemann.

Cunningham, P W, Slabbert, J A, & De Villiers, A S. 1990. 'The historic development of industrial relations', in *Managing Industrial Relations in South Africa*, eds Slabbert, J A, Prinsloo, J J & Backer, W. Pretoria: Digma.

Cushway, B. 1994. *Human Resource Management*. London: Kogan Page.

Dalton, G W, Thompson, P H & Price, R L. 1986. *Innovations: Strategies for Career Management*. Glenview, Illinois: Scott, Foresman & Company.

Daniel, J, Lutchman, J & Comninos, A. 2007. 'South Africa in Africa: Trends and forecasts in a changing African political economy', in *State of the Nation – South Africa 2007*, eds Buhlungu, S, Daniel, J, Southall, R & Lutchman, J. Cape Town: HSRC Press, 508–532.

Daniel, J, Southall, R & Lutchman, J. 2005. 'Introduction: President Mbeki's second term: Opening the golden door', in *State of the Nation – South Africa 2004–2005*, eds Daniel, J, Southall, R & Lutchman. Cape Town: HSRC Press.

Davidson, P. & Griffin, R W. 2003. *Management: An Australian Perspective*, 2nd ed. Milton: John Wiley & Sons.

Davis, P. 2007. 'The performance paradox'. *HR Professional*, April/May 2007, 26–27.

De Beer, E. 2007. 'The quest for career success', *People Dynamics*, 25(3), 16–19.

De Cieri, H. 2007. 'Transnational firms and cultural diversity', in *The Oxford Handbook of Human Resource Management,* eds Boxall, P, Purcell, J & Wright, P. New York: Oxford University Press, 509–532.

De Cieri, H & Kramar, R. 2005. *Human Resource Management in Australia : Strategy, People, Performance*, 2nd ed. Australia: McGraw-Hill.

De Meuse, K P & Marks, M L. 2003. *Resizing the Organisation.* San Francisco: Jossey-Bass.

De Vries, F. 2007. 'Looking up for a way forward', <www.africanleadershipgroupcom/Portals/89/Documents/FredDeVries_article_12May07.doc>

De Vries, G. 2008. 'Top 10 wellness trends for 2008 and beyond'. *Compensation & Benefits Review*, April, 60–64.

De Wit, B & Meyer, R. 2005. *Strategy Synthesis: Resolving Strategy Paradoxes to Create Competitive Advantage – Text and Readings*, 2nd ed. London: Thomson Learning.

De Witt, D. 1998. 'HR challenges for organisational transformation'. *Management Today*, 13(10), 33–35.

De Witt, D. 1998. 'HR challenges for organisational transformation'. *Management Today*, 14(1), 28–31.

Debrah, Y A. 2004. 'HRM in Tanzania', in *Managing Human Resources in Africa*, eds Kamoche, K , Debrah, Y, Horwitz, F. & Muuka, G N. London: Routledge.

DeCenzo, D A & Robbins, S P. 1994. *Human Resource Management: Concepts and Practices*. New York: John Wiley & Sons.

DeCenzo, D. & Robbins, S P. 2007. *Fundamentals of Human Resource Management*, 9th ed. Danvers, MA: Wiley.

Deloitte & Touche. 2002. *Human Capital Benchmarking Report*, generic report 22. Human Capital Corporation (Pty) Ltd.

Department of Labour. 2004. *Human Resource Development Strategy for South Africa*. Pretoria, <www.labour.gov.za>

Department of Labour. 2005. *Labour Market Review, 2005*. Pretoria: Department of Labour.

Department of Labour. 2005. *National Skills Development Strategy, 1 April 2005–31 March 2010*. Pretoria: Government Printer.

Department of Labour. 2005. *State of Skills in South Africa, 2005*. Pretoria: Department of Labour.

Department of Labour. 2006. *Industrial Action 2006 Annual Report*. Pretoria: Department of Labour.

Desai, A. 1997. 'Lean production and labour relations: The case of South Africa's motor industry'. *South African Journal of Labour Relations*, 21, 41–49.

Dessler, G. 1984. *Personnel Management*, 3rd ed. Boston: Prentice Hall International.

Dessler, G. 1988. *Personnel Management*. New Jersey: Prentice Hall, Inc.

Dessler, G. 1997. *Human Resource Management*, 7th ed. Upper Saddle River, NJ: Prentice Hall.

Dickenson, J. 1974. 'The linkman: Selection and training of the black personnel officer'. *People & Profits*, 1(7), 8–19.

Dickinson, D. 2006. 'Fighting for life: South African HIV/Aids peer educators as a new industrial relations actor?', *British Journal of Industrial Relations*, 44(4), 697–718.

Diessnack, C H. 1980. 'Financial impact of effective human resources management'. *People & Profits*, 7(10), 5.

'Doing business gets easier in Africa'. n.d. <www.sagoodnews.co.za/index2.php>

Dolan, S L & Schuler, R S. 1987. *Personnel and Human Resource Management in Canada*. New York: West Publishing Company.

Douwes Dekker, L. 1974. 'Workers' education: A prerequisite for effective works committees'. *People & Profits*, 1 (7), 5–7.

Dowling, P J & Welch, D E. 2004. *International Human Resource Management: Managing People in a Multinational Context*, 4th ed. London: Thomson Learning.

Dresser, N. 1996. *Multicultural Manners: Essential Rules of Etiquette for the 21st Century*. New Jersey: John Wiley & Sons.

Driver, M J. 1979. 'Career concepts and career management in organizations', in *Behavioral Problems in Organizations,* ed Cooper, C L. 79–139. Englewood Cliffs, NJ: Prentice Hall, Inc.

'Driving supply chain success through capacity building'. 2008. <www.accenture. com/Countries/South_Africa/About_Accenture/Newsroom/News_Releases/ DrivingBuilding.htm>

Du Plessis, J V, Fouché, M A, Jordaan, B & Van Wyk, M W. 1996. *A Practical Guide to Labour Law*, 2nd ed. Durban: Butterworths.

Dunlop, J T. 1958. *Industrial Relations Systems*. London & Amsterdam: Southern Illinois University Press.

Dunphy, D, Griffiths, A & Benn, S. 2003. *Organizational Change for Corporate Sustainability: A Guide for Leaders and Change Agents of the Future*. London: Routledge.

Dunphy, D, Griffiths, A & Benn, S. 2007. *Organizational Change for Corporate Sustainability: A Guide for Leaders and Change Agents of the Future,* 2nd ed. London: Routledge.

Dunphy, D. & Stace, D. 1993. 'The strategic management of corporate change'. *Human Relations*, 46(8), 905–920.

Dyer, W G, Dyer, W G & Dyer, J H. 2007. *Team Building*, 4th ed. San Francisco: Jossey-Bass.

Eaton, J. 1990/91. 'Human resource management and business policy'. *Human Resource Management Journal*, 1(2), 66–67.

Economic Profile South Africa. 2007. Johannesburg: Standard Bank.

Editorial: *Aids Analysis Africa* (southern African edition), December 1996/January 1997, 7(4).

Edwards, T & Rees, C. 2006. *International Human Resource Management: Globalization, National Systems and Multinational Companies*. Essex: Pearson Education.

Effron, M, Gandossy, R & Goldsmith, M. 2003. *Human Resources in the 21st Century*. New Jersey: John Wiley & Sons.

Einhorn, L J, Bradley, H P & Baird, J E. 1982. *Effective Employment Interviewing*. Illinois: Scott Foresman & Company.

Elvira, M M & Davila, A. 2005. *Managing Human Resources in Latin America.* Oxon: Routledge.

Erasmus, B J & Van Dyk, P S. 2003. *Training Management in South Africa*, 3rd ed. Cape Town: Oxford University Press.

Erasmus, B J, Loedolff, P v Z, Mda, T & Nel, P S. 2006. *Managing Training and Development in South Africa*, 4th ed. Cape Town: Oxford University Press.

Erasmus, P & Arumugam, S. 1998. 'Psychometric testing is dead ...'. *People Dynamics*, 16(9), 39–41.

Erwee, R. 1991. 'Accommodating dual-career couples'. *IPM Journal*, 9, 29–34.

Everingham, G K & Kana, S P. 2008. *Corporate Reporting,* 8th ed. Lansdowne: Juta.

Fairris, D. 2006. 'Union voice effects in Mexico'. *British Journal of Industrial Relations*, 44(4), 781–800.

Falcone, P. 1992. 'Reference checking: Revitalize a critical selection tool'. *HR Focus*, December 1992, 19.

Fear, R A & Chiron, R J. 1990. *The Evaluation Interview.* New York: McGraw-Hill Publishing Company.

Feldman, D C. 1988. *Managing Careers in Organisations.* Boston: Scott Foresman & Company.

Fenton, B. 1993. 'Honest workplace conversations at South African Breweries'. *People Dynamics*, 11(7), 15–17.

Financial Mail Corporate Report. 1998. 'Unilever SA: Leader of the pack?' *Financial Mail*, 23 October, 1–56.

Finnemore, M & Van der Merwe, R. 1992. *Introduction to Industrial Relations in South Africa*, 3rd ed. Johannesburg: Lexicon

Finnemore, M & Van der Merwe, R. 1996. *Introduction to Labour Relations in South Africa*, 4th ed. Durban: Butterworths

Fisher, C D, Schoenfelt, L F & Shaw, J B. 1993. *Human Resource Management.* Boston: Houghton Mifflin.

Fisher, J G. 2000. *How to Run Successful Incentive Schemes*, 3rd ed. London: Kogan Page.

Fisher, R & Brown, S. 1988. *Getting Together: Building a Relationship that Gets to Yes.* Boston: Houghton Mifflin.

Fisher, R & Ury, W. 1981. *Getting to Yes.* London: Hutchinson.

Fisher, S. 1999. 'Company alcohol and drug policy and intervention'. *Management Today,* 15(2), 10.

Fitz-enz, J. 1984. *How to Measure Human Resources Management.* New York: McGraw-Hill.

Fitz-enz, J. 2000. *The ROI of Human Capital.* New York: AMACOM.

Flamholtz, E G. 1985. *Human Resource Accounting.* San Francisco: Jossey-Bass.

Flamholtz, E G. 2005. 'Human resource accounting, human capital management, and the bottom line', in *The Future of Human Resource Management – 64 Thought Leaders Explore the Critical HR Issues of Today and Tomorrow*, eds Losey, M, Meisinger, S & Ulrich, D. New Jersey: John Wiley & Sons.

Flanders, A. 1965. *Industrial Relations: What is Wrong with the System?* London: Institute of Personnel Management

Fombrun, C J, Devanna, M A & Tichy, N M. 1899. 'The human resource management audit', in *The Strategic Human Resource Management Sourcebook,* eds Baird, L S, Schneier, C E & Beatty, R W. Amherst, Mass: HRD Press.

'Food crisis could destroy progress in Africa'. 2008. <www.prinththis.clickability.com/pt/cpt?action=cpt&title=%27Food+crisis+could...>

French, W & Bell, C H. 1984. *Organisation Development: Behavioral Science Interventions for Organisation Improvement*, 3rd ed. Englewood Cliffs, NJ: Prentice Hall.

French, W. 1994. *Human Resource Management,* 3rd ed. Boston: Houghton Mifflin.

Friedman, S. 1987. *Building Tomorrow Today: African Workers in Trade Unions 1970– 1984.* Johannesburg: Raucon Press.

FSA-Contact. 1998. *Paying for Performance: A Special Survey of Trends in Performance-based Pay Strategies*. May.

Fullinwider, R K. 1980. *The Reverse Discrimination Controversy – A Moral and Legal Analysis*. Totowa, NJ: Rowman and Littlefield.

Galvao, P. 2006. 'Increasing the productivity of the South African workforce'. *People Dynamics*, 24(11), 5.

Gatewood, R D & Field, H S. 1987. *Human Resources Selection.* New York: The Dryden Press.

Gathiram, V. 1999. 'The age of the great Aids plague'. *The Mercury*, 15 July, 9.

Gaye, A. 2008. 'China in Africa: Why the West is worried'. *New African*, 471,13–18.

Gebert, D. 1996. 'Organisation development', in *International Encyclopaedia of Business and Management,* 4th ed, ed Warner, M. New York and London: Routledge.

Gennard, J & Judge, G. 2005. *Employee Relations*, 4th ed. London: CIPD.

Gerardy, J. 2008. 'Border control disaster', *Weekend Argus*, 22 March, 1.

Gerber, P D, Nel, P S & Van Dyk, P S. 1992. *Human Resources Management*, 2nd ed. Halfway House: Southern Books.

Gerhart, B. 2000. 'Remuneration strategy and organizational performance', in *Remuneration in Organizations: Current Research and Practice*, eds Rynes, S L & Gerhart, B. San Francisco: Jossey-Bass.

Gerhart, B. 2007. 'Modeling HRM and performance linkages', in *The Oxford Handbook of Human Resource Management*, eds Boxall, P, Purcell, J & Wright, P. New York: Oxford University Press, 552–580.

Ghebregiorgis, F & Karsten, L. 2007. 'Employee reactions to human resource management and performance in a developing country: evidence from Eritrea'. *Personnel Review*, 36(5), 727–738.

Gibbon, T. 2004. 'Employer branding – the last legal advantage in winning the war for talent', in *On Staffing: Advice and Perspectives from HR Leaders*, eds Burkholder, N C, Edwards, P J & Sartain, L. Hoboken, NJ: John Wiley & Sons Inc.

Gibson, J L, Ivancevich, J M & Donnelly, J H. 1994. *Organizations: Behavior, Structure, Processes*, 8th ed. Burr Ridge, Illinois: Irwin.

Ginsberg, S W, Axelrad, S & Herman, J L. 1951. *Occupational Choice: An Approach to a General Theory*. New York: Columbia University Press.

Ginzberg, E. 1984. 'Career development', in *Career Choice and Development*, eds Brown, D & Brooks, L. Washington: Jossey-Bass Publishers, 169–191.

Giugni, S. 2004. 'Nurturing imagination: fostering creativity in your organisation' in *Innovation and Imagination at Work*, 2nd ed. North Ryde, NSW: AIM/McGraw-Hill.

Gleason, D. 1996. 'Fighting for survival in a shrinking market'. *Financial Mail,* 4 October, 22.

Godard J & Delaney, J T. 2000. 'Reflections on the "high performance" paradigm's implications for industrial relations as field'. *Industrial and Labor Relations Review*, 53, 482–502.

Goetsch, D L & Davis, S. 1995. *Implementing total quality.* Englewood Cliffs: Prentice Hall.

Gómez-Mejía, L R, Balkin, D B & Cardy, R L. 1998. *Managing Human Resources*, 2nd ed. New Jersey: Prentice Hall.

Gómez-Mejía, L R, Balkin, D B & Cardy, R L. 2001. *Managing Human Resources,* 3rd ed. Upper Saddle River, NJ: Prentice Hall.

Goodstein, L. 1991. 'Creating successful organisation change'. *Organisational Dynamics*, Spring, 5–17.

Goss, G, Pascale, R & Athos, A. 1993. 'The reinvention roller coaster: Risking the present for a powerful future'. *Harvard Business Review,* November–December, 7–108.

Gould, C. 2005. 'Change dominates global HR agenda'. *Worldlink*, 15(3), 1–3.

Gould, C. 2007. 'Trends in international long-term assignment remuneration', <www.worldlink.com> (accessed July 2007).

Graetz, F. 2002. 'Strategic thinking versus strategic planning: Towards understanding the complementarities'. *Management Decision*, 40(5/6), 456.

Grant, R M. 1998. *Contemporary Strategy Analysis*, 3rd ed. Massachusetts: Blackwell.

Greenberg, J & Baron, R A. 1997. *Behaviour in Organisations*, 6th ed. New Jersey: Prentice Hall, Inc.

Greenblo, A. 1989. 'In praise of ESOPs'. *Finance Week*, March 23–29, 4.

Greenhaus, J H & Beutell, N J. 1985. 'Sources of conflict between work and family roles'. *Academy of Management Review*, 10, 77.

Greenhaus, J H, Callanan, G A & Godshalk, V M. 2000. *Career Management*. New York: Harcourt College Publishers.

Greenhaus, J H. 1987. *Career Management.* Orlando, Florida: Dryden Press.

Greenwood, R & Hinings, C R. 1996. 'Radical organisational change: Bringing together the old and the new institutionalism'. *Academy of Management Review,* 21(4), 1022–1054.

Greer, C R. 1995. *Strategy and Human Resources – A General Managerial Perspective.* New Jersey: Prentice Hall.

Griffen, R. 1987. *Management.* Boston: Houghton Mifflin Company

Grobler, P. 2001. 'HR practices: what does the latest research say?' *Management Today*, July, 30–33.

Grobler, P & Warnich, S. 2006. *Human Resource Management in South Africa*, 3rd ed. South Africa: Thomson Learning.

Grobler, P A. 2001. *Report on Human Resource Management Practices in South Africa.* Department of Business Management, Unisa.

Grogan, J. 2007a. *Collective Labour Law.* Cape Town: Juta.

Grogan, J. 2007b. *Dismissal, Discrimination & Unfair Labour Practices*, 2nd ed. Cape Town: Juta.

Grogan, J. 2007c. *Workplace Law*, 9th ed. Cape Town: Juta.

Guest, D. 1987. 'Human resource management and industrial relations'. *Journal of Management Studies*, 24(5).

Guest, D. 1989. 'Personnel and HRM: Can you tell the difference?'. *Personnel Management*, 21, January, 48–51.

Guion, R M. 1966. 'Employment tests and discriminatory hiring'. *Industrial Relations*, 5, 20–37.

Gumede, W M. 2007. *Thabo Mbeki and the Battle for the Soul of the ANC*. Cape Town: Zebra Press.

Gupta, N & Shaw J D. 2000. 'Let the evidence speak: Financial incentives are effective!', in *Human Resources Annual Editions*, 10th ed, ed Maidment, F H. Guilford: Dushkin/McGraw-Hill.

Guterman, M. 1991. 'Working couples: Finding a balance between family and career', in *New Directions in Career Planning and the Workplace*, ed Kummerow, J M. Palo Alto, California: Davies Black Publishing, 167–193.

Gutteridge, T G, Leibowitz, Z B & Shore, J E. 1993. 'When careers flower, organizations flourish'. *Training and Development,* 47(1), 14–29.

Hackman, J R & Lawler, E E. 1971. 'Employee reactions to job characteristics'. *Journal of Applied Psychology*, 55, 259–286

Hackman, J R & Oldham, G R. 1975. 'Development of the job diagnostic survey'. *Journal of Applied Psychology*, 60, 159–170.

Hackman, J R, Oldham, G R, Jansom, R & Purdy, K. 1975. 'A new strategy for job enrichment'. *California Management Review,* Summer, 57–71.

Hall, D T. 1976. *Careers in Organisations.* California: Goodyear Publishing Company, Inc.

Hall, D T & Mervis, P H. 1995. 'Careers as lifelong learning', in *The Changing Nature of Work*. San Francisco: Jossey-Bass.

Hall, R. 1985. 'Some changes in management practice in the Transvaal'. *Industrial Relations Journal of South Africa*, 2nd quarter, 6.

Hall, T E. 1981. 'How to estimate employee turnover costs'. *Personnel*, July–August, 43–52.

Hampden-Turner, C & Trompenaars, A. 1993. *The Seven Cultures of Capitalism*. New York: Currency/Doubleday.

Hankin, H. 2005. *The New Workforce: Five Sweeping Trends that will Shape your Company's Future.* New York: AMACOM.

Hansen, F. 2008. 'Currents in compensation and benefits'. *Compensation and Benefits Review,* March/April, 5–26.

Harder, J W. 1996. 'Search for the virtual water cooler'. *Business Day* supplement: Mastering Management Series, Part 4, 25 March, 5.

Hargroves, K & Smith, M. 2005. *The Natural Advantages of Nations.* London: Earthscan.

Harned, P J. 2005. 'When ethics calls the HR helpline', in *The Future of Human Resource Management – 64 Thought Leaders Explore the Critical HR Issues of Today and Tomorrow*, eds Losey, M, Meisinger, S & Ulrich, D. New Jersey: John Wiley & Sons.

Harper, T. 1999. 'Employee assistance programming and professional developments in South Africa'. *Employee Assistance Quarterly*, 14(3), 1–18.

Harris, H, Brewster, C & Sparrow, P. 2003. *International Human Resource Management.* London: CIPD.

Harris, P. 1986. 'Building a high performance team'. *Training and Development Journal*, 40 (April), 229.

Harris, T G. 1993. 'The post-capitalist executive: An interview with Peter F Drucker'. *Harvard Business Review*, May/June, 115–122.

Hart, E & McMillan, J. 1996. 'Leadership and organisational transformation'. *HRM*, February, 4–12.

Hart, F A. 1987. 'Computer-based training', in *Training and Development Handbook*, 3rd ed, ed Craig, R L. New York: McGraw-Hill.

Härtel, C E J, Fujimoto, Y, Strybosch, V E & Fitzpatrick, K. 2007. *Human Resource Management: Transforming Theory into Innovative Practice*. Frenchs Forest, NSW: Pearson.

Harvey, D & Brown, D R. 2001. *An Experiential Approach to Organization Development*, 6th ed. Upper Saddle River, NJ: Prentice Hall.

Harvey, M, Myers, M & Novicevic, M M. 2002. 'The role of MNCs in balancing the human capital "books" between African and developed countries'. *International Journal of Human Resource Management*, 13(7), 1060–1076.

Harvey, M. 2002. 'Human resource management in Africa: Alice's adventures in Wonderland'. *International Journal of Human Resource Management,* 13(7), 1119–1145.

Harzing, A & Van Ruysseveldt, J. 2004. *International Human Resource Management*, 2nd ed. London: Sage.

Hattingh, S. 1992. 'Occupational safety', in *Occupational Health*, ed Kotzé, A J. Cape Town: Juta, 55.

Havenga, R. 2007. 'Executive pay: There must be a better option'. *Management Today*, February, 45–49.

Hay Group. 2005. 'Total reward preliminary report'. Available at <www.haygroup.com>

Heaton, N & Ackah, C. 2007. 'Changing HR careers: Implications for management education', *Journal of Management Development*, 26(10), 951–961.

Heckscher, C & Carre, F. 2006. 'Strength in networks: Employment rights organizations and the problem of co-ordination', *British Journal of Industrial Relations*, 44(4), 605–628.

Heery, E & Frege, C. 2006. 'New actors in industrial relations', *British Journal of Industrial Relations*, 44(4), 601–604.

Heller, F A. 1968. 'Human resources in the office', *Management International Review*, 6, 65–66.

Hemson, D & O'Donovan, M. 2006. 'Putting numbers to the scorecard: Presidential targets and the state of delivery', in *State of the Nation – South Africa 2005–2006,* eds Buhlungu, S, Daniel, J, Southall, R & Lutchman, J. Cape Town: HSRC Press.

Hemson, D & Owusu-Ampomah, K. 2005. 'A better life for all? Service delivery and poverty alleviation', in *State of the Nation – South Africa 2004–2005*, eds Daniel, J, Southall, R & Lutchman, J. Cape Town: HSRC Press.

Henderson, M. 2007. 'South Africa: 2005 through to 2014', *People Dynamics,* 25(7), 23–27.

Henderson , R L. 2000. *Remuneration Management in a Knowledge-based World*, 8th ed. Upper Saddle River, NJ: Prentice Hall.

Heneman, H G, Schwab, D P, Fossum, J A & Dyer, L D. 1986. *Personnel/Human Resource Management.* Homewood, Illinois: Irwin Inc.

Heneman, R L, Ledford, G E & Gresham, M T. 2000. 'The changing nature of work and its effects on remuneration design and delivery', in *Remuneration in Organizations: Current Research and Practice*, eds Rynes, S L & Gerhart, B. San Francisco: Jossey-Bass.

Hercus, T. 1993. 'Workforce planning in eight British organisations: A Canadian perspective', in *Handbook of Workforce Management*, ed Bran Towers. Oxford: Blackwell, 405.

Hermanus, M. 1991. 'Occupational health and safety: A NUM perspective'. *IPM Journal*, 9(9), 17.

Herzberg, F. 1968. 'One more time: How do you motivate employees?'. *Harvard Business Review*, January–February, 57.

Hesselbein, F. 2002. 'The key to cultural change', in *On Leading Change*, eds Hesselbein, F & Johnston, R. San Francisco, CA: Jossey-Bass.

Heyns, A. 1996. 'Internet as HR's new assistant'. *People Dynamics*, 14(7), 21–22.

Hill, S K & Bahniuk M. 1998. 'Promoting career success through mentoring' in *Review of Business*, 19(3), 4–7.

Hilliard, V. 1996. 'Transforming the public service – no room for despondency'. *HRM*, April, 9–14.

Hirschohn, P A. 1988. *Management Ideology and Environmental Turbulence: Understanding Labour Policies in the South African Gold Mining Industry*. MSc dissertation, Oxford University.

Hirschohn, P. 1998. 'Responding to globalisation and lean production: implementing training policy in the South African auto assembly sector'. *South African Journal of Labour Relations*, 22, 44–58.

Hitt, M A, Black, J S, Porter, L W & Hanson, D. 2007. *Management*. Australia: Pearson Education.

Hlope, S. 2007. *Are Share-based Incentive Schemes an Effective Way of Increasing BEE Empowerment?* Paper delivered at 16th PayCon Conference, Midrand, 29 August 2007.

Höck, C. 1991/92. 'Interest bargaining: The way ahead?'. *IPM Journal*, 10(4), 15–18.

Hodge, B J, Anthony, W P & Gales, L M. 2003. *Organization Theory – A Strategic Approach*, 6th ed. New Jersey: Pearson Education.

Hodson, R. & Sullivan, T A. 2002. *The Social Organization of Work,* 3rd ed. Toronto: Wadsworth.

Hofmeyr, K. 1997a. 'Employee attitudes: a key dimension in organisational success'. *People Dynamics,* 15(8), 31–35.

Hofmeyr, K. 1997b. *SA Employee Attitudes: A Key Factor in Organisational Change.* Unpublished paper delivered at the IPM Convention, Sun City, October.

Hofmeyr, K, Rall, J & Templer, A. 1995. 'The future challenges facing South African human resource managers'. *South African Journal of Business Management*, 26(3), 108–114.

Holburn, P. 1992. 'Psychometric assessment – identify appropriate assessment techniques for specific jobs to ensure that the right person is elected'. Johannesburg: Congress on Culture, Fair Assessment Techniques. International Executive Communications.

Holland, J L. 1973. *Making Vocational Choices: A Theory of Careers.* Englewood Cliffs, New Jersey: Prentice Hall, Inc.

Holland, J L. 1985. *Making Vocational Choices: A Theory of Careers*. Englewood Cliffs, New Jersey: Prentice Hall, Inc.

Honnet, M. 2004. Incentive design trends presentation at the 15th Annual PayCon Conference, Vodaworld, Midrand.

Honnet, M. 2006. PayCon presentation.

Hornsby, J S & Kuratko, D F. 2005. *Frontline HR – a Handbook for the Emerging Manager*. USA: Thomson.

Horwitz, F. 1988. 'Ownership issues: How employee share participation schemes can be made to work'. *Finance Week*, February, 4–10, 27.

Horwitz, F M. 2006. 'Industrial relations in Africa', in *Global Industrial Relations*, eds Morley, M J, Gunnigle, P & Collings, D G. Oxon: Routledge, 178–198.

Horwitz, F & Frost, P. 1992. 'Flexible rewards: Critical success factors'. *People Dynamics* June, 27–33.

Horwitz, F M, Browning, V, Jain, H & Steenkamp, A J. 2002. 'Human resource practices and discrimination in South Africa: Overcoming the apartheid legacy'. *International Journal of Human Resource Management*, 13(7), 1105–1118.

Horwitz, F M & Franklin, E. 1996. 'Flexibility is the name of the game'. *Business Day* supplement: Mastering Management Series, Part 7, 15 April, 15.

Horwitz, F M, Kamoche, K & Chew, I K H. 2002. 'Looking East: Diffusing high performance work practices in the southern Afro-Asian context'. *The International Journal of Human Resource Management*, 13(7), 1019–1041.

Horwitz, F M, Nkomo, S M & Rajah, M. 2004. 'HRM in South Africa', in *Managing Human Resources in Africa,* eds Kamoche, K, Debrah, Y, Horwitz, F & Muuka, G N. London: Routledge.

Horwitz, F M & Townsend, M. 1993. 'Elements in participation, teamwork and flexibility in South Africa'. *International Journal of Human Resource Management*, 4(4), 917–932.

Horwitz, F W. 1988. 'Personnel management or human resource management – euphemism or new paradigm?'. *IPM Journal*, 6(12), 6–7.

Hough, J, Neuland, E & Bothma, N. 2003. *Global Business: Environments and Strategies – Managing for Global Competitive Advantage*, 2nd ed. New York: Oxford.

Houldsworth, E. 2004. 'Managing performance', in *People Management: Challenges and Opportunities*, eds Rees, D & McBain, R. New York: Palgrave Macmillan.

House, R J, Hanges, P J, Javidan, M, Dorfman, P W & Gupta, V (eds). 2004. *Culture, Leadership, and Organizations: The GLOBE Study of 62 Societies*. Thousand Oaks: Sage.

Hubbart, W S. 1993. *Personnel Policy Handbook: How to Develop a Manual that Works*. New York: McGraw-Hill.

Hudson, M. 1999. 'AZT: Alles of niks'. *Insig*, June, 30–31.

Huffcutt, A I & Woehr, D J. 1995. *A Further Analysis of Employment Interview Validity*. Paper presented at the 10th Annual Meeting of the Society for Industrial and Organisational Psychology, Orlando.

Hughes, R L & Beatty, K C. 2005. *Becoming a Strategic Leader*. San Francisco: Jossey-Bass.

Human Capital Management. 2006/7. *The Balanced Scorecard: A Sound Performance Management Tool.* Norwood: Shorten Publications.

Human Resource Management. 1993. 'Healthcare needs total company involvement'. *Human Resource Management,* May, 27.

Human Resources Professions Bill. 2006. <www.sabpp.co.za/news/l1/Act-ArevisionbyRayEberleinendMay2006.doc>

Human, L. 1993. *Affirmative Action and the Development of People: A Practical Guide*. Kenwyn: Juta & Co, Ltd.

Human, P & Horwitz, F W. 1992. *On the Edge: How South African Companies Cope with Change*. Kenwyn: Juta & Co Ltd.

Humphrey, J & Smith, P. 1991. *Looking after Corporate Health.* London: Pitman.

Hunt, S. 2007. *Hiring Success*. San Francisco CA: Wiley.

Hurst, D K. 1991. 'Cautionary tales from the Kalahari: How hunters become herders (and may have trouble changing back again)'. *Academy of Management Executive*, 5(3), 74–86.

Huselid, M A & Becker, B E. 2005. 'Improving human resources' analytical literacy: Lessons from Moneyball', in *The Future of Human Resource Management – 64 Thought Leaders Explore the Critical HR Issues of Today and Tomorrow*, eds Losey, M, Meisinger, S & Ulrich, D. New Jersey: John Wiley & Sons.

Huselid, M A, Becker, B E & Beatty, R W. 2005. *The Workforce Scorecard – Managing Human Capital to Execute Strategy*. USA: Harvard Business School.

Hussain, S & Toure, A. 2008. 'Africa's progress on development goals linked to growth, environment'. <http://web.worldbank.org/WBSITE/EXTERNAL/COUNTRIES/AFRICAEXT/0,,print...>

Ibarra, H. 2003. *Working Identity: Unconventional Strategies for Reinventing your Career.* Boston, MA: HBS Press.

Incomes Data Services. 1994. *Multiskilling:* Study 558, 1–32.

Industrial Action 2006 Annual Report. 2006. Pretoria: Department of Labour.

Industrial Action 2006 Annual Report. 2007. Department of Labour, Pretoria.

Inyang, B J. 2007. 'Managing workforce diversity and inclusiveness in the public service: going beyond the Nigeria Federal Character Principles (FCP)'. *South African Journal of Labour Relations*, 31(2), 85–101.

'IPM and SABPP: How do they differ?' (IPM in interview with Gary Whyte). 1990. *IPM Journal*, 8(7), 33–34.

IPM Manpower Journal. 1983. 'News update – South African Board for Personnel Practice'. *IPM Manpower Journal,* 2(2), 4.

IPM. 1991. *Human Resource Management Kits: Analysing Training Needs.* Braamfontein: IPM.

Ivancevich, J M & Glueck, W F. 1983. *Foundations of Personnel/Human Resource Management*, rev ed. Plano, Texas: Business Publication.

Ivancevich, J M & Matteson, M T. 2002. *Organizational Behavior and Management,* 6th ed. New York: McGraw-Hill.

Ivancevich, J M. 1998. *Human Resource Management,* 7th ed. Boston, Mass: Irwin/McGraw-Hill.

Jackson, T. 2002. 'Reframing human resource management in Africa: A cross-cultural perspective'. *International Journal of Human Resource Management*, 13(7), 998–1018.

Jaffee, G. 1990. 'Worker co-operatives: Their emergence, problems and potential', in *Worker Participation*, ed Anstey M. Kenwyn: Juta.

Jaire, S A, Leon, J S, Simpson, D B, Holley, C H & Frye, R L. 1989. 'Stress: The pressure cooker of work'. *Personnel Administrator,* March, 92–95.

Jarrell, D W. 1993. *Human Resource Planning: Business Planning Approach*. New Jersey: Prentice Hall.

Jarvis, D. 1998. 'The organiser's dilemma: Union responses to industrial restructuring'. *South African Labour Bulletin,* 22(5), 27–33.

Jauch, H. 2005. 'Searching for scapegoats – the Ramatex saga continues'. *New Era*, 8 April, LaRRI.

Jauch, H. 2007. *Gold Mining Companies in Africa: Workers' Experiences*. ALRN (African Labour Research Network).

Jick, T D (ed). 1993a. *Managing Change, Cases and Concepts*. Boston: Richard D Irwin, Inc.

Jick, T D. 1993b. 'Implementing change', in *Managing Change, Cases and Concepts*, ed Jick, T D. Boston: Richard D. Irwin, Inc.

Johnson, C. 1986. 'An outline for team building: Cooperation, collaboration and communication are the key ingredients of an effective team'. *Training: The Magazine of Human Resource Development*, 23 (January), 48.

Johnson, D W. 2006. *Reaching out: Interpersonal Effectiveness and Self-actualization*, 9th ed. Boston: Allyn & Bacon.

Johnson, G & Scholes, K. 2002. *Exploring Corporate Strategy: Text and Cases.* 6th ed. London: Prentice Hall.

Johnson, G, Scholes, K & Whittington, R. 2008. *Exploring Corporate Strategy: Text and Cases*. UK: Prentice Hall.

Johnson, R & Redmond, D. 1998. *The Art of Empowerment.* London: Financial Times/Pitman Publishing.

Johnston, R & Clark, G. 2005. *Service Operations Management: Improving Service Delivery,* 2nd ed. Pearson Education, Essex.

Jones, B. 1996. 'Poor pay keeps mine safety inspectors away'. *Sunday Times*, 14 April, 6.

Jones, H. 2007. 'Educate staff on careers'. *People Dynamics,* 25(5), 7–11.

Jones, T H & Kleiner, B H. 1990. 'Smoking and the work environment'. *Employee Relations,* 12 (6), 29.

Kamoche K N, Nyambegera, S M & Mulinge, M M. 2004. 'HRM in Kenya', in *Managing Human Resources in Africa*, eds Kamoche, K, Debrah, Y, Horwitz, F & Muuka, G N. London: Routledge.

Kamoche, K N, Debrah, Y, Horwitz, F & Muuka, G N (eds). 2004. *Managing Human Resources in Africa*. London: Routledge.

Kamoche, K N. 2000. *Sociological Paradigms and Human Resources: An African Context.* Hampshire: Ashgate Publishing Ltd.

Kane-Berman, J. 2004. *Fast Facts – Partial Smiles for the Previously Hopeless*. South African Institute of Race Relations, no. 2.

Kane-Berman, J. 2007. 'Adding up sad figures of education after liberation'. <www.sairr.org.za/press-office/institute-opinion/adding-up-sad-figures-of-educat...>

Kanter, R M. 1990. *When Giants Learn to Dance*. New York: Simon & Schuster.

Kaplan, R M & Saccuzzo, D P. 1993. *Psychological Testing*. Belmont, California: Wadsworth Inc.

Kaplan, R S & Norton, D P. 1996. *The Balanced Scorecard: Translating Strategy into Action.* Boston: Harvard Business School Press.

Kaufman, B E. 2007. 'The development of HRM in historical and international perspective', in *The Oxford Handbook of Human Resource Management*, eds Boxall, P, Purcell, J & Wright, P. New York: Oxford University Press.

Kaufman, H G. 1974. *Obsolescence and Professional Career Development.* New York: AMACOM.

Kaufman. B E. 2007. 'The development of HRM in historical and international perspective', in *The Oxford Handbook of Human Resource Management,* eds Boxall, P, Purcell, J & Wright, P. New York: Oxford University Press, 19–47.

Kavanagh, M J, Guetal, H G & Tannenbaum S I. 1990. *Human Resource Information Systems: Development and Application.* Boston: PWS-Kent.

Kemp, N. 1992. *Labour Relations Strategies: An Interactional Approach*. Kenwyn: Juta.

Kemp, N. 1999. 'Psychometric testing is not dead'. *People Dynamics,* 17(3), 14–17.

Kerr, S (ed). 1997. *Ultimate Rewards: What Really Motivates People to Achieve?* Boston: Harvard Business School Press.

'Kgalagadi Breweries Limited launches driver-empowerment scheme in all Africa', Mmegi/*The Reporter* (Gaborone), posted to the web on 24 July 2007, at <http://palapye.wordpress.com/2007/07/25/kgalagadi-breweries-limited-launches-driver-empowerment-scheme/>

Khoza, R. 2007a. 'Values dominate the African leadership paradigm'. *Management Today,* 23(6), 24–27.

Khoza, R. 2007b. 'Sustainability: to make the world a better place'. *Management Today,* 23(9), 10.

Kieffer, M. 1991. 'The reference check: What you need to know'. *Health Care Executive*, 6(6), 18–19.

Kiel, G & Nicholson, G. 2003. *Boards that work.* Australia: McGraw-Hill.

Kiel, G, Nicholson, G & Barclay, M A. 2005. *Board, Director and CEO Evaluation.* Sydney: McGraw-Hill.

Killen, R. 2002. *Outcomes-based Education: Principles and Possibilities to Consider in the South African Context.* Unpublished report. University of Newcastle, Australia.

King Committee on Corporate Governance. 2002. *King Report on Corporate Governance for South Africa.* Institute of Directors.

King Committee Report on Corporate Governance. 1994. Johannesburg: The Institute of Directors in Southern Africa, 29 November 1994.

Kinicki, A & Kreitner, R. 2006. *Organizational Behavior: Key Concepts, Skills & Best Practice,* 2nd ed. New York: Mc Graw-Hill Irwin.

Klasen, N & Clutterbuck, D. 2002. *Implementing Mentoring Schemes: A Practical Guide to Successful Programmes.* London: Butterworth/Heinemann.

Kleiman, L S. 2000. *Human Resource Management: A Managerial Tool for Competitive Advantage,* 2nd ed. London: International Thomson.

Kniveron, B H. 1974. 'Industrial negotiating: Some training implications'. *Industrial Relations Journal,* 5(3), 27–37.

Kochan, T A. 2007, 'Social legitimacy of the HRM profession: A US perspective', *The Oxford Handbook of Human Resource Management,* eds Boxall, P, Purcell, J & Wright, P. New York: Oxford University Press, 599–619.

Korman, A K. 1977. *Organizational Behaviour.* Englewood Cliffs, NJ: Prentice Hall Inc.

Kotler, J P. 1998. 'Why change?'. *Executive Excellence,* January, 15(1), 5.

Kotter, J P. 1995. 'Leading change: why transformation efforts fail'. *Harvard Business Review,* March–April, 59–67.

Kotter, J P. 1996. *Leading Change.* Boston: Harvard Business School Press.

Kotter, J P & Schlesinger, L A. 1969. 'Choosing strategies for change'. *Harvard Business Review,* January–February.

Kriek, H J. 1991. 'Die bruikbaarheid van die takseersentrum: 'n Oorsig van resente literatuur'. *Tydskrif vir Bedryfsielkunde,* 17(3), 34–37.

Kriek, H J. 1993. *Fair Assessment Techniques: General Remarks and Conclusions.* Johannesburg: Conference on Culture-Fair Assessment Techniques. International Executive. Communications

Kriek, H J & Von der Ohe, H. 1996. *Managerial Assessment Methods Survey.* Unpublished report, Unisa.

Kriek, H J, Hurst, D N & Charoux, J A E. 1994. 'The assessment centre: Testing the fairness hypothesis'. *Journal of Industrial Psychology,* 20(2), 21–25.

Krige, P. 1999. Information systems as strategic human resources tools. *People Dynamics,* 17(6), 15–21.

Kruger, L. 2007. *Share incentive schemes: Tax implications.* PayCon conference, August.

Kulik, C T & Bainbridge, H T J. 2006. 'HR and the line: The distribution of HR activities in Australian organisations'. *Asia Pacific Journal of Human Resources,* 44(2), 240–256.

Landy, F J, Shankster-Cawley, L & Moran, S K. 1995. 'Advancing personnel selection and placement methods', in *The Changing Nature of Work,* ed Howard, A. San Francisco: Jossey-Bass, 252–281.

Langbert, M. 2005. 'The Master's degree in HRM: Midwife to a new profession?'. *Academy of Management Learning & Education,* 4(4), 434–450.

Langenhoven, H P & Verster, R. 1969. *Survey of Personnel Management in South Africa.* Bloemfontein: Personnel Research Division, University of the Orange Free State.

Langenhoven, H P. 1975. *The Present State of Black Personnel Management in South Africa.* Bloemfontein: Personnel Research Division, University of the Orange Free State.

Langenhoven, H P. 1978. 'Industrial psychology and personnel management do not mean the same thing'. *People & Profits*, 5(12), 14–15.

Lansbury, R D & Baird, M. 2004. 'Broadening the horizons of HRM: Lessons for Australia from the US experience'. *Asia Pacific Journal of Human Resources*, 42(2), 147–155.

Latham, G P. 1989. 'Behavioral approaches to the learning process', in *Training and Development in Organizations*, ed Goldstein, I L. San Francisco: Jossey-Bass.

Lawler, E E. 1987. 'The design of effective reward systems', in *Handbook of Organisation Behaviour*, ed Lorsch, J W. Englewood Cliffs, NJ: Prentice Hall.

Lawler, E E. 1990. *Strategic Pay: Aligning Organisational Strategy and Pay Systems*. San Francisco: Jossey-Bass.

Lawler, E E. 2005. 'From human resources management to organizational effectiveness', in *The Future of Human Resource Management: 64 Thought Leaders Explore the Critical HR Issues Today and Tomorrow*, eds Losey, M, Meisinger, S & Ulrich, D. Hoboken, NJ: John Wiley & Sons.

Lawler, E E, Levenson, A & Boudreau, J W. 2004. 'HR metrics and analytics: Use and impact'. *Human Resource Planning*, 27, 27–35.

Leana, C R & Feldsman, D C. 1988. 'Individual responses to job loss. Perceptions, reactions and coping behaviours'. *Journal of Management*, 14(3).

Leavitt, H J. 1964. 'Applied organisation change in industry: Structural, technical and human approaches', in *New Perspectives in Organization Research*, eds Cooper, W W, Leavitt, H J & Shelly, M W. New Jersey: Wiley, 55–71.

Lee, T. 2006. 'A primer on Internet recruiting', in *On Staffing*, eds Burkholder, N C, Edwards, P Sr & Sartain, L. New Jersey: Wiley.

Leibowitz, Z B, Kaye, B L & Farren, C. 1990. 'Career gridlock'. *Training and Development Journal*, April, 29–35.

Leigh, A. 1988. *Effective Change: Twenty Ways to Make it Happen.* London: Institute of Personnel Management.

Leopold, J, Harris, L & Watson, T. 2005. *The Strategic Managing of Human Resources.* UK: Prentice Hall.

Letsoalo, M. 2008. 'Zuma faces ANC rebellion'. *Mail & Guardian*, 26 September–2 October, 2.

Levy, A & Associates. 1995. *Annual Report on Labour Relations in South Africa: 1995–1996.* Johannesburg: Andrew Levy and Associates.

Levy, P E. 2003. *Industrial/organizational Psychology – Understanding the Workplace.* USA: Houghton Mifflin Company.

Levy, P E. 2006. *Industrial/Organizational Psychology,* 2nd ed. Boston: Houghton Mifflin.

Lewicki, R J, Saunders, D M & Barry, B. 2006. *Negotiation*, 5th ed. New York: McGraw-Hill.

Lewin, D. 2005. 'The dual theory of human resource management and business performance: Lessons for HR executives', in *The Future Of Human Resource Management – 64 Thought Leaders Explore the Critical HR Issues of Today and Tomorrow*, eds Losey, M, Meisinger, S & Ulrich, D (eds). New Jersey: John Wiley & Sons.

Lewin, K. 1951. *Field theory in social science.* London: Harper & Row.

Lewis, G. 1988. *Corporate Strategy in Action.* London: Routledge.

Lewis, P & Jeebhay, M. 1996. 'The Mines Health and Safety Bill 1996: A new era for health and safety in the mining industry'. *Industrial Law Journal*, 17, 429–447.

Liberty Group Limited sustainability report. 2005.

Lickson, C P & Maddux, R B. 2005. *Negotiation Basics: Win–Win Strategies for Everyone*, 4th ed, Boston: Thomson.

Liedtka, J M. 1998. 'Strategic thinking: Can it be taught?'. *Long Range Planning*, 31(1), 120–129.

Lippitt, R, Watson, J & Westley, B. 1985. *The Dynamics of Planned Change.* New York: Harcourt Brace Jovanovich.

Lloyd, C. 1994. *Work Organisation and World Class Management: A Critical Guide.* Senderwood: Red Earth Publications.

Logan, J. 2006. 'The union avoidance industry in the United States'. *British Journal of Industrial Relations*, 44(4), 651–676.

Lombard, B U. 1978. 'Human resources management: A new approach for South Africa'. *SA Journal of Labour Relations*, December, 12–24.

Losey, M, Meisinger, S & Ulrich, D. 2005. *The Future of Human Resource Management – 64 Thought Leaders Explore the Critical HR Issues of Today and Tomorrow.* New Jersey: John Wiley & Sons.

Louw, L & Venter, P (eds). 2006. *Strategic Management: Winning in the Southern African Workplace.* Cape Town: Oxford.

Lundy, O & Cowling, A. 1996. *Strategic Human Resource Management,* UK: Thomson.

Lussier, R N & Achua, C F. 2004. *Leadership: Theory, Application, Skill Development*, 2nd ed. US: Thomson.

Luthans, F. 2002. *Organizational Behavior*, 9th ed. New York: McGraw-Hill.

Luthans, F. 2005. *Organizational Behavior,* 10th ed. New York: McGraw-Hill.

Lynn, A I. 1993. 'Managing the challenges of trigger events: The mindsets governing adaptation to change', in *Managing Change, Cases and Concepts*, ed Jick, T D. Boston: Richard D Irwin, Inc.

MacFarlane, M. 2005. *Fast Facts – The poor get poorer.* South African Institute of Race Relations, no. 9.

MacFarlane, M. 2007. *Fast Facts – South Africa in brief.* South African Institute of Race Relations, no. 7.

MacFarlane, M. 2008. *Fast Facts – The target keeps moving.* South African Institute of Race Relations, no. 1.

Machin, A. 1998. 'The workplace challenge reportback: the plastics sector'. *South African Labour Bulletin*, 22(5), 47–48.

MacKenzie, K. 2004. 'Surviving in the corporate jungle: strategies for becoming an innovative organisation', in *Innovation and Imagination at Work*, 2nd ed. North Ryde, NSW: AIM/McGraw-Hill.

Macun, I. 1998. 'Democratising companies? Union representation on company boards'. *South African Labour Bulletin*, 22(4), 61–66.

Mafu, T. 2007. *Pretoria News*, 3 July.

Magnum, G L & Magnum, S L. 1986. 'Temporary work: the flip side of job security'. *International Journal of Manpower*, 7(1), 12–20.

Maiden, R P. 1999. 'Substance abuse in the new South Africa: implications for the workplace'. *Employee Assistance Quarterly,* 14(3), 41–60.

Management Today editorial. 1999. 'South African scores world first with labour dispute system'. *Management Today*, 15(4), 34.

Mangaliso, M P. 2001. 'Building competitive advantage from *ubuntu*: Management lessons from South Africa'. *Academy of Management Executive,* 15(3), 23–33.

Manning, T. 1996. 'Transformation or profit checkmate for SA businesses? Part 1'. *People Dynamics*, November/December, 16–20.

Manning, T. 1997. 'Profit through transformation. Part 2'. *People Dynamics*, January, 16–19.

Manpower Inc. 2006. 'Engaging the total workforce. Manpower White Paper'. <www.manpower.com>

Marchington, M & Wilkinson, A. 2005. *Human Resource Management at Work: People Management and Development,* 3rd ed. London: Chartered Institute of Personnel and Development.

Margerison, C J. 1991. *Making Management Development Work: Achieving Success in the Nineties*. New York: The McGraw-Hill Training Series.

Marks, M L. 2003. *Charging back up the Hill: Workplace Recovery after Mergers, Acquisitions, and Downsizings*. San Francisco: Jossey-Bass.

Marrow, A J. 1969. *The Practical Theorist: The Life and Work of Kurt Lewin*. New York: Basic Books.

Marshall, V. 2000. 'The management of performance management: A macro appraisal', in *Human Resource Strategies: An Applied Approach,* eds Travaglione, A. & Marshall, V. Roseville, NSW: McGraw-Hill.

Marston, C. 2007. *Motivating the 'What's in it for me' Workforce – Manage across the Generational Divide and Increase Profits*. New Jersey: John Wiley & Sons.

Martinez, M. 1993. 'Family support makes business sense'. *HR Magazine,* January, 38–43.

Marx, A E. 1992. *A Practical Guide on Implementing Suggestion Systems*. Kenwyn: Juta.

Marx, F W. 1969. *Aspects of Personnel Management*. Pretoria: University of Pretoria.

Massey, C. 2000. 'Strategic reward systems – flexible pay', in *Strategic Reward Systems*, ed Thorpe, T & Homan, G. London: Prentice Hall.

Matlala, S. 1999. 'Prioritising health promotion and employee wellness'. *People Dynamics*, 17(6), 22–25.

Mawejje, F N. 2005. 'Africa focuses on "triple bottom line"', *Worldlink*, 15(2), 1.

McBeath, G. 1992. *The Handbook of Human Resource Planning: Practical Manpower Analysis Techniques for HR Professionals*. Oxford: Blackwell Business.

McBride, E. 2008. 'A ravenous dragon'. *The Economist*, 15–21 March, 3–5.

McCalman, S. & Paton, R A. 1992. *Change Management: A Guide to Effective Implementation*. London: PCP.

McCarthy, J P. 1980. 'Memo to senior management: Is your personnel department effective?'. *Best's Review*, July, 101–105

McGee, J, Thomas, H & Wilson, D. 2005. *Strategy: Analysis & Practice*. Berkshire: McGraw-Hill.

McGregor, D. 1957. 'An uneasy look at performance appraisal'. *Harvard Business Review*, 35(3), 89–94.

McGregor, D. 1960. *The Human Side of Enterprise*. New York: McGraw-Hill Brook Company, Inc.

McKnight, R. 1991. 'Creating the future after job loss'. *Training and Development*, 45, 69–72.

McNabb, R. & Whitfield, K. 2007. 'The impact of varying types of performance-related pay and employee participation on earnings'. *International Journal of Human Resource Management*, June, 1004–1025.

McRae, H. 1996. 'Seismic forces of global change'. *Strategy and Leadership*, November/December, 6–11.

Mekonnen, S & Mamman, A. 2004. 'HRM in Ethiopia', in *Managing Human Resources in Africa,* eds Kamoche, K, Debrah, Y, Horwitz, F & Muuka, G N. London: Routledge.

Mello, J A. 2006. *Strategic Human Resource Management*, 2nd ed. USA: Thomson – South-Western.

Messmer, M & Bogardus, A. 2008. *Human Resource Management.* New Jersey: John Wiley & Sons.

Metz, J T. 1992. 'Occupational medicine and occupational diseases', in *Occupational Health*, ed Kotzé, A J Cape Town: Juta, 91.

Meyer, J B, Brown, M & Kaplan, D. 2000. *Assessing the South African Brain Drain: A Statistical Comparison.* Development Policy Research Unit Working Paper. Cape Town: University of Cape Town.

Meyer, M. 2005. *Third annual ASTD state of the South African Training and HR Industry Report.* University of South Africa.

Meyer, M (ed). 2007. *Managing Human Resource Development: An Outcomes-based Approach*, 3rd ed. Durban: LexisNexis.

Meyer, M & Bushney, M. 2007. *Annual ASTD State of the South African Training Industry Report: 2007.* Johannesburg: Knowres.

Meyer, M & Kirsten, M. 2005. *Introduction to Human Resource Management.* Claremont: NAE, an imprint of New Africa Books (Pty) Ltd.

Mgibisa, M. 2007. 'New labour giant maps its way forward', *City Press, Business,* 10 November, posted to the web: <www.news24.com/City_Press/Finance/0,186-246_2218863,00.html>

Michelson, G. 2006. 'The role of workplace chaplains in industrial relations: Evidence from Australia'. *British Journal of Industrial Relations*, 44(4), 677–696.

Miles, R & Snow, C. 1984. 'Designing strategic human resources systems'. *Organizational Dynamics*, Summer, 36–52.

Miles, R E, Miles, G & Snow, C C. 2005. 'Creating the capability for collaborative entrepreneurship: HR's role in the development of a new organizational form', in *The Future of Human Resource Management – 64 Thought Leaders Explore the Critical HR Issues of Today and Tomorrow,* eds Losey, M, Meisinger, S & Ulrich, D. New Jersey: John Wiley & Sons.

Milkovich, G T & Boudreau, J W. 1994. *Human Resource Management,* 7th ed. Homewood, Ill: Irwin.

Millward, L. 2005. *Understanding Occupational & Organisational Psychology.* London: Sage.

Ministerial Committee for Development on the NQF. 1996. *Discussion Document on Lifelong Learning through a National Qualifications Framework.* Department of Education.

Mischke, C & Garbers, C. 1994. *Safety at Work.* Kenwyn: Juta.

Mitrani, A, Dalziel, M & Fitt, D. 1992. *Competency-based Human Resource Management.* London: Kogan Page.

Mkhabela, M. 2008. '"Africa code" for SA firms urged'. *Business Times*, 6 April, 5.

Mlambo-Ngcuka, P. 2006. Media briefing by the Deputy President. *Background Document: A Catalyst for Accelerated and Shared Growth – South Africa (AsgiSA).*

Momberg, J P & Langenhoven, H P. 1974. *Die Indiensnemingsonderhoud in die Suid-Afrikaanse Bedryf.* University of the Orange Free State, Bloemfontein.

Mondy, R V & Noe, R M. 2005. *Human Resource Management,* 9th ed. Upper Saddle River, NJ: Pearson Prentice Hall.

Moorhead, G & Griffin, R W. 2000. *Organizational behaviour: Managing people and organizations,* 6th ed. Boston: Houghton Mifflin.

Morley, M J, Gunnigle, P & Collings, D G. 2006. *Global Industrial Relations.* Oxon: Routledge.

Morris, M H, Kuratko, D F & Covin, J G. 2008. *Corporate Entrepreneurship & Innovation,* 2nd ed. Mason, OH: Thomson/South-Western.

Mpabanga, D. 2004. 'HRM in Botswana', in *Managing Human Resources in Africa,* eds Kamoche, K, Debrah, Y, Horwitz, F & Muuka, G N. London: Routledge.

Muchinsky, P M, Kriek, H J & Schreuder, D. 2002. *Personnel Psychology,* 2nd ed. Cape Town: Oxford University Press.

Muchinsky, P M, Kriek, H J & Schreuder, D. 2005. *Personnel Psychology,* 3rd ed. London: Oxford.

Muller, J. 1988. 'Employee assistance programmes – a new approach to workplace productivity?' IPM *Journal,* 6(12), 21.

Mullins, L J. 2002. *Management and Organisational Behaviour,* 6th ed. Harlow: Pearson.

Munchus, G. 1992. 'Check references for safer selection'. *HR Magazine,* 1992, 75–77.

Murlis, H. 2004. 'Managing rewards', in *People Management: Challenges and Opportunities,* eds Rees, D & McBain, R. London: Palgrave Macmillan.

Musa, T. 2008. 'African poor expect leaders to unwind food price spiral'. *Business Report,* 3 April, 2.

Mutedi, A. 2006. *Industrial Action 2006 Annual Report.* Pretoria: Department of Labour.

Muuka, G N & Mwenda, K K. 2004. 'HRM in Tanzania', in *Managing Human Resources in Africa,* eds Kamoche, K , Debrah, Y, Horwitz, F & Muuka, G N. London: Routledge.

Myburgh, A. 2004. 'Codetermination in the enterprise – a proven institution in a consensual society'. Article published in German in *ifo Schnelldienst*. No. 22/2004.

Myers, I B & McCauley, M H. 1992. *A Guide to the Development and Use of the Myers-Briggs Type Indicator*. Palo Alto, California: Consulting Psychologists Press, Inc.

Nadler, D. 1983. *Concepts for the Management of Organisation Change. Section V: Organisation Adaptation and Change.* New York: Delta Consulting Group.

Nadler, D & Tushman, M. 1988. 'Organisational frame bending: Principles for managing reorientation.' *Academy of Management Executive,* August, 194–204.

Nadler, D A, Behan, B A & Nadler, M B. 2006. *Building Better Boards: A Blueprint for Effective Governance*. San Francisco: Jossey-Bass.

Nadler, L & Nadler, Z. 1989. *Developing Human Resource,* 3rd ed. San Francisco: Jossey-Bass.

Naidu, L. 2003. 'Executive pay trends'. *People Dynamics,* 21(6), 30.

Nakanyane, S. 2005. *Labour Market Review.* Department Labour RSA, 1–67.

Nankervis, A, Compton, R & Baird, M. 2002. *Strategic Human Resource Management,* 4th ed. Victoria: Thomson Learning.

Nankervis, A, Compton, R & Baird, M. 2008. *Human Resource Management: Strategies & Processes,* 6th ed. Australia: Thomson.

Nare, G. 2008. 'Zimbabweans treated like slaves by SA farmers'. *Weekend Argus,* 16 March, 12.

National Training Board. 1994. *A Discussion Document on a National Training Strategy Initiative*. Pretoria: NTB.

Ndletyana, M. 2007. 'Municipal elections 2006: Protests, independent candidates and cross-border municipalities', in *State of the Nation – South Africa 2007,* eds Buhlungu, S, Daniel, J, Southall, R & Lutchman, J. Cape Town: HSRC Press, 95–113.

Nel, J. 1999. Personal discussion on the future development of the National Training Initiative.

Nel, P S & Van Rooyen, P H. 1993. *South African Industrial Relations: Theory and Practice.* Pretoria: JL van Schaik.

Nel, P S, Erasmus, B J & Swanepoel, B J. 1993. *Successful Labour Relations: Guidelines for Practice*. Pretoria: Van Schaik.

Nel, P S, Kirsten, M, Swanepoel, B J, Erasmus, B J & Poisat, P. 2008. *South African Employment Relations: Theory and Practice,* 6th ed. Pretoria: Van Schaik.

Nel, P S, Werner, A, Haasbroek, G D, Poisat, P, Sono, T & Schultz, H B. 2008. *Human Resources Management*, 7th ed. South Africa: Oxford University Press.

Nelson, D L & Quick, J B. 2002. *Understanding Organizational Behavior: A Multimedia Approach.* Cincinnati: South-Western.

Nelson, D L & Quick, J B. 2006. *Organizational Behavior: Foundations, Realities and Challenges*, 5th ed. Mason, Ohio: Thomson South-Western.

Newenham, A K. 2005. 'Management in HR by foreign-owned bank in Tanzania: The impact of country-of-origin'. *South African Journal of Labour Relations*, 29(2), (3) & (4), 59–97.

Newmarch, J. 2008. 'Fear hits the bottom line: businesses are paying the price in lost staff and increased security costs'. *Mail & Guardian,* 14–19 March, 2.

Newstrom, J W & Davis, K. 2002. *Organizational Behavior: Human Behavior at Work*, 11th ed. New York: McGraw-Hill.

Newstrom, J W & Scannel, E E. 1980. *Games Trainers Play: Experiential Learning Exercises*. New York: McGraw-Hill.

Nieuwmeijer, L. 1988. *Negotiation: Methodology and Training.* Pretoria: Owen Burgess.

Noble, R. 2007. 'South Africa HIV & Aids statistics'. <www.avert.org/safricastats. htm>

Noe, R A, Hollenbeck, J R, Gerhart, B & Wright, P M. 1994. *Human Resource Management: Gaining a Competitive Advantage.* Boston: Irwin.

Noe, R A. Hollenbeck, J R, Gerhart, B & Wright P M. 2003. *Human Resource Management: Gaining a Competitive Advantage*, 4th ed. New York: McGraw-Hill.

Noe, R A, Hollenbeck, J R, Gerhart, B & Wright, P M. 2004. *Fundamentals of Human Resource Management*. New York: McGraw-Hill.

Noon, M & Blyton, P. 2007. *The Realities of Work – Experiencing Work and Employment in Contemporary Society,* 3rd ed. New York: Palgrave Macmillan.

Norman, P. 1998. 'Critical challenges ahead for HR in business transformation'. *Management Today*, 14(2), 14–16.

NOSA. 1995. NOSA information brochure.

Nyambegera, S M. 2002. 'Ethnicity and human resource management practice in sub-Saharan Africa: the relevance of the managing diversity discourse'. *The International Journal of Human Resource Management,* 13(7), 1077–1090.

Nyfield, G, Gibbons, P J, Baron, H & Robertson, I. 1995. *The Cross-cultural Validity of Management Assessment Methods*. Paper presented at the 5th Annual Conference on Fairness in Personnel Decisions of the Department of Industrial Psychology, Pretoria.

O'Doherty, D. 1995. 'Towards human resource planning?', in *Human Resource Management: A Contemporary Perspective*, eds Beardwell, I & Holden, L. London: Pitman, 119.

Okpara, J O & Wynn, P. 2008. 'Human resource management practices in a transition economy – challenges and prospects'. *Management Research News*, 31(1), 57–76.

Oppenheimer, N. 2007. 'No more the "hopeless continent"'. *International Herald Tribune*, 1 June.

Orlikowski, W J & Hofman, J D. 1997. 'An improvisational model for change management: The case of groupware technologies'. *Sloan Management Review*, Winter, 11–21.

Osterman, P. 2006. 'Community organizing and employee representation'. *British Journal of Industrial Relations*, 44(4), 629–650.

Otte, F L & Hutcheson, P G. 1992. *Helping Employees Manage Careers*. Englewood Cliffs, NJ: Prentice Hall.

Owens, W A. 1976. 'Background data', in *Handbook of Industrial and Organizational Psychology*, ed Dunnette, M D. Chicago: Rand McNally.

Paauwe, J & Boselie, P. 2007. 'HRM and societal embeddedness', in *The Oxford Handbook of Human Resource Management*, eds Boxall, P, Purcell, J & Wright, P. New York: Oxford University Press, 166–186.

Pandor, N. 2005. Address by the Minister of Education at the Launch of 'Trends in Public Higher Education 1995 to 2004', an analysis of the SAQA National Learners. Record Database. Pretoria: SAQA.

Pansegrouw, G. 1985. 'Strategic human resource management – an emerging dimension, parts 1 & 2'. *IPM Journal*, 4(5), 22–30; 4(6), 8–15.

PayCon 2006 conference papers. Sandton, August.

P-E Corporate Services SA (Pty) Ltd. 2006. *Top Executive Remuneration In South Africa – September 2006* (proprietary report).

P-E Corporate Services. 2006. *Policy Trends: P-E Top executive remuneration survey – South Africa*. P-E Corporate Services SA (Pty) Ltd.

Peacock B. 2008. 'A new culture of care needed'. *Business Times*, 17 February, 17.

Pearce, J A & Robinson, R B. 1991. *Strategic Management: Formulation, Implementation and Control*. Homewood, Illinois: Irwin.

Pearce, J A & Robinson, R B. 2005. *Strategic Management – Formulation, Implementation, and Control*, 9th ed. Boston: McGraw-Hill, Irwin.

Peel, M. 1988. *Ready-made Interview Questions*. London: Kogan Page Limited.

Peiperl, M A. 2001. 'Getting 360-degree feedback right'. *Harvard Business Review*, January 2001, 142–147.

People & Profits. 1973. 'Anglo sticks its neck out – Dr Alex Boraine plans for black advancement'. *People & Profits*, 1(1), July, 3–28.

Peters, T & Waterman, B. 1982. *In Search of Excellence*. New York: Harper & Row.

Pfeffer, J. 1997. 'Pitfalls on the road to measurement: The dangerous liaison of human resources with ideas of accounting and finance'. *Human Resource Management*, 36, Fall, 357–365.

Pfeiffer, J W. 1994. *Pfeiffer and Company on Experiential Learning Activities. Training Technologies*, vol 21. San Diego: Pfeiffer Company.

Phillips, J. 1996. 'Measuring the HR contribution: A survey of approaches', in *Accountability in Human Resource Management*. Houston: Gulf Publishing Co, 33–50.

Phillips, J J. 1996. 'The need for a results-based approach', in *Accountability in Human Resource Management*. Houston, Texas: Gulf Publishing Co, 1–5, 21–5.

Phillips, J J & Seers, A. 1989. 'Twelve ways to evaluate HR management'. *Personnel Administrator*, April, 54–58.

Philp, R. 2008. 'SA in 2025: Take your pick'. *Sunday Times* (Business Times Special Report), 28 September, 8.

Pienaar, W E & Spoelstra, H J. 1991. *Negotiation, Theory Strategy and Skills.* Cape Town: Juta.

Pieper, R. 1990. *Human Resource Management: An International Comparison*. Berlin: Walter de Gouyter.

Piliso, S. 2007. 'Local firms lay on gyms, shops and masseurs for staff'. *Sunday Times*, 22 July.

Piskyrich, G M. 1993. *ASTD Handbook of Instructional Technology.* New York: McGraw-Hill.

Plug, C, Meyer, W F, Louw, D A & Gouws, L A. 1986. *Psigologiewoordeboek.* Johannesburg: McGraw-Hill.

Plumbley, P. 1991. *Recruitment and Selection*. Worcester: Billing & Sons Ltd.

Pollard, E & Hillage J. 2001. 'Report 376: Exploring e-learning'. <www.employ-ment-studies.co.uk>

Pondy, L R. 1969. 'Organisation conflict, concepts and models'. *Administrative Science Quarterly*, 12 , 27–36.

Pons, A & Deale, P. 1998. *Labour Relations Handbook: A Practical Guide on Effective Labour Relations Policies, Procedures and Practices for South African Management.* Cape Town: Juta.

Poole, M. 1986. 'Managerial strategies and "styles" in industrial relations: A comparative analysis'. *Journal of General Management,* 12(1), 40–53.

Porter, M E. 1980. *Competitive Strategy.* New York: Free Press.

Porter, M E. 1985. *Competitive Advantage: Creating and Sustaining Superior Performance.* New York: The Free Press.

Posthuma, R A & Campion, M A. 2008. 'Twenty best practices for just employee performance reviews'. *Compensation and Benefits Review,* January/February 2008, 47–55.

Powell, A. 2008. 'A new face of hunger as food prices spiral', *The Star*, 3 April, 4.

Power, D F. 1991. 'Target-specific bargaining'. *IPM Journal*, 9(8), 15–20.

Pretorius, B. 2007. 'Effective leadership: Key driver of sustainable growth'. *Management Today,* 23(9), 6–10.

Price, A. 2004. *Human Resource Management in a Business Context*, 2nd ed. London: Thomson.

Professionalising HR: A time for action. The South African Board of Personnel Practice (SABPP), The Castle, Kyalami, 8th June 2007.

'Protecting your people'. 2007. *People Dynamics*, 25(1), 25.

Purcell, J & Ahlstrand, B. 1994. *Human Resource Management in the Multi-dimensional Company.* Oxford: Oxford University Press.

Purcell, J & Hutchinson, S. 2007. 'Front-line managers as agents in the HRM-performance causal chain: Theory, analysis and evidence'. *Human Resource Management Journal*, 17(1), 3–20.

Purcell, J & Hutchinson, S. 2007. *Rewarding Work: The Vital Role of Line Managers.* London: CIPD.

Purcell, J & Kinnie, N. 2007. 'HRM and business performance', in *The Oxford Handbook of Human Resource Management*, eds Boxall, P, Purcell, J & Wright, P. New York: Oxford University Press, 533–551.

Purcell, J. 1987. 'Mapping management styles in employee relations'. *Journal of Management Studies*, 24(5), 533–548.

Quinlan, T & Willan, S. 2005. 'HIV/Aids: finding ways to contain the pandemic', in *State of the Nation – South Africa 2004–2005*, eds Daniel, J, Southall, R & Lutchman, J. Cape Town: HSRC Press.

Rademan, D J & Vos, H D. 2001. 'Performance appraisals in the public sector: Are they accurate and fair?'. *Journal of Industrial Psychology*, 27(1), 54–60.

Ramgutty-Wong, A. 2004. 'HRM in Ivory Coast', in *Managing Human Resources in Africa,* eds Kamoche, K, Debrah, Y, Horwitz, F & Muuka, G N. London: Routledge.

Ramgutty-Wong, A. 2004. 'HRM in Mauritius', in *Managing Human Resources in Africa,* eds Kamoche, K, Debrah, Y, Horwitz, F & Muuka, G N. London: Routledge.

Ramphele, M 2007, 'Trailblazers: champions of change'. *Management Today*, 23(5), 38–43.

Ray, M. 1997. 'Weza Sawmill'. *South African Labour Bulletin*, 21(2), 51–54.

'Reconstruct'. 1999. Supplement to *Sunday Independent*, 13 June.

Reece, B L & Brandt, R. 2006. *Human Relation: Principles and Practices,* 6th ed. Boston: Houghton Mifflin.

Regulations for the period 01 April 2000 to 31 March 2001 regarding the Funding and Related Issues. *Government Gazette* no. 6729.

Reid, M A, Barrington, H & Kenney, J. 1992. *Training Interventions: Managing Employee Development*, 3rd ed. London: IPM.

Republic of South Africa, 2007. *State-owned Enterprises Remuneration Guidelines Part A.* Department of Public Enterprises. <www.dpe.gov.za>

Republic of South Africa. 1995. *South African Qualifications Authority Act 58 of 1995.* Pretoria: Government Printer.

Republic of South Africa. 1996. *Green Paper: Policy Proposals for a New Employment and Occupational Equity Statute.* Notice 804 of 1996, *Government Gazette* 17303. Pretoria: Government Printer.

Republic of South Africa. 1997. *Green Paper: Skills Development Strategy for Economic and Employment Growth in South Africa.* Department of Labour, March 1997. Pretoria: Department of Labour.

Republic of South Africa. 1997. *Higher Education Act, 1997.* Pretoria: Government Printer.

Republic of South Africa. 1998a. *Regulations under the South African Qualifications Authority Act 58 of 1995.* Pretoria: Government Printer.

Republic of South Africa. 1998b. *Further Education and Training Act 98 of 1998.* Pretoria: Government Printer.

Republic of South Africa. 1998c. *Skills Development Act 97 of 1998.* Pretoria: Government Printer.

Republic of South Africa. 1999. *Skills Development Levies Act 9 of 1999.* Pretoria: Government Printer.

Republic of South Africa. 2005. *State of Skills in South Africa, 2005.* Department of Labour. Pretoria: Government Printer.

Republic of South Africa. 2008. *General Notice* (256 of 2008). Department of Education. Call for Comment on National Qualifications Bill, 2008; Higher Education Act Amendment Bill, 2008; General and Further Education and Training Quality Assurance Act Amendment Bill, 2008. *Government Gazette*, 15 February 2008. Pretoria: Government Printer.

Republic of South Africa. 2008. *Kha Ri Gude: Literacy Campaign South Africa. A Guide to Partnerships in the Kha Ri Gude Literacy Campaign.* Department of Education. Pretoria. <www.gov.za>

Republic of South Africa. 2008. *Skills Development Act 97 of 1998 – Skills Development Amendment Bill, 2008* no. 30823. Department of Labour. Pretoria: Government Printer.

Richards, J. 2007. *Total Reward.* CIPD factsheet, available at <www.cipd.co.uk> (accessed 28 July 2007).

Richardson, B. 1994. 'The political-aware leader'. *Leadership and Organisation Development Journal,* 16(2), 27–35.

Robbins, P R. 1997. *Managing Today!* New Jersey: Prentice Hall.

Robbins, S P. 1994. *Essentials of Organizational Behavior,* 4th ed. New Jersey: Prentice Hall Inc.

Robbins, S P. 1996. *Organizational Behavior,* 7th ed. Englewood Cliffs, NJ: Prentice Hall Inc.

Robbins, S P. 2001. *Organizational Behavior: Concepts, Controversies, Applications,* 9th ed. Upper Saddle River, NJ: Prentice Hall.

Robbins, S P & Barnwell, N. 2002. *Organisation Theory: Concepts and Cases,* 4th ed. Australia: Pearson Education.

Robbins, S P & Barnwell, N. 2006. *Organisation Theory: Concepts and Cases,* 5th ed. Australia: Pearson Education.

Robbins, S P, Judge, T A, Millett, B & Waters-Marsh, T. 2008. *Organizational Behaviour,* 5th ed. Frenchs Forest NSW: Pearson.

Roberts, B. 2005. 'Empty stomachs, empty pockets': Poverty and inequality in post-apartheid South Africa', in *State of the Nation – South Africa 2004–2005,* eds Daniel, J, Southall, R & Lutchman, J (eds). Cape Town: HSRC Press.

Ronen, S. 1989. 'Training the international assignee', in *Training and Development in Organizations,* ed. Goldstein, I L. San Francisco: Jossey-Bass.

Rosenthal, T & Nolingo, W. 1998. 'Defend, empower, advance: CWIU's approach to company restructuring'. *South African Labour Bulletin,* 22(1), 63–69.

Rothwell, J D. 2007. *In Mixed Company – Communicating in Small Groups and Teams,* 6th ed. USA: Thomson.

Rothwell, W J & Kazanas, H C. 1994. *Planning and Managing Human Resources: Strategic Planning for Personnel Management.* Amherst: HRD Press.

Rousseau, P M & Wade-Benzoni, K A. 1995. 'Changing individual-organisational attachments: A two-way street', in *The Changing Nature of Work,* ed Haward, A. San Francisco: Jossey-Bass, 305.

Royle, T. 2006. 'The dominance effect? Multinational corporations in the Italian quick-food service sector'. *British Journal of Industrial Relations,* 44(4), 757–780.

Rugege S. 2001. 'A summary of some cases on HIV/Aids'. *Law, Democracy & Development,* 5(2), 237–241.

Rumney, R. 2005. 'Who owns South Africa: An analysis of state and private ownership patterns', in *State of the Nation – South Africa 2004–2005,* eds Daniel, J, Southall, R & Lutchman, J. Cape Town: HSRC Press.

Ryan, C. 1993. 'By comparison, SA lags behind on most counts'. *Sunday Times,* Johannesburg, 18 July.

'SA firms play vital role in Africa'. n.d. <www.sagoodnews.co.za/index2/php>

'SA is a significant engine of growth for Africa. South Africa: The Good News'. <http://www.sagoodnews.co.za/index2.php> (accessed 30 April 2008).

Sachs, A. 1991. *Affirmative Action and Good Government*. Alistair Berkeley Memorial Lecture, November, 14–15.

Sackmann, S A, Flamholtz, E G & Bullen, M L. 1989. 'Human resource accounting: A state-of-the-art review'. *Journal of Accounting Literature,* 8, 235–264.

Salaman, G, Storey, J & Billsberry, J. 2005. *Strategic Human Resource Management – Theory and Practice,* 2nd ed, London: Sage.

Salamon, M. 1992. *Industrial Relations: Theory and Practice,* 2nd ed. New York: Prentice Hall.

Salamon, M. 2000. *Industrial Relations: Theory and Practice,* 4th ed. Essex: Pearson Education.

Samson, D & Daft, R L. 2005. *Management*, 2nd ed. Australia: Thomson.

Sanderson, G. 1992. 'Objectives and evaluation', in *Handbook of Training and Development*, ed Truelove, S. Massachusetts: Fielden House.

Santhey, C. 1993. 'Medical costs: Optimise your diagnosis'. *People Dynamics*, 11(7), 14–15.

Saratoga Institute (South Africa). 1998. *South African Human Resource Effectiveness Report*. Cape Town.

Sartain, L 2005, 'Branding from the inside out: HR's role as brand builder', in *The Future of Human Resource Management – 64 Thought Leaders Explore the Critical HR Issues of Today and Tomorrow,* eds Losey, M, Meisinger, S & Ulrich, D. New Jersey: John Wiley & Sons.

Sathe, V J. 1983. 'Implications of corporate culture: A manager's guide to action'. *Organisational Dynamics,* 12(2), Autumn, 5–23.

Saunders, R. 1992. *Taking Care of Safety.* London: Pitman.

Scarpello, V G & Ledvinka, J. 1988. *Personnel/Human Resource Management*. Boston: PWS-Kent Publishing Company.

Schein, E H. 1972. *Organizational Psychology*, 2nd ed. Englewood Cliffs, NJ: Prentice Hall, Inc.

Schein, E H. 1978. *Career Dynamics: Matching Individual and Organisational Needs*. Philippines: Addison Wesley Publishing Co.

Schein, E H. 1980. *Organizational Psychology*, 3rd ed. Englewood Cliffs, NJ: Prentice Hall.

Schein, E H. 1990. *Career Anchors: Discover Your Real Values*. San Diego: University Associates.

Schein, E H. 1993. *Career Survival: Strategic Job and Role Planning*. California: Pfeifer & Company.

Schein, E H. 1996. 'Career anchors revisited: Implications for career development in the 21st century'. *Academy of Management Executive,* 80–88.

Schendel, D. 1992. 'Introduction to the summer 1992 special issue on "strategy process research"'. *Strategic Management Journal*, 13, 1–4.

Schmidt, F L & Rader M. 1999. 'Exploring the boundary condition for interview validity: Meta-analytic validity findings for a new interview type'. *Personnel Psychology,* 52, 445–464.

Schreuder, A M G & Coetzee, M. 2006. *Careers: An Organisational Perspective*, 3rd ed. Kenwyn: Juta & Co Ltd.

Schreuder, A M G & Theron, A L. 2001. *Careers: An Organisational Perspective*. Kenwyn: Juta & Co Ltd.

Schuler, R D, Dowling, P J, Smart, J P & Huber, V L. 1993. *Human Resource Management in Australia*, 2nd ed. Melbourne, Australia: Harper Educational.

Schuler, R S. 1987. *Personnel and Human Resource Management,* 3rd ed. St Paul: West.

Schuler, R S & Jackson, S E. 1996. *Human Resource Management: Positioning for the 21st Century*, 6th ed. Minneapolis/St Paul: West Publishing Company.

Schuler, R S & Jackson, S E. 2007. *Strategic Human Resource Management,* 2nd ed. Oxford: Blackwell Publishing.

Schuler, R S, Jackson, S E & Luo, Y. 2004. *Managing Human Resources in Cross-Border Alliances.* London: Routledge.

Schultz, D P & Schultz, S E. 1986. *Psychology and Industry Today.* New York: Macmillan Publishing Company.

Schultz, D P & Schultz, S E. 1994. *Psychology and Industry Today: An Introduction to Industrial and Organisational Psychology.* New York: Macmillan Publishing Company.

Schweyer, A & McGrath, D. 2004. 'Managing your workforce', in *On Staffing: Advice and Perspectives from HR Leaders*, eds Burkholder, N C, Edwards, P J & Sartain, L. Hoboken, NJ: John Wiley & Sons Inc,

Scullion, H & Collings, D G. 2006. *Global Staffing.* Oxon: Routledge.

Selby, K & Sutherland, M. 2006. '"Space creation": A strategy for achieving employment equity at senior management level'. *South African Journal of Labour Relations*, 30(2), 42–65.

Senge, P M. 1990. *The Fifth Discipline.* New York: Doubleday.

Senior, B. 2002. *Organisational Change.* London: Prentice Hall.

Seo, M & Hill, N S 2005, 'Understanding the human side of merger and acquisition: An integrative framework', *The Journal of Applied Behavioral Science,* 41(4), 422–443.

Shani, A B & Lau, J B. 1995. *Behavior in Organizations: An Experiential Approach,* 6th ed. Chicago: Irwin.

Sherman, A W & Bohlander, G W. 1992. *Managing Human Resources,* 9th ed. Cincinnati, Ohio: South-Western.

Shirley, R C. 1982. 'Limiting the scope of strategy: A decision-based approach'. *Academy of Management Review,* 7(2), 262.

Sibson, R E. 1992. *Strategic Planning for Human Resources Management.* New York: AMACOM.

Singer, M C. 1990. *Human Resource Management.* Boston: PWS-Kent Publishing Company.

Singer, M. 1993. *Fairness in Personnel Selection.* Aldershot: Avebury.

Sisson, K. 1989. 'Personnel management in perspective', in *Personnel Management in Britain*, ed Sisson, K, Oxford: Basil Blackwell, 3–21.

Smit, A & Venter, E. 1996. 'Life in a pressure cooker'. *Productivity SA*, 22(1), 10–12.

Smit, P J & Cronje, G J de J. 1992. *Management Principles.* Cape Town: Juta & Co Ltd.

Smit, P J, Cronje, G J de J, Brevis, T & Vrba, M J. 2007. *Management Principles – a Contemporary Edition for Africa*, 4th ed. Cape Town: Juta.

Smith, G D, Arnold, D R & Bizell, B G. 1988. *Business Strategy and Policy*, 2nd ed. Boston: Houghton Mifflin.

Smith, G. 2007. 'Online recruitment a growing international trend'. *People Dynamics*, 25(10), 33.

Smith, M, Gregg, M & Andrews, D. 1989. *Selection and Assessment: A New Appraisal.* London: Pitman Publishing.

Smith, N. 2000. 'New job-evaluation techniques: Don't paint yourself into a corner'. *People Dynamics* 18(5), 34–36.

Smither, R D. 1988. *The Psychology of Work and Human Performance*. New York: Harper & Row.

Solomon, J. 2007. *Corporate Governance and Accountability*. Chichester, UK: John Wiley & Sons Ltd.

'South Africa in brief', 2007. <www.sairr.org.za/research-and-publications/fast-stats-online/fast-facts-2007/fast-facts-no-7-july-2007.html>

South African Board for Personnel Practice. 2002. *Annual report 2002*. Johannesburg.

South African Board for Personnel Practice. 2008. *Annual Report 2007–2008*. Parktown.

South African Reserve Bank. 2008. *Quarterly Bulletin,* no. 247, March 2008.

Southall, R. 2005. 'Black empowerment and corporate capital', in *State of the Nation – South Africa 2004–2005.* eds Buhlungu, S, Daniel, J, Southall, R & Lutchman, J. Cape Town: HSRC Press.

Southall, R. 2006a. 'Introduction: Can South Africa be a developmental state?', in *State of the Nation – South Africa 2005–2006,* eds Buhlungu, S, Daniel, J, Southall, R & Lutchman, J. Cape Town: HSRC Press.

Southall, R. 2006b. 'Black empowerment and present limits to a more democratic capitalism in South Africa', in *State of the Nation – South Africa 2005–2006,* eds Buhlungu, S, Daniel, J, Southall, R & Lutchman, J. Cape Town: HSRC Press.

Southall, R. 2007. 'The ANC, black economic empowerment and state-owned enterprises: A recycling of history?', in *State of the Nation – South Africa 2007,* eds Buhlungu, S, Daniel, J, Southall, R & Lutchman, J. Cape Town: HSRC Press, 201–225.

Southall, R. 2007. 'The ANC state, more dysfunctional than developmental?', in *State of the Nation – South Africa 2007,* eds Buhlungu, S, Daniel, J, Southall, R & Lutchman, J. Cape Town: HSRC Press, 1–24.

SPA Consultants. 1992. *Human Resources Survey in 23 Well-known South African Organisations*, 6–24.

SPA Consultants. 1994. *Literacy Training in South Africa: A Critical Ingredient for World-Class Performance.* Johannesburg.

Spangenberg, H H, Esterhuyse, J J, Visser, J H, Briedenhann, J E & Calitz, C J. 1989. 'Construction of behaviourally anchored rating scales (BARS) for the measurement of managerial performance'. *Journal of Industrial Psychology*, 15(1) 22–27.

Spangenberg, H. 1991. 'New guidelines and ethical considerations for assessment centre operations'. *IPM Journal,* June, 29–32.

Spangenberg, H. 1993. 'A managerial view on performance management'. *People Dynamics*, October, 30–34.

Spangenberg, H. 1994. *Understanding and Implementing Performance Management.* Kenwyn: Juta.

Spearing, S. 1996. 'Mining safety: Put your fingers away'. *Productivity SA*, 22(3), 21.

Spector, P E. 2006. *Industrial and Organizational Psychology: Research and Practice,* 4th ed. Hoboken NJ: Wiley.

Spirig, J E. 1988. 'Selling the HRIS'. *Personnel*, October, 26–34.

'Spreading and sustaining growth in Africa, 2007. South Africa: The Good News'. <http://www.sagoodnews.co.za/index2.php> (accessed 30 April 2008).

Stacey, RD. 2007. *Strategic Management and Organisation Dynamics*, 5th ed. Essex: Pearson Education.

Staehle, W H. 1990. 'Human resource management and corporate strategy', in *Human Resource Management: An International Comparison*. Pieper, R. Berlin: Walter de Gouyter.

Starkey, K & McKinlay, A. 1993. *Strategy and the Human Resource – Ford and the Search for Competitive Advantage.* UK: Blackwell.

Starks, S L. 1992. 'Understanding government affirmative action and *Metro Broadcasting Inc v FCC*'. *Duke Law Journal,* 41, 993–975.

Steers, R M & Porter, L W. 1991. *Motivation and Work Behaviour*, 5th ed. New York: McGraw-Hill.

Steiner, G A & Miner, J B. 1982. *Management Policy and Strategy,* 2nd ed. New York: Macmillan.

Stengel, R. 2008. 'Mandela: His 8 lessons of leadership', *Time*, July 2008, 16–22.

Stevenson, M. 1998. 'Career transition counselling'. *People Dynamics*, 16(10), 40–46.

Stewart, G L & Brown, K G. 2006. *Human Resource Management: Linking Strategy to Practice.* New Jersey: John Wiley & Sons.

Stone, R J. 1998. *Human Resource Management,* 3rd ed. Brisbane: Wiley.

Stone, R J. 2002. *Human Resource Management*, 4th ed. Milton Qld: John Wiley & Sons.

Stone, R J. 2005. *Human Resource Management*, 5th ed. Milton, Qld: John Wiley & Sons, Australia.

Stoner, J & Wankel, C. 1986. *Management,* 3rd ed. New Jersey: Prentice Hall.

Storey, J (ed). 1989. *New Perspective on Human Resource Management.* London: Routledge.

Storey, J (ed). 1995. *Human Resource Management: A Critical Text.* London: Routledge.

Storey, J. 1992. *Developments in the Management of Human Resources.* Oxford: Blackwell.

Storey, J. 2001. *Human Resource Management: A critical text,* 2nd ed. London: Thomson Learning.

Stott, K & Walker, A. 1995. *Team, Teamwork & Teambuilding.* New York: Prentice Hall.

Strategic Planning for Personnel Management. Amherst: HRD Press.

Strauss, G. 1992. 'Human resource management in the USA', in *The Handbook of Human Resource Management,* ed Towers, S. Oxford: Blackwell, 27–29.

Strebel, P. 1996. 'Why do employees resist change?'. *Harvard Business Review,* May–June, 86–92.

'Sub-Saharan Africa: Regional economic outlook 2007'. <www.imf.org/external/np/sec/pr/2007/pr07237.htm>

Sunday Times supplement: Primary Health. 1994. 'Alcohol and drugs exact their grim toll'. 24 March, 10.

Sunday Times, 22 July 2007, 8.

Sunday Times. 2008. As summarised/reported by Philp. 'South Africa scenarios 2025: The future we chose?', 8. Also posted on <http://www.thepresidency.gov.za/>

Sunday Times: Business Times Careers, 22 June 2008.

Sunter, C & Ilbury, C. 2008. 'Back to the future'. *Leadership*, March 2008, 27–33.

Super, D E. 1992. 'Toward a comprehensive theory of career development', in *Career Development: Theory and Practice,* eds Montross, D H & Shinkman, C J. Illinois: Charles C. Thomas Publisher, 35–61.

'Supporting workplace learning for high performance working'. 2002. <http://www.ilo.org/public/english/employment/skills/workplace/case/case7.htm>

'Survey of global HR challenges: Yesterday, today and tomorrow'. 2005. Conducted by Pricewaterhouse Coopers on behalf of the World Federation of Personnel Management Associations (WFPMA).

Swanepoel, B J. 1992. 'Affirmative action and employee empowerment in Namibia: Southern African research perspective on some pieces of the jigsaw puzzle'. *South African Journal of Labour Relations*, 16(3), 23–36.

Swanepoel, B J. 1995. *'n Strategiese Benadering tot die Bestuur van die Diensverhouding*. Unpublished doctoral dissertation, Pretoria, Unisa.

Swanepoel, B. 2005. 'People puzzle: Is HRM out and leadership in?'. *Human Capital*, 3(7).

Tapscott, D & Caston, A. 1993. *Paradigm Shift*. New York: McGraw-Hill.

Taylor, B R. 1991. *Affirmative Action at Work – Law, Politics, and Ethics*. Pittsburgh, Pa; University of Pittsburgh Press.

Taylor, H C & Russell, J T. 1939. 'The relationship of validity coefficients to the practical effectiveness of tests in selection: Discussion and tables'. *Journal of Applied Psychology*, 23, 565–578.

Taylor, S. 2005. *People Resourcing*, 3rd ed. London: Chartered Institute of Personnel and Development.

Teicher, J, Holland, P & Gough, R. 2002. *Employee Relations Management – Australia in a Global Context*. Australia: Pearson Education.

'The Africa Competitiveness Report 2007'. <www.weforum.org/en/initiatives/gcp/ Africa%20Competitiveness%20Report/200...>

'The Global Competitiveness Report'. <www.gcr.weforum.org/pages/home.aspx>

The SABPP's Guide Registration, June 1992.

The Supply and Demand of Personnel Practitioners in South Africa. Pretoria: Human Sciences Research Council.

'The World Competitiveness Scoreboard 2007'. <www.imd.ch/research/publications/ wcy/competitiveness_scoreboard.cfm>

Theron, D. 2000. '360-degree performance assessment helps provide direction'. *People Dynamics*, 18(6), 15–19.

Thomas, A. 1996. *Beyond Affirmative Action – Managing Diversity for Competitive Advantage in South Africa*. Johannesburg: Knowledge Resources.

Thompson, A A & Strickland, A J. 1999. *Strategic Management: Concepts and Cases*, 11th ed. New York: McGraw-Hill.

Thompson, A A, Strickland, A J, Gamble, J E. 2007. *Crafting & Executing Strategy – The Quest for Competitive Advantage, Concepts and Cases*. Boston: McGraw-Hill Irwin.

Thompson, P & McHugh, D. 2002. *Work Organisations,* 3rd ed. New York: Palgrave.

Thompson, S H, Ghee, S L & Sherin, A F. 2007. 'The adoption and diffusion of human resources information systems in Singapore'. *Asia Pacific Journal of Human Resources*, 45(1), 44–62.

Torrington, D & Hall, L. 1991. *Personnel Management: A New Approach*. London: Prentice Hall.

Tovey, M D & Lawlor, D R. 2004. *Training in Australia: Design, Delivery, Evaluation, Management*, 2nd ed. Australia: Pearson Education.

Tovey, M D & Uren, M. 2006. *Managing Performance Improvement,* 2nd ed. Australia: Pearson Education.

Trade Unions in Africa. n.d. *African Labour Researchers Network,* 1–25.

'Trailblazers: Champions of change'. 2007. *Management Today*, 23(5), 38–43.

Trengove-Jones, T. 2008. 'South Africa: Orgy of violence spotlighted our social fault lines'. <http://allafrica.com/stories/200806060398.html>

'True democracy requires greater fairness: Mandela'. n.d. <www.sagoodnews.co.za. index2.php>

Truelove, S. 2007. *Training in Practice*. London: CIPD.

Tulgan, B. 2004, 'Generational shift', in *On Staffing: Advice and Perspectives from HR Leaders*, eds Burkholder, N C, Edwards, P J & Sartain, L. Hoboken, NJ: John Wiley & Sons Inc.

Tushman, M L, Newman, W H & Romanelli, E. 1988. 'Convergence and upheaval: Managing the unsteady pace of organizational evolution', in *Readings in the Management of Innovation*, eds Tushman, M L & Moore, W L. New York: Ballinger.

Tushman, M L, Newman, W H & Romanelli, E. 1986. 'Convergence and upheaval: Managing the unsteady pace of organisation evolution. Section V: Organisation adaptation and change'. Reprinted from the *California Management Review*, 29(1), 477–489.

Tyson, S. & Fell, A. 1986. *Evaluating the Personnel Function*. London: Hutchinson.

Tyson, S. 1987. 'The management of the personnel function'. *Journal of Management Studies,* 24(5), 523–532.

Tyson, S. 1995a. *Human Resource Strategy – Towards a General Theory of Human Resource Management*. London: Pitman.

Tyson, S. 1995b. *Strategic Prospects for HRM*. London: Institute of Personnel and Development.

Ueckermann, H. 2008. 'Stres maak al hoe meer werkers siek'. *Rapport* – Loopbane 24, 6 April, 1.

Ulrich, D & Smallwood, N. 2005. 'Human resources' new ROI: Return on intangibles', in *The Future of Human Resource Management – 64 Thought Leaders Explore the Critical HR Issues of Today and Tomorrow,* eds Losey, M, Meisinger, S & Ulrich, D. New Jersey: John Wiley & Sons.

Ulrich, D. 1997. *Human Resource Champions: The Next Agenda for Adding Value and Delivering Results*. Boston: Harvard Business School.

Ulrich, D (ed). 1998. *Delivering Results: A New Mandate for HR Professionals*. Boston: Harvard Business School Publishing.

UNAIDS. 2008. *Report on the Global Aids Epidemic*. UNAIDS.

Uttal, B. 1983. 'The corporate culture vultures'. *Fortune*, 17 October, 66–72.

Uys, J S. 1993. *The Organisation of the Future*. Paper presented at the SATBT Congress, Grahamstown.

Van Aardt, C. 2004. *A Projection of the South African Population, 2001 to 2021*. Pretoria: Buro of Market Research (Report 330).

Van der Horst, H & McDonald, R. 1997. *Outcomes-based Education: A Teacher's Manual*. Pretoria: Kagiso Publishers.

Van der Walt, R. 1999. 'Workplace forums: efficiency and democracy?' *South African Labour Bulletin*, 23(1), 69–71.

Van der Walt, S. 1982. *Work Motives of Women in the Retail Business*. Pretoria: Raad vir Geesteswetenskaplike Navorsing.

Van der Westhuizen, C. 2007. *White Power & the Rise and Fall of the National Party*. Cape Town: Zebra Press.

Van Rensburg, G. 2007a. *The Leadership Challenge in Africa*. Pretoria: Van Schaik.

Van Rensburg, G. 2007b. 'Leadership and vision: A dream for Africa', *Management Today*, 23(10), 44–48.

Van Rooyen, M S. 1969. *Aspekte van die Beroepskeuse Struktuur van 'n Generasie St X-Leerlinge*. Unpublished MA thesis, University of Port Elizabeth, Port Elizabeth.

Van Schalkwijk, O. 1997. 'Global competition, demanding clients, limited resources challenges for 1997'. *HRM Yearbook*, 4–6.

Van Wyk, C. 1989. 'The human resource practitioner's changing role'. *IPM Journal*, 7(9), 13–14.

Vecchio, R P. 1996. *Organizational Behavior*, 3rd ed. Orlando: The Dryden Press.

Veldsman, T H. 1999. *Profiling the High Performance, High Commitment, High Flexibility Organisation*. Paper presented at the Best Human Resource Practices in Southern Africa conference of the Institute for International Research, Johannesburg.

Veldsman, T. 1998. 'The making of a people miracle'. *Management Today*, 14(2), 35.

Vermaak, T. 1996. 'Revitalising South African organisation's. *Boardroom*, 1, 14–16.

Verster, R. 1979. *Personnel Management in South Africa*. Bloemfontein: Personnel Research Division, University of the Orange Free State.

Viedge, C. 2004. 'The psychology of performance management', in *Building Human Capital: South African Perspectives*, eds Boninelli, I & Meyer, T. Randburg: Knowres.

Vinton, D E. 1992. 'A new look at time, speed and the manager'. *Academy of Management Executive*, 6(4), 7–16.

Visser, C J du T. 1995. *Corporate Accountability on Human Resources – A Review of Human Resources Accounting Practices as Reflected in Corporate Annual Reports*. Harrismith: PiERD Resources.

Visser, P, Douwes Dekker, L, Majola, A & Brenner, D. 1991. 'Community conflict and violence: A human needs perspective'. *IPM Journal*, 10(2), 22.

Visser, W P. 2006. 'From MWU to solidarity – a trade union reinvesting itself'. *South African Journal of Labour Relations*, 30(2), 19–41.

Von Holdt, K & Murphy, M. 2007. 'Public hospitals in South Africa: Stressed institutions, disempowered management', in *State of the Nation – South Africa 2007*, eds Buhlungu, S, Daniel, J, Southall, R & Lutchman, J. Cape Town: HSRC Press, 312–341.

Vorster, H J S. 1977. *Die Wenslikheid van die Rekenkundige Verantwoordings van Menslike Hulpbronne in die Gepubliseerde Finansiële Jaarstate van Ondernemings*. DCom thesis, PU for CHO, Potchefstroom.

Waddell, D M, Cummings, T G & Worley, C G. 2007. *Organisation Development & Change, Asia-Pacific*, 3rd ed. Melbourne: Cengage Learning.

Waddell, D, Devine, J, Jones, G R & George, J M. 2007. *Contemporary Management*. North Ryde: McGraw-Hill.

Walsh, J. 2007. 'Experiencing part-time work: Temporal tensions, social relations and the work–family interface'. *British Journal of Industrial Relations*, 45(1), 155–177.

Walton, R E & McKersie, R B. 1965. *A Behavioral Theory of Labour Negotiation*. New York: McGraw-Hill.

Wanous, J P. 1980. *Organizational Entry: Recruitment Selection and Socialization of Newcomers*. Massachusetts: Addison-Wesley.

Warner, M & Witzel, M. 2004. *Managing in Virtual Organizations*. UK: Thomson Learning.

Warren W. 1992. 'Changing corporate culture or corporate behaviour? How to change your company'. *Academy of Management Executive*, 6(4), 72–77.

'Wat het van ESOPs geword?'. 1996. *Finansies en Tegniek*, 19 April.

Watson Wyatt. 2005. *European Total Reward Survey – 2005*.

Watson, S, Maxwell, G A & Farquharson, L. 2007. 'Line managers' view on adopting human resource roles: The case of Hilton (UK) hotels'. *Employee Relations*, 29(1), 30–49.

Watson, T. 2007. 'Organization theory and HRM', in *The Oxford Handbook of Human Resource Management*, eds Boxall, P, Purcell, J & Wright, P. New York: Oxford University Press.

Webster, E & Macun, I. 1998. 'A trend towards co-determination? Case studies of South African enterprises'. *Law, Democracy and Development,* 63–84.

Webster, E & Wood, G. 2005. 'Human resource management practice and institutional constraints – the case of Mozambique'. *Employee Relations*, 27(4), 369–385.

Weiner, M. 1993. *Affirmative Action: The International Experience: Development and Democracy.* Urban Foundation publication, 4 May, 1–15.

Weitzul, J B. 1992. *Evaluating Interpersonal Skills in the Job Interview.* New York: Quorum Books.

Wentworth, J. 2006. 'Contract recruiting', in *On Staffing*, eds Burkholder, N C, Edwards, P Sr & Sartain, L. New Jersey: Wiley.

Westcott, M. 1999. 'Now for the real transformation'. *Management Today*, 15(2), 20–40.

Wheeler, BJ. 1984. 'Nutrition programs', in *Health Promotion in the Workplace*, eds O'Donnell, P O & Ainsworth, T H. 294. New York: John Wiley & Sons.

White, I H B. 1944/45. 'Personnel management in South Africa'. *Labour Management* (Journal of the UK Institute of Personnel Management), 144.

White, I H B. 1945. 'Personnel management in industry', in *Personnel Research in South Africa*, 313. Grahamstown: Personnel Research Section: Leather Industries Research Institute.

White, I H B. 1955. *The Effect of the Changing Social and Economic Situation on the Training and Experience Demanded of the Personnel Manager.* Address delivered at a one-day conference of the Port Elizabeth branch of the SA Institute of Personnel Management on Tuesday 9 August 1955.

Whitford, C M & Coetsee, W J. 2006. 'A model of the underlying philosophy and criteria for the effective implementation of performance management'. *SA Journal of Human Resource Management*, 4(1), 63–73.

Whyte, G S. 1978. 'The professionalism of personnel management'. *People & Profits*, 5(12), 9–10.

Whyte, G. 1990. 'IPM and SABPP: How do they differ?'. (IPM in interview with Gary Whyte). *IPM Journal*, 8(7), 33–34.

Wilkinson, A. 2007. 'Total Reward is helping to define a new era of benefits'. *Employee Benefits.* <www.employeebenefits.co.uk>

Willcoxson, L. 2003. 'Creating the HRM context for knowledge management', in *Human Resource Management: Challenges & Future Directions*, eds Wiesner, R & Millett, B. Australia: John Wiley & Sons.

Williams, C. 2007. *Trends and Developments in International Assignments.* Paper delivered at 16th PayCon Conference, Midrand, 29 August 2007.

Wills, B. 1993. *Distance Education: A Practical Guide.* New Jersey: Educational Technology.

Wilson, T B. 2003. *Innovative Reward Systems for the Changing Workplace,* 2nd ed. New York: McGraw-Hill.

Wingrove, T. 1993. *Affirmative Action.* Randburg: Knowledge Resources.

Wood, J D. 1996. 'The nature of ideology'. *Business Day* supplement – Mastering Management (part 16), 10 June, 2–4.

Woolard, I & Woolard, C. 2006. 'Earnings inequality in South Africa 1995–2003'. <www.hsrcpress.ac.za>.

World Competitiveness Yearbook. 1996. Lausanne, Switzerland: International Institute for Management Development.

WorldatWork Total Rewards Model: A Framework for Strategies to Attract, Motivate and Retain Employees. <www.worldatwork.org> (accessed July 2008).

Wray, Q. 2008. 'Shares bonanza for Sasol staff'. *Business Report,* 12 March, 19–20.

Yadavalli, L. 1999. 'Labour problems in the next century'. *Management Today*,15(4), 25–27.

Yagoubi, M. 2004. 'HRM in Tunisia', in *Managing Human Resources in Africa*, eds Kamoche, K, Debrah, Y, Horwitz, F & Muuka, G N. London: Routledge.

Yukl, G. 2006. *Leadership in Organizations,* 6th ed. Upper Saddle River, NJ: Pearson.

INDEX

Entries are listed in letter-by-letter alphabetical order. Page numbers in *italics* refer to tables, figures and exhibits.

A

ABET *see* Adult Basic Education and Training (ABET)
abilities of employees, 19
absenteeism, 749-52, *752*
absolute rating techniques, 384-86
AC *see* assessment centres
Accelerated and Shared Growth Initiative for South Africa (AsgiSA), 77-78, *78*, *428-29*, *441*
Accenture South Africa, 13
accidents *see* occupational incidents
accountability, 737-40, 766-67
acquisitions, 720-21
action learning, 466-67, *466*
action research model, 709-10
Adams' equity theory, 330-33, *332*, *333*
administrative expert role, 218
Adult Basic Education and Training (ABET), 442-43
advertisements, 265-67
advisers role, 215
affirmative action, 105-7, *106*, 108-9, 245
application forms, 284-85
   attitudes and, 117
   Employment Equity Act, 98, *114*
   fears regarding, 119, 123
   implementation of, 110-24
   job analysis and, 237
   modalities of, 107
   organisational culture and, 117
   selection of new employees, 296
   statistics, *111*
   see also employment equity
Africa, 49-61
   career choice, 403, 414
   China and, *60*
   employee benefits, 525

gender equality, 356
HIV/Aids, 559-61
information communication technology, 764
international human resource management (IHRM), 790
performance evaluations, 389
recruitment, 268
remuneration, 502
selection of new employees, 296
South Africa and, 59-61
statistics, 52, *54-58*
trade unions, 589, 663
training, 431, 448
triple bottom line, 727
Africa Competitiveness Report, The, 75
African Labour Researchers Network (ALRN), 593
African National Congress *see* ANC
African workers, 41
Afrocentricity, 353-54
afrocentric leadership, 358-63, *359-60*, 365-67
agency shop agreements, 652-53
agency strategy, 184-85
AIDA formula, 265-67
AIDS Foundation South Africa, 556-57
alcoholism, 547
   see also substance abuse
Alderfer's ERG theory, 327, *336*
all-comers approach, 650
ALRN *see* African Labour Researchers Network (ALRN)
alternative dispute resolution, 617-19
AMIHRP *see* Association of Mining Industries Human Resource Practitioners (AMIHRP)
analyser strategy, 144
ANC, 76-80, 795-97
andragogy, 458
Anglo American, 42, 513, 514, 556-57
Anglo Platinum, 640, 671, *724-26*

Angola, *55*
annual reports, 768, 770-71, 773-84
antiretroviral (ARV) therapy, 552
anxiety, *324*
apartheid, 40-41, 42
application forms, 282-85
appointment of new employees, 14, 297-303
appraisal interviews, 393
aptitudes of employees, 19
aptitude tests, 285
arbitration, 615-17, 619
architects role, 215
artisan development, 439
artistic environment, 403
artistic personality type, 402
Art of War, The, 138
ARV therapy *see* antiretroviral (ARV) therapy
AsgiSA *see* Accelerated and Shared Growth Initiative for South Africa (AsgiSA)
assessment centres, 292-93, 387-88
assimilation, 130-32
Association for Personnel Service Organisations of South Africa, 81
Association of Mining Industries Human Resource Practitioners (AMIHRP), 81
attitude, 19, 117
attraction strategies, 123
auditing, 753
   see also organisational audits; safety audits; skills audits

B

Baby Boom Echo Generation, 32
Baby Boomers, 31-32
Bakke, E Wight, 4, 29
balanced scorecard, 391-93, *391*, *392*
   see also HR Scorecard
bargaining councils, 608-11, *611*, *612*
BARS *see* behaviourally anchored rating scales (BARS)
Basic Conditions of Employment Act, 91-92, 480, 522, 551

Basic Conditions of Employment Amendment Act, 92
BAT SA *see* British American Tobacco South Africa (BAT SA)
BBBEE Act *see* Broad-Based Black Economic Empowerment Act
BCEA *see* Basic Conditions of Employment Act
Beaty, Professor David, 362-63, 365-67
behavioural checklists, 384, *385*
behavioural leadership theory paradigm, 342-44
behaviourally anchored rating scales (BARS), 385-86, *386*
behavioural-modelling training, 465
benefits *see* employee benefits
BESTmed, 203
Beyond Affirmative Action - Managing Diversity for Competitive Advantage in South Africa, 129
BHAG, 143
biases, 130-32
    in performance appraisals, 377
Biesheuvel, Professor Simon, 492
black economic empowerment, 514
    see also Broad-Based Black Economic Empowerment Act
Black Economic Empowerment Commission, 101
Black Labour Relations Regulation Amendment Act, 41
Black Labour (Settlement of Disputes) Act, 40
black workers *see* African workers
BMW, 211
boards of directors, 516-18, 792-95
border control in South Africa, 65
Botswana, *55*, 127
boundaryless organisation design, 210
brand identity, 260-61
briefing groups, 636-37, *637*
British American Tobacco South Africa (BAT SA), 501
broadbanding, 498, *498*
Broad-Based Black Economic Empowerment Act, 100-104
    see also black economic empowerment
budgets, 249, 262
bullying, 550

bureaucratic organisation structures, 209, *209*
business plans, 175-78
business strategies, 141
business units *see* strategic business units (SBUs)

C
career anchors, 407-10, *410*
career centres, 419-20
career choice, 399-403
career, definition of, 399
career development, 264, 399, 417-22, *422*
career discussions, 419
career exploration, 399
career invention model, 404-7, *406, 407*
career management
    change and, 397, *397-98*
    definition of, 399
    education and, 419-20
    models of, 404-7, *405, 406, 407*
    policy, 418
career movements, 413-16
career paths, 399
career patterns, 410-11
career planning, 399
career planning workshop, 419
career plateaus, 411-12
case studies, 465
Castellion Job Evaluation method, 492
CCMA, 594-95, 609, 613-17
    see also dispute resolution
CEE *see* Commission for Employment Equity (CEE)
centralisation, 221-25, *223*
chance factors, 403
change *see* organisational change
change leader role, 218
changemakers role, 217
charismatic leadership theory, 349-50, *350*
Chartered Institute of Personnel and Development (CIPD), *169*, 220, *221*
charters (BBBEE), 103
checklists for job analysis, 233
chemical industry, *732*
childcare, 539-40
China, 50-51, *60*
CIPD *see* Chartered Institute of Personnel and Development (CIPD)
Citibank, 791
City Lodge Hotels, 205
clerks of works role, 215
closed-shop agreements, 652, 653
closed systems, 10

clothing and textile sector, 50-51
coaching, 463
Codes of Good Practice (BBBEE), 103
cognitive ability (intelligence) tests, 285
cognitive dissonance theory, 330, *331*
COIDA *see* Compensation for Occupational Injuries and Diseases Act
collective agreements, 610, *610*, 650, 652-53
collective bargaining, 97, 582, 604, *604*
collective negotiation, 653-63, *657, 659*
Commission for Conciliation, Mediation and Arbitration *see* CCMA
Commission for Employment Equity (CEE), 111-12
commission plans, 510, *511*
committee assignments, 463-64
committees, 637
common law, 89-91
communication, 22, 119
    barriers, 639
    barriers to, 639
    importance of, 634-35
    methods of, 635-39
    policy, 500-501
Compensation for Occupational Injuries and Diseases Act, 94-95, 548
competency profiling, 234, *234*
competitiveness, 73
competitive strategies, 141
complexity of jobs, 318
complex-man view, 322-23, *322*
computers *see* information communication technology
con-arb *see* conciliation-arbitration (con-arb)
concentrated growth strategies, 140
concentric diversification strategies, 140
conciliation, 618
    see also dispute resolution
conciliation-arbitration (con-arb), 617, 619
concurrent validity, 281
conference method, 233
conglomerate diversification, 141
Congress of South African Trade Unions *see* Cosatu
Congress of the People *see* COPE
consortia strategies, 140
constitutional law, 88-89

exploitation of, 158-60
independent contractors vs,
    90-91, *90*
involvement of, 642-43
new, 297-303, *300-303*
orientation of, 297-303, *300-303*
participation of, 642-43
potential, 262-63
rights of, 585
wellness of, 535-52
employee share ownership plans
    (ESOPs), 514-15
employer brand, 260-61
employers, duties of, *91*, 113
employment agencies, 264
Employment Conditions
    Commission, 92
employment costs, 743-46, *744,
    745, 746*
employment equity, 120-21, *120,
    246*
    see also affirmative action
Employment Equity Act
    Commission for Employment
        Equity (CEE), 112
    enforcement of, 113, 115, *116*
    implementation of, 113
    job analysis, 237
    monitoring of, 113, 115, *116*
    organisational audits, 118
    pay structuring, 496
    people with disabilities, 550-51
    performance appraisal, 374
    physical examinations, 294, 561
    psychological testing, 286, 414
    recruitment, 259-60, 265
    reporting, 765-66
    who is covered by, *114*
employment equity plans, 113, *115*
employment interviews, 287-92
employment opportunities, 105
employment relations, 580-82
    see also labour relations
employment relationship, 88,
    582-83
    see also work relationship
employment tests, 285-86
empowerment, 14, 105-6, 109-10,
    124, 162-63, 183
engagement strategy, 184
engine room staff, 520
enlargement of jobs, 189
enterprising environment, 403
enterprising personality type, 402
entrepreneurship, 124-27
environmental influences on
    career choice, 403
environmental scanning, 142-43,
    153-54

environmental types, 402-3
EoI's *see* expressions of interest
    (EoI's)
equality of opportunity, 107
equitable equality, 107-9, *108*, 128
equity in remuneration, 478
equity theory (Adams), 330-33,
    332, 333
e-recruiting *see* online recruitment
ergonomics, 190, 537
ERG theory (Alderfer), 327, *327*
Eritrea, 414
Eskom, 208, *224*, 636
ESOPs *see* employee share
    ownership plans (ESOPs)
espoused policies, 167
essay method, 384
essential services, 626
ethics, 794-95
ethnic diversity *see* diversity
eurocentric leadership, 363, 365-67
evaluation
    of human resource
        management, 740-58
    of training, 468-70, *469*
    of workforce planning, 252
evolutionary perspective of human
    resource management, 27-33
execution of strategy, 144
executive remuneration, 516-18
executive searchers, 264-65
expatriate employees, 518-19
expectancy theory (Vroom), 333-
    34, *333*
experienced meaningfulness,
    186-87
expressions of interest (EoI's), 276
external environment, 153
external venturing, 126

F
face-to-face communication,
    637-38
facilitators, 174
factor comparison, 488
fairness
    labour practices, 645-47
    personnel selection, 295-97
    see also unfair discrimination
fears, 110, 119, 123, 130
Federation of Unions of South
    Africa (Fedusa), 602-3
feminine leadership style, *358*
    see also gender
Festinger's cognitive dissonance
    theory, 330
Fiedler's contingency model, 345-
    46, *346*
fine tuning, 707
fitness programmes, 538-39

flexibility, 196-99
flexible organisations, 192, *193*
flexitime, 197, *198-99*
FOCAC *see* Forum on China-
    Africa Cooperation (FOCAC)
food prices, *74*
forced distribution, 383-84, *384*
Fordism, 187-88, 191
forecasting workforce supply,
    243-44
formalisation of work design, 185
Forum on China-Africa
    Cooperation (FOCAC), *60*
freedom of association, 593-95,
    595
FTSE4Good Index, 570
functional flexibility, 196-97
functionally designed organisation
    structures, 208
functional strategies, 141
future of human resource
    management, 795-805

G
gain-sharing plans, 512-13
Gallatin, Albert, 28
GDP, 71-72, *72*
GDS *see* growth and development
    summit (GDS)
GEAR *see* Growth, Employment
    and Redistribution (GEAR)
gender
    career anchors and, *410*
    leadership and, 355-58, *358*
General and Further Education
    and Training Quality Assurance
    Act, 433
General Electric, 210
generations in workforce, 31-33
Generation X, 32
Generation Y, 32
generic scorecards (BBBEE), 103
generic strategies, 141, 156-58, *157*
Ghana, 502, 589, 790
Global Competitiveness Index,
    74-75
global economy, 73
globalisation, 23-25, 33, 49-50
    see also international human
        resource management
        (IHRM)
GLOBE project, 341
goal programming, 250
goal-setting theory (Locke), 329-
    30
governance *see* corporate
    governance
government policies, 259
government, role of, 583
grade overlap, 499

Saville and Holdsworth Work
  Profiling System, 232
scanning the environment *see*
  environmental scanning
scenarios for South Africa, 795-
  805
Schein, E H, 316-23
screening, 273
SDA *see* Skills Development Act
SDLA *see* Skills Development
  Levies Act
SDWTs *see* self-directed work
  teams (SDWTs)
secondary strikes, 628
second economy, 48
Sector Education and Training
  Authorities (SETAs), 46-47,
  437-38
selection *see* personnel selection
self-actualisation man, 162, 320-
  22, *321*
self-appraisal, 388
self-directed work teams
  (SDWTs), 204-5
self-employment, 105, 126-27
self-reports, 232
senior executives, 516-18
senior managerial employees, 663
sensitivity training, 464
service level agreements (SLAs),
  304
SETAs *see* Sector Education and
  Training Authorities (SETAs)
seven-step process (Kotter), 728-
  29
severance pay, 696-97, *697*
sexual harassment, 550
sexually transmitted diseases
  (STDs), 552
  see also HIV/Aids
Seychelles, *57*
SGB *see* standards generating
  body (SGB)
shared HR services centres
  (SHRSCs), 223-25
shift work *see* working time
Shoprite, 24
shop stewards, 651-52
SHRSCs *see* shared HR services
  centres (SHRSCs)
Silent Generation, 31
simple design, 207-8
simulation methods for training,
  465-66
simulation (statistical technique),
  250
situational interview, 291
situational theory (Hersey and
  Blanchard), 347-48, *348*
skills audits, 454

Skills Development Act, 99-100,
  433, 436-39, 442
Skills Development Levies Act, 99,
  100, 439-41, 442
skills inventories, 264
Skinner, B F, 334
SLAs *see* service level agreements
  (SLAs)
slavery, 36
smoking policies, 540-41
social environment, 402
socialisation programme *see*
  orientation of employees
Socially Responsible Investment
  Index (SRI), 570
social-man view, 319-20, *319*
social personality type, 402
social responsibility *see* corporate
  social responsibility
societal-corporatist perspective,
  588
societal embeddedness, 8-10
socio-political economy of South
  Africa, 49-80
soft change situations, 707
South Africa
  Africa and, 59-61
  economic performance, 72-76
  economy of, 71-76
  first decade of democracy,
    45-47
  human resource management
    in, 35-48
  labour relations era, 41-45
  politics in, 76-80
  population of, 61-71, *64*
  second decade of democracy,
    47-48
  socio-political economy, 49-80
  statistics, *57, 64, 70*
  structure of economy, 71-72
South African Airways, *558-59*
South African Board of Personnel
  Practice (SABPP), 43, 81-82,
  82-84
South African Confederation of
  Trade Unions (Sacotu), 602-3
South African Forum of ASTD, 81
South African Institute of
  Personnel Management
  see Institute of Personnel
  Management (Southern
  Africa)
South African Qualifications
  Authority Act, 99, 431, 432
South African Qualifications
  Authority (SAQA), 434
South African Trades and Labour
  Council, 37

*South Africa Scenarios 2025: The
  future we chose?*, 797-801
Southern African Development
  Community (SADC), 52, *55-58*
special-event recruiting, 267
specialisation and work design,
  185, 187-88
specialist human resource
  practitioners *see* human
  resource practitioners
special publications, 635-36
SRI *see* Socially Responsible
  Investment Index (SRI)
stakeholders, 6, 7, 118
Stanbic, 791
standardisation of work design,
  185
standards generating body (SGB),
  46
STAR, 284
state contracts, 116
State of Skills in South Africa 2005,
  430
*State of the Nation: South Africa
  2004-2005*, 77
*State of the South African Training
  Industry Report (2007)*, 467
state tenders, 116
statistical techniques, 247, 250-51
statistics
  Africa, *53, 54*
  HIV/Aids, 552, 553, *554-55*
  South Africa, *57, 70*
  Southern African Development
    Community (SADC), *55-58*
status symbols, *326*
statutory councils, 611-13
statutory workplace forums *see*
  workplace forums
stayaways *see* protest action
STDs *see* sexually transmitted
  diseases (STDs)
Stengel, Richard, 354-55
stereotypes, 130-32
stochastic analysis, 248
Storey, J, 215-17
strategic alliances strategies, 140
strategic business units (SBUs),
  208
strategic choices, 141-42, 143
strategic human resource
  management, 148-49, 151-53
strategic management, 141-44
strategic partner role, 218
strategic position, 141-42
strategic thinking, 145, *146*
strategy, 13-14, 21
  affirmative action and, 118
  choices, 154-65
  definition of, 138-40, *139*